PROPERTY

A Local Paradise, No. 4
by Tony Berlant, 1992
House: Collage of found metal on plywood
with steel brads $8\frac{1}{4} \times 8\frac{1}{4} \times 7''$

[A]t the very roots of the symbol of the American
house lies the fact of property. —

Jan Cohn,
The Palace or the Poorhouse: The
American House as a Cultural Symbol 244 (1979)

PROPERTY

Third Edition

Jesse Dukeminier

Richard C. Maxwell Professor of Law
University of California
Los Angeles

James E. Krier

Earl Warren DeLano Professor of Law
University of Michigan

Little, Brown and Company
Boston   Toronto   London

Library of Congress Catalog Card No. 92-82982

ISBN 0-316-19523-5

Third Edition

Third Printing

MV-NY

Published simultaneously in Canada
by Little, Brown & Company (Canada) Limited
Printed in the United States of America

For David,
and for
Wendy, Jennifer, Amy, Andrew, and Patrick

Summary of Contents

Contents

List of Illustrations

Chapter 10

Chapter 11

Chapter 12

Preface to the Third Edition

The institution of property proves to be extraordinarily vital. We first published this book in 1981, then revised it very substantially in 1988 to take account of many important developments in law and scholarship alike. Now we revise again, for the same reasons and in the same spirit as before. As with the Second Edition, we have tried not simply to update and (as necessary) reorganize the material in the book, but also to enlarge, enrich, and enliven it. Our general aims and methods, however, remain essentially what they were when we started out a dozen years ago. We stated them then in the Preface to the First Edition, reprinted below.

We owe an enormous debt of gratitude to the students, teachers, and other friends who have made this book a much more collaborative enterprise than its title page suggests. Mary Beth Britton, Steve Fink, Marisa Gomez, Jim Green, Leo O'Brien, and Lou Orbach worked hard and well as research assistants; Lisa Wehrle did likewise as our editor at Little, Brown. And Margaret Kiever was invaluable in preparing the manuscript, with assists from Beth Colaner, Eeva Joensuu, and Shanta Ness. To mention everyone else by name would result in a list so long as to read like a cold accounting. Instead we extend a warm word of thanks.

Jesse Dukeminier
James E. Krier

January 1993

From the Preface to the First Edition

Property is a thoroughly modern subject of thoroughly antiquated origins. Probably in no other area of law does one see more, or even as many, strains of the old in the new. As an institution for allocating resources and distributing wealth and power, property bears in fundamentally important ways on central issues in contemporary life; as a body of doctrine, it discharges these modern-day tasks with rules and concepts drawn from age-old ways of looking at social relations in an ordered society. Property law has, to be sure, undergone constant change, but — at least in Anglo-American experience — it has not been revolutionized. Its enduring mix of old and new, rife with uneasy tensions, reflects more than an institution that has evolved over centuries and across cultures; it reflects as well two often conflicting objectives — promoting stability and accommodating change — that property systems must serve. To study property is to study social history, social relations, and social reform.

It is also, of course, to study law. The primary objective of this coursebook is to help students learn the complicated structure and functions of property doctrine and something of legal method, legal reasoning, and legal analysis. We have, however, secondary objectives as well, suggested by our opening remarks. How, why, and with what implications does the property system order relations in present-day America? What sorts of incentives does it create in terms of constructive use of scarce, valuable resources? How fairly does it confer benefits and impose burdens? To what extent is today's system a valuable, or a useless, legacy of the past? What sorts of reforms are suggested, and what might they achieve?

To pursue such secondary questions as these, and especially to accomplish the primary end of learning law and legal method, we need large doses of doctrine, but also a sense of history and of methods of critiquing institutional performance. There is, then, lots of law in what follows — in cases, statutes, text, and problems. There is also a consistent effort to trace historical antecedents. Finally, there is a fairly systematic, but by no means dominating, attempt to critique — often through an economic lens. Economics, like property, is in large part about resources. The economics in the book can be managed easily, we think, even by the totally uninitiated; it can also be ignored or even scorned. So too for the history, if one likes.

Jesse Dukeminier
James E. Krier

February 1, 1981

Acknowledgments

The authors acknowledge the permissions kindly granted to reproduce excerpts from, or illustrations of, the materials indicated below.

Books and Articles

American Law Institute, Restatement (Second) of Property, Landlord & Tenant (1977); Restatement (Third) of Property, Servitudes (1989 & 1991). Copyright © 1977, 1989 & 1991 by the American Law Institute. Reprinted with permission from The American Law Institute.

American Law of Property (A. James Casner ed. 1952 & 1977 Supp.). Copyright © 1952, 1977. Reprinted with permission from Little, Brown and Company.

Associated Press, Wilderness Subdivision OK's Nudity, Bans Mowers, Los Angeles Times, June 28, 1992.

Baird, Douglas G., Common Law Intellectual Property and the Legacy of *International News Service v. Associated Press,* 40 U. Chi. L. Rev. 411 (1983). Copyright © 1983 by University of Chicago Law Review.

Barnett, Walter, Marketable Title Acts — Panacea or Pandemonium?, 53 Cornell L. Rev. 45 (1967). Reprinted with permission from the Cornell Law Review and Fred B. Rothman & Co.

Berger, Lawrence, The Public Use Requirement in Eminent Domain, 57 Or. L. Rev. 203 (1978).

Demsetz, Harold, Toward a Theory of Property Rights, 57 Am. Econ. Rev. 347 (Pap. & Proc. 1967). Reprinted with permission from the American Economic Association.

Ellickson, Robert C., Alternatives to Zoning: Covenants, Nuisance Rules, and Fines as Land Use Controls, 40 U. Chi. L. Rev. 681 (1973). Copyright © 1973 by University of Chicago Law Review.

Ellickson, Robert C., & A. Dan Tarlock, Land-Use Controls (1981 & Supp. 1984). Copyright © 1981 & 1984. Reprinted with permission from Little, Brown and Company.

Fischel, William, The Economics of Zoning Laws (1985). Reprinted with permission from Johns Hopkins Press.

Krier, James E., The Regulation Machine, 1 Sup. Ct. Econ. Rev. 1 (1982). Copyright © 1982, Supreme Court Economic Review.

Kushner, James A., The Fair Housing Amendments of 1988: The Second Generation of Fair Housing, 42 Vand. L. Rev. 1049 (1989).

Leach, W. Barton, Perpetuities in Perspective: Ending the Rule's Rc of Terror, 65 Harv. L. Rev. 721 (1952). Copyright © 1952 by Harvard Law Review Association.

Los Angeles Times, Woman Faces Fine for Kissing Her Date, by Davi Willman, June 16, 1991. Copyright © 1991, Los Angeles Times. Reprinted by permission.

Mandelker, Daniel R., Delegation of Power and Function in Zoning Administration, 1963 Wash. U. L.Q. 60. Copyright © 1963 by the Washington University Law Quarterly.

Mandelker, Daniel R., The Zoning Dilemma (1971). Reprinted with permission from Bobbs-Merrill.

McDougal, Myres S., & John W. Brabner-Smith, Land Title Transfer: A Regression, 48 Yale L.J. 1125 (1939). Reprinted with permission from The Yale Law Journal Company and Fred B. Rothman & Co.

Michelman, Frank, Property, Utility, and Fairness: Comments on the Ethical Foundations of "Just Compensation" Law, 80 Harv. L. Rev. 1168 (1967). Copyright © 1967 by the Harvard Law Review Association.

New York Times, Rehnquist Alters Restrictive Deed, Nov. 16, 1986; U.S. Giving Certain Boat Owners Exclusive Rights to Fish Off Coast, Apr. 22, 1991; White Tilt to Balance a Project in Canarsie, Aug. 4, 1992.

Oldham, J. Thomas, Putting Asunder in the 1990s, 80 Cal. L. Rev. 1091 (1992).

Payne, John C., A Typical House Purchase Transaction in the United States, 30 Conv. & Prop. Law. (n.s.) 194 (1966). Reprinted with permission from Sweet & Maxwell, Ltd.

Perry, Sandra White, Letter to editors regarding Jessie Lide's house (1988).

Philadelphia Inquirer, Despite Ruling, Affordable Homes Still Scarce in N.J., Nov. 25, 1990.

Posner, Richard A., Economic Analysis of Law (4th ed. 1992). Copyright © 1992. Reprinted with permission from Little, Brown and Company.

Powell, Richard R., The Law of Real Property (rev. ed. 1992). Copyright © 1992 by Matthew Bender & Co., Inc., and reprinted with permission.

Schill, Michael H., Privatizing Federal Low Income Housing Assistance: The Case of Public Housing, 75 Cornell L. Rev. 878 (1990). Reprinted with permission from the Cornell Law Review and Fred B. Rothman & Co.

Siegan, Bernard H., Non-Zoning in Houston, 13 J.L. & Econ. 71 (1970). Reprinted with permission from the Journal of Law and Economics. Copyright © 1970 by the University of Chicago.

Singer, Joseph W., The Reliance Interest in Property, 40 Stan. L. Rev. 611 (1988).

Illustrations

Berlant, Tony, House: Collage of found metal on plywood (1982), photograph. Reproduced with permission from Tony Berlant.

Blackstone, Sir William, portrait by Sir Joshua Reynolds, from the National Portrait Gallery, London.

Day, Robert, drawing. Copyright © 1958, 1986. Reprinted with permission from The New Yorker Magazine, Inc.

Development Rights Transfer, from John J. Costonis, Space Adrift (1974). Copyright © 1974 by the University of Illinois Press.

Duck Decoy, drawing, from Tony Cook & R.E.M. Pilcher, The History of Borough Fen Decoy (1982). Reproduced with permission of Providence Press.

Giant Tire, Detroit, Michigan, photograph by Wendy L. Wilkes.

Gray, John Chipman, portrait by F.P. Vinton. Reproduced by permission of the Harvard Law School Art Collection.

Green Lawn Subdivision, Detroit, Michigan, photograph by Wendy L. Wilkes.

Gwernhaylod House, Overton-on-Dee, Shropshire, photograph, courtesy of John Riddell.

Haunted House, Nyack, New York, photograph. Reproduced with permission from AP/Wide World Photos.

House, Berkley Hills Addition, Emporia, Kansas, photograph by Chad Johnson.

Houses in Neponsit, New York, photographs by Jesse Dukeminier.

Ink Park, Canton, Ohio, photographs, courtesy of Albert B. Arbaugh.

Jessie Lide's House, Knoxville, Tennessee, photograph, courtesy of Sandra White Perry.

Kenyon, the First Baron, portrait by George Romney. Reproduced with permission from the Fifth Baron Kenyon.

Klimt, Gustav, painting entitled "Schloss Kammer am Attersee II." Reproduced with permission from Galerie St. Etienne, New York, and Michael S. Gruen.

Laguna Royale Condominium, Laguna Beach, California, photograph by Don Romero.

Lakeside Village Condominium, Culver City, California, photograph by Jesse Dukeminier.

Lake Naomi, Pennsylvania, photograph from Emma Miller Waygood, Changing Times in the Poconos (1972). Reprinted with permission from Mary Brower.

Leicester Square, London, etching, from the British Museum, London.

Loretto's Apartment House, New York, photograph by Michael S. Gruen.

Marshall, John, portrait by Chester Harding. Reproduced with permission from the Boston Athenaeum.

Martin, H., drawing. Copyright © 1970. Reprinted with permission from The New Yorker Magazine, Inc.

Odd Fellows Building, Los Banos, California, photographs by Todd Benjamin.

O'Keeffe, Georgia, painting entitled "Seaweed." Copyright © 1987 by Juan Hamilton. Reproduced with permission from Juan Hamilton.

O'Keeffe, Georgia, photograph by Philippe Halsman. Copyright © 1987 by Yvonne Halsman. Reprinted with permission from Yvonne Halsman.

Pierre Apartments, Hackensack, New Jersey, photograph by David S. Sanders.

River View Towers, Fort Lee, New Jersey, photograph by David S. Sanders.

Starke, drawing. Copyright © 1947, 1975. Reprinted with permission from The New Yorker Magazine, Inc.

Starrett City, Brooklyn, photograph by Ozier Muhammad. Copyright © 1991 New York Newsday.

Stoyanoff House, Ladue, Missouri, imaginative drawing by Shinji Isozaki.

Van Pelt, J.F., photograph from The Steve Hill Collection, Mitchell Community College, North Carolina. Reproduced with permission from Bill Moose.

Van Pelt Residence, Statesville, North Carolina, etching, courtesy of Bill Moose.

Weber, drawing. Copyright © 1977. Reprinted with permission from The New Yorker Magazine, Inc.

Woburn Independent Baptist Church, Woburn, Massachusetts, photograph. Reprinted with permission from the Woburn Public Library, Glennon Archives.

PROPERTY

I
An Introduction to Some Fundamentals

The first two chapters of this book pursue a common theme — how someone might acquire property other than by purchase — across a wide range of legal terrain. One purpose of the exercise is to lay down the chief doctrinal foundations of property law. Another is to introduce some basic concepts, issues, and analytic methods of ongoing importance.

1
First Possession: Acquisition of Property by Discovery, Capture, and Creation

Qui prior est tempore potior est jure.
(Who is first in point of time is stronger in right.) —

Maxim of Roman Law

First come, first served. —

Henry Brinklow,
Complaynt of Roderick Mors, Ch. 17 (c. 1545)

How does property come to be, and why, and so what? Most of us most of the time take these questions for granted, which is to say that we take property for granted. But taking something for granted is not exactly the best path to understanding it. So we begin with the genesis of our subject.

A. Acquisition by Discovery

Thus in the beginning all the world was *America* —

John Locke
Two Treatises of Government,
Book II, Ch. V ("Of Property") (c. 1690)

Johnson v. M'Intosh
Supreme Court of the United States, 1823
21 U.S. (8 Wheat.) 543

Error to the District Court of Illinois. This was an action of ejectment for lands in the State and District of Illinois, claimed by the plaintiffs under a purchase and conveyance from the Piankeshaw Indians, and by the defendant, under a [later] grant from the United States. It came up on a case stated, upon which there was a judgment below for the defendant. . . .

MR. CHIEF JUSTICE MARSHALL delivered the opinion of the Court. The plaintiffs in this cause claim the land, in their declaration mentioned, under two grants, purporting to be made, the first in 1773, and the last in 1775, by the chiefs of certain Indian tribes, constituting the Illinois and the Piankeshaw nations; and the question is, whether this title can be recognised in the Courts of the United States?

The facts, as stated in the case agreed, show the authority of the chiefs who executed this conveyance, so far as it could be given by their own people; and likewise show, that the particular tribes for whom these chiefs acted were in rightful possession of the land they sold. The inquiry, therefore, is, in a great measure, confined to the power of Indians to give, and of private individuals to receive, a title which can be sustained in the Courts of this country.

As the right of society, to prescribe those rules by which property may be acquired and preserved is not, and cannot be drawn into question; as the title to lands, especially, is and must be admitted to depend entirely on the law of the nation in which they lie; it will be necessary, in pursuing this inquiry, to examine, not singly those principles of abstract justice, which the Creator of all things has impressed on the mind of his creature man, and which are admitted to regulate, in a great degree, the rights of civilized nations, whose perfect independence is acknowledged; but those principles also which our own government has adopted in the particular case, and given us as the rule for our decision.

On the discovery of this immense continent, the great nations of Europe were eager to appropriate to themselves so much of it as they could respectively acquire. Its vast extent offered an ample field to the ambition and enterprise of all; and the character and religion of its inhabitants afforded an apology for considering them as a people over whom the superior genius of Europe might claim an ascendency. The potentates of the old world found no difficulty in convincing themselves that they made ample compensation to the inhabitants of the new, by bestowing on them civilization and Christianity, in exchange for unlimited independence. But, as they were all in pursuit of nearly the same object, it was necessary, in order to avoid conflicting settlements, and consequent war with each other, to establish a principle, which all should acknowledge as the law by which the right of acquisition, which they all asserted, should be regulated as between themselves. This principle was, that discovery gave title to the government by whose subjects, or by whose authority, it was made, against all other European governments, which title might be consummated by possession.

The exclusion of all other Europeans, necessarily gave to the nation making the discovery the sole right of acquiring the soil from the natives, and establishing settlements upon it. It was a right with which no Europeans could interfere. It was a right which all asserted for themselves, and to the assertion of which, by others, all assented.

Those relations which were to exist between the discoverer and the natives, were to be regulated by themselves. The rights thus acquired being exclusive, no other power could interpose between them.

In the establishment of these relations, the rights of the original inhabitants were, in no instance, entirely disregarded; but were necessarily, to a considerable extent, impaired. They were admitted to be the rightful occupants of the soil, with a legal as well as just claim to retain possession of it, and to use it according to their own discretion, but their rights to complete sovereignty, as independent nations, were necessarily diminished, and their power to dispose of the soil at their own will, to whomsoever they pleased, was denied by the original fundamental principle, that discovery gave exclusive title to those who made it.

While the different nations of Europe respected the right of the natives, as occupants, they asserted the ultimate dominion to be in themselves; and claimed and exercised, as a consequence of this ultimate dominion, a power to grant the soil, while yet in possession of the natives. These grants have been understood by all, to convey a title to the grantees, subject only to the Indian right of occupancy.

The history of America, from its discovery to the present day, proves, we think, the universal recognition of these principles.

Spain did not rest her title solely on the grant of the Pope. Her discussions respecting boundary, with France, with Great Britain, and with the United States, all show that she placed it on the rights given by discovery. Portugal sustained her claim to the Brazils by the same title.

France, also, founded her title to the vast territories she claimed in America on discovery. However conciliatory her conduct to the natives may have been, she still asserted her right of dominion over a great extent of country not actually settled by Frenchmen, and her exclusive right to acquire and dispose of the soil which remained in the occupation of Indians. . . .

The States of Holland also made acquisitions in America, and sustained their right on the common principle adopted by all Europe. . . .

The claim of the Dutch was always contested by the English; not because they questioned the title given by discovery, but because they insisted on being themselves the rightful claimants under that title. Their pretensions were finally decided by the sword.

No one of the powers of Europe gave its full assent to this principle, more unequivocally than England. The documents upon this subject are ample and complete. So early as the year 1496, her monarch granted a commission to the Cabots, to discover countries then unknown to *Christian people,* and to take possession of them in the name of the king of England. Two years afterwards, Cabot proceeded on this voyage, and discovered the continent of North America, along which he sailed as far south as Virginia. To this discovery the English trace their title.

In this first effort made by the English government to acquire territory on this continent, we perceive a complete recognition of the principle which has been mentioned. The right of discovery given by this commission, is confined to countries "then unknown to all Christian people"; and of these countries Cabot was empowered to take possession in the name of the king of England. Thus asserting a right to take possession, notwithstanding the occupancy of the natives, who were heathens, and, at the same time, admitting the prior title of any Christian people who may have made a previous discovery.

The same principle continued to be recognised. [Omitted here is a discussion of various charters from the English crown, granting lands in America.]

Thus has our whole country been granted by the crown while in the occupation of the Indians. These grants purport to convey the soil as well as the right of dominion to the grantees. In those governments which were denominated royal, where the right to the soil was not vested in individuals, but remained in the crown, or was vested in the colonial government, the king claimed and exercised the right of granting lands, and of dismembering the government at his will. The grants made out of the two original colonies, after the resumption of their charters by the crown, are examples of this. The governments of New-England, New-York, New-Jersey, Pennsylvania, Maryland, and a part of Carolina, were thus created. In all of them, the soil, at the time the grants were made, was occupied by the Indians. Yet almost every title within those governments is dependent on these grants. In some instances, the soil was conveyed by the crown unaccompanied by the powers of government, as in the case of the northern neck of Virginia. It has never been objected to this, or to any other similar grant, that the title as well as possession was in the Indians when it was made, and that it passed nothing on that account.

These various patents cannot be considered as nullities; nor can they be limited to a mere grant of the powers of government. A charter intended to convey political power only, would never contain words expressly granting the land, the soil, and the waters. Some of them purport to convey the soil alone; and in those cases in which the powers of government, as well as the soil, are conveyed to individuals, the crown has always acknowledged itself to be bound by the grant. Though the power to dismember regal governments was asserted and exercised, the power to dismember proprietary governments was not claimed; and, in some instances, even after the powers of government were revested in the crown, the title of the proprietors to the soil was respected. . . .

Further proofs of the extent to which this principle has been recognised, will be found in the history of the wars, negotiations, and treaties, which the different nations, claiming territory in America, have carried on, and held with each other. . . .

Thus, all the nations of Europe, who have acquired territory on this continent, have asserted in themselves, and have recognised in others, the exclusive right of the discoverer to appropriate the lands occupied by the Indians. Have the American States rejected or adopted this principle?

By the treaty which concluded the war of our revolution, Great Britain relinquished all claim, not only to the government, but to the "propriety and territorial rights of the United States," whose boundaries were fixed in the second article. By this treaty, the powers of government, and the right to soil, which had previously been in Great Britain, passed definitively to these States. We had before taken possession of them, by declaring independence; but neither the declaration of independence, nor the treaty confirming it, could give us more than that which we before possessed, or to which Great Britain was before entitled. It has never been doubted, that either the United States, or the several States, had a clear title to all the lands within the boundary lines described in the treaty, subject only to the Indian right of occupancy, and that the exclusive power to extinguish that right, was vested in that government which might constitutionally exercise it.

Virginia, particularly, within whose chartered limits the land in controversy lay, passed an act, in the year 1779, declaring her

> exclusive right of pre-emption from the Indians, of all the lands within the limits of her own chartered territory, and that no person or persons whatsoever, have, or ever had, a right to purchase any lands within the same, from any Indian nation, except only persons duly authorized to make such purchase; formerly for the use and benefit of the colony, and lately for the Commonwealth.

The act then proceeds to annul all deeds made by Indians to individuals, for the private use of the purchasers.

Without ascribing to this act the power of annulling vested rights, or admitting it to countervail the testimony furnished by the marginal note opposite to the title of the law, forbidding purchases from the Indians, in the revisals of the Virginia statutes, stating that law to be repealed, it may safely be considered as an unequivocal affirmance, on the part of Virginia, of the broad principle which had always been maintained, that the exclusive right to purchase from the Indians resided in the government.

In pursuance of the same idea, Virginia proceeded, at the same session, to open her land office, for the sale of that country which now constitutes Kentucky, a country, every acre of which was then claimed and possessed by Indians, who maintained their title with as much persevering courage as was ever manifested by any people.

The States, having within their chartered limits different portions of territory covered by Indians, ceded that territory, generally, to the United States, on conditions expressed in their deeds of cession, which demonstrate the opinion, that they ceded the soil as well as jurisdiction, and that in doing so, they granted a productive fund to the government of the Union. The lands in controversy lay within the chartered limits of Virginia, and were ceded with the whole country northwest of the river Ohio. This grant contained reservations and stipulations, which could only be made by the owners of the soil; and concluded with a stipulation, that "all the lands in the ceded territory, not reserved, should be considered as a common fund, for the use and benefit of such of the United States as have become, or shall become, members of the confederation," &c. "according to their usual respective proportions in the general charge and expenditure, and shall be faithfully and *bona fide* disposed of for that purpose, and for no other use or purpose whatsoever."

The ceded territory was occupied by numerous and warlike tribes of Indians; but the exclusive right of the United States to extinguish their title, and to grant the soil, has never, we believe, been doubted. . . .

Our late acquisitions from Spain are of the same character; and the negotiations which preceded those acquisitions, recognise and elucidate the principle which has been received as the foundation of all European title in America.

The United States, then, have unequivocally acceded to that great and broad rule by which its civilized inhabitants now hold this country. They hold, and assert in themselves, the title by which it was acquired. They maintain, as all others have maintained, that discovery gave an exclusive right to extinguish the Indian title of occupancy, either by purchase or by conquest; and gave also a right to such a degree of sovereignty, as the circumstances of the people would allow them to exercise.

The power now possessed by the government of the United States to grant lands, resided, while we were colonies, in the crown, or its grantees. The validity of the titles given by either has never been questioned in our Courts. It has been exercised uniformly over territory in possession of the Indians. The existence of this power must negative the existence of any right which may conflict with, and control it. An absolute title to lands cannot exist, at the same time, in different persons, or in different governments. An absolute must be an exclusive title, or at least a title which excludes all others not compatible with it. All our institutions recognise the absolute title of the crown, subject only to the Indian right of occupancy, and recognise the absolute title of the crown to extinguish that right. This is incompatible with an absolute and complete title in the Indians.

We will not enter into the controversy, whether agriculturists, merchants, and manufacturers, have a right, on abstract principles, to expel hunters from the territory they possess, or to contract their limits. Conquest gives a title which the Courts of the conqueror cannot deny, whatever the private and speculative opinions of individuals may be, respecting the original justice of the claim which has been successfully asserted. The British government, which was then our government, and whose rights have passed to the United States, asserted a title to all the lands occupied by Indians, within the chartered limits of the British colonies. It asserted also a limited sovereignty over them, and the exclusive right of extinguishing the title which occupancy gave to them. These claims have been maintained and established as far west as the river Mississippi, by the sword. The title to a vast portion of the lands we now hold, originates in them. It is not for the Courts of this country to question the validity of this title, or to sustain one which is incompatible with it.

Although we do not mean to engage in the defence of those principles which Europeans have applied to Indian title, they may, we think, find some excuse, if not justification, in the character and habits of the people whose rights have been wrested from them.

The title by conquest is acquired and maintained by force. The conqueror prescribes its limits. Humanity, however, acting on public opinion, has established, as a general rule, that the conquered shall not be wantonly oppressed, and that their condition shall remain as eligible as is compatible with the objects of the conquest. Most usually, they are incorporated with the victorious nation, and become subjects or citizens of the government with which they are connected. The new and old members of the society mingle with each other; the distinction between them is gradually lost, and they make one people. Where this incorporation is practicable, humanity demands, and a wise policy requires, that the rights of the conquered to property should remain unimpaired; that the new subjects should be governed as equitably as the old, and that confidence in their security should gradually banish the painful sense of being separated from their ancient connexions, and united by force to strangers.

When the conquest is complete, and the conquered inhabitants can be blended with the conquerors, or safely governed as a distinct people, public opinion, which not even the conqueror can disregard, imposes these restraints upon him; and he cannot neglect them without injury to his fame, and hazard to his power.

But the tribes of Indians inhabiting this country were fierce savages, whose occupation was war, and whose subsistence was drawn chiefly from the forest. To leave them in possession of their country, was to leave the country a wilderness; to govern them as a distinct people, was impossible, because they were as brave and as high spirited as they were fierce, and were ready to repel by arms every attempt on their independence.

What was the inevitable consequence of this state of things? The
Europeans were under the necessity either of abandoning the country,
and relinquishing their pompous claims to it, or of enforcing those
claims by the sword, and by the adoption of principles adapted to the
condition of a people with whom it was impossible to mix, and who could
not be governed as a distinct society, or of remaining in their neighbourhood, and exposing themselves and their families to the perpetual hazard of being massacred.

Frequent and bloody wars, in which the whites were not always the
aggressors, unavoidably ensued. European policy, numbers, and skill
prevailed. As the white population advanced, that of the Indians necessarily receded. The country in the immediate neighbourhood of agriculturists became unfit for them. The game fled into thicker and more
unbroken forests, and the Indians followed. The soil, to which the crown
originally claimed title, being no longer occupied by its ancient inhabitants, was parcelled out according to the will of the sovereign power,
and taken possession of by persons who claimed immediately from the
crown, or mediately, through its grantees or deputies.

That law which regulates, and ought to regulate in general, the relations between the conqueror and conquered, was incapable of application to a people under such circumstances. The resort to some new
and different rule, better adapted to the actual state of things, was un-
avoidable. Every rule which can be suggested will be found to be attended with great difficulty.

However extravagant the pretension of converting the discovery of
an inhabited country into conquest may appear; if the principle has been
asserted in the first instance, and afterwards sustained; if a country has
been acquired and held under it; if the property of the great mass of the
community originates in it, it becomes the law of the land, and cannot
be questioned. So, too, with respect to the concomitant principle, that
the Indian inhabitants are to be considered merely as occupants, to be
protected, indeed, while in peace, in the possession of their lands, but to
be deemed incapable of transferring the absolute title to others. However this restriction may be opposed to natural right, and to the usages
of civilized nations, yet, if it be indispensable to that system under which
the country has been settled, and be adapted to the actual condition of
the two people, it may, perhaps, be supported by reason, and certainly
cannot be rejected by Courts of justice. . . .

It has never been contended, that the Indian title amounted to
nothing. Their right of possession has never been questioned. The claim
of government extends to the complete ultimate title, charged with
this right of possession, and to the exclusive power of acquiring that
right. . . .

After bestowing on this subject a degree of attention which was
more required by the magnitude of the interest in litigation, and the able

and elaborate arguments of the bar, than by its intrinsic difficulty, the Court is decidedly of opinion, that the plaintiffs do not exhibit a title which can be sustained in the Courts of the United States; and that there is no error in the judgment which was rendered against them in the District Court of Illinois.

Judgment affirmed, with costs.

NOTES AND QUESTIONS

1. *A logical place to begin.* Our concern here is not the complexities of title to land once occupied exclusively by Native Americans.[1] We are interested, instead, in getting a study of property under way, and Johnson v. M'Intosh provides an apt point of departure for several reasons.

First, how better to start a course in the American law of property than with the foundations of landownership in the United States? Land, you will learn, plays an important part in property law, and not just because so much of that law aims to resolve — better yet, avoid — conflicts over real property (as land is called). Landownership also commonly determines the ownership and control of a host of other natural resources, such as wild animals, water and minerals, peace and quiet, clean air, and open space. Moreover, many of the general legal principles pertaining to real property also apply to personal property (that is, property in other than land). So landownership is important, and, as Johnson v. M'Intosh suggests, most landowners in the United States trace their ownership — their title — back to grants (or patents, as they are called in the case of conveyances of public land out of the government) from the United States. The United States, in turn, traces its title, by grant and otherwise, all the way back to the discovery of America by the white man.[2]

2. *Discovery . . . or conquest?* Discovery and conquest, both of which are mentioned in Chief Justice Marshall's[3] opinion in the *Johnson* case,

1. Students wishing to pursue these and other issues regarding the legal situation of Native Americans might well begin their inquiries with Felix Cohen's Handbook of Federal Indian Law (rev. ed. 1982). Cohen (1907-1953), a man of great heart and energy, made important contributions to a number of fields, including legal philosophy. He was the son of another leading philosopher, Morris Cohen (1880-1947), whose views on "Property and Sovereignty" will be considered shortly.

2. Mention of tracing introduces the idea of a *chain of title;* the links in the chain are the transactions (conveyances) by which a parcel of land moves from owner to owner over time. The significance and operation of chain of title are examined in Chapters 7 and 8 of this book.

3. John Marshall (1755-1835), the third Chief Justice of the United States (from 1801 to 1835), is one of the great figures in the constitutional history of the United States. Marshall had little formal education (and only six weeks of formal legal training!) but had a remarkable mind and character. He was prominent as a diplomat, as a legislator, and as Secretary of State before being nominated as Chief Justice by President John Adams. A strong defender of the Constitution, the architect of the doctrine of judicial review, "Mar-

are terms of art referring to methods of acquiring territory in international law. Acquisition by *discovery* essentially entails just what you would suppose: "the sighting or 'finding' of hitherto unknown or uncharted territory; it is frequently accompanied by a landing and the symbolic taking of possession," acts that give rise to an inchoate title that must (on one view) subsequently be perfected, within a reasonable time, by settling in and making an effective occupation. 10 Encyclopedia of Public International Law 504 (1987). *Conquest* is the taking of possession of enemy territory through force, followed by formal annexation of the defeated territory by the conqueror. See Parry & Grant Encyclopaedic Dictionary of International Law 72 (1986).

Neither of these two modes of territorial acquisition has much immediate relevance today. As to discovery, there are virtually no unknown territories on earth (what about a new volcanic island emerging in the high seas?), and territories beyond the earth are governed by special treaties and agreements placing the moon and other celestial bodies outside the reach of national appropriation. As to conquest, it has come to be proscribed by contemporary international law as a method of territorial acquisition.

In earlier times, though, discovery and conquest were of great importance, as Johnson v. M'Intosh suggests. In that case the two doctrines worked in concert. Discovery, Marshall wrote, "gave an exclusive right to extinguish the Indian title of occupancy, either by purchase or by conquest."[4] See page 8. The first "discoverer" had a preemptive right to deal with the Indians, as against subsequent "discoverers." But why did discovery play any role at all? In principle, only a *res nullius* or *terra nullius* (a thing or territory belonging to no one), a "hitherto unknown territory," can be discovered. See 10 Encyclopedia of Public International Law, supra, at 504. North America in the fifteenth century was not unknown to its indigenous occupants. Why didn't it *belong* to them?

The answer is discomfiting. During the so-called classical era of discovery (1450-1600), prior possession by aboriginal populations (which were sometimes called savage populations, or semi-civilized ones) was commonly thought not to matter. "In previous centuries European international lawyers were sometimes reluctant to admit that non-European societies could constitute states for the purposes of interna-

---

shall raised the office [of Chief Justice] and the Supreme Court to stature and power previously lacking." Under his leadership, the practice of individual opinions by individual justices largely ceased, dissents were discouraged, and the "Court came to speak with one voice. Usually the voice was Marshall's." The quotations are from Robert Faulkner's essay on Marshall in 3 Encyclopedia of the American Constitution 1205-1209 (1986). See also Biographical Dictionary of the Common Law 354-355 (A.W.B. Simpson ed. 1984).

4. Note that the modern indictment of acquisition by conquest is not "regarded as being retroactive to titles made by conquest in an earlier period." Robert Y. Jennings, The Acquisition of Territory in International Law 56 (1963).

John Marshall
Chief Justice of the United States, 1801-1835
by Chester Harding (1828)
Collection of the Boston Athenaeum

13

tional law, and territory inhabited by non-European peoples was sometimes regarded as *terra nullius*." Michael B. Akehurst, A Modern
Introduction to International Law 145 (6th ed. 1987). Marshall was al-
luding to this attitude when he said of North America that "the character
and religion of its inhabitants afforded an apology for considering them
as a people over whom the superior genius of Europe might claim an
ascendency."[5] See page 4.

More on this shortly, after we consider some additional reasons to
begin a study of property with Johnson v. M'Intosh.

3. *Occupancy theory and the principle of first in time.* The doctrine of
discovery at work in *Johnson* may be of little importance today, but exactly the opposite is true of the doctrine's foundation — the principle of
first in time.

"The notion that being there first somehow justifies ownership
rights is a venerable and persistent one." Lawrence C. Becker, Property
Rights: Philosophical Foundations 24 (1977). The theory of first occupancy, or first possession, dates back to Roman law and played a considerable part in the writings of Hugo Grotius and Samuel Pufendorf in
the seventeenth century (you will soon bump into these figures again;
see pages 21-22, 24). As Grotius saw it, the riches of the earth were initially held in common (nothing belonged to any one individual). But
because avarice eventually led to scarcity, the institution of private property became necessary to preserve peace. Private ownership was imagined to have developed according to agreements, explicit ones or those
implied by occupation; it was to be "supposed" that whatever each person had taken possession of should be that person's property. Eventually, systems of government were introduced (how?), and the original
rules of acquisition were modified. Still, though, the government had to
recognize the pre-established property rights of its citizens.

> [T]he institution of private property really protected men's natural
> equality of rights. "Now property ownership was introduced for the purpose
> of preserving equality to this end, in fact, that each should enjoy his own."
> But what is this "own" to which each man has an equal right? . . . In fact, the
> "own" which the laws of property protect is whatever an individual has man-
> aged to get hold of, and equality of right, applied to property, means only
> that every man has an equal right to grab. The institution of property was an
> agreement among men legalizing what each had already grabbed, without

5. The sarcasm and irony seen here and elsewhere in Marshall's opinion suggest his
embarrassment with what he had to write, and there is independent evidence that he was
sympathetic to the plight of Native Americans. In an 1828 letter to Justice Joseph Story,
for example, Marshall mentioned some reasons to be forgiving of the "conduct of our
forefathers in expelling the original occupants of the soil," but went on to state his view
that "every oppression now exercised on a helpless people depending on our magnanimity
and justice for the preservation of their existence impresses a deep stain on the American
character." Quoted in The Political and Economic Doctrines of John Marshall 124-125
(John E. Oster ed. 1914).

any right to do so, and granting, for the future, a formal right of ownership to the first grabber. As a result of this agreement, which, by a remarkable oversight, puts no limit on the amount of property any one person may occupy, everything would soon pass into private ownership, and the equal right to grab would cease to have any practical value. [Richard Schlatter, Private Property: The History of an Idea 130-131 (1951).][6]

Occupancy fares rather well as a positive (descriptive or explanatory) theory of the origins of property. Sir William Blackstone put it to that use in his famous Commentaries on the Laws of England, completed a few years before the American Revolution (see pages 24-26). See also Richard A. Epstein, Possession as the Root of Title, 13 Ga. L. Rev. 1221, 1222 (1979) (the common and civil law alike adopted the proposition that "taking possession of unowned things is the only possible way to acquire ownership of them"; the universal principle is "original possession"). And, as Becker observed above, the idea that being prior in time matters is not only "venerable" but "persistent." You will see it running throughout the materials in this book, particularly in the next section on Acquisition by Capture. For an overview of its active role in contemporary property law, see Lawrence Berger, An Analysis of the Doctrine that "First in Time Is First in Right," 64 Neb. L. Rev. 349 (1985).

Despite its persistence, however, the normative case for first possession — its force as a justification — is commonly thought to be rather weak. See Morris Cohen, Property and Sovereignty, 13 Cornell L.Q. 8, 15-16 (1927). But Cohen was not single-minded; he did find "a kernel of value" in the principle. Epstein provides a more spirited defense in his essay on Possession as the Root of Title, supra. See also Richard A. Epstein, Past and Future: The Temporal Dimension in the Law of Property, 64 Wash. U. L.Q. 667 (1986). Can you anticipate the arguments in these articles, constructing for yourself a list of the pros and cons of first in time?

4. *Labor theory and John Locke.* The famous philosopher John Locke (1632-1704) drew first occupancy into his labor theory of property, but in a way that was thought to give it greater moral weight. The problem is this: So what if someone possesses something first; why should anyone else be obliged to respect the claim of the first possessor? As suggested earlier, theorists like Pufendorf "could not see how that obligation could

6. We will be making brief reference to various philosophical perspectives on property from time to time. The literature on the general subject is vast, but the following short list might prove useful to interested students: Becker, supra; C.B. Macpherson, Property: Mainstream and Critical Positions (1978); Stephen R. Munzer, A Theory of Property (1990); Alan Ryan, Property (1987); Alan Ryan, Property and Political Theory (1984); Schlatter, supra; Jeremy Waldron, The Right to Private Property (1988); Theories of Property (Anthony Parel & Thomas Flanagan eds. 1979); and the essays collected in Property, 22 Nomos (1980).

exist unless mankind had agreed to assume it. Locke discovered that it was imposed by the law of nature, and bound all men fast long before mere human conventions had been thought of." Schlatter, supra, at 154. Here is a slightly modernized statement of the core of Locke's argument:

> Though the earth and all inferior creatures be common to all men, yet every man has a property in his own person. This nobody has any right to but himself. The labor of his body, and the work of his hands, we may say, are properly his. Whatsoever then he removes out of the state that nature has provided, and left it in, he has mixed his labor with, and joined to it something that is his own, and thereby makes it his property. It being by him removed from the common state nature placed it in, has by this labor something annexed to it, that excludes the common right of other men. For this labor being the unquestionable property of the laborer, no man but he can have a right to what that is once joined to, at least where there is enough, and as good left in common for others. [John Locke, Two Treatises of Government, Book II, Ch. V (c. 1690).]

Locke's labor theory appears in several versions, most of them deficient in one respect or another. Like what? See Cohen, supra, at 16-18; Epstein, Possession as the Root of Title, supra, at 1225-1230; Carol M. Rose, Possession as the Origin of Property, 52 U. Chi. L. Rev. 73-74 (1985). Still, though, labor theory has its appeal, and the law of property continues to feel its influence (just as with its forerunner, occupancy theory). We mention a few examples here as an aside and ask you to watch for others as your studies progress.

Consider, then, the law of *accession,* which comes into play when one person adds to the property of another: by labor alone, *A* chopping *B*'s trees and making flower boxes from them; by labor and the addition of new material, *C* using her own oils and *D*'s canvas to produce a valuable painting. In the case of *A,* courts generally award the final product to the owner of the raw material *(B), unless A*'s efforts have sufficiently increased their value (and *A* has not acted willfully). Just how much is "sufficient" is difficult to determine. A six-fold increase was insufficient in one case, a three-fold increase sufficient in another. The doctrine, in short, is a bit arbitrary in application.

In the case of *C,* the final product is generally awarded to the owner of the principal material, even if that happens to be one who willfully and wrongfully took the other's material and transformed it by adding her own. (Some courts hold that when attached material can be separated harmlessly from the principal material, the doctrine of accession does not apply.) Needless to say, in a case like that of the painting posed above, a determination of the "principal" material will hardly be easy, and arbitrary results can again be expected.

What are the rights of the owner if a court awards the final product to the accessioner, and what are the rights of the accessioner should the final product be awarded to the owner? In the first instance, the owner can generally recover damages equal to the value of her material before the transformation. The rule sounds simple but can be complicated in application by such issues as whether the accessioner acted willfully or negligently. In the second instance, the general rule is that the accessioner is denied any recovery for the value of her labor or material, but once again exceptions turning on the bona fides of the accessioner (as well as the owner) are common. See generally Ray A. Brown, The Law of Personal Property 49-62 (Walter B. Raushenbush 3d ed. 1975).

For another illustration, see Haslem v. Lockwood, 37 Conn. 500 (1871), where the plaintiff had raked into heaps manure that had accumulated in a public street, intending to carry it away the next day. Before he could do so, the defendant found the heaps of manure and hauled them off in his cart. In an action in trover for the value of the manure, the court held for the plaintiff. The manure belonged originally to the owners of the animals that dropped it, but had been abandoned. As abandoned property, it belonged to the first occupant, the plaintiff, who "had changed its original condition and greatly enhanced its value by his labor. . . ." 37 Conn. at 506. The defendant argued that the plaintiff had lost his rights when he left the heaps unattended overnight. The court asked, "if a party finds property comparatively worthless . . . and greatly increases its value by his labor and expense, does he lose his right if he leaves it a reasonable time to procure the means to take it away, when such means are necessary for its removal?" Answer: No. 37 Conn. at 507.

5. *John Locke and Johnson v. M'Intosh.* Return now to the *Johnson* case where we left it at the end of Note 2 above. Locke appears to have shared the common European view that the Native Americans had no substantial claim to the New World they had so long occupied. He

> reasoned that the Indians' occupancy of their aboriginal lands did not involve an adequate amount of "labor" to perfect a "property" interest in the soil. His argument helped frame and direct later liberal debates in colonial America on the natural rights of European agriculturists to dispossess tribal societies of their land base. [Robert A. Williams, Jr., The Medieval and Renaissance Origins of the Status of the American Indian in Western Legal Thought, 57 S. Cal. L. Rev. 1, 3 n.4 (1983).]

See generally Robert A. Williams, Jr., The American Indian in Western Legal Thought (1990).

The European settlers had the power to impose a point of view on the Indians, to privilege an ideology and then use the privilege to justify the power. They could regard Native American tribes, first in time though they were, as something less than legitimate claimants by righteous reference to their own ethnocentric conception of what amounted to actual possession. Possessors, in the white man's view, cultivated and improved their land, mixed their labor with it, but the Indians had done none of this. The rationalization was remarkably weak, but it was the only one at hand, and it was enough. See William Cronon, Changes in the Land 57 (1983); Rose, supra, at 85-87.

So the epigraph from Locke with which this section began: "Thus in the beginning all the world was *America*." America was a commons, up for grabs by the first "possessor."

6. *Property and power.* Property confers and rests upon power. It bestows on owners a form of sovereignty over others, because property means that the sovereign state stands behind the owners' assertions of right.[7] But as Morris Cohen observed:

---

7. See Gregory S. Alexander, Time and Property in the American Republican Legal Culture, 66 N.Y.U. L. Rev. 273, 277 (1991):

> [W]hile the liberal vision underlying individual property rights depicts the self as separated from politics, it is politics that defines the personal sphere — individual property rights depend on state power. Moreover, property is inescapably relational. When the state recognizes and enforces one person's property right, it simultaneously denies property rights in others. Thus the owner's security as to particular assets comes at the expense of others being vulnerable to the owner's control over those assets. Ownership is power over persons, not merely things.

These remarks suggest a perspective on property that has come to be associated with Critical Legal Studies (CLS), though some of the core Critical ideas date back 50 years and more to the Legal Realists (of whom Morris Cohen was one). Commonly called a movement, CLS is nevertheless extraordinarily heterogeneous in terms of the points of view represented by its affiliates. If there is a common denominator, it is leftist disenchantment with existing social and legal institutions, with "liberal legalism," and with the idea that law transcends politics and is or can be objective or politically neutral. Most Critics essentially regard as empty the distinction between the "public" realm of coercive sovereign authority vested in government and the "private" realm of individual autonomy and voluntary transactions. They reject the notion that legal principles can be neutral and argue that all legal principles are indeterminate, such that the choices of legal decisionmakers can never truly be based on them. Choices are mere exercises of power and ideology, justified in terms that invariably beg central questions.

An instructive introduction to some of the methodology underlying the Critical approach can be found in Jack Balkin, Deconstructive Practice and Legal Theory, 96 Yale L.J. 743 (1987). Balkin notes, id. at 744, that "deconstructive techniques can show how doctrinal arguments are informed by and disguise ideological thinking." Recall in this connection the discussion in Note 5 above. On Critical Legal Studies generally, see, e.g., Mark Kelman, A Guide to Critical Legal Studies (1987); Roberto Unger, The Critical Legal Studies Movement (1986); The Politics of Law (David Kairys ed. 1982); Critical Legal Studies Symposium, 36 Stan. L. Rev. i, 1 (1984). Professor Joseph W. Singer presents a critical perspective on the situation of Native Americans in Sovereignty and Property, 86 Nw. U. L. Rev. 1 (1991), and on property law more generally in The Reliance Interest in Property, 40 Stan. L. Rev. 611 (1988).

Consider also the viewpoint of Critical Race Theory, defined by one of its practitioners as "the work of progressive legal scholars of color who are attempting to develop a jurisprudence that accounts for the role of racism in American law and that works toward the elimination of racism as part of a larger goal of eliminating all forms of oppression." Mari J. Matsuda, Pragmatism Modified and the False Consciousness Problem, 63 S. Cal. L. Rev. 1763 n.3 (1990) (citing representative works, including Professor Williams's study on The American Indian in Western Legal Thought, supra).

the recognition of private property as a form of sovereignty is not itself an argument against it [for] some form of government we must always have. . . . While, however, government is a necessity, not all forms of it are of equal value. At any rate it is necessary to apply to the law of property all those considerations of social ethics and enlightened public policy which ought to be brought to the discussion of any just form of government. [Cohen, supra, at 14.]

In this respect, the ongoing history of relations between Native Americans and the U.S. government is heated and unhappy. On one view, the government treats Native Americans differently than other Americans, conferring "less protection on American Indian property than it does on non-Indian property." Singer, Sovereignty and Property, supra footnote 7, at 43. The pattern is said to constitute "a continuing conquest of American Indian nations," id. at 8, that perhaps can be righted only by granting complete independence to Native American tribes. See, e.g., Williams, The American Indian in Western Legal Thought, supra, at 326-327. But others argue that such an "absolutist position ignores the compelling role that settled expectations play in any non-anarchic society and the importance of ensuring some degree of certainty in whatever system a society adopts. That, in fact, was one of the main points of Chief Justice Marshall's opinion in *Johnson*." Kevin J. Worthen, Book Review, 104 Harv. L. Rev. 1372, 1382 (1991). "Conquest gives a title which the Courts of the conqueror cannot deny," Marshall said, citing expediency as his reason. "However extravagant the pretension of converting the discovery of an inhabited country into conquest may appear; . . . if a country has been acquired and held under it; if the property of the great mass of the community originates in it, it becomes the law of the land, and cannot be questioned." See pages 9-10.

Johnson, foremost a case about the survival of one nation as against others, was also a statement of the justifications that might be offered in defense of property and power. Does it suffice?

7. *Epilogue and prologue.* See Rose, supra, at 87-88:

But perhaps the deepest aspect of the common law text of possession lies in the attitude that this text strikes with respect to the relationship between human beings and nature. At least some Indians professed bewilderment at the concept of owning the land. Indeed they prided themselves on not marking the land but rather on moving lightly through it, living with the land and with its creatures as members of the same family rather than as strangers who visited only to conquer the objects of nature. The doctrine of first possession, quite to the contrary, reflects the attitude that human beings are outsiders to nature. It gives the earth and its creatures over to those who mark them so clearly as to transform them, so that no one else will mistake them for unsubdued nature.

We may admire nature and enjoy wildness, but those sentiments find
little resonance in the doctrine of first possession. Its texts are those of cultivation, manufacture, and development. We cannot have our fish both loose
and fast, as Melville might have said, and the common law of first possession
makes a choice. The common law gives preference to those who convince the
world that they have caught the fish and hold it fast. This may be a reward to
useful labor, but it is more precisely the articulation of a specific vocabulary
within a structure of symbols approved and understood by a commercial people. It is this commonly understood and shared set of symbols that gives significance and form to what might seem the quintessentially individualistic act:
the claim that one has, by "possession," separated for oneself property from
the great commons of unowned things.

B.   Acquisition by Capture

Pierson v. Post
Supreme Court of New York, 1805
3 Cai. R. 175, 2 Am. Dec. 264

This was an action of trespass on the case commenced in a justice's court,
by the present defendant against the now plaintiff.

The declaration stated that Post, being in possession of certain dogs
and hounds under his command, did, "upon a certain wild and uninhabited, unpossessed and waste land, called the beach, find and start one of
those noxious beasts called a fox," and whilst there hunting, chasing and
pursuing the same with his dogs and hounds, and when in view thereof,
Pierson, well knowing the fox was so hunted and pursued, did, in the
sight of Post, to prevent his catching the same, kill and carry it off. A
verdict having been rendered for the plaintiff below, the defendant
there sued out a *certiorari*, and now assigned for error, that the declaration and the matters therein contained were not sufficient in law to
maintain an action. . . .

TOMPKINS, J., delivered the opinion of the court. This cause comes
before us on a return to a *certiorari* directed to one of the justices of
Queens county.

The question submitted by the counsel in this cause for our determination is, whether Lodowick Post, by the pursuit with his hounds in
the manner alleged in his declaration, acquired such a right to, or property in, the fox, as will sustain an action against Pierson for killing and
taking him away?

The cause was argued with much ability by the counsel on both
sides, and presents for our decision a novel and nice question. It is admitted that a fox is an animal *ferae naturae*, and that property in such

animals is acquired by occupancy only. These admissions narrow the discussion to the simple question of what acts amount to occupancy, applied to acquiring right to wild animals?

If we have recourse to the ancient writers upon general principles of law, the judgment below is obviously erroneous. Justinian's Institutes, lib. 2, tit. 1, s.13, and Fleta, lib. 3, c.2, p.175, adopt the principle, that pursuit alone vests no property or right in the huntsman; and that even pursuit, accompanied with wounding, is equally ineffectual for that purpose, unless the animal be actually taken. The same principle is recognised by Bracton, lib. 2, c.1, p.8.

Puffendorf, lib. 4, c.6, s.2, and 10, defines occupancy of beasts *ferae naturae,* to be the actual corporal possession of them, and Bynkershoek is cited as coinciding in this definition. It is indeed with hesitation that Puffendorf affirms that a wild beast mortally wounded, or greatly maimed, cannot be fairly intercepted by another, whilst the pursuit of the person inflicting the wound continues. The foregoing authorities are decisive to show that mere pursuit gave Post no legal right to the fox, but that he became the property of Pierson, who intercepted and killed him.

It therefore only remains to inquire whether there are any contrary principles, or authorities, to be found in other books, which ought to induce a different decision. Most of the cases which have occurred in England, relating to property in wild animals, have either been discussed and decided upon the principles of their positive statute regulations, or have arisen between the huntsman and the owner of the land upon which beasts *ferae naturae* have been apprehended; the former claiming them by title of occupancy, and the latter *ratione soli.* Little satisfactory aid can, therefore, be derived from the English reporters.

Barbeyrac, in his notes on Puffendorf, does not accede to the definition of occupancy by the latter, but, on the contrary, affirms, that actual bodily seizure is not, in all cases, necessary to constitute possession of wild animals. He does not, however, *describe* the acts which, according to his ideas, will amount to an appropriation of such animals to private use, so as to exclude the claims of all other persons, by title of occupancy, to the same animals; and he is far from averring that pursuit alone is sufficient for that purpose. To a certain extent, and as far as Barbeyrac appears to me to go, his objections to Puffendorf's definition of occupancy are reasonable and correct. That is to say, that actual bodily seizure is not indispensable to acquire right to, or possession of, wild beasts; but that, on the contrary, the mortal wounding of such beasts, by one not abandoning his pursuit, may, with the utmost propriety, be deemed possession of him; since, thereby, the pursuer manifests an unequivocal intention of appropriating the animal to his individual use, has deprived him of his natural liberty, and brought him within his certain control. So also, encompassing and securing such animals with nets and toils, or otherwise intercepting them in such a manner as to deprive them of their natural liberty, and render escape impossible, may justly be deemed to give possession of them to those persons who, by their industry and labour, have used such means of apprehending them. Barbeyrac seems to have adopted, and had in view of his notes, the more accurate opinion of Grotius, with respect to occupancy. . . . The case now under consideration is one of mere pursuit, and presents no circumstances or acts which can bring it within the definition of occupancy by Puffendorf, or Grotius, or the ideas of Barbeyrac upon that subject.

The case cited from 11 Mod. 74-130, I think clearly distinguishable from the present; inasmuch as there the action was for maliciously hindering and disturbing the plaintiff in the exercise and enjoyment of a private franchise; and in the report of the same case, (3 Salk. 9) Holt, Ch. J., states, that the ducks were in the plaintiff's decoy pond, and so in his possession, from which it is obvious the court laid much stress in their opinion upon the plaintiff's possession of the ducks, *ratione soli.*

We are the more readily inclined to confine possession or occupancy of beasts *ferae naturae,* within the limits prescribed by the learned authors above cited, for the sake of certainty, and preserving peace and order in society. If the first seeing, starting, or pursuing such animals, without having so wounded, circumvented or ensnared them, so as to deprive them of their natural liberty, and subject them to the control of their pursuer, should afford the basis of actions against others for intercepting and killing them, it would prove a fertile source of quarrels and litigation.

However uncourteous or unkind the conduct of Pierson towards Post, in this instance, may have been, yet his act was productive of no injury or damage for which a legal remedy can be applied. We are of opinion the judgment below was erroneous, and ought to be reversed.

LIVINGSTON, J. My opinion differs from that of the court. Of six exceptions, taken to the proceedings below, all are abandoned except the third, which reduces the controversy to a single question.

Whether a person who, with his own hounds, starts and hunts a fox on waste and uninhabited ground, and is on the point of seizing his prey, acquires such an interest in the animal, as to have a right of action against another, who in view of the huntsman and his dogs in full pursuit, and with knowledge of the chase, shall kill and carry him away?

This is a knotty point, and should have been submitted to the arbitration of sportsmen, without poring over Justinian, Fleta, Bracton, Puffendorf, Locke, Barbeyrac, or Blackstone, all of whom have been cited; they would have had no difficulty in coming to a prompt and correct conclusion. In a court thus constituted, the skin and carcass of poor *reynard* would have been properly disposed of, and a precedent set, interfering with no usage or custom which the experience of ages has sanctioned, and which must be so well known to every votary of Diana. But the parties have referred the question to our judgment, and we must dispose of it as well as we can, from the partial lights we possess, leaving to a higher tribunal, the correction of any mistake which we may be so unfortunate as to make. By the pleadings it is admitted that a fox is a "wild and noxious beast." Both parties have regarded him, as the law of nations does a pirate, *"hostem humani generis,"* and although *"de mortuis nil nisi bonum,"* be a maxim of our profession, the memory of the deceased has not been spared. His depredations on farmers and on barn yards have not been forgotten; and to put him to death wherever found, is allowed to be meritorious, and of public benefit. Hence it follows, that our decision should have in view the greatest possible encouragement to the destruction of an animal, so cunning and ruthless in his career. But who would keep a pack of hounds; or what gentleman, at the sound of the horn, and at peep of day, would mount his steed, and for hours together, *"sub jove frigido,"* or a vertical sun, pursue the windings of this wily quadruped, if, just as night came on, and his stratagems and strength were nearly exhausted, a saucy intruder, who had not shared in the honours or labours of the chase, were permitted to come in at the death, and bear away in triumph the object of pursuit? Whatever Justinian may have thought of the matter, it must be recollected that his code was compiled many hundred years ago, and it would be very hard indeed, at the distance of so many centuries, not to have a right to establish a rule for ourselves. In his day, we read of no order of men who made it a business, in the language of the declaration in this cause, "with hounds and dogs to find, start, pursue, hunt, and chase," these animals, and that, too, without any other motive than the preservation of Roman poultry; if this diversion had been then in fashion, the lawyers who composed his institutes would have taken care not to pass it by, without suitable encouragement. If any thing, therefore, in the digests or pandects shall appear to militate against the defendant in error, who, on this occasion, was the foxhunter, we have only to say *tempora mutantur;* and if men themselves change with the times, why should not laws also undergo an alteration?

It may be expected, however, by the learned counsel, that more particular notice be taken of their authorities. I have examined them all, and feel great difficulty in determining, whether to acquire dominion over a thing, before in common, it be sufficient that we barely see it, or know where it is, or wish for it, or make a declaration of our will respecting it; or whether, in the case of wild beasts, setting a trap, or lying in wait, or starting, or pursuing, be enough; or if an actual wounding, or killing, or bodily tact and occupation be necessary. Writers on general law, who have favoured us with their speculations on these points, differ on them all; but, great as is the diversity of sentiment among them, some conclusion must be adopted on the question immediately before us.

After mature deliberation, I embrace that of Barbeyrac, as the most rational, and least liable to objection. If at liberty, we might imitate the courtesy of a certain emperor, who, to avoid giving offence to the advocates of any of these different doctrines, adopted a middle course, and by ingenious distinctions, rendered it difficult to say (as often happens after a fierce and angry contest) to whom the palm of victory belonged. He ordained, that if a beast be followed with *large dogs and hounds,* he shall belong to the hunter, not to the chance occupant; and in like manner, if he be killed or wounded with a lance or sword; but if chased with *beagles only,* then he passed to the captor, not to the first pursuer. If slain with a dart, a sling, or a bow, he fell to the hunter, if still in chase, and not to him who might afterwards find and seize him.

Now, as we are without any municipal regulations of our own, and the pursuit here, for aught that appears on the case, being with dogs and hounds of *imperial stature,* we are at liberty to adopt one of the provisions just cited, which comports also with the learned conclusion of Barbeyrac, that property in animals *ferae naturae* may be acquired without bodily touch or manucaption, provided the pursuer be within reach, or have a *reasonable* prospect (which certainly existed here) of taking, what he has *thus* discovered an intention of converting to his own use.

When we reflect also that the interest of our husbandmen, the most useful of men in any community, will be advanced by the destruction of a beast so pernicious and incorrigible, we cannot greatly err, in saying, that a pursuit like the present, through waste and unoccupied lands, and which must inevitably and speedily have terminated in corporal possession, or bodily *seisin,* confers such a right to the object of it, as to make any one a wrongdoer, who shall interfere and shoulder the spoil. The justice's judgment ought, therefore, in my opinion, to be affirmed.

Judgment of reversal.

NOTES AND QUESTIONS

1. The majority and dissenting opinions in Pierson v. Post are peppered with references to a number of obscure legal works and legal scholars. Justinian's Institutes is a Roman law treatise of the sixth century; Bracton was the author of a thirteenth century tome on English law; Fleta refers to a Latin textbook on English law written in 1290 or thereabouts, supposedly in Fleet prison and possibly by one of the corrupt judges Edward I put there. Barbeyrac, Bynkershoek, Grotius, and Pufendorf (sometimes spelled Puffendorf) were civil law scholars who wrote in the seventeenth and eighteenth centuries; the last two of them figured in our discussion of Johnson v. M'Intosh, as did John Locke, the English philosopher (1632-1704), and William Blackstone (1723-1780). See pages 14-18. Blackstone was the first professor of English law at an

Sir William Blackstone
attributed to Sir Joshua Reynolds
National Portrait Gallery, London

English university. His famous Commentaries on the Laws of England (1765-1769), the first accessible general statement of English law, was popular and influential in both England and the United States, despite being scorned by the likes of Jeremy Bentham (on whom see pages 56-57) for uncritical acceptance of previous writers and blind admiration of the past. After resigning a professorship at Oxford, Blackstone was appointed to the bench, where in a famous opinion in Perrin v. Blake he concisely formulated the conservative creed of property lawyers of his time: "The law of real property in this country, wherever its materials were gathered, is now formed into a fine artificial system, full of unseen connexions and nice dependencies; and he that breaks one link of the chain, endangers the dissolution of the whole." 1 Francis Hargrave, Tracts Relative to the Law of England 489, 498 (1787).

2. The discussion in Note 3 on page 14 introduced the principle of first in time and suggested the dominant role it plays in the law of property. Did the majority and dissenting justices in Pierson v. Post agree that first in time was the governing principle? Note that the majority held as it did "for the sake of certainty, and preserving peace and order in society." See page 22. How did its opinion (that mere chase is insufficient to confer the rights of first possession) advance those goals? The benefits of peace and order seem obvious enough. What are the advantages of certainty in a property system? Are there any disadvantages in promoting certainty? Consider in this regard the dissenting opinion of Justice Livingston, who wanted to promote the destruction of "pernicious beasts." He believed that his rule would do that more effectively than the rule of the majority opinion. Was he right?

3. Livingston was also of the view that the question in Pierson v. Post "should have been submitted to the arbitration of sportsmen."[8] See page 22. In that event, Post probably would have won, because "it appeared from the record that all hunters in the region regarded hot pursuit as giving rights to take an unimpeded first possession." Richard A. Epstein, Possession as the Root of Title, 13 Ga. L. Rev. 1221, 1231

8. Arbitration would no doubt have been cheaper but maybe not so satisfying to the real contestants (who seem to have been the fathers of the plaintiff and defendant). The following recollection of Pierson v. Post is quoted in James T. Adams, Memorials of Old Bridgehampton 166 (1916, 1962):

Jesse Pierson, son of Capt. David, . . . saw a fox run down an unused well near Peter's Pond, and killed and took the fox. Lodowick Post and a company with him were in pursuit and chasing the fox, and saw Jesse with it and claimed it as theirs, while Jesse persisted in his claim. Capt. Pierson said his son Jesse should have the fox and Capt. Post said the same of his son Lodowick and hence the law suit contested and appealed to the highest court in the State. . . . This became the leading case often cited. . . . To the public the decision was worth its cost. To the parties, who each expended over a thousand pounds, the fox cost very dear.

But this only went to show that "the love of law suits had not entirely disappeared, although, as by this time lawyers were employed, they were much more in the nature of luxuries." Id. at 165.

(1979). The local custom, in short, was contrary to the rule adopted by the majority. Should the majority have abided by the custom? Consider the following case.

Ghen v. Rich

United States District Court
District of Massachusetts, 1881
8 F. 159

NELSON, J. This is a libel to recover the value of a fin-back whale. The *plaintiff* libellant lives in Provincetown and the respondent in Wellfleet. The facts, as they appeared at the hearing, are as follows:

> In the early spring months the easterly part of Massachusetts bay is frequented by the species of whale known as the fin-back whale. Fishermen from Provincetown pursue them in open boats from the shore, and shoot them with bomb-lances fired from guns made expressly for the purpose. When killed they sink at once to the bottom, but in the course of from one to three days they rise and float on the surface. Some of them are picked up by vessels and towed into Provincetown. Some float ashore at high water and are left stranded on the beach as the tide recedes. Others float out to sea and are never recovered. The person who happens to find them on the beach usually sends word to Provincetown, and the owner comes to the spot and removes the blubber. The finder usually receives a small salvage for his services. Tryworks are established in Provincetown for trying out the oil. The business is of considerable extent, but, since it requires skill and experience, as well as some outlay of capital, and is attended with great exposure and hardship, few persons engage in it. The average yield of oil is about 20 barrels to a whale. It swims with great swiftness, and for that reason cannot be taken by the harpoon and line. Each boat's crew engaged in the business has its peculiar mark or device on its lances, and in this way it is known by whom a whale is killed.
>
> The usage on Cape Cod, for many years, has been that the person who *custom* kills a whale in the manner and under the circumstances described, owns it, and this right has never been disputed until this case. The libellant has been engaged in this business for ten years past. On the morning of April 9, 1880, in Massachusetts bay, near the end of Cape Cod, he shot and instantly killed with a bomb-lance the whale in question. It sunk immediately, and on the morning of the 12th was found stranded on the beach in Brewster, within the ebb and flow of the tide, by one Ellis, 17 miles from the spot where it was killed. Instead of sending word to Provincetown, as is customary, Ellis advertised the whale for sale at auction, and sold it to the respondent, who shipped off the blubber and tried out the oil. The libellant heard of the finding of the whale on the morning of the 15th, and immediately sent one of his boat's crew to the place and claimed it. Neither the respondent nor Ellis knew the whale had been killed by the libellant, but they knew or might have known, if

they had wished, that it had been shot and killed with a bomb-lance, by some person engaged in this species of business.

The libellant claims title to the whale under this usage. The respondent insists that this usage is invalid. It was decided by Judge Sprague, in Taber v. Jenny, 1 Sprague, 315, that when a whale has been killed, and is anchored and left with marks of appropriation, it is the property of the captors; and if it is afterwards found, still anchored, by another ship, there is no usage or principle of law by which the property of the original captors is diverted, even though the whale may have dragged from its anchorage. The learned judge says:

> When the whale had been killed and taken possession of by the boat of the Hillman, (the first taker,) it became the property of the owners of that ship, and all was done which was then practicable in order to secure it. They left it anchored, with unequivocal marks of appropriation.

In Bartlett v. Budd, 1 Low. 223, the facts were these: The first officer of the libellant's ship killed a whale in the Okhotsk sea, anchored it, attached a waif [9] to the body, and then left it and went ashore at some distance for the night. The next morning the boats of the respondent's ship found the whale adrift, the anchor not holding, the cable coiled round the body, and no waif or irons attached to it. Judge Lowell held that, as the libellants had killed and taken actual possession of the whale, the ownership vested in them. In his opinion the learned judge says:

> A whale, being *feræ naturæ,* does not become property until a firm possession has been established by the taker. But when such possession has become firm and complete, the right of property is clear, and has all the characteristics of property.

He doubted whether a usage set up but not proved by the respondents, that a whale found adrift in the ocean is the property of the finder, unless the first taker should appear and claim it before it is cut in, would be valid, and remarked that "there would be great difficulty in upholding a custom that should take the property of A. and give it to B., under so very short and uncertain a substitute for the statute of limitations, and one so open to fraud and deceit." Both the cases cited were decided without reference to usage, upon the ground that the property had been acquired by the first taker by actual possession and appropriation.

In Swift v. Gifford, 2 Low. 110, Judge Lowell decided that a custom among whalemen in the Arctic seas, that the iron holds the whale, was

---

9. Worry not! To a whaler a "waif" is not a homeless child but a pole with a little flag on top. — Eds.

reasonable and valid. In that case a boat's crew from the respondent's ship pursued and struck a whale in the Arctic ocean, and the harpoon and the line attached to it remained in the whale, but did not remain fast to the boat. A boat's crew from the libellant's ship continued the pursuit and captured the whale, and the master of the respondent's ship claimed it on the spot. It was held by the learned judge that the whale belonged to the respondents. It was said by Judge Sprague, in <u>Bourne v. Ashley</u>, an unprinted case referred to by Judge Lowell in Swift v. Gifford, that the usage for the first iron, whether attached to the boat or not, to hold the whale was fully established; and he added that, although local usages of a particular port ought not to be allowed to set aside the general maritime law, this objection did not apply to a custom which embraced an entire business, and had been concurred in for a long time by every one engaged in the trade.

In Swift v. Gifford, Judge Lowell also said:

> The rule of law invoked in this case is one of very limited application. The whale fishery is the only branch of industry of any importance in which it is likely to be much used, and if a usage is found to prevail generally in that business, it will not be open to the objection that it is likely to disturb the general understanding of mankind by the interposition of an arbitrary exception.

I see no reason why the usage proved in this case is not as reasonable as that sustained in the cases cited. Its application must necessarily be extremely limited, and can affect but a few persons. It has been recognized and acquiesced in for many years. It requires in the first taker the only act of appropriation that is possible in the nature of the case. <u>Unless it is sustained, this branch of industry must necessarily cease, for no person would engage in it if the fruits of his labor could be appropriated by any chance finder</u>. It gives reasonable salvage for securing or reporting the property. That the rule works well in practice is shown by the extent of the industry which has grown up under it, and the general acquiescence of a whole community interested to dispute it. It is by no means clear that without regard to usage the common law would not reach the same result. That seems to be the effect of the decisions in Taber v. Jenny and Bartlett v. Budd. If the fisherman does all that it is possible to do to make the animal his own, that would seem to be sufficient. Such a rule might well be applied in the interest of trade, there being no usage or custom to the contrary. Holmes, Com. Law, 217. But be that as it may, I hold the usage to be valid, and that the property in the whale was in the libellant.

The rule of damages is the market value of the oil obtained from the whale, less the cost of trying it out and preparing it for the market, with interest on the amount so ascertained from the date of conversion.

As the question is new and important, and the suit is contested on both sides, more for the purpose of having it settled than for the amount involved, I shall give no costs.

Decree for libellant for $71.05, without costs. split.

NOTES AND QUESTIONS

1. A libel is the admiralty law equivalent of a lawsuit, and the libellant (or libelant) is the equivalent of the plaintiff in an action at law. Was the custom or usage relied upon in Ghen v. Rich essential to the libellant's case, or would the rule in Pierson v. Post, page 20, have served as well?

2. Ghen v. Rich describes several whaling customs, and evidence of others can be found in a surprising array of sources, including Herman Melville's Moby-Dick Ch. 89 (1851),[10] Oliver Wendell Holmes's famous lectures on The Common Law 212 (1881), a number of court reports, and various journals and historical accounts. Much of the literature is considered in Professor Robert C. Ellickson's recent essay, A Hypothesis of Wealth-Maximizing Norms: Evidence from the Whaling Industry, 5 J. Law, Econ. & Org. 83 (1989), part of a larger study on relationships between formal law and informal norms. See Robert C. Ellickson, Order Without Law: How Neighbors Settle Disputes (1991).

Ellickson concludes that all the supposed and actual whaling norms boiled down to essentially three. One usage entailed the fast-fish/loose-fish understanding "that a claimant owned a whale, dead or alive, so long as the whale was fastened by line or otherwise to the claimant's boat or ship." Another usage, iron-holds-the-whale, "conferred an exclusive right to capture upon the whaler who had first affixed a harpoon or other whaling craft to the body of the whale. . . . [T]he iron did not have to be connected by a line or otherwise to the claimant," so long as the claimant remained in fresh pursuit. The third usage, illustrated in Ghen v. Rich, "called for the value of the carcass to be split between the first harpooner and the ultimate seizer." Ellickson, Wealth-Maximizing Norms, supra; at 89-93. Each usage, Ellickson argues, "was adapted to

---

10. Chapter 89 bears the title "Fast-Fish and Loose-Fish." "A Fast-Fish belongs to the party fast to it," Melville wrote. "A Loose-Fish is fair game for anybody who can soonest catch it." The issue in Ghen v. Rich was when a fish was to be considered fast and when loose.

Recall that Professor Rose alluded to all of this in the excerpt that concluded our discussion of Johnson v. M'Intosh and the "discovery" of America (see pages 19-20). In Moby-Dick one can find, in turn, Melville's own ironic allusion to the question of that discovery, again in Chapter 89: "What was America in 1492 but a Loose-Fish, in which Columbus struck the Spanish standard by way of waifing it for his royal master and mistress?" And "What is the great globe itself but a Loose-Fish? And what are you, reader, but a Loose-Fish and a Fast-Fish, too?"

its particular context" — to the disparate circumstances of various whales and waters — and all of them were developed and observed by whalers (and observed by courts, too) as informal or extralegal property rights regimes that maximized the whalers' aggregate wealth.

So should a usage of whalers have determined the outcome of Ghen v. Rich?[11] And to get back to where we began all of this (in Note 3 on pages 26-27), should the norms of hunters have decided Pierson v. Post? More generally, when and why should custom matter, and when and why not? See id. at 95-96 (risk of overwhaling); Richard A. Epstein, Possession as the Root of Title, 13 Ga. L. Rev. 1221, 1231-1236 (1979); Benjamin van Drimmelen, The International Mismanagement of Whaling, 10 UCLA Pac. Basin L.J. 240 (1991). Cf. Richard A. Posner, Economic Analysis of Law 168-169 (4th ed. 1992).

3. The conservation organization Greenpeace tries to frustrate the capture of whales by interposing its own boats between whalers and their prey. Suppose conservationists as a group can demonstrate that this is their shared custom and that they have adopted it because they figure that it maximizes the aggregate wealth of the world by preventing overwhaling. Should the custom count? The case that follows, though decided almost three centuries ago, bears directly on the question.

underlying policy has changed

Keeble v. Hickeringill

Queen's Bench, 1707
11 East 574, 103 Eng. Rep. 1127
11 Mod. 74, 130 (as Keble v. Hickringill)
3 Salk. 9 (as Keeble v. Hickeringhall)

Action upon the case. Plaintiff declares that he was, 8th November in the second year of the Queen, lawfully possessed of a close of land called Minott's Meadow, [containing] a decoy pond, to which divers wildfowl used to resort and come: and the plaintiff had at his own costs and charges prepared and procured divers decoy ducks, nets, machines and other engines for the decoying and taking of the wildfowl, and enjoyed the benefit in taking them: the defendant, knowing which, and intending to damnify the plaintiff in his vivary, and to fright and drive away the wildfowl used to resort thither, and deprive him of his profit, did, on the 8th of November, resort to the head of the said pond and vivary, and did discharge six guns laden with gunpowder, and with the noise

11. In Ghen v. Rich, Judge Nelson worried that unless he sustained the usage in question, "this branch of industry must necessarily cease, for no person would engage in it if the fruits of his labor could be appropriated by any chance finder." See page 29. Recall that when Justice Livingston expressed the same concern (but with respect to foxes) in his dissenting opinion in Pierson v. Post, we questioned his reasoning. See pages 23, 26. Should we question Judge Nelson's? And by the way, do you agree with Nelson's statement (on page 29) that whaling customs "can affect but a few persons"?

**Rendering of a duck decoy of the sort involved
in Keeble v. Hickeringill**

The drawing of the decoy is taken from Tony Cook and R.E.M. Pilcher, The History of Borough Fen Decoy (1982), which explains the operations of the decoys. By one method (pictured), ducks that had molted and thus could not fly were driven into the conoidal nets and captured. By another method, a specially trained decoy dog (traditionally named "Piper") would appear at the front of a net, and this would attract the ducks, which are both curious and aggressive, to come closer. The dog would then move into the net and the ducks would usually follow. If they did not, still another method was used: The decoys were designed such that the dog could suddenly disappear, then reappear ("show") further along in the net. This excited the ducks and provoked them to pursue the dog. Eventually, the decoyman would step in behind the ducks and drive them to their end.

The use of duck decoys in the English fens, which dates back at least to the thirteenth century, died out in the mid-1900s. The decoy at Minnot's Meadow silted up long ago, but our colleague Brian Simpson recently visited the area and he reports that the site of the decoy can still be identified, though not with absolute precision. The site of another decoy, at Pond Hall, can also be made out. The Pond Hall Decoy was owned by Hickeringill. Simpson gathers from his research that the Minnot's Meadow Decoy was contructed after Hickeringill's decoy at Pond Hall, and unusually close to it. This might have provoked Hickeringill, "a very eccentric parson," to retaliate as he did. Hickeringill, after all, had been first in time.

and stink of the gunpowder did drive away the wildfowl then being in the pond: and on the 11th and 12th days of November the defendant, with design to damnify the plaintiff, and fright away the wildfowl, did place himself with a gun near the vivary, and there did discharge the said gun several times that was then charged with the gunpowder against the said decoy pond, whereby the wildfowl were frighted away, and did forsake the said pond. Upon not guilty pleaded, a verdict was found for the plaintiff and 20*l.* damages.

HOLT, C.J.[12] I am of opinion that this action doth lie. It seems to be new in its instance, but is not new in the reason or principle of it. For, 1st, this using or making a decoy is lawful. 2dly, this employment of his ground to that use is profitable to the plaintiff, as is the skill and management of that employment. As to the first, every man that hath a property may employ it for his pleasure and profit, as for alluring and procuring decoy ducks to come to his pond. To learn the trade of seducing other ducks to come there in order to be taken is not prohibited either by the law of the land or the moral law; but it is as lawful to use art to seduce them, to catch them, and destroy them for the use of mankind, as to kill and destroy wildfowl or tame cattle. Then when a man useth his art or his skill to take them, to sell and dispose of for his profit; this is his trade; and he that hinders another in his trade or livelihood is liable to an action for so hindering him. . . .

[W]here a violent or malicious act is done to a man's occupation, profession, or way of getting a livelihood, there an action lies in all cases. But if a man doth him damage by using the same employment; as if Mr. Hickeringill had set up another decoy on his own ground near the plaintiff's, and that had spoiled the custom of the plaintiff, no action would lie, because he had as much liberty to make and use a decoy as the plaintiff. This is like the case of 11 H. 4, 47.[13] One schoolmaster sets up a new school to the damage of an antient school, and thereby the scholars are allured from the old school to come to his new. (The action was held there not to lie.) But suppose Mr. Hickeringill should lie in the way with his guns, and fright the boys from going to school, and their parents

12. Chief Justice Holt was one of the greatest English judges. After the flight of James II to France, abandoning the throne, Holt, as a member of the House of Commons, played a leading role in establishing a constitutional monarchy under William and Mary, a system that survives today. Subsequently he was appointed Chief Justice, which office he held from 1689 to 1710. He was noted for his integrity and independence and for his common sense as well as his deep learning in the law. Holt laid down the rule that the status of slavery could not exist in England; as soon as a slave breathed the air of England he was free. Smith v. Brown & Cooper, 2 Salk. 666, 90 Eng. Rep. 1172 (1703). Chief Justice Holt was the first of a line of enlightened judges who, in the eighteenth century, shaped English law to accommodate the needs of a mercantile society that would dominate world trading. Lord Mansfield, who served as Chief Justice from 1756 to 1788, was perhaps the most notable of these. — EDS.

13. The citation indicates a case decided in the 11th year of the reign of Henry IV (1410). A variant is Y.B. 11 H.IV, 47. Y.B. refers to one of the Year Books, a collection (running from 1283 to 1535) of anonymous notes reporting cases. — EDS.

would not let them go thither; sure that schoolmaster might have an action for the loss of his scholars. 29 E. 3, 18. A man hath a market, to which he hath toll for horses sold: a man is bringing his horse to market to sell: a stranger hinders and obstructs him from going thither to the market: an action lies, because it imports damage. . . .

And when we do know that of long time in the kingdom these artificial contrivances of decoy ponds and decoy ducks have been used for enticing into those ponds wildfowl, in order to be taken for the profit of the owner of the pond, who is at the expence of servants, engines, and other management, whereby the markets of the nation may be furnished; there is great reason to give encouragement thereunto; that the people who are so instrumental by their skill and industry so to furnish the markets should reap the benefit and have their action. But, in short, that which is the true reason is that this action is not brought to recover damage for the loss of the fowl, but for the disturbance; as 2 Cro. 604, Dawney v. Dee. So is the usual and common way of declaring.

NOTES AND QUESTIONS

1. *Early English reports.* There were no official reports of judicial decisions in England prior to the nineteenth century; entrepreneurs gathered up information about cases in one way or another and published them on their own. Students of the matter consider some of these unofficial sources to be more reliable then others. We have not indicated all the reports of *Keeble.* That from East (reprinted in Volume 103 of the English Reports), which we have used, is thought to be particularly trustworthy, the reporter claiming that his account came directly from a copy of Chief Justice Holt's manuscript. Modern (Mod.) is not esteemed, nor is the third volume of Salkeld (Salk.). See generally John W. Wallace, The Reporters (4th ed. 1882).

2. Keeble *and* Pierson. Go back to page 22 and you will see that the court in Pierson v. Post reckoned with *Keeble,* though it referred to it not by name but only by citation — the "case cited from 11 Mod. 74-130" and "the report of the same case, (3 Salk. 9)." The report in 3 Salk. suggested to the court that the result in *Keeble* was influenced by the fact that the ducks were in the plaintiff's decoy pond, such that the plaintiff had possession of the ducks *"ratione soli." Ratione soli* refers to the conventional view that an owner of land has possession — *constructive* possession, that is — of wild animals on the owner's land; in other words, landowners are regarded as the prior possessors of any animals *ferae naturae* on their land, until the animals take off.[14]

_____

14. The word *constructive,* a modifier familiar to all lawyers, will appear recurringly in this and other courses. One could say that the word is a way of pretending that whatever

We shall return to property *ratione soli* shortly. The point for now is that it appears to have had little, if any, bearing on the final decision in *Keeble*, the statement of the court in Pierson v. Post to the contrary notwithstanding. The *Keeble* case was argued several times, and there was indeed a stage at which Chief Justice Holt seemed to be of the view that the plaintiff had (constructive) possession of the ducks in question. The arguments of counsel led him to change his mind, however, and to rest the judgment on the theory spelled out in the opinion from East that you have read — the theory of malicious interference with trade.

But the East report was unavailable at the time of Pierson v. Post; it was not published until 1815, a decade after the decision in *Pierson* was handed down. Hence the court had to rely on the accounts in Modern and Salkeld, which, as we saw, are probably untrustworthy.

3. *Interference with capture.* Suppose East had been available. Would the outcome of *Pierson* have been different? Should it have been? Was it essential to the outcome in *Keeble* that the plaintiff was engaged in something like a trade, as opposed to mere sport? Suppose X is an avid hunter who tracks down a deer on a piece of open hunting land during the hunting season. The deer is at very close range and just as X is about to shoot it another hunter, Y, appears and does so. Who gets the deer? And was it essential to the outcome in *Keeble* that the ducks were frightened off, rather than captured by a competitor of the plaintiff? Suppose that Y is not a hunter but a zealous animal lover who at the last instant frightens the deer away. Does X have any recourse?[15]

The second of the two situations described above gets us back to the activities of Greenpeace and other conservation groups mentioned in Note 3 on page 31. An article in the N.Y. Times, Nov. 23, 1990, at A22, reports that interference with the capture or killing of wild animals has become such a problem that 37 states have enacted legislation outlawing hunter harassment on state-owned land, and a "bill introduced in Congress would make it a Federal crime to obstruct the hunter or scare the animals being hunted." A typical harassment campaign employs groups

---

word it modifies depicts a state of affairs that actually exists when actually it does not. The pretense is made whenever judges wish, usually for good but often undisclosed reasons, a slightly different reality than the one confronting them. One might call this reasoning by strict analogy: Situation *A* is magically transformed into Situation *B* by incantation of the word *constructive*. Then the rule governing Situation *B* is applied to Situation *A* because the two situations are, after all, identical! Why might judges wish to pretend that a landowner actually possesses the wild animals on his land when actually he does not? See Problem 1 on page 36.

15. An illuminating way to begin thinking about both of these questions is this: Try to imagine what instrumental ends — or objectives, or policies — the decisions in *Pierson* and *Keeble* might have aimed to serve. Consider the schoolmaster of the "antient school" discussed in *Keeble*. A subsequent schoolmaster *scares* away the first school's students. Cause of action. *Lures* away the first school's students. No cause of action. Why the difference in results, especially given that the "antient school" was in each instance first in time? See Harold Demsetz, Wealth Distribution and the Ownership of Rights, 1 J. Legal Stud. 223, 231-232 (1972).

policy for a competitive market

of "loud leaf-rustling animal rights protesters" who "stalk behind those wearing camouflage gear and carrying rifles." " 'We believe we have the same right to protect wildlife as they do to shoot wildlife,' " said the leader of one group. So far, most challenges to the antiharassment laws have succeeded on grounds of unconstitutional vagueness and violation of the First Amendment's protection of free speech.[16]

PROBLEMS: MORE ON THE RULE OF CAPTURE AND WILD ANIMALS

1. A trespasser who captures a wild animal on the land of another might still have no rights to the animal as against the landowner, even though the landowner never had actual physical possession or control and even though the trespasser does. The court might say that the landowner had "constructive" possession of the animal. See footnote 14 on pages 34-35. Why? See Ray A. Brown, The Law of Personal Property 17 (Walter B. Raushenbush 3d ed. 1975).

Suppose that *T*, a trespasser, captures a wild animal on the land of *O*, a landowner, and carries it off to her own land where she confines it in a cage. Subsequently, *T1* trespasses on *T*'s land and takes away the animal. In a suit by *T* against *T1* for return of the animal, *T1* defends on the ground that *T* had no rights of ownership in the animal. How would you respond, and why? Would your response be different if *O* had gone on to the land of *T* and taken the animal back, and *T* is now suing *O* for its return?

2. *F* has established a herd of deer that she keeps for pleasure and an occasional roast of venison. The deer roam about on open government grazing land during the day, but are sufficiently tame and domesticated that they return to a large shelter on *F*'s land in the evening. *H*, a hunter, shoots one of *F*'s deer one day during the hunting season. *F*

16. The harassment measures described in the N. Y. Times article, and even those of Greenpeace, are moderate compared to the "ecotage" of the radical environmental group Earth First! In an effort to protect the old-growth forests of Northern California and the Pacific Northwest, Earth First!ers have among other things blocked roads, vandalized logging equipment, sat in trees scheduled to be cut, and buried spikes in them (which resulted in injury to at least one worker when a chain saw shattered). Even staunch environmentalists regularly condemn these "terrorist tactics," arguing, for example, that humans, though part of Nature, "are the only species capable of self-imposed restraint to save the Earth. . . . By breaking the law in defense of the Earth and by undermining the moral superiority of humankind that is the foundation of law, radical environmentalists engage in the ultimate sabotage." Mark Van Putten, Earth First!: Environmentalists or Saboteurs?, Detroit News, Dec. 19, 1990, at A11 (reviewing Christopher Manes, Green Rage: Radical Environmentalism and the Unmaking of Civilization (1990)).

But radical environmentalists seem not to be alone in the lack-of-restraint department. James Watt, a former Secretary of the Department of the Interior, is reported to have told the diners at a cattle ranchers' banquet, "If the troubles from environmentalists cannot be solved in the jury box or at the ballot box, perhaps the cartridge box should be used." The Animals' Agenda, News Shorts, Jan./Feb. 1992, at 28.

sues *H* for return of the carcass. Who prevails? See Brown, supra, at 18. What policies might be served by holding for *F*? For *H*? [17]

3. *P* imports two silver gray foxes, a male and a female, from Canada for breeding purposes on her Mississippi ranch. The natural habitat of the animals is the north central United States and Canada. The foxes are wild and once having escaped any captivity have no inclination to return. For this reason, *P* keeps her pair securely confined in a floored pen with plank walls five feet high. Despite these measures, the male gnaws his way out. *P* sets traps to recapture him, but to no avail. Some time later the fox is killed by *D* in a pine thicket 15 miles from *P*'s ranch. *D* skins the fox and preserves the hide. *P*, learning of this, sues for return of the hide. Who should prevail, and why? See Brown, supra, at 18.

4. *F*, a farmer, is bothered by wild migrating geese on her land and shoots them in violation of the fish and game laws. The government confiscates the carcasses, and *F* sues for their return. The government wins, the court explaining that the government owns wild animals, may regulate their taking, and may confiscate animals taken in violation of regulations. See State ex rel. Visser v. State Fish & Game Commn., 150 Mont. 525, 437 P.2d 373 (1968). So when the geese return the next year, *F* sues the government for damage to her cornfield caused by the geese the government has been said to own. The government wins again, the court holding that the government does not own wild fowl and is not liable for damage caused by them. See Sickman v. United States, 184 F.2d 616 (7th Cir. 1950), cert. denied, 341 U.S. 939, reh'g denied, 342 U.S. 874 (1951). Can you square these two holdings? See Douglas v. Seacoast Prods., Inc., 431 U.S. 265, 284 (1977). [18]

NOTES, QUESTIONS, AND PROBLEMS: THE RULE OF CAPTURE AND OTHER "FUGITIVE" RESOURCES

[I]nquiries into the acquisition of title to wild animal . . . may seem purely academic; how often, after all, do we expect to get into disputes about

---

17. As an aside — but a revealing one — suppose that *F* has a neighbor who also keeps a herd of deer. A doe belonging to *F* roams onto the neighbor's land, takes up with a buck in the neighbor's herd, is fed by the neighbor, and eventually bears a fawn sired, presumably, by the neighbor's buck. Who owns the fawn, and why? (Every legal culture seems to answer the question the same way.) See Carruth v. Easterling, 247 Miss. 364, 150 So. 2d 852 (1963), and the marvelous essay by Felix Cohen, Dialogue on Private Property, 9 Rutgers L. Rev. 357, 365-369 (1954).

18. Suppose the geese that damage *F*'s field had been attracted to the area by a pond that *N*, *F*'s neighbor, had built for the very purpose of luring the birds to earth. Does *F* have a cause of action against *N*? See Andrews v. Andrews, 242 N.C. 382, 88 S.E.2d 88 (1955). Or suppose that the geese just happen to gather on *N*'s land (there is no pond). When *N* drives the geese off, they move to *F*'s field and cause damage. Does *F* have a cause of action against *N*? See Glave v. Michigan Terminix Co., 159 Mich. App. 537, 407 N.W.2d 36 (1987).

the ownership of wild pigs . . . ? These cases are not entirely silly, though. . . . [A]nalogies to the capture of wild animals show up time and again when courts have to deal on a nonstatutory basis with some "fugitive" resource that is being reduced to property for the first time. . . . [Carol M. Rose, Possession as the Origin of Property, 52 U. Chi. L. Rev. 73, 75 (1985).]

1. *Oil and gas.* Oil and natural gas commonly collect in reservoirs that underlie many acres of land owned by many different people.[19] The resources have a fugitive character in that they wander from place to place. Oil or gas once under the land of *A* might migrate to space under the land of *B* as the result of natural circumstances or because *B* drops a well and mines a common pool beneath *A*'s and *B*'s land. The oil or gas mined by *B* may even have been placed in the pool by *A* (gas and oil extracted elsewhere are often reinjected for storage or secondary recovery).

When these obviously problematic situations first led to litigation — usually (but not always) a suit by someone like *A* to recover the value of gas or oil drawn away by someone like *B* — the courts were induced by the fugitive nature of the resources in question to liken them to wild animals. And because ownership of wild animals had long been settled in terms of the rule of capture, the courts reasoned that ownership of oil and gas should be determined in the same manner. The resources, one early case said,

may be classed by themselves, if the analogy be not too fanciful, as minerals *ferae naturae*. In common with animals, and unlike other minerals, they have the power and the tendency to escape without the volition of the owner. . . . They belong to the owner of the land, and are part of it, so long as they are on or in it, and are subject to his control; but when they escape, and go into other land, or come under another's control, the title of the former owner is gone. Possession of the land, therefore, is not necessarily possession of the gas. If an adjoining, or even a distant, owner, drills his own land, and taps your gas, so that it comes into his well and under his control, it is no longer

---

19. Or located in several countries, a point you should bear in mind when we come eventually to consider the implications of the rule of capture. See, e.g., Thomas C. Hayes, Confrontation in the Gulf: The Oilfield Lying Below the Iraq-Kuwait Dispute, N.Y. Times, Sept. 3, 1990, §1 at 7:

At the heart of Iraq's dispute with Kuwait over oil, money and boundaries lies a huge banana-shaped oil formation some 10,200 feet below the desert sands.

One of the world's largest oil reservoirs, the Rumaila field runs beneath the Iraq-Kuwait border, and the bulk of the 50-mile-long formation lies under Iraq. Yet much of the oil pumped from Rumaila in the last decade was taken by the Kuwaitis. Just as the pump at the edge of a lake can pull water from the entire lake, Kuwait's wells could eventually, in theory, bring up oil from the entire Rumaila pool.

As Iraq sees it, Kuwait has been stealing its oil. And the Rumaila field is a rich prize, estimated by some American oil experts to still contain more than 30 billion barrels, or three times the original size of the Prudhoe Bay formation in Alaska.

yours, but his. [Westmoreland & Cambria Natl. Gas Co. v. DeWitt, 130 Pa. 235, 249-250, 18 A. 724, 725 (1889).][20]

Go back to the examples involving *A* and *B* above and consider the following:

(a) Does *A* have any remedy at all if *B* starts draining the pool? See Barnard v. Monongahela Natural Gas Co., 216 Pa. 362, 65 A. 801 (1907) (*A* can go and do likewise). Compare Union Gas & Oil Co. v. Fyffe, 219 Ky. 640, 294 S.W. 176 (1927) (suggesting that *A* might be able to get an injunction against excessive drilling or nonratable extraction). Which of these approaches is better, and why?

(b) Suppose *B*'s well starts on her land but angles down such that it "bottoms" underneath land owned by *A*. Does the rule of capture still apply? See 1 Howard R. Williams & Charles J. Meyers, Oil and Gas Law 55-59 (1986); John D. McKinnis, Directional Drilling, Subsurface Trespass, and Conversion, 4 J. Min. L. & Policy 235 (1988-1989).

(c) Suppose that *A* has reinjected gas (it could as well be oil) that moves under *B*'s land. *B* sues to recover damages for the use and occupation of her land by *A*'s gas. What result? See Hammonds v. Central Kentucky Natural Gas Co., 255 Ky. 685, 75 S.W.2d 204 (1934).

Unsurprisingly, perhaps, the court in the *Hammonds* case just cited held that *A* was not liable because, under the rule of capture, the gas was no longer hers. Because fugitive resources are to be treated like "wild animals," when they "escape" or are "restored to their natural wild and free state, the dominion and individual proprietorship of any person over them is at an end and they resume their status as common property." 255 Ky. at 689-690, 75 S.W.2d at 206. (Compare the situation discussed in connection with the *Glave* case in footnote 18, page 37.)

Hammonds has been criticized and rejected by a number of jurisdictions on the grounds that the analogy to wild animals is silly, that reinjected gas or oil has not really "escaped," and that in any event it is not "returned to its natural habitat" by reinjection. The Supreme Court of Kentucky has itself just recently agreed and overruled *Hammonds*. See Texas American Energy Corp. v. Citizens Fidelity Bank & Trust Co., 736 S.W.2d 25 (Ky. 1987). We presume it is also the case today that reinjection does not ordinarily give rise to liability for the use and occupation of parts of a reservoir underlying the land of neighbors, even though ownership of the reinjected minerals remains intact. See, e.g., Railroad Commn. of Texas v. Manziel, 361 S.W.2d 560 (Tex. 1962).

There is a reason independent of strained analogies to discard the rule in *Hammonds*: It denied society at large the benefits of economical

---

20. Just as minerals such as oil can roam like wild animals, so wild animals such as oysters can stay put like iron ore. Who owns *them*? See McKee v. Gratz, 260 U.S. 127 (1922).

underground storage. (Do you see why?) There are also reasons —
again independent of strained analogies — to discard the rule of capture
altogether, yet it still applies to so-called native, or pre-severed, gas and
oil. Should it? For that matter, should the rule of capture even be applied to wild animals themselves? We shall consider all of this a little
later, in the course of examining some consequences of the rule and
some means of mitigating them. See pages 54-55.

2. *Water.* The rule of capture has played a formative role in the case
of another migratory resource — water. *Groundwater* (water found in
underground aquifers), for example, was governed early on by the English rule of absolute ownership, which allowed each landowner over an
aquifer to withdraw freely without regard to effects on neighbors.[21]
"[F]ramed in property language, the rule was in reality a rule of capture,
for a landowner's pump could induce water under the land of his neighbor to flow to his well — water that was in theory the neighbor's property
while it remained in place." Restatement (Second) of Torts ch. 41, commentary at 256 (1977). Whoever first captured the water, then, was
really its owner. The so-called English rule was adopted by a number of
states, but virtually all others followed the American rule of reasonable
use, itself a rule of capture but with the slight addition that wasteful uses
of water, if they actually harmed neighbors, were considered unreasonable and hence unlawful. As with the English rule, there was no principle of apportionment among overlying users. Today groundwater
extraction is commonly governed by legislative and administrative programs.

In the Western states, *surface waters* are allocated according to an
explicit rule of first in time, called prior appropriation. The basic principle is that the person who first appropriates (captures) water and puts
it to reasonable and beneficial use has a right superior to later appro-
priators. (Obviously, complications can arise. Suppose that *A* begins efforts to appropriate water from a stream — starts building diversion
works — before *B,* but that *B* finishes her works and puts the water to
beneficial use before *A.* Who is prior to whom? What would Pierson v.
Post say?) Prior appropriation doctrine developed as a direct conse-

21. What sorts of effects? In Friendswood Dev. Co. v. Smith-Southwest Indus., Inc.,
576 S.W.2d 21 (Tex. 1978), defendant pumped large amounts of groundwater from a
common aquifer, causing severe subsidence of neighboring lands. The neighbors sued for
damages, showing that the defendant knew subsidence would occur but nevertheless
drilled excessive wells and operated them in a negligent manner. Judgment for the defendant. The court followed the English rule: To the extent one is not liable for withdrawing
the water to begin with, he is not liable for any subsidence that follows. Stare decisis, the
court said; Texas had long before adopted the English rule and the court felt constrained
to follow it — while acknowledging that it was harsh and outmoded — because it had become a rule of property in the state, relied upon by thousands of citizens. As to future
subsidence caused by drilling subsequent to its decision, however, the court said it would
apply the law of negligence. See generally the Note on Lateral and Subjacent Support on
page 962.

quence of the scarcity of water in the arid West. Eastern states, where water is abundant, use one or another variant of riparian rights, the thrust of which is that each owner of land along a water source (riparian land) has a right to use the water, subject to the rights of other riparians. At first glance, riparian rights have no relation to a rule of capture, or first in time, but consider the argument in Richard A. Epstein, Possession as the Root of Title, 13 Ga. L. Rev. 1221, 1234 (1979):

> The riparian's ownership claims rest securely upon the ownership of lands at the edge of the river, which in turn can be originally acquired only by first possession. The rules of first possession are therefore extended by a kind of imputation rule (such as that applicable for the minerals under the earth) which says whoever takes first possession of the shore has an undivided interest in the water flowing in the watercourse. The principle is then modified to take into account the further point that many persons are riparians, such that a full specification of rights requires that limitations on use be created in order to respect the correlative rights of others.

The extraordinarily low ratio of streams to land in the West made riparian law a poor means by which to allocate water there; hence prior appropriation. Neither system is perfect. Riparian rights, for example, take little or no account of the relative productivity of the land the water services, encourage the development of uneconomical "bowling-alley" parcels of land perpendicular to the banks of a stream, and ration poorly when stream levels are low. Prior appropriation encourages premature development and excessive diversion. It also rations poorly when supplies dwindle periodically. See generally Mason Gaffney, Economic Aspects of Water Resource Policy, 28 Am. J. Econ. & Soc. 131, 137-141 (1969).

   3. *Analogies and their consequences.* The rule of capture follows directly from the powerful principle of first in time and finds support in Locke's theory of labor. See Notes 3 and 4, pages 14-16. It was applied early on to wild animals and then later, by analogy, to other fugitive resources of the sorts we have considered. Reasoning by analogy from the familiar to the new is a common human tendency and a handy problem-solving technique; it is also standard practice among lawyers and judges faced with cases of first impression. See generally Edward H. Levi, An Introduction to Legal Reasoning (1948). Rather than undertaking a general inquiry into the matter, we want to focus on the particular analogy drawn in the materials we have been discussing. What might be the consequences of applying the rule of capture to wild animals — and then to oil, gas, water, and other natural resources? What might those consequences have to do with the concept of "common property" mentioned in the quotation from *Hammonds* on page 39? The following reading addresses these fundamentally important questions.

Harold Demsetz, Toward a Theory of Property Rights

57 Am. Econ. Rev. 347-357 (Pap. & Proc. 1967)

The Concept and Role of Property Rights

In the world of Robinson Crusoe property rights play no role. Property rights are an instrument of society and derive their significance from the fact that they help a man form those expectations which he can reasonably hold in his dealings with others. These expectations find expression in the laws, customs, and mores of a society. An owner of property rights possesses the consent of fellowmen to allow him to act in particular ways. An owner expects the community to prevent others from interfering with his actions, provided that these actions are not prohibited in the specifications of his rights.

It is important to note that property rights convey the right to benefit or harm oneself or others. Harming a competitor by producing superior products may be permitted, while shooting him may not. A man may be permitted to benefit himself by shooting an intruder but be prohibited from selling below a price floor. It is clear, then, that property rights specify how persons may be benefited and harmed, and, therefore, who must pay whom to modify the actions taken by persons. The recognition of this leads easily to the close relationship between property rights and externalities.

Externality is an ambiguous concept.[22] For the purposes of this paper, the concept includes external costs, external benefits, and pecuniary as well as nonpecuniary externalities. No harmful or beneficial effect is external to the world. Some person or persons always suffer or enjoy these effects. What converts a harmful or beneficial effect into an externality is that the cost of bringing the effect to bear on the decisions of one or more of the interacting persons is too high to make it worthwhile, and this is what the term shall mean here. "Internalizing" such effects refers to a process, usually a change in property rights, that enables these effects to bear (in greater degree) on all interacting persons.

A primary function of property rights is that of guiding incentives to achieve a greater internalization of externalities. Every cost and benefit associated with social interdependencies is a potential externality. One condition is necessary to make costs and benefits externalities. The cost of a transaction in the rights between the parties (internalization) must exceed the gains from internalization. In general, transacting costs can be large relative to gains because of "natural" difficulties in trading

22. If you find this paragraph and the three that follow it difficult, skip ahead to the Note on "Externalities" on page 49, then return to the Demsetz essay. — Eds.

or they can be large because of legal reasons. In a lawful society the prohibition of voluntary negotiations makes the cost of transacting infinite. Some costs and benefits are not taken into account by users of resources whenever externalities exist, but allowing transactions increases the degree to which internalization takes place. . . .

The Emergence of Property Rights

If the main allocative function of property rights is the internalization of beneficial and harmful effects, then the emergence of property rights can be understood best by their association with the emergence of new or different beneficial and harmful effects.

Changes in knowledge result in changes in production functions, market values, and aspirations. New techniques, new ways of doing the same things, and doing new things — all invoke harmful and beneficial effects to which society has not been accustomed. It is my thesis in this part of the paper that the emergence of new property rights takes place in response to the desires of the interacting persons for adjustment to new benefit-cost possibilities.

The thesis can be restated in a slightly different fashion: property rights develop to internalize externalities when the gains of internalization become larger than the cost of internalization. Increased internalization, in the main, results from changes in economic values, changes which stem from the development of new technology and the opening of new markets, changes to which old property rights are poorly attuned. A proper interpretation of this assertion requires that account be taken of a community's preferences for private ownership. Some communities will have less-developed private ownership systems and more highly developed state ownership systems. But, given a community's tastes in this regard, the emergence of new private or state-owned property rights will be in response to changes in technology and relative prices.

I do not mean to assert or to deny that the adjustments in property rights which take place need be the result of a conscious endeavor to cope with new externality problems. These adjustments have arisen in Western societies largely as a result of gradual changes in social mores and in common law precedents. At each step of this adjustment process, it is unlikely that externalities per se were consciously related to the issue being resolved. These legal and moral experiments may be hit-and-miss procedures to some extent but in a society that weights the achievement of efficiency heavily, their viability in the long run will depend on how well they modify behavior to accommodate to the externalities associated with important changes in technology or market values.

A rigorous test of this assertion will require extensive and detailed empirical work. . . . In this part of the discussion, I shall present one group of such examples in some detail. They deal with the development of private property rights in land among American Indians. . . .

The question of private ownership of land among aboriginals has held a fascination for anthropologists. It has been one of the intellectual battlegrounds in the attempt to assess the "true nature" of man unconstrained by the "artificialities" of civilization. In the process of carrying on this debate, information has been uncovered that bears directly on the thesis with which we are now concerned. What appears to be accepted as a classic treatment and a high point of this debate is Eleanor Leacock's memoir on The Montagnes "Hunting Territory" and the Fur Trade. Leacock's research followed that of Frank G. Speck who had discovered that the Indians of the Labrador Peninsula had a long-established tradition of property in land. This finding was at odds with what was known about the Indians of the American Southwest and it prompted Leacock's study of the Montagnes who inhabited large regions around Quebec.

Leacock clearly established the fact that a close relationship existed, both historically and geographically, between the development of private rights in land and the development of the commercial fur trade. The factual basis of the correlation has gone unchallenged. However, to my knowledge, no theory relating privacy of land to the fur trade has yet been articulated. The factual material uncovered by Speck and Leacock fits the thesis of this paper well, and in doing so, it reveals clearly the role played by property right adjustments in taking account of what economists have often cited as an example of an externality — the overhunting of game.

Because of the lack of control over hunting by others, it is in no person's interest to invest in increasing or maintaining the stock of game. Overly intensive hunting takes place. Thus a successful hunt is viewed as imposing external costs on subsequent hunters — costs that are not taken into account fully in the determination of the extent of hunting and of animal husbandry.

Before the fur trade became established, hunting was carried on primarily for purposes of food and the relatively few furs that were required for the hunter's family. The externality was clearly present. Hunting could be practiced freely and was carried on without assessing its impact on other hunters. But these external effects were of such small significance that it did not pay for anyone to take them into account. There did not exist anything resembling private ownership in land. . . .

We may safely surmise that the advent of the fur trade had two immediate consequences. First, the value of furs to the Indians was increased considerably. Second, and as a result, the scale of hunting activity rose sharply. Both consequences must have increased considerably the importance of the externalities associated with free hunting. The property right system began to change, and it changed specifically in the direction required to take account of the economic effects made important by the fur trade. The geographical or distributional evidence collected by Leacock indicates an unmistakable correlation between early centers of fur trade and the oldest and most complete development of the private hunting territory. . . . An anonymous account written in 1723 states that the "principle of the Indians is to mark off the hunting ground selected by them by blazing the trees with their crest so that they may never encroach on each other. . . . By the middle of the century these allotted territories were relatively stabilized."

The principle that associates property right changes with the emergence of new and reevaluation of old harmful and beneficial effects suggests in this instance that the fur trade made it economic to encourage the husbanding of fur-bearing animals. Husbanding requires the ability to prevent poaching and this, in turn, suggests that socioeconomic changes in property in hunting land will take place. The chain of reasoning is consistent with the evidence cited above. Is it inconsistent with the absence of similar rights in property among the southwestern Indians?

Two factors suggest that the thesis is consistent with the absence of similar rights among the Indians of the southwestern plains. The first of these is that there were no plains animals of commercial importance comparable to the fur-bearing animals of the forest, at least not until cattle arrived with Europeans. The second factor is that animals of the plains are primarily grazing species whose habit is to wander over wide tracts of land. The value of establishing boundaries to private hunting territories is thus reduced by the relatively high cost of preventing the animals from moving to adjacent parcels. Hence both the value and cost of establishing private hunting lands in the Southwest are such that we would expect little development along these lines. The externality was just not worth taking into account.

The lands of the Labrador Peninsula shelter forest animals whose habits are considerably different from those of the plains. Forest animals confine their territories to relatively small areas, so that the cost of internalizing the effects of husbanding these animals is considerably reduced. This reduced cost, together with the higher commercial value of fur-bearing forest animals, made it productive to establish private hunting lands. Frank G. Speck finds that family proprietorship among the Indians of the Peninsula included retaliation against trespass. Animal resources were husbanded. Sometimes conservation practices were carried on extensively. Family hunting territories were divided into quarters. Each year the family hunted in a different quarter in rotation, leaving a tract in the center as a sort of bank, not to be hunted over unless forced to do so by a shortage in the regular tract. . . .

The Coalescence and Ownership of Property Rights

I have argued that property rights arise when it becomes economic for those affected by externalities to internalize benefits and costs. But I have not yet examined the forces which will govern the particular form of right ownership. Several idealized forms of ownership must be distinguished at the outset. These are communal ownership, private ownership, and state ownership.

By communal ownership, I shall mean a right which can be exercised by all members of the community. Frequently the rights to till and to hunt the land have been communally owned. The right to walk a city sidewalk is communally owned. Communal ownership means that the community denies to the state or to individual citizens the right to interfere with any person's exercise of communally owned rights. Private ownership implies that the community recognizes the right of the owner to exclude others from exercising the owner's private rights. State ownership implies that the state may exclude anyone from the use of a right as long as the state follows accepted political procedures for determining who may not use state-owned property. I shall not examine in detail the alternative of state ownership. The object of the analysis which follows is to discern some broad principles governing the development of property rights in communities oriented to private property.

It will be best to begin by considering a particularly useful example that focuses our attention on the problem of land ownership. Suppose that land is communally owned. Every person has the right to hunt, till, or mine the land. This form of ownership fails to concentrate the cost associated with any person's exercise of his communal right on that person. If a person seeks to maximize the value of his communal rights, he will tend to overhunt and overwork the land because some of the costs of his doing so are borne by others. The stock of game and the richness of the soil will be diminished too quickly. It is conceivable that those who own these rights, i.e., every member of the community, can agree to curtail the rate at which they work the lands if negotiating and policing costs are zero. Each can agree to abridge his rights. It is obvious that the costs of reaching such an agreement will not be zero. What is not obvious is just how large these costs may be.

Negotiating costs will be large because it is difficult for many persons to reach a mutually satisfactory agreement, especially when each hold-out has the right to work the land as fast as he pleases. But, even if an agreement among all can be reached, we must yet take account of the costs of policing the agreement, and these may be large, also. After such an agreement is reached, no one will privately own the right to work the land; all can work the land but at an agreed upon shorter workweek. Negotiating costs are increased even further because it is not possible under this system to bring the full expected benefits and expected costs of future generations to bear on current users.

If a single person owns land, he will attempt to maximize its present value by taking into account alternative future time streams of benefits and costs and selecting that one which he believes will maximize the present value of his privately-owned land rights. We all know that this means that he will attempt to take into account the supply and demand conditions that he thinks will exist after his death. It is very difficult to see how the existing communal owners can reach an agreement that takes account of these costs.

In effect, an owner of a private right to use land acts as a broker whose wealth depends on how well he takes into account the competing claims of the present and the future. But with communal rights there is no broker, and the claims of the present generation will be given an uneconomically large weight in determining the intensity with which the land is worked. Future generations might desire to pay present generations enough to change the present intensity of land usage. But they have no living agent to place their claims on the market. Under a communal property system, should a living person pay others to reduce the rate at which they work the land, he would not gain anything of value for his efforts. Communal property means that future generations must speak for themselves. No one has yet estimated the costs of carrying on such a conversation.

The land ownership example confronts us immediately with a great disadvantage of communal property. The effects of a person's activities on his neighbors and on subsequent generations will not be taken into account fully. Communal property results in great externalities. The full costs of the activities of an owner of a communal property right are not borne directly by him, nor can they be called to his attention easily by the willingness of others to pay him an appropriate sum. . . .

The state, the courts, or the leaders of the community could attempt to internalize the external costs resulting from communal property by allowing private parcels owned by small groups with similar interests. The logical groups in terms of similar interests, are, of course, the family and the individual. Continuing with our use of the land ownership example, let us initially distribute private titles to land randomly among existing individuals and, further, let the extent of land included in each title be randomly determined.

The resulting private ownership of land will internalize many of the external costs associated with communal ownership, for now an owner, by virtue of his power to exclude others, can generally count on realizing the rewards associated with husbanding the game and increasing the fertility of his land. This concentration of benefits and costs on owners creates incentives to utilize resources more efficiently.

But we have yet to contend with externalities. Under the communal property system the maximization of the value of communal property rights will take place without regard to many costs, because the owner of a communal right cannot exclude others from enjoying the fruits of his efforts and because negotiation costs are too high for all to agree jointly on optimal behavior. The development of private rights permits the owner to economize on the use of those resources from which he has the right to exclude others. Much internalization is accomplished in this way. But the owner of private rights to one parcel does not himself own the rights to the parcel of another private sector. Since he cannot exclude others from their private rights to land, he has no direct incentive (in the absence of negotiations) to economize in the use of his land in a way that takes into account the effects he produces on the land rights of others. If he constructs a dam on his land, he has no direct incentive to take into account the lower water levels produced on his neighbor's land.

This is exactly the same kind of externality that we encountered with communal property rights, but it is present to a lesser degree. Whereas no one had an incentive to store water on any land under the communal system, private owners now can take into account directly those benefits and costs to their land that accompany water storage. But the effects on the land of others will not be taken into account directly.

The partial concentration of benefits and costs that accompany private ownership is only part of the advantage this system offers. The other part, and perhaps the most important, has escaped our notice. The cost of negotiating over the remaining externalities will be reduced greatly. Communal property rights allow anyone to use the land. Under this system it becomes necessary for all to reach an agreement on land use. But the externalities that accompany private ownership of property do not affect all owners, and, generally speaking, it will be necessary for only a few to reach an agreement that takes these effects into account. The cost of negotiating an internalization of these effects is thereby reduced considerably. The point is important enough to elucidate.

Suppose an owner of a communal land right, in the process of plowing a parcel of land, observes a second communal owner constructing a dam on adjacent land. The farmer prefers to have the stream as it is, and so he asks the engineer to stop his construction. The engineer says, "Pay me to stop." The farmer replies, "I will be happy to pay you, but what can you guarantee in return?" The engineer answers, "I can guarantee you that I will not continue constructing the dam, but I cannot guarantee that another engineer will not take up the task because this is communal property; I have no right to exclude him." What would be a simple negotiation between two persons under a private property arrangement turns out to be a rather complex negotiation between the farmer and everyone else. This is the basic explanation, I believe, for the preponderance of single rather than multiple owners of property. Indeed, an increase in the number of owners is an increase in the communality of property and leads, generally, to an increase in the cost of internalizing.

The reduction in negotiating cost that accompanies the private right ~clude others allows most externalities to be internalized at rather ~ Those that are not are associated with activities that generate ~ects impinging upon many people. The soot from smoke affects many homeowners, none of whom is willing to pay enough to the factory to get its owner to reduce smoke output. All homeowners together might be willing to pay enough, but the cost of their getting together may be enough to discourage effective market bargaining. The negotiating problem is compounded even more if the smoke comes not from a single smoke stack but from an industrial district. In such cases, it may be too costly to internalize effects through the marketplace.

NOTE: "EXTERNALITIES"

"Externality," Demsetz says, "is an ambiguous concept." It is also an important one that you will be confronting more than occasionally in this book and elsewhere.[23] Let us try to explain.

Externalities exist whenever some person, say X, makes a decision about how to use resources without taking full account of the effects of the decision. X ignores some of the effects — some of the costs or benefits that would result from a particular activity, for example — because they fall on others. They are "external" to X, hence the label *externalities*. As a consequence of externalities, resources tend to be misused or "misallocated," which is to say used in one way when another would make society as a whole better off. It is not difficult to see why this is so. We will suggest the reasons in the abstract, leaving you to find concrete examples in Demsetz's discussion and your own experience. As the course develops, many instances of externalities and their consequences will become apparent.

Suppose that X is currently using his land in a way that imposes a total annual cost of $1,000 on people living in the surrounding area (the "neighbors"). Suppose too that X could change his use to one that would impose no costs on the neighbors, but the change would cost X $500 a year (in time and trouble or lost profits, for instance; construct a concrete example of our abstract hypothetical in your mind). The likelihood is that X will continue his current use, even though the alternative would make the *aggregate* of the people in question $500 better off annually (a $1,000 gain to the neighbors minus the $500 cost to X).[24] We could ex-

23. The concept of externalities is at the heart of a large and growing body of work on the relationships between law and economics. Early studies in law and economics focused mostly on taxation, trade regulation, and antitrust; more recent research covers the spectrum of legal concerns, as can be gathered from any of a number of instructive textbooks on the general subject. See, e.g., Robert Cooter & Thomas Ulen, Law and Economics (1988); Werner Z. Hirsch, Law and Economics: An Introductory Analysis (1979); Robin P. Malloy, Law and Economics: A Comparative Approach to Theory and Practice (1990); Mitchell A. Polinsky, An Introduction to Law and Economics (2d ed. 1989); Richard A. Posner, Economic Analysis of Law (4th ed. 1992); Frank A. Stephen, The Economics of the Law (1988). For a collection of readings on the economics of property in particular, see Bruce A. Ackerman, Economic Foundations of Property Law (1975).

24. The technical terminology is to say the current use is "inefficient" because another

pect X to continue his current use because the alternative would make *him* worse off, notwithstanding the net gain it would yield in the aggregate.

The example is one of external costs — costly effects of X's current land use that, because they fall on others, X does not consider in making the decision to use his land in that way. However, the example also illustrates the problem of external benefits. Once X's current use is the prevailing situation, a change by X to a use imposing no costs on the neighbors would confer a benefit on them — the removal of the costs. Because these benefits fall on others, X ignores them in considering whether to change to the alternative. A more typical example of external benefits would be a situation in which X is using his land in a way that imposes no costs and confers no benefits on the neighbors. X could change to an alternative use that would increase his costs by $500 but confer benefits of $1,000 on the neighbors. The likelihood, again, is that he would not make the change because he would not take account of the external effects — here the benefits — of his decision. All the examples illustrate how external costs and benefits encourage the misuse of resources.

No doubt the discussion thus far leads you to suggest that if the alternative use of X's land would cost him $500 but make the neighbors $1,000 better off, then obviously it is in the neighbors' self-interest to offer, and X's self-interest to accept, some payment between $500 and $1,000 in exchange for X's agreement to pursue the alternative land use. Since any payment in that range would appear to make all parties concerned better off in their own terms, offer and acceptance — and thus a correction in the misuse or misallocation of X's land — seem likely to take place. The suggestion is a good one, and it gets us to the core of the externalities problem. Notice what the offer of payment from the neighbors to X would accomplish. It would force X, in deciding how to use his land, to take account of the effect of his decision on others. It would do so because X, confronted with the offer, must now consider that if he continues his present use he forgoes payment from the neighbors, and the forgone payment is a cost to X of his decision — a cost X previously ignored because it was not brought to bear on him (it was external).[25]

---

use would increase the value of the resources involved and make all the parties better off, measured in their own terms (and given their own wealth). The use that would make them best off in those terms is the "efficient" or value-maximizing one — X's alternative use in all of our examples. For reasons that will perhaps become clear as you read this Note, the foregoing definitions should not be taken to suggest that efficient outcomes are necessarily preferred to inefficient alternatives. Or, to put the point more broadly, the economic ctive is useful but should hardly be an exclusive or conclusive way of looking at the

versely, of course, if X changes his present use, he gets the payment, and this of his decision, one he had ignored before the offer because — again — it im. For obvious reasons, economists say that the process of offers just

An offer from the neighbors, then, would appear to resolve the problem, but it is hardly clear that an offer will be forthcoming. Suppose there are 100 neighbors affected to some degree by X's land-use decisions, but none greater than $150. Notice that it is not in the self-interest of any one neighbor to offer X even the minimum amount (say $501) necessary to encourage X to begin thinking about changing his ways. Some sort of group offer is needed, but it may not come about. In particular, it is very unlikely to take place if the costs of *arranging* an offer to X ("transaction costs") are sufficiently high that they, combined with the amount required to induce X to alter his land use, add up to more than $1,000. Payment under these circumstances would be highly unlikely simply because the neighbors would be worse off if they paid than if they did not.

There are a number of reasons why transaction costs might be high. We have been assuming that X's identity is known. But what if instead, and not unrealistically, the neighbors are simply aware of effects but not their cause? Investigation will be necessary for the neighbors to find the person (X) with whom they must bargain, and this could be expensive. Efforts must also be made to raise money in the neighborhood, and these too might be costly. There are, after all, 100 neighbors involved. Dealing with so many people can be expensive, especially if they are spread over a large area, have infrequent contacts with one another, or are difficult to identify and approach because they are indistinguishable from other, unaffected people in the area.

One other factor can make matters even worse. If the effects of X's alternative land use are such that a change to that use necessarily confers a benefit (to some degree) on all 100 neighbors, then each has an incentive to take a "free ride."[26] The freerider reasons that no contribution to a group payment is necessary because the contributions of others will amount to enough to induce X to change, so that the freerider benefits at no cost. Since each neighbor tends to reason this way, none is inclined to contribute much, if anything. The reasoning is not made explicit, of course. The freerider claims to be one of the unaffected or one only slightly affected (contributing a token dollar to get rid of the nagging fund raiser). The costs of overcoming freeriding can be high; if many people are involved, they can be prohibitive.[27]

---

discussed "internalizes" externalities. But offers or bargains are not the only means of internalization, as the excerpt from Demsetz shows.

26. Under what sorts of circumstances would a change in land use by X "necessarily" confer benefits on others?

27. The freeriding problem arises when efforts are made to extract contributions *from* members of a group in order to carry out transactions that will confer collective or nonexclusive benefits on the group — on contributors and noncontributors alike. Collective or nonexclusive effects are typical of many (but not all) externalities.

A problem similar to freeriding — and one that, like freeriding, occasions high transaction costs — arises when payments must be made *to* a group in order to carry out a

There are other reasons why transaction costs might be high (for example, lawyers' fees if legal advice is necessary in the course of transacting), but those discussed above are probably the typically most important ones. The general point is this: When transaction costs become sufficiently high, the external effects of using resources are unlikely to be taken into account through any sort of bargaining process, and the resources are likely to be misused.

This is virtually all we have to understand for now: Externalities are, in essence, a function of transaction costs and they encourage the misuse (the inefficient use) of resources. Very shortly, we will begin considering the range of ways a legal system (a property system in particular) might respond to the presence of high transaction costs. Before doing so, however, it might be useful to note a few points by way of summary:

(a) An externality is not simply an effect of one person's activity on another person; rather, it is an effect that the first person is not forced to take into account. X's activity benefits X \$100 and costs A \$50. A offers X \$50 to change his activity, and X refuses. The harmful or costly effect on A will thus continue, but it is not an "externality" because X has taken account of it in deciding to forgo the payment offered by A. This hardly means you should rest easy (especially if you are A!); notice that X is benefiting at A's expense. It simply means you should not call the effect on A an externality. You might want to call it "unfair," but you should have a reason for doing so. Suppose A has the legal right to stop X's activity and will only permit it to continue if X pays A \$75. X will probably do so because to stop would cost him \$100. Now A is benefitting at X's expense. The two situations have affected the distribution of wealth or income between X and A, but not the efficiency of the resource use. In considering which situation is "fair," do you agree that you might want to know something about the wealth of each party, the nature of the conduct of each, and so forth, as well as just what "fair" means in your system of values?

(b) Externalities do not necessarily lead to inefficient resource use. X, in the example above, will continue his conduct whether or not he takes account of its effects on A and the conduct in the example happens

_____

transaction, and where, unless each member of the group accepts payment, the transaction fails entirely. Suppose X wishes to change to a land use that will increase his profits by \$1,000 but impose \$50 in costly effects on each of ten neighbors. Suppose, too, that X is prohibited by law from engaging in the use unless he first obtains the permission of each person affected. X will be inclined to offer payments (between \$50 and \$100) to each neighbor, but each has an incentive to "hold out" for an exorbitantly higher amount, knowing that without his permission X cannot pursue a venture worth far more to X than ⟨9⟩00. Holding out can frustrate transactions the completion of which would, as in the ⟨examp⟩le posed, be beneficial to all concerned.

⟨No⟩ne of the foregoing discussion should be taken to imply that transaction costs are ⟨always⟩ low when only a few parties are involved in a conflict over the use of a resource. ⟨A c⟩omplication for later. See, e.g., footnote 17 on page 137, and Note 3 on page

to be efficient. Externalities do *encourage* inefficient use of resources, however, for the reasons we discussed. This is why we have said throughout this Note that they "tend" or are "likely" to lead to misuse of resources.

(c) It would be unwise for a society simply to ban all activities with (costly) external effects or to make all those engaging in them pay for the effects.[28] First of all, whose activity is to be banned? But for the presence of *both* X and A in the example above, there would be no external effect. Externalities are reciprocal; they arise from interactions or conflicts among people in the use of resources.[29] Secondly, if your intuition insists that X is responsible, notice that banning X's conduct would foreclose the efficient use of the resource. So too would a requirement that X pay A a negotiated sum as a condition to continuing his activity, if the transaction costs involved in X paying A were sufficiently high. On the other hand, permitting X to continue without compensating A does impose a hardship on A, and this might offend one's sense of justice. We can seldom merely say, then, "Down with external effects," or "Damn the consequences, let external effects go on." Unfortunately, the problem is rather more complicated than that, and it will be troubling us in one form or another to the very end of this book. Try to be sensitive to its complications in considering how the property system has dealt and should deal with the problem in various contexts.

NOTES AND QUESTIONS

1. *Demsetz.* According to Demsetz, a system of communal ownership (common property)[30] tends to increase externalities, and a system of private ownership (private property) tends to reduce them. How?

---

28. Failure to see this leads to much of the confusion on the subject of externalities; yet, unhappily, the *externality* label contributes to the problem. The term can quite understandably, but also quite misleadingly, be taken to suggest that the best response to external costs is always to ban or otherwise control the activities seen to give rise to them.

29. See in this regard the classic essay by Ronald Coase, The Problem of Social Cost, 3 J.L. & Econ. 1 (1960). The essay develops the Coase Theorem (though nowhere in his essay does Coase call it such), which holds that in the absence of transaction costs it is irrelevant from the standpoint of efficiency whether X is liable to A for costly effects or not. Resources will be put to efficient use in either event. Do you see why? And does "efficient use in either event" necessarily mean "the *same* use in either event"? You should be able to work out the answer to the first question. On the second, see, e.g., Richard Craswell, Passing On the Costs of Legal Rules: Efficiency and Distribution in Buyer-Seller Relationships, 43 Stan. L. Rev. 361, 385-391 (1991) (discussing wealth effects and framing effects).

The Problem of Social Cost is reprinted in Ronald Coase, The Firm, the Market, and the Law (1988), which collects (together with some fresh commentary) most of Coase's chief articles over the years. The book is, at 213 pages, a slim volume — but only in that one respect. In 1991 Ronald Coase was awarded the Nobel Memorial Prize in Economic Science.

30. We consider common (or concurrent) ownership at length in Chapter 5.

Notice Demsetz's observation on page 42: "Harming a competitor by producing superior products may be permitted, while shooting him may not." Why? (Recall in this connection the discussion of "interference with capture" in Note 3 on page 35.)

The law aims to discourage trespass (see Problem 1 on page 36). A trespasser, it is typically said, "should not be allowed to profit from his wrong." Cf. Ray A. Brown, The Law of Personal Property 17 (Walter B. Raushenbush 3d ed. 1975). But why is trespass considered "wrong"? Demsetz gives some hints — of an economic sort, at least. See, e.g., pages 45-47. See also Richard A. Posner, Economic Analysis of Law 32-34, 56-57 (4th ed. 1992).

2. *Consequences of the rule of capture.* Return to a question raised earlier: What are the likely consequences of applying the rule of capture to wild animals and, by analogy, to such other "fugitive" resources as oil, gas, and water? The essay by Demsetz suggests some general answers. For a more particular treatment — one that applies to all of the resources mentioned above, and others as well — see Alan E. Friedman, The Economics of the Common Pool: Property Rights in Exhaustible Resources, 18 UCLA L. Rev. 855 (1971).

3. *Mitigation.* How might the adverse consequences of the rule of capture be mitigated? Demsetz would suggest private property rights in many instances. Would he suggest them in all? An alternative is legislative and administrative regulation of one form or another.[31] *Groundwater* extraction, for example, is commonly regulated through well-spacing requirements, limitations on the drilling of new wells, controls on quantities withdrawn, and so on. Some jurisdictions establish groundwater management districts under the direction of an administrative agency. Regarding *oil and gas,* most if not all producing states control well spacing and rates of extraction. One interesting technique is compulsory unitization: Upon vote of some proportion (usually two-thirds) of the owners of land or drilling leases overlying an oil or gas field, a unit of *all* owners is formed. All members of the unit share in production no matter whose well extracts the resource, with the result that the field is managed as though it had only a single owner trying to maximize its value — a kind of private property solution. See 2 American Law of

---

31. Do not assume that government regulation is a magic solution to resource mismanagement. The government can fail just as the market can, particularly where the costs of regulation would fall on small, intensely interested groups and the benefits would flow to the public at large and to future generations. (Do you see the problem?) The U.S. Forest Service, Bureau of Reclamation, and Bureau of Land Management, for example, are routinely said to waste the resources over which they have jurisdiction, sometimes by regulating too much but more commonly by regulating too little in favor of special interest groups favoring agriculture and the timber and cattle industries. See, e.g., Terry L. Anderson and Leal, Free Market Environmentalism (1991). We shall examine the problem of failure most closely in Chapter 11 when we consider some alleged abuses over.

Property 723-755 (1952 & Supp. 1977). As to *wildlife,* fish and game laws
are familiar to everyone, and their justification should now be apparent.
See generally Michael J. Bean, The Evolution of National Wildlife Law
(rev. ed. 1983); Thomas A. Lund, American Wildlife Law (1980).

Chapter 13 of Bean's book discusses efforts to conserve ocean fisheries. Can you see why that problem (like the problem of huge oilfields
discussed in footnote 19 on page 38) is an especially difficult one? Consider Peter Passell, U.S. Starts to Allot Fishing Rights in Coastal Waters
to Boat Owners, N.Y. Times, Apr. 22, 1991, at A1, reporting that the
U.S. government, in "response to catastrophic overfishing by foreigners
in the 1960's," enacted legislation "extending an 'exclusive economic
zone' from the traditional three-mile coastal limit to 200 miles. . . . As
intended, the act has served the interests of the American fishing industry at the expense of foreigners." But how to deal with the difficulty of
overfishing by American boats? Rather than regulate directly, the government has started using a property rights approach:

> Without fanfare, Washington has begun to turn over to private interests
> the exclusive rights to the multibillion dollar harvest of fish off the United
> States coast.
>
> Since 1976 the Federal Government has controlled the right to fish up to
> 200 miles off the coast, and in most cases it has allowed any American with a
> boat to do so. Washington is now allowing eight regional councils dominated
> by local fishing interests to hand out exclusive rights to the catch, transferra-
> ble rights that could be worth tens of billions of dollars.
>
> Many scientists, economists and industry leaders stoutly defend the
> change from collective ownership of fishing rights to private. The current
> policy, they say, has led to too many boats chasing too few fish, undermining
> efforts to preserve fisheries for future generations and helping to transform
> once-plentiful seafood into a luxury.
>
> But for all the enthusiasm over doing away with open access, there is
> deep division over who should financially benefit from the distribution of the
> rights. The regional councils seem determined to bestow this windfall on
> owners of fishing boats.
>
> Other analysts say the fishing rights should be auctioned, with the pro-
> ceeds going to the United States Treasury, much as Federal mineral rights
> are sold to the highest bidder. [Id.][32]

32. Do the implications of the rule of capture for wildlife conservation provide a
reason to rethink the conventional approach to "interference with capture" discussed in
Note 3 on page 35? To the extent that cases like Keeble v. Hickeringill and Pierson v. Post
represent fundamental legal principles, acts of harassment look to be unlawful. But are
they so clearly undesirable? Might the policy in favor of productive activity that underlies
Keeble and *Pierson* suggest that what harassers do should at times be condoned precisely
because it increases the value of resources in the long run? To do this would not change
the apparent policy of maximizing the value of production; rather it would acknowledge
the changed context in which the policy is put to work. The rule of capture and the prohibition of interference might make sense in a state of abundance but not in a state of
scarcity. Shouldn't courts and other lawmakers consider this?

4. *Pollution*. Pollution and other environmental problems have important relationships to property, and we shall be discussing them from time to time throughout this book. For now, consider what the foregoing materials have to say about some core causes of environmental problems and about their solutions. By and large, the materials are concerned with taking things (like animals, oil and gas, water) *out of* the environment; they also suggest, however, why people put things *into* the environment — why they litter the countryside, operate factories in ways that pollute the air and water, abstain from voluntarily driving cleaner cars (or driving any cars with less frequency), and so on. The problem, again, is common property. See the classic essay by Garrett Hardin, The Tragedy of the Commons, 162 Science 1243 (1968).

Are there property rights solutions to pollution problems? See generally Anderson & Leal, supra footnote 31, and the discussion at pages 986-989 of this book.

5. *The utilitarian theory of property*. Demsetz's essay provides a utilitarian account of property, the theoretical foundations of which trace back to the work of David Hume in the eighteenth century. According to Richard Schlatter, Private Property: The History of an Idea 239-242 (1951):

> Against all theories of formal right Hume urged the principle of utility — the rules of justice are conventions which experience has shown to be useful for the promotion of happiness. We obey them, not because we are obligated, but because our self-interest leads us to promote our own happiness in promoting that of the public. Applying this general principle to society, Hume argued that private ownership and its laws had no other origin or justification than utility. If we suppose a society in which nature granted an unlimited supply of goods, we can see that there no laws of property would arise. . . .
>
> The laws of property, then, are conventions which men obey because it is to their common interest to do so. . . .
>
> Jeremy Bentham and his disciples added little to the theory of property propounded by Hume. . . . But it was their writings which made it popular.

See Jeremy Bentham, Theory of Legislation 111-113 (4th ed. 1882):

> Property is nothing but a basis of expectation; the expectation of deriving certain advantages from a thing which we are said to possess, in consequence of the relation in which we stand towards it.
>
> There is no image, no painting, no visible trait, which can express the relation that constitutes property. It is not material, it is metaphysical; it is a ̃e conception of the mind.
>
> ̃ have a thing in our hands, to keep it, to make it, to sell it, to work it ̃mething else; to use it — none of these physical circumstances, nor ̃nvey the idea of property. A piece of stuff which is actually in

the Indies may belong to me, while the dress I wear may not. The aliment which is incorporated into my very body may belong to another, to whom I am bound to account for it.

The idea of property consists in an established expectation; in the persuasion of being able to draw such or such an advantage from the thing possessed, according to the nature of the case. Now this expectation, this persuasion, can only be the work of law. I cannot count upon the enjoyment of that which I regard as mine, except through the promise of the law which guarantees it to me. It is law alone which permits me to forget my natural weakness. It is only through the protection of law that I am able to inclose a field, and to give myself up to its cultivation with the sure though distant hope of harvest.

But it may be asked, What is it that serves as a basis to law, upon which to begin operations, when it adopts objects which, under the name of property, it promises to protect? Have not men, in the primitive state, a *natural* expectation of enjoying certain things, — an expectation drawn from sources anterior to law?

Yes. There have been from the beginning, and there always will be, circumstances in which a man may secure himself, by his own means, in the enjoyment of certain things. But the catalogue of these cases is very limited. The savage who has killed a deer may hope to keep it for himself, so long as his cave is undiscovered; so long as he watches to defend it, and is stronger than his rivals; but that is all. How miserable and precarious is such a possession! If we suppose the least agreement among savages to respect the acquisitions of each other, we see the introduction of a principle to which no name can be given but that of law. A feeble and momentary expectation may result from time to time from circumstances purely physical; but a strong and permanent expectation can result only from law. That which, in the natural state, was an almost invisible thread, in the social state becomes a cable.

Property and law are born together, and die together. Before laws were made there was no property; take away laws, and property ceases.

As regards property, security consists in receiving no check, no shock, no derangement to the expectation founded on the laws, of enjoying such and such a portion of good. The legislator owes the greatest respect to this expectation which he has himself produced. When he does not contradict it, he does what is essential to the happiness of society; when he disturbs it, he always produces a proportionate sum of evil.

Utilitarian theory marked the break of philosophies of property from their earlier natural rights foundations. Suddenly the concept of property was, just as any man-made object is, merely an artifact — a human invention, a social institution, a means of organization. Utilitarian theory is, without doubt, the dominant view of property today, at least among lawyers and especially among those working in law and economics.

6. *The meanings and functions of property.* What does "property" *mean?* The first two paragraphs of Demsetz's essay contain an implicit definition from an economist's point of view (which is to say from a utilitarian's

point of view; observe how closely Demsetz tracks Bentham). Felix Cohen, a lawyer and legal philosopher (but not an economist), saw the institution of property in much the same way. Property, he said, "is a relationship among human beings such that the so-called owner can exclude others from certain activities or permit others to engage in those activities and in either case secure the assistance of the law in carrying out his decision." Felix Cohen, Dialogue on Private Property, 9 Rutgers L. Rev. 357, 373 (1954).[33]

Is this a definition of property generally, or of private property in particular? For example, does common ownership fit the definition? If it does, then what, if any, are the significant differences between common and private ownership? What about state ownership, which Demsetz mentions but sets aside? (See page 46. The discussion in footnote 31 above is about government property. Would the account surprise Demsetz?)

Does a list of private property, common property, and state property exhaust all the possibilities? What about anti-common property, as to which everybody has the right to exclude everybody else, and nobody has the right to include anybody? Any examples? What about collective property, to be used only in ways determined to be in the collective social interest? Any examples? See Jeremy Waldron, What is Private Property?, 5 Oxford J. Legal Stud. 313 (1985). Isn't it likely that any culture will reflect a mix of all or most of these, implying that each is good for something?

Such as what? What are the *functions* of property? Demsetz's essay focuses on economic ordering; Cohen's horizons were hardly so confined, yet he came up with a vision of property almost identical in substance to Demsetz's. (Notice that Demsetz and Cohen alike stress the right of property owners to harm or benefit — exclude or include — other people. Do you see how this relates to the so-called *alienability*, or *transferability*, of property rights? Why is transferability important?)

Demsetz says more or less explicitly, and Cohen more or less implicitly, that a primary function of property rights is to promote the efficient use of resources, but surely there is more to property than that. Property systems are a means of distributing and redistributing the wealth of a society, a point pursued through two volumes in Richard T. Ely, Property and Contract in Their Relations to the Distribution of Wealth (1914) (see id. at 79-93 for "Illustrations Showing the Importance of Property in Wealth Distribution"). And property — private property at any rate — is said to nourish individuality and healthy diversity: It "performs the function of maintaining independence, dignity and pluralism

Cohen maintained that this way of defining property is more useful than a definition talks about property as a relationship between a person and a thing. What has h Demsetz's observation on page 42 that in the world of Robinson Crusoe putting Friday aside) property would play no role?

in society by creating zones within which the majority has to yield to the owner. Whim, caprice, irrationality and 'antisocial' activities are given the protection of law; the owner may do what all or most of his neighbors decry." Charles A. Reich, The New Property, 73 Yale L.J. 733, 771 (1964).

A related point is the view that private property is essential to political freedom. See, e.g., Milton Friedman, Capitalism and Freedom (1962). Friedman, like many classical (and modern) liberal theorists, stresses the importance of free transferability in his account. Modern civic republicans, pursuing the Jeffersonian tradition, argue in contrast that a tension arises from unfettered alienability. Alienability promotes political freedom because it "liberates individuals from one form of dependency, feudal hierarchy, but exposes them to another dependency, markets and manufacturing. By debasing the moral personality of individuals and the polity, the free transferability policy would create a new form of dependency. Individuals would be subjects of the market, and the common welfare would be subordinated to the limitless pursuit of self-interest." So property should be transferable in order to avoid privilege and inequality, but also stable, nontransferable, "to avoid being reduced to a mere commodity, the object of acquisitive pursuit that would destroy republican virtue." Gregory S. Alexander, Time and Property in the American Republican Legal Culture, 66 N.Y.U. L. Rev. 273, 293-294, 300 (1991). See also William H. Simon, Social Republican Property, 38 UCLA L. Rev. 1335 (1991).

We return to the question of free transferability at the end of this chapter. Note for now that a concern with restraints on alienation runs throughout the law of property.

7. *On accounting for private property.* Demsetz's theory of the rise of private property rights has been sharply criticized on several grounds. A *logical* objection is that the theory makes an unjustified "leap from assuming efficiency-maximizing behavior of individuals to assuming efficiency-maximizing behavior of a society."[34] The point is this: How does a *society* reorganize itself out of a system of common property and into one of private property? It seems that the *members* of the society must somehow *agree* to the reorganization, but agreement requires cooperation and Demsetz argues that the absence of cooperation in a regime of common ownership is the problem to begin with. Thus, how the transformation to private property comes about remains a mystery.[35]

34. Richard A. Posner, Some Uses and Abuses of Economics in Law, 46 U. Chi. L. Rev. 281, 289 (1979). But Posner has also praised Demsetz's essay, describing it as "one of the pathbreaking articles in the 'new' law and economics." Posner, Economic Analysis of Law, supra, at 36 n.2.

35. A move from common ownership to private property is hardly costless. A regime of some sort has to be established to run the private property system; property rights have to be defined and distributed; once distributed, they must be protected against invasion. Even in its simplest conception, then, the institution of private property is relatively elab-

A related point is this: Given that cooperation seems absolutely essential to establishing and maintaining a system of private property, and given that we have and maintain such a system, it follows that cooperation must be possible. If cooperation is possible, why do we need private property? See Frank Michelman, Ethics, Economics, and the Law of Property, 24 Nomos 3 (1982). At least as a matter of principle, couldn't resources be managed as effectively through cooperation in a commons as through cooperation in a system of private ownership?

Historical evidence on this question is mixed, but the very fact that it *is* mixed, as opposed to uniformly dreary, suggests that a well-managed commons is something more than a dream. Thus while one can find all sorts of literature documenting abuses of common property resources, there are also studies to the contrary. Common pastures in seventeenth century England were protected from overgrazing through a system of annual allocation. "But how many beasts and sheep everie tenement may keep is uncertain and left as ye Neighbors may agree among themselves," a survey from 1664 tells us, as quoted in Susan J. Cox, No Tragedy of the Commons, 7 Envtl. Ethics 49, 55 (1985). Cox did find abuses of the commons, but they were clearly illegal; in other words, they were the sorts of abuses — say, theft — so commonplace in a private property system. There were also abuses of power: The wealthy used their resources and standing in the community to take more than their share. Id. at 56-58. Cox concludes: "Perhaps what existed in fact was not a 'tragedy of the commons' but rather a triumph: that for hundreds of years — and perhaps thousands, although written records do not exist to prove the longer era — land was managed successfully by communities." Id. at 60.[36]

---

orate, or costly. At the same time, the benefits that Demsetz sees in the institution of private property are necessarily *collective* — they run in principle to *all* members of the society, including members who don't help bear the costs of setting up and maintaining the system. So why doesn't everyone take a free ride, meanwhile using the time and energy thereby saved to consume the commons that might soon fall under the discipline of private property? For discussion, see James E. Krier, The Tragedy of the Commons, Part Two, 15 Harv. J.L. & Pub. Policy 325 (1992); James E. Krier & W. David Montgomery, Resource Allocation, Information Cost and the Form of Government Intervention, 13 Natural Resources J. 89, 94-95 (1973); Carol M. Rose, Property as Storytelling: Perspectives from Game Theory, Narrative Theory, Feminist Theory, 2 Yale J.L. & Human. 37 (1990).

None of this is to say that societies can never manage to get organized and change from one form of ownership (say common property) to another (say private property). Obviously they can! Under what sorts of circumstances is this most likely to occur, and with what implications? Recall the discussion of whaling customs in Note 2 on page 30 and the works by Professor Ellickson cited there. See also Robert C. Ellickson, Property in Land, 102 Yale L.J. No. 6 (1993) (forthcoming).

36. But Cox continues by saying, "[t]hat the system failed to survive the industrial revolution, agrarian reform, and transfigured farming practices, is hardly to be wondered at." Id. at 60-61. Does this defeat the force of her earlier observations? Could not one argue, à la Demsetz, that common ownership worked well enough until economic development brought on the acute pressures of scarcity, at which point a private property system — most immediately the enclosure movement in England — began to develop in

See also Carol M. Rose, The Comedy of the Commons: Custom, Commerce, and Inherently Public Property, 53 U. Chi. L. Rev. 711 (1986), which traces among other alternatives the role of custom in managing common resources. Rose discusses the enclosure of the manorial commons in particular and notes the existence of customary limits that helped constrain the rate of exploitation. Id. at 743-744. Her larger point, based on a number of examples, is that custom can help form an effective means of resource management that is quite distinct from either private ownership or government control, and also advantageous because it is less costly than either of those alternatives, increases the value of some kinds of resources, and can "enhance the sociability of the members of an otherwise atomized society." Id. at 723. A similar argument is presented in Barry C. Field, The Evolution of Property Rights, 42 Kyklos 319 (1989). Field agrees with Demsetz that population growth and increases in demand can induce a shift from common to private ownership. Under some circumstances, however, developmental pressures encourage a shift in the opposite direction, from private to common ownership: The nature of a resource may be such that costs are lower when it is exploited by people acting together; moreover, people may have a taste for working in groups.

Two excellent works on common ownership are Elinor Ostrom, Governing the Commons: The Evolution of Institutions for Collective Action (1990); and The Question of the Commons: The Culture and Ecology of Communal Resources (Bonnie J. McCay & James M. Acheson eds. 1987).

Demsetz's *anthropological* account has been criticized by legal scholars as "extraordinarily naive" and as "an attempt to support conclusions on property ownership and property use from incomplete historical data on primitive societies."[37] William Cronon, an ecological historian and the author of Changes in the Land (1983), an important study of the impact of the colonists on the culture and natural environment of New England Native Americans, says that the account "miscontrue[s] the social and ecological nature of property rights." Id. at 184 n.7. The essence of all the criticism is that Demsetz ignores how value-laden might be the processes that lead from common to private ownership, picturing the matter, rather, as more or less mechanical and value-neutral. Cronon's study in particular makes it abundantly clear that private ownership might have developed in American Indian cultures — in the course of their exposure to European settlement — for reasons quite apart from realizing efficiency gains. Ideology was also at work. The colonists

response? For a brief description of English enclosure, including its rather tawdry politics, see pages 788-790.

37. See, respectively, Arthur A. Leff, Economic Analysis of Law: Some Realism About Nominalism, 60 Va. L. Rev. 451, 473 n.61 (1974); Eric T. Freyfogle, Land Use and the Study of Early American History, 94 Yale L.J. 717, 740 n.73 (1985).

brought with them their "more exclusive sense of property and their involvement in a capitalist economy. . . ." Id. at viii. The Native Americans were drawn into trade, with a variety of destructive consequences. One consequence, ironically, had to do with the environment. Demsetz would argue that private property ordinarily enhances environmental quality; Cronon finds that "capitalism and environmental degradation went hand in hand." Id. at 161. The colonists raised cattle; their need for pastures led to deforestation; the cattle compacted the soil, altering drainage patterns and even climate (without forests the land was sunnier, windier, hotter, colder, and drier).

One should not, of course, have an unduly romantic image of Native American culture prior to the arrival of "civilization." There is considerable evidence that some American Indian tribes, rather than being natural ecologists who lived in respectful harmony with the land, exploited the environment ruthlessly by overhunting and extensive burning of forests. See, e.g., Albert E. Cowdrey, This Land, This South: An Environmental History (1983); Malcolm W. Browne, New Findings Reveal Ancient Abuse of Lands, N.Y. Times, Jan. 13, 1987, at C1. Nor should one conclude from the foregoing that Demsetz's general account of the emergence of private property can find no evidence in its behalf. To the contrary, there are studies whose findings tend to support the lines of the argument. See, e.g., Douglas C. North & Robert P. Thomas, The Rise of the Western World (1973); John R. Umbeck, A Theory of Property Rights, With Application to the California Gold Rush (1981); Terry L. Anderson & P.J. Hill, The Evolution of Property Rights: A Study of the American West, 18 J.L. & Econ. 163 (1975); David E. Ault & Gilbert L. Rutman, Land Scarcity, Economic Efficiency, and African Common Law, 12 Res. L. & Econ. 33 (1989); D. Bruce Johnsen, The Formation and Protection of Property Rights Among the Southern Kwakiutl Indians, 15 J. Legal Stud. 41 (1986).

C. Acquisition by Creation

An observer from abroad has argued that the following principle "is part of the common law":

> Any expenditure of mental or physical effort, as a result of which there is created an entity, whether tangible or intangible, vests in the person who brought the entity into being, a proprietary right to the commercial exploitation of that entity, which right is separate and independent from the ownership of that entity. [D.F. Libling, The Concept of Property: Property in Intangibles, 94 L.Q. Rev. 103, 104 (1978).]

The assertion is that if you create something — if in that sense you are first in time — then that something is most certainly yours (and presumably yours alone) to exploit, because, Libling argues, "the foundation of proprietary rights is the expenditure of labour and money (which merely represents past effort)." Id. at 119. So the underlying idea seems to derive from John Locke, who reasoned that you own the fruits of your labor in consequence of having "a property in your own person." See Note 4 beginning on page 15.

The trouble is that the fruits of your labor are *not* always yours alone to exploit, and you do *not* always have full rights of property in your own person. Why?

Consider the following materials.

Cheney Brothers v. Doris Silk Corp.
United States Court of Appeals
Second Circuit, 1929
35 F.2d 279, cert. denied, 281 U.S. 728 (1930)

LEARNED HAND, J. The plaintiff, a corporation, is a manufacturer of silks, which puts out each season many new patterns, designed to attract purchasers by their novelty and beauty. Most of these fail in that purpose, so that not much more than a fifth catch the public fancy. Moreover, they have only a short life, for the most part no more than a single season of eight or nine months. It is in practice impossible, and it would be very onerous if it were not, to secure design patents upon all of these; it would also be impossible to know in advance which would sell well, and patent only those. Besides, it is probable that for the most part they have no such originality as would support a design patent. Again, it is impossible to copyright them under the Copyright Act or at least so the authorities of the Copyright Office hold. So it is easy for any one to copy such as prove successful, and the plaintiff, which is put to much ingenuity and expense in fabricating them, finds itself without protection of any sort for its pains.

Taking advantage of this situation, the defendant copied one of the popular designs in the season beginning in October, 1928, and undercut the plaintiff's price. This is the injury of which it complains. The defendant, though it duplicated the design in question, denies that it knew it to be the plaintiff's, and there thus arises an issue which might be an answer to the motion. However, the parties wish a decision upon the equity of the bill, and since it is within our power to dismiss it, we shall accept its allegation, and charge the defendant with knowledge.

The plaintiff asks for protection only during the season, and needs no more, for the designs are all ephemeral. It seeks in this way to disguise the extent of the proposed innovation, and to persuade us that, if we interfere only a little, the solecism, if there be one, may be pardonable. But the reasoning which would justify any interposition at all demands that it cover the whole extent of the injury. A man whose designs come to harvest in two years, or in five, has prima facie as good right to protection as one who deals only in annuals. Nor could we consistently stop at designs; processes, machines, and secrets have an equal claim. The upshot must be that, whenever anyone has contrived any of these, others may be forbidden to copy it. That is not the law. In the absence of some recognized right at common law, or under the statutes — and the plaintiff claims neither — a man's property is limited to the chattels which embody his invention. Others may imitate these at their pleasure. . . .

Of the cases on which the plaintiff relies, the chief is International News Service v. Associated Press, 248 U.S. 215, 39 S. Ct. 68, 63 L. Ed. 211, 2 A.L.R. 293. Although that concerned another subject-matter — printed news dispatches — we agree that, if it meant to lay down a general doctrine, it would cover this case; at least, the language of the majority opinion goes so far. We do not believe that it did. While it is of course true that law ordinarily speaks in general terms, there are cases where the occasion is at once the justification for, and the limit of, what is decided. This appears to us such an instance; we think that no more was covered than situations substantially similar to those then at bar. The difficulties of understanding it otherwise are insuperable. We are to suppose that the court meant to create a sort of common-law patent or copyright for reasons of justice. Either would flagrantly conflict with the scheme which Congress has for more than a century devised to cover the subject-matter. . . .

It appears to us incredible that the Supreme Court should have had in mind any such consequences. To exclude others from the enjoyment of a chattel is one thing; to prevent any imitation of it, to set up a monopoly in the plan of its structure, gives the author a power over his fellows vastly greater, a power which the Constitution allows only Congress to create. . . .

True, it would seem as though the plaintiff had suffered a grievance for which there should be a remedy, perhaps by an amendment of the Copyright Law, assuming that this does not already cover the case, which is not urged here. It seems a lame answer in such a case to turn the injured party out of court, but there are larger issues at stake than his redress. . . . Whether these would prove paramount we have no means of saying; it is not for us to decide. Our vision is inevitably contracted, and the whole horizon may contain much which will compose a very different picture.

The order is affirmed, and, as the bill cannot in any event succeed, it may be dismissed, if the defendant so desires.

International News Service v. Associated Press, 248 U.S. 215 (1918). The case involved copying by the INS of news gathered by the AP. The Court protected the AP against pirating by developing a branch of unfair competition law known as misappropriation: AP had a "quasi-property" interest in the news it had gathered and could stop competitors from using it "until its commercial value as new had passed away." In the Court's view, the INS was "endeavoring to reap where it has not sown, and . . . appropriating to itself the harvest of those who have sown." Unless such practices were stopped, the Court reasoned, no news service could manage to stay in business.

Douglas G. Baird, Common Law Intellectual Property and the Legacy of *International News Service v. Associated Press,* **50 U. Chi. L. Rev. 411, 413-414 (1983).** "That an individual has the right to reap what he has sown . . . is far from self-evident even as applied to tangible property. . . . We typically can reap only the wheat we sow on our own land, and how land becomes private property in the first place remains a mystery. In any event, wheat and information are fundamentally different from one another. It is the nature of wheat or land or any other tangible property that possession by one person precludes possession by anyone else. . . . Many people, however, can use the same piece of information. . . .

"The value of information to AP derived in part from its ability to keep its rivals from copying the information it gathered. But deciding that it could not enjoy its news exclusively is not the same as telling a farmer he must hand over wheat he has grown to someone who merely watched him grow it. Deciding against AP would not mean that it would lose all revenue from its news-gathering efforts. People would still pay for the AP's news, and its rights would be entirely unaffected in the towns that the AP served exclusively.

"That the analogy between wheat and information does not apply with full force, however, does not mean that it should not apply at all. One can still argue that individuals have the right to enjoy the fruits of their labors, even when the labors are intellectual. But granting individuals exclusive rights to the information they gather conflicts with other rights in a way that granting exclusive rights to tangible property does not. In a market economy, granting individuals exclusive rights to property is an effective way of allocating scarce resources. Saying that someone should be able to own a particular good or piece of land and should be able to keep others from getting it unless they pay him is unobjectionable once one accepts the desirability of a market economy. Granting exclusive rights to information does not, however, necessarily promote a market economy. Competition depends upon imitation. One person invests labor and money to create a product, such as a food processor, that people will buy. Others may imitate him and take advantage of the new market by selling their own food processors. Their machines may incorporate their own ideas about how such machines should be made. As a result, the quality of the machines may rise and their price may fall. The first person is made worse off than he would be if he had had an exclusive right to his idea, because his competitors are enjoying the fruits of his labor and are not paying for it. Nevertheless, the public as a whole may be better off, as long as this freedom to imitate does not destroy the incentive for people to come up with new devices."

Smith v. Chanel, Inc., 402 F.2d 562, 567-568 (9th Cir. 1968). The court held that a perfume company could claim in advertisements that its product was the equivalent of the more expensive Chanel No. 5. "Since appellees' perfume [Chanel No. 5] was unpatented, appellants had a right to copy it. . . . There was a strong public interest in their doing so, '[f]or imitation is the life blood of competition. It is the unimpeded availability of substantially equivalent units that permits the normal operation of supply and demand to yield the fair price society must pay for a given commodity.' . . . But this public benefit might be lost if appellants could not tell potential purchasers that appellants' product was the equivalent of appellees' product. . . . The most effective way . . . in which this can be done is to identify the copied article by its trademark or trade name. . . .

"[The district court stated] that the creation of the other values inherent in the trademark require 'the expenditure of great effort, skill and ability,' and that the competitor should not be permitted 'to take a free ride' on the trademark owner's 'widespread goodwill and reputation.'

"A large expenditure of money does not in itself create legally protectable rights. Appellees are not entitled to monopolize the public's desire for the unpatented product, even though they themselves created that desire at great effort and expense. . . .

"Disapproval of the copyist's opportunism may be an understandable first reaction, '[b]ut this initial response to the problem has been curbed in deference to the greater public good.' . . . By taking his 'free ride,' the copyist, albeit unintentionally, serves an important public interest by offering comparable goods at lower prices."

NOTES AND QUESTIONS

1. *Copying and the common law. Cheney Brothers* states the general rule: "In the absence of some recognized right at common law, or under the statutes . . . a man's property is limited to the chattels which embody his invention. Others may imitate these at their pleasure."

Regarding the common law, notice that Judge Hand confined International News Service v. Associated Press to its facts, thinking it "incredible" that the Supreme Court intended a broad reading. "[T]here are larger issues at stake than [plaintiff's] redress," Hand said, and the materials that follow *Cheney Brothers* suggest what they are. What goes into the argument in favor of property rights in creations? The argument against? How is one to assess and balance the pros and cons?

2. *Legislation.* The absence of property rights can dampen production, but recognition of them can create costly monopoly power. Difficult trade-offs have to be made, and — with regard to property in ideas and information in particular — they are made, in the main, by Congress through legislation on *patents* and *copyrights* (there are also common law copyrights, and, in the United States, *trademarks* are regulated through a mixed system of state common law rules and optional federal registration).

These are specialized subjects, studied in advanced courses. At bottom, though, the approach in each instance is to grant a limited monopoly: a monopoly in order to encourage productive incentives, but a limited one in order to promote competition. You should be able to understand, then, why we have patent rights, copyrights, and trademark rights, and also why: patents are of short duration (17 years; see the patent pictured on page 71); obvious inventions and fundamental ideas (such as the laws of physics) cannot be patented; copyrights are not infringed by fair use (such as quotations in a book review); the property right in a trademark terminates when the mark becomes generic (as with "aspirin"). See Richard A. Posner, Economic Analysis of Law 38-45 (4th ed. 1992).

3. *Persona as property.* According to George M. Armstrong, Jr., The Reification of Celebrity: Persona as Property, 51 La. L. Rev. 443 (1991):

> Only two decades ago a celebrity had no cause of action against an advertiser who imitated her voice. Until the 1970's any commercial value associated with celebrity was personal to the star and entered the public domain at death. As recently as the early 1950's celebrities could not assign the right to use their name and likeness. At the beginning of this century the law denied relief even to the living person whose name or likeness was the object of illicit appropriation.

Things are different now. A celebrity's "right of publicity" is widely recognized as a kind of property interest, assignable during life, descendible at death. See, e.g., State ex rel. Elvis Presley Intl. Memorial Found. v. Crowell, 733 S.W.2d 89 (Tenn. App. 1987). The property interest includes name, likeness, and other aspects of one's "identity." In 1988, for example, a U.S. Court of Appeals held that Bette Midler stated a good cause of action when she alleged that Ford Motor Company and its advertising agency had hired a singer to perform "Do You Want To

Dance" in a voice and style intended to "sound as much as possible like the Bette Midler record"; the defendants had appropriated Midler's identity. Midler v. Ford Motor Co., 849 F.2d 460, 461 (9th Cir. 1988). (At trial in 1989, Midler was awarded $400,000 in damages against the advertising agency. Midler v. Young & Rubicam, Inc., 944 F.2d 909 (9th Cir. 1991), cert. denied, 112 S. Ct. 1513 (1992).) In 1990 blues singer Tom Waits won almost $2.5 million in a lawsuit (unreported) against the Frito-Lay company and its advertising agency; the defendants had impersonated Waits's voice in a radio ad for corn chips. And Vanna White v. Samsung Electronics America, Inc., 971 F.2d 1395 (9th Cir. 1992), held that Vanna White had a cause of action against a firm that created a *robot* resembling her. (No deception had been intended.) White has a "marketable celebrity identity value," which the firm had used for commercial profit. 971 F.2d at 1399.

The right of publicity seems to be rooted in the right of privacy. See generally Note, How Much of You Do You Really Own? A Property Right in Identity, 37 Clev. St. L. Rev. 499 (1989). Richard Posner observes that the courts first recognized an explicit right of privacy in a case where the defendant, without consent, used the plaintiff's name and picture in an advertisement. "Paradoxically, this branch of the right of privacy is [now] most often invoked by celebrities avid for publicity (and therefore is sometimes called the 'right of publicity'); they just want to make sure they get the highest possible price for the use of their name and picture in advertising." Posner, supra, at 43.

In the view of Armstrong, the right of publicity developed for the same reasons that property rights generally are thought to develop: technological advance and social change generated new demands, new scarcity, and new opportunities:[38]

> pictorial and representational graphics and celebrity endorsements increased considerably in the period 1890 to 1930. . . . In the process the advertising community created a legitimate market for items such as name and likeness which had previously been out of commerce. The rapid evolution of legal doctrine during this period demonstrates the growing acceptance [by] judges [of] the notion that the persona might be a commodity, and the individual's right to exclude others from his name and likeness was well established by the second decade of this century. In later years the further expansion of this market encouraged judges to endow the persona with other characteristics of property: alienability and heritability. [Armstrong, supra, at 457.]

Judging at least from judicial statements, the purposes of a property right in one's persona are similar to some of the purposes of property

---

38. Recall Demsetz's theory of property rights, which we considered earlier (see page 43): "Changes in knowledge result in changes in production functions, market values, and aspirations. . . . It is my thesis . . . that the emergence of new property rights takes place in response to the desires of the interacting persons for adjustment to new benefit-cost possibilities."

rights that we have seen mentioned in other connections. For example, the court in the *Elvis Presley* case echoed the opinion in International News Service v. Associated Press (see page 65) when it said that "one of the basic principles of Anglo-American jurisprudence [is] that 'one may not reap where another has sown nor gather where another has strewn.' " 733 S.W.2d at 98. And the Supreme Court itself has likened the right of publicity to "the patent and copyright laws long enforced by this Court." Protection of the right "provides an economic incentive" to make investments in activities valued by the public. Zacchini v. Scripps-Howard Broadcasting Co., 433 U.S. 562, 576 (1977).

4. *Property in one's person?* The *Bette Midler* case referred to in Note 3 above held "that when a distinctive voice of a professional singer is widely known and is deliberately imitated in order to sell a product, the sellers have appropriated what is not theirs and have committed a tort. . . ." 849 F.2d at 463. But why is the appropriation wrongful, given that imitation is ordinarily allowed? See Note 1 above. How far does this notion of wrongful appropriation of another's self reach? Suppose what is at issue is not a piece of the persona but a piece of the person — tissue, blood, cells, an embryo? Are *these* to be regarded as "property"? The following materials address that question.

Moore v. Regents of the University of California

Supreme Court of California, 1990
51 Cal. 3d 120, 793 P.2d 479, 271 Cal. Rptr. 146, cert. denied,
111 S. Ct. 1388 (1991)

[*Background*: In 1976 John Moore sought treatment for hairy-cell leukemia at the Medical Center of the University of California, Los Angeles. (We shall at times refer to the doctors at the Center and to the Regents of the University who own the Center collectively as "defendants.") The defendants conducted tests, took blood and tissue samples, confirmed the diagnosis, and told Moore that his condition was life-threatening and that his spleen should be removed. What they did not tell Moore was that his cells were unique and that access to them was of great scientific and commercial value.

Moore consented to the splenectomy and to some seven years of follow-up tests and procedures that he was led to believe were important to his treatment. His spleen was retained for research purposes without his knowledge or consent, and during the post-operative period samples of tissue and blood and other fluids were taken on each of Moore's visits. At some point Moore was informed that his bodily substances were being used for research, but he was never informed of the commercial value of the research or of the defendants' financial interest in it. The defendants subsequently established a cell line from Moore's cells (named the

Mo cell line, after Moore), received a patent for it, and entered into various commercial agreements. Hundreds of thousands of dollars had been paid to the defendants under these agreements by the mid-1980s, and the potential market for products from Moore's cell line is estimated to run into the billions of dollars.

Moore sued for damages in 1984, his complaint stating a number of causes of action, including conversion (wrongful exercise of ownership rights over the personal property of another; Moore alleged that his blood and bodily substances, and the cell line derived from them, were "his tangible personal property"), lack of informed consent, breach of fiduciary duty, fraud and deceit, unjust enrichment, intentional infliction of emotional distress, negligent misrepresentation, and others. The trial court sustained the defendants' demurrers to the conversion cause of action and held that because the conversion cause of action was incorporated into all the other causes of action, those too were defective.

The court of appeal reversed, finding that Moore had adequately stated a cause of action for conversion. Moore v. Regents of the University of California, 249 Cal. Rptr. 494 (Ct. App. 1988). The court could find "no legal authority, public policy, nor universally known facts of biological science . . . which compel a conclusion that this plaintiff cannot have a sufficient legal interest in his own bodily tissues amounting to personal property. Absent plaintiff's consent to defendants' disposition of the tissues, or lawful justification, such as abandonment, the complaint adequately pleads all the elements of a cause of action for conversion."

"We have approached this issue with caution," the court said. "The evolution of civilization from slavery to freedom, from regarding people as chattels to recognition of the individual dignity of each person, necessitates prudence in attributing the qualities of property to human tissue. There is, however, a dramatic difference between having property rights in one's own body and being the property of another. . . . We are not called on to determine whether use of human tissue or body parts ought to be 'gift based' or subject to a 'free market.' That question of policy must be determined by the Legislature. In the instant case, the cell line has already been commercialized by defendants. We are presented a *fait accompli,* leaving only the question of who shares in the proceeds. . . ."

The court then considered the meaning of property and concluded that the essential element is dominion, or rights of use, control, and disposition. It went on to discuss the "many cases" (involving search and seizure, consent to medical procedures, rights to dead bodies, and other instances) that recognize "rights of dominion over one's own body, and the interests one has therein. . . . These rights and interests are so akin to property interests that it would be a subterfuge to call them something else."

4438032

THE UNITED STATES OF AMERICA

TO ALL TO WHOM THESE PRESENTS SHALL COME:

Whereas, THERE HAS BEEN PRESENTED TO THE

Commissioner of Patents and Trademarks

A PETITION PRAYING FOR THE GRANT OF LETTERS PATENT FOR AN ALLEGED NEW AND USEFUL INVENTION THE TITLE AND DESCRIPTION OF WHICH ARE CONTAINED IN THE SPECIFICATION OF WHICH A COPY IS HEREUNTO ANNEXED AND MADE A PART HEREOF, AND THE VARIOUS REQUIREMENTS OF LAW IN SUCH CASES MADE AND PROVIDED HAVE BEEN COMPLIED WITH, AND THE TITLE THERETO IS, FROM THE RECORDS OF THE PATENT AND TRADEMARK OFFICE IN THE CLAIMANT(S) INDICATED IN THE SAID COPY, AND WHEREAS, UPON DUE EXAMINATION MADE THE SAID CLAIMANT(S) IS (ARE) ADJUDGED TO BE ENTITLED TO A PATENT UNDER THE LAW.

NOW, THEREFORE, THESE Letters Patent ARE TO GRANT UNTO THE SAID CLAIMANT(S) AND THE SUCCESSORS, HEIRS OR ASSIGNS OF THE SAID CLAIMANT(S) FOR THE TERM OF SEVENTEEN YEARS FROM THE DATE OF THIS GRANT, SUBJECT TO THE PAYMENT OF ISSUE FEES AS PROVIDED BY LAW, THE RIGHT TO EXCLUDE OTHERS FROM MAKING, USING OR SELLING THE SAID INVENTION THROUGHOUT THE UNITED STATES.

In testimony whereof I have hereunto set my hand and caused the seal of the Patent and Trademark Office to be affixed at the City of Washington this twentieth day of March in the year of our Lord one thousand nine hundred and eighty-four, and of the Independence of the United States of America the two hundred and eighth.

Commissioner of Patents and Trademarks

United States Patent [19]
Golde et al.

[11] 4,438,032
[45] Mar. 20, 1984

[54] UNIQUE T-LYMHOCYTE LINE AND PRODUCTS DERIVED THEREFROM

[75] Inventors: David W. Golde; Shirley G. Quan, both of Los Angeles, Calif.

[73] Assignee: The Regents of the University of California, Berkeley, Calif.

[21] Appl. No.: 456,17

[22] Filed: Jan. 6, 1983

Related U.S. Application Data

[63] Continuation of Ser. No. 229,900, Jan. 30, 1981, abandoned.

[51] Int. Cl.³ C12P 21/00; C12N 15/00; C12R 1/91; C07G 7/00
[52] U.S. Cl. .... 260/112 R; 260/112 B; 424/85, 424 177; 435/68, 435/172; 435/240; 435/241; 435/948
[58] Field of Search .... 260/112 R, 112 B, 435/68, 172, 240, 241, 948

[56] References Cited

U.S. PATENT DOCUMENTS

4,338,397 7/1982 Gilbert 435/68

OTHER PUBLICATIONS

Saxon et al. Annals of Internal Medicine. (1978), 58:323–326.
Weisbart et al. Clin. Immunology & Immunopathology. (1979), 14:441–448.
Weisbart et al. J. Lab. Clin. Med., (1979), 93:622–626.
Lusis et al. In Vivo and In Vitro Erythropoiesis, 1980, pp. 97–106.
Golde et al. Blood, (1978), 51:1068–1071.
Golde et al., PNAS, USA, (1980), 77:593–596.
Golde et al., Annals of Internal Medicine, (1980), 92:650–662.

Primary Examiner—Howard E. Schain
Attorney, Agent, or Firm—Bertram I. Rowland

[57] ABSTRACT

Human T-lymphoblast cell line. Proteinaceous products produced therefrom, messenger RNA and DNA expressing the proteinaceous products. A human T-lymphoblast cell line (Mo) maintained as a continuous culture constitutively produces proteins, including immune interferon, neutrophil migration inhibition factor, granulocyte-macrophage colony-stimulating activity and erythroid-potentiating activity, as well as other proteins produced by T-cells.

22 Claims, No Drawings

Pages from the Mo Cell Line Patent

The court concluded by dealing with a series of contentions by defendants. There were no grounds to infer that Moore had abandoned his tissue or consented to its use in research unrelated to his treatment. And the fact that the defendants' skill and effort had enhanced the value of Moore's tissue went not to the issue of conversion but to the measure of damages for the conversion. "Plaintiff's cells and genes are a part of his person," the court said, citing the right of publicity cases that "'afford legal protection to an individual's proprietary interest in his own identity.'"[39] To hold that patients do not have the ultimate power to control the destiny of their tissues "would open the door to a massive invasion of human privacy and dignity in the name of medical progress." The court saw no reason to believe that medical research would suffer by requiring the consent of the donor of tissue before it can be appropriated. True, a potential donor, once informed, might refuse consent, but the court "would give the patient that right. As to defendants' concern that a patient might seek the greatest economic gain for his participation, this argument is unpersuasive because it fails to explain why defendants . . . are any more to be trusted with these momentous decisions than the person whose cells are being used." If giving patients a financial interest in their tissues inhibited donations and increased the costs of medical care, that problem could be addressed by the legislature.

Upon petition by the defendants, the court of appeal's judgment was reviewed by the California Supreme Court. Of particular interest here are the views of the various justices regarding the cause of action for conversion.]

PANELLI, J. We granted review in this case to determine whether plaintiff has stated a cause of action against his physician and other defendants for using his cells in potentially lucrative medical research without his permission. . . . We hold that the complaint states a cause of action for breach of the physician's disclosure obligations, but not for conversion. . . .

A. Breach of Fiduciary Duty and Lack of Informed Consent

Moore repeatedly alleges that Golde [the attending physician] failed to disclose the extent of his research and economic interests in Moore's cells before obtaining consent to the medical procedures by which the cells were extracted. These allegations, in our view, state a cause of action against Golde for invading a legally protected interest of his patient. This cause of action can properly be characterized either as the breach of a fiduciary duty to disclose facts material to the patient's consent or,

---

39. On the right of publicity, recall the discussion in Note 3 on page 67. — EDS.

alternatively, as the performance of medical procedures without first having obtained the patient's informed consent. . . .

B. *Conversion*

Moore also attempts to characterize the invasion of his rights as a conversion — a tort that protects against interference with possessory and ownership interests in personal property. He theorizes that he continued to own his cells following their removal from his body, at least for the purpose of directing their use, and that he never consented to their use in potentially lucrative medical research. Thus, to complete Moore's argument, defendants' unauthorized use of his cells constitutes a conversion. As a result of the alleged conversion, Moore claims a proprietary interest in each of the products that any of the defendants might ever create from his cells or the patented cell line.

No court, however, has ever in a reported decision imposed conversion liability for the use of human cells in medical research. While that fact does not end our inquiry, it raises a flag of caution. In effect, what Moore is asking us to do is to impose a tort duty on scientists to investigate the consensual pedigree of each human cell sample used in research. To impose such a duty, which would affect medical research of importance to all of society, implicates policy concerns far removed from the traditional, two-party ownership disputes in which the law of conversion arose. Invoking a tort theory originally used to determine whether the loser or the finder of a horse had the better title, Moore claims ownership of the results of socially important medical research, including the genetic code for chemicals that regulate the functions of every human being's immune system.

We have recognized that, when the proposed application of a very general theory of liability in a new context raises important policy concerns, it is especially important to face those concerns and address them openly. . . .

Accordingly, we first consider whether the tort of conversion clearly gives Moore a cause of action under existing law. We do not believe it does. Because of the novelty of Moore's claim to own the biological materials at issue, to apply the theory of conversion in this context would frankly have to be recognized as an extension of the theory. Therefore, we consider next whether it is advisable to extend the tort to this context.

1. Moore's Claim Under Existing Law

"To establish a conversion, plaintiff must establish an actual interference with his *ownership* or *right of possession*. . . . Where plaintiff neither has title to the property alleged to have been converted, nor possession thereof, he cannot maintain an action for conversion." . . .

Since Moore clearly did not expect to retain possession of his cells following their removal, to sue for their conversion he must have retained an ownership interest in them. But there are several reasons to doubt that he did retain any such interest. First, no reported judicial decision supports Moore's claim, either directly or by close analogy. Second, California statutory law drastically limits any continuing interest of a patient in excised cells. Third, the subject matters of the Regents' patent — the patented cell line and the products derived from it — cannot be Moore's property.

Neither the Court of Appeal's opinion, the parties' briefs, nor our research discloses a case holding that a person retains a sufficient interest in excised cells to support a cause of action for conversion. We do not find this surprising, since the laws governing such things as human tissues, transplantable organs,[40] blood, fetuses, pituitary glands, corneal tissue, and dead bodies deal with human biological materials as objects sui generis, regulating their disposition to achieve policy goals rather than abandoning them to the general law of personal property. It is these specialized statutes, not the law of conversion, to which courts ordinarily should and do look for guidance on the disposition of human biological materials.

Lacking direct authority for importing the law of conversion into this context, Moore relies, as did the Court of Appeal, primarily on decisions addressing privacy rights. One line of cases involves unwanted publicity. (Lugosi v. Universal Pictures (1979) 25 Cal. 3d 813, 160 Cal. Rptr. 323, 603 P.2d 425; Motsehenbacher v. R.J. Reynolds Tobacco Company (9th Cir. 1974) 498 F.2d 821.) These opinions hold that every person has a proprietary interest in his own likeness and that unauthorized, business use of a likeness is redressible as a tort. But in neither opinion did the authoring court expressly base its holding on property law. Each court stated, following Prosser, that it was "pointless" to debate the proper characterization of the proprietary interest in a likeness. For purposes of determining whether the tort of conversion lies, however, the characterization of the right in question is far from pointless. Only property can be converted.

Not only are the wrongful-publicity cases irrelevant to the issue of conversion, but the analogy to them seriously misconceives the nature of the genetic materials and research involved in this case. Moore, adopting the analogy originally advanced by the Court of Appeal, argues that "[i]f the courts have found a sufficient proprietary interest in one's per-

40. See the Uniform Anatomical Gift Act, Health and Safety Code section 7150 et seq. The act permits a competent adult to "give all or part of [his] body" for certain designated purposes, including "transplantation, therapy, medical or dental education, research, or advancement of medical or dental science." (Health & Saf. Code, §§7151, 7153.) The act does not, however, permit the donor to receive "valuable consideration" for the transfer. (Health & Saf. Code §7155.)

sona, how could one not have a right in one's own genetic material, something far more profoundly the essence of one's human uniqueness than a name or a face?" However, as the defendants' patent makes clear — and the complaint, too, if read with an understanding of the scientific terms which it has borrowed from the patent — the goal and result of defendants' efforts has been to manufacture lymphokines. Lymphokines, unlike a name or a face, have the same molecular structure in every human being and the same important functions in every human being's immune system. Moreover, the particular genetic material which is responsible for the natural production of lymphokines, and which defendants use to manufacture lymphokines in the laboratory, is also the same in every person; it is no more unique to Moore than the number of vertebrae in the spine or the chemical formula of hemoglobin.

. . . [T]he Court of Appeal in this case concluded that "[a] patient must have the ultimate power to control what becomes of his or her tissues. To hold otherwise would open the door to a massive invasion of human privacy and dignity in the name of medical progress." Yet one may earnestly wish to protect privacy and dignity without accepting the extremely problematic conclusion that interference with those interests amounts to a conversion of personal property. Nor is it necessary to force the round pegs of "privacy" and "dignity" into the square hole of "property" in order to protect the patient, since the fiduciary-duty and informed-consent theories protect these interests directly by requiring full disclosure.

The next consideration that makes Moore's claim of ownership problematic is California statutory law, which drastically limits a patient's control over excised cells. Pursuant to Health and Safety Code section 7054.4, "[n]otwithstanding any other provision of law, recognizable anatomical parts, human tissues, anatomical human remains, or infectious waste following conclusion of scientific use shall be disposed of by interment, incineration, or any other method determined by the state department [of health services] to protect the public health and safety." Clearly the Legislature did not specifically intend this statute to resolve the question of whether a patient is entitled to compensation for the nonconsensual use of excised cells. A primary object of the statute is to ensure the safe handling of potentially hazardous biological waste materials. Yet one cannot escape the conclusion that the statute's practical effect is to limit, drastically, a patient's control over excised cells. By restricting how excised cells may be used and requiring their eventual destruction, the statute eliminates so many of the rights ordinarily attached to property that one cannot simply assume that what is left amounts to "property" or "ownership" for purposes of conversion law.

. . . A fully informed patient may always withhold consent to treatment by a physician whose research plans the patient does not approve.

That right, however, as already discussed, is protected by the fiduciary-duty and informed-consent theories.

Finally, the subject matter of the Regents' patent — the patented cell line and the products derived from it — cannot be Moore's property. This is because the patented cell line is both factually and legally distinct from the cells taken from Moore's body. Federal law permits the patenting of organisms that represent the product of "human ingenuity," but not naturally occurring organisms. . . . It is this *inventive effort* that patent law rewards, not the discovery of naturally occurring raw materials. Thus, Moore's allegations that he owns the cell line and the products derived from it are inconsistent with the patent, which constitutes an authoritative determination that the cell line is the product of invention. . . .

2. Should Conversion Liability Be Extended?

. . . There are three reasons why it is inappropriate to impose liability for conversion based upon the allegations of Moore's complaint. First, a fair balancing of the relevant policy considerations counsels against extending the tort. Second, problems in this area are better suited to legislative resolution. Third, the tort of conversion is not necessary to protect patients' rights. For these reasons, we conclude that the use of excised human cells in medical research does not amount to a conversion.

Of the relevant policy considerations, two are of overriding importance. The first is protection of a competent patient's right to make autonomous medical decisions. That right, as already discussed, is grounded in well-recognized and long-standing principles of fiduciary duty and informed consent. . . . This policy weighs in favor of providing a remedy to patients when physicians act with undisclosed motives that may affect their professional judgment. The second important policy consideration is that we not threaten with disabling civil liability innocent parties who are engaged in socially useful activities, such as researchers who have no reason to believe that their use of a particular cell sample is, or may be, against a donor's wishes.

To reach an appropriate balance of these policy considerations is extremely important. In its report to Congress the Office of Technology Assessment emphasized that

> [u]ncertainty about how courts will resolve disputes between specimen sources and specimen users could be detrimental to both academic researchers and the infant biotechnology industry, particularly when the rights are asserted long after the specimen was obtained. The assertion of rights by sources would affect not only the researcher who obtained the original specimen, but perhaps other researchers as well.

Biological materials are routinely distributed to other researchers for experimental purposes, and scientists who obtain cell lines or other specimen-derived products, such as gene clones, from the original researcher could also be sued under certain legal theories [such as conversion]. Furthermore, the uncertainty could affect product developments as well as research. Since inventions containing human tissues and cells may be patented and licensed for commercial use, companies are unlikely to invest heavily in developing, manufacturing, or marketing a product when uncertainty about clear title exists. . . .

Indeed, so significant is the potential obstacle to research stemming from uncertainty about legal title to biological materials that the Office of Technology Assessment reached this striking conclusion: "[R]egardless of the merit of claims by the different interested parties, resolving the current uncertainty may be more important to the future of biotechnology than resolving it in any particular way." . . .

We need not, however, make an arbitrary choice between liability and nonliability. Instead, an examination of the relevant policy considerations suggests an appropriate balance: Liability based upon existing disclosure obligations, rather than an unprecedented extension of the conversion theory, protects patients' rights of privacy and autonomy without unnecessarily hindering research.

To be sure, the threat of liability for conversion might help to enforce patients' rights indirectly. This is because physicians might be able to avoid liability by obtaining patients' consent, in the broadest possible terms, to any conceivable subsequent research use of excised cells. Unfortunately, to extend the conversion theory would utterly sacrifice the other goal of protecting innocent parties. Since conversion is a strict liability tort, it would impose liability on all those into whose hands the cells come, whether or not the particular defendant participated in, or knew of, the inadequate disclosures that violated the patient's right to make an informed decision. In contrast to the conversion theory, the fiduciary-duty and informed-consent theories protect the patient directly, without punishing innocent parties or creating disincentives to the conduct of socially beneficial research.

Research on human cells plays a critical role in medical research. This is so because researchers are increasingly able to isolate naturally occurring, medically useful biological substances and to produce useful quantities of such substances through genetic engineering. These efforts are beginning to bear fruit. Products developed through biotechnology that have already been approved for marketing in this country include treatments and tests for leukemia, cancer, diabetes, dwarfism, hepatitis-B, kidney transplant rejection, emphysema, osteoporosis, ulcers, anemia, infertility, and gynecological tumors, to name but a few. . . .

The extension of conversion law into this area will hinder research by restricting access to the necessary raw materials. Thousands of human cell lines already exist in tissue repositories. . . . At present, human cell lines are routinely copied and distributed to other researchers for experimental purposes, usually free of charge. This exchange of scientific materials, which still is relatively free and efficient, will surely be compromised if each cell sample becomes the potential subject matter of a lawsuit.

To expand liability by extending conversion law into this area would have a broad impact. The House Committee on Science and Technology of the United States Congress found that "49 percent of the researchers at medical institutions surveyed used human tissues or cells in their research." . . . In addition, "there are nearly 350 commercial biotechnology firms in the United States actively engaged in biotechnology research and commercial product development and approximately 25 to 30 percent appear to be engaged in research to develop a human therapeutic or diagnostic reagent. . . . Most, but not all, of the human therapeutic products are derived from human tissues and cells, or human cell lines or cloned genes." . . .

In deciding whether to create new tort duties we have in the past considered the impact that expanded liability would have on activities that are important to society, such as research. . . .

[T]he theory of liability that Moore urges us to endorse threatens to destroy the economic incentive to conduct important medical research. If the use of cells in research is a conversion, then with every cell sample a researcher purchases a ticket in a litigation lottery. Because liability for conversion is predicated on a continuing ownership interest, "companies are unlikely to invest heavily in developing, manufacturing, or marketing a product when uncertainty about clear title exists." . . .

If the scientific users of human cells are to be held liable for failing to investigate the consensual pedigree of their raw materials, we believe the Legislature should make that decision. . . .

[T]here is no pressing need to impose a judicially created rule of strict liability, since enforcement of physicians' disclosure obligations will protect patients against the very type of harm with which Moore was threatened. So long as a physician discloses research and economic interests that may affect his judgment, the patient is protected from conflicts of interest. Aware of any conflicts, the patient can make an informed decision to consent to treatment, or to withhold consent and look elsewhere for medical assistance. As already discussed, enforcement of physicians' disclosure obligations protects patients directly, without hindering the socially useful activities of innocent researchers.

For these reasons, we hold that the allegations of Moore's third amended complaint state a cause of action for breach of fiduciary duty or lack of informed consent, but not conversion. . . .

Lucas, C. J., Eagleson, J., and Kennard, J., concurred.

ARABIAN, J., concurring. I join in the views cogently expounded by the majority. I write separately to give voice to a concern that I believe informs much of that opinion but finds little or no expression therein. I speak of the moral issue.

Plaintiff has asked us to recognize and enforce a right to sell one's own body tissue *for profit*. He entreats us to regard the human vessel — the single most venerated and protected subject in any civilized society — as equal with the basest commercial commodity. He urges us to commingle the sacred with the profane. He asks much. . . .

It is true, that this court has not often been deterred from deciding difficult legal issues simply because they require a choice between competing social or economic policies. . . . The difference here, however, lies in the nature of the conflicting moral, philosophical and even religious values at stake, and in the profound implications of the position urged. The ramifications of recognizing and enforcing a property interest in body tissues are not known, but are greatly feared — the effect on human dignity of a marketplace in human body parts, the impact on research and development of competitive bidding for such materials, and the exposure of researchers to potentially limitless and uncharted tort liability. . . .

Whether, as plaintiff urges, his cells should be treated as property susceptible to conversion is not, in my view, ours to decide. . . .

Where then shall a complete resolution be found? Clearly the Legislature, as the majority opinion suggests, is the proper deliberative forum. Indeed, a legislative response creating a licensing scheme, which establishes a fixed rate of profit sharing between researcher and subject, has already been suggested. Such an arrangement would not only avoid the moral and philosophical objections to a free market operation in body tissue, but would also address stated concerns by eliminating the inherently coercive effect of a waiver system and by compensating donors regardless of temporal circumstances. . . .

BROUSSARD, J., concurring and dissenting. . . . I dissent from the majority opinion insofar as it rejects plaintiff's conversion cause of action. . . .

If this were a typical case in which a patient consented to the use of his removed organ for general research purposes and the patient's doctor had no prior knowledge of the scientific or commercial value of the patient's organ or cells, I would agree that the patient could not maintain a conversion action. In that common scenario, the patient has abandoned any interest in the removed organ and is not entitled to demand compensation if it should later be discovered that the organ or cells have some unanticipated value. I cannot agree, however, with the majority that a patient may *never* maintain a conversion action for the unauthorized use of his excised organ or cells, even against a party who knew of the value of the organ or cells before they were removed and breached a duty to disclose that value to the patient. Because plaintiff alleges that defendants wrongfully interfered with his right to determine, prior to the removal of his body parts, how those parts would be used after removal, I conclude that the complaint states a cause of action under traditional, common law conversion principles. . . .

The majority opinion fails to recognize . . . that, in light of the allegations of the present complaint, the pertinent inquiry is not whether a patient generally retains an ownership interest in a body part after its removal from his body, but rather whether a patient has a right to determine, before a body part is removed, the use to which the part will be put after removal. Although the majority opinion suggests that there are "reasons to doubt" that a patient retains "any" ownership interest in his organs or cells after removal, the opinion fails to identify any statutory provision or common law authority that indicates that a patient does not generally have the right, before a body part is removed, to choose among the permissible uses to which the part may be put after removal. On the contrary, the most closely related statutory scheme — the Uniform Anatomical Gift Act (Health & Saf. Code, §7150 et seq.) — makes it quite clear that a patient does have this right.

The Uniform Anatomical Gift Act is a comprehensive statutory scheme that was initially adopted in California in 1970 and most recently revised in 1988. Although that legislation, by its terms, applies only to a donation of all or part of a human body which is "to take effect upon or after [the] death [of the donor]" (§7150.1 subd. (a)) — and thus is not directly applicable to the present case which involves a living donor — the act is nonetheless instructive with regard to this state's general policy concerning an individual's authority to control the use of a donated body part. The act, which authorizes an anatomical gift to be made, inter alia, to "[a] hospital [or a] physician[,] . . . for transplantation, therapy, medical or dental education, research or advancement of medical or dental science" (§7153, subd. (a)(1)), expressly provides that such a gift "may be made to a designated donee or without designating a donee" (§7153, subd. (b)) and also that the donor may make such a gift "for any of the purposes [specified in the statute or may] limit an anatomical gift to one or more of those purposes. . . ." (§7150.5, subd. (a).) Thus, the act clearly recognizes that it is the donor of the body part, rather than the hospital or physician who receives the part, who has the authority to designate, within the parameters of the statutorily authorized uses, the particular use to which the part may be put.

Although, as noted, the Uniform Anatomical Gift Act applies only to anatomical gifts that take effect on or after the death of the donor, the general principle of "donor control" which the act embodies is clearly not limited to that setting. In the transplantation context, for example, it is common for a living donor to designate the specific donee — often a relative — who is to receive a donated organ. If a hospital, after removing an organ from such a donor, decided on its own to give the organ to a different donee, no one would deny that the hospital had violated the legal right of the donor by its unauthorized use of the donated organ. Accordingly, it is clear under California law that a patient has the right, prior to the removal of an organ, to control the use to which the organ will be put after removal.

It is also clear, under traditional common law principles, that this right of a patient to control the future use of his organ is protected by the law of conversion. As a general matter, the tort of conversion protects an individual not only against improper interference with the right of possession of his property but also against unauthorized use of his property or improper interference with his right to control the use of his property. . . .

[T]he majority maintains that plaintiff's conversion action is not viable because "the subject matter of the Regents' patent — the patented cell line and the products derived from it — cannot be Moore's property." Even if this is an accurate statement of federal patent law, it does not explain why plaintiff may not maintain a conversion action for defendants' unauthorized use of his own body parts, blood, blood serum, bone marrow, and sperm. Although the damages which plaintiff may recover in a conversion action may not include the value of the patent and the derivative products, the fact that plaintiff may not be entitled to all of the damages which his complaint seeks does not justify denying his right to maintain any conversion action at all. Similarly, although the question whether plaintiff's cells are "unique" may well affect the amount of damages plaintiff will be able to recover in a conversion action, the question of uniqueness has no proper bearing on plaintiff's basic right to maintain a conversion action; ordinary property, as well as unique property, is, of course, protected against conversion.

Thus, unlike the majority, I conclude that under established common law principles the facts alleged in the complaint state a cause of action for conversion. . . .

Finally, the majority's analysis of the relevant policy considerations tellingly omits a most pertinent consideration. In identifying the interests of the patient that are implicated by the decision whether to recognize a conversion cause of action, the opinion speaks only of the "patient's right to make autonomous medical decisions" and fails even to mention the patient's interest in obtaining the economic value, if any, that may adhere in the subsequent use of his own body parts. Although such economic value may constitute a fortuitous "windfall" to the patient, the fortuitous nature of the economic value does not justify the creation of a novel exception from conversion liability which sanctions the intentional misappropriation of that value from the patient.

This last point reveals perhaps the most serious flaw in the majority's public policy analysis in this case. It is certainly arguable that, as a matter of policy or morality, it would be wiser to prohibit any private individual or entity from profiting from the fortuitous value that adheres in a part of a human body, and instead to require all valuable excised body parts to be deposited in a public repository which would make such materials freely available to all scientists for the betterment of society as a whole. The Legislature, if it wished, could create such a system, as it has done with respect to organs that are donated for transplantation. (See §7155, subd. (a); Pen. Code §367f. See also 42 U.S.C. §274e.) To date, however, the Legislature has not adopted such a system for organs that are to be used for research or commercial purposes, and the majority opinion, despite some oblique suggestions to the contrary, emphatically does not do so by its holding in this case. Justice Arabian's concurring opinion suggests that the majority's conclusion is informed by the precept that it is immoral to sell human body parts for profit. But the majority's rejection of plaintiff's conversion cause of action does *not* mean that body parts may not be bought or sold for research or commercial purposes or that *no* private individual or entity may benefit economically from the fortuitous value of plaintiff's diseased cells. Far from elevating these biological materials above the marketplace, the majority's holding simply bars *plaintiff,* the source of the cells, from obtaining the benefit of the cells' value, but permits *defendants,* who allegedly obtained the cells from plaintiff by improper means, to retain and exploit the full economic value of their ill-gotten gains free of their ordinary common law liability for conversion.

Because I conclude that plaintiff's complaint states a cause of action for conversion under traditional common law principles, I dissent from the majority opinion insofar as it rejects such a claim.

MOSK, J. I dissent. Contrary to the principal holding of the Court of Appeal, the majority conclude that the complaint does not — in fact cannot — state a cause of action for conversion. I disagree with this conclusion for all the reasons stated by the Court of Appeal, and for additional reasons. . . .

The concepts of property and ownership in our law are extremely broad. . . .

Being broad, the concept of property is also abstract: rather than referring directly to a material object such as a parcel of land or the tractor that cultivates it, the concept of property is often said to refer to a "bundle of rights" that may be exercised with respect to that object — principally the rights to possess the property, to use the property, to exclude others from the property, and to dispose of the property by sale or by gift. . . . But the same bundle of rights does not attach to all forms of property. For a variety of policy reasons, the law limits or even forbids the exercise of certain rights over certain forms of property. For example, both law and contract may limit the right of an owner of real property to use his parcel as he sees fit. Owners of various forms of personal property may likewise be subject to restrictions on the time, place, and manner of their use. Limitations on the disposition of real property, while less common, may also be imposed. Finally, some types of personal property may be sold but not given away,[41] while others may be given away but not sold,[42] and still others may neither be given away nor sold.[43]

In each of the foregoing instances, the limitation or prohibition diminishes the bundle of rights that would otherwise attach to the property, yet what remains is still deemed in law to be a protectible property interest. . . . The same rule applies to Moore's interest in his own body tissue. . . . Above all, at the time of its excision he at least had *the right to do with his own tissue whatever the defendants did with it:* i.e., he could have contracted with researchers and pharmaceutical companies to develop and exploit the vast commercial potential of his tissue and its products. . . .

Having concluded — mistakenly, in my view — that Moore has no cause of action for conversion under existing law, the majority next consider whether to "extend" the conversion cause of action to this context. Again . . . I respectfully disagree with [their reasoning].

. . . [O]ur society acknowledges a profound ethical imperative to respect the human body as the physical and temporal expression of the unique human persona. One manifestation of that respect is our prohibition against direct abuse of the body by torture or other forms of cruel or unusual punishment. Another is our prohibition against indirect abuse of the body by its economic exploitation for the sole benefit of another person. The most abhorrent form of such exploitation, of course, was the institution of slavery. Lesser forms, such as indentured servitude or even debtor's prison, have also disappeared. Yet their specter haunts the laboratories and boardrooms of today's biotechnological research-industrial complex. It arises wherever scientists or industrialists claim, as defendants claim here, the right to appropriate and exploit a patient's tissue for their sole economic benefit — the right, in other words, to freely mine or harvest valuable physical properties of the patient's body. . . .

A second policy consideration adds notions of equity to those of ethics. Our society values fundamental fairness in dealings between its members, and condemns the unjust enrichment of any member at the expense of another. This is particularly true when, as here, the parties are not in equal bargaining positions. . . . Yet defendants deny that Moore is entitled to any share whatever in the proceeds of this cell line. This is both inequitable and immoral. . . .

41. A person contemplating bankruptcy may sell his property at its "reasonably equivalent value," but he may not make a gift of the same property. (See 11 U.S.C. §548(a).)

42. A sportsman may give away wild fish or game that he has caught or killed pursuant to his license, but he may not sell it. (Fish & G. Code, §§3039, 7121.)

The transfer of human organs and blood is a special case that I discuss below.

43. E.g., a license to practice a profession, or a prescription drug in the hands of the person for whom it is prescribed.

There will be . . . equitable sharing if the courts recognize that the patient has a legally protected property interest in his own body and its products: "property rights in one's own tissue would provide a morally acceptable result by giving effect to notions of fairness and preventing unjust enrichment. . . ."

I do not doubt that the Legislature is competent to act on this topic. The fact that the Legislature may intervene if and when it chooses, however, does not in the meanwhile relieve the courts of their duty of enforcing — or if need be, fashioning — an effective judicial remedy for the wrong here alleged. . . .

The inference I draw from the current statutory regulation of human biological materials, moreover, is the opposite of that drawn by the majority. By selective quotation of the statutes [see page 74, footnote 40] the majority seem to suggest that human organs and blood cannot legally be sold on the open market — thereby implying that if the Legislature were to act here it would impose a similar ban on monetary compensation for the use of human tissue in biotechnological research and development. But if that is the argument, the premise is unsound: contrary to popular misconception, it is not true that human organs and blood cannot legally be sold.

As to organs, the majority rely on the Uniform Anatomical Gift Act (Health & Saf. Code, §7150 et seq., hereafter the UAGA) for the proposition that a competent adult may make a post mortem gift of any part of his body but may not receive "valuable consideration" for the transfer. But the prohibition of the UAGA against the sale of a body part is much more limited than the majority recognize: by its terms (Health & Saf. Code, §7155, subd. (a)) the prohibition applies only to sales for "transplantation" or "therapy." Yet a different section of the UAGA authorizes the transfer and receipt of body parts for such additional purposes as "medical or dental education, research, or advancement of medical or dental science." (Health & Saf. Code, §7153, subd. (a)(1).) No section of the UAGA prohibits anyone from selling body parts for any of those additional purposes; by clear implication, therefore, such sales are legal.[44] Indeed, the fact that the UAGA prohibits *no* sales of organs other than sales for "transplantation" or "therapy" raises a further implication that it is also legal for anyone to sell human tissue to a biotechnology company for research and development purposes. . . .

It follows that the statutes regulating the transfers of human organs and blood do not support the majority's refusal to recognize a conver-

44. "By their terms . . . the statutes in question forbid only sales for transplantation and therapy. In light of the rather clear authorization for donation for research and education, one could conclude that sales for these non-therapeutic purposes are permitted. Scientists in practice have been buying and selling human tissues for research apparently without interference from these statutes." (Note, "She's Got Bette Davis['s] Eyes": Assessing the Nonconsensual Removal of Cadaver Organs Under the Takings and Due Process Clauses (1990) 90 Colum. L. Rev. 528, 544, fn. 75.)

sion cause of action for commercial exploitation of human blood cells without consent. On the contrary, because such statutes treat both organs and blood as property that can legally be sold in a variety of circumstances, they impliedly support Moore's contention that his blood cells are likewise property for which he can and should receive compensation, and hence are protected by the law of conversion.

The majority's final reason for refusing to recognize a conversion cause of action on these facts is that "there is no pressing need" to do so because the complaint also states another cause of action that is assertedly adequate to the task. . . .

I disagree, however, with the majority's further conclusion that in the present context a nondisclosure cause of action is an adequate — in fact, a superior — substitute for a conversion cause of action. . . .

The majority do not spell out how those obligations will be "enforced"; but because they arise from judicial decision (the majority opinion herein) rather than from legislative or administrative enactment, we may infer that the obligations will primarily be enforced by the traditional judicial remedy of an action for damages for their breach. . . .

The remedy is largely illusory. "[A]n action based on the physician's failure to disclose material information sounds in negligence. As a practical matter, however, it may be difficult to recover on this kind of negligence theory because the patient must prove a *causal connection* between his or her injury and the physician's failure to inform." (Martin & Lagod, Biotechnology and the Commercial Use of Human Cells: Toward an Organic View of Life and Technology (1989) 5 Santa Clara Computer & High Tech L.J. 211, 222, fn. omitted, italics added.) There are two barriers to recovery. First, "the patient must show that if he or she had been informed of all pertinent information, he or she would have declined to consent to the procedure in question." (Ibid.) . . .

The second barrier to recovery is still higher, and is erected on the first: it is not even enough for the plaintiff to prove that he personally would have refused consent to the proposed treatment if he had been fully informed; he must also prove that in the same circumstances *no reasonably prudent person* would have given such consent. . . .

The second reason why the nondisclosure cause of action is inadequate for the task that the majority assign to it is that it fails to solve half the problem before us: it gives the patient only the right to *refuse* consent, i.e., the right to prohibit the commercialization of his tissue; it does not give him the right to *grant* consent to that commercialization on the condition that he share in its proceeds. . . .

Reversing the words of the old song, the nondisclosure cause of action thus accentuates the negative and eliminates the positive: the patient can say no, but he cannot say yes and expect to share in the proceeds of his contribution. . . .

Third, the nondisclosure cause of action fails to reach a major class of potential defendants: all those who are outside the strict physician-

patient relationship with the plaintiff. Thus the majority concede that
here only defendant Golde, the treating physician, can be directly liable
to Moore on a nondisclosure cause of action. . . .

In sum, the nondisclosure cause of action (1) is unlikely to be successful in most cases, (2) fails to protect patients' rights to share in the
proceeds of the commercial exploitation of their tissue, and (3) may allow the true exploiters to escape liability. It is thus not an adequate substitute, in my view, for the conversion cause of action. . . .

NOTES AND QUESTIONS: PROPERTY RIGHTS IN BODIES

1. *More to* Moore *than meets the eye.* The excerpts from *Moore* reproduced above are only a fraction (but the essential fraction) of the opinions in the case, which consume in their entirety 65 pages of the official
reporter. (The pages of law review and other commentary run many
times that number. A selected bibliography, including literature related
to but not directly about the case, appears in footnote 46 below.)

There's more to *Moore* in another, more substantial sense, as Justice
Arabian makes plain when he addresses in his concurring opinion (see
pages 78-79) "a concern that . . . informs much of [the majority] opinion
but finds little or no expression therein." The concern in question is
actually twofold: recognition of property rights in one's cells would (a)
necessarily entail "a right to sell one's own body tissue *for profit*" and (b)
thereby give rise to the grave difficulties Arabian suggests.

2. *A bundle of rights.* But (a) is incorrect, as one can gather from the
first few paragraphs of Justice Mosk's dissenting opinion (see pages 82-
83). For lawyers, if not lay people, property is an abstraction. It refers
not to things, material or otherwise, but to rights or relationships among
people with respect to things. And the abstraction we call property is
multi- not monolithic. It consists of a number of disparate rights, a "bundle" of them: the right to possess, the right to use, the right to exclude,
the right to transfer.

Regarding the latter, note that while property may usually be transferred by sale or by gift, this is not always the case. As Justice Mosk
explains, sometimes gifts alone are permitted, sometimes only sales,
sometimes neither. Notwithstanding, we can still be talking about property.[45]

45. When sales are prohibited but gifts allowed, property is sometimes said to be
"market-inalienable." When the situation is reversed, one might say that the property is
only market-alienable. When neither mode of transfer is permitted, the property is inalienable. Justice Mosk gives examples of each in footnotes 41-43. Can you think of others? See
generally Susan Rose-Ackerman, Inalienability and the Theory of Property Rights, 85
Colum. L. Rev. 931 (1985). Rose-Ackerman concludes that the various restrictions on

Could not the majority in *Moore* have used these observations to craft a more satisfactory opinion? The majority held that Mr. Moore's body parts, once wrongfully excised, were no longer his property but rather the defendants', and that seems odd. Surely the cells were Mr. Moore's prior to excision. Why not after? If the majority had used Justice Mosk's approach, it could first have held the cells still to be Moore's property and then gone on to consider the question of alienability. Framing the matter in this way would readily allow the conclusion that because the cells were Moore's, they were not some doctor's to take, but neither were they Moore's *to sell in a market transaction.* In other words, the majority could have limited Moore's property rights but nevertheless acknowledged and protected them through the cause of action for conversion. Concerns about the impact of conversion liability on medical research and development could in turn have been eased by an appropriately tailored measure of damages. The literature cited in footnote 46 mentions any number of alternatives, such as royalties, a percentage of profits, or a lump sum.

Still, a problem remains. "The ramifications of recognizing and enforcing a property interest in body tissues are not known, but are greatly feared," Justice Arabian says. The subject is so fraught with difficulties that even the first step is dangerous — and beyond the competence of courts. "Clearly the Legislature, as the majority opinion suggests, is the proper deliberative forum."

3. *Gifts versus sales: point/counterpoint.* Actually, there has been legislative deliberation regarding some of the issues and concerns underlying *Moore.* State legislation varies, but the matter is largely governed in any event by a federal statute making it "unlawful for any person to knowingly acquire, receive, or otherwise transfer any human organ for valuable consideration for use in human transplantation if the transfer affects interstate commerce." 42 U.S.C. §274e (1988). Notice that this provision implicitly recognizes property rights in body parts. It permits gifts from living or cadaveric donors and even permits sales, unless the sales are for transplantation. To use the terminology introduced in footnote 45, the regime is one of partial market-inalienability (a fact that tends to undermine the result in *Moore*).

Is the ban on sale of organs for transplantation appropriate? We saw earlier (for example, footnote 38 on page 68) that property rights and markets commonly come to mind when changes in knowledge cre-

---

transferability rest on no single principle. Instead, depending on the case, a particular restriction might be justified in terms of any number of concerns, such as distributive goals, externalities, imperfections in information, problems of coordination. You will see some of these considerations at work in the dialogue on pages 88-91.

Should it matter that the plaintiff in the *Moore* case was a monopolist (his cell line was unique and very valuable)? And is there anything to be made of the law of accession (sketched on pages 16-17)? Bear these two questions in mind as you return to the discussion in the text.

ate new opportunities, new demands, and a new scarcity. Body parts are no exception. Recent advances in medical technology have increased demand for organs to the point that supplies are inadequate, and this in turn has moved some observers to suggest market-based approaches as a means to augment (and perhaps allocate) the stock. Unsurprisingly, the idea is contentious, the subject of ongoing — and at times passionate — debate. Imagine a dialogue between two people named *Pro* and *Con*.[46]

PRO.   Cadavers are essentially the only source for many transplantable organs, such as hearts, lungs, and livers. Approximately 20,000 Americans die every year under conditions such that their organs could be used to help others. That's a small number in the first place, but what makes matters worse is that the donation rate is only about 15 percent, probably in part because people don't like to think about dying.

CON.   They don't have to think about it; in most jurisdictions next of kin can donate the deceased's organs.

PRO.   But by and large they don't, as the modest donation rate indicates. Removal of organs is an obviously troubling thing for a family to think about right after the loss of a loved one, and you can't expect doctors to urge donations at such a time either. Yet the decision has to be made quickly or the organs aren't suitable.

CON.   There are ways to deal with these problems. You could require doctors to make requests, for example. Better yet, you could presume that a deceased person's organs are available, absent some

---

46. A large literature stands behind the dialogue. For excellent overviews, see Henry B. Hansmann, The Economics and Ethics of Markets for Human Organs, 14 J. Health Pol., Poly. & L. 57 (1989), and Keith N. Hylton, The Law and Economics of Organ Procurement, 12 Law & Poly. 197 (1990). On the *Moore* case and property rights in body parts generally, see, e.g., Russell Scott, The Body as Property (1981); Richard M. Titmuss, The Gift Relationship (1971); Mary T. Danforth, Cells, Sales, and Royalties: The Patient's Right to a Portion of the Profits, 6 Yale L. & Poly. Rev. 179 (1988); Jesse Dukeminier, Supplying Organs for Transplantation, 68 Mich. L. Rev. 811 (1970); Leon R. Kass, Organs for Sale? Propriety, Property, and the Price of Progress, The Pub. Interest, Spring 1992, at 65; Thomas H. Murray, On the Human Body as Property: The Meaning of Embodiment, Markets, and the Meaning of Strangers, 20 U. Mich. J.L. Ref. 1055 (1987); Case Comment, *Moore v. Regents of the University of California:* Insufficient Protection of Patients' Rights in the Biotechnological Market, 25 Ga. L. Rev. 489 (1991); Note, Ownership of Human Tissue: Life After *Moore v. Regents of the University of California,* 75 Va. L. Rev. 1363 (1989); Note, Personalizing Personalty: Toward a Property Right in Human Bodies, 69 Tex. L. Rev. 209 (1990); Note, Reconsidering Inalienability for Commercially Valuable Biological Materials, 29 Harv. J. Legis. 223 (1992); Comment, Spleen for Sale: *Moore v. Regents of the University of California* and the Right to Sell Parts of Your Body, 51 Ohio St. L.J. 473 (1990); Comment, Toward the Right of Commerciality: Recognizing Property Rights in the Commercial Value of Human Tissue, 34 UCLA L. Rev. 207 (1986); Bibliography, Genetics and the Law, 39 Emory L.J. 875 (1990); Developments in the Law — Medical Technology and the Law, 103 Harv. L. Rev. 1519 (1990); Recent Developments, 104 Harv. L. Rev. 808 (1991); U.S. Congress, Office of Technology Assessment, 1 New Developments in Biotechnology, Ownership of Human Tissues and Cells (1987); Forum: Sacred or for Sale?, Harper's Mag., Oct. 1990, at 47.

kind of formal indication to the contrary by the decedent prior to death or by the family at the time of death. Opinion surveys indicate that most people actually favor organ donation. A system of presumed consent would turn inertia in favor of altruism.

PRO.   I doubt it. Both of the approaches you mention are in use, the first in over half the states and the second in Europe, but neither has made a significant dent in the donation rate. Some observers recommend a third approach. At a given time, say when applying for a driver's license, everyone would have to make a decision one way or another about organ donation. But if presumed consent hasn't made much of a difference, why would mandated choice?

CON.   So what would you do?

PRO.   I'd think about going beyond altruism and offering payment. In the case of cadaveric organs, for example, the mandated-choice approach could be modified to include payment to people who choose to be donors, made at the time they registered that choice. Under one such proposal, health insurance companies would be the buyers and there would be a centralized clearing system to match donors and recipients. Compensation could be in the form of reduced health insurance premiums.

CON.   I'd be very reluctant to participate in a scheme like that, for two reasons. First, I'd worry that if I chose to be a donor and then later was badly injured in an accident, the doctors might not give me the best care, figuring I was likely to die in any event and that my organs could save someone else.

PRO.   That's a strange thing for you to say, because you seem to favor gifts of organs. Don't gifts raise exactly the same difficulty?

CON.   Well, maybe you're right about that, but they avoid my second concern. If you pay people for organs the cost is going to be passed on, making transplants and medical research much more expensive than they are now.

PRO.   I'm surprised you're so sure about that. You said earlier that people favor donating their organs at death, that the chief problem is inertia. The payment needed to overcome inertia could be quite modest. Living donors, of course, would command a considerable premium.

CON.   Living donors? You are talking about organs from living donors?

PRO.   We already use organs from living donors — kidneys, for example.

CON.   But those are gifts, not sales.

PRO.   So what? People can sell semen, skin tissue, and blood. Why shouldn't someone be able to sell a kidney? If sales by living donors were allowed, the potential supply would be sufficient to satisfy all medical needs, unlike the situation with cadavers. People can live with a single kidney, donation isn't particularly hazardous, and transplants can save lives, so why not allow sales? The price might be high, but the alternative to a kidney transplant, hemodialysis, is itself very costly.

CON.   The poor can't afford either.

PRO.   Exactly, so the system wouldn't make them any worse off, and it promises to improve their situation. First of all, using a market system to obtain organs doesn't dictate exclusive reliance on the same system to distribute them, especially if the supply is abundant. Organs could be made freely available to the poor, as many medical services already are. Second, low-income people would have an income opportunity that they don't have now.

CON.   So you would force the poor to provide, in this tragic way, for the well-to-do.

PRO.   I wouldn't force anybody to do anything. This would be a voluntary system.

CON.   Right! And if you were poor, could you resist the temptation?

PRO.   I don't know. But if I did succumb, it would be because I thought doing so, all things considered, improved my situation. Would you want to set up a system that allowed sales but excluded participation by the impoverished? Low-income people have few enough choices and few enough means to better themselves as it is. Ideally we should redistribute wealth to the poor, period, and let them choose from there. But this isn't an ideal world. Poor people take dirty, risky jobs like coal mining. Should we prohibit that?

CON.   You can always quit a job, but the decision to sacrifice a kidney is irreversible.

PRO.   I hope you see that that argument applies only to living donors. Even as to them, kidney donors who later suffered kidney failure could get transplants. Moreover, *giving* a kidney during life is no more reversible than selling one, but you seem to feel comfortable with gifts from living donors.

CON.   Gifts are different. Consider the studies showing that commercially obtained blood is of lower quality than blood freely donated. When people give, their altruism provides some assurance that they at least think what they give is good. When people sell, however, narrow self-interest takes over. People would sell faulty organs.

PRO.   People know less about the quality of their organs than they do the quality of their blood, so they couldn't corrupt the system in the same way. Moreover, it's probably feasible to measure the quality of organs.

CON.   Probably isn't for sure. In any event, the blood studies also suggest that if compensation were offered, the rate of altruistic giving might decrease so much that we'd end up with a reduction in the supply. And even if the supply of organs increased, the amount of altruism would no doubt decline, and altruism is a good in and of itself. It bonds people; it strengthens a sense of community, of interdependence and reciprocal obligation. And, particularly in the setting we are talking about here, it expresses the ideal of life's sanctity.

PRO. If life is so sacred, why are you willing to let people die unnecessarily? There must be better ways to foster altruism, such as education.

CON. And what sort of education would you be providing? A market in body parts would corrupt our sense of what it is to be human. Everybody — every body — would tend to be viewed as just another commodity. Some things just don't belong in markets.

PRO. But body parts are already in markets; they can be sold for research.

CON. Right, and maybe that shouldn't be. Immanuel Kant, for example, was of the view that people are not entitled to sell parts of themselves for money, essentially because it degrades them to the level of mere objects; they would lose their freedom, dignity, and self-respect.

PRO. Kant's views are widely regarded as problematic. In his view, for example, a poor mother couldn't sell a body part to get the wherewithal to pay for an operation to save her child. In any event, Kant lived in a different time. Moral visions change. Human dignity, the sanctity of life, and the sacredness of bodies were offered as objections to life insurance and autopsy in the nineteenth century and to abdominal surgery and artificial insemination earlier in this century. Do you find those morally objectionable?

CON. But now you want to carry matters another step further. Next you'll want to experiment with markets in babies.

PRO. There are those who think we should consider the idea.

CON. See what I mean? It's a slippery slope.

PRO. Every decision is a slippery slope. We nevertheless have to decide, and usually we do so in a disciplined way. History shows that it is possible to maintain appropriate normative boundaries regarding market activity. Indeed, in many instances we have rightly narrowed the role of markets and commodification, as with slavery and child labor. And the debate about body parts suggests, if anything, that the move to property rights and markets is often the result of a hard climb, not a slippery slope. We protect our sense of human dignity very zealously, sometimes counterproductively. Human dignity is about autonomy and self-determination. The freedom to sell body parts no more reduces human dignity than the freedom to sell one's labor or the freedom to sell the intellectual products of one's mind.

Perhaps you can now understand why the majority in *Moore* wished the property rights issue onto the legislature. If you were a legislator, how would you decide? Going beyond *Moore,* can you see how aspects of the debate between *Pro* and *Con* might bear on such issues as frozen embryos, surrogate motherhood, baby-selling, and even prostitution?[47]

4.   Moore *and the right to exclude.* Note 6 on pages 57-58 introduced Felix Cohen's notion of property as a relationship that entitles so-called owners to *include* or *exclude* other people with respect to the things owned, and suggested what this has to do with transferability. We have focused thus far on the right to include, the right to give or sell to another, but, interestingly enough, that right does not of itself result in a fully effective power of transfer: The right to exclude is needed as well. The two rights together are the necessary and sufficient conditions of transferability. (Do you see why?)

The law of trespass, introduced in Note 1 on pages 53-54, protects the right to exclude, but then so too does the law of conversion at issue in *Moore.* Indeed, conversion developed in part as a substitute for the old action of trespass to chattels (chattels are personal property; the word derives from cattle, a significant item of personal property in earlier times). So *Moore* can be seen to involve the right to exclude as well as the right to include, as Justice Broussard perhaps recognized in his concurring and dissenting opinion (see pages 79, 82). One of the commentators participating in the Harper's Magazine Forum, supra footnote 46, seems to object to such a right with respect to body parts on the ground that it would result in "enclosure of the genetic commons." Is enclosure a bad idea? Recall the preceding section of this chapter and consider the view that property rights in body parts are governed at present by "something like a 'rule of capture' under which the organs effectively become the property of the hospital that harvests them." Hansmann, supra footnote 46, at 82-83. Doesn't that sound like *Moore?*

The right to exclude, like the right to include, is not unlimited. Consider the following case.

State v. Shack
Supreme Court of New Jersey, 1971
58 N.J. 297, 277 A.2d 369

WEINTRAUB, C.J. Defendants entered upon private property to aid migrant farmworkers employed and housed there. Having refused to de-

47. On these and related matters, see, e.g., R.G. Hammond, Personal Property (1990); Stephen R. Munzer, A Theory of Property (1990); J. Robert Prichard, A Market for Babies?, 34 U. Toronto L.J. 341 (1984); Margaret J. Radin, Market-Inalienability, 100 Harv. L. Rev. 1849 (1987); John A. Robertson, Technology and Motherhood: Legal and Ethical Issues in Human Egg Donation, 39 Case W. Res. L. Rev. 1 (1988-1989); Ownership of Life (collection of articles on surrogacy), 13 Harv. J.L. & Pub. Poly. 125 (1990); Note, Evolving Conceptualizations of Property: A Proposal to De-Commercialize the Value of Fetal Tissue, 99 Yale L.J. 169 (1989); Note, Frozen Embryos — Persons or Property?: *Davis v. Davis,* 23 Creighton L. Rev. 807 (1990); Forum: Adoption and Market Theory, 67 B.U. L. Rev. 59-175 (1987).

part upon the demand of the owner, defendants were charged with violating N.J.S.A. 2A:170-31 which provides that "[a]ny person who trespasses on any lands . . . after being forbidden so to trespass by the owner . . . is a disorderly person and shall be punished by a fine of not more than $50." Defendants were convicted in the Municipal Court of Deerfield Township and again on appeal in the County Court of Cumberland County on a trial *de novo*. We certified their further appeal before argument in the Appellate Division.

Before us, no one seeks to sustain these convictions. The complaints were prosecuted in the Municipal Court and in the County Court by counsel engaged by the complaining landowner, Tedesco. However Tedesco did not respond to this appeal, and the county prosecutor, while defending abstractly the constitutionality of the trespass statute, expressly disclaimed any position as to whether the statute reached the activity of these defendants.

Complainant, Tedesco, a farmer, employs migrant workers for his seasonal needs. As part of their compensation, these workers are housed at a camp on his property.

Defendant Tejeras is a field worker for the Farm Workers Division of the Southwest Citizens Organization for Poverty Elimination, known by the acronym SCOPE, a nonprofit corporation funded by the Office of Economic Opportunity pursuant to an act of Congress, 42 U.S.C.A. §§2861-2864. The role of SCOPE includes providing for the "health services of the migrant farm worker."

Defendant Shack is a staff attorney with the Farm Workers Division of Camden Regional Legal Services, Inc., known as "CRLS," also a nonprofit corporation funded by the Office of Economic Opportunity pursuant to an act of Congress, 42 U.S.C.A. §2809(a)(3). The mission of CRLS includes legal advice and representation for these workers.

Differences had developed between Tedesco and these defendants prior to the events which led to the trespass charges now before us. Hence when defendant Tejeras wanted to go upon Tedesco's farm to find a migrant worker who needed medical aid for the removal of 28 sutures, he called upon defendant Shack for his help with respect to the legalities involved. Shack, too, had a mission to perform on Tedesco's farm; he wanted to discuss a legal problem with another migrant worker there employed and housed. Defendants arranged to go to the farm together. Shack carried literature to inform the migrant farmworkers of the assistance available to them under federal statutes, but no mention seems to have been made of that literature when Shack was later confronted by Tedesco.

Defendants entered upon Tedesco's property and as they neared the camp site where the farmworkers were housed, they were confronted by Tedesco who inquired of their purpose. Tejeras and Shack stated their missions. In response, Tedesco offered to find the injured worker, and as to the worker who needed legal advice, Tedesco also offered to locate the man but insisted that the consultation would have to take place in Tedesco's office and in his presence. Defendants declined, saying they had the right to see the men in the privacy of their living quarters and without Tedesco's supervision. Tedesco thereupon summoned a State Trooper who, however, refused to remove defendants except upon Tedesco's written complaint. Tedesco then executed the formal complaints charging violations of the trespass statute.

I

The constitutionality of the trespass statute, as applied here, is challenged on several scores.

It is urged that the First Amendment rights of the defendants and of the migrant farmworkers were thereby offended. Reliance is placed on Marsh v. Alabama, 326 U.S. 501 (1946), where it was held that free speech was assured by the First Amendment in a company-owned town which was open to the public generally and was indistinguishable from any other town except for the fact that the title to the property was vested in a private corporation. Hence a Jehovah's Witness who distributed literature on a sidewalk within the town could not be held as a trespasser. Later, on the strength of that case, it was held that there was a First Amendment right to picket peacefully in a privately owned shopping center which was found to be the functional equivalent of the business district of the company-owned town in Marsh. Amalgamated Food Employees Union Local 590 v. Logan Valley Plaza, Inc., 391 U.S. 308 (1968). Those cases rest upon the fact that the property was in fact opened to the general public. There may be some migrant camps with the attributes of the company town in Marsh and of course they would come within its holding. But there is nothing of that character in the case before us, and hence there would have to be an extension of Marsh to embrace the immediate situation.

Defendants also maintain that the application of the trespass statute to them is barred by the Supremacy Clause of the United States Constitution, Art. VI, cl. 2, and this on the premise that the application of the trespass statute would defeat the purpose of the federal statutes, under which SCOPE and CRLS are funded, to reach and aid the migrant farmworker. The brief of the United States, amicus curiae, supports that approach. Here defendants rely upon cases construing the National Labor Relations Act, 29 U.S.C.A. §151 et seq., and holding that an employer may in some circumstances be guilty of an unfair labor practice in violation of that statute if the employer denies union organizers an opportunity to communicate with his employees at some suitable place upon the employer's premises. See NLRB v. Babcock and Wilcox Co., 351 U.S. 105 (1956), and annotation, 100 L. Ed. 984 (1956). The brief of New Jersey State Office of Legal Services, amicus curias, asserts the workers'

Sixth Amendment right to counsel in criminal matters is involved and suggests also that a right to counsel in civil matters is a "penumbra" right emanating from the whole Bill of Rights under the thinking of Griswold v. Connecticut, 381 U.S. 479 (1965), or is a privilege of national citizenship protected by the privileges and immunities clause of the Fourteenth Amendment, or is a right "retained by the people" under the Ninth Amendment, citing a dictum in United Public Workers v. Mitchell, 330 U.S. 75, 94 (1947).

These constitutional claims are not established by any definitive holding. We think it unnecessary to explore their validity. The reason is that we are satisfied that under our State law the ownership of real property does not include the right to bar access to governmental services available to migrant workers and hence there was no trespass within the meaning of the penal statute. The policy considerations which underlie that conclusion may be much the same as those which would be weighed with respect to one or more of the constitutional challenges, but a decision in nonconstitutional terms is more satisfactory, because the interests of migrant workers are more expansively served in that way than they would be if they had no more freedom than these constitutional concepts could be found to mandate if indeed they apply at all.

II

Property rights serve human values. They are recognized to that end, and are limited by it. Title to real property cannot include dominion over the destiny of persons the owner permits to come upon the premises. Their well-being must remain the paramount concern of a system of law. Indeed, the needs of the occupants may be so imperative and their strength so weak, that the law will deny the occupants the power to contract away what is deemed essential to their health, welfare, or dignity.

Here we are concerned with a highly disadvantaged segment of our society. We are told that every year farmworkers and their families numbering more than one million leave their home areas to fill the seasonal demand for farm labor in the United States. The migrant farmworkers come to New Jersey in substantial numbers. . . .

The migrant farmworkers are a community within but apart from the local scene. They are rootless and isolated. Although the need for their labors is evident, they are unorganized and without economic or political power. It is their plight alone that summoned government to their aid. In response, Congress provided under Title III-B of the Economic Opportunity Act of 1964 (42 U.S.C.A. §2701 et seq.) for "assistance for migrant and other seasonally employed farmworkers and their families." Section 2861 states "the purpose of this part is to assist migrant and seasonal farmworkers and their families to improve their living conditions and develop skills necessary for a productive and self-sufficient life in an increasingly complex and technological society." Section 2862(b)(1) provides for funding of programs "to meet the immediate needs of migrant and seasonal farmworkers and their families, such as day care for children, education, health services, improved housing and sanitation (including the provision and maintenance of emergency and temporary housing and sanitation facilities), legal advice and representation, and consumer training and counseling." As we have said, SCOPE is engaged in a program funded under this section, and CRLS also pursues the objectives of this section although, we gather, it is funded under §2809(a)(3), which is not limited in its concern to the migrant and other seasonally employed farmworkers and seeks "to further the cause of justice among persons living in poverty by mobilizing the assistance of lawyers and legal institutions and by providing legal advice, legal representation, counseling, education, and other appropriate services."

These ends would not be gained if the intended beneficiaries could be insulated from efforts to reach them. It is in this framework that we must decide whether the camp operator's rights in his lands may stand between the migrant workers and those who would aid them. The key to that aid is communication. Since the migrant workers are outside the mainstream of the communities in which they are housed and are unaware of their rights and opportunities and of the services available to them, they can be reached only by positive efforts tailored to that end. The Report of the Governor's Task Force on Migrant Farm Labor (1968) noted that "One of the major problems related to seasonal farm labor is the lack of adequate direct information with regard to the availability of public services," and that "there is a dire need to provide the workers with basic educational and informational material in a language and style that can be readily understood by the migrant" (pp. 101-102). The report stressed the problem of access and deplored the notion that property rights may stand as a barrier, saying "In our judgment, 'no trespass' signs represent the last dying remnants of paternalistic behavior" (p. 63).

A man's right in his real property of course is not absolute. It was a maxim of the common law that one should so use his property as not to injure the rights of others. Although hardly a precise solvent of actual controversies, the maxim does express the inevitable proposition that rights are relative and there must be an accommodation when they meet. Hence it has long been true that necessity, private or public, may justify entry upon the lands of another.

The subject is not static. As pointed out in 5 Powell, Real Property (Rohan 1970) §745, pp. 493-494, while society will protect the owner in his permissible interests in land, yet

. . . [S]uch an owner must expect to find the absoluteness of his property rights curtailed by the organs of society, for the promotion of the best interests of others for whom these organs also operate as protective agencies. The necessity for such curtailments is greater in a modern industrialized and urbanized society than it was in the relatively simple American society of fifty, 100, or 200 years ago. The current balance between individualism and dominance of the social interest depends not only upon political and social ideologies, but also upon the physical and social facts of the time and place under discussion.

Professor Powell added in §746, pp. 494-496:

> As one looks back along the historic road traversed by the law of land in England and in America, one sees a change from the viewpoint that he who owns may do as he pleases with what he owns, to a position which hesitatingly embodies an ingredient of stewardship; which grudgingly, but steadily, broadens the recognized scope of social interests in the utilization of things. . . .
>
> To one seeing history through the glasses of religion, these changes may seem to evidence increasing embodiments of the golden rule. To one thinking in terms of political and economic ideologies, they are likely to be labeled evidences of "social enlightenment," or of "creeping socialism" or even of "communistic infiltration," according to the individual's assumed definitions and retained or acquired prejudices. With slight attention to words or labels, time marches on toward new adjustments between individualism and the social interests.

This process involves not only the accommodation between the right of the owner and the interests of the general public in his use of his property, but involves also an accommodation between the right of the owner and the right of individuals who are parties with him in consensual transactions relating to the use of the property. Accordingly substantial alterations have been made as between a landlord and his tenant.

The argument in this case understandably included the question whether the migrant worker should be deemed to be a tenant and thus entitled to the tenant's right to receive visitors, or whether his residence on the employer's property should be deemed to be merely incidental and in aid of his employment, and hence to involve no possessory interest in the realty. [Citing cases.] These cases did not reach employment situations at all comparable with the one before us. Nor did they involve the question whether an employee who is not a tenant may have visitors notwithstanding the employer's prohibition. Rather they were concerned with whether notice must be given to end the employee's right to remain upon the premises, with whether the employer may remove the discharged employee without court order, and with the availability of a particular judicial remedy to achieve his removal by process. We of course are not concerned here with the right of a migrant worker to remain on the employer's property after the employment is ended.

We see no profit in trying to decide upon a conventional category and then forcing the present subject into it. That approach would be artificial and distorting. The quest is for a fair adjustment of the competing needs of the parties, in the light of the realities of the relationship between the migrant worker and the operator of the housing facility.

Thus approaching the case, we find it unthinkable that the farmer-employer can assert a right to isolate the migrant worker in any respect significant for the worker's well-being. The farmer, of course, is entitled to pursue his farming activities without interference, and this defendants readily concede. But we see no legitimate need for a right in the farmer to deny the worker the opportunity for aid available from federal, State, or local services, or from recognized charitable groups seeking to assist him. Hence representatives of these agencies and organizations may enter upon the premises to seek out the worker at his living quarters. So, too, the migrant worker must be allowed to receive visitors there of his own choice, so long as there is no behavior hurtful to others, and members of the press may not be denied reasonable access to workers who do not object to seeing them.

It is not our purpose to open the employer's premises to the general public if in fact the employer himself has not done so. We do not say, for example, that solicitors or peddlers of all kinds may enter on their own; we may assume for the present that the employer may regulate their entry or bar them, at least if the employer's purpose is not to gain a commercial advantage for himself or if the regulation does not deprive the migrant worker of practical access to things he needs.

And we are mindful of the employer's interest in his own and in his employees' security. Hence he may reasonably require a visitor to identify himself, and also to state his general purpose if the migrant worker has not already informed him that the visitor is expected. But the employer may not deny the worker his privacy or interfere with his opportunity to live with dignity and to enjoy associations customary among our citizens. These rights are too fundamental to be denied on the basis of an interest in real property and too fragile to be left to the unequal bargaining strength of the parties.

It follows that defendants here invaded no possessory right of the farmer-employer. Their conduct was therefore beyond the reach of the trespass statute. The judgments are accordingly reversed and the matters remanded to the County Court with directions to enter judgments of acquittal.

NOTES AND QUESTIONS:
THE RIGHT TO EXCLUDE

1. William Blackstone (see pages 24-26) grandly defined the right of property as "that sole and despotic dominion which one man claims and exercises over the external things of the world, in total exclusion of the right of any other individual in the universe." 2 Commentaries *2. Two centuries later, the U.S. Supreme Court described "the right to exclude others" as "one of the most essential sticks in the bundle of rights that are commonly characterized as property." Kaiser Aetna v. United States, 444 U.S. 164, 176 (1979).

Notwithstanding all of this, there were limitations on the right to exclude even in Blackstone's time, and there are many more in ours. Here is a list of just some of the examples you will encounter as you work your way through this book (watch for others): civil rights legislation forbidding various forms of discrimination; rent controls and other limitations on a landlord's right to evict tenants; the law of adverse possession; bodies of doctrine granting public rights of access to private beaches; legislation protecting homeowners who have defaulted on mortgage payments.

2. As *Shack* and the foregoing examples suggest, limitations on the right to exclude might find their source in federal or state constitutional provisions, in federal, state, or local legislation, or in the common law. The same is generally true of limitations on the right to include, or transfer, studied in connection with the *Moore* case. We saw earlier that the various limitations on the right to transfer seem to reflect a range of considerations rather than one overarching principle. See footnote 45 on pages 86-87. Is this true as well of the right to exclude?

For the view that it is not, see Joseph W. Singer, The Reliance Interest in Property, 40 Stan. L. Rev. 611 (1988). Professor Singer argues that the "wide variety of current legal rules" limiting the right to exclude, some of them mentioned in Note 1 above, can all be justified in terms of a single "underlying moral principle" — "the reliance interest in property." Id. at 622. The reliance interest can be formally stated as follows:

(1) When owners grant rights of access to their property to others, they are not unconditionally free to revoke such access. Non-owners who have relied on a relationship with the owner that made such access possible in the past may be granted partial or total immunity from having such access revoked when this is necessary to achieve justice.

(2) When people create relations of mutual dependence involving joint efforts, and the relationship ends, property rights (access to or control of valued resources) must be redistributed (shared or shifted) among the parties to protect the legitimate interests of the more vulnerable persons.

(3) Property rights are redistributed from owners to non-owners:
(a) to protect the interests of the more vulnerable persons in reasonably relying on the continuation of the relationship;
(b) to distribute resources earned by the more vulnerable party for contributions to joint efforts; and
(c) to fulfill needs of the more vulnerable persons. [Id. at 699.]

Singer sees the reliance interest at work in State v. Shack; the general proposition, he says, is that "non-owners have a right of access to property based on need or on some other important public policy." Id. at 675. How would you bound that right of access, or the reliance interest generally? Suppose a gambling casino in Atlantic City, New Jersey, wants to exclude card counters (card counting is a blackjack strategy that entails keeping track of playing cards as they are dealt — no simple feat — and adjusting betting patterns when the odds are favorable). Does "need or . . . some other important public policy" foreclose the casino from having its way? See Uston v. Resorts Intl. Hotel, Inc., 89 N.J. 163, 445 A.2d 370 (1982), and Singer, supra, at 676 (no right to exclude). May Princeton University in Princeton, New Jersey, deny access to off-campus organizations that wish, without first seeking permission, to distribute political campaign materials on university property? See State v. Schmid, 84 N.J. 535, 423 A.2d 615 (1980) (no). May an abortion clinic keep "right-to-life" demonstrators off of its property? See Right to Life Advocates, Inc. v. Aaron Women's Clinic, 737 S.W.2d 564 (Tex. Ct. App. 1987) (yes).[48]

3. The court in State v. Shack said "[w]e of course are not concerned here with the right of a migrant worker to remain on the employer's property after the employment is ended." See page 97. Consider a related matter. Suppose a company wishes after many years in a particular location to close its plant, and the workers, through their union, seek an order requiring the company to keep the plant open or, in the alternative, sell it to the workers. Does the long relationship between the company and its employees (more broadly, between the company and the local area that has come to depend on the plant's existence) give rise to some sort of property right in the workers that supports the relief they request?

In Local 1330, United Steel Workers v. United States Steel Corp.,

48. The *Schmid* and *Right to Life Advocates* cases involved First Amendment (free expression) claims, which were also asserted in *Shack*. (See the discussion of Marsh v. Alabama and the *Logan Valley* case on page 94 of the *Shack* opinion. *Logan Valley* was overruled by Hudgens v. NLRB, 424 U.S. 507 (1976). The line of cases is discussed at some length in *Schmid*.)

The Fifth Amendment also figures regularly in right-to-exclude cases, the claim being that denial of the right by government action amounts to a "taking" of property without just compensation. *Kaiser Aetna*, cited in Note 1 above, is an example. Another is Prune-Yard Shopping Center v. Robins, 447 U.S. 74 (1980). It involved First Amendment and Fifth Amendment claims alike. We take up the takings issue in Chapter 12.

631 F.2d 1264 (6th Cir. 1980), the court concluded that no such right exists and that it is inappropriate for the judiciary, as opposed to the legislature, to create it. Singer, who considers the case at length, disagrees. He grounds his argument on the reliance interest and its underlying precedents and principles:

> [T]he judges in the *United Steel Workers* case failed to find these precedents and principles in the rules in force because they asked the wrong questions. They wrongly defined the issue as a search for the "owner" of the property. They then assumed that, in the absence of specific doctrinal exceptions to the contrary, owners are allowed to do whatever they want with their property. . . . [T]his approach takes our attention away from the relations of mutual dependence that develop within industrial enterprises and between those enterprises and the communities in which they are situated. Legitimate reliance on such relationships constitutes a central aspect of our social and economic life — so central that numerous rules in force protect reliance on those relationships. . . . Consideration of competing interests in access to resources and past reliance on relationships granting such access should be a central component of any legal determination of how to allocate lawful power over those resources. [Singer, supra, at 621-622.][49]

4. Singer's views rest on a long and distinguished tradition of property scholarship. Recall Morris Cohen, who addressed the relationships between property and power in his essay on Property and Sovereignty, published on the eve of the great depression (see Note 6 on pages 18-19). Acknowledging that "the essence of private property is always the right to exclude others," Cohen nevertheless maintained that it should not be regarded as inviolable. To the contrary:

> [W]e can no longer maintain Montesquieu's view that private property is sacrosanct and that the general government must in no way interfere with or retrench its domain. . . . To be really effective . . . , the right of property must be supported by restrictions or positive duties on the part of owners, enforced by the state as much as the right to exclude others which is the essence of property. . . . [I]f the large property owner is viewed, as he ought to be, as a wielder of power over the lives of his fellow citizens, the law should not hesitate to develop a doctrine as to his positive duties in the public interest. [Morris Cohen, Property and Sovereignty, 13 Cornell L.Q. 12, 21, 26 (1927).]

Some 50 years later, C.B. Macpherson, a political theorist, argued in a similar vein that the right to exclude is no more the essence of property — as a matter of logic or as a matter of propriety — than *the right*

---

49. Notice that the *United Steel Workers* case concerns a matter that was also at the heart of Moore v. Regents of the University of California on page 69: the authority of common law courts to recognize or create new property rights in response to changes in social conditions and values. Does Singer's reliance interest have a bearing on *Moore?*

not to be excluded (as in the case of common property, which figured throughout the preceding section of this chapter). And when property is so understood, he said, the problem is no longer one "of putting limits on the property right, but of supplementing the individual right to exclude others by the individual right not to be excluded by others." This latter right "may provisionally be stated as the individual right to equal access to the means of labour and/or the means of life." C.B. Macpherson, Property: Mainstream and Critical Positions 201 (1978).[50]

5. There is, of course, an opposing point of view with its own considerable pedigree and modern-day proponents. Richard A. Epstein, for example, speaks in defense of a firm right to exclude in two recent essays: Rights and "Rights Talk" (Book Review), 105 Harv. L. Rev. 1106 (1992) and Property and Necessity, 13 Harv. J.L. & Pub. Poly. 2 (1990). "What is wrong," Professor Epstein asks, "with a system of absolute rights that allows individuals to exclude some persons on a whim and admit others only by mutual consent?" His answer: "By and large, nothing," because by and large absolute rights simply establish the conditions for subsequent market transactions. Buyers and sellers may deal as they see fit, but so long as there are many buyers and sellers market forces will check abuse. "Those who exercise absolute rights in a capricious fashion pay for their folly by losing their markets." Epstein, Rights and "Rights Talk," supra, at 1109.

On occasion, however, narrow limitations on the right to exclude are appropriate because "the preconditions that make absolute rights workable are not satisfied." Id. at 1110.

> Under certain localized circumstances, . . . conferring these absolute rights to exclude does not advance competition in ordinary markets, but rather it creates bilateral monopoly, holdout problems, and transaction-cost obstacles of one sort or another. At common law it is just these various situations in which there is a systematic, intuitive willingness to back off the comprehensive ideal of property in favor of a system that is a little bit frayed at the edges. [Epstein, Property and Necessity, supra, at 7.]

Epstein concludes that "it is not sufficient to condemn all systems of absolute rights on the ground that they sometimes leave some people out in the cold. A strong critique must also consider the dangers of forcing individuals to open their property to persons whom they would prefer, for whatever reason, to exclude." Epstein, Rights and "Rights Talk," supra, at 1110.

---

50. Standing between Cohen and Macpherson in time, but with them in outlook, was Robert Hale, whose work is enjoying renewed attention. See, e.g., Robert L. Hale, Freedom Through Law: Public Control of Private Governing Power (1952), and Singer, supra, at 647 n.128.

2

Subsequent Possession: Acquisition of Property by Find, Adverse Possession, and Gift

Possession, as we saw in the preceding chapter, is a powerful concept in the law of property. By virtue of *first* possession one can make an unowned thing, or a thing before enjoyed only by all in common, one's own. But suppose the principle of first in time so dominant in Chapter 1 no longer holds. Suppose that something *already* owned by someone else, say *A*, *subsequently* comes into the possession of *B*, and without *A*'s consent. Surprisingly enough, *B* might still become the thing's "owner," as the first two sections of this chapter make clear. Even without being declared owner, *B* might nevertheless be granted considerable protection by the legal system. But when does *B* have "possession," so as to enjoy this favored position, and why are possessors favored anyway? These important questions figured in the last chapter and they do so again in this one.

Another common theme persists. Chapter 1 was concerned among other things with acquisition of property other than by purchase, and this chapter is as well — right through to its final section, where we examine the law of gifts. Possession plays a role there, too.

A. Acquisition by Find

Possession is eleven points in the law. —

Colley Cibber,
Woman's Wit, Act I (1697)

Possession is very strong; rather more than nine points of the law. —

Lord Mansfield,
Corporation of Kingston-upon-Hull v. Horner,
98 Eng. Rep. 807, 815 (1774)

Finders keepers, losers weepers. —

Old Scottish Proverb

Armory v. Delamirie
King's Bench, 1722
1 Strange 505

The plaintiff being a chimney sweeper's boy found a jewel and carried it to the defendant's shop (who was a goldsmith)[1] to know what it was, and delivered it into the hands of the apprentice, who under pretence of weighing it, took out the stones, and calling to the master to let him know it came to three halfpence, the master offered the boy the money, who refused to take it, and insisted to have the thing again; whereupon the apprentice delivered him back the socket without the stones. And now in trover against the master these points were ruled:

1. That the finder of a jewel, though he does not by such finding acquire an absolute property or ownership, yet he has such a property as will enable him to keep it against all but the rightful owner, and consequently may maintain trover.

2. That the action well lay against the master, who gives a credit to his apprentice, and is answerable for his neglect.

3. As to the value of the jewel several of the trade were examined to prove what a jewel of the finest water that would fit the socket would be worth; and the Chief Justice (Pratt) directed the jury, that unless the defendant did produce the jewel, and shew it not to be of the finest water, they should presume the strongest against him, and make the value of the best jewels the measure of their damages: which they accordingly did.

1. Two points about the defendant in this case: First, his surname — de Lamerie, given name Paul — was misspelled by the court reporter. Second, although he was a goldsmith, he made his name working in silver. Indeed, Paul de Lamerie was perhaps the most celebrated and prolific silversmith of the finest period of English silver, the first half of the eighteenth century.

> His flawless technique and mastery of brilliant rococo exuberance were accompanied by a cheeky nose-thumbing at authority. In 1713, with his maker's mark entered at the Assay Office at Goldsmith Hall, he was fined for not using it, the first of a number of such penalties. Probably for a fee, de Lamerie would generously pass off as his own the work of other silversmiths who were working without a maker's mark. [Claire Frankel, 200 Rare Pieces by de Lamerie Under One Roof, Intl. Herald Tribune, June 16-17, 1990, at 6.]

For a catalog of de Lamerie's work, see Paul de Lamerie: At the Sign of The Golden Ball — An Exhibition of the Work of England's Master Silversmith (1688-1751) (Goldsmith's Hall, London, June 1990, Susan Hare ed.).

We have to wonder how the plaintiff in *Armory*, a poor "chimney sweeper's boy," managed to get a lawyer to plead and try his case against such a formidable adversary. Was this an early example of pro bono lawyering? — Eds.

NOTES AND QUESTIONS

1. Based on judicial statements like that in the *Armory* case, it is often said "that the title of the finder is good as against the whole world but the true owner. . . ." Ray A. Brown, The Law of Personal Property 26 (Walter B. Raushenbush 3d ed. 1975). To test the generalization, suppose that *F1* loses a watch he had earlier found, and that it is subsequently found by *F2*. *F1* sues *F2* for return of the watch. Who wins? See Clark v. Maloney, 3 Harr. 68 (Del. 1840). *Prior possessor prevails* [handwritten: *First in time*]

We saw in the last chapter that lawyers conceive of property as referring to relationships among people with respect to things, not to a relationship between a person and a thing. See Note 6 on pages 57-58. The *F1-F2* problem provides an illustration of that proposition. The meaning of the phrase *true owner* depends upon who the other claimants are. Title, or ownership, is *relative: B* can have title as against *C* but not as against *A*.

The rule that a prior possessor prevails over a subsequent possessor applies in cases involving land as well as in cases involving personal property. Tapscott v. Cobbs, 52 Va. (11 Gratt.) 172 (1854); Percy Bordwell, Ejectment Takes Over, 55 Iowa L. Rev. 1089 (1970).

2. In Armory v. Delamirie the plaintiff sued defendant in trover. *Trover* is a common law action for money damages resulting from the defendant's conversion to his own use of a chattel owned or possessed by the plaintiff. The plaintiff waives his right to obtain the return of the chattel and insists that the defendant be subjected to a forced purchase of the chattel from him. If the defendant loses, he must pay money damages to the plaintiff. What is the measure of damages: the value of the chattel at the time the conversion occurs or the value of the plaintiff's interest (i.e., the value of the chattel discounted by the probability that the true owner will appear and reclaim it)? Which measure did the court adopt? Is it sound? [handwritten: *Value of the chattel at the time.*]

3. Suppose that in 1723 the true owner of the jewel involved in the *Armory* case appeared at the goldsmith's shop and demanded return of the jewel. What are the rights of the goldsmith and the true owner as against each other and as against the chimney sweeper's boy? See the case of The Winkfield, [1902] P. 42 (1901), involving a voluntary bailment,[2]

[handwritten: *still has to pay*]

2. A bailment is the rightful possession of goods by a person (the bailee) who is not the owner. A voluntary bailment occurs when the owner of the goods (the bailor) gives possession to the bailee, as when you leave your clothes with a laundry or check your coat at a restaurant or turn over your car keys to a parking lot attendant or deposit mail in the post office. In the case of found goods, the bailment is involuntary from the standpoint of the owner but not from that of the finder, who has, after all, chosen to take possession; by doing so, the finder assumes the obligations of a bailee. Which are what? Traditionally, the answer to that question has turned on an elaborate scheme of classification according to which some bailees were held to a standard of great care, some (such as finders) to a standard of minimal care, and the balance to an ordinary negligence standard of reason-

where the court said: "The wrongdoer, having once paid full damages to the bailee, has an answer to any action by the bailor."

In voluntary bailment situations, as in The Winkfield, the courts usually bar an action by the true owner against the present possessor if the bailee has recovered from the present possessor. See Note, Bailment: The Winkfield Doctrine, 34 Cornell L.Q. 615 (1949). Should they bar an action by the true owner against the present possessor where a *finder* or *prior wrongful possessor* has recovered from the present possessor? Why might this case be treated differently? See Brown, supra, at §11.11.

4. Would it have made any difference in Armory v. Delamirie if the chimney sweeper's boy had taken the jewel off a dressing table in the house where he was cleaning the chimney? In Anderson v. Gouldberg, 51 Minn. 294, 53 N.W. 636 (1892), the plaintiffs trespassed upon the timber land of a third party, cut logs, and hauled them to a mill, where the defendants took them. In an action of *replevin* (a lawsuit to obtain return of the goods, not damages), the court ruled for the plaintiffs and said:

> Therefore the only question is whether bare possession of property, though wrongfully obtained, is sufficient title to enable the party enjoying it to maintain replevin against a mere stranger, who takes it from him. We had supposed that this was settled in the affirmative as long ago, at least, as the early case of Armory v. Delamirie, 1 Strange 505, so often cited on that point. When it is said that to maintain replevin the plaintiff's possession must have been lawful, it means merely that it must have been lawful as against the person who deprived him of it; and possession is good title against all the world except those having a better title.
>
> Counsel says that possession only raises a presumption of title, which, however, may be rebutted. Rightly understood, this is correct; but counsel misapplies it. One who takes property from the possession of another can only rebut this presumption by showing a superior title in himself, or in some way connecting himself with one who has. One who has acquired the possession of property, whether by finding, bailment, or by mere tort, has a right to retain that possession as against a mere wrongdoer who is a stranger to the property. Any other rule would lead to an endless series of unlawful seizures and reprisals in every case where property had once passed out of the possession of the rightful owner. [51 Minn. at 295-296, 53 N.W. at 637.]

But see Richard H. Helmholz, Wrongful Possession of Chattels: Hornbook Law and Case Law, 80 Nw. U. L. Rev. 1221 (1986), noting that cases like *Anderson,* involving two wrongdoers, seldom arise. After surveying a number of substantive areas (including the law of finders), Helmholz concludes that in the more common case of disputes between

---

able care under the circumstances. The modern view is that the latter standard should apply across the board. See, e.g., Note, Bailment Liability: Toward a Standard of Reasonable Care, 61 S. Cal. L. Rev. 2117 (1988).

a prior wrongful possessor and an honest subsequent one, courts regularly prefer the latter — in quiet defiance of the hornbook rule. The rule of prior possession is said to be explicitly invoked only in support of honest claimants.

5. Should the courts be more willing to grant replevin to the prior possessor than to grant money damages? See Annot., 150 A.L.R. 163 (1944). Should it matter whether the true owner is known?

Replevin and trover are actions involving personal property. The action similar to replevin in real property cases[3] is an action for possession (ejectment) and the action similar to trover is an action for damages (trespass).[4] The courts appear to be more reluctant to give the prior possessor of land, who has no title, permanent damages than to put the prior possesor back into possession. Compare Tapscott v. Cobbs, 52 Va. (11 Gratt.) 172 (1854) (prior possessor wins in ejectment), with Winchester v. City of Stevens Point, 58 Wis. 350, 17 N.W. 3 (1883) (possessor denied damages for permanent reduction in value of the land), and with Illinois & St. Louis Railroad & Coal Co. v. Cobb, 94 Ill. 55 (1879) (possessor allowed to recover from trespasser damages up to the commencement of action; language of court indicates possessor can recover full damages for permanent injury to the land, even though defendant can prove an outstanding title in some third person).

Hannah v. Peel

King's Bench Division, 1945
[1945] K.B. 509

Action tried by BIRKETT, J. On December 13, 1938, the freehold of Gwernhaylod House, Overton-on-Dee, Shropshire, was conveyed to the defendant, Major Hugh Edward Ethelston Peel, who from that time to the end of 1940 never himself occupied the house and it remained unoccupied until October 5, 1939, when it was requisitioned [for quartering soldiers], but after some months was released from requisition.

3. Real property is that sort of property for which a "real action," as distinct from a "personal action," could be brought in the king's courts in feudal times. The word *real* is derived from the Latin *res* meaning "thing" and was applied to actions concerning land because, if an owner had been wrongfully deprived of land, the remedy was restoration of the land (i.e., the thing) itself, whereas in a "personal action" (which was, in early times, all that could be brought in respect of movable goods), the court would allow payment of the value of the goods instead of compelling their return. After considerable hesitancy, the law finally developed the action of replevin for the specific return of movable goods, but by this time the name personal property had become stuck to them.

4. The common law actions of trover, replevin, ejectment, and trespass, which were complicated by numerous procedural niceties, have in most states been simplified and in many renamed. We leave these details for your course in civil procedure, but note that the essential difference in remedies afforded by these actions — the return of the thing as opposed to damages — is preserved in modern codes of civil procedure.

Gwernhaylod House, Overton-on-Dee

Gwernhaylod, a Welsh word, means sunny marsh. Gwernhaylod House was
originally built in 1460, rebuilt in 1740, and torn down in 1950.

Thereafter it remained unoccupied until July 18, 1940, when it was
again requisitioned, the defendant being compensated by a payment at
the rate of 250*l*. a year. In August, 1940, the plaintiff, Duncan Hannah,
a lance-corporal, serving in a battery of the Royal Artillery, was stationed
at the house and on the 21st of that month, when in a bedroom, used as
a sick-bay, he was adjusting the black-out curtains when his hand
touched something on the top of a window-frame, loose in a crevice,
which he thought was a piece of dirt or plaster. The plaintiff grasped it
and dropped it on the outside window ledge. On the following morning
he saw that it was a brooch covered with cobwebs and dirt. Later, he took
it with him when he went home on leave and his wife having told him it
might be of value, at the end of October, 1940, he informed his commanding officer of his find and, on his advice, handed it over to the
police, receiving a receipt for it. In August, 1942, the owner not having
been found the police handed the brooch to the defendant, who sold it
in October, 1942, for 66*l*., to Messrs. Spink & Son, Ltd., of London, who
resold it in the following month for 88*l*. There was no evidence that the
defendant had any knowledge of the existence of the brooch before it
was found by the plaintiff. The defendant had offered the plaintiff a
reward for the brooch, but the plaintiff refused to accept this and maintained throughout his right to the possession of the brooch as against all
persons other than the owner, who was unknown. By a letter, dated
October 5, 1942, the plaintiff's solicitors demanded the return of the

108

brooch from the defendant, but it was not returned and on October 21, 1943, the plaintiff issued his writ claiming the return of the brooch, or its value, and damages for its detention. By his defence, the defendant claimed the brooch on the ground that he was the owner of Gwernhaylod House and in possession thereof. . . .

BIRKETT, J. There is no issue of fact in this case between the parties. As to the issue in law, the rival claims of the parties can be stated in this way. The plaintiff says: "I claim the brooch as its finder and I have a good title against all the world, save only the true owner." The defendant says: "My claim is superior to yours inasmuch as I am the freeholder. The brooch was found on my property, although I was never in occupation, and my title, therefore, ousts yours and in the absence of the true owner I am entitled to the brooch or its value." Unhappily the law on this issue is in a very uncertain state and there is need of an authoritative decision of a higher court. Obviously if it could be said with certainty that this is the law, that the finder of a lost article, wherever found, has a good title against all the world save the true owner, then, of course, all my difficulties would be resolved; or again, if it could be said with equal certainty that this is the law, that the possessor of land is entitled as against the finder to all chattels found on the land, again my difficulties would be resolved. But, unfortunately, the authorities give some support to each of these conflicting propositions. . . .

The case of Bridges v. Hawkesworth, 21 L.J. (Q.B.) 75, 15 Jur. 1079, was . . . an appeal against a decision of the county court judge at Westminster. The facts appear to have been that in the year 1847 the plaintiff, who was a commercial traveller, called on a firm named Byfield & Hawkesworth on business, as he was in the habit of doing, and as he was leaving the shop he picked up a small parcel which was lying on the floor. He immediately showed it to the shopman, and opened it in his presence, when it was found to consist of a quantity of Bank of England notes, to the amount of 65l. The defendant, who was a partner in the firm of Byfield & Hawkesworth, was then called, and the plaintiff told him he had found the notes, and asked the defendant to keep them until the owner appeared to claim them. Then various advertisements were put in the papers asking for the owner, but the true owner was never found. No person having appeared to claim them, and three years having elapsed since they were found, the plaintiff applied to the defendant to have the notes returned to him, and offered to pay the expenses of the advertisements, and to give an indemnity. The defendant refused to deliver them up to the plaintiff, and an action was brought in the county court of Westminster in consequence of that refusal. The county court judge decided that the defendant, the shopkeeper, was entitled to the custody of the notes as against the plaintiff, and gave judgment for the defendant. Thereupon the appeal was brought which came before the court composed by Patteson, J., and Wightman, J. Patteson, J., said:

"The notes which are the subject of this action were incidentally dropped, by mere accident, in the shop of the defendant, by the owner of them. The facts do not warrant the supposition that they had been deposited there intentionally, nor has the case been put at all upon that ground. The plaintiff found them on the floor, they being manifestly lost by someone. The general right of the finder to any article which has been lost, as against all the world, except the true owner, was established in the case of Armory v. Delamirie, 1 Str. 505, which has never been disputed. This right would clearly have accrued to the plaintiff had the notes been picked up by him outside the shop of the defendant and if he once had the right, the case finds that he did not intend, by delivering the notes to the defendant, to waive the title (if any) which he had to them, but they were handed to the defendant merely for the purpose of delivering them to the owner should he appear." Then a little later: "The case, therefore, resolves itself into the single point on which it appears that the learned judge decided it, namely, whether the circumstance of the notes being found inside the defendant's shop gives him, the defendant, the right to have them as against the plaintiff, who found them." After discussing the cases, and the argument, the learned judge said: "If the discovery had never been communicated to the defendant, could the real owner have had any cause of action against him because they were found in his house? Certainly not. The notes never were in the custody of the defendant, nor within the protection of his house, before they were found, as would have been had they been intentionally deposited there; and the defendant has come under no responsibility, except from the communication made to him by the plaintiff, the finder, and the steps taken by way of advertisement. . . . We find, therefore, no circumstances in this case to take it out of the general rule of law, that the finder of a lost article is entitled to it as against all persons except the real owner, and we think that that rule must prevail, and that the learned judge was mistaken in holding that the place in which they were found makes any legal difference. Our judgment, therefore, is that the plaintiff is entitled to these notes as against the defendant."

It is to be observed that in Bridges v. Hawkesworth, which has been the subject of immense disputation, neither counsel put forward any argument on the fact that the notes were found in a shop. Counsel for the appellant assumed throughout that the position was the same as if the parcel had been found in a private house, and the learned judge spoke of "the protection of his" (the shopkeeper's) "house." The case for the appellant was that the shopkeeper never knew of the notes. Again, what is curious is that there was no suggestion that the place where the notes were found was in any way material; indeed, the judge in giving the judgment of the court expressly repudiates this and said in terms "The learned judge was mistaken in holding that the place in which they were found makes any legal difference." It is, therefore, a little remarkable that in South Staffordshire Water Co. v. Sharman, [1896] 2 Q.B. 44, Lord Russell of Killowen, C.J., said: "The case of Bridges v. Hawkesworth stands by itself, and on special grounds; and on those grounds it seems to me that the decision in that case was right. Someone had accidentally dropped a bundle of banknotes in a public shop. The shopkeeper did not know they had been dropped, and did not in any sense exercise control over them. The shop was open to the public, and they were invited to come there." That might be a matter of some doubt. Customers were invited there, but whether the public at large was, might be open to some question. Lord Russell continued: "A customer picked up the notes and gave them to the shopkeeper in order that he might advertise them. The owner of the notes was not found, and the finder then sought to recover them from the shopkeeper. It was held that he was entitled to do so, the ground of the decision being, as was pointed out by Patteson, J., that the notes, being dropped in the public part of the shop, were never in the custody of the shopkeeper, or 'within the protection of his house.' " Patteson, J., never made any reference to the public part of the shop and, indeed, went out of his way to say that the learned county court judge was wrong in holding that the place where they were found made any legal difference. . . .

With regard to South Staffordshire Water Co. v. Sharman, [1896] 2 Q.B. 44, the first two lines of the headnote are: "The possessor of land is generally entitled, as against the finder, to chattels found on the land." I am not sure that this is accurate. The facts were that the defendant Sharman, while cleaning out, under the orders of the plaintiffs, the South Staffordshire Water Company, a pool of water on their land, found two rings embedded in the mud at the bottom of the pool. He declined to deliver them to the plaintiffs, but failed to discover the real owner. In an action brought by the company against Sharman in detinue it was held that the company was entitled to the rings. Lord Russell of Killowen, C.J., said: "The plaintiffs are the freeholders of the locus in quo, and as such they have the right to forbid anybody coming on their land or in any way interfering with it. They had the right to say that their pool should be cleaned out in any way that they thought fit, and to direct what should be done with anything found in the pool in the course of such cleaning out. It is no doubt right, as the counsel for the defendant contended, to say that the plaintiffs must show that they had actual control over the locus in quo and the things in it; but under the circumstances, can it be said that the Minster Pool and whatever might be in that pool were not under the control of the plaintiffs? In my opinion they were. . . . The principle on which this case must be decided, and the distinction which must be drawn between this case and that of Bridges v. Hawkesworth, is to be found in a passage in Pollock and Wright's Essay on Possession in the Common Law, p. 41: 'The possession of land carries with it in general, by our law, possession of everything

never in cust. or within the protection of his house

[locus in quo — place in question]

which is attached to or under that land, and, in the absence of a better title elsewhere, the right to possess it also. . . .'" And it makes no difference that the possessor is not aware of the thing's existence. . . .

Then Lord Russell cited the passage which I read earlier in this judgment and continued: "It is somewhat strange" — I venture to echo those words — "that there is no more direct authority on the question; but the general principle seems to me to be that where a person has possession of house or land, with a manifest intention to exercise control over it and the things which may be upon or in it, then, if something is found on that land, whether by an employee of the owner or by a stranger, the presumption is that the possession of that thing is in the owner of the locus in quo." It is to be observed that Lord Russell there is extending the meaning of the passage he had cited from Pollock and Wright's essay on Possession in the Common Law, where the learned authors say that the possession of "land carries with it possession of everything which is attached to or under that land." Then Lord Russell adds possession of everything which may be on or in that land. South Staffordshire Water Co. v. Sharman, which was relied on by counsel for the defendant, has also been the subject of some discussion. It has been said that it establishes that if a man finds a thing as the servant or agent of another, he finds it not for himself, but for that other, and indeed that seems to afford a sufficient explanation of the case. The rings found at the bottom of the pool were not in the possession of the company, but it seems that though Sharman was the first to obtain possession of them, he obtained them for his employers and could claim no title for himself.

The only other case to which I need refer is Elwes v. Brigg Gas Co., 33 Ch. D. 562, in which land had been demised to a gas company for ninety-nine years with a reservation to the lessor of all mines and minerals. A pre-historic boat embedded in the soil was discovered by the lessees when they were digging to make a gasholder. It was held that the boat, whether regarded as a mineral or as part of the soil in which it was embedded when discovered, or as a chattel, did not pass to the lessees by the demise, but was the property of the lessor though he was ignorant of its existence at the time of granting the lease. Chitty, J., said: "The first question which does actually arise in this case is whether the boat belonged to the plaintiff at the time of the granting of the lease. I hold that it did, whether it ought to be regarded as a mineral, or as part of the soil within the maxim above cited, or as a chattel. If it was a mineral or part of the soil in the sense above indicated, then it clearly belonged to the owners of the inheritance as part of the inheritance itself. But if it ought to be regarded as a chattel, I hold the property in the chattel was vested in the plaintiff, for the following reasons." Then he gave the reasons, and continued: "The plaintiff then being thus in possession of the chattel, it follows that the property in the chattel was vested in him. Obviously the right of the original owner could not be established; it had for centuries been lost or barred, even supposing that the property had not been abandoned when the boat was first left on the spot where it was found. The plaintiff, then, had a lawful possession, good against all the world, and therefore the property in the boat. In my opinion it makes no difference, in these circumstances, that the plaintiff was not aware of the existence of the boat."[5]

A review of these judgments shows that the authorities are in an unsatisfactory state. . . .

It is fairly clear from the authorities that a man possesses everything which is attached to or under his land. Secondly, it would appear to be the law from the authorities I have cited, and particularly from Bridges v. Hawkesworth, that a man does not necessarily possess a thing which is lying unattached on the surface of his land even though the thing is not possessed by someone else. A difficulty, however, arises . . . because the rule which governs things an occupier possesses as against those which he does not, has never been very clearly formulated in our law. . . .

There is no doubt that in this case the brooch was lost in the ordinary meaning of that term, and I should imagine it had been lost for a very considerable time. Indeed, from this correspondence it appears that at one time the predecessors in title of the defendant were considering making some claim. But the moment the plaintiff discovered that the brooch might be of some value, he took the advice of his commanding officer and handed it to the police. His conduct was commendable and meritorious. The defendant was never physically in possession of these premises at any time. It is clear that the brooch was never his, in the ordinary acceptation of the term, in that he had the prior possession. He had no knowledge of it, until it was brought to his notice by the finder. A discussion of the merits does not seem to help, but it is clear on the facts that the brooch was "lost" in the ordinary meaning of that word, that it was "found" by the plaintiff in the ordinary meaning of that word, that its true owner has never been found, that the defendant was the owner of the premises and had his notice drawn to this matter by the plaintiff, who found the brooch. In those circumstances I propose

5. "Thus the case ended," says a comment on *Elwes* written a century later. "Mr. Elwes, having gained possession of the boat, exhibited it in a specially constructed brick building in the estate yard, near Brigg Station. There for twenty-three years many thousands of visitors paid for admission to see it." Subsequently Elwes gave the boat to a public museum at Hull. "[I]t was carefully removed to Hull, via the River Ancholme (appropriately enough), though in a rather different method from the trip it made on the same river some two thousand or more years ago. Would that it had remained in Brigg! In 1943 the boat was destroyed in an air raid on the museum premises. . . ." Michael L. Nash, Are Finders Keepers? One Hundred Years Since *Elwes v. Brigg Gas Co.*, 137 New L.J. 118, 119 (1987). — EDS.

to follow the decision in Bridges v. Hawkesworth, and to give judgment in this case for the plaintiff for 66*l*.

Judgment for plaintiff.

NOTES AND QUESTIONS

1. Did Major Peel lose because he did not have prior possession, or did he not have prior possession because he lost?

2. How effective was the court's marshalling of precedent to support its decision? Was its reasoning persuasive? Was the court relying upon horse sense? Do the words of the court act as a guide for the prediction of the outcome of similar, but not too similar, cases?

3. Suppose Major Peel had resided in Gwernhaylod House from December 1938 until the first requisition in October 1939. Would the result in Hannah v. Peel be the same? See Parker v. British Airways Bd., [1982] 2 W.L.R. 503, 516-517: "I would be inclined to say that the occupier of a house will almost invariably possess any lost article on the premises. He may not have taken any positive steps to demonstrate his *animus possidendi*, but so firm is his control that the *animus* can be seen to attach to it" (per Eveleigh, L.J.). Cf. Margaret J. Radin, Property and Personhood, 34 Stan. L. Rev. 957, 987, 991-996 (1982) (sanctity of the home).

Or suppose (as was the fact) that the house had never been occupied by Peel but also never requisitioned by the government. Hannah, while stationed at a nearby military base, went for a walk in the woods around Gwernhaylod House, was intrigued by the imposing mansion, entered by the unlocked front door, and found the brooch. Would the result in Hannah v. Peel be the same? Recall Problem 1 on page 36, and see Favorite v. Miller, 176 Conn. 310, 315, 407 A.2d 974, 977 (1978) (owner of locus prevails as against trespassing finder unless trespass "trivial or merely technical"); Bishop v. Ellsworth, 91 Ill. App. 2d 386, 391, 234 N.E.2d 49, 52 (1968) ("if the discoverer is a trespasser such trespasser can have no claim to possession of such property even if it might otherwise be considered lost"). But see Hendle v. Stevens, 224 Ill. App. 3d 1046, 1054, 586 N.E.2d 826, 832 (1992) ("we think the *Bishop* court's statement that a trespasser has no claim to possession of lost property is erroneous").

McAvoy v. Medina
Supreme Judicial Court of Massachusetts, 1866
93 Mass. (11 Allen) 548

Tort to recover a sum of money found by the plaintiff in the shop of the defendant.

At the trial in the superior court, before Morton, J., it appeared that the defendant was a barber, and the plaintiff, being a customer in the defendant's shop, saw and took up a pocket-book which was lying upon a table there, and said, "See what I have found." The defendant came to the table and asked where he found it. The plaintiff laid it back in the same place and said, "I found it right there." The defendant then took it and counted the money, and the plaintiff told him to keep it, and if the owner should come to give it to him; and otherwise to advertise it; which the defendant promised to do. Subsequently the plaintiff made three demands for the money, and the defendant never claimed to hold the same till the last demand. It was agreed that the pocket-book was placed upon the table by a transient customer of the defendant and accidentally left there, and was first seen and taken up by the plaintiff, and that the owner had not been found.

The judge ruled that the plaintiff could not maintain his action, and a verdict was accordingly returned for the defendant; and the plaintiff alleged exceptions. . . .

DEWEY, J. It seems to be the settled law that the finder of lost property has a valid claim to the same against all the world except the true owner, and generally that the place in which it is found creates no exception to this rule. 2 Parsons on Con. 97. Bridges v. Hawkesworth, 7 Eng. Law & Eq. R. 424.

But this property is not, under the circumstances, to be treated as lost property in that sense in which a finder has a valid claim to hold the same until called for by the true owner. This property was voluntarily placed upon a table in the defendant's shop by a customer of his who accidentally left the same there and has never called for it. The plaintiff also came there as a customer, and first saw the same and took it up from the table. The plaintiff did not by this acquire the right to take the property from the shop, but it was rather the duty of the defendant, when the fact became thus known to him, to use reasonable care for the safe keeping of the same until the owner should call for it. In the case of Bridges v. Hawkesworth the property, although found in a shop, was found on the floor of the same, and had not been placed there voluntarily by the owner, and the court held that the finder was entitled to the possession of the same, except as to the owner. But the present case more resembles that of Lawrence v. The State, 1 Humph. (Tenn.) 228, and is indeed very similar in its facts. The court there take a distinction between the case of property thus placed by the owner and neglected to be removed, and property lost. It was there held that "to place a pocket-book upon a table and to forget to take it away is not to lose it, in the sense in which the authorities referred to speak of lost property."

We accept this as the better rule, and especially as one better adapted to secure the rights of the true owner.

In view of the facts of this case, the plaintiff acquired no original right to the property, and the defendant's subsequent acts in receiving and holding the property in the manner he did does not create any.

Exceptions overruled.

NOTES AND QUESTIONS

1. *The rule in* McAvoy. An essay by Walter Wheeler Cook, Ownership and Possession, in 11 Encyclopedia of the Social Sciences 521, 524 (1937), says this: "It is obvious . . . that from the point of view of social policy the shopkeeper ought to be preferred to the customer, as in that event the article would be more likely to get back into the possession of the real owner." Do you agree? Are you sure?

2. *Mislaid, lost, and abandoned property.* A typical summary of the common law rules on finders runs like this: "A finder of property acquires no rights in mislaid property, is entitled to possession of lost property against everyone except the true owner, and is entitled to keep abandoned property." Michael v. First Chicago Corp., 139 Ill. App. 3d 374, 382, 487 N.E.2d 403, 409 (1985).

Like many typical summaries, this one is a bit misleading. The statement regarding mislaid property is correct, but the statement regarding lost property is not — at least in some jurisdictions. Notice, for example, that the statement neglects the distinctions, suggested in Hannah v. Peel, having to do with the circumstances under which lost goods are found: Embedded in the soil, or not? Found in a public place, or a private one? Such considerations can matter. Should they?

The statement is also probably inaccurate as to abandoned property, meaning items intentionally and voluntarily relinquished, with no intent to reclaim. The dominant concern of the law of finders — to protect true owners — drops out in the case of abandoned property because the true owner has renounced any claim, but the interests of the owner of the place of the find remain. Should they count? (It seems that they did in *South Staffordshire* and *Elwes*, the two abandoned-goods cases mentioned in Hannah v. Peel. And what of *Hannah*? Was the brooch involved there in fact abandoned? How do you tell? Is passage of time itself sufficient? Was the brooch perhaps mislaid? Again, how do you tell, and why should any of this matter?)

3. *Employees and other agents.* A janitor cleaning up in a hotel finds a sum of money and turns it in to the manager. After a year the money is unclaimed, and the janitor sues for its return. Who wins? The law here sprawls all over the lot, with decisions commonly turning on the lost-mislaid-abandoned distinction, or on the place of the find, or on the law of principal and agent. See, e.g., Kalyvakis v. The T.S.S. Olympia, 181 F. Supp. 32 (S.D.N.Y. 1960) ($3,000 found by ship steward on floor of

ship's public men's room awarded to finder on ground that it was lost or abandoned; court rejected English master-servant (principal-agent) exception as not in accord with the weight of American authority); Erickson v. Sinykin, 223 Minn. 232, 26 N.W.2d 172 (1947) (money found by interior decorator held abandoned, and decorator, unlike a maid or janitor, has no duty to report find to employer); Jackson v. Steinberg, 186 Or. 129, 200 P.2d 376 (1948), reh'g denied, 186 Or. 140, 205 P.2d 562 (1949) ($800 found by chambermaid under paper lining in dresser drawer awarded to hotel owner on theory that maid had a duty to deliver the money to her employer).

Was the crown entitled to the brooch found by its employee, Corporal Hannah? Compare Morrison v. United States, 492 F.2d 1219 (Ct. Cl. 1974), where an American infantry sergeant found $150,000 in United States currency and $950,000 in South Vietnamese piasters in a cave while on a search-and-destroy patrol in South Vietnam. Applying common law concepts, the court said the money was mislaid but held that under the Uniform Code of Military Justice the sergeant was acting as an agent of the United States and the money belonged to it as "captured" or "abandoned" property taken from the enemy.

4. *Treasure trove.* At English common law treasure trove (derived from the Old French *tresor trové*, found treasure) belonged to the king. Treasure trove was any money or coin, gold, silver plate, or bullion hidden in the earth. When the Romans were driven out of England and northern Europe, they concealed their money and treasures underground, and the kings or conquering generals, knowing this, seized the goods for themselves and punished severely any person who did not deliver up found treasures. The law drew a distinction between treasures hidden with the intention of returning to reclaim them, which went to the king, and abandoned property, which went to the finder.

A contemporary case of treasure trove was reported in Time, Mar. 24, 1980, at 40. An Irishman, with the aid of a metal detector and a history book, found in a bog near the ruins of several medieval monasteries in County Tipperary a complete set of communion vessels, including a choice silver communion chalice, dating from the eighth or early ninth century. Said Time:

> The chalice, paten and strainer, when found, were covered with a beaten bronze bowl; experts presume that monks had deliberately hidden them in the bog, probably to protect them from marauding Irishmen or even Vikings. The circumstances of concealment are important under Irish law. If the buried treasure was intended for later recovery, then it becomes state property. But if the courts hold that the vessels were lost or abandoned, then the operative rule is "finders keepers"; in that case, the [finder] could go home with his afternoon's discoveries, which have been conservatively valued at $4 million.

*"The way I see it, we divvy up—a third for you, a third for me, and a third for Sam—
and what the George A. Fuller Company doesn't know won't hurt them."*

Drawing by Robert Day; © 1958, 1986
The New Yorker Magazine, Inc.

The general reader, as well as the finder, must think it exceedingly odd
to go to law on terms such as these.

Under modern American cases, treasure trove — which today includes money hidden in places above ground and is not limited to money
and gold and silver buried underground — is usually awarded to the
finder and not to the state or the owner of the premises (occasionally, it
appears, even if the finder is a trespasser). See generally Comment,
Property Owners' Constructive Possession of Treasure Trove: Rethinking the Finders Keepers Rule, 38 UCLA L. Rev. 1659 (1991). Some
states, however, treat treasure trove like any other found property. See,
e.g., Schley v. Couch, 155 Tex. 195, 284 S.W.2d 333 (1955) ($1,000 in a
buried glass jar held to be mislaid property possessed by owner of locus).
Compare Willsmore v. Township of Oceola, 106 Mich. App. 671, 308
N.W.2d 796 (1981), arising in a jurisdiction that has never recognized
the law of treasure trove. A hunter lawfully present on unposted land
discovered a buried suitcase containing a large sum of money. After he
notified the police, a man asserting that he was both the purchaser of
the land and the owner of the money made a claim but refused to disclose where the money had come from. The court refused to recognize
the claim. It was not unmindful of the suspicious nature of the buried
money, nor of the finder's honest behavior. For discussion, see Richard
H. Helmholz, Wrongful Possession of Chattels: Hornbook Law and Case
Law, 80 Nw. U. L. Rev. 1221, 1232 (1986).

The English common law of treasure trove has been criticized for
giving insufficient attention to the government's interest in protecting
antiquities. See N.E. Palmer, Treasure Trove and the Protection of Antiquities, 44 Mod. L. Rev. 178 (1981). American law affords even less
protection. For a comparative treatment, see Roman Krys, Treasure
Trove Under Anglo-American Law, 11 Anglo-Amer. L. Rev. 214 (1982).

5. *Shipwrecks.* Under English common law, "wreck" — which referred very narrowly to cargo washed ashore from a ship lost at sea with
no survivors — went to the crown. Blackstone claimed that this right in
the king was "grounded on the consideration of his guarding and protecting the seas from pirates and robbers." 1 William Blackstone, Commentaries *290. Under traditional maritime law, a ship lost at sea and
settled on the ocean floor remained the owner's property — unless title
to the vessel had been abandoned — but anyone subsequently reducing
the ship or its cargo to possession was entitled to a salvage award. See
Columbus-America Discovery Group v. Atlantic Mutual Ins. Co., 974
F.2d 450 (4th Cir. 1992) (holding that the insurers of the *Central America,*
which had sunk in 1857, had not abandoned their title and were still
owners of $1 billion in gold on board; the salvors who had found the
ship were entitled to a salvage award).

In this country, the law of finders has usually been applied to ships
lost in territorial waters, and the finder held entitled to an abandoned

shipwreck unless the wreck was embedded in land owned or possessed by another. Given this, the United States and individual states have successfully asserted claims to shipwrecks embedded in their territorial waters and thus constructively possessed. In the Abandoned Shipwreck Act of 1987, 43 U.S.C. §§2101-2106 (1988), the United States asserts title to any abandoned shipwreck embedded in submerged lands of a state and simultaneously transfers its title to the state in which the wreck is located. The purpose is to turn over management of embedded shipwrecks in state waters to the states and permit them to develop their own rules for salvage or preservation unimpeded by the general law. (The act provides that the law of finds and the law of salvage shall not apply to abandoned shipwrecks covered by its provisions.)

Maritime law and its principle of salvage awards, mentioned above, contrasts sharply with property law, which awards a finder all or nothing.[6] Should the law of finders be changed such that the finder is entitled to an award (a reward) if the property in question is returned to its owner or held to be in possession of the owner of the locus?[7] Or should the law be changed so that in hard cases, where no clear policy objective seems to dominate, the value of the find should be split between the finder and the owner of the locus?[8] See Richard H. Helmholz, Equitable Division and the Law of Finders, 52 Fordham L. Rev. 313 (1983).

6. All, that is, subject to the rights of the true owner. But, as mentioned in Note 6 below, legislation in some states abrogates the true owner's title in favor of a finder if no claim is made within a specified period. You will see in the next section that the law of adverse possession can have a similar effect.

7. There is no common law right to a reward, though statutes in some states may confer such a right. Moreover, finders and custodians may claim any reward that the owner of the goods has offered, as well as reimbursement for reasonable expenses incurred in securing and caring for the property in question — this as a consequence of the law of bailments. See footnote 2 on page 105.

The right to a reward seems to be more common among civil law jurisdictions in Europe (civil law here meaning codified law that derives from the Roman law tradition). An example is Article 971 of the German Civil Code:

(1) The finder may demand a finder's fee from the person entitled to receive the thing. The finder's fee amounts to five per cent of the value of the thing up to one thousand Deutsch marks, three per cent of the value above this figure, and in the case of animals three per cent. If the thing represents value only to the person entitled to receive it, the finder's fee shall be fixed in an equitable manner.

(2) The claim is not allowed if the finder violates the duty of reporting or hides the found property when inquiry is made.

8. Another kind of division — between custody and eventual ownership — is also possible: "[W]here the article is found in a quasi-public place, the occupier will be allowed to hold it, but he must relinquish it to the finder if the owner remains unascertained after a reasonable time." David Riesman, Jr., Possession and the Law of Finders, 52 Harv. L. Rev. 1105, 1125 (1939) (a classic essay well worth reading in its entirety; its author is the lawyer and social scientist David Riesman, perhaps best known for his book The Lonely Crowd (1950)).

What do you think of Riesman's suggestion? What is it supposed to accomplish? Could it at times be fruitfully combined with Helmholz's idea of equitable division? Can you

6. *Legislation.* Many states have legislation covering lost, mislaid, and abandoned property — sometimes very lengthy and complicated legislation. A typical statute might require finders to deposit the property at a designated place, provide for notice to possible owners, and provide for an award of title — say to the finder — if the property owner does not appear within a specified period. Provision is sometimes also made for property found by public and private employees in the course of their duties and for property found within the enclosed safe deposit area of banks.

Why not just enact into law the old folk-saying, "Finders keepers, losers weepers"?

B.   Acquisition by Adverse Possession

This section continues the inquiry begun in the last, on finders. Something is owned by A; subsequently, and without A's consent, it comes into the possession of B. B might become the thing's owner; short of that, B still has some rights. But, again, when is B in "possession," and why is B's possession — which might be openly adverse to the claims of A — even recognized by the legal system? These are exactly the questions considered in the last section, examined now in a new setting.

1.   The Theory and Elements of Adverse Possession

7 Richard R. Powell, The Law of Real Property ¶1012
(rev. ed. 1992)

"Adverse possession" functions as a method of transferring interests in land without the consent of the prior owner, and even in spite of the

---

imagine how the concept of possession underlying the common law of finders probably led the courts to neglect various sorts of division (in time or value or both) in favor of the all-or-nothing approach that characterizes the law of finders?

•   For an example of a decision recognizing the important but regularly overlooked distinction between custody of the found item for now and ownership of the found item eventually, see Paset v. Old Orchard Bank & Trust Co., 62 Ill. App. 3d 534, 378 N.E.2d 1264 (1978) (making locus owner temporary custodian and then vesting ownership in finder). *Paset* was influenced in part by Illinois legislation on lost goods, a so-called estray statute. *Estray* refers to stray beasts whose owner is unknown, and early estray legislation applied to lost property generally the common law principles applicable to lost animals.

dissent of such owner. It rests upon social judgments that there should be a restricted duration for the assertion of "aging claims," and that the elapse of a reasonable time should assure security to a person claiming to be an owner. The theory upon which adverse possession rests is that the adverse possessor may acquire title at such time as an action in eject-ment by the record owner would be barred by the statute of limita-tions. . . .

Every American jurisdiction has statutory provisions fixing the pe-riod of time beyond which the owner of land can no longer bring an action, or undertake self-help, for the recovery of his land from a person in possession of the land. These statutes differ substantially in the estab-lished periods, in their provision for extending the normally operative period, and in other particulars. These statutes are complemented by a large body of case law as to the kind of possession by another which is sufficient to cause the statutory period to begin to run, and to continue running, against the true owner. Thus, the law of adverse possession is a composite of statutory and decisional law.

These statutes of limitation have a long history extending back into the thirteenth and earlier centuries. In a 1275 statute, the practice began of naming past events, beyond which no suitor in an action affecting land could go for evidence supporting his title. This permitted recent seisin, even if tortiously acquired, to become protected ownership. As time passed, and the statutorily named historical event receded into an-tiquity, this sort of statute became increasingly valueless. A statute of 1540 adopted the more modern procedure of stipulating a period of years within which various land actions had to be commenced. This type of statute matured into one of 1623,[9] which furnished the pattern for many American enactments. Statutes patterned on the English proto-types of 1540 and 1623 are, in most particulars, similarly construed by American courts. The language of these statutes stresses their negative and procedural importance, namely, the barring of an action, or of con-duct, designed to recover land, when the plaintiff has delayed too long. Their chief importance in the law of property, however, rests on their proprietary and affirmative consequences, in constituting one means for the acquisition of ownership.

---

9. 21 Jac. I, Ch. 16, §§1, 2 (1623): "For quieting of men's estates and avoiding of suits [described types of action] shall be sued and taken within twenty years next after the title and cause of action first descended or fallen, and at no time after the said twenty years; . . . and that no person or persons shall at any time hereafter make any entry into any lands, tenements or hereditaments, but within twenty years next after his or their right of title which shall hereafter first descend or accrue to the same, and in default thereof, such persons, so not entering and their heirs, shall be utterly excluded and disabled from such entry after to be made. . . ."

Henry W. Ballantine, Title
by Adverse Possession
32 Harv. L. Rev. 135 (1918)

Title by adverse possession sounds, at first blush, like title by theft or robbery, a primitive method of acquiring land without paying for it. When the novice is told that by the weight of authority not even good faith is a requisite, the doctrine apparently affords an anomalous instance of maturing a wrong into a right contrary to one of the most fundamental axioms of the law.

> For true it is, that neither fraud nor might
> Can make a title where there wanteth right.[10]

The policy of statutes of limitation is something not always clearly appreciated. Dean Ames, in contrasting prescription in the civil law with adverse possession in our law, remarks: "English lawyers regard not the merit of the possessor, but the demerit of the one out of possession." It has been suggested, on the other hand, that the policy is to reward those using the land in a way beneficial to the community. This takes too much account of the individual case. The statute has not for its object to reward the diligent trespasser for his wrong nor yet to penalize the negligent and dormant owner for sleeping upon his rights; the great purpose is automatically to quiet all titles which are openly and consistently asserted, to provide proof of meritorious titles, and correct errors in conveyancing.

Oliver Wendell Holmes, The Path of the Law
10 Harv. L. Rev. 457, 476-477 (1897)

Let me now give an example to show the practical importance, for the decision of actual cases, of understanding the reasons of the law, by taking an example from rules which, so far as I know, never have been explained or theorized about in any adequate way. I refer to statutes of limitation and the law of prescription. The end of such rules is obvious, but what is the justification for depriving a man of his rights, a pure evil as far as it goes, in consequence of the lapse of time? Sometimes the loss of evidence is referred to, but that is a secondary matter. Sometimes the desirability of peace, but why is peace more desirable after twenty years than before? It is increasingly likely to come without the aid of legislation. Sometimes it is said that, if a man neglects to enforce his rights, he cannot complain if, after a while, the law follows his example. . . .

---

10. Quoted in Altham's Case, 8 Coke Rep. 153, 77 Engl. reprint, 707.

I should suggest that the foundation of the acquisition of rights by lapse of time is to be looked for in the position of the person who gains them, not in that of the loser. Sir Henry Maine has made it fashionable to connect the archaic notion of property with prescription. But the connection is further back than the first recorded history. It is in the nature of man's mind. A thing which you have enjoyed and used as your own for a long time, whether property or an opinion, takes root in your being and cannot be torn away without your resenting the act and trying to defend yourself, however you came by it. The law can ask no better justification than the deepest instincts of man. It is only by way of reply to the suggestion that you are disappointing the former owner, that you refer to his neglect having allowed the gradual dissociation between himself and what he claims, and the gradual association of it with another. If he knows that another is doing acts which on their face show that he is on the way toward establishing such an association, I should argue that in justice to that other he was bound at his peril to find out whether the other was acting under his permission, to see that he was warned, and, if necessary, stopped.

NOTES AND QUESTIONS

1. What do you make of the passage from Oliver Wendell Holmes (written a few years before he joined the U.S. Supreme Court)? Does it suggest that adverse possession is motivated by economic concerns, or psychological ones, or moral ones? As it happens, each view finds some support. See, e.g., Richard A. Posner, Economic Analysis of Law 79 (4th ed. 1992) (Holmes was suggesting an economic explanation, based on diminishing marginal utility of income); Robert C. Ellickson, Bringing Culture and Human Frailty to Rational Actors: A Critique of Classical Law and Economics, 65 Chi.-Kent L. Rev. 23, 39 (1989) (Holmes "is more faithfully interpreted as anticipating (in a primitive way)" much later developments in cognitive psychology — in particular, prospect theory, which holds that people regard loss of an asset in hand as more significant than forgoing the opportunity to realize an apparently equivalent gain); Joseph W. Singer, The Reliance Interest in Property, 40 Stan. L. Rev. 611, 667 (1988) ("The possessor has come to expect continued access to the property and the true owner has fed those expectations by her actions (or her failure to act). It is morally wrong for the true owner to allow a relationship of dependence to be established and then to cut off the dependent party," citing the passage from Holmes.).

2. The excerpt from Powell says that adverse possession functions as a means of "transferring" ownership, and so it does, but not so straightforwardly as you might think. The running of the statute of limitations not only bars an action by the erstwhile owner but also vests a

new title, created by operation of law, in the adverse possessor. Once acquired, this new title "relates back" to the date of the event that started the statute of limitations running, and the law acts as though the adverse possessor were the owner from that date. With what implications? Consider the rule of increase, introduced in footnote 17 on page 37. By the rule of increase, the offspring of animals belong to the owner of the mother. Suppose that at point 1 in time *A* takes possession of *B*'s cow without *B*'s consent; that at point 2 in time a calf is born to the cow; and that at point 3 in time *A* gets title to the cow by adverse possession. *A*'s title relates back to point 1 in time. Given that it is now *as though A* owned the cow since that time, *A* owns the calf too, even though *A* might not have possessed *the calf* for the statutory period. (Notice that adverse possession applies to personal property as well as land — sometimes, however, with special twists that we take up later.)

3. How (if at all) might one reconcile adverse possession with the principle of first in time that figured so prominently in Chapter 1? See Richard A. Epstein, Past and Future: The Temporal Dimension in the Law of Property, in Symposium, Time, Property Rights, and the Common Law, 64 Wash. U. L.Q. 667, 673, 676 (1986).

4. In the case of adverse possession, what considerations should influence the *length* of the statute of limitations? A period of 20 years was once commonplace, but the modern trend is to shorten this to something on the order of 6 to 10 years. See, e.g., Epstein, supra, at 680-682, where the author endorses this pattern. If shorter periods are a good thing, why not have a very short statute, one with a period, say, of one year? See Robert C. Ellickson, Adverse Possession and Perpetuities Law: Two Dents in the Libertarian Model of Property Rights, in Symposium, supra, at 723, 725-734. Ellickson's discussion suggests the various interests at stake in settling on a statutory period — the interests of landowners, adverse possessors, buyers of land, and society at large.

Van Valkenburgh v. Lutz

Court of Appeals of New York, 1952
304 N.Y. 95, 106 N.E.2d 28

[*Prologue: Background information taken by the editors from the record and briefs submitted to the New York Court of Appeals.* Shortly after their marriage in 1912, Mary and William Lutz bought at auction two wooded lots in Yonkers, a suburb of New York, taking title in the husband's name. The lots, numbered 14 and 15, were situated high on a hill above Leroy Avenue, at the time an unimproved "paper" street. To the west was a wooded triangular tract — consisting of lots 19, 20, 21, and 22 — the ownership of which is at issue in this case. (Lots 19-22 appear as one lot — lot 19 — on the current Yonkers tax map reproduced as Figure

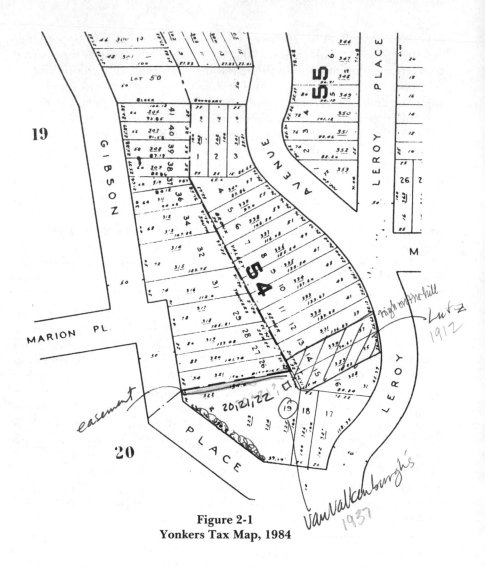

Figure 2-1
Yonkers Tax Map, 1984

2-1.) Instead of climbing the steep grade from Leroy Avenue to reach lots 14 and 15, the Lutzes found it easier to cross the triangular tract which they did not own; Lutz cleared a "traveled way" near the northern boundary of the tract to reach Gibson Place on the west.

With the help of his brother Charlie and his wife Mary, William Lutz cleared lots 14 and 15 and built a house for his family on them. The Lutzes also partially cleared the triangular tract and built for Charlie a one-room structure on lot 19. By 1920 the buildings were occupied. In 1921 Mary's fifth and last child was born to her in the main house.

In 1928 the city graded Leroy Avenue and broke the private water line leading to the main Lutz house. Lutz, who was working in New York

126

City at the time, went home to repair it. As a result, he lost his job; thereafter Lutz stayed home tending a garden on the triangular property, selling vegetables, and doing odd jobs for neighbors. The Lutz children grew up, and all except the youngest son, Eugene, moved away.

In 1937 Joseph and Marion Van Valkenburgh bought lots west of Gibson Place and built a new home there. Some nine years later, in 1946, bad blood developed between the Lutzes and the Van Valkenburghs. In April of that year Mary Lutz was annoyed by the presence of the Van Valkenburgh children in her garden, and she called her husband over. The Van Valkenburgh children ran home, Lutz behind them brandishing an iron pipe and crying, "I'll kill you." Van Valkenburgh then appeared and began a heated argument with Lutz. He subsequently swore out a complaint of criminal assault, and Lutz was arrested, jailed, then released on bail.

A year later, in April 1947, the Van Valkenburghs bought lots 19, 20, 21, and 22 from the City of Yonkers at a foreclosure sale for nonpayment of taxes; no personal notice of the proceedings was given the Lutzes. The purchase price was $379.50. On the following July 6, Van Valkenburgh, accompanied by two policemen, visited the triangular tract and, in his words, "took possession" of it. He called to Mrs. Lutz to come out of her house and told her that the Lutzes were to clear from the property all buildings that belonged to them. On July 8 the Van Valkenburghs' attorney sent Lutz a registered letter informing him that the triangular tract was now owned by the Van Valkenburghs and that he should remove any of his property from the land. A few days later Lutz went to see the attorney and told him he wanted proof of the Van Valkenburghs' ownership and time to harvest his vegetable crop. Then, on July 13, Lutz failed to appear for the trial on the charge of criminal assault, for which he had been arrested a year earlier. A bench warrant was issued, and Lutz was again arrested, jailed, and released on bail. Subsequently he was convicted of criminal assault.

In the meantime Van Valkenburgh had the property surveyed. In response to another letter from the Van Valkenburghs' attorney, Lutz returned to the attorney's office on July 21, this time accompanied by his own lawyer. At this meeting Lutz agreed to remove his sheds, junk, and garden within thirty days, but he claimed a prescriptive right[11] to use the traveled way to reach his property. Lutz then removed the chicken coops and junk. Shortly thereafter the Van Valkenburghs invited legal action by erecting a fence across the traveled way that Lutz

---

11. Prescription differs from adverse possession in terms of the sorts of interests acquired. By adverse possession one may acquire the title or ownership, and the exclusive possession, of land formerly belonging to someone else, say X, whereas prescription gives rise to rights of use, such as rights of way and other easements, but title to the land remains in X. In some jurisdictions the elements of the two doctrines are essentially identical, in others not, as we shall see in Chapter 9.

claimed a right to use. Lutz joined battle by bringing an action against the Van Valkenburghs to enjoin them from interfering with his right of way. In the suit Lutz alleged that Marion Van Valkenburgh was the owner of the property, but that Lutz had a right of way over it. In January 1948 the trial court handed down a judgment in Lutz's favor, awarding him a right of way over the traveled way; this judgment was affirmed in June 1948 (Lutz v. Van Valkenburgh, 274 A.D. 813, 81 N.Y.S.2d 161).

The action in this case was commenced against the Lutzes on April 8, 1948. Perhaps realizing the blunder made in the prior lawsuit (the admission that Marion Van Valkenburgh owned lots 19-22), Lutz fired his Yonkers lawyer and hired one from Wall Street. Not to be outdone, the Van Valkenburghs also sought out and employed a Wall Street firm. In August 1948 William Lutz died, devising all his property to his wife Mary. The Van Valkenburghs' suit was tried in June 1950. The testimony in the case totaled some 250 pages, and in addition there were 56 exhibits consisting of deeds, surveys, and photographs. Several neighbors who had lived in the area a long time testified for the Lutzes. Not one testified for the Van Valkenburghs, who lost in the trial court and appealed.]

DYE, J. These consolidated actions were brought to compel the removal of certain encroachments upon plaintiffs' lands, for delivery of possession and incidental relief. The subject property consists of four unimproved building lots designated as 19, 20, 21 and 22 in block 54 on the official tax map of the city of Yonkers, N.Y. These lots together form a parcel somewhat triangular in shape with dimensions of approximately 150 by 126 by 170 feet fronting on Gibson Place, a street to be laid out within the subdivision running in a northwesterly direction from Leroy Avenue and now surfaced for automobile travel as far as lots 26, 27 and 28. The subject premises were purchased by the plaintiffs from the city of Yonkers by deed dated April 14, 1947. At that time the defendants were, and had been since 1912, owners of premises designated as lots 14 and 15 in block 54, as shown on the same map. The defendants' lots front on Leroy Avenue and adjoin lot 19 owned by the plaintiffs at the rear boundary line. All of these lots, though differently numbered, appear on a map of the subdivision of the Murray Estate opened prior to 1912 and numbering 479 lots. At that time that part of the Murray subdivision was covered with a natural wild growth of brush and small trees.

The defendants interposed an answer denying generally the allegations of the complaint and alleging as an affirmative defense, and as a counterclaim, that William Lutz had acquired title to the subject premises by virtue of having held and possessed the same adversely to plaintiffs and predecessors for upwards of thirty years.

The issue thus joined was tried before Hon. Frederick P. Close, Official Referee, who found that title to said lots "was perfected in William

Lutz by virtue of adverse possession by the year 1935" and not thereafter disseized. The judgment entered thereon in favor of the defendants was affirmed in the Appellate Division, Second Department, without opinion, one Justice dissenting on the ground that the evidence was insufficient to establish title by adverse possession.

To acquire title to real property by adverse possession not founded upon a written instrument, it must be shown by clear and convincing proof that for at least fifteen years (formerly twenty years) there was an "actual" occupation under a claim of title, for it is only the premises so actually occupied "and no others" that are deemed to have been held adversely (Civ. Prac. Act, §§34, 38, 39). The essential elements of proof being either that the premises (1) are protected by a substantial inclosure, or are (2) usually cultivated or improved (Civ. Prac. Act, §40).[12]

Concededly, there is no proof here that the subject premises were "protected by a substantial inclosure" which leaves for consideration only whether there is evidence showing that the premises were cultivated or improved sufficiently to satisfy the statute.

We think not. The proof concededly fails to show that the cultivation incident to the garden utilized the whole of the premises claimed. Such lack may not be supplied by inference on the showing that the cultivation of a smaller area, whose boundaries are neither defined nor its location fixed with certainty, "must have been . . . substantial" as sev-

---

12. At the time of the *Lutz* case, N.Y. Civil Practice Act §§34, 38, 39, and 40 provided:

§34. An action to recover real property or the possession thereof cannot be maintained by a party other than the people, unless the plaintiff, his ancestor, predecessor or grantor, was seized or possessed of the premises in question within fifteen years before the commencement of the action. . . .

§38. For the purpose of constituting an adverse possession, by a person claiming a title founded upon a written instrument or a judgment or decree, land is deemed to have been possessed and occupied in either of the following cases:

1. Where it has been usually cultivated or improved.
2. Where it has been protected by a substantial inclosure.
3. Where, although not inclosed, it has been used for the supply of fuel or of fencing timber, either for the purposes of husbandry or for the ordinary use of the occupant.

Where a known farm or single lot has been partly improved, the portion of the farm or lot that has been left not cleared or not inclosed, according to the usual course and custom of the adjoining country, is deemed to have been occupied for the same length of time as the part improved and cultivated.

§39. Where there has been an actual continued occupation of premises under a claim of title, exclusive of any other right, but not founded upon a written instrument or a judgment or decree, the premises so actually occupied, and no others, are deemed to have been held adversely.

§40. For the purpose of constituting an adverse possession by a person claiming title not founded upon a written instrument or a judgment or decree, land is deemed to have been possessed and occupied in either of the following cases, and no others:

1. Where it has been protected by a substantial inclosure.
2. Where it has been usually cultivated or improved.

These provisions were subsequently revised, among other ways, by reducing the statutory period from 15 to 10 years. — EDS.

eral neighbors were "supplied . . . with vegetables." This introduces an element of speculation and surmise which may not be considered since the statute clearly limits the premises adversely held to those "actually" occupied "and no others" (Civ. Prac. Act, §39) which we have recently interpreted as requiring definition by clear and positive proof (St. William's Church v. People, 296 N.Y. 861, revg. 269 App. Div. 874, motion for reargument denied 296 N.Y. 1000).

Furthermore, on this record, the proof fails to show that the premises were improved (Civ. Prac. Act, §40). According to the proof the small shed or shack (about 5 by 10½ feet) which, as shown by survey map, was located on the subject premises about 14 feet from the Lutz boundary line, . . . was built in about the year 1923 and, as Lutz himself testified, he knew at the time it was not on his land, and his wife, a defendant here, also testified to the same effect.

The statute requires as an essential element of proof, recognized as fundamental on the concept of adversity since ancient times, that the occupation of premises be "under a claim of title" (Civ. Prac. Act, §39), in other words, hostile (Belotti v. Bickhardt, 228 N.Y. 296), and when lacking will not operate to bar the legal title (Doherty v. Matsell, 119 N.Y. 646), no matter how long the occupation may have continued (La Frombois v. Jackson, 8 Cow. 589; Colvin v. Burnet, 17 Wend. 564).

Similarly, the garage encroachment, extending a few inches over the boundary line, fails to supply proof of occupation by improvement. Lutz himself testified that when he built the garage he had no survey and thought he was getting it on his own property, which certainly falls short of establishing that he did it under a claim of title hostile to the true owner. The other acts committed by Lutz over the years, such as placing a portable chicken coop on the premises which he moved about, the cutting of brush and some of the trees, and the littering of the property with odds and ends of salvaged building materials, cast-off items of house furnishings and parts of automobiles which the defendants and their witnesses described as "personal belongings," "junk," "rubbish" and "debris," were acts which under no stretch of the imagination could be deemed an occupation by improvement within the meaning of the statute, and which, of course, are of no avail in establishing adverse possession.

We are also persuaded that the defendant's subsequent words and conduct confirm the view that his occupation was not "under a claim of title." When the defendant had the opportunity to declare his hostility and assert his rights against the true owner, he voluntarily chose to concede that the plaintiffs' legal title conferred actual ownership entitling them to the possession of these and other premises in order to provide a basis for establishing defendant's right to an easement by adverse possession — the use of a well-defined "traveled way" that crossed the said premises. In that action (Lutz v. Van Valkenburgh, 274 App. Div. 813),

William Lutz, a defendant here (now deceased), chose to litigate the issue of title and possession and, having succeeded in establishing his
claim of easement by adverse possession, he may not now disavow the
effect of his favorable judgment (Goebel v. Iffla, 111 N.Y. 170), or prevent its use as evidence to show his prior intent. Declarations against
interest made by a prescriptive tenant are always available on the issue
of his intent (6 Wigmore on Evidence, §1778).

On this record we do not reach the question of disseisin by oral
disclaimer, since the proof fails to establish actual occupation for such
time or in such manner as to establish title. What we are saying is that
the proof fails to establish actual occupation for such a time or in such a
manner as to establish title by adverse possession (Civ. Prac. Act, §§39,
40; St. William's Church v. People, supra).

The judgments should be reversed, the counterclaim dismissed and
judgment directed to be entered in favor of plaintiff Joseph D. Van Valkenburgh for the relief prayed for in the complaint subject to the existing easement (Lutz v. Van Valkenburgh, 274 App. Div. 813), with costs
in all courts.

FULD, J. (dissenting). In my judgment, the weight of evidence lies
with the determination made by the court at Special Term and affirmed
by the Appellate Division. But whether that is so or not, there can be no
doubt whatsoever that the record contains some evidence that the premises here involved were occupied by William Lutz, defendant's late husband, for fifteen years under a claim of title — and that, of course,
should compel an affirmance.

The four lots in suit, located in the city of Yonkers, comprise a fairly
level parcel of land, triangular in shape, with approximate dimensions
of 150 by 126 by 170 feet. It is bounded on the north by a "traveled
way," on the west and south by Gibson Place, an unopened street, and
on the southeast by a vacant lot. Immediately to the east of the parcel,
the land descends sharply to Leroy Avenue, forming a steep hill; on the
hill are situated two lots, purchased by Lutz in 1912, upon which his
family's home has stood for over thirty years.

Wild and overgrown when the Lutzes first moved into the neighborhood, the property was cleared by defendant's husband and had
been, by 1916, the referee found, developed into a truck farm "of substantial size." Lutz, together with his children, worked the farm continuously until his death in 1948; indeed, after 1928, he had no other
employment. Each year, a new crop was planted and the harvest of vegetables was sold to neighbors. Lutz also raised chickens on the premises,
and constructed coops or sheds for them. Fruit trees were planted, and
timber was cut from that portion of the property not used for the farm.
On one of the lots, Lutz in 1920 built a one-room dwelling, in which his
brother Charles has lived ever since.

Although disputing the referee's finding that the dimensions of Lutz's farm were substantial, the court's opinion fails to remark the plentiful evidence in support thereof. For instance, there is credible testimony in the record that "nearly all" of the property comprised by the four lots was cultivated during the period to which the referee's finding relates. A survey introduced in evidence indicates the very considerable extent to which the property was cultivated in 1950, and many witnesses testified that the farm was no larger at that time than it had ever been. There is evidence, moreover, that the cultivated area extended from the "traveled way" on *one side* of the property to a row of logs and brush — placed by Lutz for the express purpose of marking the farm's boundary — at the *opposite end* of the premises.

According to defendant's testimony, she and her husband, knowing that they did not have record title to the premises, intended from the first nevertheless to occupy the property as their own. Bearing this out is the fact that Lutz put down the row of logs and brush, which was over 100 feet in length, to mark the southwestern boundary of his farm; this marker, only roughly approximating the lot lines, extended beyond them into the bed of Gibson Place. The property was, moreover, known in the neighborhood as "Mr. Lutz's gardens," and the one-room dwelling on it as "Charlie's house"; the evidence clearly indicates that people living in the vicinity believed the property to be owned by Lutz. And it is undisputed that for upwards of thirty-five years — until 1947, when plaintiffs became the record owners — no other person ever asserted title to the parcel.

With evidence such as that in the record, I am at a loss to understand how this court can say that support is lacking for the finding that the premises had been occupied by Lutz under a claim of title. The referee was fully justified in concluding that the character of Lutz's possession was akin to that of a true owner and indicated, more dramatically and effectively than could words, an intent to claim the property as his own. Recognizing that "A claim of title may be made by acts alone, quite as effectively as by the most emphatic assertions" (Barnes v. Light, 116 N.Y. 34, 39), we have often sustained findings based on evidence of actual occupation and improvement of the property in the manner that "owners are accustomed to possess and improve their estates." (La Frombois v. Jackson, 8 Cow. 589, 603. . . .)

That Lutz knew that he did not have the record title to the property — a circumstance relied upon by the court — is of no consequence, so long as he intended, notwithstanding that fact, to acquire and use the property as his own. As we stated in Ramapo Mfg. Co. v. Mapes (216 N.Y. 362, 370-371), "the bona fides of the claim of the occupant is not essential and it will not excuse the negligence of the owner in forbearing to bring his action until after the time in the Statute of Limitations shall have run against him to show that the defendant knew all along that he was in the wrong. (Humbert v. Rector, etc., of Trinity Church, 24 Wend. 587.)"

Quite obviously, the fact that Lutz alleged in the 1947 easement action — twelve years after the title had, according to the referee, vested in him through adverse possession — that one of the plaintiffs was the owner of three of the lots, simply constituted evidence pointing the other way, to be weighed with the other proof by the courts below. While it is true that a disclaimer of title by the occupant of property, made before the statutory period has run, indelibly stamps his possession as nonadverse and prevents title from vesting in him . . . , a disclaimer made after the statute has run carries with it totally different legal consequences. Once title has vested by virtue of adverse possession, it is elementary that it may be divested, not by an oral disclaimer, but only by a transfer complying with the formalities prescribed by law. . . .

Hence, an oral acknowledgment of title in another, made after the statutory period is alleged to have run, "is only evidence tending to show the character of the previous possession." (Smith v. Vermont Marble Co., 99 Vt. 384, 394. . . .)

Here, Official Referee Close, of the opinion that the 1947 admission was made by Lutz under the erroneous advice of his attorney (cf. Shirey v. Whitlow, 80 Ark. 444, 446-447), chose to rest his decision rather on evidence of Lutz's numerous and continual acts of dominion over the property — proof of a most persuasive character. Even if we were to feel that the referee was mistaken in so weighing the evidence, we would be powerless to change the determination, where, as we have seen, there is some evidence in the record to support his conclusion.

In view of the extensive cultivation of the parcel in suit, there is no substance to the argument that the requirements of sections 39 and 40 of the Civil Practice Act were not met. Under those provisions, only the premises "actually occupied" in the manner prescribed — that is, "protected by a substantial inclosure" or "usually cultivated or improved" — are deemed to have been held adversely. The object of the statute, we have recognized, "is that the real owner may, by unequivocal acts of the usurper, have notice of the hostile claim and be thereby called upon to assert his legal title." (Monnot v. Murphy, 207 N.Y. 240, 245; see, also, Trustees of Town of East Hampton v. Kirk, 84 N.Y. 215, 220.) Since the character of the acts sufficient to afford such notice "depends upon the nature and situation of the property and the uses to which it can be applied," it is settled that the provisions of sections 39 and 40 are to be construed, not in a narrow or technical sense, but with reference to the nature, character, condition, and location of the property under consideration. . . .

Judge Dye considers it significant that the proof "fails to show that the cultivation incident to the garden utilized the whole of the premises claimed" [see page 129]. There surely is no requirement in either statute or decision that proof of adverse possession depends upon cultivation of *"the whole"* plot or of *every foot* of the property in question. And, indeed, the statute — which, as noted, reads *"usually* cultivated or improved" — has been construed to mean only that the claimant's occupation must "consist of acts such as are usual in the ordinary cultivation and improvement of similar lands by thrifty owners." (Ramapo Mfg. Co. v. Mapes, supra, 216 N.Y. 362, 373.) The evidence demonstrates that by far the greater part of the four lots was regularly and continuously used for farming, and, that being so, the fact that a portion of the property was not cleared should not affect the claimant's ability to acquire title by adverse possession: any frugal person, owning and occupying lands similar to those here involved, would have permitted, as Lutz did, some of the trees to stand — while clearing the bulk of the property — in order to provide a source of lumber and other tree products for his usual needs. The portion of the property held subservient to the part actively cultivated is as much "occupied" as the portion actually tilled. The nature of the cultivation engaged in by Lutz was more than adequate, as his neighbors' testimony establishes, to give the owner notice of an adverse claim and to delimit the property to which the claim related. The limits of the parcel in suit were indicated in a general way by boundaries natural as well as man-made: the declivity to Leroy Avenue, the "traveled way," and Gibson Place. Apart from that, however, the evidence discloses that the bulk of each of the four lots was cultivated, and — even putting to one side the fact that the cottage, called "Charlie's house," had been actually occupied and lived in for upwards of thirty years — such substantial use was enough to put the owner on notice that his whole lot was claimed.

In short, there is ample evidence to sustain the finding that William Lutz actually occupied the property in suit for over fifteen years under a claim of title. Since, then, title vested in Lutz by 1935, the judgment must be affirmed. To rule otherwise, on the ground that the weight of evidence is against that finding — a view which I do not, in any event, hold — is to ignore the constitutional provision that limits our jurisdiction to the review of questions of law (N.Y. Const., art. VI, §7; see, also, Civ. Prac. Act, §605).

I would affirm the judgment reached by both of the courts below.

Lewis, Conway and Froessel, JJ., concur with Dye, J.; Fuld, J., dissents in opinion in which Loughran, Ch. J., and Desmond, J., concur.

[*Epilogue*: Litigation between the Van Valkenburghs and the Lutzes did not end with the principal case. The Van Valkenburghs' judgment included costs and disbursements, and an execution was issued directing the sale of lots 14 and 15 (the Lutz home) to pay the judgment. In the meantime Mary Lutz had transferred all her interest in her home to her son Eugene, who resided there with his mother, his wife, and his child. Eugene moved to set aside the execution, and the motion was granted; the Van Valkenburghs moved for a rehearing, and this was denied. The Van Valkenburghs then appealed the order denying the rehearing instead of appealing, as they should have, the order granting Eugene's motion. They lost. Van Valkenburgh v. Lutz, 6 A.D.2d 812, 175 N.Y.S.2d 203 (1958). By a lawyer's procedural error, the Lutz home was saved for Mary and Eugene. (*Query*: Was the lawyer liable to the Van Valkenburghs for malpractice?)

William Lutz's brother Charlie was mentally incompetent; after the principal case, Eugene was appointed as his guardian. Charlie had not been a party to the prior proceedings, so he was in position to contest them. Through his guardian he brought an action against the Van Valkenburghs to enjoin removal of "his" house from lot 19. Charlie claimed that he and his brother William had constructed the house over 20 years earlier and that when this house was being constructed he believed he was building it on William's land. He further claimed that, since 1917, he had been in possession of the house as the tenant of William, the owner, and that he paid rent to William for the house. This lawsuit wound its way up and down the courts (11 A.D.2d 746, 205 N.Y.S.2d 956 (1960); 13 A.D.2d 1014, 218 N.Y.S.2d 979 (1961); 247 N.Y.S.2d 1012 (1964); 27 A.D.2d 735, 277 N.Y.S.2d 42 (1967)) until 1968, when the Court of Appeals unanimously ruled for the Van Valkenburghs on the ground that Charlie's occupation was not under a claim of title. Lutz v. Van Valkenburgh, 21 N.Y.2d 937, 237 N.E.2d 844, 289 N.Y.S.2d 767 (1968). By this time Charlie was well into his eighties.

Van Valkenburgh v. Lutz, 304 N.Y. 95, is noted in 17 Alb. L. Rev. 181 (1953), 19 Brooklyn L. Rev. 145 (1952), and 27 St. John's L. Rev. 151 (1953).]

NOTES AND QUESTIONS

1. The excerpt from Powell on Real Property that began this section observed that "the law of adverse possession is a composite of statutory and decisional law," with judicial rules supplementing the statutes of limitation that make up the core of adverse possession. On its surface, Van Valkenburgh v. Lutz barely hints at this legislative-judicial teamwork; the majority and dissenting opinions could well be taken to suggest that the only requirements of adverse possession in New York are those set out in the Civil Practice Act. Despite this suggestion, the reality is that in most if not all jurisdictions, New York included, the courts have developed a series of requirements of their own. These are stated in

various ways, but their essence is this: There must be (1) an actual entry giving exclusive possession that is (2) open and notorious, (3) adverse[13] and under a claim of right,[14] and (4) continuous for the statutory period.[15] What might be the substance and purpose of each of these requirements? Which were in issue in Van Valkenburgh v. Lutz?

2. In the leading case of Ewing v. Burnet, 36 U.S. (11 Pet.) 41 (1837), adverse possession of an unimproved lot in Cincinnati, used principally for digging sand and gravel, was established when the claimant under color and claim of title paid taxes on the lot, from time to time dug sand and gravel from it, permitted others to do so, and brought actions of trespass against others for doing so without his permission. Notice then that adverse possession may exist even if the occupant does not reside on the property and for long periods does not use it at all.[16]

A commonly stated generalization that follows from cases like Ewing is this: The sort of entry and exclusive possession that will ripen into title by adverse possession is use of the property in the manner that an average true owner would use it under the circumstances, such that neighbors and other observers would regard the occupant as a person exercising exclusive dominion. But generalizations are dangerous, as Lutz itself suggests. In Pettis v. Lozier, 217 Neb. 191, 349 N.W.2d 372 (1984), adverse possession of an eight-acre suburban wooded tract was not established notwithstanding that the claimant occasionally used the land for a variety of purposes throughout the statutory period — kept geese and livestock there, put up three large packing crates to serve as sheds for

13. The word *hostile* is sometimes inserted here as an element of adverse possession. It does not necessarily mean animosity, but rather that possession is adverse as opposed to subordinate to the true owner. The entire question of hostility and claim of right is, however, fraught with difficulty — as we shall see shortly.

14. The New York statutes call this a claim of title, not to be confused with the concept of color of title, discussed in the Note at page 142.

15. In several states, principally in the West, the adverse possessor must pay taxes on the land in order to prevail. This requirement probably owes to the influence of railroad companies on state legislatures in the nineteenth century. Owning vast tracts of undeveloped land, the companies found it difficult to discover squatters who might adversely possess their holdings. The requirement that taxes be paid — and recorded in the tax assessor's office — provided the railroads some protection. See Comment, Payment of Taxes as a Condition of Title by Adverse Possession: A Nineteenth Century Anachronism, 9 Santa Clara Law. 244 (1969). Compare Lawrence M. Friedman, A History of American Law 413-414 (2d ed. 1985).

16. Distinguish the adverse possessor's absence from the property, on the one hand, and *abandonment* on the other. If the adverse possessor abandons the property — leaves with no intention to return — before the statute has run, the statute stops, a new entry is required, and the whole process must begin anew. Distinguish also *interruption* by the true owner before the statute has run — say by bringing a successful ejectment action against the adverse possessor, or by re-entering the property. In the latter event, the true owner's entry must be open and hostile. In some states, possession must continue for a year after entry, or entry must be followed by an ejectment action within that period. See 3 American Law of Property §15.9 (1952). All of these remarks pertain to the *continuity* requirement, considered further in Howard v. Kunto (beginning on page 144) and the materials that follow it.

his animals, planted native grass and 25 pine trees (all the trees died), did some vegetable gardening, built a watering tank, set out a beehive, dumped trash and junk and old cars, did some fencing, used the property for recreation, posted "No Hunting" and "No Trespassing" signs, twice removed "For Sale" signs, and once told a prospective purchaser of the tract that it belonged to him.

The *notoriety* requirement of adverse possession doctrine is usually straightforward, but not always. Consider an instance where adverse possession goes underground. Suppose that *A* and *B* are neighbors whose parcels of land lie over a cave, the entrance to which is on *A*'s land. *A* discovers the entrance, explores the full domain of the cave, and then opens it up to the public for a fee. *A*'s business, well-known to *B*, runs for many years. After the statute of limitations has expired, *B* learns that part of the cave is under his land and brings suit to quiet his title to that part; *A* in turn claims title to all the cave by adverse possession. Was *A*'s possession open and notorious? No, according to Marengo Cave Co. v. Ross, 212 Ind. 624, 10 N.E.2d 917 (1937).[17]

(An aside: It is implicit in *Marengo* that the owner of a surface parcel

---

17. The court in *Marengo* held that open possession of an underground cave is not notorious. Could this ever be said with respect to open possession of the *surface* of a piece of land? See Problem 1 on page 141.

Of *Marengo*, Professor A. Dan Tarlock says in Bill of Particulars, a publication of the University of Indiana School of Law, Winter 1977-1978, at 7, that "most property scholars think the decision was wrong, although modern property theory would suggest that the result in the case should have no impact on the use of the cave since the loser would buy out the winner." The first half of this statement is probably correct, but what of the second half? It rests implicitly on the Coase Theorem, and it assumes that because the dispute between the winner and the loser in the case involved few parties, transaction costs would be low and hence the value-maximizing use of the cave would be achieved in any event. (Review the discussion in footnote 29 on page 53 and recall the qualification at the end of footnote 27 on page 52. We are addressing the latter here.)

What the low-transaction-cost assumption overlooks is a problem that economists call *bilateral monopoly*. Bilateral monopolies, which arise when two parties are locked into dealing with each other (as the winner and loser in *Marengo* were), can give rise to high negotiation costs that foreclose efficient transfers. Because there is no competitive pressure from outsiders, each party is likely to bargain "strategically" — asking much, offering little, bluffing, threatening to walk away from the deal — in an effort to get as much as possible. "Indeed, each party may be so determined to engross the greater part of the potential profits from the transaction that they never succeed in coming to terms." Richard A. Posner, Economic Analysis of Law 62 (4th ed. 1992). See also Stewart E. Sterk, Neighbors in American Land Law, 87 Colum. L. Rev. 55, 69-74 (1987). Tarlock reports that Ross, the winner in *Marengo*, "stood by his principles and refused to deal with the various owners of the cave company. . . . [He] built a wall between the sections, and visitors were denied access to one of the most geologically interesting parts of the cave." Nevertheless, after Ross died his heirs sold the surface, "and the cave company was able to acquire the subsurface rights." So bilateral monopolies and strategic behavior don't always kill beneficial bargains. "But still bilateral monopoly is a social problem, because the transaction costs incurred by each party in an effort to engross as much of the profit of the transaction as possible are a social waste. They alter the relative wealth of the parties but do not increase the aggregate wealth of society. A major thrust of the common law, as we shall see [and as you shall see], is to mitigate bilateral-monopoly problems." Posner, supra, at 62.

We return to these matters later. See, e.g., Note 3 on page 974.

also owns the part of a common cave underlying the parcel. This follows from the so-called *ad coelum* doctrine: *Cujus est solum, ejus est usque ad coelum et ad infernos* (to whomsoever the soil belongs, he owns also to the sky and to the depths). Obviously, the *ad coelum* doctrine cannot be taken too seriously (think of airplanes), but it sometimes is in the case of caves. Is that sensible? Consider some alternative approaches: The owner of land on which sits the entrance to a cave owns the cave; whoever discovers a cave and opens it to access owns the cave; all the overlying landowners own the cave together, in common. Given *ad coelum* and the three alternatives, which is best? For contending views on that question, see the majority, concurring, and dissenting opinions in Edwards v. Sims, 232 Ky. 791, 24 S.W.2d 619 (1929), and Edwards v. Lee's Admr., 265 Ky. 418, 96 S.W.2d 1028 (1936).)

Claim of title. One of the matters at issue in *Lutz* — that adverse possession be accompanied by a "claim of title" — was embodied in New York legislation early in the last century and continues to the present day. The statutes of some other states express the same requirement; even when they do not, a considerable number of courts have read the requirement in, whether in terms of claim of title, claim of right, or hostility. But what does this requirement mean? A fruitful way to approach the question is in terms of the state of mind required of the adverse possessor, and here existing doctrine reflects three different views: "(1) state of mind is irrelevant; (2) the required state of mind is, 'I thought I owned it'; (3) the required state of mind is, 'I thought I did *not* own it [and intended to take it.]' These can roughly be thought of as the objective standard, the good-faith standard, and the aggressive trespass standard." Margaret J. Radin, Time, Possession, and Alienation, 64 Wash. U. L.Q. 739, 746-747 (1986).

The first view is firmly held in England, where the statute of limitations begins to run as soon as the true owner is dispossessed by someone taking possession inconsistent with — not subordinate to — his title. See Robert Megarry & H.W.R. Wade, The Law of Real Property 1034 (5th ed. 1984). The point behind this view is simple: Once there is an entry against the true owner, she has a cause of action. Given that, shouldn't the statute of limitations be running, *whatever* the entrant's state of mind? See 3 American Law of Property §15.4 (1952), endorsing the view and suggesting it is the majority position in the United States; Tioga Coal Co. v. Supermarkets Gen. Corp., 519 Pa. 66, 546 A.2d 1 (1988) (if all other requirements of adverse possession have been met, hostility will be implied, regardless of the subjective state of mind of the adverse possessor); Chaplin v. Sanders, 100 Wash. 2d 853, 861, 676, P.2d 431, 436 (1984) (adverse possessor's "subjective belief regarding his true interest in the land and his intent to dispossess or not dispossess another is irrelevant").

The second view, requiring a good-faith claim, is voiced from time to time in American decisions. A recent example is Halpern v. Lacy Inv. Corp., 259 Ga. 264, 379 S.E.2d 519 (1989), where the court said:

> We hold that the correct rule is that one must enter upon the land claiming in good faith the right to do so. To enter upon the land without any honest claim of right to do so is but a trespass and can never ripen into prescriptive title. In the language used in Hannah v. Kenny, 210 Ga. 824, 83 S.E.2d 1 (1954), such a person is called a "squatter." . . . Here there was evidence that the Halperns knew the parcel of land was owned by another yet they simply took possession when their offer to purchase was declined. There was evidence to support a finding that this possession never changed its character.
>
> One may maintain hostile possession of land in good faith. . . . [H]ostile possession and claim of right are legal equivalents for all practical purposes. The holding is that most who have hostile possession of land do so with a good faith claim of right and therefore a jury or other factfinder may, in the absence of a contrary showing, infer from hostile possession that it is done in good faith that a claim of right exists. [259 Ga. at 265, 379 S.E.2d at 521.][18]

Professor Helmholz claims that the good-faith requirement plays a larger role than might at first appear. Based on an extensive survey of recent cases, he concludes that many courts do take account of state of mind — though they might not say as much — in cases where the evidence strongly suggests that the adverse possessor was well aware he was trespassing. Manipulating the hostility and claim-of-right requirements, the courts "regularly award title to the good faith trespasser, where they will not award it to the trespasser who knows what he is doing at the time he enters the land in dispute." Richard H. Helmholz, Adverse Possession and Subjective Intent, 61 Wash. U. L.Q. 331, 356-358 (1983). A reply to Helmholz's article argues that the cases surveyed provide no basis for his conclusions. Roger A. Cunningham, Adverse Possession and Subjective Intent: A Reply to Professor Helmholz, 64 Wash. U. L.Q. 1 (1986). Helmholz's response? Cunningham has misinterpreted the case law. Richard H. Helmholz, More on Subjective Intent: A Response to Professor Cunningham, in id. at 65. For Cunningham's rejoinder, see Roger A. Cunningham, More on Adverse Possession: A Rejoinder to Professor Helmholz, in id. at 1167.

The third view, that of the aggressive trespasser, is perhaps reflected in Patterson v. Reigle, 4 Pa. 201, 45 Am. Dec. 684 (1846). Reigle

---

18. Notice the reference to "squatters," who, the court suggests, cannot become adverse possessors. Why should that be? In any event, and especially given the increasingly apparent problem of homelessness in the United States (to which we shall return), should squatters have rights — say to occupy vacant and abandoned buildings? See Note, Homelessness and the Uses of Theory: An Analysis of Economic and Personality Theories of Property in the Context of Voting Rights and Squatting Rights, 45 U. Miami L. Rev. 701 (1990-1991); Comment, Urban Homesteading: A Compromise Between Squatters and the Law, 35 N.Y.L. Sch. L. Rev. 709 (1990).

and Shingledecker entered upon land and for over 20 years used it as the average owner would, never claiming ownership. Shingledecker testified, "We intended to leave when the real owner, with a good deed, that is, the old soldier, who had a good deed, should come for it, but not till then. We settled it to hold it until a better owner came for it, and then to give it up." The court held this established adverse possession, saying:

[T]here is a presumption which lasts till it is rebutted, that an intruder enters to hold for himself; and it is not to be doubted that a trespasser entering to gain a title, though conscious that he is a wrongdoer, will accomplish his object, if the owner do not enter or prosecute his claim within the prescribed period. But to do so, it is necessary that his possession be adverse from the first; and to infer that he intended it to be otherwise, would impute to him an inconsistency of purpose. Was there evidence to rebut the presumption that the entry and possession of Reigle and Shingledecker were adverse to the title? No declaration by them was inconsistent with an intention to hold the land as long as they could, or evincive of a design to give it up before they should be compelled to do so by the appearance of a claimant whom they could not resist. They were conscious they had no title themselves, and they said so; they were conscious they could not resist him who had it, and they said so; but they did not say that they meant not to acquire a title to it for themselves. Whatever they did say, was predicated on the expected appearance of the owner while he continued to be so; for they certainly did not mean to purchase the land from any one else. Shingledecker himself testified that he and Reigle settled on the land "to hold it till a better owner came for it"; but the holder of the title would lose it, and cease to be the better owner at the end of one-and-twenty years. They intended to hold adversely to all the world till the title should be produced to them, and consequently as adversely to the owner before he disclosed himself as to any one else. The sum of the evidence is that they entered to hold the land as long as they could; and they consequently gained the title to it by the statute of limitations. [4 Pa. at 204-205, 45 Am. Dec. at 685-686.][19]

19. In the case of aggressive (bad-faith) adverse possession, consider the possibility of awarding title to the adverse possessor only upon his payment of fair market value to the former owner. Title would go to the adverse possessor for some of the reasons we have adverse possession to begin with — for example, to protect the interests of third parties who relied upon the appearance of ownership. But the obligation to compensate would be imposed to punish and deter the consciously wrongful activity. For discussion, see Thomas W. Merrill, Property Rules, Liability Rules, and Adverse Possession, 79 Nw. U. L. Rev. 1122 (1984-1985). See also Comment, Compensation for the Involuntary Transfer of Property Between Private Parties: Application of a Liability Rule to the Law of Adverse Possession, 79 Nw. U. L. Rev. 759 (1984), advancing the same idea for *all* adverse possession cases. Both articles were provoked by Warsaw v. Chicago Metallic Ceilings, Inc., 35 Cal. 3d 564, 676 P.2d 584, 199 Cal. Rptr. 773 (1984), concerning a prescriptive easement, where the court considered, but ultimately rejected, a compensation requirement (we take up prescriptive easements in Chapter 9). The compensation requirement is criticized in Richard A. Epstein, Past and Future: The Temporal Dimension in the Law of Property, 64 Wash. U. L.Q. 667, 688-689 (1986) (favoring instead a two-tier statute of limitations with a longer period for bad-faith possessors).

Notice in the title of the first two articles above the mention of *property rules* and *liability*

Which of the three approaches surveyed above do you favor, and why? In answering this question, you will probably have to settle on just what you regard as the purposes of adverse possession doctrine. Recall the discussion on pages 121-125. You may also have to deal with the fact that some of the purposes conflict with others.

Which approach was applied by the majority in the *Lutz* case? Or should we say, rather, which approach*es*? On the reasoning of *Lutz*, could anyone ever adversely possess anything?

PROBLEM AND NOTE: BOUNDARY DISPUTES

1. The adverse possessor's state of mind has played an especially dominant role in boundary disputes. Suppose *A* and *B* own adjacent lots. *A* erects a fence on what she mistakenly assumes to be the true boundary line dividing the lots; in fact the fence is erected on *B*'s lot three feet beyond the boundary. *A* thereafter acts as the owner of all the land on her side of the fence for the statutory period. Subsequently, *B* learns the truth and sues to eject *A*. What result? Does it matter whether *A*, in erecting the fence in the belief that it was on the true line, had an intention to claim title to that line whatever the reality or had an intention only to claim title to her land and not that of her neighbor? See Mannillo v. Gorski, 54 N.J. 378, 255 A.2d 258 (1969).[20]

Suppose that as a consequence of the facts above *A* did in fact acquire title by adverse possession. Later, after the statute has run, a survey by *B* reveals the mistake. *B* tells this to *A*, and *A*, "to avoid a hassle," tears down her fence and erects a new fence on the original true boundary. Three years later *A* talks to a lawyer, changes her mind, and sues to eject *B* from the three feet. What result? See Kline v. Kramer, 179 Ind.

A — no such thing as an unwritten transfer . B has possession. A|P starts all over again .

---

rules. These have become terms of art after an influential article by Guido Calabresi & A. Douglas Melamed, Property Rules, Liability Rules and Inalienability: One View of the Cathedral, 85 Harv. L. Rev. 1089 (1972). When a property interest is protected by a property rule, the interest cannot be taken from its owner without the owner's consent; all transfers are voluntary. When a property interest is protected by a liability rule, the interest can be taken without the owner's consent but only upon payment of judicially determined damages. Ordinary adverse possession doctrine protects (1) the owner's interest with a property rule before the statute of limitations has run, then (2) the adverse possessor's interest with a property rule after the statute has run. The compensation approach discussed above would observe (1) but as to (2) would leave in the owner — after the statute has run — an interest protected by a liability rule. Transfer of the owner's interest to the adverse possessor could be forced but only upon payment of compensatory damages by the latter.

We shall exploit the property rule-liability rule dichotomy in various places throughout this book. See in particular Note 3 on page 985.

20. Does a problem of notoriety lurk in the facts as outlined? And what happens if an adverse possessor's occupation is *not* open and notorious, but the true owner nevertheless knows of it?

App. 592, 386 N.E.2d 982 (1979); Mugaas v. Smith, 33 Wash. 2d 429, 206 P.2d 332 (1949).

2. Boundary disputes may also be resolved by the doctrines of agreed boundaries, acquiescence, and estoppel. The doctrine of agreed boundaries provides that if there is uncertainty between neighbors as to the true boundary line, an oral agreement to settle the matter is enforceable, at least if subsequent conduct by the parties confirms the agreement. The doctrine of acquiescence provides that long acquiescence — though perhaps for a period of time shorter than the statute of limitations — is evidence of an agreement between the parties fixing the boundary line. The doctrine of estoppel comes into play when one neighbor makes representations about (or engages in conduct that tends to indicate) the location of a common boundary, and the other neighbor then changes her position in reliance on the representations or conduct. The first neighbor is then estopped to deny the validity of his statements or acts. Estoppel has also been applied when one neighbor remains silent in the face of expenditures by another that suggest the latter's notion of the boundary's location. The three doctrines are commonly interwoven by the courts, leaving the law vague and tricky to apply. See Olin L. Browder, Jr., The Practical Location of Boundaries, 56 Mich. L. Rev. 487 (1958); Annot., 7 A.L.R.4th 53 (1981).

NOTE: COLOR OF TITLE AND CONSTRUCTIVE ADVERSE POSSESSION

The "claim of title" required by the New York statutes, and at issue in Van Valkenburgh v. Lutz, is quite different from "color of title." Claim of title is simply one way of expressing the requirement of hostility or claim of right on the part of an adverse possessor. Color of title, on the other hand, refers to a claim founded on a written instrument (a deed, a will) or a judgment or decree that is for some reason defective and invalid (as where the grantor does not own the land conveyed by deed or is incompetent to convey, or the deed is improperly executed). Claim under color of title was not required by English law and is not required in most American jurisdictions. In a few states, color of title is essential to acquiring title by adverse possession. What might be the rationale for the concept of color of title? Should it be required in all cases? Dispensed with in all?

Even though color of title is not a prerequisite for adverse possession in most states, it has important advantages for the adverse possessor. Notice, for example, that the statutes involved in Van Valkenburgh v. Lutz set out different requirements for claims of title "founded upon a written instrument or a judgment or decree" and those not so founded. The requirements in the first case are slightly more lenient than those in the second. In some states a shorter statute of limitations is applicable to adverse possessors with color of title than to those without. In all states entry with color of title may have an advantage where the adverse possessor enters into possession of only a part of the property. Actual possession under color of title of only a part of the land covered by the defective writing is *constructive* possession of all that the writing describes. The advantage that a person may gain from constructive possession is that the activities relied upon to establish adverse possession reach not only the part of the premises actually occupied but the entire premises described in a deed to the claimant. This doctrine of constructive adverse possession under color of title, established by judicial rule in some states and by statute in others, is, however, subject to some limitations. Several of them are explored in the Problems that follow.

PROBLEMS

1. In 1977 Opal Corporation owned four contiguous lots — 1, 2, 3, and 4. In that year the secretary of Opal executed a deed conveying the four lots to A. The deed was invalid because under the corporation's charter only the president has authority to execute deeds. A entered on lot 1 and has occupied and improved it in the usual fashion for the period prescribed by the statute of limitations. B recently entered lot 2. What rights has A against B and against Opal under N.Y. Civ. Prac. Act §38 (quoted in footnote 12 on page 129)? At common law? Would A have the same rights if the tract deeded to her had not been divided into lots? If the lots had not been contiguous? See 3 American Law of Property §15.11 (1952).

2. O owns and has been in possession of a 100-acre farm since 1960. In 1975 A entered the back 40 acres under color of an invalid deed from Z (who had no claim to the land) for the entire 100 acres. Since her entry, A has occupied and improved the back 40 in the usual manner for the period required by the statute of limitations. A brings suit to evict O from the farm, claiming title by constructive adverse possession. What result? See Patrick v. Goolsby, 158 Tenn. 162, 11 S.W.2d 677 (1928). Suppose that in 1960 O took title to the farm under an invalid deed and has been in possession for a period sufficient to satisfy the statute of limitations. Would the result in the suit by A be different? *NO*

3. Two contiguous lots, 1 and 2, are owned by X and Y respectively. (X and Y are not in possession.) The lots are conveyed by an invalid deed from Z to A, who enters lot 1 and occupies it in the usual manner for the period required by the statute of limitations. Subsequently A sues X and Y to quiet title to lots 1 and 2. What result? Would it matter if X had executed the deed? If X had executed the deed and A had entered lot

2? See Wheatley v. San Pedro, Los Angeles & Salt Lake Railroad, 169 Cal. 505, 147 P. 135 (1915); Brock v. Howard, 304 Ky. 311, 200 S.W.2d 734 (1947).

2.   The Mechanics of Adverse Possession

Howard v. Kunto
Court of Appeals of Washington, 1970
3 Wash. App. 393, 477 P.2d 210

PEARSON, J. Land surveying is an ancient art but not one free of the errors that often creep into the affairs of men. In this case, we are presented with the question of what happens when the descriptions in deeds do not fit the land the deed holders are occupying. Defendants appeal from a decree quieting title in the plaintiffs of a tract of land on the shore of Hood Canal in Mason County.

At least as long ago as 1932 the record tells us that one McCall resided in the house now occupied by the appellant-defendants, Kunto. McCall had a deed that described a 50-foot wide parcel on the shore of Hood Canal. The error that brings this case before us is that the 50 feet described in the deed is not the same 50 feet upon which McCall's house stood. Rather, the described land is an adjacent 50-foot lot directly west of that upon which the house stood. In other words, McCall's house stood on one lot and his deed described the adjacent lot. Several property owners to the west of defendants, not parties to this action, are similarly situated.

Over the years since 1946, several conveyances occurred, using the same legal description and accompanied by a transfer of possession to the succeeding occupants. The Kuntos' immediate predecessors in interest, Millers, desired to build a dock. To this end, they had a survey performed which indicated that the deed description and the physical occupation were in conformity. Several boundary stakes were placed as a result of this survey and the dock was constructed, as well as other improvements. The house as well as the others in the area continued to be used as summer recreational retreats.

The Kuntos then took possession of the disputed property under a deed from the Millers in 1959. In 1960 the respondent-plaintiffs, Howard, who held land east of that of the Kuntos, determined to convey an undivided one-half interest in their land to the Yearlys. To this end, they undertook to have a survey of the entire area made. After expending considerable effort, the surveyor retained by the Howards discovered that according to the government survey, the deed descriptions and the land occupancy of the parties did not coincide. Between the Howards and the Kuntos lay the Moyers' property. When the Howards' survey was completed, they discovered that they were the record owners of the land occupied by the Moyers and that the Moyers held record title to the land occupied by the Kuntos. Howard approached Moyer and in return for a conveyance of the land upon which the Moyers' house stood, Moyer conveyed to the Howards record title to the land upon which the Kunto house stood. Until plaintiffs Howard obtained the conveyance from Moyer in April, 1960, neither Moyer nor any of his predecessors ever asserted any right to ownership of the property actually being possessed by Kunto and his predecessors. This action was then instituted to quiet title in the Howards and Yearlys. The Kuntos appeal from a trial court decision granting this remedy.

At the time this action was commenced on August 19, 1960,[21] the defendants had been in occupance of the disputed property less than a year. The trial court's reason for denying their claim of adverse possession is succinctly stated in its memorandum opinion: "In this instance, defendants have failed to prove, by a preponderance of the evidence, a continuity of possession or estate to permit tacking of the adverse possession of defendants to the possession of their predecessors."

Finding of fact 6,[22] which is challenged by defendants, incorporates the above concept and additionally finds defendant's possession not to have been "continuous" because it involved only "summer occupancy."

Two issues are presented by this appeal:

(1) Is a claim of adverse possession defeated because the physical use of the premises is restricted to summer occupancy?

(2) May a person who receives record title to tract A under the mistaken belief that he has title to tract B (immediately contiguous to tract

---

21. The inordinate delay in bringing this matter to trial appears from the record to be largely inexcusable. However, neither counsel who tried the case was at fault in any way. We have intentionally declined to consider defendant's motion (probably well founded) to dismiss this case for want of prosecution . . . for the reason that a new trial of the same issues would be inevitable and in light of our disposition of the case on the merits, defendants are not prejudiced by disregarding the technical grounds.

22. "In the instant case the defendants' building was not simply over the line, but instead was built wholly upon the wrong piece of property, not the property of defendants, described in Paragraph Four (4) of the complaint herein, but on the property of the plaintiffs, described in Paragraph Three of the complaint and herein. That the last three deeds in the chain of title, covering and embracing defendants' property, including defendants' deed, were executed in other states, specifically, California and Oregon. And there is no evidence of pointing out to the grantees in said three deeds, aforesaid, including defendants' deed, of any specific property, other than the property of defendants, described in their deed, and in Paragraph Four (4) of the complaint, and herein; nor of any immediate act of the grantees, including defendants, in said three (3) deeds, aforesaid, of taking possession of any property, other than described in said three (3) deeds, aforesaid; and the testimony of husband defendant, was unequivocally that he had no intention of possessing or holding anything other than what the deed called for; and, that there is no showing of any continuous possession by defendants or their immediate predecessors in interest, since the evidence indicates the property was in the nature, for use, as a summer occupancy, and such occupancy and use was for rather limited periods of time during comparatively short portions of the year, and was far from continuous."

A) and who subsequently occupies tract B, for the purpose of establishing title to tract B by adverse possession, use the periods of possession of tract B by his immediate predecessors who also had record title to tract A?

In approaching both of these questions, we point out that the evidence, largely undisputed in any material sense, established that defendant or his immediate predecessors did occupy the premises, which we have called tract B, as though it was their own for more than the 10 years as prescribed in RCW 4.16.020.[23]

We also point out that finding of fact 6 is not challenged for its factual determinations but for the conclusions contained therein to the effect that the continuity of possession may not be established by summer occupancy, and that a predecessor's possession may not be tacked because a legal "claim of right" did not exist under the circumstances.

We start with the oft-quoted rule that: "[T]o constitute adverse possession, there must be actual possession which is *uninterrupted,* open and notorious, hostile and exclusive, and under a *claim of right* made in good faith for the statutory period." (Italics ours.) Butler v. Anderson, 71 Wash. 2d 60, 64, 426 P.2d 467, 470 (1967).[24]

We reject the conclusion that summer occupancy only of a summer beach home destroys the continuity of possession required by the statute. It has become firmly established that the requisite possession requires such possession and dominion "as ordinarily marks the conduct of owners in general in holding, managing, and caring for property of like nature and condition." Whalen v. Smith, 183 Iowa 949, 953, 167 N.W. 646, 647 (1918). . . .

We hold that occupancy of tract B during the summer months for more than the 10-year period by defendant and his predecessors, together with the continued existence of the improvements on the land and beach area, constituted "uninterrupted" possession within this rule. To hold otherwise is to completely ignore the nature and condition of the property. . . .

We find such rule fully consonant with the legal writers on the subject. In F. Clark, Law of Surveying and Boundaries, §561 (3d ed. 1959)

---

23. This statute provides:

   4.16.020 Actions to be commenced within ten years. The period prescribed in RCW 4.16.010 for the commencement of actions shall be as follows:
      Within ten years;
      Actions for the recovery of real property, or for the recovery of the possession thereof; and no action shall be maintained for such recovery unless it appears that the plaintiff, his ancestor, predecessor or grantor was seized or possessed of the premises in question within ten years before the commencement of the action.
   24. In 1984 the Washington Supreme Court overruled Howard v. Kunto to the extent that the case suggests a *good-faith* requirement for adverse possession. See Chaplin v. Sanders, cited and quoted in this book at page 138. — EDS.

at 565: "Continuity of possession may be established although the land is used regularly for only a certain period each year." Further, at 566:

> This rule . . . is one of substance and not of absolute mathematical continuity, provided there is no break so as to sever two possessions. It is not necessary that the occupant should be actually upon the premises continually. If the land is occupied during the period of time during the year it is capable of use, there is sufficient continuity.

We now reach the question of tacking. The precise issue before us is novel in that none of the property occupied by defendant or his predecessors coincided with the property described in their deeds, but was contiguous.

In the typical case, which has been subject to much litigation, the party seeking to establish title by adverse possession claims *more* land than that described in the deed. In such cases it is clear that tacking is permitted.

In Buchanan v. Cassell, 53 Wash. 2d 611, 614, 335 P.2d 600, 602 (1959), the Supreme Court stated: "This state follows the rule that a purchaser may tack the adverse use of its predecessor in interest to that of his own where the land was intended to be included in the deed between them, but was mistakenly omitted from the description." El Cerito, Inc. v. Ryndak, 60 Wash. 2d 847, 376 P.2d 528 (1962).

The general statement which appears in many of the cases is that tacking of adverse possession is permitted if the successive occupants are in "privity." See Faubion v. Elder, 49 Wash. 2d 300, 301 P.2d 153 (1956). The deed running between the parties purporting to transfer the land possessed traditionally furnishes the privity of estate which connects the possession of the successive occupants. Plaintiff contends, and the trial court ruled, that where the deed does not describe *any* of the land which was occupied, the actual transfer of possession is insufficient to establish privity.

To assess the cogency of this argument and ruling, we must turn to the historical reasons for requiring privity as a necessary prerequisite to tacking the possession of several occupants. Very few, if any, of the reasons appear in the cases, nor do the cases analyze the relationships that must exist between successive possessors for tacking to be allowed. See W. Stoebuck, The Law of Adverse Possession in Washington in 35 Wash. L. Rev. 53 (1960).

The requirement of privity had its roots in the notion that a succession of trespasses, even though there was no appreciable interval between them, should not, in equity, be allowed to defeat the record title. The "claim of right," "color of title" requirement of the statutes and cases was probably derived from the early American belief that the squatter should not be able to profit by his trespass.[25]

However, it appears to this court that there is a substantial difference between the squatter or trespasser and the property purchaser, who along with several of his neighbors, as a result of an inaccurate survey or subdivision, occupies and improves property exactly 50 feet to the east of that which a survey some 30 years later demonstrates that they in fact own. It seems to us that there is also a strong public policy favoring early certainty as to the location of land ownership which enters into a proper interpretation of privity.

On the irregular perimeters of Puget Sound exact determination of land locations and boundaries is difficult and expensive. This difficulty is convincingly demonstrated in this case by the problems plaintiff's engineer encountered in attempting to locate the corners. It cannot be expected that every purchaser will or should engage a surveyor to ascertain that the beach home he is purchasing lies within the boundaries described in his deed. Such a practice is neither reasonable nor customary. Of course, 50-foot errors in descriptions are devastating where a group of adjacent owners each hold 50 feet of waterfront property.

The technical requirement of "privity" should not, we think, be used to upset the long periods of occupancy of those who in good faith received an erroneous deed description. Their "claim of right" is no less persuasive than the purchaser who believes he is purchasing *more* land than his deed described.

In the final analysis, however, we believe the requirement of "privity" is no more than judicial recognition of the need for some reasonable connection between successive occupants of real property so as to raise their claim of right above the status of the wrongdoer or the trespasser. We think such reasonable connection exists in this case.

Where, as here, several successive purchasers received record title to tract A under the mistaken belief that they were acquiring tract B, immediately contiguous thereto, and where possession of tract B is transferred and occupied in a continuous manner for more than 10 years by successive occupants, we hold there is sufficient privity of estate to permit tacking and thus establish adverse possession as a matter of law.

We see no reason in law or in equity for differentiating this case from Faubion v. Elder, 49 Wash. 2d 300, 301 P.2d 153 (1956), where the appellants were claiming *more* land than their deed described and where successive periods of occupation were allowed to be united to each other to make up the time of adverse holding. . . .

This application of the privity requirement should particularly per-

25. The English common law does not require privity as a prerequisite for tacking. See F. Clark, Law of Surveying and Boundaries, §561 (3d ed. 1959) at 568.

tain where the holder of record title to tract B acquired the same with knowledge of the discrepancy.

Judgment is reversed with directions to dismiss plaintiffs' action and to enter a decree quieting defendants' title to the disputed tract of land in accordance with the prayer of their cross-complaint.

QUESTION

The possession in Howard v. Kunto was obviously open, but was it "notorious"? Recall footnote 20 on page 141 and bear in mind that Mannillo v. Gorski, cited in Problem 1 on the same page, suggests that intrusions discoverable only by survey do not of themselves satisfy the notoriety requirement. But the court in *Mannillo* was speaking with reference to a minor encroachment, whereas *Howard* involved a major one. Should that matter?

PROBLEMS: TACKING

An important (though not the only) issue in Howard v. Kunto concerns so-called tacking and the requirement of privity among a series of adverse possessors. The following problems explore these matters, as well as issues that arise when adverse possession is asserted against a series of owners. Assume in each problem that the jurisdiction has a 10-year statute of limitations.

1. In 1982 A enters adversely upon Blackacre,[26] owned by O. In 1989 B tells A, "Get out of here, I'm taking over." A leaves, and B enters into possession. In 1992 who owns Blackacre? Can O or A eject B? See 3 American Law of Property §15.10 (1952). For the contrary English law, see footnote 25 and Robert Megarry & H.W.R. Wade, Real Property 1036 (5th ed. 1984) ("time runs against the true owner from the time when adverse possession began, and so long as adverse possession continues unbroken it makes no difference who continues it"). Which view is better? To what extent does your answer turn on what you see as the purposes of adverse possession?

[handwritten margin note: Brits allow tacking w/out privity]

Suppose that in 1989 A leaves under threat of force, but six months later A recovers possession from B. If O does nothing, will A own Blackacre 10 years from the date of his entry in 1982, or 10 years and six

---

26. Hypothetical tracts of land traditionally have been referred to as Blackacre, Whiteacre, and Greenacre — just why no one knows for sure. One of the earliest law treatises written in English, Coke on Littleton 148b (1628), refers to Blackacre and Whiteacre. The Oxford English Dictionary suggests the terms indicate lands growing different crops (peas and beans are black, corn and potatoes are white, hay is green). Or the terms might originally have referred to lands receiving different rents (black rents are payable in produce, white rents in silver).

months from the date of his entry in 1982, or in 1999? See 3 American Law of Property, supra, §15.10.

Suppose that in 1989 *A* abandons Blackacre and *B* immediately goes into possession. If *O* does nothing, will *B* own Blackacre in 1992?

2. In 1976 *A* enters adversely upon Blackacre, owned by *O*. In 1977 *O* dies, leaving a will that devises Blackacre to *B* for life, remainder to *C*. In 1992 *B* dies. Who owns Blackacre?　*A*

3. *O*, owner of Blackacre, dies in 1977 leaving a will that devises Blackacre to *B* for life, remainder to *C*. In 1978 *A* enters adversely upon the land. In 1992 *B* dies. Who owns Blackacre? See 3 American Law of Property, supra, §15.8; Harper v. Paradise, 233 Ga. 194, 210 S.E.2d 710 (1974), reproduced at page 745; Piel v. Dewitt, 53 Ind. Dec. 663, 351 N.E.2d 48 (Ind. App. 1976). But cf. Wallace v. Magie, 214 Kan. 481, 522 P.2d 989 (1974).　*C*

A ad/p'd B's interest

NOTE:　IMPROVEMENTS AND ENCROACHMENTS

Suppose that the court in Howard v. Kunto had held that the Kuntos were *not* adverse possessors. Their house would then be on land adjudged to be the Howards'. What relief would be granted the Kuntos?

The common law on this question was, and still is in some jurisdictions, a bit harsh (though subject, of course, to the usual exceptions for delay, acquiescence, and estoppel). Buildings or fixtures erected without right, whether in good faith or not, became the property of the landowner — in our example, the Howards. The modern tendency is to soften the impact of this rule on innocent improvers like the Kuntos, either by granting them compensation equal to the market value of the improvements or permitting removal of the improvements. In some states the first sort of relief is found in legislation called "occupying claimant" or "betterment" acts (usually restricted to good-faith improvers). Many jurisdictions give the landowner a choice either to pay for the improvements or convey the land at market value to the improver. See Kelvin H. Dickinson, Mistaken Improvers of Real Estate, 64 N.C. L. Rev. 37 (1985).

If the building is not entirely on the neighboring land, as it was in Howard v. Kunto, but is only partially on the wrong lot, the building is usually not treated as a fixture on the wrong lot. If the encroachment is the result of an innocent mistake, courts tend to look at the relative hardships to the parties of granting or denying injunctive relief. If removal of the encroachment is difficult or expensive for the intruder compared to the inconvenience it causes the landowner, injunctive relief is usually denied and only damages awarded. Where the inconvenience caused by the encroachment is so minor as to be trivial, some courts simply deny all relief. In addition, the right to relief may be defeated by acquiescence, estoppel, or delay.

If the encroachment is willful or intentional, most courts issue an injunction requiring removal of the encroachment regardless of the balance of convenience or relative hardships. A party who intentionally encroaches does so at his peril. See the discussion in Stuttgart Elec. Co. v. Riceland Seed Co., 33 Ark. App. 108, 802 S.W.2d 484 (1991). Why treat the intentional encroachment differently? See Richard A. Posner, Economic Analysis of Law 56 (4th ed. 1992).

PROBLEMS: DISABILITIES

In every state the statute of limitations is extended if specified disabilities are present. Disability provisions differ, but the following example is typical:

> An action to recover the title to or possession of real property shall be brought within twenty-one years after the cause thereof accrued, but if a person entitled to bring such action, at the time the cause thereof accrues, is within the age of minority, of unsound mind, or imprisoned, such person, after the expiration of twenty-one years from the time the cause of action accrues, may bring such action within ten years after such disability is removed.

Particularly note two matters: A disability is immaterial unless it existed at the time when the cause of action accrued. And after the words "such person" you should insert, as a result of judicial construction, the words "or anyone claiming from, by, or under such person." (Do you see why a court would read those words into the statute?)

When in the following examples would the adverse possessor acquire title under the statute set out above? In each case, O is the owner in 1967, and A enters adversely on May 1, 1967. The age of majority is 18.

1. O is insane in 1967. O dies insane and intestate in 1990.
    (a) O's heir, H, is under no disability in 1990.
    (b) O's heir, H, is six years old in 1990.   *doesn't matter*

2. O has no disability in 1967. O dies intestate in 1985. O's heir, H, is two years old in 1985.

3. O is five years old in 1967. In 1977 O becomes mentally ill, and O dies intestate in 1992. O's heir, H, is under no disability. Does the adverse possessor here acquire title in 1988, 1990, or at some later date? If the answer is 1988 or 1990, how are O's interests to be protected?

Consider again the purposes of adverse possession and note how some of them conflict in the case of disabilities. Does reflection on Problem 3 suggest that disability doctrine is unnecessary?

NOTE: ADVERSE POSSESSION AGAINST THE GOVERNMENT

Under the common law rules, adverse possession does not run against the government — local, state, or federal. In England the maxim *nullum tempus occurit regis* (no time runs against the king) barred the running of the statute of limitations against the sovereign. In barring adverse possession against the government, American courts have relied on this rule as well as state constitutional provisions restricting the alienation of state lands. Courts often say, in justification, that the state owns its land in trust for all the people, who should not lose the land because of the negligence of a few state officers or employees.

A number of states, however, have changed the common law rules, whether by legislation or judge-made law.[27] A few permit adverse possession against government land on the same terms as against private land. Others permit it only if possession continues for a period much longer than that applied in the case of private lands. Still others permit it only against government lands held in a proprietary (as opposed to a public or governmental) capacity. See, e.g., American Trading Real Estate Properties, Inc. v. Town of Trumbull, 215 Conn. 68, 574 A.2d 796 (1990); Devins v. Borough of Bogota, 124 N.J. 570, 592 A.2d 199 (1991).

Are there good reasons to treat government lands differently from those privately owned? What types of land might justifiably be subjected to adverse possession and what types not? In 1970 the Public Land Law Review Commission recommended that the Congress enact a general statute of limitations running against the United States. For criticism, see John R. Call, Adverse Possession of Public Land: A Look at the Recommendation of the Public Land Law Review Commission, 1971 Law & Soc. Ord. 131; Elmer M. Million, Adverse Possession Against the United States — A Treasure for Trespassers, 26 Ark. L. Rev. 467 (1973). See also Symposium, Time, Property Rights, and the Common Law, Round Table Discussion, 64 Wash. U. L.Q. 793, 832-833 (1986) (comments of Professor Robert Ellickson regarding sensible reasons for favorable treatment of government lands).

---

27. Even absent such changes, the government may be estopped from asserting any right to land where a person improves the land with the knowledge and acquiescence of government officials. See, e.g., Clinton Natl. Bank v. City of Camanche, 251 N.W.2d 248 (Iowa 1977).

Given that a private party may not be able to get government property by adverse possession, is it fair that the government is nevertheless able to get private property by adverse possession?

3.   Adverse Possession of Chattels

O'Keeffe v. Snyder

Supreme Court of New Jersey, 1980
83 N.J. 478, 416 A.2d 862

POLLOCK, J. This is an appeal from an order of the Appellate Division granting summary judgment to plaintiff, Georgia O'Keeffe, against defendant, Barry Snyder, d/b/a Princeton Gallery of Fine Arts, for replevin of three small pictures painted by O'Keeffe. In her complaint, filed in March, 1976, O'Keeffe alleged she was the owner of the paintings and that they were stolen from a New York art gallery in 1946. Snyder asserted he was a purchaser for value of the paintings, he had title by adverse possession, and O'Keeffe's action was barred by the expiration of the six-year period of limitations . . . pertaining to an action in replevin. Snyder impleaded third party defendant, Ulrich A. Frank, from whom Snyder purchased the paintings in 1975 for $35,000

The trial court granted summary judgment for Snyder on the ground that O'Keeffe's action was barred because it was not commenced within six years of the alleged theft. The Appellate Division reversed and entered judgment for O'Keeffe. A majority of that court concluded that the paintings were stolen, the defenses of expiration of the statute of limitations and title by adverse possession were identical, and Snyder had not proved the elements of adverse possession. Consequently, the majority ruled that O'Keeffe could still enforce her right to possession of the paintings.

. . . We reverse and remand the matter for a plenary hearing in accordance with this opinion.

The record, limited to pleadings, affidavits, answers to interrogatories, and depositions, is fraught with factual conflict. Apart from the creation of the paintings by O'Keeffe and their discovery in Snyder's gallery in 1976, the parties agree on little else.

O'Keeffe contended the paintings were stolen in 1946 from a gallery, An American Place. The gallery was operated by her late husband, the famous photographer Alfred Stieglitz.

An American Place was a cooperative undertaking of O'Keeffe and some other American artists identified by her as Marin, Hardin, Dove, Andema, and Stevens. In 1946, Stieglitz arranged an exhibit which included an O'Keeffe painting, identified as Cliffs. According to O'Keeffe, one day in March, 1946, she and Stieglitz discovered Cliffs was missing from the wall of the exhibit. O'Keeffe estimates the value of the painting at the time of the alleged theft to have been about $150.

About two weeks later, O'Keeffe noticed that two other paintings, Seaweed and Fragments, were missing from a storage room at An American Place. She did not tell anyone, even Stieglitz, about the missing paintings, since she did not want to upset him.

Before the date when O'Keeffe discovered the disappearance of Seaweed, she had already sold it (apparently for a string of amber beads) to a Mrs. Weiner, now deceased. Following the grant of the motion for summary judgment by the trial court in favor of Snyder, O'Keeffe submitted a release from the legatees of Mrs. Weiner purportedly assigning to O'Keeffe their interest in the sale.

O'Keeffe testified on depositions that at about the same time as the disappearance of her paintings, 12 or 13 miniature paintings by Marin also were stolen from An American Place. According to O'Keeffe, a man named Estrick took the Marin paintings and "maybe a few other things." Estrick distributed the Marin paintings to members of the theater world who, when confronted by Stieglitz, returned them. However, neither Stieglitz nor O'Keeffe confronted Estrick with the loss of any of the O'Keeffe paintings.

There was no evidence of a break and entry at An American Place on the dates when O'Keeffe discovered the disappearance of her paintings. Neither Stieglitz nor O'Keeffe reported them missing to the New York Police Department or any other law enforcement agency. Apparently the paintings were uninsured, and O'Keeffe did not seek reimbursement from an insurance company. Similarly, neither O'Keeffe nor Stieglitz advertised the loss of the paintings in Art News or any other publication. Nonetheless, they discussed it with associates in the art world and later O'Keeffe mentioned the loss to the director of the Art Institute of Chicago, but she did not ask him to do anything because "it wouldn't have been my way." O'Keeffe does not contend that Frank or Snyder had actual knowledge of the alleged theft.

Stieglitz died in the summer of 1946, and O'Keeffe explains she did not pursue her efforts to locate the paintings because she was settling his estate. In 1947, she retained the services of Doris Bry to help settle the estate. Bry urged O'Keeffe to report the loss of the paintings, but O'Keeffe declined because "they never got anything back by reporting it." Finally, in 1972, O'Keeffe authorized Bry to report the theft to the Art Dealers Association of America, Inc., which maintains for its members a registry of stolen paintings. The record does not indicate whether such a registry existed at the time the paintings disappeared.

In September, 1975, O'Keeffe learned that the paintings were in the Andrew Crispo Gallery in New York on consignment from Bernard Danenberg Galleries. On February 11, 1976, O'Keeffe discovered that Ulrich A. Frank had sold the paintings to Barry Snyder, d/b/a Princeton Gallery of Fine Art. She demanded their return and, following Snyder's refusal, instituted this action for replevin.

Frank traces his possession of the paintings to his father, Dr. Frank, who died in 1968. He claims there is a family relationship by marriage

Georgia O'Keeffe
Seaweed (1926)
Collection of Juan Hamilton

between his family and the Stieglitz family, a contention that O'Keeffe disputes. Frank does not know how his father acquired the paintings, but he recalls seeing them in his father's apartment in New Hampshire as early as 1941-1943, a period that precedes the alleged theft. Consequently, Frank's factual contentions are inconsistent with O'Keeffe's allegation of theft. Until 1965, Dr. Frank occasionally lent the paintings to Ulrich Frank. In 1965, Dr. and Mrs. Frank formally gave the paintings to Ulrich Frank, who kept them in his residences in Yardley, Pennsylvania and Princeton, New Jersey. In 1968, he exhibited anonymously Cliffs and Fragments in a one day art show in the Jewish Community Center in Trenton. All of these events precede O'Keeffe's listing of the paintings as stolen with the Art Dealers Association of America, Inc. in 1972.

Frank claims continuous possession of the paintings through his father for over thirty years and admits selling the paintings to Snyder. Snyder and Frank do not trace their provenance, or history of possession of the paintings, back to O'Keeffe.

As indicated, Snyder moved for summary judgment on the theory that O'Keeffe's action was barred by the statute of limitations and title had vested in Frank by adverse possession. For purposes of his motion, Snyder conceded that the paintings had been stolen. On her cross motion, O'Keeffe urged that the paintings were stolen, the statute of limitations had not run, and title to the paintings remained in her. . . .

The Appellate Division accepted O'Keeffe's contention that the paintings had been stolen. However, in his deposition, Ulrich Frank traces possession of the paintings to his father in the early 1940s, a date that precedes the alleged theft by several years. The factual dispute about the loss of the paintings by O'Keeffe and their acquisition by Frank, as well as the other subsequently described factual issues, warrant a remand for a plenary hearing. . . .

Without purporting to limit the scope of the trial, other factual issues include whether . . . the paintings were not stolen but sold, lent, consigned, or given by Stieglitz to Dr. Frank or someone else without O'Keeffe's knowledge before he died; and [whether] there was any business or family relationship between Stieglitz and Dr. Frank so that the original possession of the paintings by the Frank family may have been under claim of right.

On the limited record before us, we cannot determine now who has title to the paintings. The determination will depend on the evidence adduced at trial. Nonetheless, we believe it may aid the trial court and the parties to resolve questions of law that may become relevant at trial.

Our discussion begins with the principle that, generally speaking, if the paintings were stolen, the thief acquired no title and could not transfer good title to others regardless of their good faith and ignorance of the theft. Proof of theft would advance O'Keeffe's right to possession of the paintings absent other considerations such as expiration of the statute of limitations.

Another issue that may become relevant at trial is whether Frank or his father acquired a "voidable title" to the paintings under N.J.S.A. 12A:2-403(1). That section, part of the Uniform Commercial Code (U.C.C.),[28] does not change the basic principle that a mere possessor cannot transfer good title. Nonetheless, the U.C.C. permits a person with voidable title to transfer good title to a good faith purchaser for value in certain circumstances. If the facts developed at trial merit application of that section, then Frank may have transferred good title to Snyder, thereby providing a defense to O'Keeffe's action. . . .

On this appeal, the critical legal question is when O'Keeffe's cause of action accrued. The fulcrum on which the outcome turns is the statute of limitations . . . , which provides that an action for replevin of goods or chattels must be commenced within six years after the accrual of the cause of action.

The trial court found that O'Keeffe's cause of action accrued on the date of the alleged theft, March, 1946, and concluded that her action was barred. The Appellate Division found that an action might have accrued more than six years before the date of suit if possession by the defendant or his predecessors satisfied the elements of adverse possession. As indicated, the Appellate Division concluded that Snyder had not established those elements and that the O'Keeffe action was not barred by the statute of limitations. . . .

The purpose of a statute of limitations is to "stimulate to activity and punish negligence" and "promote repose by giving security and sta-

---

28. Uniform Commercial Code §2-403 provides:

§2-403. *Power to Transfer; Good Faith Purchase of Goods; "Entrusting."*
    (1) A purchaser of goods acquires all title which his transferor had or had power to transfer except that a purchaser of a limited interest acquires rights only to the extent of the interest purchased. A person with voidable title has power to transfer a good title to a good faith purchaser for value. When goods have been delivered under a transaction of purchase the purchaser has such power even though
        (a) the transferor was deceived as to the identity of the purchaser, or
        (b) the delivery was in exchange for a check which was later dishonored, or
        (c) it was agreed that the transaction was to be a "cash sale," or
        (d) the delivery was procured through fraud punishable as larcenous under the criminal law.
    (2) Any entrusting of possession of goods to a merchant who deals in goods of that kind gives him power to transfer all rights of the entruster to a buyer in the ordinary course of business.
    (3) "Entrusting" includes any delivery and any acquiescence in retention of possession regardless of any condition expressed between the parties to the delivery or acquiescence and regardless of whether the procurement of the entrusting or the possessor's disposition of the goods have been such as to be larcenous under the criminal law. — EDS.

bility to human affairs." Wood v. Carpenter, 101 U.S. 135, 139, 25 L. Ed. 807, 808 (1879). A statute of limitations achieves those purposes by barring a cause of action after the statutory period. In certain instances, this Court has ruled that the literal language of a statute of limitations should yield to other considerations.

To avoid harsh results from the mechanical application of the statute, the courts have developed a concept known as the discovery rule. The discovery rule provides that, in an appropriate case, a cause of action will not accrue until the injured party discovers, or by exercise of reasonable diligence and intelligence should have discovered, facts which form the basis of a cause of action. The rule is essentially a principle of equity, the purpose of which is to mitigate unjust results that otherwise might flow from strict adherence to a rule of law. . . .

[W]e conclude that the discovery rule applies to an action for replevin of a painting. . . . O'Keeffe's cause of action accrued when she first knew, or reasonably should have known through the exercise of due diligence, of the cause of action, including the identity of the possessor of the paintings.

In determining whether O'Keeffe is entitled to the benefit of the discovery rule, the trial court should consider, among others, the following issues: (1) whether O'Keeffe used due diligence to recover the paintings at the time of the alleged theft and thereafter; (2) whether at the time of the alleged theft there was an effective method, other than talking to her colleagues, for O'Keeffe to alert the art world; and (3) whether registering paintings with the Art Dealers Association of America, Inc. or any other organization would put a reasonably prudent purchaser of art on constructive notice that someone other than the possessor was the true owner.

The acquisition of title to real and personal property by adverse possession is based on the expiration of a statute of limitations. . . .

To establish title by adverse possession to chattels, the rule of law has been that the possession must be hostile, actual, visible, exclusive, and continuous. . . . There is an inherent problem with many kinds of personal property that will raise questions whether their possession has been open, visible, and notorious. . . . For example, if jewelry is stolen from a municipality in one county in New Jersey, it is unlikely that the owner would learn that someone is openly wearing that jewelry in another county or even in the same municipality. Open and visible possession of personal property, such as jewelry, may not be sufficient to put the original owner on actual or constructive notice of the identity of the possessor.

The problem is even more acute with works of art. Like many kinds of personal property, works of art are readily moved and easily concealed. O'Keeffe argues that nothing short of public display should be sufficient to alert the true owner and start the statute running. Although there is merit in that contention from the perspective of the original owner, the effect is to impose a heavy burden on the purchasers of paintings who wish to enjoy the paintings in the privacy of their homes. . . .

The problem is serious. According to an affidavit submitted in this matter by the president of the International Foundation for Art Research, there has been an "explosion in art thefts" and there is a "worldwide phenomenon of art theft which has reached epidemic proportions."

The limited record before us provides a brief glimpse into the arcane world of sales of art, where paintings worth vast sums of money sometimes are bought without inquiry about their provenance. There does not appear to be a reasonably available method for an owner of art to record the ownership or theft of paintings. Similarly, there are no reasonable means readily available to a purchaser to ascertain the provenance of a painting. It may be time for the art world to establish a means by which a good faith purchaser may reasonably obtain the provenance of a painting. An efficient registry of original works of art might better serve the interests of artists, owners of art, and bona fide purchasers than the law of adverse possession with all of its uncertainties. Although we cannot mandate the initiation of a registration system, we can develop a rule for the commencement and running of the statute of limitations that is more responsive to the needs of the art world than the doctrine of adverse possession.

We are persuaded that the introduction of equitable considerations through the discovery rule provides a more satisfactory response than the doctrine of adverse possession. The discovery rule shifts the emphasis from the conduct of the possessor to the conduct of the owner. The focus of the inquiry will no longer be whether the possessor has met the tests of adverse possession, but whether the owner has acted with due diligence in pursuing his or her personal property.

For example, under the discovery rule, if an artist diligently seeks the recovery of a lost or stolen painting, but cannot find it or discover the identity of the possessor, the statute of limitations will not begin to run. The rule permits an artist who uses reasonable efforts to report, investigate, and recover a painting to preserve the rights of title and possession.

Properly interpreted, the discovery rule becomes a vehicle for transporting equitable considerations into the statute of limitations for replevin. . . .

It is consistent also with the law of replevin as it has developed apart from the discovery rule. In an action for replevin, the period of limitations ordinarily will run against the owner of lost or stolen property from the time of the wrongful taking, absent fraud or concealment. Where the chattel is fraudulently concealed, the general rule is that the statute is tolled. . . .

A purchaser from a private party would be well-advised to inquire whether a work of art has been reported as lost or stolen. However, a bona fide purchaser who purchases in the ordinary course of business a painting entrusted to an art dealer should be able to acquire good title against the true owner. Under the U.C.C. entrusting possession of goods to a merchant who deals in that kind of goods gives the merchant the power to transfer all the rights of the entruster to a buyer in the ordinary course of business. In a transaction under that statute, a merchant may vest good title in the buyer as against the original owner. The interplay between the statute of limitations as modified by the discovery rule and the U.C.C. should encourage good faith purchases from legitimate art dealers and discourage trafficking in stolen art without frustrating an artist's ability to recover stolen art works.

The discovery rule will fulfill the purposes of a statute of limitations and accord greater protection to the innocent owner of personal property whose goods are lost or stolen. . . .

By diligently pursuing their goods, owners may prevent the statute of limitations from running. The meaning of due diligence will vary with the facts of each case, including the nature and value of the personal property. For example, with respect to jewelry of moderate value, it may be sufficient if the owner reports the theft to the police. With respect to art work of greater value, it may be reasonable to expect an owner to do more. In practice, our ruling should contribute to more careful practices concerning the purchase of art.

The considerations are different with real estate, and there is no reason to disturb the application of the doctrine of adverse possession to real estate. Real estate is fixed and cannot be moved or concealed. The owner of real property knows or should know where his property is located and reasonably can be expected to be aware of open, notorious, visible, hostile, continuous acts of possession on it.

Our ruling not only changes the requirements for acquiring title to personal property after an alleged unlawful taking, but also shifts the burden of proof at trial. Under the doctrine of adverse possession, the burden is on the possessor to prove the elements of adverse possession. Under the discovery rule, the burden is on the owner as the one seeking the benefit of the rule to establish facts that would justify deferring the beginning of the period of limitations. . . .

Read literally, the effect of the expiration of the statute of limitations . . . is to bar an action such as replevin. The statute does not speak of divesting the original owner of title. By its terms the statute cuts off the remedy, but not the right of title. Nonetheless, the effect of the expiration of the statute of limitations, albeit on the theory of adverse possession, has been not only to bar an action for possession, but also to vest title in the possessor. There is no reason to change that result although the discovery rule has replaced adverse possession. History, reason, and common sense support the conclusion that the expiration of the statute of limitations bars the remedy to recover possession and also vests title in the possessor. . . . Before the expiration of the statute, the possessor has both the chattel and the right to keep it except as against the true owner. The only imperfection in the possessor's right to retain the chattel is the original owner's right to repossess it. Once that imperfection is removed, the possessor should have good title for all purposes. . . .

We next consider the effect of transfers of a chattel from one possessor to another during the period of limitation under the discovery rule. Under the discovery rule, the statute of limitations on an action for replevin begins to run when the owner knows or reasonably should know of his cause of action and the identity of the possessor of the chattel. Subsequent transfers of the chattel are part of the continuous dispossession of the chattel from the original owner. The important point is not that there has been a substitution of possessors, but that there has been a continuous dispossession of the former owner. . . .

For the purpose of evaluating the due diligence of an owner, the dispossession of his chattel is a continuum not susceptible to separation into distinct acts. Nonetheless, subsequent transfers of the chattel may affect the degree of difficulty encountered by a diligent owner seeking to recover his goods. To that extent, subsequent transfers and their potential for frustrating diligence are relevant in applying the discovery rule. An owner who diligently seeks his chattel should be entitled to the benefit of the discovery rule although it may have passed through many hands. Conversely an owner who sleeps on his rights may be denied the benefit of the discovery rule although the chattel may have been possessed by only one person.

We reject the alternative of treating subsequent transfers of a chattel as separate acts of conversion that would start the statute of limitations running anew. At common law, apart from the statute of limitations, a subsequent transfer of a converted chattel was considered to be a separate act of conversion. . . . Adoption of that alternative would tend to undermine the purpose of the statute in quieting titles and protecting against stale claims.

The majority and better view is to permit tacking, the accumulation of consecutive periods of possession by parties in privity with each other. . . .

We reverse the judgment of the Appellate Division in favor of O'Keeffe and remand the matter for trial in accordance with this opinion.

A NOTE ON GEORGIA O'KEEFFE

Georgia O'Keeffe, born on a dairy farm in 1887 in Sun Prairie, Wisconsin, grew up in the rural Midwest. After studying art under various teachers in Chicago and New York, she decided to paint to please herself. In 1915 she sent some of her drawings — of budding and organic shapes, reflecting an intense feminine sensibility — to a friend in New York, admonishing her to show them to no one. The friend, disregarding O'Keeffe's wishes, showed them to Alfred Stieglitz, the noted New York photographer and gallery owner. Upon seeing the drawings, Stieglitz remarked, "At last, a woman on paper," and promptly displayed them in his gallery. When, shortly thereafter, O'Keeffe came to New York and learned of this, she was furious. She rushed to the gallery and demanded that her private work, shown without her permission, be taken down. Stieglitz refused. To keep her work from being seen, he told her, would be like depriving the world of a child about to be born (with Stieglitz as midwife). The drawings remained on the wall, provoking much controversy about O'Keeffe's sexual symbolism, which she denied was there.

Stieglitz, obsessed with this woman 20 years his junior, soon left his wife and daughter and moved in with her. "He photographed me until I was crazy," O'Keeffe — with a mischievous chuckle — recalled in her nineties. Many of the photographs were nudes, which Stieglitz exhibited in a show, creating a scandal and bringing O'Keeffe instant fame.

Soon thereafter, O'Keeffe began to produce many of her spectacular flower paintings, which critics once again found full of Freudian symbolism. O'Keeffe replied to them:

> Well — I made you take time to look at what I saw and when you took time to really notice my flower you hung all your own associations with flowers on my flower and you write about my flower as if I think and see what you think and see of the flower — and I don't.[29]

O'Keeffe, now established in the New York art world, became the embodiment of Stieglitz's belief that women could turn out art as powerful as any man's.

O'Keeffe and Stieglitz married in 1924. When, many years later, in his sixties, Stieglitz entered into a liaison with a woman half O'Keeffe's age, O'Keeffe began summering in New Mexico, where she had some affairs of her own. She found that New Mexico was where she belonged, but she could not leave Stieglitz, to whom she remained intensely devoted. She returned to New York every fall to renew her bond with him, though she never answered amiably when addressed as "Mrs. Stieglitz."

When Stieglitz died in 1946, at age 82, O'Keeffe first kicked his mistress out of his gallery, and then she moved to New Mexico for good. In the isolated Penitente village of Abiquiu (pop. 150), on a rise overlooking the green Chama river valley and barren pink and white and

---

29. Or O'Keeffe might have replied — as Freud, who loved cigars, is reputed to have said — "Sometimes a cigar is just a cigar." Attributed to Freud in Bartlett's Familiar Quotations 570 (Justin Kaplan ed., 16th ed. 1992).

Georgia O'Keeffe, 1967
by Philippe Halsman

orange hills beyond, she found a roofless adobe building with a door she "just had to paint" and had to own. After 10 years, she was able to wrest title away from the local Catholic church. O'Keeffe fixed up the adobe (though never flooring the room used as a dining room), fitted it sparingly with simple furniture, walled it in with garden and orchard, and lived there, mostly alone, with some chow dogs she described as "good biters," until her death in 1986 at age 99.

After her move to Abiquiu the imagery in O'Keeffe's paintings gradually shifted to doors and patios and to bleached animal skulls and New Mexico's vast, sere landscape (which she painted as "My Backyard"). She led a quiet life observing and painting a land that, to her, was not empty but full of shapes and colors and vibrant life. She used the land, captured it on her canvases, and, like the Southwest Indians before her, left it unscathed. (Is an artist the only sort of person who can capture property while leaving it for others?) In her old age, Georgia O'Keeffe became an icon of the American Southwest.

Though she became what Stieglitz had envisioned — the first great American woman artist — Georgia O'Keeffe never liked to be called a *woman* artist. "Write about women. Or write about artists. I don't see how they're connected," she told a journalist. Yet she took immense satisfaction in knowing that she was one of the richest self-made women in America and in having made her fortune in a field traditionally dominated by males (unlike Elizabeth Arden and Helena Rubenstein). When O'Keeffe died she left most of her estate of $70 million (comprised largely of 400 works of art she had created) to a handsome young man by the name of Juan Hamilton, who, when O'Keeffe was 86, knocked on her door at Abiquiu looking for work. Hamilton bore an uncanny resemblance to the youthful Stieglitz. He moved in with O'Keeffe soon after being admitted at her door, becoming her indispensable companion and, some say, lover. When her old friend of many years, the mother of Harvard's former president Derek Bok, called Hamilton a fortune hunter, O'Keeffe icily rebuffed her and cut Harvard out of her will.

O'Keeffe left her letters, and Stieglitz's, to the Beinecke Library at Yale. The outer envelope of one packet of Alfred's accusatory letters to his first wife, written shortly after he had abandoned her for Georgia, bears a note by O'Keeffe in the shaky handwriting of old age: "Art is a wicked thing. It is what we are."

See Jack Cowart & Juan Hamilton, Georgia O'Keeffe, Art and Letters (1987); Benita Eisler, O'Keeffe & Stieglitz, An American Romance (1991); Roxana Robinson, Georgia O'Keeffe: A Life (1989); and the video cassette, Portrait of an Artist: Georgia O'Keeffe (Home Vision, originally produced for the series Women in Art, WNET-TV, New York 1977). For details about O'Keeffe's estate and its estate tax valuation, see Estate of O'Keeffe v. Commissioner, T.C. Memo 1992-210, 63 T.C. Mem. (CCH) 2699 (1992).

NOTES AND QUESTIONS

1. Back to the case of O'Keeffe v. Snyder. The parties subsequently settled before a retrial. The paintings were divided. O'Keeffe took "Seaweed," Snyder took another painting, and the third was sold at auction at Sotheby's to pay lawyers' bills.

2. Note that the opinion in *O'Keeffe* permits tacking of periods of possession, but — it appears — only so long as the possessors are in privity with each other. See page 161. Given the focus in *O'Keeffe* on the conduct of the owner, and given that the "important point is not that there has been a substitution of possessors, but that there has been a continuous dispossession of the former owner," why is privity required?

For an analysis of O'Keeffe v. Snyder, see Paula A. Franzese, "Georgia on My Mind" — Reflections on *O'Keeffe v. Snyder*, 9 Seton Hall L. Rev. 1, 14-15 (1989).

3. New York, which is probably the site of most purchases of major works of art in the United States, has rejected the discovery rule of *O'Keeffe* on the ground that it provides insufficient protection for owners of stolen artwork. See Solomon R. Guggenheim Found. v. Lubell, 77 N.Y.2d 311, 569 N.E.2d 426, 567 N.Y.S.2d 623 (1991). The *Guggenheim* case held that the statute of limitations for replevin does not begin to run in favor of a good-faith purchaser until the true owner makes a demand for return and the good-faith purchaser refuses. Until demand is made, possession of the stolen property by a good-faith purchaser for value is not considered wrongful. The court thought it inappropriate to put a duty of reasonable diligence on the true owner, reasoning that such an approach would encourage illicit trafficking in stolen art by putting the burden on the true owner to demonstrate that it had undertaken a reasonable search. Moreover, the court believed that it would be difficult, if not impossible, to craft a reasonable diligence requirement that could take into account all the variables in a particular situation and not unduly burden the true owner. The better rule, the court said, is to protect true owners by requiring potential purchasers to investigate the provenance of works of art. The true owner's diligence remains relevant, however, in that unreasonable delay, if it works to the prejudice of the good-faith purchaser, might permit the latter to assert the equitable defense of laches.

Oddly enough, in New York the statute of limitations begins running in favor of *a thief* at the time of the theft, because the thief's possession is wrongful from the time of the theft. Does *that* make sense?

See generally Patty Gerstenblith, The Adverse Possession of Personal Property, 37 Buffalo L. Rev. 119 (1988-1989).

4. *Autocephalous Greek-Orthodox Church of Cyprus v. Goldberg & Feldman Fine Arts, Inc., 917 F.2d 278 (7th Cir. 1990), cert. denied, 112 S. Ct.*

377 (1991). In 1979, a few years after Turkish forces invaded Cyprus and established their own government on the northern part of the island, some Byzantine mosaics were stolen from the Kanakaria Greek-Orthodox church situated in the area under Turkish rule. In 1988 the mosaics resurfaced. Peg Goldberg, an art dealer in Indiana, who was unaware that the mosaics were stolen, bought the mosaics from one Aydin Dikman, a German national, for $1,080,000. Dikman brought the mosaics from Munich to the Geneva airport, where they were delivered to Goldberg.

When Goldberg returned to Indiana with the mosaics, she worked up sales brochures about them, and contacted other dealers to help her find a buyer. The mosaics were offered to the Getty Museum in Los Angeles. A curator there contacted the Cypriot officials to see if the mosaics had been lawfully exported. Thereafter, the Republic of Cyprus and the Kanakaria Church sued Goldberg in replevin. The court awarded the mosaics to the Republic and the Church. The court held that Indiana law applied, even though the place of wrong was Switzerland, because Indiana had more significant contacts with and interest in the action than did Switzerland. Indiana follows the discovery rule applied in *O'Keeffe*. The court noted that the due diligence determination is "highly 'fact-sensitive and must be decided on a case-by-case basis.'" 917 F.2d at 289. The court concluded, after vigorous arguments to the contrary by Goldberg, that the Cypriot owners were duly diligent in notifying the art world of the theft. Therefore, the statute of limitations had not run on them.

See Note, Evaluating the Effectiveness of Foreign Laws on National Ownership of Cultural Property in United States Courts, 30 Colum. J. Transnatl. L. 179 (1992); Note, International Art Theft and the Illegal Import and Export of Cultural Property: A Study of Relevant Values, Legislation, and Solutions, 15 Suffolk Transnatl. L.J. 609 (1992).

5. *Purchasing from a thief: conflicting views.* In the United States (and adverse possession aside), a purchaser cannot obtain good title from a thief — a point implicit in the first sentence of subsection (1) of Uniform Commercial Code §2-403, set out in footnote 28 on page 157. Notice, however, that a purchaser might be able to obtain good title from other sorts of scoundrels, as the court in *O'Keeffe* suggests on page 157. If Frank had a "voidable title" for one of the reasons suggested in subsections (a) through (d) of the Code provision (for example, paying for the paintings by a check that bounced), then Frank could convey good title to Snyder if Snyder was "a good faith purchaser for value," meaning, essentially, a buyer not on notice that matters are amiss. If O'Keeffe had entrusted the paintings to Stieglitz's gallery for appraisal but not for sale, Stieglitz — being "a merchant who deals in goods of that kind" — could transfer a good title to a good-faith buyer in the ordinary course of business. See §2-403(2).

Some countries in Europe and elsewhere follow similar rules, but not all of them do. Several recognize the doctrine of market overt, according to which a bona fide purchaser may acquire good title from a thief if the sale in question takes place in an open market. Opportunities for the laundering of stolen objects arise as a result. The problem has not gone unnoticed in the art world (nor, we presume, the underworld). See, e.g., Note, International Transfers of Stolen Cultural Property: Should Thieves Continue to Benefit from Domestic Laws Favoring Bona Fide Purchasers?, 13 Loy. L.A. Intl. & Comp. L.J. 427 (1990).

Whom should the law protect in instances like those discussed, the innocent owner or the innocent bona fide purchaser? What interests are in conflict? Does reflection on the voidable-title and entrusting exceptions contained in Uniform Commercial Code §2-403 suggest a way to resolve the conflict? See Robert Cooter & Thomas Ulen, Law and Economics 152-154 (1988); John F. Dolan, The U.C.C. Framework: Conveyancing Principles and Property Interests, 59 B.U. L. Rev. 811, 813-815 (1979).

NOTE: THE NATIVE AMERICAN GRAVES PROTECTION AND REPATRIATION ACT OF 1990

Return for a moment to the events with which this book began, the so-called discovery of America. Native Americans were dispossessed of more than a homeland as a consequence of European settlement; over the years they have also lost human remains, funerary objects, sacred objects, and other items of enormous importance to their culture. Many of these are now in museums, and the Native American Graves Protection and Repatriation Act of 1990, codified at 25 U.S.C. §§3001-3013 (Supp. 1991), seeks to repatriate them — send them back to their erstwhile custodians.

The act requires museums to inventory their Native American sacred objects and objects of cultural patrimony and return them, upon request, to a "direct lineal descendant of an individual who owned the sacred object" or to an Indian tribe that "can show that the object was owned or controlled by the tribe." The museum must return the object unless it can prove that it has "a right of possession" to the object. "Right of possession" is defined to mean "possession obtained with the voluntary consent of an individual or group that had authority of alienation." In short, the burden is on the museum to show that the object was obtained with the consent of the earlier Native American owners or possessors.

Of course, as you have learned, a person can obtain title to objects — even stolen objects — through the law of adverse possession. But title by adverse possession does not give the possessor a "right of possession" under the Repatriation Act. What, then, is the impact of the Repatriation Act on the law of adverse possession of chattels? Should Native American cultural objects (like government land, dead bodies, and cemeteries) be exempt from the law of adverse possession? Should the disability exemptions be extended to Native Americans? Has the government "taken" property, for which it must pay, when it orders property acquired by adverse possession to be returned to the original owner?[30] (See Chapter 12, discussing the government's right of eminent domain.) These are fascinating questions, going to the power of government to move property from one person or group to another. For a discussion of the Repatriation Act, written before it became law but attentive to the then-proposed legislation, see Thomas H. Boyd, Disputes Regarding the Possession of Native American Religious and Cultural Objects and Human Remains: A Discussion of the Applicable Law and Proposed Legislation, 55 Mo. L. Rev. 883 (1990). For commentary on the Repatriation Act as finally enacted, see the articles in Symposium, The Native American Graves Protection and Repatriation Act of 1990 and State Repatriation-Related Legislation, 24 Ariz. St. L.J. xi-562 (1992).

C.   Acquisition by Gift

To complete our study of possession, we turn to gifts of personal property, where possession plays a most important role. The law has long required that, to make a gift of personal property, the donor must transfer possession ("hand over the property") to the donee unless it is not practicable to do so. If manual delivery is not practicable because of the size or weight of the object, or its inaccessibility, constructive or symbolic delivery may be permitted. *Constructive* delivery is handing over a key or some object that will open up access to the subject matter of the gift. *Symbolic* delivery is handing over something symbolic of the property given. The usual case of symbolic delivery involves handing over a written instrument declaring a gift of the subject matter; for example, Joe hands to Marilyn a paper reading, "I give my grand piano to Marilyn.

---

30. The definition of "right of possession" in §2 (13) of the act provides that "right of possession" means acquired with consent of the Native Americans, "unless the phrase so defined would . . . result in a Fifth Amendment taking by the United States." This language was inserted to meet the concerns of the Justice Department about the possibility that the act effected a governmental taking of property of museums. If the act is judicially declared by the U.S. Claims Court to effect a taking, then the right of possession is to be as provided under the applicable state property law.

[s] Joe." But the general rule of gifts is: ⌈If an object can be handed over, it must be.⌉

The requirement of transfer of possession is feudal in origin. In feudal times, when few could read or write, a symbolic ceremony transferring possession was an important ritual signifying the transfer. Land could only be transferred by delivering a clod of dirt to the grantee on the land itself. The ceremony was called "livery of seisin" (see page 235). Chattels had to be handed over. In 1677 the Statute of Frauds abolished livery of seisin and initiated the requirement of a deed to pass title to land. However, the visual ceremony of transferring possession still survives if the object transferred is on top of the land. Some years ago, Professor Mechem suggested the following reasons for the survival of the delivery requirement in gifts of personal property:

1. Handing over the object makes vivid and concrete to the donor the significance of the act performed. By feeling the "wrench of delivery," the donor realizes an irrevocable gift has been made.

2. The act is unequivocal evidence of a gift to the actual witnesses of the transaction.

3. Delivery of the object to the donee gives the donee, after the act, prima facie evidence in favor of the alleged gift. [Philip Mechem, Gifts of Chattels and of Choses in Action Evidenced by Commercial Instruments, 21 Ill. L. Rev. 341, 348-349 (1926).]

In re Cohn

Supreme Court of New York
Appellate Division, First Department, 1919
187 A.D. 392, 176 N.Y.S. 225

SHEARN, J. This appeal involves the validity of a gift of certificates of stock, effected by the execution and delivery of an instrument of gift, unaccompanied by actual delivery of the certificates. On September 20, 1911, the decedent, Leopold Cohn, a resident of the city of New York, but then temporarily residing with his family at West End, N.J., wrote out and delivered to his wife, in the presence of his entire family, on his wife's birthday, the following paper:

West End, N.J., Sept. 20, 1911

I give this day to my wife, Sara K. Cohn, as a present for her (46th) forty-sixth birthday (500) five hundred shares of American Sumatra Tobacco Company common stock.

Leopold Cohn

The donor died six days after the delivery of this instrument. At the time of the gift, the donor was the owner of 7,213 shares of the common stock of the American Sumatra Tobacco Company, but the stock was in the name and possession of his firm of A. Cohn & Co. and deposited in a safe deposit box in the city of New York, which was in the name of and belonged to the firm. This firm consisted of the donor, his brother, Abraham, and his nephew, Leonard A. Cohn and was dissolved by the death of Abraham Cohn on August 30, 1911. Prior to that time, the firm had 18,033 shares of the Sumatra stock, in certificates of 100 shares each, standing in the firm name. On December 20, 1910, the stock had been charged off on the books and was not an asset of the firm after that time. The testator was entitled to 40 per cent., or 7,213 shares, of the stock held in the firm name, but there had never been an actual delivery of the certificates by the firm to the donor in his lifetime. Just prior to his death the donor had agreed to enter into a new partnership, and he was to contribute some of the shares to a new firm as an asset. On September 22, 1911, two days after the delivery of the instrument of gift, the donor directed his counsel to hurry the new partnership agreement, because he wished to get the Sumatra stock belonging to him, which was to be delivered when the new partnership agreement was signed, which matter was to be closed on September 26, 1911, the day the donor died. The execution and delivery of the instrument of gift was established by the testimony of the two daughters of the donor, who were present at the time of its delivery, and their testimony is to the effect that their father handed the paper to the mother, in the presence of the whole family, and said he gave it to her as a birthday present; that he had not possession of the stock, but as soon as he got it he would give it to her.

Some stress is laid by the appellants upon the testimony that the donor "said that he could not give her the stock, because it was in the company, but as soon as he could get it he would give it to her," which it is claimed evidences an intent to make a gift in the future, instead of a present gift. This contention is completely overborne by the wording of the instrument itself, which reads, "I give this day"; also by the plain intention of the donor to make a birthday gift to his wife, the birthday being the day on which the instrument of gift was executed and delivered. When the donor explained that he could not "give" her the stock that day, "because it was in the company," and said that "as soon as he could get it he would give it to her," it is quite obvious that he meant that he could not deliver the stock that day, but would as soon as he could get it.

There being no rights of creditors involved, no suggestion of fraud, the intention to make the birthday gift being conclusively established, the gift being evidenced by an instrument of gift executed and delivered to the donee on her birthday, and ever since retained by her, and the circumstances surrounding the making of the gift affording a reason-

able and satisfactory excuse for not making actual delivery of the certif- *valid*
icates at the time the gift was made, there was in my opinion a valid and *gift*
effectual gift of the certificates mentioned in the instrument of gift.

There is no doubt that it had been held in a long line of cases in this
state that delivery of the thing given is, as a general rule, one of the *precedent*
essential elements to constitute a valid gift. Beaver v. Beaver, 117 N.Y.
421, 22 N.E. 940, 6 L.R.A. 403, 15 Am. St. Rep. 531; Young v. Young,
80 N.Y. 422, 36 Am. Rep. 634. But it is equally true that the rule requir- *flexible*
ing actual delivery is not inflexible. Matter of Van Alstyne, 207 N.Y. 298,
100 N.E. 802; McGavic v. Cossum, 72 App. Div. 35, 76 N.Y. Supp. 305;
Matter of Mills, 172 App. Div. 530, 158 N.Y. Supp. 1100, affirmed 219
N.Y. 642, 114 N.E. 1072. In Beaver v. Beaver, supra, it was said that the *symbolic*
delivery may be symbolical, as where the donor gives to the donee a
symbol which represents possession. It was held in McGavic v. Cossum,
supra, where an instrument of gift of bonds was delivered, that actual
delivery of the bonds was excused where the only reason for not making
delivery was the feeble condition of the donor and the fact that the
bonds were in the custody of a bank in a nearby city. It was said in Matter
of Van Alstyne:

> The delivery necessary to consummate a gift must be as perfect as the
> nature of the property and the circumstances and surroundings of the parties
> will reasonably permit. . . . It is true that the old rule requiring an actual
> delivery of the thing given has been very largely relaxed, but a symbolical
> delivery is sufficient only when the conditions are so adverse to actual delivery
> as to make a symbolical delivery as nearly perfect and complete as the circum-
> stances will allow.

As the rule requiring delivery is clearly subject to exceptions, in order to apply it correctly in varying circumstances resort should be had
to the reason for the rule. Under the civil law delivery was not requisite
to a valid gift, but it was made a requisite by the common law as a matter
of public policy, to prevent mistake and imposition. Noble v. Smith, 2
Johns. 52, 56, 3 Am. Dec. 399; Brinckerhoff v. Lawrence, 2 Sandf. Ch.
400, 406. The necessity of delivery where gifts resting in parol are asserted against the estates of decedents is obvious; but it is equally plain
that there is no such impelling necessity when the gift is established by
the execution and delivery of an instrument of gift. An examination of
a large number of cases in this state discloses the significant facts that (1)
in every case where the gift was not sustained, the gift rested upon parol
evidence; and (2) in every case of a gift evidenced by the delivery of an
instrument of gift, the gift has been sustained. . . .

. . . It is interesting to note that in Matson v. Abbey, 70 Hun. 475,
24 N.Y. Supp. 284, affirmed as to the gift, 141 N.Y. 179, 36 N.E. 11,
sustaining a gift evidenced by an instrument of assignment without de-

livery of the property assigned, the court quotes with approval the statement of the English law in Irons v. Smallpiece, 2 Barn. & Ald. 551, 552, made by Abbott, C.J.:

> I am of opinion that by the law of England, in order to transfer property by gift, there must either be a deed or instrument of gift, or there must be an actual delivery of the thing to the donee.

. . . [I]n view of the decision of this court in McGavic v. Cossum, supra, it seems to me beyond serious question that the delivery of the instrument of gift in the instant case constituted a good symbolical delivery. In the *McGavic* Case a woman owning bonds which had been deposited by her in a bank for safe-keeping during an illness from which she died three weeks later gave to her niece the original memorandum of the purchase of the bonds indorsed with the following statement:

Poughkeepsie, November 23, 1901

I have this day given my niece, Fannie H. McGavic, bond 2000 Reg. 4 per cent.

Delia C. Robinson

Mr. Justice McLaughlin said:

> We are of the opinion that the plaintiff was entitled to the bonds; that what was done constituted a good gift inter vivos. Actual delivery, by reason of the illness of the owner of the bonds and their possession at that time by the bank, was physically impossible; but there was present, as evidenced by the writing of the deceased, not only the intention to then give, but also the intention to then deliver the thing given. The owner did all she could do in this respect. It was a good constructive or symbolical delivery, and this, under the circumstances, was sufficient to vest good title in the plaintiff. 14 Am. & Eng. Ency. of Law (2d Ed.) 1021, and cases cited.

In the instant case, on the day the gift was made at West End, N.J., the certificates of stock were in a safe deposit box in New York City. Furthermore, there were the complications above referred to in the partnership relations and in the fact that the certificates were in the partnership strong box, made out in the name of the firm. These were circumstances and surroundings tending to excuse manual delivery and to make a symbolical delivery effective. In addition, as was said by Justice McLaughlin in the *McGavic* Case:

> There was present, as evidenced by the writing of the deceased, not only the intention to then give, but also the intention to then deliver the thing given. . . . It was a good constructive or symbolical delivery.

The instrument of gift was a symbol which represented the donee's right of possession. It was no more revocable than an assignment. A gift has been judicially defined as a voluntary transfer of property by one to another, without any consideration or compensation therefor. Gray v. Barton, 55 N.Y. 68, 14 Am. Rep. 181. A voluntary transfer or assignment unaccompanied by manual delivery was upheld, as we have seen, in Matson v. Abbey, supra. It must therefore have been held irrevocable. There is no apparent reason why a gift evidenced by an instrument of gift duly delivered is any more revocable than an assignment without consideration. Both strip the donor of dominion over the subject of the gift and place in the hands of the donee evidence of right to possession.

Therefore, applying the rule of delivery in the light of the reason which gave birth to it, and finding here no possibility of fraud or imposition, and no doubt whatever concerning the intention of the donor, and finding full support in the precedent of McGavic v. Cossum, supra, it is my opinion that there was a good constructive or symbolical delivery, consisting of the delivery of the instrument of gift, and that the gift should be sustained. . . .

The decree of the surrogate should be affirmed, with costs and disbursements to the respondents executrix and trustees, and disbursements of the special guardian, respondent. Order filed.

PAGE, J. (dissenting). In my opinion there was not a valid gift inter vivos of the 500 shares of stock of the American Sumatra Tobacco Company by the testator to Sara K. Cohn. . . .

. . . The shares were not physically delivered nor transferred on the books of the corporation, but remained in the safe deposit box in the city of New York in the firm name. Any one of the partners however, at any time, could have taken his proportion of the stock, which was in certificates of $100 each, and caused the same to be transferred to himself, individually; but by reason of the desire to control the election of directors, from which they obtained a business advantage, they allowed the stock to remain in the firm name. Abraham Cohn died in August, 1911, and the two surviving partners began liquidation of the firm's business. Negotiations were opened for the organization of a copartnership, consisting of the testator, Leonard J. Cohn, and one Lichtenstein. The testator agreed to contribute some of this stock as an asset to the new copartnership, and, as it required 7,000 shares to secure the election of a director, the testator's holdings were to be kept intact, so that the new copartnership should have the benefit thereof.

. . . When the paper was delivered to his wife, the daughters testified that the testator said:

> That he could not give her the stock because it was in the company, but as soon as he could get it he would give it to her.

From the foregoing fact, I am of opinion that the attempted gift was invalid. There was no delivery of the stock, either actual or constructive. The testator still retained dominion and control over it, for use in the business of the new copartnership.

In the present case, the writing, taken alone, would seem to show the intention of the donor to make an actual present gift, for he says, "I give this day to my wife." Yet the delivery of the writing was accompanied by the statement "that he could not give her the stock, because it was in the company, but as soon as he could get it he would give it." There is, therefore, a clearly expressed intention to give at a future day, and the acts of the testator showed an intention to retain the dominion and control of the stock, meanwhile, in himself.

. . . Until the donor has divested himself absolutely and irrevocably of the title, dominion, and control of the subject of the gift, he has the power to revoke, and a court of equity will not compel him to complete his gift. . . .

The respondent claims, however, that the delivery of this paper writing was a constructive delivery of the stock, and argues that the above rules only apply to gifts inter vivos where the evidence of the gifts rests in parol, and that, where there is a writing which evidences the donor's intention, the courts will give effect to the delivery of the writing as a constructive delivery of the subject of the gift. This, however, in my opinion, is not the law. The writing must be such as to transfer the right of possession. There may be a symbolic delivery, or there may be a constructive delivery; but, whether it be symbolic or constructive, it must be such a delivery as divests the donor with title, dominion, and right of possession, and it must be the best delivery that can be made under the circumstances of the case, having due regard to the character of the property. . . .

In the instant case there was no physical or other impossibility to the actual delivery of the stock; it stood in the name of the company, but the stock to the extent of 7,213 shares was the property of the testator, and it had been so held merely as a matter of business convenience of the old copartnership, and at the time was so held, pending the formation of a new copartnership, when it might be desirable to hold all the certificates of the stock in solido for the same business advantages. This latter consideration, in my opinion, was the controlling cause of the failure to make an immediate delivery of the stock, and the reason why the testator retained possession, dominion, and control of the certificates. . . .

I have been unable to find that the courts in this jurisdiction have held, heretofore, that it is only where a parol gift is sought to be established that delivery is essential, and that, where the intention to give is evidenced by a writing, delivery is not necessary. Among the cases cited in the prevailing opinion as tending to sustain the proposition that the

requirement for delivery of the thing given is limited to oral gifts will be
found cases where gifts evidenced by a writing have been declared invalid. It will also be found that many of those cases relate to gifts causa
mortis, and not to gifts inter vivos. . . .

The writing given to Mrs. Cohn did not purport to assign, transfer,
or set over to her the stock. It was not a deed or instrument of gift that
divested the testator of possession over and dominion of the stock. That
it was not intended that it should do so is clearly shown by the subsequent acts of the testator.

In my opinion the decree should be modified, by declaring the attempted gift void, and sustaining the objections to the account to that
extent, and the executors and trustees be surcharged with the proceeds
of the said 500 shares of stock, and that the same forms a part of the
principal of the trust estate.

NOTES AND PROBLEMS

1. Under the law of contracts, a gratuitous promise is not enforceable. A promise is enforceable only if given in exchange for consideration. (Love and affection is not consideration; consideration is a
bargained-for exchange or the price of the promise.) How does Leopold
Cohn's act differ from a gratuitous, unenforceable promise?

2. In addition to recognizing gifts by manual delivery or by constructive or symbolic delivery, the common law also permitted a gift to
be made by a sealed instrument. A sealed instrument was called a deed.
Today in almost all states the necessity for a deed to have a seal has been
abolished, and unsealed and sealed instruments conveying land generally have the same effect. Nonetheless, courts today may not recognize
delivery of personal property by an unsealed (informal) instrument
where physical delivery cannot be excused.

Suppose that O, while wearing a wristwatch, hands A a signed writing saying: "I hereby give A my wristwatch (identified as the same one O
is wearing)." Is this a valid gift? *no, watch could be delivered*

3. O owned 100 shares of stock in Legend Corporation, which split
3 for 1. O wanted to give one-half of her new shares (150 shares) to A. O
executed an assignment to A, on the back of her stock certificate, of 150
of the new shares. She turned this over to her stock agent, B, directing
B to have the company issue 150 of the new shares to A when the new
certificates were available. Before the new shares were issued to A, O
died. Is there a valid gift to A? See In re Szabo, 10 N.Y.2d 94, 176 N.E.2d
395, 217 N.Y.S.2d 593 (1961).

4. Robert Hocks rented a safe deposit box jointly with his sister
Joan. He planned to give her everything he put in the box. At a restau-

rant, Robert handed Joan four $5,000 bearer bonds, saying, "I want to give these to you." Joan put the bonds in the safe deposit box. Subsequently, Robert clipped the coupons and collected the interest on the bonds.

During the next several years, Robert added 22 more bonds to the box, as well as a diamond ring. Only Robert, not Joan, went into the box, though Joan had a right to do so. To avoid "a lot of hassle" from Robert's wife, Joan suggested to Robert that he should leave a note in the box indicating her interest. Robert placed a handwritten note in the box: "Upon my death, the contents of this safety deposit box #7069 will belong to and are to be removed only by my sister Joan Jeremiah." Upon Robert's death, is Joan entitled to the contents of the box? See Hocks v. Jeremiah, 92 Or. App. 549, 759 P.2d 312 (1988) (holding Joan entitled only to the first four bonds that were hand delivered to her; the remaining contents were not delivered even though Joan was a joint tenant of the box).

Newman v. Bost

Supreme Court of North Carolina, 1898
122 N.C. 524, 29 S.E. 848

Action tried before Coble, J., and a jury. . . .

The plaintiff alleged in her complaint that the intestate of the defendant, while in his last sickness, gave her all the furniture and other property in his dwelling-house as a gift causa mortis. Among other things claimed, there was a policy of insurance of $3,000 on the life of intestate and other valuable papers, which she alleged were in a certain bureau drawer in intestate's bedroom. She alleged that defendant administrator has collected the policy of life insurance and sold the household and kitchen furniture, and this suit is against *defendant as administrator* to recover the value of the property alleged to have been converted by him. There are other matters involved, claims for services, claim for fire insurance collected by intestate in his lifetime, etc.

On the trial it appeared that the intestate's wife died about ten years before he died, and without issue; that the intestate lived in his dwelling, after his wife's death, in Statesville until his death, and died without issue; that about the last day of March, 1896, he was stricken with paralysis and was confined to his bed in his house and was never able to be out again till he died on 12 April, 1896, that shortly after he was stricken he sent for Enos Houston to nurse him in his last illness; that while helpless in his bed soon after his confinement and *in extremis* he told Houston he had to go — could not stay here — and asked Houston to call plaintiff into his room; he then asked the plaintiff to hand him his private keys, which plaintiff did, she having gotten them from a place over the mantel in intestate's bedroom in his presence and by his direction; he then handed plaintiff the bunch of keys and told her to take them and keep them, that he desired her to have them and everything in the house; he then pointed out the bureau, the clock and other articles of furniture in the house and asked his chamber door to be opened and pointed in the direction of the hall and other rooms and repeated that everything in the house was hers — he wanted her to have everything in the house; his voice failed him soon after the delivery of the keys and these declarations, so that he could never talk again to be understood, except to indicate yes and no, and this generally by a motion of the head; the bunch of keys delivered to the plaintiff, amongst others, included one which unlocked the bureau pointed out to plaintiff as hers (and other furniture in the room), and the bureau drawer which this key unlocked, contained in it a life insurance policy, payable to intestate's estate, and a few small notes, a large number of papers, receipts, etc., etc., and there was no other key that unlocked this bureau drawer; this bureau drawer was the place where intestate kept all his valuable papers; plaintiff kept the keys as directed from time given her and still has them; at the death of intestate's wife he employed plaintiff, then an orphan about eighteen years old, to become his housekeeper, and she remained in his service for ten years and till his death, and occupied rooms assigned her in intestate's residence; in 1895 the intestate declared his purpose to marry plaintiff within twelve months; nobody resided in the house with them; immediately after the death of intestate, Houston told of the donation to Mr. Burke, and the plaintiff informed her attorney, Mr. Burke, of it, and she made known her claim to the property in the house and kept the keys and forbade the defendant from interfering with it in any way, both before and after he qualified as administrator.

Other facts in relation to the plaintiff's claim appear in the opinion. There was a verdict, followed by judgment for the plaintiff, and defendant appealed.

FURCHES, J. The plaintiff in her complaint demands $3,000 collected by defendant, as the administrator of J.F. Van Pelt,[31] on a life

---

31. J.F. Van Pelt was a man of some standing in Statesville, North Carolina. He moved there in 1859 and entered the grocery business. When the Civil War broke out, his partner joined the Confederate army, and Van Pelt stayed at home to run their business. He was mayor of the town from 1873 to 1877 and from 1883 to 1885. He was also manager of Statesville's Opera Hall. His obituary in the Statesville Semi-Weekly Landmark, April 14, 1896, printed under the heading "Called to Account," noted:

> With limited education, he was possessed of splendid business judgment and had, by judicious management, accumulated a good property. He had been retired from active business for several years.

Van Pelt was 62 years old when he died in his home on Front Street, having moved there when his Walnut Street residence burned. (In the Walnut Street house was a piano,

insurance policy, and now in his hands; $300, the value of a piano upon which said Van Pelt collected that amount of insurance money; $200.94, the value of household property sold by defendant as belonging to the estate of his intestate, and $45, the value of property in the plaintiff's bedroom and sold by the defendant as a part of the property belonging to the intestate's estate.

The $3,000, money collected on the life insurance policy, and the $200.94, the price for which the household property sold, plaintiff claims belonged to her by reason of a donatio causa mortis from said Van Pelt. The $45, the price for which her bedroom property sold, and the $300 insurance money on the piano, belonged to her also by reason of gifts inter vivos.

The rules of law governing all of these claims of the plaintiff are in many respects the same, and the discussion of one will be to a considerable extent a discussion of all.

To constitute a donatio causa mortis, two things are indispensably necessary: an intention to make the gift, and a delivery of the thing given. Without both of these requisites, there can be no gift causa mortis. And both these are matters of fact to be determined by the jury, where there is evidence tending to prove them.

The intention to make the gift need not be announced by the donor in express terms, but may be inferred from the facts attending the delivery — that is, what the donor said and did. But it must always clearly appear that he knew *what he was doing*, and that he intended a gift. So far, there was but little diversity of authority, if any.

As to what constitutes or may constitute delivery, has been the subject of discussion and adjudication in most or all the courts of the Union and of England, and they have by no means been uniform — some of them holding that a symbolical delivery — that is, some other article delivered in the name and stead of the thing intended to be given, is sufficient; others holding that a symbolical delivery is not sufficient, but that

---

which the plaintiff, Julia Newman, claimed had been given her and on which Van Pelt had collected the fire insurance proceeds.) Van Pelt died intestate. His heirs were a sister living in China Grove, North Carolina, and a brother living in Alabama.

The trial in Newman v. Bost occupied four days. The attorneys for the parties took over one day making their closing arguments to the jury. Julia Newman's lawyer, in closing, "spoke for about two and a half hours, finishing at 2 o'clock, when court adjourned for dinner." Id., January 18, 1898. (O, for the days when eloquent lawyering could produce a hungry jury!) After dinner and lengthy deliberation, the jury unanimously found for Julia.

Sometime after the trial Julia Newman left Statesville. About a month before Van Pelt's death, Julia had bought 36 acres of land from him. She sold the land in 1907, at a nice profit. The deed listed Julia, still unmarried, as living in Maryland. The information in this footnote was furnished the editors by Bill Moose of Mitchell Community College, Statesville, N.C. The photograph of Van Pelt is from the collection of Steve Hill in Statesville. — EDS.

a constructive delivery — that is, the delivery of a key to a locked house, trunk or other receptacle is sufficient. They distinguish this from a symbolical delivery, and say that this is in *substance* a delivery of the thing, as it is the means of using and enjoying the thing given; while others hold that there must be an actual manual delivery to perfect a gift causa mortis.

This doctrine of donatio causa mortis was borrowed from the Roman Civil Law by our English ancestors. There was much greater need for such a law at the time it was incorporated into the civil law and into the English law than there is now. Learning was not so general, nor the facilities for making wills so great then as now. . . .

It seems to us that, . . . after the statute of fraud and of wills, this doctrine of causa mortis is in direct conflict with the spirit and purpose of those statutes — the prevention of fraud. It is a doctrine, in our opinion, not to be extended but to be strictly construed and confined within the bounds of our adjudged cases. We were at first disposed to confine it to cases of actual *manual* delivery, and are only prevented from doing so by our loyalty to our own adjudications. , , .

Many of the cases cited by the plaintiff are distinguishable from ours, if not all of them. Thomas v. Lewis (a Virginia case), 37 Am. St., 878, was probably more relied on by the plaintiff than any other case cited, and for that reason we mention it by name. This case, in its essential facts, is distinguishable from the case under consideration. There, the articles present were taken out of the bureau drawer, handed to the donor, and then delivered by him to the donee. According to all the authorities, this was a good gift causa mortis. The box and safe, the key to which the donor delivered to the donee, were not present but were deposited in the vault of the bank; and so far as shown by the case it will be presumed, from the place where they were and the purpose for which things are usually deposited in a bank vault, that they were only valuable as a depository for such purposes, as holding and preserving money and valuable papers, bonds, stocks and the like. This box and safe would have been of little value to the donee for any other purpose. But more than this, the donor expressly stated that all you find *in this box and this safe is yours.* There is no mistake that it was the intention of the donor to give what was contained in the box and in the safe.

As my Lord Coke would say: "Note the diversity" between that case and the case at bar. There, the evidence of debt contained in the bureau, which was present, was taken out, given to the donor, and by him delivered to the donee. This was an actual manual delivery, good under all the authorities. But no such thing was done in this case as to the life insurance policy. It was neither taken out of the drawer nor mentioned by the donor, unless it is included in the testimony of Enos Houston who, at one time, in giving his testimony says that Van Pelt gave her the keys, saying "what is in this house is yours," and at another time on cross-examination, he said to Julia, "I intend to give you this furniture in this house," and at another time, "What property is in this house is yours." The bureau in which was found the life insurance policy, after the death of Van Pelt, was present in the room where the keys were handed to Julia, and the life insurance policy could easily have been taken out and handed to Van Pelt, and by him delivered to Julia, as was done in the case of Thomas v. Lewis, supra. But this was not done. The safe and box, in Thomas v. Lewis, were not present, so that the contents could not have been taken out and delivered to the donee by the donor. The ordinary use of a stand of bureaus is not for the purpose of holding and securing such things as a life insurance policy, though they may be often used for that purpose, while a safe and a box deposited in the vault of a bank are. A bureau is an article of household furniture, used for domestic purposes, and generally belongs to the ladies' department of the household government, while the safe and box, in Thomas v. Lewis, are not. The bureau itself, mentioned in this case, was such property as would be valuable to the plaintiff. . . .

It is held that the law of delivery in this State is the same in gifts inter vivos and causa mortis. Adams v. Hayes, 24 N.C., 361. . . . [T]here can be no gift of either kind without both the intention to give and the delivery. . . .

The leading case in this State is Adams v. Hayes. . . .

Following this case, . . . we feel bound to give effect to *constructive delivery,* where it plainly appears that it was the intention of the donor to make the gift, and where the things intended to be given are *not* present, or, where present, are incapable of *manual* delivery from their size or weight. But where the articles are present and are capable of manual delivery, *this must be had.* This is as far as we can go. It may be thought by some that this is a hard rule — that a dying man cannot dispose of his own. But we are satisfied that when properly considered, it will be found to be a just rule. But it is not a hard rule. The law provides how a man can dispose of all his property, both real and personal. To do this, it is only necessary for him to observe and conform to the requirements of these laws. . . . The law provides that every man may dispose of all of his property by will, when made in writing. And it is most singular how guarded the law is to protect the testator against fraud and impositions by requiring that every word of the will must be written and signed by the testator, or, if written by someone else, it must be attested by at least *two* subscribing witnesses who shall sign the same in his presence and at his request, or the will is void. . . .

In gifts causa mortis it requires but one witness, probably one servant as a witness to a gift of all the estate a man has; no publicity is to be given that the gift has been made, and no probate or registration is required.

The statute of wills is a statute against fraud, considered in England

and in this State to be demanded by public policy. And yet, if symbolical deliveries of gifts causa mortis are to be allowed, or if constructive deliveries be allowed to the extent claimed by the plaintiff, the statute of wills may prove to be of little value. For such considerations, we see every reason for restricting and none for extending the rules heretofore established as applicable to gifts causa mortis.

It being claimed and admitted that the life insurance policy was present in the bureau drawer in the room where it is claimed the gift was made, and being capable of actual manual delivery, we are of the opinion that the title of the insurance policy did not pass to the plaintiff, but remained the property of the intestate of the defendant.

But we are of the opinion that the bureau and any other article of furniture, locked and unlocked by any of the keys given to the plaintiff, did pass and she became the owner thereof. This is upon the ground that while these articles were present, from their size and weight they were incapable of actual manual delivery; and that the delivery of the keys was a constructive delivery of these articles, equivalent to an actual delivery if the articles had been capable of manual delivery.

[W]e are of the opinion that the other articles of household furniture (except those in the plaintiff's private bed chamber) did not pass to the plaintiff, but remained the property of the defendant's intestate.

We do not think the articles in the plaintiff's bed chamber passed by the donatio causa mortis for the same reason that the other articles of household furniture did not pass — want of delivery — either constructive or manual. But as to the furniture in the plaintiff's bedroom ($45) it seems to us that there was sufficient evidence of both gift and delivery to support the finding of the jury, as a gift inter vivos. The intention to give this property is shown by a number of witnesses and contradicted by none.

The only debatable ground is as to the sufficiency of the delivery. But when we recall the express terms in which he repeatedly declared that it was hers; that he had bought it for her and had given it to her; that it was placed in her private chamber, her bedroom, where we must suppose that she had the entire use and control of the same, it would seem that this was sufficient to constitute a delivery. There was no evidence, that we remember, disputing these facts. But, if there was, the jury have found for the plaintiff, upon sufficient evidence at least to go to the jury, as to this gift and its delivery. As to the piano there was much evidence tending to show the intention of Van Pelt to give it to the plaintiff, and that he had given it to her, and we remember no evidence to the contrary. And as to this, like the bedroom furniture, the debatable ground, if there is any debatable ground, is the question of delivery. It was placed in the intestate's parlor where it remained until it was burned. The intestate insured it as his property, collected and used the insurance money as his own, often saying that he intended to buy the

Residence of Mr. J.F. Van Pelt, Walnut Street
from The (Statesville, N.C.) Landmark Trade Edition, May 22, 1890

This house, and with it "Miss Julia's piano," burned between 1890 and 1896.

————————————

plaintiff another piano, which he never did. It must be presumed that the parlor was under the dominion of the intestate, and not of his cook, housekeeper, and hired servant. And unless there is something more shown than the fact that the piano was bought by the intestate, placed in his parlor, and called by him "Miss Julia's piano," we cannot think this constituted a delivery. But, as the case goes back for a new trial, if the plaintiff thinks she can show a delivery she will have an opportunity of doing so. But she will understand that she must do so according to the rules laid down in this opinion — that she must show actual or constructive delivery equivalent to actual manual delivery. We see no ground upon which the plaintiff can recover the insurance money, if the piano was not hers.

We do not understand that there was any controversy as to the plaintiff's right to recover her services, which the jury have estimated to be $125. The view of the case we have taken has relieved us from a discussion of the exceptions to evidence, and as to the charge of the Court. There is no such thing in this State as *symbolical delivery* in gifts either inter vivos or causa mortis. . . .

New trial.

NOTES AND PROBLEMS

1. A gift causa mortis, that is, a gift made in contemplation of and in expectation of immediate approaching death, is a substitute for a will.

182

If the donor lives, the gift is revoked. Because the courts see upholding gifts causa mortis as undercutting the safeguards of the Statute of Wills, they have more strictly applied the requirements for a valid gift causa mortis than for a gift inter vivos. They also have placed restrictions on gifts causa mortis not applicable to inter vivos gifts. For example, if the donee already is in possession of the property, there must be a redelivery to effect a valid gift causa mortis but not if the gift is inter vivos. If Van Pelt had put a small cinnabar box in Julia's bedroom, he could during his lifetime, before death drew near, declare that he was giving the box to Julia. But if he waited until he was on his deathbed, he would have to deliver the box to her again.

2. Suppose that Van Pelt had said to Julia, "I want to give you my insurance policy in that bureau over there, so Enos please get it and give it to her." Enos, however, leaves the policy where it was. Is there a valid gift? See Wilcox v. Matteson, 53 Wis. 23, 9 N.W. 814 (1881). What if Van Pelt instead had said, "I want to give you my bureau there. Enos, move it into her room." Enos does so. The bureau contains the life insurance policy. On the reasoning of Newman v. Bost, is there a valid gift?

3. Suppose that Van Pelt had called in Julia and said, "I want to give you my bureau and the insurance policy locked in it. Here is the key." Julia takes the key but the bureau stays where it was. On the reasoning of Newman v. Bost, has a valid gift been made?

4. Suppose that Van Pelt had called in Julia and said, "I want to give you my little strong box here and the insurance policy locked in it. Here is the key." Julia takes the key but the box stays where it was. On the reasoning of Newman v. Bost, has a valid gift been made? See Bynum v. Fidelity Bank of Durham, 221 N.C. 101, 19 S.E.2d 121 (1942).

5. If Van Pelt had said to his wife before he died, "Dear, I give you the piano," would there be a gift? See Robinson v. Hoalton, 213 Cal. 370, 2 P.2d 344 (1931).

6. Read the last sentence of the opinion in Newman v. Bost and then answer these questions:

(a) If Van Pelt had handed Julia a signed instrument reading, "Dear, I give you the piano," would there be a gift?

(b) If Van Pelt had written a book and had copyright royalties, could he assign a share of these royalties to Julia by an instrument of gift?

Gruen v. Gruen

Court of Appeals of New York, 1986
68 N.Y.2d 48, 496 N.E.2d 869, 505 N.Y.S.2d 849

SIMONS, J. Plaintiff commenced this action seeking a declaration that he is the rightful owner of a painting which he alleges his father, now deceased, gave to him. He concedes that he has never had possession of the painting but asserts that his father made a valid gift of the title in 1963 reserving a life estate for himself. His father retained possession of the painting until he died in 1980. Defendant, plaintiff's stepmother, has the painting now and has refused plaintiff's requests that she turn it over to him. She contends that the purported gift was testamentary in nature and invalid insofar as the formalities of a will were not met or, alternatively, that a donor may not make a valid inter vivos gift of a chattel and retain a life estate with a complete right of possession. Following a seven-day nonjury trial, Special Term found that plaintiff had failed to establish any of the elements of an inter vivos gift and that in any event an attempt by a donor to retain a present possessory life estate in a chattel invalidated a purported gift of it. The Appellate Division held that a valid gift may be made reserving a life estate and, finding the elements of a gift established in this case, it reversed and remitted the matter for a determination of value (104 A.D.2d 171, 488 N.Y.S.2d 401). That determination has now been made and defendant appeals directly to this court, pursuant to CPLR 5601(d), from the subsequent final judgment entered in Supreme Court awarding plaintiff $2,500,000 in damages representing the value of the painting, plus interest. We now affirm.

The subject of the dispute is a work entitled "Schloss Kammer am Attersee II" painted by a noted Austrian modernist, Gustav Klimt.[32] It was purchased by plaintiff's father, Victor Gruen, in 1959 for $8,000. On April 1, 1963 the elder Gruen, a successful architect with offices and residences in both New York City and Los Angeles during most of the time involved in this action,[33] wrote a letter to plaintiff, then an undergraduate student at Harvard, stating that he was giving him the Klimt painting for his birthday but that he wished to retain the possession of it for his lifetime. This letter is not in evidence, apparently because plaintiff destroyed it on instructions from his father. Two other letters were received, however, one dated May 22, 1963 and the other April 1, 1963. Both had been dictated by Victor Gruen and sent together to plaintiff

32. A portrait by Gustav Klimt sold in May 1987 at Sotheby's in New York for $3.85 million, a record at auction for a painting by Klimt. N.Y. Times, May 12, 1987, §1, at 23. — Eds.

33. Victor Gruen, born in Vienna, was an urban designer and architect who came to this country in 1933. His firm, Victor Gruen Associates, has been one of the most influential in shaping the urban environment since World War II. It designed the first regional shopping center, Northland in Detroit, which inspired similar plans for enormous enclosed shopping malls in other cities. Gruen was the author of several books on urban planning, in which he said his main aim was to design cities that were worthwhile to live in as well as functional. "Some say there is no need for a city, a center," Gruen once said. "They say you can communicate in the future with television phones. You may be able eventually to talk to your girl friend by television, but you can't kiss her that way." His best book is The Heart of Our Cities (1964).

Gruen viewed Vienna as the most livable of cities, largely because the automobile — which he disliked — had been banned from downtown. In the last years of his life he returned to live in Vienna, where he died in 1980. — Eds.

Gustav Klimt
Schloss Kammer am Attersee II
Courtesy The Galerie St. Etienne, New York

on or about May 22, 1963. The letter dated May 22, 1963 reads as follows:

> Dear Michael:
>
> I wrote you at the time of your birthday about the gift of the painting by Klimt. Now my lawyer tells me that because of the existing tax laws, it was wrong to mention in that letter that I want to use the painting as long as I live. Though I still want to use it, this should not appear in the letter. I am enclosing, therefore, a new letter and I ask you to send the old one back to me so that it can be destroyed.
>
> I know this is all very silly, but the lawyer and our accountant insist that they must have in their possession copies of a letter which will serve the purpose of making it possible for you, once I die, to get this picture without having to pay inheritance taxes on it.
>
> Love,
> s/*Victor*

Enclosed with this letter was a substitute gift letter, dated April 1, 1963, which stated:

> Dear Michael:
>

> The 21st birthday, being an important event in life, should be celebrated accordingly. I therefore wish to give you as a present the oil painting by Gustav Klimt of Schloss Kammer which now hangs in the New York living room. You know that Lazette and I bought it some 5 or 6 years ago, and you always told us how much you liked it.
>
> Happy birthday again.
>
> Love
> s/*Victor*

Plaintiff never took possession of the painting nor did he seek to do so. Except for a brief period between 1964 and 1965 when it was on loan to art exhibits and when restoration work was performed on it, the painting remained in his father's possession, moving with him from New York City to Beverly Hills and finally to Vienna, Austria, where Victor Gruen died on February 14, 1980. Following Victor's death plaintiff requested possession of the Klimt painting and when defendant refused, he commenced this action.

   The issues framed for appeal are whether a valid inter vivos gift of a chattel may be made where the donor has reserved a life estate in the chattel and the donee never has had physical possession of it before the donor's death and, if it may, which factual findings on the elements of a valid inter vivos gift more nearly comport with the weight of the evidence in this case, those of Special Term or those of the Appellate Division. The latter issue requires application of two general rules. First, to make a valid inter vivos gift there must exist the intent on the part of the donor to make a present transfer; delivery of the gift, either actual or constructive to the donee; and acceptance by the donee (Matter of Szabo, 10 N.Y.2d 94, 98, 217 N.Y.S.2d 593, 176 N.E.2d 395; Matter of Kelly, 285 N.Y. 139, 150, 33 N.E.2d 62 [dissenting in part opn.]). Second, the proponent of a gift has the burden of proving each of these elements by clear and convincing evidence.

Donative Intent

There is an important distinction between the intent with which an inter vivos gift is made and the intent to make a gift by will. An inter vivos gift requires that the donor intend to make an irrevocable present transfer of ownership; if the intention is to make a testamentary disposition effective only after death, the gift is invalid unless made by will.

Defendant contends that the trial court was correct in finding that Victor did not intend to transfer any present interest in the painting to plaintiff in 1963 but only expressed an intention that plaintiff was to get the painting upon his death. The evidence is all but conclusive, however, that Victor intended to transfer ownership of the painting to plaintiff in 1963 but to retain a life estate in it and that he did, therefore, effectively transfer a remainder interest in the painting to plaintiff at that time. Although the original letter was not in evidence, testimony of its contents was received along with the substitute gift letter and its covering letter dated May 22, 1963. The three letters should be considered together as a single instrument (see Matter of Brandreth, 169 N.Y. 437, 440, 62 N.E. 563) and when they are they unambiguously establish that Victor Gruen intended to make a present gift of title to the painting at that time. But there was other evidence for after 1963 Victor made several statements orally and in writing indicating that he had previously given plaintiff the painting and that plaintiff owned it. Victor Gruen retained possession of the property, insured it, allowed others to exhibit it and made necessary repairs to it but those acts are not inconsistent with his retention of a life estate. . . . Victor's failure to file a gift tax return on the transaction was partially explained by allegedly erroneous legal advice he received, and while that omission sometimes may indicate that the donor had no intention of making a present gift, it does not necessarily do so and it is not dispositive in this case.

Defendant contends that even if a present gift was intended, Victor's reservation of a lifetime interest in the painting defeated it. . . .

Defendant recognizes that a valid inter vivos gift of a remainder interest can be made not only of real property but also of such intangibles as stocks and bonds. Indeed, several of the cases she cites so hold. That being so, it is difficult to perceive any legal basis for the distinction she urges which would permit gifts of remainder interests in those properties but not of remainder interests in chattels such as the Klimt painting here. The only reason suggested is that the gift of a chattel must include a present right to possession. The application of *Brandreth* to permit a gift of the remainder in this case, however, is consistent with the distinction, well recognized in the law of gifts as well as in real property law, between ownership and possession or enjoyment. Insofar as some of our cases purport to require that the donor intend to transfer both title and possession immediately to have a valid inter vivos gift (see Gannon v. McGuire, 160 N.Y. 476, 481, 55 N.E. 7; Young v. Young, 80 N.Y. 422, 430), they state the rule too broadly and confuse the effectiveness of a gift with the transfer of the possession of the subject of that gift. The correct test is " 'whether the maker intended the [gift] to have *no effect* until after the maker's death, or whether he intended it to transfer *some present interest*' " (McCarthy v. Pieret, 281 N.Y. 407, 409, 24 N.E.2d 102 [emphasis added]; see also 25 N.Y. Jur., Gifts, §14, at 156-157). As long as the evidence establishes an intent to make a present and irrevocable transfer of title or the right of ownership, there is a present transfer of some interest and the gift is effective immediately. Thus, in Speelman v. Pascal, [10 N.Y.2d 313, 222 N.Y.S.2d 324, 178 N.E.2d 723], we held valid a gift of a percentage of the future royalties to the play "My Fair Lady" before the play even existed. There, as in this case, the donee received title or the right of ownership to some property immediately upon the making of the gift but possession or enjoyment of the subject of the gift was postponed to some future time.

Defendant suggests that allowing a donor to make a present gift of a remainder with the reservation of a life estate will lead courts to effectuate otherwise invalid testamentary dispositions of property. The two have entirely different characteristics, however, which make them distinguishable. Once the gift is made it is irrevocable and the donor is limited to the rights of a life tenant not an owner. Moreover, with the gift of a remainder title vests immediately in the donee and any possession is postponed until the donor's death whereas under a will neither title nor possession vests immediately. Finally, the postponement of enjoyment of the gift is produced by the express terms of the gift not by the nature of the instrument as it is with a will (see Robb v. Washington & Jefferson Coll., 185 N.Y. 485, 493, 78 N.E. 359).

Delivery

In order to have a valid inter vivos gift, there must be a delivery of the gift, either by a physical delivery of the subject of the gift or a construc-

tive or symbolic delivery such as by an instrument of gift, sufficient to
divest the donor of dominion and control over the property. As the
statement of the rule suggests, the requirement of delivery is not rigid
or inflexible, but is to be applied in light of its purpose to avoid mistakes
by donors and fraudulent claims by donees. Accordingly, what is sufficient to constitute delivery "must be tailored to suit the circumstances of
the case" (Matter of Szabo, supra, 10 N.Y.2d at p.98, 217 N.Y.S.2d 593,
176 N.E.2d 395). The rule requires that " '[t]he delivery necessary to
consummate a gift must be as perfect as the nature of the property and
the circumstances and surroundings of the parties will reasonably permit' " (id.).

Defendant contends that when a tangible piece of personal property
such as a painting is the subject of a gift, physical delivery of the painting
itself is the best form of delivery and should be required. Here, of
course, we have only delivery of Victor Gruen's letters which serve as
instruments of gift. Defendant's statement of the rule as applied may be
generally true, but it ignores the fact that what Victor Gruen gave plaintiff was not all rights to the Klimt painting, but only title to it with no
right of possession until his death. Under these circumstances, it would
be illogical for the law to require the donor to part with possession of
the painting when that is exactly what he intends to retain.

Nor is there any reason to require a donor making a gift of a remainder interest in a chattel to physically deliver the chattel into the
donee's hands only to have the donee redeliver it to the donor. As the
facts of this case demonstrate, such a requirement could impose practical
burdens on the parties to the gift while serving the delivery requirement
poorly. Thus, in order to accomplish this type of delivery the parties
would have been required to travel to New York for the symbolic transfer and redelivery of the Klimt painting which was hanging on the wall
of Victor Gruen's Manhattan apartment. Defendant suggests that such
a requirement would be stronger evidence of a completed gift, but in
the absence of witnesses to the event or any written confirmation of the
gift it would provide less protection against fraudulent claims than have
the written instruments of gift delivered in this case.

Acceptance

Acceptance by the donee is essential to the validity of an inter vivos gift,
but when a gift is of value to the donee, as it is here, the law will presume
an acceptance on his part. Plaintiff did not rely on this presumption
alone but also presented clear and convincing proof of his acceptance of
a remainder interest in the Klimt painting by evidence that he had made
several contemporaneous statements acknowledging the gift to his
friends and associates, even showing some of them his father's gift letter,
and that he had retained both letters for over 17 years to verify the gift
after his father died. Defendant relied exclusively on affidavits filed by

plaintiff in a matrimonial action with his former wife, in which plaintiff failed to list his interest in the painting as an asset. These affidavits were made over 10 years after acceptance was complete and they do not even approach the evidence in Matter of Kelly (285 N.Y. 139, 148-149, 33 N.E.2d 62 [dissenting in part opn.], supra) where the donee, immediately upon delivery of a diamond ring, rejected it as "too flashy." We agree with the Appellate Division that interpretation of the affidavit was too speculative to support a finding of rejection and overcome the substantial showing of acceptance by plaintiff.

Accordingly, the judgment appealed from and the order of the Appellate Division brought up for review should be affirmed, with costs.

NOTES AND QUESTIONS

1. If Victor Gruen had wanted to give Michael the complete ownership of the painting and not reserve a life estate, could he have done so by a letter sent to Michael at Harvard? *no*

2. Suppose that Victor Gruen had written Michael: "I give you the Klimt painting when I die." Would this be a valid lifetime gift? The answer is "No, this is a will. The instrument shows no intention to give Michael any rights *now*, but only when Victor dies. As a will, the instrument is not valid unless properly executed as a will, with witnesses."[34]

Carefully distinguish a will from what Victor actually did. He wrote: "I give you the Klimt painting, reserving possession for my life." This gives Michael a present ownership interest in the painting, with possession postponed until Victor's death.

Gruen v. Gruen introduces you to the concept of a life estate (in Victor) and a remainder (in Michael). Each of these estates is a separate interest in the same property, entitling first the life tenant to possession, and then, after his death, the remainderman. We will closely examine these estates in Chapters 3 and 4.

3. Return to In re Cohn, page 169. If Leopold Cohn's instrument of gift had read, "I give to my wife 500 shares of tobacco stock, but I retain possession of the stock pending the formation of the new copartnership," would there be a valid gift? If not, how can this case be distinguished from Gruen v. Gruen? Inasmuch as *Gruen* held that a person can transfer ownership of a chattel by an instrument of gift, while retaining possession for life, why cannot a person use an instrument of gift and retain possession for a shorter period?

---

34. In states permitting holographic wills (unwitnessed wills written in the testator's handwriting), the letter might be probated as a holograph. New York does not permit holographic wills.

II
The System of Estates (Leaseholds Aside)

For property law, the system of estates represents the most obvious of many links between past and present. The very word *estate,* drawn from and implying *status,* signifies the feudal origins of the system — origins that we will consider on brief occasions in the following chapters. So does the distinction, still current, between *freehold* and *nonfreehold* estates — the first referring to normal tenures of feudal times, the second to mere leases.

From its feudal origins the system of estates evolved into an elaborate hierarchy of interests in land, accompanied by an equally elaborate taxonomy by which to classify them. Those who held estates in land, free or otherwise, found it to their advantage to create new estates and new interests, or they managed to do as much without knowing they had.[1] It became commonplace for two or more persons to have interests in the same land — for example, one person with a right to possession now (present interest) and another person with a right to possession later (future interest), or two or more persons with rights to concurrent possession, now or in the future (co-ownership or cotenancy). The various estates developed as a consequence of the language or other facts giving rise to their creation, and each estate carried with it characteristics different from the others. It was necessary, it must have been thought, to have some grand scheme to keep everything straight. Hence the taxonomy that you will be studying.

Regarding that taxonomy, you should come to see that much of it is obsolete today, dealing with distinctions that have, or should have, lost their relevance. Nevertheless, the unduly elaborate classification of the estate system persists. (Why do you suppose that is so?) Justice Holmes once said, "It is revolting to have no better reason for a rule than that it was laid down in the time of Henry IV. It is still more revolting if the grounds upon which it was laid down have vanished

1. Actually, this process still goes on. We might, for example, regard the condominium as a new sort of estate, though one whose line goes back to classical times, and we acknowledge today nonfreehold estates that were unknown at common law.

long since, and the rule simply persists from imitation of the past."
Oliver Wendell Holmes, The Path of the Law, 10 Harv. L. Rev. 457, 469
(1897). Holmes was speaking in another context, but he might as well
have been talking about the system of estates. Here rules persist that
have lost their purpose (though the situation is much better now than it
was in Holmes's time and likely to improve still more). Labels have been
even more enduring — a good example of the triumph of form over
substance.

Leaseholds — the landlord-tenant estates — are an element of the
estate system, but the rules governing landlord-tenant relations are
sufficiently distinct to merit separate treatment. Accordingly, we save the
topic for close study in Part III.

3

Possessory Estates

A. *Up from Feudalism*

In January 1066, Edward the Confessor, saintly and celibate, died childless. Three contenders claimed the English crown: Harold Godwinson, the most powerful earl in England, who had been granted the kingdom by Edward on his deathbed; Harald Hardraade, king of Norway, an adventurer assisted by Harold Godwinson's exiled brother Tostig; and William of Normandy, Edward's cousin, who claimed Edward had earlier promised him the throne. Harold Godwinson was crowned king, defeated Harald of Norway in September, and on October 14 was himself defeated by William of Normandy in the Battle of Hastings on the south coast of England. This fateful event — the conquest of England by the Normans from across the channel — determined the whole future course of English, and consequently American, law. Never again was an alien conqueror able to cross the English channel. Thus insulated from disruption, but much influenced by Norman, French, and Roman thought, the English developed one of the two great legal systems of the western world, the other being Roman. This indigenous creation, which spread throughout the English-speaking world, grew out of the social system imposed by the Norman conquerors.

Here we trace in broad outline the development of property law, emphasizing that part of history still important in understanding modern concepts. You will understand that a synopsis such as this can describe only approximately the social reality of the times. Indeed, to lay all the cards on the table, scholars are not always sure what was the reality of feudal times; feudalism, like other periods of history, is an unfinished excavation.

1. Tenure

To consolidate his power and raise revenues, William, an unusually intelligent and strong, often ruthless, king, imposed a more strictly organized social and military hierarchy than had previously existed in England. This was the first planned society since the Roman Empire, and some say it represents the beginning of the modern bureaucratic state. The underlying social principle was that fighters and priests should govern society, supported by a large mass of laborers. A central feature of the system was land tenure; each person's position was defined in terms of his relationship to land. Each person, save the king, was deliberately made subservient to another, his land lord. And all were subservient to the crown, from whom all land titles derived.

   Though history calls him William the Conqueror, William claimed to be king as of right. Those Anglo-Saxons who resisted forfeited their lands, which were parceled out to William's supporters, usually Norman warriors, who became his tenants in chief. By 1086 there were around 1500 tenants in chief. Each tenant in chief held the land assigned under an agreement to render the king specific *services,* usually military in nature, such as furnishing 40 knights to fight for the king. The tenant in chief could provide knights by paying them and keeping them in his household ready to fight, but more frequently he provided his quota by *subinfeudation.* This took the form of the tenant in chief granting a parcel of his land to a subtenant in exchange for the service of one or more knights or for some other service necessary to support the land lord. A tenant in chief and a lesser tenant could not shift a service from the land, which was forfeited if the service was not performed, but they could, as between themselves, determine who would perform it. The lesser tenants might also subinfeudate, so that a feudal pyramid was built up, with services flowing to the king at the top and protection extending downward to the actual occupants of the land at the bottom. The title to one tract of land might look like this:

King
|
Tenant in chief
|
Mesne lord[1]
|
Tenant in demesne

The tenant in demesne had *seisin* or possessory use of the land; the lords above him had the rights to services.

   To assist in the collection of feudal services, William ordered the royal clerks to prepare Domesday Book (so called because there was no appeal therefrom), in which was recorded the holder of each tract of

---

1. *Mesne* (law French, pronounced mean) means intermediate; a mesne lord was lord to those who stood below him in the feudal ladder and tenant to those above. A tenant in chief could be a mesne lord, but the king, standing at the top, could not be.

land in England and the services by which the land was held. This remarkable survey, which attempted to enumerate every town, mill, church, woodland, and tenement in the kingdom, was completed in 1086 and still exists in the Public Records Office in London.

2. Feudal Tenures and Services

a. Free Tenures

In establishing their rule, the Norman conquerors had principally in view military security, economic support, and support of the church. Accordingly, they developed three major tenurial structures to organize three social orders: men who fight, men who work, and men who pray. Within each tenure there was tremendous variety and heterogeneity, but the general structures are as follows:

(1) Military Tenures

Knight service. The mounted knight was the central figure in warfare in those days, and the tenant by knight service was required to provide a specified number of men to fight for the king for 40 days each year. Almost all land granted by William was in knight service, including large tracts of land given the church.

Knight service was effective in defending the borders against Wales and Scotland, a kind of guard duty, but for continuous wars in France it proved ineffective.[2] Within a hundred years after the Conquest, with England pacified, the king had begun to take money payment (scutage or shield money) in its stead and to employ mercenaries to fight foreign wars. At this point tenants by knight service lost their military function and were slowly transformed into country gentlemen.

Grand sergeanty. To create a splendid court life and pageantry to

2. The French wars resulted in no small part from the marriage to Henry Plantagenet of Eleanor, the high-spirited duchess of Aquitaine, who owned as her feudal fiefs all of southwestern France from the Spanish border to the Loire. In 1137 Eleanor had married Louis VII of France, a pious and ascetic king. After 13 years of marriage, Eleanor, bored with Louis, in an act that scandalized Christendom, had her marriage annulled on the ground of consanguinity. A few months later she married Louis's chief enemy, the lusty Henry, duke of Normandy and count of Anjou, to whom she bore eight children including Richard the Lionhearted and "wicked" King John. This was more than a personal insult to Louis. Henry had as his feudal fiefs all of northwestern France from the Loire to the English channel, and when, four years later, he ascended the English throne as Henry II, Henry and Eleanor controlled from the Scottish border to the Spanish frontier. Although the king of the French was their nominal overlord in France, a deadly political rivalry ensued and the next 300 years were to witness almost continual war as the successive kings of France tried to regain their kingdoms. See Marion Meade, Eleanor of Aquitaine: A Biography (1977), and the film, The Lion in Winter (1968) (with Katharine Hepburn and Peter O'Toole).

accompany the knights and to secure personal services from the warrior class to the king, the tenure by grand sergeanty was created. These services might include carrying the royal banner or safeguarding the royal treasury. Several sergeanties survive today in connection with coronation services. (Petty sergeanty existed too, for nonpersonal services, but in time it came to be regarded as socage in effect.)

(2) Economic Tenure (or Socage)

To provide subsistence and maintenance for the overlords, the tenure of socage developed. It was the most common form of tenure; any kind of service could be reserved, such as money rent or 10 days of ploughing or keeping a bridge in repair or delivering a dish of mushrooms fresh for the king's breakfast in London. So strong was the notion of tenure that, upon a grant, some service — even if merely symbolic — was thought due. A father granting land to a younger son might require yearly an arrow, feathered with eagle's feathers, or from a daughter a red rose at midsummer. One Rowland is recorded as having held 110 acres for which on Christmas Day, every year, he was to perform before the king "altogether, and once, a leap, a puff, and a fart."[3] These nominal services were not as silly as they seem. They provided evidence of the tenurial relationship and thus were important for establishing the lord's right to incidents, which we shall discuss momentarily.

(3) Religious Tenures

For a society ruled by the sword and the cross, it was important to bestow land on the church. But here again, the notion that land must be held to enhance the power of a temporal lord required some service from the ecclesiastics, which might be knight service or socage or singing mass every Friday or, if no specific services were retained, to pray for the repose of the grantor's soul. This last service was called frankalmoign.

The military tenures, socage, and the religious tenures were free tenures held by free men. Free men were vassals but not peasants; they were men of power, almost always in uneasy tension with the crown.

b. Unfree Tenure: Villeinage

The king and the greater lords almost always kept possession of some choice portion of their lands for a castle or a manor house, with

---

3. Thomas Blount, Ancient Tenures 60 (2d ed. 1784).

surrounding farm and pasturage. Peasants who worked the manorial lands were called villeins (from *vill,* a settlement often but not always coinciding with a manorial unit).[4] In the early years after the Conquest, these peasants, comprising the vast majority of the tenant population, held their land at the will of the lord of the manor and were denied protection by the king's courts. In this sense villeins were not part of the feudal system based upon personal loyalty and service contracts, but held their land by a much more precarious relationship. Nonetheless, in time villein tenants came to hold "by the custom of the manor"; their rights were set forth on manorial records and a copy given to the tenants. With this change their holdings came to be called copyhold. By the fifteenth century copyholders had gained entry into the royal courts, which assisted any tenant ejected by the lord in any manner not in accordance with the custom of the manor. By the civil wars of the seventeenth century their holdings had become as secure as freeholds; copyhold had lost its taint of servility and had become merely another form of landholding.[5]

It is unclear and disputed what role townsfolk or burghers played in feudal society. Traditional theory only accounts for the 95 percent of the population that lived on and from the land. Some of the burghers did become rich in trade, but they played no large part in government outside the walls of their cities. Land, not commerce, was power.

3. Feudal Incidents

Besides the services, a tenant owed other duties and was subject to several liabilities benefitting his lord. These were called *incidents.* Feudal services were fixed obligations. In the course of the Middle Ages, the economic importance of services declined because they could not be changed when social conditions or money values made them outmoded. Many of the services were commuted into money rents, which lost value with inflation, particularly during the thirteenth and fourteenth centuries. On the other hand, feudal incidents, which gave the lord possession of the land or its equivalent, kept pace with inflation and maintained their value. Thus the feudal incidents, jealously guarded by the crown, lasted long after the feudal services disappeared.

The feudal incidents were as follows:

4. From the medieval mind, with its strong class bias, comes the modern meaning of a villain as an unprincipled scoundrel.

5. Copyhold land was finally made freehold by the Law of Property Act of 1922. Copyhold tenure has never been of any importance in the United States, where all land either is held as freehold from the state or is held allodially, i.e., with no notion of holding from anyone.

a. Homage and Fealty

In these turbulent times, when it was considered normal and just to kill a man in a fair fight, protection lay in the strength and backing of a powerful overlord. Hence homage, binding man to man, was one of the most significant features of feudal society.

Each military tenant did homage to his lord in a solemn ceremony. He knelt, put his hands between the lord's hands, swore a binding oath of loyalty, and thereby became the lord's man. William and his successors shrewdly required a separate oath of loyalty to the crown. Therefore the tenant might say: "I become your man from this day forward for the tenement which I hold of you, and I will bear you faith in life and limb and earthly worship against all men, saving only the faith I owe to our sovereign lord the king." Since a man gave his allegiance to the king, he deserved the king's protection in a dispute with his lord.[6]

b. Aids

In a financial emergency a lord could demand aid from his tenants. At first, the occasions for aids were many, but in 1215 Magna Carta limited aids to three occasions: the ransoming of the lord from his captors, the knighting of his eldest son, and the marriage of his eldest daughter.

c. Forfeiture

Although the lords had accepted by the thirteenth century the principle of hereditary succession (i.e., a tenant's son inherited his position), they insisted on the principle of revocability or forfeiture. Above all the lord needed loyal vassals. If a tenant breached his oath of loyalty or refused to perform feudal services, his land was forfeited to the lord. If a tenant were guilty of high treason, the king was entitled to seize and keep the tenant's land, whether held from the king or a mesne lord.

---

6. The rise of the royal courts was largely due to the king's acts to protect free tenants from their lords, who used self-help to dispossess their tenants unjustly. In 1166 Henry II issued an ordinance giving the dispossessed free tenant a speedy remedy to recover possession; this was called the *assize of novel disseisin*. A jury was summoned to determine whether the tenant had been in prior possession and had been ousted without a judgment; if so, the tenant was entitled to be put back in possession. Some ten years later the *assize of mort d'ancestor* was instituted to permit an heir to claim, on the death of his ancestor, possession of land from which he was unjustly excluded by the lord. Thus the lords could not vindicate their claims by self-help, but were required to get a judgment to dispossess free tenants. Compare the treatment of leasehold tenants at pages 489-499.

d. Liabilities at Death of Tenant

Wardship and marriage. When a tenant died, leaving an heir under 21, the tenant's lord was the heir's guardian. As guardian he was entitled to possession and to the rents and profits from the land for his own use; he had only to provide the heir subsistence and not commit waste. The lord also had the right to sell the heir in marriage. If the heir refused a suitable marriage, he had to pay a fine. Wardship and marriage ended when the tenant came of age.

Wardship and marriage applied only to the military tenures. These incidents were justified originally on the grounds that the lord had to be compensated for his loss of military services while the heir was a minor; it was also said that the lord would protect the young heir from malevolent relatives ("keep the lamb from the wolves"). Control over marriage of a female heir may have been necessary to keep her from marrying the son of an enemy who, as husband, gained control of the wife's lands,[7] but it was extended to control of marriage of male heirs as well. After land became alienable, and knight's service was transformed into a money payment, wardship and marriage were simply windfalls to the lord. Since the lord was not accountable for the profits, he could — and often did — sell the wardship or the marriage.

Relief. When a tenant died, the heir had to pay the lord an appropriate sum, perhaps a year's rent, to come into his inheritance. The sum paid was called a relief, to "relieve" the land from the lord's grasp.

Given that the life expectancy of males in the centuries after the Conquest was hardly more than 35 years — such was the effect of disease and violence — the overlord might reasonably expect to have wardship and marriage one out of every four years over any substantial period of time. A relief might become payable once a decade. These incidents were thus very lucrative.

Escheat. If a tenant died without heirs, the land returned to the lord from whom it was held. Similarly, if a tenant were convicted of a felony, the land escheated to the lord after the king had exercised his right to waste the criminal's land for a year and a day. A modified form of escheat is in force today: When a person dies intestate without heirs, the person's property escheats to the state.

---

7. Control of marriage of a female heir led, in some cases, to the practice of ravishment. If the lord turned down the man preferred by the female heir, she might be abducted kicking and screaming (but not too much) and ravished by the man. The law then gave the pair a choice: marry or the ravisher must die. Thus did the female heir get her chosen mate, but the lord extracted a fine for their playing fast and loose with his rights.

4. Avoidance of Taxes (i.e., Feudal Incidents)

One of the persistent themes of English and American legal history is the continuing effort of the rich to avoid taxes. As we shall see, some very important statutes and doctrines had the purpose or effect of curbing tax avoidance, with mixed results.

In early feudal times there were two ways to transfer possession of land. A tenant in demesne could *substitute* for himself some new tenant who would hold the land from his lord. Substitution required the lord's consent and homage to the lord from the new tenant. Or the tenant could add, without the lord's consent, a new rung to the bottom of the feudal ladder, becoming a mesne lord himself and having a tenant who rendered him services. As we saw at page 194, this was called *subinfeudation*.[8] The feudal system was originally built on the principle of subinfeudation; in a society where land was almost the sole form of capital wealth, it was normal for the seller to take payment in the form of continuing rent or services charged upon the land.

Subinfeudation could not diminish the feudal services because a lord could proceed directly against the tenant in possession, using the remedies of distraint and distress and, ultimately, expulsion. But subinfeudation could be used to avoid the feudal incidents. Suppose that T, holding of L by knight service, subinfeudated to the church in frankalmoign or to $T1$, reserving as service one rose at midsummer. Knight service must still be rendered L, but this subinfeudation seriously devalued L's incidents of wardship, marriage, relief, and escheat. Instead of L getting possession of the land when T died with a minor heir or without heirs, L was entitled to whatever service T could claim from the church or $T1$ — prayers, one rose, whatever.

5. Statute Quia Emptores (1290)

The king and the barons, with much to lose by subinfeudation, took steps to curb this practice. In 1272 Edward I ascended the throne, ruling until 1307. Edward, who is remembered largely because of important reform legislation passed during his reign, made Parliament so important that after him no king could rule without it. One of the first great enactments was the Statute De Viris Religiosis (Statute of Mortmain), which in 1279 provided that any land conveyed to the church was forfeited to the lord. This statute, which was directed only toward subinfeudations to the church, was too narrowly conceived. In 1290 a broader attack was mounted. The Statute Quia Emptores prohibited subinfeu-

---

8. The distinction between substitution and subinfeudation is very similar to the distinction between assignment and subleasing in landlord-tenant law. See pages 475-476.

dation altogether, and thus the mischief of devaluing feudal incidents by this route was stopped.

Quia Emptores (taking its name from the first two words of the statute, written in Latin) was a great statute which attempted to shore up the feudal system but actually marked the beginning of the end. It prohibited subinfeudation in fee simple.[9] But as a price for putting an end to subinfeudation, the great lords had to concede to all free tenants the right to substitute a new tenant for all or part of their land without the lord's consent. The new tenant would hold of the lord by the same services as the old, and if only part of the land were conveyed to a new tenant the feudal services were to be apportioned. The major historic consequences of Quia Emptores were two. The statute established a principle of free alienation of land, which turned out to be a major force in the development of property law. Second, in time, with the working of escheat and forfeiture, existing mesne lordships tended to disappear and most land came to be held directly from the crown. As it turned out, the one person who had nothing to lose and all to gain by the statute was the king. By the time of the Tudors, mesne lords had become uncommon, and Henry VIII, perceiving that feudal incidents could be sources of substantial revenue, doggedly pursued their collection. He forced through the Statute of Uses (1536), designed primarily to prevent evasions of these incidents, and set up the Court of Wards and Liveries to collect them. We shall return to this thread of the story later at page 277.

6. The Decline of Feudalism

After Quia Emptores, with free substitution permitted, the relation between tenant and lord was basically an economic one. The tenant was now the "owner"; services and incidents were a form of taxes. The personal relationship — a key feature of the feudal system — was dying.

Feudalism atrophied with the rise of an economy based upon wages and not upon rendering services. Sixty years after Quia Emptores, a sequence of plagues beginning with the Black Death in 1349 wiped out a huge number of villein tenants. The survivors could obtain well-paid work outside the manor; many became wage earners who rented their dwellings. The manors had to turn to hired labor. When wages rose swiftly, the landlords and employers of labor attempted to freeze wages by a parliamentary act, the Statute of Labourers, but the laws of supply and demand proved stronger than those of Parliament. Wages continued to rise, and peasants, welcoming independence, continued to escape from the communal obligations of manorial life.

Yet so important a social system as feudalism, which governed peo-

9. The fee simple — the greatest estate known to law — is discussed beginning at page 205. Subinfeudation of lesser estates was not prohibited, and Quia Emptores proved no block to the development of modern landlord-tenant law.

ple's lives for several centuries, did not perish outright. Feudalism has its continuations in the law, as we shall see.

William Cunningham, The Growth of English Industry and Commerce
462-466 (5th ed. 1910)

Medieval economy with its constant regard to the *relations of persons* was giving place to modern economy which treats the *exchange of things* as fundamental; and this has introduced an extraordinary simplification in the structure of society; the whole of the complicated industrial orga- nisations of the middle ages have passed away, and the strong *espirit- de-corps*, which gave so much healthy life in many cities, has also disappeared. Economically we have only three broad divisions in society, for men arrange themselves according to the things they own and ex- change; they may exchange their labour for wages, or they may ex- change the use of their capital for interest, or they may exchange the use of their land for rent. In modern societies Labourers, Capitalists and Landlords are the three classes which group themselves round the pos- session of the power to labour, the possession of wealth and the posses- sion of land. This is the social structure we habitually assume, but it is strangely unlike the municipal and manorial life it has superseded.

The change which has so altered the structure of society has also affected the individuals who compose it; the old burgess society has doubtless been idealised to an absurd extent; but it had this striking characteristic, that the ordinary object of ambition was not so much that of rising out of one's grade, but of standing well in that grade; the citizen did not aim at being a knight, but at being warden and master of his gild, or alderman and mayor of his town. For good or for evil we have but little sympathy with these humble ambitions; everyone desires to rise in the world himself; and the philanthropic construct social ladders by which the poorest child may climb to the highest rank, as was done by ecclesiastics in the middle ages. And with this changed social structure, and changed social ambition, money has come to have a new importance for the individual who possesses it. In the older days coinage had given a unit for the comparison of one kind of wares with another; but it was not an object which men were likely to seek after, except in so far as they desired to lay by for a rainy day. If they had large sums at command they could not invest them; and, so far as the greater part of the popu- lation were concerned, their food and clothing were practically deter- mined by their status in the social system. So long as prices were arranged by calculation, there must have been comparatively little vari- ation in the real reward which a man got for his labour; and while pay- ments were partly made in kind, attention was not directed forcibly to money as a purchasing power. But with competition prices all this changed; the amount of comforts a man could procure no longer depended on the regulations of his gild, but on the purchasing power of the money he obtained by the sale of his wares. Statesmen aimed at something more than regulating the coinage so as to have a definite unit for the comparison of wares; money had come to be a thing for which everyone sought, not exactly for its own sake, but because of its *purchasing power;* it was a convenient representative of all other objects of wealth, and, as such, a thing of which each man desired to have as much as possible. From this time forward the *desire of wealth,* as the means of gratifying the desire of social distinction and all else, became a much more important factor in economic affairs than it had been before.

These changes had a very important bearing on all questions of commercial morality; so long as economic dealings were based on a system of personal relationships they all had an implied moral character. To supply a bad article was morally wrong, to demand excessive payment for goods or for labour was extortion, and the right or wrong of every transaction was easily understood; but when all dealings are considered as so many instances of exchange in an open market, the case is different. No compulsion was put upon either party to the exchange; and if either of them came badly off, it might be regarded as his fault or his misfortune; but it was not always easy to say that the other party to the transaction was to blame. In every case of exchange one party has an advantage; he may have superior knowledge, or he may be less anxious to come to terms, and he can therefore afford to wait; in either case he is able to drive the better bargain. There are extreme limits which define whether any transaction shall take place or no; and though the advantage which accrues within these limits is not often equally divided, there is no apparent moral wrong in taking full advantage of the power of driving a good bargain under conditions of free competition. In many · cases the weaker has gone to the wall; and some writers have even formulated an iron law of wages which states the existence of an irresistible tendency on the part of the employer to drive down the labourer. Though this appears to be a decided overstatement, the fact remains that there is really no means of applying moral judgments to economic affairs at present; "supply and demand" are taken as ultimate; and so long as transactions are above-board and in accordance with market rates, the ordinary modern conscience is unable to go behind these circumstances and discuss how far they are right or wrong.

Henry Maine, Ancient Law
180-182 (10th ed. 1906, Frederick Pollock new ed. 1930)
(1st ed. London 1861)

The movement of progressive societies has been uniform in one respect. Through all its course it has been distinguished by the gradual dissolution of family dependency, and the growth of individual obligation in its place. The Individual is steadily substituted for the Family, as the unit of which civil laws take account. . . .

The word *Status* may be usefully employed to construct a formula expressing the law of progress thus indicated, which, whatever be its value, seems to me to be sufficiently ascertained. All the forms of Status taken notice of in the Law of Persons were derived from, and to some extent are still coloured by, the powers and privileges anciently residing in the Family. If then we employ Status, agreeably with the usage of the best writers, to signify these personal conditions only, and avoid applying the term to such conditions as are the immediate or remote result of agreement, we may say that the movement of the progressive societies has hitherto been a movement *from Status to Contract.*

NOTES AND QUESTIONS

1. In feudal times, possession of land gave security and sustenance. The land tenancy was the focus of obligations and benefits. Today a job gives income security, health insurance, pensions, and other benefits. In the United States, most workers are governed by the common law rule, developed in the nineteenth century, that workers can be discharged at the will of the employer unless the worker has contracted for a different rule. It has been argued that workers should be dischargeable only for just cause. Would this be a good idea? Would this be a return from contract to status? Would it mean that a job is "property"? In thinking about these questions, consider the following:

> We have become a nation of employees. We are dependent upon others for our means of livelihood, and most of our people have become completely dependent upon wages. If they lose their jobs they lose every resource, except for the relief supplied by the various forms of social security. Such dependence of the mass of the people upon others for *all* of their income is something new in the world. *For our generation, the substance of life is in another man's hands.* [Frank Tannenbaum, A Philosophy of Labor 9 (1951) (emphasis in original).]

For discussion, see Jack M. Beermann & Joseph W. Singer, Baseline Questions in Legal Reasoning: The Example of Property in Jobs, 23 Ga. L. Rev. 911 (1989); Matthew P. Bergman, Status, Contract, and History: A Dialectical View, 13 Cardozo L. Rev. 171, 203–216 (1991); Richard A. Epstein, In Defense of the Contract at Will, 51 U. Chi. L. Rev. 947 (1984).

2. The Fifth Amendment to the U.S. Constitution provides that "[n]o person shall . . . be deprived of life, liberty, or property, without

due process of law." The government provides numerous benefits in accordance with status — public assistance, for example, and unemployment compensation, social security, and the like. These benefits are not alienable and may not be contracted away. Should they be treated as "property" and accorded procedural due process protection against arbitrary actions of the bureaucracy? Would this enhance individual autonomy and independence? Would it mark a return to linking rights with status (a "new feudalism")? See Charles A. Reich, The New Property, 73 Yale L.J. 733 (1964); Note, Government Promises and Due Process: An Economic Analysis of the New Property, 77 Va. L. Rev. 1053 (1991); Symposium: The New Property and the Individual — 25 Years Later, 24 U.S.F. L. Rev. 221 (1990).

3. Occasionally in this country one runs across feudal services reserved by a grantor before the American Revolution. Here's one instance. In 1772 Henry William Stiegel and his wife conveyed to their fellow Lutherans in Manheim, Pennsylvania, a plot of ground on which to build a church — for five shillings and "in the month of June yearly forever hereafter the rent of one red rose if the same shall be lawfully demanded." On the second Sunday in June, each year, the Zion Evangelical Lutheran Church of Manheim continues to pay the feudal obligation of one red rose to a Stiegel descendant.

See also the quit rents reserved by the Dutch patroons and other great landowners in New York, Pennsylvania, and Maryland, discussed in footnote 31 on page 887.

B. The Fee Simple

Out of feudalism developed a system of estates in land. A tenant had a *status* as a tenant of the fee or a tenant for life. In the course of time status became *estate*. Each estate is defined by the length of time it may endure. A fee simple may endure forever; a life estate, for the life of a person; a term of years, for some period of time measured by the calendar. The estate system is central to our laws, both in theory and in practice.

1. How the Fee Simple Developed

a. Rise of Heritability

One of the key features of feudalism after the Conquest was that land was not owned by the possessor but was held by the possessor as tenant of someone else. Because of the highly personal nature of the lord-tenant relationship, in the period immediately following the Conquest the tenant's holding (called his fee or fief) could not be inherited by his heir; in effect the tenant had only lifetime tenure. Upon the tenant's death his time on the land ceased, and the lord was under no obligation to recognize the tenant's heir as his successor. After all, the heir might be a weakling and useless as a knight. Customarily, though, for an appropriate sum (a relief) the lord would regrant the land to the heir, securing from him homage and an oath of fealty. In time the lord recognized an obligation to admit the dead tenant's son, and so, in advance, would consent to descent. This advance consent was denoted by a conveyance from the lord "to A and his heirs." Still later, by the beginning of the thirteenth century, inheritance of a fee became a matter of right, but the payment of a relief to the lord continued.

b.   Rise of Alienability

In the first 200 years after the Conquest the fee was not freely alienable inter vivos and was not devisable by will; hence the practical effect of a conveyance "to A and his heirs" was to give A a fee that would pass to A's heir, to the heir's heir, and so on down the centuries. But time soon worked a change. The great expansion of the rural population in the thirteenth century resulted in land hunger. Increasingly men sought land; its value rose; and landholders were frequently tempted to sell before they died and cut off the heirs' rights to succession. With this increasing demand for land, the idea that a tenant should be able to convey the fee to another during his life openly and without the lord's consent began to gain currency. By the end of the thirteenth century, Quia Emptores settled that the fee was freely alienable.

c.   Rise of the Fee Simple Estate

Once the fee became alienable, the feudal realities behind a conveyance to A "and his heirs" became meaningless. This transformation is vividly illustrated in connection with escheat. Suppose that L conveys land "to A and his heirs" and subsequently A conveys the land "to B and his heirs." Then A dies without heirs. Will the land escheat to L? Soon after Quia Emptores the judges answered no; the land will escheat only if the current tenant of the fee dies without heirs. Thus the fee, which started out as simply a *holding*, became an alienable fee simple, a *freehold estate* not terminable at the will of the lord, with an existence all its own.

The development of the fee simple estate is an example of that most striking phenomenon of English land law, the reification of abstractions, a process of thinking that still pervades our law. Instead of thinking of the land itself, the lawyer thinks of an *estate in land,* which is imagined as almost having a real existence apart from the land.[10] *O,* owner of Blackacre, has an estate known as a *fee simple,* which is given the qualities and characteristics of a thing. During life, *O* can convey his fee simple to another; if he owns the fee simple at death, it passes under his will or descends to his heirs. Creditors may reach the fee simple and sell it to pay debts in default. Note how, in the preceding two sentences, we have spoken of a fee simple as a thing. In the next chapter we shall talk of future estates in land as things: They vest, divest, merge, are destroyed, shift, spring. These estates are almost visible entities. Imagining estates was a wonderful flight of the judicial mind in the thirteenth century, and now, after hundreds of years, it seems a quite natural way of regarding that which we cannot see. (Bear in mind, however, that modern analysis insists that an estate is "a bundle of rights," that is, estate is a word denoting legal relations between persons with respect to a thing.[11] What rights are in the bundle involves issues of public policy, not merely an analysis of qualities of imagined objects, and rights in the bundle have varied from century to century and from place to place.)

The fee simple is absolute ownership, so far as our law recognizes absolute ownership. It is the largest estate in terms of duration. It may endure forever.

Interests in personal property. Although the law of estates grew out of dispositions of land, courts permitted the same kinds of interests to be created in personal property. For historical reasons there is a fee simple only in land, not in personal property. The analogue to a fee simple is "absolute ownership" of personalty. But occasionally people speak of a fee simple in personal property, and no great harm is done.

2. Creation of a Fee Simple

At early common law a fee simple was created by the grantor conveying land "to *A and his* [or her] *heirs.*" As noted above, the words "and his heirs," inserted in a conveyance, indicated that *A*'s interest in the land was inheritable by his heirs, but such words did not give *A*'s prospective heirs any interest in the land. *A*'s son would inherit the land from *A* if *A*

___

10. Professor Reed Powell of Harvard, in a penetrating quip, thus described this attitude: "If you think you can think about something which is attached to something else without thinking about what it is attached to, then you have what is called a legal mind." Quoted in Thurman Arnold, Criminal Attempts — The Rise and Fall of an Abstraction, 40 Yale L.J. 53, 58 (1930).

11. Analyzing rights in land to be legal relations between persons with respect to land, and not — as older analysis had it — legal relations of a person to the land, was given systematic exposition by Wesley N. Hohfeld in the first quarter of the twentieth century, and was adopted by Restatement of Property §§1-10 (1936).

still owned the land at his death, but A's son had no interest during A's lifetime.

The judges reached this result by construing the words "and his heirs" as *words of limitation,* which define the estate granted to A, to wit, a fee simple. The heirs do not take as "purchasers," an old common law word referring to persons who are given an interest in land by an instrument (as opposed to persons who inherit land by intestate succession). In a conveyance "to A and his heirs," then, the words "to A" are *words of purchase,* identifying A as the grantee, and the words "and his heirs" are words of limitation indicating that A takes a fee simple.

At common law, words indicating that the land was inheritable, such as to A "and his heirs," were necessary to create a fee simple.[12] This remained true long after the original reason for inserting "and his heirs" in feudal conveyances disappeared. But it is no longer necessary to put words of inheritance in a deed, except possibly in Maine and South Carolina. Statutes and judicial decisions now provide that a grantor is presumed, in the absence of words indicating otherwise, to transfer the grantor's entire estate. A grant by O "to A," without more, conveys a fee simple to A. Although the phrase "and his heirs" is no longer required, lawyers, being creatures of habit, continue to insert it.

PROBLEMS

1. In 1600 O conveys Blackacre "to A for life, then to B forever." What estates do A and B have? If A dies and then B dies, who owns Blackacre? Suppose the conveyance takes place in 1992?

2. In 1600 O conveys Whiteacre "to A for life, remainder to the heirs of B." B is alive in 1600 but dies soon thereafter. B's heir is C. Subsequently A dies. What estate does C have?

3. O conveys Greenacre "to A and her heirs." A's only child, B, is a spendthrift and runs up large, unpaid bills. B's creditors can attach B's property to satisfy their claims. Does B have an interest in Greenacre, reachable by B's creditors? Suppose A wishes to sell Greenacre and use the proceeds to take a trip around the world. Can B prevent A from doing this?

---

12. A conveyance "to A, his successors and assigns forever" or "to A in fee simple" gave A a life estate only. In a will "and his heirs" was never necessary. In earlier times any words indicating that the testator intended a fee simple would suffice, e.g., "to A absolutely." Today it is assumed that the testator intends to dispose of as large an estate as the testator had.

3.   Inheritance of a Fee Simple

Now you are going to have to master some technical terms often used imprecisely by nonlawyers, but if you pay close attention you will not find them difficult. They are the common coinage of hundreds of problems relating to inheritance.

Heirs.   If a person dies intestate (that is, without a will), the decedent's real property descends to his or her heirs.[13] Heirs are persons who survive the decedent and are designated as intestate successors under the state's statute of descent. No one is heir of the living; a living person has no heirs (yet!). Hence, if there is a conveyance to "the heirs of A, a living person," we do not know who will take until A dies and A's heirs are ascertained.

A spouse was not an heir at common law; a spouse was given only dower or curtesy in land (see pages 400-401). Today in almost all states the surviving spouse is designated as an intestate successor of some share in the decedent's land; the size of the share often depends on who else survives. For example, the surviving spouse might take one-half if the decedent leaves one child, one-third if the decedent leaves two or more children, and all if the decedent leaves no children, no more remote issue, and no parents.

Under modern statutes of descent, classes of kindred are usually preferred as heirs in the following manner: first issue; and if no issue, then parents; and if none, then collaterals.

Issue.   If the decedent leaves issue, they take to the exclusion of all other kindred. The word issue is synonymous with descendants. Despite its physiological specificity, issue does not refer to children only but includes further descendants. The distribution is made among the decedent's issue per stirpes ("by the stocks"), which generally means that if any child of the decedent dies before the decedent leaving children who survive the decedent, such child's share goes to his or her children by right of representation.

After the Norman Conquest, until 1925, the rule of primogeniture applied to most of the land in England. The eldest son inherited the land. If the eldest son predeceased the decedent, leaving issue, his issue represented him under some rather complex rules always preferring males over females of equal degree of kinship. Only if there were no sons would the decedent's daughters inherit. Once appropriate for the military tenures, primogeniture — the law of the great folk — became

---

13. The persons who succeed to an intestate's personal property are called next of kin. At common law, where primogeniture applied to land but not to personal property, heir and next of kin were not necessarily the same. Today in most states the same persons succeed to land and to personal property.

the common law for almost all. Primogeniture was followed in some American states before the Revolution, but was completely abolished by the end of the eighteenth century. Children now share equally.

A child born out of wedlock was *filius nullius,* the child of no one, and could inherit from neither mother nor father at common law. Today a child born out of wedlock inherits from the mother and, if paternity is acknowledged or proved, from the father. Adoption was unknown in England until 1926. Today, in American states, adopted children inherit from their adoptive parents and sometimes from their natural parents as well.

Ancestors.   By statute parents usually take as heirs if the decedent leaves no issue.

Collaterals.   All persons related by blood to the decedent who are neither descendants nor ancestors are collateral kin. This includes brothers, sisters, nephews, nieces, uncles, aunts, and cousins. If a decedent leaves no spouse, no issue, and no parents, the decedent's brothers and sisters (and their descendants by representation) take in all jurisdictions. The rules for determining which of the more remote collateral kindred take were rather complicated at common law and remain so today.

Escheat.   If a person died intestate without any heirs, the person's real property escheated to the overlord in feudal times. Now such property escheats to the state where the property is located. If no next of kin could be found, the personal property of an intestate went to the crown under the principle of *bona vacantia* (goods without an owner). Today such property goes to the state.

NOTES AND PROBLEMS

1. In early feudal England it was common in many manors for villein tenements to descend to the youngest rather than the eldest son. Forced to choose one child as heir, why would the king and barons prefer the eldest son while many of the lower class preferred the youngest son? Some persons have imagined a connection with the *jus prima nox* (the right of the lord to spend the first night with his tenant's bride), but Blackstone says this custom never existed in England, though it did in Scotland until abolished by Malcolm III, successor to Macbeth. 2 William Blackstone, Commentaries *83.

2. *O,* owner of Blackacre, has two children, *A* (daughter) and *B* (son). Subsequently *B* dies testate, devising all his property to his wife, *W. B* is survived by three children, *B1* (daughter), *B2* (son), and *B3*

(daughter). *A1* (son) is born to *A*. Then *O* dies intestate. Who owns Blackacre in England in 1800? Under modern American law?

3. *O* conveys Blackacre "to *A* and her heirs." If *A* dies intestate without issue, will Blackacre escheat to the state? *parents or collaterals*

4. *O* conveys Blackacre "to *A* for life, remainder to *B* and her heirs." *B ancestors or collaterals* *B* then dies intestate without heirs. *A* then dies. Who owns Blackacre?

5. Once the estates system developed, judges decided that standardization of estates furthered alienability by facilitating subsequent transactions in the same resources. Hence, a fee simple, which is defined as an estate capable of being inherited by whoever turns out to be the heirs of the fee simple owner, can have no limitations put upon its inheritability. This distinguishes the fee simple from the fee tail (below). Except for a limitation that creates a fee tail, a limitation that purports to limit inheritance to a particular class of heirs creates a fee simple, inheritable by heirs generally. Example: Royal Whiton, not overly fond of his daughter-in-law and her family, devises land "to my granddaughter Sarah and her heirs on her father's side." Sarah takes a fee simple. It can be inherited by her heirs on her mother's side. Johnson v. Whiton, 159 Mass. 424, 34 N.E. 542 (1893) ("A man cannot create a new kind of inheritance," per Holmes, J.). If your client does not want his granddaughter's heirs on her mother's side to inherit the land, how should his will be drafted?

C. The Fee Tail

One of the great and continuing conflicts in the development of English property law arose out of the desire of the heads of rich families to make land inalienable. In a real sense, land was family power, status, and wealth, and those who controlled it wanted to make it impossible — or, if not impossible, at least very difficult — for their descendants to alienate it. The family bond was strong; the family was thought of as a chain of ancestors and descendants extending through time, with the primogenitary heir as current head.

The medieval dynasts sought an estate where the current owner could not cut off the inheritance rights of his issue. In the earliest period after the Conquest, they attempted to create such an estate by a conveyance "to *A* and the heirs of his body." The purpose was to give the land to *A* and his descendants, generation after generation. The courts, however, held that if issue were born to *A*, *A* could transfer a fee simple, cutting off the inheritance rights of his issue. Hence the estate was known as a *fee simple conditional*, a fee simple conditional upon having issue.

The judicial construction of this kind of grant was much resented by the barons, who in 1258 petitioned Parliament to redress their grievances. In 1285 Parliament responded by enacting the Statute de Donis Conditionalibus, which replaced the fee simple conditional with the *fee tail*.[14] A fee tail, like the superseded fee simple conditional, is an estate in land created by a conveyance "to A and the heirs of his body."[15] It is an estate precisely tailored to the desires of the medieval dynasts. The fee tail descends to *A*'s lineal descendants ("heirs of the body") generation after generation,[16] and it expires when the original tenant in fee tail, *A*, and all of *A*'s descendants are dead. When *A*'s bloodline runs out and the fee tail ends, the land will revert to the grantor or the grantor's heirs by way of reversion or, if specified in the instrument, will go to some other branch of the family. For example, *O* might convey land "to my son *A* and the heirs of his body, and if *A* dies without issue, to my daughter *B* and her heirs." By this conveyance *A* is given a fee tail and *B* is given a remainder in fee simple to become possessory when and if the fee tail expires. Every fee tail has a reversion or a remainder after it.

As originally authorized by the Statute de Donis, the tenant in fee tail could alienate his possessory interest, which ends upon his death, but he could not affect the rights of his issue to succeed to the land upon his death. In the 200 years after de Donis, the king and the judges began to perceive many mischiefs in the inability of the fee tail tenant to cut out succession by his issue. As Blackstone noted,

> Children grew disobedient when they knew they could not be set aside: farmers were ousted of their leases made by tenants in tail; for, if such leases had been valid, then under colour of long leases the issue might have been virtually disinherited: creditors were defrauded of their debts; for, if a tenant in tail could have charged his estate with their payment, he might also have defeated his issue, by mortgaging it for as much as it was worth: innumerable latent entails were produced to deprive purchasers of the lands they had fairly bought; of suits in consequence of which our ancient books are full: and treasons are encouraged; as estates-tail were not liable to forfeiture longer than for the tenant's life. [2 William Blackstone, Commentaries *116.]

The king was interested primarily in the last item on Blackstone's list. Soon after the enactment of De Donis, the great barons over-

---

14. In Iowa and South Carolina, courts have held that the Statute de Donis is not in force because its purpose of maintaining a landed aristocracy is contrary to American institutions. Hence a fee simple conditional, obsolete in England since 1285, can be created in these two states. See 2 Richard R. Powell, The Law of Real Property ¶195 (rev. ed. 1992).

15. A conveyance "to *A* and his issue" or "to *A* and his children" might create a fee tail, but the law was complicated by the necessity for the word *heirs* in a deed and by rules laid down in Wild's Case. See 5 American Law of Property §§22.15-22.28 (1952).

16. A *fee tail male* could also be created, limiting descent to male heirs of the body. Or a *fee tail special* might be created in a marriage settlement, limiting descent to issue of the husband by a named (special) wife.

whelmed the monarchy and became the ruling class contending for the crown. There followed the anarchic period in English history culminating in the Wars of the Roses. When Edward IV took the throne in 1461 he observed how the great families had developed in the fee tail a secure land base from which they could challenge the king, a sanctuary on which attainder for high treason had little effect. Common law forfeiture for high treason was *in personam*. It was imposed as punishment; the traitor's interest in land was forfeited to the crown. A traitorous fee tail tenant thus forfeited only his fee tail in land, not the land itself; after his death, his eldest son retook possession as the successor fee tail tenant and often renewed the challenge to the crown.

After defeating the Lancastrian forces in 1471, Edward IV began the reconstruction of the monarchy into a great power, which was achieved when Henry Tudor (head of the house of Lancaster) married Edward's daughter Elizabeth of York and acceded to the throne as Henry VII in 1485. In Taltarum's Case, Y.B. 12 Edw. IV, 19 (1472), with Edward's countenance, the judges approved a method by which a tenant in tail could "bar the entail." By bringing a collusive lawsuit known as a common recovery, the fee tail tenant in possession could obtain a court decree awarding him a *fee simple*, cutting off all rights of his issue and extinguishing any reversion or remainder.[17] The fee tail tenant thereby became the sole owner. If a fee tail were forfeited to the king thereafter, the king could suffer a common recovery, thereby converting the fee tail into a fee simple, removing the land from the traitorous family forever.

The common recovery was an expensive legal procedure, benefitting lawyers, but it did make the land alienable. After 400 years, in the nineteenth century, the common recovery was finally abolished, and a fee tail tenant was given power to disentail simply by conveying a fee simple by deed to another.[18]

Thwarted in Taltarum's Case, which approved a means of barring entails, lawyers for the dynastic landed gentry, who continued to desire to control inheritance, began to create life estates in one generation followed by remainders in the next generation, whence developed the modern law of future interests, discussed in the next chapter.

---

17. If you really want to get into the details of the common recovery, with all its legal hocus pocus, see A.W.B. Simpson, A History of the Land Law 125-138 (2d ed. 1986).

18. The power to disentail did not end the usefulness of the fee tail in England. Only a fee tail tenant *in possession* could disentail. Some 200 years after Taltarum's Case, lawyers for landowners seized upon this requirement to create what became known as a "strict settlement." In brief, land was limited to *A* for life, than to *A*'s eldest son in tail, then to *A*'s second son in tail, and so forth. When *A*'s eldest son, *B*, became of age or married, *A* surrendered possession to *B*, who suffered a common recovery, giving *B* a fee simple. *B* then turned around and made a new limitation to *A* for life, then to *B* for life, then to *B*'s eldest son in tail, and so forth. Thus inalienability was pushed forward generation by generation. The fee tail was abolished in England in 1925.

Abolition of the Fee Tail

For Thomas Jefferson, the fee tail and primogeniture were odious means of perpetuating a hereditary aristocracy. Jefferson persuaded the Virginia legislature to abolish both around the time of the American Revolution, and other legislatures soon followed suit. Today the fee tail can be created only in Delaware, Maine, Massachusetts, and Rhode Island. In these states, a fee tail tenant can bar the entail by conveying a fee simple by deed. Because the fee tail can no longer be used effectively to control inheritance of land, it is rarely encountered.

About the only problem related to the fee tail that arises in modern times is this: When an instrument uses language that would have created a fee tail at common law, what estate is thereby created today? Suppose that O conveys "to my son A and the heirs of his body, and if A dies without issue to my daughter B and her heirs." What interests are created under modern law?

In each state in which the fee tail is abolished, a statute specifies what estate is created in A by the language of O's conveyance and what interest, if any, is created in B. Although a few states provide that A takes a life estate, and A's issue take a remainder in fee simple, the large majority of states fall into one of two categories. In states falling into the first category, statutes provide that a limitation "to A and the heirs of his body" creates a fee simple in A, and that any gift over on A's death without issue is void. Neither A's issue nor B takes anything under the above conveyance. The justification for this type of statute is that inasmuch as A could disentail and destroy the interests of A's issue and B, the statute does it automatically.

In states in the second category, statutes provide that a limitation "to A and the heirs of his body" creates a fee simple in A, but they further provide that a gift over to B if A dies without issue will be given effect in one circumstance. B will take the fee simple if, and only if, *at A's death*, A leaves no surviving issue (and not, as at common law, when A's whole line of issue runs out).[19] If A leaves surviving issue at his death, B's interest fails, and A's fee simple cannot be divested thereafter. In such case, A can devise his fee simple to whomever he chooses.

In these states, does abolition of the fee tail make land more alienable or less alienable than it was at common law? If the latter, what is the justification for abolishing the fee tail in the manner provided by statute? If you want details on these and other statutory substitutes, see 2 Richard R. Powell, The Law of Real Property ¶198 (rev. ed. 1992).

---

19. B's future interest is known as a divesting executory interest, which will shift the fee simple to B if A leaves no issue at his death. Executory interests are explained beginning at page 274.

NOTES AND PROBLEMS

1. *Shakespeare's dream of a male dynasty.* William Shakespeare's will illustrates perfectly the lawyer's art of creating one fee tail after another in an attempt to keep land in the hands of descendants indefinitely. It also reflects the hopes of members of the English landed class, to which Shakespeare aspired, to establish a male dynasty, a wish not granted the great dramatist.

Shakespeare died in 1616, leaving two daughters, one granddaughter, and no son. He devised his lands to his elder daughter Susanna for life; thereafter his will was driven by his desire for male descendants. On Susanna's death, the will provided that the lands were to go to Susanna's first-born son in fee tail male, and if the first-born son died without male issue, to Susanna's second-born son in fee tail male, and if the second-born son died without male issue, to Susanna's third-, fourth-, fifth-, sixth-, and seventh-born sons successively in fee tail male. If Susanna and all of these contemplated sons died without male issue, the lands were to go to Susanna's daughter Elizabeth in fee tail male, and if she died without male issue, to Shakespeare's younger daughter Judith in fee tail male, and if she died without male issue, to Shakespeare's heirs (Susanna and Judith) in fee simple. Alas, Susanna had no more children, and Elizabeth and Judith died without issue; Shakespeare's line expired upon his granddaughter Elizabeth's death in 1670. Thus none of these seven fees tail in remainder ever materialized.

Why do you suppose Shakespeare created seven successive fees tail male in remainder in Susanna's hoped-for sons, rather than two or ten? Could it be that Shakespeare had in the back of his mind the seven royal sons of Edward III who, with their progeny, were immortalized by Shakespeare in his history plays?

2. In England in 1800, *O* conveys Blackacre "to *A* and his heirs male." What estate does *A* have?

3. *O* conveys Blackacre, located in Massachusetts, "to *A* and the heirs of her body." *A* dies leaving her only child *B* as her sole heir. *B* dies without having had children, devising all her property to *C*. What is the state of the title? How should *B* have arranged her affairs to carry out her wishes?

4. *O* conveys Whiteacre "to *A* and the heirs of her body, and if *A* dies without issue to *B* and his heirs." *A* then makes a conveyance of Whiteacre "to *C* and his heirs." *A* then marries *D* and has a son *E*. *A* dies intestate. *A* is survived by *O, B, C, D,* and *E*. Who owns Whiteacre in Massachusetts? In each of the two categories of states noted above? If *E* had predeceased *A*, who would now own Whiteacre in these states?

5. *Robins Island Preservation Fund, Inc. v. Southold Development Corp., 959 F.2d 409 (2d Cir.), cert. denied, 113 S. Ct. 603 (1992).* In 1779 Parker

Wickham owned in fee tail male Robins Island, a 445-acre island in the Peconic Bay of Long Island. In that year, New York enacted an Act of Attainder, providing for forfeiture of any property owned by loyalists to the British Crown. Parker Wickham was a loyalist, and the Act of Attainder specifically convicted him of "adherence" to the British and declared all his property forfeited to the State of New York. In 1782 New York abolished the fee tail estate, converting every existing fee tail into a fee simple. Thereafter, in 1784, New York took possession of Robins Island and sold it in fee simple to Benjamin Tallmedge and Caleb Brewster from whom it passed by mesne conveyances into the hands of Southold Development Corporation, which planned to develop it.

The plaintiff, an environmental fund dedicated to the preservation of Robins Island in its natural state, bought up 75 percent of the interests, if any, held by the descendants of Parker Wickham. Plaintiff asserted that the 1779 confiscation of Parker Wickham's fee tail in Robins Island was invalid because New York then had no sovereignty over Robins Island, which was still under British control. New York took physical possession of Robins Island only after the enactment of the Treaty of Peace of 1783 between Great Britain and the United States, which prohibited future confiscations of British and loyalist property. The court rejected this contention, holding that the 1779 Act of Attainder was self-executing, automatically divesting Parker Wickham of title upon the date of passage, even though possession was not obtained until five years later. The court also found the plaintiff's claim was barred by the statute of limitations and laches.

If you want to learn more about the abolition of the fee tail in the United States and forfeiture of loyalists' property, you will find this readable opinion illuminating.

D.   The Life Estate

Because the early feudal relation between lord and tenant involved only lifetime tenure, the law had little problem recognizing an *estate for life.* Judicial recognition of a life estate had two important consequences. First, it meant that the grantor of a life estate can control who takes the property at the life tenant's death. The life estate ultimately supplanted the fee tail as a device to control inheritance. Second, as land and stocks and bonds came to be viewed as income-producing capital, trust management for the life tenant developed. Under modern trust management, one person (often a corporate person such as a bank) manages property for the benefit of the life tenant, paying the life tenant the income therefrom. Today most life estates are created in trust. The amount of property in private trusts benefitting life tenants exceeds several hundred billion dollars in this country.

A conveyance "to *A* for life" gives *A* a life estate that lasts for the duration of *A*'s life. *A* can transfer his life estate to *B*, in which case *B* has a life estate *pur autre vie* — that is, an estate that is measured by *A*'s lifespan, not *B*'s. If *B* dies during *A*'s lifetime, the life estate passes to *B*'s heirs or devisees until *A* dies. See Collins v. Held, 174 Ind. App. 584, 369 N.E.2d 641 (1977). Every life estate is followed by a future interest — either a reversion in the transferor or a remainder in a transferee.

White v. Brown
Supreme Court of Tennessee, 1977
559 S.W.2d 938

BROCK, J. This is a suit for the construction of a will. The Chancellor held that the will passed a life estate, but not the remainder, in certain realty, leaving the remainder to pass by inheritance to the testatrix's heirs at law. The Court of Appeals affirmed.

Mrs. Jessie Lide died on February 15, 1973, leaving a holographic will which, in its entirety, reads as follows:

> April 19, 1972
>
> I, Jessie Lide, being in sound mind declare this to be my last will and testament. I appoint my niece Sandra White Perry to be the executrix of my estate. I wish Evelyn White to have my home to live in and not to be sold.
> I also leave my personal property to Sandra White Perry. My house is not to be sold
>
> Jessie Lide
> (Underscoring by testatrix)

Mrs. Lide was a widow and had no children. Although she had nine brothers and sisters, only two sisters residing in Ohio survived her. These two sisters quitclaimed any interest they might have in the residence to Mrs. White. The [twelve] nieces and nephews of the testatrix, her heirs at law [other than her two sisters and Sandra White Perry], are defendants in this action.

Mrs. White, her husband, who was the testatrix's brother, and her daughter, Sandra White Perry, lived with Mrs. Lide as a family for some twenty-five years. After Sandra married in 1969 and Mrs. White's husband died in 1971, Evelyn White continued to live with Mrs. Lide until Mrs. Lide's death in 1973 at age 88.

Jessie Lide's House, 1956
Jessie Lide on right, Sandra White in middle

Mrs. White, joined by her daughter as executrix, filed this action to obtain construction of the will, alleging that she is vested with a fee simple title to the home. The defendants contend that the will conveyed only a life estate to Mrs. White, leaving the remainder to go to them under our laws of intestate succession. The Chancellor held that the will unambiguously conveyed only a life interest in the home to Mrs. White and refused to consider extrinsic evidence concerning Mrs. Lide's relationship with her surviving relatives. Due to the debilitated condition of the property and in accordance with the desire of all parties, the Chancellor ordered the property sold with the proceeds distributed in designated shares among the beneficiaries.[20]

I

Our cases have repeatedly acknowledged that the intention of the testator is to be ascertained from the language of the entire instrument when read in the light of surrounding circumstances. But, the practical difficulty in this case, as in so many other cases involving wills drafted by lay

20. The brief for the appellee states that the chancellor ordered the proceeds divided between the life tenant, Evelyn White, and the testatrix's heirs, as remaindermen, according to the value of their respective interests ascertained from life expectancy tables. See pages 225-226. — EDS.

persons, is that the words chosen by the testatrix are not specific enough to clearly state her intent. Thus, in our opinion, it is not clear whether Mrs. Lide intended to convey a life estate in the home to Mrs. White, leaving the remainder interest to descend by operation of law, or a fee interest with a restraint on alienation. Moreover, the will might even be read as conveying a fee interest subject to a condition subsequent (Mrs. White's failure to live in the home).

In such ambiguous cases it is obvious that rules of construction, always yielding to the cardinal rule of the testator's intent, must be employed as auxiliary aids in the courts' endeavor to ascertain the testator's intent.

In 1851 our General Assembly enacted two such statutes of construction, thereby creating a statutory presumption against partial intestacy.

Chapter 33 of the Public Acts of 1851 (now codified as T.C.A. §§64-101 and 64-501) reversed the common law presumption[21] that a life estate was intended unless the intent to pass a fee simple was clearly expressed in the instrument. T.C.A. §64-501 provides:

> Every grant or devise of real estate, or any interest therein, shall pass all the estate or interest of the grantor or devisor, unless the intent to pass a less estate or interest shall appear by express terms, or be necessarily implied in the terms of the instrument.

Chapter 180, Section 2 of the Public Acts of 1851 (now codified as T.C.A. §32-301) was specifically directed to the operation of a devise. In relevant part, T.C.A. §32-301 provides:

> A will . . . shall convey all the real estate belonging to [the testator] or in which he had any interest at his decease, unless a contrary intention appear by its words and context.

Thus, under our law, unless the "words and context" of Mrs. Lide's will clearly evidence her intention to convey only a life estate to Mrs. White, the will should be construed as passing the home to Mrs. White in fee. " 'If the expression in the will is doubtful, the doubt is resolved against the limitation and in favor of the absolute estate.' " Meacham v.

---

21. Because the feudal lord granted land solely as compensation for personal services, the grant was for no longer than the life of the grantee. Later the grant was extended to the sons and other issue of the grantee under the designation of "heirs." Heirs were thus entitled to stand in the place of their ancestor after his death if mentioned in the grant — but only if specifically mentioned. Thereafter, the word "heirs," when used in a conveyance to a man "and his heirs," came to include collateral as well as lineal heirs, ultimately indicating that such grantee took an estate which would pass to his heirs or the heirs of anyone to whom he aliened it. That is, "heirs," ceased to be a word of purchase and became a word of limitation. 1 Tiffany, Real Property §28 (3d ed. 1939).

Graham, 98 Tenn. 190, 206, 39 S.W. 12, 15 (1897) (quoting Washbon v. Cope, 144 N.Y. 287, 39 N.E. 388).

Several of our cases demonstrate the effect of these statutory presumptions against intestacy by construing language which might seem to convey an estate for life, without provision for a gift over after the termination of such life estate, as passing a fee simple instead. In Green v. Young, 163 Tenn. 16, 40, S.W.2d 793 (1931), the testatrix's disposition of all of her property to her husband "to be used by him for his support and comfort during his life" was held to pass a fee estate. Similarly, in Williams v. Williams, 167 Tenn. 26, 65 S.W.2d 561 (1933), the testator's devise of real property to his children "for and during their natural lives" without provision for a gift over was held to convey a fee. And, in Webb v. Webb, 53 Tenn. App. 609, 385 S.W.2d 295 (1964), a devise of personal property to the testator's wife "for her maintenance, support and comfort, for the full period of her natural life" with complete powers of alienation but without provision for the remainder passed absolute title to the widow.

II

Thus, if the sole question for our determination were whether the will's conveyance of the home to Mrs. White "to live in" gave her a life interest or a fee in the home, a conclusion favoring the absolute estate would be clearly required. The question, however, is complicated somewhat by the caveat contained in the will that the home is "not to be sold" — a restriction conflicting with the free alienation of property, one of the most significant incidents of fee ownership. We must determine, therefore, whether Mrs. Lide's will, when taken as a whole, clearly evidences her intent to convey only a life estate in her home to Mrs. White.

Under ordinary circumstances a person makes a will to dispose of his or her entire estate. If, therefore, a will is susceptible of two constructions, by one of which the testator disposes of the whole of his estate and by the other of which he disposes of only a part of his estate, dying intestate as to the remainder, this Court has always preferred that construction which disposes of the whole of the testator's estate if that construction is reasonable and consistent with the general scope and provisions of the will. A construction which results in partial intestacy will not be adopted unless such intention clearly appears. It has been said that the courts will prefer any reasonable construction or any construction which does not do violence to a testator's language, to a construction which results in partial intestacy.

The intent to create a fee simple or other absolute interest and, at the same time to impose a restraint upon its alienation can be clearly expressed. If the testator specifically declares that he devises land to *A* "in fee simple" or to *A* "and his heirs" but that *A* shall not have the power to alienate the land, there is but one tenable construction, viz., the testator's intent is to impose a restraint upon a fee simple. To construe such language to create a life estate would conflict with the express specification of a fee simple as well as with the presumption of intent to make a complete testamentary disposition of all of a testator's property. By extension, as noted by Professor Casner in his treatise on the law of real property:

> Since it is now generally presumed that a conveyor intends to transfer his whole interest in the property, it may be reasonable to adopt the same construction [conveyance of a fee simple], even in the absence of words of inheritance, if there is no language that can be construed to create a remainder. [6 American Law of Property §26.58 (A. J. Casner ed. 1952).]

In our opinion, testatrix's apparent testamentary restraint on the alienation of the home devised to Mrs. White does not evidence such a clear intent to pass only a life estate as is sufficient to overcome the law's strong presumption that a fee simple interest was conveyed.

Accordingly, we conclude that Mrs. Lide's will passed a fee simple absolute in the home to Mrs. White. Her attempted restraint on alienation must be declared void as inconsistent with the incidents and nature of the estate devised and contrary to public policy.

The decrees of the Court of Appeals and the trial court are reversed and the cause is remanded to the chancery court for such further proceedings as may be necessary, consistent with this opinion. Costs are taxed against appellees.

HARBISON, J., dissenting. With deference to the views of the majority, and recognizing the principles of law contained in the majority opinion, I am unable to agree that the language of the will of Mrs. Lide did or was intended to convey a fee simple interest in her residence to her sister-in-law, Mrs. Evelyn White.

The testatrix expressed the wish that Mrs. White was "to have my home to live in and *not* to be sold." The emphasis is that of the testatrix, and her desire that Mrs. White was not to have an unlimited estate in the property was reiterated in last sentence of the will, to wit: "My house is not to be sold."

The testatrix appointed her niece, Mrs. Perry, executrix and made an outright bequest to her of all personal property.

The will does not seem to me to be particularly ambiguous, and like the Chancellor and the Court of Appeals, I am of the opinion that the testatrix gave Mrs. White a life estate only, and that upon the death of Mrs. White the remainder will pass to the heirs at law of the testatrix.

The cases cited by petitioners in support of their contention that a fee simple was conveyed are not persuasive, in my opinion. Possibly the strongest case cited by the appellants is Green v. Young, 163 Tenn. 16, 40 S.W.2d 793 (1931), in which the testatrix bequeathed all of her real and personal property to her husband "to be used by him for his support and comfort during his life." The will expressly stated that it included all of the property, real and personal, which the testatrix owned at the time of her death. There was no limitation whatever upon the power of the husband to use, consume, or dispose of the property, and the Court concluded that a fee simple was intended.

In the case of Williams v. Williams, 167 Tenn. 26, 65 S.W.2d 561 (1933), a father devised property to his children "for and during their natural lives," but the will contained other provisions not mentioned in the majority opinion which seem to me to distinguish the case. Unlike the provisions of the present will, other clauses in the *Williams* will contained provisions that these same children were to have "all the residue of my estate personal or mixed of which I shall die possessed or seized, or to which I shall be entitled at the time of my decease, to have and to hold the same to them and their executors and administrators and assigns forever."

Further, following some specific gifts to grandchildren, there was another bequest of the remainder of the testator's money to these same three children. The language used by the testator in that case was held to convey the fee simple interest in real estate to the children, but its provisions hardly seem analogous to the language employed by the testatrix in the instant case.

In the case of Webb v. Webb, 53 Tenn. App. 609, 385 S.W.2d 295 (1964), the testator gave his wife all the residue of his property with a clear, unqualified and unrestricted power of use, sale or disposition. Thereafter he attempted to limit her interest to a life estate, with a gift over to his heirs of any unconsumed property. Again, under settled rules of construction and interpretation, the wife was found to have a fee simple estate, but, unlike the present case, there was no limitation whatever upon the power of use or disposition of the property by the beneficiary. . . .

In the present case the testatrix knew how to make an outright gift, if desired. She left all of her personal property to her niece without restraint or limitation. As to her sister-in-law, however, she merely wished the latter have her house "to live in," and expressly withheld from her any power of sale.

The majority opinion holds that the testatrix violated a rule of law by attempting to restrict the power of the donee to dispose of the real estate. Only by thus striking a portion of the will, and holding it inoperative, is the conclusion reached that an unlimited estate resulted.

In my opinion, this interpretation conflicts more greatly with the apparent intention of the testatrix than did the conclusion of the courts below, limiting the gift to Mrs. White to a life estate. I have serious doubt that the testatrix intended to create any illegal restraint on alienation or to violate any other rules of law. It seems to me that she rather emphatically intended to provide that her sister-in-law was not to be able to sell the house during the lifetime of the latter — a result which is both legal and consistent with the creation of a life estate.

In my opinion the judgment of the courts below was correct and I would affirm.

NOTES AND QUESTIONS

1. The rule against direct restraints on alienation is an old one, going back to the fifteenth century or perhaps even earlier. It owes something to the Statute Quia Emptores (1290), which stripped the mesne lords, but not the king, of the power to block transfers of the land by their tenants without their consent.

The objections to restraints on alienation are mainly four. First, such restraints make property unmarketable. The particular land may be made unavailable for its highest and best use. Second, restraints tend to perpetuate the concentration of wealth by making it impossible for the owner to sell property and consume the proceeds of sale. The restrained owner cannot dissipate the capital and, perhaps, fall out of the ranks of the rich. Third, restraints discourage improvements on land. An owner is unlikely to sink his money into improvements on land that he cannot sell. If a mortgage cannot be placed on the land (giving the moneylender the right to sell the land if the borrower defaults on the loan), lenders will not make money available to finance improvements. Fourth, restraints prevent the owner's creditors from reaching the property, working hardship on creditors who rely on the owner's enjoyment of the property in extending credit. See 6 American Law of Property §26.3 (1952).

It is sometimes said that a restraint on alienation is "repugnant" to a fee simple and void for that reason. This argument begs the question. Do you see why? If not, see Percy Bordwell, Alienability and Perpetuities II, 23 Iowa L. Rev. 1, 14 (1937).

Restraints on alienation have traditionally been classified as disabling restraints, forfeiture restraints, and promissory restraints. A *disabling restraint* withholds from the grantee the power of transferring his interest (e.g., O conveys Blackacre "to A and his heirs but any transfer hereafter in any manner of an interest in Blackacre shall be null and void"). A disabling restraint was involved in White v. Brown. A *forfeiture restraint* provides that if the grantee attempts to transfer his interest, it is forfeited to another person (e.g., O conveys Blackacre "to A and his heirs, but if A attempts to transfer the property by any means whatsoever, then to B and her heirs"). A *promissory restraint* provides that the grantee promises not to transfer his interest (e.g., *O* conveys Blackacre "to *A* and his heirs, and *A* promises for himself, his heirs and successors in interest that Blackacre will not be transferred by any means"). A promissory restraint, if valid, is enforceable by the contract remedies of damages or an injunction.

The Restatement (Second) of Property, Donative Transfers, ch. 4 (1983) generally treats all these restraints alike when they are imposed on a fee simple. Following overwhelming authority, the Restatement provides that an absolute restraint on a fee simple is void. But with respect to partial restraints on a fee simple, the Restatement takes a more tolerant position than do most courts. The Restatement provides that a partial restraint (e.g., limiting conveyance to certain persons or putting a time limit on the restraint) is valid if, under all the circumstances of the case, the restraint is found to be reasonable in purpose, effect, and duration. For example, Illustration 9 to section 4.1 of the Restatement provides:

> 9. *O,* owning the family home in fee simple absolute, makes an otherwise effective devise thereof to *S* (*O*'s son) and his heirs "provided, however, that *S* shall permit *W* (*O*'s seventy year old wife) to reside in the family home as long as she desires to do so and any transfer of the family home without *W*'s consent during the time that *W* resides there shall be null and void." The property subject to the restraint is currently transferable by *S* with the consent of *W*. The purpose of the restraint is to assure *W* of a place of residence; the restraint can last no longer than *W*'s lifetime; and *O* could have achieved a similar result by creating a legal or equitable life estate in *W* with a remainder to *S* in fee simple absolute. In the absence of countervailing factors, the legal policy favoring freedom of alienation does not reasonably apply. The disabling restraint is valid, and any transfer of the family residence without *W*'s consent while she is residing therein is null and void.

With respect to restraints on a life estate, the Restatement provides that an absolute disabling restraint is void (§4.1(1)), but a forfeiture restraint is valid (§4.2(1)). This different treatment of disabling and forfeiture restraints follows the majority of cases. What is the justification for this different treatment of disabling and forfeiture restraints? See 6 American Law of Property §§26.48-26.50 (1952).

2. More about Jessie Lide's house from her niece Sandra White Perry:

> I moved to that house when I was nine months old along with my parents (my father was Jessie Lide's brother). I lived in that house until I married at age 22. The house originally had 4 rooms — living room, dining room, kitchen, and one bedroom. Mama, Daddy, and I lived in one room of Jessie's four-room house. She also lived in one room — originally the kitchen. Jessie

cleaned the living room every day. We never sat in it. The only time Jessie unlocked it was for a death in the family. In 1957, after renting the house for $3 a week for 38 years, Jessie purchased the house from her landlord for a price of $3,000 cash. At that time, the house had no hot water and no electrical plugs. After she purchased the house, three more rooms were added on — a bedroom for me, a kitchen for my mother, and a room to be used for storing things.

In 1964 the Chrysler Corporation offered her a price of $35,000 for the property. The company had purchased more than half the block and this house stood in the way. She refused to sell, stating this was her home.

[Jessie died in 1973.]

In 1976 my mother had a serious stroke, therefore making it impossible for her to live alone anymore. I had her move into my home and we rented out the Gratz Street house — after spending $8,000 on improvements.

In 1981 my mother died. My husband and I were unemployed at the time. We put the house up for sale. Being desperate along with threats from the bank (regarding the home improvement loan on the house), we were forced to sell to anyone that would have it. We sold it to a fellow named Brewster for $10,000. In 1986 he sold the house to the Chrysler Company next door for a price of $40,000. I had contacted the Chrysler Company in 1981, but they were not interested at that time in buying the property. [Letter from Sandra White Perry to the editors, dated Aug. 1, 1988.]

NOTE: VALUATION OF LIFE ESTATE AND REMAINDER

In White v. Brown the chancellor found that Evelyn White had a life estate in Jessie Lide's house. He ordered the house sold and the proceeds divided between the life tenant and the remaindermen. How can we determine the value of the life estate and of the remainder?

Assume that the house is worth $10,000. Since we do not know how long the life tenant will actually live, to value the life estate we assume the life tenant will die at the time predicted by a life expectancy (mortality) table. We also need an interest rate; we will assume the market interest rate is 6 percent. Now we can value the life estate and remainder.

To value the life estate, we need to ascertain the present value of the right to receive $600 annually (6 percent of $10,000) for the life tenant's life expectancy. We seek a sum that, invested for the life tenant's life expectancy at 6 percent, will pay $600 for the given number of years and exhaust itself on final payment — in short, the price of an annuity. To simplify the problem let us assume that the life tenant has a life expectancy of only three years. The right to $1 one year from now is not worth $1 now, but only $1 less the amount of interest that can be earned on it. Assuming a 6 percent rate of interest, 94 cents will grow to $1 a year from today. A dollar due in two years is worth 89 cents today (at 6 percent interest); by reinvesting interest, 89 cents today will grow into 94 cents one year from now, which will grow into $1 two years from now. The present value of the right to receive $1 per year for three years is the sum of 94 cents and 89 cents and 84 cents, or $2.67.

Now what is the present value of the right to receive $600 a year for the next three years? $600 × 2.67 = $1,600, which is the present value of the life estate.

In order to value a remainder we must know the number of years the right to receive the sum will be deferred. If we assume that the life tenant has a life expectancy of three years, 84 cents invested at 6 percent with interest compounded annually will be worth $1 at the end of three years. Therefore $8,400 will grow to $10,000 at the end of three years, when the remainder is due to fall in. Hence the remainder has a present value of $8,400.

For lack of a better method, courts, taxing authorities, and insurance companies value life estates and remainders by resort to life expectancy tables. Under Treasury regulations applicable at the time of Jessie Lide's death, if the life tenant is 10 years old, the life estate is worth 96 percent of the total asset value, and the remainder is worth 4 percent. If the life tenant is 70 years old, the life estate is worth 48 percent of the asset value, and the remainder is worth 52 percent. Treas. Reg. §25.2512-9 (f), Table A2. If Evelyn White had been given a life estate in White v. Brown and were 70 years old, why might she and the remaindermen not be willing to sell the house voluntarily and divide the proceeds 48 percent-52 percent? *Because remainder men could wait until she died & get it all.*

Baker v. Weedon

Supreme Court of Mississippi, 1972
262 So. 2d 641, 57 A.L.R.3d 1183

PATTERSON, J. This is an appeal from a decree of the Chancery Court of Alcorn County. It directs a sale of land affected by a life estate and future interests with provision for the investment of the proceeds. The interest therefrom is to be paid to the life tenant for her maintenance. We reverse and remand.

John Harrison Weedon was born in High Point, North Carolina. He lived throughout the South and was married twice prior to establishing his final residence in Alcorn County. His first marriage to Lula Edwards resulted in two siblings, Mrs. Florence Weedon Baker and Mrs. Delette Weedon Jones. Mrs. Baker was the mother of three children, Henry Baker, Sarah Baker Lyman and Louise Virginia Baker Heck, the appellants herein. Mrs. Delette Weedon Jones adopted a daughter Dorothy Jean Jones, who has not been heard from for a number of years and whose whereabouts are presently unknown.

John Weedon was next married to Ella Howell and to this union there was born one child, Rachel. Both Ella and Rachel are now deceased.

Subsequent to these marriages John Weedon bought Oakland Farm in 1905 and engaged himself in its operation. In 1915 John, who was then 55 years of age, married Anna Plaxico, 17 years of age. This marriage, though resulting in no children, was a compatible relationship. John and Anna worked side by side in farming this 152.95-acre tract of land in Alcorn County. There can be no doubt that Anna's contribution to the development and existence of Oakland Farm was significant. The record discloses that during the monetarily difficult years following World War I she hoed, picked cotton and milked an average of fifteen cows per day to protect the farm from financial ruin.

While the relationship of John and Anna was close and amiable, that between John and his daughters of his first marriage was distant and strained. He had no contact with Florence, who was reared by Mr. Weedon's sister in North Carolina, during the seventeen years preceding his death. An even more unfortunate relationship existed between John and his second daughter, Delette Weedon Jones. She is portrayed by the record as being a nomadic person who only contacted her father for money, threatening on several occasions to bring suit against him.

With an obvious intent to exclude his daughters and provide for his wife Anna, John executed his last will and testament in 1925. It provided in part:

> Second; I give and bequeath to my beloved wife, Anna Plaxico Weedon all of my property both real, personal and mixed during her natural life and upon her death to her children, if she has any, and in the event she dies without issue then at the death of my wife Anna Plaxico Weedon I give, bequeath and devise all of my property to my grandchildren, each grandchild sharing equally with the other.
>
> Third; In this will I have not provided for my daughters, Mrs. Florence Baker and Mrs. Delette Weedon Jones, the reason is, I have given them their share of my property and they have not looked after and cared for me in the latter part of my life.

Subsequent to John Weedon's death in 1932 and the probate of his will, Anna continued to live on Oakland Farm. In 1933 Anna, who had been urged by John to remarry in the event of his death, wed J. E. Myers. This union lasted some twenty years and produced no offspring which might terminate the contingent remainder vested in Weedon's grandchildren by the will.

There was no contact between Anna and John Weedon's children or grandchildren from 1932 until 1964. Anna ceased to operate the farm in 1955 due to her age and it has been rented since that time.

Anna's only income is $1000 annually from the farm rental, $300 per year from sign rental and $50 per month by way of social security payments. Without contradiction Anna's income is presently insufficient and places a severe burden upon her ability to live comfortably in view of her age and the infirmities therefrom.

In 1964 the growth of the city of Corinth was approaching Oakland Farm. A right-of-way through the property was sought by the Mississippi State Highway Department for the construction of U.S. Highway 45 bypass. The highway department located Florence Baker's three children, the contingent remaindermen by the will of John Weedon, to negotiate with them for the purchase of the right-of-way. Dorothy Jean Jones, the adopted daughter of Delette Weedon Jones, was not located and due to the long passage of years, is presumably dead. A decree pro confesso was entered against her.

Until the notice afforded by the highway department the grandchildren were unaware of their possible inheritance. Henry Baker, a native of New Jersey, journeyed to Mississippi to supervise their interests. He appears, as was true of the other grandchildren, to have been totally sympathetic to the conditions surrounding Anna's existence as a life tenant. A settlement of $20,000 was completed for the right-of-way bypass of which Anna received $7500 with which to construct a new home. It is significant that all legal and administrative fees were deducted from the shares of the three grandchildren and not taxed to the life tenant. A contract was executed in 1970 for the sale of soil from the property for $2500. Anna received $1000 of this sum which went toward completion of payments for the home.

There was substantial evidence introduced to indicate the value of the property is appreciating significantly with the nearing completion of U.S. Highway 45 bypass plus the growth of the city of Corinth. While the commercial value of the property is appreciating, it is notable that the rental value for agricultural purposes is not. It is apparent that the land can bring no more for agricultural rental purposes than the $1000 per year now received.

The value of the property for commercial purposes at the time of trial was $168,500. Its estimated value within the ensuing four years is placed at $336,000, reflecting the great influence of the interstate construction upon the land. Mr. Baker, for himself and other remaindermen, appears to have made numerous honest and sincere efforts to sell the property at a favorable price. However, his endeavors have been hindered by the slowness of the construction of the bypass.

Anna, the life tenant and appellee here, is 73 years of age and although now living in a new home, has brought this suit due to her economic distress. She prays that the property, less the house site, be sold by a commissioner and that the proceeds be invested to provide her with an adequate income resulting from interest on the trust investment. She prays also that the sale and investment management be under the direction of the chancery court.

The chancellor granted the relief prayed by Anna under the theory of economic waste. His opinion reflects:

> . . . [T]he change of the economy in this area, the change in farming conditions, the equipment required for farming, and the age of this complainant leaves the real estate where it is to all intents and purposes unproductive when viewed in light of its capacity and that a continuing use under the present conditions would result in economic waste.[22]

The contingent remaindermen by the will, appellants here, were granted an interlocutory appeal to settle the issue of the propriety of the chancellor's decree in divesting the contingency title of the remaindermen by ordering a sale of the property.

The weight of authority reflects a tendency to afford a court of equity the power to order the sale of land in which there are future interests. Simes, Law of Future Interests, section 53 (2d ed. 1966), states:

> By the weight of authority, it is held that a court of equity has the power to order a judicial sale of land affected with a future interest and an investment of the proceeds, where this is necessary for the preservation of all interests in the land. When the power is exercised, the proceeds of the sale are held in a judicially created trust. The beneficiaries of the trust are the persons who held interests in the land, and the beneficial interests are of the same character as the legal interests which they formally held in the land.

See also Simes and Smith, The Law of Future Interests, §1941 (2d ed. 1956).

This Court has long recognized that chancery courts do have jurisdiction to order the sale of land for the prevention of waste. Kelly v. Neville, 136 Miss. 429, 101 So. 565 (1924). In Riley v. Norfleet, 167 Miss. 420, 436-437, 148 So. 777, 781 (1933), Justice Cook, speaking for the Court and citing *Kelly*, supra, stated: ". . . The power of a court of equity on a plenary bill, with adversary interest properly represented, to sell contingent remainders in land, under some circumstances, though the contingent remaindermen are not then ascertained or in being, as, for instance, to preserve the estate from complete or partial destruction, is well established."

While Mississippi and most jurisdictions recognize the inherent power of a court of equity to direct a judicial sale of land which is subject to a future interest, nevertheless the scope of this power has not been

---

22. What does the chancellor mean by "economic waste"? Is it the same as the legal concept of waste? See Note 1 on page 231. — EDS.

clearly defined. It is difficult to determine the facts and circumstances which will merit such a sale.

It is apparent that there must be "necessity" before the chancery court can order a judicial sale. It is also beyond cavil that the power should be exercised with caution and only when the need is evident. Lambdin v. Lambdin, 209 Miss. 672, 48 So. 2d 341 (1950). These cases, *Kelly, Riley* and *Lambdin,* supra, are all illustrative of situations where the freehold estate was deteriorating and the income therefrom was insufficient to pay taxes and maintain the property. In each of these this Court approved a judicial sale to preserve and maintain the estate. The appellants argue, therefore, that since Oakland Farm is not deteriorating and since there is sufficient income from rental to pay taxes, a judicial sale by direction of the court was not proper.

The unusual circumstances of this case persuade us to the contrary. We are of the opinion that deterioration and waste of the property is not the exclusive and ultimate test to be used in determining whether a sale of land affected by a future interest is proper, but also that consideration should be given to the question of whether a sale is necessary for the best interest of all the parties, that is, the life tenant and the contingent remaindermen. This "necessary for the best interest of all parties" rule is gleaned from Rogers, Removal of Future Interest Encumbrances — Sale of the Fee Simple Estate, 17 Vanderbilt L. Rev. 1437 (1964); Simes, Law of Future Interests, supra; Simes and Smith, The Law of Future Interests, §1941 (1956); and appears to have the necessary flexibility to meet the requirements of unusual and unique situations which demand in justice an equitable solution.

Our decision to reverse the chancellor and remand the case for his further consideration is couched in our belief that the best interest of all the parties would not be served by a judicial sale of the entirety of the property at this time. While true that such a sale would provide immediate relief to the life tenant who is worthy of this aid in equity, admitted by the remaindermen, it would nevertheless under the circumstances before us cause great financial loss to the remaindermen.

We therefore reverse and remand this cause to the chancery court, which shall have continuing jurisdiction thereof, for determination upon motion of the life tenant, if she so desires, for relief by way of sale of a part of the burdened land sufficient to provide for her reasonable needs from interest derived from the investment of the proceeds. The sale, however, is to be made only in the event the parties cannot unite to hypothecate the land for sufficient funds for the life tenant's reasonable needs. By affording the options above we do not mean to suggest that other remedies suitable to the parties which will provide economic relief to the aging life tenant are not open to them if approved by the chancellor. It is our opinion, shared by the chancellor and acknowledged by the appellants, that the facts suggest an equitable remedy. However, it is our further opinion that this equity does not warrant the remedy of sale of all of the property since this would unjustly impinge upon the vested rights of the remaindermen.

Reversed and remanded.

NOTES AND QUESTIONS

1. *Waste.* The law of waste can become relevant whenever two or more persons — suppose two here, called *A* and *B* — have rights to possess property at the same time (as in concurrent ownership, considered in Chapter 5) or consecutively (as in Baker v. Weedon or in the case of present and future interests generally). The central idea of the waste concept is that *A* should not be able to use the property in a manner that *unreasonably* interferes with the expectations of *B*. In this regard, the law of waste is aptly named, because it is designed to avoid just that — uses of property that fail to maximize the property's value. See Richard A. Posner, Economic Analysis of Law 73 (4th ed. 1992):

> [T]he law of waste emerged to reconcile the competing interests of life tenants and remaindermen. A life tenant will have an incentive to maximize not the value of the property, that is, the present value of the entire stream of future earnings obtainable from it, but only the present value of the earnings stream obtainable during his expected lifetime. He will therefore want to cut timber before it has attained its mature growth — even though the present value of the timber would be greater if the cutting of some or all of it were postponed — if the added value from waiting would enure to the remainderman. The law of waste forbade this. There might seem to be no need for a law of waste, because the life tenant and the remainderman would negotiate an optimal plan for exploiting the property. But since the tenant and remainderman . . . [are locked into dealing with each other — a so-called bilateral monopoly], transaction costs may be high. Also, the remaindermen may be children, who do not have the legal capacity to make binding contracts; they may even be unborn children.

The law of waste began developing in the twelfth century and evolved over time into a complex set of rules for reconciling the conflicting interests of people like *A* and *B*. The precise application of waste doctrine turns on a number of variables — the nature of the property interests of the competing parties, the conduct in question, the remedy sought — and easy generalizations are likely to prove inaccurate. Here we simply underscore some central points and interesting quirks and problems. For a fuller treatment see 5 Richard R. Powell, The Law of Real Property ¶¶636-647 (rev. ed. 1992).

Suppose that *A* has a present possessory interest in property and that *B* has a future interest — a future right to possession. *A*'s interest might be of short or possibly long duration — a month-to-month tenancy at one extreme, or at the other a long term of years or (as in Baker v. Weedon) a life estate. Similarly, *B*'s interest might be certain to come into possession (as with the landlord's reversion following a tenancy) or tenuous. As to tenuous future interests, ones that may or may not become possessory, we will see a number of examples in Chapter 4. You should note, though, that Baker v. Weedon is a case in point. If Anna had children, John Weedon's grandchildren would not get the farm. With the foregoing in mind, we can simply say that typically the greater *A*'s interest, the more freedom *A* has in using the property in question; correspondingly, the more tenuous *B*'s interest, the less protection given *B*. (Keeping in mind Posner's discussion of the economic functions of waste, how would you justify these distinctions?)

What sort of conduct amounts to waste, then, turns in part on the nature of the interests involved. It also turns on the conduct in question. Here, the courts have created two general categories: affirmative waste, arising from voluntary acts, and permissive waste, arising from a failure to act. As to *affirmative waste*, liability results from injurious acts that have more than trivial effects. Generally, *injurious* has meant acts that substantially reduce the value of the property in question — but with some exceptions. Usually, for example, minerals can be extracted, even though doing so reduces the value of the property for holders of future interests, *if* the minerals were being extracted when the future interests were created.[23] Trees can be cut if clearing the land is regarded as good husbandry.

Suppose that voluntary actions by the possessory tenant change the property in question substantially but increase its value. Is this waste? Taking Baker v. Weedon as an example, suppose Anna had torn down the farm buildings and replaced them with a valuable commercial structure. Could the grandchildren seek damages for waste? Probably they would not prevail in the United States today. England for some time did grant a cause of action, on the notion that the grantor intended the remaindermen to receive the *identical* thing granted (a notion that also underlies the court's opinion in Baker v. Weedon). The leading case in this country, Melms v. Pabst Brewing Co., 104 Wis. 7, 79 N.W. 738 (1899), established that life tenants can make substantial alterations or even demolish a structure when conditions change, provided the value of the remainder is not diminished by these actions. Such an outcome is virtually certain if the life tenant has a long life expectancy.

Permissive waste is essentially a question of negligence — failure to take reasonable care of the property. Moore v. Phillips, 6 Kan. App. 2d

23. This is known as the "open mines" doctrine. If the mines were opened by the grantor before he created the life estate, it is presumed that the grantor intended the life tenant to be able to continue mining. But if the mines were not open before the life estate was created, the life tenant cannot open them.

94, 627 P.2d 831 (1981), is illustrative. In that case, the life tenant of a
farm leased the farm, but the lessees did not occupy the farmhouse. The
vacant farmhouse fell into disrepair. When the life tenant died, the remaindermen sued her estate for waste and recovered damages for the
deterioration of the farmhouse. See also Hausmann v. Hausmann, 231
Ill. App. 3d 361, 596 N.E.2d 216 (1992), holding that a life tenant's
failure to pay real estate taxes is waste, remediable by injunctive relief
and punitive damages.

2. *Wisdom of creating a legal life estate.* Is it wise to create a legal life
estate, as John Weedon did? What problems might arise during the life
tenant's life that the life tenant cannot adequately solve? How would you
handle the following problems in drafting John Weedon's will?

Sale. Circumstances might change so that a sale of the property is
advantageous. The life tenant cannot sell a fee simple unless *all* other
persons having an interest in the property consent or unless a court of
equity orders sale and reinvestment of the proceeds.

Lease. It might be advantageous for the life tenant to lease the property for a period extending beyond the life tenant's death.

Mortgage. If the life tenant has no capital of her own, she may be
unable to improve the property without borrowing from a bank and
giving the bank a mortgage on the property. A bank ordinarily does not
lend money if the security is a life estate rather than a fee simple.

Waste. The life tenant may want to take minerals out of the land or
cut timber or take down a still usable building. The actions may constitute waste, entitling the remaindermen to an injunction or damages. See
Note 1 above.

Insurance. The life tenant is under no duty to insure buildings on
the land. If the life tenant does insure buildings and the buildings are
destroyed by fire, the life tenant has been held entitled to the whole
proceeds and the remaindermen nothing.

The person creating a legal life estate can draft the instrument so as
to give the life tenant a power to sell or mortgage a fee simple or to lease
beyond the duration of the life estate. A life estate can be coupled with
any number of powers to do specific acts not otherwise permitted the
life tenant. However, if the life tenant is given the power to sell a fee
simple, the drafter should consider what is to be done with the proceeds
of sale and draft appropriate provisions. Should the proceeds be given
outright to the life tenant or held by a trustee in trust for the life tenant's
life?

3. *Protecting the life tenant by creating a trust.* A trust, which you have
not yet studied, should always be considered by a lawyer when a client
proposes to create a life estate. A trust is a more flexible and usually
more desirable property arrangement than a legal life estate. *A trustee
holds the legal fee simple* and as the "manager" of the property may be
directed to pay all the income to the life tenant or to let the life tenant

into possession. As manager, the trustee will have powers spelled out in the instrument creating the trust, or supplied by law, to administer the trust for the benefit of the life tenant and remaindermen. These powers usually give the trustee power to sell, lease, mortgage, remove minerals, or do whatever a prudent person would do with respect to the property. If the trustee sells the property, the trustee invests the proceeds of sale, paying the income therefrom to the life tenant.

The life tenant can be made trustee. For example, John Weedon could have devised his land to his wife Anna as trustee in trust for Anna for life, remainder to his grandchildren. As trustee, Anna would have a legal fee simple and would be the manager of the land, owing fiduciary duties to herself and to the remaindermen. She would also have an equitable life estate entitling her to possession of the land or to net rental income for her life. As trustee, Anna could sell the fee simple to the property if desirable, say for $168,500. She could then invest the $168,500 in stocks and bonds or other assets, and pay herself the income from them. On her death the remaindermen would be entitled to the assets owned by the trust, in whatever form those assets then took.

If John Weedon did not think Anna was capable of acting as a trustee, he could have named some other person trustee. Or he could have provided in his will that if Anna ever wanted to sell the land a trust would come into existence at that time and the court would appoint a suitable person as trustee.

The conceptual framework of the trust is detailed in the next chapter, at pages 283-284, but we want to introduce you to the trust early because, in our judgment, a legal life estate, as was created in Baker v. Weedon, should almost always be avoided. It was a property arrangement suited to the great landed families of England in an age when land was the chief form of wealth, the basis of the family dynasty and the stately homes that passed from generation to generation, and when urban development proceeded slowly and land values remained relatively stable.[24] A legal life estate is unsuited to a modern economy that regards land as just another form of income-producing wealth, which can swiftly appreciate in value under pressure for development and which must be managed effectively.

24. The legal life estate can no longer be created in England. It was abolished by the Law of Property Act of 1925. A life estate can exist only as an equitable interest, that is to say, someone must hold the legal fee simple in trust whenever a life estate is created. The purpose of this legislation was to ensure that a fee simple owner is always available with authority to deal effectively with the land. See C. Dent Bostick, Loosening the Grip of the Dead Hand: Shall We Abolish Legal Future Interests in Land?, 32 Vand. L. Rev. 1061, 1090-1097 (1979), recommending that America follow the English lead.

NOTE: SEISIN *possession +* (handwritten)

The fee simple, the fee tail, and the life estate are *freehold estates*. The chief significance of this, at common law, was that a freeholder had *seisin*. Seisin was possession, of a particular kind and with peculiar consequences. Tenants seised of the land were responsible for feudal services, and feudal land law decreed that someone must always be seised. Dower and curtesy were given only to spouses of persons seised of the land (see pages 400-401). Before 1536, a freehold estate could be created or transferred only by a ceremonial known as feoffment with *livery of seisin*. This usually included both the grantor and the grantee going on the land and the grantor, before witnesses, delivering seisin to the grantee by some symbolic act such as handing over a clod of dirt or putting the grantee's hand on the ring of the door and uttering such words as "Know ye that I have given this land to (the grantee)." Even though livery was often accompanied by a written charter of feoffment, the act of turning over possession before witnesses attested a change of ownership in the clearest possible way.[25]

Seisin was endowed by the medieval mind with a real existence, illustrating again the philosophical tendency during that period to reify abstract ideas. Bracton, for example, writing between 1250 and 1268, regarded the lord of an English manor as seised of the estate until his corpse was carried from the manor house, when seisin passed to the heir. Henry de Bracton, De Legibus et Consuetudinibus Angliae, f. 41b.

E. *Leasehold Estates* *tenant = possession* (handwritten) *no seisin — nonfreehold* (handwritten) *landlord has seisen* (handwritten)

Leasehold estates are nonfreehold possessory estates. Leasehold tenants do not have seisin. Leases originally were regarded as personal contracts between lessor and lessee outside the tenurial system. Leases were classed as personal property ("chattels real"). It was natural, then, that the law regarded the freeholder (landlord) as still seised of the land even after he had granted a term of years and given up physical possession to the leasing tenant. When a lease is involved, the landlord holds seisin; the tenant merely has possession. Fortunately, this distinction is of little importance today. It is usually not necessary to distinguish seisin from possession.

25. If this ceremony strikes you as quaint, consider that manual delivery may still be required for gifts of tangible personal property. See pages 168-169. And with respect to modern transfers by will, just the right things must be said and done when the will is executed, or the will cannot be probated. See Jesse Dukeminier & Stanley M. Johanson, Wills, Trusts, and Estates 203-206 (4th ed. 1990).

In the course of time, leaseholders were held to have an estate in land and were brought into the tenurial system. Modern leasehold estates include the term of years, the periodic tenancy, and the tenancy at will. Historically, the *term of years* was the most important of these. A term of years is an estate ending on a fixed calendar date, such as a term of five years or one year or six months. Terms of years are very common today in commercial and residential leasing. We shall consider leasehold estates at length in Chapter 6.

PROBLEM

O conveys "to *A* for 99 years if *A* so long live." What estate does *A* have? Who has seisin?

[handwritten: leasehold estate]
[handwritten: landlord has seisin]
[handwritten: fee simple determinable]

F. Defeasible Estates

Any estate can be created so as to be defeasible upon the happening of a future event, but the most common kind of defeasible freehold estate is a fee simple defeasible.

A fee simple may be *absolute*, meaning that it cannot be divested nor will it end if any event happens in the future. Or a fee simple may be *defeasible*. A defeasible fee simple is one that may last forever or may come to an end upon the happening of an event in the future. Distinguish carefully between a fee simple determinable and a fee simple subject to condition subsequent, two types of defeasible fees.

A *fee simple determinable* is a fee simple so limited that it will end *automatically* when a stated event happens. Example: *O* conveys Blackacre "to the Hartford School Board, its successors and assigns, so long as the premises are used for school purposes." The fee simple may continue forever, but if the land ceases to be used for school purposes, the fee simple will come to an end or, using the old word, determine, and the fee simple will revert back to *O*, the grantor. A fee simple determinable is sometimes called a fee simple on a special limitation, indicating that the fee simple will expire by this limitation if it occurs.

A fee simple determinable is created by language connoting that the transferor is conveying a fee simple only until an event happens. In the example above, the words "so long as the premises are used for school purposes" connotes a determinable fee. Other language that would create a determinable fee includes "while used for school purposes," "during the continuance of said school," "until the Board no longer uses the land for a school," or any words with a durational aspect. Words that merely state the motive of the transferor in making a gift do not create a determinable fee; for example, a conveyance "to the Hartford School Board for school purposes" gives the Board a fee simple absolute and not a fee simple determinable.[26]

Every fee simple determinable is accompanied by a future interest. In the ordinary case the future interest is retained by the transferor, *O* in the above example, or his heirs, and called a *possibility of reverter*.[27] The possibility of reverter may be expressly retained or, as in the above example, arise by operation of law. It arises by operation of law because *O* has transferred less than his entire interest in Blackacre when he creates a determinable fee in the School Board.

A *fee simple subject to condition subsequent* is a fee simple that does not automatically terminate but *may be cut short* or divested at the transferor's election when a stated condition happens. Example: *O* conveys White-acre "to the Hartford School Board, its successors and assigns, but if the premises are not used for school purposes, the grantor has a right to re-enter and retake the premises." Observe that we have used a different verbal formula than that creating a determinable fee. The Board's fee simple may be cut short if *O* elects to exercise the right of entry, but it is not automatically terminated when the stated event happens. Unless and until entry is made, the fee simple continues. That is the essential difference between these two defeasible fees.

A fee simple on condition subsequent is created by a conveyance of fee simple, followed by language providing that the fee simple may be divested by the transferor if a specified event happens. In the above example, the clause beginning with "but if . . ." states a condition subsequent. Other language creating a condition subsequent, after conveying a fee simple, includes "provided, however, that when the premises . . . ," "on condition that if the premises . . . ," or other words indicating that the estate may be cut short at the transferor's election. The difference between language creating a determinable fee and language creating a fee simple subject to condition subsequent is extremely subtle, but millions of dollars have turned on whether the estate expires by its own limitation or may be cut short at the election of the transferor.

The future interest retained by the transferor to divest a fee simple subject to condition subsequent is called a *right of entry* (also known as a *power of termination*).[28] The right of entry may be expressly retained or it

---

26. This rule seems to be honored almost as often in the breach as in the observance. See Forsgren v. Sollie, 659 P.2d 1068 (Utah 1983), holding (3 to 2) that a deed providing, "This property is conveyed to be used as and for a church or residence purposes only," created a fee simple subject to condition subsequent.

27. When a future interest following a determinable fee is created in a *transferee*, it is called an *executory interest*. See pages 280-281.

28. A right of entry, like a possibility of reverter, may be retained only by the transferor or his heirs. It may not be created in a transferee.

If the grantor wants to put the right to enforce forfeiture in a transferee, the grantor

may be implied if the words of the instrument are reasonably susceptible to the interpretation that this type of forfeiture estate was contemplated by the parties. For example, depending upon the circumstances of the transaction, a conveyance "to A and his heirs, provided always, and upon this condition, that the aforesaid premises shall not be used for a tavern," might be construed by a court to create either a fee simple subject to condition subsequent (enforceable by forfeiture) or a covenant imposed to benefit the grantor's retained land (enforceable by injunction or damages). It is always wise, of course, to avoid litigation by expressly including a right of entry if that is intended.

Mahrenholz v. County Board of School Trustees

Appellate Court of Illinois, 1981
93 Ill. App. 3d 366, 417 N.E.2d 138

JONES, J. This case involves an action to quiet title to real property located in Lawrence County, Illinois. Its resolution depends on the judicial construction of language in a conveyance of that property. The case is before us on the pleadings, plaintiffs' third amended complaint having been dismissed by a final order. The pertinent facts are taken from the pleadings.

On March 18, 1941, W.E. and Jennie Hutton executed a warranty deed in which they conveyed [1½ acres out of 40 acres they owned], to be known here as the Hutton School grounds, to the Trustees of School District No. 1, the predecessors of the defendants in this action. The deed provided that "this land to be used for school purpose only; otherwise to revert to Grantors herein." W.E. Hutton died intestate on July 18, 1951, and Jennie Hutton died intestate on February 18, 1969. The Huttons left as their only legal heir their son Harry E. Hutton.

The property conveyed by the Huttons became the site of the Hutton School. Community Unit School District No. 20 succeeded to the grantee of the deed and held classes in the building constructed upon the land until May 30, 1973. After that date, children were transported to classes held at other facilities operated by the District. The District has used the property since then for storage purposes only. . . .

[In July 1941, W.E. and Jennie Hutton conveyed to Earl and Madeline Jacqmain the remaining 38½ acres of the 40-acre tract from which

---

can create a fee simple subject to an executory limitation. Thus: "to the Hartford School Board, but if it ceases to use the land as a school, to City Library." City Library has an executory interest that will automatically divest the School Board if the event happens. Executory interests are treated in the next chapter (on future interests) because they developed out of the Statute of Uses (1536), long after the right of entry was recognized, and are most easily understood in that context.

the 1½ acres conveyed to the school board were taken. In addition to the land surrounding the school, this deed purported to convey to the Jacqmains the reversionary interest the Huttons held in the school land. On October 9, 1959, the Jacqmains executed a warranty deed conveying the 38½ acres adjacent to the school grounds to the plaintiffs, Herbert and Betty Mahrenholz. This deed also purported to convey to the plaintiffs the reversionary interest in the school land.]

On May 7, 1977, Harry E. Hutton, son and sole heir of W.E. and Jennie Hutton, conveyed to the plaintiffs all of his interest in the Hutton School land. This document was filed in the recorder's office of Lawrence County on September 7, 1977. On September 6, 1977, Harry Hutton disclaimed his interest in the property in favor of the defendants. The disclaimer was in the form of a written document entitled "Disclaimer and Release." It contained the legal description of the Hutton School grounds and recited that Harry E. Hutton disclaimed and released any possibility of reverter or right of entry for condition broken, or other similar interest, in favor of the County Board of School Trustees for Lawrence County, Illinois, successor to the Trustees of School District No. 1 of Lawrence County, Illinois. The document further recited that it was made for the purpose of releasing and extinguishing any right Harry E. Hutton may have had in the "interest retained by W.E. Hutton and Jennie Hutton . . . in that deed to the Trustees of School District No. 1, Lawrence County, Illinois dated March 18, 1941, and filed on the same date. . . ." The disclaimer was filed in the recorder's office of Lawrence County on October 4, 1977.

The plaintiffs filed a complaint in the circuit court of Lawrence County . . . in which they sought to quiet title to the school property in themselves. . . . On March 21, 1979, the trial court entered an order dismissing this complaint. In the order the court found that the

[W]arranty deed dated March 18, 1941, from W.E. Hutton and Jennie Hutton to the Trustees of School District No. 1, conveying land here concerned, created a fee simple subject to a condition subsequent followed by the right of entry for condition broken, rather than a determinable fee followed by a possibility of reverter.

Plaintiffs have perfected an appeal to this court.

The basic issue presented by this appeal is whether the trial court correctly concluded that the plaintiffs could not have acquired any interest in the school property from the Jacqmains and Harry Hutton. Resolution of this issue must turn upon the legal interpretation of the language contained in the March 18, 1941, deed from W.E. and Jennie Hutton to the Trustees of School District No. 1: "this land to be used for school purpose only; otherwise to revert to Grantors herein." In addition to the legal effect of this language we must consider the alienability of the interest created and the effect of subsequent deeds.

The parties appear to be in agreement that the 1941 deed from the Huttons conveyed a defeasible fee simple estate to the grantee, and gave rise to a future interest in the grantors, (see Restatement of the Law, Property, sec. 153), and that it did not convey a fee simple absolute, subject to a covenant. The fact that provision was made for forfeiture of the estate conveyed should the land cease to be used for school purposes suggests that this view is correct. Dunne v. Minsor (1924), 312 Ill. 333, 143 N.E. 842; Newton v. Village of Glen Ellyn (1940), 374 Ill. 50, 27 N.E.2d 821. Restatement of the Law, Property, secs. 44, 45.

The future interest remaining in this grantor or his estate can only be a possibility of reverter or a right of re-entry for condition broken. As neither interest may be transferred by will or by inter vivos conveyance (Ill. Rev. Stat., ch. 30, par. 37b), and as the land was being used for school purposes in 1959 when the Jacqmains transferred their interest in the school property to the plaintiffs, the trial court correctly ruled that the plaintiffs could not have acquired any interest in that property from the Jacqmains by the deed of October 9, 1959.

Consequently this court must determine whether the plaintiffs could have acquired an interest in the Hutton School grounds from Harry Hutton. The resolution of this issue depends on the construction of the language of the 1941 deed of the Huttons to the school district. As urged by the defendants and as the trial court found, the deed conveyed a fee simple subject to a condition subsequent followed by a right of reentry for condition broken. As argued by the plaintiffs, on the other hand, the deed conveyed a fee simple determinable followed by a possibility of reverter. In either case, the grantor and his heirs retain an interest in the property which may become possessory if the condition is broken. We emphasize here that although sec. 1 of An Act relating to Rights of Entry or Reentry for breach of condition subsequent and possibilities of reverter effective July 21, 1947 (Ill. Rev. Stat., ch. 30, par. 37b) provides that rights of re-entry for condition broken and possibilities of reverter are neither alienable or devisable, they are inheritable. (Deverick v. Bline (1950), 404 Ill. 302, 89 N.E.2d 43.) The type of interest held governs the mode of reinvestment with title if reinvestment is to occur. If the grantor had a possibility of reverter, he or his heirs become the owner of the property by operation of law as soon as the condition is broken. If he has a right of re-entry for condition broken, he or his heirs become the owner of the property only after they act to retake the property.

It is alleged, and we must accept, that classes were last held in the Hutton School in 1973. Harry Hutton, sole heir of the grantors, did not act to legally retake the premises but instead conveyed his interest in that land to the plaintiffs in 1977. If Harry Hutton had only a naked right of re-entry for condition broken, then he could not be the owner of that property until he had legally re-entered the land. Since he took no steps for a legal re-entry, he had only a right of re-entry in 1977, and that right cannot be conveyed inter vivos. On the other hand, if Harry Hutton had a possibility of reverter in the property, then he owned the school property as soon as it ceased to be used for school purposes. Therefore, assuming (1) that cessation of classes constitutes "abandonment of school purposes" on the land, (2) that the conveyance from Harry Hutton to the plaintiffs was legally correct, and (3) that the conveyance was not pre-empted by Hutton's disclaimer in favor of the school district, the plaintiffs could have acquired an interest in the Hutton School grounds if Harry Hutton had inherited a possibility of reverter from his parents.

The difference between a fee simple determinable (or, determinable fee) and a fee simple subject to a condition subsequent, is solely a matter of judicial interpretation of the words of a grant. . . . [T]he Huttons would have created a fee simple determinable if they had allowed the school district to retain the property *so long as* or *while* it was used for school purposes, or *until* it ceased to be so used. Similarly, a fee simple subject to a condition subsequent would have arisen had the Huttons given the land *upon condition that* or *provided that* it be used for school purposes. In the 1941 deed, though the Huttons gave the land "to be used for school purpose only, otherwise to revert to Grantors herein," no words of temporal limitation, or terms of express condition, were used in the grant.

The plaintiffs argue that the word "only" should be construed as a limitation rather than a condition. The defendants respond that where ambiguous language is used in a deed, the courts of Illinois have expressed a constructional preference for a fee simple subject to a condition subsequent. (Storke v. Penn Mutual Life Ins. Co. (1954), 390 Ill. 619, 61 N.E.2d 552.) Both sides refer us to cases involving deeds which contain language analogous to the 1941 grant in this case.

We believe that a close analysis of the wording of the original grant shows that the grantors intended to create a fee simple determinable followed by a possibility of reverter. Here, the use of the word "only" immediately following the grant "for school purpose" demonstrates that the Huttons wanted to give the land to the school district only as long as it was needed and no longer. The language "this land to be used for school purpose only" is an example of a grant which contains a limitation within the granting clause. It suggests a limited grant, rather than a full grant subject to a condition, and thus, both theoretically and linguistically, gives rise to a fee simple determinable.

The second relevant clause furnishes plaintiff's position with additional support. It cannot be argued that the phrase "otherwise to revert to grantors herein" is inconsistent with a fee simple subject to a condition subsequent. Nor does the word "revert" automatically create a possibility of reverter. But, in combination with the preceding phrase, the provisions by which possession is returned to the grantors seem to trigger a mandatory return rather than a permissive return because it is not stated that the grantor "may" re-enter the land. See City of Urbana v. Solo Cup Co. (4th Dist. 1979), 66 Ill. App. 3d 45, 22 Ill. Dec. 786, 383 N.E.2d 262.

The terms used in the 1941 deed, although imprecise, were designed to allow the property to be used for a single purpose, namely, for "school purpose." The Huttons intended to have the land back if it were ever used otherwise. Upon a grant of exclusive use followed by an express provision for reverter when that use ceases, courts and commentators have agreed that a fee simple determinable, rather than a fee simple subject to a condition subsequent, is created. (1 Simes and Smith, The Law of Future Interests (2nd ed. 1956) sec. 286 n.58.) Our own research has uncovered cases from other jurisdictions and sources in which language very similar to that in the Hutton deed has been held to create a fee simple determinable:

> A conveyance "for the use, intent and purpose of a site for a School House [and] whenever the said School District removes the School House from said tract of land or whenever said School House ceases to be used as the Public School House . . . then the said Trust shall cease and determine and the said land shall revert to the grantor and his heirs" [Consolidated School District v. Walter (1954), 243 Minn. 159, 66 N.W.2d 881, 882.]
>
> [I]t being absolutely understood that when said land ceases to be used for school purposes it is to revert to the above grantor, his heirs. [U.S. v. 1119.15 Acres of Land (E.D. Ill. 1942), 44 F. Supp. 449.]
>
> That I, S. S. Gray (Widower), for and in consideration of the sum of Donation to Wheeler School District to be used by said Wheeler Special School District for school and church purposes and to revert to me should school and church be discontinued or moved. [Williams v. Kirby School District (Ark. 1944), 181 S.W.2d 488, 490.]
>
> It is understood and agreed that if the above described land is abandoned by the said second parties and not used for school purposes then the above described land reverts to the party of the first part. [School District No. 6 v. Russell (1964), 156 Colo. 75, 396 P.2d 929, 930.]
>
> [T]o B and C [trustees of a school district] and their heirs and successors for school purposes and to revert to the grantor when it ceases to be so used. [Restatement of Property, sec. 44, comment 1, illustration V (1936).]

Thus, authority from this state and others indicates that the grant in the Hutton deed did in fact create a fee simple determinable. We are not persuaded by the cases cited by the defendants for the terms of conveyance in those cases distinguish them from the facts presented here. . . .

The estate created in Latham v. Illinois Central Railroad Co. (1912), 253 Ill. 93, 97 N.E. 254, was held to be a fee simple subject to a condition subsequent. Land was conveyed to a railroad in return for the railroad's agreement to erect and maintain a passenger depot and a freight depot on the premises. The deed was made to the grantee, "their successors and assigns forever, for the uses and purposes hereinafter mentioned and for NONE other." Those purposes were limited to "railroad purposes only." The deed provided "that in case of non-user of said premises so conveyed for the uses and purposes aforesaid, that then and in that case the title to said premises shall revert back to [the grantors], their heirs, executors, administrators and assigns." The property was granted to the railroad to have and hold forever, "subject, nevertheless, to all the conditions, covenants, agreements and limitations in this deed expressed." The estate in *Latham* may be distinguished from that created here in that the former was a grant "forever" which was subjected to certain use restrictions while the Hutton deed gave the property to the school district only as long as it could use it. . . .

The defendants also direct our attention to the case of McElvain v. Dorris (1921), 298 Ill. 377, 131 N.E. 608. There, land was sold subject to the following condition: "This tract of land is to be used for mill purposes, and if not used for mill purposes the title reverts back to the former owner." When the mill was abandoned, the heirs of the grantor brought suit in ejectment and were successful. The Supreme Court of Illinois did not mention the possibility that the quoted words could have created a fee simple determinable but instead stated,

> Annexed to the grant there was a condition subsequent, by a breach of which there would be a right of re-entry by the grantor or her heirs at law. [Citations.] A breach of the condition in such a case does not, of itself, determine the estate, but an entry, or some act equivalent thereto, is necessary to revest the estate, and bringing a suit in ejectment is equivalent to such reentry. [298 Ill. at 379, 131 N.E. 608.]

It is urged by the defendants that McElvain v. Dorris stands for the proposition that the quoted language in the deed creates a fee simple subject to a condition subsequent. We must agree with the defendants that the grant in *McElvain* is strikingly similar to that in this case. However, the opinion in *McElvain* is ambiguous in several respects. First, that portion of the opinion which states that "Annexed to the grant there was a condition subsequent . . ." may refer to the provision quoted above, or it may refer to another provision not reproduced in the opinion. Second, even if the court's reference is to the quoted language, the holding may reflect only the court's acceptance of the parties' construction of the grant. (A similar procedure was followed in Trustees of Schools v. Batdorf (1955), 6 Ill. 2d 486, 130 N.E.2d 111, as noted by defendants.) After all, as an action in ejectment was brought in *McElvain*, the difference between a fee simple determinable and a fee simple subject to a

condition subsequent would have no practical effect and the court did
not discuss it.

To the extent that *McElvain* holds that the quoted language establishes a fee simple subject to a condition subsequent, it is contrary to the
weight of Illinois and American authority. A more appropriate case with
which to resolve the problem presented here is North v. Graham (1908),
235 Ill. 178, 85 N.E. 267. Land was conveyed to trustees of a church
under a deed which stated that "said tract of land above described to
revert to the party of the first part whenever it ceases to be used or
occupied for a meeting house or church." Following an extended discussion of determinable fees, the court concluded that such an estate is legal
in Illinois and that the language of the deed did in fact create that estate.

North v. Graham, like this case, falls somewhere between those cases
in which appears the classic language used to create a fee simple determinable and that used to create a fee simple subject to a condition subsequent. . . .

Although the word "whenever" is used in the North v. Graham
deed, it is not found in a granting clause, but in a reverter clause. The
court found this slightly unorthodox construction sufficient to create a
fee simple determinable, and we believe that the word "only" placed in
the granting clause of the Hutton deed brings this case under the rule
of North v. Graham.

We hold, therefore, that the 1941 deed from W.E. and Jennie Hutton to the Trustees of School District No. 1 created a fee simple determinable in the Trustees followed by a possibility of reverter in the
Huttons and their heirs. Accordingly, the trial court erred in dismissing
plaintiffs' . . . complaint which followed its holding that the plaintiffs
could not have acquired any interest in the Hutton School property
from Harry Hutton. We must therefore reverse and remand this cause
to the trial court for further proceedings.

We refrain from deciding the following issues: (1) whether the 1977
conveyance from Harry Hutton was legally sufficient to pass his interest
in the school property to the plaintiffs, (2) whether Harry Hutton effectively disclaimed his interest in the property in favor of the defendants
by virtue of his 1977 disclaimer, and (3) whether the defendants have
ceased to use the Hutton School grounds for "school purposes." . . .

Reversed and remanded.

NOTES, QUESTIONS, AND PROBLEM

1. Several possible situations exist where different legal consequences might result from classifying an estate as a fee simple determinable with a possibility of reverter rather than a fee simple subject to a

right of entry. The first situation relates to <u>transferability of the future interest</u> — the problem in the *Mahrenholz* case.

At common law a possibility of reverter and a right of entry descended to heirs upon the death of the owner of such interests. But, curiously enough, neither interest was transferable during life. A possibility of reverter was not transferable during life because it was not thought of as a property interest (a "thing") you could transfer but as a "<u>mere possibility of becoming an estate</u>" (as, before we understood the nature of matter, we would think of gas which might pass into a solid). A right of entry was not transferable because it too was not a "thing"; rather it was thought of as a special right in the grantor to forfeit the grantee's estate. It was like a chose in action (a right to sue), and choses in action were inalienable until modern times. You might assume that because we now think of these interests as things, and because these interests are inheritable by heirs and devisable by will, we would discard the rule that they cannot be transferred during life. But history has left curious traces in our law.

In most American states the <u>possibility of reverter and the right of entry, like other property interests, are transferable inter vivos</u>. This is the modern trend. <u>But some states continue to follow the common law rule; the interests are not transferable inter vivos except to the owner of the possessory fee</u> (called a release). A few states appear to draw a distinction between the two interests and hold that the possibility of reverter is transferable, but the right of entry is not. In a couple of states the right of entry has been given even harsher treatment: <u>The mere attempt to transfer a right of entry during life destroys it.</u> For discussion of these various positions, with citations to states, see 2A Richard Powell, The Law of Real Property ¶275[2] & [3] (rev. ed. 1992).

In the second situation where different legal consequences might flow from the fact that a possibility of reverter becomes possessory automatically whereas a right of entry requires a positive act by the grantor to terminate the fee simple, adverse possession is involved. <u>The statute of limitations starts running on the possibility of reverter as soon as the determinable fee ends.</u> With respect to the right of entry, theoretically the statute of limitations should not begin to run until the grantor attempts to exercise the right and is rebuffed, giving rise to a cause of action. However, this may be more theory than reality. <u>In many states the statute begins to run on the right of entry when the condition occurs.</u> Or, analogizing to the equitable doctrine of laches which bars relief when delay works injury, prejudice, or disadvantage to the defendant, <u>courts in other states may require the right of entry to be exercised within a reasonable time, which in turn may be defined as the period of the statute of limitations.</u>

In a third situation, the difference between a determinable fee and a fee subject to condition subsequent may be crucial. If the forfeiture interest is not retained by the transferor but is created in a transferee (and called an executory interest), it is subject to the Rule against Perpetuities. Startlingly different results turn on the classification of the preceding possessory fee simple. We save the discussion of this until we take up the Rule against Perpetuities in the next chapter. See page 302.

For discussion of these and other possible differences, see Allison Dunham, Possibility of Reverter and Powers of Termination — Fraternal or Identical Twins?, 20 U. Chi. L. Rev. 215 (1953); Comment, Equivalence of Right of Entry and Right of Reverter, 18 Ohio St. L.J. 120 (1957).

In view of the fact that scriveners often do not resort to the precise classical language used to create the determinable fee and the fee on condition subsequent, thereby giving rise to much litigation (as the *Mahrenholz* case indicates), why do we continue to have these two estates? Should different consequences turn on fine distinctions in language often unwittingly chosen? California and Kentucky have abolished the fee simple determinable with statutes providing that language creating a fee simple determinable at common law creates a fee simple subject to condition subsequent. Cal. Civ. Code §885.020 (West Supp. 1992); Ky. Rev. Stat. Ann. §381.218 (1970).

2. *O* conveys Blackacre "to *A* and her heirs so long as the premises are not used for sale of beer, wine, or liquor, and if beer, wine, or liquor is sold on the premises *O* retains a right to re-enter the premises." Subsequently *A* opens a restaurant on Blackacre that serves several dishes cooked with wine or flamed with brandy and at Sunday brunch offers a complimentary glass of champagne. *A*'s restaurant is successful, and 11 years after its opening *B* wants to buy it and add a bar. Advise *B*.

3. In *Mahrenholz* the land was given for "school purpose" only. What is a school purpose? In a sequel to *Mahrenholz,* the court held that use of the Hutton School property to store school equipment and supplies, primarily used desks, was for a school purpose, and therefore the Mahrenholzes were not entitled to the property. Mahrenholz v. County Bd. of School Trustees, 188 Ill. App. 3d 260, 544 N.E.2d 128 (1989).

Suppose that the school board permits the school auditorium to be used by various community groups, including Planned Parenthood, or suppose it rents the auditorium to a promoter who stages various entertainments, including a touring ballet company and a rock band. Would the land revert? Or suppose that the school board executes an oil and gas lease and oil wells are drilled, striking oil. Would the land revert to the grantors' successors? Could the grantors' successors obtain an injunction to prevent taking oil from the land on the theory that such would constitute waste and a destruction of the value of the possibility of reverter? See Davis v. Skipper, 125 Tex. 364, 83 S.W.2d 318 (1935).

4. *Covenants distinguished.* Conditions imposed by the grantor in creating defeasible fees must be distinguished from covenants (promises) made by a grantee. A condition is much more onerous than a covenant. If a condition is breached, the land is or may be *forfeited* to the holder of the future interest. A covenant is a promise by the grantee that a specified act will or will not be performed. If a covenant is breached, the promisee may sue for an *injunction* or *damages.* Example: *O* conveys Blackacre to *A,* who promises on behalf of himself, his heirs, and assigns that Blackacre will be used only for residential purposes. If *A* erects a slaughterhouse on Blackacre, *O* can sue *A* for an injunction to have the slaughterhouse removed or *O* can sue *A* for damages. We discuss covenants in Chapter 9.

Mountain Brow Lodge No. 82, Independent Order of Odd Fellows v. Toscano

Court of Appeal of California, Fifth District, 1968
257 Cal. App. 2d 22, 64 Cal. Rptr. 816

CARGANO, J. This action was instituted by appellant, a non-profit corporation, to quiet its title to a parcel of real property which it acquired on April 6, 1950, by gift deed from James V. Toscano and Maria Toscano, both deceased. Respondents are the trustees and administrators of the estates of the deceased grantors and appellant sought to quiet its title as to their interest in the land arising from certain conditions contained in the gift deed.

The matter was submitted to the court on stipulated facts and the court rendered judgment in favor of respondents. However, it is not clear from the court's findings of fact and conclusions of law whether it determined that the conditions were not void and hence refused to quiet appellant's title for this reason, or whether it decided that appellant had not broken the conditions and then erroneously concluded that "neither party has a right to an anticipatory decree" until a violation occurs. Thus, to avoid prolonged litigation the parties have stipulated that when the trial court rendered judgment refusing to quiet appellant's title it simply decided that the conditions are not void and that its decision on this limited issue is the only question presented in this appeal. We shall limit our discussion accordingly.

The controversy between the parties centers on the language contained in the habendum clause of the deed of conveyance which reads as follows:

Said property is restricted for the use and benefit of the second party, only; and in the event the same fails to be used by the second party or in the event

**Odd Fellows Building, Los Banos,
erected 1919, meeting rooms above, stores below**

**The tract of land given the lodge by the Toscanos,
adjacent to the rear of the building, is used as a parking lot**

of sale or transfer by the second party of all or any part of said lot, the same is to revert to the first parties herein, their successors, heirs or assigns.

Respondents maintain that the language creates a fee simple subject to a condition subsequent and is valid and enforceable. On the other hand, appellant contends that the restrictive language amounts to an absolute restraint on its power of alienation and is void. It apparently asserts that, since the purpose for which the land must be used is not precisely defined, it may be used by appellant for any purpose and hence the restriction is not on the land use but on who uses it. Thus, appellant concludes that it is clear that the reversionary clause was intended by grantors to take effect only if appellant sells or transfers the land.

Admittedly, the condition of the habendum clause which prohibits appellant from selling or transferring the land under penalty of forfeiture is an absolute restraint against alienation and is void. The common law rule prohibiting restraint against alienation is embodied in Civil Code section 711 which provides: "Conditions restraining alienation, when repugnant to the interest created, are void." However, this condition and the condition relating to the use of the land are in the disjunctive and are clearly severable. In other words, under the plain language of the deed the grantors, their successors or assigns may exercise their power of termination "if the land is not used by the second party" or "in the event of sale or transfer by the second party." Thus, the invalid restraint against alienation does not necessarily affect or nullify the condition on land use (Los Angeles Investment Company v. Gary, 181 Cal. 680, 186 P. 596, 9 A.L.R. 115).

The remaining question, therefore, is whether the use condition created a defeasible fee as respondents maintain or whether it is also a restraint against alienation and nothing more as appellant alleges. Significantly, appellant is a non-profit corporation organized for lodge, fraternal and similar purposes. Moreover, decedent, James V. Toscano, was an active member of the lodge at the time of his death. In addition, the term "use" as applied to real property can be construed to mean a "right which a person has to use or enjoy the property of another according to his necessities" (Mulford v. LeFranc (1864), 26 Cal. 88, 102). Under these circumstances it is reasonably clear that when the grantors stated that the land was conveyed in consideration of "love and affection" and added that it "is restricted for the *use* and benefit of the second party" they simply meant to say that the land was conveyed upon condition that it would be used for lodge, fraternal and other purposes for which the non-profit corporation was formed. Thus, we conclude that the portion of the habendum clause relating to the land use, when construed as a whole and in light of the surrounding circumstances, created a fee subject to a condition subsequent with title to revert to the grantors, their successors or assigns if the land ceases to be used for lodge, fraternal and similar purposes for which the appellant is formed.[29] No formal language is necessary to create a fee simple subject to a condition subsequent as long as the intent of the grantor is clear. It is the rule that the object in construing a deed is to ascertain the intention of the grantor from words which have been employed and from surrounding circumstances (Brannan v. Mesick, 10 Cal. 95; Aller v. Berkeley Hall School Foundation, 40 Cal. App. 2d 31, 103 P.2d 1052; Schofield v. Bany, 175 Cal. App. 2d 534, 346 P.2d 891).

It is of course arguable, as appellant suggests, that the condition in appellant's deed is not a restriction on land use but on who uses it. Be this as it may, the distinction between a covenant which restrains the alienation of a fee simple absolute and a condition which restricts land use and creates a defeasible estate was long recognized at common law and is recognized in this state.[30] Thus, conditions restricting land use have been upheld by the California courts on numerous occasions even though they hamper, and often completely impede, alienation. A few examples follow: Mitchell v. Cheney Slough Irrigation Co., 57 Cal. App. 2d 138, 134 P.2d 34 (irrigation ditch); Aller v. Berkeley Hall School Foundation, 40 Cal. App. 2d 31, 103 P.2d 1052 (exclusively private dwellings); Rosecrans v. Pacific Electric Railway Co., 21 Cal. 2d 602, 134 P.2d 245 (to maintain a train schedule); Schultz v. Beers, 111 Cal. App. 2d 820, 245 P.2d 334 (road purposes); Firth v. Marovich, 160 Cal. 257, 116 P. 729 (residence only).

Moreover, if appellant's suggestion is carried to its logical conclusion it would mean that real property could not be conveyed to a city to be used only for its own city purposes, or to a school district to be used only for its own school purposes, or to a church to be used only for its own church purposes. Such restrictions would also be restrictions upon who uses the land. And yet we do not understand this to be the rule of this state. For example, in Los Angeles Investment Company v. Gary, supra, 181 Cal. 680, 186 P. 596, land had been conveyed upon condition that it was not to be sold, leased, rented or occupied by persons other than those of Caucasian race. The court held that the condition against alienation of the land was void, but upheld the condition restricting the land use. Although a use restriction compelling racial discrimination is no longer consonant with constitutional principles under more recent

29. It is arguable that the gift deed created a fee simple determinable. However, in doubtful cases the preferred construction is in favor of an estate subject to a condition subsequent (2 Witkin, Summary Calif. Law., Real Prop. §97, pp. 949-950).

30. The distinction between defeasible estates and future interests which also curtail alienation was recognized at common law. In fact, the creation of future interests, through trusts and similar devises, whose vesting could be indefinitely postponed, resulted in the development of the rule against perpetuities. Significantly, the rule against perpetuities has no application to defeasible estates because reversions, possibilities of reverter and powers of termination are inherently vested in nature (Strong v. Shatto, 45 Cal. App. 29, 187 P. 150; Caffroy v. Fremlin, 198 Cal. App. 2d 176, 17 Cal. Rptr. 668).

decisions, the sharp distinction that the court drew between a restriction on land use and a restriction on alienation is still valid. For further example, in the leading and often cited case of Johnston v. City of Los Angeles, 176 Cal. 479, 168 P. 1047, the land was conveyed to the City of Los Angeles on the express condition that the city would use it for the erection and maintenance of a dam, the land to revert if the city ceased to use it for such purposes. The Supreme Court held that the condition created a defeasible estate, apparently even though it was by necessity a restriction on who could use the land.

Our independent research indicates that the rule is the same in other jurisdictions. In Regular Predestinarian Baptist Church of Pleasant Grove v. Parker, 373 Ill. 607, 27 N.E.2d 522, 137 A.L.R. 635, a condition " 'To have and to hold . . . as long as the same is used by the Regular Predestinarian Baptist Church as a place of meeting . . .' " was deemed to have created a defeasible estate by the Supreme Court of Illinois.

In Frensley v. White, 208 Okl. 209, 254 P.2d 982, 983, the deed to the trustees of a religious organization contained the following language:

> To Have And To Hold said above described premises unto the said Trustees and their successors in office, as aforesaid, in trust, so long as said premises shall be held, kept and used by said church or any branch thereof, or any successor thereto for a place of divine worship, for the use of the ministry and membership of said church, subject to the usages, discipline and ministerial appointments of said church as from time to time authorized and declared by the General Council of the Assemblies of God Church and by the Annual Council within whose bounds said premises are, or may hereafter be situated.

The Supreme Court of Oklahoma treated the estate as a fee determinable, notwithstanding the extreme language of the deed which not only limited the land use but who could use it.

In Merchants Bank and Trust Company v. New Canaan Historical Society, 133 Conn. 706, 54 A.2d 696, 172 A.L.R. 1275, a parcel of real property was willed to the New Canaan Library Association " 'upon the condition and provided, however, that if said property shall not be used by said Library Association for the purposes of its organization, this devise shall terminate and the property become a part of my residuary estate. . . .' " There, as here, the language of the condition did not precisely define the restricted use but expressly permitted any use for which the library association was formed. The Supreme Court of Errors of Connecticut clearly indicated that the will had created a fee determinable.

For the reasons herein stated, the first paragraph of the judgment below is amended and revised to read:

1. That at the time of the commencement of this action title to the parcel of real property situated in the City of Los Banos, County of Merced, State of California, being described as Lot 20 Block 72 according to the Map of the Town of Los Banos, was vested in the MOUNTAIN BROW LODGE NO. 82, INDEPENDENT ORDER OF ODD FELLOWS, subject to the condition that said property is restricted for the use and benefit of the second party only; and in the event the same fails to be used by the second party the same is to revert to the first parties herein, their successors, heirs or assigns.

As so modified the judgment is affirmed. Respondents to recover their costs on appeal.

STONE, J. I dissent. I believe the entire habendum clause which purports to restrict the fee simple conveyed is invalid as a restraint upon alienation. . . .

If the words "sale or transfer," which the majority find to be a restraint upon alienation, are expunged, still the property cannot be sold or transferred by the grantee because the property may be used by only the I.O.O.F. Lodge No. 82, upon pain of reverter. This use restriction prevents the grantee from conveying the property just as effectively as the condition against "sale or transfer . . . of all or any part of said lot."

Certainly, if we are to have realism in the law, the effect of language must be judged according to what it does. When two different terms generate the same ultimate legal result, they should be treated alike in relation to that result.

Section 711 of the Civil Code expresses an ancient policy of English common law. The wisdom of this proscription as applied to situations of this kind is manifest when we note that a number of fraternal, political and similar organizations of a century ago have disappeared, and others have ceased to function in individual communities. Should an organization holding property under a deed similar to the one before us be disbanded one hundred years or so after the conveyance is made, the result may well be a title fragmented into the interests of heirs of the grantors numbering in the hundreds and scattered to the four corners of the earth.

[I]t seems to me that . . . the entire habendum clause is repugnant to the grant in fee simple that precedes it. I would hold the property free from restrictions, and reverse the judgment.

NOTES

1. Falls City, Nebraska, conveyed land to the Missouri Pacific Railway Company as long as the land was used as a site for the railroad company's divisional headquarters, and in case it should be abandoned

for such use the land was to revert to the city. Subsequently the railroad company moved its divisional headquarters from Falls City. In a quiet title action by the railroad against the city, the court held that the reverter provision was invalid as a restraint on alienation and that the railroad had a fee simple absolute:

> We find that the recent decision of the Nebraska Supreme Court in Cast v. National Bank of Commerce, Trust and Savings Association of Lincoln, 183 N.W.2d 485 (Neb. 1971), is controlling. In *Cast,* the court held, upon rehearing, that a condition attached to a defeasible fee simple is an [unenforceable] indirect restraint against alienation "if it materially affects marketability adversely." . . . If the condition subsequent in the conveyance expressly limits alienation of the property to an impermissibly small number of persons, it is void and unenforceable. Conversely, most use restrictions are valid and enforceable unless they also have the practical effect of "affecting marketability adversely" by unreasonably limiting the class of persons to whom it may be alienated. . . . In limiting the use of the property by the Railroad to use as its divisional headquarters only, the City, in practical effect, completely restricted alienation of the land to other grantees. Thus, even though the conditional restriction is couched in terms of the use of the property, like the conditional limitation in *Cast,* it unreasonably affects the marketability of the land adversely by completely restricting alienation. [Falls City v. Missouri Pacific Railway Co., 453 F.2d 771, 773-774 (8th Cir. 1971).]

2. Testators sometimes attempt to control, after their deaths, the use of their houses by family members. The results are mixed. In Cast v. National Bank of Commerce, Trust & Sav. Assn. of Lincoln, 186 Neb. 385, 183 N.W.2d 485 (1971), the testator left a farm to Richard Cast in fee simple on condition that "Richard or one of his children shall occupy the farm as his or her residence for 25 years," with forfeiture for breach of condition. The court held the condition void as a restraint on alienation. See also Wills v. Pierce, 208 Ga. 417, 67 S.E.2d 239 (1951), holding invalid a condition that a house "shall be used [by the grantee and his heirs] as a residence," with reverter to the grantor in case of breach.

Compare Casey v. Casey, 287 Ark. 395, 700 S.W.2d 46 (1985), where the testator devised land to his son with a provision for forfeiture if the son's daughter were ever to own, possess, or be a guest on the land for more than one week a year. The court held the condition unreasonable and void because capricious and imposed for spite or malice.

Compare also Babb v. Rand, 345 A.2d 496 (Me. 1975), where the testator left a summer home "to John Freeman Rand in fee simple with the proviso that he shall never deny access or occupation to [the testator's other children] during their lifetime." The court held that this created a fee simple in John subject to a valid condition subsequent that continued until the death of the testator's last child.

Ink v. City of Canton
Supreme Court of Ohio, 1965
4 Ohio St. 2d 51, 212 N.E.2d 574

This cause originated in 1959 as an action in the Common Pleas Court of Stark County for a declaratory judgment with respect to the rights of the parties in a 33½-acre tract of land known as Ink Park.

By two deeds, one in 1936 and the other in 1941, the lineal descendants of Harry H. Ink conveyed that tract to the city of Canton.[31] The second deed was given to correct the description but otherwise the two deeds are substantially identical.

Plaintiffs are the grantors or the heirs of deceased grantors in those deeds.

In each deed, the granting clause reads:

. . . for the use and purpose of a public park, but for no other use or purpose whatsoever.

In each deed, the habendum clause reads:

To have and to hold said premises, with the appurtenances thereof, unto the said grantee and its successors, for so long a time as said grantee, and its successors, shall use and maintain said above described premises as and for a public park, and for no other use and purpose whatsoever; and in case said premises shall at any time hereafter cease to be occupied and used as a public park, or in case the restrictions, conditions, reservations and exceptions above mentioned shall be violated, then all the right, title and interest of said grantee and its successors in and to said premises shall be forfeited and shall cease and terminate, and said premises shall revert to and be vested in the above grantors, their heirs, successors and assigns, and said grantors, their heirs, successors and assigns, or any of them, may thereupon enter and take possession of all or any part of the aforesaid premises without notice. . . .

Each deed also provides:

The property hereby conveyed shall be known and designated as the "Harry H. Ink Park" in memory of the man who purchased it in 1914, with the idea of donating the same at some future date to the city of Canton . . . for park purposes.

31. Canton, Ohio (pop. 100,000), a pleasant factory town 50 miles south of Cleveland, was the home of William McKinley, the President who used the "full dinner pail" to forge an alliance between the Republican party and blue-collar workers at the turn of the century. Canton, laid out in 1805, probably derived its name from Canton, China, the great eighteenth-century trading port through which millions of pieces of porcelain, furniture, and art objects flowed from China to Europe and America. How lucky that the Ohio city received its name before the name of Canton, China, was changed in the 1970s, by pinyin romanization, to Guangzhou! — EDS.

The conveyance was accepted by the city, the tract was improved and developed as a public park, was named "Ink Park" and was used as a public park until 1961 when the state instituted proceedings to appropriate perpetual easements for highway and related purposes over all but 6½ of the 33½ acres. . . .

In the appropriation proceedings, the Director of Highways stated that the value of land taken was $96,247, that the value of structures was $2,875, and that the damages to the residue of the property not taken was $31,700, and deposited a total of $130,822 to be distributed to those having interests in the property. . . .

[The Common Pleas Court awarded the whole sum to the city. The Court of Appeals affirmed.]

TAFT, C.J. Plaintiffs . . . raise questions as to the effect of the state's appropriation of a substantial part of the Ink Park property on the respective rights of the city and of the plaintiffs to (1) the portion of that property still usable for park purposes and (2) the money paid by the state for the portions thereof appropriated and for damages to the residue.

Until the latter part of the Nineteenth Century, there were no reported cases which dealt with such questions. See Courter and Maskery, The Effect of Condemnation Proceedings upon Possibilities of Reverter and Powers of Termination, 38 University of Detroit Law Journal (1960) 46, 47.

Where property is conveyed in fee with a proviso that it is to be used only for a specified use and that the property shall revert to the grantor if such specified use ceases, it would appear reasonable to conclude that the property would so revert when its appropriation by eminent domain proceedings prevents that specified use. Such a conclusion would appear to be especially reasonable where, as in the instant case, the grantee paid nothing for what had been conveyed to him. A few cases have so held. Crow, Admr. v. Tidnam (1947), 198 Okla. 650, 181 P.2d 549; Lancaster School District v. Lancaster County (1929), 295 Pa. 112, 144 A. 901; Pedrotti v. Marin County (CCA 9-1946), 152 F.2d 829. However, the great weight of authority has held that there is no reverter in such an instance, and that the grantee takes the whole of the amount paid for the property appropriated. Courter and Maskery, supra; 46 Cornell Law Quarterly (1961) 631 et seq.; The Value of Possibilities of Reverter and Powers of Termination in Eminent Domain, Illinois Law Forum (1963) 693; Condemnation of Future Interests, 48 Virginia Law Review (1962) 461, 472 et seq.; Condemnation of Future Interests, 43 Iowa Law Review (1958) 241, 247.

This court's opinion in Board of County Commissioners v. Thormyer, Dir. (1959), 169 Ohio St. 291, 159 N.E.2d 612, 75 A.L.R.2d 1373, recognizes that such a holding may give a windfall to the grantee. He not only gets the value of what he had, i.e., the value of the property

Ink Park, April 1959, looking south

Ink Park, August 1963, looking north

with the restriction as to its use, but he gets what may be a greater value than the property would have without any such restriction. At the same time, the grantor's right of reverter is destroyed and he gets nothing for it.

There may be some justification for such a conclusion where the grantee paid the grantor the full value of the property for the determinable fee. In such an instance, giving the grantor any part of the eminent domain award would represent a windfall to the grantor. Also, since the grantee would have paid the full value of the property, it is reasonably arguable that giving the whole of the award to the grantee would give him the value of no more than what the grantee had paid for when he acquired the determinable fee. See concurring opinion in McMechan v. Board of Edn. of Richland Twp. (1952), 157 Ohio St. 241, 253, 105 N.E.2d 270. However, where, as in the instant case, the grantee paid nothing to the grantor for the determinable fee, it seems apparent that, at the very least, the amount, if any, by which the value of an unrestricted fee exceeds the value of the restricted fee, is something that should go to the grantor. Before the appropriation, the grantee had no right to the greater value of the property, if it had a greater value without out the restrictions imposed upon the grantee. The difference between that greater value and what the grantee lost as a result of the appropriation, i.e., the value of what the grantee had, would seem logically to belong to the grantor. That difference certainly represents the value of something which the grantor expressly refrained from conveying to the grantee. Where the amount of that difference can be determined, as it frequently can, and where the grantee had paid nothing for his determinable fee, there would appear to be no basis whatever for the reason usually advanced for giving the whole of the award in the appropriation proceedings to the grantee. That reason is that the right of reverter of the grantor is too remote and contingent to be capable of valuation.

The other reason sometimes advanced for giving the whole of the appropriation award to the grantee is that, since the law (i.e., the legal taking in eminent domain) has made it impossible to perform the condition under which the property is held, performance of that condition is excused. This is a statement of the conclusion reached rather than any reason for reaching that conclusion. The most that might be said for such a conclusion is that the provision for reverter on breach of the condition as to use is intended by the grantor to compel the grantees to make the specified use of the property. After the property is appropriated in eminent domain proceedings, such provision can no longer have any influence in compelling such use. Hence, the only justification for its existence has disappeared. However, this does not represent a reason for giving the grantee the value of something he has not lost (i.e., the amount, if any, by which the value of the property taken exceeds its lesser value for the restricted use that the grantee could have made of it) where the grantor expressly refrained from conveying that something to him.

As stated in Simes and Smith, Law of Future Interests, 2 Ed. (1956) Section 2013:

> . . . in the usual case the testator [grantor] neither thought of eminent domain nor provided therefor. Now, in fact it may be said that in most other cases of impossibility, the testator [grantor] did not foresee the situation which occurred, nor provide for it; and that is probably true. But it does not follow that this should be treated like the ordinary case of an impossible condition subsequent. It must be remembered that in the usual case the court must give the property either to the devisee [grantee] or to the devisor's [grantor's] heirs. There is no third alternative; whereas in the eminent domain case, the court may divide the award between them. . . .

In apparent recognition of the harshness of the majority rule giving the whole of the appropriation award to the owner of the determinable fee and nothing to the owner of the right of reverter, the American Law Institute Restatement of the Law of Property (1936) 188, Section 53, comment C, provides for a division of the eminent domain award between the owner of that determinable fee and the owner of the right of reverter where,

> viewed from the time of commencement of an eminent domain proceeding, and not taking into account any changes in the use of the land sought to be condemned which may result as a consequence of such proceeding, the event upon which a possessory estate in fee simple defeasible [determinable fee] is to end is an event the occurrence of which, within a reasonably short period of time, is probable.

Although not supported by any authority prior to its promulgation in 1936, this rule has received some support. See annotation, 81 A.L.R.2d 568, entitled Rights in Condemnation Award where Land Taken was Subject to Possible Rights of Reverter or Re-entry, which endeavors to explain the authorities with reference to this rule.

In the instant case, there was no event imminent, other than the impending appropriation proceedings, that could amount to a failure to use the Ink Park property for the purposes specified in the deeds conveying it to the city. Hence, this rule of the Restatement would not be applicable in the instant case. However, this limited departure by the Restatement and the authorities following it from the harsh majority rule, giving the whole of the appropriation award to the owner of the determinable fee, encourages us to consider whether some greater departure from that harsh rule should be made in the instant case.

We have already pointed out that the grantee paid nothing to the grantor for the determinable fee involved in the instant case; and that the reasons for giving any of the eminent domain award to the grantee are not the same in such a situation as where the grantee paid for what was conveyed to him.

There is another significant and, we believe, a decisive factor that should be considered in the instant case. The deeds conveying Ink Park to the city expressed an intention to impose upon the city a duty to use the property conveyed "as and for a public park . . ." to "be known and designated as" Ink Park. By accepting that conveyance, the city undertook a fiduciary obligation to use such property only for such purpose. Ohio Society for Crippled Children and Adults, Inc. v. McElroy, Atty. Genl. (1963), 175 Ohio St. 49, 191 N.E.2d 543, 100 A.L.R.2d 1202. Thus, until a court of equity in appropriate proceedings may give authority to do otherwise, the city must hold any interests in the Ink Park property not taken from it subject to the fiduciary obligations imposed upon it by the two deeds conveying that property to the city. . . .

Likewise, whatever money the city received in the eminent domain proceedings for the Ink Park land taken or on account of damages to the Ink Park land not taken can only be held by the city so long as it proposes to use, can reasonably use, and does use that money for Ink Park purposes; and any of that money which the city either does not propose to use, cannot reasonably use, or does not use for Ink Park purposes should revert to the plaintiffs. . . .

It follows that so long as the city proposes to, can reasonably and does use for Ink Park purposes the part of the Ink Park property not taken in eminent domain proceedings and the money it receives for the Ink Park land taken and on account of damages to such land not taken, neither such land nor money will revert to plaintiffs although plaintiffs will retain their rights of reverter both with respect to that land and that money.

However, for reasons hereinbefore stated, since the money paid for the land taken in the eminent domain proceedings represents its value for any use and the conveyance to the city was for a specific use only, the amount, if any, by which the value of that land for any use exceeds its value for the specific use only should be paid to the plaintiffs. The grantor never intended to convey for park or any other purposes the interests in the Ink Park property represented by such difference between its unrestricted value and its value for the uses specified in the two deeds. . . .

Part of the eminent domain award is for structures taken. To the extent that this part of the award represents payment for structures built by the city, this part should go to the city without being subject to any fiduciary obligation imposed by or right of reverter provided for in the deeds conveying Ink Park to the city.

For the foregoing reasons, the judgment of the Court of Appeals is reversed, and the cause is remanded to the Court of Appeals for further proceedings in accordance with this opinion.

Judgment reversed.

NOTES AND QUESTIONS

1. The city of Canton and the Ink heirs, acting together to sell their separate interests to a purchaser, can receive the full market value of the land from the purchaser. Thus, in that sense, the total value of their interests equals the full market value of the land.

Valuation of the interests separately, however, results in the paradox that the sum of the parts does not equal the whole. The value of the city's fee simple determinable is the value of the land as a public park discounted by the probability of cessation of park use. Since cessation of park use is solely within the control of the city (absent exercise of eminent domain by the state), the probability of cessation of park use — and the discount — is negligible. How is the value of land limited to public park use measured? There is no market in land parcels that can be used only for a public park from which we can ascertain what comparable properties sell for. How much would you give to own a public park?

The value of the possibility of reverter is the full market value of the land discounted by the probability that the reverter will never become possessory. Since cessation of park use lies in the discretion of the city, which is likely never to cease such use, the possibility of reverter is substantially worthless on the market.

The court appears to get out of the dilemma by saying that the city's determinable fee should be valued first and "the amount, if any, by which the value of that land for any use [full market value] exceeds its value for the specific use only [value for park use] should be paid to the plaintiffs." If the court really means this, who will end up with the lion's share of the condemnation proceeds?

Does a better solution appear to you than any solution considered by the court? See Victor P. Goldberg, Thomas W. Merrill & Daniel Unumb, Bargaining in the Shadow of Eminent Domain: Valuing and Apportioning Condemnation Awards Between Landlord and Tenant, 34 UCLA L. Rev. 1083, 1133-1135 (1987). The *Ink* case is followed in Leeco Gas & Oil Co. v. County of Nueces, 736 S.W.2d 629 (Tex. 1987).

2. The valuation problem aside, were the plaintiffs in *Ink* paid for their future interest but also allowed to keep it?

3. *Postscript.* The decision in Ink v. City of Canton was handed down in December 1965 and remanded to the trial court. The city and the Ink heirs could not agree on how to divide the money according to the rule laid down in the *Ink* case, nor could they find the relevant evi-

dence that would help the trial court fix the values of their respective interests. Perhaps responding to pressure from the city, which had agreed not to contest running the interstate highway through Ink Park, the state reconsidered its valuation of the Ink Park land and paid an additional $137,000 into the pot to be divided. In 1973 the city and the Ink heirs were finally able to come to a settlement. The pot had now grown, with interest, to $293,000. The settlement gave the city $130,000, the Ink heirs $160,000, and the lawyer for the Inks $3,000. In this settlement the Ink heirs released to the city their possibility of reverter in the remaining 6½ acres of Ink Park. The trial court approved the settlement. The city of Canton put its $130,000 in an Ink Park Land Fund, for the purpose of buying park land. In 1979, the city used this money to help pay for a replacement park of 24 acres, which cost $200,000. (This information was furnished the editors by Professor William Roth, who investigated the aftermath of the *Ink* case.)

NOTE: DEFEASIBLE LIFE ESTATES

In former years it was not uncommon to run across a life estate defeasible upon marriage. For example, a husband might devise property to his widow for life with a proviso that she loses it if she remarries. Such a provision is now rarely encountered, for several reasons. First, the provision rests upon a notion that a second husband is liable for support of his wife for her lifetime, even after divorce, so the wife will not need support from her first husband, but the common law liability of husbands (second as well as first) to support their wives after divorce has almost passed from the American scene (see pages 383-384). Second, at the death of one spouse, modern law has increased the protection of the surviving spouse, giving her an elective share of fee simple ownership in her deceased husband's estate and not, as at common law, merely support for her life. If dissatisfied with a life estate defeasible upon remarriage given her by her husband's will, the surviving wife can renounce the will and claim a share of outright ownership. Third, a proviso for forfeiture upon remarriage has lost favor since the 1940s, when the marital deduction was introduced into the Internal Revenue Code, because the proviso disqualifies the devise for the federal estate tax marital deduction. For a life estate to qualify for the marital deduction and pass free of estate taxation, the surviving spouse must be entitled to all the income for her entire life. Internal Revenue Code §2056(a)(5) & (7) (1986).

In addition, provisions calling for forfeiture of property upon marriage may violate the common law rule against restraints on marriage. The common law favors marriage and is jealous of provisions that hinder it. In determining whether a particular provision violates this policy favoring marriage, courts have said that the fundamental question is whether the provision has the *purpose* (1) of coercing abstention from marriage or (2) of providing support until marriage, without any desire to hinder marriage. If the transferor has the first purpose in mind, the provision is invalid. If the second purpose is his objective, the provision will be upheld.

A number of courts have taken the position that the purpose of the grantor can be discerned from the form of the limitation. A devise "to *A* for life so long as *A* remains unmarried, then to *B*," is thought to have the dominant motive of providing support until marriage, when presumably *A*'s spouse will provide support, and not the purpose of discouraging marriage. A devise "to *A* for life, but if *A* marries, then to *B*," on the other hand, is thought to have the purpose of penalizing marriage. See Lewis v. Searles, 452 S.W.2d 153 (Mo. 1970). Is this reasoning sound? Restatement (Second) of Property, Donative Transfers, §6.1, Comment e (1983), says a determinable limitation has "some slight evidentiary value as indicative of a motive to provide support."

PROBLEM

H's will devises Blackacre "to my wife, *W*, for her use and benefit, so long as she remains unmarried." *H* devises the residue of his property to his daughter, *D*, a child by his first wife. *W* does not remarry but moves into the apartment of her male friend, *A*. *W* subsequently dies, devising all her property to *A*. Who owns Blackacre? See Eller v. Wages, 220 Ga. 58, 136 S.E.2d 730 (1964); Saunders v. Saunders, 260 Or. 480, 490 P.2d 1260 (1971). See also Restatement (Second) of Property, supra, §6.1, Comment f: "A restraint against marriage is construed as narrowly as possible, consistent with the language employed in describing the restraint and, hence, does not automatically include within it a restraint against cohabitation without marriage."

4

Future Interests

A. *Introduction*

We now turn to future interests, which confer rights to the enjoyment of property at a future time. After the courts held that the fee tail could be destroyed by a common recovery, cutting off the rights of issue and converting the fee tail into a fee simple, lawyers began to create life estates followed by one or more future interests. Thus a testator might devise land "to my son *A* for life, and on *A*'s death to *A*'s daughter *B* and her heirs." By creating a future interest in his granddaughter, *B*, to become possessory upon his son *A*'s death, the testator is able to control inheritance of the land not only at his death but also at his son's death. Today, life estates followed by future interests are the foundation blocks of wills and estate planning.

Future interests are limited in number, but the ones permitted are quite enough. In fact, we are willing to bet that, before we are through, you will have a candidate or two for the discard file.

Future interests recognized in our legal system are:

(1) Interests retained by the transferor, known as:
    (a) Reversion
    (b) Possibility of reverter
    (c) Right of entry (also known as power of termination)
(2) Interests created in a transferee, known as:
    (a) Vested remainder
    (b) Contingent remainder
    (c) Executory interest

A future interest is not a mere expectancy, like the hope of a child to inherit from a parent. A future interest gives legal rights to its owner. It is a presently existing property interest, protected by the court as such. Take this case: *O* conveys Blackacre "to *A* for life, then to *B* and her heirs." *B* has present legal rights and liabilities. *B* can sell or give away her remainder. She can enjoin *A* from committing waste. She can sue third parties who are injuring the land or are claiming the title hostilely. If *B* dies during the life of *A*, *B*'s remainder will be transmitted to *B*'s heirs or devisees, and a federal estate tax or state inheritance tax may be levied upon its value. Although a future interest does not entitle its owner to present possession, it is a *presently existing interest* that may become possessory in the future.

B.   Future Interests in the Transferor

1.   Reversion

Historically, the earliest future interest to develop was a reversion. If *O*, a fee simple owner, granted the land to *A* for life, the land would revert ("come back") to *O* at *A*'s death. *O*'s right to future possession is called a reversion. If *O* dies during *A*'s life, *O*'s reversion passes under his will or to his heirs, and at *A*'s death whoever owns the reversion is entitled to possession of the land.

In a general sense, then, a reversion is the interest left in an owner when he carves out of his estate a lesser estate and does not provide who is to take the property when the lesser estate expires. But more precise definition is necessary. "A reversion is," in the words of Professor Lewis Simes, "the interest remaining in the grantor, or in the successor in interest of a testator, who transfers a *vested estate of a lesser quantum* than that of the vested estate which he has." 1 American Law of Property §4.16 (1952) (emphasis added). The hierarchy of estates determines what is a lesser estate. The fee simple is a greater estate than a fee tail, which is a greater estate than a life estate, which is a greater estate than the leasehold estates. Hence if *O*, owning a fee simple, creates a fee tail, a life estate, or a term of years, and does not at the same time convey away a vested remainder in fee simple, *O* has a reversion. If *A*, owning a life estate, creates a term of years, *A* has a reversion.

Because reversions result from the hierarchy of estates, they are thought of as the remnant of an estate that has not entirely passed away from the transferor. Hence all reversions are retained interests, which remain vested in the transferor.

When a reversion is retained, it may or may not be certain to become possessory in the future. Thus:

> *Example 1.* *O* conveys Blackacre "to *A* for life." *O* has a reversion in fee simple that is certain to become possessory. At *A*'s death, either *O* or *O*'s successor in interest will be entitled to possession.
>
> *Example 2.* *O* conveys Whiteacre "to *A* for life, then to *B* and her heirs if *B* survives *A*." *O* has a reversion in fee simple that is not certain to become

possessory. If *B* dies before *A, O* will be entitled to possession at *A*'s death. On the other hand, if *A* dies before *B, O*'s reversion is divested on *A*'s death and will never become possessory.

In the above examples, the *value* of the reversions may differ, because one is certain to become possessory and the other is not, but the *name* of *O*'s interest in both examples — a reversion — is the same. *Note well*: In *Example 2, O* has a reversion, not a possibility of a reversion. There is no such interest as a "possibility of reversion," and you should never use that phrase. Such talk is likely to produce confusion of a reversion with an entirely different interest, the possibility of reverter which follows a determinable fee. Remember that the names of future interests are names arbitrarily given, like first names to children. Call the future interest by its correct name.

At common law a reversion was transferable during life and descendible and devisable at death. It remains so today.

PROBLEMS AND NOTE

1. *O* owns a fee simple and makes the following transfers. In which cases is there a reversion?

(a) *O* conveys "to *A* for life, then to *B* and her heirs."

(b) *O* conveys "to *A* for life, then to *B* and the heirs of her body."

(c) *O* conveys "to *A* for life, then to *B* and her heirs if *B* attains the age of 21 before *A* dies." At the time of the conveyance *B* is 15 years old. (If there is a reversion, what happens to it if *B* reaches 21 during *A*'s life?)

(d) *O* conveys "to *A* for 20 years."

2. Under the hierarchy of estates, *A*, owner of a life estate, can carve out of it a term of years of any length, even 999 years, but of course the term ends if *A* dies before the set period of years since *A* cannot convey more than *A* has.

Suppose that *B*, owner of a 10-year term, transfers it to *A* for life; then *A* dies intestate two years later. Does the property revert to *B* for the remainder of the term *or* go to *A*'s heirs for the remainder of the term on the theory that *A*, who was granted a life estate that is greater than the whole term of years, took the whole term? After much hemming and hawing, the English courts finally rose above principle and held that *A* had the whole term but that upon *A*'s death the remainder of the term, if any, reverted to *B*. Eyres v. Faulkland, 1 Salk. 231, 91 Eng. Rep. 204 (K.B. 1697). So much for the logic of estates!

3. *O* conveys Blackacre "to *A* for life, then to *B* for life." *O* subsequently dies with a will devising all of *O*'s property to *C*. Then *A* dies and *B* dies. Who owns Blackacre?

2. Possibility of Reverter

A possibility of reverter arises when an owner carves out of his estate a *determinable* estate of the same quantum. Theoretically a possibility of reverter can be retained when a life tenant conveys his life estate to another determinable on the happening of an event, but the cases, almost without exception, deal with carving a fee simple determinable out of a fee simple absolute. Thus for all practical purposes a possibility of reverter is a future interest remaining in the transferor or his heirs when a fee simple determinable is created. Example: O conveys Blackacre "to Town Library Board so long as used for library purposes." O has a possibility of reverter.

The possibility of reverter has been previously discussed in connection with its correlative possessory estate, the fee simple determinable. See pages 236-237.

3. Right of Entry

When an owner transfers an estate subject to condition subsequent and retains the power to cut short or terminate the estate, the transferor has a right of entry. Example: O conveys Whiteacre "to Town Library Board, but if it ceases to use the land for library purposes, O has the right to re-enter and retake the premises."

The right of entry has been previously discussed in connection with the fee simple subject to condition subsequent. See pages 237-238.

C. Future Interests in Transferees

There are three types of future interests in transferees: vested remainders, contingent remainders, and executory interests. A remainder or executory interest cannot be retained by the transferor; these interests are created only in transferees. Once created, a remainder or executory interest can be transferred back to the grantor, but the name originally given the interest does not change.

1. Introduction

In early law an owner of land might provide, when creating a life estate, that the land would not revert to the donor but would "remain out" for some third person. Hence developed the concept of a remainder. The earliest form of a remainder was a future interest in a transferee that is certain to become possessory upon the expiration of the prior estate created at the same time. An example is "to *A* for life, then to *B* and her heirs." In this conveyance *B* has a vested remainder in fee simple. Upon *A*'s death, *B* or *B*'s successor in interest is entitled to possession in fee simple.

Although a vested remainder was recognized with little difficulty, it took several centuries for the law to approve a contingent remainder. In the case of the vested remainder above, the transferor has decided at the outset who is to take the property upon the life tenant's death. A contingent remainder permits the transferor to let future events determine this question. For example, upon *A*'s marriage, *O* (*A*'s father) might convey "to *A* for life, then to *A*'s eldest son and his heirs." If *A* has a son born thereafter, such son will take on *A*'s death; but if a son is not born, the land will revert to *O*. The contingent remainder gave difficulty to the judges because it left uncertain who would take the land upon *A*'s death, and the old law disliked uncertainty in succession to land titles (much as people disliked uncertainty in succession to the crown). After several hesitant starts, the contingent remainder finally, in the middle of the sixteenth century, was admitted as a valid future interest.

A remainder is, as the above examples illustrate, a future interest that waits politely until the termination of the preceding possessory estate, at which time the remainder moves into possession if it is then vested. A remainder is a future interest that is capable of becoming possessory at the termination of the prior estate. It is not required that the future interest be certain of future possession, only that it be possible for the interest to become possessory when the prior estate ends. If, at the time the future interest is created, it is not possible for it to become possessory upon the termination of the prior estate, the future interest is not a remainder.

> *Example 3.* *O* conveys "to *A* for life, then to *B* and her heirs if *B* lives to attain the age of 21." *B* is 15 years old at the time of the conveyance. *B*'s future interest can become possessory upon the termination of the life estate because *B* may reach 21 before that time. On the other hand, it may not become possessory then, because *A* may die before *B* reaches 21.[1] *B* has a remainder, contingent upon reaching 21.

Observe that the full state of *B*'s title in *Example 3* is "*B* has a contingent remainder in fee simple absolute." "Remainder" tells us the kind of future interest; "in fee simple absolute" tells us the kind of estate held as a

---

1. If *A* dies before *B* reaches 21, at common law *B*'s remainder was destroyed at *A*'s death. Under modern law, *B*'s remainder is not destroyed, and *B* can take after *A*'s death when *B* reaches the age of 21. See pages 295-299.

future interest (and what kind of possessory estate the remainder will become if it becomes possessory).

Not long after the contingent remainder was recognized by the courts, the executory interest arose to complicate matters further. The executory interest, made possible by the Statute of Uses (1536), developed to do what a remainder cannot do: divest or cut short the preceding interest. An executory interest is a future interest in a transferee that can take effect only by divesting another interest. Thus suppose that the conveyance in *Example 3* had read, "to A for life, but if B attains 21 during A's life, to B upon attaining 21." In this case B would have an executory interest because B can take only by divesting A's life estate. The difference between taking possession as soon as the prior estate ends and divesting the prior estate is the essential difference between a remainder and an executory interest.

PROBLEM

O conveys Blackacre "to A for life, then to B if B gives A a proper funeral." Does B have a remainder or an executory interest? If it is an executory interest, whose interest will be divested if B gives A a proper funeral?

2.   Remainders

Now that you have a general idea of what a remainder is, we must explore the technical aspects of remainders further.

Remainders are classified into two general types: vested and contingent. A remainder is *vested* if (1) it is given to an ascertained person and (2) it is not subject to a condition precedent (other than the natural termination of the preceding estates). A remainder is *contingent* if (1) it is given to an unascertained person or (2) it is subject to a condition precedent. Or, to quote Gray's famous definition,

> A remainder is vested in A, when, throughout its continuance, A, or A and his heirs, have the right to immediate possession, whenever and however the preceding freehold estates may determine. A remainder is contingent if, in order for it to come into possession, the fulfillment of some condition precedent other than the determination of the preceding freehold estates is necessary. [John C. Gray, The Rule Against Perpetuities §101 (4th ed. 1942).]

About vested remainders. A remainder may be indefeasibly vested, meaning that the remainder is certain of becoming possessory in the future and cannot be divested. Thus:

Example 4. O conveys "to *A* for life, then to *B* and her heirs." *B* has an indefeasibly vested remainder certain to become possessory upon termination of the life estate. If *B* dies during *A*'s life, on *B*'s death *B*'s remainder passes to *B*'s devisees, or, if *B* dies intestate, passes to *B*'s heirs, or, if *B* dies intestate without heirs, escheats to the state. *B* or *B*'s successor in interest is certain to take possession upon *A*'s death.

A remainder may be vested but not certain of becoming possessory. *Example 9,* below, is an illustration.

A remainder created in a class of persons (such as in *A*'s children) is vested if one member of the class is ascertained and there is no condition precedent. The remainder is *vested subject to open* or *vested subject to partial divestment* if later-born children are entitled to share in the gift. Thus:

Example 5. O conveys "to *A* for life, then to *A*'s children and their heirs." *A* has one child, *B*. The remainder is vested in *B* subject to open to let in later-born children. *B*'s exact share cannot be known until *A* dies. If *A* has no child at the time of the conveyance, the remainder is contingent because no taker is ascertained.

About contingent remainders. A remainder that is contingent because its takers are unascertained is illustrated by the following example:

Example 6. O conveys "to *A* for life, then to the heirs of *B*." *B* is alive. The remainder is contingent because the heirs of *B* cannot be ascertained until *B* dies.[2] No living person has heirs, only heirs apparent. If *B*'s heirs apparent do not survive *B*, they will not be *B*'s heirs. The words "heirs of *B*" refer only to persons who survive *B* and are designated as *B*'s intestate successors by the applicable statute of intestate succession.

A remainder that is contingent because it is subject to a condition precedent is illustrated in *Examples 7* and *8* below:

Example 7. O conveys "to *A* for life, then to *B* and her heirs if *B* survives *A*." The language "if *B* survives *A*" subjects *B*'s remainder to a condition precedent.

Example 8. O conveys "to *A* for life, then to *B* and her heirs if *B* survives *A*, and if *B* does not survive *A* to *C* and his heirs." The language "if *B* survives *A*" subjects *B*'s remainder to a condition precedent, and the language "and if

2. Who owns this remainder? Can unborn persons own property? Restatement of Property §153, Comment a (1936), says we cannot accurately say that an unborn person has a future interest. Yet it is quite clear that the law treats the limitation as if a future interest has been created.

This paradox has a long history. Robert Megarry & H.W.R. Wade, The Law of Real Property 1177 (5th ed. 1984), report that after the validity of contingent remainders had become firmly established in the sixteenth century, "the problem of the ownership of the inheritance remained unsolved. Some said that under the above remainder to the heirs of *B*, the fee simple was in abeyance, or *in nubibus* (in the clouds) or *in gremio legis* (in the bosom of the law)."

B does not survive *A*" subjects *C*'s remainder to a condition precedent. Here we have *alternative contingent remainders* in *B* and *C*. If the remainder in *B* vests, the remainder in *C* cannot, and vice versa.

Before divesting executory interests were recognized, it could be said that a vested remainder in fee simple, unless subject to a right of entry or possibility of reverter in the grantor, was a remainder certain to become possessory whereas a contingent remainder in fee simple was uncertain of possession. But the simple logic of turning classification on the certainty of possession was shattered by the Statute of Uses (1536), which permitted the creation of a shifting interest in a transferee that can divest a vested remainder before it becomes possessory. *Example 9* illustrates the fine distinction in modern law between a contingent remainder and a remainder vested subject to divestment.

> *Example 9. O* conveys "to *A* for life, then to *B* and her heirs, but if *B* does not survive *A* to *C* and his heirs." Note carefully: *B* does *not* have a contingent remainder. *B* has a *vested remainder* in fee simple subject to divestment; *C* has a shifting executory interest which can become possessory only by divesting *B*'s remainder.

The different classification of *B*'s remainder in *Example 8* and in *Example 9* results solely from the way the conveyance is phrased. *O*'s intent is exactly the same in both cases, but it is expressed differently. Expressing intent in different ways can produce stunning differences in result. *Examples 8* and *9* should make you keenly aware that, in the law of future interests, much turns on the exact language of the conveyance.

The key to understanding why *B*'s interest is contingent in *Example 8* and vested in *Example 9* is this: You must classify interests in sequence as they are written. Gray put it this way: "Whether a remainder is vested or contingent depends upon the language employed. If the conditional element is incorporated into the description of, or into the gift to, the remainder-man, then the remainder is contingent; but if, after words giving a vested interest, a clause is added divesting it, the remainder is vested." Gray, supra, §108. We have made it easy for you to see what language is "incorporated" into the gift by inserting commas in the conveyance indicating where you should stop and classify, before moving on to the next interest. In *Example 9*, stopping at the comma after the phrase "then to *B* and her heirs," you find that *B* has a vested remainder because there is no condition precedent within the commas setting off *B*'s gift. The phrase "but if *B* does not survive *A*," coming after the comma marking the end of *B*'s gift, is language incorporated into *C*'s gift, not *B*'s. The phrase thus states a condition subsequent (or divesting condition) with respect to *B*'s interest; it states a condition precedent with respect to *C*'s interest.

NOTES, QUESTIONS, AND PROBLEM

1. In *Example 8* above there is a reversion in *O*; in *Example 9* there is no reversion. In *Example 8* under what circumstances will the property revert to *O*? The key to answering this question is to realize that the life estate can terminate prior to the death of the life tenant. At early common law, a life estate was destroyed if the life tenant made a tortious conveyance (that is, breached his oath of homage to his lord by purporting to convey more than he had, for example, a fee simple). The life estate was not forfeited to the lord; the life estate simply ended, and seisin passed on to the holder of the next vested estate. Although life estates can no longer end for breach of feudal obligations, for purposes of classifying remainders *the law has continued to assume that a life estate can end prior to the death of the life tenant.* Can you think of any modern instances where this might happen? See Jesse Dukeminier, Perpetuities: The Measuring Lives, 85 Colum. L. Rev. 1648, 1690-1692 (1985).

2. In classifying future interests after a life estate, you can bet on this rule: If the first future interest created is a contingent remainder in fee simple (as in *Example 8* above), the second future interest in a transferee will also be a contingent remainder. If the first future interest created is a vested remainder in fee simple (as in *Example 9* above), the second future interest in a transferee will be a divesting executory interest. Do you see why this is a good bet?

3. *O* conveys "to *A* for life, then to *B* for life, then to *C* and his heirs." What interests are created?

The owner of a vested or contingent remainder may transfer the remainder during life, or the owner may transfer the remainder by will or intestacy if he dies during the life tenant's life, unless the instrument creating the remainder expressly requires the remainderman to survive the life tenant. The general rule is that a requirement of survivorship is not implied.

PROBLEMS

1. *T* devises Blackacre "to my son *A* for life, then to *A*'s children and their heirs." At the time of *T*'s death, *A* has one child, *B*. Two years later *C* is born to *A*. Then *B* dies, leaving a husband, *D*, and a child, *E*; *B*'s will devises all her property to her husband, *D*. Then *A* dies, survived by *C*, *D*, and *E*. Who owns Blackacre?

2. *T* devises Blackacre "to my son *A* for life, then to *A*'s children and their heirs, and if any child dies in the lifetime of *A*, such child's share shall go to his or her issue who survive *A*." At the time of *T*'s death,

A has two children *B* and *C*. Then *B* dies, leaving a husband, *D*, and a child, *E*; *B*'s will devises all her property to her husband, *D*. Then *C* dies, leaving a wife, *F*, and no issue; *C*'s will devises all his property to his wife, *F*. Then another child, *G*, is born to *A*. Then *A* dies, survived by *D*, *E*, *F*, and *G*. Who owns Blackacre?

The law has a preference for a vested remainder, and, where an instrument is ambiguous, the courts construe it in favor of a vested remainder. As Chief Justice Coke put it, "the law always delights in the vesting of estates, and contingencies are odious in the law, and are the causes of troubles, and vesting and settling of estates, the cause of repose and certainty." Roberts v. Roberts, 2 Bulst. 123, 131, 80 Eng. Rep. 1002, 1009 (K.B. 1613).

What difference does it make whether a remainder is vested or contingent? There are four great historic differences. First, a vested remainder *accelerates* into possession whenever and however the preceding estate ends — either at the life tenant's death or earlier if the life estate ends before the life tenant's death. A contingent remainder cannot become possessory so long as it remains contingent. Hence where there is a conveyance "to *A* for life, then to *B*, but if *B* dies under 21 to *C*," *B*, holding a vested remainder, is entitled to possession at *A*'s death, even though *B* is under 21. If *B* is under 21, *B*'s possessory estate remains subject to divestment until *B* reaches 21. If, on the other hand, the conveyance had read "to *A* for life, then to *B* if *B* reaches 21," *B* would not be entitled to possession at *A*'s death prior to *B*'s reaching 21.

Second, at early common law a contingent remainder, with a few exceptions, was *not assignable* during the remainderman's life and hence was unreachable by creditors. A contingent remainder was thought of as a mere possibility of becoming an interest and not as an interest ("thing") that could be transferred. (But oddly enough, when the question was whether the heirs of a dead remainderman inherited the remainder, the courts saw the remainder as an interest passing to them, if survivorship was not required by the instrument.) Inasmuch as today we regard contingent remainders as interests in property, in most states contingent remainders are now transferable during life and reachable by creditors. In a handful of states, the old common law is still followed. Vested remainders have always been transferable during life as well as at death.

The third difference between vested and contingent remainders is that at common law contingent remainders were *destroyed* if they did not vest upon termination of the preceding life estate, whereas vested remainders were not destructible in this manner. We shall consider the modern law on this later in this chapter.

The fourth difference is that contingent remainders are subject to the *Rule against Perpetuities,* whereas vested remainders are not. In applying this rule, which is very much alive and kicking, the distinction between vested and contingent remainders remains all-important. We consider the Rule against Perpetuities at the end of this chapter.

In addition to the major common law differences, under some state statutes the owner of a contingent remainder may not have standing to sue for waste, or for partition, or for a trust accounting, whereas a vested remainderman has such standing. Legislatures have sometimes assumed that a vested interest is more worthy of protection than a contingent interest. (Does this make sense when the vested interest is held subject to divestment? Would it be better to distinguish between remainders certain to become possessory and remainders not certain of possession?)

There is also a very important difference under the *federal estate tax* between a remainder that is transmissible at the death of the remainderman and one that is not transmissible. The federal government imposes an estate tax (similar to an inheritance tax) upon the estates of decedents who die owning property in excess of $600,000. The estate tax is a tax upon the transfer of property at death; any property interest that is transferred by the decedent by will or intestacy to another person is subject to taxation. The general principle is that *transmissible* interests are taxable. The federal government also levies a gift tax on inter vivos gifts in excess of $600,000. The gift and estate taxes are integrated; the rates are the same (currently 37 to 50 percent), and generally there is little estate or gift tax advantage in making an inter vivos gift rather than a transfer at death.

A future interest is a property interest, and if it can be transmitted by its owner at death by will or intestacy it is subject to estate taxation. Thus:

> *Example 10.* As a gift, O conveys Blackacre "to A for life, and then to B and her heirs." O pays a gift tax on the value of Blackacre. During A's life, B dies. B's remainder passes under B's will to B's devisees or by intestacy to B's heirs. This is a *transmissible* remainder. At B's death, the value of B's remainder is subject to estate taxation even though B is not enjoying possession of Blackacre. (On how the remainder is valued, see pages 225-226.) If B had a remainder contingent upon surviving A ("then to B and her heirs if B survives A"), B's remainder would not be transmissible at B's death during A's lifetime, and no federal estate tax would be paid.

From *Example 10* you should discern an important tax planning precept: Do not create transmissible future interests; make every future interest contingent upon surviving to the time of possession. If you do, no federal estate tax will be imposed if the owner of the future interest dies before the life tenant. (States have gift and inheritance taxes too, but their application to vested and contingent future interests varies so much that useful generalizations cannot be made.)

PROBLEMS

1. *T* devises $1 million "to my son *A* for life, then to my grand-daughter *B* and her heirs." At *T*'s death a federal estate tax is payable on the transfer of $1 million. When *A* dies, is any federal estate tax payable by *A*'s estate?

2. *T* devises property "to *A* for life, then to *B* and her heirs, but if *B* does not survive *A*, then to *C* and his heirs." If *B* dies first, leaving *A* and *C* surviving, is the value of *B*'s remainder subject to federal estate taxation upon *B*'s death? If *C* dies first, intestate, leaving *A* and *B* surviving, is the value of *C*'s future interest subject to federal estate taxation upon *C*'s death? If so, *C*'s administrator must pay the tax out of *C*'s estate. If a tax is paid and subsequently *A* dies leaving *B* surviving, are *C*'s heirs entitled to a tax refund?

3.   Executory Interests

An executory interest is a future interest in a transferee that must, in order to become possessory,

(1) divest or cut short some interest in another *transferee* (this is known as a shifting executory interest), or

(2) divest the *transferor* in the future (this is known as a springing executory interest).[3]

Executory interests grew out of the more or less accidental circumstance that England had, in addition to courts of law, a separate Court of Equity (known also as the Court of Chancery). After the Conquest, every king had his chancellor, who had custody of the great seal and was head of all the king's clerks. The chancellor was almost always a cleric, often a high ecclesiastical official. He was also a member of the king's council — indeed, the specially learned member. When relief was not forthcoming from the common law courts, petitioners asked the king's council to interfere on behalf of the king for the love of God and in the way of charity. Because of the chancellor's learning and his position as "Keeper of the King's Conscience," the council more and more referred petitions to the chancellor, and by the end of the reign of Henry V (1413-1422) the Court of Chancery had become an established court of the realm.

The law courts adjudicated title, declaring who had rights in land.

---

3. We differentiate here between a shifting executory interest and a springing executory interest because we think it helps the student better understand what an executory interest is, but there is no difference in legal consequences between the two.

The chancellor did what conscience required by enforcing personal duties. The chancellor could not declare rights, but he could, if conscience demanded, punish those who insisted upon enforcing their rights. Thus he could bring powerful pressure on persons to obey him while not altering their legal rights. Quite naturally lawyers appealed to the chancellor's conscience to impart a much needed element of elasticity into the rigidity of the land law and hence give to landowners wider powers over their property than they possessed at common law. The chancellor's rules also offered the possibility of avoiding taxation, and it was this that brought on the Statute of Uses.

a.   Two Prohibitory Rules: No Shifting Interests; No Springing Interests

Prior to 1536 common law courts laid down two rules based upon their ideas of estates and of conveyancing. The first of these was that *no future interest could be created in favor of a transferee if the interest could operate to cut short a freehold estate.* Thus:

> *Example 11.* Prior to the Statute of Uses (1536), *O* conveys Whiteacre, a small tract of land, "to my eldest son *A* and his heirs, but if *A* inherits Blackacre (the family manor), then Whiteacre is to go to my second son *B* and his heirs." Under this conveyance, *A* takes a fee simple absolute and *B* takes nothing. *O* cannot shift title and thus is prevented from planning in this manner for contingent events.

The reason for the rule was that *O* could not create a right of entry in a stranger,[4] which a shifting interest resembled.

The second rule was that *no freehold estate could be created to spring up in the future.* This was a rule against interests springing out of the grantor at some future date. Thus:

> *Example 12.* Prior to the Statute of Uses, *O* conveys "to *A* and her heirs when *A* marries *B*." Under this conveyance, *A* takes nothing; *O* is left with the fee simple.

The reason for this rule? A freehold estate could not be created unless a feoffment with livery of seisin took place on the land. In *Example 12, A* could not take seisin at the time of the conveyance because *O* did not intend it to pass to *A* until *A* married. So *A* took nothing.

This rule did not prevent the creation of a remainder to commence in the future, provided there was a freehold estate in a transferee to

---

4. See footnote 28, page 237.

support it. Thus in a grant "to A for life, then to B and her heirs," livery of seisin to A was sufficient to create A's freehold life estate, and also to sustain B's remainder. A held seisin for his life, and on A's death seisin immediately passed to B according to the terms of the original grant.

b. The Rise of the Use

The chancellor was concerned with conscience, not seisin, and paid no attention to the seisin rules of the law courts. When he thought persons should be required to perform their moral duties, the chancellor would step in and protect a transferee, regardless of what his legal rights might be. Hence there developed in equity a protected interest known as a "use" (meaning benefit).

>   *Example 13.* Before the Statute of Uses, O goes on the land and enfeoffs "X and his heirs to hold to the use of A and his heirs, but if A inherits the family manor, then to the use of O's second son B and his heirs." (Compare *Example 11.*)

So far as the law courts were concerned, the feoffment with livery of seisin created a fee simple absolute in X; the law courts refused to compel the feoffee to uses, X, to hold the land for the benefit of A. The chancellor, however, thought that X had a good faith duty to hold seisin for the benefit of A, the *cestui que use*, a corruption of *cestui a que use le feoffment fuit fait* (the one for whose benefit the feoffment was made). If the shifting event happened, X had the duty to hold for the benefit of the other *cestui que use*, B. The chancellor enforced this duty. He would issue an order for the feoffee to uses to appear before him and, if satisfied that there was a just complaint, order the feoffee to perform some definite act, such as paying the rent to the *cestui que use* or letting the *cestui* into possession. The chancellor made no order concerning the title to the land in question, which was within the jurisdiction of the law courts, but he could coerce the legal owner by threatening him with imprisonment.

In *Example 13* we have a feoffment to uses. Another common method of creating a use was the bargain and sale deed.[5] Suppose that O and his grantee did not want to go out to the land (perhaps many

---

5. Where no consideration was given, a covenant to stand seised could raise a use in favor of family members. For example, O might covenant to stand seised in favor of his daughter A. Love and affection for relatives sufficed as good consideration to raise a use. The covenant to stand seised developed after the Statute of Uses as the normal method of making a family settlement. Unlike livery, it was secret, an advantage still sought by the rich today.

miles removed from London) and perform livery of seisin; instead, in the London office of his solicitor, *O* sold Blackacre to *A* for £50 and gave a bargain and sale deed to "*A* and his heirs." Because there had been no feoffment with livery of seisin, legal title and seisin were still in *O*. But here again, to enforce the bargain the chancellor stepped in and required *O* to hold legal title to Blackacre for the benefit of *A*.

Springing uses as well as shifting uses might be created in equity. For example, *O* might wish to endow his daughter *A* with a suitable tract of land upon her marriage to *B*. A conveyance "when *A* marries *B*" — in the form of *Example 12* — violated the law courts' rule against springing interests. But *O* could avoid this rule by enfeoffing "*X* and his heirs to the use of *O* and his heirs and then to the use of *A* and her heirs when *A* marries *B*." Equity would enforce the springing use.

As time passed, it became evident that all sorts of benefits could be accomplished by "raising a use." For example, until 1540 land could not be devised by will — but *O* could obtain the practical equivalent of a will by enfeoffing "*X* and his heirs to the use of *O* during *O*'s lifetime and then to the use of such persons as *O* shall appoint by will." By this device *O* could effectively circumvent the doctrine of primogeniture and leave land to a younger son or a daughter. Particularly because of its success in avoiding those medieval taxes known as feudal incidents, the use became universally popular.[6] By the time of the Wars of the Roses the greater part of the land in England was held in use.

c.   Abolition of the Use: The Statute of Uses

Shortly after his break with Rome, Henry VIII ran short of money. Parliament was reluctant to increase taxation, and the king did not want to add to his subjects' discontent by pushing the matter. Henry resolved to meet his needs by restoring his feudal revenues, which had been depleted by the prevalence of uses. After various maneuvers, including threats, lawsuits, and cajolery, "the Statute of Uses was forced upon an unwilling Parliament by an extremely strong-willed king."[7] The statute was enacted in 1535, to become effective in 1536 (just when the dissolution of the monasteries was greatly increasing the estates at Henry's disposition). The principle of the statute was brilliantly simple: The stat-

6. Feudal incidents were levied when seisin descended to the heir upon death (see page 199). This catastrophe to family finances could be avoided by preventing the descent of seisin. How was this done? *O* simply enfeoffed a large group of persons as joint tenants who held seisin to *O*'s own use. Under the theory of joint tenancy (page 326), upon the death of one joint tenant, seisin does not descend to his heir nor pass to the surviving tenants, who are viewed as seised of the whole property from the beginning of the tenancy. When the number of joint tenants holding seisin grew dangerously low, others could be enfeoffed jointly with them.

7. Frederic W. Maitland, Equity 34 (John Brunyate rev. ed. 1947).

Henry VIII
by Cornelis Matsys, 1544

ute provided that if any person or persons were seised to the use of any other person or persons, the legal estate (seisin) would be taken away from the feoffee to uses and given to the *cestui que use*. In the language of the time, the statute "executed" the use, that is, converted it into a legal interest.

One effect of the statute was to expand legal future interests by converting what were "shifting uses" and "springing uses" in equity before 1536 into legal "shifting executory interests" and "springing executory interests." Thus:

> *Example 14.* After 1536 *O* bargains and sells "to *A* and his heirs, but if *B* returns from Rome, then to *B* and his heirs." Here the bargain and sale conveyance raised a use in *A* and a shifting use in *B*. These were immediately "executed" by the statute, leaving as the state of *legal* title: Fee simple in *A* subject to a shifting executory interest in *B* in fee simple.

> *Example 15.* After 1536 *O* covenants to stand seised for the benefit "of *A* and her heirs when *A* marries *B*." Here the covenant to stand seised raised a use — which was immediately "executed" by the statute, leaving as the state of *legal* title: Fee simple in *O* subject to a springing executory interest in *A* in fee simple.

For a time after the Statute of Uses, in order to create these new types of legal future interests it was necessary to "employ the machinery of the statute." A use had to be raised on which the statute could operate. *O* had to employ a certain kind of conveyance, such as a bargain and sale deed, which would raise a use. This requirement is no longer a part of our law. Today, in any jurisdiction, springing and shifting future interests can be created by deed, trust, or will; no special form of conveyance has to be employed.

That is the story of how executory interests came to be recognized. What are called executory interests today are interests that would have been void at law prior to the Statute of Uses because they violated the two rules stated above.

The Statute of Uses had many important consequences besides making legal what was formerly equitable. The statute seemed to destroy the power to devise land in equity because it converted equitable interests into legal interests, and land could not be devised at law. To mollify the landowners, who rebelled against restoration of forced primogeniture, the Statute of Wills, permitting wills of land, was enacted in 1540. The Statute of Uses also made legally valid those deeds of land that had previously been valid only in equity. Deeds were found to have many advantages over livery of seisin, and in 1677 the Statute of Frauds was enacted, abolishing livery of seisin and requiring a written instrument for passing title to real property.

And how did Henry VIII's plan to restore his feudal revenues fare?

In 1540 he set up the Court of Wards and Liveries to supervise the collection of these dues. This court operated very efficiently, and the royal revenue from the landowning class was substantial. In the struggle between crown and Parliament which led to the Civil War, the feudal dues permitted the king to operate without parliamentary taxes. When Charles I was eventually forced to summon the Long Parliament, it abolished the feudal incidents and brought the crown's revenues under parliamentary control. At the Restoration in 1660 this abolition was confirmed by the Tenures Abolition Act. The crown was compensated for loss of feudal revenues from the rich by a tax on beer and other beverages.

On the Statute of Uses, see A.W.B. Simpson, A History of the Land Law 173-207 (2d ed. 1986).

d. Modern Executory Interests

The effect of the Statute of Uses was to permit the creation of a new estate: *a fee simple subject to an executory limitation.* This is a fee simple that, upon the happening of a stated event, is automatically divested by an executory interest in a *transferee.* Here are some examples that occur in modern law:

(1) *O* conveys "to Hartford School Board, its successors and assigns, but if the premises are not used for school purposes during the next 20 years, to *C* and his heirs."[8]

(2) *O* conveys "to *A* and his heirs, but if *A* dies without issue surviving him, to *C* and his heirs."

(3) *O* conveys "to *A* for life, then to *B* and her heirs, but if *B* dies without issue surviving her, to *C* and his heirs."

(4) *O* conveys "to *C* upon my death."[9]

In all these examples *C* has an executory interest that will become possessory only by divesting a preceding vested fee simple. In examples (1), (2), and (4), the preceding vested fee simple is a possessory fee simple. In example (3), the preceding vested fee simple is a fee simple in remainder.

Exception: The label *executory interest* is applied in one situation where

---

8. Compare the fee simple subject to condition subsequent with a right of entry in the *transferor.* See pages 237-238. An executory interest divests automatically, not — like a right of entry — at the option of the transferor.

9. This conveyance runs some risk of being struck down as an unattested, invalid will, because the divesting event is the death of the grantor. To some courts, it looks like a will, and requires a ceremonial required of wills. See pages 652-656.

the future interest is not a divesting interest, and that is where a future interest in a transferee follows a fee simple determinable. Thus:

> *Example 16.* O conveys "to Town Library Board so long as the premises are used for library purposes, then to Children's Hospital." The Library Board has a determinable fee. Children's Hospital has an executory interest.

The interest given to Children's Hospital should logically be classified as a remainder. It stands ready to *succeed* on the natural expiration of the preceding estate; it does *not divest* the preceding estate. But the future interest cannot be a remainder because of the rule, laid down before the Statute of Uses, that a remainder cannot follow a vested fee simple. On the other hand, the future interest does not fit into our definition of an executory interest as a divesting interest. Forced to violate one rule or the other, courts chose to give the future interest the label of executory interest, but it is not a divesting interest.

PROBLEMS

1. *O*, owner of Blackacre, comes to you to draft an instrument of gift. *O* tells you he wants to convey Blackacre to his son *A* for life, and upon *A*'s death *O* wants Blackacre to go to *A*'s children if any are alive or, if none are then alive, to *O*'s daughter *B*. Consider the following conveyances, all carrying out *O*'s intent, but each creating different future interests.

(a) *O* conveys "to *A* for life, then to *A*'s children and their heirs, but if at *A*'s death he is not survived by any children, then to *B* and her heirs." At the time of the conveyance, *A* is alive and has no children. What is the state of the title?

Two years after the conveyance, twins, *C* and *D*, are born to *A*. What is the state of the title?

Suppose that *C* dies during *A*'s lifetime, and that *A* is survived by *B* and *D*. What is the state of the title?

(b) *O* conveys "to *A* for life, then to such of *A*'s children as survive him, but if none of *A*'s children survives him, to *B* and her heirs." At the time of the conveyance, *A* is alive and has two children, *C* and *D*. What is the state of the title?

(c) *O* conveys "to *A* for life, then to *B* and her heirs, but if *A* is survived at his death by any children, then to such surviving children and their heirs." At the time of the conveyance, *A* is alive and has two children, *C* and *D*. What is the state of the title?

2. All the conveyances in Problem 1 contain a serious drafting flaw. What is it? Consider the following case: *T* devises land "to my son *A* for life, then to *A*'s children, and if *A* dies without surviving children to my

daughter *B* and her heirs." *A* has a child, *C*, and *C* has a child, *D*. *C* dies. *A* dies, survived by his grandchild *D* and his sister *B*. Who takes the land? In Clark v. Strother, 238 Va. 533, 385 S.E.2d 578 (1989), it was held that *B* takes the land.

3. *T* devises $10,000 "to my cousin, Don Little, if and when he survives his wife." What does Don Little have? In re Little's Estate, 403 Pa. 534, 170 A.2d 106 (1961). Why do you suppose that the testator would make such a devise?

4. *O* conveys Blackacre "to *A* and his heirs one year from now." By this conveyance *A* is given a springing executory interest that will divest *O*'s fee simple one year from now. But after this conveyance, how can *O* have a fee simple, which is an estate that by definition has a potentially infinite duration? (Hint: The Statute of Uses made possible new interests, which were overlaid upon the existing law.)

Almost all executory interests are subject to a condition precedent and are treated as contingent interests. On the other hand, an executory interest that is to become possessory upon an event certain to happen, as above, may be treated as a vested interest. See 6 American Law of Property §24.20 (1952); Restatement (Second) of Property, Donative Transfers, §1.4, Illustration 18 (1983). Cf. Williams v. Watt, 668 P.2d 620 (Wyo. 1983) (learned examination of future interests in minerals, treating executory interest as a vested remainder on theory it was certain to become possessory).

A caveat on proper labelling. In the preceding text, we have divided future interests in transferees into separate categories of remainders and executory interests. These historical categories are part of the current vocabulary of judges and lawyers and are the standard analytical tools of all the treatises. But the question must be asked: Do any different legal consequences follow from labelling a future interest an executory interest rather than a remainder? At common law there were differences. Executory interests were not subject to destruction by a gap in seisin, as were contingent remainders (see pages 295-296). And executory interests possibly were not caught within the web of Shelley's Case (see page 292). These rules have been abolished in all but a handful of states, and where abolished, there may be no significant differences in legal consequences between executory interests and remainders. See Jesse Dukeminier & Stanley M. Johanson, Wills, Trusts, and Estates 694-698 (3d ed. 1984); Jesse Dukeminier, Contingent Remainders and Executory Interests: A Requiem for the Distinction, 43 Minn. L. Rev. 13 (1958); John Makdisi, The Vesting of Executory Interests, 59 Tul. L. Rev. 366 (1984).

Modern statutes often include executory interests in an all-inclusive definition of a remainder. See, e.g., N.Y. Est., Powers & Trusts Law §6-3.2 (McKinney 1967).

D. The Trust

Although the purpose of the Statute of Uses was to abolish the use, within a century the use was re-established. Common law judges as well as chancellors strictly construed the statute. It is hard to say why, but they held that the statute did not operate if the feoffee to uses (trustee in modern language) was given *active duties.* An active trust was regarded as something quite different from an ordinary use where the feoffee had only the duty of protecting the property and conveying it to the beneficiary or as the beneficiary directed. It is fortunate that the judges read the statute this way, for after the feudal incidents were abolished in 1660, the trust came into its own. The trust, a brilliant invention of English jurisprudence, is an extremely flexible form of property management. See pages 233-234.

In the usual trust the trustee manages the property for the benefit of the beneficiaries. The trustee takes the entire legal interest in personal property and, if necessary to carry out the purposes of the trust, as is ordinarily the case, the legal fee simple in land. The trustee has the power to sell trust assets and reinvest the proceeds in other assets unless it appears from the trust instrument and the surrounding circumstances that the settlor intended that the particular property be retained in the trust. The net income of the trust is paid to the beneficiaries, and upon termination of the trust the trust assets as they then exist are handed over to the beneficiaries entitled thereto.

The concept of the trust is easy enough to understand. Most systems of law provide some method by which a trustworthy person is made responsible for managing property for the benefit of a person who needs protection. But the Anglo-American trust at first seems perplexing, because one person is called the "legal owner" of land while others are the "equitable owners" of the same parcel of land at the same time. This duality of ownership grew, of course, as a result of separate courts of law and equity — with equity being superior. In a trust, an equity court enforces duties against the legal owner of property for the benefit of persons who are said to hold equitable interests.

A person can create equitable interests in property corresponding to the legal possessory estates and future interests you have studied. Thus:

> *Example 17.* O conveys Blackacre "to X in trust for A for life, and then for A's children who survive A." X has the express power to sell Blackacre. X has the legal fee simple in Blackacre; A has an equitable life estate, A's children have an equitable contingent remainder, and O has an equitable reversion. If X sells Blackacre for $50,000 and reinvests the $50,000 in Whiteacre and General Motors stock, the trust property then consists of these latter items. Upon A's death X conveys the trust property to the persons entitled thereto, A's children if any are alive or O if A has no surviving children.

The trustee is a fiduciary and is held to a high standard of conduct in managing the trust property. The trustee is under a duty to administer the trust solely in the interest of the beneficiaries; self-dealing (for example, selling or lending the trust property to the trustee in his individual capacity) is prohibited. The trustee must preserve the property, make it productive, and dispose of the income in the manner specified in the trust instrument. Other important duties of a trustee include the duty to keep the trust property separate from the trustee's own property, to keep accurate accounts, to invest prudently, and not to delegate trust powers. If the trustee breaches a fiduciary duty, the trustee is subject to personal liability to the beneficiaries; if the misfeasance renders the trustee unfit to serve, the trustee can be removed by a court and another trustee appointed.

Although a trust is a useful method of separating the burdens of property management from the benefits of ownership, there is a dark side to the development of trust law. Owners of property, seeking to avoid some legal restriction on what they can do with property, sometimes create a trust, hoping modern chancellors will prove as tolerant as those ancient chancellors who developed the use.

Broadway National Bank v. Adams
Supreme Judicial Court of Massachusetts, 1882
133 Mass. 170

MORTON, C.J. The object of this bill in equity is to reach and apply in payment of the plaintiff's debt due from the defendant Adams the income of a trust fund created for his benefit by the will of his brother. The eleventh article of the will is as follows:

> I give the sum of seventy-five thousand dollars to my said executors and the survivors or survivor of them, in trust to invest the same in such manner as to them may seem prudent, and to pay the net income thereof, semiannually, to my said brother Charles W. Adams, during his natural life, such payments to be made to him personally when convenient, otherwise, upon his order or receipt in writing; in either case free from the interference or control of his creditors, my intention being that the use of said income shall not be anticipated by assignment. At the decease of my said brother Charles, my will is that the net income of said seventy-five thousand dollars shall be paid to his present wife, in case she survives him, for the benefit of herself and all the children of said Charles, in equal proportions, in the manner and upon the conditions the same as herein directed to be paid him during his life, so long as she shall remain single. And my will is, that, after the decease of said Charles and the decease or second marriage of his said wife, the said seventy-five thousand dollars, together with any accrued interest or income thereon which may remain unpaid, as herein above directed, shall be divided equally

among all the children of my said brother Charles, by any and all his wives, and the representatives of any deceased child or children by right of representation.

There is no room for doubt as to the intention of the testator. It is clear that, if the trustee was to pay the income to the plaintiff under an order of the court, it would be in direct violation of the intention of the testator and of the provisions of his will. The court will not compel the trustee thus to do what the will forbids him to do, unless the provisions and intention of the testator are unlawful.

The question whether the founder of a trust can secure the income of it to the object of his bounty, by providing that it shall not be alienable by him or be subject to be taken by his creditors, has not been directly adjudicated in this Commonwealth. The tendency of our decisions, however, has been in favor of such a power in the founder. . . . Sparhawk v. Cloon, 125 Mass. 263.

It is true that the rule of the common law is, that a man cannot attach to a grant or transfer of property, otherwise absolute, the condition that it shall not be alienated; such condition being repugnant to the nature of the estate granted. Co. Lit. 223 a. Blackstone Bank v. Davis, 21 Pick. 42.

Lord Coke gives as the reason of the rule, that "it is absurd and repugnant to reason that he, that hath no possibility to have the land revert to him, should restrain his feoffee in fee simple of all his power to alien," and that this is "against the height and puritie of a fee simple." By such a condition, the grantor undertakes to deprive the property in the hands of the grantee of one of its legal incidents and attributes, namely, its alienability, which is deemed to be against public policy. But the reasons of the rule do not apply in the case of a transfer of property in trust. By the creation of a trust like the one before us, the trust property passes to the trustee with all its incidents and attributes unimpaired. He takes the whole legal title to the property, with the power of alienation; the *cestui que trust* takes the whole legal title to the accrued income at the moment it is paid over to him. Neither the principal nor the income is at any time inalienable.

The question whether the rule of the common law should be applied to equitable life estates created by will or deed, has been the subject of conflicting adjudications by different courts, as is fully shown in the able and exhaustive arguments of the counsel in this case. As is stated in Sparhawk v. Cloon, above cited, from the time of Lord Eldon the rule has prevailed in the English Court of Chancery, to the extent of holding that when the income of a trust estate is given to any person (other than a married woman) for life, the equitable estate for life is alienable by, and liable in equity to the debts of, the *cestui que trust,* and that this quality is so inseparable from the estate that no provision, however express, which does not operate as a cesser or limitation of the estate itself, can protect it from his debts. . . .

The English rule has been adopted in several of the courts of this country. Tillinghast v. Bradford, 5 R.I. 205. Heath v. Bishop, 4 Rich. Eq. 46. Dick v. Pitchford, 1 Dev. & Bat. Eq. 480. Mebane v. Mebane, 4 Ired. Eq. 131.

Other courts have rejected it, and have held that the founder of a trust may secure the benefit of it to the object of his bounty, by providing that the income shall not be alienable by anticipation, nor subject to be taken for his debts. Holdship v. Patterson, 7 Watts 547. Shankland's Appeal, 47 Penn. St. 113. Rife v. Geyer, 59 Penn. St. 393. White v. White, 30 Vt. 338. Pope v. Elliott, 8 B. Mon. 56. Nichols v. Eaton, 91 U.S. 716. Hyde v. Woods, 94 U.S. 523.

The precise point involved in the case at bar has not been adjudicated in this Commonwealth; but the decisions of this court which we have before cited recognize the principle, that, if the intention of the founder of a trust, like the one before us, is to give to the equitable life tenant a qualified and limited, and not an absolute, estate in the income, such life tenant cannot alienate it by anticipation, and his creditors cannot reach it at law or in equity. It seems to us that this principle extends to and covers the case at bar. The founder of this trust was the absolute owner of his property. He had the entire right to dispose of it, either by an absolute gift to his brother, or by a gift with such restrictions or limitations, not repugnant to law, as he saw fit to impose. His clear intention, as shown in his will, was not to give his brother an absolute right to the income which might hereafter accrue upon the trust fund, with the power of alienating it in advance, but only the right to receive semiannually the income of the fund, which upon its payment to him, and not before, was to become his absolute property. His intentions ought to be carried out, unless they are against public policy. There is nothing in the nature or tenure of the estate given to the *cestui que trust* which should prevent this. The power of alienating in advance is not a necessary attribute or incident of such an estate or interest, so that the restraint of such alienation would introduce repugnant or inconsistent elements.

We are not able to see that it would violate any principles of sound public policy to permit a testator to give to the object of his bounty such a qualified interest in the income of a trust fund, and thus provide against the improvidence or misfortune of the beneficiary. The only ground upon which it can be held to be against public policy is, that it defrauds the creditors of the beneficiary.

It is argued that investing a man with apparent wealth tends to mislead creditors, and to induce them to give him credit. The answer is, that creditors have no right to rely upon property thus held, and to give him credit upon the basis of an estate which, by the instrument creating it, is declared to be inalienable by him, and not liable for his debts. By the exercise of proper diligence they can ascertain the nature and extent of his estate, especially in this Commonwealth, where all wills and most deeds are spread upon the public records. There is the same danger of their being misled by false appearances, and induced to give credit to the equitable life tenant when the will or deed of trust provides for a cesser or limitation over, in case of an attempted alienation, or of bankruptcy or attachment, and the argument would lead to the conclusion that the English rule is equally in violation of public policy. We do not see why the founder of a trust may not directly provide that his property shall go to his beneficiary with the restriction that it shall not be alienable by anticipation, and that his creditors shall not have the right to attach it in advance, instead of indirectly reaching the same result by a provision for a cesser or a limitation over, or by giving his trustees a discretion as to paying it. He has the entire *jus disponendi,* which imports that he may give it absolutely, or may impose any restrictions or fetters not repugnant to the nature of the estate which he gives. Under our system, creditors may reach all the property of the debtor not exempted by law, but they cannot enlarge the gift of the founder of a trust, and take more than he has given.

The rule of public policy which subjects a debtor's property to the payment of his debts, does not subject the property of a donor to the debts of his beneficiary, and does not give the creditor a right to complain that, in the exercise of his absolute right of disposition, the donor has not seen fit to give the property to the creditor, but has left it out of his reach.

Whether a man can settle his own property in trust for his own benefit, so as to exempt the income from alienation by him or attachment in advance by his creditors, is a different question, which we are not called upon to consider in this case. But we are of opinion that any other person, having the entire right to dispose of his property, may settle it in trust in favor of a beneficiary, and may provide that it shall not be alienated by him by anticipation, and shall not be subject to be seized by his creditors in advance of its payment to him.

It follows that, under the provisions of the will which we are considering, the income of the trust fund created for the benefit of the defendant Adams cannot be reached by attachment, either at law or in equity, before it is paid to him.

Bill dismissed.

John C. Gray, Restraints on the Alienation of Property
242-247 (2d ed. 1895)

[The fallacy of Broadway National Bank v. Adams] is, that the only objection to such inalienable life estates is that they defraud the creditors of the life tenant; and the courts labor, with more or less success, to show that these creditors are not defrauded.[10] . . . But, with submission, this is not the ground why equitable life estates cannot be made inalienable and free from debts. The true ground is that on which the whole law of property, legal and equitable, is based: — that inalienable rights of property are opposed to the fundamental principles of the common law; that it is against public policy that a man "should have an estate to live on, but not an estate to pay his debts with," Tillinghast v. Bradford, 5 R.I. 205, 212, . . . and should have the benefits of wealth without the responsibilities. The common law has recognized certain classes of persons who may be kept in pupilage, viz. infants, lunatics, married women; but it has held that sane grown men must look out for themselves, — that it is not the function of the law to join the futile effort to save the foolish and the vicious from the consequences of their own vice and folly. It is wholesome doctrine, fit to produce a manly race, based on sound morality and wise philosophy. . . .

That grown men should be kept all their lives in pupilage, that men not paying their debts should live in luxury on inherited wealth, are doctrines as undemocratic as can well be conceived. They are suited to the times in which the Statute De Donis was enacted, and the law was administered in the interest of rich and powerful families. The general introduction of spendthrift trusts would be to form a privileged class, who could indulge in every speculation, could practise every fraud, and yet, provided they kept on the safe side of the criminal law, could roll in wealth. They would be an aristocracy, though certainly the most contemptible aristocracy with which a country was ever cursed.

NOTES AND QUESTIONS

1. John Chipman Gray was one of the towering figures of American property law. A teacher of property at Harvard from 1869 to 1913, Gray assembled six volumes of cases on property, which law students painstakingly dissected. Famed for his erudition, rigorous logic, and oracular style, Gray was so outraged by judicial approval of the spendthrift trust that he wrote Restraints on the Alienation of Property (1st ed. 1883) denouncing the spendthrift trust on all scores: precedent, policy, and logic. Despite Gray's fulmination, the spendthrift trust is now accepted in a large majority of states. See generally 2A Austin W. Scott,

10. In Nichols v. Eaton, 91 U.S. 716, 726, and Broadway National Bank v. Adams, 133 Mass. 170, it is said that by means of the public records creditors can learn the existence of these trusts. But (1.) Deeds settling personal property, e.g., marriage settlements, are not recorded. (2.) In what registry is a creditor to look to see whether there is a will creating a spendthrift trust in favor of his debtor? That a debtor lives in a certain county is no reason why a trust may not be created for him by a will recorded in some other county or State.

John Chipman Gray
by F.P. Vinton
Collection of Harvard Law School

The Law of Trusts §§151-163 (William F. Fratcher 4th ed. 1987); Gregory S. Alexander, The Dead Hand and the Law of Trusts in the Nineteenth Century, 37 Stan. L. Rev. 1189 (1985).

Although Gray's views on spendthrift trusts were rejected, his second book, the great Rule against Perpetuities (1st ed. 1886), was enormously influential. It became *the* authority on perpetuities law, one of the few American law books to be accepted as authority on English law by English courts. We shall meet the Rule against Perpetuities later in this chapter.

2. Why is a disabling restraint upon an equitable life estate valid when a disabling restraint upon a legal life estate (see page 224) is void? Why can wages be garnished by creditors of the wage earner, but income from a spendthrift trust cannot be reached by creditors?

3. The spendthrift trust is only allowed for inherited wealth. A person can set up a spendthrift trust for another but not for himself. (Why not?) Thus persons who inherit wealth can be protected against creditors but persons who earn wealth cannot be. Does this make sense?

E. Rules Furthering Marketability by Destroying Contingent Future Interests

The late sixteenth and early seventeenth centuries may aptly be called the age of the great conveyancers. During the reign of Elizabeth I, when England rose from a second-class nation to become one of the dominant powers of the seventeenth-century world, enormous fortunes were accumulated by the mercantile class. These parvenus were eager to purchase land, build stately homes, and become squires, entrenched against forfeiture, prodigal issue, and other catastrophes. The Statute of Uses, riding roughshod over common law rules, opened up new possibilities of legal arrangements previously unattainable. It was as if a miracle-working force had been loosened on the land — waiting to be harnessed by ingenious lawyers. Legal shifting and springing interests were now possible; contingent remainders were waiting to be explored. Prior to the sixteenth century contingent remainders had been given scant recognition, and, because they were destructible by the life tenant (see page 296), they were little used. Now the most ambitious conveyancers began to draft extremely complicated documents creating an elaborate series of future interests.[11] The judges, jealous of any limitation that made

11. One of the most celebrated conveyancers was Sir Orlando Bridgman (1606-1674), who practiced during the time of the Civil War. Even his enemies did not feel secure in their estates until they had consulted him. He invented the strict settlement (see footnote

land inalienable, threw up new obstacles or firmed up existing ones. This is not to say that the cerebral sap was running all in one direction in the judges' heads; judges, after all, were usually financially successful lawyers who had become squires by purchase themselves. Nonetheless, with all their conflicting desires and vacillations, they did finally check the dynastic urge.

The judges were most wary of contingent interests. These interests made land unmarketable — either legally or practically — whereas vested interests did not. Where *O* conveyed Blackacre "to *A* for life, remainder to *B* and his heirs," a fee simple could be conveyed to a purchaser if *A* and *B* joined in the deed. Of course, *A* and *B* might have a disagreement about how to divide the proceeds of sale; *A* might believe he was going to live longer than his life expectancy, and *B* might think *A* could drop dead tomorrow. Disagreement on how to divide the proceeds might inhibit sale, but at least it was legally possible to convey a fee simple where the life tenant and the holder of an indefeasibly vested remainder in fee agreed.

With respect to contingent interests, obstacles to sale were greater. If *O* conveyed land "to *A* for life, then to *A*'s heirs," the land could not be sold during *A*'s life because the heirs could not be ascertained until *A*'s death. If *T* devised land "to *A* for life, then to *B* if *B* survives *A*," *A* and *B* and *T*'s heir (who had a reversion) would have to agree to sell the land and how to divide the proceeds. Agreement was not likely. In addition to the practical difficulties, the legal alienability of contingent interests was a clouded matter. See Richard A. Epstein, Past and Future: The Temporal Dimension in the Law of Property, 64 Wash. U. L.Q. 667, 699-707 (1986).

To destroy contingent interests and make land marketable, the judges invented a number of rules, to which we now turn.

1.   The Rule in Shelley's Case

One of the earliest rules favoring marketability, recognized in Abel's Case, Y.B. 18 Edw. 2, f.577 (1324), was given definite form in Shelley's

---

18 on page 213), created the trust to preserve contingent remainders (see Note 3 on page 297), and, to deal with an insane first son and heir of the Earl of Arundel, drew a daring series of instruments, the most important of which was upheld in the landmark Duke of Norfolk's Case, 3 Ch. Cas. 1, 22 Eng. Rep. 931 (Ch. 1681) (see page 299). Although Bridgman's gamble succeeded in this case, his instrument raised the spectre of a perpetuity and from the case evolved the Rule against Perpetuities.

In the Duke of Norfolk's Case, Lord Chancellor Nottingham said of Bridgman: "I think it is due to the memory of so great a man, whenever we speak of him, to mention him with great reverence and veneration for his learning and integrity." But such is the nature of our profession that two centuries later Lord Campbell dismissed Bridgman as "a mere lawyer." 4 John Campbell, Lives of the Lord Chancellors 154 (4th ed. 1857).

Case, 1 Co. Rep. 93b (1581), which gave its name to the rule. In addition to furthering alienability, the rule prevented feudal tax evasion; feudal incidents (wardship, marriage, relief) were due only if land descended to the heir, not if the heir took as purchaser.[12] It is reported that Queen Elizabeth I, assiduous in collecting her feudal dues, took a personal interest in Shelley's Case. After the abolition of feudal incidents in 1660, the only reason that can be given for the rule is that it promotes alienability of land. For this reason, the rule in Shelley's Case survived and was greatly extended long after it became a feudal anachronism.

A simplified statement of the rule[13] is: If

(1)   one instrument
(2)   creates a life estate in land in *A*, and
(3)   purports to create a remainder in persons described as *A*'s heirs (or the heirs of *A*'s body), and
(4)   the life estate and remainder are both legal or both equitable,

the remainder becomes a remainder in fee simple (or fee tail) in *A*. (*Note well*: This is all that the rule in Shelley's Case does.) The doctrine of merger may then come into play. According to this doctrine, a life estate merges into a next vested remainder in fee (a larger estate). Thus:

> *Example 18: O* conveys Blackacre "to *A* for life, then to *A*'s heirs." The rule in Shelley's Case gives *A* a vested remainder in fee simple. *A*'s life estate then merges into the remainder, leaving *A* with a fee simple in possession. The land is immediately alienable by *A* and not tied up for *A*'s lifetime.

The life estate cannot merge into a vested remainder in fee simple if there is an intervening vested life estate, blocking merger. For more on merger, see page 296.

The rule in Shelley's Case, as traditionally stated, applies only to remainders and not to executory interests, but case authority on this point is slight. The rule in Shelley's Case is not a rule of construction. It is a rule of law and applies regardless of the intent of the transferor.

---

12. See A.W.B. Simpson, A History of the Land Law 96-102 (2d ed. 1986). For other conjectures about the reasons for the rule in Shelley's Case, see Bruce Ziff & M.M. Litman, Shelley's Rule in a Modern Context: Clearing the "Heir," 34 U. Toronto L.J. 170, 170-185 (1984).

13. In Van Grutten v. Foxwell, [1897] A.C. 658, 671, Lord MacNaghten said, "It is one thing to put a case like Shelley's in a nutshell and another thing to keep it there." If you want a more expanded treatment, take a look at the long annotation in 29 L.R.A. (n.s.) 965 (1911), where it is said of Shelley's Case, "as in the case of Goldsmith's village parson, . . . those who come to scoff remain to pray."

PROBLEMS

1. State the effect of the rule in Shelley's Case upon each of the following transfers of land:

(a) *O* conveys "to *A* for life, then to *A*'s children and their heirs."

(b) *O* conveys "to *A* for life, then to *B* for life, then to *A*'s heirs."

(c) *O* conveys "to *A* for life, then to *A*'s heirs if *A* survives *B*."

(d) *O* conveys "to *A* for life." *O* subsequently devises the reversion to *A*'s heirs.

2. The rule in Shelley's Case does not apply to a transfer "to *A* for life, then to *A*'s issue." Suppose *O* deeds Whiteacre to his daughter Estella "during her life, then to her heirs and if she dies without issue then to her nephews and nieces." Does the rule in Shelley's Case apply? See Arnold v. Baker, 26 Ill. 2d 131, 134-135, 185 N.E.2d 844, 847 (1962):

> The rule applies . . . only when the gift in remainder refers to an indefinite line of succession, rather than to a specific class of takers. The remainder must be to the heirs of the first taker by the name of heirs as meaning a class of persons to succeed to the estate from generation to generation, and not to heirs as meaning or explained to be individuals. Where to the word *heirs* other words are added which so limit its meaning that it does not include the whole line of inheritable succession but only designates the individuals who are at the death of the life tenant to succeed to the estate, and who are themselves to constitute the source of future descent, then the rule in Shelley's case does not apply.

For further explanation, see Restatement (Second) of Property, Donative Transfers, §30.1, Comment g (1988).

Abolition of the Rule in Shelley's Case

The rule in Shelley's Case has been abolished in an overwhelming majority of states. Only in Arkansas, Colorado, Delaware, and Indiana is it reasonably certain the rule still lives. See Lewis M. Simes & Allan F. Smith, The Law of Future Interests §1563 (2d ed. 1956 & Supp. 1991). In a few states, however, abolition by statute is fairly recent and does not apply retroactively; litigation of old instruments will continue for some time. See, e.g., City Bank & Trust Co. v. Morrissey, 118 Ill. App. 3d 640, 454 N.E.2d 1195 (1983) (litigating 1952 will; rule abolished in 1953); Society Natl. Bank v. Jacobson, 54 Ohio St. 3d 15, 560 N.E.2d 217 (1990) (applying rule to 1931 trust of personal property; rule abolished in 1941). See John V. Orth, Requiem for the Rule in Shelley's Case, 67 N.C. L. Rev. 681 (1989) (North Carolina abolished rule in 1987).

2.   The Doctrine of Worthier Title

The old common law drew a distinction between titles acquired by inheritance and titles acquired by purchase (that is, other than by inheritance). Title by inheritance was deemed worthier, reflecting among other things the preference of the ruling class for old money over new. Therefore, the law forbade a person's heir to take by purchase from his own ancestor.

The common law doctrine of worthier title provides that where there is an inter vivos conveyance of land by a grantor to a person, with a limitation over to the *grantor's own heirs* either by way of remainder or executory interest, no future interest in the heirs is created but a reversion is retained by the grantor. Thus:

> *Example 19.* O conveys Blackacre "to A for life, then to O's heirs." The remainder to O's heirs is void; O has a reversion.

The reasons for this doctrine are obscure, but probably it was motivated by the same policies as underlay the rule in Shelley's Case. The doctrine furthers alienability; O can convey a reversion, whereas O's heirs, not being ascertained, cannot convey the future interest. The doctrine also prevented feudal tax evasion; the feudal incidents were due only if O's heir acquired his interest by descent from O and not by purchase. Because these reasons were inapplicable to personal property, the common law doctrine was a rule of law applying only to land.[14]

In order to do justice on the particular facts arising in Doctor v. Hughes, 225 N.Y. 305, 122 N.E. 221 (1919), Judge Cardozo revived this doctrine from innocuous desuetude and changed it in two important respects. First, he applied it as a *rule of construction,* not as a rule of law. Under the doctrine, as thus changed, it is presumed that the grantor, in providing for a limitation to his heirs, did not intend to give the heirs anything by the conveyance, but this presumption can be overcome by evidence of a contrary intent. Second, Cardozo extended the application of the doctrine to *personal property* as well as to real property, thus severing the doctrine completely from its original policy base. As a rule of construction, the doctrine produced a large volume of litigation in New York. It gave little predictability; ingenious counsel could usually find elsewhere in the instrument arguably contradictory indicia of the grantor's intent. Because it bred litigation, the doctrine was abolished by

---

14. A similar rule applied to devises of land to testator's heirs. The heirs took by way of descent rather than by devise. Because it rarely makes any difference whether the heirs take by descent or by devise, the rule is of no substantial importance today. Restatement (Second) of Property, Donative Transfers, §30.2(2), Comment j (1988), says no such rule exists as applied to devises. See In re Campbell, 319 N.W.2d 275 (Iowa 1982), abolishing the testamentary branch of the worthier title doctrine.

the legislature in New York. See 2A Richard R. Powell, The Law of Real Property ¶381 (rev. ed. 1992). As reformulated by Cardozo, the doctrine of worthier title may be followed in some American jurisdictions, but modern cases on the topic are scarce. The doctrine has been abolished in California, Illinois, Massachusetts, Minnesota, New York, North Carolina, Texas, and a number of other states. See Restatement (Second) of Property, Donative Transfers, §30.2 (1988).

PROBLEMS

1. *O* conveys Blackacre "to my friend *A* for life, then to the heirs of *O*." Thereafter during *A*'s life *O* dies, devising all his property to the American Red Cross. Upon *A*'s death, *O*'s heir, *B,* and the American Red Cross claim Blackacre. Who owns it?

Suppose that at *O*'s death *O* had creditors who were not paid. Could the creditors reach any interest in Blackacre?

2. *O* conveys property to the First National Bank in trust "to pay the income to *O* for life, and on *O*'s death to distribute the trust property to *O*'s heirs." Assume that the rule in Shelley's Case has been abolished. Do *O*'s heirs have a remainder?

A trust can be terminated by the grantor if all beneficially interested parties agree. Can *O* terminate the trust? See Hatch v. Riggs Natl. Bank, 361 F.2d 559 (D.C. Cir. 1966).

Suppose that the conveyance had directed the trustee to distribute the trust property on *O*'s death "to *O*'s surviving issue." Could the trust be terminated?

3. Destructibility of Contingent Remainders

Moved by the requirement that someone must always be seised of the land, and hence responsible for the feudal dues, the judges laid down this rule: A remainder in land is destroyed if it does not vest at or before the termination of the preceding freehold estate. If the remainderman is not ready to take seisin when it is offered, he is wiped out and seisin moves on to the next vested estate.

Although this rule apparently grew out of the feudal need for continuity of seisin, another reason arose to support it: It furthered alienability. Contingent remainders made land less alienable and were thus objectionable.

Under the doctrine of destructibility, contingent remainders were destroyed if they did not vest upon the natural termination of the life estate. Thus:

Example 20. O conveys Blackacre "to *A* for life, then to *B* and her heirs if *B* reaches 21." If at *A*'s death *B* is under the age of 21, *B*'s remainder is destroyed. Seisin returns to *O*. It will take a new conveyance by *O* to give *B* anything.

Contingent remainders could also be destroyed if they did not vest upon the artificial termination of the life estate. English courts held that the life estate could be terminated before the life tenant's death by forfeiture or merger. The life tenant therefore had the power to destroy contingent remainders whenever he wished. Thus:

Example 21. O conveys Whiteacre "to *A* for life, then to *B* and her heirs if *B* survives *A*." *A* conveys his life estate to *O*; the life estate merges into the reversion, destroying *B*'s contingent remainder.

This idea of merger requires some explanation. Suppose there is a conveyance "to *A* for life, remainder to *B* and her heirs." If *A* conveys his life estate to *B*, the life estate and remainder merge, giving *B* a fee simple. This makes good sense, as there is no reason for keeping the estates separate. From this situation the courts extracted a rule: If the life estate and the next vested estate in fee simple come into the hands of one person, the lesser estate is merged into the larger. Having so laid it down, the courts extended it to a situation where the life estate was followed by a contingent remainder and a reversion.[15] Merger of the life estate into the reversion was not required by the axiom forbidding abeyance of seisin; the judges could just as well have said in *Example 21*, for instance, that *O* took a life estate *pur autre vie* and was seised until *A*'s death, when seisin would pass to *B* if she were then living. But deference to the merger rule and the policy of furthering alienability led the judges to extend merger to this situation. Applying the destructibility doctrine in *Example 21* makes land alienable now rather than at *A*'s death.

The destructibility doctrine does not apply to executory interests, which, in taking effect, do not put seisin in abeyance; instead, the holder of an executory interest grabs seisin from some other person. To give the destructibility doctrine as extensive a reach as possible, however, it was held in Purefoy v. Rogers, 2 Wms. Saund. 380, 35 Eng. Rep. 1181 (K.B. 1670), that you must construe a limitation as creating a contingent remainder rather than an executory interest if that construction is possible.

15. *Exception:* If a life estate and the next vested estate are created simultaneously in the same person they do not merge at that time so as to destroy intervening contingent remainders. However, if the life estate and next vested estate are thereafter conveyed to another person, they will then merge and destroy intervening contingent remainders. What was the reason for this exception?

NOTES AND PROBLEMS

1. *T* devises Blackacre "to *A* for life, then in fee simple to *B*'s children who survive *B*." In a jurisdiction following the destructibility doctrine, what is the state of the title after each of the following events, considered independently of the others?

(a) *B* dies during *A*'s lifetime, leaving children; then *A* dies.

(b) *A* dies during *B*'s lifetime; *B* has children at *A*'s death.

(c) *A* dies during *B*'s lifetime; *B* has no children at *A*'s death.

(d) While *A* and *B* are alive, *A* conveys his life estate to *B*.

2. *O* conveys Whiteacre "to *A* for life, then to *A*'s first son and his heirs." *A* dies without having a son born during his life, but a son is born to *A*'s widow six months after *A*'s death.[16] Is the son's remainder destroyed at common law? In Reeve v. Long, 3 Lev. 408, 83 Eng. Rep. 754 (K.B. 1695), the House of Lords, refusing to follow the rule established by Purefoy v. Rogers, supra, held that the son took. Their lordships applied the principle, accepted today for determining all questions of property rights, that where it is for the child's benefit, a child will be treated retroactively as in being from the time of conception if the child is later born alive.

3. The great conveyancer Sir Orlando Bridgman invented the trust to preserve contingent remainders from destruction, thus: *O* conveys "to *A* for life, then to *B, C,* and *D,* trustees, for the life of *A* and to preserve contingent remainders, then to *A*'s children who survive *A*." Do you see why this device works by preventing the passage of seisin until *A*'s death?

In a jurisdiction where destructibility of contingent remainders has not been clearly abolished by statute or judicial decision, is it malpractice for a lawyer, who creates a legal contingent remainder in land, not to create a trust to preserve the contingent remainder from destruction? See Jesse Dukeminier, Cleansing the Stables of Property: A River Found at Last, 65 Iowa L. Rev. 151, 168-169 (1979).

4. If the life tenant does not hold seisin, the destructibility doctrine does not apply. Hence the doctrine does not apply to interests in personal property, in which there is no seisin, nor to equitable interests in trust, where the trustee holds seisin.

---

16. *A*'s widow, claiming to be pregnant with an heir, could be subjected to a rather rude procedure by those who would be cut out by the birth. They could obtain a writ *de ventre inspiciendo.* "The writ directs that, in the presence of knights and women, the female *tractari per uberem et ventrum,* — the presumed necessity of the case dispensing at once with common decency and with respectful deference to sex." 1 William Blackstone, Commentaries *456 n.15.

Abolition of the Destructibility Doctrine

Although destructibility of contingent remainders furthered alienability, it proved incapable of curbing what Lord Nottingham called "naughty" future interests, those that endure for an unreasonably long time. First, the exemption of executory interests meant land could be tied up for long periods of time by creating those interests rather than contingent remainders. To curb executory interests the judges invented the Rule against Perpetuities. Second, future interests created in a trust were not subject to the destructibility doctrine. As time passed, more future interests were created in trust than as legal interests; today the great majority of future interests are equitable rather than legal. Equitable future interests are controlled by the Rule against Perpetuities.

After the Rule against Perpetuities was fully developed in the nineteenth century, it appeared to be a good idea to subject all contingent future interests in transferees to one rule, the Rule against Perpetuities, and abolish the destructibility doctrine. Destructibility of contingent remainders has been abolished in about three-fourths of the American states, either by statute or judicial decision. Restatement of Property §240 (1936) declares that the doctrine ought not to be, and is not, part of American law. See Jesse Dukeminier, Contingent Remainders and Executory Interests: A Requiem for the Distinction, 43 Minn. L. Rev. 13, 31-41 (1958); Samuel M. Fetters, Destructibility of Contingent Remainders, 21 Ark. L. Rev. 145 (1967) (suggesting doctrine might exist in Arkansas); Jack D. Jones & William R. Heck, Destructibility of Contingent Remainders in Tennessee, 42 Tenn. L. Rev. 761 (1975) (suggesting doctrine exists in Tennessee).

There has been practically no litigation on destructibility of contingent remainders in more than 50 years. Perhaps the doctrine is dying from lack of use or lack of knowledge of it, and no formal pronouncement of death will ever be made. In the only case clearly raising the issue in modern times, the New Mexico court flatly rejected the destructibility doctrine. Abo Petroleum Corp. v. Amstutz, 93 N.M. 332, 600 P.2d 278 (1979).

PROBLEM

In a jurisdiction in which the destructibility rule has been abolished by statute, O conveys Blackacre "to A for life, then to such of A's children as attain the age of 21."

(a) Suppose that two years later A dies leaving two children: C, aged 8, and D, aged 4. What is the state of the title? When C reaches 21 will he take any interest in Blackacre?

(b) Suppose that during *A*'s life, child *C* reaches 21, then dies. Then *A* dies, survived by child *D*, aged 17. What is the state of the title?

4. The Rule against Perpetuities

a. The Common Law Rule

The culmination of the long struggle between landowners who wanted to keep land within the family and the royal judges who for centuries had tried to stand firm against these efforts is the Rule against Perpetuities. The Rule originated in the Duke of Norfolk's Case, 3 Ch. Cas. 1, 22 Eng. Rep. 931 (Ch. 1681), and as fleshed out in the next 200 years it took the form of a compromise between the landed class and the judges. At the time of the formulation of the Rule against Perpetuities, heads of families — the fathers — were much concerned about securing family land, perhaps acquired only a couple of generations earlier, from incompetent sons. In the Duke of Norfolk's Case, the Earl of Arundel and his lawyer, Sir Orlando Bridgman,[17] created trust indentures to protect the family from the consequences of the insanity of the Earl's eldest son. Lord Chancellor Nottingham recognized this concern as legitimate, and he and his successor judges developed an appropriate period during which the father's judgment could prevail. The father could realistically and perhaps wisely assess the capabilities of *living* members of his family, and so, with respect to them, the father's informed judgment, solemnly inscribed in an instrument, was given effect. But the head of family could know nothing of unborn persons. Hence, the father was permitted to control only so long as his judgment was informed with an understanding of the capabilities and needs of persons alive when the judgment was made. Subsequently, the judges permitted the testator to extend his control beyond lives in being if any of the persons in the next generation was actually a minor. Finally, after about 150 years, the judges fixed the period as lives in being plus 21 years thereafter.

In the elegant and concise theorem made famous by John Chipman Gray, the Rule against Perpetuities is: "No interest is good unless it must vest, if at all, not later than twenty-one years after some life in being at the creation of the interest." John C. Gray, The Rule Against Perpetuities §201 (4th ed. 1942). The compromise it strikes is that property may be tied up with contingent interests for lives in being plus 21 years thereafter, but no longer. Professor Leach observed that the balance struck by the courts permitted "a man of property . . . [to] provide for all of those in his family whom he personally knew and the first generation

---

17. For more on Orlando Bridgman, see footnote 11 on pages 290-291.

after them upon attaining majority." 6 American Law of Property §24.16 (1952). When you think about it, permitting this extensive period of dead hand control represents a considerable victory for the rich desirous of controlling their fortunes after death.

The Rule against Perpetuities is a rule that strikes down contingent interests that *might* vest too remotely. The essential thing to grasp about the Rule is that *it is a rule of logical proof.* You must prove that a contingent interest will *necessarily vest or fail* within 21 years after some life in being at the creation of the interest.[18] If you cannot prove that, the contingent interest is void from the outset. What you are looking for is a person who will enable you to prove that the contingent interest will vest within the life of, or at the death of, the person, or within 21 years after the death of the person. This person, if found, is called the *validating life.*

Inasmuch as a validating life will be found, if found at all, among persons who can affect vesting, you look only at them in searching for a validating life. These include the preceding life tenant, the taker or takers of the contingent interest, anyone who can affect the identity of the takers (such as *A* in a gift to *A*'s children), and anyone who can affect a condition precedent. If you find that there is a person in this group who enables you to make the necessary proof, you have found a validating life. If there is no person among this group of relevant lives by whom the requisite proof can be made, the interest is void unless it must vest or fail within 21 years. Thus:

> *Example 22. O* conveys "to *A* for life, then to *A*'s first child to reach 21." *A* is the validating life. You can prove that any child of *A* who reaches 21 will necessarily reach 21 within 21 years of *A*'s death. The gift must vest or fail within this period; it cannot possibly vest more than 21 years after *A* dies.

> *Example 23. O* conveys "to *A* for life, then to *A*'s first child to reach 25." *A* has no child age 25 or older. There is no validating life; the contingent remainder is void.[19] You cannot prove that *A*'s first child to reach 25 will do so within 21 years after *A*'s death. Here is what might happen: *A*'s presently living children (all under 25) die; *A* has another child, *B,* a year later; *A* dies, leaving *B,* age 3, alive. *B* will not reach 25 within 21 years after *A*'s death. If the gift vests in *B,* it will vest 22 years after *A*'s death, and this is too remote. No other life enables you to make the proof required. Since the contingent

18. If the contingent interest is created by will, the life in being must be a person alive at the testator's death. If the contingent interest is created by an irrevocable inter vivos transfer, the life in being must be a person alive at the time of the transfer. In case of a revocable transfer, the Rule against Perpetuities does not apply until the transfer becomes irrevocable, and hence the life in being must be a person alive when the power of revocation ceases.

19. If the old common law doctrine of destructibility of contingent remainders is in force, the contingent remainder is valid. It will either vest before *A* dies or it will be destroyed at *A*'s death. In no case can it vest after *A*'s death. It is doubtful that this doctrine survives in any jurisdiction. See page 298.

remainder is void, it is struck from the instrument, leaving a life estate in *A*, with a reversion in *O*.

The validating lives do not have to be persons mentioned in the instrument, but they must be persons who can affect vesting of the interest. Thus:

> *Example 24.* *T* devises property "to my grandchildren who reach 21." *T* leaves two children and three grandchildren under 21. The validating lives are *T*'s two children;[20] all of *T*'s grandchildren must reach 21, if at all, within 21 years after the death of *T*'s two children.

Since an interest satisfies the Rule if it is vested upon creation, you should classify the interests initially to see if any interest is then vested. Thus:

> *Example 25.* *O* conveys "to *A* for life, then to *A*'s children for their lives, then to *B*." The remainder to *B* is vested upon creation; *B* is the life that enables you to prove the remainder is vested and valid. Observe that *B*'s remainder may *vest in possession* at the death of *A*'s afterborn children, which may be too remote; but the remainder is valid because it is *vested in interest* now.

If you understand how to find the validating life, you have mastered the fundamental working principle of the Rule.

For abbreviated treatments of the Rule, but quite enough for the beginning student, see Jesse Dukeminier, A Modern Guide to Perpetuities, 74 Cal. L. Rev. 1867 (1986); W. Barton Leach, Perpetuities in a Nutshell, 51 Harv. L. Rev. 638 (1938); W. Barton Leach, Perpetuities: The Nutshell Revisited, 78 Harv. L. Rev. 973 (1965).

PROBLEMS

1. *O* conveys "to *A* for life, then to *B* if *B* attains the age of 30." *B* is now 2 years old. Is the conveyance good?

2. *O* conveys "to *A* for life, then to *A*'s children for their lives, then to *B* if *B* is then alive, and if *B* is not then alive, to *B*'s heirs." Is the conveyance good?

3. *O*, a teacher of property law, declares that she holds in trust $1,000 "for all members of my present property class who are admitted to the bar." Is the gift good? Suppose that *O* had said "for the first child of *A* who is admitted to the bar." Would the gift be good?

---

20. Here, as elsewhere in property law, a child is considered as in being from the time of conception if later born alive. Hence a child in the womb at *T*'s death is a life in being.

Future interests retained by the *transferor* — reversions, possibilities of reverter, and rights of entry — are not subject to the Rule against Perpetuities. They are treated as vested as soon as they arise. This exemption leads to some startling differences in result when the transferor attempts to create an equivalent interest — an executory interest — in a transferee. Compare these two cases involving future interests in the grantor:

> *Example 26.* O conveys Blackacre "to the school board so long as used for a school." The school board has a fee simple determinable; O has a possibility of reverter exempt from the Rule against Perpetuities.

> *Example 27.* O conveys Blackacre "to the school board, but if it ceases to use Blackacre for school purposes, O has a right to re-enter." The school board has a fee simple subject to condition subsequent; O has a right of entry exempt from the Rule against Perpetuities.

Now hold on to your seats and compare these two cases involving future interests in *transferees:*

> *Example 28.* O conveys Blackacre "to the school board so long as used for a school, then to A and his heirs." A's executory interest violates the Rule against Perpetuities. It will not necessarily vest within A's lifetime or within 21 years after A's death. It may become possessory centuries from now. When an interest violates the Rule against Perpetuities, it is struck out and the remaining valid interests stand. Take a pencil and line out the void gift, "then to A and his heirs." This leaves a fee simple determinable in the school board. Since O has not given away O's entire interest, O has a possibility of reverter.

> *Example 29.* O conveys Blackacre "to the school board, but if it ceases to use Blackacre for school purposes to A and his heirs." The school board has a fee simple subject to a (purported) executory interest. A's executory interest violates the Rule against Perpetuities for the reason given in *Example 28.* Strike it out, beginning with "but if it ceases. . . ." This leaves standing a conveyance "to the school board." The school board has a fee simple absolute!

If you were counsel for O in *Examples 28* and *29* how would you carry out O's desires exactly, using two pieces of paper rather than one? Would a lawyer be liable for malpractice if the lawyer failed to use two pieces of paper?

Brown v. Independent Baptist Church of Woburn

Supreme Judicial Court of Massachusetts, 1950
325 Mass. 645, 91 N.E.2d 922

Qua, C.J. The object of this suit in equity, originally brought in this court, is to determine the ownership of a parcel of land in Woburn and the persons entitled to share in the proceeds of its sale by a receiver.

Sarah Converse died seised of the land on July 19, 1849, leaving a will in which she specifically devised it

> to the Independent Baptist Church of Woburn, to be holden and enjoyed by them so long as they shall maintain and promulgate their present religious belief and faith and shall continue a Church; and if the said Church shall be dissolved, or its religious sentiments shall be changed or abandoned, then my will is that this real estate shall go to my legatees hereinafter named, to be divided in equal portions between them. And my will further is, that if my beloved husband, Jesse Converse, shall survive me, that then this devise to the aforesaid Independent Church of Woburn, shall not take effect till from and after his decease; and that so long as he shall live he may enjoy and use the said real estate, and take the rents and profits thereof to his own use.

Then followed ten money legacies in varying amounts to different named persons, after which there was a residuary clause in these words,

> The rest and residue of my estate I give and bequeath to my legatees above named, saving and except therefrom the Independent Baptist Church; this devise to take effect from and after the decease of my husband; I do hereby direct and will that he shall have the use and this rest and residue during his life.

The husband of the testatrix died in 1864. The church named by the testatrix ceased to "continue a church" on October 19, 1939.

The parties apparently are in agreement, and the single justice ruled, that the estate of the church in the land was a determinable fee. We concur. First Universalist Society of North Adams v. Boland, 155 Mass. 171, 174. Institution for Savings v. Roxbury Home for Aged Women, 244 Mass. 583, 585-586. Dyer v. Siano, 298 Mass. 537, 540. The estate was a fee, since it might last forever, but it was not an absolute fee, since it might (and did) "automatically expire upon the occurrence of a stated event." Restatement: Property, §44. It is also conceded, and was ruled, that the specific executory devise over to the persons "hereinafter named" as legatees was void for remoteness. This conclusion seems to be required by Proprietors of the Church in Brattle Square v. Grant, 3 Gray, 142, 152, 155-156, First Universalist Society of North Adams v. Boland, 155 Mass. 171, 173, and Institution for Savings v. Roxbury Home for Aged Women, 244 Mass. 583, 587. See Restatement: Property, §44, illustration 20. The reason is stated to be that the determinable fee might not come to an end until long after any life or lives in being and twenty-one years, and in theory at least might never come to an end, and for an indefinite period no clear title to the entire estate could be given.

Since the limitation over failed, it next becomes our duty to consider what became of the possibility of reverter which under our decisions remained after the failure of the limitation. First Universalist Society of

Independent Baptist Church of Woburn in the 1930s
(chapel located over Durward's Market)
from Woburn Public Library, Glennon Archives

North Adams v. Boland, 155 Mass. 171, 175. Institution for Savings v. Roxbury Home for Aged Women, 244 Mass. 583, 587. . . . A possibility of reverter seems, by the better authority, to be assignable inter vivos (Restatement: Property, §159; Simes, Future Interests, §715; see Tiffany, Real Property [3d ed.] §314, note 31) and must be at least as readily devisable as the other similar reversionary interest known as a right of entry for condition broken, which is devisable, though not assignable. . . . It follows that the possibility of reverter passed under the residuary clause of the will to the same persons designated in the invalid executory devise. It is of no consequence that the persons designated in the two provisions were the same. The same result must be reached as if they were different.

The single justice ruled that the residuary clause was void for remoteness, apparently for the same reason that rendered the executory devise void. With this we cannot agree, since we consider it settled that the rule against perpetuities does not apply to reversionary interests of is general type, including possibilities of reverter. Proprietors of the rch in Brattle Square v. Grant, 3 Gray, 142, 148. . . . For a full un- nding of the situation here presented it is necessary to keep in mind the fundamental difference in character between the attempted executory devise to the legatees later named in the will and the residuary gift to the same persons. The executory devise was in form and substance an attempt to limit or create a new future interest which might not arise or vest in anyone until long after the permissible period. It was obviously not intended to pass such a residuum of the testatrix's existing estate as a possibility of reverter, and indeed if the executory devise had been valid according to its terms the whole estate would have passed from the testatrix and no possibility of reverter could have been left to her or her devisees. The residuary devise, on the other hand, was in terms and purpose exactly adapted to carry any interest which might otherwise remain in the testatrix, whether or not she had it in mind or knew it would exist. Thayer v. Wellington, 9 Allen, 283, 295. Wellman v. Carter, 286 Mass. 237, 249-250.

We cannot accept the contention made in behalf of Mrs. Converse's heirs that the words of the residuary clause "saving and except therefrom the Independent Baptist Church" were meant to exclude from the operation of that clause any possible rights in the *land* previously given to the church. We construe these words as intended merely to render the will consistent by excluding the church which also had been "above named" from the list of *"legatees"* who were to take the residue.

The interlocutory decree entered December 16, 1947, is reversed, and a new decree is to be entered providing that the land in question or the proceeds of any sale thereof by the receiver shall go to the persons named as legatees in the will, other than the Independent Baptist Church of Woburn, or the successors in interest. Further proceedings are to be in accord with the new decree. Costs and expenses are to be at the discretion of the single justice.

So ordered.

NOTES AND QUESTIONS

1. *Brown v. Independent Baptist Church of Woburn* has been criticized on doctrinal grounds by Professors Simes and Smith. They say that the court failed to recognize the essential distinction between possibilities of reverter retained by deed and possibilities of reverter retained by will. In the latter case, they cannot be retained by the transferor, who is dead, but are retained by the transferor's heirs, who are substituted for the dead person. Inasmuch as Sarah Converse had no possibility of reverter at the time of her death (she had a fee simple) and she could retain none by will, she had no possibility of reverter to transfer to her residuary legatees. They sum this up by saying that the court assumed the testator died twice — once to give effect to the specific devise to the church leaving a possibility of reverter in the revived Sarah, and a sec-

ond time to pass the possibility of reverter by her residuary clause to the residuary devisees. Lewis M. Simes & Allan F. Smith, The Law of Future Interests §1241 (2d ed. 1956). Orthodox doctrine would hold that there is a possibility of reverter in Sarah's heirs, not in the residuary devisees. So held in In re Pruner's Estate, 400 Pa. 629, 162 A.2d 626 (1960).

2. Professor Leach was highly critical of the *Woburn Baptist Church* case on policy grounds. He objected to possibilities of reverter escaping the Rule while comparable executory interests were subject to it. W. Barton Leach, Perpetuities in Perspective: Ending the Rule's Reign of Terror, 65 Harv. L. Rev. 721, 741-745 (1952).

Professor Leach delved into the aftermath of the decision in *Woburn Baptist Church*. He reports:

A receiver sold Sarah Converse's land for $34,000 under a court order. By 1929 all of Sarah's ten residuary legatees and twenty-five heirs (as of 1849) had been dead for decades. The process of rounding up the parties to the litigation was a formidable one. Did this heir leave a will? Whom did that legatee marry? Where did she go, and is she still alive? There had been three or four devolutions of the fractional shares in Sarah's possibility of reverter, with split-ups into subfractions and sub-subfractions. To handle this situation counsel agreed that a professional genealogist and searcher for missing heirs should be employed and that his charges should be paid out of the fund; this arrangement was approved by Spalding, J. The prevailing counsel, Mr. Guy Newhall, has described in a letter to me his problem of finding out who his clients were: "As to two of the legatees, mother and daughter, my list of modern descendants looks like a genealogy of the descendants of Methuselah, scattered all the way from California to Buenos Aires. Their shares will be very small, hardly worth bothering about. The other lines vary from a few to a lot." As a consequence of the litigation the court awarded a total of $9,091.25 for counsel fees and disbursements, $1,500 for the genealogist, $4,017.50 for a receiver, and divided the balance into more than one hundred shares ranging from $774.20 to $6.25.

. . . No one can believe that this distribution of small fractional sums to remote descendants of residuary devisees was expected by Sarah Converse or would be desired by her if she could control the matter. Above all she wanted to benefit her church. In 1849 the land devised was on the village street in Woburn — just the place for a church. The church building was erected on the lot. But as time passed Woburn grew. The village street became Main Street in a busy, noisy commercial center. Other churches sold their land, greatly increased in value for commercial use, and with the proceeds of sale erected church buildings in areas more appropriate to religious services. But not Sarah Converse's church, for it had no marketable title to sell. It tried to struggle along at the same old location by renting the first floor to a tailor and a grocery and living off the rents; the second floor provided adequate space for the shrinking congregation. A church cannot live unless it attracts new members; and new members are not attracted to a makeshift place of worship over a block of stores in a commercial district. As early as 1898 the end of the

Church's useful life was in sight. During the last years services were held every fifth Sunday, for the rents could not support more frequent services. Finally in 1939, at the death of an elderly lady who seemed the last of those to whom the church had a real meaning, the organization simply passed out of existence. It is at least possible that the dissolution of this church, where others survived, is directly attributable to the unmarketable title of the Church caused jointly by Sarah's determinable fee and the exemption of her possibility of reverter from the Rule against Perpetuities. [Id. at 743-745.]

3.   Should the Rule against Perpetuities apply to possibilities of reverter and rights of entry? In England these interests are subject to the Rule by statute. English Perpetuities and Accumulations Act, 1964, §12. In this country a number of states have limited these interests to a specified number of years, usually 30, after which the possessory fee becomes absolute. See Mass. Ann. Laws ch. 184A, §7 (Law. Co-op. 1987);[21] Simes & Smith, supra, §1994. Some of these statutes permit a possibility of reverter or right of entry to be preserved for additional periods by recording in the courthouse, before the end of the allowable period, a notice of intent to preserve the future interest. Most of the statutes operate retroactively, so as to terminate existing possibilities of reverter and rights of entry if they have lasted longer than the allowable period or if no notice of intent to preserve is recorded within a few years after the statute is enacted. The retroactive provisions raise the question whether a property interest is unconstitutionally taken (see Chapter 12). Most courts have upheld the retroactive provisions as justifiable legislative attempts to eliminate ancient clogs on title. See, e.g., Walton v. City of Red Bluff, 2 Cal. App. 4th 117, 3 Cal. Rptr. 2d 275 (1991); Ludington & Northern Railway v. The Epworth Assembly, 188 Mich. App. 25, 468 N.W.2d 884 (1991). Contra, Board of Education v. Miles, 15 N.Y.2d 364, 207 N.E.2d 181, 259 N.Y.S.2d 129 (1965) (striking down retroactive application as unconstitutional).

4.   If O makes a gift to Charity A followed by a gift over to Charity B if a specified event happens, the executory interest in Charity B is exempt from the Rule against Perpetuities. Thus in a deed of Blackacre to the Board of Education so long as it is used as a school, and then to City Library, the executory interest in City Library is valid. This exemption applies only if both the possessory estate and the future interest are in

---

21. This statute, enacted in 1954 largely as a result of Professor Leach's criticism of the *Woburn Baptist Church* case, supersedes that case. The statute terminates possibilities of reverter, rights of entry, and *equivalent executory interests* after 30 years, making the fee simple then indefeasible. Oak's Oil Serv., Inc. v. Massachusetts Bay Transp. Auth., 15 Mass. App. 593, 447 N.E.2d 27 (1983). Cal. Civ. Code §885.030 (West Supp. 1992) and Ky. Rev. Stat. §381.218 (1972) are similar. But the differences between the application of the Rule against Perpetuities to executory interests and to interests in the transferor, as exemplified in the *Woburn Baptist Church* case, remains the law in almost all other jurisdictions.

charitable organizations. It does not apply if either the possessory estate
or the future interest is in a noncharity.

Is this exemption sound? In California an executory interest in a
charity to enforce a restriction on the use of real property is subject to
the same 30-year limitation as is an executory interest in a noncharity.
Cal. Civ. Code §§885.010, 885.030 (West Supp. 1992).

Central Delaware County Authority
v. Greyhound Corp.
Supreme Court of Pennsylvania, 1991
527 Pa. 47, 588 A.2d 485

FLAHERTY, J. In 1941 and 1950 the Baldwin Locomotive Works conveyed to the Central Delaware County Authority ("Authority") two parcels of land. The Authority paid $5,500 for the parcel conveyed in 1941
and $2,970 for the parcel conveyed in 1950. The deeds in both cases
conveyed a fee simple interest subject to a restrictive covenant appearing
in the encumbrance clause. The 1941 deed contains the following provision:

> It is specifically covenanted, stipulated, and agreed between the parties
> hereto that the said tract of land, while in the ownership and possession of
> the said Central Delaware County Authority and its successors, shall be kept
> available for and shall be used only for public purposes by the said Central
> Delaware County Authority and its successor or any other public instrumen-
> tality or other agency which may hereafter acquire title to the same. In the
> event that at any time hereafter said use shall be abandoned so that the said
> tract shall cease to be used for said public purposes, then and in such event
> the Baldwin Locomotive Works, its successors and assigns, shall have the right
> to repurchase, retake and reacquire the same upon the payment, either to
> the Central Delaware County Authority if owner thereof, or to any successor
> in right thereto, or to the municipalities for which the said vendee or its suc-
> cessors shall be acting, the sum of fifty-five hundred dollars ($5,500.00) above
> mentioned and herein provided to be paid therefor; or in the event of dis-
> pute, the said sum may be paid into Court in any appropriate proceeding for
> the benefit of any and all parties entitled to the same. In any such case, vendee
> shall have the right to remove all improvements.
>
> PROVIDED, HOWEVER, that if the Baldwin Locomotive Works does
> not pay the sum of fifty-five hundred dollars ($5,500.00) to the said Author-
> ity, or otherwise as above provided, within six months after the date when the
> authority or its successors in title abandons the said property for public pur-
> poses, or the date when notified by the Authority of its intention to abandon
> the property, then and in such event this covenant shall become void and of
> no effect.

The encumbrance clause of the 1950 deed is substantially the same as that of the 1941 deed, except that . . . repurchase is conditioned upon payment of $2,970 instead of $5,500.

The Authority operated a sewage treatment plant on this land for approximately twenty-six years. In 1980, the Authority ceased operation of the sewage treatment facility, but the Authority continues to maintain and possess the land. In 1983, it brought an action to quiet title in the land, alleging that the deed's public use, ownership and repurchase restrictions are void as violative of the rule against perpetuities.

The parties stipulated to evidence on each claim regarding the chain of title of the Baldwin tract and corporate successorship to Baldwin, and, accordingly, to the persons who may assert the right to repurchase. . . . [Greyhound Corporation is a successor to Baldwin.]

Superior Court . . . held that the restriction in the deed was an option to purchase, not an interest subject to a condition subsequent. 386 Pa. Super. 423, 563 A.2d 139. Since options to purchase are subject to the rule against perpetuities, and since this restriction allowed for the possibility that the option might vest later than twenty-one years after a life in being at the creation of the restriction, Superior Court held that the restrictions violated the rule. Superior Court determined that the restrictions were not invalid, however, on public policy grounds: "were we to find the rule against perpetuities applicable to this particular option contract, we would be creating a climate in which grantors would not freely give their properties for public use." At 434, 563 A.2d 139. The Authority petitioned for allowance of appeal and we granted allocatur. The principal issue on this appeal is whether Superior Court erred in determining that the rule against perpetuities did not invalidate the restrictive covenants.

The first question is whether Superior Court was correct in holding that the estate created was a repurchase option rather than an estate subject to a condition subsequent. A fee simple subject to a condition subsequent arises where the provision is that upon the happening of a certain event, the grantor has the right and power to terminate the conveyed estate. See Emrick v. Bethlehem Twp., 506 Pa. 372, 379, 485 A.2d 736, 739 (1984). This estate is not subject to the rule against perpetuities because the right of reentry or power of termination which it creates is exempt from the rule. However, a repurchase option, as the restriction in the present case was held to be by Superior Court, is subject to the rule, for an option is not a vested estate.

The initial inquiry, then, is whether Superior Court was correct in deciding that the interest in this case was a repurchase option rather than a fee simple subject to a condition subsequent. We concur with Superior Court's analysis. While it is true that the deeds may be read to create a fee simple subject to a condition subsequent (the condition subsequent would be abandonment of public use followed by the payment of certain sums of money), the deeds can also be read to create a repurchase option conditioned upon the termination of public use. Like Superior Court, to resolve this ambiguity, we turn to the Restatement of Property for guidance.

> If the language and circumstances of a conveyance of an estate in fee simple are otherwise reasonably susceptible of two constructions, under one of which it creates either a possibility of reverter or power of termination, . . . and under the other of which it creates an option to repurchase, . . . the latter of the two constructions is preferred. The fact that the exercise of the reserved privilege requires the parting with money or other consideration, by the reserving conveyor is sufficiently indicative of the intent of the conveyor to create an option. . . . The finding of the option, under these facts, furthers the protective policy which underlies the rule against perpetuities, and is in accord with the general constructional preference for covenants rather than conditions. [4 Restatement of Property §394, Comment c (1944).]

We believe that section 394 accurately reflects the law of this Commonwealth in favoring interpretations of deed restrictions which bring the restriction within the ambit of the rule. See Barton v. Thaw, 246 Pa. 348, 364, 92 A. 312, 316 (1914). Superior Court was not in error, therefore, in finding that the interest created was a repurchase option.

[Pennsylvania has modified the common law rule against perpetuities by providing that the court will not judge the validity of an interest by what might happen but will wait and see whether the interest actually vests within the common law perpetuities period. Pa. Cons. Stat. Ann. §6104(b) (Purdon 1975). In an omitted portion of the opinion, the court held that because the options were not in fact exercised within 21 years after 1941 and 1950, respectively, the options could not be saved by the wait-and-see rule.]

It remains to be considered, however, whether Superior Court was correct in also determining that the rule against perpetuities does not apply to the repurchase option on the grounds of public policy, viz., that grantors would not freely give their properties for public use.

. . . In Barton v. Thaw, 246 Pa. 348, 92 A. 312 (1914), this court addressed the policy underlying the rule and the nature of the legal obligation which the rule imposes. In that case, this court voided a covenant in the deed which granted [the purchaser of the minerals] the option to purchase the surface in fee "at any future time whatsoever . . . at a price not exceeding one hundred dollars per acre." Id. at 350, 92 A. at 313.[22] The court held that the rule against perpetuities applied to this

22. The language in the *Barton* deed read as follows:

And in case the said parties of the second part, their heirs and assigns, should at any future time whatsoever desire to purchase any of said land in fee simple, then the said

repurchase option which was unlimited in time, and the interest was, therefore, void. The rationale for this holding was that the rule against perpetuities is a "peremptory command of law," and thus is not subject to negation by a countervailing statement of public policy:

> "The rule against perpetuities is not a rule of construction, but a peremptory command of law. It is not, like a rule of construction, a test, more or less artificial to determine intention. Its object is to defeat intention. Therefore every provision in a will or settlement is to be construed as if the rule did not exist, and then to the provision so construed the rule is to be remorselessly applied." Gray on Rule Against Perpetuities (2nd Ed.), sec 629; Gerber's Est., 196 Pa. 366, 46 A. 497 (1900); Bender v. Bender, 225 Pa. 434, 74 A. 246 (1909). "We must be careful not to strain the law so as to avoid this rule. It is founded upon a sound principle of public policy and should be rigidly enforced." Coggins' App., 124 Pa. 10, 16 A. 579 (1889). [246 Pa. at 354, 92 A. at 314.]

The court described the policy underlying the rule as follows:

> Such an impress on land [one that violates the rule] ought not to be sustained, and it cannot be. It isolates the property. It takes it out of commerce. It removed [sic] it from the market. It halts improvements. It prevents the land from answering to the needs of growing communities. No homes can be built or towns laid out on land so encumbered, because the land always remains subject to be taken under the option. It is not a matter which affects the rights of individuals only. The entire community is interested. The welfare of the public is at stake. It is contrary to the well settled public policy of the state that such an option or right to purchase land should be held to be good. It was for the express purpose of destroying such serious hindrances to material and social prosperity and progress that the rule against perpetuities was brought forth. And the rule must be rigidly enforced. [246 Pa. at 364, 92 A. at 316.]

These considerations are as valid today as they were in 1914, when Barton v. Thaw was written. Now, as then, economic development and prosperity depends in important part upon the free alienability of land. It is for this reason that the rule against perpetuities is a "peremptory command of law" that "is to be remorselessly applied." The repurchase option is, therefore, void.

Order of Superior Court is reversed. Title is quieted in the Central Delaware County Authority and the option to repurchase, which constitutes a cloud upon the title, is hereby declared void and is removed by cancellation.

---

parties of the first part, for themselves, their heirs or assigns, hereby covenant and agree to sell and convey the same to the said parties of the second part, their heirs or assigns, at a price not exceeding one hundred dollars per acre.

NOTE

In recent years the large majority of cases finding violations of the Rule against Perpetuities involve options and rights of first refusal (preemptive options). An option, which is specifically enforceable in equity, creates an interest in the property involved. An option is treated like a future interest, contingent upon exercise of the option. If an option can be exercised beyond the perpetuities period, it is generally held void. For example, an option granted to A and her heirs, which is assignable and exercisable by A's successor more than 21 years after A is dead, is void. See Otter Creek Dev. Co. v. Friesenhahn, 295 Ark. 318, 748 S.W.2d 344 (1988) (dissent criticizes the application of the Rule to options); Lawrence & Grant Ave. Trust v. Robinson, 596 A.2d 1378 (Del. 1991) (voiding right of first refusal); Ferraro Constr. Co. v. Dennis Rourke Corp., 311 Md. 560, 536 A.2d 1137 (1988); but see Wildenstein & Co. v. Wallis, 79 N.Y.2d 641, 595 N.E.2d 828, 584 N.Y.S.2d 753 (1992) (holding art dealer's preemptive rights to sell art collection if owners decided to sell not subject to Rule against Perpetuities). The extensive litigation indicates that lawyers drafting commercial agreements often overlook the need to limit the duration of an option to the permissible perpetuities period.

Options given a lessee to renew the lease or purchase the land have been held not subject to the Rule against Perpetuities. Such options do not inhibit, but rather encourage, improvement of the property.

In cooperatives and condominiums, the governing board sometimes seeks to control admission of new occupants by retaining a right of first refusal when the sitting occupant wants to sell. After some initial uncertainty, it now seems settled that preemptive options in condominiums and cooperatives are not subject to the Rule against Perpetuities. They are subject to the rule against unreasonable restraints on alienation. See Note 1 on pages 933-934.

See generally 5A Richard R. Powell, The Law of Real Property ¶771 (rev. ed. 1992).

Jee v. Audley
Court of Chancery, 1787
1 Cox 324, 29 Eng. Rep. 1186

Edward Audley, by his will, bequeathed as follows,

> Also my will is that £1000 shall be placed out at interest during the life of my wife, which interest I give her during her life, and at her death I give the said £1000 unto my niece Mary Hall and the issue of her body lawfully begotten, and to be begotten, and in default of such issue I give the said £1000 to be

equally divided between the daughters then living of my kinsman John Jee
and his wife Elizabeth Jee.

   It appeared that John Jee and Elizabeth Jee were living at the time
of the death of the testator, had four daughters and no son, and were of
a very advanced age. Mary Hall was unmarried and of the age of about
40; the wife was dead. The present bill was filed by the four daughters
of John and Elizabeth Jee to have the £1000 secured for their benefit
upon the event of the said Mary Hall dying without leaving children.
And the question was, whether the limitation to the daughters of John
and Elizabeth Jee was not void as being too remote; and to prove it so, it
was said that this was to take effect on a general failure of issue of Mary
Hall; and though it was to the daughters of John and Elizabeth Jee, yet
it was not confined to the daughters living at the death of the testator,
and consequently it might extend to after-born daughters, in which case
it would not be within the limit of a life or lives in being and 21 years
afterwards, beyond which time an executory devise is void.

   On the other side it was said, that though the late cases had decided
that on a gift to children generally, such children as should be living at
the time of the distribution of the fund should be let in, yet it would be
very hard to adhere to such a rule of construction so rigidly, as to defeat
the evident intention of the testator in this case, especially as there was
no real possibility of John and Elizabeth Jee having children after the
testator's death, they being then 70 years old; that if there were two ways
of construing words, that should be adopted which would give effect to
the disposition made by the testator; that the cases, which had decided
that afterborn children should take, proceeded on the implied intention
of the testator, and never meant to give an effect to words which would
totally defeat such intention. . . .

   MASTER OF THE ROLLS [SIR LLOYD KENYON].[23] Several cases . . . have
settled that children born after the death of the testator shall take a share
in these cases; the difference is, where there is an immediate devise, and
where there is an interest in remainder; in the former case the children
living at the testator's death only shall take; in the latter those who are
living at the time the interest vests in possession; and this being now a

----

23. The Master of the Rolls, originally keeper of the chancery records, became the
chief deputy of the Lord Chancellor. Until 1827 the Master of the Rolls sat in the evening
from six to ten o'clock, when the Lord Chancellor was not sitting.
   In 1788 Sir Lloyd Kenyon was created Baron Kenyon and succeeded the great Lord
Mansfield as Lord Chief Justice of England, which office he held until 1802. Kenyon was
a narrow-minded judge who openly sneered at the equitable doctrines introduced into the
law by Mansfield. Standing by the ancient technicalities of the law, Kenyon was testy to
advocates in his court, blazing into anger when a word or sentence not in harmony with
his sentiments was uttered. It was alleged that Lord Kenyon invariably stiffed waiters by
not tipping, not even a half penny. But "he had the glory of dying very rich." 4 John
Campbell, Lives of the Chief Justices of England 1, 101 (1873). See also 1 William Townsend, The Lives of Twelve Eminent Judges 33-128 (1846).

Lloyd, First Baron Kenyon
Lord Chief Justice of England, 1788-1802
by George Romney
Collection of the Fifth Baron Kenyon

settled principle, I shall not strain to serve an intention at the expense of removing the landmarks of the law; it is of infinite importance to abide by decided cases, and perhaps more so on this subject than any other. The general principles which apply to this case are not disputed: the limitations of personal estate are void, unless they necessarily vest, if at all, within a life or lives in being and 21 years or 9 or 10 months afterwards. This has been sanctioned by the opinion of judges of all times, from the time of the Duke of Norfolk's Case to the present: it is grown reverend by age, and is not now to be broken in upon; I am desired to do in this case something which I do not feel myself at liberty to do, namely to suppose it impossible for persons in so advanced an age as John and Elizabeth Jee to have children; but if this can be done in one case it may in another, and it is a very dangerous experiment, and introductive of the greatest inconvenience to give a latitude to such sort of conjecture. Another thing pressed upon me, is to decide on the events which have happened; but I cannot do this without overturning very many cases. The single question before me is, not whether the limitation is good in the events which have happened, but whether it was good in its creation; and if it were not, I cannot make it so. Then must this limitation, if at all, necessarily take place within the limits prescribed by law? The words are "in default of such issue I give the said £1000 to be equally divided between the daughters then living of John Jee and Elizabeth his wife." If it had been to "daughters now living," or "who should be living at the time of my death," it would have been very good; but as it stands, this limitation may take in after-born daughters; this point is clearly settled by Ellison v. Airey, 1 Ves. 111, and the effect of law on such limitation cannot make any difference in construing such intention. If then this will extended to after-born daughters, is it within the rules of law? Most certainly not, because John and Elizabeth Jee might have children born ten years after the testator's death, and then Mary Hall might die without issue 50 years afterwards; in which case it would evidently transgress the rules prescribed. I am of opinion therefore, though the testator might possibly mean to restrain the limitation to the children who should be living at the time of his death, I cannot, consistently with decided case, construe it in such restrained sense, but must intend it to take in after-born children. This therefore not being within the rules of law, and as I cannot judge upon subsequent events, I think the limitation void. Therefore dismiss the bill, but without costs.

NOTES AND QUESTIONS

1. Jee v. Audley is the most famous (or infamous) case involving the Rule against Perpetuities. It settled several principles that rule us yet. Two technical aspects require some explanation. First, Edward Audley

left £1000 "unto my niece Mary Hall and the issue of her body lawfully begotten." This language would create a fee tail in Mary Hall if land were involved, but a fee tail could not be created in personal property. The Statute De Donis, which authorized the fee tail, applied only to land. Language that would create a fee tail in land was construed to create the equivalent of a fee simple in personal property. Hence, Mary Hall was given the equivalent of a fee simple.

Second, the gift over to the Jee daughters is to divest Mary's fee simple "in default of such issue" of Mary Hall. The court construed this to mean upon a general failure of issue of Mary Hall. A general failure of issue, more commonly called an *indefinite failure of issue,* means "when Mary's bloodline runs out." Mary's bloodline might run out at her death, if she leaves no descendants then living, or it might run out centuries hence, when her descendants disappear from the face of the earth. It is this second possibility that leads to a gift that might vest too remotely.

A gift over to B when A's bloodline runs out is a very strange gift to the modern mind. But it was what the grantor had in mind when he created a fee tail in A with a gift over to B. Thus if O conveyed land "to A and the heirs of her body, and if A dies without issue to B and her heirs," O created a fee tail in A and intended B's remainder to become possessory upon the expiration of the fee tail, that is, when A's bloodline runs out. In Jee v. Audley, a fee tail was not created and it is hard to believe Edward Audley had in mind shifting possession of £1000 when Mary Hall's whole line of descendants expired. But this is what Lord Kenyon held. What arguments can you make that Audley had no such remote event in mind?

When the fee tail was abolished, courts and legislatures decided that a gift over to B "if A dies without issue" should not be construed to mean a gift to B when A's bloodline expires but rather should be construed to mean a gift to B "if, at A's death, A has no issue living." If Edward Audley's will had been construed to give the £1000 to the Jee daughters if, and only if, Mary Hall were to die without leaving issue at her death, the gift over to the Jee daughters would be valid because it would vest or fail at Mary's death.

Although gifts over on the expiration of a bloodline rarely occur in modern times, the principles involved in Jee v. Audley remain fundamental. A gift over upon failure of a bloodline is the equivalent of a gift over upon any remote event that may happen more than 21 years after the death of all living persons.

2. Why were not the following persons validating lives in being under the Rule against Perpetuities: Mary Hall; John and Elizabeth Jee; the four Jee daughters living at testator's death?

The answer, of course, is that the gift to "the daughters then living of my kinsman John Jee and his wife Elizabeth Jee" will not necessarily vest or fail within 21 years after the death of any or all of these persons. The gift might vest in an afterborn daughter of the Jees more than 21 years after these persons are dead. See if you can write the scenario for remote vesting. Because the gift is not invalid unless you assume Elizabeth Jee can have a child, the scenario must include Elizabeth Jee bearing a daughter after Audley's death as well as Mary Hall giving birth to a child after Audley's death.[24]

3. Lord Kenyon says: "If it [the gift over] had been to 'daughters now living,' or 'who should be living at the time of my death,' it would have been very good." Standing alone, this statement is wrong. Do you see why? On the other hand, if Lord Kenyon was adding words to Edward Audley's will and meant to say, "if the gift over had been to the daughters now living who are then living, it would have been very good," the statement would be correct. Do you see why?

NOTE: GIFTS TO CLASSES

In Jee v. Audley it was tacitly assumed by the court that a gift to a class (the Jee daughters) was invalid if it might vest in one member of the class (an afterborn daughter) too remotely. The court could have held that the shares given to the four living Jee daughters were valid since the living daughters would have to take their shares of the £1000 within their own lives or the gifts to them would fail. But Lord Kenyon was not so inclined. Later it became firmly established that a class gift must stand or fall as a unit. If the gift to one member of the class might vest too remotely, the whole class gift is void. Or, to put it another way, a class gift is not vested *in any member* of the class until the interests of *all members* have vested. A gift that is vested subject to open (see page 269) is *not* vested under the Rule against Perpetuities. For a class gift to be vested under the Rule, the class must be closed (that is, each and every member of the class must be identified) and all conditions precedent for each and every member of the class must be satisfied within the perpetuities period. Thus suppose a gift "to A for life, then to A's children," and A has living one child, B. B's remainder is vested subject to open, but it is not vested under the Rule against Perpetuities until A dies and all of A's children are then identified. Because the remaindermen will all be ascertained at A's death, the remainder is valid.

---

24. The Guinness Book of World Records 14 (1991) says the oldest mother by authenticated records is Ruth Alice Kistler of Portland, Oregon, who gave birth in 1956 at age 57. The Biblical record is set by Sarah, who is said to have given birth to Isaac at the age of 90. Gen. 17:15-19. When God said to Abraham he would have a son by Sarah, the Bible says Abraham fell on his face and laughed, but a son, Isaac, was born to Sarah within a year.

PROBLEMS AND NOTE

1. *O* conveys "to *A* for life, then to *A*'s children who reach 25." *A* has a child, *B*, age 26, living at the time of the conveyance. Is the remainder valid?

2. *O* conveys "to *A* for life, then to *A*'s widow, if any, for life, then to *A*'s issue then living." Is the gift to *A*'s issue valid? See Dickerson v. Union Natl. Bank of Little Rock, 268 Ark. 292, 595 S.W.2d 677 (1980).

3. *T* devises property "to *A* for life, and on *A*'s death to *A*'s children for their lives, and upon the death of *A* and *A*'s children, to [   ]." *A* and *B* survive *T*. Is the devise of the remainder in fee simple valid or void if the following words are inserted in the bracket?

(a) [*B* if *A* dies childless]
(b) [*B* if *A* has no grandchildren then living]
(c) [*B*'s children]
(d) [*B*'s children then living]
(e) [*A*'s grandchildren]
(f) [*T*'s grandchildren]

4. *Saving clause in a trust.* In drafting a trust creating future interests, experienced lawyers almost always include a perpetuities saving clause. A saving clause is designed to terminate the trust, and distribute the assets, at the expiration of specified measuring lives plus 21 years, if the trust has not earlier terminated. Suppose that the testator wants to create a trust paying income to her only child *A* for life, then income to *A*'s children for their lives, then distributing the principal to *A*'s grandchildren. Here is a saving clause that might be inserted in the trust:

> Notwithstanding any other provision in this instrument, this trust shall terminate, if it has not previously terminated, 21 years after the death of the survivor of *A* and *A*'s issue living at my death. In case of such termination, the then remaining principal and undistributed income of the trust shall be distributed to *A*'s issue then living per stirpes, or, if no issue of *A* is then living, to the American Red Cross.

If *A* actually has an afterborn child who lives more than 21 years after the death of *A* and all *A*'s issue living at the testator's death (the possibility that causes the gift of trust principal to violate the Rule), the trust will terminate under the saving clause and the principal will then be distributed.

b. The Wait-and-See Doctrine

The court's opinion in Jee v. Audley states that the court was urged "to decide on the events which have happened" between the testator's death and the lawsuit. Perhaps John or Elizabeth Jee had died, so that there was no longer the possibility of their having another daughter. The court refused to take into account actual events happening after the testator's death; it determined the validity of the gift by what might happen.

The approach to perpetuities questions exemplified by Jee v. Audley — not construing the instrument so as to make it valid, voiding the interest because of the absurd possibility that a woman of 70 might bear another child — has fallen into considerable disfavor in the second half of the twentieth century. In 1952 Professor W. Barton Leach of Harvard, with memorable wit and high scorn, mounted an all-out attack on the what-might-happen test. W. Barton Leach, Perpetuities in Perspective: Ending the Rule's Reign of Terror, 65 Harv. L. Rev. 721 (1952). Leach approved the wait-and-see idea rejected by Lord Kenyon. Leach argued that we should wait and see whether a contingent interest actually vests within the perpetuities period; if it does, it should be valid. Leach's article provoked a great controversy about the merits of a wait-and-see approach, resulting in a flood of law review articles pro and con.

The virtue of the what-might-happen test is that it gives certainty; we do not wait and see whether an interest turns out to be valid or void. Interests of questionable validity may cause practical problems. On the other hand, the what-might-happen test usually strikes down interests (as in Jee v. Audley) that common sense indicates will vest within the perpetuities period. Practically all perpetuities violations could be avoided by appropriate drafting or the insertion of a saving clause. The wait-and-see doctrine serves the same function as a saving clause. Hence the wait-and-see approach promotes equality of treatment of persons who consult unskilled lawyers, "by placing the validity of all non-vested interests on the same plane, whether the interest is created by a skilled draftsman or one not so skilled." Restatement (Second) of Property, Donative Transfers, §1.4 at 13 (1983), adopting wait-and-see. For an account of the debate before the American Law Institute and a bibliography of articles on wait-and-see, see 5A Richard R. Powell, The Law of Real Property ¶¶827F, 827G, and 827H (rev. ed. 1992). See also Jeffrey E. Stake, Darwin, Donations, and the Illusion of Dead Hand Control, 64 Tulane L. Rev. 705 (1990).

(1) Wait-and-See for the Common Law Perpetuities Period

The wait-and-see doctrine has now been adopted in a majority of states, but the reform has branched generally into two different forms of wait-and-see. Some of the states adopting wait-and-see provide that a contingent interest is valid if it actually vests within the common law perpetuities period. To say that an interest is void because it will not necessarily vest or fail within the perpetuities period means it will not vest or fail within the lives of persons who can affect vesting of the particular interest plus 21 years thereafter. Each interest thus has an inherent perpetuities period applicable to it alone, measured by the persons who can affect vesting. These include the preceding life tenant, the taker or takers of the contingent interest, anyone who can affect the identity of the takers, and anyone who can affect a condition precedent. Here's how wait-and-see for the common law perpetuities period works:

> *Example 30.* T devises property "to A for life, then to A's children who reach 25." The lives in being who can affect vesting are A and all of A's children alive at T's death. A can affect vesting in possession of the remainder because A is the preceding life tenant; A can affect vesting in interest because A, by having another child, can affect the identity of the beneficiaries. A's presently living children can affect vesting because they answer the description of the beneficiaries. Hence, the common law perpetuities period is 21 years after the death of A and all A's living children. If the contingent remainder vests within that period, it is valid.

One of the virtues of waiting to see for the common law perpetuities period is that the perpetuities period remains the same, and the basic policy of permitting donors to tie up property for the lives of persons they know and can judge remains unchanged. For a full treatment of how wait-and-see for the common law perpetuities period applies, see Jesse Dukeminier, Perpetuities: The Measuring Lives, 85 Colum. L. Rev. 1648 (1985); Jesse Dukeminier, Wait-and-See: The Causal Relationship Principle, 102 L.Q. Rev. 250 (1986).

States adopting wait-and-see for the common law perpetuities period, by statute or judicial decision, include Alaska, Kentucky, Mississippi, New Hampshire, Ohio, Pennsylvania, Rhode Island, South Dakota, Vermont, and Virginia. In Illinois, Maine, Maryland, and Washington, statutes provide for waiting to see what happens during the life tenants' lives. Iowa has adopted wait-and-see for the lives of persons on a statutory list resembling the common law measuring lives. A few of these statutes are retroactive. Lake of the Woods Assn. v. McHugh, 238 Va. 1, 380 S.E.2d 872 (1989), struck down the retroactive application of the wait-and-see statute on the ground that it was an unconstitutional taking of property.

PROBLEM

Apply the wait-and-see doctrine to the following transfers. How long do we wait and see?

(a) The devise in Jee v. Audley.

(b) A devise "to the first child of A to become a lawyer."

(c) A devise "to *A* for life, then to *A*'s children for their lives, then to *A*'s grandchildren."

(d) Right of first refusal given *A* and his heirs by *O*. North Bay Council, Inc., Boy Scouts of America v. Grinnell, 123 N.H. 321, 461 A.2d 114 (1983), held that an option is valid under wait-and-see for the optionee's (beneficiary's) life plus 21 years. See also Ryland Group, Inc. v. Wills, 229 Va. 459, 463, 331 S.E.2d 399, 402 (1985) (where the parties are corporate entities and do not contract with reference to a life or lives in being, the determinative period is 21 years from the date of creation of the interest). Accord, Central Delaware County Auth. v. Greyhound Corp., page 308.

(e) A devise "to Baptist Church so long as used for a church, then to *A* and his heirs." (Brown v. Independent Baptist Church of Woburn, page 302.)

(2) Wait-and-See for 90 Years

The Uniform Statutory Rule Against Perpetuities (USRAP), promulgated in 1986, provides for wait-and-see, but it rejects waiting for the common law perpetuities period. Although there does not seem to be any case where the measuring lives for the common law perpetuities period do not manifest themselves, the Uniform Act was drafted on the assumption that, at least in some cases, the measuring lives of the common law perpetuities period might be disputed. See Lawrence W. Waggoner, Perpetuities: A Perspective on Wait-and-See, 85 Colum. L. Rev. 1714 (1985). Hence the Uniform Act drafting group decided not to wait and see for lives in being but to wait and see for 90 years, which is a fair approximation of the period that a skilled lawyer could provide using some very young persons as measuring lives (compare the saving clause on page 318). If an interest does not become valid within 90 years, US-RAP goes on to provide that at the end of 90 years the contingent interest will be reformed by the court so as to most closely approximate the dispositive plan of the donor and vest within 90 years. See Lawrence W. Waggoner, The Uniform Statutory Rule Against Perpetuities: The Rationale of the 90-Year Waiting Period, 73 Cornell L. Rev. 157 (1988).

Unlike wait-and-see for the common law perpetuities period, which replaces the what-might-happen test with an actualities test, leaving one perpetuities rule (wait-and-see) measured by the traditional period, US-RAP adopts two rules against perpetuities: the common law what-might-happen rule and a 90-year wait-and-see rule. If a contingent interest satisfies either rule, it is valid.

In saving run-of-the-mill perpetuities violations, a 90-year wait-and-see period will probably work just as well as waiting for the common law perpetuities period. The large majority of potential violations will vest or fail within either period. See Mary L. Fellows, Testing Perpetuity Reforms: A Study of Perpetuity Cases 1984-89, 25 Real Prop., Prob. & Tr.

J. 597 (1991). The 90-year wait-and-see period is controversial, however, because it provides an alternative perpetuities period to that of the common law. A lawyer can use either the common law period or a 90-year period to govern the vesting of interests and the duration of a trust.

Some commentators object to a 90-year perpetuities period because it abandons the centuries-old common law policy of permitting donors to control property only during the lives of persons they know and whose abilities they can judge (plus 21 years thereafter). The dead hand is permitted to control for 90 years, for the entire lives of afterborn persons unknown to the donor. A 90-year perpetuities period makes it easy for donors to create trusts for this extended period of time, which far exceeds the time most trusts, governed by the common law Rule, presently endure. See Ira M. Bloom, Perpetuities Refinement: There Is an Alternative, 62 Wash. L. Rev. 23 (1987); Jesse Dukeminier, The Uniform Statutory Rule Against Perpetuities: Ninety Years in Limbo, 34 UCLA L. Rev. 1023 (1987).

USRAP relaxes the rules against fettering property in an additional way. The statute abolishes the application of the Rule against Perpetuities to options and other commercial transactions. The drafters believed that lives in being plus 21 years is not a suitable period for controlling commercial transactions. But instead of subjecting them to a different period, USRAP simply exempted them from the Rule.

Although options may endure forever in USRAP jurisdictions, courts may subject them to the rule against unreasonable restraints upon alienation and invalidate those deemed unreasonable. See JLJ Assocs., Inc. v. Persiani, 41 Conn. Supp. 79, 550 A.2d 650 (Super. Ct. 1988).

USRAP has been adopted in California, Colorado, Connecticut, Florida, Georgia, Hawaii, Indiana, Kansas, Massachusetts, Michigan, Minnesota, Montana, Nebraska, Nevada, New Jersey, New Mexico, North Dakota, Oregon, South Carolina, and West Virginia.

PROBLEM

Apply USRAP to the following transfers:

(a) The devise in Jee v. Audley.

(b) A devise "to Baptist Church so long as used for a church, then to A and his heirs." (Brown v. Independent Baptist Church of Woburn, page 302.)

(c) A conveyance by O "to the city, but if it ceases to use the land as a park, to A and his heirs if A pays the city $1,000 (which the city paid O for the property)." (Cf. Central Delaware County Auth. v. Greyhound Corp., page 308.)

(d) A trust created by the testator "to pay the income to my descendants per stirpes from time to time living for 90 years, and then to pay the principal to my descendants then living per stirpes."

NOTE: USRAP AND THE GENERATION-SKIPPING TRANSFER TAX

In 1986 Congress decided to plug the big loophole in the federal estate tax law: the exemption from taxation upon the death of a life tenant (see Problem 1, page 274). In that year Congress enacted a new tax on any generation-skipping transfer, which generally is defined as a transfer to a person two or more generations removed from the donor. When a donor avoids estate taxation at the death of his children by creating a life estate in them, a generation-skipping transfer tax (levied at the highest estate tax rate — currently 50 percent) is payable at the death of the children. Thus:

> *Example 31. T* devises $2 million in trust "for my son *A* for life, then to my granddaughter *B* and her heirs." A federal estate tax is payable at *T*'s death. At *A*'s death, no federal estate tax is payable because *A* does not have a transmissible interest. However, at *A*'s death, a generation-skipping transfer occurs (a transfer from *T* to his grandchild). And so, at *A*'s death, a 50 percent generation-skipping transfer tax is levied on the value of the (nonexempt) corpus of the trust.[25]

It is now congressional policy that a wealth transfer tax — either an estate tax or a generation-skipping transfer tax — be levied on every generation. The generation-skipping transfer tax is not retroactive. Irrevocable trusts established before 1986 are "grandfathered" in. For transfers after 1986, Congress provided a $1 million exemption from the generation-skipping transfer tax for each transferor. See Jesse Dukeminier & Stanley M. Johanson, Wills, Trusts, and Estates 1022-1037 (4th ed. 1990).

Lawyers may attempt to avoid transfer taxes by prolonging pre-1986 trusts and creating new exempt $1 million trusts, with successive life estates, for as long as local perpetuities law allows. Because USRAP gives trust drafters a choice of the common law perpetuities period or a 90-year period, the Treasury Department has decided that USRAP creates an unfair advantage for taxpayers in USRAP states if lawyers attempt to secure whichever period turns out to be longer. Treasury has ruled that the exemption from the generation-skipping transfer tax will be denied if the settlor attempts, directly or indirectly, to extend the duration of a trust for the common law perpetuities period *or* for 90 years, whichever proves longer. To qualify for the tax exemption, the settlor must choose one of these two perpetuities periods at the outset; the tax exemption will be lost if the trust is changed over to the other

---

25. The history buff will observe that the generation-skipping transfer tax has a feudal antecedent in the rule in Shelley's Case (page 291). Both have the purpose of exacting a transfer tax on the death of the life tenant.

perpetuities period when it appears to be longer. See Dukeminier & Johanson, supra, at 838 (Supp. 1992).

If a lawyer in a USRAP jurisdiction violates the Rule against Perpetuities, bringing into play the 90-year wait-and-see period, this may be deemed, under some circumstances, an indirect attempt to secure the longer of the two perpetuities periods. If the generation-skipping transfer tax exemption is thereby lost, the lawyer may be liable for a large malpractice judgment. This danger of losing tax exemption is not present in jurisdictions requiring interests to vest within the common law perpetuities period, in either its what-might-happen or wait-and-see form.

c. Judicial Reformation and Other Legislation

Although a majority of states has opted for some form of wait-and-see, several have adopted other perpetuities reforms. Idaho, Missouri, Oklahoma, and Texas have authorized courts to reform interests violating the Rule so as to carry out most closely the intent of the transferor within the perpetuities period. Reformation takes place at the time the violation is called to the attention of the court. The advantage of immediate judicial reformation is that it preserves the certainty of the common law Rule and gives relief through judicial reformation to those who unwittingly fall victim to it. The disadvantage, compared to wait-and-see, is that it may require a lawsuit to cure a perpetuities violation, which might be resolved without a lawsuit under wait-and-see.

Illinois and New York have more limited reformation statutes that cure the large majority of perpetuities violations with specific remedies. They presume that a woman over 55 is incapable of bearing children and admit evidence of incapacity to bear children in any case (eliminating the conclusive presumption of fertility), presume that a gift to a person's spouse is a gift to a person in being (eliminating the unborn widow), and reduce to age 21 any age contingency in excess of 21 that causes a violation of the Rule. Ill. Ann. Stat. ch. 30, ¶194(c) (Smith-Hurd Supp. 1991); N.Y. Est., Powers & Trusts Law §§9-1.2, 9-1.3 (1967).

As a result of the different kinds of reform statutes, governing only within the enacting jurisdiction, we now have considerable diversity in perpetuities law. In view of this, how should you draft instruments so as to make them valid in all states? Why would you want them valid in all states? See Robert J. Lynn, Perpetuities Literacy for the 21st Century, 50 Ohio St. L.J. 219 (1989).

5

Co-ownership and Marital Interests

As we have seen, ownership may be divided among two or more persons in the sense that they have *consecutive* rights of possession. The division results in possessory and future interests, not co-ownership. The latter term refers to situations where two or more persons have *concurrent* rights of present or future possession, and those situations are the central subject of this chapter.[1]

Actually, we shall not be looking here at all modes of co-ownership, nor shall we be looking only at concurrent interests. Partnerships, for example, involve co-ownership of partnership assets, but we ignore the subject because it is studied in detail in such courses as business associations. Similarly, some marital interests are not concurrent, but we nevertheless study them in Section B of this chapter. We do so because several important marital interests are concurrent or do involve forms of co-ownership and thus are conveniently studied here. Since we open the subject, we might as well give it unified treatment.

A. Common Law Concurrent Interests

1. Types, Characteristics, Creation

The common law has known at least five types of concurrent interests. We can ignore two of these, one because it is of no importance and the other because it is of too much importance.[2] The three remaining

---

1. The concurrent and consecutive concepts can be and often are combined. *A* and *B* can have a concurrent life estate to last for their joint lives, with a remainder in *C*; or *A* and *B* can have concurrent interests in a remainder following a life estate in *C*.

2. The one of no importance is coparceny. At common law under the system of primogeniture the eldest son was the heir. If a decedent had only daughters, the daughters took as coparcenors. Coparceny was similar to, but not identical with, a tenancy in common. Primogeniture never took hold in the American colonies and was early eliminated, as was coparceny. See 2 American Law of Property §6.7 (1952).

The common law concurrent interest of too much importance is the tenancy in partnership, which, as already noted, we leave to other courses. Today the common

are the tenancy in common, the joint tenancy, and the tenancy by the entirety. We shall take them up in turn.

Tenants in common have separate but undivided interests in the property; the interest of each is descendible and may be conveyed by deed or will. There are no survivorship rights between tenants in common. Example: *T* devises Blackacre to *A* and *B*. *A* and *B* are tenants in common. If *A* conveys his interest to *C*, *B* and *C* are tenants in common. If *B* then dies intestate, *B*'s heir is a tenant in common with *C*. Each tenant in common owns an undivided whole (a situation that, whatever its conceptual difficulties, gives rise to a host of practical ones).

Unlike tenants in common, *joint tenants* have the right of survivorship, the outstanding characteristic of a joint tenancy. The theory underlying this right is rather peculiar but still important in several instances. By a common law fiction, joint tenants together were regarded as one entity; each tenant was seised *per my et per tout* (by the share or moiety and by the whole). In theory, then, each owns the undivided whole of the property; this being so, when one joint tenant dies *nothing passes* to the surviving joint tenant or tenants. Rather, the estate simply continues in survivors freed from the participation of the decedent, whose interest is extinguished.

Since the original notion was that all joint tenants were seised together as one, the common law insisted that their interests be equal in all respects. In particular, four "unities" were essential to a joint tenancy — time, title, interest, and possession. The meaning of each unity is as follows:

Time	The interest of each joint tenant must be acquired or vest at the same time.
Title	All joint tenants must acquire title by the same instrument or by a joint adverse possession. A joint tenancy can never arise by intestate succession or other act of law.
Interest	All must have equal undivided shares and identical interests measured by duration.
Possession	Each must have a right to possession of the whole. After a joint tenancy is created, however, one joint tenant can voluntarily give exclusive possession to the other joint tenant. (The unity of possession is essential to a tenancy in common as well; none of the other three unities is.)

At common law, and in many states today, if these four unities do not exist, a joint tenancy is not created; instead, a tenancy in common is created. Statutes in some jurisdictions abolish the requirement of the

---

law of partnership has been largely superseded by the Uniform Partnership Act or other statutory partnership law.

four unities and provide that a joint tenancy may be created simply by stating explicitly the intent to do so.

If the four unities exist at the time the joint tenancy is created but are later severed, the joint tenancy turns into a tenancy in common when the unities cease to exist. Hence, joint tenants can change their interests into a tenancy in common by a mutual agreement destroying one of the four unities. Indeed, any one joint tenant can convert a joint tenancy into a tenancy in common unilaterally by conveying his interest to a third party; this *severs* the joint tenancy as between the third party and his cotenants because it destroys one or more of the unities. (Which one or ones?)

If tenants in common or joint tenants cannot solve their problems by mutual agreement, any one of them can bring an action for judicial partition. In a partition action, a court will either physically partition the tract of land into separately owned parts or order the land sold and divide the proceeds among the tenants.

A *tenancy by the entirety* can be created only in husband and wife. The tenancy by the entirety is like the joint tenancy in that the four unities (plus a fifth — the unity of marriage) are required, and the surviving tenant has the right of survivorship. However, husband and wife are considered to hold as one person at common law. They do not hold by the moieties; rather, both are seised of the entirety, *per tout et non per my*. As a result, neither husband nor wife can defeat the right of survivorship of the other by a conveyance of a moiety to a third party; only a conveyance by husband and wife together can do so. Neither husband nor wife, acting alone, has the right to judicial partition of property held as tenants by the entirety. Divorce terminates the tenancy by the entirety because it terminates the marriage, which is a requisite for a tenancy by the entirety; absent some agreement to the contrary, the parties usually become tenants in common.

The tenancy by the entirety exists today in somewhat less than half the states. Because the tenancy by the entirety gives rise to marital interests of importance in many states, we will be investigating it further in Section B of this chapter, where we treat marital property.

Presumptions. The discussion thus far has hinted at how the various sorts of concurrent interests are created; let us now be more explicit. The English common law favored joint tenancies over tenancies in common. If an instrument conveying property to two or more persons were ambiguous, a joint tenancy resulted. Today the situation is reversed; the presumption favoring joint tenancies has been abolished in all states (with an exception in a few states where the conveyance is to husband and wife). Usually the abolition has been accomplished by statutes providing that a grant or devise to two or more persons creates a tenancy in common unless an intent to create a joint tenancy is expressly declared. Under such statutes, a conveyance "to A and B as joint tenants and not as tenants in common" will create a joint tenancy; something even a little bit less, such as "to A and B jointly," might not. Courts have sometimes thought a conveyance to A and B "jointly" merely indicates an intent to create some type of concurrent estate but not necessarily a joint tenancy. Some states require an express provision for survivorship in order to create a joint tenancy. Under these statutes, to create a joint tenancy it is necessary to say "to A and B as joint tenants with the right of survivorship."[3] A few states have done away with the joint tenancy entirely. See 4A Richard R. Powell, The Law of Real Property ¶616 (rev. ed. 1992).

What of conveyances to husband and wife? The common law presumed an intention to create a tenancy by the entirety, absent some clear indication to the contrary. The presumption still has considerable force in those states that retain the tenancy, though in some of these a conveyance to husband and wife will be presumed to create a tenancy in common or joint tenancy.

PROBLEMS AND NOTE

1. O conveys Blackacre to A, B, and C as joint tenants. Subsequently A conveys his interest to D. Then B dies intestate, leaving H as his heir. What is the state of the title? See Cortelyou v. Dinger, 62 Misc. 2d 1007, 310 N.Y.S.2d 764 (1970). What if B had died leaving a will devising his interest to H?

2. T devises Blackacre "to A and B for their joint lives, remainder to the survivor." What interests are created by the devise? How does a joint tenancy in fee simple differ?

3. A and B are planning to be married. Two weeks before the ceremony, they buy a house and take title in "A and B as tenants by the entirety." Several years after the marriage, A moves out of the house and conveys his interest in the house to his brother C. C brings an action to partition the property. What result? See Morgan v. Morgan, 111 A.D.2d 790, 490 N.Y.S.2d 539 (1985); Annot. 9 A.L.R.4th 1189 (1981).

4. In Germaine v. Delaine, 294 Ala. 443, 318 So. 2d 681 (1975), the court was called upon to construe a deed to the grantees "jointly, as tenants in common, with equal rights and interest in said land, and to the survivor thereof, in fee simple. . . . To Have and to Hold the same unto the said parties hereto, equally, jointly, as tenants in common, with equal rights and interest for the period or term of their lives, and to the

---

3. On the other hand, in a few states it is dangerous to include expressly a right of survivorship. In Michigan, a grant "to A and B as joint tenants with right of survivorship" or "to A and B as joint tenants and to the survivor" creates a joint life estate in A and B, with a contingent remainder in the survivor (see Problem 2 on this page). Albro v. Allen, 434 Mich. 271, 454 N.W.2d 85 (1990). So too in Kentucky. See Sanderson v. Saxon, 834 S.W.2d 676 (Ky. 1992).

survivor thereof at the death of the other." The court held that the deed created a joint tenancy because it provided for survivorship.

Avoidance of probate. Joint tenancies are popular, particularly between husband and wife, because a joint tenancy is the practical equivalent of a will but at the joint tenant's death probate is avoided. Probate is the judicial supervision of the administration of the decedent's property at death: The probate court appoints an administrator or executor who collects the decedent's assets, pays debts and taxes, and distributes or changes title to the property to the beneficiaries. Probate is costly; administrators, lawyers, and court costs must be paid. And property may be tied up in probate for months, even years. A joint tenancy avoids probate because *no interest passes* on the joint tenant's death. Under the theory of joint tenancy, the decedent's interest vanishes at death and the survivor's ownership of the whole continues without the decedent's participation. For other ways of avoiding probate, see Note 2 on page 656.

The idea that no interest passes at the death of a joint tenant, which shaped the historical development of the joint tenancy, was originally a clever ruse to bypass the medieval prohibition of wills of land. In order to pass land to a person other than the primogenitary heir, a landowner could enfeoff himself and his intended successor as joint tenants. When the landowner died, no interest passed by will from the landowner to the surviving tenant. See Anne L. Spitzer, Joint Tenancy with Right of Survivorship: A Legacy from Thirteenth Century England, 16 Texas Tech. L. Rev. 629 (1985).

A joint tenant cannot pass his interest in a joint tenancy by will. Inasmuch as the joint tenant's interest ceases at death, a joint tenant has no interest that can pass by will.

The idea that a joint tenant's interest ceases at death also has important consequences for creditors. If a creditor acts during a joint tenant's life, the creditor can seize and sell the joint tenant's interest in property, severing the joint tenancy. If the creditor waits until after the joint tenant's death, the decedent joint tenant's interest has disappeared and there is nothing the creditor can seize. See Rembe v. Stewart, 387 N.W.2d 313 (Iowa 1986) (criticizing but upholding the rule).

Although the theory that "nothing passes" at the joint tenant's death controls private law questions, it does not control federal estate taxation. Ignoring the fiction and looking at reality, Congress has provided that when a joint tenant dies, his share of the jointly held property is subject to federal estate taxation. If the joint tenants are husband and wife, one-half is subject to taxation when one spouse dies (though no taxes are paid on it because any amount of property passing to the surviving spouse qualifies for the marital deduction and passes tax-free). If the joint tenants are not husband and wife, when one joint tenant dies the portion of the value of the jointly held property attributable to the consideration furnished by the decedent is subject to federal estate taxation. See Internal Revenue Code §2040 (1986). Under most state inheritance taxes, the fractional share of a joint tenancy owned by the decedent is taxed; the federal who-furnished-the-consideration test is not followed.

Unequal shares. One of the four unities of a joint tenancy is equal shares. At common law if *A* owned a one-third share and *B* a two-thirds share, *A* and *B* could not hold as joint tenants. They would hold as tenants in common. This result is justifiable solely on historical grounds and makes no sense today. It is increasingly ignored by courts in situations where it counts. If *A* and *B* take title as joint tenants and *A* furnishes one-third of the purchase price and *B* two-thirds, and the parties intend the proceeds from sale of the joint tenancy property to be divided one-third and two-thirds if sold during their joint lives, a joint tenancy is created and, if the property is sold, the court will divide the proceeds according to their intent. See Moat v. Ducharme, 28 Mass. App. Ct. 749, 555 N.E.2d 897 (1990) (cohabitants with unequal contributions); Jezo v. Jezo, 23 Wis. 2d 399, 127 N.W.2d 246 (1964); but see Cunningham v. Hastings, 556 N.E.2d 12 (Ind. App. 1990).

There are other instances in which the law pays no attention to the requirement of unity of interest. In most states joint and survivor bank accounts are owned by the parties during life in proportion to the net contributions by each (see page 343). And, as stated above, Internal Revenue Code §2040 provides that a decedent joint tenant (other than a spouse) is deemed to own, and is taxed on, a fractional share of the property proportionate to the decedent's contributions.

2. Severance of Joint Tenancies

Riddle v. Harmon
Court of Appeal of California, First District, 1980
102 Cal. App. 3d 524, 162 Cal. Rptr. 530

Poché, J. We must decide whether Frances Riddle, now deceased, unilaterally terminated a joint tenancy by conveying her interest from herself as joint tenant to herself as tenant in common. The trial court determined, via summary judgment quieting title to her widower, that she did not. The facts follow.

Mr. and Mrs. Riddle purchased a parcel of real estate, taking title as joint tenants. Several months before her death, Mrs. Riddle retained an attorney to plan her estate. After reviewing pertinent documents, he advised her that the property was held in joint tenancy and that, upon her death, the property would pass to her husband. Distressed upon learning this, she requested that the joint tenancy be terminated so that she could dispose of her interest by will. As a result, the attorney prepared a grant deed whereby Mrs. Riddle granted to herself an undivided one-half interest in the subject property. The document also provided that "The purpose of this Grant Deed is to terminate those joint tenancies formerly existing between the Grantor, FRANCES P. RIDDLE, and JACK C. RIDDLE, her husband. . . ." He also prepared a will disposing of Mrs. Riddle's interest in the property. Both the grant deed and will were executed on December 8, 1975. Mrs. Riddle died 20 days later.

The court below refused to sanction her plan to sever the joint tenancy and quieted title to the property in her husband. The executrix of the will of Frances Riddle appeals from that judgment.

The basic concept of a joint tenancy is that it is one estate which is taken jointly. Under the common law, four unities were essential to the creation and existence of an estate in joint tenancy: interest, time, title and possession. (Tenhet v. Boswell (1976) 18 Cal. 3d 150, 155, 133 Cal. Rptr. 10, 554 P.2d 330.) If one of the unities was destroyed, a tenancy in common remained. (Id.) Severance of the joint tenancy extinguishes the principal feature of that estate, the *jus accrescendi* or right of survivorship. This "right" is a mere expectancy that arises "only upon success in the ultimate gamble — survival — and then only if the unity of the estate has not theretofore been destroyed by voluntary conveyance . . . , by partition proceedings . . . , by involuntary alienation under an execution . . . , or by any other action which operates to sever the joint tenancy." (Id. at pp.155-156, citations omitted.)

An indisputable right of each joint tenant is the power to convey his or her separate estate by way of gift or otherwise without the knowledge or consent of the other joint tenant and to thereby terminate the joint tenancy. (Delanoy v. Delanoy (1932) 216 Cal. 23, 26, 13 P.2d 513; Estate of Harris (1937) 9 Cal. 2d 649, 658, 72 P.2d 873; Walk v. Vencill (1947) 30 Cal. 2d 104, 108-109, 180 P.2d 351.) If a joint tenant conveys to a stranger and that person reconveys to the same tenant, then no revival of the joint tenancy occurs because the unities are destroyed. (Hammon v. McArthur (1947) 30 Cal. 2d 512, 183 P.2d 1; Comment, Severance of Joint Tenancy in California (1957) 8 Hastings L.J. 290, 291.) The former joint tenants become tenants in common.

At common law, one could not create a joint tenancy in himself and another by a direct conveyance. It was necessary for joint tenants to acquire their interests at the same time (unity of time) and by the same conveyancing instrument (unity of title). So, in order to create a valid joint tenancy where one of the proposed joint tenants already owned an interest in the property, it was first necessary to convey the property to a disinterested third person, a "strawman," who then conveyed the title to the ultimate grantees as joint tenants. This remains the prevailing practice in some jurisdictions. Other states, including California, have disregarded this application of the unities requirement "as one of the obsolete 'subtle and arbitrary distinctions and niceties of the feudal common law,' [and allow the creation of a valid joint tenancy without the use of a strawman]." (4A Powell on Real Property (1979) [¶]616, p.670, citation omitted.)

By amendment to its Civil Code,[4] California became a pioneer in allowing the *creation* of a joint tenancy by direct transfer. Under authority of Civil Code section 683, a joint tenancy conveyance may be made from a "sole owner to himself and others," or from joint owners to themselves and others as specified in the code. (See Bowman, Real Estate Law in Cal. (4th ed. 1975) p.105.) The purpose of the amendment was to "avoid the necessity of making a conveyance through a dummy" in the statutorily enumerated situations. (Third Progress Rep. to the Legislature (Mar. 1955) p.54, 2 Appen. to Sen. J. (1955 Reg. Sess.).) Accordingly, in California, it is no longer necessary to use a strawman to *create* a joint tenancy. (Donovan v. Donovan (1963) 223 Cal. App. 2d 691, 697, 36 Cal. Rptr. 225.) This court is now asked to reexamine whether a strawman is required to *terminate* a joint tenancy.

Twelve years ago, in Clark v. Carter (1968) 265 Cal. App. 2d 291, 295, 70 Cal. Rptr. 923, the Court of Appeal considered the same question and found the strawman to be indispensable. As in the instant case, the joint tenants in *Clark* were husband and wife. The day before Mrs. Clark died, she executed two documents without her husband's knowledge or consent: (1) a quitclaim deed conveying her undivided half interest in certain real property from herself as joint tenant to herself as tenant in common, and (2) an assignment of her undivided half interest in a deed of trust from herself as joint tenant to herself as tenant in common. These documents were held insufficient to sever the joint tenancy.

After summarizing joint tenancy principles, the court reasoned that

> [U]nder California law, a transfer of property presupposes participation by at least two parties, namely, a grantor and a grantee. Both are essential to the efficacy of a deed, and they cannot be the same person. A transfer of property requires that title be conveyed by one living person to another (Civ. Code, §1039.) . . .
>
> Foreign authority also exists to the effect that a person cannot convey to himself alone, and if he does so, he still holds under the original title.

---

4. Civil Code section 683, as amended in 1955, provides in relevant part that: "A joint interest is one owned by two or more persons in equal shares, by a title created by a single will or transfer, when expressly declared in the will or transfer to be a joint tenancy, or by transfer from a sole owner to himself and others, or from tenants in common or joint tenants to themselves or some of them, or to themselves or any of them and others, or from a husband and wife, when holding title as community property or otherwise to themselves or to themselves and others or to one of them and to another or others, when expressly declared in the transfer to be a joint tenancy, or when granted or devised to executors or trustees as joint tenants."

Similarly, it was the common law rule that in every property conveyance there be a grantor, a grantee, and a thing granted. Moreover, the grantor could not make himself the grantee by conveying an estate to himself. (*Clark, supra,* at pp.295-296, citations omitted.)

That "two-to-transfer" notion stems from the English common law feoffment ceremony with livery of seisin. (Swenson & Degnan, Severance of Joint Tenancies (1954) 38 Minn. L. Rev. 466, 467.) If the ceremony took place upon the land being conveyed, the grantor (feoffor) would hand a symbol of the land, such as a lump of earth or a twig, to the grantee (feoffee). (Burby, Real Property (3d ed. 1966) p.281.) In order to complete the investiture of seisin it was necessary that the feoffor completely relinquish possession of the land to the feoffee. (Moynihan, Preliminary Survey of the Law of Real Property (1940) p.86.) It is apparent from the requirement of livery of seisin that one could not enfeoff oneself — that is, one could not be both grantor and grantee in a single transaction. Handing oneself a dirt clod is ungainly. Just as livery of seisin has become obsolete,[5] so should ancient vestiges of that ceremony give way to modern conveyancing realities.

"We are given to justifying our tolerance for anachronistic precedents by rationalizing that they have engendered so much reliance as to preclude their liquidation. Sometimes, however, we assume reliance when in fact it has been dissipated by the patent weakness of the precedent. Those who plead reliance do not necessarily practice it." (Traynor, No Magic Words Could Do It Justice (1961) 49 Cal. L. Rev. 615, 622-623.) Thus, undaunted by the *Clark* case, resourceful attorneys have worked out an inventory of methods to evade the rule that one cannot be both grantor and grantee simultaneously.

The most familiar technique for unilateral termination is use of an intermediary "strawman" blessed in the case of Burke v. Stevens (1968) 264 Cal. App. 2d 30, 70 Cal. Rptr. 87. There, Mrs. Burke carried out a secret plan to terminate a joint tenancy that existed between her husband and herself in certain real property. The steps to accomplish this objective involved: (1) a letter written from Mrs. Burke to her attorney directing him to prepare a power of attorney naming him as her attorney in fact for the purpose of terminating the joint tenancy; (2) her execution and delivery of the power of attorney; (3) her attorney's execution and delivery of a quitclaim deed conveying Mrs. Burke's interest in the property to a third party, who was an office associate of the attor-

---

5. It was not until 1845 that a statute was enacted in England making it possible for a freehold estate to be conveyed by grant deed. In America, livery of seisin was done away with long before legislative reforms were effected in the mother country. (Moynihan, op. cit. supra, at p.87).

Maitland tells us that the physical acts involved in a feoffment grew out of a "mental incapacity, an inability to conceive that mere rights can be transferred." (Maitland, The Mystery of Seisin (1886) 2 L.Q. Rev. 481, 489.)

ney in fact; (4) the third party's execution and delivery of a quitclaim deed reconveying that interest to Mrs. Burke on the following day. The *Burke* court sanctioned this method of terminating the joint tenancy, noting at one point: "While the actions of the wife, from the standpoint of a theoretically perfect marriage, are subject to ethical criticism, and her stealthy approach to the solution of the problems facing her is not to be acclaimed, the question before the court is not what should have been done ideally in a perfect marriage, but whether the decedent and her attorneys acted in a legally permissible manner." (*Burke,* supra, at p.34.)

Another creative method of terminating a joint tenancy appears in Reiss v. Reiss (1941) 45 Cal. App. 2d 740, 114 P.2d 718. There a trust was used. For the purpose of destroying the incident of survivorship, Mrs. Reiss transferred bare legal title to her son, as trustee of a trust for her use and benefit. The son promised to reconvey the property to his mother or to whomever she selected at any time upon her demand. (Id., at p.746.) The court upheld this arrangement, stating, "We are of the opinion that the clearly expressed desire of Rosa Reiss to terminate the joint tenancy arrangement was effectively accomplished by the transfer of the legal title to her son for her expressed specific purpose of having the control and the right of disposition of her half of the property." (Id., at p.747.)

In view of the rituals that are available to unilaterally terminate a joint tenancy, there is little virtue in steadfastly adhering to cumbersome feudal law requirements. "It is revolting to have no better reason for a rule of law than that so it was laid down in the time of Henry IV. It is still more revolting if the grounds upon which it was laid down have vanished long since, and the rule simply persists from blind imitation of the past." (Holmes, Collected Legal Papers (1920) p.187.) Common sense as well as legal efficiency dictate that a joint tenant should be able to accomplish directly what he or she could otherwise achieve indirectly by use of elaborate legal fictions.

Moreover, this will not be the first time that a court has allowed a joint tenant to unilaterally sever a joint tenancy without the use of an intermediary. In Hendrickson v. Minneapolis Federal Sav. & L. Assn. (1968) 281 Minn. 462, 161 N.W.2d 688, decided one month after *Clark,* the Minnesota Supreme Court held that a tenancy in common resulted from one joint tenant's execution of a "Declaration of Election to Sever Survivorship of Joint Tenancy." No fictional transfer by conveyance and reconveyance through a strawman was required.[6]

---

6. In its reasoning the *Hendrickson* court recognized a policy disfavoring survivorship in Minnesota, noting that in modern times survivorship came to be regarded " 'as an "odious thing" that too often deprived a man's heirs of their rightful inheritance [fn. omitted].' " (*Hendrickson,* supra, at p.690.)

Construing the grant deed as effecting a termination of the joint tenancy will result in the concurrent estate becoming a tenancy in common. This outcome is consistent with

Our decision does not create new powers for a joint tenant. A universal right of each joint tenant is the power to effect a severance and destroy the right of survivorship by conveyance of his or her joint tenancy interest to another "person." (Swenson & Degnan, op. cit. supra, at p.469.) "If an indestructible right of survivorship is desired — that is, one which may not be destroyed by one tenant — that may be accomplished by creating a joint life estate with a contingent remainder in fee to the survivor; a tenancy in common in fee simple with an executory interest in the survivor; or a fee simple to take effect in possession in the future." (Swenson & Degnan, supra, at p.469, fn. omitted.)

We discard the archaic rule that one cannot enfeoff oneself which, if applied, would defeat the clear intention of the grantor. There is no question but that the decedent here could have accomplished her objective — termination of the joint tenancy — by one of a variety of circuitous processes. We reject the rationale of the *Clark* case because it rests on a common law notion whose reason for existence vanished about the time that grant deeds and title companies replaced colorful dirt clod ceremonies as the way to transfer title to real property. One joint tenant may unilaterally sever the joint tenancy without the use of an intermediary device.

The judgment is reversed.

NOTES, QUESTIONS, AND PROBLEMS

1. Is it fair to permit one joint tenant to sever the tenancy without giving notice to the other joint tenant? Should a deed such as the wife used in Riddle v. Harmon be effective without recordation? See Carmack v. Place, 188 Colo. 303, 535 P.2d 197 (1975); Cal. Civ. Code §683.2 (West Supp. 1992).

Suppose that the wife writes out the deed in her own handwriting: "I convey my interest in [Blackacre] to myself, to terminate the joint tenancy with my husband." Telling only her daughter of it, the wife puts the deed under some papers in her desk drawer. Subsequently the husband dies, and the wife destroys the deed. What result? How would you,

---

California's statutorily decreed preference for recognizing tenancies in common. (See Civ. Code, §§683, 686; Tenhet v. Boswell, supra, 18 Cal. 3d 150, 157.)

Contrary to the modern preference, at common law there was a presumption in favor of joint tenancy. This presumption was based on a desire to avoid the splitting of the feudal services due to the lord of the fee. (Moynihan, Preliminary Survey of the Law of Real Property (1940) p.130.) Land was kept in larger tracts and thus facilitated the rendering of services to the lord. Tenancy in common, on the other hand, resulted in constant subdivision. (Swenson & Degnan, Severance of Joint Tenancies (1954) 38 Minn. L.R. 466, 503.) Another possible reason that joint tenancy was favored is that it is easier to rely on the loyalty of one man than two. (Id.) As the age of feudalism ended, the reasons for the presumption in favor of joint tenancies also ended. (Id.)

as lawyer for the husband's estate, find out these facts? See Samuel M. Fetters, An Invitation to Commit Fraud: Secret Destruction of Joint Tenant Survivorship Rights, 55 Fordham L. Rev. 173 (1986).

2. If *A* and *B,* joint tenants, die in a common disaster and there is "no sufficient evidence" of the order of death, Uniform Simultaneous Death Act §3 (1953) provides that one-half the property is distributed as if *A* survived and one-half as if *B* survived. Suppose that *A* and *B* are killed while riding in a car struck by a train. When witnesses arrive, there are no signs of life in *A*; *B* is decapitated and blood is gushing from her neck in spurts. Does *B* survive *A*? See Gray v. Sawyer, 247 S.W.2d 496 (Ky. 1952).

If *A* murders *B,* Uniform Probate Code §2-803(c)(2)(1990) provides that murder severs the joint tenancy and converts it into a tenancy in common. The killer loses his right of survivorship in the decedent's share.

Harms v. Sprague
Supreme Court of Illinois, 1984
105 Ill. 2d 215, 473 N.E.2d 930

MORAN, J. Plaintiff, William H. Harms, filed a complaint to quiet title and for declaratory judgment in the circuit court of Greene County. Plaintiff had taken title to certain real estate with his brother John R. Harms, as a joint tenant, with full right of survivorship. The plaintiff named, as a defendant, Charles D. Sprague, the executor of the estate of John Harms and the devisee of all the real and personal property of John Harms. Also named as defendants were Carl T. and Mary E. Simmons, alleged mortgagees of the property in question. Defendant Sprague filed a counterclaim against plaintiff, challenging plaintiff's claim of ownership of the entire tract of property and asking the court to recognize his (Sprague's) interest as a tenant in common, subject to a mortgage lien. At issue was the effect the granting of a mortgage by John Harms had on the joint tenancy. Also at issue was whether the mortgage survived the death of John Harms as a lien against the property.

The trial court held that the mortgage given by John Harms to defendants Carl and Mary Simmons severed the joint tenancy. Further, the court found that the mortgage survived the death of John Harms as a lien against the undivided one-half interest in the property which passed to Sprague by and through the will of the deceased. The appellate court reversed, finding that the mortgage given by one joint tenant of his interest in the property does not sever the joint tenancy. Accordingly, the appellate court held that plaintiff, as the surviving joint tenant, owned the property in its entirety, unencumbered by the mortgage lien.

(119 Ill. App. 3d 503.) Defendant Sprague filed a petition for leave to appeal in this court. (87 Ill. 2d R. 315.) Subsequently, defendants Carl and Mary Simmons petitioned this court to supplement Sprague's petition for leave to appeal. That motion was granted and the petition for leave to appeal was allowed.

Two issues are raised on appeal: (1) Is a joint tenancy severed when less than all of the joint tenants mortgage their interest in the property? and (2) Does such a mortgage survive the death of the mortgagor as a lien on the property?

A review of the stipulation of facts reveals the following. Plaintiff, William Harms, and his brother John Harms, took title to real estate located in Roodhouse, on June 26, 1973, as joint tenants. The warranty deed memorializing this transaction was recorded on June 29, 1973, in the office of the Green County recorder of deeds.

Carl and Mary Simmons owned a lot and home in Roodhouse. Charles Sprague entered into an agreement with the Simmonses whereby Sprague was to purchase their property for $25,000. Sprague tendered $18,000 in cash and signed a promissory note for the balance of $7,000. Because Sprague had no security for the $7,000, he asked his friend, John Harms, to co-sign the note and give a mortgage on his interest in the joint tenancy property. Harms agreed, and on June 12, 1981, John Harms and Charles Sprague, jointly and severally, executed a promissory note for $7,000 payable to Carl and Mary Simmons. The note states that the principal sum of $7,000 was to be paid from the proceeds of the sale of John Harms' interest in the joint tenancy property, but in any event no later than six months from the date the note was signed. The note reflects that five monthly interest payments had been made, with the last payment recorded November 6, 1981. In addition, John Harms executed a mortgage, in favor of the Simmonses, on his undivided one-half interest in the joint tenancy property, to secure payment of the note. William Harms was unaware of the mortgage given by his brother.

John Harms moved from his joint tenancy property to the Simmons property which had been purchased by Charles Sprague. On December 10, 1981, John Harms died. By the terms of John Harms' will, Charles Sprague was the devisee of his entire estate. The mortgage given by John Harms to the Simmonses was recorded on December 29, 1981.

Prior to the appellate court decision in the instant case (119 Ill. App. 3d 503) no court of this State had directly addressed the principal question we are confronted with herein — the effect of a mortgage, executed by less than all of the joint tenants, on the joint tenancy. Nevertheless, there are numerous cases which have considered the severance issue in relation to other circumstances surrounding a joint tenancy. All have necessarily focused on the four unities which are fundamental to both the creation and the perpetuation of the joint tenancy. These are the unities of interest, title, time, and possession. (Jackson v. O'Connell (1961), 23 Ill. 2d 52, 55; Tindall v. Yeats (1946), 392 Ill. 502, 507.) The voluntary or involuntary destruction of any of the unities by one of the joint tenants will sever the joint tenancy. Van Antwerp v. Horan (1945), 390 Ill. 449, 451.

In a series of cases, this court has considered the effect that judgment liens upon the interest of one joint tenant have on the stability of the joint tenancy. In Peoples Trust & Savings Bank v. Haas (1927), 328 Ill. 468, the court found that a judgment lien secured against one joint tenant did not serve to extinguish the joint tenancy. As such, the surviving joint tenant "succeeded to the title in fee to the whole of the land by operation of law." 328 Ill. 468, 471.

Citing to *Haas* for this general proposition, the court in Van Antwerp v. Horan (1945), 390 Ill. 449, extended the holding in *Haas* to the situation where a levy is made under execution upon the interest of the debtor joint tenant. The court found that the levy was "not such an act as can be said to have the effect of a divestiture of title . . . [so as to destroy the] identity of interest or of any other unity which must occur before . . . the estate of joint tenancy has been severed and destroyed." 390 Ill. 449, 455.

In yet another case involving the attachment of a judgment lien upon the interest of a joint tenant, Jackson v. Lacey (1951), 408 Ill. 530, the court held that the estate of joint tenancy had not been destroyed. As in *Van Antwerp*, the judgment creditor had levied on the interest of the joint tenant debtor. In addition, that interest was sold by the bailiff of the municipal court to the other joint tenant, who died intestate before the time of redemption expired. While the court recognized that a conveyance, even if involuntary, destroys the unity of title and severs the joint tenancy, it held that there would be no conveyance until the redemption period had expired without a redemption. As such, title was not as yet divested and the estate in joint tenancy was unaltered.

Clearly, this court adheres to the rule that a lien on a joint tenant's interest in property will not effectuate a severance of the joint tenancy, absent the conveyance by a deed following the expiration of a redemption period. (See Johnson v. Muntz (1936), 364 Ill. 482.) It follows, therefore, that if Illinois perceives a mortgage as merely a lien on the mortgagor's interest in property rather than a conveyance of title from mortgagor to mortgagee, the execution of a mortgage by a joint tenant, on his interest in the property, would not destroy the unity of title and sever the joint tenancy.

Early cases in Illinois, however, followed the title theory of mortgages. In 1900, this court recognized the common law precept that a mortgage was a conveyance of a legal estate vesting title to the property in the mortgagee. (Lightcap v. Bradley (1900), 186 Ill. 510, 519.) Consistent with this title theory of mortgages, therefore, there are many cases which state, in dicta, that a joint tenancy is severed by one of the joint tenants mortgaging his interest to a stranger. (Lawler v. Byrne (1911), 252 Ill. 194, 196; Hardin v. Wolf (1925), 318 Ill. 48, 59; Partridge v. Berliner (1927), 325 Ill. 253, 258-59; Van Antwerp v. Horan (1945), 390 Ill. 449, 453; Tindall v. Yeats (1946), 392 Ill. 502, 511; Illinois Public Aid Com. v. Stille (1958), 14 Ill. 2d 344, 353 (personal property).) Yet even the early case of Lightcap v. Bradley, cited above, recognized that the title held by the mortgagee was for the limited purpose of protecting his interests. The court went on to say that "the mortgagor is the owner for every other purpose and against every other person. The title of the mortgagee is anomalous, and exists only between him and the mortgagor. . . ." Lightcap v. Bradley (1900), 186 Ill. 510, 522-23.

Because our cases had early recognized the unique and narrow character of the title that passed to a mortgagee under the common law title theory, it was not a drastic departure when this court expressly characterized the execution of a mortgage as a mere lien in Kling v. Ghilarducci (1954), 3 Ill. 2d 455. In *Kling,* the court was confronted with the question of when a separation of title, necessary to create an easement by implication, had occurred. The court found that title to the property was not separated with the execution of a trust deed but rather only upon execution and delivery of a master's deed. The court stated:

> In some jurisdictions the execution of a mortgage is a severance, in others, the execution of a mortgage is not a severance. In Illinois the giving of a mortgage is not a separation of title, for the holder of the mortgage takes only a lien thereunder. After foreclosure of a mortgage and until delivery of the master's deed under the foreclosure sale, purchaser acquires no title to the land either legal or equitable. Title to land sold under mortgage foreclosure remains in the mortgagor or his grantee until the expiration of the redemption period and conveyance by the master's deed. [3 Ill. 2d 455, 460.]

Kling and later cases rejecting the title theory (Department of Transportation v. New Century Engineering & Development Corp. (1983), 97 Ill. 2d 343; Kerrigan v. Unity Savings Association (1974), 58 Ill. 2d 20; Mutual Life Insurance Co. of New York v. Chambers (1980), 88 Ill. App. 3d 952; Commercial Mortgage & Finance Co. v. Woodcock Construction Co. (1964), 51 Ill. App. 2d 61) do not involve the severance of joint tenancies. As such, they have not expressly disavowed the dicta of joint tenancy cases which have stated that the act of mortgaging by one joint tenant results in the severance of the joint tenancy. We find, however, that implicit in *Kling* and our more recent cases which follow the lien theory of mortgages is the conclusion that a joint tenancy is not severed when one joint tenant executes a mortgage on his interest in the property, since the unity of title has been preserved. As the appellate court in the instant case correctly observed: "If giving a mortgage creates only a lien, then a mortgage should have the same effect on a joint tenancy as a lien created in other ways." (119 Ill. App. 3d 503, 507.) Other jurisdictions following the lien theory of mortgages have reached the same result. People v. Nogarr (1958); 164 Cal. App. 2d 591, 330 P.2d 858; D.A.D., Inc. v. Moring (Fla. App. 1969), 218 So. 2d 451; American National Bank & Trust Co. v. McGinnis (Okla. 1977), 571 P.2d 1198; Brant v. Hargrove (Ariz. Ct. App. 1981), 129 Ariz. 475, 632 P.2d 978.

A joint tenancy has been defined as "a present estate in all the joint tenants, each being seized of the whole. . . ." (Partridge v. Berliner (1927), 325 Ill. 253, 257.) An inherent feature of the estate of joint tenancy is the right of survivorship, which is the right of the last survivor to take the whole of the estate. (In re Estate of Alpert (1983), 95 Ill. 2d 377, 381; Bonczkowski v. Kucharski (1958), 13 Ill. 2d 443, 451.) Because we find that a mortgage given by one joint tenant of his interest in the property does not sever the joint tenancy, we hold that the plaintiff's right of survivorship became operative upon the death of his brother. As such plaintiff is now the sole owner of the estate, in its entirety.

Further, we find that the mortgage executed by John Harms does not survive as a lien on plaintiff's property. A surviving joint tenant succeeds to the share of the deceased joint tenant by virtue of the conveyance which created the joint tenancy, not as the successor of the deceased. (In re Estate of Alpert (1983), 95 Ill. 2d 377, 381.) The property right of the mortgaging joint tenant is extinguished at the moment of his death. While John Harms was alive, the mortgage existed as a lien on his interest in the joint tenancy. Upon his death, his interest ceased to exist and along with it the lien of the mortgage. (Merchants National Bank v. Olson (1975), 27 Ill. App. 3d 432, 434.) . . .

In their petition to supplement defendant Sprague's petition for leave to appeal, the Simmonses argue that the application of section 20-19 of the Probate Act of 1975 (Ill. Rev. Stat. 1981, ch. 110½, par. 20-19) to the facts of this case would mandate a finding that their mortgage on the subject property remains as a valid encumbrance in the hands of the surviving joint tenant. Section 20-19 reads in relevant part:

> (a) When any real estate or leasehold estate in real estate subject to an encumbrance, or any beneficial interest under a trust of real estate or leasehold estate in real estate subject to an encumbrance, is specifically bequeathed or passes by joint tenancy with right of survivorship or by the terms of a trust agreement or other nontestamentary instrument, the legatee, surviving tenant or beneficiary to whom the real estate, leasehold estate or beneficial interest is given or passes, takes it subject to the encumbrance and is not entitled to have the indebtedness paid from other real or personal estate of the decedent. [Ill. Rev. Stat. 1981, ch. 110½, par. 20-19.]

While the Simmonses have maintained from the outset that their mortgage followed title to the property, they did not raise the applicability of section 20-19 of the Probate Act of 1975 at the trial level, and thus the issue is deemed waived. (Board of Education v. Kusper (1982), 92 Ill. 2d 333, 343; Snow v. Dixon (1977), 66 Ill. 2d 443, 453.) Moreover, because we have found that the lien of mortgage no longer exists against the property, section 20-19 is inapplicable, since plaintiff, as the surviving joint tenant, did not take the property subject to an encumbrance.

For the reasons stated herein, the judgment of the appellate court is affirmed.

Judgment affirmed.

QUESTIONS AND PROBLEMS

1. Instead of analyzing the problem in Harms v. Sprague in terms of the four unities, a court might ask: Should the lender take the risk of losing its security if all the joint tenants do not agree to the mortgage? If the court had held that the mortgage severed the joint tenancy, what would be the result if the note had been paid and the mortgage released during John Harms's life?

Suppose that William Harms had died first, Sprague had not paid the note, and the Simmonses foreclosed the mortgage. Would the entire land be subject to the mortgage or only a one-half interest in it? See B. Taylor Mattis, Joint Tenancy: Notice of Severance; Mortgages and Survivorship, 7 N. Ill. U. L. Rev. 41 (1987).

On the difference between the "title theory" and the "lien theory" of mortgages, see footnote 17 on page 670.

2. A and B own Blackacre in joint tenancy. A conveys a 10-year term of years in Blackacre to C. After five years, A dies, devising all of his property to D. What are B's rights? See Tenhet v. Boswell, 18 Cal. 3d 150, 554 P.2d 330, 133 Cal. Rptr. 10 (1976); Robert W. Swenson & Ronan E. Degnan, Severance of Joint Tenancies, 38 Minn. L. Rev. 466 (1954).

Suppose that A and B sign a written agreement giving B the rentals from and possession of the land for her life. Does the agreement destroy the unity of possession? Upon A's subsequent death, who owns the land? See Tindall v. Yeats, 392 Ill. 502, 64 N.E.2d 903 (1946).

3. H and W, owners of Blackacre in joint tenancy, are getting a divorce. They sign a divorce agreement providing that Blackacre will be sold and the proceeds divided equally between H and W. Before Blackacre is sold, W dies. Does H have survivorship rights in Blackacre? See Sondin v. Bernstein, 126 Ill. App. 3d 703, 467 N.E.2d 926 (1984); In re Estate of Violi, 65 N.Y.2d 392, 482 N.E.2d 29, 492 N.Y.S.2d 550 (1985).

3.   Joint Tenancy Bank Accounts

Joint and survivor bank accounts have been the subject of much litigation. The primary reason is that the joint bank account is used by depositors with different intentions and for a variety of purposes. Suppose that O deposits $5,000 in a joint and survivor bank account with O and A as joint tenants. O may intend to make a present gift to A of one-half the sum deposited in addition to survivorship rights to the whole sum on deposit. Courts sometimes refer to this as a "true joint tenancy" bank account. Or O may intend to make a gift to A only of survivorship rights. This may be called a "payable-on-death" account. Or O may intend that A only have power to draw on the account to pay O's bills and not have survivorship rights. This is often called a "convenience" account. The bank card signed by O and A usually says either O or A has the right to withdraw all money on deposit during their joint lives, and the balance goes to the survivor.

Why do you suppose banks usually do not offer depositors an account tailored to specific desires but instead suggest the all-purpose joint bank account? An account expressly giving A survivorship rights only is in reality a will; A's name is put on the account solely for the purpose of passing the property at death. In some jurisdictions a payable-on-death account is not permitted because it is viewed as a testamentary instrument that is not signed and witnessed in accordance with the requirements of the Statute of Wills. Only in recent years have payable-on-death accounts become legally acceptable, largely because of the influence of the Uniform Probate Code, which first authorized them in 1969 in its original version. In jurisdictions that do not permit payable-on-death accounts, depositors sometimes create a joint tenancy with the intention that it be a payable-on-death account in disguise.

If O wants a convenience account, what O really intends is an account owned by O with a power in A to draw on the account during O's life. Because a power of attorney expires at the death of the principal, many banks are wary of power-of-attorney accounts and prefer joint tenancy accounts. With a joint tenancy account, the bank is safe in paying all the money on deposit to any joint tenant or to the survivor. For the bank, a joint tenancy account has little risk.

Because the joint tenancy account is an all-purpose account, it invites litigation to establish the true intention of the depositor. The agreement signed with the bank, providing that the account belongs to the survivor, is, in most states, not controlling. It is viewed as intended merely to protect the bank if it makes payment to the survivor. It does not determine the realities of ownership between the joint tenants. After the death of the depositor, disappointed heirs may claim that the joint tenant's name was put on the account merely for the purpose of paying the decedent's bills; if they can establish this, the money in the account belongs to the decedent's estate and not to the surviving joint tenant.

A majority of jurisdictions holds that the surviving joint tenant takes the sum remaining on deposit in a joint account unless there is clear and convincing evidence that a convenience account was intended. The burden of proof is placed upon persons challenging the surviving joint tenant. In some jurisdictions, to prevent litigation, statutes provide that the presumption that survivorship rights were intended in a joint bank account is conclusive.

During the lifetime of the parties, litigation may arise over what present rights the parties to a joint account have in the sum on deposit. In most jurisdictions, during the lifetime of the parties the presumption is that the joint account belongs to the parties in proportion to the net contribution of each party. Hence if *O* deposits $5,000 in a joint bank account with *A*, it is presumed that *O* does not intend a gift to *A* of $2,500 but intends *A* to have survivorship rights only. If *A* withdraws from this account without *O*'s permission or later ratification, *O* can force *A* to return the amount withdrawn. The presumption that *O* did not intend a gift to *A* can be overcome by clear and convincing evidence of a different intent. In a few jurisdictions, the parties to a joint account own, during the lifetime of the parties, equal fractional shares in the account (as in a joint tenancy in real property).

PROBLEMS

1. *O*, a widower, opens a joint bank account with his niece, *A*. *O* tells *A*, "I'll want your name on this account so that in case I am sick you can go and get the money for me." *O* dies. Is *A* entitled to the money in the bank account? See Franklin v. Anna Natl. Bank of Anna, 140 Ill. App. 3d 533, 488 N.E.2d 1117 (1986). Suppose that *O* also gives *A* a right of access to *O*'s safe deposit box by adding *A*'s name to the signature card giving access; the lease agreement signed with the bank provides that the contents of the box are owned in joint tenancy with right of survivorship. The box contains $324,000 in U.S. savings bonds and $4,000 in cash. Is *A* entitled to the bonds and cash? See Newton County v. Davison, 289 Ark. 109, 709 S.W.2d 810 (1986).

2. *H* and *W* and their son, *S*, open a joint savings account. *H* and *W* are in their sixties. The money deposited in the savings account comes from savings from *H*'s salary that *H* formerly had in a separate savings account. *H* dies. *W*, claiming that the entire amount in the savings account is hers, withdraws the balance. Does *S* have any rights to the money? See Allen v. Gordon, 429 So. 2d 369 (Fla. App. 1983).

3. *A* and *B* have a joint savings account of $40,000. *A* applies for medicaid. The state welfare authorities turn down *A*'s application on the ground that *A* is not sufficiently poor. They claim that *A* owns $20,000 in the joint savings account and must use that up before qualifying for medicaid. What should *A* do? See Anderson v. Iowa Dept. of Human Servs., 368 N.W.2d 104 (Iowa 1985); Phelps v. Kramer, 102 A.D.2d 908, 477 N.Y.S.2d 743 (1984). Compare University of Montana v. Coe, 704 P.2d 1029 (Mont. 1985) (parol evidence not admissible to contradict joint account agreement with bank; when student defaulted on loan, university could levy on one-half of a joint savings account student had with his sister).

4. *A* opens a joint bank account with *B*, depositing $10,000 therein. *A* week before *A*'s death, as *A* lies dying, *B* withdraws the $10,000 and transfers it to a new account in *B*'s sole name. At *A*'s death, what portion of the $10,000 does *B* own? See Wiggins v. Parson, 446 So. 2d 169, 171-172 (Fla. App. 1984):

> Where there is a real joint tenancy account, and one joint tenant withdraws the full amount of the account or more than his moiety, and a death occurs before suit is brought to settle rights to the funds, the view espoused by most of the New York state courts is that the survivor takes all, whether the survivor happens to be the wrongful withdrawer, or the joint owner who did not withdraw the funds. Other jurisdictions follow this view. . . .
>
> The rationale appears to be that one joint owner cannot rightfully withdraw more than his moiety, and if he does so, his act of withdrawal is a nullity, which does not destroy the right of survivorship. . . . Strangely, these same jurisdictions hold that a joint owner *may* withdraw his share and destroy the other's survivorship rights in it. . . .
>
> A better view is that withdrawal of jointly-owned funds by a joint owner and placement of the funds in other persons' names terminates the joint tenancy nature of the property and severs the right of survivorship as to the funds withdrawn. . . .
>
> An act which destroys one of the unities of the joint ownership is generally held to transform the ownership to a tenancy in common. In the context of joint accounts the withdrawal of all or some funds from the joint account, and the placement of such funds in an account in different names or in other property the other joint owner has no power or right of control over, destroys the unity of time, title, possession and interest. . . . The withdrawal severed the joint tenancy ownership of the account and transformed it into funds owned as tenants in common.

Suppose that after withdrawing the $10,000 *B* had died survived by *A*. What result?

Would your answers be different if *A* and *B* had each contributed $5,000 to the joint account?

4. Relations among Concurrent Owners

Suppose that *A* and *B* are the concurrent owners of a piece of property. What are their rights and liabilities as to the property and as to each other? In Swartzbaugh v. Sampson, at pages 357, 359, you will find the court making these announcements: "Each tenant owns an equal interest in all of the fee and each has an equal right to possession of the whole. . . . 'Neither a joint tenant nor a tenant in common can do any act to the prejudice of his cotenants in their estate.' " Even if these statements were not misleading, they would not be very helpful. If *A* cannot do as he wishes because it would prejudice *B*, then *B* in having her way harms *A*. "By definition, each tenant is entitled to possession of the entire parcel of land yet he cannot exercise that possession without coming into conflict with the reciprocal right of his cotenant." John E. Cribbet, Principles of the Law of Property 104 (2d ed. 1975). The point was put more succinctly in Mastbaum v. Mastbaum, 126 N.J. Eq. 366, 372, 9 A.2d 51, 55 (1939), where the court observed that "Two men cannot plow the same furrow." How should the inherent conflict of reciprocal rights be resolved?

The question is an important one. We saw in Chapter 1 that communal ownership — and that is what we are dealing with here — encourages inefficient use of common property resources. See pages 42-62. See also Richard A. Posner, Economic Analysis of Law 71-75 (4th ed. 1992). Presumably, thoughtfully devised legal rules can help avoid inefficiency, but this can hardly be their sole objective. The rules governing co-ownership should also distribute in a fair manner the benefits and burdens of co-ownership. Keep efficiency and fairness in mind as we consider first the action of partition — the privilege of each co-owner to transform a concurrent estate into estates held in severalty — and next some of the rules that govern the sharing of benefits and burdens of ownership during the life of concurrent interests. (The latter rules, as you will see, are often applied in partition actions to take account of events occurring prior to partition; but the rules on the sharing of benefits and burdens are applicable independent of partition as well.)

a. Partition

Concurrent owners might decide for any number of reasons to terminate a cotenancy. If they can agree on a division of the property or the proceeds from its sale, no problem arises; the termination can be accomplished through a voluntary agreement. But in the not unlikely event that such an arrangement is impossible, recourse to the equitable action of partition is necessary. The action is available to any joint tenant or tenant in common; it is unavailable to tenants by the entirety. The following materials explore some of the dimensions of partition.

Delfino v. Vealencis
Supreme Court of Connecticut, 1980
181 Conn. 533, 436 A.2d 27

HEALEY, J. The central issue in this appeal is whether the Superior Court properly ordered the sale, pursuant to General Statutes §52-500,[7] of property owned by the plaintiffs and the defendant as tenants in common.

The plaintiffs, Angelo and William Delfino, and the defendant, Helen C. Vealencis, own, as tenants in common, real property located in Bristol, Connecticut. The property consists of an approximately 20.5 acre parcel of land and the dwelling of the defendant thereon. The plaintiffs own an undivided 99/144 interest in the property, and the defendant owns a 45/144 interest. The defendant occupies the dwelling and a portion of the land, from which she operates a rubbish and garbage removal business.[8] Apparently, none of the parties is in actual possession of the remainder of the property. The plaintiffs, one of whom is a residential developer, propose to develop the property, upon partition, into forty-five residential building lots.

In 1978, the plaintiffs brought an action in the trial court seeking a partition of the property by sale with a division of the proceeds according to the parties' respective interests. The defendant moved for a judgment of in-kind partition[9] and the appointment of a committee to

7. General Statutes §52-500 states: "Sale of Real or Personal Property Owned by Two or More. Any court of equitable jurisdiction may, upon the complaint of any person interested, order the sale of any estate, real or personal, owned by two or more persons, when, in the opinion of the court, a sale will better promote the interests of the owners. The provisions of this section shall extend to and include land owned by two or more persons, when the whole or a part of such land is vested in any person for life with remainder to his heirs, general or special, or, on failure of such heirs, to any other person, whether the same, or any part thereof, is held in trust or otherwise. A conveyance made in pursuance of a decree ordering a sale of such land shall vest the title in the purchaser thereof, and shall bind the person entitled to the life estate and his legal heirs and any other person having a remainder interest in the lands; but the court passing such decree shall make such order in relation to the investment of the avails of such sale as it deems necessary for the security of all persons having any interest in such land."

8. The defendant's business functions on the property consist of the overnight parking, repair and storage of trucks, including refuse trucks, the repair, storage and cleaning of dumpsters, the storage of tools, and general office work. No refuse is actually deposited on the property.

9. Such a partition is authorized by General Statutes §52-495 which states: "Partition of Joint and Common Estates. Courts having jurisdiction of actions for equitable relief may, upon the complaint of any person interested, order partition of any real estate held in joint tenancy, tenancy in common or coparcenary, and may appoint a committee for that purpose, and may in like manner make partition of any real estate held by tenants in

conduct said partition. The trial court, after a hearing, concluded that a partition in kind could not be had without "material injury" to the respective rights of the parties, and therefore ordered that the property be sold at auction by a committee and that the proceeds be paid into the court for distribution to the parties.

On appeal, the defendant claims essentially that the trial court's conclusion that the parties' interests would best be served by a partition by sale is not supported by the findings of subordinate facts, and that the court improperly considered certain factors in arriving at that conclusion. In addition, the defendant directs a claim of error to the court's failure to include in its findings of fact a paragraph of her draft findings.

General Statutes §52-495 authorizes courts of equitable jurisdiction to order, upon the complaint of any interested person, the physical partition of any real estate held by tenants in common, and to appoint a committee for that purpose.[10] When, however, in the opinion of the court a sale of the jointly owned property "will better promote the interests of the owners," the court may order such a sale under §52-500. See Kaiser v. Second National Bank, 123 Conn. 248, 256, 193 A. 761 (1937); Johnson v. Olmsted, 49 Conn. 509, 517 (1882).

It has long been the policy of this court, as well as other courts, to favor a partition in kind over a partition by sale. See Harrison v. International Silver Co., 78 Conn. 417, 420, 62 A. 342 (1905); Johnson v. Olmsted, supra; 2 American Law of Property, Partition §6.26, pp.112-14; 4A Powell, Real Property ¶612, p.650; 59 Am. Jur. 2d, Partition §118, pp.864-65; 68 C.J.S., Partition §125. The first Connecticut statute that provided for an absolute right to partition by physical division was enacted in 1720; Statutes, 1796, p.258; the substance of which remains virtually unchanged today. Due to the possible impracticality of actual division, this state, like others, expanded the right to partition to allow a partition by sale under certain circumstances. See Penfield v. Jarvis, 175 Conn. 463, 470-71, 399 A.2d 1280 (1978); see also Restatement, 2 Property c. 11, pp.658-61. The early decisions of this court that considered the partition-by-sale statute emphasized that "[t]he statute giving the power of sale introduces . . . no new principles; it provides only for an emergency, when a division cannot be well made, in any other way. The Earl of Clarendon v. Hornby, 1 P. Wms., 446.4 Kent's Com., 365." Richardson v. Monson, 23 Conn. 94, 97 (1854); see Penfield v. Jarvis, supra, 471, 399 A.2d 1280; Harrison v. International Silver Co., 78 Conn. 417, 420, 62 A. 342 (1905); Vail v. Hammond, 60 Conn. 374, 379, 22 A. 954 (1891). The court later expressed its reason for preferring partition in

---

tail; and decrees aparting entailed estates shall bind the parties and all persons who thereafter claim title to such estate as heirs of their bodies."

10. If the physical partition results in unequal shares, a money award can be made from one tenant to another to equalize the shares. 4A Powell, Real Property ¶612, pp.653-54; 2 American Law of Property, Partition §6.26, p.113.

kind when it stated: "[A] sale of one's property without his consent is an extreme exercise of power warranted only in clear cases." Ford v. Kirk, 41 Conn. 9, 12 (1874). See also 59 Am. Jur. 2d, Partition §118, p.865. Although under General Statutes §52-500 a court is no longer required to order a partition in kind even in cases of extreme difficulty or hardship; see Scovil v. Kennedy, 14 Conn. 349, 360-61 (1841); it is clear that a partition by sale should be ordered only when two conditions are satisfied: (1) the physical attributes of the land are such that a partition in kind is impracticable or inequitable; Johnson v. Olmsted, supra; and (2) the interests of the owners would better be promoted by a partition by sale. Kaiser v. Second National Bank, supra; see Gold v. Rosenfeld, Conn. (41 Conn. L.J., No. 4, p.18) (1979). Since our law has for many years presumed that a partition in kind would be in the best interests of the owners, the burden is on the party requesting a partition by sale to demonstrate that such a sale would better promote the owners' interests. Accord, 4A Powell, Real Property ¶612, p.651; 59 Am. Jur. 2d, Partition §118, p.865.

The defendant claims in effect that the trial court's conclusion that the rights of the parties would best be promoted by a judicial sale is not supported by the findings of subordinate facts. We agree.

Under the test set out above, the court must first consider the practicability of physically partitioning the property in question. The trial court concluded that due to the situation and location of the parcel of land, the size and area of the property, the physical structure and appurtenances on the property, and other factors,[11] a physical partition of the property would not be feasible. An examination of the subordinate findings of facts and the exhibits, however, demonstrates that the court erred in this respect.

It is undisputed that the property in question consists of one 20.5 acre parcel, basically rectangular in shape, and one dwelling, located at the extreme western end of the property. Two roads, Dino Road and Lucien Court, abut the property and another, Birch Street, provides access through use of a right-of-way. Unlike cases where there are numerous fractional owners of the property to be partitioned, and the practicability of a physical division is therefore drastically reduced; see, e.g., Penfield v. Jarvis, 175 Conn. 463, 464-65, 399 A.2d 1280 (1978); Lyon v. Wilcox, 98 Conn. 393, 394-95, 119 A. 361 (1923); Candee v. Candee, 87 Conn. 85, 89-90, 86 A. 758 (1913); in this case there are only two competing ownership interests: the plaintiffs' undivided 99/144 interest and the defendant's 45/144 interest. These facts, taken together, do not support the trial court's conclusion that a physical partition of the

---

11. These other factors included the present use and the expected continued use by the defendant of the property, the property's zoning classification, and the plaintiff's proposed subdivision plans. We consider these factors later in the opinion.

property would not be "feasible" in this case. Instead, the above facts demonstrate that the opposite is true: a partition in kind clearly would be practicable under the circumstances of this case.

Although a partition in kind is physically practicable, it remains to be considered whether a partition in kind would also promote the best interests of the parties. In order to resolve this issue, the consequences of a partition in kind must be compared with those of a partition by sale.

The trial court concluded that a partition in kind could not be had without great prejudice to the parties since the continuation of the defendant's business would hinder or preclude the development of the plaintiffs' parcel for residential purposes, which the trial court concluded was the highest and best use of the property. The court's concern over the possible adverse economic effect upon the plaintiffs' interest in the event of a partition in kind was based essentially on four findings: (1) approval by the city planning commission for subdivision of the parcel would be difficult to obtain if the defendant continued her garbage hauling business; (2) lots in a residential subdivision might not sell, or might sell at a lower price, if the defendant's business continued; (3) if the defendant were granted the one-acre parcel, on which her residence is situated and on which her business now operates, three of the lots proposed in the plaintiffs' plan to subdivide the property would have to be consolidated and would be lost; and (4) the proposed extension of one of the neighboring roads would have to be rerouted through one of the proposed building lots if a partition in kind were ordered. The trial court also found that the defendant's use of the portion of the property that she occupies is in violation of existing zoning regulations. The court presumably inferred from this finding that it is not likely that the defendant will be able to continue her rubbish hauling operations from this property in the future. The court also premised its forecast that the planning commission would reject the plaintiffs' subdivision plan for the remainder of the property on the finding that the defendant's use was invalid. These factors basically led the trial court to conclude that the interests of the parties would best be protected if the land were sold as a unified unit for residential subdivision development and the proceeds of such a sale were distributed to the parties.

Before we consider whether these reasons are sufficient as a matter of law to overcome the preference for partition in kind that has been expressed in the applicable statutes and our opinions, we address first the defendant's assignment of error directed to the finding of subordinate facts relating to one of these reasons. The defendant claims that the trial court erred in finding that the defendant's use of a portion of the property is in violation of the existing zoning regulations, and in refusing to find that such use is a valid nonconforming use. . . . [The court concluded that there was insufficient evidence to support the trial court's finding that the defendant would be unable lawfully to continue her garbage hauling operation as a nonconforming use begun before the zoning ordinance was enacted.] We are left, then, with an unassailed finding that the defendant's family has operated a "garbage business" on the premises since the 1920s and that the city of Bristol has granted the defendant the appropriate permits and licenses each year to operate her business. There is no indication that this practice will not continue in the future.

Our resolution of this issue makes it clear that any inference that the defendant would probably be unable to continue her rubbish hauling activity on the property in the future is unfounded. We also conclude that the court erred in concluding that the city's planning commission would probably not approve a subdivision plan relating to the remainder of the property. Any such forecast must be carefully scrutinized as it is difficult to project what a public body will decide in any given matter. See Rushchak v. West Haven, 167 Conn. 564, 569, 356 A.2d 104 (1975). In this case, there was no substantial evidence to support a conclusion that it was reasonably probable that the planning commission would not approve a subdivision plan for the remainder of the property. Cf. Budney v. Ives, 156 Conn. 83, 90, 239 A.2d 482 (1968). Moreover, there is no suggestion in the statute relating to subdivision approval; see General Statutes §8-25; that the undeveloped portion of the parcel in issue, which is located in a residential neighborhood, could not be the subject of an approved subdivision plan notwithstanding the nearby operation of the defendant's business. The court's finding indicates that only garbage trucks and dumpsters are stored on the property; that no garbage is brought there; and that the defendant's business operations involve "mostly containerized . . . dumpsters, a contemporary development in technology which has substantially reduced the odors previously associated with the rubbish and garbage hauling industry." These facts do not support the court's speculation that the city's planning commission would not approve a subdivision permit for the undeveloped portion of the parties' property. See Rogers Co. v. F.W. Woolworth, 161 Conn. 6, 12, 282 A.2d 882 (1971); White v. Herbst, 128 Conn. 659, 661, 25 A.2d 68 (1942).

The court's remaining observations relating to the effect of the defendant's business on the probable fair market value of the proposed residential lots, the possible loss of building lots to accommodate the defendant's business and the rerouting of a proposed subdivision road, which may have some validity, are not dispositive of the issue. It is the interests of all of the tenants in common that the court must consider; see Lyon v. Wilcox, 98 Conn. 393, 395-96, 119 A. 361 (1923); 59 Am. Jur. 2d, Partition §118, p.865; and not merely the economic gain of one tenant, or a group of tenants. The trial court failed to give due consideration to the fact that one of the tenants in common has been in actual and exclusive possession of a portion of the property for a substantial period of time; that the tenant has made her home on the property; and that she derives her livelihood from the operation of a business on this portion of the property, as her family before her has for many years. A partition by sale would force the defendant to surrender her home and, perhaps, would jeopardize her livelihood. It is under just such circumstances, which include the demonstrated practicability of a physical division of the property, that the wisdom of the law's preference for partition in kind is evident.

As this court has many times stated, conclusions that violate "law, logic, or reason or are inconsistent with the subordinate facts" cannot stand. Russo v. East Hartford, 179 Conn. 250, 255, 425 A.2d 1282 (1979); Connecticut Coke Co. v. New Haven, 169 Conn. 663, 675, 364 A.2d 178, 185 (1975). Since the property in this case may practicably be physically divided, and since the interests of all owners will better be promoted if a partition in kind is ordered, we conclude that the trial court erred in ordering a partition by sale, and that, under the facts as found, the defendant is entitled to a partition of the property in kind.

There is error, the judgment is set aside and the case is remanded for further proceedings not inconsistent with this opinion.

NOTES, QUESTIONS, AND PROBLEMS

1. *Johnson v. Hendrickson, 71 S.D. 392, 24 N.W.2d 914 (1946).* In 1904 Henry Bauman died intestate. His 160-acre farm passed one-third to his widow, Katie, and two-ninths to each of his three children. In 1908 Katie married Karl Hendrickson and had twin sons by him. The whole family lived in the homestead on a corner of the farm. The Bauman children grew up and left home. Karl and his sons bought an adjacent farm across the road from the family homestead. In 1944 Katie died, devising her one-third interest in the Bauman farm to Karl and his two sons.

The Bauman children brought an action for partition, requesting sale of the whole farm. Karl and his two sons asked for partition in kind, and particularly for allocation to them of the homestead where they lived, which was across the road from their adjacent farm. The court ordered a partition sale under a statute authorizing sale if physical partition "cannot be made without great prejudice to the owners."

> The language of this statute means that a sale may be ordered if it appear to the satisfaction of the court that the value of the share of each cotenant, in case of partition, would be materially less than his share of the money equivalent that could probably be obtained for the whole. . . . Under the terms of the statute quoted above a sale is justified if it appears to the satisfaction of the court that the value of the land when divided into parcels is substantially

less than its value when owned by one person. This land is now owned by six persons. The largest individual interest is two-ninths and the smallest is one-twelfth. Partition in kind would require the division of the land into not less than four parcels: Two-ninths to each of the three respondents, and one-third to appellants, collectively. It is a matter of common knowledge in this state that the division of this quarter section of land, located as it is, into four or more separate tracts would materially depreciate its value, both as to its salability and as to its use for agricultural purposes. The fact that it would be an advantage to appellants to have the farm partitioned according to their demands because of their ownership of adjoining land is immaterial. [71 S.D. at 396, 24 N.W.2d at 916.]

The court gave no weight to the interest of Karl and his sons in remaining in the family homestead.

In Gray v. Crotts, 58 N.C. App. 365, 293 S.E.2d 626, 32 A.L.R.4th 903 (1982), one of the four cotenants argued that, upon physical partition, he should be awarded the part of the common property adjacent to his home. The court held that the property should be divided into four parcels of equal value, and then the cotenants should draw lots to determine who received which parcel. Why do courts not take into consideration the advantage to one cotenant of acquiring the portion of the tract adjacent to his other land?

2. Although it is usually said, as in Delfino v. Vealencis, that partition in kind is preferred, the modern practice is to decree a sale in partition actions in a great majority of cases, either because the parties all wish it or because courts are easily convinced that sale is the fairest method of resolving the conflict. See Note, Partitions in Kind: A Preference Without Favor, 7 Cardozo L. Rev. 855 (1986).

A recent Note, Acquiring Property Through Forced Partitioning Sales: Abuses and Remedies, 27 B.C. L. Rev. 755 (1986), argues that partition sales have worked to the disadvantage of poor black farmers, who farm land owned by many cotenants representing several generations and do not have the financial resources to buy the property at partition sale. The cotenants have often disappeared or are unaware of their ownership. The sale is often brought on by one cotenant selling his share to a third party, who brings a partition action. The Note suggests that partition sales have been a major cause of the dramatic decrease of black ownership of farm land in the South. The Note further suggests that a court should not order sale if a majority of the cotenants objects and should fashion other equitable relief to help poor cotenants bid effectively at sale.

Partition obviously has much to do with fair and equitable treatment of the interests of cotenants. Has it anything to do with efficient use of the property involved? See Richard A. Posner, Economic Analysis of Law 75 (4th ed. 1992).

3. Suppose that, before the decision in Delfino v. Vealencis, Helen

Vealencis had conveyed to Superior Refuse Disposers, Inc., by a metes and bounds description, her undivided interest in the portion of the land devoted to the garbage removal business. Superior Refuse Disposers then took over her garbage business. Upon physical partition, would Superior Refuse Disposers be awarded the land devoted to the garbage business? See Kean v. Dench, 413 F.2d 1 (3d Cir. 1969) (*A*, cotenant with *B*, conveyed his undivided interest by metes and bounds to *C*; upon partition suit by *C*, the court awarded to *C* the land conveyed to *C* on the theory this did not prejudice or injure *B*); Landskroner v. McClure, 107 N.M. 773, 765 P.2d 189 (1988) (dicta to same effect); 2 American Law of Property §6.10 (1952).

4. *A* and *B* are heirs of their father, who owned one item both *A* and *B* very much want — his old rocking chair. They cannot agree who is to have the chair. *A* brings a partition action. What relief should the court award? See In re McDowell, 74 Misc. 2d 663, 345 N.Y.S.2d 828 (Sur. Ct. 1973).

5. *A* and *B* own Blackacre as tenants in common. Each agrees in writing with the other never to bring an action to partition the land. *A* subsequently brings a partition action. What result? Suppose instead that the agreement provides for no partition until certain clouds on the title to the land are resolved in a pending lawsuit. Same result? On both questions, see Raisch v. Schuster, 47 Ohio App. 2d 98, 352 N.E.2d 657 (1975).

b. Sharing the Benefits and Burdens of Co-ownership

Concurrent owners might enter into an agreement concerning their rights and duties with respect to use, maintenance, and improvement of the property. These matters would then be governed by the law of contracts. Suppose, however, that there arises some problem not touched upon by the agreement or that the rights of third parties are in question or that there was never any agreement in the first place. Then there is a need for independent (property) rules to determine how the benefits and burdens of ownership are to be shared by the co-owners. The following materials explore some of these rules.

Spiller v. Mackereth
Supreme Court of Alabama, 1976
334 So. 2d 859

[John Spiller and Hettie Mackereth owned a building in downtown Tuscaloosa as tenants in common. When a lessee, Auto-Rite, which had been renting the building, vacated, Spiller entered and began using the structure as a warehouse. Mackereth then wrote a letter demanding that Spiller either vacate half of the building or pay half of the rental value, and, when Spiller did neither, she brought suit. The trial court awarded Mackereth $2,100 in rent. Spiller appealed.][12]

JONES, J. . . . On the question of Spiller's liability for rent, we start with the general rule that in absence of an agreement to pay rent or an ouster of a cotenant, a cotenant in possession is not liable to his cotenants for the value of his use and occupation of the property. Fundaburk v. Cody, 261 Ala. 25, 72 So. 2d 710, 48 A.L.R.2d 1295 (1954); Turner v. Johnson, 246 Ala. 114, 19 So. 2d 397 (1944). Since there was no agreement to pay rent, there must be evidence which establishes an ouster before Spiller is required to pay rent to Mackereth. The difficulty in this determination lies in the definition of the word "ouster." Ouster is a conclusory word which is used loosely in cotenancy cases to describe two distinct fact situations. The two fact situations are (1) the beginning of the running of the statute of limitations for adverse possession and (2) the liability of an occupying cotenant for rent to other cotenants. Although the cases do not acknowledge a distinction between the two uses of "ouster," it is clear that the two fact situations require different elements of proof to support a conclusion of ouster.

The Alabama cases involving adverse possession require a finding that the possessing cotenant asserted complete ownership of the land to support a conclusion of ouster. The finding of assertion of ownership may be established in several ways. Some cases find an assertion of complete ownership from a composite of activities such as renting part of the land without accounting, hunting the land, cutting timber, assessing and paying taxes and generally treating the land as if it were owned in fee for the statutory period. See Howard v. Harrell, 275 Ala. 454, 156 So. 2d 140 (1963). Other cases find the assertion of complete ownership from more overt activities such as a sale of the property under a deed purporting to convey the entire fee. Elsheimer v. Parker Bank & Trust Co., 237 Ala. 24, 185 So. 385 (1938). But whatever factual elements are present, the essence of the finding of an ouster in the adverse possession cases is a claim of absolute ownership and a denial of the cotenancy relationship by the occupying cotenant.

In the Alabama cases which adjudicate the occupying cotenant's liability for rent, a claim of absolute ownership has not been an essential element. The normal fact situation which will render an occupying cotenant liable to out of possession cotenants is one in which the occupying cotenant refuses a demand of the other cotenants to be allowed into use and enjoyment of the land, regardless of a claim of absolute ownership.

12. The facts have been slightly altered to eliminate extraneous issues. — EDS.

Judd v. Dowdell, 244 Ala. 230, 12 So. 2d 858 (1943); Newbold v. Smart, 67 Ala. 326 (1880).

The instant case involves a cotenant's liability for rent. Indeed, the adverse possession rule is precluded in this case by Spiller's acknowledgment of the cotenancy relationship as evidenced by filing the bill for partition. We can affirm the trial Court if the record reveals some evidence that Mackereth actually sought to occupy the building but was prevented from moving in by Spiller. To prove ouster, Mackereth's attorney relies upon the letter of November 15, 1973, as a sufficient demand and refusal to establish Spiller's liability for rent. This letter, however, did not demand equal use and enjoyment of the premises; rather, it demanded only that Spiller either vacate half of the building or pay rent. The question of whether a demand to vacate or pay rent is sufficient to establish an occupying cotenant's liability for rent has not been addressed in Alabama; however, it has been addressed by courts in other jurisdictions. In jurisdictions which adhere to the majority and Alabama rule of nonliability for mere occupancy, several cases have held that the occupying cotenant is not liable for rent notwithstanding a demand to vacate or pay rent. Grieder v. Marsh, 247 S.W.2d 590 (Tex. Civ. App. 1952); Brown v. Havens, 17 N.J. Super. 235, 85 A.2d 812 (1952).

There is a minority view which establishes liability for rents on a continued occupancy after a demand to vacate or pay rent. Re Holt's Estate, 14 Misc. 2d 971, 177 N.Y.S.2d 192 (1958). We believe that the majority view on this question is consistent with Alabama's approach to the law of occupancy by cotenants. As one of the early Alabama cases on the subject explains:

> Tenants in common are seized *per my et per tout*. Each has an equal right to occupy; and unless the one in actual possession denies to the other the right to enter, or agrees to pay rent, nothing can be claimed for such occupation. [Newbold v. Smart, supra.]

Thus, before an occupying cotenant can be liable for rent in Alabama, he must have denied his cotenants the right to enter. It is axiomatic that there can be no denial of the right to enter unless there is a demand or an attempt to enter. Simply requesting the occupying cotenant to vacate is not sufficient because the occupying cotenant holds title to the whole and may rightfully occupy the whole unless the other cotenants assert their possessory rights.

Besides the November 15 letter, Mackereth's only attempt to prove ouster is a showing that Spiller put locks on the building. However, there is no evidence that Spiller was attempting to do anything other than protect the merchandise he had stored in the building. Spiller testified that when Auto-Rite moved out they removed the locks from the building. Since Spiller began to store his merchandise in the building thereafter, he had to acquire new locks to secure it. There is no evidence that either Mackereth or any of the other cotenants ever requested keys to the locks or were ever prevented from entering the building because of the locks. There is no evidence that Spiller intended to exclude his cotenants by use of the locks. Again, we emphasize that as long as Spiller did not deny access to his cotenants, any activity of possession and occupancy of the building was consistent with his rights of ownership. Thus, the fact that Spiller placed locks on the building, without evidence that he intended to exclude the other cotenants, is insufficient to establish his liability to pay rent.

After reviewing all of the testimony and evidence presented at trial, we are unable to find any evidence which supports a legal conclusion of ouster. We are, therefore, compelled to reverse the trial Court's judgment awarding Mackereth $2,100 rental.

NOTES AND QUESTIONS

1. When a cotenant is in exclusive possession of concurrently owned property, the majority holds that, unless there has been an ouster, the cotenant in possession does not have to pay a proportionate share of the rental value to the cotenants out of possession. A few jurisdictions take the view that a cotenant in exclusive possession must pay rent to cotenants out of possession even in the absence of ouster. See Cohen v. Cohen, 157 Ohio St. 503, 106 N.E.2d 77, 51 A.L.R.2d 383 (1952). Which view makes better sense?

2. What constitutes an ouster? Does *Spiller* set too high a threshold? Would it be better to trigger liability for rental value rather quickly and easily, on grounds of fairness? Efficiency? Suppose a brother and sister inherit a house from their mother, and the sister moves in. The brother writes, as in *Spiller*, asking for rent. Should a refusal to pay, or even a failure to respond, amount to ouster? What if the sister's occupation makes occupation by the brother infeasible? Suppose a husband and wife own a home as joint tenants. The wife moves out because of abusive treatment by the husband. Ouster?

If the cotenants are holding the property for capital gain and neither wants to sell, what are the rights of the tenant out of possession against the tenant in exclusive possession in a jurisdiction following *Spiller*?

3. *Fiduciary duties.* Generally, cotenants are not fiduciaries with respect to each other. Each cotenant is expected to look after his or her interest. Nonetheless, in some situations the courts treat the cotenants as having fiduciary duties. If, for example, A and B are members of the

same family (say brother and sister), courts may find that the relationship of familial trust and confidence requires that each act as a fiduciary with respect to the other.

A fiduciary duty is imposed most commonly in one of two situations. The first is where one cotenant buys in concurrently owned property at a mortgage foreclosure or tax sale and then asserts a superior title against cotenants. Here courts normally compel the buyer to hold the superior title for the benefit of all the cotenants, provided they reimburse the buyer. See 4A Richard R. Powell, The Law of Real Property ¶603[2] (rev. ed. 1992).

The second situation in which a fiduciary duty may arise involves a claim of adverse possession by the cotenant in exclusive possession. Where cotenants are kindred, courts often treat the cotenant in possession as a fiduciary, who can claim adverse possession only where his claim of sole ownership is so unequivocal and notorious as to put his cotenants on actual notice of a hostile claim. In any event, adverse possession against cotenants is not easily achieved. See Quates v. Griffin, 239 So. 2d 803 (Miss. 1970); In re Estate of Neil, 152 Vt. 124, 565 A.2d 1309 (1989).

In a few jurisdictions, sole possession by one cotenant for a long period of time without any claim to possession by other cotenants gives rise to a presumption that there has been an ouster starting the statute of limitations running. This view is criticized as being in conflict with the treatment of cotenants as fiduciaries in Note, Adverse Possession Between Tenants in Common and the Rule of Presumptive Ouster, 10 Wake Forest L. Rev. 300 (1974).

Swartzbaugh v. Sampson

Court of Appeal of California
Fourth District, 1936
11 Cal. App. 2d 451, 54 P.2d 73

MARKS, J. This is an action to cancel two leases executed by John Josiah Swartzbaugh,[13] as lessor, to Sam A. Sampson, as lessee, of two adjoining

---

13. "John J. Swartzbaugh is well known as one of the oldest and most extensive walnut growers in Orange County, and his splendid estate, in West Orange precinct, is a testimonial to his industry and good management. . . . [He was born in Maryland in 1858, married Lola Desirra Knott, daughter of an Ohio farmer, in 1887, and came to California in 1888.] Soon afterwards he purchased a squatter's claim in West Orange precinct, and made valuable improvements and additional purchases, being now the owner of one hundred and ten acres of good land. Ninety acres are devoted to the growing of walnuts, of which he has made a specialty for the past thirty years, and he has gained a high reputation for his ability and success in this line of effort.

". . . Mr. and Mrs. Swartzbaugh became the parents of nine children. . . . He belongs to the Garden Grove Walnut Association and is regarded by his associates as a man of sound and dependable judgment in practical things, while, socially, he is well liked by all

parcels of land in Orange County. A motion for nonsuit was granted at the close of plaintiff's case and this appeal followed.

Defendant Swartzbaugh and plaintiff are husband and wife. They owned, as joint tenants with the right of survivorship, sixty acres of land in Orange County planted to bearing walnuts. In December, 1933, defendant Sampson started negotiations with plaintiff and her husband for the leasing of a small fraction of this land fronting on Highway 101 for a site for a boxing pavilion. Plaintiff at all times objected to making the lease and it is thoroughly established that Sampson knew she would not join in any lease to him.

The negotiations resulted in the execution of an option for a lease, dated January 5, 1934, signed by Swartzbaugh and Sampson. The lease, dated February 2, 1934, was executed by the same parties. A second lease of property adjoining the site of the boxing pavilion was signed by Swartzbaugh and Sampson. This was also dated February 2, 1934, but probably was signed after that date. Plaintiff's name does not appear in any of the three documents and Sampson was advised that she would not sign any of them.

The walnut trees were removed from the leased premises. Sampson went into possession, erected his boxing pavilion and placed other improvements on the property.

Plaintiff was injured in February, 1934, and was confined to her bed for some time. This action was started on June 20, 1934. Up to the time of the trial plaintiff had received no part of the rental of the leased property. Sampson was in possession of all of it under the leases to the exclusion of plaintiff.

There is but one question to be decided in this case which may be stated as follows: Can one joint tenant who has not joined in the leases executed by her cotenant and another maintain an action to cancel the leases where the lessee is in exclusive possession of the leased property? This question does not seem to have been decided in California and there is not an entire uniformity of decision in other jurisdictions. In decisions on analogous questions where courts reached like conclusions they did not always use the same course of reasoning in reaching them. It seems necessary, therefore, that we consider briefly the nature of the estate in joint tenancy and the rights of the joint tenants in it. . . .

An estate in joint tenancy can be severed by destroying one or more of the necessary unities, either by operation of law, by death, by voluntary or certain involuntary acts of the joint tenants, or by certain acts or omissions of one joint tenant without the consent of the other. It seems to be the rule in England that a lease by one joint tenant for a term of

---

with whom he comes in contact." 2 Mrs. J.F. Pleasants, History of Orange County, California, 193-194 (1931). — Eds.

years will effect a severance, at least during the term of the lease. (Napier v. Williams, [1911] 1 Ch. 361; Doe v. Read, 12 East, 57, 104 Reprint, 23; Roe v. Lonsdale, 12 East, 39, 104 Reprint, 16; Palmer v. Rich, [1897] 1 Ch. 134. See Thompson on Real Property, p.929, sec. 1715.) We have found no case in the United States where this rule has been applied. From the reasoning used and conclusions reached in many of the American cases its adoption in this country seems doubtful.

One of the essential unities of a joint tenancy is that of possession. Each tenant owns an equal interest in all of the fee and each has an equal right to possession of the whole. Possession by one is possession by all. Ordinarily one joint tenant out of possession cannot recover exclusive possession of the joint property from his cotenant. (Jamison v. Graham, 57 Ill. 94.) He can only recover the right to be let into joint possession of the property with his cotenant. He cannot eject his cotenant in possession. (Noble v. Manatt, 42 Cal. App. 496 [183 Pac. 823].)

Ordinarily one joint tenant cannot maintain an action against his cotenant for rent for occupancy of the property or for profits derived from his own labor. He may, however, compel the tenant in possession to account for rents collected from third parties. . . .

The case of Stark v. Barrett, 15 Cal. 361, discusses the rights of a grantee of one cotenant of a specific parcel of property. It is there said:

> The case has been argued as though the question presented was to be determined by the rules of the common law, and in that view we have examined it. For its determination, considered by the common law, it is immaterial whether the grantees took the land embraced in their grant as joint tenants or as tenants in common. During the lives of the tenants, the rules regulating the transfer of their interest are substantially the same, whether they hold in joint tenancy or in common. Neither a joint tenant nor a tenant in common can do any act to the prejudice of his cotenants in their estate. This is the settled law, and hence a conveyance by one tenant of a parcel of a general tract, owned by several, is inoperative to impair any of the rights of his cotenants. The conveyance must be subject to the ultimate determination of their rights, and upon obvious grounds. One tenant cannot appropriate to himself any particular parcel of the general tract; as, upon a partition, which may be claimed by the cotenants at any time, the parcel may be entirely set apart in severalty to a cotenant. He cannot defeat this possible result whilst retaining his interest, nor can he defeat it by the transfer of his interest. He cannot, of course, invest his grantee with rights greater than he possesses. The grantee must take, therefore, subject to the contingency of the loss of the premises, if, upon the partition of the general tract, they should not be allotted to the grantor. Subject to this contingency, the conveyance is valid, and passes the interest of the grantor. And this, we consider the result of the several cases cited by the counsel of the appellants. They go to the extent that the conveyance can have no legal effect to the prejudice of the cotenant, not that it is absolutely void, that it is ineffectual against the assertion of his interest in a

suit for partition of the general tract, but is good against all others. Until such partition, the grantee will be entitled to the use and possession as cotenant, in the parcel conveyed, with the other owners. . . .

It is a general rule that the act of one joint tenant without express or implied authority from or the consent of his cotenant cannot bind or prejudicially affect the rights of the latter. . . .

In the application of the foregoing rule the courts have imposed a limitation upon it which, in effect, is a qualification of its broad language. This perhaps is due to the nature of the estate which is universally held to be joint in enjoyment and several upon severance. This limitation arises in cases where one joint tenant in possession leases all of the joint property without the consent of his cotenant and places the lessee in possession. It seems to be based upon the theory that the joint tenant in possession is entitled to the possession of the entire property and by his lease merely gives to his lessee a right he, the lessor, had been enjoying, puts the lessee in the enjoyment of a right of possession which he, the lessor, already had and by so doing does not prejudicially affect the rights of the cotenant out of possession, it being conceded that the joint tenant not joining in the lease is not bound by its terms and that he can recover from the tenant of his cotenant the reasonable value of the use and enjoyment of his share of the estate, if the tenant under the lease refuses him the right to enjoy his moiety of the estate. (See Codman v. Hall, 9 Allen (91 Mass.), 335; Eagle Brewing Co. v. Netzel, 159 Ill. App. 375; Frans v. Young, 24 Iowa, 375.)

It has been held that each joint tenant, during the existence of the joint estate, has the right to convey, mortgage or subject to a mechanic's lien an equal share of the joint property. (People v. Varel, 351 Ill. 96 [184 N.E. 209].) It has also been held that one joint tenant in possession of personal property may pledge his interest in the property to another; that the pledgee's rights are valid to the extent of the pledgor's interest; that each joint tenant has an equal right of possession and so the pledgee has the same right of possession that the pledgor had; that the joint tenant out of possession can maintain no action against the pledgee that he could not maintain against the pledgor. . . .

In 2 Thompson on Real Property, page 929, section 1715, it is said: "One joint tenant may make a lease of the joint property, but this will bind only his share of it." The same rule is thus stated in 1 Landlord and Tenant, Tiffany, 405: "One of two or more joint tenants cannot, by making a lease of the whole, vest in the lessee more than his own share, since that is all to which he has an exclusive right. Such a lease is, however, valid as to his share."

The foregoing authorities support the conclusion that a lease to all of the joint property by one joint tenant is not a nullity but is a valid and supportable contract in so far as the interest of the lessor in the joint property is concerned. . . .

In the case of Lee Chuck v. Quan Wo Chong & Co., 91 Cal. 593 [28 Pac. 45], the plaintiff, a tenant in common, brought an action to oust defendant who was holding under a lease from another tenant in common. The Supreme Court reversed the judgment in favor of plaintiff and said: . . .

> One tenant in common may, "by either lease or license, . . . confer upon another person the right to occupy and use the property of the co-tenancy as fully as such lessor or licensor himself might have used or occupied it if such lease or license had not been granted. If either co-tenant expel such licensee or lessee, he is guilty of a trespass. If the lessee has the exclusive possession of the premises, he is not liable to any one but his lessor for the rent, unless the other co-tenants attempt to enter and he resists or forbids their entry, or unless, being in possession with them, he ousts or excludes some or all of them." (Freeman on Cotenancy and Partition, sec. 253.) There is no evidence tending to show that the defendant ever refused to allow the plaintiff to enjoy the use of the premises with him. The judgment does not confine the plaintiff's right of recovery to his own moiety, but provides that the plaintiff shall have and recover from defendant the restitution and possession of the premises described in the complaint. . . .

As far as the evidence before us in this case is concerned, the foregoing authorities force the conclusion that the leases from Swartzbaugh to Sampson are not null and void but valid and existing contracts giving to Sampson the same right to the possession of the leased property that Swartzbaugh had. It follows they cannot be cancelled by plaintiff in this action.

Plaintiff expresses the fear that as one of the leases runs for five years, with an option for an additional five years, she may lose her interest in the leased premises by prescription. It is a general rule that a lessee in possession of real property under a lease cannot dispute his landlord's title nor can he hold adversely to him while holding under the lease. If, as held in numerous cases, the lessee of one cotenant holds the possession of his lessor and that a cotenant in possession holds for the other cotenant and not adversely, Sampson would have great difficulty in establishing any holding adverse to plaintiff without a complete and definite ouster. As a general rule an adverse possessor must claim the property in fee and a lessee holding under a lease cannot avail himself of the claim of adverse possession. There are certain exceptions to this rule which do not seem to be applicable to this case. There is no showing that plaintiff ever demanded that Sampson let her into possession of her moiety of the estate nor is there anything to indicate that he is holding adversely to her.

Judgment affirmed.

A petition by appellant to have the cause heard in the Supreme Court, after judgment in the District Court of Appeal, was denied by the Supreme Court on March 26, 1936.

NOTES AND QUESTIONS

1. At the trial in the principal case the plaintiff, Lola Desirra Swartzbaugh, testified that the land was set out in walnut trees by the Swartzbaughs in 1912, that she did not want the walnut trees taken out, that the rent payable by Sampson was $15 a month which she regarded as too little when Sampson was to spend around $10,000 on building and equipping the boxing arena, that she had never received any part of the rent, and that she did not want prizefighting on her land because "women and liquor followed," and "I worked too hard for that place to have everybody against me bringing such a place there."

Mrs. Swartzbaugh also testified with respect to the signing of the lease by her husband on February 2, 1934:

A.   Mr. Swartzbaugh said it was an option or lease, but I am not sure which he said, because I felt so bad that I wasn't sure of anything, but I said "you had better take that to a lawyer, or see a lawyer before you sign anything like that. You don't know what it is," and Mr. Sampson said he read, or "I read it to him."

Q.   [Then what happened?]

A.   Well, when I saw Mr. Swartzbaugh go to the desk to sign it, I gathered up my crutches and left the room, fearing they would ask me —

A week or so later Mrs. Swartzbaugh telephoned Sampson that she was going to get an injunction against him and stop him. Sampson came to see her. Her daughter Arvilla and her son John were there. The meeting was inconclusive. John testified:

A.   . . . After mother objected and told him she would get an injunction against him and we would stop him, and I shook my fist in Sampson's face and said "you can't get away with it," and he said "forget it," and he started to tell about his previous experience [in conducting prizefighting] at Delhi and how orderly it was conducted and all [the fighters were] high school boys, and I told him to "come outside," and then I said "Sampson, get this straight, you are dealing with an old man in his dotage and my mother is lying in her bed, and nobody but a damned dirty rat would attempt to put this over," and he said "forget it, John, we will not say anything more about it," and Sampson left immediately after that, and the next time we heard anything from him, Sampson was working over there [cutting the trees and erecting the boxing pavilion] and my mother was on her back and in bed and couldn't get out an injunction.

Appellant's Opening Brief at 6-11, Swartzbaugh v. Sampson, 11 Cal. App. 2d 451, 54 P.2d 73 (1936).

2. Consider the remedies available to Mrs. Swartzbaugh.

(a) *Partition.* Mrs. Swartzbaugh could bring an action to partition the entire 60 acres or to partition the fraction leased to Sampson for the duration of the lease. If she brought an action to partition the fraction leased for a five-year term, with an option to renew for an additional five years, and the court ordered sale of the leasehold term, how would the court divide up the proceeds of the sale?

(b) *Ouster.* Another remedy for Mrs. Swartzbaugh is to enter, or try to enter, into possession with the lessee. If the lessee resists, the remedies of an ousted cotenant are then available. As the decision in the *Swartzbaugh* case points out, those remedies would allow Mrs. Swartzbaugh to recover from the lessee one-half the reasonable rental value of the leased land (a remedy called, for historical reasons, the recovery of mesne profits). Does the mere presence of the boxing pavilion work an ouster? If the lessee ousts Mrs. Swartzbaugh and becomes liable to her for one-half the fair rental value, is the lessee still liable to Mr. Swartzbaugh for the full amount of the agreed rental?

(c) *Accounting.* Mrs. Swartzbaugh can sue her husband for an accounting of the rents received by him. The Notes below discuss this and some related matters.

NOTES: ACCOUNTING FOR BENEFITS, RECOVERING COSTS

1. Concurrently owned property can yield a variety of benefits to the cotenants: rents realized from leases to third parties; profits realized from using the property for business purposes; value realized by one or more of the cotenants in occupying the property as a residence. Of course, concurrent ownership can also give rise to a variety of expenditures — for taxes and mortgage payments, maintenance and repairs, improvements — and a cotenant making such expenditures might seek to recoup some or all of them through a partition action or an action for an accounting (brought independently or incident to a partition action) or an action for contribution from the other cotenants.

Accounting is an equitable proceeding, and, although the rules given below ordinarily apply, particular facts may compel a departure from the usual rules in order to be fair to the cotenants.

2. *Rents and profits.* In all states, a cotenant who collects from third parties rents and other payments arising from the co-owned land must account to cotenants for the amounts received. Thus if one cotenant leases a farm to a third party, or executes a mineral lease, or cuts and sells timber, he must account for net rents, royalties, and other proceeds in excess of his share. See 2 American Law of Property §6.14 (1952).[14] Absent ouster, however, the accounting is usually based only on actual receipts, not fair market value. Suppose the lease signed by one cotenant claims to bind only that cotenant's share and not to give the lessee exclusive occupancy, and that the agreed rent is equal to one-half the fair rental value. Would this affect the rights of the other cotenant to an accounting? See Annot., 51 A.L.R.2d 388, 407-408 (1957).

On payment of rent by a tenant in exclusive possession, see Spiller v. Mackereth, page 353, and the Notes and Questions that follow it.

3. *Taxes, mortgage payments, and other carrying charges.* A cotenant paying more than his share of taxes, mortgage payments, and other necessary carrying charges generally has a right to contribution from the other cotenants, at least up to the amount of the value of their share in the property. (Similarly, the cotenant paying more than his share receives a credit for the excess payments in an accounting or partition action.) The principle behind this result "is that the protection of the interest of each cotenant from extinction by a tax or foreclosure sale imposes on each the duty to contribute to the extent of his proportionate share the money required to make such payments." 2 American Law of Property, supra, §6.17 at 73-74. However, "[i]f the tenant who has paid taxes or interest has been in sole possession of the property, and the value of the use and enjoyment which he has had equals or exceeds such payments, no action in any form for contribution will lie against the others." Id. at 76.

The qualification just quoted is not uniformly applied. See Annot., supra, 51 A.L.R.2d at 455-459. Is it inconsistent with the principle behind the general rule? With the rule (followed in most jurisdictions) that a cotenant in possession need not account to cotenants out of possession for the reasonable rental value of the property?

4. *Repairs and improvements.* As to *necessary repairs,* a cotenant making or paying for them has no affirmative right to contribution from the other cotenants in the absence of an agreement. This is considered the rule by "weight of authority and of reason. . . ." 2 American Law of Property, supra, §6.18 at 77. The "reason" behind the rule is said to be

---

14. In some jurisdictions extraction of minerals or cutting of timber is deemed waste, even though such operations are permitted to the owners of a fee simple. One cotenant is entitled to an injunction forbidding the extraction of minerals, even though a majority of cotenants favor extraction. See Chosar Corp. v. Owens, 235 Va. 660, 370 S.E.2d 305 (1988) (also denying judicial partition of mineral rights because not authorized by statute).

that the questions "of how much should be expended on repairs, their character and extent, and whether as a matter of business judgment such expenditures are justified," are ones too uncertain for the law to settle. Id. at 78. Given this, how is it that the cotenant receives a credit for reasonable repairs in a partition or accounting action (subject to the same qualifications as apply to taxes and mortgage payments)?

Improvements. As with repairs, a cotenant has no right to contribution from other cotenants for expenditures for improvements; beyond this (and unlike the case of repairs), no credit for the cost of the improvements is given as such in an accounting or partition action. This does not mean, however, that an improving cotenant is always without means to recapture the costs or realize the value of improvements. The general rule is that the interests of the improver are to be protected if this can be accomplished without detriment to the interests of the other cotenants. Thus, if property is physically divided pursuant to a partition action, the improved portion is awarded to the improving cotenant if such a distribution would not diminish the interests of the other cotenants as they stood prior to the making of the improvements. If physical partition is impossible or would result in injustice to one of the cotenants, the property is sold and the proceeds distributed in such a way as to award to the improver the added value (if any) resulting from his improvements. See Graham v. Inlow, 302 Ark. 414, 790 S.W.2d 428 (1990). An alternative remedy — where physical partition is possible but would jeopardize the interests of the improver by awarding improvements to cotenants who did not contribute to their cost — is to divide the property but order payment (called owelty) from noncontributing cotenants to the improver in an amount equal to the former's share of the enhanced value of the property resulting from the improvements. In an accounting for rents and profits, the improver is allowed all increments in value (if any) attributable to the improvements.

Notice that these results pay heed only to the value of improvements, not their cost. They imply that, in cases where "improvements" cost more than they yield in terms of increased sale or rental value (or, indeed, where they actually diminish value), the improver bears this full "downside" risk. Similarly, the results discussed above imply that an improver is to enjoy the full "upside" of the improvements — that is, he is to be awarded the total increase in value rather than being required to share it with the other co-owners.

Assume that the dual objectives of rules governing concurrently owned property are (or should be) to achieve a fair distribution of the benefits and burdens of co-ownership and to promote the efficient use of the property in question. Do the rules on improvements advance these ends? See generally Lawrence Berger, An Analysis of the Economic Relations Between Cotenants, 21 Ariz. L. Rev. 1015 (1979).

Recall that the law treats repairs differently than it does improvements. Is that sensible?

B. Marital Interests

Out of the medieval period in Europe emerged two different systems of marital property. One was the English system. Its fundamental principle is that husband and wife have separate property; ownership is given to the spouse who acquires the property. The other was the continental system of community property. Community property rests on the notion that husband and wife are a marital partnership (a "community") and should share their acquests equally. In Europe, community property originated among the Germanic tribes and was carried by the Visigoths into Spain in the fifth century. Gradually, over hundreds of years, community property customs grew and spread throughout the continent of Europe but never took root in England. Under the pressure of a militaristic feudalism with a powerful king on top, the English royal judges suppressed any tendencies toward community property. The presumed necessities of the great lords dictated the effacement of the wife, which became the common law for all. See Charles Donahue, Jr., What Causes Fundamental Legal Ideas? Marital Property in England and France in the Thirteenth Century, 78 Mich. L. Rev. 59 (1979).

The common law marital property system was accepted in the large majority of American states. In eight states influenced by French or Spanish law (Arizona, California, Idaho, Louisiana, Nevada, New Mexico, Texas, and Washington), a community property system exists. In the late twentieth century, the common law marital property system has come under pressure to reform itself so that the results resemble those reached under a community property system. The community property idea of treating husband and wife as an economic unit has more or less triumphed when spousal property is divided upon divorce or at the death of one spouse. But great differences between these marital property systems remain and cause complications when a couple moves from a common law property state to a community property state, or vice versa. See generally Mary Ann Glendon, The Transformation of Family Law (1989).

For exploration of an interesting hypothesis that women have less property than men because they have a greater taste for cooperation than men, see Carol M. Rose, Women and Property: Gaining and Losing Ground, 78 Va. L. Rev. 421 (1992).

"They have this arrangement. He earns the money and she takes care of the house."

Drawing by Weber; © 1977
The New Yorker Magazine, Inc.

1. The Common Law Marital Property System

a. During Marriage (The Fiction that Husband and Wife Are One)

The English marital property system, feudal in origin, mirrored the need of the patriarchal landed class to keep their estates intact and under the control of a single male. A married woman was to be supported and maintained for her entire life, but she was not entitled, by and large, to exercise powers of ownership. Her property relationship to her husband was one of dependency.

At the instant of marriage, a woman moved under her husband's protection or *cover* (becoming a *feme covert*). She ceased to be a legal person for the duration of the marriage. Husband and wife were regarded as one, and that one was the husband. Except for clothes and ornaments (known as the wife's *paraphernalia*), all personal property owned by the wife at the time of the marriage or acquired thereafter, including her earnings, became the property of the husband. Although the notion that husband and wife were one flesh was not pushed to the logical extreme

367

of depriving the wife of title to her real property, the husband had the right of possession to all the wife's lands during marriage, including land acquired after marriage. That right, known as *jure uxoris,* was alienable by the husband and reachable by his creditors. In addition, the wife had the duty of rendering services within the home. In exchange for all this, and a marriage vow to obey her husband, the wife received the benefit of the husband's support and protection.[15]

Beginning with Mississippi in 1839, all common law property states had, by the end of the nineteenth century, enacted Married Women's Property Acts. These statutes removed the disabilities of coverture and gave a married woman, like a single woman, control over all her property. Such property was her separate property, immune from her husband's debts. The wife also gained control of all her earnings outside the home.

The Married Women's Property Acts, prompted by a desire to protect a wife's property from her husband's creditors, as well as to give her legal autonomy, did not give the wife full equality. Husband and wife were expected to play complementary roles. The husband, employed outside the home, remained head of the family and owed his wife a duty of support; his wife, mistress of the household and in charge of rearing the children, owed him domestic services. Although the wife was given control over her property, it was unlikely that — as an unpaid homemaker — she would have much of that commodity.

PROBLEM

After having a stroke, *H,* anxious to avoid going into a nursing home or being cared for by professional nurses, entered into an agreement with *W. H* promised *W* that if *W* personally cared for him at home for the rest of his life, *H* would devise her certain property by will. In compliance with the agreement, *W* personally cared for *H* at home until his death. When he died, *H* devised the property promised his wife to his daughter by a prior marriage. Can *W* enforce the contract? See Borelli v. Brusseau, 12 Cal. App. 4th 647, 16 Cal. Rptr. 2d 16 (1993), holding the contract unenforceable for lack of consideration. The court reasoned: *W* owes *H* the marital duty of personally caring for him when ill; performance of a pre-existing legal duty cannot serve as consideration. Is this sound?

---

15. At common law a husband was liable for the torts of his wife, for the law supposed that a wife acts under her husband's direction. " 'If the law supposes that,' said Mr. Bumble, squeezing his hat emphatically in both hands, 'the law is a ass — a idiot. If that's the eye of the law, the law's a bachelor; and the worst I wish the law is, that his eye may be opened by experience — by experience.' " Charles Dickens, Oliver Twist ch. 51, at 394 (Everyman Lib. ed. 1940).

Sawada v. Endo

Supreme Court of Hawaii, 1977
57 Hawaii 608, 561 P.2d 1291

MENOR, J. This is a civil action brought by the plaintiffs-appellants, Masako Sawada and Helen Sawada, in aid of execution of money judgments in their favor, seeking to set aside a conveyance of real property from judgment debtor Kokichi Endo to Samuel H. Endo and Toru Endo, defendants-appellees herein, on the ground that the conveyance as to the Sawadas was fraudulent.

On November 30, 1968, the Sawadas were injured when struck by a motor vehicle operated by Kokichi Endo. On June 17, 1969, Helen Sawada filed her complaint for damages against Kokichi Endo. Masako Sawada filed her suit against him on August 13, 1969. The complaint and summons in each case was served on Kokichi Endo on October 29, 1969.

On the date of the accident, Kokichi Endo was the owner, as a tenant by the entirety with his wife, Ume Endo, of a parcel of real property situate at Wahiawa, Oahu, Hawaii. By deed, dated July 26, 1969, Kokichi Endo and his wife conveyed the property to their sons, Samuel H. Endo and Toru Endo. This document was recorded in the Bureau of Conveyances on December 17, 1969. No consideration was paid by the grantees for the conveyance. Both were aware at the time of the conveyance that their father had been involved in an accident, and that he carried no liability insurance. Kokichi Endo and Ume Endo, while reserving no life interests therein, continued to reside on the premises.

On January 19, 1971, after a consolidated trial on the merits, judgment was entered in favor of Helen Sawada and against Kokichi Endo in the sum of $8,846. 46. At the same time, Masako Sawada was awarded judgment on her complaint in the amount of $16,199.28. Ume Endo, wife of Kokichi Endo, died on January 29, 1971. She was survived by her husband, Kokichi. Subsequently, after being frustrated in their attempts to obtain satisfaction of judgment from the personal property of Kokichi Endo, the Sawadas brought suit to set aside the conveyance which is the subject matter of this controversy. The trial court refused to set aside the conveyance, and the Sawadas appeal.

The determinative question in this case is, whether the interest of one spouse in real property, held in tenancy by the entireties, is subject to levy and execution by his or her individual creditors. This issue is one of first impression in this jurisdiction.

A brief review of the present state of the tenancy by the entirety might be helpful. Dean Phipps, writing in 1951,[16] pointed out that only nineteen states and the District of Columbia continued to recognize it as

---

16. Phipps, Tenancy by Entireties, 25 Temple L.Q. 24 (1951).

a valid and subsisting institution in the field of property law. Phipps divided these jurisdictions into four groups. He made no mention of Alaska and Hawaii, both of which were then territories of the United States.

In the Group I states (Massachusetts, Michigan, and North Carolina) the estate is essentially the common law tenancy by the entireties, unaffected by the Married Women's Property Acts. As at common law, the possession and profits of the estate are subject to the husband's exclusive dominion and control. . . . In all three states, as at common law, the *husband* may convey the entire estate subject only to the possibility that the wife may become entitled to the whole estate upon surviving him. . . . As at common law, the obverse as to the wife does not hold true. Only in Massachusetts, however, is the estate in its entirety subject to levy by the husband's creditors. . . . In both Michigan and North Carolina, the use and income from the estate is not subject to levy during the marriage for the separate debts of either spouse. . . .

In the Group II states (Alaska, Arkansas, New Jersey, New York, and Oregon) the interest of the debtor spouse in the estate may be sold or levied upon for his or her separate debts, subject to the other spouse's contingent right of survivorship. . . . Alaska, which has been added to this group, has provided by statute that the interest of a debtor spouse in any type of estate, except a homestead as defined and held in tenancy by the entirety, shall be subject to his or her separate debts. . . .

In the Group III jurisdictions (Delaware, District of Columbia, Florida, Indiana, Maryland, Missouri, Pennsylvania, Rhode Island, Vermont, Virginia, and Wyoming) an attempted conveyance by either spouse is wholly void, and the estate may not be subjected to the separate debts of one spouse only. . . .

In Group IV, the two states of Kentucky and Tennessee hold that the contingent right of survivorship appertaining to either spouse is separately alienable by him and attachable by his creditors during the marriage. . . . The use and profits, however, may neither be alienated nor attached during coverture.

It appears, therefore, that Hawaii is the only jurisdiction still to be heard from on the question. Today we join that group of states and the District of Columbia which hold that under the Married Women's Property Acts the interest of a husband or a wife in an estate by the entireties is not subject to the claims of his or her individual creditors during the joint lives of the spouses. In so doing, we are placing our stamp of approval upon what is apparently the prevailing view of the lower courts of this jurisdiction.

Hawaii has long recognized and continues to recognize the tenancy in common, the joint tenancy, and the tenancy by the entirety, as separate and distinct estates. See Paahana v. Bila, 3 Haw. 725 (1876). That the Married Women's Property Act of 1888 was not intended to abolish the tenancy by the entirety was made clear by the language of Act 19 of the Session Laws of Hawaii, 1903 (now HRS §509-1). See also HRS §509-2. The tenancy by the entirety is predicated upon the legal unity of husband and wife, and the estate is held by them in single ownership. They do not take by moieties, but both and each are seized of the whole estate. Lang v. Commissioner of Internal Revenue, 289 U.S. 109, 53 S. Ct. 534, 77 L. Ed. 1066 (1933).

A joint tenant has a specific, albeit undivided, interest in the property, and if he survives his cotenant he becomes the owner of a larger interest than he had prior to the death of the other joint tenant. But tenants by the entirety are each deemed to be seized of the entirety from the time of the creation of the estate. At common law, this taking of the "whole estate" did not have the real significance that it does today, insofar as the rights of the wife in the property were concerned. For all practical purposes, the wife had no right during coverture to the use and enjoyment and exercise of ownership in the marital estate. All she possessed was her contingent right of survivorship.

The effect of the Married Women's Property Acts was to abrogate the husband's common law dominance over the marital estate and to place the wife on a level of equality with him as regards the exercise of ownership over the whole estate. The tenancy was and still is predicated upon the legal unity of husband and wife, but the Acts converted it into a unity of equals and not of unequals as at common law. . . . No longer could the husband convey, lease, mortgage or otherwise encumber the property without her consent. The Acts confirmed her right to the use and enjoyment of the whole estate, and all the privileges that ownership of property confers, including the right to convey the property in its entirety, jointly with her husband, during the marriage relation. Jordan v. Reynolds, 105 Md. 288, 66 A. 37 (1907); Hurd v. Hughes, 12 Del. Ch. 188, 109 A. 418 (1920). They also had the effect of insulating the wife's interest in the estate from the separate debts of her husband. Jordan v. Reynolds, supra.

Neither husband nor wife has a separate divisible interest in the property held by the entirety that can be conveyed or reached by execution. Fairclaw v. Forrest, 76 U.S. App. D.C. 197, 130 F.2d 829 (1942). A joint tenancy may be destroyed by voluntary alienation, or by levy and execution, or by compulsory partition, but a tenancy by the entirety may not. The indivisibility of the estate, except by joint action of the spouses, is an indispensable feature of the tenancy by the entirety. Ashbaugh v. Ashbaugh, 273 Mo. 353, 201 S.W. 72 (1918); Newman v. Equitable Life Assur. Soc., 119 Fla. 641, 160 So. 745 (1935); Lang v. Commissioner of Internal Revenue, supra.

In Jordan v. Reynolds, supra, the Maryland court held that no lien could attach against entirety property for the separate debts of the husband, for that would be in derogation of the entirety of title in the spouses and would be tantamount to a conversion of the tenancy into a joint tenancy or tenancy in common. In holding that the spouses could jointly convey the property, free of any judgment liens against the husband, the court said:

> To hold the judgment to be a lien at all against this property, and the right of execution suspended during the life of the wife, and to be enforced on the death of the wife, would, we think, likewise encumber her estate, and be in contravention of the constitutional provision heretofore mentioned, protecting the wife's property from the husband's debts.
>
> It is clear, we think, if the judgment here is declared a lien, but suspended during the life of the wife, and not enforceable until her death, if the husband should survive the wife, it will defeat the sale here made by the husband and wife to the purchaser, and thereby make the wife's property liable for the debts of her husband. [105 Md. at 295, 296, 66 A. at 39.]

In Hurd v. Hughes, supra, the Delaware court, recognizing the peculiar nature of an estate by the entirety, in that the husband and wife are the owners, not merely of equal interests but of the whole estate, stated:

> The estate [by the entireties] can be acquired or held only by a man and woman while married. Each spouse owns the whole while both live; neither can sell any interest except with the other's consent, and by their joint act; and at the death of either the other continues to own the whole, and does not acquire any new interest from the other. There can be no partition between them. From this is deduced the indivisibility and unseverability of the estate into two interests, and hence that the creditors of either spouse cannot during their joint lives reach by execution any interest which the debtor had in land so held. . . . One may have doubts as to whether the holding of land by entireties is advisable or in harmony with the spirit of the legislation in favor of married women; but when such an estate is created due effect must be given to its peculiar characteristics. [12 Del. Ch. at 190, 109 A. at 419.] . . .

We are not persuaded by the argument that it would be unfair to the creditors of either spouse to hold that the estate by the entirety may not, without the consent of both spouses, be levied upon for the separate debts of either spouse. No unfairness to the creditor is involved here. We agree with the court in Hurd v. Hughes, supra: "But creditors are not entitled to special consideration. If the debt arose prior to the creation of the estate, the property was not a basis of credit, and if the debt arose subsequently the creditor presumably had notice of the characteristics of the estate which limited his right to reach the property." 12 Del. Ch. at 193, 109 A. at 420.

We might also add that there is obviously nothing to prevent the creditor from insisting upon the subjection of property held in tenancy by the entirety as a condition precedent to the extension of credit. Further, the creation of a tenancy by the entirety may not be used as a device to defraud existing creditors. In re Estate of Wall, 142 U.S. App. D.C. 187, 440 F.2d 215 (1971).

Were we to view the matter strictly from the standpoint of public policy, we would still be constrained to hold as we have done here today. In Fairclaw v. Forrest, supra, the court makes this observation: "The interest in family solidarity retains some influence upon the institution [of tenancy by the entirety]. It is available only to husband and wife. It is a convenient mode of protecting a surviving spouse from inconvenient administration of the decedent's estate and from the other's improvident debts. It is in that protection the estate finds its peculiar and justifiable function." 130 F.2d at 833.

It is a matter of common knowledge that the demand for single-family residential lots has increased rapidly in recent years, and the magnitude of the problem is emphasized by the concentration of the bulk of fee simple land in the hands of a few. The shortage of single-family residential fee simple property is critical and government has seen fit to attempt to alleviate the problem through legislation. When a family can afford to own real property, it becomes their single most important asset. Encumbered as it usually is by a first mortgage, the fact remains that so long as it remains whole during the joint lives of the spouses, it is always available in its entirety for the benefit and use of the entire family. Loans for education and other emergency expenses, for example, may be obtained on the security of the marital estate. This would not be possible where a third party has become a tenant in common or a joint tenant with one of the spouses, or where the ownership of the contingent right of survivorship of one of the spouses in a third party has cast a cloud upon the title of the marital estate, making it virtually impossible to utilize the estate for these purposes.

If we were to select between a public policy favoring the creditors of one of the spouses and one favoring the interests of the family unit, we would not hesitate to choose the latter. But we need not make this choice for, as we pointed out earlier, by the very nature of the estate by the entirety as we view it, and as other courts of our sister jurisdictions have viewed it, "[a] unilaterally indestructible right of survivorship, an inability of one spouse to alienate his interest, and, importantly for this case, a broad immunity from claims of separate creditors remain among its vital incidents." In re Estate of Wall, supra, 440 F.2d at 218.

Having determined that an estate by the entirety is not subject to the claims of the creditors of one of the spouses during their joint lives, we now hold that the conveyance of the marital property by Kokichi Endo and Ume Endo, husband and wife, to their sons, Samuel H. Endo and Toru Endo, was not in fraud of Kokichi Endo's judgment creditors. Cf. Jordan v. Reynolds, supra.

Affirmed.

KIDWELL, J., dissenting. . . . The majority reaches its conclusion by holding that the effect of the Married Women's Act was to equalize the positions of the spouses by taking from the husband his common law right to transfer his interest, rather than by elevating the wife's right of alienation of her interest to place it on a position of equality with the husband's. I disagree. I believe that a better interpretation of the Married Women's Acts is that offered by the Supreme Court of New Jersey in King v. Greene, 30 N.J. 395, 412, 153 A.2d 49, 60 (1959):

> It is clear that the Married Women's Act created an equality between the spouses in New Jersey, insofar as tenancies by the entirety are concerned. If, as we have previously concluded, the husband could alienate his right of survivorship at common law, the wife, by virtue of the act, can alienate her right of survivorship. And it follows, that if the wife takes equal rights with the husband in the estate, she must take equal disabilities. Such are the dictates of common equality. Thus, the judgment creditors of either spouse may levy and execute upon their separate rights of survivorship.

One may speculate whether the courts which first chose the path to equality now followed by the majority might have felt an unexpressed aversion to entrusting a wife with as much control over her interest as had previously been granted to the husband with respect to his interest. Whatever may be the historical explanation for these decisions, I feel that the resultant restriction upon the freedom of the spouses to deal independently with their respective interests is both illogical and unnecessarily at odds with present policy trends. Accordingly, I would hold that the separate interest of the husband in entireties property, at least to the extent of his right of survivorship, is alienable by him and subject to attachment by his separate creditors, so that a voluntary conveyance of the husband's interest should be set aside where it is fraudulent as to such creditors, under applicable principles of the law of fraudulent conveyances.

NOTES AND PROBLEMS

1. As the court in Sawada v. Endo points out, divergent views have been taken in various jurisdictions as to the effect of the Married Women's Property Acts on the tenancy by the entirety. Pushed by serious doubts as to the constitutionality of unequal treatment of husband and wife in the common law tenancy by the entirety, and the modern move-

ment to eradicate gender-based differences in the law, Massachusetts, Michigan, and North Carolina (the last three adherents to the classic tenancy by the entirety) have enacted legislation to give equal rights to husband and wife in a tenancy by the entirety. See Mass. Ann. Laws ch. 209, §§1, 1A (1981 & Supp. 1991), giving husband and wife equal rights in tenancies by the entireties created after February 11, 1980, and providing that husband and wife may agree, in writing, to equal rights in tenancies by the entireties created before that date; and also providing that creditors of one tenant by the entirety cannot seize and sell the entirety property if it is the principal residence of the nondebtor spouse. See also Mich. Comp. Laws Ann. §557.71 (West 1988); N.C. Gen. Stat. §39-13-6 (1991).

Interpretive variations regarding the effect of the Married Women's Property Acts on the tenancy by the entirety have important consequences for general creditors because a creditor can reach only such property as the debtor can voluntarily assign. In a majority of states a creditor of one spouse cannot reach a tenancy by the entirety because one spouse cannot assign his or her interest. Doubtless this exemption from creditors is one of the main reasons for the survival of the tenancy by the entirety. The tenancy serves to protect the family home as well as other property from transfer by one spouse and from creditors of one spouse. The tenancy by the entirety, where recognized, can be created in any amount of real property and, in many states, in any amount of personal property.

Property owned by a bankrupt debtor in tenancy by the entirety is exempt from bankruptcy creditors if the debtor chooses the state law exemptions from creditors rather than the exemptions provided in the bankruptcy code and state law exempts the debtor spouse's interest from creditors. See In re Garner, 952 F.2d 232 (8th Cir. 1991); Note, Bankruptcy and Tenancy by the Entirety Property, 58 UMKC L. Rev. 501 (1990).

2. *H* and *W* owned their home in New York as tenants by the entirety. *H* abandoned *W*. *X*, a judgment creditor of *H*, levied on *H*'s interest in the dwelling and purchased it at execution sale. *X* demanded from *W* one-half the reasonable rental value of the house. *W* refused. What are *X*'s rights? See Lover v. Fennell, 14 Misc. 2d 874, 179 N.Y.S.2d 1017 (1958).

In New York, *X* steps into *H*'s shoes. Though the tenancy between *W* and *X* is labelled a "tenancy in common" (because a tenancy by the entirety can exist only between married persons), the rights of the parties are essentially the same as tenants by the entirety. Neither party can unilaterally sever the tenancy by partition. If *H* dies first, *W* owns the house free of *X*'s interest. If *W* dies first, *X* owns the house free of *W*'s interest. If *H* and *W* divorce, the tenancy becomes a tenancy in common in reality as well as in name, and *X*'s and *W*'s survivorship interests cease to exist. See V.R.W., Inc. v. Klein, 68 N.Y.2d 560, 503 N.E.2d 496, 510 N.Y.S.2d 848 (1986).

3. At common law, a husband took title to all his wife's chattels and choses in action, and for this reason a tenancy by the entirety could not be created in personal property. Today many of the states recognizing the tenancy by the entirety permit it in personal as well as in real property.

Suppose that a jurisdiction recognizes the tenancy by the entirety only in real property. *H* and *W* own their home as tenants by the entirety. The house burns down, and *H* dies five days later. The insurance company is now ready to pay $100,000 on the policy insuring the house. To whom should the company pay the $100,000? See Regnante v. Baldassare, 15 Mass. App. 718, 448 N.E.2d 775 (1983); 4A Richard R. Powell, The Law of Real Property ¶621[6] (rev. ed. 1992); Annot., 22 A.L.R.4th 459 (1983).

United States v. 1500 Lincoln Avenue
United States Court of Appeals, Third Circuit, 1991
949 F.2d 73

ALITO, J. The United States appeals from an order dismissing its complaint seeking civil forfeiture of property containing a pharmacy that was used for the illegal distribution of prescription drugs. The pharmacy was owned as a tenancy by the entireties by a husband, who was convicted for the illegal activities, and his wife, who did not know about or consent to this use of the property. The district court held that the United States was not entitled at this time to forfeiture of any interest in the property. We will reverse.

I

In 1989, the United States filed a complaint seeking civil forfeiture under 21 U.S.C. §881 of property in Pittsburgh, Pennsylvania, on which the Pentown Pharmacy, Inc., was located. The complaint alleged that the property in question was transferred to A. Leonard Bernstein and his wife, Linda M. Bernstein, in October 1979. The complaint asserted that A. Leonard Bernstein, the president of the pharmacy, had used the property for the illegal diversion of various pharmaceutical drugs from 1984 to 1987. The affidavit submitted in support of the complaint asserted the following facts. . . . [Mr. Bernstein was indicted by a federal grand jury for 51 drug-related offenses, mainly selling prescription drugs without a prescription.] He eventually pled guilty to nine counts and was sentenced to ten years' imprisonment.

Mr. and Mrs. Bernstein filed an answer to the forfeiture complaint. Mrs. Bernstein averred that she had "no knowledge of any of the activity that took place at [the pharmacy] in that, even though she is a title owner of the property, she did not occupy the premises." Mr. Bernstein asserted that "the record of his conviction speaks for itself."

In a letter-brief submitted at the court's direction, the government conceded that Mrs. Bernstein had "a valid innocent owner defense" under 21 U.S.C. §881(a)(7), which permits forfeiture of any real property used in drug offenses except for any interest of an innocent owner. The government then discussed the extent of the interest in the property that it believed Mrs. Bernstein was entitled to retain. The government first observed that since Mr. Bernstein's interest was forfeitable and since a tenancy by the entireties is an "indivisible" "unitary" estate, the "logical conclusion" was that Mrs. Bernstein had no severable interest that she was entitled to retain. The government did not advocate this result, however, but instead maintained that her husband's illegal use of the property resulted in the severance of the entireties estate (i.e., conversion of the estate into a tenancy in common) and that Mrs. Bernstein was therefore entitled to keep a one-half interest in the property. Counsel for Mrs. Bernstein contended that the complaint should simply be dismissed.

The district court dismissed the complaint, holding "that a spouse's innocent owner defense bars a civil *in rem* forfeiture action against property held in a tenancy by the entirety." The court noted that under Pennsylvania law a tenant by the entireties has title to the whole property, not to a share of the property. Relying on United States v. 15621 S.W. 209th Avenue, 894 F.2d 1511 (11th Cir. 1990), the court reasoned that Mrs. Bernstein, as an innocent owner, was entitled to retain her interest in the property. Because she had "an interest in all of [the property]," the court concluded, no interest in the property was subject to forfeiture by the government. The court also held that Mr. Bernstein's illegal use of the property did not result in a severance of the estate under either Pennsylvania law or federal common law. The court accordingly entered an order dismissing the government's forfeiture complaint.

The government then moved to alter or amend the judgment and argued that the court should enter an order granting forfeiture of the property except to the extent of the interest of the innocent owner, Mrs. Bernstein. Relying on the Sixth Circuit's recent decision in United States v. 2525 Leroy Lane, 910 F.2d 343 (6th Cir. 1990), cert. denied, — U.S. — , 111 S. Ct. 1414, 113 L. Ed. 2d 467 (1991), the government contended that it should at least be able to obtain "any separate interest which [Mr. Bernstein] would be entitled to should he survive or divorce [Mrs. Bernstein] or should the entireties be severed in any other manner." The government maintained that its approach would "protect

[Mrs. Bernstein's] interest in the property to the fullest extent" because it would give her a life estate in the property and preserve her right of survivorship.

The district court denied the motion to alter or amend the judgment but noted in its opinion that the government could file a *lis pendens* against the property and thereby preserve its ability to seek forfeiture of any separate interest in the property that Mr. Bernstein might subsequently acquire as a result of the death of his wife or the severance of the tenancy. The government then filed this appeal.

II

On appeal, the government relies on the same argument advanced in its motion to alter or amend the judgment of the district court. The Bernsteins, on the other hand, appear to insist that nothing short of outright dismissal of the government's complaint would fully protect Mrs. Bernstein's interests.

In order to determine whether any interest in the property is subject to forfeiture, we first turn to the language of 21 U.S.C. §881(a)(7). That section states in pertinent part:

> The following shall be subject to forfeiture to the United States and no property right shall exist in them. . . . (7) All real property, including any right, title and interest . . . in the whole of any lot or tract of land and any appurtenances or improvements, which is used, or intended to be used, in any manner or part, to commit, or to facilitate the commission of, a violation of this title punishable by more than one year's imprisonment, except that no property shall be forfeited under this paragraph, to the extent of an interest of an owner, by reason of any act or omission established by that owner to have been committed or omitted without the knowledge or consent of that owner.

In short, if property is used to commit or facilitate a drug offense, the statute calls for forfeiture of any interest in that property except for the interest of an innocent owner.

Unfortunately, the statutory language does not clearly reveal what interest, if any, is subject to forfeiture in a case such as this. Indeed, the statutory language is susceptible to diametrically opposed interpretations. Because each spouse in a tenancy by the entireties is regarded as owning the whole estate, it may be argued, as the government initially suggested in the district court, that forfeiture of the guilty spouse's interest means forfeiture of the whole estate and consequently leaves nothing for the innocent spouse. On the other hand, it may be argued, as the district court reasoned, that the innocent spouse's retention of his or her interest in the tenancy means retention of the whole estate and therefore leaves nothing for the government to obtain by forfeiture. Intermediate interpretations — such as the government's contention earlier in this case that one-half of the property should be forfeited — are also possible.

Looking beyond the statutory language, we find nothing in the legislative history that provides an answer to the specific question presented here. The legislative history does show clearly that 21 U.S.C. §881(a)(7) and other new forfeiture provisions were added in 1984 because Congress felt that strong forfeiture laws were badly needed to combat rampant drug offenses. The Senate Report stated:

> Profit is the motivation for [drug trafficking] and it is through economic power that it is sustained and grows. . . . Today, few in Congress or the law enforcement community fail to recognize that the traditional sanctions of fine and imprisonment are inadequate to deter or punish the enormously profitable trade in dangerous drugs which, with its inevitable attendant violence is plaguing the country. Clearly, if law enforcement efforts to combat . . . drug trafficking are to be successful, they must include an attack on the economic aspects of these crimes. Forfeiture is the mechanism through which such an attack may be made. [S. Rep. 98-225, 98th Cong., 2d Sess. 191 (1983), reprinted in 1984 U.S.C.C.A.N. 3182, 3374.]

Thus, Congress clearly felt that "there is a strong governmental interest in obtaining full recovery of all forfeitable assets." Caplain & Drysdale Chartered v. United States, 491 U.S. 617, 631, 109 S. Ct. 2646, 2655, 105 L. Ed. 2d 528 (1989). At the same time, however, the insertion of the innocent owner defense in 21 U.S.C. §881(a)(7) shows that Congress did not want to extinguish the interests of innocent owners, and nothing in the legislative history discloses precisely how Congress wanted to balance the interest in forfeiture and the interest of an innocent owner in the circumstances presented by the case now before us.

Without any definitive guidance in the statutory language or the legislative history, we believe that we should adopt the interpretation that best serves the two goals that 21 U.S.C. §881(a)(7) was intended to promote: forfeiture of the property used in committing drug offenses and preservation of the property rights of innocent owners. In the present case, the innocent owner held title as a tenant by the entireties. As a tenant by the entireties, Mrs. Bernstein has the right to possess and use the whole property during her life and the right to obtain title in fee simple absolute if her cotenant predeceased her. Similarly, she had protection against a unilateral conveyance by her cotenant of his interest in the estate, as well as protection against a levy upon the property by any creditor of her cotenant. Clingerman v. Sadowski, 513 Pa. 179, 183-84, 519 A.2d 378, 380-81 (1986); Klebach v. Mellon Bank, N.A., 388 Pa. Super. 203, 208, 565 A.2d 448, 450 (1989), appeal granted, 527 Pa. 647, 593 A.2d 420 (Pa. 1990).

The range of possible interpretations that we must consider has been substantially narrowed as a result of the position taken by the government in its motion to alter or amend the judgment and on appeal. The government maintains that it is now entitled to forfeiture of Mr. Bernstein's interest in the tenancy by the entireties but that Mrs. Bernstein may retain full and exclusive use of the property during her life, protection against any alienation without her consent or any attempt to levy upon her husband's former interest, and the right to obtain title in fee simple absolute if her husband predeceases her. In light of the government's position, we need not consider possible interpretations of the statute that would result in a greater degree of forfeiture. Instead, we may limit our consideration to the interpretation now advanced by the government and those interpretations that would result in a lesser degree of forfeiture.

Two such interpretations have been suggested. As noted earlier, the Bernsteins argue that the complaint should simply be dismissed, and thus they appear to contend that the government may not obtain forfeiture of any interest in the property either now or at any future time. The district court and the Eleventh Circuit decision on which the district court relied, concluded that in a situation such as this the government is not entitled to the forfeiture of any interest from the tenants by the entireties but that the government may file a *lis pendens* and thereby preserve its right to seek forfeiture of any separate interest in the property that might later be acquired by the guilty spouse due to either the death of the innocent spouse or the severance of the estate. See United States v. 15621 S.W. 209th Avenue, 894 F.2d at 1516 n.6.

We believe that the interpretation advanced by the government best serves the dual purposes of 21 U.S.C. §881(a)(7). This interpretation permits the immediate forfeiture of the interest of the guilty spouse and thus serves the goal of forfeiting property used in illegal drug activities. At the same time, this interpretation fully protects all of the property rights that the innocent owner enjoyed under the tenancy by the entireties. The innocent owner retains full use and possession (indeed, *exclusive* use and possession) of the property during his or her lifetime. The innocent owner is also protected against any conveyance without his or her consent or any attempt to levy upon the interest formerly held by the guilty spouse. In addition, the innocent owner retains the right to obtain title in fee simple absolute if he or she is predeceased by the guilty spouse.

Neither the interpretation urged by the Bernsteins nor that adopted by the district court and the Eleventh Circuit serves the dual purposes of 21 U.S.C. §881(a)(7). The interpretation recommended by the Bernsteins — outright denial of forfeiture — completely frustrates the strong interest in forfeiture of property used in committing drug offenses. The approach adopted by the district court and the Eleventh Circuit — denial of forfeiture but recognition of the government's ability to file a *lis pendens* and seek forfeiture at a later time — likewise frustrates the strong governmental interest in forfeiture since it permits a guilty spouse during his or her lifetime to retain title as a tenant by the entireties in property that he or she has used in illegal drug activities. Moreover, this interpretation would create substantial procedural difficulties because it requires the government to postpone prosecution of civil forfeiture proceedings until the guilty spouse acquires a separate interest in the property, an event that may not occur until many years after the criminal conduct. Suppose, for example, that the government filed a complaint seeking forfeiture of the property interest of a spouse who it believed had used the property in illegal drug activities but who had not been convicted on criminal charges. Under the approach taken by the district court and the Eleventh Circuit, the complaint would be dismissed, but the government could file a *lis pendens*. Suppose that many years later the innocent spouse died or the tenancy by the entireties was severed by divorce. In order to prevent the guilty spouse from taking title in fee simple absolute or as a tenant in common, the government would have to refile its forfeiture complaint and prove the underlying criminal conduct long after it occurred. Proof of the relevant facts after such delay would often be extremely difficult if not impossible. Moreover, we do not see what purpose would be served by postponing adjudication of the government's right to forfeiture of the interest of the guilty spouse until this time, rather than adjudicating that issue when the evidence was still fresh.

Accordingly, we hold that the district court erred in dismissing the complaint in this case. On remand, the district court should determine whether Mr. Bernstein's interest is subject to forfeiture irrespective of Mrs. Bernstein's innocent owner defense. If the court decides that it is, the court should enter an order forfeiting that interest but preserving Mrs. Bernstein's right to full and exclusive use and possession of the property during her life, her protection against conveyance of or execution by third parties upon her husband's former interest, and her survivorship right.

NOTES AND QUESTION

1. The Drug Abuse Prevention and Control Act provides for a civil forfeiture proceeding in rem. 21 U.S.C. §881 (Supp. 1992). Upon proof that the property is used in an illegal drug transaction, the property itself is forfeited, except for any interest in an innocent owner. The act also provides for criminal forfeiture of property by a person convicted of illegal drug activity (id. §853). Each element of the criminal offense must be proved beyond a reasonable doubt. Criminal forfeiture is in

personam; it is imposed as punishment and only the defendant's interest in the property is forfeited. The federal RICO statute also provides for criminal forfeiture of property used in dealing in drugs or acquired with funds from the activity. 18 U.S.C. §1963 (Supp. 1992). See Note, Real Property Forfeitures as a Weapon in the Government's War on Drugs: A Failure to Protect Innocent Ownership Rights, 72 B.U. L. Rev. 217 (1992); Comment, The Scope of Real Property Forfeiture for Drug-Related Crimes Under the Comprehensive Forfeiture Act, 137 U. Pa. L. Rev. 303 (1988).

2. Suppose that the Bernsteins had owned the pharmacy as joint tenants. What result?

3. In State v. One 1984 Toyota Truck, 311 Md. 171, 533 A.2d 659, 84 A.L.R.4th 601 (1987), the court held that a Toyota truck, owned by husband and wife in tenancy by the entirety and used by the husband, without the wife's knowledge, to deliver drugs was not subject to forfeiture under the state's Controlled Substances Act. The court reasoned that "neither tenant holds a separate interest, there are no divisible parts, and therefore but one owner," and the tenancy cannot be severed without the consent of both parties.

b. Termination of Marriage by Divorce

At common law, upon divorce property of the spouses remained the property of the spouse holding title. Property held by the spouses as tenants in common or as joint tenants remained in such co-ownership. Because the unity of marriage was severed by divorce, property held in tenancy by the entirety was converted into a tenancy in common. Inasmuch as the husband owed the wife a duty of support, a duty undertaken upon marriage, the wife was usually entitled to a continuation of support (called alimony), though it might be denied her if she was at fault.

The common law, then, placed great emphasis on the way title was held. Where the wage earner was the husband, probably most property other than the family home was held in the husband's name. The husband's wages (and what he bought with them) belonged to the husband unless he voluntarily made a gift to the wife. The common law largely ignored the wife's contribution of services in the home, although to some extent the wife was compensated by giving her continuing support in the form of alimony. There was, however, no recognition at common law of marriage as a partnership of shared assets acquired during the marriage.

In the last 20 years, dramatic changes have taken place in divorce law. Before 1970, divorce could be granted only if one party was found to have committed some marital fault, such as extreme cruelty or adultery. In 1970, California introduced no-fault divorce and in the years since, no-fault divorce has swept through the legislatures of almost every state. No-fault divorce brought with it changes in property division upon divorce. The common law division of property (according to how title is held) has been abrogated in every common law property state. Legislatures have replaced it with a rule of "equitable distribution." Under the rule of equitable distribution, property is divided by the court, in its discretion, on equitable principles. Although there are many differences in detail among the states, section 307 (Alternative A) of the Uniform Marriage and Divorce Act (1973) is representative of equitable division statutes. It provides:

> [T]he court, without regard to marital misconduct, shall . . . finally equitably apportion between the parties the property and assets belonging to either or both however and whenever acquired, and whether the title thereto is in the name of the husband or wife or both. In making apportionment the court shall consider the duration of the marriage, and prior marriage of either party, antenuptial agreement of the parties, the age, health, station, occupation, amount and sources of income, vocational skills, employability, estate, liabilities, and needs of each of the parties, custodial provisions, whether the apportionment is in lieu of or in addition to maintenance, and the opportunity of each for future acquisition of capital assets and income. The court shall also consider the contribution or dissipation of each party in the acquisition, preservation, depreciation, or appreciation in value of the respective estates, and the contribution of a spouse as a homemaker or to the family unit.

The concept of fault is sometimes expressly included, or ignored, or, as in the Uniform Act, expressly excluded as a factor to guide equitable division.

Many equitable division statutes authorize a court to divide all property owned by the spouses, regardless of the time and manner of acquisition. Other statutes authorize a court to divide only "marital property." Marital property is defined in some states to include all property acquired during marriage by whatever means (earnings, gifts, or inheritances); in others it includes only property acquired from earnings of either spouse during marriage. This last approach is based on the principle underlying community property — that marriage is a partnership and property acquired from earnings of the spouses during marriage should be equally divided upon dissolution of the partnership.[17]

The idea that marriage involves a lifelong obligation of the husband to support the wife after divorce has also been discarded in modern

17. On the community property system, which is the law in eight states, see pages 404-411. Wisconsin has adopted the Uniform Marital Property Act (1983), which is based on community property principles. See pages 403-404.

divorce legislation. Alimony is largely viewed today as support for a limited period of time until the spouse can enter the job market and become self-sufficient (called "rehabilitative alimony"). Section 308(a) of the Uniform Marriage and Divorce Act, for example, provides that maintenance shall be granted only if the spouse seeking maintenance

(1) lacks sufficient property to provide for his reasonable needs; and
(2) is unable to support himself through appropriate employment or is the custodian of a child whose condition or circumstances make it appropriate that the custodian not be required to seek employment outside the home.

In almost all states providing for equitable distribution of property upon divorce, alimony (or maintenance) may also be granted where special needs exist. In some states permanent alimony may be granted after a long marriage where it is appropriate to balance an inequity in the distribution of the property.

In equitably dividing property, there is a movement toward equal distribution of marital property upon divorce. In some states equal division is required, in others it is a presumptive rule, in still others it is the starting point for the application of the factors enumerated in the statute (such as special need), and in a few states equal division is a presumptive rule only in a long marriage. Equal division presumptively gives full valuation to the home-making services of one spouse. For an examination of cases making awards upon divorce, see Suzanne Reynolds, The Relationship of Property Division and Alimony: The Division of Property to Address Need, 56 Fordham L. Rev. 827 (1988); Symposium, Equitable Distribution in New York: Results and Reform, 57 Brooklyn L. Rev. 621 (1991); Symposium, Property Division at Divorce, 23 Fam. L.Q. 147 (1989). For a state-by-state analysis of equitable distribution statutes, see J. Thomas Oldham, Divorce, Separation and the Distribution of Property (1989).

One of the earliest advocates of equal division of marital property upon divorce in accordance with gender-neutral rules, Professor Lenore Weitzman, discovered in an empirical study of no-fault divorce that equal division at divorce has not worked to put divorcing wives in as good a position as their husbands. See Lenore J. Weitzman, The Divorce Revolution (1985). The fundamental reason, she suggests, is that most wives give priority to their family roles, while husbands enhance their careers.

If the divorce rules do not give her a share of his enhanced earning capacity (through alimony and child support awards), and if divorce rules expect her to enter the labor market as she is, with few skills, outdated experience, no seniority, and no time for retraining, and if she continues to have the major burden of caring for young children after divorce, it is easy to

> understand why the divorced woman is likely to be much worse off than her
> former husband. [Id. at xi.]

Dean Herma Hill Kay argues that the law should encourage women's economic independence and discourage women from assuming the traditional homemaker's role. To that end, while Kay favors support awards for older women whose expectations arose under a different marital property system, she opposes support awards in divorce proceedings for women who now make "economically disabling" choices, such as homemaking. She favors joint custody decrees making fathers equally responsible with mothers for child-rearing after divorce. If these positions are taken by courts, Dean Kay believes, the "large disparity between men's and women's household standard of living that Weitzman discovered . . . should be greatly reduced." Herma H. Kay, Equality and Difference: A Perspective on No-Fault Divorce and Its Aftermath, 56 U. Cin. L. Rev. 1, 86 (1987). For a collection of essays on divorce reform laws, see Divorce Reform at the Crossroads (Stephen D. Sugarman & Herma H. Kay eds. 1990), reviewed by J. Thomas Oldham in Putting Asunder in the 1990s, 80 Cal. L. Rev. 1091 (1992).

See also Grace G. Blumberg, Reworking the Past, Imagining the Future: On Jacob's Silent Revolution, 16 Law & Soc. Inquiry 115 (1991); June Carbone & Margaret F. Brinig, Rethinking Marriage: Feminist Ideology, Economic Change, and Divorce Reform, 65 Tul. L. Rev. 953 (1991).

In re Marriage of Graham
Supreme Court of Colorado, 1978
574 P.2d 75

Lee, J. This case presents the novel question of whether in a marriage dissolution proceeding a master's degree in business administration (M.B.A.) constitutes marital property which is subject to division by the court. In its opinion in Graham v. Graham, Colo. App., 555 P.2d 527, the Colorado Court of Appeals held that it was not. We affirm the judgment.

The Uniform Dissolution of Marriage Act requires that a court shall divide marital property, without regard to marital misconduct, in such proportions as the court deems just after considering all relevant factors. The Act defines marital property as follows:

> For purposes of this article only, "marital property" means all property acquired by either spouse subsequent to the marriage except:
>   (a) Property acquired by gift, bequest, devise, or descent;
>   (b) Property acquired in exchange for property acquired prior to the

marriage or in exchange for property acquired by gift, bequest, devise, or descent;

(c) Property acquired by a spouse after a decree of legal separation; and

(d) Property excluded by valid agreement of the parties. [Section 14-10-113(2), C.R.S. 1973.]

The parties to this proceeding were married on August 5, 1968, in Denver, Colorado. Throughout the six-year marriage, Anne P. Graham, wife and petitioner here, was employed full-time as an airline steward-ess. She is still so employed. Her husband, Dennis J. Graham, respon-dent, worked part-time for most of the marriage, although his main pur-suit was his education. He attended school for approximately three and one-half years of the marriage, acquiring both a bachelor of science de-gree in engineering physics and a master's degree in business adminis-tration at the University of Colorado. Following graduation, he obtained a job as an executive assistant with a large corporation at a starting salary of $14,000 per year.

The trial court determined that during the marriage petitioner con-tributed seventy percent of the financial support, which was used both for family expenses and for her husband's education. No marital assets were accumulated during the marriage. In addition, the Grahams to-gether managed an apartment house and petitioner did the majority of housework and cooked most of the meals for the couple. No children were born during the marriage.

The parties jointly filed a petition for dissolution, on February 4, 1974, in Boulder County District Court. Petitioner did not make a claim for maintenance or for attorney fees. After a hearing on October 24, 1974, the trial court found, as a matter of law, that an education ob-tained by one spouse during a marriage is jointly-owned property to which the other spouse has a property right. The future earnings value of the M.B.A. to respondent was evaluated at $82,836 and petitioner was awarded $33,134 of this amount, payable in monthly installments of $100.[18]

The court of appeals reversed, holding that an education is not itself "property" subject to division under the Act, although it was one factor

18. The appellee's brief states that, at trial, an expert for the wife testified that an M.B.A. degree holder could expect to earn $178,000 more than the holder of a B.A. over his lifetime. The court discounted this to a present value of $82,836. The trial court awarded Anne 40 percent of $82,836, arrived at this way: Dennis pursued education 40 hours a week and worked part-time 20 hours a week, while Anne worked 40 hours a week. Thus Anne's contribution of the total time the couple invested in acquiring the M.B.A. degree was 40 percent. The trial court ordered Anne to be paid $33,134 over 27½ years at a rate of $100 a month. See Note, Graduate Degree Rejected as Marital Property Subject to Division Upon Divorce: In re Marriage of Graham, 11 Conn. L. Rev. 62, 65 n.12 (1978); Case Comment, 12 J. Marshall J. Prac. & Proc. 709, 713 n.27 (1979).

Do you have any criticism of the trial court's valuation method? — EDS.

to be considered in determining maintenance or in arriving at an equitable property division.

I

The purpose of the division of marital property is to allocate to each spouse what equitably belongs to him or her. See H. Clark, Domestic Relations §14.8. The division is committed to the sound discretion of the trial court and there is no rigid mathematical formula that the court must adhere to. Carlson v. Carlson, 178 Colo. 283, 497 P.2d 1006; Greer v. Greer, 32 Colo. App. 196, 510 P.2d 905. An appellate court will alter a division of property only if the trial court abuses its discretion. This court, however, is empowered at all times to interpret Colorado statutes.

The legislature intended the term "property" to be broadly inclusive, as indicated by its use of the qualifying adjective "all" in section 14-10-113(2). Previous Colorado cases have given "property" a comprehensive meaning, as typified by the following definition: "In short it embraces anything and everything which may belong to a man and in the ownership of which he has a right to be protected by law." Las Animas County High School District v. Raye, 144 Colo. 367, 356 P.2d 237.

Nonetheless, there are necessary limits upon what may be considered "property," and we do not find any indication in the Act that the concept as used by the legislature is other than that usually understood to be embodied within the term. One helpful definition is "everything that has an exchangeable value or which goes to make up wealth or estate." Black's Law Dictionary 1382 (rev. 4th ed. 1968). In Ellis v. Ellis, Colo., 552 P.2d 506, this court held that military retirement pay was not property for the reason that it did not have any of the elements of cash surrender value, loan value, redemption value, lump sum value, or value realizable after death. The court of appeals has considered other factors as well in deciding whether something falls within the concept, particularly whether it can be assigned, sold, transferred, conveyed, or pledged, or whether it terminates on the death of the owner. In re Marriage of Ellis, 36 Colo. App. 234, 538 P.2d 1347, aff'd, Ellis v. Ellis, supra.

An educational degree, such as an M.B.A., is simply not encompassed even by the broad views of the concept of "property." It does not have an exchange value or any objective transferable value on an open market. It is personal to the holder. It terminates on death of the holder and is not inheritable. It cannot be assigned, sold, transferred, conveyed, or pledged. An advanced degree is a cumulative product of many years of previous education, combined with diligence and hard work. It may not be acquired by the mere expenditure of money. It is simply an intellectual achievement that may potentially assist in the future acquisition of property. In our view, it has none of the attributes of property in the usual sense of that term.

II

Our interpretation is in accord with cases in other jurisdictions. We have been unable to find any decision, even in community property states, which appears to have held that an education of one spouse is marital property to be divided on dissolution. This contention was dismissed in Todd v. Todd, 272 Cal. App. 2d 786, 78 Cal. Rptr. 131 (Ct. App.), where it was held that a law degree is not a community property asset capable of division, partly because it "cannot have monetary value placed upon it." Similarly, it has been recently held that a person's earning capacity, even where enhanced by a law degree financed by the other spouse, "should not be recognized as a separate, particular item of property." Stern v. Stern, 66 N.J. 340, 331 A.2d 257.

Other cases cited have dealt only with related issues. For example, in awarding alimony, as opposed to dividing property, one court has found that an education is one factor to be considered. Daniels v. Daniels, 20 Ohio Op. 2d 458, 185 N.E.2d 773 (Ct. App.). In another case, the wife supported the husband while he went to medical school. Nail v. Nail, 486 S.W.2d 761 (Tex.). The question was whether the accrued goodwill of his medical practice was marital property, and the court held it was not, inasmuch as goodwill was based on the husband's personal skill, reputation, and experience. Contra, Mueller v. Mueller, 144 Cal. App. 2d 245, 301 P.2d 90; see Annot., 52 A.L.R.3d 1344.

III

The trial court relied on Greer v. Greer, 32 Colo. App. 196, 510 P.2d 905, for its determination that an education is "property." In that case, a six-year marriage was dissolved in which the wife worked as a teacher while the husband obtained a medical degree. The parties had accumulated marital property. The trial court awarded the wife alimony of $150 per month for four years. The court of appeals found this to be proper, whether considered as an adjustment of property rights based upon the wife's financial contribution to the marriage, or as an award of alimony in gross. The court there stated that ". . . [i]t must be considered as a substitute for, or in lieu of, the wife's rights in the husband's property. . . ." We note that the court did not determine that the medical education itself was divisible property. The case is distinguishable from the instant case in that here there was no accumulation of marital property and the petitioner did not seek maintenance [alimony].

IV

A spouse who provides financial support while the other spouse acquires an education is not without a remedy. Where there is marital property to be divided, such contribution to the education of the other spouse may be taken into consideration by the court. Greer v. Greer, supra. See also Carlson v. Carlson, 178 Colo. 283, 497 P.2d 1006. Here, we again note that no marital property had been accumulated by the parties. Further, if maintenance is sought and a need is demonstrated, the trial court may make an award based on all relevant factors. Section 14-10-114(2). Certainly, among the relevant factors to be considered is the contribution of the spouse seeking maintenance to the education of the other spouse from whom the maintenance is sought. Again, we note that in this case petitioner sought no maintenance from respondent.

The judgment is affirmed.

CARRIGAN, J. I respectfully dissent.

As a matter of economic reality the most valuable asset acquired by either party during this six-year marriage was the husband's increased earning capacity. There is no dispute that this asset resulted from his having obtained Bachelor of Science and Master of Business Administration degrees while married. These degrees, in turn, resulted in large part from the wife's employment which contributed about 70% of the couple's total income. Her earnings not only provided her husband's support but also were "invested" in his education in the sense that she assumed the role of breadwinner so that he would have the time and funds necessary to obtain his education.

The case presents the not-unfamiliar pattern of the wife who, willing to sacrifice for a more secure family financial future, works to educate her husband, only to be awarded a divorce decree shortly after he is awarded his degree. The issue here is whether traditional, narrow concepts of what constitutes "property" render the courts impotent to provide a remedy for an obvious injustice.

In cases such as this, equity demands that courts seek extraordinary remedies to prevent extraordinary injustice. If the parties had remained married long enough after the husband had completed his postgraduate education so that they could have accumulated substantial property, there would have been no problem. In that situation abundant precedent authorized the trial court, in determining how much of the marital property to allocate to the wife, to take into account her contributions to her husband's earning capacity. Greer v. Greer, 32 Colo. App. 196, 510 P.2d 905 (1973) (wife supported husband through medical school); In re Marriage of Vanet, 544 S.W.2d 236 (Mo. App. 1976) (wife was breadwinner while husband was in law school).

A husband's future income earning potential, sometimes as indicated by the goodwill value of a professional practice, may be considered in deciding property division or alimony matters, and the wife's award may be increased on the ground that the husband probably will have substantial future earnings. Todd v. Todd, 272 Cal. App. 2d 786, 78

Cal. Rptr. 131 (1969) (goodwill of husband's law practice); Golden v. Golden, 270 Cal. App. 2d 401, 75 Cal. Rptr. 735 (1969) (goodwill of husband's medical practice); Mueller v. Mueller, 144 Cal. App. 2d 245, 301 P.2d 90 (1956) (goodwill of husband's dental lab); In re Marriage of Goger, 27 Or. App. 729, 557 P.2d 46 (1976) (potential earnings of husband's dental practice); In re Marriage of Lukens, 16 Wash. App. 481, 558 P.2d 279 (1976) (goodwill of husband's medical practice indicated future earning capacity).

Similarly, the wife's contributions to enhancing the husband's financial status or earning capacity have been considered in awarding alimony and maintenance. Kraus v. Kraus, 159 Colo. 331, 411 P.2d 240 (1966); Shapiro v. Shapiro, 115 Colo. 505, 176 P.2d 363 (1946). The majority opinion emphasizes that in this case no maintenance was requested. However, the Colorado statute would seem to preclude an award of maintenance here, for it restricts the court's power to award maintenance to cases where the spouse seeking it is unable to support himself or herself. Section 14-10-114, C.R.S. 1973.[19]

While the majority opinion focuses on whether the husband's master's degree is marital "property" subject to division, it is not the degree itself which constitutes the asset in question. Rather it is the increase in the husband's earning power concomitant to that degree which is the asset conferred on him by his wife's efforts. That increased earning capacity was the asset appraised in the economist's expert opinion testimony as having a discounted present value of $82,000.

Unquestionably the law, in other contexts, recognizes future earning capacity as an asset whose wrongful deprivation is compensable. Thus one who tortiously destroys or impairs another's future earning capacity must pay as damages the amount the injured party has lost in anticipated future earnings. Nemer v. Anderson, 151 Colo. 411, 378 P.2d 841 (1963); Abram, Personal Injury Damages in Colorado, 35 Colo. L. Rev. 332, 338 (1963).

Where a husband is killed, the widow is entitled to recover for loss of his future support damages based in part on the present value of his anticipated future earnings, which may be computed by taking into account probable future increases in his earning capacity. See United

19. Colo. Rev. Stat. §14-10-114(1) (1973) provides that in a proceeding for dissolution of marriage,

> the court may grant a maintenance order for either spouse only if it finds that the spouse seeking maintenance:
>
> (a) Lacks sufficient property, including marital property apportioned to him, to provide for his reasonable needs; and
>
> (b) Is unable to support himself through appropriate employment or is the custodian of a child whose condition or circumstances make it appropriate that the custodian not be required to seek employment outside the home.

Uniform Marriage and Divorce Act §308(a) is substantially identical — Eds.

States v. Sommers, 351 F.2d 354 (10th Cir. 1965); Good v. Chance, 39
Colo. App. 70, 565 P.2d 217 (1977). See also Colo. J.I. (Civil) 10:3.

The day before the divorce the wife had a legally recognized interest in her husband's earning capacity. Perhaps the wife might have a
remedy in a separate action based on implied debt, quasi-contract, unjust enrichment, or some similar theory. See, e.g., Dass v. Epplen, 162
Colo. 60, 424 P.2d 779 (1967). Nevertheless, the law favors settling all
aspects of a dispute in a single action where that is possible. Therefore I
would affirm the trial court's award.

NOTES

1. In Mahoney v. Mahoney, 91 N.J. 488, 453 A.2d 527 (1982), the
New Jersey court declined to recognize a professional degree as marital
property. It found such an item too speculative to value. In addition, the
court thought the idea of a spousal investment in human capital de-
meaned the concept of marriage. Instead, the court ordered that the
working spouse be given "reimbursement alimony."

> To provide a fair and effective means of compensating a supporting
> spouse who has suffered a loss or reduction of support, or has incurred a
> lower standard of living, or has been deprived of a better standard of living
> in the future, the Court now introduces the concept of reimbursement ali-
> mony into divorce proceedings. The concept properly accords with the
> Court's belief that regardless of the appropriateness of permanent alimony
> or the presence or absence of marital property to be equitably distributed,
> there will be circumstances where a supporting spouse should be reimbursed
> for the financial contributions he or she made to the spouse's successful pro-
> fessional training. Such reimbursement alimony should cover *all* financial
> contributions towards the former spouse's education, including household
> expenses, educational costs, school travel expenses and any other contribu-
> tions used by the supported spouse in obtaining his or her degree or li-
> cense. . . .

If reimbursement is the remedy to the "diploma dilemma," is the
amount of reimbursement determined by adding the actual cost of education to the opportunity costs incurred in forgoing other employment
during the period in professional school? For example, assume that the
actual cost of a legal education for a spouse is $5,000 and that the spouse
could have earned over a three-year period, had he or she not gone to
law school, $36,000; the total sum is $41,000. This sum equals the cost
of the investment in expected future earnings attributable to the law
degree. Assuming that the spouses during marriage combined their
earning power through the division of labor to maximize total utility in

the provision of mutual consumption and savings in the form of human capital, each spouse contributed equally to the cost of investment in the degree. After divorce the lawyer spouse will receive returns from an investment costing $41,000. The lawyer spouse could be required to compensate the other spouse $20,500 for the latter's contribution in making the investment. Such a remedy deprives the nonlawyer spouse of the particular investment made by the couple but gives such spouse capital to make a similar investment if desired (for example, the nonlawyer spouse may acquire a professional degree). See Deborah A. Batts, Remedy Refocus: In Search of Equity in "Enhanced Spouse/Other Spouse" Divorces, 63 N.Y.U. L. Rev. 751 (1988).

    2. Almost all courts that have ruled on the issue agree either with *Graham* or *Mahoney*. New York is one of the exceptions. In O'Brien v. O'Brien, 66 N.Y.2d 576, 489 N.E.2d 712, 498 N.Y.S.2d 743 (1985), the court had before it the question whether a husband's medical license constituted marital property within the meaning of the state's equitable distribution law. New York Domestic Relations Law §236 (McKinney 1986) provides that in making an equitable distribution of marital property

> the court shall consider: . . . (6) any equitable claim to, interest in, or direct or indirect contribution made to the marital property by the party not having title, including joint efforts or expenditures and *contributions and services as a spouse*, parent, wage earner and homemaker, and *to the career or career potential of the other party* [and] . . . (9) the impossibility or difficulty of evaluating any component asset or any interest in a business, corporation or *profession*. [Emphasis added.]

The court held that these italicized words

> mean exactly what they say: that an interest in a profession or professional career potential is marital property which may be represented by direct or indirect contributions of the non-title-holding spouse, including financial contributions and nonfinancial contributions made by caring for the home and family. . . . The Legislature has decided, by its explicit reference in the statute to the contributions of one spouse to the other's profession or career . . . , that these contributions represent investments in the economic partnership of the marriage and that the product of the parties' joint efforts, the professional license, should be considered marital property. [66 N.Y.2d at 584, 489 N.E.2d at 716, 498 N.Y.S.2d at 747.]

The court rejected the argument that reimbursement was an adequate remedy. The court viewed reimbursement of financial contributions as inequitable to the supporting spouse. "By parity of reasoning, a spouse's down payment on real estate or contribution to the purchase of securities would be limited to the money contributed, without any remuneration for any incremental value in the asset because of price appreciation." 66 N.Y.2d at 588, 489 N.E.2d at 718, 498 N.Y.S.2d at 749.

Elkus v. Elkus

Supreme Court of New York, Appellate Division,
First Department, 1991
169 A.D.2d 134, 572 N.Y.S.2d 901

ROSENBERGER, J. In this matrimonial action, the plaintiff, Frederica von Stade Elkus, moved for an order determining, prior to trial, whether her career and/or celebrity status constituted marital property subject to equitable distribution. The parties have already stipulated to mutual judgments of divorce terminating their seventeen year marriage and to joint custody of their two minor children. The trial on the remaining economic issues has been stayed pending the outcome of this appeal from the order of the Supreme Court, which had determined that the enhanced value of the plaintiff's career and/or celebrity status was not marital property subject to equitable distribution. Contrary to the conclusion reached by the Supreme Court, we find that to the extent the defendant's contributions and efforts led to an increase in the value of the plaintiff's career, this appreciation was a product of the marital partnership, and, therefore, marital property subject to equitable distribution.

At the time of her marriage to the defendant on February 9, 1973, the plaintiff had just embarked on her career, performing minor roles with the Metropolitan Opera Company. During the course of the marriage, the plaintiff's career succeeded dramatically and her income rose accordingly. In the first year of the marriage, she earned $2,250. In 1989, she earned $621,878. She is now a celebrated artist with the Metropolitan Opera, as well as an international recording artist, concert and television performer. She has garnered numerous awards, and has performed for the President of the United States.

During the marriage, the defendant travelled with the plaintiff throughout the world, attending and critiquing her performances and rehearsals, and photographed her for album covers and magazine articles. The defendant was also the plaintiff's voice coach and teacher for ten years of the marriage. He states that he sacrificed his own career as a singer and teacher to devote himself to the plaintiff's career and to the lives of their young children, and that his efforts enabled the plaintiff to become one of the most celebrated opera singers in the world. Since the plaintiff's career and/or celebrity status increased in value during the marriage due in part to his contributions, the defendant contends that he is entitled to equitable distribution of this marital property.

The Supreme Court disagreed, refusing to extend the holding in O'Brien v. O'Brien, 66 N.Y.2d 576, 498 N.Y.S.2d 743, 489 N.E.2d 712, in which the Court of Appeals determined that a medical license constituted marital property subject to equitable distribution, to the plaintiff's career as an opera singer. The court found that since the defendant enjoyed a substantial life style during the marriage and since he would be sufficiently compensated through distribution of the parties' other assets, the plaintiff's career was not marital property.

There is a paucity of case law and no appellate authority in New York governing the issue of whether a career as a performing artist, and its accompanying celebrity status, constitute marital property subject to equitable distribution. The plaintiff maintains that since her career and celebrity status are not licensed, are not entities which are owned like a business, nor are protected interests which are subject to due process of law, they are not marital property. In our view, neither the Domestic Relations Law, nor relevant case law, allows for such a limited interpretation of the term marital property.

Domestic Relations Law §236[B][1][c] broadly defines marital property as property acquired during the marriage "regardless of the form in which title is held." In enacting the Equitable Distribution Law (L. 1980, ch. 281, §9), the Legislature created a radical change in the traditional method of distributing property upon the dissolution of a marriage (Price v. Price, 69 N.Y.2d 8, 14, 511 N.Y.S.2d 219, 503 N.E.2d 684). By broadly defining the term "marital property," it intended to give effect to the "economic partnership" concept of the marriage relationship (id. at 15, 511 N.Y.S.2d 219, 503 N.E.2d 684; Majauskas v. Majauskas, 61 N.Y.2d 481, 474 N.Y.S.2d 699, 463 N.E.2d 15). It then left it to the courts to determine what interests constitute marital property.

Things of value acquired during marriage are marital property even though they may fall outside the scope of traditional property concepts (O'Brien v. O'Brien, supra; Florescue, "Market Value," Professional Licenses and Marital Property: A Dilemma in Search of a Horn, 1982 NY St Bar Assn Fam L Rev 13 [Dec.]). The statutory definition of marital property does not mandate that it be an asset with an exchange value or be salable, assignable or transferable. (Freed, Brandes and Weidman, "What is Marital Property?," NYLJ, December 5, 1990, p.3, col. 1.) The property may be tangible or intangible (Id.).

Medical licenses have been held to enhance the earning capacity of their holders, so as to enable the other spouse who made direct or indirect contributions to their acquisition, to share their value as part of equitable distribution (O'Brien v. O'Brien, supra; Maloney v. Maloney, 137 A.D.2d 666, 524 N.Y.S.2d 758; Raff v. Raff, 120 A.D.2d 507, 501 N.Y.S.2d 707). A Medical Board Certification (Savasta v. Savasta, 146 Misc. 2d 101, 549 N.Y.S.2d 544 (Sup. Ct. Nassau Co.)), a law degree, (Cronin v. Cronin, 131 Misc. 2d 879, 502 N.Y.S.2d 368 (Sup. Ct. Nassau

Co.), an accounting degree (Vanasco v. Vanasco, 132 Misc. 2d 227, 503 N.Y.S.2d 480 (Sup. Ct. Nassau Co.), a podiatry practice (Morton v. Morton, 130 A.D.2d 558, 515 N.Y.S.2d 499), the licensing and certification of a physician's assistant (Morimando v. Morimando, 145 A.D.2d 609, 536 N.Y.S.2d 701), a Masters degree in teaching (McGowan v. McGowan, 142 A.D.2d 355, 535 N.Y.S.2d 990) and a fellowship in the Society of Actuaries (McAlpine v. McAlpine, 143 Misc. 2d 30, 539 N.Y.S.2d 680 (Sup. Ct. Suffolk Co.) have also been held to constitute marital property.

Although the plaintiff's career, unlike that of the husband in *O'Brien*, is not licensed, the *O'Brien* court did not restrict its holding to professions requiring a license or degree. In reaching its conclusion that a medical license constitutes marital property, the *O'Brien* court referred to the language contained in Domestic Relations Law §236 which provides that in making an equitable distribution of marital property,

> the court shall consider: . . . (6) any equitable claim to, interest in, or direct or indirect contribution made to the acquisition of such marital property by the party not having title, including joint efforts or expenditures and contributions and services as a spouse, parent, wage earner and homemaker, and *to the career or career potential* of the other party [and] . . . (9) the impossibility or difficulty of evaluating any component asset or any interest in a business, corporation or profession (Domestic Relations law §236[B][5][d][6], [9]) (emphasis added).

The court also cited §236[B][5][e] which provides that where equitable distribution of marital property is appropriate, but "the distribution of an interest in a business, corporation or profession would be contrary to law," the court shall make a distributive award in lieu of an actual distribution of the property (O'Brien v. O'Brien, supra, 66 N.Y.2d at 584, 498 N.Y.S.2d 743, 489 N.E.2d 712).

The Court of Appeals' analysis of the statute is equally applicable here. "The words mean exactly what they say: that an interest in a profession or professional career potential is marital property which may be represented by direct or indirect contributions of the non-title-holding spouse, including financial contributions and nonfinancial contributions made by caring for the home and family" (O'Brien v. O'Brien, supra at 584, 498 N.Y.S.2d 743, 489 N.E.2d 712). Nothing in the statute or the *O'Brien* decision supports the plaintiff's contention that her career and/or celebrity status are not marital property. The purpose behind the enactment of the legislation was to prevent inequities which previously occurred upon the dissolution of a marriage. Any attempt to limit marital property to professions which are licensed would only serve to discriminate against the spouses of those engaged in other areas of employment. Such a distinction would fail to carry out the premise upon which equitable distribution is based, i.e., that a marriage is an economic partnership to which both parties contribute, as spouse, parent, wage earner or homemaker (Assembly Memorandum, 1980 NY Legis Ann, at 130; Governor's Memorandum of Approval, 1980 McKinney's Session Laws of NY, at 1863; O'Brien v. O'Brien, supra at 585, 498 N.Y.S.2d 743, 489 N.E.2d 712).

In Golub v. Golub, 139 Misc. 2d 440, 527 N.Y.S.2d 946 (Sup. Ct. New York Co.), the Supreme Court agreed with the defendant husband that the increase in value in the acting and modeling career of his wife, Marisa Berenson, was marital property subject to equitable distribution as a result of his contributions thereto. Like Ms. von Stade, Ms. Berenson claimed that since her celebrity status was neither "professional" nor a "license," and, since her show business career was subject to fluctuation, it should not be considered "marital property."

The court disagreed, concluding at p.447, 527 N.Y.S.2d 946 that "the skills of an artisan, actor, professional athlete or any person whose expertise in his or her career has enabled him or her to become an exceptional wage earner should be valued as marital property subject to equitable distribution." (See, also, Getz v. Getz, NYLJ, March 2, 1989, p.28, col. 6 [Sup. Ct. Westchester Co.].) As the *Golub* court found, it is the enhanced earning capacity that a medical license affords its holder that the *O'Brien* court deemed valuable, not the document itself. There is no rational basis upon which to distinguish between a degree, a license, or any other special skill that generates substantial income.

As further noted by the *Golub* court, there is tremendous potential for financial gain from the commercial exploitation of famous personalities. While the plaintiff insists that she will never be asked to endorse a product, this is simply speculation. More and more opportunities have presented themselves to her as she continues to advance in her career. The career of the plaintiff is unique, in that she has risen to the top in a field where success is rarely achieved.

Like the parties here, after Joe Piscopo and his wife married in 1973, they focused on one goal — the facilitation of his rise to stardom (Piscopo v. Piscopo, 231 N.J. Super. 576, 555 A.2d 1190, aff'd, 232 N.J. Super. 559, 557 A.2d 1040, certification denied, 117 N.J. 156, 564 A.2d 875). The defendant wife claimed that her husband's celebrity goodwill was a distributable asset and that she was entitled to a share in his excess earning capacity to which she contributed as homemaker, caretaker of their child, and sounding board for his artistic ideas.

Rejecting Mr. Piscopo's argument that celebrity goodwill is distinguishable from professional goodwill since professional goodwill had educational and regulatory requirements while celebrity goodwill requires ineffable talent, the court held that "it is the person with particular and uncommon aptitude for some specialized discipline whether law, medicine or entertainment that transforms the average professional or entertainer into one with measurable goodwill" (Piscopo v. Piscopo, supra at 555 A.2d 1191). We agree with the courts that have considered the issue, that the enhanced skills of an artist such as the plaintiff, albeit growing from an innate talent, which have enabled her to become an exceptional earner, may be valued as marital property subject to equitable distribution.

The plaintiff additionally contends that her career is not marital property because she had already become successful prior to her marriage to the defendant. As noted, supra, during the first year of marriage, the plaintiff earned $2,250. By 1989, her earnings had increased more than 275 fold. Further, in Price v. Price, supra, 69 N.Y.2d at 11, 511 N.Y.S.2d 219, 503 N.E.2d 684, the Court of Appeals held that

> under the Equitable Distribution Law an increase in the value of separate property of one spouse, occurring during the marriage and prior to the commencement of matrimonial proceedings, which is due in part to the indirect contributions or efforts of the other spouse as homemaker and parent, should be considered marital property (Domestic Relations Law §236[B][1][d][3]).

In this case, it cannot be overlooked that the defendant's contributions to plaintiff's career were direct and concrete, going far beyond child care and the like, which he also provided.

While it is true that the plaintiff was born with talent, and, while she had already been hired by the Metropolitan Opera at the time of her marriage to the defendant, her career, at this time, was only in the initial stages of development. During the course of the marriage, the defendant's active involvement in the plaintiff's career, in teaching, coaching, and critiquing her, as well as in caring for their children, clearly contributed to the increase in its value. Accordingly, to the extent the appreciation in the plaintiff's career was due to the defendant's efforts and contributions, this appreciation constitutes marital property.

In sum, we find that it is the nature and extent of the contribution by the spouse seeking equitable distribution, rather than the nature of the career, whether licensed or otherwise, that should determine the status of the enterprise as marital property. . . .

Accordingly, the order of the Supreme Court, New York County (Walter M. Schackman, J.), entered September 26, 1990, which determined that the plaintiff's career and/or celebrity status was not "marital property" subject to equitable distribution, should be reversed, on the law, without costs, and the matter should be remitted to the Supreme Court for further proceedings.

All concur.

J. Thomas Oldham, Putting Asunder in the 1990s
80 Cal. L. Rev. 1091, 1121 (1992)

Could we keep the current system and add a new dimension for human capital accumulations during marriage? This is what New York state appears to be doing. Note, however, that this "double counts" wages earned by an employee, if (as is quite likely) the employee remarries. For example, in New York, one spouse may earn a medical degree during marriage. Upon divorce, the degree is included in the marital estate and its value is determined by the increased lifetime earning capacity that will be generated by that degree. If the educated spouse then remarries, the wages generated by the degree during the second marriage will be included in the second marital estate: no deduction is received for the amount included in the first marital estate. Under normal marital-partnership theory, property is deemed earned only once. As an illustration, assume that an employee works for forty years, during which time he has two twenty-year marriages. Half of the accumulated pension rights will be deemed part of the marital estate of the first marriage, and half will be part of the second marital estate. Similarly, if a lawyer-spouse works on a contingent fee case during the first marriage and settles the case during the second marriage, most courts would apportion the fee between both marriages in some manner, such as the relative amount of time spent on the case during the two marriages. By treating professional degrees and licenses earned during marriage as marital property, and by valuing the degree in terms of the lifetime earning capacity of the spouse, the New York system counts a professional's accumulations twice.

NOTES

1. Professional goodwill is a divisible marital asset in most jurisdictions, even in those that do not treat enhanced earning capacity from a professional degree as a marital asset subject to equitable distribution. In Dugan v. Dugan, 92 N.J. 423, 457 A.2d 1 (1983), the court defined goodwill as "essentially reputation that will probably generate future business" and said:

> ... [Goodwill] does not exist at the time professional qualifications and a license to practice are obtained. A good reputation is earned after accomplishment and performance. Field testing is an essential ingredient before goodwill comes into being. Future earning capacity per se is not goodwill. However, when that future earning capacity has been enhanced because reputation leads to probable future patronage from existing and potential

clients, goodwill may exist and have value. When that occurs the resulting goodwill is property subject to equitable distribution. [92 N.J. at 433; 457 A.2d at 6.]

Goodwill results from the ability to generate above-average earnings and is usually valued by capitalizing earnings in excess of the average. Here is one way to value goodwill, suggested in Dugan v. Dugan. Take the professional's average net income for the previous five years and deduct from it (a) the average salary of a comparable professional, and (b) a reasonable rate of return on the professional's invested capital. The resulting amount represents annual excess earnings, or goodwill. Capitalize this sum, taking into account the risk of realization and the expected life of the goodwill. The capitalization factor is rather arbitrary, but 25 to 50 percent is usually acceptable. See Case Comment, 11 Harv. Women's L.J. 147 (1988).

In a story on celebrity goodwill in the N.Y. Times, Apr. 15, 1988, §1, at 17, Marvin Mitchelson, the well-known divorce lawyer, was quoted as saying the value of celebrity goodwill would not be hard to measure. He speculated about an actor who, on his wedding day, was being paid scale but who, when the marriage ended, was commanding $1 million a movie:

> "A court can determine the goodwill value of that actor at that moment," Mr. Mitchelson said, "based on his past earnings, current earnings and what he gets for just initialing a contract. Say he has a two- or three-picture deal on the books when the divorce occurs. Even though he hasn't made the pictures, the compensation he'll get was bargained for during the marriage and reflects what he's worth at the box office. The movie actor argues he has to go out and make the movie. But Dr. O'Brien [O'Brien v. O'Brien, discussed in Note 2 on page 392] argued this unsuccessfully. He said he had to go out and practice medicine."

2. *Gastineau v. Gastineau, 151 Misc. 2d 813, 573 N.Y.S.2d 819 (1991).* The wife of Marc Gastineau, a professional football player, filed for divorce. Gastineau had a contract with the New York Jets to play 16 games in 1988 for $775,000, or $48,437 a game. After playing 6 games, Gastineau broke his contract, forfeiting a salary of $484,375 for the ten remaining games. He took off for Arizona to be with his girlfriend Brigitte Nielsen, thus ending his professional career.

The court held that the $484,375 that Gastineau forfeited was a marital asset dissipated by Gastineau. The court awarded the wife one-third of all the marital assets, including the $484,375, which equalled the equity the couple had in their New York home, their only other marital asset. Thus the wife was given the home, and the husband was given the broken and worthless contract.

c.   Termination of Marriage by Death of One Spouse

(1)   Common Law

The surviving spouse's rights at English common law reflected the desires of the landed class. Land should stay in the partriarchal family, but surviving spouses should be supported for their lives. The law accommodated these desires by the institutions of dower and curtesy.

With respect to personal property, the common law gave a surviving widow one-third if there were surviving issue and one-half otherwise.[20] A surviving widower took all his wife's personal property absolutely.

Dower. Dower originally was a gift made by the bridegroom to the bride at the wedding; hence the importance of including in the marriage ceremony the words, "With all my worldly goods I thee endow." As time would have it, dower became fixed by law and was granted regardless of what was said at the wedding.

The law gave dower to a surviving wife in all *freehold land of which her husband was seised during marriage and which was inheritable by the issue of husband and wife.* Thus any land owned in fee simple by the husband alone or as a tenant in common during marriage was subject to dower. Dower was a life estate in one-third of each parcel of qualifying land. In a feudal society that looked upon land as the resource to support a military state, dower was a generous concession to the widow of a rich man. But to the widow of a man who owned only a home and no farm acreage, dower (one-third for life) was small protection indeed.

Dower attaches to land at the moment of marriage, if the land is then owned, or thereafter when the land is acquired. It is "inchoate" until the husband dies. If the wife predeceases the husband, or they are divorced, her inchoate dower is extinguished. If she survives the husband, the wife becomes entitled to her dower in possession. After inchoate dower has attached, the husband is powerless to defeat it. Any purchaser from, or creditor of, the husband takes subject to it, unless the wife releases her dower.

Curtesy. At his wife's prior death, a widower was, at common law, entitled to a life estate in each piece of the wife's real property if certain

---

20. An exception was made for heirlooms, which were chattels that, by ancient custom, descended to the primogenitary heir under the rules applicable to real property. Heirlooms did not pass to the surviving spouse and the other children; nor could they be separated from the land by will. Heirlooms included the crown jewels, title deeds, and, in some localities, the best bed. Co. Litt. 18b (1628). The evidence indicates that in Warwickshire, where Shakespeare lived, the best bed was an heirloom, going with the house to the new head of family. Hence Shakespeare, devising his house to his elder daughter Susanna, could, and did, bequeath only his second-best bed to his wife. See Robert Megarry & H.W.R. Wade, The Law of Real Property 547 (5th ed. 1984); O. Hood Phillips, Shakespeare and the Lawyers 16 (1972).

conditions were fulfilled. This was known as curtesy, or, more fully, an estate by the Curtesy of England. Curtesy, like dower, attached to all freehold land of which the wife was seised during marriage and which was inheritable by the issue of husband and wife. Unlike dower, however, curtesy did not attach to land unless issue of the marriage capable of inheriting the estate were born alive.

Dower and curtesy have been abolished in all but six American jurisdictions. In four of these, curtesy has been abolished and dower has been extended to husbands. Ark. Code Ann. §28-11-301 (Supp. 1991); D.C. Code Ann. §19-102 (1981); Ky. Rev. Stat. §§392.020, 392.080 (1984); Ohio Rev. Code Ann. §2103.02 (Baldwin 1987). In Michigan, curtesy has been abolished, but dower is still given to wives. Mich. Comp. Laws §558.1 (1988). The statute is of doubtful constitutionality. See Boan v. Watson, 281 S.C. 516, 316 S.E.2d 401 (1984), striking down a similar statute as violative of the Equal Protection Clause. In Iowa, dower has been changed to give the surviving spouse a fractional fee simple interest, rather than a life estate, in the decedent's lands owned during marriage. Iowa Code Ann. §§633.212, 633.238 (Supp. 1991). Virginia abolished dower and curtesy in 1990, preserving any dower or curtesy rights vested before 1991. Va. Code §64.1-19.2 (1991).

The important consequence of dower in modern times is that both husband and wife must sign deeds to land to release dower, even though title is in only one of them.

PROBLEMS

1. *O* conveys Blackacre to *A* and *B* as joint tenants.

(a) *A* dies survived by his wife *W*. Is *W* entitled to dower in Blackacre?

(b) *A* conveys his interest in Blackacre to *C*. *A* dies survived by his wife, *W*, who did not join in the deed to *C*. Is *W* entitled to dower in Blackacre? If *C* dies, is *C*'s widow entitled to dower in Blackacre?

2. *H* desires to purchase Brownacre. He wants to be able to deal with the property after the purchase without any interference from his wife. In what way should he take title to Brownacre in a jurisdiction that has common law dower?

(2) The Modern Elective Share

After the Civil War, with the great growth in wealth in personal property (principally stocks and bonds) and the rise of a large class of urban renters, it appeared that dower and curtesy were no longer effective to protect the surviving spouse. Legislatures began to enact "forced share" legislation, giving the surviving spouse an elective forced share in all property — real and personal — that the decedent spouse owned at death. The surviving spouse is not entitled only to support, as dower and curtesy provided, but to an ownership share in the decedent spouse's property. This is a form of deferred community property; one spouse does not receive a property interest in the other spouse's property during marriage, but only at the other spouse's death.

All common law property states except Georgia have elective forced share statutes. The surviving spouse can renounce the will, if any, and elect to take a statutory share, which is usually one-half or one-third or some other fractional share. States retaining dower give the surviving spouse the right to elect dower or a statutory forced share; the statutory share is usually larger.

The elective forced share ordinarily applies only to property that the decedent spouse owns at death. The elective forced share usually does not apply to property held by the decedent and another in joint tenancy nor to life insurance proceeds. The elective share can be defeated by lifetime gifts of property, but a word of caution is appropriate here. Courts and statutes in many states permit the surviving spouse to set aside gifts made with the intent to defeat the elective share, or transfers where the donor spouse retained control (for example, a revocable trust). The law on this is subject to considerable variation from state to state. See Sullivan v. Burkin, 390 Mass. 864, 460 N.E.2d 572 (1984); Jesse Dukeminier & Stanley M. Johanson, Wills, Trusts, and Estates 388-402 (4th ed. 1990).

PROBLEM

H dies in a state that gives the surviving spouse an elective forced share of one-half of the decedent's property passing by will or intestacy. During his life *H* took out a life insurance policy in the face amount of $60,000 payable to *W*. *H* and *W* also bought a house, worth $60,000 at *H*'s death, and took title as joint tenants. *H* dies owning Blackacre worth $90,000, stocks and bonds worth $20,000, and a $10,000 savings account. *H*'s will bequeaths all his estate to his daughter by a first marriage, *D*. How is *H*'s estate distributed?

If you were advising *H* before he died, how would you advise him to carry out his wishes?

Community property (which divides earnings equally between the spouses) generally offers rewards to the nonworking spouse commensurate with the duration of the marriage. A surviving spouse of a five-year marriage receives half of the property acquired from five years of earnings; a surviving spouse of a 30-year marriage gets half of the property from 30 years of earnings. Under the typical forced share statute, length of the marriage is irrelevant. The spouse has a claim to the same forced share whether married to the decedent for 1 hour or 50 years.[21]

In 1990, the Uniform Probate Code was amended to achieve results closer to those of a community property system. Section 2-201 provides for a sliding scale percentage ranging from 3 percent for marriages of one year to 50 percent for marriages of 15 years or more. Section 2-202 was amended to give the surviving spouse a percentage of the value of the decedent's newly defined "augmented estate." The augmented estate concept is complicated, but basically it totals up the couple's combined assets — including nonprobate property such as life insurance, joint tenancies, and property transferred during life in which the spouse retained a life estate or power to revoke — and gives the survivor a percentage of the total based on the length of the marriage. The Uniform Probate Code augmented estate attempts to divide all property of the couple half and half if the marriage has lasted more than 15 years. If the survivor owns more than 50 percent of the couple's combined assets, the elective share gives the survivor nothing from the decedent spouse's estate. Section 2-207 provides that the surviving spouse's share is collectible out of probate assets first and, if insufficient, then out of nonprobate assets. See Lawrence W. Waggoner, Spousal Rights in Our Multiple-Marriage Society: The Revised Uniform Probate Code, 26 Real Prop., Prob. & Tr. J. 683 (1992).

NOTE: THE UNIFORM MARITAL PROPERTY ACT (1983)

In 1983 the National Conference of Commissioners on Uniform State Laws promulgated a Uniform Marital Property Act. This act is based on community property principles, though the phrase "community property" is avoided and "marital property" used instead. The root concept is that property acquired during marriage from earnings of the spouses is marital property. Property acquired before marriage and property acquired by gift, devise, or inheritance is "individual property."

---

21. In Estate of Neiderhiser, 2 Pa. D.&C.3d 302, 59 Westmoreland County L.J. 60 (1977), these facts occurred at the wedding ceremony. The groom answered "I will" to the question, "Wilt thou have this woman to be thy wife, etc."; the bride answered affirmatively to a similar question; the groom then placed a ring on the bride's finger, saying "With this ring I thee wed, In the name of the Father, and of the Son, and of the Holy Spirit. Amen." The minister began to pray and, during the prayer, the groom dropped dead; whereupon the minister cut the ceremony short and pronounced the groom and bride man and wife. The court held that marriage is a contract and the contract becomes binding at the moment the couple exchange their vows (by saying "I will"); the subsequent pronouncement of the minister that they are man and wife is merely recognition of the marriage in a solemn way. The bride — made widow at her wedding — was entitled to a forced share in her husband's estate.

With respect to marital property, each spouse owns a one-half undivided interest in such property as soon as it is acquired. For example, if the husband earns $1,000, one-half belongs to the wife. If the husband subsequently buys 10 shares of stock with the money, taking title in his name alone, the stock is marital property and the wife owns one-half of it. Sharing in marital property is not deferred until the marriage ends, as is provided in statutes calling for equitable distribution upon divorce and a forced share at death.

In drafting the Uniform Act, the commissioners compared the often differing rules developed in community property states to solve the major problems; they selected the rule that appeared to them most sound and equitable. In our treatment of community property, which follows, where important subsidiary rules differ we note in footnotes which choice the commissioners have made.

Upon divorce, marital property is distributed in accordance with the state's existing division system, which in almost all states is equitable division. Upon death, the decedent owns one-half of the marital property and can dispose of it by will; the surviving spouse owns the other one-half of the marital property.

Wisconsin adopted the Uniform Marital Property Act in 1984. Wis. Stat. Ann. §§766.001-766.97 (Supp. 1991). The Commissioner of Internal Revenue has ruled that under the provisions of the Wisconsin Marital Property Act the rights of the spouses are community property rights for purposes of federal income taxation. Rev. Rul. 87-13, I.R.B. 1987-6, 4. See Howard S. Erlanger & June M. Weisberger, From Common Law Property to Community Property: Wisconsin's Marital Property Act Four Years Later, 1990 Wis. L. Rev. 769.

2. The Community Property System

a. Introduction

Eight states — Arizona, California, Idaho, Louisiana, Nevada, New Mexico, Texas, and Washington — have a system of community property traceable to French or Spanish influence among the early settlers in the South and West. Although there are substantial differences in details among the community property states, the fundamental idea of community property is that *earnings* of each spouse during marriage should be owned equally in undivided shares by both spouses. The basic assumption is that both husband and wife contribute equally to the material success of the marriage, and thus each should own an equal share of property acquired during the marriage by their joint efforts. In these eight states community property includes earnings during marriage and the rents, profits, and fruits of earnings.[22] Whatever is bought with earnings is community property. All property that is not community is separate. Separate property is property acquired before marriage and property acquired during marriage by gift, devise, or descent. In Idaho, Louisiana, and Texas, the income from all property — separate as well as community — is community property. In the other states the income from separate property retains its separate character.[23]

Property acquired or possessed during marriage by either husband or wife is presumed to be community property. This is a strong presumption and can be overcome only by a preponderance of the evidence. Where there has been a commingling of separate and community property, the party contending for separate property may have a very difficult tracing burden. Recitals in a deed prepared by one spouse that property is separate property are not controlling; otherwise a self-serving spouse could take his or her earnings and unilaterally convert them into separate property.

In most states the husband and wife can freely change ("transmute") the character of their property by written agreement and, in some states, by oral agreement. They can convert community property into separate property, or vice versa.

If marriage is terminated by divorce, California, New Mexico, and Louisiana require an equal division of community property. The other community property states authorize a divorce court to make equitable division of community property.

b.   Community Property Compared with Common Law Concurrent Interests

None of the eight community property states recognizes dower or curtesy; none recognizes the tenancy by the entirety. These marital interests developed out of the subjugation of the wife to the husband at common law and were deemed inconsistent with the principles of a marital community based on sharing. However, a tenancy in common or a joint tenancy can be created between husband and wife in community property states. These concurrent estates are permitted as separate property, but husband and wife cannot simultaneously hold property both as community property and as a tenancy in common or a joint ten-

---

22. For an extended treatment of community property, see Grace G. Blumberg, Community Property in California (2d ed. 1993); William S. McClanahan, Community Property Law in the United States (1982); William Reppy, Jr. & Cynthia A. Samuel, Community Property in the United States (2d ed. 1982).

23. Uniform Marital Property Act §4(d) adopts the Texas rule.

ancy. These cotenancies have different characteristics from community property.

Community property, compared with tenancies in common and joint tenancies, has these significant differences:

Husband and wife. Community property can exist only between husband and wife, whereas a tenancy in common or a joint tenancy can exist between any two or more persons.

Conveyance of share. Unlike tenants in common or joint tenants, neither spouse acting alone can convey his or her *undivided* one-half share of community property, except to the other spouse. It follows from this principle that neither spouse can change community property into separate property without the consent of the other. A tenant in common or a joint tenant acting alone can convey his or her undivided share to a third party, can change the form of estate (for example, from a joint tenancy into a tenancy in common), and has the right to partition; all these actions are unavailable to an owner of community property acting alone.

At death. Each spouse has the power to dispose by will of one-half the community property at death. There is no survivorship feature, as with joint tenancy. If a spouse dies intestate in California, Idaho, Nevada, New Mexico, or Washington, his or her share of the community property passes to the surviving spouse. In the other states community property passes to the descendants of the decedent.

Sale after death. At the death of one spouse, the entire community property receives a "stepped-up" tax basis for federal income tax purposes. (The difference between "basis," which is usually what the item cost, and selling price is income to the taxpayer.) The new basis is the value of the property upon the date of the decedent's death. Internal Revenue Code §§1014(a), 1014(b)(6). Thus suppose that H and W buy a house for \$100,000, taking title in community property. At H's death several years later, the house is worth \$300,000. The house receives a new tax basis of \$300,000. If W thereafter sells the house for \$325,000, W realizes taxable income of only \$25,000. If H and W had taken title to the house as joint tenants, only H's one-half would receive a stepped-up basis at H's death, and W's basis after H's death would be \$200,000 (\$50,000 for her cost plus \$150,000 for H's stepped-up basis). When W sells the house for \$325,000, she would realize \$125,000 in taxable income. Hence there is a possible considerable income tax advantage in holding property as community property rather than in a common law concurrent ownership form.

PROBLEM

H, married to W, saves $5,000 out of his earnings, which he deposits in a savings account in his name only. Subsequently H withdraws the $5,000 and buys a lot, taking title in H and W as joint tenants. H then dies, devising all his separate and community property to his son, S. Who owns the lot?

c. Management of Community Property

In a tenancy in common or a joint tenancy each tenant separately can convey his or her undivided interest, but this cannot be done with community property. Because it can exist only between husband and wife and cannot be converted into separate property without the consent of both spouses, community property can be conveyed to a third person only as an undivided whole. As a result, special management problems arise. Can the husband or the wife or only both of them make a conveyance of community property? Prior to the 1960s, the husband was deemed to be manager of the community, but beginning in the late 1960s, all eight community property states enacted statutes giving the husband and wife equal management powers. These statutes, however, differ in many details. In Texas, for example, the wife has sole management power over her earnings kept separate, and the husband has sole power over his. If the earnings are commingled, they are subject to individual management by either spouse. In California and the other community property states husband and wife are equal managers. Either the husband or the wife, acting alone, has the power to manage community property. However, statutory exceptions in some of these states empower only one spouse to act in certain situations. If title is in the name of only one spouse, only that spouse may be able to manage the property.[24] If a spouse is operating a business that is community property, exclusive control of the business may be given to that spouse. In most states, however, statutes require both spouses to join in transfers or mortgages of community real property.

The manager of community property is a kind of fiduciary. The community property must be managed for the benefit of the community. Each spouse must act in good faith in exercising authority, but good judgment is not necessary. The manager can sell community personal property and, if joinder of the other spouse is not required by statute,

---

24. Uniform Marital Property Act §5 gives management power to the titleholder of property. If title is held in the name of "H and W," both spouses manage and joinder of both is required to convey. If title is held in the name of "H or W," either spouse can manage the property. Where no title document exists, either spouse acting alone can manage the property. Bona fide purchasers from the managing spouse are protected.

community real property. Under the Spanish law of community property the manager (formerly the husband) could validly make reasonable gifts, for good cause, of community property. This law persists in some states, for example, Texas. In California and Washington any gift of community property by the managing spouse can be set aside by the other spouse.[25] Any bona fide purchaser from the spouse having the right to manage is protected. Thus if husband and wife are equal managers of an oil painting, either can sell it to a bona fide purchaser.

In most community property states liability to creditors follows management and control. The creditors of a managing spouse can reach whatever community property the creditor spouse is legally entitled to manage. Hence if the husband and wife are equal managers of the property, creditors of either the husband or the wife can reach the property.[26]

PROBLEM

W.C. Fields, who married Harriett Fields in 1900, subsequently earned large sums of money as a movie star. All of these earnings were community property.[27] Although depicted on the screen as a skinflint, Fields bestowed handsome gifts of money upon various persons, including several "lady friends," without his wife's knowledge or consent. These gifts totaled $482,450. After Fields died in 1946,[28] his wife found out about these transfers and sued Fields's executor. She alleged:

25. Uniform Marital Property Act §6 permits gifts by the managing spouse if "the gift is reasonable in amount considering the economic position of the spouses." Any gift beyond this amount can be set aside by the other spouse.
26. Uniform Marital Property Act §8 does not follow the managerial system, but adopts the community debt system followed in Arizona, New Mexico, and Washington. Debts incurred for a family purpose or to benefit the community are obligations of the community; debts incurred for personal purposes can be satisfied only out of the debtor spouse's separate property and share of community property.
27. Fields was long separated from his wife, but under the California law then applicable earnings were community property until divorce. This rule is still followed in most community property states. But today in three states — Arizona, California, and Washington — earnings cease to be community property at the time the spouses live separate and apart. Uniform Marital Property Act §4(d) provides that all income is marital property until divorce.
28. Fields's estate, valued at around $800,000, was all community property since it had all been earned after his marriage to Harriett. In his will Fields left his wife and his son each $10,000, but Harriett, his wife, owned half of the $800,000 community property, and this attempt to cut her off with very little failed. After providing small legacies of a few hundred or a few thousand dollars for various friends and relatives, Fields left the residue of his property to establish an orphans' home to be called "the W.C. Fields College . . . where no religion of any sort is to be preached." See Robert L. Taylor, W.C. Fields 283 (1967). This final bequest came from a man who, playing Gus, wrote his own dialogue in the movie Tillie and Gus (1933):

Tillie.   Do you like children?

many of said donees are deceased and that those remaining alive reside at divers places, some of them away from the State of California, and that they have used up and dissipated the sums of money by way of gift transferred and set over to them as aforesaid, and would not be able to pay a judgment, if one were rendered against them for return to plaintiff of said gifts or some part thereof. Plaintiff is without any means of collecting in full from said donees those portions of said gifts which she is entitled to.

Should the court direct Fields's executor to pay Harriett Fields $241,225? See Fields v. Michael, 91 Cal. App. 2d 443, 205 P.2d 402 (1949).

d.   Mixing Community Property with Separate Property

Where community property is mixed with separate property, the community property states are not all in agreement as to the consequences. This situation sometimes arises where property is acquired before marriage but part of the purchase price is paid after marriage with community funds. In this situation some states, including Texas, follow the "inception of right" rule, a few follow the "time of vesting" rule, and still others, including California, follow a pro rata apportionment. The differences are easily seen if you think of a house bought on an installment land contract by the wife paying one-third down before marriage, with the remaining two-thirds of the installments paid after marriage from community funds. Under the "inception of right" rule, the character of the property is determined at the time the wife signed the contract of purchase; the house is her separate property. The community is entitled only to a return of community payments plus interest. Under the "time of vesting" rule, title does not pass to the wife until all the installments are paid, and hence the house is community property. Under the pro rata sharing rule, the community payments "buy in" a pro rata share of the title.[29]

PROBLEMS

1. During marriage *H* takes out a $50,000 life insurance policy on his life, paying premiums out of his earnings. The named beneficiary is

---

Gus.   I do if they're properly cooked.

Whatever Fields's motive in pitting his wife — a religious woman — against the orphans, her claims were satisfied first, leaving insufficient funds for an orphanage.

29. Uniform Marital Property Act §14 generally adopts pro rata sharing of ownership where marital property or a spouse's labor is mixed with separate property.

H's son, *S*. At *H*'s death, who is entitled to the $50,000? Suppose that *H* had taken out the policy before marriage and that $3,000 in premiums had been paid before marriage and $7,000 in premiums had been paid after marriage from community funds. At *H*'s death who is entitled to the $50,000? See McCurdy v. McCurdy, 372 S.W.2d 381 (Tex. Civ. App. 1963).

2. During his marriage to *W*, *H* purchases land for $20,000, using $5,000 of his separate funds as a down payment and giving a note secured by a mortgage to the seller for the balance. *H* pays off the principal and interest of the note from community funds, and then sells the land for $40,000. Who is entitled to the proceeds? Should the $5,000 be considered a gift to the community if title is taken in the name of *H* and *W* (that is, a voluntary contribution to the purchase price)? See Grace G. Blumberg, Community Property in California 202-229 (2d ed. 1993); William Reppy, Jr. & Cynthia A. Samuel, Community Property in the United States 99-111 (2d ed. 1982).

3. Suppose *W* owns and operates a jewelry store before marriage. At marriage to *H* it is worth $100,000. Five years after marriage the jewelry store is sold for $250,000. Who is entitled to the proceeds? Should *W* receive $100,000 plus a fair rate of return on that sum for five years, and the community receive the rest? Or should the community receive a fair salary for *W*'s labors in the store over five years, and *W* receive the rest? In California the answer turns on whether the increase in value is primarily due to *W*'s personal activity and ability or due to the character of the investment in a jewelry store. Suppose that instead of managing a jewelry store, *W* manages her separate stock portfolio and increases its value to $250,000 after five years. What part of the increase is community? See Beam v. Bank of America, 6 Cal. 3d 12, 490 P.2d 257, 98 Cal. Rptr. 137 (1971). See also Jensen v. Jensen, 665 S.W.2d 107 (Tex. 1984); J. Thomas Oldham, Separate Property Businesses that Increase in Value During Marriage, 1990 Wis. L. Rev. 585.

e.   Migrating Couples

Whether property is characterized in accord with the community property system or in accord with the common law property system depends upon the domicile of the spouses when the property is acquired. Suppose that the wife earns $1,000 and buys a horse with it. If the parties are domiciled in New York, the horse belongs to the wife alone. If domiciled in Texas, the horse is community property. Once the property has been initially characterized, *the ownership does not change when the parties change their domicile* unless both parties consent to the change in ownership. If, after the wife earns the $1,000, the spouses move from New

York to Texas, the horse remains the wife's separate property. On the other hand, if the parties had been domiciled in Texas when the wife earned the money, and then had moved from Texas to New York, the horse would remain community property unless the parties agreed to change the ownership to another form. Common law property states generally recognize community property when it is brought into the state from a community property state. This point is frequently overlooked by lawyers or real estate agents in common law property states who advise immigrating husbands and wives to take the proceeds from the sale of their house in a community property state and buy a new house as joint tenants or tenants by the entirety, thereby losing the tax advantage of community property (explained on page 406). See Stanley M. Johanson, The Migrating Client: Estate Planning for the Couple from a Community Property State, 9 U. Miami Inst. Est. Plan. ¶800 (1975).

When a person dies, the law of the decedent's domicile at death governs the disposition of personal property and the law where land is located governs the disposition of land. A move from a common law property state to a community property state may leave a nonworking spouse of a retired worker at a disadvantage. The nonworking spouse loses the protection of the forced share given by the common law property state and gains the protection of the law of the community property state. The community property laws in most states do not give the surviving spouse a forced share in the decedent spouse's property owned at death.[30]

PROBLEM

H and *W* marry and live in Ohio. From *H*'s earnings during marriage, *H* accumulates personal property worth $500,000. Under Ohio law, *W* has, at *H*'s death, an elective share of one-half of *H*'s property. After retirement, *H* and *W* move to Texas, a community property state. *H* dies leaving a will devising all his property to a daughter by a prior marriage. Texas does not have an elective share statute. What are *W*'s rights? See Estate of Hanau v. Hanau, 730 S.W.2d 663 (Tex. 1987). By moving to Texas, *W* lost the protection of the Ohio elective share and gained no substitute protection. What advice would you give *W* before moving from Ohio?

30. California attempts to put immigrating couples in somewhat the same marital property position as they would have been in had they been domiciled in California all along. Upon divorce or death of a spouse, one-half of that spouse's property that would have been community property had the couple been domiciled in California when the property was acquired belongs to the other spouse. This is called "quasi-community property." Cal. Civ. Code §4800 (West 1983); Cal. Prob. Code §§66, 6401 (West 1991).

3. Status and Contract

a. Contracts between Spouses

In some European and Latin American countries, spouses must elect at the time of marriage how they will hold their property. Three property regimes are usually available. They may choose (1) to hold all their property in separate ownership (as under the American common law system); (2) to hold property acquired from earnings as community property, and inherited property as separate property (the American community property system); or (3) to hold all their property from whatever source as community property (universal community property). A variation on the separate property option might include a provision that the surviving spouse takes a share of the decedent's property upon his or her death. Since the existence of optional marital property regimes within one foreign jurisdiction does not seem to have caused substantial difficulties, one wonders why married couples in the United States are not given similar options.

These choices are available in American community property states because the spouses can make an agreement to hold their property in any one of these forms. But in the past these choices have not been easily available in common law property states. Courts have been hesitant in permitting rights conferred by marital status to be varied by contract. Antenuptial agreements attempting to limit the husband's duty of support upon *divorce* have been, until recent years, almost always held invalid in most states. Such agreements were thought to give an incentive for divorce either to the husband, if the agreed payments were small, or to the wife, if the agreed payments exceeded those ordinarily awarded by a court. Antenuptial contracts providing for a division of property upon *death* of one of the spouses traditionally have been enforced only if the agreement makes a fair and reasonable provision for the surviving spouse (typically the wife) *or* if the decedent spouse (typically the husband) made a full, accurate, and specific disclosure of his property.

In the last quarter century, some commentators on marital property, unhappy with rights conferred by status, have urged that spouses and prospective spouses be free to contract with respect to their property. See Marjorie M. Schultz, Contractual Ordering of Marriage: A New Model for State Policy, 70 Cal. L. Rev. 204 (1982); Faith H. Spencer, Expanding Marital Options: Enforcement of Premarital Contracts During Marriage, 1989 U. Chi. Leg. Forum 281. A growing number of cases hold that antenuptial agreements dividing property upon divorce are valid, provided the agreement is fair and reasonable or — or perhaps *and* — it is based upon full knowledge of each other's property. A few courts have even indicated a willingness to enforce a reasonable agreement regarding spousal support. Nonetheless, in specific cases it is not easy to predict with assurance whether the particular premarital contract regarding division of property and support rights upon divorce will be enforced by courts. Decisions tend to be ad hoc. See E. Allan Farnsworth, Contracts §5.4 (1982); Theodore F. Haas, The Rationality and Enforceability of Contractual Restrictions on Divorce, 66 N.C. L. Rev. 879 (1988); J. Thomas Oldham, Premarital Contracts are Now Enforceable, Unless . . . , 21 Hous. L. Rev. 757 (1984); June M. Weisberger, Spousal Property Agreements: An Evolving Concept in Wisconsin and Elsewhere, 5 Wis. Women's L.J. 43 (1990); Judith T. Younger, Perspectives on Antenuptial Agreements, 40 Rutgers L. Rev. 1059 (1988).

Uniform Marital Property Act §10(g) (1983) and Uniform Premarital Agreement Act §6 (1983) both provide for enforcement of antenuptial property agreements unless there was insufficient disclosure of wealth *and* the agreement was unconscionable when made. Most states have not gone so far in permitting freedom of antenuptial contract. Indeed, the comment to section 3 of the Uniform Marital Property Act admits as much: "The Act permits a couple to move its marital economics from status to contract and encourages a type of interpersonal contractual freedom little known in common law states."

PROBLEMS

1. Terry and Chris are domiciled in a common law property state. They plan to get married and do not like the property rights accorded spouses under the local law. Terry and Chris sign an antenuptial agreement providing that after marriage all their property rights shall be governed by the Uniform Marital Property Act (which basically provides for community property). After their marriage, is this agreement enforceable during marriage? Upon divorce? Upon death? See Stein-Sapir v. Stein-Sapir, 52 A.D.2d 115, 382 N.Y.S.2d 799 (1976) (enforcing on divorce an antenuptial agreement for community property, one of the marital property regimes a couple may select in Mexico, where the couple married); Richard W. Bartke, Marital Sharing — Why Not Do It By Contract?, 67 Georgetown L.J. 1131 (1979).

2. Suppose that Terry and Chris, husband and wife domiciled in a community property state, sign an agreement that all their property acquired from earnings during marriage shall be community property. Subsequently they move to a common law property state. What result?

b.   Contracts between Unmarried Cohabitants

Marvin v. Marvin

Supreme Court of California, 1976
18 Cal. 3d 660, 557 P.2d 106, 134 Cal. Rptr. 815

TOBRINER, J. During the past 15 years, there has been a substantial increase in the number of couples living together without marrying. Such
nonmarital relationships lead to legal controversy when one partner dies
or the couple separates. . . . We take this opportunity to . . . declare the
principles which should govern distribution of property acquired in a
nonmarital relationship.

We conclude: . . . [1] The courts should enforce express contracts
between nonmarital partners except to the extent that the contract is
explicitly founded on the consideration of meretricious sexual services.
[2] In the absence of an express contract, the courts should inquire into
the conduct of the parties to determine whether that conduct demonstrates an implied contract, agreement of partnership or joint venture,
or some other tacit understanding between the parties. The courts may
also employ the doctrine of quantum meruit, or equitable remedies such
as constructive or resulting trusts, when warranted by the facts of the
case.

In the instant case plaintiff and defendant lived together for seven
years without marrying; all property acquired during this period was
taken in defendant's name. When plaintiff sued to enforce a contract
under which she was entitled to half the property and to support payments, the trial court granted judgment on the pleadings for defendant,
thus leaving him with all property accumulated by the couple during
their relationship. Since the trial court denied plaintiff a trial on the
merits of her claim, its decision conflicts with the principles stated above,
and must be reversed.

1. The Factual Setting of this Appeal

. . . Plaintiff avers that in October of 1964 she and defendant "entered
into an oral agreement" that while "the parties lived together they would
combine their efforts and earnings and would share equally any and all
property accumulated as a result of their efforts whether individual or
combined." Furthermore, they agreed to "hold themselves out to the
general public as husband and wife" and that "plaintiff would further
render her services as a companion, homemaker, housekeeper and cook
to . . . defendant."

Shortly thereafter plaintiff agreed to "give up her lucrative career
as an entertainer [and] singer" in order to "devote her full time to defen-

dant . . . as a companion, homemaker, housekeeper and cook"; in return defendant agreed to "provide for all of plaintiff's financial support and needs for the rest of her life."

Plaintiff alleges that she lived with defendant from October of 1964 through May of 1970 and fulfilled her obligations under the agreement. During this period the parties as a result of their efforts and earnings acquired in defendant's name substantial real and personal property, including motion picture rights worth over $1 million. In May of 1970, however, defendant compelled plaintiff to leave his household. He continued to support plaintiff until November of 1971, but thereafter refused to provide further support.

On the basis of these allegations plaintiff asserts two causes of action. The first, for declaratory relief, asks the court to determine her contract and property rights; the second seeks to impose a constructive trust upon one half of the property acquired during the course of the relationship. . . .

2. Plaintiff's Complaint States a Cause of Action for Breach of an Express Contract

In Trutalli v. Meraviglia (1932) 215 Cal. 698, 12 P.2d 430, we established the principle that nonmarital partners may lawfully contract concerning the ownership of property acquired during the relationship. We reaffirmed this principle in Vallera v. Vallera (1943) 21 Cal. 2d 681, 685, 134 P.2d 761, 763, stating that "If a man and woman [who are not married] live together as husband and wife under an agreement to pool their earnings and share equally in their joint accumulations, equity will protect the interests of each in such property."

In the case before us plaintiff, basing her cause of action in contract upon these precedents, maintains that the trial court erred in denying her a trial on the merits of her contention. . . .

Defendant first and principally relies on the contention that the alleged contract is so closely related to the supposed "immoral" character of the relationship between plaintiff and himself that the enforcement of the contract would violate public policy. . . . [But] California decisions . . . disclose a narrower and more precise standard: a contract between nonmarital partners is unenforceable only to the extent that it explicitly rests upon the immoral and illicit consideration of meretricious sexual services.

. . . The fact that a man and woman live together without marriage, and engage in a sexual relationship, does not in itself invalidate agreements between them relating to their earnings, property, or expenses. Neither is such an agreement invalid merely because the parties may have contemplated the creation or continuation of a nonmarital relation-

ship when they entered into it. Agreements between nonmarital partners fail only to the extent that they rest upon a consideration of
meretricious sexual services. . . .

In summary, we base our opinion on the principle that adults who
voluntarily live together and engage in sexual relations are nonetheless
as competent as any other persons to contract respecting their earnings
and property rights. Of course, they cannot lawfully contract to pay for
the performance of sexual services, for such a contract is, in essence, an
agreement for prostitution and unlawful for that reason. But they may
agree to pool their earnings and to hold all property acquired during
the relationship in accord with the law governing community property;
conversely they may agree that each partner's earnings and the property
acquired from those earnings remains the separate property of the earning partner.[31] So long as the agreement does not rest upon illicit meretricious consideration, the parties may order their economic affairs as
they choose, and no policy precludes the courts from enforcing such
agreements.

In the present instance, plaintiff alleges that the parties agreed to
pool their earnings, that they contracted to share equally in all property
acquired, and that defendant agreed to support plaintiff. The terms of
the contract as alleged do not rest upon any unlawful consideration. We
therefore conclude that the complaint furnishes a suitable basis upon
which the trial court can render declaratory relief. (See 3 Witkin, Cal.
Procedure (2d ed.) pp.2335-2336.) The trial court consequently erred in
granting defendant's motion for judgment on the pleadings.

3. Plaintiff's Complaint Can Be Amended to State a Cause of Action Founded upon Theories of Implied Contract or Equitable Relief

As we have noted, both causes of action in plaintiff's complaint allege an
express contract; neither assert any basis for relief independent from
the contract. . . . [Upon argument to dismiss the complaint before the
trial court], the parties to the present case realized that plaintiff's alleged
relationship with defendant might arguably support a cause of action
independent of any express contract between the parties. The parties
have therefore briefed and discussed the issue of the property rights of
a nonmarital partner in the absence of an express contract. Although
our conclusion that plaintiff's complaint states a cause of action based

---

31. A great variety of other arrangements are plausible. The parties might keep their
earnings and property separate, but agree to compensate one party for services which
benefit the other. They may choose to pool only part of their earnings and property, to
form a partnership or joint venture, or to hold property acquired as joint tenants or tenants in common, or agree to any other such arrangement. (See generally Weitzman, Legal
Regulation of Marriage: Tradition and Change (1974) 62 Cal. L. Rev. 1169.)

on an express contract alone compels us to reverse the judgment for defendant, resolution of the [implied contract] issue will serve both to guide the parties upon retrial and to resolve a conflict presently manifest in published Court of Appeal decisions. . . .

The principal reason why the . . . [older] decisions [denying relief to a nonmarital partner] result in an unfair distribution of property inheres in the court's refusal to permit a nonmarital partner to assert rights based upon accepted principles of implied contract or equity. We have examined the reasons advanced to justify this denial of relief, and find that none have merit.

First, we note that the cases denying relief do not rest their refusal upon any theory of "punishing" a "guilty" partner. Indeed, to the extent that denial of relief "punishes" one partner, it necessarily rewards the other by permitting him to retain a disproportionate amount of the property. Concepts of "guilt" thus cannot justify an unequal division of property between two equally "guilty" persons.

Other reasons advanced in the decisions fare no better. The principal argument seems to be that "[e]quitable considerations arising from the reasonable expectation of . . . benefits attending the status of marriage . . . are not present [in a nonmarital relationship]." (Vallera v. Vallera, supra, 21 Cal. 2d at p.685, 134 P.2d 761, 763). But, although parties to a nonmarital relationship obviously cannot have based any expectations upon the belief that they were married, other expectations and equitable considerations remain. The parties may well expect that property will be divided in accord with the parties' own tacit understanding and that in the absence of such understanding the courts will fairly apportion property accumulated through mutual effort. We need not treat nonmarital partners as putatively married persons in order to apply principles of implied contract, or extend equitable remedies; we need to treat them only as we do any other unmarried persons.

The remaining arguments advanced from time to time to deny remedies to the nonmarital partners are of less moment. There is no more reason to presume that services are contributed as a gift than to presume that funds are contributed as a gift; in any event the better approach is to presume, as Justice Peters suggested, "that the parties intend to deal fairly with each other." (Keene v. Keene (1962) 57 Cal. 2d 657, 674, 21 Cal. Rptr. 593, 603, 371 P.2d 329, 339 (dissenting opn.) . . .)

The argument that granting remedies to the nonmarital partners would discourage marriage must fail; as [In re Marriage of] Cary pointed out, "with equal or greater force the point might be made that . . . [denying the homemaking partner any relief] was calculated to cause the income producing partner to avoid marriage and thus retain the benefit of all of his or her accumulated earnings." ((1973) 34 Cal. App. 3d 345, 353, 109 Cal. Rptr. 862, 866.) Although we recognize the well-established public policy to foster and promote the institution of marriage (see Deyoe v. Superior Court (1903) 140 Cal. 476, 482, 74 P. 28), perpetuation of judicial rules which result in an inequitable distribution of property accumulated during a nonmarital relationship is neither a just nor an effective way of carrying out that policy.

In summary, we believe that the prevalence of nonmarital relationships in modern society and the social acceptance of them, marks this as a time when our courts should by no means apply the doctrine of the unlawfulness of the so-called meretricious relationship to the instant case. As we have explained, the nonenforceability of agreements expressly providing for meretricious conduct rested upon the fact that such conduct, as the word suggests, pertained to and encompassed prostitution. To equate the nonmarital relationship of today to such a subject matter is to do violence to an accepted and wholly different practice.

We are aware that many young couples live together without the solemnization of marriage, in order to make sure that they can successfully later undertake marriage. This trial period, preliminary to marriage, serves as some assurance that the marriage will not subsequently end in dissolution to the harm of both parties. We are aware, as we have stated, of the pervasiveness of nonmarital relationships in other situations.

The mores of the society have indeed changed so radically in regard to cohabitation that we cannot impose a standard based on alleged moral considerations that have apparently been so widely abandoned by so many. Lest we be misunderstood, however, we take this occasion to point out that the structure of society itself largely depends upon the institution of marriage, and nothing we have said in this opinion should be taken to derogate from that institution. The joining of the man and woman in marriage is at once the most socially productive and individually fulfilling relationship that one can enjoy in the course of a lifetime.

We conclude that the judicial barriers that may stand in the way of a policy based upon the fulfillment of the reasonable expectations of the parties to a nonmarital relationship should be removed. As we have explained, the courts now hold that express agreements will be enforced unless they rest on an unlawful meretricious consideration. We add that in the absence of an express agreement, the courts may look to a variety of other remedies in order to protect the parties' lawful expectations.[32]

The courts may inquire into the conduct of the parties to determine whether that conduct demonstrates an implied contract or implied

---

32. We do not seek to resurrect the doctrine of common law marriage, which was abolished in California by statute in 1895. (See Norman v. Thomson (1898) 121 Cal. 620, 628, 54 P. 143; Estate of Abate (1958) 166 Cal. App. 2d 282, 292, 333 P.2d 200.) Thus we do not hold that plaintiff and defendant were "married," nor do we extend to plaintiff the rights which the Family Law Act grants valid or putative spouses: we hold only that she has the same rights to enforce contracts and to assert her equitable interest in property acquired through her effort as does any other unmarried person.

agreement of partnership or joint venture (see Estate of Thornton (1972) 81 Wash. 2d 72, 499 P.2d 864), or some other tacit understanding between the parties. The courts may, when appropriate, employ principles of constructive trust (see Omer v. Omer (1974) 11 Wash. App. 386, 523 P.2d 957) or resulting trust (see Hyman v. Hyman (Tex. Civ. App. 1954) 275 S.W.2d 149). Finally, a nonmarital partner may recover in quantum meruit for the reasonable value of household services rendered less the reasonable value of support received if he can show that he rendered services with the expectation of monetary reward. (See Hill v. Estate of Westbrook (1952) 39 Cal. 2d 458, 462, 247 P.2d 19.)

Since we have determined that plaintiff's complaint states a cause of action for breach of an express contract, and, as we have explained, can be amended to state a cause of action independent of allegations of express contract,[33] we must conclude that the trial court erred in granting defendant a judgment on the pleadings.

The judgment is reversed and the cause remanded for further proceedings consistent with the views expressed herein.

NOTES AND QUESTION

1. In Morone v. Morone, 50 N.Y.2d 481, 407 N.E.2d 438, 429 N.Y.S.2d 592 (1980), the New York Court of Appeals held that a contract to share earnings and assets may not be implied between unmarried cohabitants, but that an express contract of such a couple is enforceable. An implied contract was thought to be so amorphous as to defy equitable enforcement and to be inconsistent with the legislative policy abolishing common law marriage.

In Hewitt v. Hewitt, 77 Ill. 2d 49, 394 N.E.2d 1204, 3 A.L.R.3d 1 (1979), the court rejected Marvin v. Marvin and refused to enforce a contract between unmarried partners to share acquisitions on the ground that this would revive common law marriage, abolished by the legislature. The court thought that the issue in *Marvin* involved complex public policy considerations best left to the legislature.

In Ayala v. Fox, 206 Ill. App. 3d 538, 564 N.E.2d 920 (1990), Anita Ayala moved in with Lawrence Fox in July 1976, and soon thereafter Fox proposed that they jointly pay to construct a new dwelling on his property. Fox promised Ayala that title to the property would be changed to joint tenancy and that, if they split up, Ayala would receive one-half the equity. Ayala and Fox both signed a note and mortgage for

---

33. We do not pass upon the question whether, in the absence of an express or implied contractual obligation, a party to a nonmarital relationship is entitled to support payments from the other party after the relationship terminates.

$48,000, which was used to construct the new house. From 1978 to 1981, while Fox was unemployed, Ayala made the mortgage payments. From 1981 to 1988, Fox and Ayala jointly contributed to the mortgage payments. Fox and Ayala ceased living together in 1988. Fox never transferred title into joint tenancy and refused to pay Ayala her half of the equity in the property. Upon suit by Ayala, the court held she was not entitled to any relief under *Hewitt.*

2. Professor Grace Blumberg is critical of the contract approach to cohabitants' rights and its reliance on the express or implied intent of the parties. She points out that status rights (such as common law marriage) can create benefits and entitlements under federal tax and welfare laws that contract law cannot now achieve. She proposes using the behavior of the parties (as did common law marriage) as the criterion of cohabitants' rights and liabilities between themselves, third parties, and the state. She would grant status rights to persons who have a "stable cohabitation," giving the cohabitants the same rights to opt out of the statutory scheme as formally married persons have. Grace G. Blumberg, Cohabitation Without Marriage: A Different Perspective, 28 UCLA L. Rev. 1125 (1981). See also William Reppy, Jr., Property and Support Rights of Unmarried Cohabitants: A Proposal for Creating a New Legal Status, 44 La. L. Rev. 1677 (1984), arguing for the revival of common law marriage; Note, Looking for a Family Resemblance: The Limits of the Functional Approach to the Legal Definition of Family, 104 Harv. L. Rev. 1640 (1991).

See Equality for All: Minutes of Proceedings and Evidence of the Sub-Committee on Equality Rights of the Standing Committee on Justice and Legal Affairs, 33d Canadian Parliament, 1st Sess., 37 (1985), recommending that all individuals living in heterosexual relationships for one year or more be treated as married for all purposes.

3. Should *Marvin*'s contractual and equitable remedies extend to cohabiting couples of the same sex? See Whorton v. Dillingham, 202 Cal. App. 3d 447, 248 Cal. Rptr. 405 (1988); Comment, Applying Marvin v. Marvin to Same-Sex Couples: A Proposal for a Sex-Preference Neutral Cohabitation Contract Statute, 25 U.C. Davis L. Rev. 1029 (1992). See also Crooke v. Gilden, 262 Ga. 122, 414 S.E.2d 645 (1992) (enforcing an express contract made by a lesbian couple on the theory that an illegal or immoral relationship was not part of the contract).

4. No American state recognizes marriages between homosexuals. They cannot acquire status rights by marriage. In Denmark, registered partnerships between same-sex couples are recognized. A registered partnership confers the same legal rights and obligations on two persons of the same sex as marriage confers on a man and a woman. See Henning Bech, Report from a Rotten State: Marriage and Homosexuality in Denmark, in Modern Homosexualities 134 (Ken Plummer ed. 1992). For discussion of whether substantially the same rights conferred on a

couple by marriage can be acquired in this country by contract between same-sex couples, see Note, Family, Marriage, and the Same-Sex Couple, 12 Cardozo L. Rev. 681 (1990); Note, Prohibiting Marital Status Discrimination: A Proposal for the Protection of Unmarried Couples, 42 Hastings L.J. 1415 (1991); Note, Property Rights of Unmarried Cohabitants in New York: Proposal for Legislative Action Towards a More Equitable Future, 7 Touro L. Rev. 229 (1990).

The block to unmarried cohabitants achieving the same federal income tax consequences by contract as married couples presently have under the federal income tax laws is Lucas v. Earl, 281 U.S. 111 (1930). In that case a husband and wife had made a contract to split equally the husband's earnings. The Supreme Court held that all the income must be taxed to the husband in spite of the wife's enforceable right to receive half of it. Hence, income tax consequences between cohabitants cannot be shifted by contract. The decision is criticized by Boris Bittker, Federal Income Taxation and the Family, 27 Stan. L. Rev. 1389, 1401-1404 (1975). The effect of Lucas v. Earl on married couples has been greatly diminished by the 1948 federal tax act permitting income splitting by married couples filing joint returns. See Patricia A. Cain, Same-Sex Couples and the Federal Tax Laws, 1 Law & Sexuality 97 (1991).

Judge Richard A. Posner, applying a cost-benefit analysis to same-sex marriages in his Sex and Reason 311-313 (1992), observes that there are significant benefits to recognizing same-sex marriages (self-esteem of lesbians and gay men, stability of same-sex relationships, reduced promiscuity lowering the HIV infection rate) while "the costs seem slight." Nonetheless, Judge Posner concludes that "public hostility to homosexuals in this country is too widespread to make homosexual marriage a feasible proposal even if it is on balance cost-justified." He suggests that "an intermediate solution" is to enact domestic partnership laws, giving limited rights. For a review of Posner's book, criticizing Posner for caving in to public opinion and failing to press economic analysis of discrimination against homosexuals relentlessly to unsettling conclusions, as he is famed for doing elsewhere, see William N. Eskridge, Jr., A Social Constructionist Critique of Posner's Sex and Reason: Steps Toward a Gaylegal Agenda, 102 Yale L.J. 333 (1992).

In a number of cities domestic partnership ordinances have been enacted that permit a cohabiting couple to register as partners and become entitled to health insurance benefits for partners of municipal employees, sick leave upon illness of a partner, and tenancy succession to an apartment. Similarly, a number of large corporations have extended health insurance benefits to same-sex partners. See Note, A More Perfect Union: A Legal and Social Analysis of Domestic Partnership Ordinances, 92 Colum. L. Rev. 1164 (1992); Note, Property Rights of Same-Sex Couples: Toward a New Definition of Family, 26 J. Fam. L. 357 (1988).

Stanford to Provide Benefits
for Partners of Gays
L.A. Times, Dec. 9, 1992, at B4

Domestic partners of gay faculty and employees at Stanford University soon will be eligible for the same benefits as spouses of heterosexuals under a policy adopted by the school's Board of Trustees on Tuesday.

Starting Feb. 1, same-sex partners can receive health insurance coverage, survivors' benefits, library privileges and the right to audit university courses.

Though not the first university or institution to institute such a policy, Stanford is thought to be among the pioneers, officials said. The University of Iowa, the Levi Strauss Co. and Bay Area Rapid Transit previously adopted similar rules for gays; other campuses and firms are studying the matter.

Between 40 and 60 Stanford employees are expected to apply for benefits for their homosexual partners, said Barbara Butterfield, vice president for faculty and staff services.

"Stanford feels it should not treat differently its gay and lesbian employees who cannot obtain a legal sanction of their enduring partnership, though their commitment to the partnership is analogous to that involved in contemporary marriage relationships," she said.

Eligible domestic partners are defined as "two individuals in an enduring relationship with exclusive mutual commitment and financial responsibilities analogous to those of marriage." The policy does not apply to unmarried heterosexuals, however. Officials contended that those couples at least have the opportunity to get married and receive benefits.

Officials say they do not intend to investigate private lives and will take the word of applicants.

Stanford raised the ire of some conservative alumni in recent years by allowing gay couples to live together in housing facilities for married students.

QUESTION

Recall Sir Henry Maine's dictum on page 204 that "the movement of the progressive societies has hitherto been a movement *from Status to Contract*." How far is this true with respect to the property rights of same-sex couples? See Symposium, The Family in the 1990s: An Exploration of Lesbian and Gay Rights, 1 Law & Sexuality 1 (1991).

III
Leaseholds:
The Law of Landlord
and Tenant

Leaseholds — or nonfreeholds, or tenancies — are a part of the larger estates system considered in Part II. Like the freehold estates, leaseholds have roots that run deep into feudal times (hence the notion of a *tenant* who holds under a *landlord*). And again like freeholds, leaseholds have been fairly static over the years in terms of their formal characteristics. In terms of relations between landlord and tenant, however, there have been regular and significant developments. The most important of these, together with the body of conventional law in the background, make up the bulk of the next chapter. The chapter considers, step by step, the nature and incidents of leaseholds, and then concludes with a selective look at the persistent problem of affordable rental housing.

6

Tradition, Tension, and Change in Landlord-Tenant Law

A. The Leasehold Estates

Tenancies, or leaseholds — of which the principal ones are the term of years, the periodic tenancy, and the tenancy at will — are nonfreehold estates.[1] Why nonfreehold? The conventional wisdom is that this implicitly disparaging conception began with the term of years, first used as a moneylender's device to avoid the church's prohibition of usury, and the termor (tenant) was thought to be not quite respectable;[2] this has, however, recently been disputed.[3] Whatever the background, the fact remains that leaseholds and leasehold tenants were low in feudal dignity.

Let us look more closely at the leasehold estates.

1. The Term of Years

A term of years is an estate that lasts for some fixed period of time or for a period computable by a formula that results in fixing calendar dates for beginning and ending, once the term is created or becomes possessory. The period can be one day, two months, five years, or 3,000 years. These are all terms of years. At common law there was no limit on the number of years permitted, but in some American

---

1. One could add the tenancy at sufferance to the list, though it is not really a tenancy at all. We consider it below.

Bear in mind that when any of the leasehold estates is created, a future interest — in the landlord or in a third party — necessarily arises. If the landlord has retained the right to possession at the end of the leasehold, the future interest is a reversion. If provision is made for some third party to take possession, ordinarily the future interest will be a remainder.

2. See, e.g., John F. Hicks, The Contractual Nature of Real Property Leases, 24 Baylor L. Rev. 443, 448-449 (1972).

3. See William M. McGovern, The Historical Conception of a Lease for Years, 23 UCLA L. Rev. 501 (1976).

states statutes limit the duration of terms of years.[4] A term must be for a fixed period, but it can be terminable earlier upon the happening of some event or condition. Because a term of years states from the outset when it will terminate, no notice of termination is necessary to bring the estate to an end.

2.   The Periodic Tenancy

A periodic tenancy is a lease for a period of some fixed duration that continues for succeeding periods until either the landlord or tenant gives notice of termination. Examples: "to A from month to month"; "to B from year to year." If notice is not given the period is automatically extended for another period. (These are examples of express periodic tenancies. As we shall see, periodic tenancies are often created by implication.)

Under common law rules, half a year's notice is required to terminate a year-to-year tenancy. For example, if T is a year-to-year tenant beginning January 1, 1988, L must receive notice of termination before July 1, 1988, or T can be held over for another term — until January 1, 1990. For any periodic tenancy less than a year, notice of termination must be given equal to the length of the period, but not to exceed six months. The notice must terminate the tenancy on the final day of the period, not in the middle of the tenancy. Thus if a month-to-month tenant who began his tenancy on January 1 decided on March 20 to terminate, the earliest termination date would be April 30. In many states, statutes have shortened the length of notice required to terminate periodic tenancies and have permitted a month-to-month tenancy to be terminated at any time following thirty days' notice.

The death of the landlord or tenant has no effect on the duration of a term of years or periodic tenancy,[5] but it does on the tenancy at will.

4. For example, in California leases of agricultural land cannot exceed 51 years, nor those of urban land 99 years, if any rent or service of some kind is reserved. Cal. Civ. Code §§717, 718 (West 1982). In many areas, though, very long leases are permitted. Yale University still receives annual rents from 999-year leases of Connecticut farmland executed in the 1700s. Fred Strebeigh, Yale's 999-Year Leases, Yale Alumni Mag., Dec. 1976, at 29. And see Trustees of First Presbyterian Church of Pittsburgh v. Oliver-Tyrone Corp., 375 A.2d 193 (Pa. Super. Ct. 1977) (999-year lease).

Why such long-term leases? Some answers are suggested in Robert Megarry & H.W.R. Wade, The Law of Real Property (5th ed. 1984). First, during early times in England long-term leases had the advantage that, because they were personalty, they could be devised, whereas wills of freehold land were not allowed before 1540. Id. at 41. Of more contemporary interest, a landlord "can control the use of land by means of covenants in the lease, and a greater variety of covenants are enforceable under a lease than under an outright conveyance of the fee simple. Such very long leases may therefore be useful when a landlord is developing an estate and wishes to keep control over its appearance and character." Id. at 629.

5. But see Annot., 42 A.L.R.4th 963 (1985), suggesting that courts sometimes termi-

PROBLEMS

1. On October 1, *L* leases Whiteacre "to *T* for one year, beginning October 1." On the following September 30, *T* moves out without giving *L* any notice. What are *L*'s rights? What if the lease had been "to *T* from year to year, beginning October 1"? What if the lease had been for no fixed term "at an annual rental of $2,400 payable $200 per month on the first of each month"?

2. *T*, a month-to-month tenant, notified *L* on November 16, 1992, that she would vacate as of November 30, 1992. *T* subsequently vacated on that date and paid no further rent to *L*. *L*, after reasonable efforts, finally relet the premises beginning April 1, 1993. The jurisdiction in question has no statute prescribing the method of terminating a month-to-month tenancy. *L* sues *T* for unpaid rent for the months of December 1992 and January through March 1993. What result? See S.D.G. v. Inventory Control Co., 178 N.J. Super. 411, 429 A.2d 394 (1981).

3. The Tenancy at Will

A tenancy at will is a tenancy of no fixed period that endures so long as both landlord and tenant desire. If the lease provides that it can be terminated by one party, it is necessarily at the will of the other as well *if* a tenancy at will has been created. (Complications in this statement are examined in the *Garner* case, below.) Note, however, that a unilateral power to terminate a lease can be engrafted on a term of years or a periodic tenancy; for example, a lease by *L* to *T* for 10 years or until *L* sooner terminates creates a term of years determinable.

The tenancy at will ends, among other ways, when one of the parties terminates it. (It also ends, as suggested above, at the death of one of the parties.) Modern statutes ordinarily require a period of notice — say 30 days or a time equal to the interval between rent payments — in order for one party or the other to terminate a tenancy at will.[6]

---

nate residential leaseholds upon the death of the tenant (absent statutes providing otherwise) on the ground that residential tenancies are "personal."

6. How, in such jurisdictions, does the tenancy at will differ from a periodic tenancy? See 1 American Law of Property §§3.28, 3.31 (1952 & Supp. 1977). Note here, by the way, that if under a tenancy for no fixed period rent is reserved or paid periodically, a periodic tenancy — rather than a tenancy at will — arises in most jurisdictions by implication. See id. §3.25.

Garner v. Gerrish

Court of Appeals of New York, 1984
63 N.Y.2d 575, 473 N.E.2d 223

WACHTLER, J. The question on this appeal is whether a lease which grants the tenant the right to terminate the agreement at a date of his choice creates a determinable life tenancy on behalf of the tenant or merely establishes a tenancy at will. The courts below held that the lease created a tenancy at will permitting the current landlord to evict the tenant. We granted the tenant's motion for leave to appeal and now reverse the order appealed from.

In 1977 Robert Donovan owned a house located in Potsdam, New York. On April 14 of that year he leased the premises to the tenant Lou Gerrish. The lease was executed on a printed form and it appears that neither side was represented by counsel. The blanks on the form were filled in by Donovan who provided the names of the parties, described the property and fixed the rent at $100 a month. With respect to the duration of the tenancy the lease provides it shall continue "for and during the term of *quiet enjoyment* from the *first* day of *May,* 1977 which term will end — *Lou Gerrish has the privilege of termination [sic] this agreement at a date of his own choice*" (emphasis added to indicate handwritten and typewritten additions to the printed form). The lease also contains a standard reference to the landlord's right of reentry if the rent is not timely paid, which is qualified by the handwritten statement: "Lou has thirty days grace for payment."

Gerrish moved into the house and continued to reside there, apparently without incident, until Donovan died in November of 1981. At that point David Garner, executor of Donovan's estate, served Gerrish with a notice to quit the premises. When Gerrish refused, Garner commenced this summary proceeding to have him evicted. Petitioner contended that the lease created a tenancy at will because it failed to state a definite term. In his answering affidavit, the tenant alleged that he had always paid the rent specified in the lease. He also contended that the lease granted him a tenancy for life, unless he elects to surrender possession during his lifetime.

The County Court granted summary judgment to petitioner on the ground that the lease is "indefinite and uncertain ... as regards the length of time accorded respondent to occupy the premises. Although the writing specifies the date of commencement of the term, it fails to set forth the duration of continuance, and the date or event of termination." The court concluded that the original landlord leased the premises to the tenant "for a month-to-month term and that petitioner was entitled to terminate the lease upon the death of the lessor effective upon the expiration of the next succeeding monthly term of occupancy."

In support of its decision the court quoted the following statement from our opinion in Western Transp. Co. v. Lansing, 49 N.Y. 499, 508: "A lease . . . for so long as the lessee shall please, is said to be a lease at will of both lessor and lessee."

The Appellate Division affirmed for the same reasons in a brief memorandum (99 A.D.2d 608, 471 N.Y.S.2d 717).

On appeal to our court, the parties concede that the agreement creates a lease. The only question is whether it should be literally construed to grant to the tenant alone the right to terminate at will, or whether the landlord is accorded a similar right by operation of law.

At early common law according to Lord Coke, "when the lease is made to have and to hold at the will of the lessee, this must be also at the will of the lessor" (1 Co. Litt., §55a). This rule was generally adopted in the United States during the 19th century and at one time was said to represent the majority view (see Ann., 137 A.L.R. 362, 367; 51C C.J.S., Landlord and Tenant, §167, p.475). However, it was not universally accepted (see, e.g., Effinger v. Lewis, 32 Pa. 367; Gunnison v. Evans, 136 Kan. 791, 18 P.2d 191; Thompson v. Baxter, 107 Minn 122, 119 N.W. 797) and has been widely criticized, particularly in this century, as an antiquated notion which violates the terms of the agreement and frustrates the intent of the parties (1 Tiffany, Real Property [3d ed.], §159; 1 American Law of Real Property [Casner ed., 1952], §3.30; Schoshinski, American Law of Landlord and Tenant, §2:7; see, also, Restatement, Property 2d, Landlord and Tenant, §1:6).

It has been noted that the rule has its origins in the doctrine of livery of seisin (Tiffany, op. cit., §159; Effinger v. Lewis, supra), which required physical transfer of a clod of earth, twig, key or other symbol on the premises in the presence of witnesses, to effect a conveyance of a fee interest (23 Blackstone's Comm., pp.315, 316; Black's Law Dictionary [Fourth ed.], p.1084). Although this ceremony was not required for leases, which were gradually limited to a specified term of years, it was necessary to create a life tenancy which was viewed as a fee interest. Thus, if a lease granting a tenant a life estate was not accompanied by livery of seisin, the intended conveyance would fail and a mere tenancy at will would result. The corollary to Lord Coke's comment is that the grant of a life estate would be enforceable if accompanied by livery of seisin and the other requisites for a conveyance. Because such a tenancy was terminable at the will of the grantee, there was in fact no general objection at common law to a tenancy at the will of the tenant. The express terms of a lease granting a life tenancy would fail, and a tenancy at will would result, only when livery of seisin, or any other requirement for a conveyance, had not been met. . . .

Because livery of seisin, like the ancient requirement for a seal, has been abandoned, commentators generally urge that there is no longer any reason why a lease granting the tenant alone the right to terminate at will, should be converted into a tenancy at will terminable by either party (Tiffany, op. cit. §159; 1 American Law of Property, op. cit., §3.30; Schoshinski, op. cit., §2:16, pp.61, 62). The Restatement adopts this view and provides the following illustration: "*L* leases a farm to *T* 'for as long as *T* desires to stay on the land.' The lease creates a determinable life estate in *T*, terminable at *T*'s will or on his death." (Restatement, Property 2d, Landlord and Tenant, §1.6, Comment g, Illustration 6.) This rule has increasingly gained acceptance in courts which have closely examined the problem. . . .

In the case now before us, the lease . . . simply grants a personal right to the named lessee, Lou Gerrish, to terminate at a date of his choice, which is a fairly typical means of creating a life tenancy terminable at the will of the tenant. . . . Thus the lease will terminate, at the latest, upon the death of the named lessee. The fact that it may be terminated at some earlier point, if the named tenant decides to quit the premises, does not render it indeterminate. Leases providing for termination upon the occurrence of a specified event prior to the completion of an otherwise fixed term, are routinely enforced even when the event is within the control of the lessee (Schoshinski, op. cit., §2:7, pp.41-42).

In sum, the lease expressly and unambiguously grants to the tenant the right to terminate, and does not reserve to the landlord a similar right. To hold that such a lease creates a tenancy terminable at the will of either party would violate the terms of the agreement and the express intent of the contracting parties.

Accordingly, the order of the Appellate Division should be reversed and the petition dismissed.

PROBLEMS

1. *L* leases Orangeacre "to *T* for as many years as *L* desires." What estate does *T* have? See Restatement (Second) of Property, Landlord and Tenant, §1.6, Comment g, Illustration 7 (1977).

2. For rent payments of $500 a month *L* leases Greenacre "to *T* for the duration of the war." What estate does *T* have? What difference does it make? National Bellas Hess, Inc. v. Kalis, 191 F.2d 739 (8th Cir. 1951), cert. denied, 342 U.S. 933 (1952); Smith's Transfer & Storage Co. v. Hawkins, 50 A.2d 267 (D.C. 1946).

Philpot v. Field, 633 S.W.2d 546 (Tex. Civ. App. 1982), involved a lease to *T* for a term of 20 years and so long thereafter as *T* used the premises for particular purposes. Thereafter the premises were used continuously by *T* for the particular purposes. *L*, sometime after the expiration of the 20-year term, wished to terminate the lease. *L* argued that because the lease had an uncertain term, it was a tenancy at will terminable by either party once the 20 years expired. The court held otherwise, saying:

> Although there is no definite ending date after the 20 year term, that date is tied to the cessation of the use of the land for certain definitely ascertainable purposes. Common sense, logic and the trend in the law supports this decision. It appears that the parties intended to create a perpetual right to lease the land. When the parties' intent is made clear, courts should enforce the agreement as written, even though perpetual rights are not favored. . . .
>
> No legitimate reason exists for us to hold that the parties cannot freely and intelligently lease land for so long as a certain definite use is made of the land. Although [T] can terminate this lease when he desires by his voluntary choice, this lease does not create a tenancy at will terminable at the will of either party. [633 S.W.2d at 548.]

See also Myers v. East Ohio Gas Co., 51 Ohio St. 2d 121, 364 N.E.2d 1369 (1977), holding that "leases which clearly and unambiguously terminate at the will of only one party are to be controlled by their express terms." But ambiguous leases — "those leases which do not clearly state whether they are terminable at the will of one or both parties" — are subject to a rebuttable presumption that they are at the will of both. 51 Ohio St. at 126-127, 364 N.E.2d at 1373. The lease in *Myers* was similar to the lease in *Philpot*. The Court found it unambiguous and enforced it according to its terms.

4.   The Tenancy at Sufferance: Holdovers

The so-called tenancy at sufferance arises when a tenant remains in possession (holds over) after termination of the tenancy. Common law rules give the landlord confronted with a holdover essentially two options — eviction (plus damages), or consent (express or implied) to creation of a new tenancy. Some jurisdictions have changed these rules. Complications arise in any event. Consider the following case.

Crechale & Polles, Inc. v. Smith
Supreme Court of Mississippi, 1974
295 So. 2d 275

RODGERS, J. This action originated in the Chancery Court of the First Judicial District of Hinds County, Mississippi. . . . The court awarded the complainants one thousand seven hundred and fifty dollars ($1,750.00) in back rent payment and seven hundred sixty dollars ($760.00) for damages to the leasehold premises, as well as costs incurred in the proceeding. From this judgment appellant files this appeal. . . .

The testimony shows that on February 5, 1964, the appellant, Crechale and Polles, Inc., a Mississippi corporation, entered into a lease agreement with appellees, John D. Smith, Jr. and Mrs. Gloria Smith, with appellant as lessor and appellees as lessees. The lease was for a term of five (5) years commencing February 7, 1964, and expiring February 6, 1969, with rental in the amount of one thousand two hundred fifty dollars ($1,250.00) per month.

Smith was informed near the end of his lease that the new building which he planned to occupy would not be complete until a month or two after his present lease expired. With this in mind, he arranged a meeting with his landlord, Crechale, in late December, 1968, or early January, 1969, for the purpose of negotiating an extension of the lease on a month-to-month basis. The outcome of this meeting is one of the focal points of this appeal and the parties' stories sharply conflict. Crechale maintains that he told Smith that since he was trying to sell the property, he did not want to get involved in any month-to-month rental. Smith asserts that Crechale informed him that he was trying to sell the building, but that he could stay in it until it was sold or Smith's new building was ready. Smith's attorney drafted a thirty (30) day extension, but Crechale refused to sign it, saying, "Oh, go ahead. It's all right." Crechale denies that he was ever given the document to sign.

The following is a chronological explanation of the events which led to the subsequent litigation:

February 4, 1969 — Smith sent a letter to Crechale confirming their oral agreement to extend the lease on a monthly basis.

February 6, 1969 — Crechale wrote Smith denying the existence of any oral agreement concerning extension of the lease and requesting that Smith quit and vacate the premises upon expiration of the term at midnight, February 6, 1969. The letter also advised Smith that he was subject to payment of double rent for any holdover.

March 3, 1969 — Smith paid rent for the period of February to March. The check was accepted and cashed by Crechale.

April 6, 1969 — Smith paid rent for the period of March to April, but the check was not accepted by Crechale, because it was for "final payment."

April 7, 1969 — Smith sent a telegram to Crechale stating that he was tendering the premises for purposes of lessor's inventory. The telegram confirmed a telephone conversation earlier that day in which Crechale refused to inventory the building.

April 19, 1969 — Approximately two and one-half (2½) months after the expiration of the lease, Crechale's attorney wrote Smith stating that since the lessee had held over beyond the normal term, the lessor was treating this as a renewal of the lease for a new term expiring February 6, 1974.

April 24, 1969 — Smith again tendered the check for the final month's occupancy and it was rejected by Crechale.

April 29, 1969 — Crechale's attorney wrote Smith again stating the lessor's intention to consider the lessee's holdover as a renewal of the terms of the lease.

There was no further communication between the parties until a letter dated May 15, 1970, from Crechale to Smith requesting that Smith pay the past-due rent or vacate the premises.

May 27, 1970 — Smith's attorney tendered the keys to the premises to Crechale.

Subsequently, this lawsuit was filed by Crechale to recover back rent and damages beyond ordinary wear and tear to the leasehold premises. From the chancellor's decision, appellant files the following assignments of error:

(1) The lower court erred in holding that the appellees were not liable as holdover tenants for an additional term of one (1) year.

(2) The lower court's award of damages to the appellant was so inadequate in its amount as to be contrary to the overwhelming evidence. . . .

The appellant, Crechale and Polles, Inc., contends that the appellees became holdover tenants for a new term under the contract at the election of the landlord appellant, and that appellees owe appellant the rent due each month up to the filing of the suit, less the rent paid. . . . This argument is based upon the general rule expressed in 3 Thompson on Real Property §1024, at 65-66 (1959), wherein it is said:

> As a general rule, a tenancy from year to year is created by the tenant's holding over after the expiration of a term for years and the continued payment of the yearly rent reserved. . . . By remaining in possession of leased premises after the expiration of his lease, a tenant gives the landlord the option of treating him as a trespasser or as a tenant for another year. . . .

In support of this rule the appellant cites Tonkel, et al. v. Riteman, 163 Miss. 216, 141 So. 344 (1932), wherein it is said:

> It is firmly established that where, without a new contract, a tenant continues to occupy the property which he has held under an annual lease, he becomes liable as tenant for another year at the same rate and under the same terms. Love v. Law, 57 Miss. 596; Usher v. Moss, 50 Miss. 208. It is the duty of a tenant when his period of tenancy has expired to surrender the premises to his landlord or else to have procured a new contract, and, if he fails to do either, the landlord may treat him as a trespasser or as a tenant under the

previous terms, according to the option of the landlord. [163 Miss. at 219, 141 So. at 344.]

An examination of the testimony in this case has convinced us that the appellant is not entitled . . . to require the appellees to pay rent for a new term of the rental contract as a holdover tenant for the following reasons.

After receiving a letter from one of the appellees in which appellee Smith confirmed an alleged agreement to extend the lease on a month-to-month basis, Crechale immediately wrote Smith and denied that there was such an agreement, and demanded that Smith quit and vacate the premises at the end of the lease.

In addition to the rule expressed in 3 Thompson on Real Property §1024, above cited, another rule is tersely expressed in American Law of Property §3.33, at 237 (1952) as follows: "When a tenant continues in possession after the termination of his lease, the landlord has an election either to evict him, treat him as a trespasser it is said, or to hold him as a tenant."

The letter from the appellant dated February 6, 1969, was an effective election on the part of appellant to terminate the lease and to treat the appellees as trespassers.

After having elected not to accept the appellees as tenants, the appellant could not at a later date, after failing to pursue his remedy to evict the tenants, change the election so as to hold the appellees as tenants for a new term.

It is pointed out by the text writer in 49 Am. Jur. 2d under the title of Landlord and Tenant that:

> After the landlord has once exercised his election not to hold the tenant for another term, his right to hold him is lost. On the other hand, if he has signified his election to hold the tenant for another term he cannot thereafter rescind such election and treat the tenant as a trespasser, *since his election when once exercised is binding upon the landlord as well as the tenant.* (Emphasis added.) [49 Am. Jur. 2d Landlord and Tenant §1116, at 1070 (1970).]

Although the landlord, appellant, expressly refused to extend the lease on a month-to-month basis, nevertheless, the appellant accepted and cashed the rent check for the month of February. The normal effect of such action by the landlord is tantamount to extension of the lease for the period of time for which the check was accepted, unless, of course, the landlord had elected to treat the tenant as a holdover tenant.

The following excerpt from Annot., 45 A.L.R.2d 827, 831 (1956) points out this rule: "It is the rule that, absent evidence to show a contrary intent on the part of the landlord, a landlord who accepts rent from his holding-over tenant will be held to have consented to a renewal or extension of the leasing."

Although there is authority to the contrary [see Annot., 45 A.L.R.2d at 842] the overwhelming weight of authority has adopted the rule above expressed.

On April 6, 1969, the tenants mailed a check for rent for the month of March accompanied by a letter stating that the enclosed check represented the final payment of rent. The next day the tenants tendered the lease premises to the landlord and requested an inventory of certain personal property described in the lease. The landlord refused to accept the tender and rejected the check as a final payment. On April 19, 1969 [two and one-half (2½) months after the expiration of the lease] the landlord attempted to change its position. It then notified the tenants that it had elected to treat them as holdover tenants so as to extend the lease for another term.

We are of the opinion that once a landlord elects to treat a tenant as a trespasser and refuses to extend the lease on a month-to-month basis, but fails to pursue his remedy of ejecting the tenant, and accepts monthly checks for rent due, he in effect agrees to an extension of the lease on a month-to-month basis. See Lally v. The New Voice, 128 Ill. App. 455 (1906); Stillo v. Pellettieri, 173 Ill. App. 104 (1912). *Rule*

There is authority to the contrary, but we believe this rule to be based on the best reasoned authority.

The appellant contends that the decree of the trial court awarded inadequate damages to the appellant. The appellant fails, however, to point out any fact which would indicate to this Court wherein the decree of the trial court is manifestly wrong. We think that this issue of damages was a question of fact for the chancellor, and from an examination of the record we cannot say that the chancellor was manifestly wrong. . . .

We hold, therefore, that the decree of the trial court should be and is hereby affirmed.

Affirmed.

NOTES AND QUESTIONS

1. The landlord's lawyer in *Crechale* initially took the position that the Smiths were liable, as holdover tenants, for an additional five-year term, but there appears to be no basis for such a claim. In most jurisdictions, holding over gives rise (at the landlord's election) to a periodic tenancy; in the balance, it results in a term. As to the basis for the length of the period or term, on one view it is the way rent is reserved in the original lease and on another view it is the length of the original term or period — but the maximum length in each case is limited to one year. See 1 American Law of Property §3.35 at 244-246 (1952 & Supp. 1977). According to the Restatement, holding over results in a periodic tenancy measured by the way rent is computed, up to a maximum period of one

year. Restatement (Second) of Property, Landlord and Tenant, §14.4, Comment f (1977). These points aside, the tenancy resulting from a holding over is usually subject to the same terms and conditions (the amount of rent, the duty to repair, and so forth) as those in the original lease, unless the parties agree otherwise or unless some term or condition is regarded as inconsistent with the new situation.

2. Many states have adopted legislation to deal with holdovers, but in widely varying ways. Some statutes specify the length of the holdover tenancy. See, e.g., Cal. Civ. Code §1945 (West 1985) ("not exceeding one month when the rent is payable monthly, nor in any case one year"). Others, probably only a few, convert the holdover tenancy into a tenancy at will and provide that the tenant shall be liable for the reasonable value of use and occupation — even though this may be less than the rent agreed upon in the original lease! Such, at least, is one judicial interpretation. See Townsend v. Singleton, 257 S.C. 1, 183 S.E.2d 893 (1971). Still other statutes provide that landlords may demand double rent from holdover tenants.

The last approach is fairly common and, as it happens, should have been mentioned in *Crechale*, because Mississippi had such a statute at the time that case was decided. See Mississippi State Dept. of Pub. Welfare v. Howie, 449 So. 2d 772 (Miss. 1984), where the Supreme Court of Mississippi acknowledged that it had been inconsistent in dealing with the state's double-rent statute. It had implicitly held in a 1932 decision that the statute did not abrogate the common law rules on holdover tenancies, explicitly held in 1937 that it did, then implicitly held once again, in *Crechale*, that it did not.

> Therefore, our opinions have been a yes you can, no you can't, yes you can, response to this issue.
>
> We now hold that [the double-rent statute] was intended by the legislature to provide the sole action for damages as the result of a tenant's holdover. The common law rule has been abrogated once and for all and may no longer be used to impose the renewal of an expired lease. [449 So. 2d at 778.][7]

---

7. The court explained in a footnote that the statute "is the exclusive remedy to a landlord only insofar as money damages. The landlord is still free to evict a holdover tenant. . . ." 449 So. 2d at 778 n.1. We take up the general topic of eviction later in this chapter. See pages 489-499.

Regarding damages, the common law measure is the fair rental value of the leased premises, plus any special damages, and the rent reserved in the original lease is usually regarded as good evidence of fair rental value (although technically the landlord is not recovering rent).

Conventional common law doctrine provides that an incoming tenant with the right to possession also has the right to evict a holdover tenant and recover damages measured as above. The Restatement goes further; it extends to the incoming tenant a right, like the landlord's, to hold a holdover tenant to a new tenancy. Restatement (Second) of Property, Landlord and Tenant, supra, §14.4, Comment h. See also pages 463-469, discussing delivery of possession.

Does this mean that the result (as opposed to some of the statements) in *Crechale* was incorrect? It does not. The court endorsed the view that if a landlord neglects to evict a holdover tenant and to demand double rent for the holdover period, choosing instead to accept monthly rent payments, the lease is extended on a month-to-month basis.

Given the common law approach to holdovers, and the various legislative alternatives, which do you prefer? In thinking about the question, consider that conventional common law holdover doctrine

> is said to be for the benefit of tenants as a class because it secures to the incoming tenants the possession of the premises on the date bargained for, and . . . since leases . . . tend to begin and end at certain periods and property values are based on continuity of rental income, it is socially and economically important for the landlord to be able to deliver possession on a stipulated date. While this is true, the penalty imposed on the tenant frequently is out of all proportion to the injury to the landlord or the incoming tenant. [1 American Law of Property, supra, §3.33 at 238.]

policy

3. Suppose a tenant vacates leased premises in a timely fashion but leaves some office equipment behind. Is the tenant liable as a holdover? See Caserta v. Action for Bridgeport Community, 34 Conn. Super. 561, 377 A.2d 856 (1976) (no holdover, because the equipment did not interfere with the landlord's use of the premises). Suppose the tenant stays on after the end of the term because her doctor has advised her that it would be dangerous, for the time being, to move her very ill child. Is the tenant liable as a holdover? See Herter v. Mullen, 159 N.Y. 28, 53 N.E. 700 (1899) (no, because the tenant did not stay on voluntarily).

B. *The Lease*

An arrangement that resembles a lease — indeed, an arrangement explicitly declaring itself, in writing, to be a "lease" — might nevertheless be held by the courts to amount to something else, such as a license (see the discussion of licenses at page 800) or a life estate (see pages 428-430).[8] Suppose, for example, that *A* (1) "rents" from *B* the right to erect

8. Similarly, an arrangement that does not announce itself as a lease might still be regarded as one. See, e.g., Township of Sandyston v. Angerman, 134 N.J. Super. 450, 341 A.2d 682 (1975), involving an agreement between the Angermans and the U.S. Department of the Interior. By the terms of the agreement, the Angermans were given exclusive possession of a single-family dwelling and adjoining land located in a national recreation area; no rent was called for, but the Angermans were obligated to restore and maintain the dwelling and watch for forest fires in the area. A New Jersey statute subjected leaseholds to a municipal tax. The Angermans claimed that their arrangement with the Department of the Interior was a license, not a lease, and hence not subject to the leasehold tax. They lost.

a billboard on land owned by *B;* (2) contracts with *B* to install and oper-ate a cosmetics concession in *B*'s department store; (3) is allowed to farm *B*'s land, the consideration being that *A* will share the crops with *B;* (4) rents a room for two months in *B*'s rustic country inn; (5) works for *B* and is given a room in *B*'s house as partial compensation. Do these ex-amples involve leases — or something else? See generally 1 American Law of Property §§3.3-3.8 (1952 & Supp. 1977), discussing the many considerations that bear on the question (such as the intention of the parties, the number of restrictions on use, the exclusivity of possession, the degree of control retained by the granting party, the presence or absence of incidental services, and so on).

Putting aside obvious instances like that suggested in footnote 8, why might it matter whether any given arrangement amounts to a lease, as opposed to something else? The answer, for now, has to be limited to a pretty empty generalization: It matters primarily whether or not an arrangement amounts to a lease because leases give rise to the landlord-tenant relationship, which carries with it certain incidents — certain rights and duties and liabilities and remedies — that do not attach to other relationships. Those incidents are the chief concern of the balance of this chapter.

Conveyance versus contract. Here is another question you will see play-ing a part in much of the material that follows: Is a lease a *conveyance* or a *contract?* Actually, of course, it is both. A lease transfers a possessory interest in land, so it is a conveyance that creates property rights. But it is also the case that leases usually contain a number of promises (or cov-enants, which originally referred to promises under seal) — such as a promise by the tenant to pay rent or a promise by the landlord to pro-vide utilities — so the lease is a contract, too, thus creating contract rights.[9]

Historically, it was lease-as-conveyance that the courts tended to stress, but this has changed over the last several decades in favor of a view emphasizing the contractual nature of leases. The objective of the new orientation was to reform the "property law" of landlord and tenant by importing into it much of the modern law of contracts.[10] Some com-

---

9. Though leaseholds eventually came to be recognized as interests in land, they were and still are classified, like contractual interests, as personal property. Their peculiar origin is indicated by their old-fashioned name, chattels real. Chattel suggests personal property; real suggests a connection with land. The reasons for classifying a lessee's interest as per-sonal property have generally disappeared, but the classification can nevertheless be of some significance. For discussion, see 1 American Law of Property, supra, §3.12.

10. Especially as to residential leases. See, e.g., Report of Subcommittee on the Model Landlord-Tenant Act of Committee on Leases, Proposed Uniform Residential Landlord and Tenant Act, 8 Real Prop. Prob. & Tr. J. 104, 105 (1973): "[T]he proposed Act departs from the traditional view that the landlord-tenant relationship is founded in property law. Instead, the Act makes it plain that the relationship of the landlord and tenant in a *residen-tial* lease arrangement should be founded in contract law." Notice the emphasis on "resi-

mentators have found the move unnecessary, or even counterproductive,[11] but the fact remains that courts today commonly rely, explicitly,
on contract principles to reshape the law of leases with respect to such
questions as the following: (1) Are the covenants in leases "mutually dependent," such that (as in contract doctrine) a material breach by one
party excuses further performance by the other party, even if the lease
does not so provide? Suppose, for example, that the landlord breaches
a promise to repair? Does the tenant's obligation to pay rent cease? If
the tenant defaults in rent payments, may the landlord terminate the
lease, absent a provision allowing him to do so? (2) If the leased premises
are destroyed, is the tenant still liable for rent (again, notwithstanding
the absence of any relevant provision in the lease)? (3) If the tenant
wrongfully abandons the leased premises, must the landlord take steps
to mitigate (reduce) the damages, say by searching for a suitable new
tenant?[12] (4) Is a warranty of quality — that the leased premises are habitable or fit for their purpose — to be implied in leases? We shall be
addressing questions like these in subsequent sections of this chapter.

   The Statute of Frauds. Every state has a Statute of Frauds (intended
to prevent just that) patterned in one way or another after the English
Statute of Frauds enacted in the seventeenth century. Commonly, the
American statutes provide that leases for more than one year must be in
writing. All but a few jurisdictions permit oral leases for a term less than
a year; those that do not usually hold that entry under an oral lease plus
payment of rent creates a periodic tenancy that is not subject to the Statute. For a discussion of the consequences of failure to comply with the
statutory requirements, see 1 American Law of Property, supra, §§3.18-
3.21. See also pages 587-593.

   Form leases and the question of "bargaining power." The written lease
can be a long document. Unlike a deed, by which (in the usual case) all
of the seller's interest is conveyed to the buyer forever, a lease contemplates a continuing relationship between landlord and tenant. Thus
deeds are commonly brief, whereas leases can be wordy, full of clauses
to handle various contingencies.

   Quite typically, landlords use form leases — standardized docu-

---

dential"; "the Act [does] not purport to apply to commercial leases." Id. at 104 n.2. See
generally Uniform Residential Landlord and Tenant Act (URLTA).
   11. See, e.g., Edward Chase, The Property-Contract Theme in Landlord and Tenant
Law: A Critical Commentary on Schoshinski's American Law of Landlord and Tenant, 13
Rutgers L.J. 189 (1982); John A. Humbach, The Common-Law Conception of Leasing:
Mitigation, Habitability, and Dependence of Covenants, 60 Wash. U. L.Q. 1213 (1983).
   Understand that contract principles have always governed agreements to make a
lease, though it can sometimes be difficult to tell whether a particular transaction amounts
to a lease (but one to commence in the future), or rather to an agreement to make a lease.
See generally 1 American Law of Property, supra, §3.17.
   12. Usually, of course, the landlord will wish to re-rent as soon as possible in any
event, for the sake of cash flow and protection of the premises. But see Sommer v. Kridel,
reproduced on page 500.

ments offered to all tenants on a take-it-or-leave-it basis, with no negotiation over terms. Does this indicate that tenants lack bargaining power, such that harsh terms can be forced upon them by landlords? Not necessarily. Consider the following, addressing form contracts generally:

> It is an easy step from the observation that there is no negotiation to the conclusion that the purchaser lacked a free choice and therefore should not be bound by onerous terms. But there is an innocent explanation: The seller is just trying to avoid the costs of negotiating and drafting a separate agreement with each purchaser. These costs, of which the largest probably is supervising the employees and agents who engage in the actual contract negotiations on the company's behalf, are likely to be very high for a large company that has many contracts. Consistent with the innocent explanation, large and sophisticated buyers, as well as individual consumers, often make purchases pursuant to printed form contracts.
>
> The sinister explanation is that the seller refuses to dicker separately with each purchaser because the buyer has no choice but to accept his terms. This assumes an absence of competition. If one seller offers unattractive terms, a competing seller, wanting sales for himself, will offer more attractive terms. The process will continue until the terms are optimal. All the firms in the industry may find it economical to use standard contracts and refuse to negotiate with purchasers. But what is important is not whether there is haggling in every transaction but whether competition forces sellers to incorporate in their standard contracts terms that protect the purchasers.
>
> Under monopoly, by definition, the buyer has no good alternatives to dealing with the seller, who is therefore in a position, within limits, to compel the buyer to agree to terms that in a competitive market would be bettered by another seller. [Richard A. Posner, Economic Analysis of Law 114-115 (4th ed. 1992).]

On this view, the underlying problem is not form leases but monopoly power — created, say, by a shortage of rental housing.[13] What, then, should be the remedy? The courts can respond by policing lease terms on grounds of "unequal bargaining power" (a theme you will see running throughout this chapter), but this case-by-case approach is thought by some to be insufficient. See, e.g., Curtis J. Berger, Hard Leases Make Bad Law, 74 Colum. L. Rev. 791 (1974), calling instead for statutory reform — legislation requiring full disclosure of landlords' and tenants' duties, rights, and remedies. A more far-reaching approach would rely on statutory leases setting out prescribed terms and conditions.[14]

---

13. If there is a glut, tenants will have enhanced "bargaining power." Form leases might still be used, but their terms — especially terms regarding the amount of rent — are likely to be attractive to tenants.

14. See, e.g., Allen R. Bentley, An Alternative Residential Lease, 74 Colum. L. Rev. 836 (1974).

Statutory leases can be problematic if landlords have political power as well as market power. See Note, Standard Form Leases in Wisconsin, 1966 Wis. L. Rev. 583, describing a program that allowed Wisconsin real estate brokers to use form leases only if the forms

Given the assumption of market (monopoly) power, would not land-lords respond to any of the foregoing measures by increasing the rents they charged? Rent controls could then be considered, but they might aggravate the underlying housing shortage. See pages 559-565.

C. Selection of Tenants (Herein of Unlawful Discrimination)

Landlords, once free to discriminate as they wished in selecting ten-ants — whether on grounds of race, gender, national origin, or what-ever — are today constrained in a number of respects. Perhaps the most significant constraints (not the only ones) are imposed by the federal Fair Housing Act, 42 U.S.C. §§3601-3619, 3631 (1988),[15] portions of which provide:

§3601. Declaration of Policy

It is the policy of the United States to provide, within constitutional lim-itations, for fair housing throughout the United States. . . .

§3603. Effective Dates of Certain Prohibitions

(a) Application to certain described dwellings
Subject to the provisions of subsection (b) of this section and section 3607 of this title [section 3607 exempts religious organizations and private clubs under certain circumstances, and also states that provisions regarding familial status do not apply to housing for older persons], the prohibitions against discrimination in the sale or rental of housing set forth in section 3604 of this title shall apply. . . .

---

were issued or approved by the Wisconsin Real Estate Commission. The Commission, charged by legislation to "safeguard the interests of the public," nevertheless approved standard forms that contained provisions and clauses in conflict with state policy; the forms were "landlords' leases." Id. at 585, 592.

15. The Act, originally enacted as Title VIII of the Civil Rights Act of 1968, was significantly expanded by the Fair Housing Amendments Act of 1988.

Attempts by the federal government to combat discrimination, *racial* discrimination in particular, date back to adoption of the Fourteenth Amendment and its guarantee of equal protection. The Fourteenth Amendment prohibits only *state action*, but the Supreme Court's 1948 decision in Shelley v. Kraemer (see page 903) effectively eliminated at least some private racial discrimination as well. A provision in the Civil Rights Act of 1866, 42 U.S.C. §1982 (1988), promised to do more, at least with respect to property transactions: "All citizens of the United States," it said, "shall have the same right, in every State and Territory, as is enjoyed by white citizens thereof to inherit, purchase, lease, sell, hold, and convey real and personal property." Despite the promise, the 1866 Act had essentially no impact on private housing discrimination during the first century of its life. More on this shortly.

(b) Exemptions

Nothing in section 3604 of this title (other than subsection (c)) shall apply to —

(1) any single-family house sold or rented by an owner: *Provided,* That such private individual owner does not own more than three such single-family houses at any one time: *Provided further,* That in the case of the sale of any such single-family house by a private individual owner not residing in such house at the time of such sale or who was not the most recent resident of such house prior to such sale, the exemption granted by this subsection shall apply only with respect to one such sale within any twenty-four month period: *Provided further,* That such bona fide private individual owner does not own any interest in, nor is there owned or reserved on his behalf, under any express or voluntary agreement, title to or any right to all or a portion of the proceeds from the sale or rental of, more than three such single-family houses at any one time: *Provided further,* That after December 31, 1969, the sale or rental of any such single-family house shall be excepted from the application of this subchapter only if such house is sold or rented (A) without the use in any manner of the sales or rental facilities or the sales or rental services of any real estate broker, agent, or salesman, or of such facilities or services of any person in the business of selling or renting dwellings, or of any employee or agent of any such broker, agent, salesman, or person and (B) without the publication, posting or mailing, after notice, of any advertisement or written notice in violation of section 3604(c) of this title; but nothing in this proviso shall prohibit the use of attorneys, escrow agents, abstractors, title companies, and other such professional assistance as necessary to perfect or transfer the title, or

(2) rooms or units in dwellings containing living quarters occupied or intended to be occupied by no more than four families living independently of each other, if the owner actually maintains and occupies one of such living quarters as his residence. . . .

§3604. Discrimination in the sale or rental of housing and other prohibited practices

As made applicable by section 3603 of this title and except as exempted by sections 3603(b) and 3607 of this title, it shall be unlawful —

(a) To refuse to sell or rent after the making of a bona fide offer, or to refuse to negotiate for the sale or rental of, or otherwise make unavailable or deny, a dwelling to any person because of race, color, religion, sex, familial status, or national origin.

(b) To discriminate against any person in the terms, conditions, or privileges of sale or rental of a dwelling, or in the provision of services or facilities in connection therewith, because of race, color, religion, sex, familial status, or national origin.

(c) To make, print, or publish, or cause to be made, printed, or published any notice, statement, or advertisement, with respect to the sale or rental of a dwelling that indicates any preference, limitation, or discrimination based on race, color, religion, sex, handicap, familial status, or national origin, or an intention to make any such preference, limitation, or discrimination.

(d) To represent to any person because of race, color, religion, sex, handicap, familial status, or national origin that any dwelling is not available for inspection, sale, or rental when such dwelling is in fact so available.

(e) For profit, to induce or attempt to induce any person to sell or rent any dwelling by representations regarding the entry or prospective entry into the neighborhood of a person or persons of a particular race, color, religion, sex, handicap, familial status, or national origin.

(f)(1) To discriminate in the sale or rental, or to otherwise make unavailable or deny, a dwelling to any buyer or renter because of a handicap of —

(A) that buyer or renter;

(B) a person residing in or intending to reside in that dwelling after it is so sold, rented, or made available; or

(C) any person associated with that buyer or renter.

(2) To discriminate against any person in the terms, conditions, or privileges of sale or rental of a dwelling, or in the provision of services or facilities in connection with such dwelling, because of a handicap of —

(A) that person; or

(B) a person residing in or intending to reside in that dwelling after it is so sold, rented, or made available; or

(C) any person associated with that person.

(3) For purposes of this subsection, discrimination includes —

(A) a refusal to permit, at the expense of the handicapped person, reasonable modifications of existing premises occupied or to be occupied by such person if such modifications may be necessary to afford such person full enjoyment of the premises except that, in the case of a rental, the landlord may where it is reasonable to do so condition permission for a modification on the renter agreeing to restore the interior of the premises to the condition that existed before the modification, reasonable wear and tear excepted;

(B) a refusal to make reasonable accommodations in rules, policies, practices, or services, when such accommodations may be necessary to afford such person equal opportunity to use and enjoy a dwelling; or

(C) in connection with the design and construction of covered multifamily dwellings for first occupancy after the date that is 30 months after September 13, 1988, a failure to design and construct those dwellings in such a manner that —

(i) the public use and common use portions of such dwellings are readily accessible to and usable by handicapped persons;

(ii) all the doors designed to allow passage into and within all premises within such dwellings are sufficiently wide to allow passage by handicapped persons in wheelchairs; and

(iii) all premises within such dwellings contain the following features of adaptive design:

(I) an accessible route into and through the dwelling;

(II) light switches, electrical outlets, thermostats, and other environmental controls in accessible locations;

(III) reinforcements in bathroom walls to allow later installation of grab bars; and

(IV) usable kitchens and bathrooms such that an individual in a wheelchair can maneuver about the space. . . .

NOTES, QUESTIONS, AND PROBLEMS

1. As enacted in 1968, the Fair Housing Act did not prohibit discrimination on the grounds of sex, handicap, or familial status. Sex discrimination was added to the Act in 1974; the 1988 amendments added the prohibitions regarding handicap and familial status.

Portions of the Fair Housing Act not set out above prohibit discrimination in the financing of housing and in the provision of brokerage services. Anyone injured by a discriminatory practice may commence a civil suit for injunctive relief and damages (including punitive damages). Other enforcement measures include conference and conciliation proceedings, suits by the U.S. Attorney General, and criminal penalties.

On the Fair Housing Act and the 1988 amendments generally, see James A. Kushner, The Fair Housing Amendments Act of 1988: The Second Generation of Fair Housing, 42 Vand. L. Rev. 1049 (1989).

2. Recall 42 U.S.C. §1982, a provision of the Civil Rights Act of 1866 mentioned in footnote 15 above. In Jones v. Alfred H. Mayer Co., 392 U.S. 409 (1968), decided the same year the original Fair Housing Act became law, the Court held that the 1866 provision bars *all* racial discrimination, private and public, in the sale or rental of property. The Court noted that the 1866 provision is narrower than the Fair Housing Act because, for example, it reaches only racial discrimination, does not deal with discrimination in the provision of services or facilities, and does not prohibit discriminatory advertising. But the provision is broader in that it contains none of the exemptions found in the Fair Housing Act.[16]

3. Mrs. Murphy has an apartment to rent in her home. She puts the following advertisement in a local newspaper:

For rent: Furnished basement apartment in private white home. Call 376-7410.

---

16. The 1866 legislation was broader in another important respect as well: It had no cap on damages, whereas the Fair Housing Act as originally enacted limited punitive damages to $1,000. The 1988 amendments did away with the limitation.

Professor Kushner predicted in 1989 that "[t]he rise in compensatory damage awards should soon generate the first one million dollar verdict. Such a symbolic award, and the publicity it is likely to spawn, may begin to carry a deterrent effect and, more importantly, open the eyes of the practicing bar to the ease and profit of litigating fair housing cases." Kushner, supra, at 1078. See in this respect Robert Pear, Accusation of Bias Against Children Leads to Big Award in Housing Suit, N.Y. Times, July 16, 1992, at A18: "Lawyers for the plaintiffs predict that the size of the verdict [$2.4 million], one of the first under a Federal housing law enacted four years ago, will prompt lawsuits nationwide against property owners and managers believed to be discriminating. . . ."

A black couple applies and is rejected by Mrs. Murphy because of race. Are there any violations of 42 U.S.C. §1982 or §3604? See United States v. Hunter, 459 F.2d 205 (4th Cir.), cert. denied, 409 U.S. 934 (1972). Suppose the advertisement had not contained the word "white." What result? See Bush v. Kaim, 297 F. Supp. 151 (N.D. Ohio 1969). Suppose the advertisement had not said "in private white home," but had said "rented only to persons speaking Polish, German, or Swedish." What result? See Holmgren v. Little Village Community Reporter, 342 F. Supp. 512 (N.D. Ill. 1971).[17]

Does the regular exclusion of black and other minority models from real estate advertisements containing human models violate 42 U.S.C. §3604(c)? See Ragin v. New York Times Co., 923 F.2d 995 (2d Cir.), cert. denied, 112 S. Ct. 81 (1991); Comment, When the Medium Becomes the Message: A Proposal for Principal Media Liability for the Publication of Racially Exclusionary Real Estate Advertisements, 40 UCLA L. Rev. 199 (1992); Note, Advertising and Title VIII: The Discriminatory Use of Models in Real Estate Advertisements, 98 Yale L.J. 165 (1988).

The following advertisement is typical of many found nowadays in campus newspapers:

> *Wanted:* Female to share lovely 2-bedrm. 2-bath apt. near campus and bus lines. $400/mo. plus half utilities. Call Pat eves. at 927-1214.

Should such ads be held to violate the Fair Housing Act? See generally Kenneth L. Karst, The Freedom of Intimate Association, 89 Yale L.J. 624 (1980).

4. Which (if any) of the following would violate the Fair Housing Act?

(a) *L* refuses to rent to a heterosexual couple because they are unmarried. See Kushner, supra, at 1106-1107; Comment, The Wages of Living in Sin: Discrimination in Housing Against Unmarried Couples, 25 U.C. Davis L. Rev. 1055 (1992).

(b) *L* refuses to rent to a gay couple because he objects to the partners' sexual orientation. See Kushner, supra, at 1108. Would it matter that *L*'s reason is a fear of AIDS? See Baxter v. City of Belleville, 720 F. Supp. 720, 728 (S.D. Ill. 1989); Michael P. Seng, Discrimination Against Families with Children and Handicapped Persons Under the 1988

---

17. See also Judy Pasternak, Housing Bias with a Twist, L.A. Times, Feb. 7, 1991, at A1 ("Complaints are increasing about immigrant landlords who close the door to renters who are not from their homeland. . . . Patricia Leigh felt the stinging suspicion that she was a victim of racism. It was an odd, unsettling thought for a white American.").

Going back to the example in the text, suppose Mrs. Murphy discriminates *against,* say, German people in renting the apartment in her home. This would not violate the Fair Housing Act. (Do you see why?) Would it violate the Civil Rights Act of 1866, 42 U.S.C. §1982? See Shaare Tefila Congregation v. Cobb, 481 U.S. 615 (1987).

Amendments to the Fair Housing Act, 22 J. Marshall L. Rev. 541, 554-555 (1989).[18]

(c) *L* rents to *T,* a single woman, and then, several weeks into the tenancy, begins harassing her with demands for sexual favors. See Grieger v. Sheets, 689 F. Supp. 835 (N.D. Ill. 1988); Comment, Home is No Haven: An Analysis of Sexual Harassment in Housing, 1987 Wis. L. Rev. 1061, 1075-1081; Comment, Landlord Sexual Harassment: A Federal Remedy, 65 Temp. L. Rev. 589 (1992).

(d) *L* regularly rents one-bedroom apartments to households consisting of two adults, and two-bedroom apartments to households of two adults and two children, but will not rent the one-bedroom units to one adult and one child, nor the two-bedroom units to one adult and three children. See Glover v. Crestwood Lake Section 1 Holding Corps., 746 F. Supp. 301 (S.D.N.Y. 1990).

(e) *L,* the owner of a large apartment complex, reserves a certain number of units for white applicants in order to maintain integrated housing conditions. Consider the following case.

United States v. Starrett City Associates
United States Court of Appeals, Second Circuit, 1988
840 F.2d 1096, cert. denied, 488 U.S. 946 (1988)

MINER, J. The United States Attorney General, on behalf of the United States ("the government"), commenced this action under Title VIII of the Civil Rights Act of 1968 ("Fair Housing Act" or "the Act") against defendants-appellants Starrett City Associates, Starrett City, Inc. and

---

18. Recall that 42 U.S.C. §3604 prohibits discrimination because of a handicap. "Handicap" is defined by §3602(h), which states that the term means,

> with respect to a person —
> (1) a physical or mental impairment which substantially limits one or more of such person's major life activities,
> (2) a record of having such an impairment, or
> (3) being regarded as having such an impairment. . . .

But §3604 goes on to add that the term "does not include current, illegal use of or addiction to a controlled substance. . . ."

Proposed amendments that would have similarly excluded alcoholism (as well as infectious, contagious, and communicable diseases) from the definition of "handicap" failed to pass. Note, however, that landlords may consider alcoholism in determining whether applicants would be suitable tenants. Note also that dwellings need not "be made available to an individual whose tenancy would constitute a direct threat to the health or safety of other individuals. . . ." 42 U.S.C. §3604(f)(9).

Regarding the meaning of "handicap," one odd provision did become law: the term does not include transvestism! See Note on Transvestism set out under §3602. "By adopting this provision, Congress was likely reacting [to a 1986 case] in which a district court held that . . . transvestites are 'handicapped' " within the meaning of the federal Rehabilitation Act. Recent Developments, 24 Harv. C.R.-C.L. L. Rev. 249, 252 (1989).

Delmar Management Company (collectively, "Starrett") in the United States District Court for the Eastern District of New York (Neaher, J.). The government maintained that Starrett's practices of renting apartments in its Brooklyn housing complex solely on the basis of applicants' race or national origin, and of making apartments unavailable to black and hispanic applicants that are then made available to white applicants, violate section 804(a), (b), (c) and (d) of the Act, 42 U.S.C. §3604(a)-(d) (1982).

The parties made cross-motions for summary judgment based on extensive documentary submissions. The district court granted summary judgment in favor of the government and permanently enjoined appellants from discriminating on the basis of race in the rental of apartments. Starrett appeals from this judgment.

Background

Appellants constructed, own and operate "Starrett City," the largest housing development in the nation, consisting of 46 high-rise buildings containing 5,881 apartments in Brooklyn, New York. The complex's rental office opened in December 1973. Starrett has made capital contributions of $19,091,000 to the project, the New York State Housing Finance Agency has made $362,720,000 in mortgage loans, and the U.S. Department of Housing and Urban Development subsidizes Starrett's monthly mortgage interest payments. The United Housing Foundation abandoned a project to build a development of cooperative apartments at the Starrett City site in 1971. Starrett proposed to construct rental units on the site on the condition that the New York City Board of Estimate approve a transfer to Starrett of the city real estate tax abatement granted to the original project. The transfer created "substantial community opposition" because "the neighborhood surrounding the project and past experience with subsidized housing" created fear that "the conversion to rental apartments would result in Starrett City's becoming an overwhelmingly minority development." United States v. Starrett City Assocs., 660 F. Supp. 668, 670 (E.D.N.Y. 1987). The transfer was approved, however, "upon the assurance of Starrett City's developer that it was intended to create a racially integrated community."

Starrett has sought to maintain a racial distribution by apartment of 64% white, 22% black and 8% hispanic at Starrett City. Starrett claims that these racial quotas are necessary to prevent the loss of white tenants, which would transform Starrett City into a predominantly minority complex. Starrett points to the difficulty it has had in attracting an integrated applicant pool from the time Starrett City opened, despite extensive advertising and promotional efforts. Because of these purported difficulties, Starrett adopted a tenanting procedure to promote and maintain

Winter Garden
Starrett City
Photograph by Ozier Muhammad
© 1991 New York Newsday

the desired racial balance. This procedure has resulted in relatively stable percentages of whites and minorities living at Starrett City between 1975 and the present.

The tenanting procedure requires completion of a preliminary information card stating, *inter alia,* the applicant's race or national origin, family composition, income and employment. The rental office at Starrett City receives and reviews these applications. Those that are found preliminarily eligible, based on family composition, income, employment and size of apartment sought, are placed in "the active file," in which separate records by race are maintained for apartment sizes and income levels. Applicants are told in an acknowledgement letter that no apartments are presently available, but that their applications have been placed in the active file and that they will be notified when a unit becomes available for them. When an apartment becomes available, applicants are selected from the active file for final processing, creating a processed applicant pool. As vacancies arise, applicants of a race or national origin similar to that of the departing tenants are selected from the pool and offered apartments.

In December 1979, a group of black applicants brought an action against Starrett in the United States District Court for the Eastern Dis-

448

trict of New York. . . . Plaintiffs alleged that Starrett's tenanting procedures violated federal and state law by discriminating against them on
the basis of race. The parties stipulated to a settlement in May 1984, and
a consent decree was entered subsequently, see Arthur v. Starrett City
Assocs., No. 79-CV-3096, slip op. at 1 (E.D.N.Y. April 2, 1985). The
decree provided that Starrett would, depending on apartment availability, make an additional 35 units available each year for a five-year period
to black and minority applicants.

The government commenced the present action against Starrett in
June 1984, "to place before the [c]ourt the issue joined but left expressly
unresolved" in the *Arthur* consent decree: the "legality of defendants'
policy and practice of limiting the number of apartments available to
minorities in order to maintain a prescribed degree of racial balance."
United States v. Starrett City Assocs., 605 F. Supp. 262, 263 (E.D.N.Y.
1985). The complaint alleged that Starrett, through its tenanting policies, discriminated in violation of the Fair Housing Act. Specifically, the
government maintained that Starrett violated the Act by making apartments unavailable to blacks solely because of race, 42 U.S.C. §3604(a),
by forcing black applicants to wait significantly longer for apartments
than whites solely because of race, id. §3604(b); by enforcing a policy
that prefers white applicants while limiting the numbers of minority applicants accepted, id. §3604(c); and by representing in an acknowledgement letter that no apartments are available for rental when in fact units
are available, id. §3604(d). . . .

Starrett maintained that the tenanting procedures "were adopted at
the behest of the [s]tate solely to achieve and maintain integration and
were not motivated by racial animus." To support their position, appellants submitted the written testimony of three housing experts. They
described the "white flight" and "tipping" phenomena, in which white
residents migrate out of a community as the community becomes poor
and the minority population increases, resulting in the transition to a
predominantly minority community. Acknowledging that " 'the tipping
point for a particular housing development, depending as it does on
numerous factors and the uncertainties of human behavior, is difficult
to predict with precision,' " one expert stated that the point at which
tipping occurs has been estimated at from 1% to 60% minority population, but that the consensus ranged between 10% and 20%. Another
expert, who had prepared a report in 1980 on integration at Starrett
City for the New York State Division of Housing and Community Renewal, estimated the complex's tipping point at approximately 40%
black on a population basis. A third expert, who had been involved in
integrated housing ventures since the 1950's, found that a 2:1 white-
minority ratio produced successful integration.

The court, however, accepted the government's contention that
Starrett's practices of making apartments unavailable for blacks, while

reserving them for whites, and conditioning rental to minorities based on a "tipping formula" derived only from race or national origin are clear violations of the Fair Housing Act. The district court found that apartment opportunities for blacks and hispanics were far fewer "than would be expected if race and national origin were not taken into account," while opportunities for whites were substantially greater than what their application rates projected. Minority applicants waited up to ten times longer than the average white applicant before they were offered an apartment. Starrett City's active file was 21.9% white in October 1985, but whites occupied 64.7% of the apartments in January 1984. Although the file was 53.7% black and 18% hispanic in October 1985, blacks and hispanics, respectively, occupied only 20.8% and 7.9% of the apartments as of January 1984. Appellants did not dispute this. Further, the court found that appellants' tipping argument was undercut by the "wide elasticity of that standard" and the lack of difficulty they had in increasing their black quota from 21% to 35% "when it became necessary to avoid litigating the private *Arthur* lawsuit which threatened their unlawful rental practices." The court also found that Starrett violated the Act by making untrue representations of apartment unavailability to qualified minority applicants in order to reserve units for whites. Finally, the court rejected Starrett's claim that the duty imposed upon government to achieve housing integration justified its actions, stating that "[d]efendants cannot arrogate to themselves the powers" of a public housing authority.

The court concluded that Starrett's obligation was "simply and solely to comply with the Fair Housing Act" by treating "black and other minority applicants . . . on the same basis as whites in seeking available housing at Starrett City." The court noted that Starrett did not dispute any of the operative facts alleged to show violations of the Fair Housing Act. Accordingly, Judge Neaher granted summary judgment for the government, enjoining Starrett from discriminating against applicants on the basis of race and "[r]equiring [them] to adopt written, objective, uniform, nondiscriminatory tenant selection standards and procedures" subject to the court's approval. The court retained jurisdiction over the parties for three years.

On appeal, Starrett presses arguments similar to those it made before the district court. We affirm the district court's judgment.

Discussion

Title VIII of the Civil Rights Act of 1968 ("Fair Housing Act" or "the Act"), 42 U.S.C. §§3601-3631 (1982), was enacted pursuant to Congress' thirteenth amendment powers "to provide, within constitutional limitations, for fair housing throughout the United States." 42 U.S.C. §3601. Section 3604 of the statute prohibits discrimination because of race, color or national origin in the sale or rental of housing by, *inter alia:* (1) refusing to rent or make available any dwelling, id. §3604(a); (2) offering discriminatory "terms, conditions or privileges" of rental, id. §3604(b); (3) making, printing or publishing "any notice, statement, or advertisement . . . that indicates any preference, limitation, or discrimination based on race, color . . . or national origin," id. §3604(c); and (4) representing to any person "that any dwelling is not available for . . . rental when such dwelling is in fact so available," id. §3604(d).

Housing practices unlawful under Title VIII include not only those motivated by a racially discriminatory purpose, but also those that disproportionately affect minorities. . . .

Starrett's allocation of public housing facilities on the basis of racial quotas, by denying an applicant access to a unit otherwise available solely because of race, produces a "discriminatory effect . . . [that] could hardly be clearer," Burney v. Housing Auth., 551 F. Supp. 746, 770 (W.D. Pa. 1982). Appellants do not contend that the plain language of section 3604 does not proscribe their practices. Rather, they claim to be "clothed with governmental authority" and thus obligated, under Otero v. New York City Housing Auth., 484 F.2d 1122 (2d Cir. 1973), to effectuate the purpose of the Fair Housing Act by affirmatively promoting integration and preventing "the reghettoization of a model integrated community." We need not decide whether Starrett is a state actor, however. Even if Starrett were a state actor with such a duty, the racial quotas and related practices employed at Starrett City to maintain integration violate the antidiscrimination provisions of the Act.

Both Starrett and the government cite to the legislative history of the Fair Housing Act in support of their positions. This history consists solely of statements from the floor of Congress. These statements reveal "that at the time that Title VIII was enacted, Congress believed that strict adherence to the anti-discrimination provisions of the [A]ct" would eliminate "racially discriminatory housing practices [and] ultimately would result in residential integration." *Burney,* 551 F. Supp. at 769. Thus, Congress saw the antidiscrimination policy as the means to effect the antisegregation-integration policy. While quotas promote Title VIII's integration policy, they contravene its antidiscrimination policy, bringing the dual goals of the Act into conflict. The legislative history provides no further guidance for resolving this conflict.

We therefore look to analogous provisions of federal law enacted to prohibit segregation and discrimination as guides in determining to what extent racial criteria may be used to maintain integration. . . . [T]he Supreme Court's analysis of what constitutes permissible race-conscious affirmative action under provisions of federal law with goals similar to those of Title VIII provides a framework for examining the affirmative use of racial quotas under the Fair Housing Act.

Although any racial classification is presumptively discriminatory, a race-conscious affirmative action plan does not necessarily violate federal constitutional or statutory provisions. However, a race-conscious plan cannot be "ageless in [its] reach into the past, and timeless in [its] ability to affect the future." Wygant v. Jackson Bd. of Educ., 476 U.S. 267, 106 S. Ct. 1842, 1848, 90 L. Ed. 2d 260 (1986) (plurality opinion). A plan employing racial distinctions must be temporary in nature with a defined goal as its termination point. See, e.g., Johnson v. Transportation Agency, 480 U.S. 616, 107 S. Ct. 1442, 1456, 94 L. Ed. 2d 615 (1987). . . . Moreover, we observe that societal discrimination alone seems "insufficient and over expansive" as the basis for adopting so-called "benign" practices with discriminatory effects "that work against innocent people," Wygant, 106 S. Ct. at 1848, in the drastic and burdensome way that rigid racial quotas do. Furthermore, the use of quotas generally should be based on some history of racial discrimination, see id. at 1847, or imbalance, see Johnson, 107 S. Ct. at 1452-53, within the entity seeking to employ them. Finally, measures designed to increase or ensure minority participation, such as "access" quotas, see Burney, 551 F. Supp. at 763, have generally been upheld, see, e.g., Johnson, 107 S. Ct. at 1456-57. However, programs designed to maintain integration by limiting minority participation, such as ceiling quotas, are of doubtful validity. . . .

Starrett's use of ceiling quotas to maintain integration at Starrett City lacks each of these characteristics. First, Starrett City's practices have only the goal of integration maintenance. The quotas already have been in effect for ten years. Appellants predict that their race-conscious tenanting practices must continue for at least fifteen more years, but fail to explain adequately how that approximation was reached. In any event, these practices are far from temporary. Since the goal of integration maintenance is purportedly threatened by the potential for "white flight" on a continuing basis, no definite termination date for Starrett's quotas is perceivable. Second, appellants do not assert, and there is no evidence to show, the existence of prior racial discrimination or discriminatory imbalance adversely affecting whites within Starrett City or appellants' other complexes. On the contrary, Starrett City was initiated as an integrated complex, and Starrett's avowed purpose for employing race-based tenanting practices is to maintain that initial integration. Finally, Starrett's quotas do not provide minorities with access to Starrett City, but rather act as a ceiling to their access. Thus, the impact of appellants' practices falls squarely on minorities, for whom Title VIII was intended to open up housing opportunities. Starrett claims that its use of quotas serves to keep the numbers of minorities entering Starrett City low enough to avoid setting off a wave of "white flight." Although the "white flight" phenomenon may be a factor "take[n] into account in the integration equation," Parent Ass'n of Andrew Jackson High School v. Ambach, 598 F.2d 705, 720 (2d Cir. 1979), it cannot serve to justify attempts to maintain integration at Starrett City through inflexible racial quotas that are neither temporary in nature nor used to remedy past racial discrimination or imbalance within the complex.

Appellants' reliance on *Otero* is misplaced. In *Otero* the New York City Housing Authority ("NYCHA") relocated over 1800 families in the Lower East Side of Manhattan to make way for the construction of new apartment buildings. Pursuant to its regulations, NYCHA offered the former site occupants first priority of returning to any housing built within the urban renewal area. However, because the response by the largely minority former site residents seeking to return was nearly seven times greater than expected, NYCHA declined to follow its regulation in order to avoid creating a "pocket ghetto" that would "tip" an integrated community towards a predominantly minority community. It instead rented up half of these apartments to non-former site occupants, 88% of whom were white.

In a suit brought by former site occupants who were denied the promised priority, the district court held as a matter of law that "affirmative action to achieve racially balanced communities was not permitted where it would result in depriving minority groups" of public housing, and thus granted summary judgment in favor of plaintiffs. This court reversed the grant of summary judgment, stating that public housing authorities had a federal constitutional and statutory duty "to fulfill, as much as possible, the goal of open, integrated residential housing patterns and to prevent the increase of segregation, in ghettos," but we recognized that "the effect in some instances might be to prevent some members of a racial minority from residing in publicly assisted housing in a particular location."

Otero does not, however, control in this case. The challenge in *Otero* did not involve procedures for the long-term maintenance of specified levels of integration, but rather, the rental of 171 of 360 new apartments to non-former site occupants, predominantly white, although former site residents, largely minority, sought those apartments and were entitled to priority under NYCHA's own regulation. The *Otero* court did not delineate the statutory or constitutional limits on permissible means of integration, but held only that NYCHA's rent-up practice could not be declared invalid as a matter of law under those limits. . . .

It is particularly important to note that the NYCHA action challenged in *Otero* only applied to a single event — the initial rent up of the new complexes — and determined tenancy in the first instance alone. NYCHA sought only to prevent the immediate creation of a "pocket ghetto" in the Lower East Side, which had experienced a steady loss of white population, that would tip the precarious racial balance there, resulting in increased white flight and inevitable "non-white ghettoization of the community." Further, the suspension of NYCHA's regulation did not operate as a strict racial quota, because the former site residents entitled to a rental priority were approximately 40% white. As a one-time measure in response to the special circumstances of the Lower East Side in the early 1970's, the action challenged in *Otero* had an impact on non-whites as a group far less burdensome or discriminatory than Starrett City's continuing practices.

Conclusion

We do not intend to imply that race is always an inappropriate consideration under Title VIII in efforts to promote integrated housing. We hold only that Title VIII does not allow appellants to use rigid racial quotas of indefinite duration to maintain a fixed level of integration at Starrett City by restricting minority access to scarce and desirable rental accommodations otherwise available to them. We therefore affirm the judgment of the district court.

NEWMAN, J., dissenting. Congress enacted the Fair Housing Act to prohibit racial segregation in housing. Starrett City is one of the most successful examples in the nation of racial integration in housing. I respectfully dissent because I do not believe that Congress intended the Fair Housing Act to prohibit the maintenance of racial integration in private housing. . . .

To reach its target of racial balance, Starrett City explicitly declined to rent on a first-come, first-served basis. Instead, reacting to the fact that Blacks and other minorities applied for apartments at Starrett City in far greater numbers than Whites, the management imposed ceilings on the number of apartments of various sizes that would be rented to Blacks and other minorities. As the number of tenants of each minority reached the ceiling for a particular size of apartment, subsequent applicants from that minority were placed on a waiting list until sufficient vacancies occurred to permit a rental to a member of that minority without exceeding the established ceiling.

As experience with this rental policy developed, Starrett City decided that it would permit the percentage of apartments rented to minorities to move above 30% and to reach approximately 35%. The components of this aggregate figure are 21% Black, 8% Hispanic, 4.5% Oriental, and 2% other or mixed. These figures have been fairly constant since 1976. During that period the minority percentage of the Starrett City *population* has been approximately 45%. In 1984, Starrett City agreed, as part of a settlement of a lawsuit brought by a class of Black applicants, to raise the minority rental unit percentage to 38% over five years.

The consequence of Starrett's policy of maintaining racial balance has been that Black applicants constitute a disproportionately larger share of the waiting list for apartments than do Whites, and remain on the list for considerably longer periods of time than do Whites. As of November 1985, Blacks made up approximately 54% of the waiting list while Whites filled approximately 22% of the places on the list. For a two-bedroom apartment, the average waiting time on the list for qualified applicants was twenty months for Blacks and two months for Whites; for a one-bedroom apartment, the comparable figures were eleven months and four months.[19]

The development of Starrett City as an apartment complex committed to a deliberate policy of maintained racial integration has at all times occurred with the knowledge, encouragement, and financial support of the agency of the United States directly concerned with housing, the Department of Housing and Urban Development (HUD). . . .

Despite its close cooperation in the development of Starrett City as an integrated housing complex, the United States now sues Starrett City to force it to abandon the rental policies that have enabled it to maintain racial integration. The bringing of the suit raises a substantial question as to the Government's commitment to integrated housing. The timing of the suit puts that commitment further in doubt. In 1979 a class of Black applicants for housing at Starrett City brought suit to challenge on federal statutory and constitutional grounds the same tenant selection policies at issue in this case. Arthur v. Starrett City Associates, 79 Civ. 3096 (ERN) (E.D.N.Y. 1979). With the federal government observing from the sidelines, the parties to the *Arthur* litigation engaged in protracted settlement negotiations. More than four years later, a mutually advantageous settlement was reached. Starrett City was permitted to continue its policy of maintaining integration through its tenant selection policies. In return, Starrett City agreed to increase by three percent over five years the proportion of rental units occupied by minority tenants. At the same time, DHCR, the state housing agency, which was also a defendant in the *Arthur* litigation, agreed to take affirmative steps to promote housing opportunities for minorities in DHCR-supervised housing projects in New York City. Specifically, the State agency agreed to give a priority in other projects to minority applicants on the Starrett City waiting list. No member of the class of minority applicants for housing at Starrett City objected to the settlement. Thus, the needs of the minority class for whose benefit the suit had been brought were met to their satisfaction by providing for more rental opportunities both at Starrett City and elsewhere. Just one month after that settlement was reached, the United States filed this suit, ostensibly concerned with vin-

19. Occasionally, the burden of Starrett City's rental policy falls on Whites. The complex designates certain buildings for senior citizens and, during periods when White seniors have applied for these units in greater numbers than Black seniors, White seniors have waited for apartments longer than Black seniors.

dication of the rights of the same minority applicants for housing who had just settled their dispute on favorable terms.

The only issue in this case is whether Starrett City's rental policies violate Title VIII of the Civil Rights Act of 1968. . . .

The defendants do not dispute that their rental policies fall within the literal language of Title VIII's prohibition on discriminatory housing practices. See 42 U.S.C. §3604. Instead they contend that they are state actors for purposes of the Fourteenth Amendment, that their policies are to be tested under both the Fourteenth Amendment and the Fair Housing Act by the strict scrutiny standard of Regents of the University of California v. Bakke, 438 U.S. 265, 98 S. Ct. 2733, 57 L. Ed. 2d 750 (1978), and that they meet this test because their race-conscious policies further the compelling state interest of promoting integrated housing and are narrowly tailored to achieve that interest. At a minimum, they contend, they are entitled to a trial on the merits to prove their claim.

In my view, the defendants are entitled to prevail simply on the statutory issue to which the Government has limited its lawsuit. Though the terms of the statute literally encompass the defendants' actions, the statute was never intended to apply to such actions. This statute was intended to bar perpetuation of segregation. To apply it to bar maintenance of integration is precisely contrary to the congressional policy "to provide, within constitutional limitations, for fair housing throughout the United States." 42 U.S.C. §3601.

We have been wisely cautioned by Learned Hand that "[t]here is no surer way to misread a document than to read it literally." Guiseppi v. Walling, 144 F.2d 608, 624 (2d Cir. 1944) (concurring opinion), aff'd sub nom. Gemsco, Inc. v. Walling, 324 U.S. 244, 65 S. Ct. 605, 89 L. Ed. 921 (1945). That aphorism is not always true with respect to statutes, whose text is always the starting point for analysis and sometimes the ending point. But literalism is not always the appropriate approach even with statutes, as the Supreme Court long ago recognized: "It is a familiar rule, that a thing may be within the letter of the statute and yet not within the statute, because not within its spirit, nor within the intent of its makers." Church of the Holy Trinity v. United States, 143 U.S. 457, 459, 12 S. Ct. 511, 512, 36 L. Ed. 226 (1892).

Title VIII bars discriminatory housing practices in order to end segregated housing. Starrett City is not promoting segregated housing. On the contrary, it is maintaining integrated housing. It is surely not within the spirit of the Fair Housing Act to enlist the Act to bar integrated housing. Nor is there any indication that application of the statute toward such a perverse end was within the intent of those who enacted the statute. . . . A law enacted to enhance the opportunity for people of all races to live next to each other should not be interpreted to prevent a landlord from maintaining one of the most successful integrated housing projects in America.

None of the legislators who enacted Title VIII ever expressed a view on whether they wished to prevent the maintenance of racially balanced housing. Most of those who passed this statute in 1968 probably could not even contemplate a private real estate owner who would deliberately set out to achieve a racially balanced tenant population. Had they thought of such an eventuality, there is not the slightest reason to believe that they would have raised their legislative hands against it.

This Circuit has previously ruled that Title VIII does not apply literally to prohibit racially based rental policies adopted to promote integration. Otero v. New York City Housing Authority, 484 F.2d 1122 (2d Cir. 1973). . . .

Acknowledging the significance of the ruling in *Otero*, the Court distinguishes it essentially on the ground that *Otero* involved a policy of limited duration, applicable only to the period in which those displaced from the site were applying for housing in the new project, whereas Starrett City seeks to pursue a long-term policy of maintaining integration. I see nothing in the text or legislative history of Title VIII that supports such a distinction. If, as the Court holds, Title VIII bars Starrett City's race-conscious rental policy, even though adopted to promote and maintain integration, then it would bar such policies whether adopted on a short-term or a long-term basis. Since the Act makes no distinction among the durations of rental policies alleged to violate its terms, *Otero*'s upholding of a race-conscious rental policy adopted to promote integration cannot be ignored simply because the policy was of limited duration.[20]

But even if Title VIII can somehow be construed to make the lawfulness of a race-conscious rental policy that promotes integration turn on the duration of the policy, Starrett City is entitled to a trial so that it can prove its contention that its policy is still needed to maintain integration. In the District Court the Government, though seeking summary judgment, contested Starrett City's factual contention that a race-conscious rental policy was currently needed to prevent the complex

---

20. The Court, drawing a parallel between Title VIII and Title VII, which bars discrimination in employment, 42 U.S.C. §2000e (1982), supports its view of Title VIII with Supreme Court decisions approving only limited use of race-conscious remedies under statutory and constitutional standards in the employment context. Though Titles VIII and VII share a common objective of combatting discrimination, their differing contexts preclude the assumption that the law of affirmative action developed for employment is readily applicable to housing. The Title VII cases have not been concerned with a "tipping point" beyond which a work force might become segregated. Yet that is a demonstrated fact of life in the context of housing. The statutory issue arising under Title VIII should be decided on the basis of what practices Congress was proscribing when it enacted this provision. . . .

from passing the "tipping point" and becoming segregated. The Government relied on a brief affidavit of a HUD employee, who made primarily the unremarkable observation that it is difficult to predict with any certainty the precise "tipping point" in a particular neighborhood. In opposing summary judgment, Starrett City presented detailed affidavits providing abundant evidence to show that abandonment of its rental policies would cause the complex to pass the "tipping point" and soon become a segregated development. This evidence was solidly based on relevant experience. Several housing developments near Starrett City, operating without a policy of integration maintenance, have become racially segregated, including one across the street from Starrett City.

Otero established for this Circuit that a race-conscious rental policy adopted to promote integration does not violate Title VIII and that a defendant must be afforded an opportunity to demonstrate at a trial that its rental policy is needed to prevent a housing complex from becoming segregated. Starrett City's affidavit evidence may well be sufficient to entitle it to summary judgment on this issue of continued need for a race-conscious rental policy to maintain integration. At a minimum it is entitled to a trial to present its evidence to a trier of fact.

Whether integration of private housing complexes should be maintained through the use of race-conscious rental policies that deny minorities an equal opportunity to rent is a highly controversial issue of social policy. There is a substantial argument against imposing any artificial burdens on minorities in their quest for housing. On the other hand, there is a substantial argument against forcing an integrated housing complex to become segregated, even if current conditions make integration feasible only by means of imposing some extra delay on minority applicants for housing. Officials of the Department of Justice are entitled to urge the former policy. Respected civil rights advocates like the noted psychologist, Dr. Kenneth Clark, are entitled to urge the latter policy, as he has done in an affidavit filed in this suit. That policy choice should be left to the individual decisions of private property owners unless and until Congress or the New York legislature decides for the Nation or for New York that it prefers to outlaw maintenance of integration. I do not believe Congress made that decision in 1968, and it is a substantial question whether it would make such a decision today. Until Congress acts, we should not lend our authority to the result this lawsuit will surely bring about. In the words of Dr. Clark:

> [I]t would be a tragedy of the highest magnitude if this litigation were to lead to the destruction of one of the model integrated communities in the United States.

Because the Fair Housing Act does not require this tragedy to occur, I respectfully dissent.

NOTES AND QUESTIONS

1. *Affirmative action and the Fair Housing Act.* Affirmative action measures were not explicitly barred by the original Fair Housing Act, at issue in the *Starrett City* case, nor are they prohibited by the amendments enacted shortly after the case was decided by the court of appeals (on the amendments, recall footnote 15 on page 441). True, the act on its face "literally prohibits any discrimination based on race, and is thus 'color-blind,'" but the federal courts have nevertheless recognized that "the policies of the Act necessarily mandate race-conscious measures in some circumstances." Comment, Fair Housing and the Constitutionality of Governmental Measures Affecting Community Ethnicity, 55 U. Chi. L. Rev. 1229, 1247 (1988). Congress appears to agree: "in the passage of the Fair Housing Amendments Act of 1988 the House rejected an amendment designed to prohibit affirmative action." James A. Kushner, The Fair Housing Amendments Act of 1988: The Second Generation of Fair Housing, 42 Vand. L. Rev. 1049, 1115 (1989).

Notice that *Starrett City* itself leaves room for race-conscious measures. Under what circumstances, and of what sorts? More generally, how, if at all, might the Fair Housing Act's goal of integrated housing be achieved without unduly (and unlawfully) compromising its antidiscrimination goal? For a discussion and evaluation of alternative approaches, see, e.g., Ankur J. Goel, Maintaining Integration Against Minority Interests: An Anti-Subjugation Theory for Equality in Housing, 22 Urb. Law. 369 (1990); Comment, Individual Rights and Demographic Realities: The Problem of Fair Housing, 82 Nw. U. L. Rev. 874 (1988); Comment, Fair Housing, supra.

Item from the news. See Sam Roberts, White Tilt to Balance a Project in Canarsie, N.Y. Times, Aug. 4, 1992, at B3:

> A school for 1,000 young Soviet émigrés will open in Canarsie, Brooklyn, next month with two goals: to assimilate the students into American and Jewish culture and to persuade their parents to apply for apartments in the adjoining Starrett City housing development, which leased the school land for its new building.
>
> "We're trying to attract a broader base, because otherwise you attract the one group that already lives in the surrounding area," said Robert C. Rosenberg, chairman of Starrett's management company. "The law does not say we cannot encourage diverse people by income and race to apply."
>
> The school is the latest lure to white applicants as Starrett City tries to mitigate the United States Supreme Court's ruling that racial quotas to maintain integration at the development violated Federal law. . . .
>
> Since the Supreme Court ruling, the number of whites among the 20,000 or so residents declined, from 62 percent to 50 percent. Blacks increased, from 25 percent to 35 percent. The proportion of Hispanic people edged up, from 9 percent to 11 percent.

"If it would continue in this trend it would invariably end up a totally minority community in five to eight years," Mr. Rosenberg said. . . .

Management hopes to accommodate its own goal of maintaining a successfully integrated community by luring more whites to the list of applicants and by expanding its base with thousands of new middle-income town houses, condominiums and cooperative apartments — much like a central city might annex a suburb.

"We can't monkey with the list," Mr. Rosenberg said, "but there are ways to change demographics."

See also Alan Finder, Brooklyn Landlord, To Keep Racial Mix, Looks to Soviet Jews, N.Y. Times, July 24, 1990, at A1 (discussing an earlier aspect of the plan, according to which the Soviet Jews might qualify for separate, shorter waiting lists; critics urged the Justice Department to reject the approach, calling it "an elaborate attempt to get around both the letter and spirit of the Supreme Court decision").

Starrett City has been the subject of considerable discussion in the legal literature. See, in addition to the material cited above, Note, Racial Integration in Urban Public Housing: The Method is Legal, the Time Has Come, 34 N.Y.L. Sch. L. Rev. 349 (1989); Note, The Legality of Integration Maintenance Quotas: Fair Housing or Forced Housing?, 55 Brooklyn L. Rev. 197 (1989); Thomas W. Simon, Double Reverse Discrimination in Housing: Contextualizing the *Starrett City* Case, 39 Buffalo L. Rev. 803 (1991). Simon says (contrary to our own impression of the literature) that "[a]lmost no legal commentator has come to the defense of Starrett City's integration maintenance policy; most scholars agree with the courts and reject the policy as discriminatory." Id. at 804.

The discrimination argument is straightforward. See, e.g., Note, The Legality of Integration Maintenance Quotas, supra, at 203, 226, 247-248:

[I]ntegration maintenance quotas represent a departure from the typical affirmative action program. The main objective of the integration maintenance quota is to promote integration in housing, not to eradicate discrimination in housing. Quotas adopted in the employment or education context differ from integration maintenance quotas; the former are access quotas used to *provide* opportunities to those previously denied of such social goods, the latter *limit* minority access to the very housing sought to be integrated. . . .

. . . Regressive racial quotas simply reinforce racial stereotypes and stigmatic harm, the enduring source of injustice. More discrimination is simply not the way to end discrimination. . . .

Despite the pragmatic allure of integration maintenance, the concept cannot be reconciled with the Fair Housing Act's ban against racial discrimination.

The opposing view, equally straightforward, is voiced as follows by Kushner, supra, at 1113, 1116-1117:

The most troubling paradox for fair housing is the identification of the movement's goals. Generally, all involved believe that people should not be denied a dwelling because of the color of their skin. However, many set as their goal an integrated society with diverse schools and neighborhoods — a society in which racially concentrated neighborhoods are not ghettos but communities like those of other ethnic minorities where inhabitants live by choice and a desire for the cultural attractions of community. Unfortunately, these goals are incompatible in the short run. In reality, policies carry either an integrative or segregative effect, and current policy is decidedly segregative. Only through affirmative action can integrated projects, neighborhoods, and communities be established and maintained. Bizarre as it may seem, only through discrimination can we get past discrimination. . . .

. . . The Second Circuit . . . failed to face the segregative effect of its ruling and the obvious need for integration maintenance policies if integration is to survive. Only Judge Newman in his dissent recognized the stark symbol of the majority's segregationist ruling.

2. *Motive and effect.* As the opinion in *Starrett City* points out (see page 451), a discriminatory motive need not be proved in order to make out a prima facie case under the Fair Housing Act; proof of discriminatory effect is sufficient.

[C]laimants in Title VIII actions need merely to demonstrate that an action or practice carries a discriminatory or segregative impact in order to shift the burden to the defendant. Alternatively, when a single plaintiff claims a housing denial without regard to a policy or pattern, the plaintiff establishes a prima facie case by proof of disparate treatment, typically a denial to an eligible minority applicant followed by a subsequent transfer to another party or the continued availability of the dwelling in the market. . . .

After the plaintiff establishes either disparate impact or disparate treatment, the defendant must then justify the action as one taken in pursuit of a bona fide, compelling governmental purpose, with no less discriminatory alternative available to achieve the goal, or in the case of private defendants, one taken pursuant to a rational and necessary business purpose. Should a defendant demonstrate a valid justification, the burden, at least in the private sector, would shift back to the plaintiff to demonstrate that the business necessity was a pretext for engaging in discrimination. [Kushner, supra, at 1074-1075.][21]

3. *State legislation.* Legislation in many states prohibits discrimination in the leasing of property. State legislation, of course, may not op-

___

21. Claims under the Civil Rights Act of 1866 (see footnote 15 on page 441) probably require proof of intentional or purposeful discrimination; claims based on the equal protection clause of the Fourteenth Amendment clearly do. See Village of Arlington Heights v. Metropolitan Hous. Dev. Corp., 429 U.S. 252 (1977); Kushner, supra, at 1073 n.96, 1076.

Brown v. Artery Org., Inc., 654 F. Supp. 1106 (D.D.C. 1987), is a lone case holding that proof of discriminatory impact is sufficient under the Fair Housing Act only if the

erate to narrow the rights and remedies available under federal law, but states are free to go beyond federal law, and in some instances they do. The prohibited grounds of discrimination vary a good deal from jurisdiction to jurisdiction, but include, among others: race, religion, national origin, sex, sexual orientation, marital status, tenants with children, handicapped children. For a description, see Restatement (Second) of Property, Landlord and Tenant, §3.1, Comments a-e (1977).

In Marina Point, Ltd. v. Wolfson, 30 Cal. 3d 721, 640 P.2d 115, 180 Cal. Rptr. 496, cert. denied, 459 U.S. 858 (1982), the issue was whether California's antidiscrimination legislation prohibited a refusal to rent to a family solely because the family included a minor child (the landlord excluded all children on the ground they were noisier, rowdier, more mischievous, and more boisterous). The court found a violation, even though the state's legislation referred only to discrimination on the basis of race, color, religion, ancestry, or national origin. The categories were regarded as illustrative; the legislature intended, the court said, to prohibit *all* arbitrary discrimination by business establishments. The landlord's discrimination was arbitrary because it aimed at children as a class, rather than looking in each instance at the individual child or children involved.

PROBLEMS

1. California's fair housing legislation prohibits discrimination based on such grounds as race and sex but does not explicitly prohibit discrimination based on wealth. *L* requires that prospective tenants have gross monthly incomes of at least three times the rent to be charged. Does this minimum income policy violate California law? See the *Marina Point* case discussed in Note 3 above, and Harris v. Capital Growth Investors XIV, 52 Cal. 3d 1142, 805 P.2d 873, 278 Cal. Rptr. 614 (1991). Does the policy violate the Fair Housing Act?

2. New York legislation prohibits discrimination on the basis of race, creed, color, national origin, sex, disability, or marital status. A

---

defendant is a governmental body; if the defendant is not a governmental body, some proof of discriminatory intent is necessary. 654 F. Supp. at 1115. The court's reasoning was as follows: The income of a disproportionate number of the members of minority groups is such that they cannot afford upgraded housing. Given this, if a disproportionate effect or impact on minorities were alone sufficient to make out a prima facie case under the Fair Housing Act, "the inhabitants of low-rent private housing largely populated by minorities would be entitled on this basis to judicial orders halting the upgrading or conversion of such housing in all or almost all circumstances. That . . . is not what Congress intended." 654 F. Supp. at 1116. For discussion, and on proof of discriminatory effect generally, see Annot., 100 A.L.R. Fed. 97 (1990).

landlord refuses to rent an apartment to Judith Pierce, a black divorced woman,who subsequently brings suit claiming unlawful discrimination. The landlord testifies that he rejected Ms. Pierce only because she is a lawyer. He found lawyers troublesome as tenants, preferring more passive people who are not attuned to their legal rights. What result? See Kramarsky v. Stahl Management, 92 Misc. 2d 1030, 401 N.Y.S.2d 943 (Sup. Ct. Special Term 1977). See also James B. Stewart, Landlords' Verdict: Lawyers as Tenants Have Little Appeal, Wall St. J., Jan. 23, 1984, at 1.

How would Ms. Pierce fare under the Fair Housing Act?[22]

D. Delivery of Possession

Suppose that L and T have entered into a lease to begin on the first of January. On that date T arrives at the premises, ready to take possession, only to find a former tenant holding over. Is this L's problem, or T's? Could there be any question?

Hannan v. Dusch

Supreme Court of Appeals of Virginia, 1930
154 Va. 356, 153 S.E. 824, 70 A.L.R. 141

PRENTIS, C.J., delivered the opinion of the court. The declaration filed by the plaintiff, Hannan, against the defendant, Dusch, alleges that Dusch had on August 31, 1927, leased to the plaintiff certain real estate in the city of Norfolk, Virginia, therein described, for fifteen years, the term to begin January 1, 1928, at a specified rental; that it thereupon became and was the duty of the defendant to see to it that the premises leased by the defendant to the plaintiff should be open for entry by him on January 1, 1928, the beginning of the term, and to put said petitioner in possession of the premises on that date; that the petitioner was willing

22. Landlords routinely use services that provide information on the credit standing of prospective tenants. Beyond this, "[i]n some housing markets, a landlord can purchase from a commercial data bank a report detailing a prospective tenant's prior involvement in housing litigation." Robert C. Ellickson, Order Without Law: How Neighbors Settle Disputes 277 (1991), citing Pam Belluck, Tenants Cry Foul as Screening Companies Help Landlords Spot "Problem" Applicants, Wall St. J., Dec. 27, 1985, at 13. See also Simson L. Garfinkel, From Database to Blacklist: Computer Records Let Employers and Landlords Discriminate Against Unsuspecting Applicants, Christian Science Monitor, Aug. 1, 1990, at 12 ("[a] pending lawsuit charges that mismatches have kept innocent tenants from securing housing").

and ready to enter upon and take possession of the leased property, and so informed the defendant; yet the defendant failed and refused to put the plaintiff in possession or to keep the property open for him at that time or on any subsequent date; and that the defendant suffered to remain on said property a certain tenant or tenants who occupied a portion or portions thereof, and refused to take legal or other action to oust said tenants or to compel their removal from the property so occupied. Plaintiff alleged damages which he had suffered by reason of this alleged breach of the contract and deed, and sought to recover such damages in the action. There is no express covenant as to the delivery of the premises nor for the quiet possession of the premises by the lessee.

The defendant demurred to the declaration on several grounds, one of which was "that under the lease set out in said declaration the right of possession was vested in said plaintiff and there was no duty upon the defendant, as alleged in said declaration, to see that the premises were open for entry by said plaintiff."

The single question of law therefore presented in this case is whether a landlord, who without any express covenant as to delivery of possession leases property to a tenant, is required under the law to oust trespassers and wrongdoers so as to have it open for entry by the tenant at the beginning of the term — that is, whether without an express covenant there is nevertheless an implied covenant to deliver possession.

For an intelligent apprehension of the precise question it may be well to observe that some questions somewhat similar are not involved.

It seems to be perfectly well settled that there is an implied covenant in such cases on the part of the landlord to assure to the tenant the legal right of possession — that is, that at the beginning of the term there shall be no legal obstacle to the tenant's right of possession. This is not the question presented. Nor need we discuss in this case the rights of the parties in case a tenant rightfully in possession under the title of his landlord is thereafter disturbed by some wrongdoer. In such case the tenant must protect himself from trespassers, and there is no obligation on the landlord to assure his quiet enjoyment of his term as against wrongdoers or intruders.

Of course, the landlord assures to the tenant quiet possession as against all who rightfully claim through or under the landlord.

The discussion then is limited to the precise legal duty of the landlord in the absence of an express covenant, in case a former tenant, who wrongfully holds over, illegally refuses to surrender possession to the new tenant. This is a question about which there is a hopeless conflict of authorities. It is generally claimed that the weight of the authority favors the particular view contended for. There are, however, no scales upon which we can weigh the authorities. In numbers and respectability they may be quite equally balanced.

It is then a question about which no one should be dogmatic, but all should seek for that rule which is supported by the better reason. . . .

It is conceded by all that the two rules, one called the English rule, which implies a covenant requiring the lessor to put the lessee in possession, and that called the American rule, which recognizes the lessee's legal right to possession, but implies no such duty upon the lessor as against wrongdoers, are irreconcilable.

The English rule is that in the absence of stipulations to the contrary, there is in every lease an implied covenant on the part of the landlord that the premises shall be open to entry by the tenant at the time fixed by the lease for the beginning of his term. . . .

It must be borne in mind, however, that the courts which hold that there is such an implied covenant do not extend the period beyond the day when the lessee's term begins. If after that day a stranger trespasses upon the property and wrongfully obtains or withholds possession of it from the lessee, his remedy is against the stranger and not against the lessor.

It is not necessary for either party to involve himself in uncertainty, for by appropriate covenants each may protect himself against any doubt either as against a tenant then in possession who may wrongfully hold over by refusing to deliver the possession at the expiration of his own term, or against any other trespasser. . . .

As has been stated, the lessee may also protect himself by having his lessor expressly covenant to put him in possession at a specified time, in which case, of course, the lessor is liable for breach of his covenant where a trespasser goes into possession, or wrongfully holds possession, and thereby wrongfully prevents the lessee from obtaining possession. . . .

King v. Reynolds, 67 Ala. 229, 42 Am. Rep. 107, has been said to be the leading case in this country affirming the English rule. In that case, after citing some of the cases which affirm the American rule, this is said:

English Rule

> . . . The authorities being in conflict, how does this question stand on principle? As was said in Coe v. Clay, 5 Bing. 440, 3 M.&P. 57, 7 L.J.C.P., O.S., 162, 30 R.R. 699 . . . , one who accepts a lease expects to enjoy the property, not a mere chance of a lawsuit. A lease for a year, or term of years, is not a freehold. It is a chattel interest. The prime motive of the contract is, that the lessee shall have possession; as much so as if a chattel were the subject of the purchase. . . .

Another case which supports the English rule is Herpolsheimer v. Christopher, 76 Neb. 352, 107 N.W. 382, 111 N.W. 359, 9 L.R.A. (N.S.) 1127, 14 Ann. Cas. 399 note. In that case the court gave these as its reasons for following the English rule:

> We deem it unnecessary to enter into an extended discussion, since the reasons pro and con are fully given in the opinions of the several courts cited. We think, however, that the English rule is most in consonance with good conscience, sound principle, and fair dealing. Can it be supposed that the plaintiff in this case would have entered into the lease if he had known at the

time that he could not obtain possession on the 1st of March, but that he would be compelled to begin a lawsuit, await the law's delays, and follow the case through its devious turnings to an end before he could hope to obtain possession of the land he had leased? Most assuredly not. It is unreasonable to suppose that a man would knowingly contract for a lawsuit, or take the chance of one. Whether or not a tenant in possession intends to hold over or assert a right to future term may nearly always be known to the landlord, and is certainly much more apt to be within his knowledge than within that of the prospective tenant. Moreover, since in an action to recover possession against a tenant holding over, the lessee would be compelled largely to rely upon the lessor's testimony in regard to the facts of the claim to hold over by the wrongdoer, it is more reasonable and proper to place the burden upon the person within whose knowledge the facts are most apt to lie. We are convinced, therefore, that the better reason lies with the courts following the English doctrine, and we therefore adopt it, and hold that, ordinarily, the lessor impliedly covenants with the lessee that the premises leased shall be open to entry by him at the time fixed in the lease as the beginning of the term.

In commenting on this line of cases, Mr. Freeman says [in a note on the subject in 134 Am. St. Rep. 916 (1909)]:

The above rule practically prohibits the landlord from leasing the premises while in the possession of a tenant whose term is about to expire, because notwithstanding the assurance on the part of the tenant that he will vacate on the expiration of his term, he may change his mind and wrongfully hold over. It is true that the landlord may provide for such a contingency by suitable provisions in the lease to the prospective tenant, but it is equally true that the prospective tenant has the privilege of insisting that his prospective landlord expressly agree to put him in possession of the premises if he imagines there may be a chance for a lawsuit by the tenant in possession holding over. It seems to us that to raise by implication a covenant on the part of the landlord to put the tenant into possession is to make a contract for the parties in regard to a matter which is equally within the knowledge of both the landlord and tenant.

So let us not lose sight of the fact that under the English rule a covenant which might have been but was not made is nevertheless implied by the court, though it is manifest that each of the parties might have provided for that and for every other possible contingency relating to possession by having express covenants which would unquestionably have protected both.

Referring then to the American rule: Under that rule, in such cases,

the landlord is not bound to put the tenant into actual possession, but is bound only to put him in legal possession, so that no obstacle in the form of superior right of possession will be interposed to prevent the tenant from obtaining actual possession of the demised premises. If the landlord gives the tenant a right of possession he has done all that he is required to do by the terms of an ordinary lease, and the tenant assumes the burden of enforcing such right of possession as against all persons wrongfully in possession, whether they be trespassers or former tenants wrongfully holding over.

tenant assumes burden

This quoted language is Mr. Freeman's. . . .

So that, under the American rule, where the new tenant fails to obtain possession of the premises only because a former tenant wrongfully holds over, his remedy is against such wrongdoer and not against the landlord — this because the landlord has not covenanted against the wrongful acts of another and should not be held responsible for such a tort unless he has expressly so contracted. This accords with the general rule as to other wrongdoers, whereas the English rule appears to create a specific exception against lessors. It does not occur to us now that there is any other instance in which one clearly without fault is held responsible for the independent tort of another in which he has neither participated nor concurred and whose misdoings he cannot control. . . .

For the reasons which have been so well stated by those who have enforced the American rule, our judgment is that there is no error in the judgment complained of. . . .

We are confirmed in our view by the Virginia statute, providing a summary remedy for unlawful entry or detainer, Code, section 5445, et seq. The adequate, simple and summary remedy for the correction of such a wrong provided by the statute was clearly available to this plaintiff. It specifically provides that it shall lie for one entitled to possession "in any case in which a tenant shall detain the possession of land after his right has expired without the consent of him who is entitled to possession."

Certainly there should be co-operation between the lessor and the lessee to impose the resulting loss upon such a trespasser, but whatever other equities may have arisen, when the plaintiff found that the premises which he had leased were occupied by a wrongdoer who unlawfully refused to surrender possession, it is manifest that he, the lessee, Hannan, had the right to oust the wrongdoer under this statute. His failure to pursue that remedy is not explained. . . .

The plaintiff alleges in his declaration as one of the grounds for his action that the defendant suffered the wrongdoer to remain in possession, but the allegations show that he it was who declined to assert his remedy against the wrongdoer, and so he it was who permitted the wrongdoer to retain the possession. Just why he valued his legal right to the possession so lightly as not to assert it in the effective way open to him does not appear. Whatever ethical duty in good conscience may possibly have rested upon the defendant, the duty to oust the wrongdoer by the summary remedy provided by the unlawful detainer statute clearly rested upon the plaintiff. The law helps those who help themselves, generally aids the vigilant, but rarely the sleeping, and never the acquiescent.

Affirmed.

NOTES AND QUESTIONS

1. Case law on the matter of delivery of possession remains divided, with substantial support for both the English and the American rule. See, e.g., Annot., 96 A.L.R.3d 1155 (1980). Restatement (Second) of Property, Landlord and Tenant, §6.2 (1977) adopts the English rule, as does URLTA §2.103. The former permits the parties to agree otherwise; the latter, it appears, does not (see URLTA §1.403).

2. Under the American rule, the tenant's remedies are against the person wrongfully in possession: He may sue to recover possession and damages. As to remedies under the English rule, see Restatement (Second) of Property, Landlord and Tenant, supra, §6.2, Reporter's Note at 246:

> It is well established that upon the landlord's default, the tenant may terminate the lease and sue for damages. . . . If the third party is in possession of only a part of the premises, the tenant may take possession of the remainder with an appropriate abatement in rent and damages. . . . Where the tenant's entry into possession is delayed beyond the date on which the term was to begin, he is not obligated to pay rent for the portion of the term during which he was kept out of possession and may collect appropriate damages. . . . See also 1 American Law of Property §3.37 (A.J. Casner ed. 1952) on the right of the tenant to continue the lease and sue for damages.
>
> It is well established that the tenant may go directly against the third party to recover possession or damages. . . .
>
> No authority has been found permitting the use of rent to defray the cost of removing the third person or withholding the rent until such person is removed. However, there is an emerging body of law, much of it statutory, which permits rent application and rent withholding when the landlord fails to maintain habitable premises.

3. It has been said that the "American rule seems to be founded on the argument that the tenant has sufficient legal and equitable remedies available to protect himself against the third party wrongfully in possession and a greater incentive to use them than the landlord would have." Restatement (Second) of Property, Landlord and Tenant, supra, §6.2, Reporter's Note at 245. What policies support the English rule? See id., Comment a at 236-237. Which rule do you prefer, and why?

PROBLEMS

1. *T* leases a large piece of open land to be used for hunting and trapping. After paying a year's rent in advance, *T* finds out that there is no public access to the land. Neighboring landowners refuse to give *T* ingress and egress. The jurisdiction follows the English rule. Has *L* satisfied the duty imposed by that rule? See Moore v. Cameron Parish School Bd., 511 So. 2d 62 (La. App. 1987). On landlocked parcels generally, see pages 813-822.

2. *L* and *T* execute a lease for a specified term. *T* takes possession and pays rent for several months. *T* then learns that *L* had earlier leased the premises to another tenant for the same term. *T* stops paying rent. *L* sues *T* for unpaid rent; *T* counterclaims for rent already paid. What result? See Campbell v. Henshey, 450 S.W.2d 501 (Ky. 1970).

3. *T* leases from *L* a building under construction; the term of the lease is three years and possession is to be delivered on a specified date. Eight months after that date the building is still under construction and not ready for occupancy. *T* sues to rescind the lease and to recover advance rent paid to *L*. The lease in question contains a clause excusing *L* from liability for failure to deliver possession if the building is still under construction. What result? See Fox Paper, Ltd. v. Schwarzman, 168 A.D.2d 604, 563 N.Y.S.2d 439 (1990); Seabrook v. Commuter Hous. Co., 72 Misc. 2d 6, 338 N.Y.S.2d 67 (Civ. Ct. 1972), aff'd, 79 Misc. 2d 168, 363 N.Y.S.2d 566 (Sup. Ct. 1973); Hartwig v. 6465 Realty Co., 67 Misc. 2d 450, 324 N.Y.S.2d 567 (Sup. Ct. 1971).

E. Subleases and Assignments

Ernst v. Conditt

Court of Appeals of Tennessee, 1964
54 Tenn. App. 328, 390 S.W.2d 703

CHATTIN, J. Complainants, B. Walter Ernst and wife, Emily Ernst, leased a certain tract of land in Davidson County, Tennessee, to Frank D. Rogers on June 18, 1960, for a term of one year and seven days, commencing on June 23, 1960.

Rogers went into possession of the property and constructed an asphalt race track and enclosed the premises with a fence. He also constructed other improvements thereon such as floodlights for use in the operation of a Go-Cart track.

We quote these paragraphs of the lease pertinent to the question for consideration in this controversy:

3. Lessee covenants to pay as rent for said leased premises the sum of $4,200 per annum, payable at the rate of $350 per month or 15% of all gross receipts, whether from sales or services occurring on the leased premises, whichever is the larger amount. The gross receipts shall be computed on a quarterly basis and if any amount in addition to the $350 per month is due, such payment shall be made immediately after the quarterly computation. All payments shall be payable to the office of Lessors' agent, Guaranty Mortgage Company, at 316 Union Street, Nashville, Tennessee, on the first day of each month in advance. Lessee shall have the first right to refusal in the event Lessors desire to lease said premises for a period of time commencing immediately after the termination date hereof. . . .

5. Lessee shall have no right to assign or sublet the leased premises without prior written approval of Lessors. In the event of any assignment or sublease, Lessee is still liable to perform the covenants of this lease, including the covenant to pay rent, and nothing herein shall be construed as releasing Lessee from his liabilities and obligations hereunder. . . .

9. Lessee agrees that upon termination of this contract, or any extensions or renewals thereof, that all improvements above the ground will be moved at Lessee's expense and the property cleared. This shall not be construed as removing or digging up any surface paving; but if any pits or holes are dug, they shall be leveled at Lessors' request.

Rogers operated the business for a short time. In July, 1960, he entered into negotiations with the defendant, A.K. Conditt, for the sale of the business to him. During these negotiations, the question of the term of the lease arose. Defendant desired a two-year lease of the property. He and Rogers went to the home of complainants and negotiated an extension of the term of the lease which resulted in the following amendment to the lease, and the sublease or assignment of the lease as amended to Conditt by Rogers:

By mutual consent of the parties, the lease executed the 18th day of June 1960, between B. Walter Ernst and wife, Emily H. Ernst, as Lessors, and Frank D. Rogers as Lessee, is amended as follows:

1. Paragraph 2 of said lease is amended so as to provide that the term will end July 31, 1962 and not June 30, 1961.

2. The minimum rent of $350 per month called for in paragraph 3 of said lease shall be payable by the month and the percentage rental called for by said lease shall be payable on the first day of the month following the month for which the percentage is computed. In computing gross receipts, no deduction or credit shall be given the Lessee for the payment of sales taxes or any other assessments by governmental agencies.

3. Lessee agrees that on or prior to April 1, 1961, the portion of the property covered by this lease, consisting of about one acre, which is not presently devoted to business purposes will be used for business purposes and the percentage rent called for by paragraph 3 of the original lease will be paid on the gross receipts derived therefrom. In the event of the failure of the Lessee to devote the balance of said property to a business purpose on or before

April 1, 1961, then this lease shall terminate as to such portion of the property.

4. Lessee agrees to save the Lessor harmless for any damage to the property of the lessor, whether included in this lease or not,which results from the use of the leased property by the Lessee or its customers or invitees. Lessee will erect or cause to be erected four (4) "No Parking" signs on the adjoining property of the Lessor not leased by it.

5. Lessor hereby consents to the subletting of the premises to A. K. Conditt, but upon the express condition and understanding that the original Lessee, Frank D. Rogers, will remain personally liable for the faithful performance of all the terms and conditions of the original lease and of this amendment to the original lease.

Except as modified by this amendment, all terms and conditions of the original lease dated the 18th day of June, 1960, by and between the parties shall remain in full force and effect.

In witness whereof the parties have executed this amendment to lease on this the 4 day of August, 1960.

> *B. Walter Ernst*
> *Emily H. Ernst*
> Lessors
> *Frank D. Rogers*
> Lessee

For value received and in consideration of the promise to faithfully perform all conditions of the within lease as amended, I hereby sublet the premises to A.K. Conditt upon the understanding that I will individually remain liable for the performance of the lease.

This 4 day of Aug, 1960.

> *Frank D. Rogers*
> Frank D. Rogers

The foregoing subletting of the premises is accepted, this the 4 day of Aug, 1960.

> *A.K. Conditt*
> A.K. Conditt

Conditt operated the Go-Cart track from August until November, 1960. He paid the rent for the months of August, September and October, 1960, directly to complainants. In December, 1960, complainants contacted defendant with reference to the November rent and at that time defendant stated he had been advised he was not liable to them for rent. However, defendant paid the basic monthly rental of $350.00 to complainants in June, 1961. This was the final payment received by complainants during the term of the lease as amended. The record is not clear whether defendant continued to operate the business after the last payment of rent or abandoned it. Defendant, however, remained in possession of the property until the expiration of the leasehold.

On July 10, 1962, complainants, through their Attorneys, notified Conditt by letter the lease would expire as of midnight July 31, 1962, and they were demanding a settlement of the past due rent and unless the improvements on the property were removed by him as provided in paragraph 9 of the original lease; then, in that event, they would have same removed at his expense. Defendant did not reply to this demand.

On August 1, 1962, complainants filed their bill in this cause seeking a recovery of $2,404.58 which they alleged was the balance due on the basic rent of $350.00 per month for the first year of the lease and the sum of $4,200.00, the basic rent for the second year, and the further sum necessary for the removal of the improvements constructed on the property.

The theory of the bill is that the agreement between Rogers, the original lessee, and the defendant, Conditt, is an assignment of the lease; and, therefore, defendant is directly and primarily liable to complainants.

The defendant by his answer insists the agreement between Rogers and himself is a sublease and therefore Rogers is directly and primarily liable to complainants.

The Chancellor heard the matter on the depositions of both complainants and three other witnesses offered in behalf of complainants and documentary evidence filed in the record. The defendant did not testify nor did he offer any evidence in his behalf.

The Chancellor found the instrument to be an assignment. A decree was entered sustaining the bill and entering judgment for complainants in the sum of $6,904.58 against defendant.

Defendant has appealed to this Court and has assigned errors insisting the Chancellor erred in failing to hold the instrument to be a sublease rather than an assignment.

To support his theory the instrument is a sublease, the defendant insists the amendment to the lease entered into between Rogers and complainants was for the express purpose of extending the term of the lease and obtaining the consent of the lessors to a "subletting" of the premises to defendant. That by the use of the words "sublet" and "subletting" no other construction can be placed on the amendment and the agreement of Rogers and the acceptance of defendant attached thereto.

Further, since complainants agreed to the subletting of the premises to defendant "upon the express condition and understanding that the original lessee, Frank D. Rogers, will remain personally liable for the faithful performance of all the terms and conditions of the original lease and this amendment to the original lease," no construction can be placed upon this language other than it was the intention of complainants to hold Rogers primarily liable for the performance of the original lease and the amendment thereto. And, therefore, Rogers, for his own protection, would have the implied right to re-enter and perform the lease in the event of a default on the part of the defendant. This being true, Rogers retained a reversionary interest in the property sufficient to satisfy the legal distinction between a sublease and an assignment of a lease.

It is then urged the following rules of construction of written instruments support the above argument:

> Where words or terms having a definite legal meaning and effect are knowingly used in a written instrument the parties thereto will be presumed to have intended such words or terms to have their proper legal meaning and effect, in the absence of any contrary intention appearing in the instrument. 12 Am. Jur., Contracts, Section 238.
>
> Technical terms or words of art will be given their technical meaning unless the context, or local usage shows a contrary intention. 3 Williston on Contracts, Section 68, Sub S. 2.

As stated in complainants' brief, the liability of defendant to complainants depends upon whether the transfer of the leasehold interest in the premises from Rogers is an assignment of the lease or a sublease. If the transfer is a sublease, no privity of contract[23] exists between complainants and defendant; and, therefore, defendant could not be liable to complainants on the covenant to pay rent and the expense of the removal of the improvements. But, if the transfer is an assignment of the lease, privity of contract does exist between complainants and defendant; and defendant would be liable directly and primarily for the amount of the judgment. . . .

The general rule as to the distinction between an assignment of a lease and a sublease is an assignment conveys the whole term, leaving no interest nor reversionary interest in the grantor or assignor. Whereas, a sublease may be generally defined as a transaction whereby a tenant grants an interest in the leased premises less than his own, or reserves to himself a reversionary interest in the term.

The common law distinction between an assignment of a lease and a sublease is succinctly stated in the case of Jaber v. Miller, 219 Ark. 59, 239 S.W.2d 760: "If the instrument purports to transfer the lessee's estate for the entire remainder of his term it is an assignment, regardless of its form or the parties' intention. Conversely, if the instrument purports to transfer the lessee's estate for less than the entire term — even for a day less — it is a sublease, regardless of its form or of the parties' intention."

The modern rule which has been adopted in this State for construing written instruments is stated in the case of City of Nashville v. Law-

---

23. In this and the next sentence, substitute the words "privity of estate" where the opinion reads "privity of contract." Privity of estate is what the court means to say; the Problems on pages 476-477 explore the distinction between the two concepts. — EDS.

rence, 153 Tenn. 606, 284 S.W. 882: "The cardinal rule to be followed in this state, in construing deeds and other written instruments, is to ascertain the intention of the parties."

In Williams v. Williams, 84 Tenn. 164, 171, it was said: "We have most wisely abandoned technical rules in the construction of conveyances in this State, and look to the intention of the instrument alone for our guide, that intention to be arrived at from the language of the instrument read in the light of the surrounding circumstances." . . .

It is our opinion under either the common law or modern rule of construction the agreement between Rogers and defendant is an assignment of the lease.

The fact that Rogers expressly agreed to remain liable to complainants for the performance of the lease did not create a reversion nor a right to re-enter in Rogers either express or implied. The obligations and liabilities of a lessee to a lessor, under the express covenants of a lease, are not in anywise affected by an assignment or a subletting to a third party, in the absence of an express or implied agreement or some action on his part which amounts to a waiver or estops him from insisting upon compliance with the covenants. This is true even though the assignment or sublease is made with the consent of the lessor. By an assignment of a lease the privity of estate between the lessor and lessee is terminated, but the privity of contract between them still remains and is unaffected. Neither the privity of estate or contract between the lessor and lessee are affected by a sublease. 32 Am. Jur., Landlord and Tenant, Sections 356, 413, pages 310, 339.

Thus the express agreement of Rogers to remain personally liable for the performance of the covenants of the lease created no greater obligation on his part or interest in the leasehold, other than as set forth in the original lease.

The argument that since the agreement between Rogers and defendant contains the words, "sublet" and "subletting" is conclusive the instrument is to be construed as a sublease is, we think, unsound.

> A consent to sublet has been held to include the consent to assign or mortgage the lease; and a consent to assign has been held to authorize a subletting. [51 C.J.S. Landlord and Tenant §36, page 552.]

Prior to the consummation of the sale of the Go-Cart business to defendant, he insisted upon the execution of the amendment to the lease extending the term of the original lease. For value received and on the promise of the defendant to perform all of the conditions of the lease as amended, Rogers parted with his entire interest in the property. Defendant went into possession of the property and paid the rent to complainants. He remained in possession of the property for the entire term. By virtue of the sale of the business, defendant became the owner of the improvements with the right to their removal at the expiration of the lease.

Rogers reserved no part or interest in the lease; nor did he reserve a right of re-entry in event of a breach of any of the conditions or covenants of the lease on the part of defendant.

It is our opinion the defendant, under the terms of the agreement with Rogers, had a right to the possession of the property for the entire term of the lease as amended, including the right to remove the improvements after the expiration of the lease. Rogers merely agreed to become personally liable for the rent and the expense of the removal of the improvements upon the default of defendant. He neither expressly, nor by implication, reserved the right to re-enter for a condition broken by defendant.

Thus, we are of the opinion the use of the words, "sublet" and "subletting" is not conclusive of the construction to be placed on the instrument in the case; it plainly appearing from the context of the instrument and the facts and circumstances surrounding the execution of it the parties thereto intended an assignment rather than a sublease.

It results the assignments are overruled and the decree of the Chancellor is affirmed with costs.

NOTES AND PROBLEMS

1. *Sublease or assignment?* The *Ernst* case indicates the two ways in which courts have gone about distinguishing between a sublease and an assignment. The first (and most commonly used) approach is formalistic: An *assignment* arises when the lessee transfers his entire interest under the lease — when, that is, he transfers the right to possession for the duration of the term. If the lessee transfers anything less than his entire interest (say two years remain on the lease and the lessee transfers for a term of one year), a *sublease* results. In the latter case, the lessee is said to have retained a reversion; the right to possession goes back (reverts) to him at the end of the period designated in the transfer. (Compare the analogous reversion in the landlord discussed in footnote 1 on page 425.) Suppose the lessee transfers all of his interest in some physical part of the premises; is this a sublease or a partial assignment? Most courts, quite correctly, say the latter. Suppose the lessee transfers his entire interest, but the instrument of transfer provides that if the transferee breaches any obligation of the lease, the original lessee may terminate the arrangement and retake possession (such a provision is called a power of termination or right of re-entry). A substantial minority of jurisdictions finds a sublease in this situation.

The second (and less common) approach to the sublease-assignment problem considers the intention of the parties. The actual words used —

sublease or *assignment* — are not conclusive (witness the *Ernst* case), though they may be persuasive (except in those cases, hardly unheard of, where both terms are used). Indeed, one occasionally gets the impression that courts claiming to honor the intention of the parties are in fact doing nothing more than inferring that "intention" from use of the words *sublease* or *assignment,* without the slightest basis for assuming that the parties knew the consequences of what they were saying. See, e.g., Jaber v. Miller, 219 Ark. 59, 239 S.W.2d 760 (1951).

Whether sublease or assignment, what happens if the primary lease between the landlord and the original tenant is prematurely terminated? It depends. If the landlord exercises a power to forfeit the primary lease because of some breach by the original tenant, then the landlord is entitled to possession as against sublessees and assignees. But if the original tenant merely gives up the primary lease voluntarily — "surrenders" it, see page 509 — the rights of possession of sublessees and assignees remain intact. In the case of a sublease, for example, surrender by the original tenant (the sublessor) leaves the sublessee holding of the landlord. They are in privity of estate. See, e.g., Parris-West Maytag Hotel Corp. v. Continental Amusement Co., 168 N.W.2d 735 (Iowa 1969).

2. *The consequences.* The *Ernst* case suggests some of the results attendant upon transferring by sublease on the one hand or assignment on the other. The following problems explore the matter further:

(a) *L* leases to *T* for a term of three years at a monthly rent of $300. One year later *T* "subleases, transfers, and assigns" to *T1* for "a period of one year from date." Thereafter neither *T* nor *T1* pays rent to *L*. What rights has *L* against *T*? Against *T1*? See 1 American Law of Property §§3.57, 3.62 (1952 & Supp. 1977). Compare Ky. Rev. Stat. §383.010(5) (1972). Suppose in the instrument of transfer *T1* had "agreed to pay the rents" reserved in the head lease. What effect might this have on *L*'s rights? See Restatement (Second) of Property, Landlord and Tenant, §16.1, Comment c at 120-121 (1977):

> At the time a transfer of an interest in the leased property is made, the transferor may exact a promise from the transferee that he will perform the promises in the lease which were made by the transferor. The exaction of such a promise does not relieve the transferor of liability on his promises. It does give him a direct remedy against his transferee if the transferee fails to perform the promises, which remedy will continue to be available even after the transferee has transferred the interest to someone else. If the holder of the benefits of the promises made by the transferor acquires enforcement rights as a third party beneficiary against the transferee by virtue of the transferee's promise to the transferor, then the transferee is in privity of contract with such third party beneficiary and a subsequent transfer by the transferee of an interest in the leased property will not affect that privity of contract liability.

(b) *L* leases to *T* for a term of three years at a monthly rent of $300; the lease provides that "*T* hereby covenants to pay said rent in advance on the first of each month." The lease also provides that "*T* shall not sublet or assign without the permission of *L*." Six months later *T*, with the permission of *L*, transfers to *T1* for the balance of the term. Thereafter *T1* pays the rent directly to *L* for several months, then defaults. *L* sues *T* for the rent due. What result, and why? See South Bay Center, Inc. v. Butler, Herrick & Marshall, 43 Misc. 2d 269, 250 N.Y.S.2d 863 (Sup. Ct. 1964); Buck v. J.M. McEntee & Sons, 275 P.2d 984 (Okla. 1954).

(c) *L* leases to *T* for a term of three years at a monthly rent of $600; in the lease *T* covenants to pay the rent in advance on the first of each month and also covenants to keep the leased premises in good repair. Six months later *T* assigns her entire interest to *T1*, who agrees in the instrument of assignment to "assume all the covenants in the lease" between *L* and *T*; three months later *T1* assigns his entire interest to *T2*, and three months after that *T2* assigns his entire interest to *T3*. *T3* defaults on rent payments and fails to keep the premises in good repair. *L* sues *T*, *T1*, *T2*, and *T3*. What are the liabilities of the four tenants to *L* and as among themselves? See 1 American Law of Property, supra, §3.61; 2 id. §§9.4, 9.5.[24]

3. Notice that the prime lease in the *Ernst* case contained a provision (paragraph 5 of the lease) prohibiting assignment or sublease without the lessors' approval. Suppose instead there had been no such provision, or suppose the provision had gone on to state that "lessors' approval shall not be unreasonably withheld." What in each case would be the rights of the parties? Consider the following materials.

Kendall v. Ernest Pestana, Inc.

Supreme Court of California, 1985
40 Cal. 3d 488, 709 P.2d 837, 220 Cal. Rptr. 818

BROUSSARD, J. This case concerns the effect of a provision in a commercial lease[25] that the lessee may not assign the lease or sublet the premises without the lessor's prior written consent. The question we address is whether, in the absence of a provision that such consent will not be unreasonably withheld, a lessor may unreasonably and arbitrarily withhold

---

24. According to the opinion in the *Ernst* case, the defendant's liability depended upon whether the transfer in question was an assignment or a sublease. Having worked through the Problems thus far, can you see grounds for disagreeing with that statement?

25. We are presented only with a commercial lease and therefore do not address the question whether residential leases are controlled by the principles articulated in this opinion.

his or her consent to an assignment.[26] This is a question of first impression in this court.

I

This case arises on appeal from an order sustaining a demurrer without leave to amend. We review the allegations of the complaint applying the established principle that a demurrer "admits the truth of all material factual allegations in the complaint. . . ." (Alcorn v. Anbro Engineering, Inc. (1970) 2 Cal. 3d 493, 496, 86 Cal. Rptr. 88, 468 P.2d 216.)

The allegations of the complaint may be summarized as follows. The lease at issue is for 14,400 square feet of hangar space at the San Jose Municipal Airport. The City of San Jose, as owner of the property, leased it to Irving and Janice Perlitch, who in turn assigned their interest to respondent Ernest Pestana, Inc. Prior to assigning their interest to respondent, the Perlitches entered into a 25-year sublease with one Robert Bixler commencing on January 1, 1970. The sublease covered an original five-year term plus four 5-year options to renew. The rental rate was to be increased every 10 years in the same proportion as rents increased on the master lease from the City of San Jose. The premises were to be used by Bixler for the purpose of conducting an airplane maintenance business.

Bixler conducted such a business under the name "Flight Services" until, in 1981, he agreed to sell the business to appellants Jack Kendall, Grady O'Hara and Vicki O'Hara. The proposed sale included the business and the equipment, inventory and improvements on the property, together with the existing lease. The proposed assignees had a stronger financial statement and greater net worth than the current lessee, Bixler, and they were willing to be bound by the terms of the lease.

The lease provided that written consent of the lessor was required before the lessee could assign his interest, and that failure to obtain such consent rendered the lease voidable at the option of the lessor. Accordingly, Bixler requested consent from the Perlitches' successor-in-interest, respondent Ernest Pestana, Inc. Respondent refused to consent to the assignment and maintained that it had an absolute right arbitrarily to refuse any such request. The complaint recites that respondent demanded "increased rent and other more onerous terms" as a condition of consenting to Bixler's transfer of interest.

The proposed assignees brought suit for declaratory and injunctive relief and damages seeking, inter alia, a declaration "that the refusal of ERNEST PESTANA, INC. to consent to the assignment of the lease is unreasonable and is an unlawful restraint on the freedom of alienation. . . ."

---

26. Since the present case involves an assignment rather than a sublease, we will speak primarily in terms of assignments. However, our holding applies equally to subleases. . . .

The trial court sustained a demurrer to the complaint without leave to amend and this appeal followed.

II

The law generally favors free alienability of property, and California follows the common law rule that a leasehold interest is freely alienable. Contractual restrictions on the alienability of leasehold interests are, however, permitted. "Such restrictions are justified as reasonable protection of the interests of the lessor as to who shall possess and manage property in which he has a reversionary interest and from which he is deriving income." (Schoshinski, American Law of Landlord and Tenant (1980) §8:15, at pp.578-579. See also 2 Powell on Real Property, ¶246[1], at p.372.97.)

The common law's hostility toward restraints on alienation has caused such restraints on leasehold interests to be strictly construed against the lessor. . . . This is particularly true where the restraint in question is a "forfeiture restraint," under which the lessor has the option to terminate the lease if an assignment is made without his or her consent. . . .

Nevertheless, a majority of jurisdictions have long adhered to the rule that where a lease contains an approval clause (a clause stating that the lease cannot be assigned without the prior consent of the lessor), the lessor may arbitrarily refuse to approve a proposed assignee no matter how suitable the assignee appears to be and no matter how unreasonable the lessor's objection. . . . The harsh consequences of this rule have often been avoided through application of the doctrines of waiver and estoppel, under which the lessor may be found to have waived (or be estopped from asserting) the right to refuse consent to assignment.

The traditional majority rule has come under steady attack in recent years. A growing minority of jurisdictions now hold that where a lease provides for assignment only with the prior consent of the lessor, such consent may be withheld *only where the lessor has a commercially reasonable objection to the assignment,* even in the absence of a provision in the lease stating that consent to assignment will not be unreasonably withheld. (See Rest. 2d Property, §15.2(2) (1977); 21 A.L.R.4th 188 (1983).)

For the reasons discussed below, we conclude that the minority rule is the preferable position. . . .

III

The impetus for change in the majority rule has come from two directions, reflecting the dual nature of a lease as a conveyance of a leasehold interest and a contract. (See Medico-Dental etc. Co. v. Horton & Con-

verse (1942) 21 Cal. 2d 411, 418, 132 P.2d 457.) The policy against restraints on alienation pertains to leases in their nature as *conveyances.*
Numerous courts and commentators have recognized that "[i]n recent
times the necessity of permitting reasonable alienation of commercial
space has become paramount in our increasingly urban society."
(Schweiso v. Williams [(1984) 150 Cal. App. 3d 883, 887, 198 Cal. Rptr.
238.)] . . .

Civil Code section 711 provides: "Conditions restraining alienation,
when repugnant to the interest created, are void." It is well settled that
this rule is not absolute in its application, but forbids only *unreasonable*
restraints on alienation. (Wellenkamp v. Bank of America (1978) 21 Cal.
3d 943, 948, 148 Cal. Rptr. 379, 582 P.2d 970.) . . . Reasonableness is
determined by comparing the justification for a particular restraint on
alienation with the quantum of restraint actually imposed by it. "[T]he
greater the quantum of restraint that results from enforcement of a
given clause, the greater must be the justification for that enforcement."
(Wellenkamp v. Bank of America, supra, 21 Cal. 3d at p.949, 148 Cal.
Rptr. 379, 582 P.2d 970.) In Cohen v. Ratinoff [(1983) 147 Cal. App. 3d
321, 195 Cal. Rptr. 84], the court examined the reasonableness of the
restraint created by an approval clause in a lease:

> Because the lessor has an interest in the character of the proposed commer-
> cial assignee, we cannot say that an assignment provision requiring the lessor's
> consent to an assignment is inherently repugnant to the leasehold interest
> created. We do conclude, however, that *if such an assignment provision is imple-
> mented in such a manner that its underlying purpose is perverted by the arbitrary or
> unreasonable withholding of consent, an unreasonable restraint on alienation is estab-
> lished.* [Id., 147 Cal. App. 3d at p.329, 195 Cal. Rptr. 84, italics added.]

One commentator explains as follows:

> The common-law hostility to restraints on alienation had a large exception
> with respect to estates for years. A lessor could prohibit the lessee from trans-
> ferring the estate for years to whatever extent he might desire. It was believed
> that the objectives served by allowing such restraints outweighed the social
> evils implicit in the restraints, in that they gave to the lessor a needed control
> over the person entrusted with the lessor's property and to whom he must
> look for the performance of the covenants contained in the lease. Whether
> this reasoning retains full validity can well be doubted. Relationships between
> lessor and lessee have tended to become more and more impersonal. Courts
> have considerably lessened the effectiveness of restraint clauses by strict con-
> struction and liberal applications of the doctrine of waiver. With the shortage
> of housing and, in many places, of commercial space as well, the allowance of
> lease clauses forbidding assignments and subleases is beginning to be cur-
> tailed by statutes. [2 Powell, supra, ¶246[1], at pp.372.97-372.98, fns. omit-
> ted.]

The Restatement Second of Property adopts the minority rule on the validity of approval clauses in leases: "A restraint on alienation without the consent of the landlord of a tenant's interest in leased property is valid, *but the landlord's consent to an alienation by the tenant cannot be withheld unreasonably,* unless a freely negotiated provision in the lease gives the landlord an absolute right to withhold consent." (Rest. 2d Property, §15.2(2) (1977), italics added.)[27] A comment to the section explains:

> The landlord may have an understandable concern about certain personal qualities of a tenant, particularly his reputation for meeting his financial obligations. The preservation of the values that go into the personal selection of the tenant justifies upholding a provision in the lease that curtails the right of the tenant to put anyone else in his place by transferring his interest, but this justification does not go to the point of allowing the landlord arbitrarily and without reason to refuse to allow the tenant to transfer an interest in leased property. [Id., com. a.]

Under the Restatement rule, the lessor's interest in the character of his or her tenant is protected by the lessor's right to object to a proposed assignee on reasonable commercial grounds. (See id., reporter's note 7 at pp.112-113.) The lessor's interests are also protected by the fact that the original lessee remains liable to the lessor as a surety even if the lessor consents to the assignment and the assignee expressly assumes the obligations of the lease. . . .

The second impetus for change in the majority rule comes from the nature of a lease as a *contract.* As the Court of Appeal observed in Cohen v. Ratinoff, supra, "[s]ince Richard v. Degan & Brody, Inc. [espousing the majority rule] was decided, . . . there has been an increased recognition of and emphasis on the duty of good faith and fair dealing inherent in every contract." (Id., 147 Cal. App. 3d at p.329, 195 Cal. Rptr. 84.) Thus, "[i]n every contract there is an implied covenant that neither party shall do anything which will have the effect of destroying or injuring the right of the other party to receive the fruits of the contract. . . ." (Universal Sales Corp. v. Cal. etc. Mfg. Co. (1942) 20 Cal. 2d 751, 771, 128 P.2d 665. . . .) "[W]here a contract confers on one party a discretionary power affecting the rights of the other, a duty is imposed to exercise that discretion in good faith and in accordance with fair dealing." (Cal. Lettuce Growers v. Union Sugar Co. (1955) 45 Cal. 2d 474, 484, 289 P.2d 785. See also, Larwin-Southern California, Inc. v. J.G.B. Inv. Co. (1979) 101 Cal. App. 3d 626, 640, 162 Cal. Rptr. 52.) Here the lessor retains the discretionary power to approve or disapprove an assignee proposed by the other party to the contract; this discretionary power

---

27. This case does not present the question of the validity of a clause absolutely prohibiting assignment, or granting absolute discretion over assignment to the lessor. We note that under the Restatement rule such a provision would be valid if freely negotiated.

should therefore be exercised in accordance with commercially reasonable standards. "Where a lessee is entitled to sublet under common law, but has agreed to limit that right by first acquiring the consent of the landlord, we believe the lessee has a right to expect that consent will not be unreasonably withheld." (Fernando v. Vazquez (Fla. App. 1981) 397 So. 2d 1171, 1174.)[28]

Under the minority rule, the determination whether a lessor's refusal to consent was reasonable is a question of fact. Some of the factors that the trier of fact may properly consider in applying the standards of good faith and commercial reasonableness are: financial responsibility of the proposed assignee; suitability of the use for the particular property; legality of the proposed use; need for alteration of the premises; and nature of the occupancy, i.e., office, factory, clinic, etc.

Denying consent solely on the basis of personal taste, convenience or sensibility is not commercially reasonable. Nor is it reasonable to deny consent "in order that the landlord may charge a higher rent than originally contracted for." (Schweiso v. Williams, supra, 150 Cal. App. 3d at p.886, 198 Cal. Rptr. 238.) This is because the lessor's desire for a better bargain than contracted for has nothing to do with the permissible purposes of the restraint on alienation — to protect the lessor's interest in the preservation of the property and the performance of the lease covenants. " '[T]he clause is for the protection of the landlord *in its ownership and operation of the particular property* — not for its general economic protection.' " (Ringwood Associates v. Jack's of Route 23, Inc. [(1977) 153 N.J. Super. 294, 379 A.2d 508, 512], quoting Krieger v. Helmsley-Spear, Inc. (1973) 62 N.J. 423, 302 A.2d 129, italics added.)

In contrast to the policy reasons advanced in favor of the minority rule, the majority rule has traditionally been justified on three grounds. Respondent raises a fourth argument in its favor as well. None of these do we find compelling.

First, it is said that a lease is a conveyance of an interest in real property, and that the lessor, having exercised a personal choice in the selection of a tenant and provided that no substitute shall be acceptable without prior consent, is under no obligation to look to anyone but the lessee for the rent. This argument is based on traditional rules of conveyancing and on concepts of freedom of ownership and control over one's property.

A lessor's freedom at common law to look to no one but the lessee

28. Some commentators have drawn an analogy between this situation and the duties of good faith and reasonableness implied in all transactions under the Uniform Commercial Code. (U. Com. Code §§1-203, 2-103(b); see also U. Com. Code §1-102, com. 1 [permitting application of the U. Com. Code to matters not expressly within its scope].) See Comment, The Approval Clause in a Lease: Toward a Standard of Reasonableness (1983) 17 U.S.F.L. Rev. 681, 695; see also Levin, Withholding Consent to Assignment: The Changing Rights of the Commercial Landlord (1980) 30 De Paul L. Rev. 109, 136.

for the rent has, however, been undermined by the adoption in California of a rule that lessors — like all other contracting parties — have a duty to mitigate damages upon the lessee's abandonment of the property by seeking a substitute lessee. (See Civ. Code, §1951.2.) Furthermore, the values that go into the personal selection of a lessee are preserved under the minority rule in the lessor's right to refuse consent to assignment on any commercially reasonable grounds. Such grounds include not only the obvious objections to an assignee's financial stability or proposed use of the premises, but a variety of other commercially reasonable objections as well. (See, e.g., Arrington v. Walter E. Heller Intl. Corp. (1975) 30 Ill. App. 3d 631, 333 N.E.2d 50 [desire to have only one "lead tenant" in order to preserve "image of the building" as tenant's international headquarters]; Warmack v. Merchants Natl. Bank of Fort Smith (Ark. 1981) 612 S.W.2d 733 [desire for good "tenant mix" in shopping center]; List v. Dahnke (Col. App. 1981) 638 P.2d 824 [lessor's refusal to consent to assignment of lease by one restaurateur to another was reasonable where lessor believed proposed specialty restaurant would not succeed at that location].) The lessor's interests are further protected by the fact that the original lessee remains a guarantor of the performance of the assignee. . . .

The second justification advanced in support of the majority rule is that an approval clause is an unambiguous reservation of absolute discretion in the lessor over assignments of the lease. The lessee could have bargained for the addition of a reasonableness clause to the lease (i.e., "consent to assignment will not be unreasonably withheld"). The lessee having failed to do so, the law should not rewrite the parties' contract for them. . . .

Numerous authorities have taken a different view of the meaning and effect of an approval clause in a lease, indicating that the clause is not "clear and unambiguous," as respondent suggests. As early as 1940, the court in Granite Trust Bldg. Corp. v. Great Atlantic & Pacific Tea Co. [(D. Mass. 1940)] 36 F. Supp. 77, examined a standard approval clause and stated: "It would seem to be the better law that when a lease restricts a lessee's rights by requiring consent before these rights can be exercised, *it must have been in the contemplation of the parties that the lessor be required to give some reason for withholding consent.*" (Id., at p.78, italics added.) The same view was expressed by commentators in the 1950s. (See Note, Landlord and Tenant — Right of Lessor to Refuse Any Settlement When Lease Prohibits Transfer Without Consent (1957) 41 Minn. L. Rev. 355, 358-359; Note, Real Property — Landlord and Tenant — Lessor's Arbitrary Withholding of Consent to Sublease (1957) 55 Mich. L. Rev. 1029, 1031; 2 Powell, supra, ¶229, n.79 (1950).) Again in 1963, the court in Gamble v. New Orleans Housing Mart, Inc. (La. App. 1963) 154 So. 2d 625, stated: "Here the lessee is simply not permitted to sublet without the written consent of the lessor. This does not *prohibit* or *interdict* subleasing. To the contrary, it permits subleasing provided only that the lessee first obtain the written consent of the lessor. *It suggests or connotes that, when the lessee obtains a subtenant acceptable or satisfactory to the lessor, he may sublet. . . .* Otherwise the provision simply would prohibit subleasing." (Id., at p.627, final italics added.) In Shaker Bldg. Co. v. Federal Lime and Stone Co. (1971) 28 Ohio Misc. 246, 277 N.E.2d 584, the court expressed the same view: "While the lease before the court clearly states that no assignment may take place without prior consent, inherent, however, in that provision is the representation that an assignment is possible. This court is of the opinion that *equally inherent in that provision is the representation that such prior consent will not be withheld under any and all circumstances, reasonable or unreasonable.*" (Id., 277 N.E.2d at p.587, italics added.)[29]

In light of the interpretations given to approval clauses in the cases cited above, and in light of the increasing number of jurisdictions that have adopted the minority rule in the last 15 years, the assertion that an approval clause "clearly and unambiguously" grants the lessor absolute discretion over assignments is untenable. It is not a rewriting of a contract, as respondent suggests, to recognize the obligations imposed by the duty of good faith and fair dealing, which duty is implied by law in every contract.

The third justification advanced in support of the majority rule is essentially based on the doctrine of stare decisis. It is argued that the courts should not depart from the common law majority rule because "many leases now in effect covering a substantial amount of real property and creating valuable property rights were carefully prepared by competent counsel in reliance upon the majority viewpoint." (Gruman v. Investors Diversified Services [(1956) 247 Minn. 502, 78 N.W.2d 377, 381.] . . .) As pointed out above, however, the majority viewpoint has been far from universally held and has never been adopted by this court. Moreover, the trend in favor of the minority rule should come as no surprise to observers of the changing state of real property law in the 20th century. The minority rule is part of an increasing recognition of the contractual nature of leases and the implications in terms of contractual duties that flow therefrom. We would be remiss in our duty if we declined to question a view held by the majority of jurisdictions simply because it is held by a majority. . . .

A final argument in favor of the majority rule is advanced by respondent and stated as follows: "Both tradition and sound public policy dictate that the lessor has a right, under circumstances such as these, to realize the increased value of his property." Respondent essentially argues that any increase in the market value of real property during the

---

29. Similar interpretations of the standard approval clause have been advanced recently by courts in support of their adoption of the minority rule. . . .

term of a lease properly belongs to the lessor, not the lessee. We reject
this assertion. One California commentator has written:

> [W]hen the lessee executed the lease he acquired the contractual right for the
> exclusive use of the premises, and all of the benefits and detriment attendant
> to possession, for the term of the contract. He took the downside risk that he
> would be paying too much rent if there should be a depression in the rental
> market. . . . Why should he be deprived of the contractual benefits of the lease
> because of the fortuitous inflation in the marketplace[?] By reaping the ben-
> efits he does not deprive the landlord of anything to which the landlord was
> otherwise entitled. The landlord agreed to dispose of possession for the lim-
> ited term and he could not reasonably anticipate any more than what was
> given to him by the terms of the lease. His reversionary estate will benefit
> from the increased value from the inflation in any event, at least upon the
> expiration of the lease. [Miller & Starr, Current Law of Cal. Real Estate (1977)
> 1984 Supp., §27:92 at p.321.]

Respondent here is trying to get *more* than it bargained for in the
lease. A lessor is free to build periodic rent increases into a lease, as the
lessor did here. . . . Any increased value of the property beyond this "belongs" to the lessor only in the sense, as explained above, that the lessor's
reversionary estate will benefit from it upon the expiration of the lease.
We must therefore reject respondent's argument in this regard.[30] . . .

IV

In conclusion, both the policy against restraints on alienation and the
implied contractual duty of good faith and fair dealing militate in favor
of adoption of the rule that where a commercial lease provides for assignment only with the prior consent of the lessor, such consent may be
withheld only where the lessor has a commercially reasonable objection
to the assignee or the proposed use. Under this rule, appellants have
stated a cause of action against respondent Ernest Pestana, Inc.

The order sustaining the demurrer to the complaint, which we have
deemed to incorporate a judgment of dismissal, is reversed.

[Two justices dissented in *Kendall*, on the ground that the provisions
of the agreement between the parties should be respected, especially
because the lessor had relied upon the rule existing at the time of the
lease. In the view of the dissent, the legislature had implicitly endorsed
the common law rule overturned in *Kendall*; it was up to the legislature,

---

30. Amicus Pillsbury, Madison & Sutro request that we make clear that, "whatever
principle governs in the absence of express lease provisions, nothing bars the parties to
commercial lease transactions from making their own arrangements respecting the allocation of appreciated rentals if there is a transfer of the leasehold." This principle we
affirm; we merely hold that the clause in the instant lease established no such arrangement.

not the court, to change the rule, and any change should be prospective only.]

NOTES AND QUESTIONS

1. Legislation enacted in California in 1989 codifies the holding in *Kendall* and resolves certain questions about the case, including the matter of retroactivity (*Kendall* is made applicable only to restrictions on transfer executed on or after September 23, 1983 — the date of Cohen v. Ratinoff, cited by the court in *Kendall*.) See Cal. Civ. Code §§1995.010-1995.270 (West 1992).

Notice the statement in footnote 27 on page 481. Section 1995.230 of the foregoing legislation provides: "A restriction on transfer of a tenant's interest in a lease may absolutely prohibit transfer." A Law Revision Commission Comment appearing after the section states that it "settles the question raised in *Kendall* . . . of the validity of a clause absolutely prohibiting assignment or sublease."

Notice also footnote 30 on page 485. In Carma Dev. v. Marathon Dev. California, Inc., 2 Cal. 4th 342, 826 P.2d 710, 6 Cal. Rptr. 2d 467 (1992), the court considered and upheld a so-called termination and recapture clause in a commercial lease entered into by "sophisticated commercial entities operating at arm's length and assisted by competent counsel." The clause provided: (1) that the tenant, before entering into any sublease or assignment, was to give the landlord written notice identifying the intended assignee or sublessee and specifying the terms of the intended transfer; (2) that the landlord could then terminate its lease with the tenant and, if the landlord elected to do so, enter into a new lease with the intended assignee or sublessee; and (3) that the tenant was not entitled to any profit realized by the landlord in consequence of the termination and reletting. The court held the clause valid under *Kendall* and the new legislation alike, notwithstanding another lease provision stating that the landlord's consent to any sublease or assignment was not to be unreasonably withheld.

2. Should the rule in *Kendall* apply to residential leases? The opinion in the case leaves the question open (see footnote 25 on page 477), and the California legislation discussed above is limited to leases for other than residential purposes, Cal. Civ. Code §1995.010, because, according to a Law Revision Commission Comment following that section, "residential real property leases involve different public policies than commercial real property leases."

See in this respect Slavin v. Rent Control Bd. of Brookline, 406 Mass. 458, 462-464, 548 N.E.2d 1226, 1228-1229 (1990):

[N]o State court has acted to create a reasonableness requirement in a case involving only a residential lease. . . .

[An important] concern that appears to have motivated the commercial lease decisions is a desire to limit restraints on alienation in light of the fact that "the necessity of reasonable alienation of commercial building space has become paramount in our ever-increasing urban society." . . . [W]e are not persuaded that there is such a "necessity of reasonable alienation of [residential] building space" that we ought to impose on residential landlords a reasonableness requirement to which they have not agreed. We are mindful that valid arguments in support of such a rule can be made, but there are also valid counter-arguments, not the least of which is that such a rule would be likely to engender a plethora of litigation about whether the landlord's withholding of consent was reasonable. The question is one of public policy which, of course, the Legislature is free to address. We note that the Legislature has spoken in at least four States [Alaska, Delaware, Hawaii, and New York].[31]

3. Notice the mention in *Kendall* (at page 483) of the landlord's duty to mitigate damages. In some jurisdictions the courts follow the common law rule that a landlord may arbitrarily and unreasonably refuse permission to sublet or assign (unless, of course, the lease provides to the contrary) but go on to say that if the tenant thereafter abandons the premises, the landlord is under a duty to mitigate damages. Is this any

---

31. This said, one might think that the Supreme Judicial Court of Massachusetts would follow *Kendall* with respect at least to commercial leases. Not so! See Merchants Row Corp. v. Merchants Row, Inc., 412 Mass. 204, 205-207, 587 N.E.2d 788, 789 (1992):

At issue [here] is whether, in a commercial lease, the requirement that the tenant must obtain the landlord's consent before assigning the lease implies, as a matter of law, an obligation on the landlord's part to act reasonably in withholding consent. We conclude that a landlord is not so obligated.

In Slavin v. Rent Control Bd. of Brookline, . . . we held that a reasonableness requirement would not be implied in the assignment clause of a residential lease. . . . We see no sound reason to depart from this rule and to grant greater protection in this regard to commercial tenants than that afforded to residential tenants, especially since we and other jurisdictions see no rational distinction between residential and commercial leases in this regard. . . .

Since the bargaining power of commercial tenants at the lease drafting stage is ordinarily greater than that of residential tenants, logic would indicate that, if we were to differentiate between residential and commercial leases, we would do so in favor of residential rather than commercial tenants.

For another recent case rejecting the rule in *Kendall*, see First Federal Sav. Bank v. Key Markets, Inc., 559 N.E.2d 600 (Ind. 1990).

In contrast to the foregoing, several states have recently followed *Kendall* in the case of commercial leases. See Newman v. Hinky Dinky Omaha-Lincoln, Inc., 229 Neb. 382, 427 N.W.2d 50 (1988) ("the rule of reasonableness, expressed in *Kendall* . . . , is the correct rule . . . where a commercial lease does not expressly permit a lessor to withhold consent . . . , even in the absence of a lease provision that the lessor's consent will not be unreasonably withheld"); Julian v. Christopher, 320 Md. 1, 575 A.2d 735, 740 (1990) (if the lease provides that tenant must obtain landlord's consent, such consent may not be unreasonably withheld; but if the parties intend to preclude any transfer, or intend to limit the right to transfer by giving landlord the right to withhold consent arbitrarily, they may do so by a freely negotiated provision indicating that intent).

On *Kendall*, see Alex M. Johnson, Jr., Correctly Interpreting Long-Term Leases Pursuant to Modern Contract Law: Toward a Theory of Relational Leases, 74 Va. L. Rev. 751 (1988).

different than saying that a landlord may not unreasonably and arbitrarily refuse permission to sublet or assign? Cf. Vasquez v. Carmel Shopping Center Co., 777 S.W.2d 532 (Tex. App. 1989). (We look more closely at abandonment and mitigation beginning at page 500.)

PROBLEMS

1. Suppose the following situations arise in a jurisdiction following the rule in *Kendall,* or in any jurisdiction under a lease providing that "there shall be no sublease or assignment without landlord's consent, and such consent shall not be unreasonably withheld." What result?

(a) *L* leases to *T* for a term of five years. After two years, *T* wishes to transfer the lease to *T1*. *L* refuses consent because *T1* is a tenant in another of *L*'s buildings under a lease that is about to expire; *L* and *T1* have been actively negotiating a new lease, and *L* wants to avoid losing *T1* as a tenant in the other building. See Krieger v. Helmsley-Spear, Inc., 62 N.J. 423, 302 A.2d 129 (1973), cited with apparent approval in *Kendall* at page 482.

Suppose instead that *T1* is not already a tenant of *L*'s, but rather is a prospective tenant who wants to use the leased property for a business that will compete with *L*'s business in the same area. See Pay 'N Pak Stores, Inc. v. Superior Court, 210 Cal. App. 3d 1404, 258 Cal. Rptr. 816 (1989).

(b) *L,* a Christian evangelical organization, owns a building that it uses as its headquarters. No religious services are held in the building. *L* leases space in the building to *T* for a term of three years. After one year, *T* wishes to transfer the lease to *T1*, an organization that proposes to use the leased space as a counselling center providing information on birth control and abortion. *L* refuses consent on the sole ground that it is fundamentally opposed to the aims and activities of *T1*. See American Book Co. v. Yeshiva Univ. Dev. Found., 59 Misc. 2d 31, 297 N.Y.S.2d 156 (1969).[32]

2. Suppose a jurisdiction following the majority rule, and a lease providing that *L* may terminate if *T* transfers without the necessary consent. Unlike the situation in Problem 1, however, the lease prohibits only assignment without *L*'s permission. *T* wishes to assign to *T1*, but *L* — because she wishes to rent to *T1* on her own for a higher rent — refuses consent. *T* then transfers the lease to *T1* for the remainder of the original term, minus one day. *L* brings suit to terminate the head lease with *T* (which would terminate *T1*'s tenancy as well), arguing that the form of the transaction should be disregarded, that it was a subterfuge, that

---

32. Is it never "commercially reasonable" to deny consent to a transfer "solely on the basis of personal taste, convenience or sensibility," as the court in *Kendall* puts it at page 482? See the discussion of leases in housing cooperatives at pages 934-935.

the parties clearly intended the transfer to be an assignment, and that the assignment was made without *L*'s consent. What result? See pages 475-476 and Walgreen Arizona Drug Co. v. Plaza Center Corp., 132 Ariz. 512, 647 P.2d 643 (1982).

3. *L* leases to *T* for a term of five years at a monthly rent of $900; in the lease, *T* covenants to pay the rent, and further covenants not to sublet or assign without *L*'s permission. Thereafter *T*, with *L*'s permission, assigns to *T1* (*T1* does not expressly assume the obligations of the lease); then *T1* assigns to *T2* without first obtaining *L*'s permission. *T2* defaults in rent payments and *L* sues *T1* for the amount due. What result? See Restatement (Second) of Property, Landlord and Tenant, §16.1, Comment g at 125 (1977) (expressing disapproval of the so-called Rule in Dumpor's Case, 4 Coke 119b, 76 Eng. Rep. 1110 (K.B. 1578), "which would terminate the prohibition against assignment when the landlord consents to an assignment unless he specifically reserves the right to prohibit future assignments").

F.   The Tenant Who Defaults

Suppose a tenant *in possession* has defaulted — say by failing to pay rent or observe some other lease obligation — or is holding over after the termination of the lease (see pages 431-437), and the landlord wishes to recover possession. Or suppose the tenant has *abandoned* the premises prior to the end of the tenancy, perhaps owing some back rent. What, in each case, may the landlord do? Consider the following materials.

1.   The Tenant in Possession

Berg v. Wiley
Supreme Court of Minnesota, 1978
264 N.W.2d 145

ROGOSHESKE, J. Defendant landlord, Wiley Enterprises,Inc., and defendant Rodney A. Wiley (hereafter collectively referred to as Wiley) appeal from a judgment upon a jury verdict awarding plaintiff tenant, A Family Affair Restaurant, Inc., damages for wrongful eviction from its leased premises. The issues for review are whether the evidence was sufficient to support the jury's finding that the tenant did not abandon or surrender the premises and whether the trial court erred in finding Wiley's reentry forcible and wrongful as a matter of law. We hold that the jury's verdict is supported by sufficient evidence and that the trial court's determination of unlawful entry was correct as a matter of law, and affirm the judgment.

On November 11, 1970, Wiley as lessor and tenant's predecessor in interest as lessee executed a written lease agreement letting land and a building in Osseo, Minnesota, for use as a restaurant. The lease provided a 5-year term beginning December 1, 1970, and specified that the tenant agreed to bear all costs of repairs and remodeling, to "make no changes in the building structure" without prior written authorization from Wiley, and to "operate the restaurant in a lawful and prudent manner." Wiley also reserved the right "at [his] option [to] retake possession" of the premises "[s]hould the Lessee fail to meet the conditions of this Lease."[33] In early 1971, plaintiff Kathleen Berg took assignment of the lease from the prior lessee, and on May 1, 1971, she opened "A Family Affair Restaurant" on the premises. In January 1973, Berg incorporated the restaurant and assigned her interest in the lease to "A Family Affair Restaurant, Inc." As sole shareholder of the corporation, she alone continued to act for the tenant. [The prior lessee referred to by the court was Phillip Berg, Kathleen's brother, who ran a pool hall and served 3.2 beer and small meals on the leased premises from December 1, 1970 (when the lease began), until February 20, 1971 (when Phillip assigned to Kathleen with the consent of Wiley). Kathleen then began remodeling the premises to make them suitable for a restaurant.]

The present dispute has arisen out of Wiley's objection to Berg's continued remodeling of the restaurant without procuring written permission and her consequent operation of the restaurant in a state of disrepair with alleged health code violations. Strained relations between the parties came to a head in June and July 1973. In a letter dated June 29, 1973, Wiley's attorney charged Berg with having breached lease items 5 and 6 by making changes in the building structure without written authorization and by operating an unclean kitchen in violation of health regulations. The letter demanded that a list of eight remodeling items be completed within 2 weeks from the date of the letter, by Friday, July 13, 1973, or Wiley would retake possession of the premises under lease item 7. Also, a June 13 inspection of the restaurant by the Minnesota Department of Health had produced an order that certain listed

33. The provisions of the lease pertinent to this case provide:

Item #5 The Lessee will make no changes to the building structure without first receiving written authorization from the Lessor. The Lessor will promptly reply in writing to each request and will cooperate with the Lessee on any reasonable request.

Item #6 The Lessee agrees to operate the restaurant in a lawful and prudent manner during the lease period.

Item #7 Should the Lessee fail to meet the conditions of this Lease the Lessor may at their [sic] option retake possession of said premises. In any such event such act will not relieve Lessee from liability for payment [of] the rental herein provided or from the conditions or obligations of this lease.

changes be completed within specified time limits in order to comply with the health code. The major items on the inspector's list, similar to those listed by Wiley's attorney, were to be completed by July 15, 1973.

During the 2-week deadline set by both Wiley and the health department, Berg continued to operate the restaurant without closing to complete the required items of remodeling. The evidence is in dispute as to whether she intended to permanently close the restaurant and vacate the premises at the end of the 2 weeks or simply close for about 1 month in order to remodel to comply with the health code. At the close of business on Friday, July 13, 1973, the last day of the 2-week period, Berg dismissed her employees, closed the restaurant, and placed a sign in the window saying "Closed for Remodeling." Earlier that day, Berg testified, Wiley came to the premises in her absence and attempted to change the locks. When she returned and asserted her right to continue in possession, he complied with her request to leave the locks unchanged. Berg also testified that at about 9:30 P.M. that evening, while she and four of her friends were in the restaurant, she observed Wiley hanging from the awning peering into the window. Shortly thereafter, she heard Wiley pounding on the back door demanding admittance. Berg called the county sheriff to come and preserve order. Wiley testified that he observed Berg and a group of her friends in the restaurant removing paneling from a wall. Allegedly fearing destruction of his property, Wiley called the city police, who, with the sheriff, mediated an agreement between the parties to preserve the status quo until each could consult with legal counsel on Monday, July 16, 1973.

Wiley testified that his then attorney advised him to take possession of the premises and lock the tenant out. Accompanied by a police officer and a locksmith, Wiley entered the premises in Berg's absence and without her knowledge on Monday, July 16, 1973, and changed the locks. Later in the day, Berg found herself locked out. The lease term was not due to expire until December 1, 1975. The premises were re-let to another tenant on or about August 1, 1973. Berg brought this damage action against Wiley and three other named defendants, including the new tenant, on July 27, 1973. A second amended complaint sought damages for lost profits, damage to chattels, intentional infliction of emotional distress, and other tort damages based upon claims in wrongful eviction, contract, and tort. Wiley answered with an affirmative defense of abandonment and surrender and counterclaimed for damage to the premises and indemnification on mechanics lien liability incurred because of Berg's remodeling. At the close of Berg's case, all defendants other than Rodney A. Wiley and Wiley Enterprises, Inc., were dismissed from the action. Only Berg's action for wrongful eviction and intentional infliction of emotional distress and Wiley's affirmative defense of abandonment and his counterclaim for damage to the premises were submitted by special verdict to the jury. With respect to the wrongful eviction claim, the trial court found as a matter of law that Wiley did in fact lock the tenant out, and that the lockout was wrongful.

The jury, by answers to the questions submitted, found no liability on Berg's claim for intentional infliction of emotional distress and no liability on Wiley's counterclaim for damages to the premises, but awarded Berg $31,000 for lost profits and $3,540 for loss of chattels resulting from the wrongful lockout. The jury also specifically found that Berg neither abandoned nor surrendered the premises. . . .

On this appeal, Wiley seeks an outright reversal of the damages award for wrongful eviction, claiming insufficient evidence to support the jury's finding of no abandonment or surrender and claiming error in the trial court's finding of wrongful eviction as a matter of law.

The first issue before us concerns the sufficiency of evidence to support the jury's finding that Berg had not abandoned or surrendered the leasehold before being locked out by Wiley. Viewing the evidence to support the jury's special verdict in the light most favorable to Berg, as we must, we hold it amply supports the jury's finding of no abandonment or surrender of the premises. While the evidence bearing upon Berg's intent was strongly contradictory, the jury could reasonably have concluded, based on Berg's testimony and supporting circumstantial evidence, that she intended to retain possession, closing temporarily to remodel. Thus, the lockout cannot be excused on the ground that Berg abandoned or surrendered the leasehold.

The second and more difficult issue is whether Wiley's self-help repossession of the premises by locking out Berg was correctly held wrongful as a matter of law.

Minnesota has historically followed the common-law rule that a landlord may rightfully use self-help to retake leased premises from a tenant in possession without incurring liability for wrongful eviction provided two conditions are met: (1) The landlord is legally entitled to possession, such as where a tenant holds over after the lease term or where a tenant breaches a lease containing a reentry clause; and (2) the landlord's means of reentry are peaceable. Mercil v. Broulette, 66 Minn. 416, 69 N.W. 218 (1896). Under the common-law rule, a tenant who is evicted by his landlord may recover damages for wrongful eviction where the landlord either had no right to possession or where the means used to remove the tenant were forcible, or both. See, e.g., Poppen v. Wadleigh, 235 Minn. 400, 51 N.W.2d 75 (1952); Sweeney v. Meyers, 199 Minn. 21, 270 N.W. 906 (1937); Lobdell v. Keene, 85 Minn. 90, 88 N.W. 426 (1901). See, also, Minn. St. 566.01 (statutory cause of action where entry is not "allowed by law" or, if allowed, is not made "in a peaceable manner").

Wiley contends that Berg had breached the provisions of the lease, thereby entitling Wiley, under the terms of the lease, to retake possession, and that his repossession by changing the locks in Berg's absence was accomplished in a peaceful manner. In a memorandum accompanying the post-trial order, the trial court stated two grounds for finding the lockout wrongful as a matter of law: (1) It was not accomplished in a peaceable manner and therefore could not be justified under the common-law rule, and (2) any self-help reentry against a tenant in possession is wrongful under the growing modern doctrine that a landlord must always resort to the judicial process to enforce his statutory remedy against a tenant wrongfully in possession. Whether Berg had in fact breached the lease and whether Wiley was hence entitled to possession was not judicially determined. That issue became irrelevant upon the trial court's finding that Wiley's reentry was forcible as a matter of law because even if Berg had breached the lease, this could not excuse Wiley's nonpeaceable reentry. The finding that Wiley's reentry was forcible as a matter of law provided a sufficient ground for damages, and the issue of breach was not submitted to the jury.

In each of our previous cases upholding an award of damages for wrongful eviction, the landlord had in fact been found to have no legal right to possession. In applying the common-law rule, we have not before had occasion to decide what means of self-help used to dispossess a tenant in his absence will constitute a nonpeaceable entry, giving a right to damages without regard to who holds the legal right to possession. Wiley argues that only actual or threatened violence used against a tenant should give rise to damages where the landlord had the right to possession. We cannot agree.

It has long been the policy of our law to discourage landlords from taking the law into their own hands, and our decisions and statutory law have looked with disfavor upon any use of self-help to dispossess a tenant in circumstances which are likely to result in breaches of the peace. We gave early recognition to this policy in Lobdell v. Keene, 85 Minn. 90, 101, 88 N.W. 426, 430 (1901), where we said:

> The object and purpose of the legislature in the enactment of the forcible entry and unlawful detainer statute was to prevent those claiming a right of entry or possession of lands from redressing their own wrongs by entering into possession in a violent and forcible manner. All such acts tend to a breach of the peace, and encourage high-handed oppression. The law does not permit the owner of land, be his title ever so good, to be the judge of his own rights with respect to a possession adversely held, but puts him to his remedy under the statutes.

To facilitate a resort to judicial process, the legislature has provided a summary procedure in Minn. St. 566.02 to 566.17 whereby a landlord may recover possession of leased premises upon proper notice and showing in court in as little as 3 to 10 days. As we recognized in Mutual

Trust Life Ins. Co. v. Berg, 187 Minn. 503, 505, 246 N.W. 9, 10 (1932), "[t]he forcible entry and unlawful detainer statutes were intended to prevent parties from taking the law into their own hands when going into possession of lands and tenements. . . ." To further discourage self-help, our legislature has provided treble damages for forcible evictions, §§557.08 and 557.09, and has provided additional criminal penalties for intentional and unlawful exclusion of a tenant, §504.25. In Sweeney v. Meyers, supra, we allowed a business tenant not only damages for lost profits but also punitive damages against a landlord who, like Wiley, entered in the tenant's absence and locked the tenant out.

In the present case, as in *Sweeney*, the tenant was in possession, claiming a right to continue in possession adverse to the landlord's claim of breach of the lease, and had neither abandoned nor surrendered the premises. Wiley, well aware that Berg was asserting her right to possession, retook possession in her absence by picking the locks and locking her out. The record shows a history of vigorous dispute and keen animosity between the parties. Upon this record, we can only conclude that the singular reason why actual violence did not erupt at the moment of Wiley's changing of the locks was Berg's absence and her subsequent self-restraint and resort to judicial process. Upon these facts, we cannot find Wiley's means of reentry peaceable under the common-law rule. Our long-standing policy to discourage self-help which tends to cause a breach of the peace compels us to disapprove the means used to dispossess Berg. To approve this lockout, as urged by Wiley, merely because in Berg's absence no actual violence erupted while the locks were being changed, would be to encourage all future tenants, in order to protect their possession, to be vigilant and thereby set the stage for the very kind of public disturbance which it must be our policy to discourage.

Consistent with our conclusion that we cannot find Wiley's means of reentry peaceable under the common-law rule is Gulf Oil Corp. v. Smithey, 426 S.W.2d 262 (Tex. Civ. App. 1968). In that case the Texas court, without departing from the common-law rule, held that a landlord's reentry in the tenant's absence by picking the locks and locking the tenant out, although accomplished without actual violence, was forcible as a matter of law.[34] The Texas courts, by continuing to embrace the common-law rule, have apparently left open the possibility that self-help may be available in that state to dispossess a tenant in some undefined circumstances which may be found peaceable.

We recognize that the growing modern trend departs completely from the common-law rule to hold that self-help is never available to dispossess a tenant who is in possession and has not abandoned or vol-

---

34. California courts similarly implied force in certain nonviolent entries made in the tenant's absence. See, e.g., Karp v. Margolis, 159 Cal. App. 2d 69, 323 P.2d 557 (1958); McNeil v. Higgins, 86 Cal. App. 2d 723, 195 P.2d 470 (1948).

untarily surrendered the premises. Annotation, 6 A.L.R.3d 177, 186; 76 Dickinson L. Rev. 215, 227. This growing rule is founded on the recognition that the potential for violent breach of peace inheres in any situation where a landlord attempts by his own means to remove a tenant who is claiming possession adversely to the landlord. Courts adopting the rule reason that there is no cause to sanction such potentially disruptive self-help where adequate and speedy means are provided for removing a tenant peacefully through judicial process. At least 16 states[35] have adopted this modern rule, holding that judicial proceedings, including the summary procedures provided in those states' unlawful detainer statutes, are the exclusive remedy by which a landlord may remove a tenant claiming possession. . . .

While we would be compelled to disapprove the lockout of Berg in her absence under the common-law rule as stated, we approve the trial court's reasoning and adopt as preferable the modern view represented by the cited cases. To make clear our departure from the common-law rule for the benefit of future landlords and tenants, we hold that, subsequent to our decision in this case, the only lawful means to dispossess a tenant who has not abandoned nor voluntarily surrendered but who claims possession adversely to a landlord's claim of breach of a written lease is by resort to judicial process. We find that Minn. St. 566.02 to 566.17 provide the landlord with an adequate remedy for regaining possession in every such case.[36] Where speedier action than provided in §§566.02 to 566.17 seems necessary because of threatened destruction of the property or other exigent circumstances, a temporary restraining

35. Annotation, 6 A.L.R.3d 177, 186, Supp. 13, shows this modern rule to have been adopted in California, Connecticut, Delaware, Florida, Georgia, Illinois, Indiana, Louisiana, Nebraska, North Carolina, Ohio, Tennessee, Texas, Utah, Vermont, and Washington.

We have examined the summary statutory procedures for repossession held exclusive in these other states and we find them comparable and on the whole no speedier than the summary judicial procedures by which a landlord may regain possession in as little as 3 to 10 days under Minn. St. 566.02 to 566.17.

36. Under §§566.05 and 566.06, a landlord may regain possession in default proceedings against a tenant personally served with process in as little as 3 to 10 days. Default judgment against a tenant not present and served by posting may be procured in a week to 10 days. §§566.05 and 566.06. Trial is by the court unless either party demands a jury trial. §566.07. Proceedings are stayed on appeal except as against a holdover tenant. §566.12. Upon execution of a writ of restitution, the tenant is allowed 24 hours to vacate the property.

We are mindful that by §566.04 the summary remedy of §§566.02 to 566.17 is made unavailable against any tenant having been "in quiet possession for three years next before the filing of the complaint. . . ." This reflects an appropriate policy choice by the legislature to require full litigation of the right to possession in a common-law ejectment action before judicially ousting a tenant of such long tenure. Our holding, disallowing self-help in such cases as well, is consistent with the legislative policy protecting the long-term tenant. The availability of temporary restraining orders, temporary injunctions against waste, and eventual damages for unlawful detainer or unpaid rent provides an adequate compensating remedy to the landlord for any delay in obtaining possession during judicial proceedings.

order under Rule 65, Rules of Civil Procedure, and law enforcement protection are available to the landlord. Considered together, these statutory and judicial remedies provide a complete answer to the landlord. In our modern society, with the availability of prompt and sufficient legal remedies as described, there is no place and no need for self-help against a tenant in claimed lawful possession of leased premises.

Applying our holding to the facts of this case, we conclude, as did the trial court, that because Wiley failed to resort to judicial remedies against Berg's holding possession adversely to Wiley's claim of breach of the lease, his lockout of Berg was wrongful as a matter of law. The rule we adopt in this decision is fairly applied against Wiley, for it is clear that, applying the older common-law rule to the facts and circumstances peculiar to this case, we would be compelled to find the lockout non-peaceable for the reasons previously stated. The jury found that the lockout caused Berg damage and, as between Berg and Wiley, equity dictates that Wiley, who himself performed the act causing the damage, must bear the loss.

Affirmed.

NOTES AND QUESTIONS

1. Under the common law, a landlord entitled to possession could resort to self-help without fear of civil liability — so long as he used no more force than reasonably necessary. Criminal prosecution was nevertheless a possibility; forcible entry was a common law crime. Thus the civil and criminal systems were a bit at odds.[37] The modern view on self-help appears to be that in Berg v. Wiley. It should be noted, however, that while a flat prohibition on self-help is the trend, it is probably not yet the majority rule. See, e.g., Restatement (Second) of Property, Landlord and Tenant, §14.2, Reporter's Note at 16 (1977). Where self-help is allowed, of course, there still arises the difficult issue of just what constitutes reasonable or permissible force. Here the courts have tended to be rather strict, so that self-help may be a theoretical but not a practical alternative. See, e.g., Annot., 6 A.L.R.3d 177, 189-194 (1966). See also Comment, Landlord Eviction Remedies Act — Legislative Overreaction

---

37. And may still be so today — to some degree. See, e.g., Restatement (Second) of Property, Landlord and Tenant, §14.1, Statutory Note at 5 (1977): "If a person makes a 'forcible' entry by using self-help, he will probably be subject to criminal liability; yet he may be entitled to retain possession of the premises which he has obtained through such force. If the law permits the party entitled to possession to keep the premises, the . . . tenant may be uninterested in pressing criminal charges against the party using self-help. Thus, in practice, such a jurisdiction may still permit self-help." But might not the tenant be interested in remedies other than regaining possession? See Berg v. Wiley and Annot., 6 A.L.R.3d 177, 182, 199-237 (1966).

to Landlord Self-Help, 18 Wake Forest L. Rev. 25, 30 (1982) (in some jurisdictions, reasonable force means any nonviolent entry; in others it means only an entry not against the tenant's will).

2. Berg v. Wiley involved a commercial lease, but the court's reasoning would appear to apply to all leases, residential and commercial alike. See also Simpson v. Lee, 499 A.2d 889 (D.C. App. 1985) (self-help prohibited in either instance). In some jurisdictions, the prohibition on self-help applies only to residential leases. Is there any reason to treat the two situations differently? See Case Note, 60 N.C. L. Rev. 885, 891-892 (1982) (loss of residence has greater psychological impact than loss of possession of place of business, and the need for immediate replacement of commercial space is less vital; moreover, in the commercial setting there is more likely to be equal bargaining power between the parties). See also Watson v. Brown, 67 Hawaii 252, 686 P.2d 12 (1984) (permits self-help in commercial tenancies, because of equality of bargaining power; expresses no opinion as to residential tenancies). Of what relevance is equal bargaining power?

In Berg v. Wiley, item 7 of the lease might be read to permit self-help by the landlord. Should such a provision make a difference in a jurisdiction otherwise prohibiting self-help? See Annot., supra, at 194-199; Restatement (Second) of Property, Landlord and Tenant, supra, §14.3; Edwards v. C.N. Inv. Co., 27 Ohio Misc. 57, 272 N.E.2d 652 (Mun. Ct. 1971).

3. Should self-help repossession by a landlord be subject to constitutional attack on the ground that it denies the tenant due process of law? Apparently no decision has ever held to that effect, although a number of state courts have invalidated a related self-help remedy — distraint, or distress for rent — on due process grounds. See Restatement (Second) of Property, Landlord and Tenant, supra, §12.1, Reporter's Note at 429; id. §14.1, Statutory Note at 6-7. Under the common law remedy of distress for rent (abolished in some states by statute), a landlord could seize a defaulting tenant's property found on the premises and retain it until payment of overdue rent, all without prior hearing. The absence of a prior hearing has proved the vulnerable point in cases invalidating modern analogues of this procedure. See also Soldal v. Cook County, 113 S. Ct. 538 (1992) (Fourth Amendment protects against unreasonable seizures, by or with the assistance of public officials, of tenant's property prior to eviction order required under state law).

PROBLEM

A local YWCA provides housing and social services to battered women and their children as part of an effort to support families seeking transition to a life independent of their former abusers. Participants are furnished with subsidized apartments and social services, in return for which they are expected to work or attend school and take part in counseling sessions. When several women who are unhappy with the way their cases are being handled refuse to attend the sessions, the YWCA gives them notice to vacate their apartments and then, shortly thereafter, changes the locks on their apartment doors. A state statute prohibits efforts by a "lessor or landlord" to regain possession of residential premises "by force without benefit of judicial process." Does the statute apply? See Serreze v. YWCA of Western Massachusetts, 30 Mass. App. Ct. 639, 572 N.E.2d 581 (1991).

NOTE: SUMMARY PROCEEDINGS

At one time, self-help was a very important remedy for the landlord who sought to recover possession of leased premises, because the only alternative was a cumbersome, time-consuming, common law procedure called ejectment (which still exists today, with statutory modifications). The time and expense associated with ejectment ill served the landlord's needs; self-help, on the other hand, was problematic from the viewpoint of landlords, tenants, and society generally. A response to this mix of shortcomings began to develop in the nineteenth century — legislative provision for summary proceedings (sometimes called forcible entry and detainer statutes). Today every state provides some form of summary proceeding. For background, description, and discussion of the variety of provisions, see Restatement (Second) of Property, Landlord and Tenant, §12.1, Statutory Note at 399-405 (1977); id. §14.1, Statutory Note at 3-11.

Summary proceedings are intended to be just what the name implies — a quick and efficient means by which to recover possession (and, in some jurisdictions, rent) after termination of a tenancy. To promote quickness, the typical statute requires only a few days' notice to the tenant prior to bringing an eviction action, and the range of issues subject to litigation is kept narrow. It is difficult to generalize about the latter point other than to say that any matter extrinsic to the issue of possession is normally excluded (for example, a tenant may not claim an earlier unrelated debt owed by the landlord as a setoff for past due rent). As we shall see later in this chapter, a number of jurisdictions are beginning to provide that failure by a landlord to maintain leased premises in a habitable condition justifies certain "self-help" measures by a tenant, including rent withholding. It seems quite logical, then, to permit a tenant to raise the condition of the premises as a defense to a summary eviction action brought for nonpayment of rent — the defense appears to go, after all, to the issue of the right to possession. Many states so provide, but not all do, and the U.S. Supreme Court has held that a failure to do so does not violate due process. Lindsey v. Normet, 405 U.S. 56 (1972).[38]

As the *Berg* case suggests, courts have quite generally relied on the availability of summary proceedings as one reason to abrogate the common law remedy of self-help. After all, if a quick and economical remedy is available to the landlord, why court the troubles to which self-help is thought to give rise? The difficulty is that typical summary eviction procedures can be time-consuming and expensive, even if uncontested. See, e.g., U.S. G.A.O., District of Columbia: Information on Court-Ordered Tenant Evictions 2 (Dec. 1990), reporting that an average of 114 days elapsed from the date landlords requested evictions to the date they were accomplished. Delay occurred for a variety of reasons: stay of eviction orders when tenants agreed (but subsequently failed) to pay the rent due; trials; failure of the marshall to evict on bad weather days, holidays, and weekends; a shortage of marshalls; landlords' failure to comply with arrangements agreed upon with the marshalls (for example, failure to have movers at the eviction sites). See also California Apartment Law Information Foundation, Unlawful Detainer Study 5 (1991), lamenting

> the failure of the state's eviction process to provide a remedy for the economic losses caused by defaulting tenants. The experience of many landlords is that they lose an inordinate amount of money through an increasingly lengthy and complicated eviction process. Reportedly, landlords try to recover these losses through higher rents from average rent-paying tenants.

Should self-help be permitted after all, even if summary proceedings are available? Is the abolition of self-help necessarily a good thing from the tenant's point of view? Cf. James J. White, The Abolition of Self-Help Repossession: The Poor Pay Even More, 1973 Wis. L. Rev. 503.

NOTE: LANDLORD'S REMEDIES IN ADDITION TO EVICTION

Usually a landlord will want to do more than simply terminate the lease and evict the defaulting tenant in possession: some back rent may be due; future rents may exceed what the landlord can obtain on a reletting; the leased premises may have been damaged in some way. But

---

38. As we shall see later, many jurisdictions today prohibit "retaliatory eviction" — eviction motivated by a landlord's desire to retaliate against a tenant who has, for example, withheld rent payments because of the condition of the leased premises. While retaliatory eviction can usually be asserted by a tenant as a defense in a summary proceeding, Lindsey v. Normet implies that this need not be the case.

the remedies in these and related respects are in many instances the same as those a landlord might wish to pursue against a tenant who has abandoned. Accordingly, we defer them until the end of the next section.

2.   The Tenant Who Has Abandoned Possession

Sommer v. Kridel

Supreme Court of New Jersey, 1977
74 N.J. 446, 378 A.2d 767

PASHMAN, J. We granted certification in these cases to consider whether a landlord seeking damages from a defaulting tenant is under a duty to mitigate damages by making reasonable efforts to re-let an apartment wrongfully vacated by the tenant. Separate parts of the Appellate Division held that, in accordance with their respective leases, the landlords in both cases could recover rents due under the leases regardless of whether they had attempted to re-let the vacated apartments. Although they were of different minds as to the fairness of this result, both parts agreed that it was dictated by Joyce v. Bauman, 113 N.J.L. 438, 174 A. 693 (E.&A. 1934), a decision by the former Court of Errors and Appeals. We now reverse and hold that a landlord does have an obligation to make a reasonable effort to mitigate damages in such a situation. We therefore overrule Joyce v. Bauman to the extent that it is inconsistent with our decision today.

I

A

Sommer v. Kridel

The case was tried on stipulated facts. On March 10, 1972 the defendant, James Kridel, entered into a lease with the plaintiff, Abraham Sommer, owner of the "Pierre Apartments" in Hackensack, to rent apartment 6-L in that building.[39] The term of the lease was from May 1, 1972 until April 30, 1974, with a rent concession for the first six weeks, so that the first month's rent was not due until June 15, 1972.

One week after signing the agreement, Kridel paid Sommer $690. Half of that sum was used to satisfy the first month's rent. The remainder was paid under the lease provision requiring a security deposit of

---

39. Among other provisions, the lease prohibited the tenant from assigning or transferring the lease without the consent of the landlord. If the tenant defaulted, the lease gave the landlord the option of re-entering or re-letting, but stipulated that failure to re-let or to recover the full rental would not discharge the tenant's liability for rent.

The Pierre Apartments
Hackensack

$345. Although defendant had expected to begin occupancy around May 1, his plans were changed. He wrote to Sommer on May 19, 1972, explaining

> I was to be married on June 3, 1972. Unhappily the engagement was broken and the wedding plans cancelled. Both parents were to assume responsibility for the rent after our marriage. I was discharged from the U.S. Army in October 1971 and am now a student. I have no funds of my own, and am supported by my stepfather.
>
> In view of the above, I cannot take possession of the apartment and am surrendering all rights to it. Never having received a key, I cannot return same to you.
>
> I beg your understanding and compassion in releasing me from the lease, and will of course, in consideration thereof, forfeit the 2 month's rent already paid.
>
> Please notify me at your earliest convenience.

Plaintiff did not answer the letter.

Subsequently, a third party went to the apartment house and inquired about renting apartment 6-L. Although the parties agreed that she was ready, willing and able to rent the apartment, the person in charge told her that the apartment was not being shown since it was already rented to Kridel. In fact, the landlord did not re-enter the apartment or exhibit it to anyone until August 1, 1973. At that time it was rented to a new tenant for a term beginning on September 1, 1973. The new rental was for $345 per month with a six week concession similar to that granted Kridel.

Prior to re-letting the new premises, plaintiff sued Kridel in August 1972, demanding $7,590, the total amount due for the full two-year term of the lease. Following a mistrial, plaintiff filed an amended complaint asking for $5,865, the amount due between May 1, 1972 and September 1, 1973. The amended complaint included no reduction in the claim to reflect the six week concession provided for in the lease or the $690 payment made to plaintiff after signing the agreement. Defendant filed an amended answer to the complaint, alleging that plaintiff breached the contract, failed to mitigate damages and accepted defendant's surrender of the premises. He also counterclaimed to demand repayment of the $345 paid as a security deposit.

The trial judge ruled in favor of the defendant. Despite his conclusion that the lease had been drawn to reflect "the 'settled law' of this state," he found that "justice and fair dealing" imposed upon the landlord the duty to attempt to re-let the premises and thereby mitigate damages. He also held that plaintiff's failure to make any response to defendant's unequivocal offer of surrender was tantamount to an acceptance, thereby terminating the tenancy and any obligation to pay rent. As a result, he dismissed both the complaint and the counterclaim. The Appellate Division reversed in a per curiam opinion, 153 N.J. Super. 1 (1976), and we granted certification. 69 N.J. 395, 354 A.2d 323 (1976).

B

Riverview Realty Co. v. Perosio

This controversy arose in a similar manner. On December 27, 1972, Carlos Perosio entered into a written lease with plaintiff Riverview Realty Co. The agreement covered the rental of apartment 5-G in a building owned by the realty company at 2175 Hudson Terrace in Fort Lee. As in the companion case, the lease prohibited the tenant from subletting or assigning the apartment without the consent of the landlord. It was to run for a two-year term, from February 1, 1973 until January 31, 1975, and provided for a monthly rental of $450. The defendant took possession of the apartment and occupied it until February 1974. At that time he vacated the premises, after having paid the rent through January 31, 1974.

The landlord filed a complaint on October 31, 1974, demanding $4,500 in payment for the monthly rental from February 1, 1974 through October 31, 1974. Defendant answered the complaint by alleging that there had been a valid surrender of the premises and that plain-

**River View Towers
2175 Hudson Terrace
Fort Lee**

tiff failed to mitigate damages. The trial court granted the landlord's motion for summary judgment against the defendant, fixing the damages at $4,050 plus $182.25 interest.[40]

The Appellate Division affirmed the trial court holding that it was bound by prior precedents, including Joyce v. Bauman, supra. 138 N.J. Super. 270, 350 A.2d 517 (App. Div. 1976). Nevertheless, it freely criticized the rule which it found itself obliged to follow:

> There appears to be no reason in equity or justice to perpetuate such an unrealistic and uneconomic rule of law which encourages an owner to let valuable rented space lie fallow because he is assured of full recovery from a defaulting tenant. Since courts in New Jersey and elsewhere have abandoned ancient real property concepts and applied ordinary contract principles in other conflicts between landlord and tenant there is no sound reason for a continuation of a special real property rule to the issue of mitigation. . . . [138 N.J. Super. at 273-74, 350 A.2d at 519; citations omitted.]

40. The trial court noted that damages had been erroneously calculated in the complaint to reflect ten months' rent. As to the interest awarded to plaintiff, the parties have not raised this issue before this Court. Since we hold that the landlord had a duty to attempt to mitigate damages, we need not reach this question.

We granted certification. 70 N.J. 145, 358 A.2d 191 (1976).

II

As the lower courts in both appeals found, the weight of authority in this State supports the rule that a landlord is under no duty to mitigate damages caused by a defaulting tenant. . . . This rule has been followed in a majority of states, Annot. 21 A.L.R.3d 534, §2[a] at 541 (1968), and has been tentatively adopted in the American Law Institute's Restatement of Property. Restatement (Second) of Property, §11.1(3) (Tent. Draft No. 3, 1975).

Nevertheless, while there is still a split of authority over this question, the trend among recent cases appears to be in favor of a mitigation requirement. . . .

The majority rule is based on principles of property law which equate a lease with a transfer of a property interest in the owner's estate. Under this rationale the lease conveys to a tenant an interest in the property which forecloses any control by the landlord; thus, it would be anomalous to require the landlord to concern himself with the tenant's abandonment of his own property. Wright v. Baumann, 239 Or. 410, 398 P.2d 119, 120-21, 21 A.L.R.3d 527 (1968).

For instance, in Muller v. Beck, [94 N.J.L. 311, 110 A. 831 (Sup. Ct. 1920)], where essentially the same issue was posed, the court clearly treated the lease as governed by property, as opposed to contract, precepts.[41] The court there observed that the "tenant had an estate for years, but it was an estate qualified by this right of the landlord to prevent its transfer," 94 N.J.L. at 313, 110 A. at 832, and that "the tenant has an estate with which the landlord may not interfere." Id. at 314, 110 A. at 832. Similarly, in Heckel v. Griese, [12 N.J. Misc. 211, 171 A. 148 (Sup. Ct. 1934)], the court noted the absolute nature of the tenant's interest in the property while the lease was in effect, stating that "when the tenant vacated, . . . no one, in the circumstances, had any right to interfere with the defendant's possession of the premises." 12 N.J. Misc. at 213, 171 A. 148, 149. Other cases simply cite the rule announced in Muller v. Beck, supra, without discussing the underlying rationale. . . .

Yet the distinction between a lease for ordinary residential purposes and an ordinary contract can no longer be considered viable. As Professor Powell observed, evolving "social factors have exerted increasing influence on the law of estates for years." 2 Powell on Real Property (1977 ed.), §221[1] at 180-81. The result has been that

> [t]he complexities of city life, and the proliferated problems of modern society in general, have created new problems for lessors and lessees and these

---

41. It is well settled that a party claiming damages for a breach of contract has a duty to mitigate his loss. . . .

have been commonly handled by specific clauses in leases. This growth in the number and detail of specific lease covenants has reintroduced into the law of estates for years a predominantly contractual ingredient. [Powell, supra, at 181.]

Thus in 6 Williston on Contracts (3 ed. 1962), §890A at 592, it is stated:

There is a clearly discernible tendency on the part of courts to cast aside technicalities in the interpretation of leases and to concentrate their attention, as in the case of other contracts, on the intention of the parties. . . .

See also Javins v. First National Realty Corp., 138 U.S. App. D.C. 369, 373, 428 F.2d 1071, 1075 (D.C. Cir. 1970), cert. den. 400 U.S. 925, 91 S. Ct. 186, 27 L. Ed. 2d 185 (1970) ("the trend toward treating leases as contracts is wise and well considered"); 57 E. 54 Realty Corp. v. Gay Nineties Realty Corp., 71 Misc. 2d 353, 335 N.Y.S.2d 872, 874 (App. Div. 1972); Parkwood Realty Co. v. Marcano, 77 Misc. 2d 690, 353 N.Y.S.2d 623, 626 (Cty. Ct. 1974); 3 Thompson on Real Property (1959 ed.), §1110 at 377; Hicks, The Contractual Nature of Real Property Leases, 24 Baylor L. Rev. 443 (1972); Note, Right of Lessor to Refuse Any Subtenant When Lease Prohibits Transfer Without Consent, 41 Minn. L. Rev. 355, 357 (1957).

This Court has taken the lead in requiring that landlords provide housing services to tenants in accordance with implied duties which are hardly consistent with the property notions expressed in Muller v. Beck, supra, and Heckel v. Griese, supra. See Braitman v. Overlook Terrace Corp., 68 N.J. 368, 346 A.2d 76 (1975) (liability for failure to repair defective apartment door lock); Berzito v. Gambino, 63 N.J. 460, 308 A.2d 17 (1973) (construing implied warranty of habitability and covenant to pay rent as mutually dependent); Marini v. Ireland, 56 N.J. 130, 265 A.2d 526 (1970) (implied covenant to repair); Reste Realty Corp. v. Cooper, 53 N.J. 444, 251 A.2d 268 (1969) (implied warranty of fitness of premises for leased purpose). In fact, in Reste Realty Corp. v. Cooper, supra, we specifically noted that the rule which we announced there did not comport with the historical notion of a lease as an estate for years. 53 N.J. at 451-52, 251 A.2d 268. And in Marini v. Ireland, supra, we found that the "guidelines employed to construe contracts have been modernly applied to the construction of leases." 56 N.J. at 141, 265 A.2d at 532.

Application of the contract rule requiring mitigation of damages to a residential lease may be justified as a matter of basic fairness.[42] Profes-

42. We see no distinction between the leases involved in the instant appeals and those which might arise in other types of residential housing. However, we reserve for another day the question of whether a landlord must mitigate damages in a commercial setting. Cf. Kruvant v. Sunrise Market, Inc., 58 N.J. 452, 456, 279 A.2d 104 (1971), modified on other grounds, 59 N.J. 330, 282 A.2d 746 (1971).

sor McCormick first commented upon the inequity under the majority rule when he predicted in 1925 that eventually

> the logic, inescapable according to the standards of a "jurisprudence of conceptions" which permits the landlord to stand idly by the vacant, abandoned premises and treat them as the property of the tenant and recover full rent, will yield to the more realistic notions of social advantage which in other fields of the law have forbidden a recovery for damages which the plaintiff by reasonable efforts could have avoided. [McCormick, The Rights of the Landlord Upon Abandonment of the Premises by the Tenant, 23 Mich. L. Rev. 211, 221-22 (1925).]

Various courts have adopted this position. See Annot., supra, §7(a) at 565, and ante at 770-771.

The pre-existing rule cannot be predicated upon the possibility that a landlord may lose the opportunity to rent another empty apartment because he must first rent the apartment vacated by the defaulting tenant. Even where the breach occurs in a multi-dwelling building, each apartment may have unique qualities which make it attractive to certain individuals. Significantly, in Sommer v. Kridel, there was a specific request to rent the apartment vacated by the defendant; there is no reason to believe that absent this vacancy the landlord could have succeeded in renting a different apartment to this individual.

We therefore hold that antiquated real property concepts which served as the basis for the pre-existing rule, shall no longer be controlling where there is a claim for damages under a residential lease. Such claims must be governed by more modern notions of fairness and equity. A landlord has a duty to mitigate damages where he seeks to recover rents due from a defaulting tenant.

If the landlord has other vacant apartments besides the one which the tenant has abandoned, the landlord's duty to mitigate consists of making reasonable efforts to re-let the apartment. In such cases he must treat the apartment in question as if it was one of his vacant stock.

As part of his cause of action, the landlord shall be required to carry the burden of proving that he used reasonable diligence in attempting to re-let the premises. We note that there has been a divergence of opinion concerning the allocation of the burden of proof on this issue. See Annot., supra, §12 at 577. While generally in contract actions the breaching party has the burden of proving that damages are capable of mitigation, see Sandler v. Lawn-A-Mat Chem. & Equip. Corp., 141 N.J. Super. 437, 455, 358 A.2d 805 (App. Div. 1976); McCormick, Damages, §33 at 130 (1935), here the landlord will be in a better position to demonstrate whether he exercised reasonable diligence in attempting to re-let the premises. Cf. Kulm v. Coast to Coast Stores Central Org., 248 Or. 436, 432 P.2d 1006 (1967) (burden on lessor in contract to renew a lease).

III

The Sommer v. Kridel case presents a classic example of the unfairness which occurs when a landlord has no responsibility to minimize damages. Sommer waited 15 months and allowed $4658.50 in damages to accrue before attempting to re-let the apartment. Despite the availability of a tenant who was ready, willing and able to rent the apartment, the landlord needlessly increased the damages by turning her away. While a tenant will not necessarily be excused from his obligations under a lease simply by finding another person who is willing to rent the vacated premises, see, e.g., Regent v. Dempsey-Tegler & Co., 70 Ill. App. 2d 32, 216 N.E.2d 500 (Ill. App. 1966) (new tenant insisted on leasing the premises under different terms); Edmands v. Rust & Richardson Drug Co., 191 Mass. 123, 77 N.E. 713 (1906) (landlord need not accept insolvent tenant), here there has been no showing that the new tenant would not have been suitable. We therefore find that plaintiff could have avoided the damages which eventually accrued, and that the defendant was relieved of his duty to continue paying rent. Ordinarily we would require the tenant to bear the cost of any reasonable expenses incurred by a landlord in attempting to re-let the premises, . . . but no such expenses were incurred in this case.[43]

In Riverview Realty Co. v. Perosio, no factual determination was made regarding the landlord's efforts to mitigate damages, and defendant contends that plaintiff never answered his interrogatories. Consequently, the judgment is reversed and the case remanded for a new trial. Upon remand and after discovery has been completed, R. 4: 17 et seq., the trial court shall determine whether plaintiff attempted to mitigate damages with reasonable diligence, . . . and if so, the extent of damages remaining and assessable to the tenant. As we have held above, the burden of proving that reasonable diligence was used to re-let the premises shall be upon the plaintiff. See Annot., supra, §11 at 575.

In assessing whether the landlord has satisfactorily carried his burden, the trial court shall consider, among other factors, whether the landlord, either personally or through an agency, offered or showed the apartment to any prospective tenants, or advertised it in local newspapers. Additionally, the tenant may attempt to rebut such evidence by showing that he proffered suitable tenants who were rejected. However, there is no standard formula for measuring whether the landlord has utilized satisfactory efforts in attempting to mitigate damages, and each case must be judged upon its own facts. Compare Hershorin v. La Vista,

---

43. As to defendant's counterclaim for $345, representing the amount deposited with the landlord as a security deposit, we note that this issue has not been briefed or argued before this Court, and apparently has been abandoned. Because we hold that plaintiff breached his duty to attempt to mitigate damages, we do not address defendant's argument that the landlord accepted a surrender of the premises.

Inc., 110 Ga. App. 435, 138 S.E.2d 703 (App. 1964) ("reasonable effort" of landlord by showing the apartment to all prospective tenants); Carpenter v. Wisniewski, 139 Ind. App. 325, 215 N.E.2d 882 (App. 1966) (duty satisfied where landlord advertised the premises through a newspaper, placed a sign in the window, and employed a realtor); Re Garment Center Capitol, Inc., 93 F.2d 667, 115 A.L.R. 202 (2 Cir. 1938) (landlord's duty not breached where higher rental was asked since it was known that this was merely a basis for negotiations); Foggia v. Dix, 265 Or. 315, 509 P.2d 412, 414 (1973) (in mitigating damages, landlord need not accept less than fair market value or "substantially alter his obligations as established in the pre-existing lease"); with Anderson v. Andy Darling Pontiac, Inc., 257 Wis. 371, 43 N.W.2d 362 (1950) (reasonable diligence not established where newspaper advertisement placed in one issue of local paper by a broker); Scheinfeld v. Muntz T.V., Inc., 67 Ill. App. 2d 8, 214 N.E.2d 506 (Ill. App. 1966) (duty breached where landlord refused to accept suitable subtenant); Consolidated Sun Ray, Inc. v. Oppenstein, 335 F.2d 801, 811 (8 Cir. 1964) (dictum) (demand for rent which is "far greater than the provisions of the lease called for" negates landlord's assertion that he acted in good faith in seeking a new tenant).

IV

The judgment in Sommer v. Kridel is reversed. In Riverview Realty Co. v. Perosio, the judgment is reversed and the case is remanded to the trial court for proceedings in accordance with this opinion.

NOTES AND QUESTIONS

1. Various justifications are given for the rule, forsaken in the *Sommer* case, that a landlord is under no obligation to mitigate damages in the event of abandonment by a tenant: The tenant cannot by his own wrongdoing impose a duty on the landlord; the tenant has "purchased" an interest in real estate (and, presumably, is stuck with it); the landlord should not be forced into a personal relationship with a new tenant he does not wish to accept; the landlord should not be required to seek out new tenants "continually." See Annot., 21 A.L.R.3d 534, 548-549 (1968). The Restatement offers another consideration in support of its surprising position against a duty of mitigation: "Abandonment of property is an invitation to vandalism, and the law should not encourage such conduct by putting a duty of mitigation of damages on the landlord." Restatement (Second) of Property, Landlord and Tenant, §12.1, Comment i at 392 (1977). Are any of these points compelling?

Yet another justification for the no-mitigation rule arises from a line of cases suggesting that efforts on the part of a landlord to mitigate damages by reletting abandoned premises "might be held to constitute an unwilling acceptance of the surrender" offered by the defaulting tenant. Wohl v. Yelen, 22 Ill. App. 2d 455, 464, 161 N.E.2d 339, 343 (1959).

Surrender is a term of art, one that connotes quite neatly a tenant's offer to end a tenancy — "here, I give up." Surrender terminates a lease, provided, of course, that the landlord accepts the tenant's offer. If he does — if the surrender is effected — this "extinguishes the lessee's liability for future rent,[44] but not for accrued rent or for past breaches of other covenants." 1 American Law of Property §3.99 at 390 (1952).

Surrender may, of course, come about explicitly — tenant expressly offers, landlord expressly accepts. In such event, and if the Statute of Frauds is complied with, the lease is unambiguously terminated. Our concern here, though, is with an implied offer and, more particularly, an implied acceptance. Suppose, then, that tenant abandons — an implied offer of surrender.[45] What acts of the landlord might be regarded as an acceptance? The answer to this question is generally said to turn on the intent of the landlord in retaking possession, without regard to whether the tenant is on notice that any reletting is on the tenant's account (the Restatement would require notice; see Restatement (Second) of Property, Landlord and Tenant, supra, §12.1). Under the intent test, one considers whether the landlord's actions are inconsistent with or repugnant to continuation of the original lease. The length of the new tenancy, whether alterations have been made, the new rent, and similar factors will be suggestive but not conclusive.

The upshot of the common law rule, still followed in a majority of jurisdictions, is that a landlord may but need not mitigate.[46] What happens if the landlord relets, on the tenant's account, for less than the fair rental value and also less than the original rent? If the landlord relets for more than the original rent? Suppose the tenant abandons, and the landlord notifies him, as the law in the jurisdiction permits, that he intends to relet on the tenant's account. The landlord then finds a new

---

44. Be cautioned that this statement does not necessarily mean what you probably think it does. To say a lessee is no longer liable for future *rent* after a surrender does not necessarily mean that there is no liability for *damages* equal to the landlord's loss of the value of the remaining portion of the original lease. This is a matter that we take up in the Notes beginning on page 510. See especially footnote 50 on page 512. — EDS.

45. "An abandonment of the leased property by the tenant occurs when he vacates the leased property without justification and without any present intention of returning and he defaults in the payment of rent." Restatement (Second) of Property, Landlord and Tenant, supra, §12.1, Comment i at 392. See generally Annot., 84 A.L.R.4th 183 (1991).

46. "[T]he landlord has the option of (1) terminating the lease, (2) obtaining another tenant while holding the original tenant liable for any deficiency that may occur, or (3) permitting the premises to remain vacant while collecting the agreed-upon rent from the original tenant." Crolley v. Crow-Childress-Mobley No. 2, 190 Ga. App. 496, 497, 379 S.E.2d 202, 204 (1989).

tenant willing to pay more than the original rent, revokes the notice to the original tenant and accepts his surrender, and relets at the higher amount. Who is entitled to the excess rent?

2. The court in *Sommer* left undecided the issue of a landlord's duty to mitigate in the case of a commercial lease.[47] Other jurisdictions recognizing a duty to mitigate do not, it appears, limit the duty to residential leases. Is there any reason they should?

The justifications for the duty to mitigate are pertinent to the question. The opinion in *Sommer* mentions "modern notions of fairness and equity." Efficiency considerations also enter in, however. Does not the mitigation duty help avoid waste of resources by giving landlords an incentive to make use of available capacity? See Richard A. Posner, Economic Analysis of Law 117-126 (4th ed. 1992). Consider in this connection the requirement announced by the court in *Sommer* that a landlord must treat an abandoned apartment as part of his "vacant stock" (page 506); presumably, then, the landlord must make (at least) the same effort to rent the abandoned premises as he makes to rent other vacant units. Is this justified by the rationale that the rent the landlord "receives from the substitute tenant is . . . a gain *enabled* by the breach of contract by the first tenant"?[48]

3. What is the consequence of a landlord's failure to mitigate? May he recover no rent subsequent to the abandonment, or may he recover the difference between the agreed rent and the amount he could reasonably have avoided? There is authority for each alternative. See, e.g., Whitehorn v. Dickerson, 419 S.W.2d 713 (Md. App. 1967) (no recovery of such damages as might have been avoided by reasonable efforts); URLTA §4.203 (failure by landlord to use reasonable efforts terminates rental agreement).

NOTES: LANDLORD'S REMEDIES AND SECURITY DEVICES

Thus far we have considered the means available to a landlord to terminate a tenancy and regain the leased premises from a defaulting

47. The New Jersey Superior Court, Appellate Division, subsequently extended the rule in *Sommer* to commercial leases but added that in such leases (as opposed to residential leases) the parties could agree to the contrary. Carisi v. Wax, 192 N.J. Super. 536, 471 A.2d 439 (1983).

48. Posner, supra, at 122 (emphasis in original). See also Note, Application of the Avoidable Consequence Rule to the Residential Leasehold Agreement, 57 Fordham L. Rev. 425, 442-443 (1988) (discussing the lost-volume problem). In one of the lower appellate court decisions reversed in *Sommer* the court remarked that the doctrine of mitigation "cuts both ways. Why should plaintiff be compelled to lease defendant's apartment in order to mitigate defendant's damages when he has other empty apartments being held for rent? We know of no sound reason, legal or equitable, why plaintiff should be required to suffer in order to mitigate defendant's damages." 153 N.J. Super. at 7, 378 A.2d at 777.

tenant (Section F1), and the question of a landlord's duty to mitigate damages (Section F2). These Notes address some related matters.

1. *Rent and damages.* Suppose the tenant has failed to pay rent when due or has breached some other lease obligation. Putting aside the question of a tenant's defenses (some of which will be suggested in Section G1), the landlord's right to sue for back rent and for damages occasioned by the tenant's breach of lease obligations is straightforward. If the tenant is in possession, the landlord may also terminate the lease and recover possession.[49]

Suppose that the landlord also wishes — in addition to collecting past rent and damages, and in addition to terminating the lease and evicting the tenant — to recover damages equal to the difference (reduced to present value) between the rent reserved in the lease for the unexpired term and the reasonable rental value of the premises for that period. Is there such a remedy?

The question has to do with the doctrine of anticipatory breach (or repudiation) familiar to contract law. In some jurisdictions, at least, the remedy is made available by statute. See, e.g., Cal. Civ. Code §1951.2 (West 1985) (if landlord terminates because of a breach of the lease, he may recover — in addition to back rent and other damages — the present value "of the amount by which the unpaid rent for the balance of the term . . . exceeds the amount of such rental loss that the lessee proves could be reasonably avoided," provided the lease either expresses such a remedy or the landlord has relet in mitigation; notice that the doctrine of anticipatory breach has mitigation built into its damage formula). Absent such a statute, it appears that the anticipatory breach remedy is generally unavailable, at least as to a failure to pay rent, perhaps on the reasoning that a failure to pay rent when due, of itself, is not a

---

49. Matters were not always so simple. At common law, the failure by the tenant to pay rent or perform some other lease obligation did not of itself permit the landlord to terminate the lease; the landlord's remedy, rather, was to sue for breach of contract and damages. (This is another way of saying that the obligations of landlord and tenant were regarded as independent, such that a material breach by one party usually did *not* excuse performance by the other absent some language in the lease providing otherwise. Modern contract law is to the contrary, and (as mentioned earlier on pages 438-439) the law of landlord and tenant is coming to be so as well.)

In response to the common law rule, landlords began putting "forfeiture" clauses in leases. Wording could be very important: If the clause were phrased so as to end the lease automatically in the event of the tenant's breach, the landlord could resort to the sort of summary proceedings discussed in the Note on page 498; if, on the other hand, the clause merely gave the landlord an election in the event of breach, eviction could only be accomplished through the cumbersome ejectment remedy. See Stephen Ross, Converting Nonpayment to Holdover Summary Proceedings: The New York Experience with Conditional Limitations Based upon Nonpayment of Rent, 15 Fordham Urb. L.J. 289, 300 n.66 (1987). Most jurisdictions today have done away with the common law technicalities; summary proceedings are usually available regardless of the wording of the forfeiture clause, or even without such a clause, at least for some kinds of breach (in particular, the tenant's failure to pay rent).

sufficient "repudiation" of the lease.[50] In the case of a tenant's abandonment, however, repudiation is clearcut, and here anticipatory breach will apply if the jurisdiction in question extends that contract doctrine to leases. (This, then, is a remedy in addition to those listed in footnote 46 on page 509, and its mention should clarify the ambiguity raised in footnote 44 on the same page.) For an overview, see Sarajane Love, Landlord's Remedies When the Tenant Abandons: Property, Contract, and Leases, 30 Kan. L. Rev. 533 (1982).

2. *Security devices.* There is an old saw that a landlord's best security is judicious selection of tenants. Most landlords want more, and they have over the years developed a number of techniques to protect themselves in the event of a tenant's default. The following summary highlights the most important of these.

(a) *Security deposits.* The first security device that occurs to most people is, we suspect, the security deposit — simply because most people have had (probably unpleasant) experience with it. The purposes of such deposits — to protect the landlord in the event a tenant defaults in rent, damages the premises, or otherwise breaches the lease — are straightforward, but there is some evidence that things get bent in practice. In principle, the landlord is obliged to return to the tenant, upon termination of the lease, the deposit less any amounts necessary to compensate for defaults by the tenant. In practice, the landlord has an incentive to imagine all sorts of reasons why he should be entitled to retain the deposit, and with money in hand he has leverage that permits abuse. This, at least, is the central concern; justified or not, it has led to a good deal of reform — most of it statutory. The following provisions are typical: limits are placed on the amount of deposits (e.g., two months' rent); deposits create a trust relationship; deposits must be placed in a trust or escrow account; deposits are not to be commingled with other funds; the tenant's claim to a deposit is made prior to other creditors, including, in some instances, a trustee in bankruptcy; the landlord must pay interest on deposits; the landlord must submit an itemized list of deductions from a deposit; penalties are levied for violations (e.g., double or treble the amount of the deposit, or some fixed sum).

(b) *Other techniques.* Landlords have tried in various ways, and with some success, to avoid the legal strictures on security deposits. Thus a lease might characterize a payment as "consideration" or a "bonus" for execution of the lease, an approach that tends to work so long as there is no provision for return of the payment upon termination. Designating

---

50. But see Lennon v. U.S. Theatre Corp., 920 F.2d 996, 1000 (D.C. Cir. 1990) (under District of Columbia law, termination — including termination by acceptance of surrender, or by re-entry for nonpayment — forecloses landlord's right to collect rent but does not eliminate an otherwise applicable right to damages; a lease covenant providing for tenant liability for lost rent after landlord's re-entry creates a right to damages, subject to a mitigation requirement).

the payment "advance rent" has been even more successful; a number of jurisdictions permit the landlord to retain such a deposit on termination for default, sometimes relying on the theory that rent is nonapportionable. Finally, a deposit may be characterized as "liquidated damages." This technique might be tolerated when the amount in question is reasonable and especially when actual damages are difficult to determine. Most often, though, the "liquidated damages" are regarded as an unenforceable penalty. A liquidated damages clause is not ideal from the landlord's standpoint in any event. With such a clause, once default has occurred the tenant has little incentive to minimize damages. If the landlord attempts to guard against this shortcoming with a provision allowing him to hold the tenant for damages over and above the deposit, the likelihood is that the liquidated damages will be regarded as a penalty.

A final device worth mention is rent acceleration — a provision that upon the tenant's default, all rent for the entire term is due and payable. Rent acceleration is accepted by a majority of courts, at least with regard to default in rent payments as opposed to other breaches. If rent is accelerated, the landlord usually cannot take possession as well.[51]

G.   Duties, Rights, and Remedies (Especially Regarding the Condition of the Leased Premises)

Leases give rise to a problem called "moral hazard," a piece of jargon first used to describe "the tendency of an insured to relax his efforts to prevent the occurrence of the risk that he has insured against because he has shifted all or part of the expected cost of the risk to an insurance company." Richard A. Posner, Economic Analysis of Law 108 (4th ed. 1992). But the moral hazard problem arises in other than strictly insurance situations, landlord-tenant relationships being an example. Once a lease is entered into, the landlord has an incentive to neglect everyday repairs because the costs of neglect are borne primarily by tenants. Tenants, in turn, have an incentive to neglect maintenance, especially toward the end of the term, because the costs of neglect will soon shift to the landlord. How might the law deal with these difficulties? That question is the subject of this section.

---

51. The result might be otherwise if the lease expressly provides that the landlord may terminate and hold the tenant liable for all the future rent. See, e.g., Nylen v. Park Doral Apts., 535 N.E.2d 178 (Ind. Ct. App. 1989) (lease of school-year residence to students!).

1. Landlord's Duties; Tenant's Rights and Remedies

The early common law was hardheaded, and hardhearted, about a tenant's rights and remedies. The law implied covenants concerning title and possession (see pages 463-468), but not concerning the condition of the premises. Absent some clause in the lease providing otherwise, the tenant took the premises "as is," and landlords were under no obligation to warrant their fitness.

Given the culture in which the early common law rules developed, perhaps they made some sense. In any event, as the culture changed, largely in the direction of urbanization and specialization, so too did the common law — but begrudgingly, usually in the language of exceptions and qualifications rather than the bold rhetoric of reform, and often with statutory prodding. The process of change began well over a century ago and led to the development of a body of conventional doctrine that was, for a long time, very stable. But with the 1960s there began a period of sweeping reform — most of it at first concerned with residential tenancies, much of it initiated by courts rather than legislatures — the implications and merits of which are still matters of dispute. The reforms have not so much replaced conventional doctrine as riddled it. A given jurisdiction might adopt one new reform but not another, or limit what it adopts to residential tenancies. A useful understanding of this area of landlord-tenant relations thus requires some attention to the older rules as well as the newer ones.

———————

Disputes between landlord and tenant regarding the condition of the premises arise in essentially two ways. First, the tenant might wish to vacate, or to stay but pay less (or no) rent. Second, the tenant (or an invitee of the tenant) might be injured by allegedly defective premises and claim damages against the landlord in tort. The materials below concentrate on the first sort of dispute, but give some attention to the second as well.

a. Quiet Enjoyment and Constructive Eviction

Reste Realty Corp. v. Cooper
Supreme Court of New Jersey, 1969
53 N.J. 444, 251 A.2d 268

FRANCIS, J. Plaintiff-lessor sued defendant-lessee to recover rent allegedly due under a written lease. The suit was based upon a charge that defendant had unlawfully abandoned the premises two and a quarter years before the termination date of the lease. The trial court, sitting without a jury, sustained tenant's defense of constructive eviction and entered judgment for defendant. The Appellate Division reversed, holding (1) the proof did not support a finding of any wrongful act or omission on the part of the lessor sufficient to constitute a constructive eviction, and (2) if such act or omission could be found, defendant waived it by failing to remove from the premises within a reasonable time thereafter. We granted defendant's petition for certification. 51 N.J. 574, 242 A.2d 378 (1968).

On May 13, 1958 defendant Joy M. Cooper leased from plaintiff's predecessor in title a portion of the ground or basement floor of a commercial (office) building at 207 Union Street, Hackensack, N.J. The term was five years, but after about a year of occupancy the parties made a new five-year lease dated April 1959 covering the entire floor except the furnace room. The leased premises were to be used as "commercial offices" and "not for any other purpose without the prior written consent of the Landlord." More particularly, the lessee utilized the offices for meetings and training of sales personnel in connection with the business of a jewelry firm of which Mrs. Cooper was branch manager at the time. No merchandise was sold there.

A driveway ran along the north side of the building from front to rear. Its inside edge was at the exterior foundation wall of the ground floor. The driveway was not part of Mrs. Cooper's leasehold. Apparently it was provided for use of all tenants. Whenever it rained during the first year of defendant's occupancy, water ran off the driveway and into the offices and meeting rooms either through or under the exterior or foundation wall. At this time Arthur A. Donigian, a member of the bar of this State, had his office in the building. In addition, he was an officer and resident manager of the then corporate-owner. Whenever water came into the leased floor, defendant would notify him and he would take steps immediately to remove it. Obviously Donigian was fully aware of the recurrent flooding. He had some personal files in the furnace room which he undertook to protect by putting them on 2 × 4's in order to raise them above the floor surface. When negotiating with defendant for the substitute five-year lease for the larger space, Donigian promised to remedy the water problem by resurfacing the driveway. (It is important to note here that Donigian told Water T. Wittman, an attorney, who had offices in the building and who later became executor of Donigian's estate, that the driveway needed "regrading and some kind of sealing of the area between the driveway which lay to the north of the premises and the wall." He also told Wittman that the grading was improper and was "letting the water into the basement rather than away from it.") The work was done as promised and although the record is not entirely clear,

Donigian actually owned bldg.

apparently the seepage was somewhat improved for a time. Subsequently it worsened, but Donigian responded immediately to each complaint and removed the water from the floor.

Donigian died on March 30, 1961, approximately two years after commencement of the second lease. Whenever it rained thereafter and water flooded into the leased floor, no one paid any attention to defendant's complaints, so she and her employees did their best to remove it. During this time sales personnel and trainees came to defendant's premises at frequent intervals for meetings and classes. Sometimes as many as 50 persons were in attendance in the morning and an equal number in the afternoon. The flooding greatly inconvenienced the conduct of these meetings. At times after heavy rainstorms there was as much as two inches of water in various places and "every cabinet, desk and chair had to be raised above the floor." On one occasion jewelry kits that had been sitting on the floor, as well as the contents of file cabinets, became "soaked." Mrs. Cooper testified that once when she was conducting a sales training class and it began to rain, water came into the room making it necessary to move all the chairs and "gear" into another room on the south side of the building. On some occasions the meetings had to be taken to other quarters for which rent had to be paid; on others the meetings were adjourned to a later date. Complaints to the lessor were ignored. What was described as the "crowning blow" occurred on December 20, 1961. A meeting of sales representatives from four states had been arranged. A rainstorm intervened and the resulting flooding placed five inches of water in the rooms. According to Mrs. Cooper it was impossible to hold the meeting in any place on the ground floor; they took it to a nearby inn. That evening she saw an attorney who advised her to send a notice of vacation. On December 21 she asked that the place be cleaned up. This was not done, and after notifying the lessor of her intention she left the premises on December 30, 1961.

Plaintiff acquired the building and an assignment of defendant's lease January 19, 1962. On November 9, 1964 it instituted this action to recover rent for the unexpired term of defendant's lease, i.e., until March 31, 1964.

At trial of the case defendant's proofs showed the facts outlined above. Plaintiff offered very little in the way of contradiction. It seemed to acknowledge that a water problem existed but as defense counsel told the court in his opening statement, he was "prepared to show that the water receded any number of times, and therefore the damage, if it was caused by an act that can be traced to the landlord, [the condition] was not a permanent interference" with the use and enjoyment of the premises. Plaintiff contended further that the water condition would not justify defendant's abandonment of the premises because in the lease she had stipulated that prior to execution thereof she had "examined the demised premises, and accept[ed] them in their [then] condition . . . , and without any representations on the part of the landlord or its agents as to the present or future condition of the said premises"; moreover she had agreed "to keep the demised premises in good condition" and to "redecorate, paint and renovate the said premises as may be necessary to keep them in good repair and good appearance."

The trial judge found that the "testimony is just undisputed and overwhelming that after every rainstorm water flowed into the leased premises of the defendant" and nothing was done to remedy the condition despite repeated complaints to the lessor. He declared also that the condition was intolerable and so substantially deprived the lessee of the use of the premises as to constitute a constructive eviction and therefore legal justification for vacating them. . . .

Since the language of the two leases is the same, except that the second one describes the larger portion of the basement taken by the tenant, evaluation of the landlord's contentions will be facilitated by first considering the original lease and the factual setting attending its execution. Although the second or substitutionary lease is the controlling instrument, we take this approach in order to focus more clearly upon the effect of the change in the factual setting when the second lease was executed. This course brings us immediately to the landlord's reliance upon the provisions of the first lease (which also appear in the second) that the tenant inspected the "demised premises," accepted them in their "present condition" and agreed to keep them in good condition. The word "premises," construed most favorably to the tenant, means so much of the ground floor as was leased to Mrs. Cooper for commercial offices. The driveway or its surfacing or the exterior wall or foundation under it cannot be considered included as part of the "premises." In any event there is nothing to show that the inspection by Mrs. Cooper of the driveway or the ground floor exterior wall and foundation under it prior to the execution of the first lease would have given or did give her notice that they were so defective as to permit rainwater to flood into the leased portion of the interior. The condition should have been and probably was known to the lessor. If known, there was a duty to disclose it to the prospective tenant. Certainly as to Mrs. Cooper, it was a latent defect, and it would be a wholly inequitable application of caveat emptor to charge her with knowledge of it. The attempted reliance upon the agreement of the tenant in both leases to keep the "demised premises" in repair furnishes no support for the landlord's position. The driveway, exterior ground floor wall and foundation are not part of the demised premises. Latent defects in this context, i.e., those the existence and significance of which are not reasonably apparent to the ordinary prospective tenant, certainly were not assumed by Mrs. Cooper. . . .

But the landlord says that whatever the factual and legal situation may have been when the original lease was made, the relationship underwent a change to its advantage when the second was executed.

This contention is based upon the undisputed fact that in April 1959, after a year of occupancy, defendant, with knowledge that the premises were subject to recurrent flooding, accepted a new lease containing the same provisions as the first one. . . . [T]he landlord's position here is not sustainable because it is asserted in disregard of certain vital facts — the agent's promise to remedy the condition and the existence of an express covenant of quiet enjoyment in the lease.

The evidence is clear that prior to execution of the substitutionary lease, the tenant complained to the owner's agent about the incursion of water whenever it rained. The agent conceded the problem existed and promised to remedy the condition. Relying upon the promise Mrs. Cooper accepted the new lease, and the landlord resurfaced the drive-way. Unfortunately, either the work was not sufficiently extensive or it was not done properly because at some unstated time thereafter the water continued to come into the tenant's offices. The complaints about it resumed, and as noted above, until the building manager died he made prompt efforts to remove the water. In our opinion the tenant was entitled to rely upon the promise of its agent to provide a remedy. Thus it cannot be said as a matter of law that by taking the second lease she accepted the premises in their defective condition. . . .

This brings us to the crucial question whether the landlord was guilty of a breach of a covenant which justified the tenant's removal from the premises on December 30, 1961. We are satisfied there was such a breach.

The great weight of authority throughout the country is to the effect that ordinarily a covenant of quiet enjoyment is implied in a lease. . . .

The early New Jersey cases laid down the strict rule that such a covenant would not be implied simply from the relationship of landlord and tenant. An express agreement to that effect or the use of words from which it could be implied was required. May v. Levy, 88 N.J.L. 351, 353, 95 A. 999 (E.&A. 1915). We need not deal here with problems of current serviceability of that rule because as has been indicated above, the lease in question contains an express covenant of quiet enjoyment for the term fixed. Where there is such a covenant, whether express or implied, and it is breached substantially by the landlord, the courts have applied the doctrine of constructive eviction as a remedy for the tenant. Under this rule any act or omission of the landlord or of anyone who acts under authority or legal right from the landlord, or of someone having superior title to that of the landlord, which renders the premises substantially unsuitable for the purpose for which they are leased, or which seriously interferes with the beneficial enjoyment of the premises, is a breach of the covenant of quiet enjoyment and constitutes a constructive eviction of the tenant. . . .

Examples of constructive eviction having close analogy to the present case are easily found. Failure to supply heat as covenanted in the lease so that the apartment was "unlivable" on cold days amounted to constructive eviction. Higgins v. Whiting, [102 N.J.L. 279, 131 A. 879 (Sup. Ct. 1926)]; Anderson v. Walker Realty Co., 1 N.J. Misc. 287 (Sup. Ct. 1923). So too, when the main waste pipe of an apartment building was permitted to become and remain clogged with sewage for a long period of time causing offensive odors and danger to health, the covenant of quiet enjoyment was breached and justified the tenant's abandonment of his premises. . . . If a landlord lets an apartment in his building to a tenant as a dwelling and knowingly permits another part to be used for lewd purposes which use renders the tenant's premises "unfit for occupancy by a respectable family," his failure to terminate the use when he has the legal power to do so constitutes a constructive eviction. . . . The same rule was applied in White v. Hannon, 11 N.J.L.J. 338 (Dist. Ct. 1888), where it appeared that the plumbing in the rooms to the rear of the demised premises became so old and worn out as to emit strong and unhealthy odors which came through into the tenant's quarters. The tenant's removal was held justified. . . .

As noted above, the trial court found sufficient interference with the use and enjoyment of the leased premises to justify the tenant's departure and to relieve her from the obligation to pay further rent. In our view the evidence was sufficient to warrant that conclusion, and the Appellate Division erred in reversing it. Plaintiff argued and the Appellate Division agreed that a constructive eviction cannot arise unless the condition interferes with the use in a permanent sense. It is true that the word "permanent" appears in many of the early cases. See e.g., Stewart v. Childs Co., 86 N.J.L. 648, 650, 92 A. 392, L.R.A. 1915C, 649 (E.&A. 1914). But it is equally obvious that permanent does not signify that water in a basement in a case like this one must be an everlasting and unending condition. If its recurrence follows regularly upon rainstorms and is sufficiently serious in extent to amount to a substantial interference with use and enjoyment of the premises for the purpose of the lease, the test for constructive eviction has been met. Additionally in our case, the defective condition of the driveway, exterior and foundation walls which permitted the recurrent flooding was obviously permanent in the sense that it would continue and probably worsen if not remedied. There was no obligation on the tenant to remedy it.

Plaintiff claims further that Stewart v. Childs Co., supra, strongly supports its right to recovery. Under the lease in that case the landlord covenanted that at all times he would keep the cellar waterproof. The cellar was known to be necessary to the conduct of the tenant's business. After the business opened, water flooded into the cellar, at times to a depth of two and three feet. There was no doubt the flooding resulted from failure of the landlord to make the place waterproof. But when the tenant moved out, a suit for rent for the unexpired term was instituted and the landlord was allowed to recover. It was held that the agreement to pay rent and the agreement to waterproof the cellar were independent covenants and breach of the covenant to waterproof was not a defense to the action for rent. We regard this holding as basically contrary to that in Higgins v. Whiting, supra, where the agreement by the landlord to heat the leased premises and the tenant's agreement to pay rent during the term were declared to be mutually dependent covenants. Thus failure to heat constituted a failure of consideration and justified vacation by the tenant without liability for further rent. We reject the rule of Stewart v. Childs Co. and espouse Higgins v. Whiting as propounding the sounder doctrine. . . .

Similarly whether the landlord's default in the present case is treated as a substantial breach of the express covenant of quiet enjoyment resulting in a constructive eviction of a tenant or as a material failure of consideration, (i.e., such failure as amounts to a substantial interference with the beneficial enjoyment of the premises) the tenant's vacation was legal. Thus it is apparent from our discussion that a tenant's right to vacate leased premises is the same from a doctrinal standpoint whether treated as stemming from breach of a covenant of quiet enjoyment or from breach of any other dependent covenant. Both breaches constitute failure of consideration. The inference to be drawn from the cases is that the remedy of constructive eviction probably evolved from a desire by the courts to relieve the tenant from the harsh burden imposed by common law rules which applied principles of caveat emptor to the letting, rejected an implied warranty of habitability, and ordinarily treated undertakings of the landlord in a lease as independent covenants. To alleviate the tenant's burden, the courts broadened the scope of the long-recognized implied covenant of quiet enjoyment (apparently designed originally to protect the tenant against ouster by a title superior to that of his lessor) to include the right of the tenant to have the beneficial enjoyment and use of the premises for the agreed term. It was but a short step then to the rule that when the landlord or someone acting for him or by virtue of a right acquired through him causes a substantial interference with that enjoyment and use, the tenant may claim a constructive eviction. In our view, therefore, at the present time whenever a tenant's right to vacate leased premises comes into existence because he is deprived of their beneficial enjoyment and use on account of acts chargeable to the landlord, it is immaterial whether the right is expressed in terms of breach of a covenant of quiet enjoyment, or material failure of consideration, or material breach of an implied warranty against latent defects.

Plaintiff's final claim is that assuming the tenant was exposed to a constructive eviction, she waived it by remaining on the premises for an unreasonable period of time thereafter. The general rule is, of course, that a tenant's right to claim a constructive eviction will be lost if he does not vacate the premises within a reasonable time after the right comes into existence. . . .

What constitutes a reasonable time depends upon the circumstances of each case. In considering the problem courts must be sympathetic toward the tenant's plight. Vacation of the premises is a drastic course and must be taken at his peril. If he vacates, and it is held at a later time in a suit for rent for the unexpired term that the landlord's course of action did not reach the dimensions of constructive eviction, a substantial liability may be imposed upon him. That risk and the practical inconvenience and difficulties attendant upon finding and moving to suitable quarters counsel caution.

Here, plaintiff's cooperative building manager died about nine months before the removal. During that period the tenant complained, patiently waited, hoped for relief from the landlord, and tried to take care of the water problem that accompanied the recurring rainstorms. But when relief did not come and the "crowning blow" put five inches of water in the leased offices and meeting rooms on December 20, 1961, the tolerance ended and the vacation came ten days later after notice to the landlord. The trial court found as a fact that under the circumstances such vacation was within a reasonable time, and the delay was not sufficient to establish a waiver of the constructive eviction. We find adequate evidence to support the conclusion and are of the view that the Appellate Division should not have reversed it. . . .

For the reasons expressed above, we hold the view that the trial court was correct in deciding that defendant had been constructively evicted from the premises in question, and therefore was not liable for the rent claimed. Accordingly, the judgment of the Appellate Division is reversed and that of the trial court is reinstated.

NOTES AND QUESTIONS

1. *The theory of constructive eviction.* The common law at one time viewed the promises expressed in leases — a promise, say, on the part of the landlord to keep the premises in repair — as independent, such that a breach by the landlord gave the tenant a cause of action for damages, but not the right to suspend rent payments or terminate the tenancy. See, e.g., 1 American Law of Property §3.11 (1952). There was, however, an important exception to the foregoing, one that led directly to the theory of constructive eviction: The obligation to pay rent was dependent upon the tenant's having possession undisturbed by the landlord (or someone claiming through the landlord). If one could characterize a shortcoming in the leased premises as an unlawful disturbance by the landlord — as a breach of the covenant of quiet enjoyment implied in all leases — and if the disturbance was so substantial as to *amount*

to eviction, and if the tenant thereafter abandoned the premises, then it is *as though* the tenant were evicted (the eviction was "constructive" — recall footnote 14 on pages 34-35). And once evicted, of course, the tenant was relieved of the obligation to pay rent. Q.E.D. In other words, the doctrine of constructive eviction "serves as a substitute for dependency of covenants." 1 American Law of Property, supra, at 204. See also the *Reste* case at page 520.

2. *Scope of the covenant of quiet enjoyment.* The covenant of quiet enjoyment was initially limited to cases in which the tenant was actually ousted physically, but with time (as *Reste* observes) it was expanded to include beneficial enjoyment. This was obviously sensible — otherwise landlords could simply make tenants miserable, without actually ousting them — but it was also obviously limited, at least in theory. The early common law, remember, imposed on landlords no duty to provide suitable premises. See page 514. As a matter of principle, then, the implied covenant of quiet enjoyment would be breached only when the landlord's conduct had "the effect of depriving the lessee of the beneficial use of the demised premises, whether by positive acts of interference or by withholding something essential to full enjoyment *and included within the terms of the lease.*" 1 American Law of Property, supra, §3.51 at 280 (emphasis added). But given the absence of a common law duty on the landlord's part, what if anything would be "included within the terms of the lease"?

One clear answer is that an explicit clause in the lease might put a duty on the landlord — say to provide heat or make repairs — and similar duties might be imposed by statute. Without the doctrines of quiet enjoyment and constructive eviction, breach of such obligations would ordinarily entitle the tenant only to sue for damages. With the doctrines, the tenant may also abandon if the breach is substantial. A less clear answer turns on the exceptions that the common law made to the general no-landlord-duty rule. One early exception, for example, concerned short-term leases of furnished dwellings; here there was an implied duty to make and keep the premises habitable. Additional exceptions developed such that landlords had the duty to disclose latent defects in the premises of which the landlord knew or should have known and as to which the tenant could not be held to have notice; to maintain common areas used by all the tenants in a building; to undertake carefully any repairs the landlord promised or volunteered to make; to abstain from fraudulent misrepresentations as to the condition of the leased premises; and, in some jurisdictions, to abate immoral conduct and other nuisances that occurred on property owned by the landlord if they affected the leased premises.

What, do you suppose, are the reasons behind each of these exceptions? On which of the exceptions could the court in *Reste* have relied? Did it rely on any, or did it rather give the covenant of quiet enjoyment a life of its own?

3. *Partial eviction — actual and constructive.* If there is an *actual eviction,* even though from a *part* of the premises only, the tenant is relieved of *all* liability for rent notwithstanding continued occupation of the balance. The landlord, it is said, may not apportion his wrong. (Restatement (Second) of Property, Landlord and Tenant, §6.1 (1977) rejects this rule and provides that the tenant may receive an abatement in the rent but may not withhold all rent.) Is a tenant relieved of the obligation to pay rent when there is not an actual but rather a *constructive* partial eviction — say where some breach by the landlord makes only a part, but not all, of the premises uninhabitable — even though the tenant remains in undisturbed possession of the balance? In most jurisdictions the answer is no. See, e.g., Brine v. Bergstrom, 4 Wash. App. 288, 480 P.2d 783 (1971). The lower courts in New York have gone back and forth on the question. See Minjak Co. v. Randolph, 140 A.D.2d 245, 528 N.Y.S.2d 554 (1988) (accepting theory); Zweighaft v. Remington, 66 Misc. 2d 261, 320 N.Y.S.2d 151 (Civ. Ct. 1971) (rejecting theory); East Haven Assocs., Inc. v. Gurian, 64 Misc. 2d 276, 313 N.Y.S.2d 927 (Civ. Ct. 1970) (accepting the theory of constructive partial eviction).

4. *Tenant's remedies.* Judicial decisions sometimes say that an eviction, actual or constructive, is necessary to constitute a *breach* of the covenant of quiet enjoyment, but they are incorrect. For discussion, see Moe v. Sprankle, 32 Tenn. App. 33, 221 S.W.2d 712 (1948). The view that eviction is necessary reflects conceptual confusion between a breach of the implied covenant on the one hand, and the remedies available for breach on the other — a confusion that probably relates back to the early common law notion that a breach occurred only in cases of actual ouster. Once the covenant of quiet enjoyment was broadened beyond that notion, it should have been understood that actionable interference by the landlord could be remedied other than by the tenant's abandoning the premises. So the tenant should be, and usually is, able to stay in possession and sue for damages equal to the difference between the value of the property with and without the breach. If the breach is substantial,[52] the tenant, as we saw, may leave on a theory of constructive eviction, in which event he is relieved of any liability for future rent and entitled (presumably) to recover damages — to compensate both for losses realized while in possession and for losses resulting from a higher rent for equivalent replacement premises.

PROBLEMS

1. *T* is a tenant at will of *L*. *L* causes a nuisance that interferes with *T*'s business on the leased premises. *T* vacates, rents equivalent space at a higher rent, and subsequently sues for damages on a theory of con-

---

52. What if it is not? See Stevan v. Brown, 54 Md. App. 235, 458 A.2d 466 (1983).

structive eviction arising from a breach of the covenant of quiet enjoyment. What result? Cf. Kent v. Humphries, 303 N.C. 675, 281 S.E.2d 43 (1981).

2. In each of the following cases, *T*, who has a term of years, vacates the leased premises prior to the end of the term and stops paying rent. In a subsequent suit by *L* for unpaid rent, *T* asserts a defense of constructive eviction, claiming that *L* breached the covenant of quiet enjoyment. What result on the facts described below?

(a) *L* fails to control excessive noise made by neighboring tenants of *T* who commonly party long and loud into the night. See Eskanos & Supperstein v. Irwin, 637 P.2d 403 (Colo. App. 1981); Bocchini v. Gorn Management Co., 69 Md. App. 1, 515 A.2d 1179 (1986); Gottdiener v. Mailhot, 179 N.J. Super. 286, 431 A.2d 851 (1981).

(b) The building in which *T* leases an apartment from *L* has been the site of criminal activity — acts of burglary and vandalism by unknown third parties. *L* installs deadbolt locks on all entrance doors and hires private security guards, but the problems continue. See Sciascia v. Riverpark Apts., 3 Ohio App. 3d 164, 444 N.E.2d 40 (1981); Annot., 43 A.L.R.3d 331 (1972).

(c) The office space leased by *T*, a gynecologist whose practice includes performing elective abortions, has been the target of ongoing demonstrations by anti-abortion protesters. During the protests, singing and chanting demonstrators picket in the parking lot and inner lobby. They approach patients to speak to them, distribute literature, discourage patients from entering, and accuse *T* of "killing babies." Despite many months of complaints by *T*, *L* has done essentially nothing. See Fidelity Mutual Life Ins. Co. v. Kaminsky, 768 S.W.2d 818 (Tex. Ct. App. 1989).

3. Suppose that *T* believes that *L* has breached the covenant of quiet enjoyment and wishes to abandon the leased premises, claiming constructive eviction. Rather than vacate, however, *T* brings suit for equitable relief in the form of a declaratory judgment that *L* has breached the covenant, that the breach is substantial, and that if *T* leaves within 30 days of the requested judgment he will have vacated within a reasonable time. Why does *T* seek this relief? May (should) the court grant it? See Charles E. Burt, Inc. v. Seven Grand Corp., 340 Mass. 124, 163 N.E.2d 4 (1959).

NOTE: THE ILLEGAL LEASE

In Brown v. Southall Realty Co., 237 A.2d 834 (D.C. App. 1968), the landlord sued to evict for nonpayment of rent. In defense, the tenant argued that no rent was due under the lease because the unsafe and unsanitary conditions of the leased premises violated the housing code. The court agreed, holding that the lease was an illegal contract made in violation of statutory prohibitions and therefore unenforceable. In a quick series of subsequent decisions, the court sketched out the contours of the illegal lease doctrine. It does not apply if code violations develop *after* the making of the lease. Saunders v. First Natl. Realty Corp., 245 A.2d 836 (D.C. App. 1968). Minor technical violations do not render a lease illegal, nor do violations of which the landlord had neither actual nor constructive notice. Diamond Hous. Corp. v. Robinson, 257 A.2d 492 (D.C. App. 1969). A tenant under an illegal lease is a tenant at sufferance, and the landlord is entitled to the reasonable rental value of the premises, given their condition. William J. Davis, Inc. v. Slade, 271 A.2d 412 (D.C. App. 1970).

From the tenant's point of view, the chief attraction of the illegal lease defense is the leverage it provides: The tenant can withhold rent and still stave off the landlord's inevitable action to evict for nonpayment. (The situation is otherwise with respect to quiet enjoyment and constructive eviction. Recall the discussion in Note 3 on page 523.) In this respect, the *Brown* case anticipated a development soon to follow, and to which we now turn.

b. The Implied Warranty of Habitability

Hilder v. St. Peter

Supreme Court of Vermont, 1984
144 Vt. 150, 478 A.2d 202

BILLINGS, C.J. Defendants appeal from a judgment rendered by the Rutland Superior Court. The court ordered defendants to pay plaintiff damages in the amount of $4,945.00, which represented "reimbursement of all rent paid and additional compensatory damages" for the rental of a residential apartment over a fourteen month period in defendants' Rutland apartment building. Defendants filed a motion for reconsideration on the issue of the amount of damages awarded to the plaintiff, and plaintiff filed a cross-motion for reconsideration of the court's denial of an award of punitive damages. The court denied both motions. On appeal, defendants raise three issues for our consideration: first, whether the court correctly calculated the amount of damages awarded the plaintiff; secondly, whether the court's award to plaintiff of the entire amount of rent paid to defendants was proper since the plaintiff remained in possession of the apartment for the entire fourteen month period; and finally, whether the court's finding that defendant Stuart St. Peter acted on his own behalf and with the apparent authority of defendant Patricia St. Peter was error.

The facts are uncontested. In October, 1974, plaintiff began occupying an apartment at defendants' 10-12 Church Street apartment building in Rutland with her three children and new-born grandson.[53] Plaintiff orally agreed to pay defendant Stuart St. Peter $140 a month and a damage deposit of $50; plaintiff paid defendant the first month's rent and the damage deposit prior to moving in. Plaintiff has paid all rent due under her tenancy. Because the previous tenants had left behind garbage and items of personal belongings, defendant offered to refund plaintiff's damage deposit if she would clean the apartment herself prior to taking possession. Plaintiff did clean the apartment, but never received her deposit back because the defendant denied ever receiving it. Upon moving into the apartment, plaintiff discovered a broken kitchen window. Defendant promised to repair it, but after waiting a week and fearing that her two year old child might cut herself on the shards of glass, plaintiff repaired the window at her own expense. Although defendant promised to provide a front door key, he never did. For a period of time, whenever plaintiff left the apartment, a member of her family would remain behind for security reasons. Eventually, plaintiff purchased and installed a padlock, again at her own expense. After moving in, plaintiff discovered that the bathroom toilet was clogged with paper and feces and would flush only by dumping pails of water into it. Although plaintiff repeatedly complained about the toilet, and defendant promised to have it repaired, the toilet remained clogged and mechanically inoperable throughout the period of plaintiff's tenancy. In addition, the bathroom light and wall outlet were inoperable. Again, the defendant agreed to repair the fixtures, but never did. In order to have light in the bathroom, plaintiff attached a fixture to the wall and connected it to an extension cord that was plugged into an adjoining room. Plaintiff also discovered that water leaked from the water pipes of the upstairs apartment down the ceilings and walls of both her kitchen and back bedroom. Again, defendant promised to fix the leakage, but never did. As a result of this leakage, a large section of plaster fell from the back bedroom ceiling onto her bed and her grandson's crib. Other sections of plaster remained dangling from the ceiling. This condition was brought to the attention of the defendant, but he never corrected it. Fearing that the remaining plaster might fall when the room was occupied, plaintiff moved her and her grandson's bedroom furniture into the living room and ceased using the back bedroom. During the summer months an odor of raw sewage permeated plaintiff's apartment. The odor was so strong that the plaintiff was ashamed to have company in her apartment. Responding to plaintiff's complaints, Rutland City workers unearthed a broken sewage pipe in the basement of defendants' building. Raw sewage littered the floor of the basement,

---

53. Between October, 1974, and December, 1976, plaintiff rented apartment number 1 for $140.00 monthly for 18 months, and apartment number 50 for $125.00 monthly for 7 months.

but defendant failed to clean it up. Plaintiff also discovered that the electric service for her furnace was attached to her breaker box, although defendant had agreed, at the commencement of plaintiff's tenancy, to furnish heat.

In its conclusions of law, the court held that the state of disrepair of plaintiff's apartment, which was known to the defendants, substantially reduced the value of the leasehold from the agreed rental value, thus constituting a breach of the implied warranty of habitability. The court based its award of damages on the breach of this warranty and on breach of an express contract. Defendant argues that the court misapplied the law of Vermont relating to habitability because the plaintiff never abandoned the demised premises and, therefore, it was error to award her the full amount of rent paid. Plaintiff counters that, while never expressly recognized by this Court, the trial court was correct in applying an implied warranty of habitability and that under this warranty, abandonment of the premises is not required. Plaintiff urges this Court to affirmatively adopt the implied warranty of habitability.

Historically, relations between landlords and tenants have been defined by the law of property. Under these traditional common law property concepts, a lease was viewed as a conveyance of real property. See Note, Judicial Expansion of Tenants' Private Law Rights: Implied Warranties of Habitability and Safety in Residential Urban Leases, 56 Cornell L.Q. 489, 489-90 (1971) (hereinafter cited as Expansion of Tenants' Rights). The relationship between landlord and tenant was controlled by the doctrine of caveat lessee; that is, the tenant took possession of the demised premises irrespective of their state of disrepair. Love, Landlord's Liability for Defective Premises: Caveat Lessee, Negligence, or Strict Liability?, 1975 Wis. L. Rev. 19, 27-28. The landlord's only covenant was to deliver possession to the tenant. The tenant's obligation to pay rent existed independently of the landlord's duty to deliver possession, so that as long as possession remained in the tenant, the tenant remained liable for payment of rent. The landlord was under no duty to render the premises habitable unless there was an express covenant to repair in the written lease. Expansion of Tenants' Rights, supra, at 490. The land, not the dwelling, was regarded as the essence of the conveyance.

An exception to the rule of caveat lessee was the doctrine of constructive eviction. Lemle v. Breeden, 51 Haw. 426, 430, 462 P.2d 470, 473 (1969). Here, if the landlord wrongfully interfered with the tenant's enjoyment of the demised premises, or failed to render a duty to the tenant as expressly required under the terms of the lease, the tenant could abandon the premises and cease paying rent. Legier v. Deveneau, 98 Vt. 188, 190, 126 A. 392, 393 (1924).

Beginning in the 1960's, American courts began recognizing that this approach to landlord and tenant relations, which had originated during the Middle Ages, had become an anachronism in twentieth century, urban society. Today's tenant enters into lease agreements, not to obtain arable land, but to obtain safe, sanitary and comfortable housing.

> [T]hey seek a well known package of goods and services — a package which includes not merely walls and ceilings, but also adequate heat, light and ventilation, serviceable plumbing facilities, secure windows and doors, proper sanitation, and proper maintenance. [Javins v. First National Realty Corp., 428 F.2d 1071, 1074 (D.C. Cir.), cert. denied, 400 U.S. 925, 91 S. Ct. 186, 27 L. Ed. 2d 185 (1970).]

Not only has the subject matter of today's lease changed, but the characteristics of today's tenant have similarly evolved. The tenant of the Middle Ages was a farmer, capable of making whatever repairs were necessary to his primitive dwelling. Green v. Superior Court, 10 Cal. 3d 616, 622, 517 P.2d 1168, 1172, 111 Cal. Rptr. 704, 708 (1974). Additionally, "the common law courts assumed that an equal bargaining position existed between landlord and tenant. . . ." Note, The Implied Warranty of Habitability: A Dream Deferred, 48 UMKC L. Rev. 237, 238 (1980) (hereinafter cited as A Dream Deferred).

In sharp contrast, today's residential tenant, most commonly a city dweller, is not experienced in performing maintenance work on urban, complex living units. The landlord is more familiar with the dwelling unit and mechanical equipment attached to that unit, and is more financially able to "discover and cure" any faults and break-downs. Confronted with a recognized shortage of safe, decent housing, today's tenant is in an inferior bargaining position compared to that of the landlord. Park West Management Corp. v. Mitchell, 47 N.Y.2d 316, 324-25, 391 N.E.2d 1288, 1292, 418 N.Y.S.2d 310, 314, cert. denied, 444 U.S. 992, 100 S. Ct. 523, 62 L. Ed. 2d 421 (1979). Tenants vying for this limited housing are "virtually powerless to compel the performance of essential services." Id. at 325, 391 N.E.2d at 1292, 418 N.Y.S.2d at 314.

In light of these changes in the relationship between tenants and landlords, it would be wrong for the law to continue to impose the doctrine of caveat lessee on residential leases.

> The modern view favors a new approach which recognizes that a lease is essentially a contract between the landlord and the tenant wherein the landlord promises to deliver and maintain the demised premises in habitable condition and the tenant promises to pay rent for such habitable premises. These promises constitute interdependent and mutual considerations. Thus, the tenant's obligation to pay rent is predicated on the landlord's obligation to deliver and maintain the premises in habitable condition. [Boston Housing Authority v. Hemingway, 363 Mass. 184, 198, 293 N.E.2d 831, 842 (1973).] . . .

Therefore, we now hold expressly that in the rental of any residential dwelling unit an implied warranty exists in the lease, whether oral or written, that the landlord will deliver over and maintain, throughout the period of the tenancy, premises that are safe, clean and fit for human habitation. This warranty of habitability is implied in tenancies for a specific period or at will. Additionally, the implied warranty of habitability covers all latent and patent defects in the essential facilities of the residential unit.[54] Essential facilities are "facilities vital to the use of the premises for residential purposes. . . ." Kline v. Burns, 111 N.H. 87, 92, 276 A.2d 248, 252 (1971). This means that a tenant who enters into a lease agreement with knowledge of any defect in the essential facilities cannot be said to have assumed the risk, thereby losing the protection of the warranty. Nor can this implied warranty of habitability be waived by any written provision in the lease or by oral agreement.

In determining whether there has been a breach of the implied warranty of habitability, the courts may first look to any relevant local or municipal housing code; they may also make reference to the minimum housing code standards enunciated in 24 V.S.A. §5003(c)(1)-5003(c)(5). A substantial violation of an applicable housing code shall constitute prima facie evidence that there has been a breach of the warranty of habitability. "[O]ne or two minor violations standing alone which do not affect" the health or safety of the tenant, shall be considered de minimis and not a breach of the warranty. In addition, the landlord will not be liable for defects caused by the tenant.

However, these codes and standards merely provide a starting point in determining whether there has been a breach. Not all towns and municipalities have housing codes; where there are codes, the particular problem complained of may not be addressed. In determining whether there has been a breach of the implied warranty of habitability, courts should inquire whether the claimed defect has an impact on the safety or health of the tenant.

In order to bring a cause of action for breach of the implied warranty of habitability, the tenant must first show that he or she notified the landlord "of the deficiency or defect not known to the landlord and [allowed] a reasonable time for its correction." King v. Moorehead, 495 S.W.2d [65, 76 (Mo. App. 1973).]

Because we hold that the lease of a residential dwelling creates a contractual relationship between the landlord and tenant, the standard contract remedies of rescission, reformation and damages are available to the tenant when suing for breach of the implied warranty of habitability. The measure of damages shall be the difference between the value

---

54. The warranty also covers those facilities located in the common areas of an apartment building or duplex that may affect the health or safety of a tenant, such as common stairways, or porches. . . .

of the dwelling as warranted and the value of the dwelling as it exists in its defective condition. In determining the fair rental value of the dwelling as warranted, the court may look to the agreed upon rent as evidence on this issue. "[I]n residential lease disputes involving a breach of the implied warranty of habitability, public policy militates against requiring expert testimony" concerning the value of the defect. [Birkenhead v. Coombs, 143 Vt. 167, 173, 465 A.2d 244, 247 (1983).] The tenant will be liable only for "the reasonable rental value [if any] of the property in its imperfect condition during his period of occupancy." Berzito v. Gambino, 63 N.J. 460, 469, 308 A.2d 17, 22 (1973).

We also find persuasive the reasoning of some commentators that damages should be allowed for a tenant's discomfort and annoyance arising from the landlord's breach of the implied warranty of habitability. See Moskovitz, The Implied Warranty of Habitability: A New Doctrine Raising New Issues, 62 Cal. L. Rev. 1444, 1470-73 (1974) (hereinafter cited as A New Doctrine); A Dream Deferred, supra, at 250-51. Damages for annoyance and discomfort are reasonable in light of the fact that

> the residential tenant who has suffered a breach of the warranty . . . cannot bathe as frequently as he would like or at all if there is inadequate hot water; he must worry about rodents harassing his children or spreading disease if the premises are infested; or he must avoid certain rooms or worry about catching a cold if there is inadequate weather protection or heat. Thus, discomfort and annoyance are the common injuries caused by each breach and hence the true nature of the general damages the tenant is claiming. [Moskovitz, A New Doctrine, supra, at 1470-71.]

Damages for discomfort and annoyance may be difficult to compute; however, "[t]he trier [of fact] is not to be deterred from this duty by the fact that the damages are not susceptible of reduction to an exact money standard." Vermont Electric Supply Co. v. Andrus, 132 Vt. 195, 200, 315 A.2d 456, 459 (1974).

Another remedy available to the tenant when there has been a breach of the implied warranty of habitability is to withhold the payment of future rent.[55] King v. Moorehead, supra, 495 S.W.2d at 77. The burden and expense of bringing suit will then be on the landlord who can

55. Because we hold that the tenant's obligation to pay rent is contingent on the landlord's duty to provide and maintain a habitable dwelling, it is no longer necessary for the tenant to first abandon the premises, Northern Terminals, Inc. v. Smith Grocery & Variety, Inc., 138 Vt. 389, 396-97, 418 A.2d 22, 26-27 (1980); Legier v. Deveneau, supra, 98 Vt. at 190, 126 A. at 393; thus, the doctrine of constructive eviction is no longer a viable or needed defense in an action by the landlord for unpaid rent. Lemle v. Breeden, supra, 51 Haw. at 435-36, 462 P.2d at 475; Boston Housing Authority v. Hemingway, supra, 363 Mass. at 199-200, 293 N.E.2d at 843; see also Expansion of Tenants' Rights, supra, at 491 (constructive eviction "[w]ith its absolute requirement of abandonment . . . is utterly unsatisfactory for a tenant faced with today's urban housing shortage").

better afford to bring the action. In an action for ejectment for nonpayment of rent, 12 V.S.A. §4773, "[t]he trier of fact, upon evaluating the seriousness of the breach and the ramification of the defect upon the health and safety of the tenant, will abate the rent at the landlord's expense in accordance with its findings." A Dream Deferred, supra, at 248. The tenant must show that: (1) the landlord had notice of the previously unknown defect and failed, within a reasonable time, to repair it; and (2) the defect, affecting habitability, existed during the time for which rent was withheld. See A Dream Deferred, supra, at 248-50. Whether a portion, all or none of the rent will be awarded to the landlord will depend on the findings relative to the extent and duration of the breach.[56] Javins v. First National Realty Corp., supra, 428 F.2d at 1082-83. Of course, once the landlord corrects the defect, the tenant's obligation to pay rent becomes due again. Id. at 1083 n.64.

Additionally, we hold that when the landlord is notified of the defect but fails to repair it within a reasonable amount of time, and the tenant subsequently repairs the defect, the tenant may deduct the expense of the repair from future rent. 11 Williston on Contracts §1404 (3d ed. W. Jaeger 1968); Marini v. Ireland, 56 N.J. 130, 146, 265 A.2d 526, 535 (1970).

In addition to general damages, we hold that punitive damages may be available to a tenant in the appropriate case. Although punitive damages are generally not recoverable in actions for breach of contract, there are cases in which the breach is of such a willful and wanton or fraudulent nature as to make appropriate the award of exemplary damages. A willful and wanton or fraudulent breach may be shown "by conduct manifesting personal ill will, or carried out under circumstances of insult or oppression, or even by conduct manifesting . . . a reckless or wanton disregard of [one's] rights. . . ." Sparrow v. Vermont Savings Bank, 95 Vt. 29, 33, 112 A. 205, 207 (1921). When a landlord, after receiving notice of a defect, fails to repair the facility that is essential to the health and safety of his or her tenant, an award of punitive damages is proper. 111 East 88th Partners v. Simon, 106 Misc. 2d 693, 434 N.Y.S.2d 886, 889 (N.Y. Civ. Ct. 1980).

> The purpose of punitive damages . . . is to punish conduct which is morally culpable. . . . Such an award serves to deter a wrongdoer . . . from repetitions of the same or similar actions. And it tends to encourage prosecution of a claim by a victim who might not otherwise incur the expense or inconve-

56. Some courts suggest that, during the period rent is withheld, the tenant should pay the rent, as it becomes due, into legal custody. See, e.g., Javins v. First National Realty Corp., supra, 428 F.2d at 1083 n.67; see also King v. Moorehead, supra, 495 S.W.2d at 77 (*King* requires the deposit of the rent into legal custody pending the litigation). Such a procedure assures the availability of that portion, if any, of the rent which the court determines is due to the landlord. King v. Moorehead, supra, 495 S.W.2d at 77; see A Dream Deferred, supra, at 248-50.

nience of private action. . . . The public benefit and a display of ethical indig-
nation are among the ends of the policy to grant punitive damages. [Davis v.
Williams, 92 Misc. 2d 1051, 402 N.Y.S.2d 92, 94 (N.Y. Civ. Ct. 1977).]

In the instant case, the trial court's award of damages, based in part
on a breach of the implied warranty of habitability, was not a misappli-
cation of the law relative to habitability. Because of our holding in this
case, the doctrine of constructive eviction, wherein the tenant must
abandon in order to escape liability for rent, is no longer viable. When,
as in the instant case, the tenant seeks, not to escape rent liability, but to
receive compensatory damages in the amount of rent already paid,
abandonment is similarly unnecessary. Under our holding, when a landlord breaches the implied warranty of habitability, the tenant may withhold future rent, and may also seek damages in the amount of rent
previously paid.

In its conclusions of law the trial court stated that the defendants'
failure to make repairs was compensable by damages to the extent of
reimbursement of all rent paid and additional compensatory damages.
The court awarded plaintiff a total of $4,945.00; $3,445.00 represents
the entire amount of rent plaintiff paid, plus the $50.00 deposit. This
appears to leave $1500.00 as the "additional compensatory damages."
However, although the court made findings which clearly demonstrate
the appropriateness of an award of compensatory damages, there is no
indication as to how the court reached a figure of $1500.00. It is "crucial
that this Court and the parties be able to determine what was decided
and how the decision was reached." Fox v. McLain, 142 Vt. 11, 16, 451
A.2d 1122, 1124 (1982).

Additionally, the court denied an award to plaintiff of punitive
damages on the ground that the evidence failed to support a finding of
willful and wanton or fraudulent conduct. The facts in this case, which
defendants do not contest, evince a pattern of intentional conduct on
the part of defendants for which the term "slumlord" surely was coined.
Defendants' conduct was culpable and demeaning to plaintiff and
clearly expressive of a wanton disregard of plaintiff's rights. The trial
court found that defendants were aware of defects in the essential facilities of plaintiff's apartment, promised plaintiff that repairs would be
made, but never fulfilled those promises. The court also found that
plaintiff continued, throughout her tenancy, to pay her rent, often in
the face of verbal threats made by defendant Stuart St. Peter. These
findings point to the "bad spirit and wrong intention" of the defendants,
Glidden v. Skinner, 142 Vt. 644, 648, 458 A.2d 1142, 1144 (1983), and
would support a finding of willful and wanton or fraudulent conduct,
contrary to the conclusions of law and judgment of the trial judge. However, the plaintiff did not appeal the court's denial of punitive damages,
and issues not appealed and briefed are waived.

We find that defendants' third claimed error, that the court erred in finding that both defendant Stuart St. Peter and defendant Patricia St. Peter were liable to plaintiff for the breach of the implied warranty of habitability, is meritless. Both defendants were named in the complaint as owners of the 10-12 Church Street apartment building. Plaintiff's complaint also alleged that defendant Stuart St. Peter acted as agent for defendant Patricia St. Peter. Defendants failed to deny these allegations; under V.R.C.P. 8(d) these averments stand as admitted.

Affirmed in part; reversed in part and remanded for hearing on additional compensable damages, consistent with the views herein.

NOTES AND QUESTIONS

1. *The implied warranty of habitability and other legal doctrines.* The implied warranty of habitability does *not* render pointless the doctrines of quiet enjoyment, constructive eviction, and illegal leases considered earlier, for a variety of reasons. First, a good handful of jurisdictions (probably about 10) have yet to adopt the warranty. Second, most — though not all — jurisdictions have refused to extend the idea to an implied warranty of fitness or suitability for purpose in commercial leases. (The usual rationales are equal bargaining power and tenant capacity to inspect and maintain.) See Annot., 76 A.L.R.4th 928 (1990). Third, the implied warranty of habitability — whether defined by legislation or judicial decisions — does not necessarily apply across the board to all residential leases: single-family residences might be excluded, for example, or agricultural leases, or long-term leases. So too for casual leases by nonmerchant landlords (as when a law professor goes off on sabbatical). See, e.g., Zimmerman v. Moore, 441 N.E.2d 690 (Ind. App. 1982) (no reason to suppose that landlord had knowledge or expertise superior to that of tenant, or that landlord was in a better position than the tenant to absorb or spread the costs of maintenance). Contrast Boudreau v. General Elec. Co., 2 Haw. App. 10, 625 P.2d 384 (1981).[57]

2. *Standard and breach of the warranty.* On the questions of the standard of the warranty and the conditions held to breach it, the jurisdictions fall into four groups:

(a) The standards are those of the housing code, and apparently any failure to comply with the code is a breach.

(b) The standards are those of the housing code, but substantial

_____

57. Most jurisdictions agree with *Hilder* that the implied warranty of habitability cannot be waived, but a few might permit a "knowing" waiver by the tenant if "bargaining power" is essentially "equal." See Restatement (Second) of Property, Landlord and Tenant, §5.6 (1977). Consistent with this, most jurisdictions apply the warranty even to patent defects, though a few appear to exclude them at least so long as they do not violate housing code provisions.

compliance is sufficient so long as habitability is unaffected. Put differently, only a substantial defect constitutes breach. The nature of the defect, its effects on habitability, how long it has existed, the age of the
building, and the amount of rent are identified by some courts as factors
relevant to the issue of breach.

(c) Housing code provisions and their violation are compelling but
not conclusive. An "adequate standard of habitability" is required, and
breach occurs when the premises are "uninhabitable in the eyes of a
reasonable person," with violation of a code provision being a relevant
factor. Berzito v. Gambino, 63 N.J. 460, 469, 470, 308 A.2d 17, 21, 22
(1973). See also Boston Hous. Auth. v. Hemingway, 363 Mass. 184, 293
N.E.2d 831 (1973) (standard is fitness for human habitation; proof of
code violation would usually compel conclusion of uninhabitability). Under this approach, a court could require less than substantial code compliance but would be unlikely to do so; requiring more than the code
might be somewhat more probable.

(d) The standard and its breach are independent of the housing
code. (The standard for example, is "fit for human habitation"; a breach
occurs if the premises are "substantially unfit.")

Compare Restatement (Second) of Property, Landlord and Tenant,
supra footnote 57, §§5.1 (not suitable for residential use on date lease
made), 5.4 (landlord obligated to keep leased premises in condition
meeting health, safety, and housing codes and to keep common areas
safe and in repair).

Where among the foregoing views does the *Hilder* case fall? In a
jurisdiction falling into group (c) above, would continued loud noise in
an apartment building constitute a breach of the implied warranty?
What about failure of a central air conditioning system during the summer months? See Millbridge Apts. v. Linden, 151 N.J. Super. 168, 376
A.2d 611 (Dist. Ct. 1977) (noise could be breach); Park Hill Terrace
Assocs. v. Glennon, 146 N.J. Super. 271, 369 A.2d 938 (App. Div. 1977)
(air conditioning failure could be breach).

3. *Remedies for breach.* The implied warranty of habitability is based
largely on contractual principles, and a number of cases agree with
Hilder that in the case of breach a tenant may avail himself of all the basic
contract remedies — damages, rescission, and reformation. There are
some unique aspects of the tenant's remedies, however. Moreover, the
remedies vary with the circumstances and also from jurisdiction to jurisdiction.

As to circumstances, the posture of the *Hilder* case is one possibility:
A tenant who has paid rent and remained in possession later sues for
reimbursement and damages, claiming breach of the implied warranty
of habitability. Perhaps more typical is the tenant who remains in possession but withholds rent. The landlord sues for possession and back
rent, whereupon the tenant asserts breach of the warranty as a defense.

Virtually all jurisdictions permit the tenant to raise the defense in a summary eviction action. If the tenant is successful, rent is reduced partially or totally (depending on the degree of breach) and the tenant may retain possession if he pays whatever reduced amount is determined.[58] Whether viewed as a rent reduction or a setoff or a counterclaim for damages, the practical result is the same: The tenant may withold rent, retain possession, and have the agreed rent reduced by virtue of the landlord's breach.

While there is general agreement on these points, there is considerable disagreement regarding calculation of the rent reduction or damages. The following are the most common approaches:

(a) The approach illustrated in *Hilder* (see pages 529-530): "[D]amages shall be the difference between the value of the dwelling as warranted and the value of the dwelling as it exists in its defective condition." The agreed rent is evidence of "fair rental value . . . as warranted." Was the apartment in *Hilder* worthless?

(b) A variant of the foregoing (how is it different?): Tenant's damages are "the difference between the agreed rent and the fair rental value of the premises as they were during their occupancy by the tenant in the unsafe, unsanitary or unfit condition." Kline v. Burns, 111 N.H. 87, 93-94, 276 A.2d 248, 252 (1971). See also Berzito v. Gambino, supra, 63 N.J. at 469, 308 A.2d at 22 ("tenant will be charged only with the reasonable rental value of the property in its imperfect condition during his period of occupancy").

(c) The percentage diminution approach: The agreed rent is reduced by a percentage equal to the percentage of use lost by the tenant in consequence of the landlord's breach. See, e.g., Academy Spires, Inc. v. Brown, 111 N.J. Super. 477, 487-488, 268 A.2d 556, 562 (Dist. Ct. 1970).

Consider also the following variants:

(d) The Restatement approach:

> If the tenant is entitled to an abatement of the rent, the rent is abated to the amount of that proportion of the rent which the fair rental value after the event giving the right to abate bears to the fair rental value before the event. Abatement is allowed until the default is eliminated or the lease terminates, whichever first occurs. [Restatement (Second) of Property, Landlord and Tenant, supra, §11.1.]

An example clarifies the formula:

---

58. The courts in several jurisdictions hold that, notwithstanding breach of warranty by the landlord, the tenant cannot defend an eviction action for nonpayment of rent unless the landlord's breach is so substantial as to have totally abated the rent (or unless, in the event a partial abatement is justified, the tenant has managed to calculate the amount to be abated and tendered the balance to the landlord!). See Foisy v. Wyman, 83 Wash. 2d 22, 515 P.2d 160 (1973).

If the fair rental value of the premises in "suitable" condition (that is, in substantial compliance with the housing code) would be $100 a month, and if at the beginning of the tenancy the fair rental value of the premises in their existing, dilapidated condition is $20 a month, and if the contract rent is $30 a month, is the tenant entitled to reduce his rent by the amount of $24 a month to the sum of $6 a month? *Answer:* yes. [Charles J. Meyers, The Covenant of Habitability and the American Law Institute, 27 Stan. L. Rev. 879, 883 (1975).]

(e) The tort approach: Several commentators (endorsed in the *Hilder* case) have suggested a tort theory of damages for breach of the implied warranty — damages for discomfort and annoyance or for infliction of emotional harm, and punitive damages. See Paul Falick, A Tort Remedy for the Slum Tenant, 58 Ill. B.J. 204 (1969); Myron Moskovitz, The Implied Warranty of Habitability: A New Doctrine Raising New Issues, 62 Cal. L. Rev. 1444 (1974); Joseph L. Sax & Fred J. Hiestand, Slumlordism as a Tort, 65 Mich. L. Rev. 869 (1967). Cases recognizing or awarding recovery for emotional distress include Simon v. Solomon, 385 Mass. 91, 431 N.E.2d 556 (1982); Fair v. Negley, 257 Pa. Super. 50, 390 A.2d 240 (1978); Beasley v. Freedman, 256 Pa. Super. 208, 389 A.2d 1087 (1978).

What problems, if any, do you see in these various approaches to damages? For good discussion, see Samuel B. Abbott, Housing Policy, Housing Codes and Tenant Remedies: An Integration, 56 B.U. L. Rev. 1, 20-25 (1976); Roger A. Cunningham, The New Implied and Statutory Warranties of Habitability in Residential Leases: From Contract to Status, 16 Urb. L. Ann. 3, 102–109 (1979).

Other remedies. The foregoing comments address a tenant's right to assert breach of the implied warranty of habitability as a *defense* justifying rent withholding, retention of possession, and rent abatement; or to stay in possession, pay rent, and bring an *affirmative cause of action* for damages — presumably measured on one of the bases (depending on the jurisdiction) described above. The tenant may also terminate the lease and sue for damages. (In this instance, some courts have complicated matters by using different measures of damages for the period the tenant was in possession and the period after termination — as to which the tenant has lost the benefit, if any, of an advantageous lease. See Cunningham, supra, at 105.) In any of these cases, special and consequential damages should also be recoverable.

The equitable remedy of specific performance — in the form of injunctive relief against violations of the warranty — has been mentioned in dicta, but by and large tenants appear to have ignored it. Another equitable remedy, application of rent to repairs, has existed in some states for many years in the form of repair-and-deduct statutes. Several cases have adopted the remedy in the event of breach of the implied warranty of habitability. See, e.g., Marini v. Ireland, 56 N.J. 130, 265 A.2d 526 (1970). See also Restatement (Second) of Property, Landlord and Tenant, supra, §11.2, and the *Hilder* case at page 531.

PROBLEMS (AND A QUESTION)

1. *L* owns a high-rise apartment building. *L*'s entire maintenance and janitorial staff goes on strike for two weeks. The building's incinerators are inoperative as a consequence of the strike; tenants must take their garbage to the curb in paper bags supplied by *L*. City sanitation workers refuse to cross the striking employees' picket lines. Trash piles up to the height of the building's first-floor windows. The garbage exudes noxious odors and results in a declaration of a health emergency by the city. Routine maintenance and extermination service is not performed during the strike, and rats and vermin become a problem. Has *L* breached the implied warranty of habitability? See Park West Management Corp. v. Mitchell, 47 N.Y.2d 316, 391 N.E.2d 1288, 418 N.Y.S.2d 310, cert. denied, 444 U.S. 992 (1979).

2. *L* offers a small run-down house for rent at $100 per month. *T* inspects the premises, finds a number of defects, and tells *L* that she will take the place, "but only at $50 a month because that's all it's worth in its condition." *L* agrees and *T* takes possession; subsequently she fails to pay any rent. In an eviction suit by *L*, may *T* assert breach of the implied warranty of habitability as a defense (and what are *T*'s damages)? See Haddad v. Gonzalez, 410 Mass. 855, 872-873, 576 N.E.2d 658, 668 (1991); Foisy v. Wyman, 83 Wash. 2d 22, 515 P.2d 160 (1973). See generally Edward H. Rabin, The Revolution in Residential Landlord-Tenant Law: Causes and Consequences, 69 Cornell L. Rev. 517, 524-525 (1984).

3. Compared to quiet enjoyment, constructive eviction, and illegal lease doctrine, what are the advantages of the implied warranty of habitability from the tenant's point of view? Should tenants regard the warranty theory as risk-free? More generally, is the warranty a good thing for tenants? (We return to this last question in Section H. See pages 562-566.)

NOTE: RETALIATORY EVICTION

Conventional common law doctrine gave landlords virtually unlimited freedom to terminate periodic tenancies and tenancies at will upon proper notice, and to refuse to renew expired terms of years. The landlord's reasons were irrelevant, and could be malevolent. This feature of the common law could easily undermine such reforms as the implied warranty of habitability: Landlords could cope with expanding tenant rights simply by getting rid of tenants who exercised them, at the same time giving a message to tenants who were thinking of doing so. So something had to change, and it did. Most jurisdictions today, commonly by statute, forbid retaliatory action by landlords. See generally Restatement (Second) of Property, Landlord and Tenant, §§14.8, 14.9 and Commentary (1977). A fairly common approach is to create a rebuttable presumption of retaliatory purpose if the landlord seeks to terminate a tenancy, increase rent, or decrease services within some given period (commonly anywhere from 90 to 180 days) after a good-faith complaint or other action by a tenant based on the condition of the premises. Retaliatory acts beyond the stated period are also usually prohibited, but the tenant bears the burden of proof.

Landlord freedom to terminate tenancies is constrained by more than retaliatory eviction prohibitions: for example, antidiscrimination legislation (see pages 441-444) and rent control laws (see pages 553-555).

> Some landlords, however, have experienced even greater restriction of their common law rights. New Jersey, for example, permits the landlord to evict a tenant at the end of the lease term only for "good cause." Under such statutes, a landlord may legally evict the tenant only for reasons specified in the statute. In effect, the tenant may arbitrarily terminate the tenancy at the end of the term, while the landlord may terminate only for just cause. [Edward H. Rabin, The Revolution in Residential Landlord-Tenant Law: Causes and Consequences, 69 Cornell L. Rev. 517, 534-535 (1984).][59]

NOTE AND PROBLEMS: LANDLORD'S TORT LIABILITY

The common law held landlords liable for tenant injuries (and perhaps for injuries to third parties on the leased premises) only when the landlord negligently breached the limited duties that arise from the handful of exceptions introduced earlier in connection with our discussion of quiet enjoyment and constructive eviction. See Note 2 on page 522. Here again, however, matters have changed somewhat in the last several decades, partly in response to the development of the implied warranty of habitability. A few jurisdictions have cited the warranty as a

---

59. See N.J. Stat. Ann. §2A:18-61.1 (West Supp. 1991). Good cause includes such things as failure to pay rent, destruction of the rental property, disturbance of neighbors, and breach of covenants in the lease. Just cause eviction statutes are commended in Joseph W. Singer, The Reliance Interest in Property, 40 Stan. L. Rev. 611, 682-684 (1988) (the statutes rightly protect the tenant's personal reliance interest in maintaining a home over the landlord's fungible investment interest; the interests protected by allowing people to stay in their homes are crucial to living a fulfilled life, and the landlord can continue to make money while those interests are protected).

reason to impose a *general* standard of care on landlords under *all* circumstances. The leading case is Sargent v. Ross, 113 N.H. 388, 308 A.2d 528 (1973). See also Pagelsdorf v. Safeco Ins. Co. of America, 91 Wis. 2d 734, 284 N.W.2d 55 (1979). And at least two states — California and Louisiana — have gone further, making landlords strictly liable for injuries caused by latent defects in the leased premises. See Becker v. IRM Corp., 38 Cal. 3d 454, 698 P.2d 116, 213 Cal. Rptr. 213 (1985); Virginia E. Nolan and Edmund Ursin, Strict Tort Liability of Landlords: *Becker v. IRM Corp.* in Context, 23 San Diego L. Rev. 125 (1986). But the conventional common law exceptions remain of paramount importance in the majority of jurisdictions, which neither impose strict liability nor recognize a general duty of care on the part of landlords. Suppose in such a jurisdiction that —

1. *L* leases land to *T* for a term of one year, knowing that *T* intends to use the land to board and rent horses and to operate a riding trail. *T* holds over at the end of the term and becomes a month-to-month tenant, from the first till the last of each month. On a rainy Fourth of July a customer of *T*'s is injured when her horse slips on a soft narrow riding trail and falls on top of her. Is *L* liable? See Pritchett v. Rosoff, 546 F.2d 463 (2d Cir. 1976).

2. *L* leases a farm to the father of the plaintiff, a young boy badly injured when he becomes entangled in a silage auger in the barn. Is *L* liable? See Thomas v. Shelton, 740 F.2d 478 (7th Cir. 1984).

3. *L* leases a unit in an apartment building to the parents of the plaintiff, a little girl badly injured when she is struck by boys racing their bikes on a parking lot owned by *L* and used by his tenants. The parking lot has no speed bumps. Is *L* liable? See Jackson v. Ray Kruse Constr. Co., 708 S.W.2d 664 (Mo. 1986).

Suppose the little girl is injured on the street, *off L*'s property (which has no fence around it). Is *L* liable? Compare Udy v. Calvary Corp., 162 Ariz. 7, 780 P.2d 1055 (Ariz. Ct. App. 1989); Brooks v. Eugene Burger Management Corp., 215 Cal. App. 3d 1611, 264 Cal. Rptr. 756 (1989).

4. *L* leases a unit in an apartment building to the *T*s, a married couple. A parking garage adjacent to the building, and owned by *L*, is available for use by tenants. Parking there one evening, the *T*s are attacked and badly injured by three men who are never caught. Is *L* liable? See Feld v. Merriam, 506 Pa. 383, 485 A.2d 742 (1984); Kline v. 1500 Massachusetts Ave. Apt. Corp., 439 F.2d 477 (D.C. Cir. 1970). See generally Note, Property Law: The Growing Accountability of Landlords for Third-Party Criminal Attacks, 1991 Ann. Surv. Am. L. 501.

5. Would it matter if in any of the foregoing the lease in question provided as follows? "Lessor shall not be liable to tenant or to any other person or to any property for damage or injury occurring on or owing to the condition of the leased premises, or any part thereof, or in the common areas thereof, and tenant agrees to hold lessor harmless from

any claims for damages no matter how caused." See Henrioulle v. Marin Ventures, Inc., 20 Cal. 3d 512, 573 P.2d 465, 143 Cal. Rptr. 247 (1978); O'Callaghan v. Waller & Beckwith Realty Co., 15 Ill. 2d 436, 155 N.E.2d 545 (1958); Cardona v. Eden Realty Co., 118 N.J. Super. 381, 288 A.2d 34 (1972). See generally William K. Jones, Private Revision of Public Standards: Exculpatory Agreements in Leases, 63 N.Y.U. L. Rev. 717 (1988).

2. Tenant's Duties; Landlord's Rights and Remedies

Back to the problem of moral hazard (see page 513). Having considered above how the law deals with a landlord's incentives to neglect the condition of the leased premises, we turn now to the flip side of the matter. Tenants too, after all, have reasons to shirk when it comes to maintenance and repair.

Actually, we have already considered some of the relevant doctrine.[60] Recall, for example, the law of *waste*, which can come into play whenever property ownership is divided such that two or more persons have consecutive rights to possession (as with present and future interests). The relationship of landlord and tenant is an instance, and our earlier discussion (in Note 1 on page 231) suggests the nature of the tenant's duties. A dated but still accurate statement is that the duty not to commit waste is breached if a tenant makes "such a change as to affect a vital and substantial portion of the premises; as would change its characteristic appearance; the fundamental purpose of the erection; or the uses contemplated, or a change of such a nature, as would affect the very realty itself, extraordinary in scope and effect, or unusual in expenditure." Pross v. Excelsior Cleaning & Dyeing Co., 110 Misc. 195, 201, 179 N.Y.S. 176, 179-180 (Mun. Ct. 1919). So not every alteration made by a tenant amounts to waste. The degree of effect on the use and value of the leased premises is relevant, as is its permanence; so too should be the length of the term remaining at the time the tenant makes the changes in question. (Do you see why?)

There is no bright line that distinguishes waste from lawful activities. For example, in Rumiche Corp. v. Eisenreich, 40 N.Y.2d 174, 352 N.E.2d 125 (1976), the tenant replaced a defective ceiling with sheetrock that did not meet code requirements, installed a light fixture and light switch, attached a wooden closet to a wall, and put a frame around a window. The court, quoting the language from the *Pross* case set out above, found no waste; a dissenting judge thought otherwise because

---

60. Including doctrine on the landlord's remedies in the event of tenant default. Recall the general treatment of this topic in Section F.

there were substantial and material changes in the structure of the leased premises, and because at least one of the changes was not up to code.

Suppose in a case like *Rumiche* that the tenant subsequently moves from the apartment and takes along some of the improvements — say, the light fixture and the window frame. Obviously the tenant might be liable for waste if removal results in substantial damage, but suppose it does not. Might the tenant be liable anyway, and for what? See Kane v. Timm, 11 Wash. App. 910, 527 P.2d 480 (1974); Ray A. Brown, The Law of Personal Property §§16.1-16.5, 16.8-16.10 (Walter B. Raushen-bush 3d ed. 1975) (discussing the law of *fixtures*). Or suppose the tenant agrees in the lease not to make any alterations in the premises without the landlord's consent, then does so without consent. Is this a breach? The cases are mixed. See, e.g., *Rumiche,* supra (making alterations with-out permission violates agreement); Garland v. Titan West Assocs., 147 A.D.2d 304, 543 N.Y.S.2d 56 (1989) (no breach absent alterations that would amount to waste independent of agreement; in other words, the agreement is read as simply restating the law of waste).

The *Rumiche* case involved acts of voluntary waste, arising from af-firmative actions, as opposed to involuntary or permissive waste arising from a failure to act. Permissive waste provided the foundation of the tenant's *duty to repair*. See, e.g., 1 American Law of Property §3.78 at 347 (1952 & Supp. 1977):

> The tenant . . . had an implied duty at common law to make minor re-pairs, a duty which arose out of his duty not to commit waste. The duty was to make such repairs as would keep the buildings windtight and watertight, thus preserving the property in substantially the same condition as at the commencement of the term, ordinary wear excepted. So the tenant was re-quired to replace broken windows and doors, repair a leaking roof, and re-store boards on the side of a building. He was not required to rebuild or restore a building, or any substantial part thereof, that had been destroyed by fire or other casualty or become so dilapidated from ordinary wear that it had to be torn down. Nor was he under any obligation to correct defects existing at the commencement of his lease.[61]

It is a common view today that the tenant's implied duty to repair no longer makes sense, the argument being that landlords, not tenants, are generally in the best position to maintain the property. See, e.g., id. at 347-348. The implied warranty of habitability — which essentially ne-gates the tenant's duty to repair — is based in part on this view, but bear in mind that the warranty does not apply across the board to all residen-tial leases, and seldom extends to commercial leases. See Note 1 on page 533.

61. Was the *landlord* under any obligation to correct defects existing at the outset of the tenancy? Recall the discussion in Note 2 on page 522.

In what respects, then, might a commercial tenant's duty to repair be altered by a covenant in the lease? The answer depends considerably on the language of the agreement in question. A covenant that excepts "fair wear and tear" amounts to no more than the common law duty. Slightly different wording (say "to keep in good repair") might be found to enlarge the tenant's obligations, and a number of vexing interpretive problems can arise. For instance, a bald promise to repair that contains no qualifications whatsoever *may* give rise to a duty to repair whatever the cause of the damage and even if repair entails rebuilding an entire structure. On the other hand, statutes in a number of jurisdictions abrogate the latter part of this rule absent an express promise to rebuild, and some courts, perhaps a majority, reach the same result by holding that "repair" does not mean "rebuild." See Amoco Oil Co. v. Jones, 467 N.W.2d 357 (Minn. Ct. App. 1991); Restatement (Second) of Property, Landlord and Tenant, §13.1, Reporter's Note at 504-505 (1977).

Explicit covenants to repair regularly except, in addition to fair wear and tear, damage by fire or other casualty. The current trend appears to be that the exception relieves the tenant from liability even with regard, say, to fire damage brought about by the tenant's negligence. See, e.g., Belden Mfg. Co. v. Chicago Threaded Fasteners, Inc., 84 Ill. App. 2d 336, 228 N.E.2d 532 (1967) (clause exculpates lessee; statute voiding exculpatory clauses applies only to landlords); Stein v. Yarnell-Todd Chevrolet, Inc., 41 Ill. 2d 32, 241 N.E.2d 439 (1969) (tenant relieved of liability for negligence despite the fact that clause in lease excepted only fire or other casualty *beyond lessee's control*). Compare U.S. Fidelity & Guaranty Co. v. Let's Frame It, Inc., 759 P.2d 819 (Colo. App. 1988) (fire damage exception held inapplicable to fire caused by tenant's negligence where other lease provisions required tenant to repair damage resulting from its negligence).

Whether or not there is a covenant to repair, must a tenant continue to pay rent after the leased premises have been destroyed? Consider the following case.

Albert M. Greenfield & Co. v. Kolea

Supreme Court of Pennsylvania, 1976
475 Pa. 351, 380 A.2d 758

MANDERINO, J. This is an appeal from an order of the Superior Court, affirming the judgment of the Court of Common Pleas of Delaware County. Appellee (lessor) had sued appellant (lessee) for breach of two lease agreements. The trial court awarded appellee $7,200.00. Appellant's motions for judgment n.o.v., arrest of judgment, and new trial were denied. The Superior Court affirmed the trial court per curiam. Greenfield v. Kolea, 232 Pa. Super. 701, 331 A.2d 824 (1975). Appellant's petition for allowance of appeal was granted by us and this appeal followed. We reverse.

The appellee's claim in this case is based on two separate, but related, lease agreements. The first lease, executed on March 20, 1971, covered ". . . all that certain one story garage building and known as 5735-37 Wayne Avenue, extending to Keyser Street in the rear [Philadelphia] . . . to be used and occupied as storage of automobiles. . . ." This lease, executed for a term of two years beginning May 1, 1971, provided for an annual rental of $4,800.00. The second lease, covering adjoining property, was also executed on March 20, 1971. The second lease covered ". . . all those certain lots or pieces of ground known as 5721-33 Wayne Avenue . . . to be used and occupied for the sale and storage of automobiles. . . ." The second lease, also executed for a two-year term beginning May 1, 1971, provided for an annual rental of $2,500.00. There was no building located on the real estate covered by the second lease. Neither lease contained a provision with respect to the tenant's obligations in the event of destruction of the building.

On May 1, 1972, after the appellant had occupied the premises for one year, fire completely destroyed the building covered by lease number one. The fire was labeled as accidental by the Fire Marshall's office. The day after the fire the remaining sections of the exterior walls were razed by the lessor, and barricades were placed around the perimeter of the premises covered by both leases. Appellant thereafter refused to pay rent under either of the leases.

The general rule has been stated that in the absence of a lease provision to the contrary, a tenant is not relieved from the obligation to pay rent despite the total destruction of the leased premises. Magaw v. Lambert, 3 Pa. 444 (1846); Hoy v. Holt, 91 Pa. 88 (1879).

The reason for the rule has been said to be that although a building may be an important element of consideration for the payment of rent, the interest in the soil remains to support the lease despite destruction of the building. It has also been said that since destruction of the building is usually by accident, it is only equitable to divide the loss; the lessor loses the property and the lessee loses the term. See generally, Sum. Pa. Jur. Landlord and Tenant, §72.

Two exceptions designed to afford relief to the tenant from the harshness of the common law principle have been created. These exceptions reflect the influence of modern contract principles as applied in the landlord-tenant relationship.

The first exception provides that where only a portion of a building is leased, total destruction of the building relieves the tenant of the obligation to pay rent. Moving Picture Co. of America v. Scottish Union & Natl. Ins. Co. of Edinburgh, 244 Pa. 258, 90 A. 642 (1914). See also Paxson & Comfort Co. v. Potter, 30 Pa. Super. 615 (1906). This exception recognizes that in the leasing of a part of a building there is no implication that any estate in land is granted. This Court, in other words, has recognized that in a landlord-tenant relationship with respect to an apartment, the parties have *bargained for* a part of a building and not the land beneath.

The influence of contract principles of bargained for exchange is also apparent in the second exception to the general common law rule. The second exception is based on the doctrine of *impossibility of performance*, and is stated in Greenburg v. Sun Shipbuilding Co., 277 Pa. 312, 313, 121 A. 63, 64 (1923):

> Where a contract relates to the use and possession of specific property, the existence of which is necessary to the carrying out of the purpose in view, a condition is implied by law, as though written in the agreement, that the impossibility of performance arising from the destruction of the property without fault of either party shall end all contractual obligations relating to the thing destroyed.

See also Rest. Contracts, §460, 6 Corbin on Contracts, §1337.

As was said in West v. Peoples First Natl. Bank & Trust Co., 378 Pa. 275, 106 A.2d 427 (1954),

> . . . where a contract relates to specific property the existence or maintenance of which is necessary to the carrying out of the purpose of the agreement, the condition is implied by law, just as though it were written into the agreement, that the impossibility of performance or the frustration of purpose arising from the destruction of the property or interference with its use, without the fault of either party, ends all contractual obligations relating to the property. Moreover, impossibility in that connection means not only strict impossibility but impracticability because of extreme and unreasonable difficulty, expense, or loss involved. (Footnote omitted.)

The Rest. Contracts, §454, also applies the test of impracticability rather than strict impossibility:

> . . . [I]mpossibility means not only strict impossibility but *impracticability* because of extreme and unreasonable difficulty, expense, injury, or loss involved. (Emphasis added.)

In the instant case, it is apparent that when the building was destroyed by fire it became impossible for the appellee to furnish the agreed consideration — ". . . all that one story garage building. . . ." Nothing in the first lease implies that any interest in the land itself was intended to be conveyed. It is also obvious that the purpose of the lease with respect to the appellant was thereby frustrated. As noted in the lease, the parties contemplated that appellant would use the building for the repair and sale of used motor vehicles. Without a building appellant could no longer carry on a used car business as contemplated by the parties at the time they entered into the lease agreement. It became extremely impracticable for the appellant to continue using the adjoining lot when his business office and repair stations were destroyed by the fire. Additionally, because of the dangerous condition created by the fire, the city required appellee to barricade the property covered by both leases, thus preventing appellant from entering the property.

In reaching our decision that the accidental destruction of the building by fire excused the parties from further performance of their obligations under the lease agreements, we are cognizant of the fact that we are allocating the risk to be assumed by the parties. Such an allocation of risk can be accomplished in one of two ways. First, the parties could specifically provide for risk assumption with respect to certain possible contingencies. In the absence of an express recognition and assumption by the parties, the court is left with the task of determining what the parties would have done had the issue arisen in the contract negotiations. See Restatement, Second, Property (Landlord and Tenant) §5.4. In reaching such a decision a court must consider many factors. As stated in 6 Corbin on Contracts §1325:

> There is no rule of law by which the issue can be deductively determined; it depends upon the practices and customs of men in like cases, upon the prevailing mores of the time.

In reaching a decision involving the landlord-tenant relationship, too often courts have relied on outdated common law property principles and presumptions and have refused to consider the factors necessary for an equitable and just conclusion. In this case, for example, if we applied the general rule and ignored the realities of the situation, we would bind the appellant to paying rent for barren ground when both parties to the lease contemplated that the building would be used for the commercial enterprise of repair and sale of used motor vehicles.

The trial court's decision to bind the lessee to the lease was simply an application of an outdated common law presumption. That presumption developed in a society very different from ours today: one where the land was always more valuable than the buildings erected on it. Buildings are critical to the functioning of modern society. When the parties bargain for the use of a building, the soil beneath is generally of little consequence. Our laws should develop to reflect these changes. As stated in Javins v. First Natl. Realty Corp., 138 U.S. App. D.C. 369, 372, 428 F.2d 1071, 1074, cert. denied, 400 U.S. 925, 91 S. Ct. 186, 27 L. Ed. 2d 185 (1970):

> Courts have a duty to reappraise old doctrines in the light of the facts and values of contemporary life — particularly old common law doctrines which the courts themselves created and developed. As we have said before,

"[T]he continued vitality of the common law . . . depends upon its ability to reflect contemporary values and ethics." (Footnote omitted.)

The presumption established in *Magaw* and *Hoy,* supra, no longer has relevance to today's landlord-tenant relationships. It is no longer reasonable to *assume* that in the absence of a lease provision to the contrary the lessee should bear the risk of loss in the event of total destruction of the building. Where the parties do not expressly provide for such a catastrophe, the court should analyze the facts and the lease agreement as any other contract would be analyzed. Following such an analysis, if it is evident to the court that the parties bargained for the existence of a building, and no provision is made as to who bears the risk of loss if the building is destroyed, the court should relieve the parties of their respective obligations when the building no longer exists.

Accordingly, we reverse the order of the Superior Court, and remand to the trial court with directions to grant the appellant's motion for judgment n.o.v.

ROBERTS, J., concurring.

I join in the opinion of the majority because the rule established reaches the same result as the Restatement, Second, Property (Landlord and Tenant) Section 5.4 (Unsuitable Condition Arises After Entry — Remedies Available) which states:

> Except to the extent the parties to a lease validly agree otherwise, there is a breach of the landlord's obligation if, after the tenant's entry and without fault of the tenant, a change in the condition of the leased property . . . caused suddenly by a nonmanmade force, makes the leased property unsuitable for the use contemplated by the parties and the landlord does not correct the situation within a reasonable time after being requested by the tenant to do so. For that breach, the tenant may:
> (1) terminate the lease. . . .

The unexpressed intent of the parties is thus irrelevant.

NIX, J., concurring.

Insofar as the majority opinion represents the adoption in this Commonwealth of Section 5.4 of the Restatement, Second, Property, I am in complete agreement. The common law rule that an accidental fire which totally destroys a building is no defense to the claim for rent for the premises, is clearly inappropriate in our present society.[62]

62. The rationale of the common law rule was stated in Paxson & Comfort Co. v. Potter, 30 Pa. Super. 615, 616 (1906): "This rule has its foundation in the fact that *the tenant is still in possession of the soil* on which the building was located and that *something remains to which the lease attaches.* He may use the land for some purposes and may reconstruct the building." (Emphasis added.) See also, Supermarkets Operating Co. v. Arkwright Mut. Ins. Co., 257 F. Supp. 273 (D.C. Pa. 1966); Solomon v. Neisner Bros., Inc., 93

As I view our holding today, it replaces a rule of law, which may have had validity in a predominantly agrarian society but is clearly outmoded today.

NOTES AND QUESTIONS

1. See, in addition to the principal case, Crow Lumber & Bldg. Materials Co. v. Washington County Library Bd., 428 S.W.2d 758 (Mo. App. 1968) (discussing the common law rule and its exceptions and legislative abrogation of the common law rule in a number of states). Compare Osterling v. Sturgeon, 156 N.W.2d 344 (Iowa 1968) (where lease is for a portion of premises, destruction of premises terminated rent obligation only where leased portion is totally destroyed as opposed to merely damaged).

2. Should the rationale of the *Greenfield* case apply if the destruction of the premises is the tenant's fault? If the tenant has covenanted to repair? If the tenant has covenanted to pay rent even if the premises are destroyed? (Would the latter covenant be unconscionable?) Cf. 1 American Law of Property §3.103 (1952 & Supp. 1977).

3. The court in *Greenfield* implies that the tenant is relieved from the obligation to pay rent on the second lease because, among other reasons, the government required that the property covered by that lease be closed off. Consider other government actions. Suppose, for example, that the government orders a building repaired. Must the tenant make the repairs if he has not covenanted to repair? If he has? Suppose government regulations adopted subsequent to the making of a lease prohibit or restrict the uses to which the leased premises were being put. Does the tenant remain liable for rent? See 1 American Law of Property, supra, §§3.80, 3.104.

NOTE: FRUSTRATION OF PURPOSE
(IMPOSSIBILITY OF PERFORMANCE)

The contract doctrine of frustration of purpose is being used increasingly by courts in landlord-tenant cases. It has been used quite commonly with respect to situations in which government regulations make the purpose of a lease illegal (see above). But its use in *Greenfield* as the basis for a "second exception" to the tenant's obligation to pay rent despite destruction of the leased premises is unusual. Notice the court's

---

F. Supp. 310 (1950), aff'd, 187 F.2d 735 (CA3d); Demas v. Laskey, 358 Pa. 633, 58 A.2d 134 (1948); 32 Am. Jur., Landlord and Tenant, §§493, 494; Sum. Pa. Jur. Landlord and Tenant, §72.

explicit acknowledgment that it was allocating risk between the parties. By what criteria did the court make its allocation? By what criteria should it have done so? On the latter question, see Richard A. Posner, Economic Analysis of Law 102-109 (4th ed. 1992) (issue should be which of the parties was intended to bear risk; in the absence of evidence of actual intention, the question can be answered by comparing the relative costs to the parties of preventing or insuring against the risk).

H.   The Problem of Affordable Housing

Homelessness is no secret, nor are slums, nor high rents in densely populated urban areas. To find affordable housing of decent quality is a challenge to many Americans, not just — but obviously most especially — the poor. The implied warranty of habitability and allied reforms, studied above, aimed to improve the situation, for low-income tenants in particular.[63] But won't landlords respond to the reforms by increasing the rents they charge, such that housing might be more decent but less affordable? Can rent controls help here? What about government-assisted housing programs?

These, as we shall see, are large and contentious questions. The materials that follow are an introduction, not an exhaustive treatment.

1.   Rent Controls

Cromwell Associates v. Mayor and Council of Newark

Superior Court of New Jersey, Law Division, 1985
211 N.J. Super, 462, 511 A.2d 1273

SIMON, J. Attacks on the facial constitutionality of rent-control ordinances have inundated the courts since Inganamort v. Borough of Fort

---

63. The late J. Skelly Wright, a U.S. Circuit Judge for the District of Columbia, played a central role in the reform of residential landlord-tenant law. In an October 1982 letter to Edward H. Rabin, professor of law at the University of California at Davis, Judge Wright said this:

[M]ost of the tenants in Washington, D.C. slums were poor and black and most of the landlords were rich and white. There is no doubt in my mind that these conditions played a subconscious role in influencing my landlord and tenant decisions.
     . . . I didn't like what I saw, and I did what I could to ameliorate, if not eliminate, the injustice involved in the way many of the poor were required to live in the nation's capital.

The letter is reprinted in full in Edward H. Rabin, The Revolution in Residential Landlord-Tenant Law: Causes and Consequences, 69 Cornell L. Rev. 517, 549 (1984).

Lee, 62 N.J. 521, 303 A.2d 298 (1973), which held that municipalities have the power to enact such ordinances in the face of critical housing shortages. However, this is a case of first impression. The issue here is whether an ordinance which places a maximum limitation on annual increases, including increases granted pursuant to the hardship provision of the ordinance, is constitutionally permissible.

The rent-control ordinance presently in effect in Newark was adopted in 1982. The ordinance permits a 6% increase annually as well as a board-approved increase in cases where the proofs demonstrate that a particular hardship forecloses on a landlord's ability to obtain a fair rate of return defined by the ordinance as an 11.5% return on investment.

On April 17, 1985, the City of Newark amended the rent control ordinance to limit the total of all increases granted in any 12-month period to 25%.

> Since an immediate rent increase of more than 25 per cent above the prior monthly rent may be considered unconscionable and imposes a hardship on a tenant, the board shall not grant increases exceeding 25 percent in any one year for any tenant.
>
> For the purpose of determining whether the rent increase exceeds 25 per cent of the monthly rent, all increases pursuant [to the sections on rent increases, capital improvements, and landlord hardship] occurring within 12 months prior to the effective date of the increase shall be added to determine if that amount exceeds 25 per cent of the prior monthly rent.

Plaintiff contends that the imposition of the 25% limitation denies it a fair rate of return as constitutionally mandated.

Plaintiff is the owner of the 294-unit Cromwell Terrace Apartments [in] Newark. On August 31, 1984, plaintiff applied to the Rent Control Board of the City of Newark (hereinafter the board) for hardship increases. Subsequently the board declared a moratorium on all hardship increases until January 31, 1985; plaintiff's application predated the declaration and therefore was exempt from the moratorium.

On November 27, 1984, the board approved plaintiff's application for hardship increases averaging 33% per tenant, but conditioned its approval on the completion of specified repairs. These conditions were substantially complied with and the hardship increases became effective March 1, 1985. The increases granted by the board were not appealed and are not disputed. In March 1985, plaintiff notified its tenants of an additional 6% increase to be effective May 1, 1985, pursuant to the automatic increase provision of the ordinance which provides:

> The establishment of rents between a landlord and tenant in all housing spaces shall hereafter be determined by the provisions of this ordinance. At the expiration of a lease or at the termination of the lease of a periodic tenant, no landlord may request or receive a percentage increase in rent which is

greater than six (6%) per cent without first petitioning the Rent Control Board.

The rental for housing space shall not be increased more than 6% in any consecutive twelve (12) month period irrespective of the number of different tenants occupying said housing space during said 12 month period, any change of ownership of the landlord or vacancy of the housing space.

As a result of the April 17, 1985 amendment to the ordinance limiting increases to 25% in a year, plaintiff was unable to obtain the 6% increase. Plaintiff then filed a verified complaint in lieu of prerogative writs against defendants, Mayor and Council of the City of Newark and the City of Newark on May 7, 1985 challenging the constitutionality of the amendment. Defendant-intervenors are tenants of Cromwell Terrace who dispute the 6% increase.

On May 31, 1985, the court placed preliminary restraints on the application of the ordinance and ordered that the 6% increase be collected and held in escrow pending determination of this matter.

The facial validity of a rent-control ordinance depends upon whether the regulatory scheme, in its entirety, permits an efficient landlord to receive a just and reasonable return on its investment. Hutton Park Gardens v. West Orange Town Council, 68 N.J. 543, 568, 350 A.2d 1 (1975). The Newark ordinance, on its face, defines a fair and reasonable return as an 11.5% return on investment. The constitutionality of this provision is not questioned.

The constitutional requirement that rent regulation permit a fair and reasonable return does not mandate any particular form for the regulation. *Hutton*, supra, 68 N.J. at 569, 350 A.2d 1. It does, however, require that the regulation serve a public purpose without arbitrariness and discrimination. Consequently, the question is whether the 25% limitation on annual increases, including hardship increases, amounts to an arbitrary or discriminatory act of legislative power.

The very nature of rent control requires that a limit be placed on rent increases. Such limits have been held valid providing a safety valve, such as a hardship mechanism, exists which can assure an efficient landlord a fair return. *Hutton*, supra at 572, 350 A.2d 1. In *Hutton*, supra, our Supreme Court mandated that "every rent control ordinance must be deemed to intend, and will so be read, to permit property owners to apply to the local administrative agency for relief on the ground that the regulation entitles the owner to a just and reasonable return." Ibid. The amendment to the Newark ordinance before this court, goes one step further than the ordinances contemplated in *Hutton* by placing a limit on the hardship relief granted by the local administrative agency. As a practical matter, it would appear that severe hardships requiring more than a 25% increase would be rare. The court agrees with plaintiff that any such limit, even a generous 25%, is arbitrary in that it cannot be read as contemplated by *Hutton,* to insure a fair return.

It is the obligation of the court to uphold the validity of the ordinance where there exists any reasonable interpretation which effectuates
the legislative intent without violating the Constitution. Consequently,
any reasonable interpretation which achieves this goal would be more
desirable than a finding of unconstitutionality. One proposed interpretation would eliminate application of the amendment to plaintiff by calculating the calendar year from the effective date of the amendment
rather than the usual anniversary date. However, the amendment specifically provides that "all increases . . . occurring within 12 months prior
to the effective date of the increase shall be added to determine if that
amount exceeds 25 per cent of the prior monthly rent."

The plain meaning of this language coupled with the conduct of
defendants who enacted the amendment and immediately applied it to
plaintiff clearly militate against such an interpretation. The 12-month
period contemplated here is no different from the base year concept
frequently employed in rent-control legislation and must be interpreted
as such. Even though this amendment considers the prior 12-month period in its calculation, it cannot be considered retroactive legislation or a
retroactive application. The present situation is unlike that considered
by the Supreme Court in South Hamilton Associates v. Mayor and
Council of Morristown, 99 N.J. 437, 493 A.2d 523 (1985) where an ordinance was specifically enacted to be effective retroactively and such
retroactive application interfered with existing contract rights.

A second proposed interpretation proferred by defendants-intervenors is that the hardship provision and the 6% annual increase provision are alternate mechanisms. As a result, even if the 25% limit is
unconstitutional, they maintain plaintiff cannot collect an additional 6%
as it made a hardship application during the same year. The court finds
that this proposed interpretation violates not only the plain meaning,
but the past implementation of the ordinance.

The 6% increase is tailored to keep a landlord current with respect
to operating income and expenses. Where the 6% increase does not give
a fair and reasonable return, a landlord may apply for relief under the
hardship provision. That the increases are not mutually exclusive is further reinforced by the fact that the notice of hardship determination
sent to plaintiff by the rent control board granting specific increases averaging 33% provided "no rent may be charged in excess of the maximum rent stated above other than the legal annual 6%. . . ." This
language indicates that the intent of the legislators is to allow a 6% increase automatically and in cases where necessary, to allow larger increases if the board approves them.

Defendants and defendants-intervenors suggest that the ordinance
might also be interpreted as merely placing a moratorium and not a cap
on total increases. They argue that the net effect of the amendment is
not to deny increases, but merely to delay them. Implicit in this argu-

ment is a recognition that the constitutional requisites are not otherwise met. While the power of municipalities to establish moratoriums is recognized, such moratoriums have been imposed under different circumstances such as land development and the granting of licenses.

Interpreting the 25% limit as a moratorium and not a ceiling not only violates the plain meaning of the ordinance, but fails to render it constitutionally valid. Hardship increases are determined yearly based on actual operating costs of the prior year. Since there is no provision to factor in a "lost" hardship increase, the limitation would cause a snowball effect of losses that might not be recouped. Whether considered a ceiling or a moratorium, the net effect of this amendment is to compel the type of subsidization by a landlord or landlords invalidated in Property Owners Association of North Bergen v. Township of North Bergen, 74 N.J. 327, 378 A.2d 25 (1977).

Municipal ordinances are presumed to be valid. . . . This presumption may only be overcome by clear and convincing evidence that the ordinance has a confiscatory effect on landlords.

Defendant contends that plaintiff has failed to meet its burden of proof in that it presented the court with no specific evidence of confiscatory effect. Plaintiff made its proofs to the administrative agency. It is not required to furnish further proofs when the language of the amendment operates to deny plaintiff the fair rate of return contemplated by the board in granting the hardship increase.

In addition, when an ordinance is so restrictive as to facially preclude any possibility of a just and reasonable return, a court may declare it invalid without considering the actual effect on a specified landlord. Orange Taxpayers Council, Inc. v. Orange, 83 N.J. 246, 256, 416 A.2d 353 (1980) and cases cited therein. The amendment in question fits into that category because no matter what circumstances are presented to the board, the board cannot grant an effective hardship increase in excess of 19% (25% cap less 6% automatic increase).

When the maximum increase allowable by the rent-control ordinance is insufficient to provide an efficient operator a fair rate of return, the ordinance is unconstitutional on its face. *Hutton,* supra. Specifically, if a landlord cannot operate efficiently without an increase in excess of 25%, the limitation precludes that landlord from realizing a just return. No "saving provision" can be read into the ordinance as required by *Hutton* because of the clear 25% limit.

Defendants further argue that the burden of proof rests with the plaintiff to show that the increases charged are not unconscionable. Cases considering the concept of unconscionability treat that concept in the context of the Anti-Eviction Act, N.J.S.A. 2A:18-61.1(f). See Edgemere at Somerset v. Johnson, 143 N.J. Super. 222, 362 A.2d 1250 (Cty. D. Ct. 1976); Hill Manor Apartments v. Broome, 164 N.J. Super. 295, 395 A.2d 1307 (Cty. Ct. 1978). It is interesting to note that, although only relevant here by way of analogy, *Hill Manor* employs a balancing test using landlord's reasonable expenses in considering whether a rent increase is "unconscionable." Ibid. In the present case, the board completed a similar test and granted plaintiff-landlord increases averaging 33%. Although the court sympathizes with those tenants who may be unable to afford higher rents, constitutionally, it cannot compel particular landlords to subsidize tenants to their own detriment. Property Owners Association of North Bergen v. Township of North Bergen, supra.

Furthermore, according to the provisions of the ordinance, landlords may effectuate the annual 6% increase without board approval, i.e., without submissions of proof of need. Compelling plaintiff to submit proofs with respect to the need for the 6% automatic increase constitutes a denial of equal protection where no other landlords are required to do so. Wilson v. City of Long Branch, 27 N.J. 360, 377, 142 A.2d 837 (1985), certif. den. 358 U.S. 873, 79 S. Ct. 113, 3 L. Ed. 2d 104 (1958); Nelson v. South Brunswick Planning Board, 84 N.J. Super. 265, 277, 201 A.2d 741 (App. Div. 1964).

The amendment to the Newark rent-control ordinance fails to comply with constitutional requisites. No reasonable interpretation of the amendment allows an efficient landlord to realize a fair and reasonable rate of return in cases where the board finds it is necessary to grant a hardship increase in excess of 19% annually. The increase is designed to be a supplement to the 6% increase, which is an automatic cost of living increase, so that a constitutional minimum return may be realized by all landlords.

The court, therefore, must find this amendment to be unconstitutional on its face and as applied to plaintiff.

Judgment for plaintiff.

NOTES AND QUESTIONS

1. *The mechanics of rent controls.* Rent control regulations vary significantly from city to city, but a few generalizations can be made. The usual approach is to set the controlled rent for a given rental unit[64] by establishing a base figured with reference to values as they existed on some specified date in the past, then adding reasonable periodic increases designed to yield a "fair" or "reasonable" rate of return (more on this in Note 3). Units are usually exempt from controls the first time they are put on the rental market; the base for these "new" units is likely

---

64. Almost always a residential unit, though commercial rent controls have been used in a few instances. See Comment, Commercial Rent Regulation: Preserving the Diversity of Neighborhood Commercial Districts, 15 Ecology L.Q. 281 (1988).

to be whatever the market will bear. What if a landlord rebuilds a bunch of previously rented apartments after their virtual destruction by fire or converts a 30-unit rooming house into a dozen 3- and 4-room apartments; may he charge the market price for these "new" apartments, or only the controlled price for "renovated" dwellings? Compare Somers Assocs., Inc. v. Gloucester Township, 241 N.J. Super. 323, 575 A.2d 20 (1990) (the fire example; what landlord did was "renovation"); Figueiredo v. Rent Control Bd. of Cambridge, 26 Mass. App. Ct. 661, 531 N.E.2d 597 (1988) (the conversion example; the dwellings were so substantially rehabilitated as to be the equivalent of new).

Some cities take a mixed approach to rent regulation. New York, for example, has a fairly typical rent control ordinance for older buildings, but also a rent stabilization ordinance for buildings constructed after 1947. Rent stabilization was adopted in 1969 as a compromise measure; it brought previously unregulated post-1947 housing under control but in a manner intended to encourage new construction by allaying builders' fears about extending the reach of the original rent control program. The stabilization regulations allow, among other things, more and higher rent increases than do the rent control regulations. See, e.g., Note, The Question of Succession in New York City: Who Has the Right to Renew a Rent-Stabilized Lease?, 9 Cardozo L. Rev. 1831 (1988).

2. *Succession rights.* Consider the question of succession referred to in the citation above, bearing in mind the following background information:

Under some ordinances, landlords may set a new market (base) rent with every change of tenant; other ordinances work only from the original base rent for a unit, without regard to tenant changes. A central purpose of the first kind of ordinance in particular would obviously be subverted if landlords could simply evict tenants at the end of a term and rent anew at the market rate, as would another purpose of both kinds of ordinance — security of tenure for tenants. So rent controls have always been accompanied by provisions requiring good cause (such as default in rent payments) for termination by the landlord.[65] But what is the reach of such protective provisions? Suppose someone has been living with T, the tenant of record whose name is on the lease, and that T then dies. Does the surviving occupant qualify for a renewal lease at the controlled rent? Does it matter whether the surviving occupant is the

---

65. Recall the similar but more encompassing New Jersey statute discussed at page 538 and footnote 59.

In some cities with rent controls, if a rent controlled apartment is not being used as a primary residence, the landlord is entitled to evict. But how is the landlord to know? "If you are a rent regulated tenant in New York City, there is a good chance that you have been, are being or will be investigated by a new subspecies of private detective — the lease police." Richard D. Lyons, Getting the Goods on Those "Nonprimary" Renters, N.Y. Times, June 22, 1986, §8, at 7. For another account, see Tom Wolfe, The Bonfire of the Vanities (1987).

spouse, son, daughter-in-law, lover, or simply the roommate of *T*? Does it matter how long the survivor has been occupying the apartment with *T*?

A general answer can't be given; the outcome turns on the wording of the ordinance in question, and on judicial interpretation of any ambiguities. For example, in Braschi v. Stahl Assocs. Co., 74 N.Y.2d 201, 543 N.E.2d 49, 544 N.Y.S.2d 784 (1989), the court read a protective provision referring to any "member of the deceased tenant's family" to include gay life-partners, reasoning that the language in question should be taken to include long-term relationships characterized by emotional and financial interdependence. New York's regulations were subsequently amended to reflect the reading in *Braschi*, and succession rights have since been extended to, for example, a man living in his great aunt's apartment, a mother and son who had lived with the deceased tenant for several years, and an orphan taken in by the tenant but never formally adopted.

Most commentators favor the "functional approach" of *Braschi*. See, e.g., Note, Looking for a Family Resemblance: The Limits of the Functional Approach to the Legal Definition of Family, 104 Harv. L. Rev. 1640 (1991) (discussing the general endorsement of the approach and noting problems with it). But see Note, The Question of Succession, supra, arguing that the expansion of succession rights tightens rental markets and places an increased burden on prospective tenants – a view apparently shared in England, where succession rights have recently been cut back as part of an overall plan to decontrol rental markets. See Note, Family Ties: A Comparison of the Changing Legal Definition of Family Succession Rights to Rent-Regulated Housing in the United States and Great Britain, 17 Brooklyn J. Intl. L. 123 (1991).

3. *Legal constraints.* Early rent control ordinances were enacted to deal with temporary emergencies and upheld on that basis. See Block v. Hirsh, 256 U.S. 135 (1921). The emergency requirement has been relaxed over the years, however, and explicitly abandoned in some jurisdictions. See the *Hutton* case cited in *Cromwell*. Today reasonable rent controls are generally considered to be justified as an exercise of the police power of state and local governments. But:

Fair return. To be reasonable, rent controls must allow landlords a fair return. Why did the regulations in *Cromwell* fail in this respect? Cf. Searle v. City of Berkeley Rent Stabilization Bd., 271 Cal. Rptr. 437 (Ct. App. 1990) (invalidating an ordinance providing for an inflation adjustment of 40 percent of the increase in the Consumer Price Index); Helmsley V. Borough of Fort Lee, 78 N.J. 200, 394 A.2d 65 (1978) (invalidating an ordinance imposing a 2.5 percent ceiling on rent increases and providing inadequate administrative relief); Birkenfeld v. City of Berkeley, 17 Cal. 3d 129, 550 P.2d 1001, 130 Cal. Rptr. 465 (1976) (invalidating an ordinance that rolled rents back to a period five years earlier with the intention of holding them as the base rents for an indefinite time). Ordinances have also been invalidated where they failed to provide for a landlord's financial hardship. Compare Pennell v. City of San Jose, 485 U.S. 1 (1988) (upholding ordinance despite provision permitting consideration of *tenant* hardship in determining rent increases).

How is "fair return" calculated? One question has to do with the *base* to be used as a point of reference. Does one figure return in light of the market value of the property, for example, or in light of the owner's investment? Each approach has proved popular, and each is problematic. The market value of property is usually a function of the rents the property generates (the rental income is "capitalized"). So if market value is the base, is it the market value as it was before enactment of rent controls? The problem is that rents (and market values) were presumably high at that time, which is why rent controls were put into operation. So does one instead use a market value calculated after rent controls? The problem is that this approach might understate the amount that should be received by owners who purchased their properties before rent controls were enacted. To deal with these difficulties, some courts have used "hypothetical" market values supposedly equal to what market values would have been, before rent controls, if supply and demand for rental property in the market were equal. Many observers think that even experts can't come up with a reliable number.

Similar quandaries arise if fair return is based on an owner's investment. Suppose the owner inherited the property and didn't pay anything for it. What then? What about the buyer who invested long ago, when dollars were worth more? See generally Kenneth K. Baar, Guidelines for Drafting Rent Control Laws: Lessons of a Decade, 35 Rutgers L. Rev. 723, 781-816 (1983).

Setting the *rate* of return can also be troublesome. The rate is supposed to allow an efficient landlord to recover reasonable expenses and earn a "fair" profit. But a fair profit (questions of the base aside) could be based on any number of considerations, such as inflation, the Consumer Price Index, yields of similar alternative investments, interest rates, and so on. The difficulties of principled judicial supervision are obvious, and it appears that as to rate issues the courts have generally accommodated the rent control authorities, in the absence of obviously confiscatory rates (see the *Helmsley* case, supra).

Takings. The Fifth Amendment provides that the government shall not "take" private property without just compensation. The prohibition is explored at length in Chapter 12; here we merely note its bearing on rent controls.

A taking might be found either if a government program works a physical invasion of the property in question, or if it unduly reduces the property's value (the latter is usually called a regulatory taking). Rent controls have been challenged on both grounds, sometimes successfully, sometimes not.[66]

In Yee v. City of Escondido, 112 S. Ct. 1522 (1992), the Court considered whether Escondido's "mobilehome" rent control ordinance, coupled with California's Mobilehome Residency Law, amounted to a taking by physical occupation.[67] Typically, mobile homes (so-called; they seldom move once in place) are owned by their occupants, but the pads on which they sit are leased from the owner of a mobile home park. California's Residency Law limits the right of a park owner to terminate a mobile home owner's tenancy and provides that while a rental agreement is in effect the park owner may not require removal of a mobile home upon its sale, charge a transfer fee, or disapprove of the buyer so long as he or she is able to pay the rent. The state law does not limit the rent a park owner may charge, but the Escondido ordinance does (so too for similar ordinances in other California communities). See generally Werner Z. Hirsch & Joel G. Hirsch, Legal-Economic Analysis of Rent Controls in a Mobile Home Context: Placement Values and Vacancy Decontrol, 35 UCLA L. Rev. 399 (1988).

The petitioners in Yee based their takings challenge "on the unusual economic relationship between park owners and mobile home owners":

> Park owners may no longer set rents or decide who their tenants will be. As a result, according to petitioners, any reduction in the rent for a mobile home pad causes a corresponding increase in the value of a mobile home, because the mobile home owner now owns, in addition to a mobile home, the right to occupy a pad at a rent below the value that would be set by the free market. . . . Because under the California Mobilehome Residency Law the park owner cannot evict a mobile home owner or easily convert the property to other uses, the argument goes, the mobile home owner is effectively a perpetual tenant of the park, and the increase in the mobile home's value thus represents the right to occupy a pad at below-market rent indefinitely. And because the Mobilehome Residency Law permits the mobile home owner to sell the mobile home in place, the mobile home owner can receive a premium from the purchaser corresponding to this increase in value. The amount of this premium is not limited by the Mobilehome Residency Law or the Escondido ordinance. As a result, petitioners conclude, the rent control ordinance has

66. Takings allegations are the prominent — but not the only — constitutional challenge to rent controls today. See, e.g., Michael D. Bergman, Property Law: Recent Developments in Rent Control and Related Laws Regulating the Landlord-Tenant Relationship, 1989 Ann. Surv. Am. L. 691, 714-724 (discussing due process, equal protection, and the contracts clause).

67. Mobile home rent controls similar to those in Yee have been implemented in several areas. Conflict between state and federal courts regarding the constitutionality of the measures — with respect to the physical takings issue in particular — was one of the considerations that prompted the U.S. Supreme Court to grant certiorari in Yee. See 112 S. Ct. at 1533. See generally Kenneth K. Baar, The Right to Sell the "Im"mobile Manufactured Home in Its Rent Controlled Space in the "Im"mobile Home Park: Valid Regulation or Unconstitutional Taking?, 24 Urb. Law. 157 (1992).

transferred a discrete interest in land — the right to occupy the land indefinitely at a sub-market rent — from the park owner to the mobile home owner. Petitioners contend that what has been transferred from park owner to mobile home owner is no less than a right of physical occupation of the park owner's land. [112 S. Ct. at 1528.]

The Court found no physical taking, because the park owners were not *required* to submit to the physical occupation of their land. They rented voluntarily in the first instance and were not compelled to continue; the state legislation permitted anyone who wished to change the use of their land to evict tenants after notice. "Put bluntly, no government has required any physical invasion of petitioners' property." 112 S. Ct. at 1528.

In *Yee* the Court conceded that the laws under review might work a regulatory taking — among other reasons, because of the wealth transfer from park owners to incumbent mobile home owners (and with no benefit to future tenants), and because of the limits placed on the park owners' freedom to choose incoming tenants. The Court declined, however, to rule on the matter because it had not been fairly included in the petition for certiorari nor fully litigated below.

Consider another recent case — this one decided by New York's highest court — finding that a local rent control ordinance worked both a physical invasion and a regulatory taking. See Seawall Assocs. v. City of New York, 74 N.Y.2d 92, 542 N.E.2d 1059, 544 N.Y.S.2d 542, cert. denied, 493 U.S. 976 (1989). The New York City ordinance at issue in *Seawall* put a five-year moratorium (renewable as the city deemed necessary) on the demolition, alteration, or conversion of single-room occupancy (SRO) properties and required their owners to restore all such units to habitable condition and lease them at controlled rents. (Owners could buy out of the moratorium at a price of $45,000 per SRO unit, or by providing replacement units, and might qualify for a reduction in the price, or in the number of replacement units, in cases of hardship.)[68]

The court held that the forced occupancy worked by the ordinance effectively denied owners their rights of possession and exclusion and

68. The ordinance reflected a 180 degree turn in New York City's housing policy. "After years of encouraging the demolition and redevelopment of SRO properties — which the City of New York considered substandard housing — the City abandoned its policy when it found that the stock of low-cost rental housing was shrinking at an alarming rate." 74 N.Y.2d at 99, 542 N.E.2d at 1061, 544 N.Y.S.2d at 544.

On conversion regulation generally, understand that landlords obviously stand to gain by changing rent controlled properties to uncontrolled uses. Conversion to condominiums has been especially popular. (In a condominium, units are sold, not leased; there is no rent, though there are periodic charges to cover such costs as maintenance of common areas of the building. See pages 922-924.) Some cities have ignored the conversion problem. Others have ordinances requiring that a stated percentage of tenants must first agree either to the conversion or to buy a unit, or prohibiting conversion unless the rental vacancy rate in the city exceeds a certain percentage, or limiting the number of conversions that can occur annually, or essentially prohibiting conversion.

therefore amounted to a per se physical taking. Ordinary rent controls are different because they do not force owners, in the first instance, to make their properties available. In any event, physical taking aside, the ordinance was invalid as a regulatory taking, for two reasons. First, it did not allow owners an economically viable use of their property. The owners, who may have purchased with the intention of tearing down and replacing the existing structures, could neither rent nor sell for amounts that let them realize on their investments. Second, the ordinance did not substantially advance legitimate state interests. New York City's own study acknowledged that a ban on converting or destroying SRO units would do little to remedy the problem of homelessness.

   4. *The homeless and the poor: the debate over rent controls, the implied warranty of habitability, and related measures.* "No one minimizes the tragic reality of homelessness," said the court in *Seawall.* "But the City's response — to foist its responsibility on certain private property owners, by requiring them to remain in the SRO business or ransom their property rights — simply does not meet the requirements of the Federal and State Constitutions." 74 N.Y.2d at 117, 542 N.E.2d at 1071-1072, 544 N.Y.S.2d at 555.

   Contrast the sentiments reflected in this statement to those expressed by Judge Wright in the letter quoted in footnote 63 on page 548. The statement and the letter alike acknowledge the plight of the poor. They differ, however, on the question of accountability and on the efficacy of various remedies. Judge Wright held landlords responsible, whereas the court in *Seawall* sees them as scapegoats. And Judge Wright thought that reforms like the implied warranty of habitability could make matters better, whereas the court in *Seawall* thinks otherwise. Which of these outlooks is, in its various respects, right? Begin your thinking on the question by considering the following case.

Chicago Board of Realtors, Inc. v. City of Chicago
United States Court of Appeals, Seventh Circuit, 1987
819 F.2d 732

[In 1986 the Chicago City Council enacted a Residential Landlord and Tenant Ordinance. The ordinance was not a rent control measure; rather, it essentially codified the implied warranty of habitability and, beyond that, established new landlord responsibilities and tenant rights in respects described below. A group of property owners challenged the constitutionality of the ordinance, arguing that it violated the contracts clause, procedural and substantive due process, void-for-vagueness doctrine, equal protection, the takings clause, and the commerce clause. The district court denied a motion for a preliminary injunction, concluding that the plaintiff property owners did not have a reasonable like-lihood of prevailing on the merits.

The plaintiffs appealed, contesting the district courts' ruling with respect to all but the takings and commerce clause issues. The court of appeals affirmed in an opinion by Cudahy, J., holding, among other things, that the ordinance was sufficiently specific and — giving due deference to the legislative judgment — sufficiently reasonable in light of its stated purpose to promote public health, safety, and welfare.

Of interest to us here is not the constitutional analysis in Judge Cudahy's opinion but the policy analysis in a separate opinion filed in the case, an opinion that moved Judge Cudahy to say: "the economic critique of the Ordinance contained in the separate opinion has not been litigated here and is, at best, superfluous." 819 F.2d at 737 n.2. That "critique" follows.]

POSNER, J., with whom EASTERBROOK, J., joins. We agree with Judge Cudahy's opinion as far as it goes, and we therefore join it. But in our view it does not go far enough. It makes the rejection of the appeal seem easier than it is, by refusing to acknowledge the strong case that can be made for the unreasonableness of the ordinance. . . . So we are led to write separately, and since this separate opinion commands the support of two members of this panel, it is also a majority opinion.

The new ordinance rewrites present and future leases of apartments in Chicago to give tenants more legal rights than they would have without the ordinance. It requires the payment of interest on security deposits; requires that those deposits be held in Illinois banks; allows (with some limitations) a tenant to withhold rent in an amount reflecting the cost to him of the landlord's violating a term in the lease; allows a tenant to make minor repairs and subtract the reasonable cost of the repair from his rent; forbids a landlord to charge a tenant more than $10 a month for late payment of rent (regardless of how much is owing); and creates a presumption (albeit rebuttable) that a landlord who seeks to evict a tenant after the tenant has exercised rights conferred by the ordinance is retaliating against the tenant for the exercise of those rights.

The stated purpose of the ordinance is to promote public health, safety, and welfare and the quality of housing in Chicago. It is unlikely that this is the real purpose, and it is not the likely effect. Forbidding landlords to charge interest at market rates on late payment of rent could hardly be thought calculated to improve the health, safety, and welfare of Chicagoans or to improve the quality of the housing stock. But it may have the opposite effect. The initial consequence of the rule will be to reduce the resources that landlords devote to improving the quality of housing, by making the provision of rental housing more costly. Landlords will try to offset the higher cost (in time value of money, less predictable cash flow, and, probably, higher rate of default) by raising rents. To the extent they succeed, tenants will be worse off, or at least no better off. Landlords will also screen applicants more carefully, because the cost of renting to a deadbeat will now be higher; so marginal tenants will find it harder to persuade landlords to rent to them. Those who do find apartments but then are slow to pay will be subsidized by responsible tenants (some of them marginal too), who will be paying higher rents, assuming the landlord cannot determine in advance who is likely to pay rent on time. Insofar as these efforts to offset the ordinance fail, the cost of rental housing will be higher to landlords and therefore less will be supplied — more of the existing stock than would otherwise be the case will be converted to condominia and cooperatives and less rental housing will be built.

The provisions of the ordinance requiring that interest on security deposits be paid and that those deposits be kept in Illinois banks are as remote as the provision on late payment from any concern with the health or safety of Chicagoans, the quality of housing in Chicago, or the welfare of Chicago as a whole. Their only apparent rationale is to transfer wealth from landlords and out-of-state banks to tenants and local banks — making this an unedifying example of class legislation and economic protectionism rolled into one. However, to the extent the ordinance seeks to transfer wealth from landlords to tenants it could readily be undone by a rent increase; the ordinance puts no cap on rents. Cf. Coase, The Problem of Social Cost, 3 J. Law & Econ. 1 (1960).

The provisions that authorize rent withholding, whether directly or by subtracting repair costs, may seem more closely related to the stated objectives of the ordinance; but the relation is tenuous. The right to withhold rent is not limited to cases of hazardous or unhealthy conditions. And any benefits in safer or healthier housing from exercise of the right are likely to be offset by the higher costs to landlords, resulting in higher rents and less rental housing.

The ordinance is not in the interest of poor people. As is frequently the case with legislation ostensibly designed to promote the welfare of the poor, the principal beneficiaries will be middle-class people. They will be people who buy rather than rent housing (the conversion of rental to owner housing will reduce the price of the latter by increasing its supply); people willing to pay a higher rental for better-quality housing; and (a largely overlapping group) more affluent tenants, who will become more attractive to landlords because such tenants are less likely to be late with the rent or to abuse the right of withholding rent — a right that is more attractive, the poorer the tenant. The losers from the ordinance will be some landlords, some out-of-state banks, the poorest class of tenants, and future tenants. The landlords are few in number (once owner-occupied rental housing is excluded — and the ordinance excludes it). Out-of-staters can't vote in Chicago elections. Poor people in our society don't vote as often as the affluent. See Filer, An Economic

Theory of Voter Turnout 81 (Ph.D. thesis, Dept. of Econ., Univ. of Chi., Dec. 1977); Statistical Abstract of the U.S., 1982-83, at pp.492-93 (tabs. 805, 806). And future tenants are a diffuse and largely unknown class. In contrast, the beneficiaries of the ordinance are the most influential group in the city's population. So the politics of the ordinance are plain enough, cf. DeCanio, Rent Control Voting Patterns, Popular Views, and Group Interests, in Resolving the Housing Crisis 301, 311-12 (Johnson ed. 1982), and they have nothing to do with either improving the allocation of resources to housing or bringing about a more equal distribution of income and wealth.

A growing body of empirical literature deals with the effects of governmental regulation of the market for rental housing. The regulations that have been studied, such as rent control in New York City and Los Angeles, are not identical to the new Chicago ordinance, though some — regulations which require that rental housing be "habitable" — are close. The significance of this literature is not in proving that the Chicago ordinance is unsound, but in showing that the market for rental housing behaves as economic theory predicts: if price is artificially depressed, or the costs of landlords artificially increased, supply falls and many tenants, usually the poorer and the newer tenants, are hurt. See e.g., Olsen, An Econometric Analysis of Rent Control, 80 J. Pol. Econ. 1081 (1972); Rydell et al., The Impact of Rent Control on the Los Angeles Housing Market, ch. 6 (Rand Corp. N-1747-LA, Aug. 1981); Hirsch, Habitability Laws and the Welfare of Indigent Tenants, 61 Rev. Econ. & Stat. 263 (1981). The single proposition in economics from which there is the least dissent among American economists is that "a ceiling on rents reduces the quantity and quality of housing available." Frey et al., Consensus and Dissension Among Economists: An Empirical Inquiry, 74 Am. Econ. Rev. 986, 991 (1984) (tab. 2). . . .

NOTE: THE DEBATE OVER LANDLORD-TENANT REFORMS

Judges Posner and Easterbrook chide Judge Cudahy for making things seem easier than they are, but one might say the same of these two former law professors (both were full-time faculty members at the University of Chicago before they became judges). To be sure, many people who have studied the matter agree with their views on such measures as the Chicago ordinance, or the implied warranty of habitability, or rent controls (notice that Posner and Easterbrook question all of these on essentially the same grounds). On the other hand, many other people disagree. Unhappily for the student, though, the vast literature bearing on the debate — a literature that we merely sample here — is unlikely to lead a disinterested observer to firm conclusions one way or the other.

Rent controls. Posner and Easterbrook pretty much capture the case against rent controls.[69] Virtually all economists, as they point out right at the end of their analysis, regard them as counterproductive. Virtually all *American* economists, that is. Fewer than 2 percent of them dissented from the proposition stated by Posner and Easterbrook. But almost 44 percent of French economists did, along with almost 20 percent of Swiss economists and 11 percent of Austrian economists, down to 6 percent of German economists. See page 991 (table 2) of the article by Frey et al. cited by Posner and Easterbrook.

A thoroughgoing study of rent controls, published by the Urban Land Institute, is Anthony Downs, Residential Rent Controls: An Evaluation (1988). Among Downs's principal conclusions are these:

> As a general rule, residential rent regulation makes economic sense if, and only if, two conditions occur simultaneously in the market and are both expected to last for some time. Demand for rental units must rise sharply at the same time that new construction of such units has been legally restricted in order to conserve resources — as during wartime. In the absence of these conditions, rent controls are neither an appropriate nor an effective response to perceived housing shortages. On the contrary, they generally exacerbate such shortages. . . .
>
> As a general rule, the more an ordinance intrudes upon the market conditions that would otherwise prevail, the more likely it is to cause dislocations in a housing market. Conversely, less intrusive rent regulations appear to cause less severe dislocations. . . .
>
> . . . Much evidence indicates that all rent controls, even temperate controls, transfer income from owners to tenants or between various classes of tenants. In addition, many of the short-term benefits of rent controls (reduced rents) aid affluent rather than poor households, and some of the costs (reduced access to vacant units) must be borne by very poor households. Where rent is eliminated as a basis for distinguishing among potential tenants, owners often use other factors such as credit-worthiness, race, sex, or ethnicity in allocating scarce rental units — even though most such discrimination is illegal. [Id. at 1-2.][70]

69. *Famous people in the rent control news.* If anybody is opposed to rent controls, it would have to be Robert Nozick, whose Anarchy, State, and Utopia (1974), winner of the National Book Award, "mocked the economic interventionism of contemporary liberals who, he said, are 'willing to tolerate every kind of behavior except capitalistic acts between consenting adults.' Alas, it now appears that like so many other advocates of the free market, Nozick is willing to make one small exception — himself." William Tucker, Anarchy, State, and Rent Control, New Republic, Dec. 22, 1986, at 20. Tucker goes on to describe the travail of Eric (Love Story) Segal as he tried to oust his tenant Nozick from the rent controlled apartment Segal owned in Cambridge, Massachusetts. Nozick had a strong position under Cambridge's strict rent control ordinance, and he (and, we presume, his lawyers) defended it successfully. He finally departed when Segal paid him $31,000.

70. "The conclusion of this study," Downs adds, "is that the social and economic costs and disadvantages of rent controls — especially over the long run — almost always outweigh any perceived short-term benefits they provide, in the absence of the two justifying conditions described earlier." Id. at 2.

On rent control and discrimination, a point mentioned by Downs, see also James A. Kushner, The Fair Housing Amendments Act of 1988: The Second Generation of Fair Housing, 42 Vand. L. Rev. 1049, 1056 (1989): "In a very tight, rent-controlled rental

Defenders of rent control respond to such conclusions in two different ways, arguing either that they are unreliable or largely irrelevant. An example of the first approach is John I. Gilderbloom & Richard P. Appelbaum, Rethinking Rental Housing (1988). Finding "little research that systematically examines the differences between restrictive, moderate, and strong rent controls in cities across the United States," the authors undertook "a comprehensive review of studies by economists, political scientists, planners, and sociologists. Such a review suggests that neither moderate nor strong forms of control have caused a decline in either the quality or supply of the rental stock. Although such findings do not, of course, prove that rent controls are without deleterious effect, they provide no warrant for drawing the conventional conclusions." Id. at 134. They add: "Rent control has *not,* however, brought average rents down to affordable levels." Id. at 149. See also Note, Reassessing Rent Control: Its Economic Impact in a Gentrifying Housing Market, 101 Harv. L. Rev. 1835 (1988) (arguing that the conclusions of economists about rent controls have little application to gentrifying markets; and that controls in such markets will not lead to abandonment, conversion, inadequate maintenance, or a decrease in future construction, but will reduce the social costs of poverty by increasing the supply of low-income housing).

An example of the second approach is Margaret J. Radin, Residential Rent Control, 15 Phil. & Pub. Affairs 350 (1986), who wonders whether economists have overlooked important nonutilitarian considerations that might "trump" the conventional analysis. Radin knows that existing tenants are usually the primary beneficiaries of most rent controls, but perhaps that's the whole point: Rent controls "make it possible for existing tenants to stay where they are, with roughly the same proportion of their income going to rent as they have become used to," a result that might be more justified in some circumstances than in others. From a moral point of view, then, judgments about rent controls must turn very much on context. Id. at 352-353. They might be justified in the easy case where a landlord is earning monopoly rents, for example, but not where the landlord lives on the premises and rents a portion to commercial tenants or transients who are not maintaining a home. (The home counts for much in Radin's analysis.) See also Mark Kelman, On Democracy-Bashing: A Skeptical Look at the Theoretical and "Empirical" Practice of the Public Choice Movement, 74 Va. L. Rev. 199, 271-273 (1988) (rent control and community); William H. Simon, Social-Republican Property, 38 UCLA L. Rev. 1355, 1361 (1991) ("the social-

---

market, landlords may be successful in renting solely through word of mouth advertising and referrals by current tenants or relatives — a scheme that carries extreme discriminatory impact."

republican argument sees rent control as protecting against loss of membership in the community").

For more on the rent control debate generally, see Symposium, Rent Control and the Theory of Efficient Regulation, 54 Brooklyn L. Rev. 727-780 (1988), and Responses [to the Symposium], 54 Brooklyn L. Rev. 1215-1304 (1989).

The implied warranty of habitability. The debate here is much the same as the rent control debate, in virtually every respect. A very large literature examines the warranty and related reforms (illegal lease doctrine, prohibition of retaliatory evictions) and reaches conclusions similar to — and mixed like — the conclusions regarding rent controls. See, for example, the review of the theoretical and empirical literature in Roger A. Cunningham, The New Implied and Statutory Warranties of Habitability in Residential Leases: From Contract to Status, 16 Urb. L. Ann. 3 (1979). Subsequent research has not changed matters. Thus there are arguments that the reforms are beneficial, from the standpoint of low-income tenants, under various circumstances. See, e.g., Duncan Kennedy, The Effect of the Warranty of Habitability on Low Income Housing: "Milking" and Class Violence, 15 Fla. St. U. L. Rev. 484 (1987) (selective enforcement of the implied warranty could increase supply more than it decreases it, thus reducing rent levels for poor tenants). But, again, there are responses questioning the assumptions of the pro-reform literature. See, e.g., Richard A. Posner, Economic Analysis of Law 470-474 (4th ed. 1992). By the same token, there is, as with Radin's contribution to the rent control debate, a normative or moral argument on behalf of tenant reforms. See, e.g., Joseph W. Singer, The Reliance Interest in Property, 40 Stan. L. Rev. 614, 659-663, 679-684 (1988). Yet others believe that the moral argument wrongly blames landlords for, and burdens them with, a social problem that is not of their making. This view was suggested by the court in *Seawall*. See the beginning of Note 4 on page 559.

Homelessness. It would be surprising to find that the problem of homelessness is any less a muddle than the matters considered above. Homelessness is a newer problem — at least, it is perceived to be — and so our understanding of it is unlikely to surpass our (limited) insights into rent controls or landlord-tenant reforms. This follows especially to the degree that homelessness is a product of our hotly debated approach to housing markets generally. So there are no surprises. Homelessness is as contentious a subject as the others. There is, in a few words, marked disagreement about the size and characteristics of the homeless population,[71] about the causes of the problem (partly rent controls, in the view

71. These matters are discussed in Robert C. Ellickson, The Homelessness Muddle, Pub. Interest, Spring 1990, at 45. Estimates of the size of the homeless population range from about 250,000 to about 4 million as of the late 1980s. Id. at 52-53.

of some),[72] about its cures (partly rent controls, in the view of others).[73] For a quick, hardheaded survey, see Robert C. Ellickson, cited in footnote 71. Book length studies include Martha R. Burt, Over the Edge: The Growth of Homelessness in the 1980s (1992); Peter H. Rossi, Down and Out in America: The Origins of Homelessness (1989); Housing the Homeless (Jon Erickson & Charles Wilhelm eds. 1986). For two recent law review symposia on the subject, see Homelessness: Problems and Solutions, 36 Vill. L. Rev. 1019-1149 (1991); Law and the Homeless, 45 U. Miami L. Rev. 261-736 (1990-1991).

2. Government-Assisted Housing Programs

Whatever the merits of the debates sketched above, it might well be that decent housing is simply beyond the reach of the poor, absent government financial support. But government support can take a number of forms: *project subsidies* tied to specific dwellings (in other words, traditional public housing — if the recipient leaves the subsidized dwelling, the subsidy is forgone); *housing allowances* distributed according to need and to be spent for housing only — the money is tied not to dwellings but to recipients, who may take the subsidy with them when they move; *income maintenance programs* involving unrestricted cash payments to needy recipients, who may spend the money as they wish. See Report of the President's Committee on Urban Housing, A Decent Home 71 (1968).

The following reading considers American low-income housing policy in terms of these alternatives. It provides an introduction, but little more, and we have to be satisfied with that. The general subject (including the related problem of homelessness) deserves a course of its own.

Michael H. Schill, Privatizing Federal Low Income Housing Assistance: The Case of Public Housing*
75 Cornell L. Rev. 878, 890-900, 948 (1990)

If, as most analysts agree, the major housing problem facing low income households today is one of affordability, why do public policymakers

---

72. See, e.g., William Tucker, Where Do the Homeless Come From?, Nat. Rev., Sept. 25, 1987, at 32, 43: "Truly widespread homelessness does not occur . . . until a city imposes rent control."

73. See, e.g., Note, Reassessing Rent Control, supra, at 1855: "Rent Control will reduce the social costs associated with poverty and homelessness" in rapidly gentrifying markets.

treat the difficulties faced by low income renters as housing problems rather than as problems of income distribution? If the problems faced by these households could be solved by increased income, why not provide low income households with unrestricted income supplements rather than subsidies earmarked for housing expenditure? If the market for housing were free of market imperfections, and the only housing problem of low income households was affordability, elementary welfare economics would indicate that an unrestricted income supplement such as a negative income tax would be the most efficient policy. Earmarked subsidies and in-kind redistribution are generally considered to be inefficient, since many households would not, if left to their own choices, spend each additional dollar of income on a dollar's worth of housing consumption. Instead, households would typically choose to spend only a portion of the increased income on housing and the remainder on other consumption items such as food and clothing. By providing low income households with in-kind assistance, the public sector's expenditure presumably results in less overall utility than would an unrestricted transfer payment.

The housing market, however, is not free from market imperfections and artificial constraints on supply. Tying public subsidies to housing is justified in circumstances where they can be utilized efficiently to overcome these market failures and constraints. Although most economists believe that housing markets are generally competitive with a large number of actual and potential consumers and sellers, absent government intervention, the housing market may fail to generate an optimal amount of housing. The supply of housing, although quite elastic in the long run, is relatively inelastic in the short run because of the length of time required for site selection, financing and construction. In addition, government regulation impedes the supply of housing, especially for low income households. Zoning and land use regulations, health and safety ordinances, as well as rent control and security of tenure laws, may restrict the supply of housing. Furthermore, discrimination against minorities in the housing market might limit their ability to purchase housing in certain neighborhoods.

Public intervention in the housing market may also be justified by the problem of substandard housing. Deteriorated housing sometimes poses an externality problem. The existence of a dilapidated structure can reduce the value of neighboring homes and may lead to disinvestment in the neighborhood. Because the owner of the deteriorated structure does not have to bear all of the costs generated by his or her property, public intervention such as slum clearance or renovation assistance might be appropriate. In much the same way that a deteriorated building might be considered a negative externality, a high quality building might be a positive externality or public good. The existence of such a structure might increase values and confidence in the community. Private entrepreneurs might avoid making the investment since they would receive only a portion of its benefit, with nearby owners free-riding on the remainder.

Another justification for government intervention in the housing market, as opposed to pure income assistance, is based on noneconomic factors. As Tobin has noted, although Americans typically accept inequality in most aspects of life, there is a rough consensus that "certain specific scarce commodities should be distributed less unequally than the ability to pay for them."[74] Society may be justified in preferring a minimum entitlement to housing, despite the desires of the recipient, for several reasons. People who prefer other goods and services to a minimum level of shelter may lack sufficient information or be unable to assess rationally the true worth of decent housing, thereby justifying societal paternalism. Furthermore, especially in light of the increasing number of children born to unmarried, teenage parents, efforts to provide a minimum level of housing consumption may be justified as necessary to protect those who do not themselves have the power to make expenditure decisions. In addition, the knowledge that people are not living in desperately deteriorated and unhealthful accommodations may itself bring taxpayers positive utility and therefore serve as a consumption item for the donors rather than the donees.

Public Housing and Housing Policy

The argument that government programs to provide housing assistance to lower income households are justified on grounds of market failure, supply constraints or societal consensus does not lead to a simple answer to the question of how that assistance should be designed. Typically, housing policies are characterized as either supply- or demand-oriented. Programs in which the government supports the construction of new dwellings, either by building them itself or by subsidizing developers, are enacted to directly increase the supply of housing. Programs that provide the recipients of assistance with the funds to purchase housing services increase the demand for housing, and indirectly, its supply. In this section, I describe and compare public housing, a supply-oriented program, with housing certificates and allowances, a demand-oriented subsidy. I contend that in the future, the public sector should primarily subsidize demand, leaving the construction of additional housing to the private sector. Nevertheless, construction of public housing may be de-

74. James Tobin, On Limiting the Domain of Inequality, 13 J.L. & Econ. 263, 264 (1970). Tobin calls this norm "specific egalitarianism." See id. The concept of specific egalitarianism is closely related to the concept of "merit goods" which is used to describe commodities that should be provided by the public sector even if market actors do not demand them. See Richard A. Musgrave, The Theory of Public Finance 13 (1959) (subsidized housing is a "merit want").

sirable under certain market conditions, including those markets subject to artificial entry barriers and discrimination.

A Short History of Public Housing

Since the mid-1930s, the federal government has funded the construction of housing for low income households. New Deal agencies such as the Public Works Administration bought land, cleared slums and built almost 22,000 housing units. Direct federal provision of housing was initially dealt a blow in 1935 when a federal appeals court upheld a lower court ruling that the federal government could not use its power of eminent domain to condemn sites for housing projects because housing was not a "public purpose." In 1937, however, Congress passed the Wagner-Steagall Housing Act of 1937, establishing the public housing program. Under the Act, public housing would be built by local public housing authorities ("PHAs") rather than by the federal government. In addition to concerns of comity, the program utilized PHAs because several state courts had held that cities and states had the power to condemn property for housing. Under the program, a PHA and the federal government execute an Annual Contributions Contract ("ACC") which sets forth the parties' rights and obligations. The PHA funds the purchase of land and the construction of housing by issuing long term bonds, typically with a forty-year maturity. The federal government undertakes an obligation to make all debt service payments on the bonds, effectively subsidizing all capital costs. The PHA, in turn, obligates itself to operate the public housing in a manner consistent with federal statutes and regulations during the term of the ACC. The municipality in which the project is located is required to grant an exemption from real property taxes for the housing development. Unlike housing built by the Public Works Administration, public housing was, from the start, limited to low income households. Due to the onset of World War II, only a modest number of units were built under the 1937 Housing Act. In 1949, however, Congress passed the Housing Act of 1949 which provided federal subsidies for slum clearance and urban redevelopment. As part of the Act, Congress authorized the construction of an additional 810,000 public housing units and established the national housing policy of "[a] decent home and a suitable living environment for every American family. . . ." It was not until 1972, however, that all of the housing units authorized by the 1949 Act were actually completed. Today, approximately 1.3 million units of public housing exist in the United States.

From its inception, public housing was controversial. In the 1930s, the private real estate lobby alleged that the program was socialistic and wasteful. Projects were frequently segregated by race and built in less desirable neighborhoods where their presence would not be "offensive" to community residents. Public housing was originally created for temporary occupancy by the "submerged middle class." As soon as residents could get themselves on their feet, they were expected to move elsewhere. During the 1950s, however, the socioeconomic character of public housing changed. Federal government policies and programs such as mortgage insurance, tax preferences for homeownership and highway construction subsidized the movement of middle and moderate income households out of the city to the suburbs. At roughly the same time, black migration from the South to northern cities accelerated. As manufacturing jobs followed the migration of households to suburban locations, central cities increasingly became home to low income and black households. Public housing no longer served as a temporary haven for upwardly mobile households, but instead became a permanent home to a very poor and disproportionately nonwhite population.

As the income of public housing residents plummeted and the age of public housing projects increased, the rents charged by PHAs to cover operating expenses became increasingly burdensome. Some PHAs deferred maintenance due to shortages of funds. In 1969, Congress's action to assist tenants by limiting maximum rents chargeable by PHAs further added to PHA burdens. The federal government enacted subsidy programs to help PHAs pay for operating and modernization expenses. Neither of these subsidies, however, was fully funded, and many PHAs further cut back on maintenance which led to structural deterioration and, in some extreme cases, the demolition of uninhabitable buildings.

Public Housing Today

At present, there are over 1.3 million units of public housing in the United States, housing 3.5 million people. Public housing constitutes 1.5% of the nation's housing stock. The average annual income of households is $6,539. Approximately 60% of nonelderly resident households have no one employed and half receive Aid to Families with Dependent Children. Thirty-eight percent of such households are composed of elderly persons. Data from a 1986 survey of PHAs indicate that 60% of all families in public housing are headed by blacks and an additional 24% by hispanics.

Over one-half of public housing developments are comprised of single family homes or garden apartments. In addition, one quarter of all units are located in suburban locations. Although several public housing developments have serious structural and social problems, most studies indicate that public housing is in much better condition than its popular image would indicate. A 1980 study of the physical condition of public housing commissioned by the federal government concluded that while the vast majority of the housing stock was in good condition, seven and two-fifths percent of all units had "chronic problems." Another study that examined social, financial, managerial and physical problems concluded that only fifteen percent of all public housing units were troubled. Furthermore, surveys indicate that residents of public housing are quite satisfied with their living conditions, and that most public housing authorities have extremely long waiting lists.

The Future Role of Public Housing in Federal Housing Assistance

Public housing is only one of several housing programs enacted by the federal government to assist low income households. Since the mid-1970s, the government has increasingly relied on the private sector to deliver housing assistance. One supply-oriented approach initiated by the federal government in 1974 is called the Section 8 New Construction and Substantial Rehabilitation Program. Under this program, the government subsidizes the rents of tenants who live in new or substantially renovated structures owned by non-profit or profit-motivated developers. The subsidy, which is tied to the units in these structures, is guaranteed for a period of twenty to forty years and covers the difference between the amount paid by the tenants (usually thirty percent of adjusted income) and a fair market rent based upon the developer's capital and operating costs. In 1974, Congress also enacted one of a series of demand-oriented subsidy programs called the Section 8 Existing Housing Certificate Program. Under this program, participating households are issued a certificate that enables them to rent dwellings owned by private landlords. Provided that they lease homes that meet minimum quality standards and that do not cost more than the federally prescribed maximum level, households participating in the Section 8 Existing Housing Certificate Program must pay no more than thirty percent of their income for rent. The difference between thirty percent of income and the dwelling's rent is paid for by the federal government. . . .

. . . [A]lthough future federal housing assistance for low income households should rely to a greater extent on the private sector for *delivery* of services, that does not mean that the federal government should cut back its role in financing such assistance or abandon its already sizable investment in public housing. To the contrary, there remains a need for the public sector to assist low income households in obtaining adequate and affordable housing. By using the private sector to deliver these housing services, it is likely that the greatest number of households can be assisted for a given level of federal expenditure. There will remain for the foreseeable future, however, a role in American housing policy for publicly owned rental housing, especially in those circumstances where artificial constraints on supply or housing discrimination exist.

QUESTION

Given the debate about the implied warranty of habitability (see page 565), what do you make of a case refusing to extend the full reach of state law on the warranty to public housing? See Conille v. Secretary of Hous. and Urban Dev., 840 F.2d 105 (1st Cir. 1988). In the event of a breach, the court held, tenants may seek restitution of rental payments but not consequential damages.

> The imposition of consequential damages upon the Secretary in this case could potentially impede the realization of the overall purpose of the NHA: the upgrading of national housing. . . . To impose upon the Secretary a consequential damages penalty for breaching duties implied under leases with his tenants would expose the federal government to unpredictable costs. This would frustrate Congress's considered judgment to allocate scarce financial resources to improve the overall quality of the nation's housing stock. We therefore cannot impose a damages remedy against the Secretary under Massachusetts law without interfering with federal purposes underlying the national housing program. [840 F.2d at 113-114.]

See generally Note, The Incorporation of the Implied Warranty of Habitability in Public Housing Programs, 38 Wash. U. J. Urb. & Contemp. L. 205 (1990).

IV
Transfers of Land

By now you should understand the premium that the legal system puts on alienability, on the easy transfer and exchange of property rights. Generally speaking, free and voluntary exchange permits resources, land included, to move to higher valued uses. But "free" here means unfettered, not costless. Exchange is never costless because it takes place in a world full of friction and imperfect information. Transferors and transferees must search out mutually beneficial opportunities for exchange, must negotiate and enforce agreements, must confront risk and uncertainty, must obtain and secure that elusive thing called "title." Presumably, the law strives to reduce these burdens — these transaction costs — but how well it succeeds is a matter of dispute, in the case of land transfers in particular. There is little question that the cost (including time expended) of transferring land ownership is greater per dollar value than the cost of transferring ownership of stocks or automobiles or diamond rings. Why?

The reasons should become apparent in the next two chapters, which focus on inter vivos transfers of land. A comprehensive survey would include transfers at death as well, but transfers at death involve the application of a separate body of doctrines taught in advanced courses in decedents' estates. Thus they are largely excluded here. So are involuntary transfers, already considered in Part I's study of conquest and adverse possession, and to be considered again in Part V's examination of zoning and the "taking" of property by government action.

7

The Land Transaction

A. Introduction

John C. Payne, A Typical House Purchase Transaction in the United States
30 Conv. (n.s.) 194, 199-211 (1966)

Normally, the *first* step in a house-buying venture is to consult a real estate agent. He will know what property is for sale in the local market and what price is being asked. Then will follow the conventional searching and haggling, culminating in a parol understanding as to the amount of the purchase price (frequently expressed merely in terms of the amount of the required down payment and the anticipated monthly mortgage amortization payments) and the time when occupancy can be given.

Second: At this point the reasonable and prudent buyer will employ his own attorney to draft a proper contract and steer him through the legal and financial shoals which lie ahead. He will know that the contract he is about to sign will have predominate influence upon what is to follow and should clearly and explicitly express the rights and responsibilities of both parties. As a matter of fact it is much more probable that the buyer is somewhat unreasonable and not very prudent, and will, instead, sign a printed form supplied by the real estate agent. In this he will be flying in the face of fortune and may suffer bitter regrets when he finds that the contract holds him to a bad bargain, does not express the intention of the parties or is unenforceable for indefiniteness. But sign it he will, for the American lay public is not yet convinced that a lawyer is needed at this juncture[1] and prefers to thrust itself into the hands of the real

1. . . . The practice of real estate agents assisting the parties in drafting instruments is of long standing in this country and stems originally from primitive conditions which existed in a pioneer community. It continues today because the average layman does not want to spend money for a lawyer and because the real estate agents would prefer not to have a lawyer in the transaction. The agents have the impression that they are not entitled to their fee until some sort of an agreement is signed and they are

estate agent. This is somewhat anomalous, for certainly the reputation of these agents is not above reproach and obviously they are the creatures of the seller. . . .

Third: . . . [After agreement is reached on the purchase price, the buyer expects to pay down a certain percentage of the purchase price and expects] to obtain the remainder of the purchase price by giving a mortgage. The loan will be liquidated by level monthly payments, covering principal and interest, over a period of approximately thirty years. . . .

After he has signed the contract, the buyer will require two things, credit and the assurance that the seller has a good title to convey. These two needs are closely linked for, if a mortgage is to be given, the mortgagee will also demand proof of title. It is entirely possible that the buyer will now himself solicit credit directly from some lender and that he may also employ his own attorney for the purpose of protecting his interests. However, this would not be the typical transaction which we are now describing. Instead, at some point in the negotiations he will have been assured by the real estate agent that he, the agent, will "take care of everything," including all details as to the loan, drafting of instruments, and closing, and that the buyer will have nothing to do except come to a designated office at an appropriate time and sign the necessary papers. This offer will have been accepted with alacrity, as the buyer at that point was uncertain as to how he should proceed and wanted, above all, to avoid any unnecessary trouble. If this arrangement is to proceed, however, he will now have to sign an application for a mortgage and make a deposit sufficient to cover all anticipated closing costs.

Fourth: Prior to this time the real estate agent will have obtained some sort of informal commitment for the necessary loan. Since credit is the lifeblood of the real estate market, every agent must be in a position to assist buyers in obtaining financing. This results in close relations between lending institutions and the realtors. This relation may range from ad hoc negotiation in each transaction to something like organic union, but there are few, if any, substantial real estate firms which cannot offer this service. In the case we are now considering, since credit has already been promised, the agent will forward the application for the loan to the lending institution. There it will be processed to determine whether the borrower is a good risk and a credit report will be obtained. An appraisal will also be ordered. The lender will then begin the preparation of the necessary papers for an F.H.A. application and,

---

eager to close a contract as quickly as possible. The time of agreement may be a very inconvenient one in so far as obtaining legal assistance is concerned and, as one judge said, you cannot expect a real estate agent to carry a lawyer around in his hip pocket. Furthermore, the agents have an idea that lawyers tend to disrupt sales by making objections of one kind or another.

simultaneously, will notify its attorney that an investigation of title will be required.

Fifth: With the investigation of title comes the most involved and time-consuming part of the transfer process. Three principal types of title assurance, each exclusive of the other, are used. None of these can be understood, however, without some preliminary grasp of the American recording system and the theories of title which have depended upon it. Unlike the mother country, the American colonist from the very beginning rejected the system of proof by muniments of title and, instead, provided for registration of assurances. The American recording statutes ordinarily provide that all documents relating to land titles may be recorded in the county courthouses. There they are entered seriatim and *in extenso* in large folio volumes. These records are open to public inspection and access to the contents is made possible through name (and sometimes tract) indices. Registration is voluntary, but a failure to register may result in an innocent purchaser for value obtaining priority. As a consequence, registration is almost universal . . . [and] we deduce title from the documents found in the courthouse. This is done by starting with the present owner and, using the indirect or grantee index, taking a "chain of title" back to a grant from the sovereign.[2] The title is then "back tracked" through the indices to determine whether any adverse interests have been created. Tracing title back to the state is, in conventional American theory, the only way in which a good marketable title can be established. However, as in some of the older sections of the country the original grants are found more than three centuries ago, it is no longer practical in these areas to make a full search of title and searches are limited to some conventional period, say sixty years. The system which I have described involves a direct search of the records by the examining attorney and culminates in the attorney giving his client a written statement, called a "certificate of title," to the effect that he has made the examination and that, on the basis of what he has found, the fee simple is vested in the vendor free and clear of any encumbrances other than those noted as exceptions. This system of direct examination still prevails in some places but is excessively laborious because the books

2. Sources of title in the United States ordinarily fall under three headings: (1) In the original 13 states and in some other areas titles in most part depend upon colonial grants made by the English, Spanish and French crowns. (2) Land not granted by the Crown and located in the original thirteen states became the property of the state governments following the Revolution, and thereafter the source of title was a state grant. In Texas, which was a sovereign state following the revolt from Mexican rule, title to ungranted land also vested in the state. (3) In most of the country title to land is derived from the federal government. Following the Revolution the several states ceded their title to their "western lands" to the federal government and it thereafter acquired title with each new accession of territory. When new states were set up they acquired "sovereignty" over these lands but title remained in the federal government.

which must be examined are quite numerous and unwieldy and indices are so primitive that most of the examiner's time must be spent in separating the relevant from the irrelevant. These objections have led to its being superseded in many areas by the system of examining abstracts.

Where abstracts are used a lay individual or corporation makes a "take-off," or copy of all of the public records, and then re-indexes them so as to make the contents readily available. This constitutes the "title plant." When an abstract is ordered the abstractor assembles all of the pertinent records, and abstracts or abbreviates their content.[3] He then "certifies" this abstract on its face as containing a reference to all instruments of record pertaining to the particular title and sells it to the purchaser of the abstract. It is then examined by an attorney, who certifies the title to his client in the same fashion as the attorney who has made a direct examination. Once the abstract has been prepared, it is passed down from seller to buyer, being merely brought up to date by addenda at the time of each transfer. . . .

Whether the title is established by direct search or by the examination of an abstract, the attorney for the vendee or mortgagee may demand, as additional security, that a certificate of title insurance be obtained from a national company. This kind of insurance is issued by a corporate insurer on the basis of a certificate furnished to it by the local attorney. It has three principal advantages — the substitution of contract for tort liability, the replacement of a mortal individual assurer by an immortal corporation and some additional protection against defects of title not appearing on the record. It simply supplements other modes of title assurance, at somewhat greater cost, and does not interfere with the conventional relationship between attorney and client.

The third major method of establishing title is by local title insurance. A company issuing this kind of a policy maintains a title plant substantially like that of the abstractor. When a title policy is ordered it assembles its records and then makes an examination by its own salaried staff. On the basis of this examination it issues a policy and this policy is used by the vendee or mortgagee in lieu of the conventional attorney's certificate. This form of insurance, then, displaces the independent attorney from the principal work in the title transaction and local title companies are in direct competition with the Bar.

I have described above the three basic forms of establishing title, and, obviously, all three are not employed simultaneously. Despite the very great expansion of local title insurance during the post-Second

---

3. An abstract of a deed, for example, will give the names of the grantor and grantee, the date of execution and recording, an exact description of the property, the consideration recited, the names of the attesting witnesses and the person before whom probate or acknowledgment were taken. It will also show whether a spouse joined in the instrument, whether the estate was limited, whether the deed contained a warranty and whether any restrictive covenants or conditions were recited.

World War period, especially in large urban areas, it is probable that the abstract system is still the most prevalent in the United States and I will, for that reason, assume its use in the typical house-buying transaction. When the mortgagee's attorney has been instructed to prepare for closing, his first step will be to get in touch with the vendor and arrange to have the abstract brought up to date. When he has received the abstract from the abstract company he will examine it and make an informal judgment as to whether curative action is required. If such action is needed, he will notify the vendor what his requirements are. Thereafter, if the vendor fails to take proper curative action, the attorney may advise his client to refuse to complete the contract. We will assume in this case, however, that the title is acceptable. . . . When he has before him the accepted abstract . . . he will then make an application for a title insurance "binder." As soon as the binder is received he will notify the mortgagee to set a date for closing and will then prepare a note (or bond) and mortgage for execution by the mortgagor. If he has been requested to do so by the vendor, he will also prepare a deed. In addition, either he or the mortgagee will prepare a closing statement.[4]

Sixth: The function of the closing is to bring all interested parties together and to permit them to execute and deliver the necessary documents simultaneously with the payment of the purchase price and the settlement of the costs of the transactions. The latter are conventionally known as closing costs, although they are generally incurred prior to the time when the closing actually takes place. A closing may be held at any convenient place — the office of the mortgagee's attorney, mortgagee's place of business, real estate agent's office or elsewhere. When the parties have assembled it is first customary to check the closing statement. The vendor (and [spouse], if necessary) will then execute the deed and will receive the adjusted purchase price by cheque drawn by the mortgagee. At the same time the vendee (and [spouse], if necessary) will execute the bond (or note) and mortgage. He will then or later receive a cheque for any amount he has paid to the mortgagee in excess of the actual closing charges.

---

4. The closing statement is got up to show the allocation of various charges to the several parties. The vendor is entitled to receive the amount of the purchase price, less the down payment, the cost of drawing the deed (unless he has had the deed drawn by his own attorney), the cost of revenue stamps placed on the deed, and the commission to be paid the real estate agent. As taxes . . . are assessed at the beginning of the year but paid at the end, he will also have to pay a pro rata part of the unpaid assessment. He may be entitled to receive from the vendee, in addition to the purchase price, the value of chattels left on the premises and sold to the vendee, such as rugs, coal, blinds, stoves and the like. If he should have a tenant in the house and the closing takes place at a time other than the rent day, he will have to account for rent paid in advance beyond the time of closing. The vendee-mortgagor will have to pay the remaining costs and, if the mortgagee agrees to take care of the details of fire insurance and taxes, the mortgagor will have to make payment in advance for these items. No particular form is required for a closing statement. It may be written on the back of an old envelope or may be a highly complex document.

Seventh: Following the closing the mortgagee's attorney will send the deed and mortgage to the courthouse for the attachment of revenue stamps and recording and will pay the necessary fees. When the instruments are returned from the courthouse he will send the deed to the vendee and the abstract, mortgage, note (or bond) and a certificate of title to the mortgagee. In the meantime he will have sent to the title insurance company a final certificate of title and an application for a mortgagee policy. His certificate will show that title is vested in the mortgagor and that the mortgage is a valid first lien against the property. When the policy is issued it will be sent by the company to the mortgagee. . . .

The vendee now has title, subject to the mortgage, and presumably is in possession. The transfer is completed, except for the repayment of the loan, and the work of the conveyancer is ended.

State v. Buyers Service Co.

Supreme Court of South Carolina, 1987
292 S.C. 426, 357 S.E.2d 15

PER CURIAM: In this action the circuit court issued a declaratory judgment that Buyers Service Company, Inc. (Buyers Service) has illegally engaged in the practice of law. Additionally, Buyers Service was enjoined from performing future acts deemed to constitute the practice of law. We affirm in part and reverse in part.

Facts

Buyers Service is a commercial title company which also assists homeowners in purchasing residential real estate. Its principal place of business is Hilton Head Island.

The State brought this action alleging Buyers Service has engaged in the unauthorized practice of law by: (1) providing reports, opinions or certificates as to the status of titles to real estate and mortgage liens; (2) preparing documents affecting title to real property; (3) handling real estate closings; (4) recording legal documents at the courthouse; and (5) advertising to the public that it may handle conveyancing and real estate closings.

Buyers Service's clients are usually prospective home purchasers referred by local real estate agents. Its general procedures for handling a real estate transaction are as follows:

After a client is referred, Buyers Service receives an executed contract of sale from the realtor. If the sale involves a mortgage, the buyer makes an application to a local lender. If the lender approves the loan, it notifies Buyers Service and sends a letter of commitment to the buyer stating the terms. Buyers Service then orders the loan package from the lender. This consists of a set of instructions, a note and mortgage, truth in lending statement, HUD-1 Statement, miscellaneous affidavits regarding employment, and other forms. The documents arrive in various degrees of completion depending upon the particular lender. Buyers Service fills in the mortgagor-mortgagee on the mortgage, the grantor-grantee on the deed, consideration, the legal description and other blank spaces.

Buyers Service sends the completed forms to the purchaser for his examination and signature. Thereafter, the lender examines the loan package and funds the loan. Buyers Service deposits the loan proceeds check in its escrow account and disburses the funds according to the HUD-1 Statement and the closing instructions. Buyers Service also prepares settlement statements after loans are closed.

When a title search is necessary, Buyers Service sends an employee to the courthouse to abstract the title. The purchaser pays $50 for this service. The abstract is reviewed by a non-attorney employee who determines if the seller has fee simple title to the property. Buyers Service gives purchasers a fact sheet describing three ways to hold fee simple title in South Carolina. If a purchaser has questions, an employee of Buyers Service elaborates. The purchasers then tell Buyers Service how they wish to hold title.

Subsequent to the commencement of the litigation, Buyers Service retained an attorney to review its closing documents. The attorney, whose name and charges appear on the settlement sheet, receives $35 for this service. Buyers Service pays this fee and passes it on to the purchaser. There is no direct contact between the attorney and the purchaser.

Buyers Service conducts closings without any attorney present. The majority are handled by mail. For these, Buyers Service sends written instructions to the parties as to the manner of signing the legal documents. When the purchaser comes to Buyers Service's office for the closing, an employee supervises the signing of the legal documents. If the purchaser has any questions, the employee answers them or refers the purchaser to the mortgage lender.

Buyers Service has legal instruments hand-carried or mailed to the courthouse for recording. It sends a form instruction letter with each set of documents but does not take responsibility for ensuring proper recording, which it maintains is the responsibility of the clerk of court.

The circuit court's order enjoins Buyers Service from the following activities:

> 1. Providing reports, opinions or certificates as to the status of real estate titles to persons other than attorneys licensed to practice law in the State of South Carolina and seeking separate compensation for performing title work in connection with [Buyers Service's] title insurance business.
> 2. Preparing deeds, mortgages, notes and other legal instruments related to transfer of real property or mortgage loans.

3. Giving legal advice during the closing of real estate transfers or real estate mortgage loan transactions.

4. Advertising to the general public that the Defendant is a full-service closing company and may handle complete real estate closings, practice law, or perform any activity constituting the practice of law.

Both Buyers Service and the State have appealed.

Discussion

This court in In re Duncan, 83 S.C. 186, 189, 65 S.E. 210, 211 (1909) held the practice of law includes ". . . conveyancing, the preparation of legal instruments of all kinds, and, in general, all advice to clients, and all action for them in matters connected with the law." See also State v. Wells, 191 S.C. 468, 5 S.E.2d 181 (1939); Matter of Easler, 275 S.C. 400, 272 S.E.2d 32 (1980). Additionally, S.C. Code Ann. §40-5-320 (1986) strictly prohibits corporations from the practice of law.

A. Preparation of Instruments

Buyers Service contends the circuit court erred in holding it may not prepare deeds, notes and other instruments related to mortgage loans and transfers of real property. It argues the forms are standard and require no creative drafting. The State counters that preparation of instruments falls within the definition of the practice of law of In re Duncan, and that Buyers Service acts as more than a mere scrivener in the process. We agree.

The practice of law is not confined to litigation, but extends to activities in other fields which entail specialized legal knowledge and ability. Often, the line between such activities and permissible business conduct by non-attorneys is unclear. However, courts of other jurisdictions considering the issue of whether preparation of instruments involves the practice of law have held that it does.

In Pioneer Title Ins. & Trust Co. v. State Bar of Nev., 74 Nev. 186, 326 P.2d 408 (1958) escrow agents were enjoined from preparation of instruments necessary to effectuate real estate sales transactions. The court reasoned that preparation of instruments, even with *preprinted forms*, involves more than a mere scrivener's duties. By necessity, the agents pass upon the legal sufficiency of the instruments to accomplish the contractual agreement of the parties. See also Arkansas Bar Ass'n v. Block, 230 Ark. 430, 323 S.W.2d 912, cert. denied, 361 U.S. 836, 80 S. Ct. 87, 4 L. Ed. 2d 76 (1959).

The reason preparation of instruments by lay persons must be held to constitute the unauthorized practice of law is not for the economic protection of the legal profession. Rather, it is for the protection of the

public from the potentially severe economic and emotional consequences which may flow from erroneous advice given by persons un-
trained in the law. This principle was stated by the Supreme Court of
Washington in Bennion, Van Camp, Hagen & Ruhl v. Kassler Escrow,
Inc., 96 Wash. 2d 443, 635 P.2d 730 (1981). There, the legislature had
enacted a statute authorizing escrow agents to perform services such as
selection, preparation and completion of instruments in real estate
transactions. The court previously had held these activities to constitute
the unauthorized practice of law. See Washington State Bar Ass'n v.
Great W. Union Fed. Sav. & Loan Ass'n, 91 Wash. 2d 48, 586 P.2d 870
(1978). The statute was held unconstitutional on the ground it violated
the court's exclusive power to regulate the practice of law:

> The statute fails to consider who is to determine whether such agents and
> employees of banks, etc., are possessed of the requisite skill, competence and
> ethics. Only the Supreme Court has the power to make that determination
> through a bar examination, yearly Continuing Legal Education require-
> ments, and the Code of Professional Responsibility. The public is also pro-
> tected against unethical attorneys by a client's security fund maintained by
> the Washington State Bar Association. [635 P.2d at 734.]

Similar protections are afforded to the public in South Carolina
through this Court's regulation of attorneys' competency and conduct.

As noted in the statement of facts, Buyers Service has retained attorneys to review the closing documents. This does not save its activities
from constituting the unauthorized practice of law. In State Bar of Ariz.
v. Arizona Land Title & Trust Co., 90 Ariz. 76, 366 P.2d 1, reheard, 91
Ariz. 293, 371 P.2d 1020 (1962), a title company employed staff counsel
to prepare legal instruments. The court cited the Arizona prohibition
against a corporation's practice of law similar to that in S.C. Code Ann.
§40-5-320 (1986). The court then noted the conflicts of interest inherent
in such an arrangement, reasoning that the adverse interests in real estate transactions make it extremely difficult for the attorney to maintain
a proper professional posture toward each party.

We agree and hold the circuit court properly enjoined Buyers Service from the preparation of deeds, mortgages, notes and other legal
instruments related to mortgage loans and transfers of real property.

B. Title Abstracts

Buyers Service next contends the circuit court erred in holding that
preparation of title abstracts for persons other than attorneys constitutes
the unauthorized practice of law. As noted in the statement of facts, the
buyer pays Buyers Service $50 for title searches. However, the resulting
title abstract is furnished not to the buyer, but to the mortgagee to certify
that fee simple title will be vested in the buyer.

The State argues that even though the buyer does not see the title abstract, he nevertheless relies upon it to determine if he receives good, marketable title. That is, because the buyer knows a title search has been conducted, he reasonably assumes title is good if nothing adverse is reported. We agree.

The same principles which render the preparation of instruments the practice of law apply equally to the preparation of title abstracts. In Beach Abstract & Guar. Co. v. Bar Ass'n of Ark., 230 Ark. 494, 326 S.W.2d 900 (1959), the court relied upon its earlier holding in Arkansas Bar Ass'n v. Block, supra, in holding that title examination, when done for another, constitutes the practice of law. The court rejected the title insurance company's arguments that the examinations were performed only incidentally to its own business and that no separate fee was charged.

We affirm the circuit court's injunction which provides Buyers Service may conduct title examinations and prepare abstracts only for the benefit of attorneys. The examination of titles requires expert legal knowledge and skill. For the protection of the public such activities, if conducted by lay persons, must be under the supervision of a licensed attorney.

C. Real Estate Closings

The terms of the circuit court's injunction permit Buyers Service to continue its practice of handling real estate and mortgage loan closings with the restriction that no legal advice be given to the parties during the closing sessions.

The State contends instructing clients in the manner in which to execute legal documents is itself the practice of law and requires a legal knowledge of statutes and case law. See, e.g., S.C. Code Ann. §§27-7-10 and 30-5-30 (1976). We agree.

Courts of other jurisdictions have recognized dangers in allowing lay persons to handle real estate closings. See, e.g., Bowers v. Transamerica Title Ins. Co., 100 Wash. 2d 581, 675 P.2d 193 (1983); Coffee County Abstract and Title Co. v. State ex rel. Norwood, 445 So. 2d 852 (Ala. 1984); Conway-Bogue Realty Inv. Co. v. Denver Bar Ass'n, 135 Colo. 398, 312 P.2d 998 (1957); Oregon State Bar v. Security Escrows, Inc., 233 Or. 80, 377 P.2d 334 (1962); New Jersey State Bar Ass'n v. Northern N.J. Mortgage Assocs., 32 N.J. 430, 161 A.2d 257 (1960).

While some of these cases hold that lay persons may conduct closings, they note that giving advice as to the effect of the various instruments required to be executed constitutes the unauthorized practice of law. Thus, in Coffee County Abstract and Title Co., supra, the title company was permitted to conduct real estate closings with the restriction that no legal advice or opinions be given. Chief Justice Torbert, concurring, gave instructions as to how such a closing should be handled: "If the parties to the transaction raise a legal question at the closing, the title company should stop the proceeding and instruct them to consult their attorneys." 445 So. 2d at 857.

We agree this approach, in theory, would protect the public from receiving improper legal advice. However, there is in practice no way of assuring that lay persons conducting a closing will adhere to the restrictions. One handling a closing might easily be tempted to offer a few words of explanation, however innocent, rather than risk losing a fee for his or her employer.

We are convinced that real estate and mortgage loan closings should be conducted only under the supervision of attorneys, who have the ability to furnish their clients legal advice should the need arise and fall under the regulatory rules of this court. Again, protection of the public is of paramount concern.

D. Recording Instruments

The circuit court's order permits Buyers Service to continue its practice of mailing or hand-carrying instruments to the courthouse for recording. The State contends this activity is the practice of law. We agree.

We do not consider the physical transportation or mailing of documents to the courthouse to be the practice of law. However, when this step takes place as part of a real estate transfer it falls under the definition of the practice of law as formulated by this court in In re Duncan, supra. It is an aspect of conveyancing and affects legal rights. The appropriate sequence of recording is critical in order to protect a purchaser's title to property.

We conclude that instructions to the Clerk of Court or Register of Mesne Conveyances as to the manner of recording, if given by a lay person for the benefit of another, must be given under the supervision of an attorney.

Both parties' remaining exceptions relating to evidentiary rulings are without merit, and we affirm pursuant to Supreme Court Rule 23.

Affirmed in part and reversed in part.

NOTES

1. Quintin Johnstone, Land Transfers: Process and Processors, 22 Val. U. L. Rev. 493 (1988), provides a comprehensive and detailed description of the land transfer process, including discussion of significant changes that have occurred in the last decade in land transfer servicing.

2. For a report detailing all the legal problems that can arise in residential land transfers, see American Bar Association's Special Committee on Residential Real Estate Transactions: The Lawyer's Proper Role, 14 Real Prop., Prob. & Tr. J. 581 (1979). Needless to say, the committee believes each party to a residential real estate sale should have a lawyer, who should be involved from the drafting of the contract of sale through the closing.

3. *The role of the broker.* Where a real estate broker has been employed to facilitate the sale of real property, the broker traditionally prepares the sales contract. The sales contract is, of course, a legally binding document, and the organized bar has sometimes accused brokers of practicing law. The line between "simple contracts," which courts have permitted real estate brokers to prepare, and unauthorized practice of law is difficult to define. But it now seems clearly established that licensed real estate brokers can complete standard form contracts for the sale of land. All the recent cases have decided that it is in the public interest to permit brokers to do this. See Cultum v. Heritage House Realtors, Inc., 103 Wash. 2d 623, 694 P.2d 630 (1985); New Jersey State Bar Assn. v. New Jersey Assn. of Realtor Bds., 93 N.J. 470, 461 A.2d 1112 (1983) (approving a form contract agreed upon by the bar and realtors, which provides, "This is a legally binding contract that will become final within three business days. During this period you may choose to consult an attorney who can review and cancel the contract.").

After the buyer signs the contract, when does the broker earn the commission? Up until the middle of this century, the standard rule was, surprisingly, that the broker earned a commission when the contract of sale was signed, whether or not the sale was actually consummated thereafter. This rule did not carry out the seller's usual intent. As Lord Denning said,

> When a house owner puts his house into the hands of an estate agent, the ordinary understanding is that the agent is only to receive a commission if he succeeds in effecting a sale. . . . The common understanding of men is . . . that the agent's commission is payable out of the purchase price. . . . The house owner wants to find a man who will actually buy his house and pay for it. He does not want a man who will only make an offer or sign a contract. He wants a purchaser "able to purchase and able to complete as well." [Dennis Reed, Ltd. v. Goody, [1950] 2 K.B. 277, 284-285.]

The old rule was first rejected in this country in Ellsworth Dobbs, Inc. v. Johnson, 50 N.J. 528, 236 A.2d 843, 30 A.L.R.3d 1370 (1967). In *Ellsworth Dobbs,* the court held that the seller's broker does not earn a commission until the purchaser completes the transaction by closing the title in accordance with the contract. If the sale falls through because of the seller's wrongful act or interference, however, the broker is entitled to a commission. The *Ellsworth Dobbs* rule has been followed by a number of courts. See Tristram's Landing, Inc. v. Wait, 367 Mass. 622, 327 N.E.2d 727 (1975). But the old rule has not yet been formally abandoned in a majority of states. See Ladd v. Coldwell Banker, 167 A.D.2d 676, 563 N.Y.S.2d 255 (1990); D. Barlow Burke, Jr., Law of Real Estate Brokers §§3.1-3.5, 4.1-4.4 (2d ed. 1992); Annot., 28 A.L.R.4th 1007 (1984).

B. The Contract of Sale

1. The Statute of Frauds

The Statute of Frauds, enacted in 1677 under the title "An Act for the Prevention of Frauds and Perjuries," sought to make people more secure in their property and their contracts by making deceitful claims unenforceable. The Statute dealt with diverse subjects, but two provisions were of particular importance for the law of real property. First, sections 1 to 3 provided that, except for leases for less than three years, no interest in land could be created or transferred except by an instrument in writing signed by the party to be bound thereby. Second, section 4 provided that no action shall be brought "upon any contract or sale of lands . . . or any interest in or concerning them . . . unless the agreement upon which such action shall be brought or some memorandum or note thereof shall be in writing, and signed by the party to be charged therewith."

    The provisions of the English Statute of Frauds have been generally re-enacted in the United States. The courts, however, when not confined by express language, have treated the Statute of Frauds as a principle rather than as a statute. Frequently, in discussing the Statute, they do not cite or quote any statutory text. As a consequence, most law relating to the Statute of Frauds is judge-made law, not statutory. Some judges, believing the requirements wise and salutary, are quite strict in enforcing the Statute. Others have relaxed the requirements, giving effect to oral agreements under circumstances where fraud seems unlikely or unfairness results. Even within a single jurisdiction there is likely to be no consistent view on the necessity for a written instrument; judges may enforce some types of oral agreements while rejecting others.

    To satisfy the Statute of Frauds a memorandum of sale must, at a minimum, be signed by the party to be bound, describe the real estate, and state the price. Where a price has been agreed upon, most courts regard it as an essential term that must be set forth. But if no price was agreed upon, a court may imply an agreement to pay a reasonable price. Under Uniform Land Transactions Act §2-203 (1975), the parties may enter into a binding contract without having agreed on the price. However, the agreement is not enforceable unless the parties refer to price and indicate the method they intend to use in fixing it. A contract for sale at "fair market value" is enforceable. Goodwest Rubber Corp. v. Munoz, 170 Cal. App. 3d 919, 216 Cal. Rptr. 604 (1985). In some states, the memorandum must contain, in addition to the above, all the material terms of the agreement, but given the extensive litigation, no accurate simple summary of "material terms" is possible. See Nelson v. Rebello, 26 Mass. App. Ct. 270, 530 N.E.2d 798 (1988).

Exceptions to the Statute of Frauds. Courts have created two principal exceptions to the Statute of Frauds: *part performance* and *estoppel*. Part performance allows the specific enforcement of oral agreements when particular acts have been performed by one of the parties to the agreement. Acts held to constitute part performance vary from jurisdiction to jurisdiction, depending primarily on how the court views the theoretical basis for the doctrine of part performance. One theory is that the acts of the parties substantially satisfy the evidentiary requirements of the Statute. Hence if the acts make sense only as having been performed pursuant to the oral contract ("unequivocally referable to a contract of sale"), they constitute part performance. Such acts include the buyer's taking possession *and* paying all or part of the purchase price or making valuable improvements. Cf. Mann v. White Marsh Properties, Inc., 321 Md. 111, 581 A.2d 819 (1990). Another theory of part performance is that it is a doctrine used to prevent injurious reliance on the contract; if the plaintiff shows that he would suffer irreparable injury if the contract were not enforced, then the buyer's taking of possession alone is sufficient to set the court in motion. The doctrine of part performance originated in equity in suits for specific performance and in most jurisdictions does not apply to actions at law for damages. See 3 American Law of Property §§11.7-11.12 (1952). In a few states, acts of part performance are not recognized. See Roger A. Cunningham, William B. Stoebuck & Dale A. Whitman, The Law of Property §10.2 (1984).

Estoppel applies where unconscionable injury would result from denying enforcement of the oral contract after one party has been induced by the other seriously to change his position in reliance on the contract. Estoppel may also apply where unjust enrichment would result if a party who has received the benefits of the other's performance were allowed to rely upon the Statute. Estoppel, though originating in equity, has long been recognized as a defense in law. See Michael Braunstein, Remedy, Reason, and the Statute of Frauds: A Critical Economic Analysis, 1989 Utah L. Rev. 383 (arguing that courts create exceptions in the Statute of Frauds when adherence to it would result in economically wasteful behavior).

Hickey v. Green
Appeals Court of Massachusetts, 1982
14 Mass. App. Ct. 671, 442 N.E.2d 37

CUTTER, J. This case is before us on a stipulation of facts (with various attached documents). A Superior Court judge has adopted the agreed facts as "findings." We are in the same position as was the trial judge (who received no evidence and saw and heard no witnesses).

Mrs. Gladys Green owns a lot (Lot S) in the Manomet section of Plymouth. In July, 1980, she advertised it for sale. On July 11 and 12, Hickey and his wife discussed with Mrs. Green purchasing Lot S and "orally agreed to a sale" for $15,000. Mrs. Green on July 12 accepted a deposit check of $500, marked by Hickey on the back, "Deposit on Lot . . . Massasoit Ave. Manomet . . . Subject to Variance from Town of Plymouth." Mrs. Green's brother and agent "was under the impression that a zoning variance was needed and [had] advised . . . Hickey to write" the quoted language on the deposit check. It turned out, however, by July 16 that no variance would be required. Hickey had left the payee line of the deposit check blank, because of uncertainty whether Mrs. Green or her brother was to receive the check, and asked "Mrs. Green to fill in the appropriate name." Mrs. Green held the check, did not fill in the payee's name, and neither cashed nor endorsed it. Hickey "stated to Mrs. Green that his intention was to sell his home and build on Mrs. Green's lot."

"Relying upon the arrangements . . . with Mrs. Green," the Hickeys advertised their house on Sachem Road in newspapers on three days in July, 1980, and agreed with a purchaser for its sale and took from him a deposit check for $500 which they deposited in their own account.[5] On July 24, Mrs. Green told Hickey that she "no longer intended to sell her property to him" but had decided to sell to another for $16,000. Hickey told Mrs. Green that he had already sold his house and offered her $16,000 for Lot S. Mrs. Green refused this offer.

The Hickeys filed this complaint seeking specific performance. Mrs. Green asserts that relief is barred by the Statute of Frauds contained in G.L. c. 259 §1. The trial judge granted specific performance.[6] Mrs. Green has appealed.

The present rule applicable in most jurisdictions in the United States is succinctly set forth in Restatement (Second) of Contracts, §129 (1981). The section reads,

---

5. On the back of the check was noted above the Hickeys' signatures endorsing the check "Deposit on Purchase of property at Sachem Rd. and First St., Manomet, Ma. Sale price, $44,000."

6. The judgment ordered Mrs. Green to convey Lot S to the Hickeys but, probably by inadvertence, it failed to include an order that it be conveyed only upon payment by the grantees of the admittedly agreed price of $15,000.

A contract for the transfer of an interest in land may be specifically enforced notwithstanding failure to comply with the Statute of Frauds if it is established that the party seeking enforcement, in *reasonable reliance on the contract* and on the continuing assent of the party against whom enforcement is sought, *has so changed his position that injustice can be avoided only by specific enforcement* (emphasis supplied).[7]

The earlier Massachusetts decisions laid down somewhat strict requirements for an estoppel precluding the assertion of the Statute of Frauds. See, e.g., Glass v. Hulbert, 102 Mass. 24, 31-32, 43-44 (1869); Davis v. Downer, 210 Mass. 573, 576-577, 97 N.E. 90 (1912); Hazelton v. Lewis, 267 Mass. 533, 538-540, 166 N.E. 876 (1929); Andrews v. Charon, 289 Mass. 1, 5-7, 193 N.E. 737 (1935), where specific performance was granted upon a consideration of "the effect of all the facts in combination;" Winstanley v. Chapman, 325 Mass. 130, 133, 89 N.E.2d 506 (1949); Park, Real Estate Law, §883 (1981). . . . Frequently there has been an actual change of possession and improvement of the transferred property, as well as full payment of the full purchase price, or one or more of these elements.

It is stated in Park, Real Estate Law, §883, at 334, that the "more recent decisions . . . indicate a trend on the part of the [Supreme Judicial C]ourt to find that the circumstances warrant specific performance." This appears to be a correct perception. See Fisher v. MacDonald, 332 Mass. 727, 729, 127 N.E.2d 484 (1955), where specific performance was granted upon a showing that the purchaser "was put into possession and . . . [had] furnished part of the consideration in money and services;" Orlando v. Ottaviani, 337 Mass. 157, 161-162, 148 N.E.2d 373 (1958), where specific performance was granted to the former holder of an option to buy a strip of land fifteen feet wide, important to the option holder, and the option had been surrendered in reliance upon an oral promise to convey the strip made by the purchaser of a larger parcel of which the fifteen-foot strip was a part; Cellucci v. Sun Oil Co., 2 Mass.

---

7. Comments a and b to §129, read (in part): "a. . . . This section restates what is widely known as the 'part performance doctrine.' Part performance is not an accurate designation of such acts as taking possession and making improvements when the contract does not provide for such acts, but such acts regularly bring the doctrine into play. The doctrine is contrary to the words of the Statute of Frauds, but it was established by English courts of equity soon after the enactment of the Statute. Payment of purchase-money, without more, was once thought sufficient to justify specific enforcement, but a contrary view now prevails, since in such cases restitution is an adequate remedy. . . . Enforcement has . . . been justified on the ground that repudiation after 'part performance' amounts to a 'virtual fraud.' A more accurate statement is that courts with equitable powers are vested by tradition with what in substance is a dispensing power based on the promisee's reliance, *a discretion to be exercised with caution* in the light of all the circumstances . . . [emphasis supplied].

"b. . . . Two distinct elements enter into the application of the rule of this Section: first, the extent to which the evidentiary function of the statutory formalities is fulfilled by the conduct of the parties; second, the reliance of the promisee, providing a compelling substantive basis for relief in addition to the expectations created by the promise."

App. 722, 727-728, 320 N.E.2d 919 (1974), S.C., 368 Mass. 811, 331 N.E.2d 813 (1975). . . .

The present facts reveal a simple case of a proposed purchase of a residential vacant lot, where the vendor, Mrs. Green, knew that the Hickeys were planning to sell their former home (possibly to obtain funds to pay her) and build on Lot S. The Hickeys, relying on Mrs. Green's oral promise, moved rapidly to make their sale without obtaining any adequate memorandum of the terms of what appears to have been intended to be a quick cash sale of Lot S. So rapid was action by the Hickeys that, by July 21, less than ten days after giving their deposit to Mrs. Green, they had accepted a deposit check for the sale of their house, endorsed the check, and placed it in their bank account. Above their signatures endorsing the check was a memorandum probably sufficient to satisfy the Statute of Frauds under A.B.C. Auto Parts, Inc. v. Moran, 359 Mass. 327, 329-331, 268 N.E.2d 844 (1971). Cf. Guarino v. Zyfers, 9 Mass. App. 874, 401 N.E.2d 857 (1980). At the very least, the Hickeys had bound themselves in a manner in which, to avoid a transfer of their own house, they might have had to engage in expensive litigation. No attorney has been shown to have been used either in the transaction between Mrs. Green and the Hickeys or in that between the Hickeys and their purchaser.

There is no denial by Mrs. Green of the oral contract between her and the Hickeys. This, under §129 of the Restatement, is of some significance.[8] There can be no doubt (a) that Mrs. Green made the promise on which the Hickeys so promptly relied, and also (b) she, nearly as promptly, but not promptly enough, repudiated it because she had a better opportunity. The stipulated facts require the conclusion that in equity Mrs. Green's conduct cannot be condoned. This is not a case where either party is shown to have contemplated the negotiation of a purchase and sale agreement. If a written agreement had been expected, even by only one party, or would have been natural (because of the participation by lawyers or otherwise), a different situation might have existed. It is a permissible inference from the agreed facts that the rapid sale of the Hickeys' house was both appropriate and expected. These are not circumstances where negotiations fairly can be seen as inchoate. Compare Tull v. Mister Donut Development Corp., 7 Mass. App. 626, 630-632, 389 N.E.2d 447 (1979).

We recognize that specific enforcement of Mrs. Green's promise to

---

8. Comment d of Restatement (Second) of Contracts, §129, reads "d. . . . Where specific enforcement is rested on a transfer of possession plus either part payment of the price or the making of improvements, it is commonly said that the action taken by the purchaser must be unequivocally referable to the oral agreement. But this requirement is not insisted on *if the making of the promise is admitted or is clearly proved.* The promisee *must act in reasonable reliance on the promise, before the promisor has repudiated* it, and the action must be such that the remedy of restitution is inadequate. If these requirements are met, *neither taking of possession nor payment of money nor the making of improvements is essential . . .*" (emphasis supplied).

convey Lot S may well go somewhat beyond the circumstances considered in the *Fisher* case, 332 Mass. 727, and in the *Orlando* case, 337 Mass. 157, 148 N.E.2d 373, where specific performance was granted. It may seem (perhaps because the present facts are less complicated) to extend the principles stated in the *Cellucci* case (see esp. 2 Mass. App. at 728, 320 N.E.2d 919). We recognize also the cautionary language about granting specific performance in comment a to §129 of the Restatement (see note 7, supra). No public interest behind G.L. c. 259, §1, however, in the simple circumstances before us, will be violated if Mrs. Green fairly is held to her precise bargain by principles of equitable estoppel, subject to the considerations mentioned below.

Over two years have passed since July, 1980, and over a year since the trial judge's findings were filed on July 6, 1981. At that time, the principal agreed facts of record bearing upon the extent of the injury to the Hickeys (because of their reliance on Mrs. Green's promise to convey Lot S) were those based on the Hickeys' new obligation to convey their house to a purchaser. Performance of that agreement had been extended to May 1, 1981. If that agreement has been abrogated or modified since the trial, the case may take on a different posture. If enforcement of that agreement still will be sought, or if that agreement has been carried out, the conveyance of Lot S by Mrs. Green should be required now.

The case, in any event, must be remanded to the trial judge for the purpose of amending the judgment to require conveyance of Lot S by Mrs. Green only upon payment to her in cash within a stated period of the balance of the agreed price of $15,000. The trial judge, however, in her discretion and upon proper offers of proof of counsel, may reopen the record to receive, in addition to the presently stipulated facts, a stipulation or evidence concerning the present status of the Hickeys' apparent obligation to sell their house. If the circumstances have changed, it will be open to the trial judge to require of Mrs. Green, instead of specific performance, only full restitution to the Hickeys of all costs reasonably caused to them in respect of these transactions (including advertising costs, deposits, and their reasonable costs for this litigation) with interest. The case is remanded to the Superior Court Department for further action consistent with this opinion. The Hickeys are to have costs of this appeal.

So ordered.

NOTES AND PROBLEMS

1. With Hickey v. Green, compare Nessralla v. Peck, 403 Mass. 757, 532 N.E.2d 685 (1989). In the latter case, *A* orally agreed to buy Blackacre for *B*, and *B* orally agreed to buy Whiteacre for *A* (to conceal the

true buyers from the respective owners of the properties); *A* bought Blackacre and conveyed it to *B*; *B* bought Whiteacre and refused to convey it to *A*. The court held that *A* did not demonstrate any detrimental reliance or part performance that would estop *B* from pleading the Statute of Frauds as a defense. *A* "points to no evidence that suggests he would have attempted to purchase the property, or would have sought out another to purchase the property on his behalf, had the oral agreement not existed." *A* had no remedy.

2. *O*, owner of Blackacre, executes and delivers a deed of Blackacre to her daughter *A* as a gift. The deed is not recorded. Subsequently *O* tells *A* that she would like Blackacre back, and *A*, a dutiful daughter, hands the deed back to *O* and says, "The land is yours again." *O* tears up the deed. Who owns Blackacre?

3. Seller and Buyer sign the following contract:

> I, Seller, agree to sell my home to Buyer for $213,000, with $5,000 down payment. A formal contract will be drawn up by attorneys for both parties within 10 days.

Buyer gives Seller a check for $5,000.

(a) Suppose that three days after signing the contract, Buyer sends in a termite inspector who finds the house riddled with termites. Can Buyer rescind the contract?

(b) Suppose that Buyer can obtain a loan secured by a mortgage on the house only in the amount of $150,000, whereas Buyer expected she would be able to obtain a $175,000 loan. Can Buyer rescind the contract?

(c) Suppose that the parties cannot quickly agree upon the terms of a formal contract. Buyer thinks a window air conditioner comes with the house; Seller does not. Seller does not want to move for 90 days; Buyer wants possession in 30 days. Buyer thinks Seller should furnish title insurance; Seller refuses. After two months of arguing back and forth, Buyer decides that she wants to rescind the contract and find another house. Can she rescind? See Blomendale v. Imbrescia, 25 Mass. App. Ct. 144, 516 N.E.2d 177 (1987); Estate of Younge v. Huysmans, 127 N.H. 461, 506 A.2d 282 (1985).

4. For a detailed analysis of forms of real estate sales contracts, both simple and complex, see Lucy A. Marsh, Real Property Transactions 168-223 (1992).

2. Marketable Title

An implied condition of a contract of sale of land is that the seller must convey to the buyer a "marketable title." If the seller cannot convey a marketable title, the buyer is entitled to rescind the contract. Marketable title is "a title not subject to such reasonable doubt as would create a just apprehension of its validity in the mind of a reasonable, prudent and intelligent person, one which such persons, guided by competent legal advice, would be willing to take and for which they would be willing to pay fair value." Seligman v. First Natl. Invs., Inc., 184 Ill. App. 3d 1053, 1057, 540 N.E.2d 1057, 1060 (1989).

Lohmeyer v. Bower

Supreme Court of Kansas, 1951
170 Kan. 442, 227 P.2d 102

[In May 1949, Dr. K.L. Lohmeyer entered into a contract to buy from the Bowers lot number 37 in the Berkley Hills Addition to the city of Emporia. The contract provided that the Bowers would convey

> By Warranty Deed with an abstract of title, certified to date showing good merchantable title or an Owners Policy of Title Insurance in the amount of the sale price, guaranteeing said title to party of the second part [Dr. Lohmeyer], free and clear of all encumbrances except special taxes subject, however, to all restrictions and easements of record applying to this property, it being understood that the first party shall have sufficient time to bring said abstract to date or obtain Report for Title Insurance and to correct any imperfections in the title if there be such imperfections.

The abstract of title showed that the original subdivider of the Berkley Hills Addition had, in 1926, imposed a restrictive covenant on lot 37 requiring any house erected on lot 37 to be two stories in height. Lot 37 had a one-story house on it.

Dr. Lohmeyer gave the abstract of title to a lawyer to examine, and from the lawyer Dr. Lohmeyer learned that the city of Emporia had a zoning ordinance providing that no frame building could be erected within three feet of a side or rear lot line. The frame house on lot 37 was located within 18 inches of the north line of the lot in violation of the ordinance. The Bowers had, in 1946, moved the house, which had been built elsewhere, onto lot 37. When Dr. Lohmeyer brought the zoning violation to the attention of the Bowers, they offered to purchase and convey to Lohmeyer two feet along the entire north side of lot 37. Dr. Lohmeyer refused their offer.

Dr. Lohmeyer brought suit to rescind the contract and demanded return of his earnest money. The Bowers answered, contesting Lohmeyer's right to rescind, and by cross-complaint asked specific performance of the contract. The trial court rendered judgment for the Bowers and decreed specific performance of the contract. Dr. Lohmeyer appealed from that judgment.]

PARKER, J. . . . From what has been heretofore related, since resort

**House on lot 37, Berkley Hills Addition,
which Dr. Lohmeyer backed out of buying, 1990**

to the contract makes it clear appellees agreed to convey the involved property with an abstract of title showing good merchantable title, free and clear of all encumbrances, it becomes apparent the all decisive issue presented by the pleadings and the stipulation is whether such property is subject to encumbrances or other burdens making the title unmerchantable and if so whether they are such as are excepted by the provision of the contract which reads "subject however, to all restrictions and easements of record applying to this property."

Decision of the foregoing issue can be simplified by directing attention early to the appellant's position. Conceding he purchased the property subject to all restrictions of record he makes no complaint of the restrictions contained in the declaration forming a part of the dedication of Berkley Hills Addition nor of the ordinance restricting the building location on the lot but bases his right to rescission of the contract solely upon presently existing violations thereof. This, we may add, limited to restrictions imposed by terms of the ordinance relating to the use of land or the location and character of buildings that may be located thereon, even in the absence of provisions in the contract excepting them, must necessarily be his position for we are convinced, although it must be conceded there are some decisions to the contrary, the rule supported by the better reasoned decisions, indeed if not by the great weight of authority, is that municipal restrictions of such character, existing at the time of the execution of a contract for the sale of real estate, are not such encumbrances or burdens on title as may be availed of by a vendee to avoid his agreement to purchase on the ground they render his title unmerchantable. For authorities upholding this conclusion see Hall v. Risley & Heikkila, 188 Or. 69, 213 P.2d 818; Miller v. Milwaukee Odd Fellows Temple, 206 Wis. 547, 240 N.W. 193; Wheeler v. Sullivan, 90 Fla. 711, 106 So. 876; Lincoln Trust Co. v. Williams Bldg. Corp., 229 N.Y. 313, 128 N.E. 209; Maupin on Marketable Title to Real Estate, (3rd Ed.) 384 §143; 175 A.L.R. anno. 1056 §2; 57 A.L.R. anno. 1424 §11(c); 55 Am. Jur. 705 §205; 66 C.J. 860, 911 §§531, 591.

On the other hand there can be no question the rule respecting restrictions upon the use of land or the location and type of buildings that may be erected thereon fixed by covenants or other private restrictive agreements, including those contained in the declaration forming a part of the dedication of Berkley Hills Addition, is directly contrary to the one to which we have just referred. Such restrictions, under all the authorities, constitute encumbrances rendering the title to land unmerchantable. . . .

There can be no doubt regarding what constitutes a marketable or merchantable title in this jurisdiction. This court has been called on to pass upon that question on numerous occasions. See our recent decision in Peatling v. Baird, 168 Kan. 528, 213 P.2d 1015, and cases there cited, wherein we held:

> A marketable title to real estate is one which is free from reasonable doubt, and a title is doubtful and unmarketable if it exposes the party holding it to the hazard of litigation.
>
> To render the title to real estate unmarketable, the defect of which the purchaser complains must be of a substantial character and one from which he may suffer injury. Mere immaterial defects which do not diminish in quantity, quality or value the property contracted for, constitute no ground upon which the purchaser may reject the title. Facts must be known at the time which fairly raise a reasonable doubt as to the title; a mere possibility or conjecture that such a state of facts may be developed at some future time is not sufficient.

Under the rule just stated, and in the face of facts such as are here involved, we have little difficulty in concluding that the violation of section 5-224 of the ordinances of the city of Emporia as well as the violation of the restrictions imposed by the dedication declaration so encumber the title to Lot 37 as to expose the party holding it to the hazard of litigation and make such title doubtful and unmarketable. It follows, since, as we have indicated, the appellees had contracted to convey such real estate to appellant by warranty deed with an abstract of title showing good merchantable title, free and clear of all encumbrances, that they cannot convey the title contracted for and that the trial court should have rendered judgment rescinding the contract. This, we may add is so, notwithstanding the contract provides the conveyance was to be made subject to all restrictions and easements of record for, as we have seen, it is the violation of the restrictions imposed by both the ordinance and the dedication declaration, not the existence of those restrictions, that render the title unmarketable. The decision just announced is not without precedent or unsupported by sound authority. . . .

Finally appellees point to the contract which, it must be conceded, provides they shall have time to correct imperfections in the title and contend that even if it be held the restrictions and the ordinance have been violated they are entitled to time in which to correct those imperfections. Assuming, without deciding, they might remedy the violation of the ordinance by buying additional ground the short and simple answer to their contention with respect to the violation of the restrictions imposed by the dedication declaration is that any changes in the house would compel the purchaser to take something that he did not contract to buy.

Conclusions heretofore announced require reversal of the judgment with directions to the trial court to cancel and set aside the contract and render such judgment as may be equitable and proper under the issues raised by the pleadings.

It is so ordered.

NOTES AND QUESTIONS

1. Look at the contract Dr. Lohmeyer signed. Would you have advised Dr. Lohmeyer not to sign it? First, it provides that Lohmeyer agrees to take the property subject to all restrictions and easements on record. Second, it provides that the sellers must provide Lohmeyer "with an abstract of title, certified to date showing good merchantable title *or* an Owners Policy of Title Insurance." Suppose that a title insurance company, of which more in Chapter 8, agreed to issue a policy of title insurance on the property, guaranteeing title, even though the title is legally unmarketable. Would Lohmeyer be entitled to rescind the contract? See Creative Living, Inc. v. Steinhauser, 78 Misc. 2d 29, 355 N.Y.S.2d 897 (1974), aff'd without opinion, 47 A.D.2d 598, 365 N.Y.S.2d 987 (1975) (contract provided seller shall have a title such as a title insurer would insure; "[t]his provision in the contract made the title company the final judge of title and when the title company was prepared to insure title in accordance with the contract no further requirement had to be met").

What is the function of the concept of "marketable title"? Why do courts not rule that the seller must produce a complete chain of title from an unimpeachable source (a sovereign) and prove that no encumbrance exists? See Roger A. Cunningham, William B. Stoebuck & Dale A. Whitman, The Law of Property §10.12 (1984).

2. Suppose there is a recorded sewage easement or easement for utility poles across the property. Does this make title unmarketable? Should it matter whether the easement is visible, or whether the easement diminishes or enhances the value of the property? See Rhodes v. Astro-Pac, Inc., 41 N.Y.2d 919, 363 N.E.2d 347, 394 N.Y.S.2d 623 (1977) (easement an encumbrance, even though it does not diminish value of property); Ziskind v. Bruce Lee Corp., 224 Pa. Super. Ct. 518, 307 A.2d 377 (1973) (knowledge of easement irrelevant; title unmarketable); Ludke v. Egan, 87 Wis. 2d 221, 274 N.W.2d 641 (1979) (easement known to purchaser, or open and obvious, does not make title unmarketable).

3. In Sinks v. Karleskint, 130 Ill. App. 3d 527, 474 N.E.2d 767 (1985), the purchasers of a 40-acre tract alleged that title was not marketable because the tract had no legal access, which the purchasers knew. The court held the title was marketable. The court reasoned that lack of access affects market value, not marketability of title. A title is marketable, said the court, if the seller has a fee simple, the title is free from any encumbrances, and the buyer is entitled to possession. The fact that the buyer may not be able to reach the property does not make title legally unmarketable. The court further held that, even if lack of access were a title defect, the purchaser entered the contract with knowledge of lack of access and had waived such a defect. For more on the problem of landlocked property, see pages 813-822. See also Hocking v. Title Ins. Co., 37 Cal. 2d 644, 234 P.2d 625 (1951) (denial of building permit on unimproved road, because of subdivider's malfeasance in failing to post bond for paving roads, only affected market value, not marketable title).

4. Why do public restrictions, such as zoning, not make title unmarketable whereas private restrictions, such as covenants, do make title unmarketable? See Allison Dunham, The Effect on Title of Violations of Building Covenants and Zoning Ordinances, 27 Rocky Mtn. L. Rev. 255 (1955); Comment, Public Land Use Regulations and Marketability of Title, 1958 Wis. L. Rev. 128; Annot., 39 A.L.R.3d 362 (1971).

Conklin v. Davi
Supreme Court of New Jersey, 1978
76 N.J. 468, 388 A.2d 598

MOUNTAIN, J. Plaintiffs contracted to sell and convey to defendants a residential property in Ridgewood. The purchasers refused to consummate the sale, alleging defects in title and misrepresentations on the part of the sellers. Plaintiffs instituted an action for specific performance; defendants counterclaimed for rescission. Before the trial commenced, plaintiffs abandoned their claim for specific performance, and the case proceeded solely as an action on the counterclaim of the defendants-purchasers, seeking rescission, in effect to secure the return of the down payment.

At the conclusion of the purchasers' case, the court granted the sellers' motion for judgment. The purchasers appealed, and the Appellate Division, in an unreported opinion, reversed the judgment of the trial court. Instead of remanding for a new trial, however, the Appellate Division ordered that judgment be entered in favor of the purchasers. . . .

Although we agree with the Appellate Division that the trial court erred in granting vendors' motion, we think its entry of judgment in purchasers' favor to have been clearly erroneous. There must be a new trial.

It would appear that the validity of the title to a portion of the premises in question is sought to be sustained by the sellers upon a claim of adverse possession. The purchasers take the position that this being so, they were justified in repudiating the agreement; that the sellers could not force such a title upon them, but should have perfected the record title prior to the date of closing. This, they add, should have been done either by securing a deed from the present record title holder, or by means of an action to quiet title. While we readily concede that the sellers would have been well advised to have followed such a course, we do not agree that their failure to do so imperiled their position to the extent urged by the purchasers.

When a prospective seller's title is grounded upon adverse possession, or contains some apparent flaw of record, he has a choice of options. He may at once take whatever steps are necessary to perfect the record title, including resort to an action to quiet title, an action to cancel an outstanding encumbrance, or whatever other appropriate step may be necessary to accomplish the purpose. In the alternative he may, believing his title to be marketable despite the fact that it rests on adverse possession or is otherwise imperfect of record, choose to enter into a contract of sale, hoping to convince the purchaser or, if necessary, a court, that his estimate of the marketability of his title is justified. That is the course the sellers seem to have followed here. It must be borne in mind that this latter course is available only where the contract of sale does not require the vendor to give a title valid of record, but provides for a less stringent requirement, such as marketability or insurability. Such is the case here. Of course "[a] buyer is entitled to the kind of title stipulated for in the contract of sale." Friedman, Contracts and Conveyances of Real Property (3rd ed. 1975) §4.2, p.259; Lounsbery v. Locander, 25 N.J. Eq. 554 (E.&J. 1874). Here the contract contained the following provision:

> Title to be conveyed shall be marketable and insurable, at regular rates, by any reputable title insurance company licensed to do business in the State of New Jersey, subject only to the encumbrances hereinabove set forth.

It will be seen at once that while the title for which the purchasers have contracted must be marketable and insurable, there is no requirement that it be a perfect title of record. Many titles, imperfect of record, are nonetheless marketable. Justice Cardozo, then Chief Judge of the New York Court of Appeals, observed: "The law assures to a buyer a title free from reasonable doubt, but not from every doubt. . . . If 'the only defect in the title' is 'a very remote and improbable contingency,' a 'slender possibility only,' a conveyance will be decreed. . . ." [Norwegian Evangelical Free Church v. Milhauser, 252 N.Y. 186, 169 N.E. 134, 135 (1929).]

Incidentally, the law will imply that title must be marketable, even where the contract is silent upon the point. LaSalle v. LaPointe, 14 N.J. 476, 479-80, 102 A.2d 761 (1954) and authorities cited. The purchasers are accordingly in error in insisting that nothing less than a good record title will suffice. A title that is marketable and insurable, though imperfect of record, will meet the terms of the contract.

Having thus chosen to rely upon marketability of the title to so much of their land as they claim by adverse possession, and upon it clearly appearing that the purchasers would not, under such conditions, perform the contract, sellers instituted an action for specific performance. . . .

Thereafter, as we have also noted, the sellers abandoned their suit for specific performance, leaving for trial only the issue raised by the purchasers' counterclaim for rescission. . . .

The criterion, in a case such as this, is the same whether the seller seeks specific performance or the purchaser sues for the return of his deposit. The determinative issue in each case is whether or not the seller had marketable title.

> The criterion of a marketable title does not vary with the form of action in which it is an issue. In a situation wherein title is sufficiently doubtful to impel a court of equity to deny specific performance to the seller, the buyer may recover his downpayment in an action at law. [Friedman, supra, §4.1, p.258.]

The purchasers also advance the contention that the validity of the title must be assessed as of the specified closing date, and not at some later time. But established doctrine refutes this contention. Where, because of an alleged title defect, vendor and vendee litigate the issue, it will be the title as it exists at the time of final decree or judgment that will control, not the title the vendor may have had when the suit was commenced.

In all cases where the vendor seeks to force a title upon the vendee, it is the latter's position, not at the commencement of the suit, but at its termination, which is to be regarded. The question is, not what kind of a title the vendor has, but what kind of a title the vendee will get if the court of chancery or the court of errors and appeals, after reviewing the decree of the court of chancery, forces the offered title upon him. [Barger v. Gery, 64 N.J. Eq. 263, 268, 53 A. 483, 485 (Ch. 1902).]. . .

To recapitulate, in an action for specific performance by a vendor or for rescission by a vendee, where the issue is marketability of title, the vendor is entitled to a judgment if, at the conclusion of the suit, the court holds title to be marketable, even though the decision in favor of marketability rests upon facts adduced for the first time at trial or upon legal rulings made during the course of the proceedings.

The purchasers have also advanced the contention that they were entitled to rescind the contract because, contrary to the contractual proviso, title was not insurable by a reputable title insurance company. Generally, provisions requiring title insurance as a condition precedent to acceptance of title are enforceable. Mackenzie v. McLean, 20 N.J. Super. 517, 90 A.2d 515 (App. Div. 1952); Brinn v. Mennen Co., 4 N.J. 610, 615, 73 A.2d 541 (1950). This condition may already have been satisfied, for a Vice-President of New Jersey Realty Title Insurance Company testified to a willingness to insure the purchasers' possession against claims of third persons. Under these circumstances it would appear that the contractual condition had probably been met, but the point can be fully explored at the retrial.

As we have said, we agree with the Appellate Division that the trial court erred in granting the sellers' motion at the conclusion of the purchasers' case. The purchasers had shown that the sellers did not have record title to one tract of the entire parcel. The contract of sale provided that title must be marketable and insurable. It did not provide, however, as many such agreements do, that the sellers would be required to produce a clear title of record, without reliance upon adverse possession. It is well settled in New Jersey that title resting in adverse possession, if clearly established, will be held marketable. This rule represents the great weight of authority. See Annot., Title by or through adverse possession as marketable, 46 A.L.R.2d 544, 548 (1956). Accordingly, if the sellers could prove that they did in fact hold title to the tract in question by virtue of adverse possession, they would have met their contractual obligation, at least insofar as marketability is concerned. Although the trial judge indicated that he believed the sellers could readily establish title by adverse possession, they had not yet done so. Therefore their motion should have been denied and they should have been directed to go forward with their proofs.

We note that it is not necessary for the sellers to join as parties all

possible claimants with outstanding interests, as would be the case in an
action to quiet title. In many, if not most, cases of this sort the claimants
who may hold adverse interests are not joined; very often they are not
known. It follows, as the purchasers here correctly point out, that a judgment in the action will not be res judicata as to such claimants. And yet
virtually all courts agree that in such a suit there may be, and often is, a
judgment of marketability leading to affirmative relief by way of specific
performance or to a denial of a vendee's claim to rescind. This result
has been reached in a number of reported cases in this state. In order to
reach this result the court must conclude (1) that the outstanding claimants could not succeed were they in fact to assert a claim, and (2) that
there is no real likelihood that any claim will ever be asserted. Such a
conclusion leads to a determination of marketability.

Although there are statements in some of the cases to the contrary,
we think that in a suit such as this, where the purchaser seeking rescission has shown that record title is outstanding in some person other than
the seller, the burden should then shift to the seller to establish his title
by adverse possession.

The judgment of the Appellate Division entering judgment in favor
of the purchasers is reversed and the cause is remanded to the Superior
Court, Chancery Division for a new trial in accordance with what has
been said above.

NOTES AND QUESTION

1. If at the new trial of Conklin v. Davi the seller cannot establish
marketable title by adverse possession, the seller can attempt to quiet
title by suing the record owners, if they can be identified and found.
The jurisdiction may have an in rem quiet-title proceeding that permits
service on unknown claimants by publication. Such proceedings have
been narrowly interpreted by the courts, however, and have many limitations. Moreover, the decree is susceptible to collateral attack by those
parties over whom adequate jurisdiction was not obtained. The due process clause of the Constitution requires reasonably diligent inquiry of the
identity and the whereabouts of unnamed persons interested in the
property before a judicial decree can bar their interests. Virtually all
quiet-title decrees barring unnamed persons are thus vulnerable. See
Comment, Enhancing the Marketability of Land: The Suit to Quiet Title, 68 Yale L.J. 1245 (1959).

2. In equity, unless the parties expressly provide that "time is of the
essence," the court will give the parties a reasonable time for performance. If the contract does not say that time is of the essence, either
party can fix the time for performance by giving notice to the other,

provided the notice leaves a reasonable time for rendering performance. Sohayegh v. Oberlander, 155 A.D.2d 436, 547 N.Y.S.2d 98 (1989).

If a contract provides that closing day is the following June 1, and further provides that time is of the essence, then the seller's title must stand or fall as it exists on June 1. Title defects cannot be cured after that date, without the purchaser's consent.

In Hays v. Coe, 88 Md. App. 491, 595 A.2d 484 (1991), four days before closing, the seller and the buyers extended the date for closing with a contract addendum providing: "Because a title problem has arisen and a complete survey is necessary, we hereby extend this contract until a good and marketable title can be transferred." The court held that this contract addendum did not violate the Rule against Perpetuities because the parties contemplated that performance would occur within a reasonable period of time, which was necessarily less than 21 years.

3. *Measure of damages.* In Conklin v. Davi the buyers counter-claimed, asking for the return of their down payment because of breach of contract. Let us suppose that, at the new trial, the buyers amend their counterclaim and ask for loss-of-bargain damages — the difference be-tween the contract price and the market value of the property on the date of breach. Let us suppose further that upon retrial the sellers can-not provide title by adverse possession to the backyard of the house. Finally, let us suppose that the contract price of the house is $90,000 and that upon the date of closing (usually deemed the date of breach for determining damages) the house without a backyard has a market value of $60,000. When the final decree is entered after retrial, some years later, the house has increased in value. At that time, the house with the backyard has a market value of $160,000, and the house without the backyard a market value of $100,000. What is the amount of the buyer's recovery?

In many states where the seller has acted in good faith but cannot convey satisfactory title, the courts will give the buyer restitution but not loss-of-bargain damages. The rule appears to rest on the notion that it is unreasonable to make a seller pay such damages when the seller may not have known of the defect in title when the contract was signed. The rule has been severely criticized, and in perhaps a majority of states, includ-ing New Jersey, is not followed. A good-faith seller is liable for loss-of-bargain damages. See Roger A. Cunningham, William B. Stoebuck & Dale A. Whitman, The Law of Property §10.3 (1984).

4. *Specific performance.* Specific performance is a remedy that a court of equity, in its sound discretion, may grant to a buyer or seller whose money-damages remedy is inadequate. When the *buyer* asks for specific performance, courts usually grant it, saying that each parcel of land is "unique" and therefore money damages cannot be an accurate substi-tute.

In asserting that the subject matter of a particular contract is unique and has no established market value, a court is really saying that it cannot obtain, at reasonable cost, enough information about substitutes to permit it to calculate an award of money damages without imposing an unacceptably high risk of undercompensation on the injured promisee. Conceived in this way, the uniqueness test seems economically sound. [Anthony T. Kronman, Specific Performance, 45 U. Chi. L. Rev. 351, 362 (1978).]

When the *seller* asks for specific performance, courts ordinarily grant it on the theory that the seller may find it difficult "to prove with reasonable certainty the difference between the contract price and the market price of the land." Restatement (Second) of Contracts §360, Comment e (1981). The property may not be easily resalable immediately. Nonetheless, specific performance is an equitable remedy and in the discretion of the court.

NOTE: EQUITABLE CONVERSION

The doctrine of equitable conversion, simply put, is that if there is a specifically enforceable contract for the sale of land, equity regards as done that which ought to be done. The buyer is viewed in equity as the owner from the date of the contract (thus having the "equitable title"); the seller has a claim for money secured by a vendor's lien on the land. The seller is also said to hold the legal title as trustee for the buyer.

Risk of loss. Equitable conversion has been used by some courts to determine whether the seller or the purchaser takes the loss when the premises are destroyed between signing the contract of sale and the closing and the contract has no provision allocating the risk of loss. Paine v. Meller, 6 Ves. Jr. 349, 31 Eng. Rep. 1088 (Ch. 1801), held that from the time of the contract of sale of real estate the burden of fortuitous loss was on the purchaser, even though the seller retains possession. This result was said to follow from equitable conversion, treating the purchaser as owner. Most courts are thought to follow this view. Some courts, however, have declined to apply equitable conversion and have held that the loss is on the seller until legal title is conveyed. In Massachusetts, the risk of loss is on the seller if the loss is substantial and the terms of the contract show that the building constituted an important part of the subject matter of the contract; if the loss is not substantial, either party can enforce the contract, though an abatement in purchase price may be given. In some other states, the risk of loss is placed on the party in possession, which view is also taken by the Uniform Vendor and Purchaser Act (1935). If the purchaser has the risk of loss, and the seller has insurance, in most states the seller holds the insurance proceeds as trustee for the buyer. See Bryant v. Willison Real Estate Co., 350 S.E.2d

748, 85 A.L.R.4th 221 (W. Va. 1986) (discussing the law of many states); Roger A. Cunningham, William B. Stoebuck & Dale A. Whitman, The Law of Property §10.13 at 703-709 (1984); 6A Richard R. Powell, The Law of Real Property ¶925[6] (rev. ed. 1992). Obviously, to avoid litigation, the parties should include a provision regarding risk of loss in the contract of sale and buy insurance accordingly.

Inheritance. Equitable conversion has been applied in situations where one of the parties to a contract for the sale of land dies and the issue arises whether the decedent's interest is real property or personal property. If equitable conversion has occurred, the seller's interest is personal property (right to the purchase price), and the buyer is treated as owner of the land. Thus suppose that *O*, owner of Blackacre, contracts to sell Blackacre to *A* for $10,000. Before closing, *O* dies intestate. By the applicable intestacy statute, *B* succeeds to *O*'s real property and *C* succeeds to *O*'s personal property. Under equitable conversion, *C* is entitled to the $10,000 when it is paid. Shay v. Penrose, 25 Ill. 2d 447, 185 N.E.2d 218 (1962).

3. The Duty to Disclose Defects

Stambovsky v. Ackley

New York Supreme Court, Appellate Division,
First Department, 1991
169 A.D.2d 254, 572 N.Y.S.2d 672

RUBIN, J. Plaintiff, to his horror, discovered that the house he had recently contracted to purchase was widely reputed to be possessed by poltergeists, reportedly seen by defendant seller and members of her family on numerous occasions over the last nine years. Plaintiff promptly commenced this action seeking rescission of the contract of sale. Supreme Court reluctantly dismissed the complaint, holding that plaintiff has no remedy at law in this jurisdiction.

The unusual facts of this case, as disclosed by the record, clearly warrant a grant of equitable relief to the buyer who, as a resident of New York City, cannot be expected to have any familiarity with the folklore of the Village of Nyack. Not being a "local," plaintiff could not readily learn that the home he had contracted to purchase is haunted. Whether the source of the spectral apparitions seen by defendant seller are parapsychic or psychogenic, having reported their presence in both a national publication (Reader's Digest) and the local press (in 1977 and 1982, respectively), defendant is estopped to deny their existence and, as a matter of law, the house is haunted. More to the point, however, no divination is required to conclude that it is defendant's promotional efforts in publicizing her close encounters with these spirits which fostered the home's reputation in the community. In 1989, the house was included in a five-home walking tour of Nyack and described in a November 27th newspaper article as "a riverfront Victorian (with ghost)." The impact of the reputation thus created goes to the very essence of the bargain between the parties, greatly impairing both the value of the property and its potential for resale. The extent of this impairment may be presumed for the purpose of reviewing the disposition of this motion to dismiss the cause of action for rescission (Harris v City of New York, 147 AD2d 186, 188-189) and represents merely an issue of fact for resolution at trial.

While I agree with Supreme Court that the real estate broker, as agent for the seller, is under no duty to disclose to a potential buyer the phantasmal reputation of the premises and that, in his pursuit of a legal remedy for fraudulent misrepresentation against the seller, plaintiff hasn't a ghost of a chance, I am nevertheless moved by the spirit of equity to allow the buyer to seek rescission of the contract of sale and recovery of his down payment. New York law fails to recognize any remedy for damages incurred as a result of the seller's mere silence, applying instead the strict rule of caveat emptor. Therefore, the theoretical basis for granting relief, even under the extraordinary facts of this case, is elusive if not ephemeral.

"Pity me not but lend thy serious hearing to what I shall unfold" (William Shakespeare, Hamlet, Act I, Scene V [Ghost]).

From the perspective of a person in the position of plaintiff herein, a very practical problem arises with respect to the discovery of a paranormal phenomenon: "Who you gonna' call?" as a title song to the movie "Ghostbusters" asks. Applying the strict rule of caveat emptor to a contract involving a house possessed by poltergeists conjures up visions of a psychic or medium routinely accompanying the structural engineer and Terminix man on an inspection of every home subject to a contract of sale. It portends that the prudent attorney will establish an escrow account lest the subject of the transaction come back to haunt him and his client — or pray that his malpractice insurance coverage extends to supernatural disasters. In the interest of avoiding such untenable consequences, the notion that a haunting is a condition which can and should be ascertained upon reasonable inspection of the premises is a hobgoblin which should be exorcised from the body of legal precedent and laid quietly to rest.

It has been suggested by a leading authority that the ancient rule which holds that mere nondisclosure does not constitute actionable misrepresentation "finds proper application in cases where the fact undisclosed is patent, or the plaintiff has equal opportunities for obtaining information which he may be expected to utilize, or the defendant has no reason to think that he is acting under any misapprehension" (Prosser, Torts §106, at 696 [4th ed 1971]). However, with respect to trans-

AP/Wide World Photos

"*. . . as a matter of law, the house is haunted.*"

actions in real estate, New York adheres to the doctrine of caveat emptor and imposes no duty upon the vendor to disclose any information concerning the premises (London v Courduff, 141 AD2d 803) unless there is a confidential or fiduciary relationship between the parties (Moser v Spizzirro, 31 AD2d 537, affd 25 NY2d 941; IBM Credit Fin. Corp. v Mazda Motor Mfg. [USA] Corp., 152 AD2d 451) or some conduct on the part of the seller which constitutes "active concealment" (see, 17 E. 80th Realty Corp. v 68th Assocs., 173 AD2d 245 [dummy ventilation system constructed by seller]; Haberman v Greenspan, 82 Misc 2d 263 [foundation cracks covered by seller]). Normally, some affirmative misrepresentation (e.g., Tahini Invs. v Bobrowsky, 99 AD2d 489 [industrial waste on land allegedly used only as farm]; Jansen v Kelly, 11 AD2d 587 [land containing valuable minerals allegedly acquired for use as campsite]) or partial disclosure (Junius Constr. Corp. v Cohen, 257 NY 393 [existence of third unopened street concealed]; Noved Realty Corp. v A.A.P. Co., 250 App Div 1 [escrow agreements securing lien concealed]) is required to impose upon the seller a duty to communicate undisclosed conditions affecting the premises (contra, Young v Keith, 112 AD2d 625 [defective water and sewer systems concealed]).

Caveat emptor is not so all-encompassing a doctrine of common law as to render every act of nondisclosure immune from redress, whether legal or equitable. . . . Where fairness and common sense dictate that an exception should be created, the evolution of the law should not be stifled by rigid application of a legal maxim.

The doctrine of caveat emptor requires that a buyer act prudently to assess the fitness and value of his purchase and operates to bar the purchaser who fails to exercise due care from seeking the equitable remedy of rescission (see, e.g., Rodas v Manitaras, 159 AD2d 341). . . . It should be apparent, however, that the most meticulous inspection and the search would not reveal the presence of poltergeists at the premises or unearth the property's ghoulish reputation in the community. Therefore, there is no sound policy reason to deny plaintiff relief for failing to discover a state of affairs which the most prudent purchaser would not be expected to even contemplate (see, Da Silva v Musso, 53 NY2d 543, 551).

The case law in this jurisdiction dealing with the duty of a vendor of real property to disclose information to the buyer is distinguishable from the matter under review. The most salient distinction is that existing cases invariably deal with the physical condition of the premises (e.g., London v Courduff, supra [use as a landfill]; Perin v Mardine Realty Co., 5 AD2d 685, affd 6 NY2d 920 [sewer line crossing adjoining property without owner's consent]), defects in title (e.g., Sands v Kisane, 282 App Div 140 [remainderman]), liens against the property (e.g., Noved Realty Corp. v A.A.P. Co., supra), expenses or income (e.g., Rodas v Manitaras, supra [gross receipts]) and other factors affecting its operation. No case has been brought to this court's attention in which the property value was impaired as the result of the reputation created by information disseminated to the public by the seller (or, for that matter, as a result of possession by poltergeists).

Where a condition which has been created by the seller materially impairs the value of the contract and is peculiarly within the knowledge of the seller or unlikely to be discovered by a prudent purchaser exercising due care with respect to the subject transaction, nondisclosure constitutes a basis for rescission as a matter of equity. Any other outcome places upon the buyer not merely the obligation to exercise care in his purchase but rather to be omniscient with respect to any fact which may affect the bargain. No practical purpose is served by imposing such a burden upon a purchaser. To the contrary, it encourages predatory business practice and offends the principle that equity will suffer no wrong to be without a remedy.

Defendant's contention that the contract of sale, particularly the merger or "as is" clause, bars recovery of the buyer's deposit is unavailing. Even an express disclaimer will not be given effect where the facts are peculiarly within the knowledge of the party invoking it (Danaan Realty Corp. v Harris, 5 NY2d 317, 322; Tahini Invs. v Bobrowsky, supra). Moreover, a fair reading of the merger clause reveals that it expressly disclaims only representations made with respect to the physical condition of the premises and merely makes general reference to representations concerning "any other matter or things affecting or relating to the aforesaid premises." As broad as this language may be, a reasonable interpretation is that its effect is limited to tangible or physical matters and does not extend to paranormal phenomena. Finally, if the language of the contract is to be construed as broadly as defendant urges to encompass the presence of poltergeists in the house, it cannot be said that she has delivered the premises "vacant" in accordance with her obligation under the provisions of the contract rider. . . .

In the case at bar, defendant seller deliberately fostered the public belief that her home was possessed. Having undertaken to inform the public-at-large, to whom she has no legal relationship, about the supernatural occurrences on her property, she may be said to owe no less a duty to her contract vendee. It has been remarked that the occasional modern cases which permit a seller to take unfair advantage of a buyer's ignorance so long as he is not actively misled are "singularly unappetizing" (Prosser, Torts §106, at 696 [4th ed 1971]). Where, as here, the seller not only takes unfair advantage of the buyer's ignorance but has created and perpetuated a condition about which he is unlikely to even inquire, enforcement of the contract (in whole or in part) is offensive to the court's sense of equity. Application of the remedy of rescission, within the bounds of the narrow exception to the doctrine of caveat emptor set forth herein, is entirely appropriate to relieve the unwitting purchaser from the consequences of a most unnatural bargain.

Accordingly, the judgment of the Supreme Court, New York

County (Edward H. Lehner, J.), entered April 9, 1990, which dismissed the complaint pursuant to CPLR 3211 (a) (7), should be modified, on the law and the facts, and in the exercise of discretion, and the first cause of action seeking rescission of the contract reinstated, without costs.

SMITH, J., dissenting.

. . . [I]f the doctrine of caveat emptor is to be discarded, it should be for a reason more substantive than a poltergeist. The existence of a poltergeist is no more binding upon the defendants than it is upon this court.

Johnson v. Davis
Supreme Court of Florida, 1985
480 So. 2d 625

ADKINS, J. [The Davises entered into a contract to buy the Johnsons' home for $310,000. The Johnsons knew that the roof leaked, but they affirmatively represented to the Davises that there were no problems with the roof. After the Davises made a $31,000 deposit, the Johnsons vacated the home. Several days later, following a heavy rain, Mrs. Davis entered the home and discovered water "gushing" in from around the windows and from the ceiling in two rooms. The Davises brought an action for rescission of the contract and return of their deposit. The court held that the affirmative representation that the roof was sound was a false representation, entitling the Davises to rescind. Then the court turned to an alternative ground for the judgment.]

In determining whether a seller of a home has a duty to disclose latent material defects to a buyer, the established tort law distinction between misfeasance and nonfeasance, action and inaction must carefully be analyzed. The highly individualistic philosophy of the earlier common law consistently imposed liability upon the commission of affirmative acts of harm, but shrank from converting the courts into an institution for forcing men to help one another. This distinction is deeply rooted in our case law. Liability for nonfeasance has therefore been slow to receive recognition in the evolution of tort law.

In theory, the difference between misfeasance and nonfeasance, action and inaction is quite simple and obvious; however, in practice it is not always easy to draw the line and determine whether conduct is active or passive. That is, where failure to disclose a material fact is calculated to induce a false belief, the distinction between concealment and affirmative representations is tenuous. Both proceed from the same motives and are attended with the same consequences; both are violative of the principles of fair dealing and good faith; both are calculated to produce the same result; and, in fact, both essentially have the same effect.

Still there exists in much of our case law the old tort notion that there can be no liability for nonfeasance. The courts in some jurisdictions, including Florida, hold that where the parties are dealing at arm's length and the facts lie equally open to both parties, with equal opportunity of examination, mere nondisclosure does not constitute a fraudulent concealment. . . .

These unappetizing cases are not in tune with the times and do not conform with current notions of justice, equity and fair dealing. One should not be able to stand behind the impervious shield of caveat emptor and take advantage of another's ignorance. . . . Thus, the tendency of the more recent cases has been to restrict rather than extend the doctrine of caveat emptor. The law appears to be working toward the ultimate conclusion that full disclosure of all material facts must be made whenever elementary fair conduct demands it.

The harness placed on the doctrine of caveat emptor in a number of other jurisdictions has resulted in the seller of a home being liable for failing to disclose material defects of which he is aware. This philosophy was succinctly expressed in Lingsch v. Savage, 213 Cal. App. 2d 729, 29 Cal. Rptr. 201 (1963):

> It is now settled in California that where the seller knows of facts materially affecting the value or desirability of the property which are known or accessible only to him and also knows that such facts are not known to or within the reach of the diligent attention and observation of the buyer, the seller is under a duty to disclose them to the buyer.

In Posner v. Davis, 76 Ill. App. 3d 638, 32 Ill. Dec. 186, 395 N.E.2d 133 (1979), buyers brought an action alleging that the sellers of a home fraudulently concealed certain defects in the home which included a leaking roof and basement flooding. Relying on *Lingsch,* the court concluded that the sellers knew of and failed to disclose latent material defects and thus were liable for fraudulent concealment. Id. 32 Ill. Dec. at 190, 395 N.E.2d at 137. Numerous other jurisdictions have followed this view in formulating law involving the sale of homes. See Flakus v. Schug, 213 Neb. 491, 329 N.W.2d 859 (1983) (basement flooding); Thacker v. Tyree, 297 S.E.2d 885 (W. Va. 1982) (cracked walls and foundation problems); Maguire v. Masino, 325 So. 2d 844 (La. Ct. App. 1975) (termite infestation); Weintraub v. Krobatsch, 64 N.J. 445, 317 A.2d 68 (1974) (roach infestation); Cohen v. Vivian, 141 Colo. 443, 349 P.2d 366 (1960) (soil defect).

We are of the opinion, in view of the reasoning and results in *Lingsch, Posner* and the aforementioned cases decided in other jurisdictions, that the same philosophy regarding the sale of homes should also be the law in the state of Florida. Accordingly, we hold that where the seller of a home knows of facts materially affecting the value of the property which are not readily observable and are not known to the buyer, the seller is under a duty to disclose them to the buyer. This duty is equally applicable to all forms of real property, new and used.

. . . Thus, we . . . find that the Johnsons' fraudulent concealment . . . entitles the Davises to the return of the . . . deposit payment plus interest. We further find that the Davises should be awarded costs and fees. It is so ordered.

NOTES

1. In Harding v. Willie, 458 N.W.2d 612 (Iowa App. 1990), when the buyer inquired about a crack in the ceiling, the seller stated there was "absolutely no problem" with the roof, because the leak had been fixed. Later the buyer found new evidence of leaking and elected to rescind the contract, either because of fraud or mutual mistake. The court permitted rescission, reasoning that when the seller stated there was "absolutely no problem" with the roof, he either knew it still leaked, which was fraud, or thought the roof had been repaired and no longer leaked, which led to a mutual mistake of fact (that the roof would not leak).

2. A majority of states has adopted variants of the duty to disclose, equating nondisclosure with fraud or misrepresentation. For discussion of the seller's obligation to disclose, see 1 Milton R. Friedman, Contracts and Conveyances of Real Property §1.2(n) (5th ed. 1991); Note, Protecting the Virginia Homebuyer: A Duty to Disclose Defects, 73 Va. L. Rev. 459 (1987); Note, Risk Allocation and the Sale of Defective Used Housing — Should Silence be Golden?, 20 Cap. U. L. Rev. 215 (1991).

In some states statutes require the seller to deliver to prospective buyers a written statement disclosing facts about the property. The statutes set forth detailed information forms. The forms vary, but the required disclosure may include known significant structural defects, soil problems, underground sewage or storage tanks, presence of hazardous materials, alterations or repairs made without necessary permits, violations of building codes or zoning ordinances, and encroachments by neighbors. See, e.g., Cal. Civ. Code §1102.6 (West Supp. 1992); Wis. Stat. Ann. §709.03 (West Supp. 1992). The disclosure statement is not a warranty by the seller and is not a substitute for any warranty or inspection the buyer may want to obtain. The statement gives the buyer information upon which the buyer may rely in deciding whether to rescind the contract.

In some states requiring disclosure, there is no duty to disclose violations of building codes, zoning regulations, or private restrictive covenants. See Eric T. Freyfogle, Real Estate Sales and the New Implied Warranty of Lawful Use, 71 Cornell L. Rev. 1 (1985), arguing that courts should go beyond requiring disclosure of unlawful use and imply a warranty of lawful use. Professor Freyfogle believes an implied warranty of lawful use would enhance compliance with public land-use regulations.

In each jurisdiction requiring disclosure, the defect must be "material" to be actionable. One of two tests of materiality is applied: (1) An objective test of whether a reasonable person would attach importance to it in deciding to buy, or (2) a subjective test of whether the defect "affects the value or desirability of the property to the buyer."

In California, the seller must disclose, among other things, any "neighborhood noise problems or other nuisances." In Alexander v. McKnight, 7 Cal. App. 4th 973, 9 Cal. Rptr. 2d 453 (1992), the Mc-Knights were bad neighbors. In violation of the subdivision covenants, they constructed a deck and two-story cabana in their backyard. They staged late-night basketball games, parked too many cars on their property, and, after complaints by neighbors, poured motor oil on the roof of their house. The Alexanders, who lived next door, sued for an injunction against the nuisances and for damages. The trial court enjoined all the objectionable behavior and awarded the Alexanders $24,000 damages on this theory: Since the Alexanders would have to disclose to prospective buyers that the McKnights were difficult neighbors, the Alexanders' property would sell for $24,000 less because of the Mc-Knights' conduct. On appeal, the appellate court agreed that the Alexanders would be legally required to disclose the offensive and noisy activities of the McKnights, if the McKnights were still living in the neighborhood.

> The fact that a neighborhood contains an overly hostile family who delights in tormenting their neighbors with unexpected noises or unending parties is not a matter which will ordinarily come to the attention of a buyer viewing the property at a time carefully selected by the seller to correspond with an anticipated lull in the "festivities." [7 Cal. App. 4th at 979, 9 Cal. Rptr. 2d at 456.]

However, the court reversed the award of damages as premature. The court assumed that the McKnights would comply with the court order and cease the objectionable activity. If the McKnights failed to comply or found other ways to offend their neighbors, so that the economic loss was not eliminated, the Alexanders could then enforce the existing judgment by an action for damages.

3. In Reed v. King, 145 Cal. App. 3d 261, 193 Cal. Rptr. 130 (1983), the seller of a house did not disclose to the buyer that a multiple murder had occurred at the house 10 years earlier. After the sale, the buyer learned of the murders from a neighbor. The buyer then sued for rescission and damages. The court held that the complaint stated a cause of action. If the buyer proved at trial that the decade-old multiple

murder had a significant effect on market value, the buyer would be entitled to relief for the seller's failure to disclose a material fact about the house.

Should the fact that the previous owner died of AIDS be disclosed? A few states (including California) have statutes declaring that it need not be disclosed. Some state officials have interpreted the 1988 amendments to the Federal Fair Housing Act prohibiting discrimination against the handicapped (see pages 442-445), which includes persons with AIDS, to prohibit disclosure that the former owner had AIDS. See Paula C. Murray, AIDS, Ghosts, Murder: Must Real Estate Brokers and Sellers Disclose?, 27 Wake Forest L. Rev. 689 (1992).

4. *Broker's duty to disclose.* In Easton v. Strassburger, 152 Cal. App. 3d 90, 199 Cal. Rptr. 383, 46 A.L.R.4th 521 (1984), the court held that a real estate broker representing the seller has an affirmative duty to conduct a reasonably competent and diligent inspection of the residential property for sale and to disclose to prospective purchasers all facts materially affecting the value or desirability of the property that such an investigation would reveal. If the broker does not disclose defects to the buyer, the buyer can sue the broker for negligence. The court stated that the buyer is not relieved of a duty to use reasonable care when the defect is so clearly apparent that, as a matter of law, a broker would not be negligent in failing expressly to disclose it. The case is noted approvingly in 99 Harv. L. Rev. 1861 (1986); 25 Santa Clara L. Rev. 651 (1985); 20 Val. U. L. Rev. 255 (1985).

On the broker's liability for misrepresentations or failure to investigate the condition of the property, see Paul Meyer, Illinois Real Estate Brokers: The Duties of Disclosure and Accuracy, 23 Loy. U. Chi. L.J. 241 (1992); Paula C. Murray, The Real Estate Broker and the Buyer: Negligence and the Duty to Investigate, 32 Vill. L. Rev. 939 (1987); Note, Potential Liability for Misrepresentations in Residential Real Estate Transactions: Let the Broker Beware, 16 Fordham Urb. L.J. 127 (1987).

5. *Disclosure of hazardous waste disposal.* In 1980 Congress enacted the Comprehensive Environmental Response Compensation and Liability Act (CERCLA), 42 U.S.C. §§9601-9675 (Supp. 1992). CERCLA imposes strict liability for cleanup costs of a hazardous waste site upon any *current owner* or operator of a site containing hazardous waste, any *prior owner* or operator of the site at the time it was contaminated, any generator of hazardous waste, and transporters of hazardous substances. 42 U.S.C. §9607(a). The principal implementing agency of CERCLA is the U.S. Environmental Protection Agency (EPA). At the time CERCLA was enacted, Congress appropriated a "superfund" of $1.6 billion to be used to pay for cleanup costs of sites contaminated with hazardous wastes. The EPA is authorized to use this money to clean up contaminated sites. Then it sues the responsible parties to recover its costs. The cleanup

costs of hazardous waste sites can run into the millions of dollars, and the liability of owners can be staggering.

In 1986 Congress amended CERCLA by enacting the Superfund Amendments and Reauthorization Act (SARA). This act provides for an "innocent landowner defense." 42 U.S.C. §9601(35). This defense is available to a person who buys the property *after* the site is contaminated and does not know and has no reason to know that any hazardous substance has been released on the property. CERCLA places a duty on the buyer to make "all appropriate inquiry" into previous ownership and uses of the property if the buyer is to escape cleanup liability.

As a result, cautious buyers have spawned a fast-growing environmental assessment industry to discover as much as they can about possible contamination before they close a deal. They want to know about all previous owners and occupants of the property for a great many years back, as well as all uses to which the property has been put. They want physical tests to discover contamination. The liability under CERCLA is so broad and the statute so open to interpretation as to make most real estate attorneys hesitant to conclude that CERCLA liability could not attach in any particular set of circumstances. See Comment, CERCLA's Innocent Landowner Defense: The Rising Standard of Environmental Due Diligence for Real Estate Transactions, 38 Buffalo L. Rev. 827 (1990); Note, Beyond Caveat Emptor: Disclosure to Buyers of Contaminated Land, 10 Stan. Envtl. L.J. 169 (1991).

In T & E Indus., Inc. v. Safety Light Corp., 123 N.J. 371, 587 A.2d 1249 (1991), the court held that a purchaser could sue a predecessor in title who had polluted the property in carrying on an abnormally dangerous activity. The predecessor is strictly liable for cleanup costs. The court observed that the seller could shift the risk of harm and cleanup costs to the buyer if the buyer knowingly and voluntarily assumed the risk. The court refused to apply caveat emptor where the prior owner had engaged in abnormally dangerous activity. Moreover, the court said, in a statement applicable to a wider range of polluting activities,

> the seller who conceals or fails to disclose any condition that involves an unreasonable risk to others can be held liable to a buyer who had no reason to know of the undisclosed condition or risk if the seller knew or should have known of the condition or risk as well as of the likelihood that the buyer would not discover that condition or risk. [123 N.J. at 388, 587 A.2d at 1257-1258.]

An "as is" clause in a purchase contract will not release the seller from liability to the buyer for response costs under CERCLA unless the contract specifically provides for a release from such costs. See Weigmann & Rose Intl. Corp. v. NL Indus., 735 F. Supp. 957 (N.D. Cal. 1990); Annot., 8 A.L.R.5th 312 (1992).

NOTE: MERGER

An old doctrine says that a contract merges into the deed, and once the deed is accepted, the deed is deemed the final act of the parties expressing the terms of their agreement. The buyer can no longer sue the seller on promises in the contract of sale not contained in the deed, but must sue the seller on the warranties, if any, contained in the deed. There are recognized exceptions to the doctrine, such as fraud and contractual promises deemed collateral to the deed. The merger doctrine principally applies to questions of title or quantity of land. If a contract, for instance, calls for marketable title, and the buyer accepts a deed with no warranties, the buyer cannot thereafter upon discovery of a title defect sue on the contract provision requiring the seller to furnish marketable title.

The merger doctrine is now in disfavor and is becoming riddled with exceptions where the buyer does not intend to discharge the seller's contractual obligations by acceptance of the deed. The usual way of avoiding the doctrine is to say the particular obligation of the seller is an independent or collateral obligation. See Lawrence Berger, Merger by Deed — What Provisions of a Contract for the Sale of Land Survive the Closing?, 21 Real Est. L.J. 22 (1992); Edwin M. Ginsburg, The Doctrine of Merger with Respect to Real Estate Transactions: Taking the Bull by the Horns, 16 Nova L. Rev. 1171 (1992).

Uniform Land Transactions Act §1-309 (1975) abolishes the doctrine of merger. Acceptance of a deed does not relieve any party of the duty to perform all his obligations under the contract.

4. The Implied Warranty of Quality

Recall the implied warranty of habitability in landlord-tenant law. (See pages 525-537.) Sales of real estate may also give rise to a similar warranty. Suits on the warranty can arise only after the closing has taken place and the plaintiff has accepted the deed. Nonetheless, because such suits are closely connected with suits against the seller for nondisclosure, we take up the implied warranty of quality at this point.

Lempke v. Dagenais
Supreme Court of New Hampshire, 1988
130 N.H. 782, 547 A.2d 290

THAYER, J. This is an appeal from the Trial Court's (Gray, J.) dismissal of the plaintiffs' complaint alleging breach of implied warranty of workmanlike quality and negligence. The primary issue before this court is whether a subsequent purchaser of real property may sue the builder/ contractor on the theory of implied warranty of workmanlike quality for latent defects which cause economic loss, absent privity of contract.

We hold that privity of contract is not necessary for a subsequent purchaser to sue a builder or contractor under an implied warranty theory for latent defects which manifest themselves within a reasonable time after purchase and which cause economic harm. Accordingly, we reverse the dismissal by the trial court, and remand.

In 1977, the plaintiffs' predecessors in title contracted with the defendant, Dagenais, to build a garage. In April, 1978, within six months after the garage's construction, the original owners sold the property to plaintiffs, Elaine and Larry Lempke. Shortly after they purchased the property, the plaintiffs began to notice structural problems with the garage — the roof line was uneven and the roof trusses were bowing out. The plaintiffs contend that the separation of the trusses from the roof was a latent defect which could not be discovered until the separation and bowing became noticeable from the exterior of the structure. Fearing a cave-in of the roof, the plaintiffs contacted the defendant and asked him to repair the defects. The defendant initially agreed to do so, but never completed the necessary repairs. The plaintiffs then brought suit against the builder. In turn, the builder filed a motion to dismiss, which the superior court granted based on our holding in Ellis v. Morris, 128 N.H. 358, 513 A.2d 951 (1986). This appeal followed.

The plaintiffs set forth three claims in their brief: one for breach of implied warranty of workmanlike quality; one for negligence; and one, in the alternative, for breach of assigned contract rights. We need address only the first two claims.

We have previously denied aggrieved subsequent purchasers recovery in tort for economic loss and denied them recovery under an implied warranty theory for economic loss. See Ellis v. Morris supra. The court in *Ellis* acknowledged the problems a subsequent purchaser faces, but declined to follow the examples of those cases which allow recovery. 128 N.H. at 361, 513 A.2d at 952. The policy arguments relied upon in *Ellis* for precluding tort recovery for economic loss, in these circumstances, accurately reflect New Hampshire law and present judicial scholarship, see generally Bertschy, Negligent Performance of Service Contracts and Economic Loss, 17 J. Mar. L. Rev. 246 (1984) (hereinafter Negligent Performance) and, as such, remain controlling on the negligence claim. However, the denial of relief to subsequent purchasers on an implied warranty theory was predicated on the court's adherence to the requirement of privity in a contract action and on the fear that to allow recovery without privity would impose unlimited liability on builders and contractors. Thus we need only discuss the implied warranty issue.

I. Privity

This case affords us an opportunity to review and reassess the issue of
privity as it relates to implied warranties of workmanlike quality. In Norton v. Burleaud, 115 N.H. 435, 342 A.2d 629 (1975), this court held that
an implied warranty of workmanlike quality applied between the builder
of a house and the first purchaser. The *Norton* court so held based on
the facts before it, and did not explicitly or impliedly limit the benefit of
implied warranties solely to the first purchaser. The question before us
today is whether this implied warranty may be relied upon by subsequent purchasers and, if so, whether recovery may be had for solely
economic loss.

There has been much judicial debate on the basis of implied warranty. Some courts find that it is premised on tort concepts. See, e.g.,
LaSara Grain v. First National Bank of Mercedes, 673 S.W.2d 558, 565
(Tex. 1984) ("implied warranties are created by operation of law and are
grounded more in tort than contract"); Berman v. Watergate West, Inc.,
391 A.2d 1351 (D.C. App. 1978).

Other courts find that implied warranty is based in contract. See,
e.g., Redarowicz v. Ohlendorf, 92 Ill. 2d 171, 183, 65 Ill. Dec. 411, 417,
441 N.E.2d 324, 330 (1982) (Implied warranty extended to subsequent
purchaser, who purchased house from original owner within first year,
for policy reason. Plaintiff could recover under implied warranty theory
for cracks in basement, chimney and adjoining wall separating, water
leakage in basement, but no recovery in negligence for economic harm.);
Aronsohn v. Mandara, 98 N.J. 92, 484 A.2d 675 (1984) (suit for implied
warranty of habitability for structurally unsound patio); Cosmopolitan
Homes, Inc. v. Weller, 663 P.2d 1041 (Colo. 1983) (en banc) (implied
warranty arises from contractual relationship).

Other authorities find implied warranty neither a tort nor a contract concept, but "a freak hybrid born of the illicit intercourse of tort
and contract. . . . Originally sounding in tort, yet arising out of the warrantor's consent to be bound, it later ceased necessarily to be consensual, and at the same time came to lie mainly in contract." Prosser,
The Assault Upon the Citadel, 69 Yale L.J. 1099, 1126 (1960); accord
Scott v. Strickland, 10 Kan. App. 2d 14, 18, 691 P.2d 45, 50 (1984) (discussing first purchaser, court found implied warranty could be tort or
contract); Edmeades, The Citadel Stands: The Recovery of Economic
Loss in American Products Liability, 27 Case W. Res. L. Rev. 647, 662
(1977).

Regardless of whether courts have found the implied warranty to
be based in contract or tort, many have found that it exists independently, imposed by operation of law, the imposition of which is a matter
of public policy. See 67A Am. Jur. 2d §690 ("Implied warranties arise by
operation of law and not by agreement of the parties, their purpose

being to protect the buyer from loss. . . ."); Elliott v. Lachance, 109 N.H. 481, 483, 256 A.2d 153, 155 (1969) ("Such warranties [referring to UCC merchantability] are not created by agreement . . . but are said to be imposed by law on the basis of public policy."); Richards v. Powercraft Homes, Inc., 139 Ariz. 242, 678 P.2d 427 (1984) (en banc) (Warranty of workmanlike quality and habitability is imposed by law. Homeowners were entitled to recover for breach of implied warranty of workmanlike quality for damages such as cracking, separation of floors from walls, regardless of privity, so long as no substantial change occurred to structure.); Terlinde v. Neely, 275 S.C. 395, 271 S.E.2d 768 (1980) (Subsequent purchaser can rely on theories of implied warranty and negligence for cracks in structure, ill-fitting doors, etc. Court allowed recovery on both theories as a matter of public policy, holding builder to industry standards.); Barnes v. Mac Brown & Co., Inc., 264 Ind. 227, 342 N.E.2d 619 (1976) (Implied warranty extended to second purchaser for latent defects which caused economic harm. Implied warranty of fitness is to real property what implied warranty of merchantability is to personal property.); *Redarowicz*, 92 Ill. 2d at 183, 65 Ill. Dec. at 417, 441 N.E.2d at 330 ("While the warranty of habitability has its roots in the execution of the contract . . . we emphasize that it exists independently.") (Citations omitted.); Petersen v. Hubschman Const. Co., 76 Ill. 2d 31, 38, 27 Ill. Dec. 746, 749, 389 N.E.2d 1154, 1157 (1979) ("implied warranty . . . is a judicial innovation . . . used to avoid the harshness of caveat emptor. . . ."); George v. Veach, 67 N.C. App. 674, 677, 313 S.E.2d 920, 922 (1984) ("An implied warranty arises by operation of law. . . ."); Woodward v. Chirco Const. Co., Inc., 141 Ariz. 514, 687 P.2d 1269 (1984) (en banc); Nastri v. Wood, 142 Ariz. 439, 690 P.2d 158 (1984).

We continue to agree with our statement in *Elliott,* supra at 483-84, 256 A.2d at 155, that

> [implied] warranties are not created by an agreement . . . between the parties but are said to be imposed by law on the basis of public policy. They arise by operation of law because of the relationship between the parties, the nature of the transaction, and the surrounding circumstances

and agree with other courts that find implied warranties, in circumstances similar to those presented here, to be creatures of public policy "that ha[ve] evolved to protect purchasers of . . . homes upon the discovery of latent defects." *Redarowicz,* 92 Ill. 2d at 183, 65 Ill. Dec. at 417, 441 N.E.2d at 330, and that, regardless of their theoretical origins, "exist independently." Id.

There are jurisdictions which have refused to extend the implied warranty to subsequent purchasers, finding privity necessary. . . .

However, numerous jurisdictions have now found privity of contract unnecessary for implied warranty. See, e.g., Tusch Enterprises v. Coffin, 113 Ida. 37, 740 P.2d 1022 (1987) (Subsequent purchasers who suffer purely economic damages from latent defects manifested within a reasonable time may maintain an action in implied warranty without privity, but not in negligence.); Richards v. Powercraft Homes, Inc., 139 Ariz. 242, 678 P.2d 427; Nastri v. Wood, 142 Ariz. 439, 690 P.2d 158; Reichelt v. Urban Investment & Development Co., 577 F. Supp. 971 (N.D. Ill., E.D. 1984); Aronsohn v. Mandara, 98 N.J. 92, 484 A.2d 675 (Subsequent purchasers could sue, on negligence and implied warranty of habitability, for defective construction of patio and recover for economic damages.); Bridges v. Ferrell, 685 P.2d 409 (Okl. App. 1984); Keyes v. Guy Baily Homes, Inc., 439 So. 2d 670 (Miss. 1983) (Overruling earlier Mississippi cases preventing recovery. Subsequent purchaser can now sue builder for breach of implied warranty of good workmanship for latent defects resulting in financial losses. The Court reasoned that an innocent purchaser should not suffer when the builder failed to construct the building in a workmanlike manner.); Briarcliffe West v. Wiseman Const. Co., 118 Ill. App. 3d 163, 73 Ill. Dec. 503, 454 N.E.2d 363 (1983) (implied warranty extended to subsequent purchaser of vacant common lot who discovers latent defect within reasonable time); Gupta v. Ritter Homes, Inc., 646 S.W.2d 168 (Tex. 1983) (implied warranty of habitability and good workmanship implicit in contract and automatically assigned to subsequent purchaser); Redarowicz v. Ohlendorf, 92 Ill. 2d 171, 65 Ill. Dec. 411, 441 N.E.2d 324; Elden v. Simmons, 631 P.2d 739 (Okl. 1981) (Suit for damages resulting from cracking, buckling; implied warranty of habitability and workmanlike manner does not necessarily terminate upon transfer of title. Court analogized situation similar to the UCC and reasoned that buyers were in chain of title.); Blagg v. Fred Hunt Co., 272 Ark. 185, 612 S.W.2d 321 (1981); Hermes v. Staiano, 181 N.J. Super. 424, 437 A.2d 925 (1981) (subsequent purchasers could recover for buckling foundation on theory of implied warranty and strict liability); Terlinde v. Neely, 275 S.C. 395, 271 S.E.2d 768; Wagner Construction Co., Inc. v. Noonan, 403 N.E.2d 1144 (Ind. App. 1st Dist. 1980) (subsequent purchasers could maintain suit in implied warranty for damages resulting from septic system backup); Moxley v. Laramie Builders, Inc., 600 P.2d 733 (Wyo. 1979) (Subsequent purchasers could sue on an implied warranty and negligence theories for latent defects in electric system.); Berman v. Watergate West, Inc., 391 A.2d 1351; Barnes v. Mac Brown & Co. Inc., 264 Ind. 227, 342 N.E.2d 619. . . .

In keeping with judicial trends and the spirit of the law in New Hampshire, we now hold that the privity requirement should be abandoned in suits by subsequent purchasers against a builder or contractor for breach of an implied warranty of good workmanship for latent defects. "To require privity between the contractor and the home owner in such a situation would defeat the purpose of the implied warranty of good workmanship and could leave innocent homeowners without a remedy. . . ." *Aronsohn,* 98 N.J. at 102, 484 A.2d at 680.

Numerous practical and policy reasons justify our holding. The essence of implied warranty is to protect innocent buyers. As such, this principle, which protects first purchasers as recognized by Norton v. Burleaud, 115 N.H. 435, 342 A.2d 629, is equally applicable to subsequent purchasers. The extension of this principle is based on "sound legal and policy considerations." *Terlinde,* 275 S.C. at 397, 271 S.E.2d at 769. The mitigation of caveat emptor should not be frustrated by the intervening ownership of the prior purchasers. As a general principle, "[t]he contractor should not be relieved of liability for unworkmanlike construction simply because of the fortuity that the property on which he did the construction has changed hands." *Aronsohn,* supra at 102, 484 A.2d at 680. . . .

First, "[c]ommon experience teaches that latent defects in a house will not manifest themselves for a considerable period of time . . . after the original purchaser has sold the property to a subsequent unsuspecting buyer." *Terlinde,* 275 S.C. at 398, 271 S.E.2d at 769.

Second, our society is rapidly changing.

> We are an increasingly mobile people; a builder-vendor should know that a house he builds might be resold within a relatively short period of time and should not expect that the warranty will be limited by the number of days that the original owner holds onto the property. [*Redarowicz,* 92 Ill. 2d at 185, 65 Ill. Dec. at 417, 441 N.E.2d at 330.]

Furthermore, "the character of society has changed such that the ordinary buyer is not in a position to discover hidden defects. . . ." *Terlinde,* supra at 397, 271 S.E.2d at 769; *Redarowicz,* supra at 184, 65 Ill. Dec. at 417, 441 N.E.2d at 330 (citation omitted).

Third, like an initial buyer, the subsequent purchaser has little opportunity to inspect and little experience and knowledge about construction. "Consumer protection demands that those who buy homes are entitled to rely on the skill of a builder and that the house is constructed so as to be reasonably fit for its intended use." *Moxley,* 600 P.2d at 735; accord *Wagner Const. Co., Inc.,* 403 N.E.2d 1144, 1147.

Fourth, the builder/contractor will not be unduly taken unaware by the extension of the warranty to a subsequent purchaser. "The builder already owes a duty to construct the home in a workmanlike manner. . . ." *Keyes,* 439 So. 2d at 673. And extension to a subsequent purchaser, within a reasonable time, will not change this basic obligation.

Fifth, arbitrarily interposing a first purchaser as a bar to recovery "might encourage sham first sales to insulate builders from liability." *Richards,* 139 Ariz. at 245, 678 P.2d at 430.

Economic policies influence our decision as well. "[B]y virtue of superior knowledge, skill, and experience in the construction of houses, a builder-vendor is generally better positioned than the purchaser to . . . evaluate and guard against the financial risk posed by a [latent defect]. . . ." George v. Veach, 67 N.C. App. 674, 313 S.E.2d 920, 923 (1984). . . .

As the *Moxley* court stated: the "purpose of [an] [implied] warranty is to protect innocent purchasers and hold builders accountable for their work . . . [and] any reasoning which would arbitrarily interpose a first buyer as an obstruction to someone equally as deserving of recovery is incomprehensible." 600 P.2d 736.

This court, as well, does not find it logical to limit protection arbitrarily to the first purchaser. Most purchasers do not have the expertise necessary to discover latent defects, and they need to rely on the skill and experience of the builder. After all, the effect of a latent defect will be equally debilitating to a subsequent purchaser as to a first owner, and the builder will be "just as unable to justify the improper or substandard work." *Richards*, 139 Ariz. at 245, 678 P.2d at 430; accord *Gupta*, 646 S.W.2d at 169.

Not only do policy and economic reasons convince us that a privity requirement in this situation is unwarranted, but analogous situations show us the soundness of this extension. Public policy has compelled a change in the law of personal property and goods, as witnessed by the adoption of UCC. The logic which compelled this change is equally persuasive for real property. . . . As one law review commentator said: the "[a]pplication of such a warranty is similar to that of implied warranty of fitness and merchantability under the Uniform Commercial Code." Comment, Builder's Liability for Latent Defects in Used Homes, 32 Stan. L. Rev. 607 (1980) (author urged that regardless of method employed, liability for latent defects occurring within a reasonable time should be placed on builder). . . .

II. Economic Loss

Finally, we address the issue of whether we should allow recovery for purely economic harm, which generally is that loss resulting from the failure of the product to perform to the level expected by the buyer and is commonly measured by the cost of repairing or replacing the product. See Comment, Manufacturers' Liability to Remote Purchasers for "Economic Loss" Damages — Tort or Contract?, 114 U. Pa. L. Rev. 539, 541 (1966) (hereinafter Remote Purchaser); Bertschy, Negligent Performance, 17 J. Mar. L. Rev. at 264-70. Much theoretical debate has taken place on whether to allow economic recovery and whether tort or contract is the most appropriate vehicle for such recovery.

It is clear that the majority of courts do not allow economic loss recovery in tort, but that economic loss is recoverable in contract, see *Remote Purchaser,* 114 U. Pa. L. Rev. 539; *Negligent Performance,* 17 J. Mar. L. Rev. 246; Note, *Economic Loss in Products Liability Jurisprudence,* 66 Colum. L. Rev. 917 (1966). . . . However, what is less clear is whether courts allow recovery for economic loss on an implied warranty theory, without privity, in situations such as ours. Some courts do not. Other courts implicitly allow recovery for economic loss, see, e.g., *Moxley,* 600 P.2d 733 (electrical wire defective); *Terlinde,* 275 S.C. 395, 271 S.E.2d 768 (ill-fitting doors, cracking); *Richards,* 139 Ariz. 242, 678 P.2d 427 (separation of walls); *Elden,* 631 P.2d 739 (faulty bricks); *Nastri,* 142 Ariz. 439, 690 P.2d 158; and other courts that have dealt directly with the issue of economic harm in implied warranty have found that an aggrieved party can recover. . . .

The courts which have allowed economic loss recovery in situations similar to ours have done so basically because the line between property damage and economic loss is not always easy to draw. . . .

We agree with the courts that allow economic recovery in implied warranty for subsequent purchasers, finding as they have that "the contention that a distinction should be drawn between mere 'economic loss' and personal injury is without merit."

> Why there should be a difference between an economic loss resulting from injury to property and an economic loss resulting from personal injury has not been revealed to us. When one is personally injured from a defect, he recovers mainly for his economic loss. Similarly, if a wife loses a husband because of injury resulting from a defect in construction, the measure of damages is totally economic loss. We fail to see any rational reason for such a distinction.
>
> If there is a defect in a stairway and the purchaser repairs the defect and suffers an economic loss, should he fail to recover because he did not wait until he or some member of his family fell down the stairs and broke his neck? Does the law penalize those who are alert and prevent injury? Should it not put those who prevent personal injury on the same level as those who fail to anticipate it? [*Barnes,* 264 Ind. at 230, 342 N.E.2d at 621.]

The vendee has a right to expect to receive that for which he has bargained. . . .

III. Limitations

We are, however, aware of the concerns that this court in *Ellis* raised about unlimited liability. As with any rule, there must be built-in limitations, which in this case would act as a barrier to the possibility of unlimited liability.

Therefore, our extension of the implied warranty of workmanlike quality is not unlimited; it does not force the builder to act as an insurer, in all respects, to a subsequent purchaser. Our extension is limited to *latent* defects "which become manifest after the subsequent owner's purchase and which were not discoverable had a reasonable inspection of the structure been made prior to the purchase." *Richards,* 139 Ariz. at 245, 678 P.2d at 430.

The implied warranty of workmanlike quality for latent defects is limited to a reasonable period of time. *Terlinde,* 275 S.C. at 398, 271 S.E.2d at 769; *Redarowicz,* 92 Ill. 2d at 185, 65 Ill. Dec. at 418, 441 N.E.2d at 331. "The length of time for latent defects to surface, so as to place subsequent purchasers on equal footing should be controlled by the standard of reasonableness and not an arbitrary time limit created by the Court." *Terlinde,* supra at 398, 271 S.E.2d at 769; accord *Barnes,* 264 Ind. at 229, 342 N.E.2d at 621; *Blagg,* 272 Ariz. at 187, 612 S.W.2d at 322.

Furthermore, the plaintiff still has the burden to show that the defect was caused by the defendant's workmanship, *Barnes,* supra at 230, 342 N.E.2d at 621; and defenses are also available to the builder. "The builder . . . can demonstrate that the defects were not attributable to him, that they are the result of age or ordinary wear and tear, or that previous owners have made substantial changes." *Richards,* 139 Ariz. at 245, 678 P.2d at 430.

Finally, we want to clarify that the duty inherent in an implied warranty of workmanlike quality is to perform in "a workmanlike manner and in accordance with accepted standards." Norton v. Burleaud, 115 N.H. at 436, 342 A.2d at 630. "The law recognizes an implied warranty that the contractor or builder will use the customary standard of skill and care." Kenney v. Medlin Const. & Realty Co., 68 N.C. App. 339, 343, 315 S.E.2d 311, 314 (1984); accord *Nastri,* 142 Ariz. at 444, 690 P.2d at 163.

In conclusion, to the extent Ellis v. Morris, 128 N.H. 358, 513 A.2d 951 (1986) suggests otherwise, we overrule it, and therefore reverse and remand this case for further proceedings.

Reversed and remanded.

SOUTER, J, dissenting.

Because I am not satisfied that there is an adequate justification to repudiate the rationale unanimously adopted by this court a mere two years ago in Ellis v. Robert C. Morris, Inc., 128 N.H. 358, 513 A.2d 951 (1986), I respectfully dissent.

NOTES

1. Caveat emptor in the sale of real estate by a vendor-builder is, if not yet dead, certainly moribund. Almost all of the recent cases imply a

warranty of quality or skillful construction in connection with the sale of homes. See Caceci v. DiCanio Constr. Corp., 72 N.Y.2d 52, 526 N.E.2d 266, 530 N.Y.S.2d 771 (1988) (citing cases from over 25 states). For discussion of its theoretical underpinnings see Paul G. Haskell, The Case for an Implied Warranty of Quality in Sales of Real Property, 53 Geo. L.J. 633 (1965) (pointing out the irony of a system of law that "offers greater protection to the purchaser of a seventy-nine cent dog leash than it does to the purchaser of a 40,000-dollar house"); E. F. Roberts, The Case of the Unwary House Buyer: The Housing Merchant Did It, 52 Cornell L.Q. 835 (1967).

In Sensenbrenner v. Rust, Orling & Neale, 236 Va. 419, 374 S.E.2d 55 (1988), the court reaffirmed the old rules that a subsequent home purchaser cannot recover against the builder for economic loss (1) on a contract theory where the purchaser is not in privity of contract with the builder, or (2) on a tort theory because the controlling policy considerations underlying tort law are the safety of persons and property and recovery of losses resulting from injury. See also Floor Craft Floor Covering, Inc. v. Parma Community Gen. Hosp. Assn., 54 Ohio St. 3d 1, 560 N.E.2d 206 (1990) (holding contractor cannot sue architect who called for installation of faulty flooring in absence of privity of contract). But see, to the contrary, Beachwalk Villas Condominium Assn., Inc. v. Martin, 406 S.E.2d 372 (S.C. 1991) (holding architect liable to home buyer for negligence and for breach of implied warranty even though no contractual privity exists).

2. Uniform Land Transactions Act §2-309(b) (1975), provides for two implied warranties against persons who are in "the business of selling" real estate: (1) a warranty of suitability and (2) a warranty of quality. What is the difference? The warranty of suitability arises in the case of used as well as new buildings, whereas the warranty of quality applies only to new construction. The warranty of quality is broader than the warranty of suitability in that defects may not be so serious as to make property unsuitable for its intended purpose, but may nonetheless breach the warranty of quality. See Evans v. J. Stiles, Inc., 689 S.W.2d 399 (Tex. 1985).

Uniform Land Transactions Act §2-311 provides that the warranties implied by law may be excluded or modified by agreement of the parties, or by including such expressions as "as is," *except* no general disclaimer is effective with respect to a buyer of a home in which the buyer intends to live. A seller may disclaim liability to such a buyer only for a specific defect and then only if the specific defect entered into and became a part of the basis of the bargain.

Uniform Land Transactions Act §2-312(b) provides that, notwithstanding any contrary agreement, the warranty of quality runs with the land to subsequent buyers. Thus a waiver by the first buyer could not prevent a subsequent buyer from suing the builder on the warranty.

Uniform Land Transactions Act §2-521 provides for a six-year statute of limitations which begins to run, regardless of the buyer's lack of knowledge of the breach, when the buyer to whom the warranty is first made enters into possession. Six years is the usual amount of time allowed for suit on an express warranty; the idea underlying the Uniform Act is that the statute of limitations applicable to express warranties should apply to implied warranties.

Although no state has yet adopted the Uniform Land Transactions Act, the act is likely to be influential on judicial decisions regarding implied warranties of quality and suitability.

New York has enacted a housing merchant warranty statute. N.Y. Gen. Bus. Law §777 (McKinney Supp. 1992). The statute implies a warranty that the house was built in a "skillful manner" in all contracts for sales of new homes, in addition to any express warranties the builder may make. The statutory warranty covers material defects for six years after the warranty date. See Note, The New York Housing Merchant Warranty Statute: Analysis and Proposals, 75 Cornell L. Rev. 754 (1990).

3. On disclaimers, see Frona M. Powell, Disclaimers of Implied Warranty in the Sale of New Homes, 34 Vill. L. Rev. 1123 (1989); Note, The Implied Warranty of Habitability in the Sale of New Homes: Disclaiming Liability in Illinois, 1987 Ill. L. Rev. 649.

4. A warranty of quality is not normally implied where the seller is not a "merchant of housing," that is, a builder, subdivider, or commercial vendor. See Stevens v. Bouchard, 532 A.2d 1028 (Me. 1987), and compare the treatment of the nonmerchant landlord discussed in Note 1 on page 533. Suits against a person who sells his home to another ordinarily must be based on fraud, misrepresentation, or failure to disclose.

C.   The Deed

1.   Warranties of Title

In the long course of English and American law, various types of deeds developed. The earliest deed of historical interest is the charter of feoffment. This deed, which evidenced the fact and terms of a feoffment, was used from the Norman Conquest until the middle of the sixteenth century. The charter of feoffment passed out of fashion after the Statute of Uses (1536) made it possible to convey a legal interest in land by a bargain and sale deed without livery of seisin (see pages 276-277). It was far more convenient to deliver a deed to the grantee in the solicitor's office than to go out on the land (perhaps many miles away) and perform the ceremony of livery of seisin. In 1677 the Statute of Frauds was enacted requiring a written instrument for the conveyance of an interest in land and abolishing livery of seisin.

In the several hundred years since, a number of different kinds of deeds came into use, each designed to transfer a particular type of interest in land. It was only in the nineteenth century that these old forms of deeds became obsolete, replaced by the modern deed. In the process of evolving one deed out of many, either because the scrivener was being paid by the word or the lawyer was overly cautious, all of the words of transfer used in earlier kinds of deeds were incorporated into one deed. A deed might contain this all-embracing language: "By these presents the grantor does give, grant, bargain, sell, remise, demise, release, and convey unto the grantee, and to his heirs and assigns forever, all that parcel of land described as follows." This lawyer's habit of coupling well-worn words represents, according to Professor Mellinkoff, "the lawyer's gamble on venial repetition against mortal omission. . . . The great mass of these coupled synonyms are simply redundancies, furnishing opportunity for argument that something beyond synonymy was intended." David Mellinkoff, Dictionary of American Legal Usage 129 (1992). "Grant, bargain, and sell," as well as longer couplings, says this doyen of the plain language movement, is "an archaic form, awaiting only interment. *Grant* is sufficient." Id. at 274.

To wean lawyers away from verbosity, many states have by statute provided a short form of deed that may be used. The short form deed contains all the essential elements required in order for an instrument to be a conveyance: grantor, grantee, words of grant, description of the land involved, signature of the grantor, and, sometimes, attestation or acknowledgment. It is a matter of local custom whether statutory short form deeds or more elaborate instruments are used.

Currently in general use in the United States are three types of deeds: general warranty deed, special warranty deed, and quitclaim deed. A *general warranty deed* warrants title against all defects in title, whether they arose before or after the grantor took title. A *special warranty deed* contains warranties only against the grantor's own acts but not the acts of others. Thus if the defect is a mortgage on the land executed by the grantor's predecessors in ownership, the grantor is not liable. A *quitclaim deed* contains no warranties of any kind. It merely conveys whatever title the grantor has, if any, and if the grantee of a quitclaim deed takes nothing by the deed, the grantee cannot sue the grantor.

Here is a general warranty deed:

GENERAL WARRANTY DEED

I, John Doe, hereby grant to Nancy Roe and her heirs and assigns forever, for $10 and other good and valuable consideration, the following real estate situated in _____ County, State of _____, described as follows:

[Insert description of land]

To have and to hold[9] the premises, with all the privileges and appurtenances belonging thereunto, to the use of the grantee and her heirs and assigns forever.

The grantor, for himself and his heirs and assigns, covenants (1) that the grantor is lawfully seized in fee simple of the premises, (2) that he has a good right to convey the fee simple, (3) that the premises are free from all encumbrances, (4) that the grantor and his heirs and assigns will forever warrant and defend the grantee and her heirs and assigns against every person lawfully claiming the premises or any part thereof, (5) that the grantor and his heirs and assigns will guarantee the quiet enjoyment of the premises to the grantee and her heirs and assigns, and (6) that the grantor and his heirs and assigns will, on demand of the grantee or her heirs or assigns, execute any instrument necessary for the further assurance of the title to the premises that may be reasonably required.

Dated this ____ day of _____, 19__.

John Doe

_____
[signature of grantor]

Acknowledgment[10]
State of _____
County of _____

I hereby certify that on this day before me, a notary public, personally appeared before me the above named John Doe, who

---

9. The clause beginning "To have and to hold" is known as the *habendum clause* (after the Latin *habendum et tenendum*). (Early deeds were written in Latin, the language of clerks (clerics).) The habendum clause had the function in feudal times of declaring of which lord the land was held and by what services. Modern deeds usually contain a habendum clause, which is unnecessary but may function to limit the estate granted in some way. See Robert G. Natelson, Modern Law of Deeds to Real Property §§9.1-9.10 (1992).

10. In almost all states, a deed signed by the grantor, and delivered, is valid without an acknowledgment before a notary public. However, in order for the deed to be recorded in the court house, giving notice to the world of the grantee's interest, the deed must be acknowledged by the grantor (in some states, witnessing is permitted in place of acknowledgment). Therefore, as a matter of practice, all deeds prepared by professionals are acknowledged.

acknowledged before me that he voluntarily signed the foregoing instrument on the day and year therein mentioned.

In testimony whereof, I hereunto subscribe my name and affix my official seal on this _____ day of _____, 19__.

[signature of notary]

Notary Public in and for
_____ County,
State of _____
My commission
[affix notarial seal]   expires _____

THE DEED: QUESTIONS AND NOTES

1. *Consideration.* It is customary to state in a deed that some consideration was paid by the grantee, in order to raise a presumption that the grantee is a bona fide purchaser entitled to the protection of the recording acts against prior unrecorded instruments. See pages 736-737. It is neither customary nor necessary to state the exact consideration given. Do you see why?

Some years ago the federal government levied a documentary stamp tax on deeds conveying land to a purchaser. When the tax was repealed, many state legislatures, at the instigation of real estate brokers who wanted to learn the sales price by counting the tax stamps, imposed state documentary stamp taxes. Can you imagine why a purchaser might affix more tax stamps to a deed than are required? Might not?

2. *Description of tract.* A deed must contain a description of the parcel of land conveyed that locates the parcel by describing its boundaries. Customary methods of description include (1) reference to natural or artificial monuments and, from the starting point, reference to directions and distances ("metes and bounds"); (2) reference to a government survey, recorded plat, or some other record; and (3) reference to the street and number or the name of the property.

There are many cases, particularly old ones, litigating the correct boundaries of a tract of land. When this country was settled, deed descriptions of land were very informal. They might refer to "Hester Quinn's farm" or to a tract "beginning at the old oak tree near the road and running 30 feet north, thence 70 feet east to the creek, thence south along the creek to an iron post, thence back to the beginning." In time, the reference points frequently disappeared.[11]

11. *Water boundaries.* When natural forces gradually shift a river and cause the adjacent land to recede or to advance by the build-up of new soil, there has been an *accre-*

Then too, the descriptions were sometimes conflicting. Using the monuments referred to in the deed might yield a tract of different dimensions than would be produced by using the metes and bounds description in the deed. Ultimately courts laid down a hierarchy of rules to decide cases of conflicting descriptions: Natural monuments (e.g., trees) prevail over artificial monuments (e.g., surveyor's stakes), which prevail over references to adjacent boundaries (e.g., "to Hunter's property line"), which prevail over directions (e.g., northwest), which prevail over distances (e.g., 30 feet), which prevail over area (e.g., 5 acres), which prevails over place names (e.g., "the Quinn farm"). These rules were designed to discover the intent of the parties, who probably relied more on specific, visible landmarks than on measurements of the eye. The hierarchy of precedence is not inflexible, however, and conflicts in boundary descriptions in a deed tend to be resolved on the particular facts of a case.

3. *Seal.* An old saw says a deed to land is effective when it is signed, sealed, and delivered. The requirement of a signed document was initiated by the Statute of Frauds in 1677. The requirement of sealing is older, going back to the Norman Conquest, when a seal replaced the sign of the cross[12] on documents. If a person had no seal, he borrowed someone else's. At common law a "deed" was defined as a sealed instrument; a sealed instrument was required for the conveyance of a freehold. Most state legislatures have abolished the distinction between sealed and unsealed instruments. Where still extant, the requirement of a seal on transfers of real property is formal in the purest sense. Almost anything can be a seal; the word *seal,* the initials L.S. (standing for *locus sigilli,* the place of the seal), a ribbon, a scrawl, a scratch.

4. *Forgery.* A forged deed is void. The grantor whose signature is forged to a deed prevails over all persons, including subsequent bona fide purchasers from the grantee who do not know the deed is forged.

On the other hand, most courts hold that a deed procured by fraud is voidable by the grantor in an action against the grantee, but a subsequent bona fide purchaser from the grantee who is unaware of the fraud prevails over the grantor. The grantor, having introduced the deed into the stream of commerce, made it possible for a subsequent purchaser to suffer loss. As between two innocent persons, one of whom must suffer by the act of the fraudulent third party, the law generally places the loss on the person who could have prevented the loss to the other. Love v. Elliott, 350 So. 2d 93 (Fla. App. 1977), illustrates this. In *Love,* one B.G. Russell sought to buy certain mineral interests from Mary Elliott, "a to-

---

tion. With accretion, the owner of the adjacent land gains or loses land as the water boundary gradually shifts. If there is a sudden change in the course of a river (as after a flood), the process is called *avulsion,* not accretion, and the boundaries do not change. See 3 American Law of Property §15.27 (1952).

12. The sign of the cross is the ancestral form of signing by the mark X.

tally illiterate 87-year-old widow." Mrs. Elliott agreed to sell Russell the mineral rights in 2 of 15 acres that she owned, but, unknown to her, the deed prepared by Russell and that Mrs. Elliott signed by her mark conveyed to him a much larger interest. Russell recorded his deed and promptly conveyed his interest to a bona fide purchaser for value, who recorded. Oil was then found under the land. The court held for the bona fide purchaser, saying a deed procured by fraud, unlike a forged deed, is effectual to pass title to a bona fide purchaser.

Determining the line between forgery and fraud is not always easy. See Cumberland Capital Corp. v. Robinette, 331 So. 2d 709 (Ala. App. 1976) (holding that a signature procured by deceiving the grantor into signing the instrument in ignorance of its true character is considered forged); Harding v. Ja Laur Corp., 20 Md. App. 209, 315 A.2d 132 (1974) (holding that where the grantor's signature was written on a paper, and the paper was thereafter made a part of a deed without her knowledge, there was a "material alteration" of the signature and hence a forgery).

5. *Indenture and deed poll.* In the days before typewriters and carbon paper, and centuries before Xerox, lawyers were faced with the problem of providing duplicate copies of deeds in certain instances where both the grantor and grantee wanted a copy (for example, in case of a mortgage). They found the solution in an *indenture.* The deed was written out twice on a single sheet of parchment (usually made from sheepskin stretched, scraped, and scoured), and signed at the end of each copy by both grantor and grantee. The parchment was then cut into two pieces in an irregular line, leaving a sawtooth or indented edge. The two halves, forming two separate deeds, one for the grantor and one for the grantee, could be fitted together to show their genuineness.

An indenture is to be contrasted with a *deed poll,* which is signed only by the grantor. It was called a deed poll because the top was not indented but polled or shaved even.

Indentures were rarely used in the United States because, from earliest times, every state had a recording system in which the county clerk copied the deed into the public records by hand, thus providing an official copy for the interested parties. We take up the recording system in the next chapter.

Do you see how the phrase "indentured servant" arose?

Read closely the warranty clause of the general warranty deed, set forth above, and you will see that it contains six express warranties:

1. *A covenant of seisin* — The grantor warrants that he owns the estate that he purports to convey.

2. *A covenant of right to convey* — The grantor warrants that he has the right to convey the property. In most instances this covenant serves

the same purpose as the covenant of seisin, but it is possible for a person who has seisin not to have the right to convey (e.g., a trustee may have legal title but be forbidden by the trust instrument to convey it).

3. *A covenant against encumbrances* — The grantor warrants that there are no encumbrances on the property. Encumbrances include, among other items, mortgages, liens, easements, and covenants.

4. *A covenant of general warranty* — The grantor warrants that he will defend against lawful[13] claims and will compensate the grantee for any loss that the grantee may sustain by assertion of superior title.

5. *A covenant of quiet enjoyment* — The grantor warrants that the grantee will not be disturbed in possession and enjoyment of the property by assertion of superior title. This covenant is, for all practical purposes, identical with the covenant of general warranty and is often omitted from general warranty deeds.

6. *A covenant of further assurances* — The grantor promises that he will execute any other documents required to perfect the title conveyed.

Observe that the first three covenants are phrased in the present tense and are called *present covenants*. The last three covenants are phrased in the future tense and are called *future covenants*. The distinction is this: A present covenant is broken, if ever, at the time the deed is delivered. Either the grantor owns the property at that time, or he does not; either there are existing encumbrances at that time, or there are none. A future covenant promises that the grantor will do some future act, such as defending against claims of third parties or compensating the grantee for loss by virtue of failure of title. A future covenant is not breached until the grantee or his successor is evicted from the property, buys up the paramount claim, or is otherwise damaged.

The statute of limitations begins to run on a breach of a present covenant at the date of delivery of the deed. It begins to run on a future covenant at the time of eviction, or when the covenant is broken in the future.

Brown v. Lober
Supreme Court Illinois, 1979
75 Ill. 2d 547, 389 N.E.2d 1188

[In 1947 the owner of 80 acres of land conveyed it to William and Faith Bost, reserving a two-thirds interest in the mineral rights. In 1957 the Bosts conveyed the 80-acre tract to James R. Brown and his wife by a

13. Carefully note the word *lawful*. The grantor is not liable for legal fees incurred by the grantee in *successfully* defending title, because the third party's losing claim is not lawful. The grantor is liable for the grantee's legal fees only if the grantee loses to a superior lawful claim. McDonald v. Delhi Sav. Bank, 440 N.W.2d 839 (Iowa 1989).

In some jurisdictions, the grantee can recover legal fees for an unsuccessful defense only if the grantee gives the grantor notice of the suit and demands that the grantor defend title. See Bloom v. Hendricks, 111 N.M. 250, 804 P.2d 1069 (1991).

general warranty deed containing no exceptions. In 1974 the Browns contracted to sell the mineral rights to Consolidated Coal Co. for $6,000, but upon finding that the Browns owned only one-third of the mineral rights the parties had to renegotiate the contract to provide for payment of $2,000 for one-third of the mineral rights. The prior grantor had never made any attempt to exercise his mineral rights. The 10-year statute of limitations barred a suit on the present covenants, so the Browns sued the executor of the Bosts, who had died, seeking $4,000 damages for breach of the covenant of quiet enjoyment. The trial court ruled in favor of the defendant. The appellate court reversed, and the case is now before the supreme court.]

UNDERWOOD, J. . . . The question is whether plaintiffs have alleged facts sufficient to constitute a constructive eviction. They argue that if a covenantee fails in his effort to sell an interest in land because he discovers that he does not own what his warranty deed purported to convey, he has suffered a constructive eviction and is thereby entitled to bring an action against his grantor for breach of the covenant of quiet enjoyment. We think that the decision of this court in Scott v. Kirkendall (1878), 88 Ill. 465, is controlling on this issue and compels us to reject plaintiffs' argument.

In Scott, an action was brought for breach of the covenant of warranty by a grantee who discovered that other parties had paramount title to the land in question. The land was vacant and unoccupied at all relevant times. This court, in rejecting the grantee's claim that there was a breach of the covenant of quiet enjoyment, quoted the earlier decision in Moore v. Vail (1855), 17 Ill. 185, 191: " 'Until that time, (the taking possession by the owner of the paramount title,) he might peaceably have entered upon and enjoyed the premises, without resistance or molestation, which was all his grantors covenanted he should do. They did not guarantee to him a perfect title, but the possession and enjoyment of the premises.' " 88 Ill. 465, 468.

Relying on this language in Moore, the Scott court concluded:

> We do not see but what this fully decides the present case against the appellant. It holds that the mere existence of a paramount title does not constitute a breach of the covenant. That is all there is here. There has been no assertion of the adverse title. The land has always been vacant. Appellant could at any time have taken peaceable possession of it. He has in no way been prevented or hindered from the enjoyment of the possession by any one having a better right. It was but the possession and enjoyment of the premises which was assured to him, and there has been no disturbance or interference in that respect. True, there is a superior title in another, but appellant has never felt "its pressure upon him." [88 Ill. 465, 468-469.]

Admittedly, Scott dealt with surface rights while the case before us concerns subsurface mineral rights. We are, nevertheless, convinced that the reasoning employed in *Scott* is applicable to the present case. While plaintiffs went into possession of the surface area, they cannot be said to have possessed the subsurface minerals. "Possession of the surface does not carry possession of the minerals. . . . To possess the mineral estate, one must undertake the actual removal thereof from the ground or do such other act as will apprise the community that such interest is in the exclusive use and enjoyment of the claiming party." Failoni v. Chicago & North Western Ry. Co. (1964), 30 Ill. 2d 258, 262, 195 N.E.2d 619, 622.

Since no one has, as yet, undertaken to remove the coal or otherwise manifested a clear intent to exclusively "possess" the mineral estate, it must be concluded that the subsurface estate is "vacant." As in *Scott,* plaintiffs "could at any time have taken peaceable possession of it. [They have] in no way been prevented or hindered from the enjoyment of the possession by any one having a better right." (88 Ill. 465, 468.) Accordingly, until such time as one holding paramount title interferes with plaintiffs' right of possession (e.g., by beginning to mine the coal), there can be no constructive eviction and, therefore, no breach of the covenant of quiet enjoyment.

What plaintiffs are apparently attempting to do on this appeal is to extend the protection afforded by the covenant of quiet enjoyment. However, we decline to expand the historical scope of this covenant to provide a remedy where another of the covenants of title is so clearly applicable. As this court stated in Scott v. Kirkendall (1878), 88 Ill. 465, 469: "To sustain the present action would be to confound all distinction between the covenant of warranty and that of seizin, or of right to convey. They are not equivalent covenants. An action will lie upon the latter, though there be no disturbance of possession. A defect of title will suffice. Not so with the covenant of warranty, or for quiet enjoyment, as has always been held by the prevailing authority." The covenant of seisin, unquestionably, was breached when the Bosts delivered the deed to plaintiffs, and plaintiffs then had a cause of action. However, despite the fact that it was a matter of public record that there was a reservation of a two-thirds interest in the mineral rights in the earlier deed, plaintiffs failed to bring an action for breach of the covenant of seisin within the 10-year period following delivery of the deed. The likely explanation is that plaintiffs had not secured a title opinion at the time they purchased the property. . . . Plaintiffs' oversight, however, does not justify us in overruling earlier decisions in order to recognize an otherwise premature cause of action. The mere fact that plaintiffs' original contract with Consolidated had to be modified due to their discovery that paramount title to two-thirds of the subsurface minerals belonged to another is not sufficient to constitute the constructive eviction necessary to a breach of the covenant of quiet enjoyment.

Accordingly, the judgment of the appellate court is reversed, and the judgment of the circuit court of Montgomery County is affirmed.

QUESTIONS AND NOTE

1. Suppose that the Browns buy up the two-thirds interest in the minerals for $10,000 and then sue the Bosts' executor on the covenant of general warranty. Can they recover?

For a proposal to change the law of warranties so that the statute of limitations begins to run when the defect is discovered, see Leonard Levin, Warranties of Title — A Modest Proposal, 29 Vill. L. Rev. 649 (1983-1984).

2. Suppose that the buyer has knowledge of an encumbrance on the property when he accepts a general warranty deed. Is the covenant against encumbrances breached?

There is considerable conflict among the authorities as to whether or not a visible or known easement is excepted from a covenant against encumbrances. A distinction is made in some cases between encumbrances which affect the title and those which simply affect the physical condition of the land. In the first class, it is universally held that the encumbrances are included in the covenant, regardless of the knowledge of the grantee. Those encumbrances relating to physical conditions of the property have, in many instances, been treated as excluded from the covenant. Some of these cases are decided upon the theory that, whenever the actual physical conditions of the realty are apparent, and are in their nature permanent and irremediable, such conditions are within the contemplation of the parties when contracting, and are therefore not included in a general covenant against encumbrances.

There seems to be a tendency toward the proposition that certain visible public easements, such as highways and railroad rights of way, in open and notorious use at the time of the conveyance, do not breach a covenant against encumbrances. However, it still seems to be the general rule, particularly in those cases involving private rights of way, that an easement which is a burden upon the estate granted and which diminishes its value constitutes a breach of the covenant against encumbrances in the deed, regardless of whether the grantee had knowledge of its existence or that it was visible and notorious.

Certainly, if the deed contains anything which would indicate that a known encumbrance was not intended to be within the covenant, the purchaser cannot complain that such an encumbrance was a breach of the covenant. However, with the possible exception of public easements that are apparent and in their nature permanent and irremediable, mere knowledge of the encumbrance is not sufficient to exclude it from the operation of the covenant. The intention to exclude an encumbrance should be manifested in the deed itself, for a resort to oral or other extraneous evidence would violate settled principles of law in regard to deeds. [Jones v. Grow Inv. & Mortgage Co., 11 Utah 2d 326, 328-329, 358 P.2d 909, 910-911 (1961).]

Frimberger v. Anzellotti

Appellate Court of Connecticut, 1991
25 Conn. App. 401, 594 A.2d 1029

LAVERY, J. The defendant appeals from the judgment of the trial court awarding the plaintiff damages for breach of the warranty against encumbrances and innocent misrepresentation of real property that the defendant conveyed to the plaintiff by warranty deed.

The defendant claims that the court was incorrect (1) in finding that she had misrepresented the property and that the plaintiff had relied on that misrepresentation to his detriment, (2) in finding that she breached the warranty deed covenant against encumbrances, and (3) in awarding damages for diminution of value to the property caused by a wetlands violation as well as damages for costs of correcting that violation. We agree with the defendant and reverse the decision of the trial court.

The record and memorandum of decision disclose the following facts. In 1978, the defendant's brother and predecessor in title, Paul DiLoreto, subdivided a parcel of land located in Old Saybrook for the purpose of constructing residences on each of the two resulting parcels. The property abuts a tidal marshland and is, therefore, subject to the provisions of General Statutes §22a-28 et seq.

DiLoreto built a bulkhead and filled that portion of the subject parcel immediately adjacent to the wetlands area, and then proceeded with the construction of a dwelling on the property. On February 21, 1984, DiLoreto transferred the subject property to the defendant by quit claim deed. On December 31, 1985, the defendant conveyed the property to the plaintiff by warranty deed, free and clear of all encumbrances but subject to all building, building line and zoning restrictions as well as easements and restrictions of record.

During the summer of 1986, the plaintiff decided to perform repairs on the bulkhead and the filled area of the property. The plaintiff engaged an engineering firm which wrote to the state department of environmental protection (DEP) requesting a survey of the tidal wetlands on the property. On March 14, 1986, working with the plaintiff's engineers, the DEP placed stakes on the wetlands boundary and noted that there was a tidal wetlands violation on the property. In a letter to the plaintiff dated April 10, 1986, the DEP confirmed its findings and indicated that in order to establish the tidal wetlands boundary, as staked for regulatory purposes, the plaintiff must provide DEP with an A-2 survey of the property. At some point after April, 1986, and before March, 1988, the plaintiff engaged a second group of engineers who met with DEP officials and completed an A-2 survey.

On March 28, 1988, members of the DEP water·resources unit met with the plaintiff's new engineers to stake out the wetlands boundary again. On April 13, 1988, as confirmation of that meeting, Denis Cunningham, the assistant director of the DEP water resources unit, wrote to the plaintiff to advise him that the filled and bulkheaded portion of the property, and possibly the northwest corner of the house were encroaching on the tidal wetlands boundary, thereby creating a violation of General Statutes §22a-30. This letter suggested that to correct the violation, the plaintiff would have to submit an application to DEP demonstrating the necessity of maintaining the bulkhead and fill within the tidal wetlands. Instead of filing the application, the plaintiff filed the underlying lawsuit against the defendant, claiming damages for breach of the warranty against encumbrances and innocent misrepresentation.

The trial court determined that the area has been filled without obtaining the necessary permits required under General Statutes §22a-32. The court found that the defendant had breached the warranty against encumbrances and had innocently misrepresented the condition of the property by allowing the plaintiff to purchase the property in reliance on the defendant's warranty against encumbrances. The court awarded the plaintiff damages and costs in the amount of $47,792.60, a figure that included the costs to correct the wetlands violation as well as the diminution of value of the property caused by the wetlands violation. The defendant brought the present appeal.

This appeal turns on a determination of whether an alleged latent violation of a land use statute or regulation, existing on the land at the time title is conveyed, constitutes an encumbrance such that the conveyance breaches the grantor's covenant against encumbrances. An encumbrance is defined as "every right to or interest in the land which may subsist in third persons, to the diminution of the value of the land, but consistent with the passing of the fee by the conveyance." H. Tiffany, Real Property (1975) §1002; Aczas v. Stuart Heights, Inc., 154 Conn. 54, 60, 221 A.2d 589 (1966). All encumbrances may be classed as either (1) a pecuniary charge against the premises, such as mortgages, judgment liens, tax liens, or assessments, or (2) estates or interests in the property less than the fee, like leases, life estates or dower rights, or (3) easements or servitudes on the land, such as rights of way, restrictive covenants and profits. H. Tiffany, supra, §§1003-1007. It is important to note that the covenant against encumbrances operates in praesenti and cannot be breached unless the encumbrance existed at the time of the conveyance. Id.

The issue of whether a latent violation of a restrictive land use statute or ordinance, that exists at the time the fee is conveyed, constitutes a breach of the warranty deed covenant against encumbrances has not been decided in Connecticut. There is, however, persuasive and authoritative weight in the legal literature and the case law of other jurisdictions to support the proposition that such an exercise of police power by the state *does not* affect the marketability of title and should not rise to the level of an encumbrance. See, e.g., Domer v. Sleeper, 533 P.2d 9 (Alaska 1975) (latent building code violation not an encumbrance); McCrae v. Giteles, 253 So. 2d 260, 261 (Fla. App. 1971) (violation of housing code noticed and known by vendor not an encumbrance); Monti v. Tangora, 99 Ill. App. 3d 575, 54 Ill. Dec. 732, 425 N.E.2d 597 (1981) (noticed building code violations not an encumbrance); Silverblatt v. Livadas, 340 Mass. 474, 164 N.E.2d 875 (1960) (contingent or inchoate lien which might result from building code violation not an encumbrance); Fahmie v. Wulster, 81 N.J. 391, 408 A.2d 789 (1979) (discussed infra); Woodenbury v. Spier, 122 App. Div. 396, 106 N.Y.S. 817 (1907) (a lis pendens filed to enforce housing code violations after conveyance not an encumbrance); Stone v. Sexsmith, 28 Wash. 2d 947, 184 P.2d 567 (1947).

Of the cases cited from other jurisdictions, Fahmie v. Wulster, supra, provides the closest factual analogue to the case before us. In *Fahmie*, a closely held corporation that originally owned certain property requested permission from the New Jersey bureau of water to place a nine foot diameter culvert on the property to enclose a stream. The bureau required instead that a sixteen and one-half foot diameter culvert should be installed. The corporation went ahead with its plan and installed the nine foot culvert.

The property was later conveyed to Wulster, the titular president of the corporation, who had no knowledge of the installation of the nine foot culvert. Nine years after the installation of the culvert, Wulster conveyed the property, by warranty deed, to Fahmie.

In anticipation of the subsequent resale of the property, Fahmie made application to the New Jersey economic development commission, division of water policy and supply, to make additional improvements to the stream and its banks. It was then that the inadequate nine foot culvert was discovered, and the plaintiff was required to replace it with a sixteen and one-half foot diameter pipe. Fahmie sued Wulster for the cost to correct the violation claiming a breach of the deed warranty against encumbrances.

The New Jersey Supreme Court concluded that it was generally the law throughout the country that a claim for breach of a covenant against encumbrances cannot be predicated on the necessity to repair or alter the property to conform with land use regulations. By so doing, the *Fahmie* court refused to expand the concept of an encumbrance to include structural conditions existing on the property that constitute violations of statute or governmental regulation. The court concluded that such a conceptual enlargement of the covenant against encumbrances would create uncertainty and confusion in the law of conveyancing and title insurance because neither a title search nor a physical examination of the premises would disclose the violation. The New Jersey court went on to state that "[t]he better way to deal with violations of governmental regulations, their nature and scope being as pervasive as they are, is by contract provisions which can give the purchaser full protection [in such situations]." Id., 81 N.J. at 397, 408 A.2d 789.

The case before us raises the same issues as those raised in *Fahmie*. Here, the court found that in 1978 the wetlands area was filled without a permit and in violation of state statute. The alleged violation was unknown to the defendant, was not on the land records and was discovered only after the plaintiff attempted to get permission to perform additional improvements to the wetlands area.

Although the DEP first advised the plaintiff of the alleged violation in 1986, it did not bring any action to compel compliance with the statute. Rather, it suggested that the violation may be corrected by submitting an application to DEP. As of the date of trial, the plaintiff had not made such an application, there had been no further action taken by the DEP to compel compliance, and no administrative order was ever entered from which the plaintiff could appeal. Thus, the plaintiff was never required by DEP to abate the violation or restore the wetlands.

Our Supreme Court has stated that for a deed to be free of all encumbrances there must be marketable title that can be sold "at a fair price to a reasonable purchaser or mortgaged to a person of reasonable prudence as a security for the loan of money." Perkins v. August, 109 Conn. 452, 456, 146 A. 831 (1929). To render a title unmarketable, the defect must present a real and substantial probability of litigation or loss at the time of the conveyance. Frank Towers Corporation v. Laviana, 140 Conn. 45, 53, 97 A.2d 567 (1953). Latent violations of state or municipal land use regulations that do not appear on the land records, that are unknown to the seller of the property, as to which the agency charged with enforcement has taken no official action to compel compliance at the time the deed was executed, and that have not ripened into an interest that can be recorded on the land records do not constitute an encumbrance for the purpose of the deed warranty. Monti v. Tangora, 99 Ill. App. 3d 575, 581-582, 54 Ill. Dec. 732, 425 N.E.2d 597 (1981). Although, under the statute, DEP could impose fines or restrict the use of the property until it is brought into compliance, such a restriction is not an encumbrance. Silverblatt v. Livadas, 340 Mass. 474, 479, 164 N.E.2d 875 (1960); Gaier v. Berkow, 90 N.J. Super. 377, 379, 217 A.2d 642 (1966).

Because the plaintiff never actually filed the application, any damages that he may have suffered were speculative. The court based its assessment of damages on a *proposed* application and the anticipated costs of complying with that *proposed* application. The fact that the alleged violation was first noted by DEP only after the plaintiff made requests to rework the bulkhead and filled area, leads us to the conclusion that no litigation or loss was imminent. This position is confirmed by the fact that, as of the date of trial, no order was entered by DEP to compel the plaintiff to rectify the violative condition and no application was made by the plaintiff to gain approval of existing conditions.

We adopt the reasoning of Fahmie v. Wulster, supra, and hold that the concept of encumbrances cannot be expanded to include latent conditions on property that are in violation of statutes or government regulations. To do so would create uncertainty in the law of conveyances, title searches and title insurance. The parties to a conveyance of real property can adequately protect themselves from such conditions by including protective language in the contract and by insisting on appropriate provisions in the deed. As the Illinois Appellate Court held in Monti v. Tangora, supra, 99 Ill. App. 3d at 582, 54 Ill. Dec. 732, 425 N.E.2d 597, "[t]he problem created by the existence of code violations is not one to be resolved by the courts, but is one that can be handled quite easily by the draftsmen of contracts for sale and of deeds. All that is required of the law on this point is that it be certain. Once certainty is achieved, parties and their draftsmen may place rights and obligations where they will. It is the stability in real estate transactions that is of paramount importance here." Monti v. Tangora, supra, at 582, 54 Ill. Dec. 732, 425 N.E.2d 597.

The plaintiff in this case is an attorney and land developer who had developed waterfront property and was aware of the wetlands requirement. He could have protected himself from any liability for wetlands violations either by requiring an A-2 survey prior to closing or by inserting provisions in the contract and deed to indemnify himself against potential tidal wetlands violations or violations of other environmental statutes.

We disagree as well with the court's finding of innocent misrepresentation. The elements of innocent misrepresentation are (1) a representation of material fact (2) made for the purpose of inducing the purchase, (3) the representation is untrue, and (4) there is justifiable reliance by the plaintiff on the representation by the defendant and (5) damages. Johnson v. Healy, 176 Conn. 97, 405 A.2d 54 (1978). From the evidence adduced at trial, *no* representation was made relating to the wetlands area. The court relied exclusively on the warranty against encumbrances as the "assertion" that the property was free and clear of all encumbrances as the material fact misrepresented. Because we have held that the warranty of a covenant against encumbrances was not violated, no misrepresentation was made.

The judgment is reversed as to the award of damages for breach of the warranty against encumbrances and for innocent misrepresentation of real property, and the case is remanded with direction to render judgment in favor of the defendant on those issues.

NOTES, QUESTIONS, AND PROBLEMS

1. Is the definition of "encumbrance" the same in a suit alleging breach of the covenant against encumbrances as in a suit on a contract of sale alleging unmarketable title? See Lohmeyer v. Bower, page 594. Compare 3 American Law of Property §12.128 (1952) with id. §11.49.

2. Suppose that B discovers that hazardous waste was deposited on the land many years ago by X Corporation, which conveyed the land to A. X Corporation is now out of business. A, unaware of the contamination, had conveyed the land by general warranty deed to B. What are B's remedies? If the EPA comes in, cleans up the land, and sues B to recover the costs, is A liable to B for the costs?

3. In Commonwealth Land Title Ins. Co. v. Stephenson, 101 N.C. App. 379, 399 S.E.2d 380 (1991), a septic tank providing sewage disposal for the property was on the neighbor's land, a fact discovered by the grantee after closing. The grantee sued the grantors on the general warranty deed. The court held that the mislocated septic tank system was not an encumbrance. "An adoption of the plaintiff's contention could result in increased liabilities and would amount to the circumventing of our present system of certifying title for real estate."

Suppose that the granted lot has, on record, an easement of access over the neighboring lot, but, after taking possession, the grantee discovers that the recorded deed granting this easement was signed by an incompetent person, now dead, whose heirs object to the use of their lot by the grantee. Is any warranty in the general warranty deed breached?

4. The measure of damages for breach of a covenant of seisin is the return of all or a portion of the purchase price. For example, if A buys a tract of 100 acres, and title fails to 20 acres, A is entitled to the return of one-fifth of the purchase price (and not to the market value of 20 acres of land). If A struck a particularly good bargain, and the market value is significantly higher than A paid, A does not get the benefit of her bargain.

The measure of damages for breach of a covenant against encumbrances is different. If the encumbrance is easily removable (for example, a mortgage), the measure of damages is the cost of removal. If the encumbrance is not easily removable (for example, a restrictive covenant or easement), the measure of damages is the difference in value between the land with the encumbrance and without the encumbrance. In all cases damages are limited by the total price received by the warrantor.

The measure of damages for breach of a covenant against encumbrances generally follows the rules of contract law by putting the grantee in as good a position as if the covenant or warranty had not been breached, thus giving the grantee the benefit of her bargain. Why does not the measure of damages for breach of a covenant of seisin do this?

See L. Smirlock Realty Corp. v. Title Guarantee Co., 97 A.D.2d 208, 469 N.Y.S.2d 415 (1983), aff'd, 63 N.Y.2d 955, 473 N.E.2d 234, 483 N.Y.S.2d 984 (1984) (mem.) (criticizing the measure of damages for breach of a covenant of seisin); Roger A. Cunningham, William B. Stoebuck & Dale A. Whitman, The Law of Property §11.13 at 817-818 (1984).

_____

Future covenants run with the land to all successors in interest of the grantee. Hence if *A* gives a general warranty deed to *B*, and *B* sells to *C*, *A* is liable to *C* on any of the future covenants in *A*'s deed. If the paramount owner, *O*, evicts *C*, *A* is liable to *C* on the covenants of general warranty and quiet enjoyment.

A present covenant, if not breached when the deed is delivered, can never be broken, and it is senseless to say it either runs or does not run with the land. It can never be sued upon. On the other hand, if a present covenant is breached when the deed is delivered, the grantee no longer has a covenant but, instead, has a cause of action for breach of the covenant. Under the older common law view, which objected to assignment of choses in action, the cause of action was not impliedly assigned. Thus *C* could not sue *A* for breach of a covenant of seisin. This view is still adhered to in a majority of states. In a number of states, however, a different view is now taken. The chose in action of *B* against *A* can be, and is impliedly, assigned to *C* when *B* sells the land to *C*. Under this latter view *C* can sue *A* for breach of the covenant of seisin. Rockafellor v. Gray explains this in greater detail.

Rockafellor v. Gray

Supreme Court of Iowa, 1922
194 Iowa 1280, 191 N.W. 107

FAVILLE, J. On October 14, 1907, one Doffing conveyed to the plaintiff, by warranty deed, the 80 acres of land in controversy in this action. At that time there was outstanding a certain mortgage to one Gray of $500 against said land, which the grantee in said deed assumed and agreed to pay. Subsequently foreclosure proceedings were instituted upon said mortgage, and the same culminated in a sheriff's deed, which was executed and delivered to the appellant Connelly on February 23, 1911. On April 20, 1911, Connelly conveyed said premises to one Dixon. The said deed contained the usual covenants of warranty and recited a consideration of $4,000. On June 26, 1911, Dixon in turn conveyed the premises to Hansen & Gregerson by a special warranty deed which recited a consideration of $7,000. On August 15, 1918, the plaintiff, who was the original grantee from Doffing, brought this suit to vacate and set aside the foreclosure sale under said mortgage, on the ground that the same was void because no jurisdiction had been acquired of the plaintiff in said action. On January 13, 1920, Hansen & Gregerson filed their cross-petition. Connelly, who acquired the title by sheriff's deed, as well as Hansen & Gregerson, the present owners, were made parties to said action. Hansen & Gregerson, in their cross-petition against Connelly, prayed that in the event the plaintiff was successful in vacating and setting aside the sheriff's deed that they have judgment against the remote grantor Connelly upon the covenants in his deed to Dixon, their immediate grantor. The court entered a decree in favor of the plaintiff adjudging that the said foreclosure proceedings were invalid and void, and that the sheriff's deed to Connelly should be vacated and set aside, and upon the cross-petition of Hansen & Gregerson entered judgment against Connelly on the covenant of seizin in his deed for the amount of $4,000 and interest, being the consideration recited in the deed from Connelly to Dixon, with interest from the date of the deed from Dixon to Hansen & Gregerson. From this portion of the decree Connelly prosecutes this appeal and the questions presented for our consideration are only those that arise between Connelly, the remote grantor, and Hansen & Gregerson, the remote grantees, in the chain of title.

The first question for our determination is whether or not the covenant of seizin runs with the land in this state, so that an action thereon may be maintained by a remote grantee. In Brandt v. Foster, 5 Iowa 287, we announced the rule that a covenant of seizin is a covenant for the title, and that if, at the time of the conveyance, the grantor did not own the land the covenant is broken immediately, and that it is not necessary, in order to recover, to allege or prove an ouster or eviction.

In Schofield v. Iowa Homestead Co., 32 Iowa 317, 7 Am. Rep. 197, the precise question now presented was before us. The opinion contains a full discussion of the proposition. The court recognized the division among the authorities and also that a majority of American courts recognize that the covenant of seizin does not run with the land. This court expressly, at that time (1871), adopted the English rule, holding that the covenant of seizin runs with the land, and is broken the instant the conveyance is delivered, and then becomes a chose in action held by the covenantee in the deed, and that a deed by said first covenantee operates as an assignment of such chose in action to a remote grantee, who can maintain an action thereon against the grantor in the original deed. This case has withstood all subsequent assaults upon it, and the rule therein announced has become thoroughly imbedded in the jurisprudence of this state. It is a rule of property, and we are disposed to adhere to it, regardless of any views we may entertain as to the soundness of the rule as originally announced. It is too well established for us to now consider any repudiation of it. . . .

However, another question confronts us, and that is the contention that the original covenantee, never having been in possession of the premises, that the covenant of seizin could not run with the land. Some of the courts which recognize the rule that the covenant of seizin runs with the land appear to base the holding upon the fact of the grantee having had possession under the deed. It is the theory that seizin in fact is what carries the covenant of seizin and causes it to run with the land. See Mecklem v. Blake, 22 Wis. 495, 99 Am. Dec. 68. This, however, is not the reason for the rule that the covenant of seizin runs with the land to a remote grantee, as recognized by this court. In the *Schofield* case, speaking by Mr. Justice Beck, this court said:

> What legal principle would be violated by holding that the deed from the first grantee operates as an assignment of this chose in action? Deeds under the laws of this state have been reduced to forms of great simplicity. Intricate technicalities have been pruned away, and they are now as brief and simple in form as a promissory note. All choses in action, as I have just remarked, may be assigned and transferred. The covenant of seizin (if it be held that such a covenant exists in a deed of the form authorized by the laws of this state), as we have seen, is intended to secure indemnity for the deprivation of the title and enjoyment of the lands conveyed. Why not brush away the "technical scruples" gathered about the covenant of seizin, as we have the like technical and cumbrous forms of the instrument itself, and enforce it for the benefit of the party who is really injured by its breach, even though, in so doing, we find it necessary to hold that a chose in action is assigned and transferred by the operation of the deed?

In the case at bar the evidence shows that the original grantor, Connelly, never had possession of the premises in question, nor did his grantee Dixon, who conveyed to the appellees Hansen & Gregerson. Neither Connelly nor Dixon paid any attention to the land. They never were in possession, nor leased the same, nor paid any taxes thereon. If in every case it must be held that the covenant of seizin only runs with the land where the original covenantee takes possession before conveyance by him to another, then it could not be said to run with the land in this case. The original covenantee, Dixon, did not take possession of the land and had no such possession when he conveyed to the appellees Hansen & Gregerson. The evidence tends to show that the latter never had actual possession of the premises. If the covenant of seizin runs with the land to a remote grantee, under the theory that subsequent deeds operate as an assignment of the chose in action that accrued to the first grantee, then there is no logical reason why the remote grantee, claiming by conveyance under the original grantee, cannot maintain the action whether or not he ever had actual possession of the land. The rights of the remote grantee are acquired by conveyance (assignment) and not by virtue of actual possession of the premises. The grantor (appellant Connelly) had neither title to nor possession of the premises at the time he executed and delivered his deed to Dixon on April 20, 1911. Dixon thereupon had a right of action against Connelly for the breach of the covenant of seizin. This right of action, under our holding in Schofield v. Iowa Homestead Co., supra, passed by assignment to the appellees Hansen & Gregerson by the deed which Dixon executed and delivered to them June 26, 1918. These grantees asserted their claim for breach of appellant's deed within the 10-year period from the date of the execution and delivery of the original deed from Connelly to Dixon, and were entitled to maintain said action and to recover against the remote grantor Connelly.

A question is raised as to the amount of the recovery of the appellees Hansen & Gregerson against Connelly. The court allowed recovery in the amount of the consideration recited in the deed from Connelly to his grantee Dixon, with interest thereon from the date of the execution of the deed from Dixon to Hansen & Gregerson. This was in accordance with the general rule in cases of a breach of the covenant of seizin.

In Brandt v. Foster, supra, we held that —

> If, at the time of the conveyance, the grantor does not own the land, the covenant is broken immediately. . . . The measure of damages for breach of this covenant is the consideration money and interest, upon the ground that this is the actual loss. If the grantee, however, has lost less, he is limited to the amount of injury sustained. . . . The consideration money with interest is the extent to which damages can, under any circumstances, be recovered, upon this covenant. As a general rule, this is the standard. They may, under some circumstances, fall below, but can never exceed.

In Shorthill v. Ferguson, 44 Iowa 249, we said: "Parol proof of consideration to contradict that expressed in the deed is admissible as between the original parties, but it is not admissible in a suit against the original grantor by one to whom his grantee has transferred the land." . . .

In Foshay v. Shafer, 116 Iowa 302, 89 N.W. 1106, we held that where the covenantee had been given possession the breach of the covenant of seizin did not entitle him to recover substantial damages until some positive injury had been suffered; and held that no more than nominal damages could be recovered so long as the grantee remains in possession, without actual injury.[14] See, also, Greenvault v. Davis, 4 Hill (N.Y.) 643.

Appellant contends that if it is held that the covenant of seizin is

14. In Hilliker v. Rueger, 228 N.Y. 11, 126 N.E. 266 (1920), the court allowed the warrantee to recover a proportionate part of the purchase price *and* remain in possession of the acreage to which title had failed (the holder of superior title had not yet appeared to claim possession). Which view is sounder? — EDS.

breached immediately upon the execution and delivery of the original deed to the immediate grantee where the grantor has no title, and that the rights of the grantee pass by assignment to a remote grantee by mesne conveyances, that the measure of damages in an action by the remote grantee would be the same as the damages which the original grantee could have recovered against the grantor. It must be conceded that there is much force in this contention of the appellant. If the consideration recited in the original deed could be attacked between the original grantor and his immediate grantee, and if a conveyance by the first grantee operates as an assignment of a chose in action for breach of the covenant of seizin to a remote grantee, it can well be argued that the remote grantee can in no event recover any greater amount than could the immediate grantee. . . . In this case it is the contention of the appellant that while the deed from him to his immediate grantee Dixon recites a consideration of $4,000 that in truth and in fact there was no consideration, or at least it was merely a nominal one, and it is his contention that the remote grantees Hansen & Gregerson can recover against him no greater amount than Dixon could have recovered.

Just what would be our ruling on this question, if it were one of first impression, we do not need to determine. We regard the question as settled by our previous decisions, and are bound by the rule of stare decisis. We have recognized and announced the rule that, as between the original parties parol proof of the actual consideration is admissible to contradict the recitals of a deed, but that such evidence is not admissible in a suit by a remote grantee against the original grantor. See cases supra. The remote grantee, in purchasing the premises, had a right to rely upon the fact that the original grantor in a prior deed was bound by the covenants of warranty and of seizin therein, and had a right to take into account the consideration recited in such prior deed in purchasing the premises. In this case Hansen & Gregerson, from an examination of the record, would have been apprised of the fact that the appellant had executed and delivered to his grantee Dixon a warranty deed containing the covenant of seizin and that said deed recited a consideration of $4,000. They likewise had a right to rely upon the law of this state that said covenant of said deed ran with the land and inured to their benefit. It is to be presumed that they took these matters into consideration in purchasing from Dixon. As to them, the original grantor is estopped to claim that the consideration recited in said deed is in fact less than the recitals therein contained. This is the rule as to the covenant of warranty and applies in this state equally to the covenant of seizin. In no event could the remote grantee recover from the remote grantor a greater amount than the consideration recited in the original deed between the remote grantor and his immediate grantee.

In this instance the recovery of Hansen & Gregerson against the appellant Connelly is limited to $4,000, the consideration recited in the deed from Connelly to his grantee Dixon. Hansen & Gregerson are entitled to interest on this amount from the date of their deed from Dixon. The recited consideration in the deed from Dixon to Hansen & Gregerson is $7,000. The evidence tends to show that this consideration was in fact paid by Hansen & Gregerson to Dixon. The amount of the recovery of Hansen & Gregerson, as before stated, is limited to the consideration recited in the deed from the original grantor to his immediate grantee, even though the remote grantee paid a larger consideration. Whether or not the remote grantee could recover from the remote grantor the amount of the consideration recited in the original deed between the remote grantor and his immediate grantee, in the event that the remote grantee had paid his grantor a less sum than the consideration recited in said original deed, is not before us, and we express no opinion thereon. . . .

The decree of the lower court was in accordance with the rules herein announced, and was correct.

The decree of the district court should be in all respects affirmed.

NOTES AND PROBLEMS

1. In Rockafellor v. Gray, why did Hansen & Gregerson not sue on the future covenants of warranty and quiet enjoyment, which do run with the land? There are two explanations. First, for a covenant to "run with the land" to a successor claimant, the covenantee must convey to the successor either title or possession, some "thing" to which the covenant can "attach" and with which it can "run." In the case, Dixon (the covenantee) transferred neither title nor possession to Hansen & Gregerson; both were in Rockafellor. Second, future covenants of warranty and quiet enjoyment are intended to secure compensation to the purchaser when his quiet possession is disturbed. These covenants are not breached unless the covenantee or his assigns is prevented from taking complete possession or is actually or constructively evicted by a person having paramount title. 3 American Law of Property §12.129 (1952).

Observe that the Iowa court, in quoting from the *Schofield* case, is careful to say that Hansen & Gregerson can sue on the covenant of seisin because the chose in action arising from its breach was assigned to them, not because the covenant runs with title or possession (seisin in fact).

2. By general warranty deed A conveys Blackacre to B for $20,000. B conveys Blackacre to C for $15,000. O, the true owner, ousts C. The jurisdiction holds that present covenants are breached, if at all, when made, and the chose in action is not assigned to subsequent grantees.

(a) The deed from B to C is a quitclaim deed. How much, if anything, can B recover from A?

(b) The deed from *B* to *C* is a general warranty deed. *C* has not sued *B* nor settled with him. How much, if anything, can *B* recover from *A*?

(c) The deed from *B* to *C* is a general warranty deed. *C* sues *B* and recovers $15,000. How much, if anything, can *B* recover from *A*?

(d) Would your answers be different if the jurisdiction follows the view of Rockafellor v. Gray?

3. By general warranty deed *A* conveys Whiteacre to *B* for $15,000. By quitclaim deed *B* conveys Whiteacre to *C* for $12,000. By general warranty deed *C* conveys Whiteacre to *D* for $20,000. *O*, the true owner, ousts *D* at a time that the land is worth $24,000. Advise *D* and *C* as to how much they can recover on the warranties.

4. How effective is a warranty deed in protecting the purchaser against defects in title? Consider the following:

(a) The maximum recovery on a warranty is the consideration received by the covenantor, plus incidental damages such as out-of-pocket expenses incurred in examining title or defending the title against a successful direct attack. This rule is continued by Uniform Land Transactions Act §2-513(2) (1975). Suppose that *B* purchases Blackacre from *A* for $10,000, and 20 years later, when paramount title is asserted by *O*, Blackacre is worth $125,000. Should *A* or *B* bear the risk of loss for increase in value?

(b) Most states have statutes authorizing a decedent's personal representative to publish notice to creditors of the decedent's death in a local newspaper and barring claims not presented to the personal representative within a specified period thereafter. These statutes, varying in detail, are thought necessary to permit distribution of the decedent's assets free and clear to the beneficiaries. Iowa Code Ann. §633.410 (1992) generally bars all claims not presented within four months after publication of the notice to creditors.

Suppose that in Rockafellor v. Gray the defendant Connelly had died in 1915 and no claim had been filed against his estate by Hansen & Gregerson within four months of publication of a creditors' notice. What result? See Arthur R. Gaudio, Title Covenants for the Iowa Homeowner — Some Good News and Much Bad News, 23 Drake L. Rev. 1, 9-13 (1973).

(c) Judgments against the covenantor may be uncollectible because the covenantor is insolvent or owns no property, or the covenantor's property is fully within statutory exemptions to creditors' claims or is fully covered by a mortgage.

2. Delivery

To be effective, a deed must be delivered by the grantor.

Merry v. County Board of Education of Jefferson County

Supreme Court of Alabama, 1956
264 Ala. 411, 87 So. 2d 821

[Shortly before her death in 1952, Lena B. Snedecor and the County Board of Education were negotiating for the sale of Snedecor's land to the Board. Snedecor executed a deed to the Board and gave it to her lawyers, so that they might deliver it if the Board accepted her written offer. On April 1, 1952, Snedecor died. Not knowing of her death, the Board thereafter voted to accept Snedecor's offer. On April 28, the Board paid the purchase money to Snedecor's lawyers, and they handed over the deed to the Board.

The executors of Snedecor's estate brought suit to cancel the deed. The Board demurred. The trial court overruled the demurrer.]

SIMPSON, J. Appellants seek cancellation on the theory that the deed executed by testatrix was never delivered. They allege that it was deposited with her attorneys, along with an offer to sell, but that during her lifetime there was no delivery. Further, they allege that the deed was given (not "delivered") to the appellee Board after testatrix' death, this however, did not amount to delivery — they maintain — because testatrix' death revoked the attorneys' power to deliver.

As we understand this aspect, the ruling on demurrer raises the question: do the facts alleged show a nondelivery as a matter of law? . . .

Delivery as a matter of law in this aspect requires consideration of two distinct phases — delivery *before* the death of the grantor and delivery *after* the death of the grantor.

Delivery before death of grantor. Appellants allege that the deed was executed and forwarded to testatrix' attorneys:

> . . . in order that said deed might be delivered to said County Board if and when such negotiations should culminate in a contract between the testatrix and said County Board for the sale of said realty and the terms of said contract should be complied with . . .

The allegations are tested by general demurrer.

Construed most strongly against the pleader, we understand him to maintain that during her lifetime the testatrix did not deliver the disputed deed: She (or her agent attorneys) were negotiating for the sale of the realty; she executed a deed to it and forwarded it to her attorneys (depositaries) along with an offer to sell at a fixed figure; she instructed them to deliver the deed ". . . if and when such negotiations should culminate in a contract . . . and the terms should be complied with. . . ." It appears that no promise was made or consideration paid by the Board prior to delivery to it of the deed, which delivery, as stated, was made by grantor's attorneys after her death.

The situation thus presented is controlled by the law with respect to escrow agreements, the determinative question being whether or not there was a valid escrow. The applicable rule is thus well stated in 19 American Jurisprudence, Escrow §5, p.421:

> In order that an instrument may operate as an escrow when delivered to one not a party to the instrument to be delivered over in turn to a party to the instrument upon the performance of certain conditions, there must be a valid contract between all the parties as to the subject matter of the instrument and the delivery, and . . . in the absence of such a contract the party making the delivery may recall the instrument. Hence, not only must there be sufficient parties, a proper subject matter, and a consideration in order for an escrow to exist, but the parties must have actually contracted. The actual contract of sale on the one side and of purchase on the other is as essential to constitute the instrument an escrow as that it be executed by the grantor; and until both parties have definitely assented to the contract, the instrument executed by the proposed grantor, though in form a deed, is neither a deed nor an escrow. It makes no difference whether the instrument remains in the possession of the nominal grantor or is placed in the hands of a third party, pending the proposals for the sale or purchase.

. . . Here, according to the allegations of the bill, the proposed grantee neither paid any consideration nor contracted to purchase the property. If this be so, then the agreement on the part of the grantor that the deed executed by her and placed in the hands of her attorneys should be delivered to the named grantee upon payment of the recited consideration was, like any other contract, unilateral and unenforceable so long as it remained executory. Therefore, the escrow was revocable at any time before it was accepted and acted upon by the grantee. If not done in the lifetime of the grantor, it was ipso facto revoked upon her death.

We are not to be understood as holding that death of the grantor alone abrogates a deposit in escrow. We are not unmindful of the rule that where death of either of the parties is not contemplated as a condition, the escrow will not be affected by the death of either or both of the parties to the instrument before the actual condition is performed or before final delivery. "The death of the parties in no way abrogates a true contract of escrow, for in such cases the escrow takes effect by constructive delivery upon the performance of the happening of the agreed condition or contingency, and such delivery by fiction of law relates back to, and is substituted for, the delivery made to the depositary in the lifetime of the grantor." 19 Am. Jur. Escrow, §10, p.426. . . .

It results as our opinion that the trial court did not err in its ruling on the demurrers to the aspect of the bill seeking cancellation.

NOTE AND QUESTIONS

1. In the *Merry* case, towards the end of its opinion, the court refers to the doctrine of relation back applied in escrows where there is a written contract. According to this doctrine, the delivery of the deed by the escrow agent to the grantee (the second delivery) is treated as if it took place at the time of delivery of the deed by the grantor to the escrow agent (the first delivery). Hence, if the County Board of Education had accepted Snedecor's offer before she died, the delivery of the deed by Snedecor's lawyers after her death would be treated as if it occurred before her death. By this fiction the rule that a will is required to pass title at death is avoided. Title would have been transferred by Snedecor during life.

The fiction of relation back is applied in a number of circumstances to carry out the parties' intention and to do equity. For example, if the grantor puts a deed in escrow and subsequently executes and delivers a second deed to a donee, and then the escrow agent delivers the first deed to the grantee, the title of the first grantee relates back to the time the deed was put in escrow, thus prevailing over the donee-grantee. On the other hand, if the second grantee is a subsequent bona fide purchaser who does not know of the prior deed in escrow, the purchaser will win.

2. Seller is ready to deliver a deed to buyer, but buyer does not yet have the money. Seller says to buyer, "I'll give you this deed now on condition that you pay me by the first of next month." Buyer takes the deed and records, but subsequently does not pay. Where delivery is made on an oral condition, the delivery is good, even though the oral condition is not complied with. What is seller's remedy? See State ex rel. Pai v. Thom, 58 Haw. 8, 563 P.2d 982 (1977).

3. De Bess Clevenger of Bartlesville, Oklahoma, agreed to exchange a building she owned for an apartment house owned by J.D. Simmons in Tulsa. Simmons told her that the apartment house had a brick front. Clevenger executed a deed to Simmons and gave it to the real estate broker, Peay, who arranged the exchange. Clevenger told Peay not to deliver the deed to Simmons until she went to Tulsa and saw that the apartment house was as represented. A week later Clevenger went to Tulsa and found the apartment house did not have a brick front. Upon returning to Bartlesville, Clevenger notified Peay that she would not trade and demanded her deed back. Peay could not give the deed back because, in violation of her instructions, Peay had given the deed to Simmons. Simmons recorded the deed and went into possession. Four

months later, Simmons sold Clevenger's building to D. F. Moore, a bona
fide purchaser. Thereafter, Clevenger bestirred herself and sued Moore
to cancel her deed to Simmons and the deed from Simmons to Moore.
What result? See Clevenger v. Moore, 126 Okla. 246, 259 P.219, 54
A.L.R.1237 (1927) (holding that whether Clevenger ratified delivery by
her subsequent conduct was a jury question), 126 Okla. 361, 298 P.248
(1931) (affirming jury finding for Moore). Would it make any difference
if Clevenger had not given the deed to Peay but had put it in her desk
drawer and Peay had stolen it from her drawer?

St. Louis County National Bank v. Fielder
Supreme Court of Missouri, 1953
364 Mo. 207, 260 S.W.2d 483

HYDE, J. Action to determine title to real estate. Plaintiff claims title as
testamentary trustee under the will of Paul A. Kessler, deceased, executed September 17, 1947. Defendant claims under a quitclaim deed,
executed by Kessler, June 2, 1949, and recorded on that date. Kessler
died July 24, 1950. The question for decision is whether the deed is void
as an invalid testamentary disposition as contended by plaintiff. The trial
court found the deed void, adjudged title in plaintiff and defendant has
appealed.

The case was tried on an agreed statement of facts. Kessler's will left
all his estate, real and personal, to plaintiff as trustee for his daughter
and three grandchildren, the corpus to go to the grandchildren at the
daughter's death. The deed conveyed Kessler's residence to defendant.
It was in regular form but contained the following reservation: "The
said party of the first part hereby reserves a Life Estate in and to said
property, with power to sell, rent, lease, mortgage or otherwise dispose
of said property during his natural lifetime." Kessler continued to reside
in the property until his death, and at no time did he sell, rent, lease,
mortgage or otherwise dispose of said property during his natural lifetime or attempt to do so.

Plaintiff contends that "a deed, in order to convey, must vest in the
grantee a present irrevocable interest"; that "retention of power to sell,
mortgage or otherwise dispose of property during lifetime, by grantor,
in deed purporting to convey an estate to commence in the future prevents an immediate and irrevocable interest from being vested in
grantee because the retention of such powers is equivalent to the power
to revoke the deed"; that the reservation of the power to revoke shows
grantor's intention to be that no estate is to pass to grantee until the
death of the grantor; and that this reservation makes the deed testamentary in character. Plaintiff relies mainly on Goins v. Melton, 343 Mo. 413,
121 S.W.2d 821, 823 and cases cited therein.

However, the reservation in the deed herein involved says nothing about postponing the passing or vesting of title until the death of the grantor, as is true in every Missouri case we have found holding a deed to be testamentary. See cases cited in article on Testamentary Character of Deeds in Missouri, Ottman, 5 Mo. Law Rev. 350; see also Deed or Will, Eckhardt, 15 Mo. Law Rev. 383. Instead, this deed unconditionally conveys the title immediately, stating "neither the said party of the first part, nor his heirs . . . will hereafter claim or demand any right or title to the aforesaid premises." It makes a clear and proper reservation of a life estate and does also reserve the right to sell, mortgage or otherwise dispose of the property during the grantor's lifetime, which plaintiff correctly says is in effect a reservation of the power to revoke to be exercised in a particular manner. See 3 Tiffany, Real Property 14, Sec. 681. Of course, the right to rent or lease is not inconsistent with the life estate; and none of these provisions prevents the immediate vesting of title in the grantee of the remainder in fee. While the grantee's estate might later be defeated by exercise of the power, that would only make it a defeasible fee but nevertheless a vested estate. See 31 C.J.S., Estates, §5, p.15; 133 Am. Jur. 544, Sec. 88. The deed in the *Goins* case, in addition to the retention of the right to sell during the grantor's lifetime, stated: "*At his death the title* to all, or whatever part thereof remains unsold, *to pass to and vest in the grantee together with all his personal property and belongings.*" Providing for personal property to thus vest in the grantee at the same time as the title to the land (at the grantor's death) was an added indication of the grantor's intention to make a testamentary disposition not found in many of the cases. This intention, as therein stated, was to be "gathered from the four corners of the instrument." For criticism of the *Goins* case see Work of Missouri Supreme Court — 1938, Property, Eckhardt, 4 Mo. Law Rev. 419. There is nothing like the above quoted provision of the *Goins* case deed in this case. Indeed the grantor had already made his testamentary disposition by his previously executed will. (For a deed more like the *Goins* case deed see Wren v. Coffey, Tex. Civ. App., 26 S.W. 142, 143, where the language was "all our right, title, and interest in and to our homestead . . . should we not sell or dispose of the same before death." While this did not prohibit the vesting of title as specifically as did the *Goins* case deed, the Court held it testamentary, saying it was "a declaration of intention that the conveyance should not have the effect to divest title out of the makers, and invest it in the son, during the lifetime of such makers.") In this case, there is only the reservation of a life estate and a power to revoke during the grantor's lifetime. There is no language indicating an intention to postpone the vesting of the remainder in fee; but instead this deed affirmatively provides for the immediate vesting of title.

For the reasons hereinafter stated, we are convinced that a grantor has the right to reserve the power to revoke and that such a reservation alone does not make a deed testamentary. Insofar as Goins v. Melton indicates this reservation alone to be a reason for declaring a deed testamentary, it should be no longer followed. In fact, it would be more logical to hold the reservation void as repugnant to the grant (see 6 Thompson on Real Property 698, Sec. 3471) and thus leave the conveyance absolute, than it would be to hold that such a reservation makes the deed testamentary. That was the result reached by the Supreme Court of Kansas in Newell v. McMillan, 139 Kan. 94, 30 P.2d 126, 127 where a deed, reserving a life estate to the grantors, provided "The right to mortgage, sell or . . . dispose of the within described real estate is hereby reserved by the grantors, until said grantee shall have attained the age of forty years." The Court held this reservation was a nullity and did not defeat the conveyance of the fee to the grantee.

Apparently that was what the early common law did before the Statute of Uses (see Farwell on Powers, p.2) for reasons stated by the Supreme Court of California, in Tennant v. John Tennant Memorial Home, 167 Cal. 570, 140 P.242, loc. cit. 244, as follows:

> Under the ancient common law, there was a rule to the effect that, where a transfer was made by feoffment and livery of seisin, any power of revocation reserved in the feoffment itself was void, on the ground that it was repugnant to the grant. The rule arose from the peculiar nature and purpose of the ceremony of livery of seisin, which was a necessary part of an alienation by feoffment. It consisted of a formal delivery of possession on the premises, symbolized by the manual delivery of a clod or piece of turf from the land, all of which was done in the presence of witnesses from the vicinage. The publicity was required because in those times there were no public records of conveyances and it was necessary in some way to preserve evidence of the transfer. For this reason the ceremony was required and the presence of witnesses was necessary. 4 Kent's Comm. 480. As this purpose would be defeated if the accompanying deed contained a reservation of power to revoke it, so that thereby the transfer could be absolutely defeated and a retransfer effected without such public ceremony or witnesses, the courts were forced to hold that such reservation in a feoffment was void. [1 Sugden on Powers, 2.]

While the Court, in the *Tennant* case, put the validity of the reservation of the right to revoke on statutory grounds, it also said: "Aside from the implied permission in the above section, . . . the reasonable conclusion would be that it was one of the inherent rights of every landowner to include such a reservation in a grant of his land." See also Smith v. Smith, 167 Ga. 368, 145 S.E. 661; Ricketts v. Louisville, St. L. & T. Ry. Co., Ky., 15 S.W. 182; Brandish v. Sullivan, 54 R.I. 434, 173 A. 117; Stamper v. Venable, 117 Tenn. 557, 97 S.W. 812; Jones v. Clifton, 101 U.S. 225, 25 L. Ed. 908.

Obviously, therefore, whether the reserved power to revoke was valid or invalid, defendant would have title to the land herein involved. That is, if the grantor had a valid right to revoke, since he did not do so, defendant's title in fee is now absolute. On the other hand, if such a provision was invalid, because the grantor could not reserve such a power, then it was a nullity and his conveyance in fee was absolute. Likewise, it seems clear that neither the existence of a power to revoke nor its validity or invalidity has any bearing whatever on the question of testamentary character of a conveyance. Thus it requires something more than the reservation of a power to revoke alone to show an intention to make a testamentary disposition and there is nothing more in this case.

However, we think we should put our decision on the ground that the reservation of a power to revoke is valid because that is the modern trend. As pointed out in the *Tennant* case, 140 P. loc. cit. 244, modern statutes for the transfer of lands by deed and the recording thereof have removed all the reasons on which the rule of the common law (holding void the reservation of such a power) was founded. . . . The Kentucky case, Ricketts v. Louisville, St. L. & T. Ry. Co., 15 S.W. 182, answered the contention that the reservation of a power to revoke was against public policy, because it would enable the parties to defeat creditors, by saying: "The deed is notice to the creditors of the reserved power. If they trust the grantee upon the credit of the estate thus granted, they do so knowing the risk, because the deed gives them notice of it."

There is both good reason and authority for holding valid the reservation of a power to revoke. In 3 Tiffany, 3rd Ed. 12, Sec. 681, it is said:

> A power of revocation in favor of the grantor himself is, even by the English authorities, perfectly valid in a conveyance by way either of bargain and sale or covenant to stand seised, though it would not have been valid at common law. In this country, as in England, a power of revocation is frequently inserted in a voluntary deed of trust and that there is no such power in a deed of that character has been regarded as an indication that the deed was obtained by undue influence. But such a power is valid in conveyances other than deeds of trust, and the reservation of such a power involves no inconsistency with the conveyance. It merely involves, as before remarked, the creation of an executory limitation in favor of the grantor himself. . . .

We, therefore, hold that the deed to defendant herein created a defeasible fee subject to a life estate and, since the life estate has terminated and the power to revoke was not exercised, defendant is now the absolute owner.

The judgment is reversed and remanded with directions to enter judgment for defendant.

All concur.

NOTES AND QUESTIONS

1. The *Fielder* case represents the majority view, but there is considerable authority holding that a power to revoke in a deed prevents a delivery. See John L. Garvey, Revocable Gifts of Legal Interests in Land, 54 Ky. L.J. 19 (1965). Butler v. Sherwood, 196 A.D. 603, 188 N.Y.S. 242 (1921), aff'd, 233 N.Y. 655, 135 N.E. 957 (1922), is the leading case for the latter view. Should revocable deeds be valid? The law permits several other types of revocable transfers, mentioned below, which are, in practical effect, substitutes for wills.

Compare gifts of personal property. As was set forth in earlier cases (at pages 169-190), revocable gifts of personal property are not generally permitted. Why should revocable deeds of land be permitted but not revocable gifts of personal property?

2. *Avoidance of probate.* After the death of a person, testate or intestate, a personal representative may be appointed to collect the decedent's assets, to pay the claims of creditors and the tax collectors, to distribute the remaining assets to the beneficiaries, and *to change the title of property from the decedent to the new owners.* This process is called "probate of the decedent's estate," and it is supervised by a probate court. Generally speaking, a probate is not required by law; it is the procedure the law makes available for settling the decedent's affairs.

The key to avoiding probate is to have title to property put in some form so that a court order changing title at death is unnecessary. A classic way of avoiding probate is to hold property in joint tenancy. Under the theory of joint tenancy, at the death of one joint tenant nothing passes to the survivor, who owned the whole all along; the survivor is merely relieved of the participation of the decedent in the tenancy (see page 329). Other ways of avoiding probate include using life insurance contracts and joint and survivor bank accounts. In many states, a death beneficiary may be put on any contract (pension plan, Keogh plan, IRA, stock account with brokerage house, partnership agreement). See Uniform Probate Code §6-101 (1990).

3. *Revocable trusts.* An increasingly popular way for the rich to avoid probate is by creating a revocable inter vivos trust. Under a simple form of this arrangement, O transfers property to X to hold in trust and pay the income to O for life, and on O's death to distribute the property to O's children. O retains the power to revoke the trust. If O desires, O can be the trustee herself under a declaration of trust; there is no necessity of having a third-party trustee. A revocable inter vivos trust — or, for that matter, an irrevocable inter vivos trust — avoids probate because O has, during life, changed the legal title from a fee simple in O to a fee simple in a trustee. There is no necessity to change the legal title at O's death. (Upon the death of a trustee, the property to which the trustee

has legal title does not go through probate. A successor trustee, either named in the trust instrument or appointed by a court, takes over the property and administers it under the terms of the trust instrument.)

Why do persons want to avoid probate? First and foremost, probate is costly. The executor gets a commission, usually a fixed percentage of the value of the assets. The lawyer for the estate also is entitled to a fee, again often a fixed percentage. In addition, there may be court costs, appraiser's fees, and fees for guardians ad litem of any minor beneficiaries. These costs can run to 10 percent of the estate or higher.

Second, probate may bring publicity. A will (including a will creating a testamentary trust) is a public record, as is the inventory of assets filed in probate court. An inter vivos trust, on the other hand, is not recorded in any public place. It is a purely private transaction involving the settlor, the trustee, and the beneficiaries. Persons desirous of secrecy — especially all the Rockefellers, Fords, and Gettys, and even the lesser millionaires — can avoid publicity about their wealth by transferring their property during life to a trustee.

There are other reasons for establishing a revocable trust besides avoiding probate, but we leave the full development of this subject to a course in trusts. For uses of revocable trusts, see Jesse Dukeminier & Stanley M. Johanson, Wills, Trusts, and Estates 532-538 (4th ed. 1990).

NOTE: DELIVERY WITHOUT HANDING OVER

To deliver a deed of land, it is not necessary that the deed be "handed over." "Delivery" means no more than an act that evinces an intent to be immediately bound. The act can be, of course, handing over the document to the grantee, but it can also be the grantor's declaration, express or implied, that he is bound by his deed. The traditional view was put by Sir Edward Coke with his usual felicity: "As a deed may be delivered to the party without words, so may a deed be delivered by words without any act of delivery." 1 Co. Litt. 36A.

The most common case of delivery without manual tradition arises where the grantor executes a deed and places it in a safe deposit box, usually with the thought that the grantee will "take" the land at the grantor's death. If the grantor intends to pass title or a future interest to the grantee *now*, there has been a delivery even though possession may be postponed until the grantor's death. On the other hand, if the grantor intends that no interest should arise until death, no delivery during life has taken place; the deed cannot take legal effect at death because the grantor intended it to be a deed, not a will, and the instrument is not executed with two witnesses in accordance with the Statute of Wills.[15] Laypersons often do not know of the sharp distinction the law draws between an *inter vivos transfer of land,* requiring the delivery of a signed instrument, and a *transfer at death,* requiring an instrument complying with the Statute of Wills.

To give effect to a deed put away for safekeeping, a court must hold that rights passed to the grantee during the grantor's life, with possession postponed. This in turn requires a court to find that the deed has been delivered. Courts have found delivery where the grantor manifests, by words, acts, or circumstances, his intention to be bound, and particularly where the grantor hands the deed to the grantee who hands it back to the grantor *or* the grantor tells the grantee or some third person of the deed. A public act is deemed important in establishing intent to be bound. These "deed-in-the-box" cases tend to be resolved on their own facts. Delivery is likely to be found if the court believes the grantee is deserving and the deed is part of a rational and wise estate plan of the grantor. See Roger A. Cunningham, William B. Stoebuck & Dale A. Whitman, The Law of Property §11.3 (1984); Annot., 87 A.L.R.2d 787 (1963).

Sweeney, Administratrix v. Sweeney
Supreme Court of Errors of Connecticut, 1940
126 Conn. 391, 11 A.2d 806

JENNINGS, J. Maurice Sweeney, plaintiff's intestate, hereinafter called Maurice, deeded his farm to his brother John M. Sweeney, hereinafter called John, and the deed was recorded. John deeded the property back to Maurice. This deed is unrecorded and was accidentally burned. The question to be decided is whether the second deed was delivered and if so, whether or not a condition claimed to be attached to the delivery is operative. This must be determined on the finding. The following statement includes such changes therein as are required by the evidence:

The plaintiff is the widow and administratrix of Maurice but had not lived with him for the twenty years preceding his death in September, 1938, at the age of seventy-three years. Maurice lived on a tract of land of some hundred and thirty-five acres which he owned in East Hampton, where he ran a tavern. John assisted him in running the tavern to some extent. On February 2, 1937, Maurice and John went to the town clerk's office in East Hampton pursuant to an appointment made the preceding day. Maurice requested the town clerk to draw a deed of his East Hampton property to John and this was done. At the same time he requested that a deed be prepared from John to himself so that he,

15. Why should a will require two witnesses (an acknowledgment before a notary public is not sufficient for a will), whereas an acknowledgment, not witnesses, is required for recordation of a deed?

Maurice, would be protected if John predeceased him. Both deeds were duly executed. The first was left for recording and the second was taken away by Maurice and never recorded. A week or two later Maurice took to John the recorded deed and a week or two after that took the unrecorded deed to John's house. John kept both deeds and gave the second deed to his attorney after the institution of this action. It was destroyed when the latter's office was burned. After the execution of the deeds, Maurice continued to occupy the property, paid the fixed charges, received the rents and exercised full dominion over it until his death. In April, 1937, Maurice made a written lease to Ernest Myers of a portion of the premises and on June 18, 1938, a written lease to Frank and Esther Fricke for twenty years. The first lease is lost but the second was recorded. The defendant never collected any money from tenants or paid any fixed charges or repairs prior to the death of Maurice. On these facts the trial court concluded that there was no intention to make present delivery of John's deed to Maurice, that there was no delivery or acceptance thereof, that it was not intended to operate until John's death and rendered judgment for the defendant.

This deed was, in effect, manually delivered. Maurice continued to occupy the property and exercised full dominion over it without interference by John. It follows that all the essentials of a good delivery were present unless there is something in the contentions of John which defeats this result. He claims that there was no intention on his part to make present delivery.

It is, of course, true that physical possession of a duly executed deed is not conclusive proof that it was legally delivered. McDermott v. McDermott, 97 Conn. 31, 34, 115 Atl. 638. This is so under some circumstances even where there has been a manual delivery. Hotaling v. Hotaling, 193 Cal. 368, 381, 224 Pac. 455, 56 A.L.R. 734, and note p.746. Delivery must be made with the intent to pass title if it is to be effective. Porter v. Woodhouse, 59 Conn. 568, 575, 22 Atl. 299; McDermott v. McDermott, supra.

The deed having been in effect actually delivered to Maurice, the execution of the attestation clause was prima facia proof that the deed was delivered. New Haven Trust Co. v. Camp, 81 Conn. 539, 542, 71 Atl. 788. There is a rebuttable presumption that the grantee assented since the deed was beneficial to him. Moore v. Giles, 49 Conn. 570, 573. No fact is found which militates against this presumption. Where deeds are formally executed and delivered, these presumptions can be overcome only by evidence that no delivery was in fact intended. Loughran v. Kummer, 297 Pa. St. 179, 183, 146 Atl. 534; Cragin's Estate, 274 Pa. St. 1, 5, 117 Atl. 445; Stewart v. Silva, 192 Cal. 405, 409, 221 Pac. 191. The only purpose in making the deed expressed by either party was the statement by Maurice that it was to protect him in case John predeceased him. Since this purpose would have been defeated had there been no delivery with intent to pass title, this conclusively establishes the fact that there was a legal delivery.

The defendant next claims that if there was a delivery, it was on condition and that the condition (the death of John before that of Maurice) was not and cannot be fulfilled. This claim is not good because the delivery was to the grantee. "A conditional delivery is and can only be made by placing the deed in the hands of a third person to be kept by him until the happening of the event upon the happening of which the deed is to be delivered over by the third person to the grantee." Porter v. Woodhouse, supra, 574; Raymond v. Smith, 5 Conn. 555, 559. Conditional delivery to a grantee vests absolute title in the latter. As is pointed out in the *Loughran* case, supra, this is one of the instances where a positive rule of law may defeat the actual intention of the parties. The safety of real estate titles is considered more important than the unfortunate results which may follow the application of the rule in a few individual instances. To relax it would open the door wide to fraud and the fabrication of evidence. Although the doctrine has been criticized (2 Tiffany, Real Property [2d Ed.] p.1764; 5 Wigmore, Evidence [2d Ed.] §§2405, 2408) no material change has been noted in the attitude of the courts in this country.

The finding does not support the conclusion. The finding shows a delivery and, even if a conditional delivery is assumed, the condition is not good for the reasons stated. Since a new trial is necessary, the one ruling on evidence made a ground of appeal is noticed. The town clerk was permitted to testify to certain statements made by Maurice when the deed was drafted. Parol evidence is not admissible to vary the terms of the deed but may be received to show the use that was to be made of it. Fisk's Appeal, 81 Conn. 433, 437, 71 Atl. 559. The ruling was correct as showing the circumstances surrounding delivery.

There is error and a new trial is ordered.

In this opinion the other judges concurred.

NOTES AND QUESTIONS

1. At the time of Maurice Sweeney's death, Conn. Gen. Stat. §5156 (1930) gave the surviving spouse a forced share of a life estate in one-third of decedent's property owned at death.[16] Dower had long been abolished. If decedent died intestate, as Maurice did, §5156 gave his surviving spouse one-third absolutely; if no issue or parent of the decedent survived, §5156 gave the surviving spouse all of the estate of the

16. The rights of a surviving spouse under Connecticut's present law are substantially the same as those set forth in this paragraph. See Conn. Gen. Stat. Ann. §§45a-436, 45a-437 (West Supp. 1992).

decedent. From the facts it appears that Maurice was survived by his estranged wife Maria and his brother John. If so, under Connecticut law Maria took all of Maurice's property.

Maurice Sweeney failed to carry out his wish that John have the land if John survived him. What would you have recommended had Maurice consulted you before engaging in the sleight-of-hand business with the two deeds?

2. The *Sweeney* case represents the prevailing view, though there are two other solutions courts have reached. Where the deed is handed over to the grantee but the extrinsic evidence shows that the deed is to "take effect" at the death of the grantor, a few courts have held that there is no delivery, that the transfer is testamentary and void. See Mueller v. Marshall, 166 Cal. App. 2d 367, 333 P.2d 260 (1958); Juel v. Doll, 51 Wash. 2d 435 319 P.2d 543 (1957); First Security Bank of Utah v. Burgi, 122 Utah 445, 251 P.2d 297 (1952).

Chillemi v. Chillemi, 197 Md. 257, 78 A.2d 750 (1951), rejected the *Sweeney* rule, on particularly compelling facts. *H,* going overseas on a dangerous military mission, delivered a deed to *W* with oral instructions that if *H* was killed *W* was to record the deed and if *H* returned from the mission the deed was to be returned to *H* and destroyed. One month after *H*'s return, and following considerable marital squabbling, *W* recorded the deed. The court upheld the oral conditions and annulled the deed, saying:

> The ancient rule that the mere transfer of a deed from the grantor to the grantee overrides the grantor's explicit declaration of intention that the deed shall not become operative immediately is a relic of the primitive formalism which attached some peculiar efficacy to the physical transfer of the deed as a symbolical transfer of the land. . . . In England in ancient times there could be no change of possession of land until a livery of seisin had taken place. A knife was produced and a piece of turf was cut, and the turf was handed over to the new owner. Later, under the Roman influence, the written document came into use. These documents, which few people had the art to manufacture, were regarded with mystical awe. Just as the sod had been taken up from the ground to be delivered, so the document was laid upon the ground and then solemnly lifted and delivered as a symbol of ownership. In this way the principle developed that the delivery of the deed was the mark of finality. . . .
>
> But there is actually no logical reason why a deed should not be held in escrow by the grantee as well as by any other person. . . . After all, conditional delivery is purely a question of intention, and it is immaterial whether the instrument, pending satisfaction of the condition, is in the hands of the grantor, the grantee, or a third person. After the condition is satisfied, there is an operative conveyance which is considered as having been delivered at the time of the conditional delivery, for the reason that it was then that it was actually delivered, although the ownership does not pass until the satisfaction of the condition. [197 Md. at 263-264, 78 A.2d at 753.]

skip ?

Ferrell v. Stinson

Supreme Court of Iowa, 1943
233 Iowa 1331, 11 N.W.2d 701

GARFIELD, J. The land in controversy is a farm of 220 acres in Franklin County, Iowa, subject to a mortgage of $2,500. Plaintiff asserts there was no valid delivery of the deed under which defendants claim. In her lifetime, the property was owned by Miss Mary Kamberling, who died on October 2, 1940, in Phoenix, Arizona. She was an only child who had inherited the farm from her parents. She had no near relatives. From early childhood Mary was a cripple, who used crutches when she attended school in Iowa Falls, her girlhood home. She developed tuberculosis and about 1917 was taken to Phoenix, where she continued to live as an invalid until her death.

In Iowa Falls, Mary formed a most intimate and enduring friendship with Mrs. Esgate, one of the defendants, a daughter of the late Justice Weaver of this court. In 1916, Mrs. Esgate also moved from Iowa Falls to Phoenix and lived there until 1932, when she moved to Washington, D.C. Mary lived with Mrs. Esgate part of that time. After moving to Washington, Mrs. Esgate returned to Phoenix for about six weeks on each of five occasions, during which she did what she could to relieve Miss Kamberling, whose condition grew progressively worse. Miss Kamberling was indebted to Mrs. Esgate and her husband for money loaned her.

The other two defendants who, with Mrs. Esgate, were grantees of the deed, are Brooks Baughman, of Cedar Falls, Iowa, a first cousin of the grantor (apparently her nearest living relative), and Mrs. I. W. Stinson, of Mason City, Iowa, a distant cousin of Mary and a first cousin of plaintiff, Mrs. Ferrell, also a distant cousin of the grantor testatrix. Miss Kamberling was also attached to these three cousins, defendants Baughman and Mrs. Stinson, and plaintiff, Mrs. Ferrell, who visited and assisted her at times.

The deed under which the three defendants claim was executed on December 2, 1939, in Phoenix. Miss Kamberling, bedridden at the time, called in a young lady notary who lived next door, gave her a copy of a quitclaim deed she had filled in with pencil, and asked her to copy it on a typewriter. As directed, the notary typed the deed on another form which was duly signed, witnessed by two witnesses, and acknowledged. The grantor then handed the executed deed to her housekeeper, Mrs. Orbison, and asked her to put it in a little metal box in a closet opening into her bedroom. The servant did as directed and the deed remained in the box in the closet during the ten months until the grantor's death. The box was not locked and there is no evidence that there was a key for it.

About the time the deed was executed Miss Kamberling talked to the same notary about making a will. The notary, as requested, asked an attorney, Mr. Karz, to get in touch with Miss Kamberling. This attorney prepared a will and it was executed the following day, December 3d. The will provides for payment of debts of the testatrix; directs the sale by her executrix of her real estate in Phoenix, describing it, in the event her debts are fully paid from her personal property; leaves two legacies of $400 each and some personal belongings; and bequeaths all the rest and residue of her estate to plaintiff, Mrs. Ferrell. Following Miss Kamberling's death the will was admitted to probate both in Arizona and Franklin County, Iowa. Plaintiff claims the farm in question as residuary devisee.

Mrs. Flora Thompson was a close friend of Miss Kamberling, who was named in the will as executrix. On December 3d, the day the will was made, Miss Kamberling told Mrs. Thompson, in substance:

> I have made a deed of my Iowa farm to Mrs. I. W. Stinson, Brooks Baughman and Mrs. A. T. Esgate [the defendants], and the deed is placed in the box in the closet with other papers and after I am gone you are to take the deed out of the box and send it to Jane [meaning Mrs. Stinson].

In this conversation Mrs. Thompson told testatrix she had always done everything she could for her while alive and would be very glad to do what she could after Miss Kamberling was gone. Mrs. Thompson had frequently seen the box in the closet before that time, but did not see it again till the day after Miss Kamberling's death. Mrs. Thompson then found the deed in the box in the closet and on October 4, 1940, as directed by the grantor, mailed it to Mrs. Stinson at Mason City, who had it placed of record in Franklin county. When opened by Mrs. Thompson the box contained the deed, the will, some old canceled mortgages and checks, and some tax receipts. The box in which the deed was kept apparently was not used for current papers. The lease to the farm and bills were kept in a folder in a table drawer in the sickroom.

There is no doubt that Miss Kamberling desired and intended defendants should have this farm and believed she had effectively conveyed the farm to them. The equity in the Iowa farm is worth approximately three times her other property, her personalty and Arizona real estate. It is plain that she intended to divide her estate in four nearly equal shares among her three cousins and her devoted friend, Mrs. Esgate. These four were the principal natural objects of her bounty.

The attorney who drew the will testified, without objection:

> At the time she gave me the information with respect to the will she told me she had disposed of her property in Iowa; that she had executed deeds to

the people she wanted to have that property and . . . it would not be necessary to insert it in the will or be bothered with probate proceedings. . . . She told me specifically at that time she had disposed of the property by deed, and that all had been taken care of long before the will was drawn, that is, the property out of the State of Arizona.

There is competent evidence that Miss Kamberling told the grantees of the making of the deed. She also told intimate friends she had deeded her Iowa farm to the three defendants. Mrs. Smith, an acquaintance of twenty years who wrote letters for the invalid, testified:

> Mary Kamberling had told me what disposition she had made of the Iowa land. . . . Shortly after Mary Kamberling made her will I was at her house and she told me she had made her will which covered her Phoenix property. She said, "Not the farm, the Iowa property," because that was deeded to Mrs. Esgate, her cousin, Brooks (Baughman), and her cousin, Mrs. Stinson. . . . that she deeded [it] because they might break a will but a deed would secure the property and insure it going to the people she wanted it to go to.

Although the grantor lived ten months after making the deed and will, it fairly appears that she made them in contemplation of impending death. She was in the advanced stages of tuberculosis, with many complications, and was failing rapidly. There is no evidence she was able to or did leave her bed except to go to the hospital in January or February 1940, for an operation in an attempt to prolong her life.

It was stipulated upon the trial that, until she died, Miss Kamberling rented the farm, received the rents, and controlled its operation.

I. The deed having been duly executed and recorded, plaintiff has the burden of proving its nondelivery by evidence that is clear, satisfactory, and convincing. This is true even though the recording was after the grantor's death. . . . Plaintiff does not question the above rule but contends the presumption of delivery has been conclusively rebutted.

II. Delivery is, of course, essential to the validity of a deed. Our own and other decisions hold that delivery depends very largely upon the intent of the grantor, to be determined by his acts or words, or both, and that a manual delivery is not essential if it appears that the grantor intended to relinquish dominion and control over the deed and have it take effect as a present conveyance of title. Annotation 129 A.L.R. 11, 12, and cases cited.

We have frequently said that actual manual transfer of the paper is not necessary and that acts and words evincing the grantor's intent to part with the deed and relinquish his right over it is a sufficient delivery. . . . We have declared time and again that the intent of the grantor is the controlling element in the delivery of a deed. . . .

This court has uniformly held that where an unrecorded deed is found in a box belonging to the grantor, after his death, without more, there is no presumption of delivery.

We have also frequently held that an effective delivery may be made by placing the deed in the hands of a third person, without reserving the right to recall it and with instructions to deliver to the grantee after the grantor's death. If the conveyance is beneficial to the grantee, the third person is presumed to act as the grantee's agent. The effect of thus placing the instrument with a third person is to reserve a life estate to the grantor with title immediately passing to the grantee but with the latter's right to possession and enjoyment postponed until the grantor's death. . . .

Davis v. John E. Brown College, 208 Iowa 480, 222 N.W. 858, and Boone Biblical College v. Forrest, 223 Iowa 1260, 275 N.W. 132, 116 A.L.R. 67, held there was a valid delivery where a deed was placed with a third party, in spite of an expressed reservation of the right to recall the instrument during the grantor's life, provided such reservation was never exercised. These decisions were contrary to the clear weight of authority and to the principles of some of our own cases, including Lathrop v. Knoop, 202 Iowa 621, 210 N.W. 764, and were overruled in Orris v. Whipple, 224 Iowa 1157, 1171, 280 N.W. 617, 624, 129 A.L.R. 1. The *Orris* case also overruled Robertson v. Renshaw, 220 Iowa 572, 261 N.W. 645, which was based largely on Davis v. John E. Brown College. The three overruled cases were said to "stand alone as supporting the rule therein announced."

The trial court's decision in plaintiff's favor here is based entirely on Orris v. Whipple, supra, upon which plaintiff mainly relies. We are unable to agree that the *Orris* case, with which we are in entire accord, is controlling here. It was a suit at law in replevin by the grantees of an unrecorded deed which had been executed and placed in the grantor's safe-deposit box, to which she alone had access. There was, to quote the opinion, "no semblance of a delivery either to the grantees or to a third person." See Lawson v. Boo, 227 Iowa 100, 103, 287 N.W. 282. No instructions were given to the banker or anyone else to deliver the deed. The only evidence in the *Orris* case having any tendency to show delivery was that the grantor told some others she wanted plaintiffs, or one of them, to have the property and had prepared papers so providing. This court properly held that plaintiffs, who had the burden, as the opinion points out, failed to prove delivery.

One important distinction between the case at bar and Orris v. Whipple is that here the deed was in the nature of a voluntary settlement among the principal natural objects of the grantor's bounty. In the cited case attention is called to the fact that the grantees were "not even collateral heirs" of the grantor.

The rule that a valid delivery may occur without actual transfer of possession of the deed is particularly true where, as here, the conveyance is one of voluntary settlement among the objects of the grantor's bounty. 26 C.J.S. 237, 239, section 42a; 18 C.J. 200, 201, section 96. In such a case, the mere fact that the grantor retains possession of the deed is not conclusive against its validity if there is no circumstance other than its retention to show the deed was not intended to be absolute. Annotation 129 A.L.R. 11, 40, and cases cited; 7 Thompson on Real Property, Perm. Ed., 638, 639, section 4170, and cases cited; Leighton v. Leighton, 196 Iowa 1191, 1201, 194 N.W. 276.

Where there is a good-faith voluntary conveyance to those who naturally have a claim upon the grantor's bounty, courts of equity are strongly inclined to uphold the deed and will do so unless impelled to the opposite conclusion by strong and convincing evidence. There is in such a case a high degree of mutual confidence between the parties. In this class of cases courts of equity do not put so much importance in the mere manual possession of the deed as in the intent of the grantor. If his intent to pass title presently to the grantee is satisfactorily shown, equity usually sustains such a conveyance, even where the grantor retained manual possession of the deed. . . .

Mary Kamberling executed this deed when she was in her last illness. By the deed and will she clearly made what she believed was a final effective disposition of her property among the principal claimants to her bounty. She handed the deed to Mrs. Orbison and instructed her to put it in a box in the closet, where it remained. It is a fair inference that the grantor, in her weakened condition, was physically unable to go to the box during the remainder of her life. The grantor, so far as shown by the evidence, never intended to exercise further control or dominion over the deed. She plainly told Mrs. Thompson where the deed was and would be at her death and asked her to mail it to Mrs. Stinson, giving the address, when the grantor died. Mrs. Thompson at least impliedly promised to do as requested and later made good her promise. The deed was found where the grantor had said it would be.

Miss Kamberling told her attorney that her will was not to include her Iowa property which had been deeded to those she wanted to have it. On the testimony of the attorney, see McKemey v. Ketchum, 188 Iowa 1081, 1082, 175 N.W. 325, and Payne v. Henderson, 340 Ill. 160, 172 N.E. 173. She later told defendants and others of the deed in a way that clearly shows she believed she had made an effective delivery and intended that what she did would so operate. Evidence of statements by the grantor that he had executed the deed has been "considered a potent factor, in connection with other circumstances, in determining whether or not there has been a delivery." Annotation 129 A.L.R. 11, 27, and cases cited. It is true the belief of the grantor is not sufficient of itself to prove delivery. Heavner v. Kading, 209 Iowa 1271, 1274, 228 N.W. 311.

Let us suppose the grantor had handed the deed to Mrs. Thompson when instructing her as to its disposition, that Mrs. Thompson had agreed to do as directed and then herself placed the deed in this same box in the closet. In the light of the evidence in the case, there would then clearly have been a valid constructive delivery of this deed, under our decisions. Even if the grantor had access to the box, this would not invalidate a previously completed delivery. . . . Since the controlling consideration is the intent of the grantor, we think the failure to hand the deed to Mrs. Thompson is not fatal to the claim of delivery. Unless we are to sacrifice substance for form, the legal effect of what was done is the substantial equivalent of the supposed case.

Plaintiff relies on one piece of testimony which it is claimed negatives delivery. The housekeeper testified:

> After she made a loan on her place of $2,000 she said she had every intention of changing her will or deed, I wouldn't say which, or if she made both, I don't know.

On this subject, however, Mrs. Smith, friend and typist, testified:

> . . . I was at Mary Kamberling's home every afternoon while the housekeeper was gone. During that time she talked to me about changing her will. She said that the way the will was worded Mrs. Thompson would be unable to give away any of the household furniture or any of her personal things . . . and that there were certain things in the house she wished to go to certain friends, and that was why she felt she should change the will so that Mrs. Thompson would have the privilege of giving those things away. She wanted to make lists of various things in the house to go to certain friends but she never got it done.

In view of Mrs. Smith's testimony about talk of changing the will, and under the entire record showing the grantor's complete satisfaction with the deed, we think the housekeeper's uncertain statement does not tend to show the deed was not delivered. We find nothing to indicate that the grantor did not intend the deed to be absolute except its retention in the box in the closet. Under the authorities heretofore cited, where the deed, as here, is a voluntary settlement, this circumstance is insufficient to establish that the deed was not delivered.

From the standpoint of equity and justice there can be no doubt that defendants are entitled to prevail unless such a decision runs counter to some established rule of law. We think there is no legal principle or no decision of this court which requires an affirmance of the lower court. We hold there was a valid delivery of the deed.

In a case of this kind a plaintiff must recover on the strength of his own title. Section 12232, Code, 1939; Bohle v. Brooks, 225 Iowa 980, 986, 282 N.W. 351; Blain v. Blain, 215 Iowa 69, 72, 244 N.W. 827. Here it appears beyond question that the grantor intended not only that defendants should have this farm but also that the plaintiff should not have it. It is undisputed that the will under which plaintiff claims was not intended to include the farm. Plaintiff is asking a court of equity to take the property from those whom the grantor intended to have it, holding as they do under a deed delivered in accordance with her expressed directions, and to vest title in one whom she intended not to have it. We hold the relief asked should be denied. — Reversed.

All Justices concur.

NOTES AND QUESTIONS

1. In Brandt v. Schucha, 250 Iowa 679, 96 N.W.2d 179 (1959), the court held that Orris v. Whipple overruled Davis v. John E. Brown College and established that in Iowa, as in most states, a reservation of a right to recall makes a delivery to an escrow agent ineffective. Why is a revocable escrow invalid but a revocable trust or a revocable deed valid? Does this rule discriminate against persons of moderate means who own a piece of real property and who do not consult a lawyer and establish a trust? In defense of the courts, it should be pointed out that the rule against revocable escrows was established long before revocable trusts became generally acceptable.

2. Why is Mrs. Thompson not a trustee? The stumbling block is the Statute of Frauds, which requires a writing where an express trust of land is created. (An agency does not have to be created in writing, nor does the Statute of Frauds require a writing for a trust of personal property.) Hence if Miss Kamberling owned a stock certificate for 100 shares of General Electric, endorsed upon it an assignment to her three friends, and asked Mrs. Thompson to take it from the metal box at her death and deliver it to the three friends, and Mrs. Thompson promised to do so, a trust would arise. See Innes v. Potter, 130 Minn. 320, 153 N.W. 604, 3 A.L.R. 896 (1915).

3. Suppose that Mrs. Thompson testified that she understood that Miss Kamberling could change her mind and cancel the deed. Same result as in the actual case? See Brown v. Hutch, 156 So. 2d 683, 687 (Fla. App. 1963) ("Testimony of the deed's depositary to the effect that he would have returned the deed upon request by its grantor has been considered in various jurisdictions through cases which concerned delivery of a deed after death of its grantor. Such statements have been repeatedly held to be opinion testimony having no legal significance. . . . [T]he only thing the court was concerned with was what the depositary had a right to do with the deed.").

Suppose that Miss Kamberling did in fact change her mind and that Mrs. Thompson took the deed out of the metal box and handed it to Miss Kamberling, who tore it up. Same result as in the actual case? See Pipes v. Sevier, 694 S.W.2d 918 (Mo. App. 1985) (deed delivered to grantor's attorney, who refused to return deed to grantor 10 years later when she asked for it back, held irrevocable); Lenhart v. Desmond, 705 P.2d 338 (Wyo. 1985) (deed put in grantor's safe deposit box, to which grantee had access; after grantor's hospitalization, grantee removed deed and recorded it; upon recovery, grantor sued to invalidate deed, saying he had no intent to divest himself irretrievably of his land; grantor won).

D. The Mortgage

It is a rare person who can pay all cash when buying real estate. Ordinarily the buyer will make a down payment of a small fraction of the purchase price and borrow the rest of the money needed. Let us assume that Bob and Betty Byar, looking for a house, find "just what they want" at a price of $100,000. They cannot pay that amount in cash and must borrow a large portion of it. Where can they borrow the money, and under what terms? Herein we treat moneylending and mortgages.

Banks, savings and loan associations, and other financial institutions are in the business of providing the money needed to finance the purchase of homes. Bob and Betty Byar may apply to such an institution, which we shall call, collectively, a lender. The Byars make a loan application, after which the lender checks their credit rating, earnings, and job security to determine if the Byars are an acceptable credit risk. If the loan is approved, the lender will issue its commitment to provide financing on specified terms within a specified period. It will require security in the form of a mortgage on the property purchased. Generally the lender will set the terms and requirements of the mortgage with strict inflexibility; the buyer is asked to sign a "standard form" used in the jurisdiction.

Although real estate credit markets have been generally integrated into the national capital market, and mortgages, after being originated by local lenders, are sold on the secondary mortgage market to capital investors more or less as just another form of investment, mortgage law has proved highly resistant to uniformity. The typical transaction sketched below is common to each of the states, but significant variations in the law and practices exist in every state. See Michael H. Schill, Uniformity or Diversity: Residential Real Estate Finance Law in the 1990s and the Implications of Changing Financial Markets, 64 S. Cal. L. Rev. 1261 (1991) (arguing that diversity of state mortgage law is an advantage).

To borrow the money from the lender, the borrower must give the lender a *note* and a *mortgage*. Let us assume that the lender will lend Bob and Betty Byar $75,000 toward the purchase of the house costing $100,000. The Byars will execute a note promising to pay the lender $75,000, with interest; the amount is usually payable in equal installments spread over a period of 20 to 30 years. Under modern financing techniques, part of each installment payment is allotted to reducing the principal sum due; another part pays the interest due on the sum. In the early years of the note most of the payment is allotted to interest, but as the principal sum is reduced more and more of the payment is allotted to principal. The final installment payment, equal to each of the preceding payments, completely pays off the note. There is no balloon payment at the end of the period.

The note creates personal liability, but in case of default the lender will want to be able to reach, with priority over other creditors of the borrowers, some specific property. To secure the note the lender will require Bob and Betty Byar to execute a mortgage on the property they are buying. The Byars are *mortgagors*, the lender is *mortgagee*. If the Byars fail to pay their note or do not otherwise perform their obligations, the lender, either at private sale or under judicial supervision, depending on the jurisdiction, can have the property sold ("foreclose the mortgage") and apply the proceeds of sale to the amount due on the note.

The mortgagor's interest in the property is known as the "equity," a shortened form of "equity of redemption" which also pays linguistic homage to the generations of chancellors who have been moved to protect debtors from overreaching moneylenders. The early classic form of the mortgage, which came into common use in the fourteenth century, was a deed in fee simple given to the moneylender by the borrower, with a condition subsequent clause providing that if the borrower paid back the sum owed on the day due, the deed would become void.[17] If the borrower did not pay the sum due on the very day set, the moneylender owned the land in fee simple absolute; the defeasance clause could no longer become operative. As the land was almost always worth more than the debt, the lender received a windfall. The chancellor, believing that prompt payment was not of sufficient importance to justify the debtor losing the property when the lender could be compensated by an

17. Under this form of mortgage the mortgagee takes legal title to the land; the mortgagor has only the equity of redemption. This approach is still retained in eight states — Alabama, Georgia, Maine, Maryland, Massachusetts, New Hampshire, Pennsylvania, and Rhode Island — and is called the "title theory" of mortgages. Most states subscribe to the "lien theory," which disregards the form and holds that the mortgagor keeps legal title and the mortgagee has only a lien on the property. Although this distinction used to count for a lot, the differences in practical application between "title theory" and "lien theory" states have almost entirely disappeared because title theory states have come to see that title passes to the mortgagee only for purposes of securing the debt and have interpreted the mortgage accordingly. See Ann M. Burkhart, Freeing Mortgages of Merger, 40 Vand. L. Rev. 283, 322-329 (1987). But cf. severance of a joint tenancy by one tenant giving a mortgage (pages 336-341).

award of money, moved to protect the debtor. At first the chancellor permitted the borrower, by paying the sum due, to redeem the property after the time set only when a great injustice would occur. But by the seventeenth century the right of the mortgagor to redeem after the day set had become a matter of course and right. The right of redemption was given all and continued until cut off by the chancellor.

The possibility of redemption after the time set meant that the lender could not rest safe in his possession after default by the debtor. The lender had title to the land, but the mortgagor could redeem at any time. To remedy this, the chancellor permitted the mortgagor's right of redemption to be foreclosed. This equity accomplished first by a *strict foreclosure,* a proceeding in which the mortgagor was ordered to pay within a given period or be forever barred. Later equity barred the right of redemption by a judicial proceeding determining the amount of the debt and ordering a *foreclosure sale.* The foreclosure decree directed an officer of the court to sell the land at a public sale, conveying title to the property to the purchaser, and, from the proceeds of sale, paying the debt to the lender and paying any amount exceeding the debt to the borrower. If the land did not bring enough to satisfy the debt, the mortgagee could recover a judgment for the deficiency against the mortgagor (subject to antideficiency legislation, which we will discuss later). The foreclosure sale became standard practice in most American states; in some jurisdictions there are variations on it.

So far we have recounted how the *courts* stepped in to protect borrowers from overreaching lenders. They ended up requiring a lawsuit ordering foreclosure sale of the property, cutting off the borrower's *equity of redemption.* Even this was not deemed enough protection of debtors by legislators, who in about half the states passed statutes giving the mortgagor a *statutory* right to buy back the title from the purchaser at a judicial foreclosure sale within a specified period *after* the foreclosure sale (ranging from three months to two years). These statutes were usually enacted in periods of depression or collapse of land values. Carefully distinguish the *judicially* created right to redeem *from the mortgagee* (the equity of redemption), on the one hand, and the *statutory* right to redeem from the *purchaser* at foreclosure sale, on the other hand. The statutory right does not come into play until the borrower's equity is extinguished at foreclosure sale. See Grant S. Nelson & Dale A. Whitman, Real Estate Finance Law §§8.4-8.8 (2d ed. 1985).

Quite naturally, lawyers for lenders cast about for a way to avoid judicial foreclosure (which requires a costly and time-consuming lawsuit) and, where enacted, the statutory right of redemption from foreclosure sale. They sought a way for the lender to sell the land and be paid soon after default. They found this in the form of a *deed of trust,* which is recognized in a majority of jurisdictions. Id. §§1.6, 7.19. Under a deed of trust, the borrower conveys title to the land to a person (who is usually a third person but may be the lender) to hold in trust to secure payment of the debt to the lender. In a deed of trust the trustee is given the power to sell the land without going to court if the borrower defaults. (A mortgage that is not a deed of trust may also have a power of sale incorporated into it.) The power of sale foreclosure is quicker and less costly than a judicial foreclosure. Except for the power to foreclose privately, the deed of trust is treated in almost all significant respects as a mortgage.

To conclude this introduction, let us return to our hypothetical couple, Bob and Betty Byar. The Byars purchase the house they want for $100,000. They make a down payment of $10,000 patched together from several sources, including savings and family help. They borrow $75,000 from a bank and give the bank a note secured by a mortgage on the house, and give the seller a note secured by a second mortgage for $15,000. The second mortgagee is subject to the prior rights of the first mortgagee; if the sum brought upon foreclosure sale is insufficient to pay off both the first and second mortgages, the first mortgage is paid off first. Because of this increased risk, a second mortgage usually carries a higher interest rate than a first mortgage. Perhaps at some future time the Byars will take out a home improvement loan and give a financing institution a third mortgage.

PROBLEMS AND NOTES

1. The Byars purchase the house and finance the purchase as stated above. Subsequently the Byars default on payments of the note secured by the first mortgage and the bank forecloses. On foreclosure sale, the house brings $50,000. How should this be distributed?

Suppose the Byars had defaulted on payments of the note secured by the second mortgage, but had kept paying the note given the bank. What would be the rights of the second mortgagee?

2. *Deficiency judgments.* If the house brings $50,000 on foreclosure sale, and the mortgage debt is $80,000, can the mortgagee obtain a deficiency judgment for $30,000 against the borrower? The answer may turn on whether $50,000, the proceeds of sale, is a fair price for the property and hence the appropriate amount to credit against the debt. If foreclosure is through a judicial proceeding, the sale price is ordinarily not challengeable (unless it shocks the conscience of the court), and the amount realized is applied to the debt. The mortgagee is entitled to a deficiency judgment for the difference, collectible out of the general assets of the borrower. Where the foreclosure is by private sale, however, courts may scrutinize the sale closely to assure that the mortgagee acted fairly, and may deny a deficiency judgment where there are sufficient grounds to set the sale aside. Thus if the mortgagee is interested in ob-

taining a deficiency judgment against the borrower, judicial foreclosure is the prudent route. See Grant S. Nelson & Dale A. Whitman, Real Estate Finance Law §8.1 (2d ed. 1985).

3. *Antideficiency statutes.* Many states have enacted legislation designed to protect some borrowers from deficiency judgments.

> Some states prohibit deficiency judgments if the mortgagor has used the proceeds of the loan to purchase a residence. Other states prohibit deficiency judgments only when a particular type of foreclosure process is utilized, most commonly power of sale foreclosure. A number of states permit mortgagees to sue mortgagors for deficiency judgments, but regulate how the judgment can be obtained and the amount of the judgment. Some states require that mortgagees seek deficiency judgments at the same time they foreclose a mortgage; others limit the amount of the deficiency judgment to the difference between the principal balance and the property's fair market value at the time of foreclosure, rather than the difference between the principal balance and the high bid at the foreclosure sale. [Michael H. Schill, An Economic Analysis of Mortgagor Protection Laws, 77 Va. L. Rev. 489, 494-495 (1991).]

Professor Schill reconceptualizes the mortgagor protection laws (including the statutory right to redeem and antideficiency legislation) as a form of insurance against the adverse effects of default and foreclosure. He suggests that a compulsory insurance program would be more efficient in ameliorating the adverse effects of foreclosure than the existing mortgagor protection laws.

Murphy v. Financial Development Corp.

Supreme Court of New Hampshire, 1985
126 N.H. 536, 495 A.2d 1245

DOUGLAS, J. The plaintiffs brought this action seeking to set aside the foreclosure sale of their home, or, in the alternative, money damages. The Superior Court (Bean, J.), adopting the recommendation of a Master (R. Peter Shapiro, Esq.), entered a judgment for the plaintiffs in the amount of $27,000 against two of the defendants, Financial Development Corporation and Colonial Deposit Company (the lenders).

The plaintiffs purchased a house in Nashua in 1966, financing it by means of a mortgage loan. They refinanced the loan in March of 1980, executing a new promissory note and a power of sale mortgage, with Financial Development Corporation as mortgagee. The note and mortgage were later assigned to Colonial Deposit Company.

In February of 1981, the plaintiff Richard Murphy became unemployed. By September of 1981, the plaintiffs were seven months in arrears on their mortgage payments, and had also failed to pay substantial amounts in utility assessments and real estate taxes. After discussing unsuccessfully with the plaintiffs proposals for revising the payment schedule, rewriting the note, and arranging alternative financing, the lenders gave notice on October 6, 1981, of their intent to foreclose.

During the following weeks, the plaintiffs made a concerted effort to avoid foreclosure. They paid the seven months' mortgage arrearage, but failed to pay some $643.18 in costs and legal fees associated with the foreclosure proceedings. The lenders scheduled the foreclosure sale for November 10, 1981, at the site of the subject property. They complied with all of the statutory requirements for notice. See RSA 479:25.

At the plaintiffs' request, the lenders agreed to postpone the sale until December 15, 1981. They advised the plaintiffs that this would entail an additional cost of $100, and that the sale would proceed unless the lenders received payment of $743.18, as well as all mortgage payments then due, by December 15. Notice of the postponement was posted on the subject property on November 10 at the originally scheduled time of the sale, and was also posted at the Nashua City Hall and Post Office. No prospective bidders were present for the scheduled sale.

In late November, the plaintiffs paid the mortgage payment which had been due in October, but made no further payments to the lenders. An attempt by the lenders to arrange new financing for the plaintiffs through a third party failed when the plaintiffs refused to agree to pay for a new appraisal of the property. Early on the morning of December 15, 1981, the plaintiffs tried to obtain a further postponement, but were advised by the lenders' attorney that it was impossible unless the costs and legal fees were paid.

At the plaintiffs' request, the attorney called the president of Financial Development Corporation, who also refused to postpone the sale. Further calls by the plaintiffs to the lenders' office were equally unavailing.

The sale proceeded as scheduled at 10:00 A.M. on December 15, at the site of the property. Although it had snowed the previous night, the weather was clear and warm at the time of the sale, and the roads were clear. The only parties present were the plaintiffs, a representative of the lenders, and an attorney, Morgan Hollis, who had been engaged to conduct the sale because the lenders' attorney, who lived in Dover, had been apprehensive about the weather the night before. The lenders' representative made the only bid at the sale. That bid of $27,000, roughly the amount owed on the mortgage, plus costs and fees, was accepted and the sale concluded.

Later that same day, Attorney Hollis encountered one of his clients, William Dube, a representative of the defendant Southern New Hampshire Home Traders, Inc. (Southern). On being informed of the sale, Mr. Dube contacted the lenders and offered to buy the property for $27,000. The lenders rejected the offer and made a counter offer of $40,000. Within two days a purchase price of $38,000 was agreed upon by Mr. Dube and the lenders and the sale was subsequently completed.

The plaintiffs commenced this action on February 5, 1982. The lenders moved to dismiss, arguing that any action was barred because the plaintiffs had failed to petition for an injunction prior to the sale. The master denied the motion. After hearing the evidence, he ruled for the plaintiffs, finding that the lenders had "failed to exercise good faith and due diligence in obtaining a fair price for the subject property at the foreclosure sale. . . ."

The master also ruled that Southern was a bona fide purchaser for value, and thus had acquired legal title to the house. That ruling is not at issue here. He assessed monetary damages against the lenders equal to "the difference between the fair market value of the subject property on the date of the foreclosure and the price obtained at said sale."

Having found the fair market value to be $54,000, he assessed damages accordingly at $27,000. He further ruled that "[t]he bad faith of the 'Lenders' warrants an award of legal fees." The lenders appealed. . . .

The . . . issue before us is whether the master erred in concluding that the lenders had failed to comply with the often-repeated rule that a mortgagee executing a power of sale is bound both by the statutory procedural requirements *and* by a duty to protect the interests of the mortgagor through the exercise of good faith and due diligence. . . .

The master found that the lenders, throughout the time prior to the sale, "did not mislead or deal unfairly with the plaintiffs." They engaged in serious efforts to avoid foreclosure through new financing, and agreed to one postponement of the sale. The basis for the master's decision was his conclusion that the lenders had failed to exercise good faith and due diligence in obtaining a fair price for the property.

This court's past decisions have not dealt consistently with the question whether the mortgagee's duty amounts to that of a fiduciary or trustee. Compare Pearson v. Gooch, 69 N.H. 208, 209, 40 A. 390, 390-91 (1897) and Merrimack Industrial Trust v. First National Bank of Boston, 121 N.H. 197, 201, 427 A.2d 500, 504 (1981) (duty amounts to that of a fiduciary or trustee) with Silver v. First National Bank, 108 N.H. 390, 391, 236 A.2d 493, 494-95 (1967) and Proctor v. Bank of N.H., 123 N.H. 395, 400, 464 A.2d 263, 266 (1983) (duty does not amount to that of a fiduciary or trustee). This may be an inevitable result of the mortgagee's dual role as seller and potential buyer at the foreclosure sale, and of the conflicting interests involved. See Wheeler v. Slocinski, 82 N.H. 211, 214, 131 A. 598, 600 (1926).

We need not label a duty, however, in order to define it. In his role as a seller, the mortgagee's duty of good faith and due diligence is essentially that of a fiduciary. Such a view is in keeping with "[t]he 'trend . . . towards liberalizing the term [fiduciary] in order to prevent unjust enrichment.' " Lash v. Cheshire County Savings Bank, Inc., 124 N.H. 435, 438, 474 A.2d 980, 981 (1984) (quoting Cornwell v. Cornwell, 116 N.H. 205, 209, 356 A.2d 683, 686 (1976)).

A mortgagee, therefore, must exert every reasonable effort to obtain "a fair and reasonable price under the circumstances," Reconstruction &c. Corp. v. Faulkner, 101 N.H. 352, 361, 143 A.2d 403, 410 (1958), even to the extent, if necessary, of adjourning the sale or of establishing "an upset price below which he will not accept any offer." Lakes Region Fin. Corp. v. Goodhue Boat Yard, Inc., 118 N.H. 103, 107, 382 A.2d 1108, 1111 (1978).

What constitutes a fair price, or whether the mortgagee must establish an upset price, adjourn the sale, or make other reasonable efforts to assure a fair price, depends on the circumstances of each case. Inadequacy of price alone is not sufficient to demonstrate bad faith unless the price is so low as to shock the judicial conscience. Mueller v. Simmons, 634 S.W.2d 533, 536 (Mo. App. 1982); Rife v. Woolfolk, 289 S.E.2d 220, 223 (W. Va. 1982); Travelers Indem. Co. v. Heim, 218 Neb. 326, 352 N.W.2d 921, 923-24 (1984).

We must decide, in the present case, whether the evidence supports the finding of the master that the lenders failed to exercise good faith and due diligence in obtaining a fair price for the plaintiffs' property.

We first note that "[t]he duties of good faith and due diligence are distinct. . . . One may be observed and not the other, and any inquiry as to their breach calls for a separate consideration of each." Wheeler v. Slocinski, 82 N.H. at 213, 131 A. at 600. In order "to constitute bad faith there must be an intentional disregard of duty or a purpose to injure." Id. at 214, 131 A. at 600-01.

There is insufficient evidence in the record to support the master's finding that the lenders acted in bad faith in failing to obtain a fair price for the plaintiffs' property. The lenders complied with the statutory requirements of notice and otherwise conducted the sale in compliance with statutory provisions. The lenders postponed the sale one time and did not bid with knowledge of any immediately available subsequent purchaser. Further, there is no evidence indicating an intent on the part of the lenders to injure the mortgagor by, for example, discouraging other buyers.

There is ample evidence in the record, however, to support the master's finding that the lenders failed to exercise due diligence in obtaining a fair price. "The issue of the lack of due diligence is whether a reasonable man in the [lenders'] place would have adjourned the sale," id. at 215, 131 A. at 601, or taken other measures to receive a fair price.

In early 1980, the plaintiffs' home was appraised at $46,000. At the time of the foreclosure sale on December 15, 1981, the lenders had not had the house reappraised to take into account improvements and appreciation. The master found that a reasonable person in the place of the lenders would have realized that the plaintiffs' equity in the property was at least $19,000, the difference between the 1980 appraised value of $46,000 and the amount owed on the mortgage totaling approximately $27,000.

At the foreclosure sale, the lenders were the only bidders. The master found that their bid of $27,000 "was sufficient to cover all monies due and did not create a deficiency balance" but "did not provide for a return of any of the plaintiffs' equity."

Further, the master found that the lenders "had reason to know" that "they stood to make a substantial profit on a quick turnaround sale." On the day of the sale, the lenders offered to sell the foreclosed property to William Dube for $40,000. Within two days after the foreclosure sale, they did in fact agree to sell it to Dube for $38,000. It was not necessary for the master to find that the lenders knew of a specific potential buyer before the sale in order to show lack of good faith or due diligence as the lenders contend. The fact that the lenders offered the property for sale at a price sizably above that for which they had purchased it, only a few hours before, supports the master's finding that the lenders had reason to know, at the time of the foreclosure sale, that they could make a substantial profit on a quick turnaround sale. For this reason, they should have taken more measures to ensure receiving a higher price at the sale.

While a mortgagee may not always be required to secure a portion of the mortgagor's equity, such an obligation did exist in this case. The substantial amount of equity which the plaintiffs had in their property, the knowledge of the lenders as to the appraised value of the property, and the plaintiffs' efforts to forestall foreclosure by paying the mortgage arrearage within weeks of the sale, all support the master's conclusion that the lenders had a fiduciary duty to take more reasonable steps than they did to protect the plaintiffs' equity by attempting to obtain a fair price for the property. They could have established an appropriate upset price to assure a minimum bid. They also could have postponed the auction and advertised commercially by display advertising in order to assure that bidders other than themselves would be present.

Instead, as Theodore DiStefano, an officer of both lending institutions testified, the lenders made no attempt to obtain fair market value for the property but were concerned *only* with making themselves "whole." On the facts of this case, such disregard for the interests of the mortgagors was a breach of duty by the mortgagees.

Although the lenders *did* comply with the statutory requirements of notice of the foreclosure sale, these efforts were not sufficient in this case to demonstrate due diligence. At the time of the initially scheduled sale, the extent of the lenders' efforts to publicize the sale of the property was publication of a legal notice of the mortgagees' sale at public auction on November 10, published once a week for three weeks in the Nashua Telegraph, plus postings in public places. The lenders did not advertise, publish, or otherwise give notice to the general public of postponement of the sale to December 15, 1981, other than by posting notices at the plaintiffs' house, at the post office, and at city hall. That these efforts to advertise were ineffective is evidenced by the fact that no one, other than the lenders, appeared at the sale to bid on the property. This fact allowed the lenders to purchase the property at a minimal price and then to profit substantially in a quick turnaround sale.

We recognize a need to give guidance to a trial court which must determine whether a mortgagee who has complied with the strict letter of the statutory law has nevertheless violated his additional duties of good faith and due diligence. A finding that the mortgagee had, or should have had, knowledge of his ability to get a higher price at an adjourned sale is the most conclusive evidence of such a violation.

More generally, we are in agreement with the official Commissioners' Comment to section 3-508 of the Uniform Land Transactions Act:

> The requirement that the sale be conducted in a reasonable manner, including the advertising aspects, requires that the person conducting the sale use the ordinary methods of making buyers aware that are used when an owner is voluntarily selling his land. Thus an advertisement in the portion of a daily newspaper where these ads are placed or, in appropriate cases such as the sale of an industrial plant, a display advertisement in the financial sections of the daily newspaper may be the most reasonable method. In other cases employment of a professional real estate agent may be the more reasonable method. It is unlikely that an advertisement in a legal publication among other legal notices would qualify as a commercially reasonable method of sale advertising. [13 Uniform Laws Annotated 704 (West 1980).]

As discussed above, the lenders met neither of these guidelines.

While agreeing with the master that the lenders failed to exercise due diligence in this case, we find that he erred as a matter of law in awarding damages equal to "the difference between the fair market value of the subject property . . . and the price obtained at [the] sale."

Such a formula may well be the appropriate measure where *bad faith* is found. See Danvers Savings Bank v. Hammer, 122 N.H. 1, 5, 440 A.2d 435, 438 (1982). In such a case, a mortgagee's conduct amounts to more than mere negligence. Damages based upon the *fair market value*, a figure in excess of a *fair* price, will more readily induce mortgagees to perform their duties properly. A "fair" price may or may not yield a figure close to fair market value; however, it will be that price arrived at as a result of due diligence by the mortgagee.

Where, as here, however, a mortgagee fails to exercise due diligence, the proper assessment of damages is the difference between a fair price for the property and the price obtained at the foreclosure sale. We have held, where lack of due diligence has been found, that "the test is not 'fair market value' as in eminent domain cases nor is the mortgagee bound to give credit for the highest possible amount which might be obtained under different circumstances, as at an owner's sale." Silver v. First National Bank, 108 N.H. 390, 392, 236 A.2d 493, 495 (1967) (quoting Reconstruction &c. Corp. v. Faulkner, 101 N.H. 352, 361, 143 A.2d 403, 410 (1958)) (citation omitted). Accordingly, we remand to the trial court for a reassessment of damages consistent with this opinion.

Because we concluded above that there was no "bad faith or obstinate, unjust, vexatious, wanton, or oppressive conduct," on the part of the lenders, we see no reason to stray from our general rule that the prevailing litigant is not entitled to collect attorney's fees from the loser. Harkeem v. Adams, 117 N.H. 687, 688, 377 A.2d 617, 617 (1977). Therefore, we reverse this part of the master's decision.

Reversed in part; affirmed in part; remanded.

Grant S. Nelson & Dale A. Whitman, Real Estate Finance Law
§7.21 at 540 (2d ed. 1985)*

All jurisdictions adhere to the recognized rule that mere inadequacy of the foreclosure sale price will not invalidate a sale, absent fraud, unfairness or other irregularity. Stating the rule in a slightly different manner, courts sometimes say that inadequacy of the sale price is an insufficient ground unless it is so gross as to shock the conscience of the court, warranting an inference of fraud or imposition.

Absent the presence of such additional circumstances, it is extremely difficult to get a sale set aside on mere price inadequacy. While some courts have found that sales for one-seventh and one-sixtieth of fair market value "shock the conscience," one commentator has noted with respect to his jurisdiction that "such sales have been upheld where the price paid for the property was only one-half, one-third, one-fourth, one-fifth, or even one-twentieth of its reasonable value." On the other hand, where other factors are present, such as chilled bidding, unusual hour of sale or any other indicia of unfairness, courts do set sales aside. For example, in a case where the mortgaged real estate sold for 3% of the fair market value, the court set aside the sale because of the additional factor that the mortgagee had informed the mortgagor of the incorrect sale date.

NOTES AND QUESTIONS

1. In the *Murphy* case, how can the mortgagee determine an appropriate upset price? Specifically, what should the lenders have done to receive a higher bid?

2. If the foreclosure sale is defective, what are the borrower's rem-

*Reprinted with permission of the West Publishing Company.

edies? Can the title of the purchaser at the sale be set aside? See Nelson & Whitman, supra, §7.22.

3. Why is the mortgagee frequently the only bidder at a foreclosure sale? See id. §8.8. What reform of the foreclosure sale system would bring a higher sale price?

4. In Crown Life Ins. Co. v. Candlewood, Ltd., 112 N.M. 633, 818 P.2d 411 (1991), Crown Life held a mortgage for $1.9 million on an apartment complex valued at $1.29 million. On foreclosure sale, Crown Life's winning bid was $200,010. Subsequently a real estate investor, learning of the sale, bought the debtor's statutory redemption rights and, proffering $200,010, petitioned the court for a certificate of redemption. At that point, Crown Life (previously unaware of the statutory right of redemption) sought to have the foreclosure sale vacated, the mortgage reinstated, and a new sale ordered. The court (3 to 2) set aside the foreclosure sale because "however insensitive the court's conscience, this disparity . . . should shock it."

5. *Transfer by the mortgagor.* Notwithstanding any agreement to the contrary, the mortgagor can transfer his interest in the land by sale, mortgage, or otherwise. The transfer will not, however, shake off the mortgage. The land remains subject to the mortgage in the hands of the transferee.

The purchaser of the equity may buy the mortgagor's equity either "subject to the mortgage" or "assuming the mortgage." If the purchaser takes subject to the mortgage, the purchaser does not assume any personal liability for the mortgage debt, for which the mortgagor remains liable. But the purchaser agrees, as between himself and the mortgagor, that the debt is to be satisfied out of the land; if the debt is not paid, the land will be sold and the debt paid from the proceeds. If the purchaser assumes the mortgage, the purchaser promises to pay off the mortgage debt. This promise does not relieve the mortgagor of the duty to pay the mortgagee, unless the lender consents to this change in the contract, but it gives the mortgagor the right to pay the debt and sue the assuming purchaser for reimbursement. The mortgagee can enforce the promise made by the purchaser of the equity in assuming the mortgage.

Although the mortgagor can transfer his interest, the mortgage contract may contain an acceleration clause that enables the mortgagee, upon transfer of the mortgagor's equity, to declare the whole amount of the mortgage debt due and, upon failure to pay, to foreclose. By enforcing the acceleration clause, thus requiring the new purchaser of the equity to refinance, the lender may use a due-on-sale clause to increase the loan interest rate to current rates upon transfer of the property.

An installment land sale contract is an arrangement whereby the seller contracts to convey title to the purchaser when the purchaser has

paid the purchase price in regular installments over a fixed period of
time. These payments may be allocated to principal and interest in a
fashion similar to amortized mortgage payments, or there may be annual payments of interest and a balloon payment at the end. If the purchaser pays the contract price in full, the seller agrees to deliver a deed
conveying legal title to the purchaser.

There is little functional difference between a purchase money
mortgage and an installment land sale contract. Both are devices to secure payment of unpaid purchase money. But the installment land sale
contract, which provides financing by the *seller,* not by an institutional
lender, is widely used in transfers of real estate, particularly low-cost
housing and vacation lots. The buyer may not have a sufficient down
payment to qualify for a loan from an institutional lender, or the buyer
may be considered by the institutional lender as a poor credit risk. With
an installment land sale contract, no bank loan is necessary; the down
payment can be minimal, and the seller may be willing to sell to persons
deemed poor credit risks by institutional lenders. Installment land contracts have also been favored by sellers in those states where judicial
foreclosure is the only method of foreclosing a mortgage.

Bean v. Walker

New York Supreme Court, Appellate Division,
Fourth Department, 1983
95 A.D.2d 70, 464 N.Y.S.2d 895

DOERR, J. Presented for our resolution is the question of the relative
rights between a vendor and a defaulting vendee under a land purchase
contract. Special Term, in granting summary judgment in favor of
plaintiffs, effectively held that the defaulting vendee has no rights. We
cannot agree.

The facts may be briefly stated. In January 1973 plaintiffs agreed to
sell and defendants agreed to buy a single-family home in Syracuse for
the sum of $15,000.[18] The contract provided that this sum would be paid
over a 15-year period at 5% interest, in monthly installments of $118.62.
The sellers retained legal title to the property which they agreed to convey upon payment in full according to the terms of the contract. The
purchasers were entitled to possession of the property, and all taxes,
assessments and water rates, and insurance became the obligation of the
purchasers. The contract also provided that in the event purchasers defaulted in making payment and failed to cure the default within 30 days,
the sellers could elect to call the remaining balance immediately due or
elect to declare the contract terminated and repossess the premises. If

18. The house now has an alleged market value of $44,000.

the latter alternative was chosen, then a forfeiture clause came into play whereby the seller could retain all the money paid under the contract as "liquidated" damages and "the same shall be in no event considered a penalty but rather the payment of rent."

Defendants went into possession of the premises in January 1973 and in the ensuing years claim to have made substantial improvements on the property. They made the required payments under the contract until August 1981 when they defaulted following an injury sustained by defendant Carl Walker. During the years while they occupied the premises as contract purchasers defendants paid to plaintiff $12,099.24, of which $7,114.75 was applied to principal. Thus, at the time of their default, defendants had paid almost one-half of the purchase price called for under the agreement. After the required 30-day period to cure the default,[19] plaintiffs commenced this action sounding in ejectment seeking a judgment "that they be adjudged the owner in fee" of the property and granting them possession thereof. The court granted summary judgment to plaintiffs.

If the only substantive law to be applied to this case was that of contracts, the result reached would be correct. However, under the facts presented herein the law with regard to the transfer of real property must also be considered. The reconciliation of what might appear to be conflicting concepts is not insurmountable.

While there are few New York cases which directly address the circumstances herein presented, certain general principles may be observed. "It is well settled that the owner of the real estate from the time of the execution of a valid contract for its sale is to be treated as the owner of the purchase money and the purchaser of the land is to be treated as the equitable owner thereof. The purchase money becomes personal property" (New York C. & H. R.R. Co. v. Cottle, 187 App. Div. 131, 144, 175 N.Y.S. 178 affd. 229 N.Y. 514, 129 N.E. 896). Thus, notwithstanding the words of the contract and implications which may arise therefrom, the law of property declares that, upon the execution of a contract for sale of land, the vendee acquires equitable title. . . . The vendor holds the legal title in trust for the vendee and has an equitable lien for the payment of the purchase price. . . . The vendee in possession, for all practical purposes, is the owner of the property with all the rights of an owner subject only to the terms of the contract. The vendor may enforce his lien by foreclosure or an action at law for the purchase price of the property — the remedies are concurrent (Flickinger v. Glass, 222 N.Y. 404, 118 N.E. 792; Zeiser v. Cohn, 207 N.Y. 407, 101 N.E. 184). . . . The conclusion to be reached, of course, is that upon the execution of a contract an interest in real property comes into existence

---

19. Defendant's offer to bring the payments up-to-date and pay a higher interest rate on the balance due were unavailing.

by operation of law, superseding the terms of the contract. An analogous result occurs in New York if an owner purports to convey title to real property as security for a loan; the conveyance is deemed to create a lien rather than an outright conveyance, even though the deed was recorded (Schulte v. Cleri, 39 A.D.2d 692, 332 N.Y.S.2d 518) and "one who has taken a deed absolute in form as security for an obligation, in order to foreclose the debtor's right to redeem, must institute a foreclosure, and is entitled to have the premises sold in the usual way" (14 Carmody-Wait 2d, §92:2, p.612).

Cases from other jurisdictions are more instructive. In Skendzel v. Marshall, 261 Ind. 226, 301 N.E.2d 641 [addressing itself to a land sale contract], the court observed that while legal title does not vest in the vendee until the contract terms are satisfied, he does acquire a vested equitable title at the time the contract is consummated. When the parties enter into the contract all incidents of ownership accrue to the vendee who assumes the risk of loss and is the recipient of all appreciation of value. The status of the parties becomes like that of mortgagor-mortgagee. Viewed otherwise would be to elevate form over substance (Skendzel v. Marshall, supra, p. 234, 301 N.E.2d 641). The doctrine that equity deems as done that which ought to be done is an appropriate concept which we should apply to the present case.

Where sale of real property is evidenced by contract only and the purchase price has not been paid and is not to be paid until some future date in accordance with the terms of the agreement, the parties occupy substantially the position of mortgagor and mortgagee at common law. In New York a mortgage merely creates a lien rather than conveying title (Moulton v. Cornish, 138 N.Y. 133, 33 N.E. 842), but this was not always so. At common law the mortgage conveyed title, and it was to protect the buyer from summary ejectment that Courts of Equity evolved the concept of "equitable" title as distinct from "legal" title (Barson v. Mulligan, 191 N.Y. 306, 313-314, 84 N.E. 75; see also, 2 Rasch, Real Property Law and Practice, §1684; 14 Carmody-Wait 2d §92:1). The doctrine of equitable conversion had important consequences. The equitable owner suffered the risk of loss (Sewell v. Underhill, 197 N.Y. 168, 171, 172, 91 N.E. 1120) as does a contract vendee in possession today (see General Obligations Law, §5-1311, subd. 1, par. [b]), but concomitantly, the equitable owner was also entitled to any increase in value; "since a purchaser under a binding contract of sale is in equity regarded as the owner of the property, he is entitled to any benefit or increase in value that may accrue to it" (6 Warren's Weed, New York Real Property, Vendee and Vendor, §6.01). Similarly, upon the parties' death, the vendor's interest is regarded as personal property (i.e., the right to receive money), while the vendee's interest is treated as real property (Barson v. Mulligan, supra, 191 N.Y. at p.313-314, 84 N.E. 75).

Because the common-law mortgagor possessed equitable title, the legal owner (the mortgagee) could not recover the premises summarily, but had to first extinguish the equitable owner's equity of redemption. Thus evolved the equitable remedy of mortgage foreclosure, which is now governed by statute (RPAPL, §1301 et seq.). In our view, the vendees herein occupy the same position as the mortgagor at common law; both have an equitable title only, while another person has legal title. We perceive no reason why the instant vendees should be treated any differently than the mortgagor at common law. Thus the contract vendors may not summarily dispossess the vendees of their equitable ownership without first bringing an action to foreclose the vendees' equity of redemption. This view reflects the modern trend in other jurisdictions (see Skendzel v. Marshall, supra; followed in Sebastian v. Floyd, 585 S.W.2d 381 [Ky. 1979]; Thomas v. Klein 99 Idaho 105, 577 P.2d 1153 [1978]; Anderson Contracting Co. v. Daugherty, 274 Pa. Super. 13, 417 A.2d 1227; H & L Land Co. v. Warner, 258 So. 2d 293 [Fla. App. 1972]), and has been recognized in New York (Hudson v. Matter, 219 App. Div. 252, 219 N.Y.S. 555; Gerder Servs. v. Johnson, 109 Misc. 2d 216, 439 N.Y.S.2d 794; 16 Carmody-Wait 2d, ch. 98; see also, 4 Pomeroy, Equity Jurisprudence, §1260-1262; and see cases collected at Anno. 4 A.L.R.4th 993; 47 S. Cal. L. Rev. 191; 41 Albany L. Rev. 71; 36 Mont. L. Rev. 110; 28 Wayne L. Rev. 239).

The key to the resolution of the rights of the parties lies in whether the vendee under a land sale contract has acquired an interest in the property of such a nature that it must be extinguished before the vendor may resume possession. We hold that such an interest exists since the vendee acquires equitable title and the vendor merely holds the legal title in trust for the vendee, subject to the vendor's equitable lien for payment of the purchase price in accordance with the terms of the contract. The vendor may not enforce his rights by the simple expedient of an action in ejectment but must instead proceed to foreclose the vendee's equitable title or bring an action at law for the purchase price, neither of which remedies plaintiffs have sought.

The effect of the judgment granted below is that plaintiffs will have their property with improvements made over the years by defendants, along with over $7,000 in principal payments on a purchase price of $15,000, and over $4,000 in interest. The basic inequity of such a result requires no further comment (see, Hudson v. Matter, 219 App. Div. 252, 219 N.Y.S. 555; Gerder Servs. v. Johnson, 109 Misc. 2d 216, 439 N.Y.S.2d 794).[20] If a forfeiture would result in the inequitable disposi-

20. Some jurisdictions refuse to enforce the forfeiture provision of a land contract if the proportion of the purchase price paid is so substantial that the amount forfeited would be an invalid "penalty" (see, e.g., Hook v. Bomar, 320 F.2d 536 (5th Cir.1963) [applying Florida law]; Rothenberg v. Follman, 19 Mich. App. 383, 172 N.W.2d 845 (1969); Morris v. Sykes, 624 P.2d 681 [Utah 1981]; Johnson v. Carman, 572 P.2d 371 [Utah 1977]; Beh-

tion of property and an exhorbitant monetary loss, equity can and should intervene (Thomas v. Klein, 99 Idaho 105, 107, 577 P.2d 1153; Ellis v. Butterfield, 98 Idaho 644, 648, 570 P.2d 1334 [1977]).

The interest of the parties here can only be determined by a sale of the property after foreclosure proceedings with provisions for disposing of the surplus or for a deficiency judgment. In arguing against this result, plaintiffs stress that in New York a defaulting purchaser may not recover money paid pursuant to an executory contract (Lawrence v. Miller, 86 N.Y. 131). Although we have no quarrel with this general rule of law (see, e.g., Dmochowski v. Rosati, 96 A.D.2d 718, 465 N.Y.S.2d 367, decided herewith), we observe that this rule has generally been applied to cases involving down payments (see Gerder Servs. v. Johnson, supra, 109 Misc. 2d at p.217, 439 N.Y.S.2d 794 and cases cited therein), or to cases wherein the vendee was not in possession (see, e.g., Leonard v. Ickovic, 55 N.Y.S.2d 727, 447 N.Y.S.2d 153, 431 N.E.2d 638 [factually distinguishable because the defaulting vendee was not in possession and was not attempting to defend his equitable title, but rather to recover money paid under a theory of joint venture]; Havens v. Patterson, 43 N.Y. 218 [the defaulting party had abandoned possession eight years earlier, whereupon the vendor retook possession and made substantial improvements]).

By our holding today we do not suggest that forfeiture would be an inappropriate result in all instances involving a breach of a land contract. If the vendee abandons the property and absconds, logic compels that the forfeiture provisions of the contract may be enforced. Similarly, where the vendee has paid a minimal sum on the contract and upon default seeks to retain possession of the property while the vendor is paying taxes, insurance and other upkeep to preserve the property, equity will not intervene to help the vendee (Skendzel v. Marshall, supra, 261 Ind. at pp.240, 241, 301 N.E.2d 641). Such is not the case before us.

Accordingly, the judgment should be reversed, the motion should be denied and the matter remitted to Supreme Court for further proceedings in accordance with this Opinion.

NOTE

In an illuminating examination of installment land contracts, Professor Freyfogle has catalogued the many uncertainties of forfeiture law. Eric T. Freyfogle, Vagueness and the Rule of Law: Reconsidering Installment Land Contract Forfeitures, 1988 Duke L.J. 609. In nearly all

---

rendt v. Abraham, 64 Cal. 2d 182, 49 Cal. Rptr. 292, 410 P.2d 828 (1966); Land Development, Inc. v. Padgett, 369 P.2d 888 [Alaska 1962]).

states, the seller must give notice of a possible forfeiture, either in a manner prescribed by statute or in a reasonable manner satisfactory to a court. Accepting late payments may waive the seller's right to forfeiture in the future, as it may mislead the purchaser into believing that promptness is not required. Purchasers in default may have the right to specific performance by paying the entire purchase price. The seller's declaration of forfeiture may bar the seller from suing for the remainder of the purchase price. The purchaser, even a willfully defaulting one, may be entitled to restitution of some payments in excess of what is fair to the seller to cover his loss. Some courts require foreclosure by the seller, but with exceptions not easy to apply. Professor Freyfogle points out that installment land contract law has developed, in the last 50 years, an ex post analysis after the breach has occurred and tried to then sort out the rights and obligations of the parties. The result has been flexibility but also extraordinary vagueness and unpredictability. See also Grant S. Nelson & Dale A. Whitman, Real Estate Finance Law §§2.26-3.37 (2d ed. 1985).

History is repeating itself. In the development of mortgage law, the chancellor protected defaulting borrowers when it was necessary to do equity. In time, the chancellor gave all borrowers a right of redemption, regardless of their merits, and the previous ad hockery disappeared. The same, it seems, is now happening with installment land contracts. See Carol M. Rose, Crystals and Mud in Property Law, 40 Stan. L. Rev. 577, 583-585 (1988).

8

Title Assurance

In this chapter we deal with the system our country has developed to assure purchasers of land that they have good title to the land purchased. At the heart of the system is the public records office, where all instruments affecting land titles (deeds, mortgages, liens, wills, and so forth) are recorded. Before buying, a purchaser should search (or, more accurately, pay a professional to search) the public records office to discover the evidence of title recorded in that office. From the evidence of title in the records office, a professional (often a lawyer) will conclude who has the fee simple title to the land, which may be encumbered with a mortgage or a servitude. Relying on the professional's opinion of title, the purchaser decides whether or not to buy the land.

In a few localities, title registration is available. Under title registration, the state registers title and issues a title certificate to the owner, which is reissued to each new purchaser of the property.

Public records are not always perfect, and purchasers might want further security. So private insurance companies sell title insurance to purchasers for a premium. In many localities, particularly in the Far West and large urban areas, title insurance companies maintain their own private record storage systems, which duplicate the public records and store the information in a computerized system.

With title insurance companies serving as backup to the recording system, security of title in the United States ought to be, and is, very high. This, however, results less from any merits in our land title transfer system than from the ingenuity of professionals in the title industry, who manage to provide security in spite of the recording system's manifest and long-recognized defects.

A. The Recording System

1. Introduction

Public recording of deeds, mortgages, leases, and other instruments affecting land title began in this country in the Plymouth and Massachusetts Bay colonies around 1640. It was not an English custom. Indeed, not until the twentieth century did England have a general public registration system; deeds and other muniments of title were handed from purchaser to purchaser and were usually kept in boxes in the office of the owner's solicitor. Today in every American state, statutes provide for land title records to be maintained by the county recorder (or other equivalent public official) in each county. The land title records include copies of documents filed with the recorder and indexes to these copied documents. (The original document presented for recordation is copied by the recorder and returned to the grantee.)

The recording acts generally do not affect the validity of a deed or other instrument. A deed is valid and good against the grantor upon delivery without recordation. The recording system serves other functions. First, it establishes a system of public recordation of land titles. Anyone — creditor, tax collector, prospective purchaser, or just plain curious — can ascertain who owns land in the county by searching the records. Second, the recording system preserves in a secure place important documents which, in private hands, may be easily lost or misplaced. In most states recorded copies of documents can be admitted directly into evidence in judicial proceedings, without producing or accounting for the original. In other states, the recorded copy can be admitted, but only after showing why the original cannot be produced. In order to increase the reliability of the public records, statutes typically require that a deed be acknowledged before a notary public or other public official before it is entitled to recordation.

Recording statutes often specify what instruments can be recorded, but generally any kind of deed, mortgage, lease, option, or other instrument creating or affecting an interest in land can be recorded. A judgment or decree affecting title to land can also be recorded. Prior to judgment in a lawsuit, any party may record a *lis pendens* (notice of pending action) which will effectively put subsequent claimants on notice of the claims being litigated. In addition, wills and affidavits of heirship of an intestate are entitled to be recorded. About one-third of the states have statutes permitting recordation of affidavits containing statements of fact relating to title.

Finally, recording acts have the function of protecting purchasers for value and lien creditors against prior unrecorded interests. At common law, as between successive grantees, priority of title was determined by priority in time of conveyance. The theory was that once the grantor conveyed his interest to a grantee, he no longer had an interest to convey to any subsequent grantee. Thus:

> *Example 1.* O mortgages Blackacre to A. O subsequently conveys Blackacre to B who does not know of the mortgage. At common law B takes the land subject to A's mortgage. (In equity, the doctrine of *bona fide purchaser* would protect B against A's mortgage if A's mortgage were purely equitable

and not a legal interest. Equity refused to enforce prior hidden equitable interests against bona fide purchasers of the legal title.)

The recording acts in general have adopted and broadened the equitable doctrine of bona fide purchaser. Under the recording acts, *a subsequent bona fide purchaser is protected against prior unrecorded interests.* Thus a purchaser of property will want to search the records to make sure that there are no adverse prior recorded claims, and a purchaser records his deed in order to prevent a subsequent purchaser from a previous owner from prevailing over him. *But remember*: The common law rule of "prior in time, prior in effect," illustrated by *Example 1*, continues to control unless a person can qualify for protection under the applicable recording act.

2. The Indexes

It is impossible for a buyer of land to search out and find all the interests in a particular tract of land without using an index to the thousands, or millions, of documents filed in the recorder's office. There are two types of indexes currently used in the United States: (1) tract index, and (2) grantor-grantee index. Both are useful in searching title. Public tract indexes, indexing documents by a parcel identification number assigned to the particular tract, do not exist in most states. The primary obstacle to establishing public tract indexes was the fact that early deeds in eastern states described land by metes and bounds (see pages 629-630). No short formula was available by which a tract of land could be described. This obstacle remains today where land has not been subdivided and conveyed by subdivision tract numbers, or conveyed by reference to a government survey, or, in recent years, has not acquired a parcel identification number in localities where such numbers are available.

The most common method of indexing is the grantor-grantee system. Under this system separate indexes are kept for grantors and grantees. In the *grantor index* all instruments are indexed alphabetically and chronologically under the grantor's surname. In the *grantee index* all instruments are indexed under the grantee's surname. Thus a deed from Able to Baker will be indexed under Able's name in the grantor index and under Baker's name in the grantee index. Usually many volumes compose the grantor index and similarly the grantee index. For example, the recorder's office may have consolidated all of its nineteenth century grantor index volumes into one volume indexing grantors prior to 1900. For twentieth century grantors, there may be one volume for each decade: 1900 to 1910, 1910 to 1920, and so forth until 1980. After 1980 there may be one volume for each year and for the most recent year a monthly and daily index. These volumes covering different time

1980 - - - - - GRANTOR INDEX FEB. 2,81 THRU FEB. 20,81 - - - - - SUFFOLK COUNTY REGISTRY OF DEEDS PAGE 180

MO-DY	GRANTOR	GRANTEE	TOWN	BOOK	PGE	INST	DESCRIPTION
02-05	SECURITY PLANNERS LTD INC EAL	RELEASE		9669	238	REL	U S TAX LIEN 8515,35
02-05	SECURITY WAREHOUSE INC EAL	RELEASE		9669	236	REL	U S TAX LIEN 8467,535
02-05	SECURITY WAREHOUSE INC EAL	RELEASE		9669	237	REL	U S TAX LIEN 8442,251
02-05	SECURITY WAREHOUSE INC EAL	RELEASE		9669	247	REL	U S TAX LIEN
02-05	SEGAL, EDITH EAL	RELEASE		9669	243	REL	U S TAX LIEN
02-05	SEGAL, MARY L. EAL	RELEASE		9669	241	REL	U S TAX LIEN
02-05	SEGAL, MARY L. EAL	RELEASE		9669	242	REL	U S TAX LIEN
02-05	SEGAL, MAX EAL	RELEASE		9669	243	REL	U S TAX LIEN
02-05	SEGAL, MICHAEL G. EAL	RELEASE		9669	243	REL	U S TAX LIEN
02-05	SEGAL, MICHAEL O. EAL	RELEASE		9669	241	REL	U S TAX LIEN
02-04	SEGAL, ROSALYN A. EAL	AMENDMENT		9663	225	AMDT	MASTER CNDMNM DEED 9344,337 PLANS
02-03	SEGALINI, ROLAND JR EAL	J R MCLAUGHLIN TR		9667	240	MTG	UNIT 400-21 OF THE CANTERBURY VILLAGE CNDMNM
02-12	SEGALINI, ROLAND JR TR	M C MAGUIRE EAL	BRI	9676	306	DEED	57 AUSTIN ST LT 45 PL 3500,5366 PEING, LT 3A PL 1932,383
02-20	SEIDNER, MICHAEL A.	HOUSEHOLD FIN CORP	BRI	9683	282	MTG	SUMMIT AVE&ALLSTON ST LT 3 PL 2306,435
02-11	SEKENSKI, EDWARD A. JR EAL	LEVY & SUSPENDED	CHE	9675	316	LES	WALTHAM DIST CT MADE FEB 11, 1981 BELLINGHAM ST 2 PCS
02-11	SEKENSKI, LINDA C. EAL	LEVY & SUSPENDED	CHE	9675	316	LES	WALTHAM DIST CT MADE FEB 11, 1981 BELLINGHAM ST 2 PCS,
02-05	SELCY AUTO SUPPLY CO INC EAL	RELEASE		9669	240	REL	U S TAX LIEN 8443,434
02-05	SELLARO, FRANK EAL	RELEASE		9669	248	REL	U S TAX LIEN
02-09	SELWYN, BARBARA E. EAL	SHAWMUT BK BOSTON N A		9671	113	MTG	19-21 RICKER TERR LT 30 PL 2436 FND WDLSX #OUT OF CO
02-13	SELYA, ANNE EAL	DISCHARGE		9677	193	DIS	MTG 8460,419
02-13	SELYA, DAVID EAL	DISCHARGE		9677	193	DIS	MTG 8460,419
02-09	SEMINERIO, SANTINA TR	A DESALVATORE EAL	BRI	9673	170	DEED	MURDOCK&SPARHAWK STS LT 4 PL D APRIL 4,1887
02-03	SENA, LAURA EAL	NOTICE PETN	S B	9665	316	NOT	A HUMPHREYS ST FCL TAX 2143,093
02-02	SENNET, CAROL EAL	C SENNETT EAL	T P	9665	234	DFED	162 SHERRIN ST LT 546 PL 4710 END
02-18	SEPULVEDA, PABLO	J A PROROK JR	ROX	9680	135	DEED	4 ESTRELLA ST
02-06	SERVICENTER LTD EAL	WESTINGHOUSE CR CORP	ROX	9670	338	MTG	BROOKLINE AVE&FRANCISE BINNEY ST&FENWOOD RD PL D 1-25-1979
02-06	SERVICENTER LTD EAL	WESTINGHOUSE CR CORP		9671	1	ASST	ASST LEASES&RENTS ETC SEE INSTR

A page from the Grantor Index, Register of Deeds, Suffolk County, Massachusetts

spans result from periodic consolidation by the recorder. The more consolidation, the easier it is to search title because there are fewer volumes to check.

There may also be separate grantor and grantee indexes for each type of instrument — one index for deeds, one for mortgages, one for wills, one for liens, and so on. In our description of searching title below, we use the term grantor index to refer comprehensively to all the volumes indexing grantors. Similarly the term grantee index refers to all volumes indexing grantees.

The reference in the index to a document sets forth its essentials: the grantor, the grantee, description of the land, kind of instrument, date of recording, and volume and page numbers where the instrument can be found set forth in full. The title searcher must, of course, examine the complete instrument; the index is merely a helpful method of locating the instrument among the many volumes in the recorder's office.

How to search title. You will more easily comprehend the issues arising under the recording system if you understand how title is searched in the grantor-grantee indexes. The best way to learn is by doing, and we recommend that you go to the court house in your county and search the title of your parents' house, the apartment where you are living, or some other property you are interested in. The records are public, and employees in the recorder's office in most localities are quite helpful in giving a law student a start. Barring a personal search, you will have to learn from the following description.[1]

Searching title bears some resemblance to what the genealogist does in establishing kindred; first, trace backward for ancestors, and then under each ancestor fill in the names and relationships of his or her descendants. Similarly, in searching title you go backward in time to an acceptable source or "root of title," then search forward from that source. Since you use the grantee index to search backwards and the grantor index to search forward, both indexes must be searched.

 `   Assume that a man named Dubek is selling to your client a tract of land called (as any astrologer might have predicted) Blackacre. Since you want to find out how Dubek received title, you look in the *grantee* index under Dubek's name from the present time backward until you find a deed to Dubek from, let us say, Cotter in 1977. Now you want to know how Cotter received title, so you look, again in the grantee index, under Cotter's name from 1977 backwards in time until you find a deed to

---

1. We describe here only the search in the recorder's office, but a title searcher typically must search in other places as well. Transfers by will may be kept in the probate court; claims of *lis pendens*, mechanics' liens, state and federal tax liens, zoning ordinances, building codes, and other pertinent items may be found in other places. See Roger A. Cunningham, William B. Stoebuck & Dale A. Whitman, The Law of Property §11.9 (1984).

Cotter from Barker in 1952. Now you want to know how Barker received title, and so you run Barker's name in the grantee index from 1952 backwards in time to his source of title. By running each grantee's name back through the grantee index you can discover the preceding source of title (the grantor) of each person who purports to own Blackacre.

Suppose you run the grantee index back to 1900, which is as far as you deem necessary, and you find that in 1900 record title was in Oliver. Now you must switch to the *grantor* index and search that index forward in time under the name of each grantor (remember: you have ascertained the names of each grantor by running the grantee index). You start with Oliver in the year 1900. You look under Oliver's name in 1900, 1901, 1902, and so forth, until you find a deed from Oliver to Anderson, executed and recorded in 1915. Having found that Oliver parted with record title to Blackacre in 1915, you stop looking under Oliver's name and start, with the volume for 1915, looking under the name of Anderson to find the first deed out from Anderson. This deed you find is a deed from Anderson to Barker executed in 1934 and recorded in 1939. You then drop Anderson's name in 1939, and run Barker's name in the grantor index from *1934* (the date of execution of the deed) until you find, in 1952, the deed from Barker to Cotter, which was executed and recorded on the same day in 1952. You next run Cotter's name in the grantor index from 1952 until you find the deed from Cotter to Dubek, executed and recorded in 1977. Finally you run Dubek's name in the grantor index from 1977 to the present.

As you can see, you have discovered a chain of title that looks like this:

1900-1915	Oliver owns; conveys to Anderson in 1915
1915-1934	Anderson owns; conveys to Barker in 1934 by deed not recorded until 1939
1934-1952	Barker owns; conveys to Cotter in 1952
1952-1977	Cotter owns; conveys to Dubek in 1977

In running the grantor index under Oliver's name from 1900 to 1915 (to the first deed out, to Anderson) you pick up any mortgages given by Oliver, any attachments or lawsuits filed against Oliver, and any conveyances by Oliver of interests less than a fee simple. Similarly, with respect to each other owner, you pick up all of the claims against the particular owner by running the grantor index under the owner's name forward from the time of the *execution* of the first deed giving title to such owner to the time of *recording* of the first deed out from such owner.

Why must you search under Barker's name from 1934 (the date of execution of the *A* to *B* deed) rather than from 1939 (the date of recording)? The deed from Anderson to Barker passed title to Barker in 1934.

Barker thus could convey title to a person after that time. Suppose that Barker mortgaged the property in 1936, which mortgage was recorded. If you ran the grantor index under Barker's name only from 1939 forward, you would not pick up the mortgage. As pointed out above, you also have to run the grantor index under the name of Anderson from 1934 to 1939, because Anderson was the record owner until 1939. If in 1937 Anderson had given a deed to Florence, a bona fide purchaser who recorded, Florence would prevail over Barker's then unrecorded deed.

recorded deed prevails over unrecorded deed

The search sketched above, the minimum required in all jurisdictions without tract indexes, is the standard title search. This search produces a chain of title going back to a source deemed satisfactory. Many jurisdictions require a more extensive search of title, however. The more extensive searches and the problems they raise are examined in the discussion of Chain of Title Problems beginning at page 721.

How far back? How far back in the abysm of time a title searcher must search to find a satisfactory root of title varies both with local custom and with the identity of the client. In some jurisdictions the practice is to go back to a sovereign, in others 60 years, in still others a shorter period. The search is not ordinarily limited to the period of the statute of limitations because the statute may not have begun to run on various types of interests (such as a remainder, an easement, a covenant, or mineral rights). Because a purchaser is liable under CERCLA for costs of cleaning up contaminated land unless the purchaser makes "all appropriate inquiry" into possible contamination and qualifies as an innocent purchaser (see page 615), purchasers of commercial properties are now making far more extensive searches to ascertain previous owners and possible polluters of the particular property they are interested in buying.

Agencies of the federal government customarily require a search back to the original source. This perfectionism led to the circulation some years ago of a spurious but delightful story. A New Orleans lawyer had searched title back to 1803 for his client, a federal agency. The agency asked who owned the land prior to that date. The lawyer replied:

Gentlemen:

I am in receipt of your letter of the fifth of this month inquiring as to the state of the title prior to the year 1803.

Please be advised that in the year 1803 the United States of America acquired the Territory of Louisiana from the Republic of France by purchase. The Republic of France previously acquired title from the Spanish Crown by conquest. Spain acquired title by virtue of the discoveries of one Christopher Columbus, a Genoese sailor who had been duly authorized to embark upon his voyage of discovery by Isabella, Queen of Spain. Before granting such authority, Isabella, a pious and cautious woman, obtained the sanction of His Holiness, the Pope. The Pope is the Vicar on earth of Jesus Christ, the only son and heir apparent of God. God made Louisiana.

Luthi v. Evans

Supreme Court of Kansas, 1978
223 Kan. 622, 576 P.2d 1064

PRAGER, J. On February 1, 1971, Grace V. Owens was the owner of interests in a number of oil and gas leases located in Coffey county. On that date Owens, by a written instrument designated "Assignment of Interest in Oil and Gas Leases," assigned to defendant International Tours, Inc. (hereinafter Tours) all of such oil and gas interests. This assignment provided as follows:

Assignment of Interest in Oil and Gas Leases

KNOW ALL MEN BY THESE PRESENTS:
    That the undersigned Grace Vannocker Owens, formerly Grace Vannocker, Connie Sue Vannocker, formerly Connie Sue Wilson, Larry R. Vannocker, sometimes known as Larry Vannocker, individually and also doing business as Glacier Petroleum Company and Vannocker Oil Company, hereinafter called Assignors, for and in consideration of $100.00 and other valuable consideration, the receipt whereof is hereby acknowledged, do hereby sell, assign, transfer and set over unto International Tours, Inc., a Delaware Corporation, hereinafter called Assignee, all their right, title, and interest (which includes all overriding royalty interest and working interest) in and to the following Oil and Gas Leases located in Coffey County, Kansas, more particularly specified as follows, to-wit:

[The court omitted the description of the leases assigned, but, to make the case more understandable, we reproduce here the description of one of the leases referred to in the actual instrument:

WILEY (Phillips CP #50098)
    Entire ⅞ Working Interest in Lease
    Dated: June 8, 1936
    From: Lillian Wiley
    To: E.L. Harrigan and T.F. Harrigan
    Recorded: Book 6L pages 137 and 138
    Insofar as lease covers NE4 Sec. 14-23-14 (160 a.)

Similar descriptions of six other leases from Rossillon, Scott, Shotwell, Vannocker, McCartney, and Cochran are set forth in the instrument of assignment.]

together with the rights incident thereto and the personal property thereon, appurtenant thereto or used or obtained in connection therewith.
    And for the same consideration the Assignors covenant with the Assignee, his heirs, successors or assigns: That the Assignors are the lawful owners of and have good title to the interest above assigned in and to said Lease, estate, rights and property, free and clear from all liens, encumbrances or adverse claims; That said Lease is valid and subsisting Lease on the land above described, and all rentals and royalties due thereunder have been paid and all conditions necessary to keep the same in full force have been duly

performed, and that the Assignor will warrant and forever defend the same against all persons whomsoever, lawfully claiming or to claim the same. *Assignors intend to convey, and by this instrument convey, to the Assignee all interest of whatsoever nature in all working interests and overriding royalty interest in all Oil and Gas Leases in Coffey County, Kansas, owned by them whether or not the same are specifically enumerated above with all oil field and oil and gas lease equipment owned by them in said County whether or not located on the leases above described,* or elsewhere in storage in said County, but title is warranted only to the specific interests above specified, and assignors retain their title to all minerals in place and the corresponding royalty (commonly referred to as land owners royalty) attributable thereto. The effective date of this Assignment is February 1, 1971, at 7:00 o'clock A.M.

/s/ *Grace Vannocker Owens*
Connie Sue Vannocker
Larry R. Vannocker

(Acknowledgment by Grace Vannocker Owens before notary public with seal impressed thereon dated Feb. 5, 1971, appears here.) (Emphasis supplied.)

This assignment was filed for record in the office of the register of deeds of Coffey county on February 16, 1971.

It is important to note that in the first paragraph of the assignment, seven oil and gas leases were specifically described. Those leases are not involved on this appeal. In addition to the seven leases specifically described in the first paragraph, Owens was also the owner of a working interest in an oil and gas lease known as the Kufahl lease which was located on land in Coffey county. The Kufahl lease was not one of the leases specifically described in the assignment.

The second paragraph of the assignment states that the assignors intended to convey, and by this instrument conveyed to the assignee, "all interest of whatsoever nature in all working interests and overriding royalty interest in all Oil and Gas Leases in Coffey County, Kansas, owned by them whether or not the same are specifically enumerated above. . . ." The interest of Grace V. Owens in the Kufahl lease, being located in Coffey county, would be included under this general description.

On January 30, 1975, the same Grace V. Owens executed and delivered a second assignment of her working interest in the Kufahl lease to the defendant, J.R. Burris. Prior to the date of that assignment, Burris personally checked the records in the office of the register of deeds and, following the date of the assignment to him, Burris secured an abstract of title to the real estate in question. Neither his personal inspection nor the abstract of title reflected the prior assignment to Tours.

The controversy on this appeal is between Tours and Burris over ownership of what had previously been Owens's interest in the Kufahl lease. It is the position of Tours that the assignment dated February 1,

COFFEY COUNTY KANSAS
GENERAL INDEX

LOCKWOOD CO., INC., ATCHISON 10414B-4-60

TIME OF RECEPTION				GRANTOR	GRANTEE
Year	Month	Day	Hour	Part	
1971	Feb.	16	8:50 A.M.	Owens, Grace Vanrocker et al	International Tours, Inc.

INSTRUMENT	RECORDED		DESCRIPTION OF PROPERTY
	Vol.	Page	
Assign. of oil	13 O+G	1/2 -115	Entire $\frac{7}{8}$ W.I. in $W^2 NE^4$ less $10a$ $12-23-14$ + $10a$, $E^2 NE^4$ $12-23-14$
& gas lease			$N^2 E^2 SW^4 SE^4$, $SE^4 SW^4 SE^4$ $14-23-14$; $N^2 SE^4$ $1-23-14$; $N^2 NW^4$ + $S^2 NW^4$ $13-23-$

Above is the entry in the grantor index of the assignment from Owens to Tours. The land involved is described by reference to the United States Government Survey. Observe that land involved in the Wiley lease, referred to in the case, is described in the index as NE4 (northeast quarter) in 14-23-14 (Section 14, Township 23, Range 14). The other tracts were described by similar references. The Kufahl land did not come within the legal descriptions mentioned in the index.

1971, effectively conveyed from Owens to Tours, Owens's working interest in the Kufahl lease by virtue of the general description contained
in paragraph two of that assignment. Tours then contends that the recording of that assignment in the office of the register of deeds of Coffey
county gave constructive notice of such conveyance to subsequent purchasers, including Burris. Hence, Tours reasons, it is the owner of
Owens's working interest in the Kufahl lease.

[Tours says]

Burris admits that the general description and language used in the
second paragraph of Owens's assignment to Tours was sufficient to effect a valid transfer of the Owens interest in the Kufahl lease to Tours
as between the parties to that instrument. Burris contends, however, that the
general language contained in the second paragraph of the assignment
to Tours, as recorded, which failed to state with specificity the names of
the lessor and lessee, the date of the lease, any legal description, and the
recording data, was not sufficient to give constructive notice to a subsequent innocent purchaser for value without actual notice of the prior
assignment. Burris argues that as a result of those omissions in the assignment to Tours, it was impossible for the register of deeds of Coffey
county to identify the real estate involved and to make the proper entries
in the numerical index. Accordingly, even though he checked the records at the courthouse, Burris was unaware of the assignment of the
Kufahl lease to Tours and he did not learn of the prior conveyance until
after he had purchased the rights from Grace V. Owens. The abstract
of title also failed to reflect the prior assignment to Tours. Burris maintains that as a result of the omissions and the inadequate description of
the interest in real estate to be assigned under the second paragraph of
the assignment to Tours, the Tours assignment, as recorded, was not
sufficient to give constructive notice to a subsequent innocent purchaser
for value. It is upon this point that Burris prevailed before the district
court. On appeal, the Court of Appeals held the general description
contained in the assignment to Tours to be sufficient, when recorded, to
give constructive notice to a subsequent purchaser for value, including
Burris.

[Burris says]

[district court for Burris]

At the outset, it should be noted that a deed or other instrument in
writing which is intended to convey an interest in real estate and which
describes the property to be conveyed as "all of the grantor's property
in a certain county," is commonly referred to as a "Mother Hubbard"
instrument. The language used in the second paragraph of the assignment from Owens to Tours in which the assignor conveyed to the assignee "all interest of whatsoever nature in all working interests . . . in
all Oil and Gas Leases in Coffey County, Kansas," is an example of a
"Mother Hubbard" clause. The so-called Mother Hubbard clauses or
descriptions are seldom used in this state, but in the past have been
found to be convenient for death bed transfers and in situations where
time is of the essence and specific information concerning the legal de-

[Mother Hubbard deed]

[best argument]

scription of property to be conveyed is not available. Instruments of conveyance containing a description of the real estate conveyed in the form of a "Mother Hubbard" clause have been upheld in Kansas for many years as between the parties to the instrument. (In re Estate of Crawford, 176 Kan. 537, 271 P.2d 240; Bryant v. Fordyce, 147 Kan. 586, 78 P.2d 32.)

The parties in this case agree, and the Court of Appeals held, that the second paragraph of the assignment from Owens to Tours, providing that the assignors convey to the assignee all interests in all oil and gas leases in Coffey County, Kansas, owned by them, constituted a valid transfer of the Owens interest in the Kufahl lease to Tours *as between the parties to that instrument.* We agree. We also agree with the parties and the Court of Appeals that a single instrument, properly executed, acknowledged, and delivered, may convey separate tracts by specific description and by general description capable of being made specific, where the clear intent of the language used is to do so. We agree that a subsequent purchaser, who has *actual* notice or knowledge of such an instrument, is bound thereby and takes subject to the rights of the assignee or grantor.

This case involves a legal question which is one of first impression in this court. As noted above, the issue presented is whether or not the recording of an instrument of conveyance which uses a "Mother Hubbard" clause to describe the property conveyed, constitutes *constructive notice to a subsequent purchaser.* The determination of this issue requires us to examine the pertinent Kansas statutes covering the conveyance of interests in land and the statutory provisions for recording the same. . . .

The recordation of instruments of conveyance and the effect of recordation is covered in part by K.S.A. 58-2221, 58-2222, and 58-2223. These statutes are directly involved in this case and are as follows:

58-2221. *Recordation of instruments conveying or affecting real estate; duties of register of deeds.* Every instrument in writing that conveys real estate, any estate or interest created by an oil and gas lease, or whereby any real estate, may be affected, proved or acknowledged, and certified in the manner hereinbefore prescribed, may be recorded in the office of register of deeds of the county in which such real estate is situated: *Provided,* It shall be the duty of the register of deeds to file the same for record immediately, and in those counties where a numerical index is maintained in his or her office the register of deeds shall compare such instrument, before copying the same in the record, with the last record of transfer in his or her office of the property described and if the register of deeds finds such instrument contains apparent errors, he or she shall not record the same until he or she shall have notified the grantee where such notice is reasonably possible.

The grantor, lessor, grantee or lessee or any other person conveying or receiving real property or other interest in real property upon recording the instrument in the office of register of deeds shall furnish the register of deeds the full name and last known post-office address of the person to whom the property is conveyed or his or her designee. The register of deeds shall forward such information to the county clerk of the county who shall make any necessary changes in address records for mailing tax statements.

58-2222. *Same; filing imparts notice*. Every such instrument in writing, certified and recorded in the manner hereinbefore prescribed, shall, from the time of filing the same with the register of deeds for record, impart notice to all persons of the content thereof; and all subsequent purchasers and mortgagees shall be deemed to purchase with notice.

58-2223. *Same; unrecorded instrument valid only between parties having actual notice*. No such instrument in writing shall be valid, except between the parties thereto, and such as have actual notice thereof, until the same shall be deposited with the register of deeds for record.

... [W]e must also consider the Kansas statutes which govern the custody and the recordation of instruments of conveyance, and the duties of the register of deeds in regard thereto, as contained at K.S.A. 19-1201 through K.S.A. 19-1219. We will discuss only those statutes which we deem pertinent in the present controversy. . . . K.S.A. 19-1205 requires the register of deeds to keep a general index, direct and inverted, in his office. The register is required to record in the general index under the appropriate heading the names of grantors and grantees, the nature of the instrument, the volume and page where recorded, and, where appropriate, *a description of the tract.*

K.S.A. 19-1207 requires the register to keep a book of plats with an index thereof. K.S.A. 19-1209 provides that the county commissioners of any county may order the register of deeds to furnish a numerical index containing "the name of the instrument, the name of the grantor, the name of the grantee, *a brief description of the property,* and the volume and page in which each instrument indexed is recorded." K.S.A. 19-1210 makes it the duty of the register to make correct entries in the numerical index, of all instruments recorded concerning real estate, under the appropriate headings, and *"in the subdivision devoted to the particular quarter section described in the instrument making the conveyance."*[2]

. . . It . . . seems obvious to us that the purpose of the statutes authorizing the recording of instruments of conveyance is to impart to a subsequent purchaser notice of instruments which affect the title to a *specific tract of land* in which the subsequent purchaser is interested at the time. From a reading of all of the statutory provisions together, we have

---

2. Observe that the Kansas statutes require each county to maintain a grantor-grantee index ("a general index, direct and inverted"). The statutes give the counties the option of establishing, in addition, a tract ("numerical") index by quarter sections of the U.S. government survey (see page 701). An index by quarter sections is better than no tract index at all, but such an index contains references to instruments affecting land in the quarter section other than the land the searcher is interested in.

Where tract indexes are available, the jurisdictions are split over whether the title searcher must search the tract index as well as the grantor-grantee index. In some states only recordation in the grantor-grantee index gives constructive notice. — EDS.

concluded that the legislature intended that recorded instruments of conveyance, to impart constructive notice to a subsequent purchaser or mortgagee, should describe the land conveyed with sufficient specificity so that the specific land conveyed can be identified. . . . A description of the property conveyed should be considered sufficient if it identifies the property or affords the means of identification within the instrument itself or by specific reference to other instruments recorded in the office of the register of deeds. Such a specific description of the property conveyed is required in order to impart constructive notice to a subsequent purchaser.

Again, we wish to emphasize that an instrument which contains a "Mother Hubbard" clause, describing the property conveyed in the general language involved here, is valid, enforceable, and effectively transfers the entire property interest as between the parties to the instrument. Such a transfer is not effective as to subsequent purchasers and mortgagees unless they have *actual* knowledge of the transfer. If, because of emergency, it becomes necessary to use a "Mother Hubbard" clause in an instrument of conveyance, the grantee may take steps to protect his title against subsequent purchasers. He may take possession of the property. Also, as soon as a specific description can be obtained, the grantee may identify the specific property covered by the conveyance by filing an affidavit or other appropriate instrument or document with the register of deeds.

We also wish to make it clear that in situations where an instrument of conveyance containing a sufficient description of the property conveyed is duly recorded but not properly indexed, the fact that it was not properly indexed by the register of deeds will not prevent constructive notice under the provisions of K.S.A. 58-2222. (See Gas Co. v. Harris, 79 Kan. 167, 100 Pac. 72.)

From what we have said above, it follows that the recording of the assignment from Owens to Tours, which did not describe with sufficient specificity the property covered by the conveyance, was not sufficient to impart constructive notice to a subsequent purchaser such as J.R. Burris in the present case. Since Burris had no *actual* knowledge of the prior assignment from Owens to Tours, the later assignment to Burris prevails over the assignment from Owens to Tours.

The judgment of the Court of Appeals is reversed and the judgment of the district court is affirmed.

NOTES AND QUESTIONS

1. Note that the Kansas court states in the third paragraph from the end of its opinion that "the fact that it [a deed] was not properly

indexed by the register of deeds will not prevent constructive notice." 4 American Law Property §17.25 (1952) states that:

> [T]he rule appears to be well established that in the absence of statutory provision to that effect, an index is not an essential part of the record. In other words, a purchaser is charged with constructive notice of a record even though there is no official index which will direct him to it.

For a recent case following this rule, see Haner v. Bruce, 146 Vt. 262, 499 A.2d 792 (1985). Is this a sound rule? See Hochstein v. Romero, 219 Cal. App. 3d 447, 268 Cal. Rptr. 202 (1990) (rejecting rule on ground purchaser cannot find instrument not indexed); Howard Sav. Bank v. Brunson, 244 N.J. Super. 571, 582 A.2d 1305 (1990) (rejecting rule).

2. Should the recorder of deeds be liable for negligence if the recorder fails to index a deed properly? "In the absence of specific statutory provisions to the contrary, the recorder has traditionally been protected by a shield of governmental immunity. Most states provide some liability, but the scope of the liability is usually below that of a common law action grounded in negligence." Paul E. Basye, A Uniform Land Parcel Identifier — Its Potential for All Our Land Records, 22 Am. U. L. Rev. 251, 262 n.29 (1973). Basye also points out that recovery on the recorder's bond is usually permitted but that the bonding limitations (typically $10,000) are inadequate to cover most claims. See Siefkes v. Waterton Title Co., 437 N.W.2d 190 (S.D. 1989) (recorder immune under doctrine of sovereign immunity).

3. In Luthi v. Evans, Grace Owens assigned her working interest in the Kufahl lease twice. The first assignee, Tours, lost to the second assignee, Burris. Does Tours have any claim against Owens? Under principles of restitution, Tours can have a constructive trust imposed upon Owens to prevent Owens's unjust enrichment. Owens must give Tours the amount Owens received from Burris. See Patterson v. Bryant, 216 N.C. 550, 5 S.E.2d 849 (1939).

NOTE: DESCRIPTION BY GOVERNMENT SURVEY

On the formation of the Union it became federal government policy, initiated by the Continental Congress in 1785, to make no disposition of lands in the public domain until the lands were surveyed and a plat of the survey was filed in the General Land Office. This great survey, using a method adapted by Thomas Jefferson[3] from earlier New

3. Thomas Jefferson, principal supporter of the L'Enfant gridiron plan for Washington, D.C., is the intellectual father of the gridiron plan of development in America. Jefferson thought that a rectangular survey was easy to lay out, comprehensible by unso-

England surveys, was as remarkable in its own time as Domesday Book had been 700 years earlier. It became the basis of land description in Alabama, Florida, Mississippi, in all states east of the Mississippi River and north of the Ohio River, in all states west of the Mississippi except Texas, and in portions of a few states that were never a part of the public domain because embraced in grants by prior governments. This survey did not include the original 13 colonies nor Kentucky, Maine, Tennessee, Vermont, and West Virginia, and land descriptions in those states are not based on the U.S. Government Survey. See 3 American Law of Property §12.100 (1952).

All of the public land in the United States in the areas above described was first surveyed into rectangular tracts by running parallel lines north and south and by crossing them at approximately right angles with other parallel lines so as to form rectangles six miles square. The first north and south line established for any surveyed area was a selected true meridian, which is called a *principal* or *prime meridian*. There are 34 such meridians in the area surveyed. Parallel to the principal meridian, running north and south, are *range lines*. They are six miles apart, and the six-mile strips bounded by the range lines are called *ranges*. For each principal meridian there is a *base line* running east and west on a true parallel of latitude. Parallel to the base line, at six-mile intervals, are *township lines*. The six-mile strips bounded by township lines are called *townships*, as also are the six-mile squares formed by the intersection of

---

phisticated settlers, and, like geometry, a thing of beauty. In addition, the imposition of a formal rectilinear order on the wilderness served social purposes. It encouraged division of land into small uniform tracts, which could be — and were — given to soldiers who had fought in the continental army. By act of Congress, section 16 of each township in the survey was granted to each of the states formed out of the territory for the purpose of supporting public schools. All this reflected Jefferson's belief that the future of the country lay with small rural landowners, coming together in townships with the school section at the center, all active in the democratic process. The grid system, as Jefferson conceived it, was a device for the promotion of an agrarian egalitarian society. As it turned out, however, the grid system also was ideally suited to the land speculation that gripped the country in the nineteenth century; nationally surveyed land was easy to describe in deeds and sell from the auctioneer's block.

Jefferson's faithful devotion to the gridiron plan also resulted in the most characteristic design of our urban environment. Unlike European cities, with their winding streets of uneven widths, American cities were, until late in the nineteenth century, built in monotonous conformance to the grid system; almost all were Jeffersonian. The most audacious application of the grid occurred in San Francisco, where streets charge straight up impossibly steep slopes and plunge down the other side, totally oblivious of the topography of the place. This led to the invention of that unique San Francisco carryall, the cable car, to take people up and down the hills.

In defense of Jefferson, in these days when the grid is looked upon by city planners as dull and unimaginative, it should be noted that he suggested a checkerboard plan, with the black squares for development and the white ones for open space. But in the few cities where this idea was followed, the open squares proved too great a temptation as building sites and in time they were obliterated. An exception is Savannah, Georgia, where the open squares still survive, providing breathing room in one of our most architecturally interesting cities. See John W. Reps, The Making of Urban America: A History of City Planning in the United States 294-324 (1965).

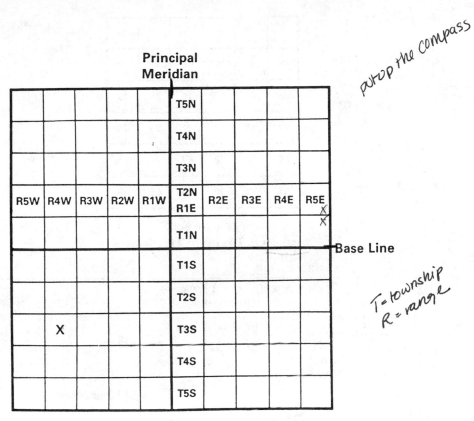

put up the compass

T = township
R = range

Figure 8-1
Range and Township Lines

range and township lines. These townships are for survey purposes only and do not necessarily coincide with any unit of political subdivision or municipality. Each survey township is numbered and located by describing its location north or south of the base line and east or west of the principal meridian. Thus on the chart (Figure 8-1) illustrating a township grid pattern, an X is placed on Township 3 South, Range 4 West of the _____ Principal Meridian. Can you spot Township 4 North, Range 1 West?

Since the curvature of the earth causes all lines running north and south to converge toward the north, correction lines are run at intervals of 24 miles north and south of the base line to avoid an accumulation of errors. As a consequence, not all townships are exactly square, and some quarter sections are slightly larger than others.

Each township was surveyed into 36 tracts called *sections*, each one-mile square and containing, as near as may be, 640 acres. The sections are numbered consecutively, beginning with section 1 in the northeast corner of the township and proceeding west to section 6; thence back to the east in the next tier down numbering 7 through 12; and so on back

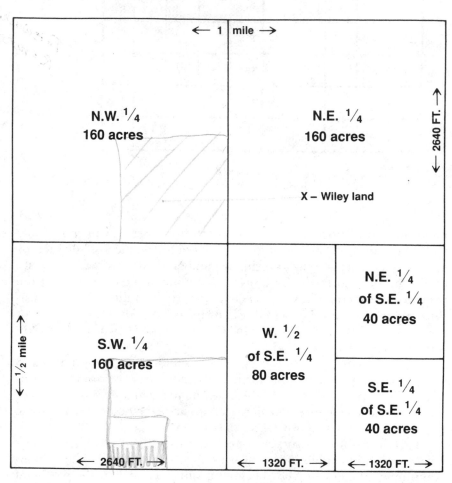

6	5	4	3	2	X1
7	8	9	10	11	12
18	17	16	15	14X	13
19	20	21	22	23	24
30	29	28	27	26	25
31	32	33	34	35	36

Figure 8-2
Sections in Township 23S, Range 14E

← 1 mile →

N.W. ¼
160 acres

N.E. ¼
160 acres

← 2640 FT. →

X – Wiley land

← ½ mile →

S.W. ¼
160 acres

W. ½
of S.E. ¼
80 acres

N.E. ¼
of S.E. ¼
40 acres

S.E. ¼
of S.E. ¼
40 acres

← 2640 FT. →   ← 1320 FT. →   ← 1320 FT. →

Figure 8-3
Enlargement of Section 14, Township 23S, Range 14E

and forth until section 36 is reached in the southeast corner. The section corners are marked by monuments or stakes, and halfway between these monuments were placed other markers called "quarter-corners." Imaginary lines drawn from these latter markers divide the section into quarter sections of 160 acres each. Quarter sections were not further subdivided by the government survey, but they may be divided further in accordance with rules laid down by the General Land Office.

Observe that in Luthi v. Evans the Wiley lease, which Owens assigned to Tours (page 694), is described as covering land in the northeast quarter of section 14, township 23, range 14. In Coffey County, Kansas, all land is located east of the sixth principal meridian and south of the baseline; the description of township 23 as *south* and range 14 as *east* is therefore omitted. On Figures 8-2 and 8-3, we have marked the location of the Wiley land with an X. The other leases mentioned in the assignment from Owens to Tours described land in quarter sections in sections 1, 12, 13, and 14. The Kufahl land was not located in any of these quarter sections. Thus Burris was not put on constructive notice that the assignment from Owens to Tours affected the Kufahl land located in another quarter section.

Orr v. Byers

Court of Appeal of California, Fourth District, 1988
198 Cal. App. 3d 666, 244 Cal. Rptr. 13

SONENSHINE, J. The question presented in this appeal is whether an abstract of judgment containing a misspelled name imparts constructive notice of its contents under the doctrine of *idem sonans*. We conclude it does not and, accordingly, affirm the trial court's ruling.

I

The facts are not in dispute. In October 1978, James Orr obtained a judgment in excess of $50,000 against William Elliott. The written judgment prepared by Orr's attorney identified Elliott erroneously as "William Duane Elliot." The following month, an abstract of judgment was recorded in the Orange County Recorder's Office, this time identifying Elliott both as "William Duane Elliot" and "William Duane Eliot." Consequently, the abstract was listed in the Orange County Combined Grantor-Grantee Index under those names only.

Elliott thereafter obtained title to a parcel of property which became subject to Orr's judgment lien. But when Elliott sold that property to Rick Byers in July 1979, a title search failed to disclose the abstract of judgment. As a result, the preliminary title report did not identify Orr's judgment lien against Elliott, and the judgment was not satisfied from the proceeds of Elliott's sale to Byers.

In February 1981, Orr filed an action against Byers, Elliott, Pomona First Federal Savings & Loan Association and Imperial Bank[4] seeking a declaration of the rights and duties of all parties. Essentially, he was requesting judicial foreclosure of his judgment lien.

At the June 1985 trial, Orr argued the defendants had constructive notice of the abstract of judgment through application of the doctrine of *idem sonans*. The trial judge acknowledged the doctrine's existence, but he concluded it was inapplicable and announced his intended decision to deny Orr's request for declaratory relief. A formal judgment was filed February 21, 1986, and this appeal followed.[5]

II

Orr takes the position his attorney did not *misspell* Elliott's name on the abstract but rather, used *alternative spellings* of the same name. And, he argues, it is imperative that a title searcher be charged with knowledge of such alternative spellings under the established doctrine of *idem sonans*.

"The doctrine of *idem sonans* is that though a person's name has been inaccurately written, the identity of such person will be presumed from the similarity of sounds between the correct pronunciation and the pronunciation as written. Therefore, absolute accuracy in spelling names is not required in legal proceedings, and if the pronunciations are practically alike, the rule of *idem sonans* is applicable." (46 Cal. Jur. 3d, Names, §4, p.110, fns. omitted; see also Napa State Hospital v. Dasso (1908) 153 Cal. 698, 701, 96 P. 355.) The rule is inapplicable, however, under circumstances "where the written name is material." (Emeric v. Alvarado (1891) 90 Cal. 444, 466, 27 P. 356.) "[T]o be material, [a variance] must be such as has misled the opposite party to his prejudice." (Black's Law Dict. (5th ed. 1979) p.671.)

Orr insists all that is required to invoke the doctrine is a similarity in pronunciation; thus, the trial court erred in refusing to do so here. We cannot agree. There is no question the names Eliot, Elliot and Elliott are *idem sonans*. But we refuse to extend the doctrine's application in the manner urged.

---

4. As part of the transaction, Byers borrowed $120,000 from Pomona First Federal which held a first trust deed on the property. Byers thereafter obtained a line of credit with Imperial Bank and delivered to Imperial a trust deed encumbering the property. Imperial ultimately acquired the property through foreclosure proceedings.

5. Respondents inform us the appellant in this case is actually the law firm which prepared the erroneous abstract of judgment. Apparently, . . . Orr's malpractice action against that firm was settled prior to trial of this case, with Orr's cause of action against Byers being assigned to the law firm in exchange for payment of a sum equal to the amount of the judgment lien.

In virtually all of the cases cited by Orr, the doctrine was applied solely to establish sameness of identity. (See, e.g., Kriste v. International Sav. etc. Bk. (1911) 17 Cal. App. 301, 119 P. 666, Galliano v. Kilfoy (1892) 94 Cal. 86, 29 P. 416, Hall v. Rice (1884) 64 Cal. 443, 1 P. 891.) Furthermore, and contrary to Orr's assertion, the rule does not have "widespread application" in the area of real property law. Simply stated, the doctrine of *idem sonans* remains viable for purposes of identification. But it has not, to our knowledge, been applied in this state to give constructive notice to good faith purchasers for value. . . .

Nor are we impressed with the reasoning behind the decision in Green v. Meyers (1903) 98 Mo. App. 438, 72 S.W. 128, a case Orr urges us to follow. In *Green,* a purchaser of property from an individual named Eleanor G. Sibert was charged with notice of a judgment against Sibert appearing in the judgment abstract as entered against E.G. Seibert. The appellate court concluded: "The names Seibert and Sibert are not only *idem sonans* — they not only sound the same in utterance — but they are, practically, the same name. Therefore, no matter which way it may be spelled by the party . . . , or by the recording officer, it is notice. It is common knowledge that proper names are spelled in a variety of ways, and everybody is presumed to have such knowledge. Thus, 'Reed,' 'Reid,' and 'Read,' are different ways of spelling one name. Manifestly, the record of a judgment against 'Reed' is notice to a subsequent purchaser from the same man signing the deed as 'Reid.' 'Persons searching the judgment docket for liens ought to know the different forms in which the same name may be spelled, and to make their searches accordingly, unless, indeed, the spelling is so entirely unusual that a person cannot be expected to think of it.' [Citation.]" (Id., 72 S.W. at p.129.)

The *Green* court recognized "[s]ome confusion has arisen in the authorities as to whether the rule as to *idem sonans* applies to records. It is said that the law of notice by record is addressed to the eye and not the ear, and that therefore the rule cannot apply to records. It is true that record notice is principally a matter of sight and not sound. Yet it is, above all, a matter for the consideration of the mind, and if the record of a name spelled in one way should directly suggest to the ordinary mind that it is also commonly spelled another way, the searcher should be charged with whatever the record showed in some other spelling under the same capital letter. It is not necessary to decide here whether this would be carried out to the extent of holding that the searcher for information in the record should look under some other capital for another mode of finding the same name, as, for instance, 'Kane' and 'Cain,' 'Phelps' and 'Felps,' etc. But that the rule of *idem sonans* has been applied to records has been too often accepted by the supreme court of this state for us to question it. [Citations.]" (Ibid.) . . .

In our view, the case at bar presents a situation where the written name is material. We therefore decline to follow *Green*'s holding which, in essence, dispenses with the formalities of record notice. Moreover, the *Green* opinion entirely ignores the added burden placed on the searcher who is charged with knowledge of the alternative spellings.

In refusing to apply the doctrine here, the trial judge found requiring a title searcher to comb the records for other spellings of the same name would place an undue burden on the transfer of property.[6] The court observed "if you put the burden on those people in addition to what comes up when the name is properly spelled, to track down and satisfy themselves about whatever comes up when the name is improperly spelled in all different ways that it might be improperly spelled, it leads to, I think, an unjustifiable burden." We agree.

Indeed, not every name disclosed by a search corresponds to the individual who is subject to the lien. Thus, if a search uncovered alternative spellings of the same name, the searcher would be required to locate every lien against every individual with a name similar to the one being searched and determine whether that lien impacted the transaction under consideration.

We reject Orr's contention "modern technology has provided a solution to the burden at relative inexpense to the title industry." He advocates use of a system known as Soundex whereby each last name is reduced to a code consisting of a letter and a three digit number. He argues use of that system here would have revealed all three spelling variations.

Testimony at trial disclosed the Soundex systems is presently utilized by two title companies in the area, and that the doctrine of *idem sonans* "is one of the reasons why some companies use [that] system." But the same witness also told of a drawback to its use: According to Donald Henley, a developer of software and computer systems for the title insurance industry, "the problem with Soundex is that you may get a lot of extraneous names if it is computer generated. And the task of going through all these names and determining which name affects your search, you know, can be lengthy if it is a popular name in a large county."

We conclude the burden is properly on the judgment creditor to

---

6. Orr asserts he "is not suggesting that a search for each and every possible misspelling of a name be undertaken." Rather, he contends "when a name consists of a double consonant (especially a name which is regularly spelled with either single or double consonants without phonetic dissimilarity, like Elliott), it is reasonable to require and simple for the searcher to look for listings under these variations in spelling."

At oral argument, Orr's attorney displayed a local telephone directory which he brought to illustrate his position the practice of searching for alternative spellings is commonplace today. Indeed, the following notations appear in the November 1987 edition of the Pacific Bell White Pages for Orange County Central & North: (1) directly above the listings for "Eliot," are the words "See Also–Elliot–Elliott," (2) preceding the listings for "Elliot," appear the words "See Also–Eliot–Elliott," and (3) before the name "Elliott," the reader is instructed to "See Also–Eliot–Elliot."

take appropriate action to ensure the judgment lien will be satisfied. The procedure is simple enough. In fact, " '[t]he judgment lien is one of the simplest and most effective means by which a judgment creditor may seek to secure payment of the judgment and establish a priority over other judgment creditors.' " (8 Witkin, Cal. Procedure (3d ed. 1986) Enforcement of Judgment, §62, p.77, quoting from 16 Cal. Law Rev. Com. Reports, p.1041.) Indeed, to rule otherwise is to grant the judgment creditor a "free ride."

As respondents succinctly state, Orr asks us "to change the law of constructive notice to accommodate [his] error in such a way that future title searches will be required to be performed only by trained individuals with elaborate and expensive equipment at their disposal or else to go uninsured in a world where prudence demands title insurance. Neither result is satisfactory, especially considering that the simple alternative is to require [judgment creditors] simply to spell the names of their judgment debtors properly."

Judgment affirmed. Respondents to receive costs.

NOTES AND PROBLEM

1. For discussion of *idem sonans* and its application to the title searcher, see 4 American Law of Property §17.18 (1952), stating that names like that of the record owner, spelled differently but pronounced alike, give constructive notice so long as they begin with the same letter. See also id. §18.30.

Judgment liens and federal tax liens become liens on all the debtor's land located in the county where the lien is filed. Such liens are filed in the index under the name of the debtor. Do you see why searching a grantor-grantee index and not a tract index is required to find judgment liens and federal tax liens?

2. Elizabeth Taylor owns Whiteacre, and the record title is in her name. Elizabeth marries Eddie Fisher and gives a mortgage on Whiteacre to Carol Burnett, signing the mortgage "Elizabeth Taylor Fisher."[7] This mortgage is recorded under the name of "Fisher." Subsequently Elizabeth divorces Eddie, resumes her maiden name, and sells Whiteacre to Woody N. Cheers, signing the deed, "Elizabeth Taylor." Cheers has no actual notice of the Burnett mortgage. In a jurisdiction where indexing is a part of the record, does Cheers prevail over Burnett?

---

7. If the real Elizabeth Taylor were involved, would the title searcher have to look under the names of all her husbands — Hilton, Wilding, Todd, Fisher, Burton, Burton again, Warner and Fortensky? How would the searcher know the dates of her marriages and the dates of her divorces or husbands' deaths? And suppose she continued to use a husband's name after his death or divorce?

Suppose that after the divorce and before the conveyance to Cheers, Taylor's landlord had obtained a judgment against Betty Taylor d/b/a Betty Taylor Jewelry. The name Betty was used in the judgment because the lease was signed that way. The judgment created a lien on all Taylor's property, and the judgment was filed and indexed under the name of "Betty Taylor." The title examiner hired by Cheers does not search under the name "Betty Taylor." Does Taylor's landlord prevail over Cheers? Is the title examiner liable? See J.I. Case Credit v. Barton, 621 F. Supp. 610 (E.D. Ark. 1985) (holding examiner must search under diminutives, and noting that documents reciting an erroneous middle initial must also be read).

3. *Computerized indexes.* In recent years, in urban counties with many daily real estate transactions, recording clerks have begun to type the indexing information into a computer (and not enter it by hand, as was done in Luthi v. Evans). This enables the title searcher to search the grantor-grantee indexes by computer back to the date computer entries began. When older index books are consolidated, they will be consolidated into the computer (much as library card catalogs have been replaced by computer retrieval systems). In a few localities, the copies of deeds are micrographically stored, and the computer system permits the deed itself to be called upon the screen.

In some localities computerized tract indexes have been established. This requires giving each parcel a parcel identification number (PIN). The tax assessor's number may be used as a PIN, or the PIN may be derived from aerial photography, surveyor's coordinates, or field inspection. Parcel identification numbers are not based on legal descriptions.

In 1973, Paul E. Basye, A Uniform Land Parcel Identifier — Its Potential for All Our Land Records, 22 Am. U. L. Rev. 251 (1973), reported that the recorder's office in Suffolk County, Massachusetts (Boston), records approximately 7,000 instruments a month; in Cook County, Illinois (Chicago), about 15,000 documents a month; and in Los Angeles County between 5,000 and 6,000 instruments a day! These data were collected before the surge in condominium sales, which has generated a significant increase in the amount of paper recorded. A transfer of one tract of land typically involves three pieces of paper (a deed, a release of the prior mortgage, a new mortgage). Development of the tract for 30 condominiums results in transfers of 30 units, each often involving a dozen pieces of paper (on condominiums, see pages 922-924). Obviously, to avoid being overwhelmed by growing amounts of paper, recording offices in urban counties will necessarily turn to computerization.

Old records will probably not be computerized in public record offices because of the high cost, and complete computerization will take a generation or two to be phased in. See U.S. Department of Housing and Urban Development, Land Title Recordation Practices: A State-of-the-Art Study (1980).

3. Types of Recording Acts

The earliest type of recording act was what we today call a *race statute*. Under a race statute, as between successive purchasers of Blackacre, the person who wins the race to record prevails. Whether a subsequent purchaser has actual knowledge of the prior purchaser's claim is irrelevant. Thus:

[handwritten margin note: race statute / first in time to record]

> *Example 2. O*, owner of Blackacre, conveys Blackacre to *A*, who does not record the deed. *O* subsequently conveys Blackacre to *B* for a valuable consideration. *B* actually knows of the deed to *A*. *B* records the deed from *O* to *B*. Under a race statute, *B* prevails over *A*, and *B* owns Blackacre.

The virtue of a race statute for the title searcher is that it limits inquiry into matters off the record. The question of who knew what (in *Example 2*, whether *B* actually knew of the deed to *A*), which is often difficult to ascertain and harder to prove, is not relevant.[8] Transfer of title is more efficient where off-record inquiries are eliminated. Race statutes applicable to conveyances generally exist today only in Louisiana and North Carolina. A few other states have race statutes applicable to mortgages, but notice or race-notice statutes for deeds.

The second type of recording statute is a *notice statute* (see the Florida statute set forth on page 713 below). It developed from judicial decisions interpreting race statutes. Early in the nineteenth century some courts held that if a subsequent purchaser had notice of a prior unrecorded instrument, the purchaser could not prevail over the prior grantee, for such would work a fraud on the prior grantee.[9] In time, legislatures amended the statutes to reflect the judicial interpretation. In *Example 2* above, if a notice statute were applicable, *B* would not prevail over *A* because *B* has notice of *A*'s prior deed.

In addition to protecting only subsequent purchasers without notice, a notice statute differs from a race statute in another respect. A race statute protects a subsequent purchaser only if the subsequent purchaser records first. A notice statute protects a subsequent purchaser against prior unrecorded instruments even though the subsequent purchaser fails to record (read the Florida statute carefully and you will see that this is so). Thus:

---

8. Although *actual* knowledge of a prior instrument by a subsequent purchaser is irrelevant under a race statute, whether a prior instrument has been "recorded" (so as to give *constructive notice* of its contents) is important. Thus the problems discussed hereafter under Chain of Title Problems, pages 721-736, can arise in a race jurisdiction as well as in notice and race-notice jurisdictions. See Lawing v. Jaynes, 285 N.C. 418, 206 S.E.2d 162 (1974); Wood v. Morvant, 321 So. 2d 914 (La. App. 1975).

9. For sharp criticism of the courts for having defeated the early race statutes by introducing the equitable doctrine of notice, see Francis S. Philbrick, Limits of Record Search and Therefore of Notice (pt. 1), 93 U. Pa. L. Rev. 125 (1944).

> *Example 3.* O, owner of Blackacre, conveys Blackacre to A, who does not record the deed. O subsequently conveys Blackacre to B for a valuable consideration. B has no knowledge of A's deed. Under a notice statute, B prevails over A even though B does not record the deed from O to B.

The virtue of a notice statute is its fairness as between two conflicting claimants, but inasmuch as the question of whether the subsequent purchaser has notice depends on facts not on record, notice statutes are less efficient than race statutes. In *Example 3,* for instance, suppose that, after the conveyance to B and before B records, A records his deed. Thereafter C desires to purchase from B. C, searching title, would find A's deed on record, and C then would have to ascertain from facts off the record whether B had notice of A's deed. If B did not have notice, B prevails over A, and C can buy from B and, standing in B's shoes, prevail over A.[10]

The third type of recording statute is a *race-notice statute* (see the California statute set forth below). Under a race-notice statute a subsequent purchaser is protected against prior unrecorded instruments only if the subsequent purchaser (1) is without notice of the prior instrument and (2) records before the prior instrument is recorded. The race-notice statute incorporates features of both a notice statute and a race statute. Thus:

> *Example 4.* O, owner of Blackacre, conveys Blackacre to A, who does not record the deed. O subsequently conveys Blackacre to B, who does not know of A's deed. Then A records. Then B records. A prevails over B because, even though B had no notice of A's deed, B did not record before A did.

The virtues of a race-notice statute, compared to a race or notice statute, are debatable. It has been suggested that a race-notice statute tends to eliminate lawsuits turning on extrinsic evidence about which deed was delivered first. In *Example 3,* for instance, whether A or B wins depends upon whether O delivered A's deed or B's deed first. Under a race-notice statute, the allegation that B's deed was delivered after A's (or A's after B's) is irrelevant if one of the deeds has been recorded; the first to record wins. It has also been suggested that a race-notice statute is preferable because, by punishing nonrecording, it provides motivation to record, making the public records complete. See B. Taylor Mattis, Recording

---

10. Why does C prevail over A in a notice jurisdiction when A records before B does? A's recordation puts C on notice as to A's deed so C cannot claim to be a subsequent purchaser without notice. The answer is: C claims protection under the *shelter rule.* A person who takes from a bona fide purchaser protected by the recording act has the same rights as his grantor. This rule is necessary if the recording act is to give B the benefit of his bargain by protecting his market. The shelter rule does not extend to B's grantor, O, however. If O repurchased Blackacre from B, O would not prevail over A. There is too much risk of undiscoverable collusion between O and B to permit B to transfer the property back to his grantor freed of A's claim.

Acts: Anachronistic Reliance, 25 Real Prop., Prob. & Tr. J. 17, 94-101 (1990) (rejecting these arguments and concluding notice statute is preferable).

About half the states have notice statutes, and half have race-notice statutes. Among the notice jurisdictions are Illinois, Massachusetts, Texas, and Virginia; among the race-notice ones are Georgia, Michigan, New Jersey, and New York. For a listing of states by types of recording acts, see 4 American Law of Property §17.5 (1952 & Supp. 1977).

Notice statute. Fla. Stat. Ann. §695.01(1) (1969):

> No conveyance, transfer or mortgage of real property, or of any interest therein, nor any lease for a term of one year or longer, shall be good and effectual in law or equity against creditors or subsequent purchasers for a valuable consideration and without notice, unless the same be recorded according to the law.

Race-notice statute. Cal. Civ. Code §1214 (West Supp. 1992):

> Every conveyance of real property or an estate for years therein, other than a lease for a term not exceeding one year, is void as against any subsequent purchaser or mortgagee of the same property, or any part thereof, in good faith and for a valuable consideration, whose conveyance is first duly recorded, and as against any judgment affecting the title, unless the conveyance shall have been duly recorded prior to the record of notice of action.

For further discussion of race, notice, and race-notice statutes, see 6A Richard R. Powell, The Law of Real Property ¶905[1] (rev. ed. 1992).

PROBLEMS

1. *O* conveys Blackacre to *A*, who does not record. *O* subsequently dies, leaving *H* as her heir. *H* then conveys Blackacre to *B*, who records. *B* purchases for a valuable consideration and without notice of the deed from *O* to *A*. Who prevails? In the leading case of Earle v. Fiske, 103 Mass. 491 (1870), it was held that *B* prevails. But how can this be? If *H* did not inherit Blackacre from *O*, how can *H* convey Blackacre to *B*? See Burnett v. Holliday Bros., 279 S.C. 222, 305 S.E.2d 238 (1983).

2. *O* conveys Whiteacre to *A*, who does not record. *O* subsequently conveys to *B*, who purchases in good faith and for a valuable consideration, but does not record. *A* then records and conveys to *C*. *C* purchases in good faith and for a valuable consideration. *B* records. *C* records. Who prevails under a notice statute? A race-notice statute?

3. *O* contracts to sell Greenacre, a subdivision lot, to *A*. The closing takes place on May 30, when *O* hands *A* a deed to Greenacre and *A*

hands O the purchase price. Subsequently, on June 3, O discovers that A intends to move a mobile home onto the lot. On June 4, O records a declaration of restrictive covenants onto all the subdivision lots, including Greenacre, prohibiting mobile homes. On June 5, A records the deed from O, and moves a mobile home onto Greenacre. On July 3, A conveys Greenacre to B, who promptly records the deed.

In late July, O sues B, asking for an injunction against use of Greenacre for a mobile home. What result? See Hair v. Hales, 95 N.C. App. 431, 382 S.E.2d 796 (1989).

4. O, owner of Blackacre, which is worth $50,000, borrows $10,000 from A and gives A a mortgage on Blackacre. A does not record. O then borrows $14,000 from B and, after telling B of the prior mortgage to A, gives B a mortgage on Blackacre. B records. O then borrows $5,000 from C and gives C a mortgage on Blackacre. C has no notice of A's mortgage. C records.

Subsequently Blackacre is discovered to be contaminated with hazardous wastes and its value plummets. O defaults. Upon foreclosure sale, Blackacre sells for $20,000. How should this amount be distributed among A, B, and C? Suppose all of the figures in this problem, except for the original worth of $50,000, were $5,000. How should the fund be distributed? The dissenting opinion of Dixon, J., in Hoag v. Sayre, 33 N. J. Eq. 552 (1881), suggesting that the parties should be given their expectations, is the starting point for discussion by most commentators. See 2 Grant Gilmore, Security Interests in Personal Property §§39.1-39.4 (1965); 4 American Law of Property §17.33 (1952).

The actual copying by the recorder of a document into the records does not necessarily mean that the document is "recorded" within the terms of the recording act. If it is not authorized, it may not be "recorded" so as to give constructive notice. Almost without exception, statutes require that, in order for an instrument to enter the records, it must be acknowledged before a notary public or other official. In addition, some states require that a transfer tax must be paid before a deed is recorded. If the record does not show that the tax has been paid, a deed actually of record may be deemed not to be legally recorded.

Messersmith v. Smith
Supreme Court of North Dakota, 1953
60 N.W.2d 276

MORRIS, C.J. This is a statutory action to quiet title to three sections of land in Golden Valley County.[11] The records in the office of the register

---

11. Golden Valley County (pop. 2,600) is located in the badlands of western North Dakota, on the Montana border. In January 1951 Amerada Petroleum Corporation, drill-

of deeds of that county disclose the following pertinent facts concerning the title: For some time prior to May 7, 1946, the record title owners of this property were Caroline Messersmith and Frederick Messersmith. On that date, Caroline Messersmith executed and delivered to Frederick Messersmith a quitclaim deed to the property which was not recorded until July 9, 1951. Between the date of that deed and the time of its recording the following occurred: On April 23, 1951, Caroline Messersmith, as lessor, executed a lease to Herbert B. Smith, Jr., lessee, which was recorded May 14, 1951. On May 7, 1951, Caroline Messersmith, a single woman, conveyed to Herbert B. Smith, Jr., by mineral deed containing a warranty of title, an undivided one-half interest in and to all oil, gas and other minerals in and under or that may be produced upon the land involved in this case. This deed was recorded May 26, 1951. On May 9, 1951, Herbert B. Smith, Jr., executed a mineral deed conveying to E.B. Seale an undivided one-half interest in all of the oil, gas and other minerals in and under or that may be produced upon the land. This deed was also recorded in the office of the Registry of Deeds of Golden Valley County, on May 26, 1951. Seale answered plaintiff's complaint by setting up his deed and claiming a one-half interest in the minerals as a purchaser without notice, actual or constructive, of plaintiff's claim. To this answer the plaintiff replied by way of a general denial and further alleged that the mineral deed by which Seale claims title is void; that it was never acknowledged, not entitled to record and was obtained by fraud, deceit and misrepresentation. The defendant Herbert B. Smith, Jr., defaulted.

For some time prior to the transactions herein noted, Caroline Messersmith and her nephew, Frederick S. Messersmith, were each the owner of an undivided one-half interest in this land, having acquired it by inheritance. The land was unimproved except for being fenced. It was never occupied as a homestead. Section 1 was leased to one tenant and Sections 3 and 11 to another. They used the land for grazing. One party had been a tenant for a number of years, paying $150 a year. The amount paid by the other tenant is not disclosed. The plaintiff lived in Chicago. Caroline Messersmith lived alone in the City of Dickinson where she had resided for many years. She looked after the renting of the land, both before and after she conveyed her interest therein to her nephew. She never told her tenants about the conveyance.

On April 23, 1951, the defendant Smith, accompanied by one King and his prospective wife, went to the Messersmith home and negotiated

---

ing a discovery well some 100 miles from Golden Valley, found a "pint of oil" which was widely reported in the press. Drilling continued and on April 4, 1951, the Clarence Iverson Well No. 1 struck oil. Brokers, oil men, and speculators began moving into western North Dakota. Soon it was realized that the Williston oil basin, with vast quantities of oil, had been discovered. Golden Valley County, smack in the middle of the basin, began to run oil fever. — Eds.

an oil and gas lease with Miss Messersmith covering the three sections of land involved herein. According to Miss Messersmith, all that was discussed that day concerned royalties. According to the testimony of Mr. Smith and Mr. King, the matter of the mineral deed was discussed.

Two or three days later, Smith and King returned. Again the testimony varies as to the subject of conversation. Miss Messersmith said it was about royalties. Smith and King say it was about a mineral deed for the purchase of her mineral rights. No agreement was reached during this conversation. On May 7, 1951, Smith returned alone and again talked with Miss Messersmith. As a result of this visit, Miss Messersmith executed a mineral deed for an undivided one-half interest in the oil, gas and minerals under the three sections of land. Smith says this deed was acknowledged before a notary public at her house. She says no notary public ever appeared there. She also says that Smith never told her she was signing a mineral deed and that she understood she was signing a "royalty transfer." The consideration paid for this deed was $1,400, which is still retained by Miss Messersmith. After leaving the house Smith discovered a slight error in the deed. The term "his heirs" was used for the term "her heirs." He returned to the home of Miss Messersmith the same day, explained the error to her, tore up the first deed, and prepared another in the same form, except that the error was corrected. According to Smith's testimony, he took the second deed to the same notary public to whom Miss Messersmith had acknowledged the execution of the first deed and the notary called Miss Messersmith for her acknowledgment over the telephone and then placed on the deed the usual notarial acknowledgment, including the notary's signature and seal. The notary, who took many acknowledgments about that time, has no independent recollection of either of these acknowledgments. It is the second deed that was recorded on May 26, 1951, and upon which the defendant, E.B. Seale, relied when he purchased from the defendant, Herbert B. Smith, Jr., the undivided one-half interest in the minerals under the land in question. . . .

The trial court found "that such deeds, or either of them, were not procured through fraud or false representation." The evidence does not warrant this court in disturbing that finding.

The determination that the mineral deed from Caroline Messersmith to Herbert B. Smith, Jr., was not fraudulently obtained by the grantee does not mean that the defendant, who in turn received a deed from Smith, is entitled to prevail as against the plaintiff in this action. At the time Miss Messersmith executed the mineral deed she owned no interest in the land, having previously conveyed her interest therein to the plaintiff. Smith in turn had no actual interest to convey to the defendant Seale. If Seale can assert title to any interest in the property in question, he must do so because the plaintiff's deed was not recorded until July 9, 1951, while the deed from Caroline Messersmith to Smith and the deed from Smith to the defendant Seale were recorded May 26, 1951, thus giving him a record title prior in time to that of the plaintiff. . . . The defendant Seale asserts that priority of record gives him a title superior to that of the plaintiff by virtue of the following statutory provision, Section 47-1941, NDRC 1943:

> Every conveyance of real estate not recorded as provided in section 47-1907 shall be void as against any subsequent purchaser in good faith, and for a valuable consideration, of the same real estate, or any part or portion thereof, whose conveyance, whether in the form of a warranty deed, or deed of bargain and sale, or deed of quitclaim and release, of the form in common use or otherwise, first is recorded, or as against an attachment levied thereon or any judgment lawfully obtained, at the suit of any party, against the person in whose name the title to such land appears of record, prior to the recording of such conveyance. The fact that such first recorded conveyance of such subsequent purchaser for a valuable consideration is in the form, or contains the terms, of a deed of quitclaim and release aforesaid, shall not affect the question of good faith of the subsequent purchaser, or be of itself notice to him of any unrecorded conveyance of the same real estate or any part thereof.

Section 47-1945, NDRC 1943, in part, provides:

> The deposit and recording of an instrument proved and certified according to the provisions of this chapter are constructive notice of the execution of such instrument to all purchasers and encumbrancers subsequent to the recording.

As against the seeming priority of record on the part of Seale's title, the plaintiff contends that the deed from Caroline Messersmith to Smith was never acknowledged and, not having been acknowledged, was not entitled to be recorded, and hence can confer no priority of record upon the grantee or subsequent purchasers from him.

It may be stated as a general rule that the recording of an instrument affecting the title to real estate which does not meet the statutory requirements of the recording laws affords no constructive notice. J.I. Case Co. v. Sax Motor Co., 64 N.D. 757, 256 N.W. 219; First National Bank v. Casselton Realty & Investment Co., 44 N.D. 353, 175 N.W. 720, 29 A.L.R. 911. The applicability of the rule is easily determined where the defect appears on the face of the instrument, but difficulty frequently arises where the defect is latent. Perhaps the most common instance of this nature arises when an instrument is placed of record bearing a certificate of acknowledgment sufficient on its face despite the fact that the statutory procedure for acknowledgment has not been followed. See Annotations 19 A.L.R. 1074; 72 A.L.R. 1039.

The certificate of acknowledgment on the mineral deed to Smith, while it is presumed to state the truth, is not conclusive as to the fact of actual acknowledgment by the grantor.

In Severtson v. Peoples, 28 N.D. 372, 148 N.W. 1054, 1055, this court, in the syllabus, said:

> 4. A certificate of acknowledgment, regular on its face, is presumed to state the truth; and proof to overthrow such certificate must be very strong and convincing, and the burden of overthrowing the same is upon the party attacking the truth of such certificate. 5. To constitute an acknowledgment, the grantor must appear before the officer for the purpose of acknowledging the instrument, and such grantor must, in some manner with a view to giving it authenticity, make an admission to the officer of the fact that he had executed such instrument. 6. Where, in fact, the grantor has never appeared before the officer and acknowledged the execution of the instrument, evidence showing such fact is admissible, even as against an innocent purchaser for value and without notice.

It avails the purchaser nothing to point out that a deed is valid between the parties though not acknowledged by the grantor — see Bumann v. Burleigh County, 74 N.D. 655, 18 N.W.2d 10 — for Caroline Messersmith, having previously conveyed to the plaintiff, had no title. The condition of the title is such that Seale must rely wholly upon his position as an innocent purchaser under the recording act.

Before a deed to real property can be recorded its execution must be established in one of the ways prescribed by Section 47-1903, NDRC 1943. No attempt was made to prove the execution of this deed other than "by acknowledgment by the person executing the same." It is the fact of acknowledgment that the statute requires as a condition precedent to recording. Subsequent sections of Chapter 47-19, NDRC 1943, prescribe before whom and how proof of the fact of acknowledgment may be made. A general form of certificate of acknowledgment is set forth in Section 47-1927. The certificate on the mineral deed follows this form and states:

> On this 7th day of May, in the year 1951, before me personally appeared Caroline Messersmith, known to me to be the person described in and who executed the within and foregoing instrument, and acknowledged to me that she executed the same.

But Caroline Messersmith did not appear before the notary and acknowledge that she executed the deed that was recorded. In the absence of the fact of acknowledgment the deed was not entitled to be recorded, regardless of the recital in the certificate. The deed not being entitled to be recorded, the record thereof did not constitute notice of its execution, Section 47-1945, or contents, Section 47-1919. The record appearing in the office of the register of deeds not being notice of the execution or

contents of the mineral deed, the purchaser from the grantee therein
did not become a "subsequent purchaser in good faith, and for a valuable consideration" within the meaning of Section 47-1941, NDRC 1943.

   In this case we have the unusual situation of having two deeds covering the same property from the same grantor, who had no title, to the
same grantee. The only difference between the two was a minor defect
in the first deed, for which it was destroyed. The evidence is conflicting
as to whether or not the first deed was acknowledged. The second deed
clearly was not. It is argued that the transaction should be considered as
a whole, with the implication that if the first deed was actually acknowledged, the failure to secure an acknowledgment of the second deed
would not be fatal to the right to have it recorded and its efficacy as
constructive notice. We must again point out that the right which the
defendant Seale attempts to assert is dependent exclusively upon compliance with the recording statutes. His claim of title is dependent upon
the instrument that was recorded and not the instrument that was destroyed. Assuming that Smith is right in his assertion that the first deed
was acknowledged before a notary public, we cannot borrow that unrecorded acknowledgment from the destroyed deed and, in effect, attach
it to the unacknowledged deed for purposes of recording and the constructive notice that would ensue. . . .

   The judgment appealed from is reversed.

On Petition for Rehearing

   MORRIS, C.J. The respondent has petitioned for a rehearing and
additional briefs have been filed. From the cases cited and statements of
counsel, it appears that there may be a misapprehension concerning the
scope of our opinion. We would emphasize the fact that at the time
Caroline Messersmith signed and delivered the deed to Herbert B.
Smith, Jr., she had no title to convey. Smith therefore obtained no title
to convey to E.B. Seale who, as grantee of Smith, claims to be an innocent purchaser. The title had already been conveyed to Frederick Messersmith. The deed to Smith had never been acknowledged and was
therefore not entitled to be recorded, although it bore a certificate of
acknowledgment in regular form. Seale, whose grantor had no title,
seeks through the operation of our recording statutes to divest Frederick
Messersmith of the true title and establish a statutory title in himself.

   We are here dealing with a prior unrecorded valid and effective
conveyance that is challenged by a subsequent purchaser to whom no
title was conveyed and who claims that the recording laws vest title in
him by virtue of a deed that was not acknowledged in fact and therefore
not entitled to be placed of record. This situation differs materially from
a case where an attack is made by a subsequent purchaser on a prior
recorded deed which actually conveyed title to the grantee but was not

entitled to be recorded because of a latent defect. The questions presented by the latter situation we leave to be determined when they arise.

The petition for rehearing is denied.

NOTES AND QUESTIONS

1. In denying the petition for rehearing, the court in *Messersmith* draws a distinction between the following two cases:

> *Example 5. O* conveys to *A*, who does not record. *O* subsequently conveys to *B*, who has no notice of *A*'s deed and gives a valuable consideration. *B*'s deed is entered into the records, but it has a defective acknowledgment. *B* conveys to *C*, who has no notice of *A*'s deed, gives a valuable consideration, and records his deed. This is the *Messersmith* case, where it is held that *B*'s deed is not "recorded" and therefore *C* is not a "subsequent purchaser in good faith . . . whose conveyance . . . first is recorded." [12]

> *Example 6. O* conveys to *A* by a deed with a defective acknowledgment. *A* records his deed. *O* subsequently conveys to *B*, who records. The court in the last paragraph of the *Messersmith* opinion says this case "differs materially" from *Example 5* and leaves open the question whether *B* would prevail over *A*. [13] (Of course, if *B* actually searched the record and found *A*'s deed, *B* would have actual notice; the issue of constructive notice arises only if *B* does not have actual notice.)

Does *B* have a more persuasive claim in *Example 6* than *C* does in *Example 5*? Which one can better protect himself against prior claims? See Richard C. Maxwell, The Hidden Defect in Acknowledgment and Title Security, 2 UCLA L. Rev. 83 (1954).

---

12. It has been held that a race-notice statute protects the subsequent purchaser who first records his own conveyance *only if* all prior conveyances in his chain of title are also recorded. Zimmer v. Sundell, 237 Wis. 270, 296 N.W. 589, 133 A.L.R. 882 (1941) (holding that a deed from *B* to *C* entered on the records was not "recorded" where the *O*-to-*B* deed, connecting the *B*-to-*C* deed to the chain of title, had not been recorded), criticized in B. Taylor Mattis, Recording Acts: Anachronistic Reliance, 25 Real Prop., Prob. & Tr. J. 17, 47-50 (1990). Is it sound to apply the *Zimmer* rule to the *Messersmith* facts?

13. The majority rule in this situation is that when the defect does not appear on the face of the acknowledgment, the deed imparts constructive notice, but if the defect is patent, the deed does not give constructive notice. Metropolitan Natl. Bank v. United States, 901 F.2d 1297 (5th Cir. 1990).

Suppose that the recording statute provides that no instrument shall be recorded unless it contains the name of the person who prepared the instrument. (What is the purpose of such a requirement?) If an instrument is recorded but does not contain the name of the preparer, does it give constructive notice to subsequent purchasers? See In re Sandy Ridge Oil Co., 510 N.E.2d 667 (Ind. 1987) (holding 3 to 2 that such an instrument gives constructive notice).

2. Would Seale have lost in *Messersmith* if North Dakota had a notice statute rather than a race-notice statute?

3. Can Seale recover damages from the notary public who took Caroline Messersmith's acknowledgment over the telephone? In Garton v. Title Ins. & Trust Co., 106 Cal. App. 3d 365, 165 Cal. Rptr. 449 (1980), the court held that a notary public who, either intentionally or negligently, took the acknowledgment of the grantors' signatures when they were not present breached her duty as a notary and the corporate employer of the notary was liable in tort for damages proximately caused by the breach.

4. Chain of Title Problems

The phrase *chain of title* refers generally to the recorded sequence of transactions by which title has passed from a sovereign to the present claimant. It also has a more technical meaning: the period of time for which records must be searched and the documents which must be examined within that time period. In this technical sense, the chain of title includes, and is coextensive with, those instruments that will be picked up by the title search required in the particular jurisdiction. Earlier, at pages 691-693, we described the standard title search required against each owner: from the date of execution of the deed granting title to the owner to the date of recordation of the first deed by such owner conveying title to someone else. Some jurisdictions require a more extended search, and in these jurisdictions the chain of title is defined to include the documents that may be found in the extended search. Thus the meaning of *chain of title* varies from jurisdiction to jurisdiction; it includes the series of recorded documents that, in the particular jurisdiction, give constructive notice to a subsequent purchaser. For discussion of chain of title problems and a listing by states of the extent of search required, see Harry M. Cross, The Record "Chain of Title" Hypocrisy, 57 Colum. L. Rev. 787 (1957). (*Caveat:* Sometimes in legal literature the phrase *chain of title* is used to refer to documents found in a standard title search and not to include documents that might be found in an extended search.)

To help you focus on the precise issue, we preface our treatment of each chain of title problem with a hypothetical example raising the issue. Thus:

> *Example 7.* O conveys to A, who does not record. A conveys to B, who records the A-to-B deed. O conveys to C, a purchaser for value who has no actual knowledge of the deeds from O to A and from A to B. C records. Who prevails, B or C? The issue is: Is the A-to-B deed properly "recorded" so as to give constructive notice to the world?

Board of Education of Minneapolis v. Hughes
Supreme Court of Minnesota, 1912
118 Minn. 404, 136 N.W. 1095

BUNN, J. Action to determine adverse claims to a lot in Minneapolis. The complaint alleged that plaintiff owned the lot, and the answer denied this, and alleged title in defendant L.A. Hughes. The trial resulted in a decision in favor of plaintiff, and defendants appealed from an order denying a new trial.

The facts are not in controversy and are as follows: On May 16, 1906, Carrie B. Hoerger, a resident of Faribault, owned the lot in question, which was vacant and subject to unpaid delinquent taxes. Defendant L.A. Hughes offered to pay $25 for this lot. His offer was accepted, and he sent his check for the purchase price of this and two other lots bought at the same time to Ed. Hoerger, husband of the owner, together with a deed to be executed and returned. The name of the grantee in the deed was not inserted; the space for the same being left blank. It was executed and acknowledged by Carrie B. Hoerger and her husband on May 17, 1906, and delivered to defendant Hughes by mail. The check was retained and cashed. Hughes filled in the name of the grantee, but not until shortly prior to the date when the deed was recorded, which was December 16, 1910. On April 27, 1909, Duryea & Wilson, real estate dealers, paid Mrs. Hoerger $25 for a quitclaim deed to the lot, which was executed and delivered to them, but which was not recorded until December 21, 1910. On November 19, 1909, Duryea & Wilson executed and delivered to plaintiff a warranty deed to the lot, which deed was filed for record January 27, 1910. It thus appears that the deed to Hughes was recorded before the deed to Duryea & Wilson, though the deed from them to plaintiff was recorded before the deed to defendant.

The questions for our consideration may be thus stated: (1) Did the deed from Hoerger to Hughes ever become operative? (2) If so, is he a subsequent purchaser whose deed was first duly recorded, within the language of the recording act?

1. The decision of the first question involves a consideration of the effect of the delivery of a deed by the grantor to the grantee with the name of the latter omitted from the space provided for it, without express authority to the grantee to insert his own or another name in the blank space. It is settled that a deed that does not name a grantee is a nullity, and wholly inoperative as a conveyance, until the name of the grantee is legally inserted. Allen v. Allen, 48 Minn. 462, 51 N.W. 473; Clark v. Butts, 73 Minn. 361, 76 N.W. 199; Id. 78 Minn. 373, 81 N.W. 11; Casserly v. Morrow, 101 Minn. 16, 111 N.W. 654. It is clear, therefore, and this is conceded, that the deed to defendant Hughes was not operative as a conveyance until his name was inserted as grantee.

Defendant, however, contends that Hughes had implied authority from the grantor to fill the blank with his own name as grantee, and that when he did so the deed became operative. This contention must, we think, be sustained. Whatever the rule may have been in the past, or may be now in some jurisdictions, we are satisfied that at the present day, and in this state, a deed which is a nullity when delivered because the name of the grantee is omitted becomes operative without a new execution or acknowledgment if the grantee, with either express or implied authority from the grantor, inserts his name in the blank space left for the name of the grantee. . . .

Unquestionably the authorities are in conflict; but this court is committed to the rule that in case of the execution and delivery of a sealed instrument, complete in all respects save that the blank for the name of the grantee is not filled, the grantee may insert his name in the blank space, provided he has authority from the grantor to do so, and, further, that this authority may be in parol, and may be implied from circumstances. We consider this the better rule, and also that it should be and is the law that when the grantor receives and retains the consideration, and delivers the deed in the condition described to the purchaser, authority to insert his name as grantee is presumed. Any other rule would be contrary to good sense and to equity. The same result could perhaps be reached by applying the doctrine of estoppel; but we prefer to base our decision on the ground of implied authority. Clearly the facts in the case at bar bring it within the principle announced, and we hold that Hughes, when he received the deed from Mrs. Hoerger, had implied authority to insert his name as grantee, in the absence of evidence showing the want of such authority. The delay in filling up the blank has no bearing on the question of the validity of the instrument when the blank was filled.

It is argued that holding that parol authority to fill the blank is sufficient violates the statute of frauds. This theory is the basis of many of the decisions that conflict with the views above expressed; but we do not think it sound. The cases in this state, and the Wisconsin, Iowa, and other decisions referred to, are abundant authority for the proposition that the authority of the grantee need not be in writing. Our conclusion is, therefore, that the deed to Hughes became operative as a conveyance when he inserted his name as grantee.

2. When the Hughes deed was recorded, there was of record a deed to the lot from Duryea & Wilson to plaintiff, but no record showing that Duryea & Wilson had any title to convey. The deed to them from the common grantor had not been recorded. We hold that this record of a deed from an apparent stranger to the title was not notice to Hughes of the prior unrecorded conveyance by his grantor. He was a subsequent purchaser in good faith for a valuable consideration, whose conveyance

was first duly recorded; that is, Hughes' conveyance dates from the time when he filled the blank space, which was after the deed from his grantor to Duryea & Wilson. He was, therefore, a "subsequent purchaser," and is protected by the recording of his deed before the prior deed was recorded. The statute cannot be construed so as to give priority to a deed recorded before, which shows no conveyance from a record owner. It was necessary, not only that the deed to plaintiff should be recorded before the deed to Hughes, but also that the deed to plaintiff's grantor should be first recorded. Webb, Record of Title, §158; 3 Washburn, Real Property, 292; Losey v. Simpson, 11 N.J. Eq. 246; Burke v. Beveridge, 15 Minn. 160 (205); Schoch v. Birdsall, 48 Minn. 443, 51 N.W. 382.

Our conclusion is that the learned trial court should have held on the evidence that defendant L.A. Hughes was the owner of the lot.

Order reversed, and new trial granted.

QUESTIONS

1. Minnesota at the time of the *Hughes* case was, and at present is, a race-notice jurisdiction. Minn. Stat. Ann. §507.34 (West 1990). Would the result in the case be different in a notice jurisdiction? Would the result in *Hughes* be different if a tract index were used? See Andy Assocs., Inc. v. Bankers Trust Co., 49 N.Y.2d 13, 399 N.E.2d 1160, 424 N.Y.S.2d 139 (1979).

2. What are the rights of the Board of Education against Duryea & Wilson and against Carrie B. Hoerger?

3. Suppose that the court had decided that the deed to Hughes became operative on May 17, 1906. What result? See Zimmer v. Sundell, 237 Wis. 270, 296 N.W. 589, 133 A.L.R. 882 (1941), discussed above in footnote 12 on page 720; B. Taylor Mattis, Recording Acts: Anachronistic Reliance, 25 Real Prop., Prob. & Tr. J. 17, 50-55 (1990).

The next chain of title problem involves interests in an adjacent or nearby lot owner created by a person who once owned the adjacent lot as well as the tract at hand. Thus:

> *Example 8. O,* owner of Blackacre and Whiteacre, conveys Blackacre to *A* by a deed that also transfers to *A* an easement over Whiteacre. *A* records the deed, and it is described in the index as a deed to Blackacre. *O* subsequently conveys Whiteacre to *B,* a purchaser for value who has no actual knowledge of the easement over Whiteacre conveyed to *A. B* records. Is Whiteacre subject to the easement? The issue is: Does the deed of Blackacre from *O* to *A* give constructive notice to purchasers of Whiteacre?

Guillette v. Daly Dry Wall, Inc.

Supreme Judicial Court of Massachusetts, 1975
367 Mass. 355, 325 N.E.2d 572

BRAUCHER, J. A recorded deed of a lot in a subdivision refers to a recorded plan, contains restrictions "imposed solely for the benefit of the other lots shown on said plan," and provides that "the same restrictions are hereby imposed on each of said lots now owned by the seller." A later deed of another lot from the same grantor refers to the same plan but not to the restrictions. The plan does not mention the restrictions, and the later grantee took without knowledge of them. We reject the later grantee's contention that it was not bound by the restrictions because they were not contained in a deed in its chain of title, and affirm a decree enforcing the restrictions.

The plaintiffs, owners of three lots in the subdivision, brought suit in the Superior Court to enjoin the defendant, owner of a lot in the same subdivision, from constructing a multifamily apartment building on its lot. The case was referred to a master, and his report was confirmed. A final decree was entered enjoining the defendant from "constructing any structures designed, intended, or suited for any purpose other than a dwelling for one family and which . . . [do] not conform to the restrictions contained in a deed from Wallace L. Gilmore to Pauline A. Guillette and Kenneth E. Guillette." The defendant appealed, and the case was transferred from the Appeals Court to this court under G.L. c.211A, §10(A). The evidence is not reported.

We summarize the master's findings. Gilmore sold lots in a subdivision called Cedar Hills Section I in Easton to the plaintiffs, the defendant, and others. Two of the plaintiffs, the Walcotts, purchased a lot in August, 1967, by a deed referring to a plan dated in July, 1967. The plaintiff Guillette and her husband, now deceased, purchased a lot in May, 1968, by a deed referring to a plan dated in March, 1968. The 1967 and 1968 plans are the same for all practical purposes; neither mentions restrictions. The plaintiffs Paraskivas purchased a lot in June, 1968, by a deed referring to the 1968 plan. Each of these deeds and five other deeds to lots in the subdivision either set out the restrictions or incorporated them by reference. Only the Guillette deed and one other contained a provision restricting lots retained by the seller.[14] It was the

---

14. Paragraph 8 of the restrictions in the Guillette deed: "The foregoing restrictions are imposed solely for the benefit of the other lots shown on said plan, and may be modified or released at any time by an instrument in writing signed by the seller herein or the legal representative of said seller, and the owner or owners for the time being of each of said lots, said written instructions to be effective immediately upon recording thereof in the proper Registry of Deeds; *and the same restrictions are hereby imposed on each of said lots now owned by the seller*" (emphasis supplied). The italicized language is found only in the Guillette deed and one other. The master found that there had been no release.

intention of the grantor and the plaintiffs to maintain the subdivision as a residential subdivision to include only dwellings for one family.

The master further found that the defendant Daly Dry Wall, Inc. (Daly), purchased its lot from Gilmore in April, 1972, and that the deed to Daly contained no reference to any restrictions but did refer to the 1968 plan. Daly made no inquiry concerning restrictions and did not know of any development pattern. It had a title examination made. It learned of the restrictions in August, 1972. Subsequently it obtained a building permit for thirty-six apartment-type units.

In similar circumstances, where the common grantor has not bound his remaining land by writing, we have held that the statute of frauds prevents enforcement of restrictions against the grantor or a subsequent purchaser of a lot not expressly restricted. G.L. c.183, §3. Houghton v. Rizzo, 361 Mass. 635, 639-642 (1972), and cases cited. Gulf Oil Corp. v. Fall River Housing Authy. 364 Mass. 492, 500-501 (1974). Where, as here, however, the grantor binds his remaining land by writing, reciprocity of restriction between the grantor and grantee can be enforced. See Snow v. Van Dam, 291 Mass. 477, 482 (1935), and cases cited. In such cases a subsequent purchaser from the common grantor acquires title subject to the restrictions in the deed to the earlier purchaser. Beekman v. Schirmer, 239 Mass. 265, 270 (1921). See Am. Law of Property, §9.31 (1952); Tiffany, Real Property, §§858, 861 (3d ed. 1939); Restatement: Property, §539, comment i (1944). Each of the several grantees, if within the scope of the common scheme, is an intended beneficiary of the restrictions and may enforce them against the others. . . .

The sole issue raised by the defendant is whether it is bound by a restriction contained in deeds to its neighbors from a common grantor, when it took without knowledge[15] of the restrictions and under a deed which did not mention them. It has, it says, only the duty to ascertain whether there were any restrictions in former deeds in its chain of title. See Stewart v. Alpert, 262 Mass. 34, 37-38 (1928). But the deed from Gilmore to the Guillettes conveyed not only the described lot but also an interest in the remaining land then owned by Gilmore. That deed was properly recorded under G.L. c.36, §12, and cannot be treated as an unrecorded conveyance under G.L. c.183, §4. As a purchaser of part of the restricted land, the defendant therefore took subject to the restrictions. See Houghton v. Rizzo, 361 Mass. 635, 642 (1972); Am. Law of Property, §17.24 (1952).

The defendant argues that to charge it with notice of any restriction put in a deed by a common grantor is to "put every title examiner to the almost impossible task of searching carefully each and every deed which a grantor deeds out of a common subdivision." But our statutes provide for indexing the names of grantors and grantees, not lot numbers or

---

15. General Laws c.183, §4, as appearing in St. 1941, c.85, denies protection to "persons having actual notice of" an unrecorded conveyance.

tracts. G.L. c.36, §§25, 26. Lot numbers or other descriptive information, even though included in an index, do not change what is recorded. Cf. Gillespie v. Rogers, 146 Mass. 610, 612 (1888), and cases cited. In such a system the purchaser cannot be safe if the title examiner ignores any deed given by a grantor in the chain of title during the time he owned the premises in question. In the present case the defendant's deed referred to a recorded subdivision plan, and the deed to the Guillettes referred to the same plan. A search for such deeds is a task which is not at all impossible. Cf. Roak v. Davis, 194 Mass. 481, 485 (1907).

Decree affirmed with costs of appeal.

NOTE AND QUESTIONS

1. 4 American Law of Property §17.24 (1952) says the cases are equally divided between the position of the Massachusetts court and the position that an easement or restrictive covenant on Whiteacre that appears in a prior deed of Blackacre from the common owner of Blackacre and Whiteacre is not in the purchaser's chain of title to Whiteacre. For cases taking the latter position, see Witter v. Taggart, 78 N.Y.2d 234, 577 N.E.2d 338, 573 N.Y.S.2d 146 (1991); Spring Lakes, Ltd. v. O.F.M. Co., 12 Ohio St. 3d 333, 467 N.E.2d 537 (1984).

If you are practicing in New York or Ohio, how would you put the subdivider's covenants in the deeds, so as to give notice to all subsequent purchasers?

2. Would the problem in *Example 8* arise if the jurisdiction had a tract index?

Does a title searcher have a duty to examine the records under the name of each owner prior to the date of the deed transferring title to the owner? Consider this hypothetical example:

Example 9. A conveys Blackacre to B by a general warranty deed. B records. A subsequently acquires title to Blackacre from O. A records the deed from O to A. A then conveys Blackacre to C, a purchaser for value who has no actual knowledge of B's deed. C records. Who prevails, B or C? The issue is: Does the A-to-B deed give C constructive notice?

Sabo v. Horvath
Supreme Court of Alaska, 1976
559 P.2d 1038

BOOCHEVER, C.J. This appeal arises because Grover C. Lowery conveyed the same five-acre piece of land twice — first to William A. Horvath and

Barbara J. Horvath and later to William Sabo and Barbara Sabo. Both conveyances were by separate documents entitled "Quitclaim Deeds." Lowery's interest in the land originates in a patent from the United States Government under 43 U.S.C. §687a (1970) ("Alaska Homesite Law"). Lowery's conveyance to the Horvaths was prior to the issuance of patent, and his subsequent conveyance to the Sabos was after the issuance of patent. The Horvaths recorded their deed in the Chitna Recording District on January 5, 1970; the Sabos recorded their deed on December 13, 1973. The transfer to the Horvaths, however, predated patent and title, and thus the Horvaths' interest in the land was recorded "outside the chain of title." Mr. Horvath brought suit to quiet title, and the Sabos counterclaimed to quiet their title.

In a memorandum opinion, the superior court ruled that Lowery had an equitable interest capable of transfer at the time of his conveyance to the Horvaths and further said the transfer contemplated more than a "mere quitclaim" — it warranted patent would be transferred. The superior court also held that Horvath had the superior claim to the land because his prior recording had given the Sabos constructive notice for purposes of AS 34.15.290.[16] The Sabos' appeal raises the following issues:

1. Under 43 U.S.C. §687a (1970), when did Lowery obtain a present equitable interest in land which he could convey?

2. Are the Sabos, as grantees under a quitclaim deed, "subsequent innocent purchaser[s] in good faith"?

3. Is the Horvaths' first recorded interest, which is outside the chain of title, constructive notice to Sabo?

We affirm the trial court's ruling that Lowery had an interest to convey at the time of his conveyance to the Horvaths. We further hold that Sabo may be a "good faith purchaser" even though he takes by quitclaim deed. We reverse the trial court's ruling that Sabo had constructive notice and hold that a deed recorded outside the chain of title is a "wild deed" and does not give constructive notice under the recording laws of Alaska.[17]

The facts may be stated as follows. Grover C. Lowery occupied land in the Chitna Recording District on October 10, 1964 for purposes of obtaining Federal patent. Lowery filed a location notice on February 24, 1965, and made his application to purchase on June 6, 1967 with the Bureau of Land Management (BLM). On March 7, 1968, the BLM field

16. AS 34.15.290 states: "A conveyance of real property in the state hereafter made, other than a lease for a term not exceeding one year, is void as against a subsequent innocent purchaser or mortgagee in good faith for a valuable consideration of the property or a portion of it, whose conveyance is first duly recorded. An unrecorded instrument is valid as between the parties to it and as against one who has actual notice of it."

17. Because we hold Lowery had a conveyable interest under the Federal statute, we need not decide issues raised by the parties regarding after-acquired property and the related issue of estoppel by deed.

examiner's report was filed which recommended that patent issue to Lowery. On October 7, 1969, a request for survey was made by the United States Government. On January 3, 1970, Lowery issued a document entitled "Quitclaim Deed" to the Horvaths; Horvath recorded the deed on January 5, 1970 in the Chitna Recording District. Horvath testified that when he bought the land from Lowery, he knew patent and title were still in the United States Government, but he did not rerecord his interest after patent had passed to Lowery.

Following the sale to the Horvaths, further action was taken by Lowery and the BLM pertaining to the application for patent and culminating in issuance of the patent on August 10, 1973.

Almost immediately after the patent was issued, Lowery advertised the land for sale in a newspaper. He then executed a second document also entitled "quitclaim" to the Sabos on October 15, 1973. The Sabos duly recorded this document on December 13, 1973.

Luther Moss, a representative of the BLM, testified to procedures followed under the Alaska Homesite Law [43 U.S.C. §687a (1970)]. After numerous steps, a plat is approved and the claimant notified that he should direct publication of his claim. In this case, Lowery executed his conveyance to the Horvaths after the BLM field report had recommended patent.

The first question this court must consider is whether Lowery had an interest to convey at the time of his transfer to the Horvaths. . . .

[W]e hold that at the time Lowery executed the deed to the Horvaths he had complied with the statute to a sufficient extent so as to have an interest in the land. . . .

Since the Horvaths received a valid interest from Lowery, we must now resolve the conflict between the Horvaths' first recorded interest and the Sabos' later recorded interest.

The Sabos, like the Horvaths, received their interest in the property by a quitclaim deed. They are asserting that their interest supersedes the Horvaths under Alaska's statutory recording system. AS 34.15.290 provides that:

> A conveyance of real property . . . is void as against a subsequent innocent purchaser . . . for a valuable consideration of the property . . . whose conveyance is first duly recorded. An unrecorded instrument is valid . . . as against one who has actual notice of it.

Initially, we must decide whether the Sabos, who received their interest by means of a quitclaim deed, can ever be "innocent purchaser[s]" within the meaning of AS 34.15.290. Since a "quitclaim" only transfers the interest of the grantor, the question is whether a "quitclaim" deed itself puts a purchaser on constructive notice. Although the authorities are in conflict over this issue, the clear weight of authority is that a quitclaim grantee can be protected by the recording system, assuming, of course, the grantee purchased for valuable consideration and did not otherwise have actual or constructive knowledge as defined by the recording laws.[18] We choose to follow the majority rule and hold that a quitclaim grantee is not precluded from attaining the status of an "innocent purchaser."

In this case, the Horvaths recorded their interest from Lowery prior to the time the Sabos recorded their interest. Thus, the issue is whether the Sabos are charged with constructive knowledge because of the Horvaths' prior recordation. Horvath is correct in his assertion that in the usual case a prior recorded deed serves as constructive notice pursuant to AS 34.15.290, and thus precludes a subsequent recordation from taking precedence. Here, however, the Sabos argue that because Horvath recorded his deed prior to Lowery having obtained patent, they were not given constructive notice by the recording system. They contend that since Horvath's recordation was outside the chain of title, the recording should be regarded as a "wild deed."

It is an axiom of hornbook law that a purchaser has notice only of recorded instruments that are within his "chain of title." If a grantor (Lowery) transfers prior to obtaining title, and the grantee (Horvath) records prior to title passing, a second grantee who diligently examines all conveyances under the grantor's name from the date that the grantor had secured title would not discover the prior conveyance. The rule in most jurisdictions which have adopted a grantor-grantee index system of recording is that a "wild deed" does not serve as constructive notice to a subsequent purchaser who duly records.

Alaska's recording system utilizes a "grantor-grantee" index. Had Sabo searched title under both grantor's and grantee's names but limited his search to the chain of title subsequent to patent, he would not be chargeable with discovery of the pre-patent transfer to Horvath.

On one hand, we could require Sabo to check beyond the chain of title to look for pretitle conveyances. While in this particular case the burden may not have been great, as a general rule, requiring title checks beyond the chain of title could add a significant burden as well as uncertainty to real estate purchases. To a certain extent, requiring title searches of records prior to the date a grantor acquired title would thus defeat the purposes of the recording system. The records as to each grantor in the chain of title would theoretically have to be checked back to the later of the grantor's date of birth or the date when records were first retained.

On the other hand, we could require Horvath to rerecord his interest in the land once title passes, that is, after patent had issued to Lowery.

18. See Note, Deeds — Quitclaim Grantee as a Bona Fide Purchaser, 28 Ore. L. Rev. 258 n.1 (1949) and the many cases cited therein.

As a general rule, rerecording an interest once title passes is less of a burden than requiring property purchasers to check indefinitely beyond the chain of title.

It is unfortunate that in this case due to Lowery's double conveyances, one or the other party to this suit must suffer an undeserved loss. We are cognizant that in this case, the equities are closely balanced between the parties to this appeal. Our decision, however, in addition to resolving the litigants' dispute, must delineate the requirements of Alaska's recording laws.

Because we want to promote simplicity and certainty in title transactions, we choose to follow the majority rule and hold that the Horvaths' deed, recorded outside the chain of title, does not give constructive notice to the Sabos and is not "duly recorded" under the Alaskan Recording Act, AS 34.15.290. Since the Sabos' interest is the first duly recorded interest and was recorded without actual or constructive knowledge of the prior deed, we hold that the Sabos' interest must prevail. The trial court's decision is accordingly reversed.

NOTES, QUESTIONS, AND PROBLEM

1. The court in *Sabo* is not concerned with whether estoppel by deed applies to a subsequent purchaser from the grantor, but the record search principle involved in *Sabo* more typically is at issue in estoppel by deed cases. In *Example 9, A* conveyed by warranty deed to *B,* and subsequently *A* acquired title from *O.* Under the doctrine of estoppel by deed, *A* is estopped to claim he did not have title when he conveyed to *B,* and title passes by virtue of the estoppel from *O* to *B.* Should a subsequent purchaser from *A, C,* likewise be estopped, or, to put the question another way, does the deed from *A* to *B* give constructive notice to *C?* The majority holds no, but an important minority holds against *C.* The leading cases for the minority view are Ayer v. Philadelphia & Boston Face Brick Co., 159 Mass. 84, 34 N.E. 177 (1893) (opinion by Holmes, J.), and Tefft v. Munson, 57 N.Y. 97 (1874). In these minority jurisdictions each owner's name must be run in the indexes prior to the time of his acquisition of title to see if the owner conveyed the land prior to acquiring it. Title searchers rarely do this in practice, however, because of the cost.

2. Would the problem in *Example 9* arise if the jurisdiction had a tract index?

3. *O* is the owner of Blackacre. *A* conveys Blackacre to *B. A* conveys Blackacre to *C,* who gives a valuable consideration and is without actual knowledge of *B*'s deed. *O* conveys Blackacre to *A. B* records. *A* records. *C* records. *C* goes into possession of Blackacre. *B* brings an action of ejectment against *C.* Judgment for whom in a notice jurisdiction? In a race-notice jurisdiction?

4. In a few jurisdictions, a purchaser by quitclaim deed cannot claim the position of a bona fide purchaser without notice. This usually rests upon the idea that a refusal of the grantor to warrant title is a sufficiently suspicious fact as to put a purchaser to further inquiry. This rule is applied only to the immediate recipient of the quitclaim deed, and not to subsequent purchasers from the recipient. See 6A Richard R. Powell, The Law of Real Property ¶905[1][B] (rev. ed. 1992).

As a final chain of title problem, we present the matter of a prior deed recorded after a later purchaser with notice has recorded a subsequent deed. Thus:

> *Example 10.* O conveys to A, who does not record. O subsequently conveys to B, who knows of the conveyance to A. B records. A records. Later B conveys to C, a purchaser for value who has no actual knowledge of the deed from O to A. C records. Who prevails, A or C? The issue is: Does the deed from O to A, when recorded, give constructive notice to C?

Woods v. Garnett

Supreme Court of Mississippi, 1894
72 Miss. 78, 16 So. 390

Bill to cancel defendant's claim to certain land and to recover possession. Decree for defendants. Complainant appeals. The opinion sufficiently states the facts. . . .

Cooper, C.J., delivered the opinion of the court.

The parties to this suit all claim title from one Riley, who, in 1891, was the owner of the land in controversy. On the ninth day of November, A.D. 1891, Riley executed a deed of trust, whereby he conveyed the land to one M.H. Trantham, as trustee, to secure the payment of a promissory note of that date for $3,500, payable to the order of C.H. Pond. This deed contained the usual power of sale if default should be made in the payment of the secured debt at maturity, and also provided that Pond, or the assignee of the note, might at pleasure substitute any other person in lieu of the trustee, Trantham. This deed was acknowledged before Trantham, the trustee, who was a justice of the peace of the county. The certificate stated only that the grantor acknowledged that he had "signed" the deed, omitting the words "and delivered," as required by law. This deed was filed for record in the proper office on the twelfth day of November.

On May 6, 1892, Riley executed a deed of trust to one Oliver, as trustee, to secure the payment of a debt to W.G. Cocke & Co. of $397.22. This deed also contained a power of sale if the debt secured should not be paid at maturity. Before accepting this security, W.D. Lester, a member of the firm of Cocke & Co., examined the records, and there saw and read the prior deed, but was of opinion that, by reason of the defective acknowledgment, and because it had been taken by the trustee therein, it was not entitled to registration, and, being of that opinion, decided to accept the deed to secure his firm.

Some time prior to October, 1892, Pond assigned the note executed by Riley payable to him to the complainant, Chas. R. Woods. About this time it was discovered that the deed of trust by which this note had been secured had not been so acknowledged as to entitle to registration, and thereupon Woods exhibited his bill in equity to enjoin Riley from disposing of the lands to his injury, and an injunction was allowed. The attorney of Woods, being of opinion that a re-execution and acknowledgment of the deed by Riley, and another registration thereof, would serve the same purpose as the injunction, sent the clerk of the chancery court to see Riley and get a re-acknowledgment of the deed, which he did on October 7, 1892, when the deed was on that day again filed for record and recorded on the twenty-fourth.

. . . On November 19, 1892, the land was sold under each of the two deeds of trust, the sales being at different places. At the sale under the deed of trust first made, but junior in record (the Pond deed), the appellant [Woods] became the purchaser. At the sale under the deed junior in date, but the first recorded, the appellee, Mrs. D.L. Garnett, purchased. The appellant exhibited his bill in this cause to cancel the title of . . . Mrs. D.L. Garnett . . . , and to recover possession of the land . . . [she] having been let into possession by Riley.

Mrs. D.L. Garnett defends the suit upon the ground that she was a bona fide purchaser, without notice of the deed of trust under which complainant claims title. . . .

1. Were Cocke & Co. bona fide incumbrancers of the land, without notice of the Pond mortgage? It has been generally held by the American courts, though with some exceptions, that, notwithstanding the registry acts, one who has notice of such facts in reference to an unrecorded conveyance, as devolves on him, as an honest man, the duty of making further inquiry, is to be held as having such knowledge as such inquiry, honestly made, would have disclosed. In those states in which this rule does not apply, it will be found that the registry acts require actual knowledge of the unrecorded conveyance. One who sees upon the record, and reads an instrument improperly recorded, because not acknowledged or proved as required by law, cannot claim to be a bona fide purchaser of the property therein described. He knows that what he sees is the copy of an instrument purporting to have been made by the grantor to the grantee. Good faith requires that he shall prosecute further inquiry, and, if he negligently or willfully neglects so to do, he is to be held to have known all the facts to which that inquiry would have led.

The notice to Lester by reading the improperly recorded mortgage, was
notice to his firm of the existence of that conveyance, and Cocke & Co.
were not bona fide purchasers of the property.[19]

2. Where a conveyance is made to one who fails to record his deed
until after another has received and recorded a conveyance from the
same grantor, but with notice of the first deed, what are the rights of the
first grantee against a purchaser from the second, where such purchaser, having no actual knowledge of the facts, buys after the record of
the prior deed? This question is determinable by a construction of our
registry act, for, at the common law, a second purchaser of the fee could
take nothing, since, by the first conveyance, the grantor would have divested himself of all his estate, and would have nothing to convey. Basset
v. Nosworthy, 2 Ldg. Cas. in Eq. and note; Coke on Littleton, 390*d*.

[The court sets forth the Mississippi recording statute, which is a
notice statute.] . . . In Massachusetts and Vermont it is held that a purchaser is not bound to examine the record, after the date of a recorded
conveyance, to discover whether the grantor therein has made another
conveyance prior in time but junior in record, but may safely purchase
from the grantee in the first recorded conveyance, if he, the purchaser,
has no actual notice of the prior deed, and no notice of facts which
makes it his duty to prosecute inquiry. Connecticut v. Bradish, 14 Mass.,
296; Trull v. Bigelow, 16 Ib., 406; Morse v. Curtis, 140 Ib., 112; Day v.
Clark, 25 Vt., 397. And this is said to be the more reasonable rule by the
annotators of the leading cases in equity (LeNeve v. LeNeve, 2 Ldg. Cas.,
p.180), and by Mr. Jones (1 Jones on Mortg., §574). The decided weight
of authority is, however, to the contrary, though Mr. Jones cites none of
them as supporting the contrary view, except the New York decisions.
Among others, the following cases may be noted: Van Rensselaer v.
Clark, 17 Wend. (N.Y.), 25; Westbrook v. Gleason, 79 N.Y., 23; Clark

---

19. In Amoskeag v. Chagnon, 133 N.H. 11, 572 A.2d 1153 (1990), the court had the
same question before it as is discussed in this paragraph. The court concluded that a subsequent *purchaser* with actual knowledge of a defectively acknowledged mortgage was obligated to investigate its validity, but a subsequent *mortgagee* with actual knowledge was not
obligated to inquire. Why not?

Prospective BFP's and attaching creditors are treated differently in this context
because of their differing commercial goals. . . . Because a potential BFP has a desire
to obtain the property free and clear of all encumbrances, such evidence is enough to
obligate him or her to investigate beyond the record to determine whether a properly
executed and acknowledged mortgage actually exists.
An attaching creditor, on the other hand, . . . simply wants to know *how many* creditors, if any, have already recorded an interest in the property. Rarely, if ever, will an
attaching creditor forego recording simply because another creditor has recorded first.
An attaching creditor in this position would likely record the attachment and then look
for additional ways to secure the underlying debt. . . .
Because of the profound differences between the goals of a BFP and an attaching
creditor, we hold that an attaching creditor need not investigate outside of the record
to determine whether a mortgage has, in fact, been properly executed and acknowledged. [133 N.H. at 16, 572 A.2d at 1155-1156.] — Eds.

v. Mackin, 30 Hun. (N.Y.), 411; Mahoney v. Middleton, 41 Cal., 41; English v. Waples, 13 Iowa, 57; Fallass v. Pierce, 30 Wis., 443; Erwin v. Lewis, 32 Ib., 276; Van Aken v. Gleason, 34 Mich., 477; Bayless v. Young, 51 Ill., 127. . . .

We think the Massachusetts decisions are erroneous, because they hold that one not bound by the registry law is protected by it. But for the registry law, where one has conveyed his legal title, he has nothing left to convey to another, and that other, with or without notice of the prior conveyance, would get nothing, for his grantor had nothing to convey. Now, the statute comes and provides that, though a conveyance of the class named in the statute may be made, it shall as to certain persons, viz., creditors and purchasers without notice, be valid only from a certain time, viz., the time when it is filed for record. . . . One who buys after that event can find no protection in the statute, for its terms have been complied with by the holder of the adverse title. It is no answer to say that it is inconvenient to the purchaser to examine a long and voluminous record, made after the record of the title of his grantor. To this the sufficient reply is that, but for the registry acts, he would not have even the protection which such records afford, but would deal at his peril with his grantor, and secure only such title as he might assert. If that grantor had good title because a purchaser for value without notice, that is a defense to his vendee; but if such grantor was not such purchaser, then the validity of the title he conveys must depend upon the character of his vendee, and if such vendee is not a bona fide purchaser under the common law or the statute, we cannot perceive from what source a principle can be deduced which will afford him protection. It seems clear to us that one who buys an estate cannot invoke the protection of the registry act as against a deed recorded under such act at the time of his purchase. . . .

The decree is reversed, and a decree will be entered here canceling the title . . . of the appellee . . . , and that the complainant be at once placed in possession of the land. The cause will then be remanded, that an account may be taken of rents and profits and of the injury done by the appellee . . . in cutting timber therefrom, for all of which the chancery court will award complainants a decree.

Reversed, and decree here.

NOTES AND QUESTIONS

1. There is substantial authority holding contrary to Woods v. Garnett. The leading case for the opposite view is Morse v. Curtis, 140 Mass. 112, 2 N.E. 929 (1885), cited by the court in Woods v. Garnett. See 4 American Law of Property §17.22 (1952); Francis S. Philbrick, Limits of Record Search and Therefore of Notice (pt. 3), 93 U. Pa. L.

Rev. 391 (1945) (pointing out, at 415, that the practice of title examiners in New York is to search only under each name to the day of the recording of the first deed out from that person, even though the law follows the principle of Woods v. Garnett).

2. Suppose that the jurisdiction follows the view of Morse v. Curtis and has a race-notice statute. In *Example 10,* will *C* prevail?

Professor Philbrick says that in *Example 10,* in a race-notice jurisdiction, *C* must always fail because *C* "can never satisfy the requirement of prior recording." Philbrick, supra, at 391. The American Law of Property agrees. "The anomaly is that the court in notice-race jurisdictions should have injected into their opinions any consideration of notice, either inquiry notice or record notice, when dealing with a problem definitely settled by the requirements of their acts relative to securing priority of record." 4 American Law of Property, supra, §17.22. Is this convincing? If *A*'s deed is not "recorded" so as to give constructive notice to *C,* why is not *C*'s deed "first recorded"? Why should the word "recorded" be given one meaning when the problem is whether *A*'s deed is recorded so as to give constructive notice and another when the problem is whether *C* has recorded first? Have the learned authors confused the fact of an instrument being entered on the records with the legal conclusion that it is recorded? See B. Taylor Mattis, Recording Acts: Anachronistic Reliance, 25 Real Prop., Prob. & Tr. J. 17, 44-45 (1990).

3. Would the problem in *Example 10* arise if the jurisdiction had a tract index?

4. *Curative acts.* Many states have curative acts which provide that, in an instrument of record for a specified number of years, technical defects in the instrument may be disregarded. Here is Mississippi's curative act:

Miss. Code §89-5-13 (1991)

Whenever a deed has been of record twenty (20) years or more in the land records of the county in which the said land is located, the same shall be presumed to have been upon lawful authority; and the acknowledgment shall be good without regard to the form of the certificate of acknowledgment.

If, in Woods v. Garnett, Riley's deed of trust to Trantham had been executed more than 20 years before the other events took place, what result?

5. Persons Protected by the Recording System

The recording statute in each state must be read carefully to see who comes within the protection of the statute. Observe that the Florida statute (page 713) protects, against unrecorded conveyances or mortgages, "creditors or subsequent purchasers[20] for a valuable consideration," and the California statute (page 713) protects "any subsequent purchaser or mortgagee" and "any judgment affecting the title." By judicial construction, the recording statutes have been held, almost universally, not to protect donees and devisees, even in race jurisdictions. As a result, it is sometimes necessary for a court to decide whether a person is a purchaser (and protected) or a donee (and not protected). This in turn may require the court to determine what is a valuable consideration for purposes of obtaining the protection of the recording act.

An examination of the cases leads to the conclusion that there is some disagreement as to how much a grantee must pay to be deemed a purchaser. Most courts require more than a nominal value, such as a "substantial" amount, or an amount "not grossly inadequate." See Roger A. Cunningham, William B. Stoebuck & Dale A. Whitman, The Law of Property §11.10 at 783-786 (1984). Why do you suppose that courts require more "consideration" here than is necessary to enforce a contract?

If a deed recites that it is for "$1 and other good and valuable consideration," this raises a presumption that the grantee is a purchaser for a valuable consideration, and places the burden of going forward to establish the falsity of the recital of consideration on the party attacking the deed.

Alexander v. Andrews

Supreme Court of Appeals of West Virginia, 1951
135 W. Va. 403, 645 S.E.2d 487

Fox, President. This is a suit in equity instituted in the Circuit Court of Ohio County in which the plaintiff seeks to have quieted his alleged title to two certain lots of land, situated in the City of Wheeling, purportedly conveyed to him by Thomas A. Alexander on May 14, 1946, and to remove, as a cloud upon his title, a deed for the same property, executed by the said Thomas A. Alexander to Sarah R. Alexander, now Andrews, dated May 8, 1946, but not recorded until July 8, 1946. The plaintiff claims this relief by reason of the allegations contained in his bill that he purchased the said real estate for valuable consideration and without notice of the deed to Sarah R. Andrews. . . .

In order to fully present the questions involved on this appeal, it is necessary to make the following statement: On June 6, 1939, Katherine B. Alexander, a sister of both the plaintiff and defendant, Sarah R. Andrews, purchased the real estate involved herein. She died intestate and without issue on June 9, 1945, and her estate passed by inheritance

---

20. The term *purchaser* is uniformly held to apply to all parties who have paid consideration for the interest acquired, including a mortgagee or a lessee.

to her father and mother, Thomas A. Alexander and Mary J. Alexander. Mary J. Alexander died testate on April 25, 1946, and devised her interest in said real estate to the plaintiff, Charles B. Alexander. On May 8, 1946, Thomas A. Alexander executed, acknowledged and presumably delivered to Sarah R. Andrews, who was his daughter, a deed for his interest in the real estate, but said deed was not recorded until July 8, 1946. On May 14, 1946, the same Thomas A. Alexander executed, acknowledged and delivered to the plaintiff, Charles B. Alexander, a deed for his interest in the real estate which he had theretofore conveyed to Sarah R. Andrews, and this second deed was recorded on the same day. The real estate involved has been occupied by Charles B. Alexander, and since the date of his deed his father, Thomas A. Alexander, lived therein until his death in October 1948. . . .

It is well to state at this time that the validity of the deed from Thomas A. Alexander to Sarah R. Andrews, dated May 8, 1946, as of the date of its execution, is not questioned. . . . But our recording Act, Code, 40-1-9, makes a perfectly valid and effective conveyance void as to creditors and subsequent purchasers for valuable consideration without notice, until such deed is duly admitted to record in the county wherein the property conveyed is situated; and, therefore, while the grantor has nothing to convey, when he executes a subsequent deed for the same property, to a different party, then by force of this statute, his grantee in the subsequent deed gets title to the land in cases where the grantee in the first deed fails to record his deed before the second deed is executed, and where the grantee in the second deed can qualify as a purchaser for value and without notice of the first deed. Probably the explanation for this illogical result is that the first purchaser, who fails to record his deed, is charged with fault in a situation where one of two persons must suffer loss, in which situation it seems just, and our statute, in effect, provides that the loss must fall upon the person who has committed a fault in failing to record his deed, and by his fault has created a situation where a subsequent innocent purchaser is induced to part with his money and thereby suffer a loss which the grantee in the first deed could have prevented. . . .

Code, 40-1-9, reads: "Every such contract, every deed conveying any such estate or term, and every deed of gift, or trust deed or mortgage, conveying real estate or goods and chattels, shall be void as to creditors, and subsequent purchasers for valuable consideration without notice, until and except from the time that it is duly admitted to record in the county wherein the property embraced in such contract, deed, trust deed or mortgage may be."

It is clear that if the plaintiff in this case purchased the real estate here involved, without notice of the execution of the prior deed, and paid in full a valuable consideration for his deed, he is entitled under the statute to the relief prayed for; but he must meet the conditions which give him the right to such relief. . . .

As stated above, there is no attack upon the deed to Sarah R. Andrews, dated May 8, 1946, as to its validity at the time it was executed and acknowledged. The consideration for that deed was stated therein to be love and affection. If the legal effect of that deed is to be avoided in this suit, it can only be done under the statutory provision quoted above, and the conditions under which that statute can be made effective must be met. There is likewise no serious attack upon the validity of the deed to the plaintiff, dated May 14, 1946, for the same property. The circumstances under which this deed was executed may have some bearing upon our decision, and will be here stated. Obviously there must have been some discussion of the matter of the execution of this deed between Charles B. Alexander and his father, Thomas A. Alexander, although the record does not so disclose such discussion in detail, and for obvious reasons could not be developed under the rule which prevented Charles B. Alexander from testifying concerning a transaction between his father and himself. (Code, 57-3-1.) Charles B. Alexander had been "keeping company" with a young lady by the name of Hazel Horner for some twenty years. According to her testimony she was his fiancee. She was and had been employed in the law office of William C. Piper as a stenographer for a long period of time, and testified that she was capable of preparing simple deeds. This being the situation, on May 14, 1946, Thomas A. Alexander called Hazel Horner to his home and asked her to have a deed prepared, conveying to Charles B. Alexander his interest in the property here involved. Piper being absent from his office, Hazel Horner, having been furnished the necessary description of the property to be conveyed, prepared such deed. A blue wrapper was placed on the deed which contained Piper's professional card, but for some reason this was obliterated by someone not known. Hazel Horner delivered the unexecuted paper to Thomas A. Alexander, and there her connection with the same ended. On the same day, Thomas A. Alexander took the deed form to Saul N. Rosenburg, a notary public, who lived near the residence of Alexander. The record shows that these two men were close friends. Rosenburg testifies that on May 14, 1946, he was present at the signing of and certified the acknowledgment to a deed conveying Alexander's interest in the property here involved to Charles B. Alexander. His statement as to what occurred on that occasion is well worth quotation, and is, we think, of some importance in the decision of this case. That statement follows: "I said, 'Tom' — I said, 'Tommie, do you know what you are doing here?' and he said, 'Yes.' I said, 'You know you are deeding your property away.' Tom and I were very friendly. 'Well,' he said, 'it is up to Chuck to bury me. He is taking care of me.' " He also testifies that Thomas A. Alexander was what he termed "in good mind," and also that when asked whether Alexander made any statement concerning his feelings towards his daughters, particularly Sarah, answered: "Well, any more than the time he signed that deed, and I questioned whether it was a wise thing to do, and he told me the girls walked out on him and it was up to Chuck to bury him." He didn't mention any names. The witness later testified: "He told me he had some money in the bank in a joint account at the time he said the girls walked out on him. He said that money was withdrawn and it was up to Chuck to bury him." The deed acknowledged by Rosenburg was recorded on the same day, which, of course, indicates prompt delivery by the grantor to the grantee. In connection with the acknowledgment of this deed, Rosenburg says it was acknowledged in his office. . . . Under all the circumstances, it seems quite clear that the May 14, 1946, deed was signed and acknowledged in the office of Rosenburg, and that at the time Alexander was warned against executing the deed, was in full possession of his faculties, and was determined to convey the property to his son Charles B. Alexander. At that time he said nothing about his former conveyance. The record, taken as a whole, does not explain the conduct of this old man in executing, within six days of each other, two deeds for the same property to different people. The will of Thomas A. Alexander, which devised and bequeathed his estate to the plaintiff, Charles B. Alexander, was not offered for probate for the reason that he had no property at the date of his death.

. . . [T]he plaintiff must, to be entitled to the benefit of the statute, be a purchaser for value or, in other words, must have paid a valuable consideration for his deed. This presents some difficulty. It is contended that plaintiff paid $1,000 in cash for this conveyance and assumed certain obligations. There was introduced in evidence a receipt, admittedly in the handwriting of Thomas A. Alexander. This receipt reads:

May 1946

> Received from C.B. Alexandre $1000.00 Cash intrest for whitch i will execute a deed to him for my right title intrest in the property known as 21 Noth front St Wheeling W V A

> TomaS Alexandre

Some question is raised as to whether or not this $1,000 was actually paid. It is testified by two or more witnesses that Thomas A. Alexander denied having received such sum from the plaintiff, but the said receipt stands as an admission on his part that he had received that sum of money, and is *prima facie* proof thereof. Hazel Horner testified that he told her that Charles B. Alexander had paid him $1,000.

There is no showing of any other consideration paid at or before the conveyance of May 14, but there are strong indications that other considerations were involved. When Rosenburg attempted to dissuade Alexander from conveying his property he was told that he had some money in a joint account and that someone had gotten that money, and that his son "Chuck", the same person as Charles B. Alexander, "is taking care of me" and that he would have to bury him. The testimony shows that he occupied with his son the property conveyed by the two deeds until his death some two and one-half years later, all leading to the inference that the plaintiff herein had agreed to provide for his burial and take care of him during his declining years. We are of the opinion that the receipt, aforesaid, and the apparent understanding as to care and burial of the grantor, constituted a sufficient consideration for the conveyance, and complies with the requirement of the statute in that respect. The value of the property is stipulated. The gross market value of the property in May, 1946 was $7,700. . . .

We do not understand that to place a person in a position to take the benefit of the recording statute there must be paid as consideration what would be termed the full value of the property. We think that what is required is a consideration which would sustain a conveyance in the ordinary transaction where consideration becomes important. Of course, in the absence of creditors, a person may convey his property on whatever terms he chooses; but in a transaction such as is now before us, we think a reasonably adequate consideration should be paid by a subsequent grantee, before the person who claims under the first deed may be deprived of the benefit of his conveyance. We are of the opinion that the consideration shown here is sufficient to give to the plaintiff the benefit of Code, 40-1-9, had it been paid in full at the time the grantee in the May 14, 1946, deed first received notice of the former deed.

Another question involved in this case, is whether there has been a complete transaction in respect to the deed of May 14, 1946. As early as 1831 in Doswell v. Buchanan's Ex'ers., 3 Leigh 365, 30 Va. 365, it was held: "To sustain a plea of purchaser without notice, the party must be a complete purchaser before notice; that is, must have obtained a conveyance and paid the whole purchase money."

This rule, slightly modified and liberalized, has been followed in this State in Webb v. Bailey, 41 W. Va. 463, 23 S.E. 644; Welch v. King and Douglas, 82 W. Va. 258, 95 S.E. 844; Heck v. Morgan, 88 W. Va. 102, 106 S.E. 413; and United Fuel Gas Company v. Morley Oil and Gas Company, 101 W. Va. 83, 131 S.E. 716. . . .

As indicated above, we are of the opinion that at the date the plaintiff obtained his deed of May 14, 1946, he was without notice of the former deed for the same property; and paid and agreed to pay a valuable consideration for such conveyance. But we are forced to conclude that we cannot grant to him the relief prayed for in his bill because the transaction was not a completed one. In United Fuel Gas Company v. Morley Oil and Gas Company, supra, this Court held: "To be protected by section 5, chapter 74, of the Code [Code, 40-1-9], against a prior unrecorded deed, one must be a complete purchaser, must have had no notice of the prior contract or deed, and have paid all the purchase money for the land purchased by him."

That case is fully supported by other authorities, and we consider it binding upon us.

The question then arises as to what are the rights of the plaintiff, if any, growing out of the peculiar circumstances of this case. The defendant, Sarah R. Andrews, recorded her deed on July 8, 1946, and from that time on, while the plaintiff herein may not have had actual notice of the deed to Sarah R. Andrews, he had constructive notice thereof, and his purchase not being complete, any payments of purchase money he may have made thereafter were at his own risk. We are of the opinion that the record shows that $1,000 was paid by the plaintiff to his father at or before the conveyance of May 14, 1946, and we think the record shows there was an agreement between the parties to that deed that the plaintiff would take care of his father and see that he had a suitable burial. However, unless it be from May 8, 1946 to July 8, 1946, when the Sarah R. Andrews deed was recorded, that part of the consideration had not been paid, and, therefore, the transaction had not been completed by the full payment of the purchase money. Assuming for the sake of argument that the plaintiff undertook to take care of his father during his lifetime, and provided for his burial, it would be no different than if he had executed a note or notes for given amounts to make up a reasonably adequate consideration for the conveyance.

On the subject of consideration, we are of the opinion that the plaintiff in order to receive the benefit of the statute must have paid a reasonably adequate one. We have a stipulation in the record that the value of the one-half interest in the property here involved, as of May, 1946, was $3,850. We do not think the $1,000 cash payment was an adequate consideration, and it is clear that the other elements of consideration which were necessary to make the deed valid in the circumstances were not paid at the date of the conveyance to the plaintiff. . . .

The plaintiff having obtained a legal advantage through the failure of Sarah R. Andrews to record her deed of May 8, 1946, promptly lost that advantage when said deed was recorded on July 8, 1946. The very terms of the statute force that conclusion. Therefore, after the deed of May 8, 1946, was recorded, it became effective for all purposes, and the grantee in the subsequent deed of May 14, not having completed his purchase, could obtain no rights based upon the payments thereafter made. His rights, whatever they are, must be based upon his situation on the date when he first had actual or constructive notice of the deed of May 8, 1946. He says that he did not have actual notice thereof until one or one and one-half years after he received his deed, but we think this immaterial because he received constructive notice thereof on July 8, 1946, when the first deed was recorded.

In the circumstances of this case, the plaintiff is entitled to have paid to him the sum of $1,000 which he had paid to his father at or before the execution of the deed of May 14, 1946, and such sums as he may have expended in the care of his father from that date until the recordation of the Andrews deed on July 8, 1946. . . . In our opinion, this principle is fully supported by the case of Webb v. Bailey, supra. That was a case involving a trust, and it was held: "Notice of a prior existing trust, received by a subsequent purchaser before the payment of all the purchase money, although it be secured and the conveyance executed, is equivalent to notice before the contract of purchase, in so far as the legal title to the trust subject is concerned."

In other words, the subsequent purchaser did not get legal title to the property involved, but was protected to the extent of any purchase money actually paid before notice. In the body of the opinion in that case, we find this language: "But, as to the purchase price in so far as paid before notice, the rule prevails that the purchaser, to that extent having acted in good faith, is entitled to be reimbursed from the rightful owner as a condition to granting him a restoration of the property. This is on the principle that he who asks equity must do equity. . . . Purchasers having no notice of any fraud when they take their deed and pay their first installment of the purchase money may be protected as to the amount paid by them on the land. But they cannot claim to be innocent purchasers until they have made the purchase, received the deed, and paid the whole of the purchase money."

Coming to a conclusion on the whole matter, we are of the opinion that the relief prayed for in plaintiff's bill must be denied, solely on the ground that the purchase of the property involved on May 14, 1946, was not a complete one, and, therefore, plaintiff is not in a position to take advantage of the provision of Code, 40-1-9; but that having in good faith paid the sum of $1,000 on the purchase price of the property conveyed to him on that date, he is entitled to have that sum returned to him, with interest; and is entitled to have paid to him any sums expended by him in caring for his father until the 8th day of July, 1946, when the deed to Sarah R. Andrews was recorded.

. . . We remand the cause to the circuit court with directions to enter a decree in accordance with this opinion. . . .

PROBLEMS AND NOTE

1. *O* conveys Blackacre for $40,000 to *A*, who does not record. *O* subsequently contracts to sell Blackacre to *B* for $50,000, with $5,000

down and $5,000 to be paid each year for nine years. The contract is not recorded. After *B* pays $20,000 to *O*, *A* records her deed. Then *B* pays *O* $10,000 more on the contract. Blackacre is now worth $80,000. *A* sues *B* in a notice jurisdiction to determine their relative priorities. What result? See Tomlinson v. Clarke, 118 Wash. 2d 498, 825 P.2d 706 (1972); Roger A. Cunningham, William B. Stoebuck & Dale A. Whitman, The Law of Property §11.10 at 795 (1984).

2. Suppose that, in Problem 1, instead of *O* financing *B*'s purchase, *B* had borrowed $50,000 from a bank. *B* gave *O* the $50,000, and *O* gave *B* a deed and *B* gave the bank a mortgage. After *B* paid the bank $20,000 on its loan, *A* recorded her deed. Then *A* sues *B*. What result? Why is an installment land contract treated differently from a mortgage? See 4 American Law of Property §17.10 at 557 n.7 (1952), citing older cases holding that a purchaser under an installment land contract is not protected as a subsequent purchaser until the purchaser acquires legal title by deed, because, until the latter time, the purchaser can rescind the purchase and recover the purchase money.

Why shouldn't *B* be entitled to the benefit of his bargain whether he buys by installment land contract *or* deed and mortgage? Suppose that, instead of borrowing from a bank, *B* borrows from *O* and gives *O* a purchase money mortgage. What result? Compare 4 Austin W. Scott, The Law of Trusts §303 (William F. Fratcher 4th ed. 1989).

3. *O*, owner of Blackacre, borrows $5,000 from a bank on an unsecured loan. *O* subsequently conveys Blackacre to *A*, who does not record. *O* defaults on her payments to the bank, which agrees not to sue *O* if *O* gives the bank a mortgage on Blackacre. *O* does so. Does the bank prevail over *A*? Would it make a difference if the bank had extended the time for payment when it took the mortgage? The issue in both cases is whether the bank, when it takes the mortgage, has given value and qualifies as a subsequent mortgagee for value. See Cunningham, Stoebuck & Whitman, supra, §11.10 at 785.

4. *Creditors.* A number of recording statutes protect "creditors" against unrecorded deeds and mortgages (see the Florida statute on page 713). Courts have interpreted these statutes to protect only creditors who have established a lien, such as by attachment or judgment, and not all creditors. Merely lending money to the record owner does not give priority over unrecorded instruments. In some states, lien creditors are construed to come within broad language extending protection to "all persons except parties to the conveyance."

In many states, a creditor is not protected until the creditor prosecutes a lawsuit to judgment and forecloses a lien or holds an execution sale. The buyer at the sale, who may be the creditor, is protected under the recording act as a subsequent bona fide purchaser for value if the buyer has no notice of the unrecorded claim at the time of sale.

In many states, special statutes give persons who provide labor or materials on a building project a lien on the property from the time such labor or material is provided.

For an examination of which creditors should be protected under the policies of the recording act, see Dan S. Schechter, Judicial Lien Creditors Versus Prior Unrecorded Transferees of Real Property: Rethinking the Goals of the Recording System and Their Consequences, 62 S. Cal. L. Rev. 105 (1988).

6. Inquiry Notice

There are three kinds of notice a person may have with respect to a prior claim: actual, record, and inquiry. The latter two are forms of constructive notice — notice that the law declares you have regardless of your actual knowledge.

Harper v. Paradise
Supreme Court of Georgia, 1974
233 Ga. 194, 210 S.E.2d 710

INGRAM, J. This appeal involves title to land. It is from a judgment and directed verdict granted to the appellees and denied to the appellants in the Superior Court of Oglethorpe County.

Appellants claim title as remaindermen under a deed to a life tenant with the remainder interest to the named children of the life tenant. This deed was delivered to the life tenant but was lost or misplaced for a number of years and was not recorded until 35 years later.

On February 1, 1922, Mrs. Susan Harper conveyed by warranty deed a 106.65-acre farm in Oglethorpe County to her daughter-in-law, Maude Harper, for life with remainder in fee simple to Maude Harper's named children. The deed, which recited that it was given for Five Dollars and "natural love and affection," was lost, or misplaced, until 1957 when it was found by Clyde Harper, one of the named remaindermen, in an old trunk belonging to Maude Harper. The deed was recorded in July, 1957.

Susan Harper died sometime during the period 1925-1927 and was survived by her legal heirs, Price Harper, Prudie Harper Jackson, Mildred Chambers and John W. Harper, Maude Harper's husband. In 1928, all of Susan Harper's then living heirs, except John W. Harper, joined in executing an instrument to Maude Harper, recorded March 19, 1928, which contained the following language:

Deed, Heirs of Mrs. Susan Harper, to Mrs. Maude Harper. Whereas Mrs. Susan Harper did on or about the . . . day of March, 1927 [1922?], make and deliver a deed of gift to the land hereinafter more fully described to Mrs. Maude Harper the wife of John W. Harper, which said deed was delivered to the said Mrs. Maude Harper and was not recorded; and Whereas said deed has been lost or destroyed and cannot be found; and Whereas the said Mrs. Susan Harper has since died and leaves as her heirs at law the grantors herein; Now therefore for and in consideration of the sum of $1.00, in hand paid, the receipt of which is hereby acknowledged, the undersigned, Mrs. Prudence Harper Jackson, Price Harper and Ben Grant as guardian of Mildred Chambers, do hereby remise, release and forever quit claim to the said Mrs. Maude Harper, her heirs and assigns, all of their right, title, interest, claim or demand that they and each of them have or may have had in and to the [described property]. To have and to hold the said property to the said Mrs. Maude Harper, her heirs and assigns, so that neither the said grantors nor their heirs nor any person or persons claiming under them shall at any time hereafter by any way or means, have, claim or demand any right, title or interest in and to the aforesaid property or its appurtenances or any part thereof. This deed is made and delivered to the said Mrs. Maude Harper to take the place of the deed made and executed and delivered by Mrs. Susan Harper during her lifetime as each of the parties hereto know that the said property was conveyed to the said Mrs. Maude Harper by the said Mrs. Susan Harper during her lifetime and that the said Mrs. Maude Harper was on said property and in possession thereof.

On February 27, 1933, Maude Harper executed a security deed, recorded the same day, which purported to convey the entire fee simple to Ella Thornton to secure a fifty dollar loan. The loan being in default, Ella Thornton foreclosed on the property, receiving a sheriff's deed executed and recorded in 1936. There is an unbroken chain of record title out of Ella Thornton to the appellees, Lincoln and William Paradise, who claim the property as grantees under a warranty deed executed and recorded in 1955. The appellees also assert title by way of peaceful, continuous, open and adverse possession by them and their predecessors in title beginning in 1940.

The appellees trace their title back through Susan Harper, but they do not rely on the 1922 deed from Susan Harper to Maude Harper as a link in their record chain of title. If appellees relied on the 1922 deed, then clearly the only interest they would have obtained would have been Maude Harper's life estate which terminated upon her death in 1972. . . .

Appellees contended that the 1928 instrument executed by three of Susan Harper's then living heirs must be treated under Code §67-2502 as having been executed by the heirs as agents or representatives of Susan Harper, thereby making both the 1922 and 1928 deeds derivative of the same source. That Code section provides:

All innocent persons, firms or corporations acting in good faith and without actual notice, who purchase for value, or obtain contractual liens, from distributees, devisees, legatees, or heirs at law, holding or apparently holding land or personal property by will or inheritance from a deceased person, shall be protected in the purchase of said property or in acquiring such a lien thereon as against unrecorded liens or conveyances created or executed by said deceased person upon or to said property in like manner and to the same extent as if the property had been purchased of or the lien acquired from the deceased person.

Appellees argue that since both deeds must be treated as having emanated from the same source, the 1928 deed has priority under Code §29-401 because it was recorded first. Code §29-401 provides:

Every deed conveying lands shall be recorded in the office of the clerk of the superior court of the county where the land lies. The record may be made at any time, but such deed loses its priority over a subsequent recorded deed from the same vendor, taken without notice of the existence of the first.

In the present case, . . . after the death of the original grantor, Susan Harper, her heirs could have joined in a deed to an innocent person acting in good faith and without actual notice of the earlier deed. If such a deed had been made, conveying a fee simple interest without making any reference to a prior unrecorded lost or misplaced deed, Code §67-2502 might well apply to place that deed from the heirs within the protection of Code §29-401.

However, the 1928 deed relied upon by appellees was to the same person, Maude Harper, who was the life tenant in the 1922 deed. The 1928 deed recited that it was given in lieu of the earlier lost or misplaced deed from Susan Harper to Maude Harper and that Maude Harper was in possession of the property. Thus Maude Harper is bound to have taken the 1928 deed with knowledge of the 1922 deed. See King v. McDuffie, 144 Ga. 318, 320, 87 S.E. 22. The recitals of the 1928 deed negate any contention that the grantors in that deed were holding or apparently holding the property by will or inheritance from Susan Harper. Indeed, the recitals of the 1928 deed actually serve as a disclaimer by the heirs that they were so holding or apparently holding the land.

Therefore, Code §67-2502 is not applicable under the facts of this case and cannot be used to give the 1928 deed priority over the 1922 deed under the provisions of Code §29-401. The recitals contained in the 1928 deed clearly put any subsequent purchaser on notice of the existence of the earlier misplaced or lost deed, and, in terms of Code §29-401, the 1928 deed, though recorded first, would not be entitled to priority.

We conclude that it was incumbent upon the appellees to ascertain through diligent inquiry the contents of the earlier deed and the interests conveyed therein. See Henson v. Bridges, 218 Ga. 6(2), 126 S.E.2d 226. Cf. Talmadge Bros. & Co. v. Interstate Building & Loan Assn., 105 Ga. 550, 553, 31 S.E. 618, holding that "a deed in the chain of title, discovered by the investigator, is constructive notice of all other deeds which were referred to in the deed discovered," including an unrecorded plat included in the deed discovered. Although the appellees at trial denied having received any information as to the existence of the interests claimed by the appellants, the transcript fails to indicate any effort on the part of the appellees to inquire as to the interests conveyed by the lost or misplaced deed when they purchased the property in 1955. "A thorough review of the record evinces no inquiry whatsoever by the defendants, or attempt to explain why such inquiry would have been futile. Thus it will be presumed that due inquiry would have disclosed the existent facts." Henson v. Bridges, supra, p.10, of 218 Ga., p.228 of 126 S.E.2d.

The appellees also contend that they have established prescriptive title by way of peaceful, continuous, open and adverse possession by them and their predecessors in title beginning in 1940. However, the remaindermen named in the 1922 deed had no right of possession until the life tenant's death in 1972. "Prescription does not begin to run in favor of a grantee under a deed from a life tenant, against a remainderman who does not join in the deed, until the falling in of the life-estate by the death of the life tenant." Mathis v. Solomon, 188 Ga. 311, 312, 4 S.E.2d 24, 25.

. . . The trial court erred in granting appellees' motion for directed verdict and in overruling the appellants' motion for directed verdict. Therefore, the judgment of the trial court is reversed with direction that judgment be entered in favor of the appellants.

Judgment reversed with direction.

PROBLEM AND QUESTIONS

1. *O* conveys a mortgage to *A*, but the typist fails to insert in the mortgage a description of the property to be bound. The mortgage is intended to secure Blackacre. The mortgage is recorded. *O* subsequently conveys a mortgage on Blackacre to *B*, who pays a valuable consideration, has no actual knowledge of *A*'s mortgage, and records. Who has priority, *A* or *B*? See Air Flow Heating & Air Conditioning, Inc. v. Baker, 326 So. 2d 449 (Fla. App. 1976).

2. Commercial leases often run on for many pages, and the lessor and lessee may not want the amount of rent payable to be made a public record. Should a recorded memorandum of lease put a subsequent purchaser to inquiry notice of the contents of a lease? Suppose that a shopping center developer leases one space to Howard Johnson for a

restaurant; the lease contains a covenant by the lessor that no other restaurant will be permitted in the shopping center. A memorandum of lease is recorded, but the full lease — including the covenant against competition — is not recorded. Subsequently the developer leases another space in the shopping center to McDonald's restaurant. Is Howard Johnson entitled to an injunction against McDonald's? See Howard D. Johnson Co. v. Parkside Dev. Corp., 169 Ind. App. 379, 348 N.E.2d 656 (1976) (holding that, even though a memorandum of lease by the common lessor to Howard Johnson is in McDonald's chain of title, the memorandum does not give constructive notice of the full contents of the lease; McDonald's not put to inquiry notice from Howard Johnson's existing restaurant together with custom of shopping center developers to use noncompetition covenants); Mister Donut of America, Inc. v. Kemp, 368 Mass. 220, 330 N.E.2d 810, 89 A.L.R.3d 896 (1975) (holding memorandum of lease gives constructive notice of contents); Genovese Drug Stores, Inc. v. Connecticut Packing Co., 732 F.2d 286 (2d Cir. 1984) (holding memorandum of lease of adjacent property (such as Howard Johnson's) in shopping center is not in chain of title of subsequent lessee (such as McDonald's)).

3. Is the doctrine of inquiry notice sound? Does it make the transfer of land more costly and title less certain? Should the courts abolish inquiry notice and require actual notice?

Waldorff Insurance and Bonding, Inc. v. Eglin National Bank

District Court of Appeal of Florida, First District, 1984
453 So. 2d 1383

SHIVERS, J. Waldorff Insurance and Bonding, Inc. (Waldorff) appeals the supplemental final judgment of foreclosure entered against it in favor of Eglin National Bank (Bank) on a condominium unit. Appellant argues that the trial court erred in not finding its interest in the condominium unit superior to the liens of two mortgages held by the Bank. We agree and reverse.

Choctaw Partnership (Choctaw) developed certain properties in Okaloosa County by constructing condominiums. On June 8, 1972, Choctaw executed a promissory note and mortgage on these properties in the amount of $850,000. This indebtedness was later increased to $1,100,000. This note and mortgage was eventually assigned to appellee Bank on January 17, 1975. At that time, the principal balance remaining on this note and mortgage was $41,562.61.

Waldorff entered into a written purchase agreement with Choctaw for condominium unit 111 on April 4, 1973. Choctaw was paid $1,000 at that time as a deposit on Unit 111. The total purchase price of Unit

111 was to be $23,550. In April or May 1973, Waldorff began occupancy of the unit. Furniture worth $5,000 was purchased by Waldorff and placed in the unit. Waldorff continually occupied the unit for about 1½ years thereafter, paying the monthly maintenance fee, the fee for maid service, the fee for garbage pick-up, and paying for repairs to the unit. At the time of the hearing in this case on February 21, 1983, the furniture was still in the unit, the utility bills and monthly maintenance fees were paid by Waldorff, and Waldorff had the keys to the unit and controlled it.

On October 10, 1973, Choctaw executed a note and mortgage for the principal sum of $600,000 in favor of the Bank. Among the properties included in this mortgage was the condominium unit involved in the instant case, Unit 111.

On June 28, 1974, Choctaw executed yet another note and mortgage, this one in favor of the Bank for the principal sum of $95,000. This mortgage secured a number of units, one of which was Unit 111.

Choctaw was apparently a client of Waldorff, and in 1974, Choctaw owed Waldorff over $35,000 for insurance premiums. Choctaw agreed to consider the purchase price of Unit 111 paid in full in return for cancellation of the debt owed by Choctaw to Waldorff. Waldorff "wrote off" the debt, and Choctaw executed a quitclaim deed to Unit 111 in favor of Waldorff. The deed was recorded in March 1975.

In 1976, the Bank brought a foreclosure action against Choctaw, Waldorff and others. A final judgment of foreclosure was entered in September 1976, but that judgment did not foreclose Waldorff's interest in Unit 111. Instead, the 1976 final judgment explicitly retained jurisdiction to determine the ownership of Unit 111. A hearing was held on February 21, 1983. The issue at this hearing was whether Waldorff's occupancy, together with the purchase agreement, was sufficient notice so as to make Waldorff's interest in Unit 111 superior to that of the Bank. At this hearing, evidence was taken concerning the agreements between Choctaw and Waldorff and Waldorff's occupancy of Unit 111. There was evidence that condominium units other than 111 were also occupied and that many of these units were occupied by persons who had no legal interest in the units, e.g., persons invited by Choctaw to occupy the units for a time as part of Choctaw's marketing campaign.

The trial court entered a supplemental final judgment of foreclosure which found that Waldorff's occupancy of Unit 111 was "equivocal" because Choctaw allowed at least 8 other condominium units to be furnished and used for occupancy by various persons. The trial court also found that Waldorff did not pay the consideration promised for Unit 111 because the debt owed by Choctaw to Waldorff was used as a bad debt write-off for federal income tax purposes rather than being credited to Choctaw. The trial court found that "even if defendant could establish some right to Unit 111 by occupancy, defendant failed to pay the agreed consideration for the quitclaim deed and, therefore, the conveyance is void." Based on these findings, the trial court held the Bank's mortgage liens superior to Waldorff's interest.

A contract to convey legal title to real property on payment of the purchase price creates an equitable interest in the purchaser. Lafferty v. Detwiler, 155 Fla. 95, 20 So. 2d 338, 343 (1944); Felt v. Morse, 80 Fla. 154, 85 So. 656 (1920). Beneficial ownership passes to the purchaser while the seller retains mere naked legal title. Arko Enterprises, Inc. v. Wood, 185 So. 2d 734 (Fla. 1st DCA 1966); Tingle v. Hornsby, 111 So. 2d 274 (Fla. 1st DCA 1959). Subsequent successors to the legal title take such title burdened with the equitable interests of which they have either actual or constructive notice. Hoyt v. Evans, 91 Fla. 1053, 109 So. 311 (1926). In the instant case, it appears clear that the April 4, 1973, Agreement to Purchase entered into between Choctaw and Waldorff vested equitable title in Waldorff. Therefore, the interests acquired by the Bank pursuant to the October 1973 and June 1974 mortgages would be subordinate to Waldorff's equitable interest if the Bank had either actual or constructive notice of that interest.

In Blackburn v. Venice Inlet Co., 38 So. 2d 43 (Fla. 1948), the court stated:

> It is settled law in Florida that actual possession is constructive notice to all the world, or anyone having knowledge of said possession of whatever right the occupants have in the land. Such possession, when open, visible and exclusive, will put upon inquiry those acquiring any title to or a lien upon the land so occupied to ascertain the nature of the rights the occupants really have in the premises. [38 So. 2d at 46.]

See generally 38 Fla. Jur. 2d Notice and Notices §7 (1982) and cases cited therein. In the instant case, Waldorff was in open, visible and exclusive possession of Unit 111 at the time of the making of the October 1973 and June 1974 mortgages.

The trial court found, however, that Waldorff's possession of Unit 111 was "equivocal" because other units in the condominium project were occupied by persons who had no interest in the units. We do not agree with this analysis. Although many of the condominium units were held by a common grantor, Choctaw, the units were separate parcels intended to be alienated individually. The mortgage executed on June 28, 1974, which secures both the $95,000 note and the $600,000 note of October 10, 1973, described the property mortgaged in terms of individual units, specifically including Unit 111. The status of other units within the condominium project, therefore, is irrelevant to the question of the possession of Unit 111. The issue in the instant case concerned only the rights of the parties involved in Unit 111, not the condominium project as a whole or any other individual units.

Appellee argues, however, that it would have been difficult to ascertain whether any person physically occupying any of the units in the project had a claim of ownership interest in the unit being occupied. Although we agree that it would be more inconvenient for a prospective lender to make several inquiries rather than a single one, we do not find this argument persuasive. We find the ancient, but oft-cited, case of Phelan v. Brady, 119 N.Y. 587, 23 N.E. 1109 (N.Y. 1890), to be instructive in this matter. On May 1, 1886, Mrs. Brady took possession of a tenement building containing 48 apartments occupied by 20 different occupants as tenants from month to month. Her possession was pursuant to a contract for sale secured for her by her attorney. Three of the apartments were occupied by Mrs. Brady and her husband, who kept a liquor store in part of the building. Mrs. Brady began collecting rents immediately upon taking possession of the premises. Mrs. Brady's deed, however, was not recorded until August 26, 1886, subsequent to the recordation of Phelan's mortgage which had been executed by the record owner of the property on July 23, 1886. The court stated:

> At the time of the execution and delivery of the mortgage to the plaintiff, the defendant Mrs. Brady was in the actual possession of the premises under a perfectly valid, but unrecorded, deed. Her title must therefore prevail as against the plaintiff. It matters not, so far as Mrs. Brady is concerned, that the plaintiff in good faith advanced his money upon an apparently perfect record title of the defendant John E. Murphy. Nor is it of any consequence, so far as this question is concerned, whether the plaintiff was in fact ignorant of any right or claim of Mrs. Brady to the premises. It is enough that she was in possession under her deed and the contract of purchase, as that fact operated in law as notice to the plaintiff of all her rights. It may be true, as has been argued by plaintiff's counsel, that, when a party takes a conveyance of property situated as this was, occupied by numerous tenants, it would be inconvenient and difficult for him to ascertain the rights or interests that are claimed by all or any of them. But this circumstance cannot change the rule. Actual possession of real estate is sufficient to a person proposing to take a mortgage on the property, and to all the world, of the existence of any right which the person in possession is able to establish. [23 N.E. at 1110-1111.]

Moreover, cases citing Phelan v. Brady have stated that the possession involved there was not equivocal. Swanstrom v. Day, 46 Misc. 311, 93 N.Y.S. 192 (N.Y. Sup. Ct. 1905); Baker v. Thomas, 61 Hun. 17, 15 N.Y.S. 359 (N.Y. Sup. Ct. 1891).

We also agree with appellant that the trial court erred in finding that the conveyance of the property from Choctaw to Waldorff was void due to lack of consideration for the quitclaim deed. Although Waldorff may have erred in attempting to take a "bad debt" tax deduction after cancelling the debt Choctaw owed to Waldorff for insurance premiums,

Choctaw was relieved from payment of that debt, and this constituted a valuable consideration flowing to Choctaw. Booth v. Bond, 56 Cal. App. 2d 153, 132 P.2d 520 (Cal. Dist. Ct. App. 1942); see generally Dorman v. Publix-Saenger-Sparks Theatres, 135 Fla. 284, 184 So. 886 (1939); 17 C.J.S. Contracts §§74, 87 (1963).

The parties agree that the 1972 mortgage lien is superior to Waldorff's interest in Unit 111. Appellee, however, stated at oral argument that it did not disagree with the proposition that a proper application of the funds from the 1976 foreclosure sale of the rest of the condominium project should first satisfy the 1972 mortgage. Our decision renders moot appellant's other points on appeal. Accordingly, the supplemental final judgment of foreclosure is reversed and the cause remanded for entry of a judgment consistent with this opinion.

Reversed and remanded.

PROBLEMS

1. A mother-in-law buys a house for herself, her daughter, and her son-in-law to live in. She takes title from the seller in her son-in-law's name because she thinks his income and credit rating will better enable them to obtain a mortgage. As the mother-in-law is the true beneficial owner, however, the son-in-law holds the property in a resulting trust in her favor undisclosed on the records. Subsequently the lender approached by the son-in-law visits the property and ascertains that the mother-in-law, daughter, and son-in-law are living in the house. The lender never asks the mother-in-law if she has any claim to the property, and on the strength of the son-in-law's record title lends him money and takes his note secured by a mortgage on the property. The son-in-law defaults on the payments, and the lender desires to foreclose. Can the lender do so? Would the result be different if the mother-in-law lived in the house by herself? See Yancey v. Harris, 234 Ga. 320, 216 S.E.2d 83 (1975).

2. You are the attorney for a prospective purchaser of a 50-unit apartment house. The present owner has shown the prospective purchaser copies of the leases on file in her office. Can the purchaser rely on these leases? Suppose that the landlord had orally extended tenant A's one-year lease for two more years and has given tenant B a written option to renew for a five-year term, which option does not appear in the landlord's records. Suppose also that tenant C has a five-year lease and has prepaid the rent, though there is nothing in the lease to indicate this. Will the prospective purchaser take subject to the aforementioned rights of tenants A, B, and C? See Gates Rubber Co. v. Ulman, 214 Cal. App. 3d 356, 262 Cal. Rptr. 630 (1989); Martinique Realty Corp. v. Hall,

64 N.J. Super. 599, 166 A.2d 803 (1960). What would you advise the prospective purchaser to do? See 4 American Law of Property §17.12 (1952).

7. Marketable Title Acts

Marketable title acts, enacted in a large number of states, have as their purpose limiting title searches to a reasonable period, typically the last 30 or 40 years. The essential idea is quite simple: When one person has a record title to land for a designated period of time, inconsistent claims or interests are extinguished. Some of the acts take the form of a statute of limitations barring a claim not recorded within the designated period. Others declare that the record owner with a clear title going back for the designated period has marketable record title that is free and clear of adverse claims. Thus, except for the interests excepted from the statute, title searches may be safely limited to the number of years specified in the statute. Under a marketable title act, all claimants of interests in land, to be safe, must file a notice of claim every 30 to 40 years after the recording of their instruments of acquisition. See Uniform Marketable Title Act (1990) (30 years); Fla. Stat. Ann. §§712.01 et seq. (West 1988); Mich. Comp. Laws §§565.101 et seq. (West 1988); N.C. Gen. Stat. §§47B-1 et seq. (1984).

Walter E. Barnett, Marketable Title Acts — Panacea or Pandemonium?
53 Cornell L. Rev. 45, 52–54 (1967)*

Marketable title acts are intended to operate in conjunction with, rather than as a substitute for, the recording acts. They seek to extinguish old title defects automatically with the passage of time. The acts provide that if a person has an unbroken chain of title from the present back to his "root of title," then he has the sort of title in favor of which their extinguishment feature will operate. His "root of title" is the most recent transaction in his chain of title that has been of record at least forty years.[21] With certain specified exceptions, claims and interests that depend on matters antedating the root of title are declared null and void. The acts seek to avoid the constitutional problems of an outright extin-

---

    21. The 40-year period is most common and is the one used for illustrative purposes throughout this article. . . .

guishment of property interests by providing, in one of the specified exceptions, that the holders of old interests and claims may preserve them by recording a notice of claim.

The acts do not require a person seeking their benefits to be a bona fide purchaser. In fact, although the acts refer to "the time when marketability is being determined," no "purchase" or other transaction affecting the land need occur to trigger the extinguishment of old defects and interests.

The following example illustrates the intended operation of a marketable title act. Suppose that in 1889 O, the owner of Blackacre, gives X a ninety-nine-year lease, which is recorded that same year. In 1890, O conveys to A, the deed reciting that it is subject to the recorded lease to X. In 1920 A conveys to B, the deed making no mention of the lease. In 1941, B conveys to C, the deed making no mention of the lease. All these deeds were recorded when executed. Under a forty-year marketable title act such as the Model Act, C's title to Blackacre would be free and clear of the ninety-nine-year lease as of 1960, when the 1920 deed from A to B had been of record for forty years. This result assumes that the lessee, X, is not in possession. It is immaterial that the recorded lease gave constructive notice to both B and C, or that both had actual knowledge of its existence. It is likewise immaterial that no transaction affecting the land has taken place between 1941 and the present. The lease is still extinguished in 1960 if X has not filed a notice of claim. C's root of title is the 1920 deed from A to B, and he has an unbroken chain of title for at least forty years since it was recorded. In 1981, C or his successor will have a new root of title — the 1941 deed from B to C — and any claims or interests antedating *its* recording will be extinguished. Thus, title to Blackacre undergoes an automatic "cleansing" whenever forty years elapse from the recording of a transaction that is capable of serving as a root of title. If one asks why the 1890 deed from O to A did not serve to extinguish the lease in 1930, the answer is that, although the 1890 deed *is* the root of title from 1930 to 1960, its reference to the lease preserves the lease from extinguishment, under one of the act's specified exceptions. If the 1920 deed had made a similar reference to the lease, it would not have been extinguished in 1960. C would have had to wait until 1981, when he could show a chain of title from a root at least forty years old, with neither the root nor any subsequent instrument in the chain referring specifically to the lease.

To ensure that his leasehold is preserved from extinction, X must file a notice of claim under the act every forty years after the date of his lease. Otherwise, he runs the risk that some recorded transaction will fail to refer to his lease and thus, forty years later, become a root of title that will cut off his rights. Actually, X could protect himself in the example given simply by filing one notice of claim in 1960, just before the 1920 deed from A to B has been of record forty years. But X may not know whether or when such transactions have occurred, unless he periodically secures an abstract of title. Regularly filing a notice of claim is his surest protection.

Heifner v. Bradford
Supreme Court of Ohio, 1983
4 Ohio St. 3d 49, 446 N.E.2d 440

In 1916, Elvira Sprague and her husband, owners in fee simple of a tract of real estate located in Monroe Township, Muskingum County, conveyed their interest by deed to Fred H. Waters. By this instrument, the grantors reserved the oil and gas rights in the land. This transaction was recorded in Muskingum County that same year.

Elvira Sprague died testate in Tuscarawas County in 1931. Her will was probated in Tuscarawas County and devised the reserved oil and gas rights in the land equally to her two daughters, Lottie E. Rogers and Sarah A. Bradford.

In 1936, Fred H. Waters and his wife, without mention of the reservation of the oil and gas rights, conveyed the property by warranty deed to Charles B. Waters, Emma M. Waters, Sarah K. Waters, and William H. Waters. This conveyance was recorded in 1936.

An authenticated copy of Elvira Sprague's will was filed in Muskingum County in 1957. In accordance with the terms of the will, an affidavit of transfer was filed and recorded in Muskingum County evidencing the transfer of the oil and gas rights by inheritance from Elvira Sprague to her daughters. However, both Lottie E. Rogers and Sarah A. Bradford had died intestate prior to this transfer. Thus, Lottie E. Rogers' one-half share in the oil and gas rights was divided equally among her four children and Sarah A. Bradford's share was equally divided among her three children. These conveyances were evidenced by affidavits of transfer which were duly recorded in Muskingum County in 1957.

In 1980, Charles B. Waters et al. conveyed their interest in the property to William H. Waters and his wife Shirley S. Waters.

Appellants, Charlotte Heifner, Jean Stewart and Doris Schaevitz, own three undivided fractional shares of the oil and gas rights in the property. Appellants instituted this action in the court of common pleas seeking to quiet title and partition the undivided fractional shares in the oil and gas rights. Defendants represent the remaining fractional oil and gas rights owners, as well as the record surface owner, William H. and Shirley S. Waters.

Relevant to this appeal, the record surface owners claim also to be owners of the oil and gas rights in the land contrary to the claim of appellants. Appellees, William H. and Shirley S. Waters, base their claim upon an operation of R.C. 5301.47 through 5301.56, Ohio's Marketable Title Act.

Upon appellants' motion for summary judgment, the trial court ruled that appellants were owners of the oil and gas rights and ordered a partition of the undivided fractional interests. The court of appeals reversed, holding that the Marketable Title Act operated to extinguish appellants' interest and vest complete ownership of the property in William H. and Shirley S. Waters.[22]

The cause is now before this court upon the allowance of a motion to certify the record.

CELEBREZZE, C.J. This case involves a controversy between independent competing claims of ownership to the oil and gas rights in a particular tract of land. For purposes of this decision, appellants are the purported owners of the oil and gas rights while appellees are the undisputed owners of the surface land. The question involved is one of first impression in this state and deals exclusively with the operation of R.C. 5301.47 through 5301.56, otherwise known as the Ohio Marketable Title Act. The issue presented by this appeal is whether appellees, who have an unbroken chain of title of record of forty years or more, have a marketable record title even though appellants' competing interest arose from an independent chain of title recorded during the forty-year period subsequent to appellees' root of title.

At the outset, the Marketable Title Act sets forth several definitions germane to the instant cause. R.C. 5301.47(A) defines "marketable record title" as a "title of record, as indicated in section 5301.48 of the Revised Code, which operates to extinguish such interests and claims, existing prior to the effective date of the root of title. . . ." A "root of title" is defined in subsection (E) as "that conveyance or other title transaction in the chain of title of a person, upon which he relies as a basis for the marketability of his title, and which was the most recent to be recorded as of a date forty years prior to the time when marketability is being determined. . . ." Subsection (F) defines "title transaction" as "any transaction affecting title to any interest in land, including title by will or descent. . . ."

---

22. The trial court distributed the oil and gas interests as follows:

Charlotte Heifner an undivided ⅛
Jean Stewart an undivided ⅛
Doris Schaevitz an undivided ⅙
Lane S. Bradford an undivided ⅙
Jean Weaver Reed an undivided 1/12
Edith Morris Rogers an undivided ¼
Charles Weaver an undivided 1/12

Further, the determination by the trial court with respect to the fractionalization of the oil and gas ownership is not before us.

R.C. 5301.48 provides that one "who has an unbroken chain of title of record to any interest in land for forty years or more, has a marketable record title to such interest . . . subject to the matters stated in section 5301.49 of the Revised Code."

In relevant part, R.C. 5301.49 states:

> Such record marketable title shall be subject to: . . .
>
> (D) Any interest arising out of a title transaction which has been recorded subsequent to the effective date of the root of title from which the unbroken chain of title of record is started; provided that such recording shall not revive or give validity to any interest which has been extinguished prior to the time of the recording. . . .

Appellants' root of title is the 1916 deed from Elvira Sprague and her husband to Fred H. Waters which reserved to the grantors the oil and gas rights in the land. Appellees' root of title is the 1936 conveyance from Fred H. Waters and his wife to Charles B. Waters, Emma M. Waters, Sarah K. Waters, and William H. Waters which failed to mention the reservation of oil and gas rights. Consequently, unless subject to R.C. 5301.49, appellees hold a marketable record title to the oil and gas rights, as well as title to the surface land, by virtue of having an "unbroken chain" of record title for over forty years which extinguishes prior claims and interests, including that of appellants. R.C. 5301.47(A) and 5301.48.

The Act defines a "title transaction" to include the passage of "title by will or descent." Thus, the 1957 conveyance of the oil and gas rights which passed under the terms of Elvira Sprague's will must be considered a "title transaction" under R.C. 5301.49(D).

Appellees argue that we should construe R.C. 5301.49(D) to require that a title transaction under that section arise from the same chain of title as that under which there is claimed to be a marketable record title. For the reasons to follow, we feel the proper construction should be otherwise.

Ohio's Marketable Title Act is taken primarily from the Model Marketable Title Act. In fact, R.C. 5301.49(D) is virtually identical to Section 2(d) of the Model Act.[23] This being the case, we are convinced that the General Assembly and the drafters of the Model Act intended that a title transaction under R.C. 5301.49(D) and Section 2(d), respectively, may be part of an entirely independent chain of title.

In Simes & Taylor, Model Title Standards (1960) 32, the drafters of the Model Act proposed comprehensive model title standards to accompany the Model Act. Standard 4.10 states:

_____

23. The Model Marketable Title Act was first proposed in Simes & Taylor, The Improvement of Conveyancing by Legislation (1960).

"The recording of an instrument of conveyance subsequent to the effective date of the root of title has the same effect in preserving any interest conveyed as the filing of the notice provided for in §4 of the Act. (See §2[d] of the Model Act.)"

Perhaps more significant is the comment to the above standard which provides that, "[t]his standard is operative both where there are claims under a single chain of title and where there are *two or more independent chains of title.*" Id. (Emphasis added.)

Moreover, the Ohio Standards of Title Examination drafted and adopted by the Ohio State Bar Association have embraced an identical approach. See 55 Ohio Bar No. 19 (May 10, 1982), at page 763.

Hence, we are satisfied that R.C. 5301.49(D) ought to be construed in the manner that Simes and Taylor, as drafters of Section 2(d) of the Model Act, intended.[24] Accordingly, a "marketable title," as defined in R.C. 5301.47(A) and 5301.48, is subject to an interest arising out of a "title transaction" under R.C. 5301.49(D) which may be part of an independent chain of title.[25] Further, the effect of R.C. 5301.49(D) is identical to that obtained by the filing of a preservation notice. R.C. 5301.51 provides for the preservation of interests by the filing of a notice of claim during the forty-year period. As a result, the recording of a "title trans-

---

24. Appellees contend, however, that under the present grantor-grantee indexing system, in order to locate title transactions in an independent chain of title, the title examiner will have to search the title to its origin and then forward to discover such transactions. It is appellees' position that the purpose of the Act is to limit title searches to forty years.

The approach taken by the court of appeals and advanced by the appellees is not without support. See Barnett, Marketable Title Acts — Panacea or Pandemonium? 53 Cornell L. Rev. 45, 54-56 (1967). However, we are left unpersuaded by Professor Barnett's analysis. Initially, Barnett concedes his approach is contrary to that of the drafters of the Model Act [Barnett, supra, at page 89, fn. 122] and, further, Barnett views the purpose of marketable title acts solely to shorten title examinations. Barnett, at page 91.

We are not inclined to view the purpose of the Marketable Title Act so narrowly. The Supreme Court of Florida in Miami v. St. Joe Paper Co. (Fla. 1978), 364 So.2d 439, 442, aptly stated that the purpose of marketable record title acts is three-fold:

The Marketable Record Title Act is a comprehensive plan for reform in conveyancing procedures. . . .

The Marketable Record Title Act is also a statute of limitations in that it requires state demands to be asserted within a reasonable time after a cause of action has accrued. . . .

The Marketable Record Title Act is also a recording act in that it provides for a simple and easy method by which the owner of an existing old interest may preserve it. If he fails to take the step of filing the notice as provided, he has only himself to blame if his interest is extinguished. The legislature did not intend to arbitrarily wipe out old claims and interests without affording a means of preserving them and giving a reasonable period of time within which to take the necessary steps to accomplish that purpose.

See, also, Semachko v. Hopko (1973), 35 Ohio App. 2d 205, 301 N.E.2d 560 [64 O.O.2d 316].

25. Facing the same issue, other courts have reached the conclusion we reach today. See, e.g., Kittrell v. Clark (Fla. App. 1978), 363 So.2d 373.

action" under R.C. 5301.47(F) and 5301.49(D) is equivalent to the filing of a notice of claim during the forty-year period as specified in R.C. 5301.51 and 5301.52.[26]

Thus, the 1957 conveyance under the terms of Elvira Sprague's will was a "title transaction" within the meaning of R.C. 5301.49(D), and appellants' interest was not extinguished by operation of the Marketable Title Act.[27] Accordingly, the judgment of the court of appeals is reversed.

Judgment reversed.

PROBLEM AND NOTES

1. The jurisdiction has a 40-year marketable title act. In 1949, O, owner of Blackacre, unimproved land, dies intestate. O's heir, H, is unaware that O owns Blackacre. In 1950 F forges H's name to a deed to Blackacre to A. This deed is recorded. In 1952, A conveys Blackacre to B.

In 1993, H's daughter and sole heir, C, discovers the 1950 forgery. C brings suit against B to establish title to Blackacre. Who prevails? See Marshall v. Hollywood, Inc., 236 So. 2d 114 (Fla. 1970); Lewis M. Simes & Clarence B. Taylor, The Improvement of Conveyancing by Legislation 295-349 (1960).

2. The marketable title acts except certain interests, which do not have to be re-recorded. These exceptions may include mineral rights, easements, interests of persons in possession, claims of the federal government, or other interests. These exceptions defeat the act's objective of limiting title search because the title examiner much check back beyond the set period of years to be sure no interest excepted exists on record.

3. Some states, without general marketable title statutes, require the periodic re-recordation of certain types of interests in order to preserve them. If not re-recorded, the interests expire. The usual re-recor-

26. This precise conclusion was reached by the Supreme Court of Oklahoma in Allen v. Farmers Union Co-Operative Royalty Co. (Okl. 1975), 538 P.2d 204, 209, in interpreting similar provisions of Oklahoma's Marketable Record Title Act.

We do recognize, as a practical matter, the difficulty faced by title examiners in locating these title transactions in a common title examination. We note that the General Assembly has mandated a "Notice Index" by which notices under R.C. 5301.51 are indexed under the description of the real estate. R.C. 5301.52. It would seem consistent to similarly require such an indexing procedure of at least the title transactions falling under R.C. 5301.49(D). See Webster, The Quest for Clear Land Titles — Making Land Title Searches Shorter and Surer in North Carolina via Marketable Title Legislation, 44 N.C.L. Rev. 89, 108-109 and 122 (1965). However, that is in the nature of a legislative determination beyond the scope of our consideration.

27. The 1957 title transaction took place only twenty-one years from appellees' root of title, obviously within the forty-year period.

dation period is 30 years. Interests affected by these special re-recordation requirements may include possibilities of reverter and rights of entry (see page 307), easements, covenants, and mineral interests. See Texaco v. Short, 454 U.S. 516 (1982) (upholding a retroactive Indiana statute requiring re-recordation of unused mineral interests every 20 years).

B. Registration of Title

Myres S. McDougal[28] & John W. Brabner-Smith, Land Title Transfer: A Regression
48 Yale L.J. 1125, 1126-1131 (1939)

It takes no prophet to foresee that fundamental reforms in land utilization are hot upon us. Yet for the achievement of such reforms without payment of undue and continued tribute to private monopolies and without fruitless bother and delay — perhaps even if they are to be achieved at all — major changes must be effected in our antiquated, pre-commerce "system" of land transfer. Cheap, expeditious, and secure methods must be designed, if they are not already available, to replace the present complicated and dilatory methods which, while costly to the individual and burdensome to the public, afford no adequate security of title. Streamlined need cannot long endure horse-and-buggy obstacles to the liquidity of land. It is an ancient query, but its relevance grows: why should not a lot or a farm be as easily acquired and as securely held as a ship or a share of stock or an automobile?

Why *cannot* a lot or a farm be so easily acquired and securely held? The answer can be found in any courthouse. It is in the wild disorder and the incompleteness of the public records. First, the disorder. Suppose a bank had been in business 100 years with 100,000 customers and had repeatedly honored some thirty different kinds of instruments against each account, copying each instrument serially into big books,

---

28. Myres S. McDougal, Yale's great angry man of property in the 1940s, assailed, with memorable invective, lawyers, judges, legislators, and scholars for failing to reform property doctrines to serve modern needs. McDougal's outrage is summed up in the final line of his evisceration of volume three of the Restatement of Property: "To make a superb inventory of Augean stables is not to cleanse them." Myres S. McDougal, Future Interests Restated: Tradition Versus Clarification and Reform, 55 Harv. L. Rev. 1077, 1115 (1942).

McDougal's casebook, Property, Wealth, Land (1948), written with David Haber, was what the French call a *succès d'estime* — a huge success with the critics but a failure at the box office. Although it found few adoptions, Property, Wealth, Land, filled with imaginative ways of looking at property and trenchant criticism of the received wisdom, greatly influenced the way property law is taught.

before returning it to the customer, and keeping only alphabetical indexes — thirty different indexes — to these books. Imagine the expense and delay which might ensue in determining a customer's balance every time he demanded a little money. Preposterous as it may seem, that is a comparison not unfair to our "indigenous" system of land title "recordation" inherited from the Pilgrim Fathers. "The fact is," Professor John R. Rood has written, "that the path of the searcher for a safe title to land . . . is beset by more traps, sirens, harpies, and temptations, than ever plagued the wandering Ulysses, the faithful Pilgrim, or the investor in gilt-edged securities." Such a searcher must go back to a good "root" of title, varying in different states from 40 to 60 or a 100 years or more, and come down to date. As he ploughs through the Joneses, Smiths, and Johnsons and through the deeds, mortgages, judgments, taxes, and mechanics' liens he can never be sure that he isn't missing something fatal to his title. Worse yet, all this laborious retracing of the tortuous path of title is perpetual motion. Every time the land is sold or mortgaged or subdivided — no matter into how small parts — it all has to be done over again; or else private title plants, better ordered than the public records, must be constructed and maintained at great expense. Furthermore, whether our searcher maintains a plant or continually retraces his steps, the accelerating fecundity of the records, added to the disorder, scarcely lessens his labors.

Next, the incompleteness of the records. Here again the perils are legion. In simple truth the notion that we have anywhere in this country (apart from the Torrens statutes) any such thing as "record title" is sheer delusion. There are too many facts affecting the validity of a title which not only do not appear in the records but which often cannot be ascertained by any reasonable search outside the records. Contributors to the literature of land transfer . . . have vied with each other in the number of such facts they could list. Among the most frequently recurring items are: adverse possession and prescriptions; forgeries and other frauds; matters of heirship, marriage, and divorce; copyists' and recorders' errors; infancy, insanity, and other disabilities; authority of corporate officers; invalidity of acknowledgments; identity of persons; invalidity of mortgage foreclosures and of judgments and decrees; want of legal delivery of instruments; violations of the usury laws; unprobated wills, praetermitted heirs, and posthumous children; falsity of affidavits; revocation of powers of attorney by death or insanity; parol partitions and dedications; inchoate mechanics' liens; extent of restrictive covenants; non-recordation of prior government patent; and facts about boundaries. Such are some of the hazards external to the records which may disturb the peace of the faithful searcher for an indefeasible title. Obviously, for even the most scant security he must go much beyond the official sources of information. Often he does not go far enough. Is it any wonder that volumes of reports are filled with cases about "marketability" of titles and that court calendars are crowded with actions to quiet title?

Let us now suppose that some reasonably prudent man — some "rational" seeker for the "good life" — were to set out to reform this mess. What steps would he take? First, he would undoubtedly make provision for getting rid of existing stale claims and threats by a cheap and expeditious procedure for quieting titles or by a short Statute of Limitations or by both. Next, once the account of any particular lot or farm or other convenient unit of land in single ownership had been balanced by such new procedure, he would require a common-sense change in the method of keeping the public books. This change would take the form of a new and improved "tract" index. So far as possible all the facts about the title to any one piece of land, whatever the convenient unit, would be entered on one page, a "register" page. Where the interests making up a "title" are unusually complicated, memorials on the register page could refer an examiner to the field documents creating such interests. For convenience a copy of the register page, called a certificate of title, would be given to the owner. On subsequent voluntary transfers of the land, for double protection against fraud, surrender of this certificate would be required in addition to the vendor's deed. Then a new register page, with all obsolete entries removed, would be opened for the purchaser and a copy handed to him. And so on. Transfers of less than the fee would be memorialized on both the register page and the certificate, and the documents effecting such transfers filed. Involuntary transfers could be made only on order of the court making the transfer.

With the public records at long last in acceptable order, our bold reformer could then proceed to kill caveat emptor, protect the bona fide purchaser, and so create a new security of title. This he would accomplish by making the public records as nearly conclusive, as nearly unimpeachable, as is constitutionally possible. He would need to except only the Federal Government and persons in actual occupation of the premises, making adverse claim, on the date of the initial registration. No other claimants to any piece of land could get their claims honored, against bona fide purchasers for value, who did not have such claims properly entered in the public register. Under such a system, there could scarcely be need of an insurance fund to protect purchasers. Yet occasionally an odd claimant of an interest less than the fee might fail to get his interest properly registered because of oversight or error by a public official. For the protection of such claimants an ample fund could be collected by imposing on the first registrant a small fee (of not more than one-tenth of 1 percent of the value of the land).

Should our estimable reformer now, by chance, turn to any of the voluminous literature on the Torrens system, he would find that his ideas had long been anticipated. Substantially the system he advocates has had an honorable history in Europe of over five hundred years. Its present use spreads wide about the world. It "prevails throughout" Germany (including Austria), Hungary, Australia, Tasmania, Papua, New Zealand, Fiji, the "great majority of the provinces of Canada," and other scattered British colonies and protectorates. It is of "large importance" in England and Ireland. In the United States at least five states — California, Illinois, Massachusetts, Minnesota, and Ohio — have had substantial experience with the system. Statutes have existed in fourteen other states. The system has had the approval of the American Bar Association and of the Commissioners on Uniform State Laws and has even been embodied in a uniform statute. It has had the blessing and active support of a long line of distinguished and disinterested scholars. Predictions have long been current that title registration must inevitably, because of its easily demonstrable superiority, supersede title "recordation" throughout the country. Dissenting voices have usually come from those whose interests were obviously served by the existing chaos.

The system of registering title is widely known as the "Torrens system," named after Sir Richard Torrens who in 1858 introduced registration of title into South Australia, from which it spread to many other parts of the world under his name. Registration of title rests upon these principles: (1) A lawsuit adjudicates title to be in the plaintiff, subject to any mortgage, easement, or other interest the court finds to exist. All other claims are wiped out. This adjudicated state of the title is officially registered on a conclusive certificate of title. (2) When the registered land is transferred, a new certificate is issued by the registrar, after making a substantive review of what has happened to the title since the last certificate was issued. (3) An insurance indemnity fund is established to compensate those who lose interests because of errors of the registrar or operation of the system. As you can see, title registration puts title assurance in the hands of the government whereas the recording system puts title assurance in private hands using the public records.

At one time, statutes in 19 states authorized voluntary registration of title, but about half of these have been repealed. Today only in five states — Hawaii, Illinois (Cook County), Massachusetts, Minnesota (Hennepin and Ramsey Counties), and Ohio (Hamilton County) — is there any substantial amount of land with registered title.

Why has the Torrens system failed to take hold in the United States? First, the initial cost of a lawsuit adjudicating title has been a substantial deterrent to widespread use. Second, although the certificate of title is supposed to be conclusive, exceptions have been provided for certain interests, either by legislatures or courts. Exceptions may include federal tax liens, statutory liens, real property tax liens, short-term leases, possessory claims, and visible easements. A fraudulent registration may make a title registration certificate unreliable. As with the early race recording statutes, courts have been reluctant to protect certificate holders against prior known unrecorded claims, though the object of title registration is to put title in the certificate holder. See Carol M. Rose, Crystals and Mud in Property Law, 40 Stan. L. Rev. 577, 588-589 (1988). Since title registration does not in fact prove conclusive, there is less incentive to go to the expense of registering title. Third, title registration has been opposed by title insurance companies, title abstract companies, and lawyers who have a financial interest in preserving the present system.

Finally, inadequate or inadequately trained personnel in the public records office have, at least in California and Illinois, brought on crises that have resulted in legislative repeal of title registration. In 1989, in Cook County, Illinois, there was a two-year backlog in the issuance of Torrens certificates in the county recorder's office. Some years earlier, an employee had been convicted of taking payments to expedite service to patrons. United States v. Thomas, 684 F.2d 433 (7th Cir. 1981). Upon the recommendation of a blue-ribbon committee appointed by the Cook County recorder, Carol Moseley Braun, now U.S. Senator from Illinois, the Illinois legislature in 1991 repealed its Torrens act, prohibiting additional title registrations under it, and closing the registration office in 1997. Ill. Stat. Ann. ch. 30, ¶¶1201 et seq. (Smith-Hurd Supp. 1992).

For a description of the Torrens system and an evaluation of its merits, see John L. McCormack, Torrens and Recording: Land Title Assurance in the Computer Age, 18 Wm. Mitchell L. Rev. 61 (1992) (citing many earlier studies). McCormack concludes that the failure of Torrens in Chicago was "mainly caused by incompetent, unsatisfactory administration. . . . This incompetence is largely due to the fiscal or political constraints which bind many county governments and is really not the fault of the people who administer and work for these governments." Id. at 113 n.220. McCormack further concludes that title insurance companies, which are establishing their own computerized title plants and have the capacity to access computerized public records where available, are more efficient and less costly to operate than a public title registration system. "[I]t is clear that Torrens or any other true registration system is more costly and difficult for government to administer than recording. This higher cost is inherent in title registration systems because much of the data consolidation, evaluation and management done by private parties under recording is done by government employees or their agents under registration." Id. at 113.

For favorable appraisals of the Torrens system, see C. Dent Bostick, Land Title Registration: An English Solution to an American Problem, 63 Ind. L.J. 55 (1987); Comment, Possessory Title Registration: An Improvement of the Torrens System, 11 Wm. Mitchell L. Rev. 825 (1985); Comment, The Torrens System of Title Registration: A New Proposal for Effective Implementation, 29 UCLA L. Rev. 661 (1982).

C.   Title Insurance

Title insurance developed because of the inadequacies and inefficiencies
of the public records in protecting private titles. Title insurance is
bought by one premium paid at the time the policy is issued. The premium is based on the amount of insurance purchased, which ordinarily,
in a homeowner's policy, is the amount of the purchase price of the
property and, in a lender's policy, the amount of the loan. Title insurance has no fixed term and continues for as long as the insured maintains an interest in the property. Title insurance creates liability to the
insured only and does not run with the land to subsequent purchasers.
A subsequent purchaser must take out a new policy if the purchaser
wants title insurance. In a nutshell, title insurance is the opinion of the
insurer concerning the validity of title, backed by an agreement to make
that opinion good if it should prove to be mistaken and loss results as a
consequence.

    In most states, title insurance companies are free to use whatever
contract forms they choose. However, under pressure by large institutional lenders and by quasi-governmental corporations operating the
secondary mortgage market (Federal National Mortgage Association,
Federal Home Loan Mortgage Corporation, Government National
Mortgage Association) — all of whom need uniform national forms —
most title insurance companies today use uniform policy forms based
upon forms developed by the American Land Title Association. ALTA
has two basic forms of title insurance policies, a mortgagee's policy and
an owner's policy. The mortgagee's policy insures the mortgage lender
and not the homeowner. The homeowner who desires title insurance
must take out a separate owner's policy.

    Basically, title insurance guarantees that the insurance company has
searched the public records and insures against any defects in the public
records, unless such defects are specifically excepted from coverage in
the policy. The standard policy excludes losses arising from government
regulations affecting the use, occupancy, or enjoyment of land (for example, zoning ordinances, subdivision regulations, and building codes),
unless a notice of enforcement or violation is recorded in the public records. The standard policy also excludes claims of persons in possession
not shown by the public records, as well as unrecorded easements, implied easements (see pages 812-813), and easements arising by prescription (see pages 822-827). Standard policies also exclude defects that
would be revealed by a survey or inspection.

    Extended coverage, adding various kinds of protection, can be pur-
chased for an increased premium.

    The American Land Title Association's standard mortgage policy insuring the mortgage lender is substantially similar to the owner's policy. It varies principally in that it insures that the mortgage lien is valid, enforceable, and a first and prior lien against all other liens, including mechanics' liens. Almost all institutional lenders require title insurance (at the borrower's expense). Because all secondary-market purchasers of mortgages also require lender's title insurance, there has been an explosive growth of title insurance in the last 30 years.

Walker Rogge, Inc. v. Chelsea Title & Guaranty Co.
Supreme Court of New Jersey, 1989
116 N.J. 517, 562 A.2d 208

[Walker Rogge, Inc., acting through its president, John Rogge, purchased a tract of land from Alexander Kosa. Kosa had acquired the property from one Aiello. Before Rogge signed the contract of sale on December 12, 1979, Kosa showed him a 1975 survey by Price Walker. This survey indicated the tract consisted of 18.33 acres. The Kosa-Rogge contract described the land by reference to the Price Walker survey and indicated that quantity of land to be "19 acres more or less." It called for a price of $363,000, which was to be adjusted on the basis of $16,000 per acre "for deviations from the amount of 19 acres." (Because the tract included a house, the actual sale price was greater than the product of the number of acres times the price per acre.) Signed on December 12, 1979, the contract called for closing on December 31, with time of the essence.

Rogge requested that the title work be handled by Chelsea Title & Guaranty Co., which insures titles, examines titles, and conducts real estate closings. Chelsea had issued two prior title policies on the property. In the deed from Aiello to Kosa the property description, based on a survey done by one Schilling, stated that the property contained 12.486 acres. A copy of this deed was in Chelsea's files.

The deed from Kosa to Rogge described the property in accordance with the 1975 Price Walker survey, but the deed did not indicate the acreage of the tract. Similarly, the title commitment or binder issued by Chelsea before closing, as well as the title insurance policy, described the property by reference to the Price Walker survey, without indicating the total acreage of the property. No one can remember why a description based on the Price Walker survey, rather than the description in the Aiello-to-Kosa deed, was inserted in Chelsea's title commitment, Kosa's deed, and Chelsea's title insurance policy.]

POLLOCK, J. After the closing, Chelsea issued a title policy, which states that

SUBJECT TO THE EXCLUSIONS FROM COVERAGE, THE EXCEP-
TIONS CONTAINED IN SCHEDULE B AND THE PROVISIONS OF
THE CONDITIONS AND STIPULATIONS HEREOF,
Chelsea Title and Guaranty Company, a New Jersey corporation herein
called the Company, insures, as of Date of Policy shown in Schedule A [Jan-
uary 10, 1980], against loss or damage, not exceeding the amount of insurance stated in Schedule A [$363,000], and costs, attorneys' fees and expenses
which the Company may become obligated to pay hereunder, sustained or
incurred by the insured [Walker Rogge] by reason of:

1. Title in the estate or interest described in Schedule A being vested
    otherwise than as stated herein;
2. Any defect in or lien or encumbrance on such title;
3. Lack of a right of access to and from the land; or
4. Unmarketability of such title.

Repeating the identical exception in Schedule B of the title commitment, that schedule in the title policy states: "This policy does not insure
against loss or damage by reason of the following: . . . 3. Encroachments,
overlaps, boundary line disputes and other matters which could be disclosed by an accurate survey and inspection of the premises." . . .

Over the six years following the closing, Walker Rogge paid off the
purchase money mortgage, but did not obtain a more recent survey.
Then in 1985 Rogge sought to acquire lots adjacent to the property in
question preparatory to subdividing the entire property. In connection
with the subdivision, Rogge hired a new surveyor, Dennis Duffy, who
concluded after extensive field work, research, and title searching that
the property in question contained not 18.33 acres, as was stated in the
1975 Price Walker survey, but 12.43 acres, a quantity much closer to the
recital of 12.486 acres in the Aiello deed. . . .

On learning from Duffy that it had acquired only twelve acres,
Walker Rogge instituted the present action. In its complaint, Walker
Rogge alleged that the 5.5 acre shortage was an insurable loss under the
policy and that Chelsea was liable in negligence in failing to disclose documents in its files revealing that the property contained fewer than eighteen acres. . . . At the conclusion of the trial, the court determined that
the policy covered the shortage in acreage. The court found that title to
the property was not vested as described in the policy, that the shortage
constituted a defect in title, and that the title was unmarketable. Furthermore, the court found the survey exception "so vague as to be meaningless."

Although Chelsea had billed Walker Rogge $75 for a title exami-
nation, the court found that Rogge had ordered only a title policy, and
not a title search. Damages were computed by deducting the 12.5 acres
actually received, as determined by the Duffy survey, from the 18 acres
for which Rogge had paid. By multiplying 5.5 acres times the $16,000

per-acre purchase price, the court calculated that damages were $88,000. Costs and prejudgment interest were awarded, but counsel fees were denied.

The Appellate Division affirmed the judgment, but remanded the matter for clarification of the damages. 222 N.J. Super. 363, 536 A.2d 1309. . . .

As we have previously stated, "[a] title insurance policy is a contract of indemnity under which the insurer for a valuable consideration agrees to indemnify the insured in a specified amount against loss through defects of title to, or liens or encumbrances upon realty in which the insured has an interest." Sandler v. New Jersey Realty Title Ins. Co., 36 N.J. 471, 478-79, 178 A.2d 1 (1962). Like other policies of insurance, title policies are liberally construed against the insurer and in favor of the insured. Id. at 479, 178 A.2d 1. Notwithstanding that principle of construction, courts should not write for the insured a better policy of insurance than the one purchased. Last v. West Am. Ins. Co., 139 N.J. Super. 456, 460, 354 A.2d 364 (App. Div. 1976).

Real estate title insurance policies, like other aspects of the transfer of real estate, are unavoidably technical. That technicality counsels a prudent purchaser to consult qualified experts such as lawyers and surveyors. The reason is that the purchase of real estate, even something as commonplace as a single-family residence, is qualitatively different from the purchase of personal property such as furniture, automobiles, and securities. Lawyers, who are familiar with the technicalities and terminology of real estate law, are not only helpful but virtually essential for the protection of the rights of anyone purchasing real property. Every home buyer knows as much. Anyone who buys real estate without the aid of a surveyor runs the risk that he or she may not receive all the land for which he or she paid. In brief, title insurance is no substitute for a survey. . . .

In the absence of a recital of acreage, a title company does not insure the quantity of land. Title companies are in the business of guaranteeing title, not acreage. See Contini v. Western Title Ins. Co., 40 Cal. App. 3d 536, 542-43, 115 Cal. Rptr. 257, 260-61 (1974). To obtain such insurance, an insured should provide the title company with an acceptable survey that recites the quantity of land described or obtain from the company an express guaranty of the quantity of land insured in the policy.

Consistent with that premise, title insurance policies generally provide either that they are subject to such state of facts as an accurate survey would disclose or to the facts shown on an acceptable survey. Thus, one of the reasons that purchasers obtain surveys is to find out how much land they are buying. Another reason for obtaining a survey is to eliminate from the title policy the exception for such state of facts as an accurate survey would disclose. . . .

At the outset, we find that the survey exception is neither vague nor unenforceable. . . . Whatever else the phrase "other matters" might mean in a survey exception, it clearly refers to the dimensions of the lot lines and the size of the lot. The size of a tract simply cannot be ascertained with any certainty from a search of public records alone. The reason is that land exists on the ground, not on paper. When a description refers to a point in the line of another, only a survey can reveal the actual size of a piece of property and the amount of land included in a deed. A shortage in acreage is one of the facts that an accurate survey and inspection would disclose.

. . . The purpose of the survey exception is to exclude coverage when the insured fails to provide the insurer with a survey. 13A M. Lieberman, New Jersey Practice §1701 at 194 (3d ed. 1966). From a search of relevant public records, a title company cannot ascertain the risks that an accurate survey would disclose. It is for this reason that the title company puts that risk on the insured, who can control it either by obtaining a survey or arranging for the elimination of the survey exception. . . . Had plaintiff obtained a survey from Duffy before the Kosa closing, instead of waiting until it wanted to subdivide the property, it could have eliminated the risk of paying for property it did not receive. . . .

We now turn to plaintiff's negligence claim against Chelsea. In support of that claim, plaintiff points to Chelsea's separate charge for "title examination" and to its reliance on Chelsea to conduct a reasonable search. Courts and commentators, like the lower courts in this case, have divided on the question whether a title company should be exposed to liability in tort for negligence in searching records as well as to liability in contract under its policy of insurance.

The basic question is whether the issuance of the title commitment and policy places a duty on a title insurance company to search for and disclose to the insured any reasonably discoverable information that would affect the insured's decision to close the contract to purchase. In this state, the rule has been that a title company's liability is limited to the policy and that the company is not liable in tort for negligence in searching records. Underlying that rule is the premise that the duty of the title company, unlike the duty of a title searcher, does not depend on negligence, but on the agreement between the parties. . . . If, however, the title company agrees to conduct a search and provide the insured with an abstract of title in addition to the title policy, it may expose itself to liability for negligence as a title searcher in addition to its liability under the policy. Trenton Potteries Co. v. Title Guar. & Trust Co., 176 N.Y. 65, 68 N.E. 132, 135 (1903). In that regard, the trial court expressly found that

it is the conclusion of this court that plaintiff did not engage Chelsea to undertake two separate functions; that is, to prepare a title report, then a policy of title insurance. The title search which was completed by Chelsea was simply an internal procedure for Chelsea's own purposes in deciding whether or not to issue a title policy. Even though plaintiff was billed for the title search, it is the conclusion of this court that the real transaction between the parties was a policy of insurance. This conclusion means that plaintiff's remedy against Chelsea lies in contract, not in negligence. Consequently, the negligence charges against Chelsea are dismissed.

Notwithstanding Chelsea's separate $75 charge for "title examination," the trial court's finding is supported by substantial credible evidence in the record. Rova Farms Resort v. Investors Ins. Co., 65 N.J. 474, 484, 323 A.2d 495 (1974). Chelsea conducted the search in conjunction with its obligation to issue the title commitment and policy. It did not prepare a separate abstract of title for plaintiff, but made the search for its own benefit.

Some out-of-state courts and commentators favor the view that a title company should be liable in tort as well as contract if it negligently fails to discover and disclose information that would be of interest to the insured. The underlying notion is that the insured has the reasonable expectation that the title company will search the title. 9 J. Appleman, Insurance Law and Practice §5212 at 72 (1981); see Note, Title Insurance: The Duty to Search, 71 Yale L.J. 1161, 1171 (1962). . . .

Other courts have acknowledged in dictum a title company's obligation to make a reasonable search. Those courts have been reluctant, however, to impose on the title companies a duty in tort. For example, in L. Smirlock Realty Corp. v. Title Guar. Co., 52 N.Y.2d 179, 437 N.Y. S.2d 57, 418 N.E.2d 650 (1981), the New York Court of Appeals . . . carefully pointed out that the basis for the imposition of liability on the company was the title policy, and the court was not reaching the question whether the company was liable in negligence. Id. 418 N.E.2d at 652. Similarly, the Illinois Appellate Court in a suit on the policy has stated that an "insurer has a duty to search the records and examine the applicable law before issuing its commitment or policy." McLaughlin v. Attorneys' Title Guar. Fund, 61 Ill. App. 3d 911, 916, 18 Ill. Dec. 891, 895, 378 N.E.2d 355, 359 (Ill. App. Ct. 1978). Although an intermediate court in Washington found a duty to search and disclose that arose by implication from the nature of the policy, Shotwell v. Transamerica Title Ins. Co., 16 Wash. App. 627, 631, 558 P.2d 1359, 1361 (1976), on appeal the Washington Supreme Court expressly reserved the question of the existence of such a duty. 91 Wash. 2d 161, 165-66, 588 P.2d 208, 211 (1978).

At one time the California courts adopted the view that a title company was subject to liability in tort similar to that of a title abstractor. Jarchow v. Transamerica Title Ins., 48 Cal. App. 3d 917, 122 Cal. Rptr. 470 (1975). In 1982, however, the California Legislature extinguished this cause of action by passing a statute that expressly stated that title commitments are not abstracts of title and that the issuance of a title commitment does not give rise to the same duties as are incurred when a company issues such an abstract. Cal. Insurance Code §12340.11 (West 1988). More recently, the California courts have distinguished title commitments from an abstract of title by stating that a title commitment "generally constitutes no more than a statement of the terms and conditions upon which the insurer is willing to issue its title policy [and] liability for negligence based upon the [title commitment] in addition to liability under the policy does not seem supportable." Lawrence v. Chicago Title Ins. Co., 192 Cal. App. 3d 70, 76, 237 Cal. Rptr. 264, 268 (1987). . . .

Similarly, the Supreme Court of New Mexico has refused to hold a title company liable when it failed to discover a recorded adverse claim. The court held that "[d]efendant clearly had no duty under the policy to search the records, and any search it may have actually undertaken, was undertaken solely for its own protection as indemnitor against losses covered by its policy." Horn v. Lawyers Title Ins. Co., 89 N.M. 709, 711, 557 P.2d 206, 208 (1976).

The Texas Court of Appeals has reached a similar result. As that court recently stated, "[t]he title insurance company is not, as is an abstract company, employed to examine title; rather, the title insurance company is employed to guarantee the status of title and to insure against existing defects. Thus, the relationship between the parties is limited to that of indemnitor and indemnitee." Houston Title Co. v. Ojeda de Toca, 733 S.W.2d 325, 327 (1978). . . .

Although we recognize that an insured expects that a title company will conduct a reasonable title examination, the relationship between the company and the insured is essentially contractual. See Spring Motors Distribs., Inc. v. Ford Motor Co., 98 N.J. 555, 579-80, 489 A.2d 660 (1985). The end result of the relationship between the title company and the insured is the issuance of the policy. . . .

From this perspective, the insured expects that in consideration for payment of the premium, it will receive a policy of insurance. The insurer's expectation is that in exchange for that premium it will insure against certain risks subject to the terms of the policy. If the title company fails to conduct a reasonable title examination or, having conducted such an examination, fails to disclose the results to the insured, then it runs the risk of liability under the policy. In many, if not most, cases conduct that would constitute the failure to make a reasonable title search would also result in a breach of the terms of the policy.

The expectation of the insured that the insurer will conduct a reasonable search does not necessarily mean that the insurer may not limit its liability in the title commitment and policy. If the company may not so limit its liability, then it would be exposed to consequential damages resulting from its negligence. Under general contract principles, however, consequential damages are not recoverable unless they were within the specific contemplation of the parties. Donovan v. Backstadt, 91 N.J. 434, 444-45, 453 A.2d 160 (1982). Another difference is that in an action under the title policy, the insured may establish a cause of action for breach of contract without establishing that the title company breached the standard of care appropriate for a reasonable title search. In an action in tort for the failure to conduct such a search, the insured would be required to establish the appropriate standard of care applicable to title searching.

Both Chelsea and amicus, New Jersey Land Title Association, recognize that negligence principles provide an alternative basis for imposing liability on Chelsea. Notwithstanding the essentially contractual nature of the relationship between a title company and its insured, the company could be subject to a negligence action if the "act complained of was the direct result of duties voluntarily assumed by the insurer in addition to the mere contract to insure title." Brown's Tie and Lumber v. Chicago Title, 115 Idaho 56, 59, 764 P.2d 423, 426 (1988). As support for its negligence claim against Chelsea, Walker Rogge points to various facts. For example, Chelsea had twice insured the property in question and on four other occasions it had opened files on the property. In addition, Chelsea's own back title plant reflected that the tract comprised twelve, not eighteen, acres. One of Chelsea's employees, moreover, supervised the closing, at which time the purchase price was computed on that basis. Because it restricted plaintiff's claim to the policy, the trial court did not determine whether Chelsea knew or should have known of the difference in acreage and of its materiality to the transaction. The court did not, therefore, determine whether Chelsea assumed an independent duty to assure the quantity of acreage, whether it breached that duty, or whether the breach caused any damage to Walker Rogge. Consequently, we are obliged to remand the matter to the trial court for a determination of those issues. In remanding, we do not decide whether Chelsea was obligated to bring the difference in acreage to the attention of its insured under an implied duty of fair dealing. That issue has played no role at the trial or appellate level. We leave to the discretion of the trial court whether the matter should be resolved on the present record or should be supplemented by additional testimony. . . .

The judgment of the Appellate Division is affirmed in part, reversed in part, and, as modified, the matter is remanded to the Law Division.

NOTES AND QUESTIONS

1. See Note, Title Insurance: The Duty to Search, 71 Yale L.J. 1161, 1164-1165 (1962):

The combination of search and insurance exists today in a variety of forms. The majority of title insurers operate as "title-plant" companies, maintaining duplicates of the public records and carrying out their own independent searches. This form of organization displaces the ordinary practitioners from the title examination process and substitutes the insurance policy for the lawyer's opinion. A second form of company, typified by the Lawyers' Title Guaranty Fund, issues what have been called "lawyer-title policies." Such policies are issued on the basis of applications from lawyers who have performed the traditional search rather than on the basis of independent investigations of title by the company itself. A third form of company, very similar to the second, insures title on the basis of an abstract furnished by an approved abstract company. "Title-plant companies" adopt both the second and third forms of organization in extending their business into geographic areas in which they do not have title plants. Still another organizational form appears to be developing: there are reports of title insurers who issue policies on the basis of little or no preliminary title search. This development reflects the ultimate in the casualty or actuarial approach.

See also D. Barlow Burke, Jr., Law of Title Insurance §§12.1-12.6 (1986) (title insurer's liability as an abstractor); Joyce D. Palomar, Title Insurance Companies' Liability for Failure to Search Title and Disclose Record Title, 20 Creighton L. Rev. 455 (1987).

In the *Walker Rogge* case, if a lawyer had been hired by Rogge to search title, would the lawyer be liable for not reporting to Rogge the discrepancy in acreage between that described in the Aiello-to-Kosa deed and that called for in the Kosa-Rogge contract?

2. In Crawford v. Safeco Title Ins. Co., 585 So. 2d 952 (Fla. App. 1991), the court held that the title insurance company was liable to the insured for failing to disclose a neighbor's boundary dispute claim on record and known to the company, even though claims arising from boundary disputes were excepted from coverage under the policy.

In Bank of California v. First American Title Ins. Co., 826 P.2d 1126 (Alaska 1992), the court allowed a suit by a bank relying on a preliminary title report stating that the seller had exclusive ownership when in fact he was a cotenant. It invalidated an exculpatory clause against negligence because title insurance is a "business affected with the public interest" and the insurance company "cannot, by an adhesory contract, exculpate itself from liability for negligence."

3. Does a grantee have less or more protection of his title under the standard title insurance policy than under a general warranty deed? See Jerome J. Curtis, Jr., Title Assurance in Sales of California Residential Realty: A Critique of Title Insurance and Title Covenants with Suggested Reforms, 7 Pac. L.J. 1 (1976); Quintin Johnstone, Title Insurance, 66 Yale L.J. 492 (1957).

One advantage title insurance has over general warranty deeds is that the title insurance company agrees to defend at its expense all litigation against the insured based upon a defect insured against in the policy. Moreover, eviction is not a prerequisite for a suit on an insurance policy, as it is to a suit for breach of a covenant of general warranty.

> By the terms of the policy the company does more than agree to warrant and defend the insured against anyone claiming adverse title. The policy contract begins by saying in emphatic type: "The Southern Title Guaranty Co., Inc. . . . [d]oes hereby guarantee to Vincent Prendergast and wife, Leola Prendergast . . . that they have good and indefeasible title to the following described real property. . . ." This is the basic assurance of the contract, and a failure of that guarantee gives rise to a cause of action for damages. It would be a substantial reduction of that assurance to make the insured bear his detriment until the owner of the superior title is found and sued to judgment; the policy will not be given that effect in the absence of language more explicit than the provision advanced by the company and quoted above. [Southern Title Guaranty Co., Inc. v. Prendergast, 494 S.W.2d 154, 156 (Tex. 1974).]

The measure of damages for breach of a title insurance contract is ordinarily analogized to the measures of damages for breaches of covenants of seisin and against encumbrances (see pages 641-642). If title fails, the insured receives the consideration paid. If the breach is by an encumbrance, the insured receives the difference in value of the property with the encumbrance and without the encumbrance. See L. Smirlock Realty Corp. v. Title Guarantee Co., 97 A.D.2d 208, 469 N.Y.S.2d 415 (1983) (rejecting analogy and holding that insured may recover for loss of bargain rather than consideration paid).

4. Suppose that a person buys a house that is partially located on a neighbor's lot. Is this defect covered by a title insurance policy? See Transamerica Title Ins. Co. v. Northwest Bldg. Corp., 54 Wash. App. 289, 773 P.2d 431 (1989): "To hold that Transamerica's title insurance coverage extends beyond the policy's specifically defined property boundaries would effectively eliminate any way of conclusively defining the reach of the insurance policy's protection. The title insurer would be exposed to potentially limitless liability in its policy." 54 Wash. App. at 293, 773 P.2d at 433. Would it be covered by covenants of title? See Commonwealth Land Title Ins. Co. v. Stephenson, 101 N.C. App. 379, 399 S.E.2d 380 (1991), discussed at page 641.

5. Suppose that in Brown v. Lober, page 632, where the purchasers received only one-third of the mineral rights, the purchasers had taken out a title insurance policy. Would the title insurance company be liable? Suppose that Paradise, the buyer in Harper v. Paradise, page 745, had purchased a title insurance policy. Would he have been protected against the old deed found in the trunk in the attic?

Lick Mill Creek Apartments v. Chicago Title Insurance Co.

Court of Appeal of California, Sixth District, 1991
231 Cal. App. 3d 1654, 283 Cal. Rptr. 231

AGLIANO, P.J. Plaintiffs Lick Mill Creek Apartments and Prometheus Development Company, Inc., appeal from a judgment of dismissal entered after the trial court sustained, without leave to amend, the demurrer of defendants Chicago Title Insurance Company and First American Title Insurance Company to plaintiffs' first amended complaint. The trial court determined, based on undisputed facts alleged in the complaint, that title insurance policies issued by defendants did not provide coverage for the costs of removing hazardous substances from plaintiffs' property. For the reasons stated below, we conclude the trial court's ruling was correct and affirm the judgment. . . .

The real property which is the subject of this case comprises approximately 30 acres of land near the Guadalupe River in Santa Clara County. Prior to 1979, various corporations operated warehouses and/ or chemical processing plants on the property. Incident to this use of the property, the companies maintained underground tanks, pumps, and pipelines for the storage, handling, and disposal of various hazardous substances. These hazardous substances eventually contaminated the soil, subsoil, and groundwater.

In 1979, Kimball Small Investments 103 (KSI) purchased the property. Between 1979 and 1981, the California Department of Health Services ordered KSI to remedy the toxic contamination of the property. KSI, however, did not comply with this order.

In early October 1986, plaintiffs acquired lot 1 of the property from KSI. In connection with this acquisition, plaintiffs purchased title insurance from Chicago Title Insurance Company (Chicago Title). The insurance policy issued was of the type known as an American Land Title Insurance Association (ALTA) policy (policy 1). Prior to issuing this policy, Chicago Title commissioned a survey and inspection of the property by Carroll Resources Engineering & Management (Carroll Resources).

Plaintiffs subsequently purchased lots 2 and 3 from KSI and secured two additional ALTA policies (policies 2 and 3) from Chicago Title and First American Title Insurance Company (First American). The entire site was surveyed and inspected. During its survey and inspection, Carroll Resources noted the presence of certain pipes, tanks, pumps, and other improvements on the property. At the time each of the policies was issued, the Department of Health Services, the Regional Water Quality Control Board, and the Santa Clara County Environmental Health Department maintained records disclosing the presence of hazardous substances on the subject property.

Following their purchase of the property, plaintiffs incurred costs for removal and clean-up of the hazardous substances in order "to mitigate plaintiffs' damages and avoid costs of compliance with government mandate." Then, claiming their expenses were a substitute, i.e., a payment made under threat of compulsion of law, for restitution to the State Hazardous Substance Account (Health & Saf. Code, §25300 et seq.) and "response costs" as defined under the Comprehensive Environmental Response, Compensation, and Liability Act (CERCLA) (42 U.S.C. §9601 et seq.), plaintiffs sought indemnity from defendants for the sums expended in their cleanup efforts. Defendants, however, denied coverage.

Discussion . . .

Here the insuring clauses of policies 1, 2, and 3 are identical and provide the following: "SUBJECT TO THE EXCLUSIONS FROM COVERAGE, THE EXCEPTIONS CONTAINED IN SCHEDULE B AND THE PROVISIONS OF THE CONDITIONS AND STIPULATIONS HEREOF [THE INSURER] INSURES, AS OF DATE OF POLICY SHOWN IN SCHEDULE A, AGAINST LOSS OR DAMAGE, NOT EXCEEDING THE AMOUNT OF INSURANCE STATED IN SCHEDULE A, AND COSTS, ATTORNEYS' FEES AND EXPENSES WHICH THE COMPANY MAY BECOME OBLIGATED TO PAY HEREUNDER, SUSTAINED OR INCURRED BY THE INSURED BY REASON OF: [¶] (1) TITLE TO THE ESTATE OR INTEREST DESCRIBED IN SCHEDULE A BEING VESTED OTHERWISE THAN AS STATED THEREIN; [¶] (2) ANY DEFECT IN OR LIEN OR ENCUMBRANCE ON SUCH TITLE; [¶] (3) LACK OF A RIGHT OF ACCESS TO AND FROM THE LAND; OR [¶] (4) UNMARKETABILITY OF SUCH TITLE."

Marketability of Title

Plaintiffs first contend the policies in the instant case expressly insured that title to the subject property was marketable and, since the presence of hazardous substances on the property impaired its marketability, defendants were obliged to pay cleanup costs. Plaintiffs' position, however, is dependent upon their view that California courts have adopted a definition of marketable title that encompasses the property's market value. Our review of relevant authority establishes no support for this position. . . .

The case of Hocking v. Title Ins. & Trust Co. (1951) 37 Cal. 2d 644 [234 P.2d 625, 40 A.L.R.2d 1238], . . . illustrates the distinction between marketability of title and marketability of the land. In *Hocking*, the plaintiff purchased unimproved property and received a grant deed, describing it as two lots in a particular block according to a recorded subdivision map. However, because the subdivider had not complied with various local ordinances regarding subdivision of land, the city would not issue building permits until the plaintiff complied with the ordinances. The plaintiff sought damages from the title insurer claiming defective title.

The *Hocking* court noted the distinction between the land and its title: "It is defendants' position that plaintiff confuses title with physical condition of the property she purchased and of the adjacent streets, and that 'One can hold perfect title to land that is valueless; one can have marketable title to land while the land itself is unmarketable.' The truth of this proposition would appear elementary. It appears to be the condition of her *land* in respect to improvements related thereto (graded and paved streets), rather than the condition of her *title* to the land, which is different from what she expected to get." (37 Cal. 2d at p.651; italics in original.) Thus, the court held that the owner's inability to make economic use of the land due to the subdivider's violations of law did not render the title defective or unmarketable within the terms of the title insurance policy. "Although it is unfortunate that plaintiff has been unable to use her lots for the building purposes she contemplated, it is our view that the facts which she pleads do not affect the marketability of her *title* to the land, but merely impair the market *value* of the property. She appears to possess fee simple title to the property for whatever it may be worth; if she has been damaged by false representations in respect to the condition and value of the land her remedy would seem to be against others than the insurers of the title she acquired." (37 Cal. 2d at p.652, italics in original.) Similarly, here plaintiffs have pled facts relating to marketability of the land rather than marketability of title.

Other jurisdictions have also recognized the distinction. In Chicago Title Ins. Co. v. Kumar (1987) 24 Mass. App. 53 [506 N.E.2d 154, 156], the defendant had purchased property on which hazardous substances were discovered. The defendant sought payment for cleanup costs from its title insurer. (Ibid.) The insurer sought a declaration as to its obligations under the policy. The defendant owner filed a counterclaim, seeking a declaration that the presence of hazardous substances constituted a defect in title and the state's statutory power to impose a lien to secure payment of cleanup costs rendered his title unmarketable. (Ibid.) Relying on Hocking v. Title Ins. & Trust Co., supra, 37 Cal. 2d 644, 651, the court found in favor of the insurer, stating "the defendant confuses economic lack of marketability, which relates to physical conditions affecting the use of the property, with title marketability, which relates to defects affecting legally recognized rights and incidents of ownership. . . . The presence of hazardous material may affect the market value of the defendant's land, but, on the present record [since no lien had been recorded], it does not affect the title to the land." (506 N.E.2d at p.157.)[29] . . .

_____

29. Plaintiffs did not purchase an environmental protection endorsement (ALTA form 8.1 policy).

We find no ambiguity in the insuring clause: defendants are obligated to insure plaintiffs against unmarketability of title on the subject property. Because marketability of title and the market value of the land itself are separate and distinct, plaintiffs cannot claim coverage for the property's physical condition under this clause of the insurance policies.

Encumbrance on Title

The policies in question insure plaintiffs against "any defect in or lien or encumbrance" on title. Although no lien had been recorded or asserted at the time the title insurance policies were issued, plaintiffs contend the presence of hazardous substances on the property constituted an encumbrance on title.

Encumbrances are defined by statute as "taxes, assessments, and all liens upon real property." (Civ. Code, §1114.) Where a property is contaminated with hazardous substances, a subsequent owner of the property may be held fully responsible for the financial costs of cleaning up the contamination. (42 U.S.C. §9607(a); Health & Saf. Code, §§25323.5, 25363.) A lien may also be imposed on the property to cover such cleanup costs. (42 U.S.C. §9607(*l*).) Plaintiffs reason that because any transfer of contaminated land carries with it the responsibility for cleanup costs, liability for such costs constitutes an "encumbrance on title" and is covered. We disagree.

In United States v. Allied Chemical Corp. (N.D. Cal. 1984) 587 F. Supp. 1205, the plaintiff alleged a breach of warranty that property conveyed was free of encumbrance where hazardous substances were present on the property at the time it was conveyed. The court dismissed the plaintiff's cause of action, stating: "Plaintiff argues that the term 'encumbrance' is broad enough to include the presence of hazardous substances. However, the only authorities cited have interpreted 'encumbrance' to include only liens, easements, restrictive covenants and other such interests in or rights to the land held by third persons. (See Evans v. Faught, 231 Cal. App. 2d 698, 706. . . .) Plaintiff has given no authority establishing its broad argument that any physical condition, including the presence of hazardous substances, is an 'encumbrance' if 'not visible or known' at the time of conveyance. The court declines to interpret 'encumbrance' as broadly as plaintiff urges. The court finds that, under current law, the term 'encumbrance' does not extend to the presence of hazardous substances alleged in this case." (Id. at p.1206.) (Accord Cameron v. Martin Marietta Corp. (E.D.N.C. 1990) 729 F. Supp. 1529, 1532.)

In Chicago Title Ins. Co. v. Kumar, supra, 506 N.E.2d 154, the court also held that the presence of hazardous substances on the land at the time title was conveyed did not constitute an encumbrance. "The mere possibility that the Commonwealth may attach a future lien . . . , as a result of the release of hazardous material (existing but unknown at the time a title insurance policy is issued) when the Commonwealth has neither expended moneys on the property requiring reimbursement nor recorded the necessary statement of claim, is insufficient to create a 'defect in or lien or encumbrance on . . . title.' " (Id. at p.156.)

In South Shore Bank v. Stewart Title Guar. Co. (D. Mass. 1988) 688 F. Supp. 803, the plaintiff sought a declaration that the title insurance company was liable for the cleanup costs related to hazardous substances on the property where there was no recorded lien at the time the policy was issued. The court held as a matter of law there was no coverage under the policy, stating "[p]laintiff has neither alleged nor offered any facts to show a defect in title. Hence, it has no cause of action against [the title insurer]." (Id. at p.806.)

In Holmes v. Alabama Title Co., Inc. (Ala. 1987) 507 So. 2d 922, the landowners' parcels contained an abandoned coal mine. Surface fractures began to appear, indicating that methane gas might eventually escape. The landowners brought suit against their title insurers and others. The reviewing court found in favor of the insurers, reasoning: "The purpose of title insurance is not to protect the insured against loss arising from physical damage to property; rather, it is to protect the insured against defects in the title." (Id. at p.925.) (Accord Title & Trust Co. of Florida v. Barrows (Fla. Dist. Ct. App. 1979) 381 So. 2d 1088, 1090; Mafetone v. Forest Manor Homes, Inc. (1970) 34 A.D.2d 566 [310 N.Y.S.2d 17, 18]; Edwards v. St. Paul Title Ins. Co. (1977) 39 Colo. App. 235 [563 P.2d 979, 980].) . . .

Exclusions in Policies 1 and 3

Plaintiffs contend the governmental regulation and police power exclusions included in policies 1 and 3 are inapplicable.[30] We need not decide this question, since we have found no coverage under the identical insuring clauses of each policy. . . .

As previously discussed, the language of the insuring clauses of all three policies unambiguously provides coverage only for defects relating to title. These clauses make no reference to the physical condition of the land. . . .

Disposition

The judgment is affirmed.

30. Policies 1 and 3 contain exclusions from coverage as follows: "Any law, ordinance or governmental regulation (including but not limited to building and zoning ordinances) restricting or regulating or prohibiting the occupancy, use or enjoyment of the land, or regulating the character, dimensions or location of any improvement now or hereafter erected on the land, or prohibiting a separation in ownership or a reduction in the dimensions or area of the land, or the effect of any violation of any such law, ordinance or

Radovanov v. Land Title Co. of America

Appellate Court of Illinois, First District, 1989
189 Ill. App. 3d 433, 545 N.E.2d 351

[The Radovanovs purchased an 88-unit apartment hotel in Chicago. Before the closing, the sellers informed the Radovanovs that they had received notice of building code violations. The parties agreed that these problems would be corrected before the sale was completed. At closing, the Radovanovs were assured that the building code violations had been resolved. Unknown to the Radovanovs, a lawsuit was pending involving a violation of the housing code.

Land Title Co. issued title insurance to the Radovanovs, but it did not disclose the pending lawsuit. However, the policy, in Exclusion 1, denied coverage for building ordinances and the effects of their violations. Nine months after the sale, the Radovanovs found out about the pending litigation, which alleged numerous violations and sought demolition or the appointment of a receiver for the building.

The Radovanovs brought suit to recover damages that resulted from the failure to disclose the existence of the pending lawsuit or to provide coverage for the resulting financial loss. The trial court ruled for Land Title Co. The Radovanovs appealed.]

Rizzi, J. On appeal, the Radovanovs argue that the trial court erred in ruling that the terms of the Title Insurance Companies' commitment and policy excluded coverage for damages incurred as a result of building code violation litigation which preexisted the date of the title insurance commitment and policy. We agree. . . .

In the present case, the Title Insurance Companies contracted to provide the Radovanovs insurance coverage for damages resulting from the "unmarketability" of their title. Since a housing code violation lawsuit clearly renders a title unmarketable, in the absence of an applicable exclusion, the Title Insurance Companies are obligated to provide coverage for damages caused by the pending lawsuit which predated the issuance of the title commitment and policy.

Next, we address the Title Insurance Companies' contention that insurance coverage was properly denied because under Exclusion 1 of the Policy, building ordinances and the effects of violations of building ordinances are not covered.

The purpose of title insurance is to protect a purchaser of real estate against title surprises. Pohrer v. Title Insurance Co. of Minnesota (N.D. Ill. 1987), 652 F. Supp. 348, 352. A prospective purchaser of real estate

---

governmental regulation." The police power exclusion states as follows: "Rights of eminent domain or governmental rights of police power unless notice of the exercise of such rights appears in the public records at Date of Policy."

relies on the title insurer's search when they decide whether or not to purchase the property. Thus, they expect the insurer to have (1) researched the applicable law, as well as the records, before issuing the commitment and (2) to provide warnings about areas in which they might find surprises. Pohrer, 652 F. Supp. 348 at 353. Moreover, when a person finalizes a real estate transaction and purchases title insurance, they expect to obtain a professional title search, legal opinion on the condition of title and a guarantee. McLaughlin v. Attorneys' Title Guaranty Fund, Inc. (1978), 61 Ill. App. 3d 911, 916, 18 Ill. Dec. 891, 895, 378 N.E.2d 355, 359. . . .

In the present case, the Title Insurance Companies urge us to construe the phrase "the effects of violations of building ordinances" in Exclusion 1 of the Policy to include building code violation litigation which was pending when the title insurance commitment and policy issued. This construction would relieve the Title Insurance Companies from any responsibility for failure to disclose many types of litigation which impair the marketability of title. Such a construction is in direct conflict with the Title Insurance Companies guarantee to insure against loss or damage sustained due to unmarketability of title. In this context, the conflict renders the phrase "the effects of violations of building ordinances" ambiguous. The purpose of title insurance would be defeated by an adoption of the statutory interpretation urged by the Title Insurance Companies. Disclosure of title surprises such as a pending lawsuit which seeks to demolish or place into receivership a parcel of real estate is just the sort of problem that a title insurance purchaser seeks to discover and/or insure against. Because ambiguities in an insurance policy are to be construed in favor of the insured, and forfeitures are disfavored, we find that Exclusion 1 of the Policy does not exclude from coverage damages caused by a housing code violation lawsuit which existed prior to issuance of the title commitment and policy. . . .

Accordingly, the judgment of the circuit court is reversed and this cause remanded for a new trial.

NOTE

In Houston Title Co. v. Ojeda de Toca, 733 S.W.2d 325 (Tex. Civ. App. 1987), the City of Houston had placed an order on a house, which had burned, authorizing the city to demolish the building and put a lien on the property for demolition costs. The order was filed for record. Thereafter Ojeda de Toca, of Mexico City, purchased the house to remodel it to live in on her trips from Mexico City. Ojeda de Toca bought a title insurance policy from the defendant, which failed to mention the order authorizing demolition. Immediately after closing, Ojeda de Toca parked her car in the garage of the house and returned to Mexico.

When she returned, she found the City of Houston had demolished the house, leaving only her car in the garage, and had placed a lien on the property for demolition costs. Ojeda de Toca sued the title insurance company for negligence in not disclosing the demolition order. The court held for the title insurer, saying it was under no duty to point out to the insured any outstanding incumbrance.

Ojeda de Toca also sued her seller for fraudulent failure to disclose the city's order. The seller argued that since the order was on record, providing constructive notice to buyers, the seller had no duty to disclose. The Supreme Court of Texas held that imputed notice under the recording statutes is not a defense to a deceptive trade practices action. Ojeda de Toca v. Wise, 748 S.W.2d 449 (Tex. 1988).

V
Control of Land Use through "Private" and "Public" Means

In Chapter 1 (see page 49) we introduced the concept of "externalities"; since then, we have considered the relevance of the concept in a number of settings. It takes only a moment's reflection to see that the presence of external costs and benefits becomes especially important to understanding the role of property institutions in controlling conflicting uses of land — the concern of this part. As the examples in Chapter 1's introduction should have suggested, land-use activities present the paradigm case of externalities, and much of the law to be studied now — the law of "private" and "public" land-use controls — can be examined usefully as responses to this central fact. But there is more to the subject than just that, and economic considerations should not provide the only perspective. History, a sense of changing times and attitudes, is especially important to understanding many of the major developments in land use. So, too, is politics, especially with regard to zoning and other "public" devices. Finally, some of the nicest (which is to say, perhaps, least tractable) issues presented in the following chapters involve fundamental questions of distributional justice and basic fairness.

In the title to this part, and in the paragraph above, we have placed "private" and "public" in quotation marks to indicate that while these labels have some categorical virtues, they are also a bit misleading, because all land-use controls contain a mix of private and public elements. It remains the fact, however, that the mixture varies across a broad continuum, characterized by essentially decentralized and voluntary arrangements on the one extreme (private), and rather highly centralized, bureaucratic, mandatory regulations on the other (public).

The materials that follow work through the continuum, beginning with the most private of land-use controls (servitudes, Chapter 9), moving next to the middle (nuisance, Chapter 10), and concluding with the most public (zoning, Chapter 11, and the related topics of eminent domain and the law of "takings," Chapter 12).

9

Private Land-Use Arrangements: A Comparative Study of Servitudes

In this chapter we study land-use arrangements arising out of private agreements. Usually, but not always, the agreements involve two or more parcels of land and the purpose of the agreements is to increase the total value of all the parcels involved. And usually, but not always, the effect of the agreements is to burden one parcel of land for the benefit of another parcel. For example, the owner of Tract 1 may have an easement to cross Tract 2 to reach a public road. Burdens and benefits are often reciprocal, as where all lots in a subdivision are restricted to residential use. These agreements create interests in land, binding and benefiting not only the parties to the agreement in question but also their successors. These interests are commonly called, as a class, servitudes.

Modern servitudes can be divided into two major types: easements and covenants.[1] Covenants can be further divided into covenants enforceable at law (real covenants) and covenants enforceable in equity (equitable servitudes). Each of these forms evolved more or less in historical succession, one after the other. When easements were hedged in during the Industrial Revolution by judges who regarded them as interfering with marketability, landowners sought enforcement in the law courts of promissory agreements (covenants) against successors to the promisor's land. But the law courts, ever jealous of fetters on land, threw up roadblocks against these "covenants running with the land." Finally, turning to equity, landowners found a more sympathetic ear. The chancellor began to enforce restrictive covenants, which came to be known as equitable servitudes. The law of servitudes thus is a study of how the tides of urbanization, and the demands of the market for efficient control of externalities, swept around the artificial barriers limiting one form of servitude and forced courts to recognize and develop other forms.

---

1. There are also two minor types: profits and licenses, both very much like easements in form, but not — as we shall see — always treated in the same fashion.

Although land-use agreements can deal with a wide variety of matters, the rights they create can generally be categorized functionally into five types:

1. *A* is given the right to enter upon *B*'s land;
2. *A* is given the right to enter upon *B*'s land and remove something attached to the land;
3. *A* is given the right to enforce a restriction on the use of *B*'s land;
4. *A* is given the right to require *B* to perform some act on *B*'s land; and
5. *A* is given the right to require *B* to pay money for the upkeep of specified facilities.

A's right in example 1 is an easement. *A*'s right in example 2 is a profit. *A*'s right in each of the other examples usually originates in a promise by *B* (or *B*'s predecessor), and the promise may be enforceable either in law as a real covenant or in equity as an equitable servitude.

A. Easements

1. Historical Background

In this chapter we put great emphasis on how and why the law of servitudes developed as it did, because we believe it is far easier to understand this rather disorderly law from the perspective of history than as a logical system. In the medieval period, manorial and village land was cultivated throughout most of England using a common field system. Arable land was divided into strips, and each tenant would be assigned possession — originally by the lord of the manor or by the village inhabitants in council — of a number of scattered, noncontiguous strips. To be fair, the allocation consisted of a little bit of the good land, a little bit of the bad, and a little bit of the middling. Communal decisions were made as to what crops were to be planted and what strips were to lie fallow in order to restore fertility. Attached to each tenant's holding were certain common rights, for instance, the right to pasture cattle after the crop was cut. Bordering the arable land was wasteland, in which were additional common rights. These rights gave to members of the community *profits à prendre* — rights, as the old French phrase indicates, to take off the land things that were thought of as "part" of the land (for example, timber, minerals, wild game, and fish). Profits were the common wealth.

"This system of agriculture," the English historian Holdsworth wrote:

came to appear more and more anomalous with the lapse of time. It was impossible to do anything without the consent of a large number of persons who were not likely to agree; and any attempts to carry through improvements were met by the decided opposition of what was in those days the most ignorant and conservative class in the community. We are not surprised, therefore, to hear that it was denounced by all writers on agriculture from the sixteenth to the nineteenth century. . . . [B]ut, though some enclosures took place in the sixteenth and seventeenth centuries, large masses of land remained unenclosed — it was so common in the seventeenth century that it was transplanted by the early colonists to New England. One reason for its long life was no doubt the fact that the attempt to alter the existing common-field system was often combined with the extensive enclosure of common land, which reasonably enough roused much popular feeling. [2 William S. Holdsworth, History of English Law 60 (4th ed. 1927).]

For a number of reasons, the common field system began to break apart during the reign of the Tudors.[2] With the growth in population and prosperity in the sixteenth century, the price of wool — commonly used for clothing — began to rise. Many landowners gave up cultivation and turned to sheep farming, with gradual dispossession of the commoners and the small farmers who lived on the produce of the strips. Some enterprising farmers wanted to experiment with new agricultural techniques to produce better and more crops. Others wanted to breed cattle selectively to increase the output of dairy produce, and this required enclosures to control access to the cows. (Selective breeding led eventually to the fine, glossy-coated herds, with extended udders, seen grazing today on the English countryside — beasts very different from the angular medieval cows.) The manorial economy had broken down. The better farmers aimed to meet the demands of the market, not the needs of a great household and the local villagers. As population grew and the price of foodstuffs increased, so did the demand for enclosure of land in separately owned tracts, thereby withdrawing some portion of open fields or wasteland from use in common.

In the sixteenth century enclosures began with small cultivators rearranging their holdings by bargaining among themselves. The movement picked up speed, ultimately catastrophic to the rural peasantry forced off the lands, when the lords of the manors began leasing the demesne lands of the manors to large farmers, evicting the customary tenants at the end of their leases and breaking up the village community. In the eighteenth century, privately sponsored acts of Parliament authorized specific enclosures when individual bargaining among those concerned failed.

Common fields and shared pastures gave way to fenced fields and consolidated farms amidst considerable outcry and social disorder, for a

2. See Richard H. Tawney, The Agrarian Problem in the Sixteenth Century (1912).

large share of the peasantry forced off the land drifted into the cities. Nonetheless, the enclosure movement proved irresistible in England as well as throughout Western Europe. By 1820 the transformation to closed fields was nearly complete in England; the only commons left were small patches of green in the middle of villages. And by that date England was well into the Industrial Revolution, which during the 70 years from 1770 to 1840 brought about the rapid growth of towns and completely altered the lives of erstwhile countryfolk.[3]

The typical modern forms of servitudes — easements, real covenants, and equitable servitudes — are products of the nineteenth century. In the days of common fields there was little need for defining rights of way; people wandered where they wished through the unfenced countryside, causing little injury. But enclosures pushed the law of *profits à prendre* off center-stage[4] and, together with the Industrial Revolution, brought about a need for the development of a new, systematic body of law dealing with easements of way as well as with other servitudes regulating interdependent land uses.[5]

The first English textbook on easements, Gale on Easements,[6] was published in 1839, just as the law of easements was quickening. Prior to Gale's book the law, recognizing only specific types of servitudes that it lumped together with other incorporeal hereditaments having nothing to do with land use,[7] had had no general theory of easements. Besides

3. See 1 William Cunningham, The Growth of English Industry and Commerce 526-533 (5th ed. 1910); 2 id. 545-561. Compare the discussion at pages 202-203.

4. The most important profits that have survived to modern times are the right to take timber from land and the right to remove sand and gravel and minerals (coal, oil, and gas). Oil, gas, and mineral law has developed into a separate and complex branch of doctrine, with unique rules applicable only to these subsurface interests. Nonmineral profits are generally governed by the same rules as easements. See Restatement of Property §450, Special Note (1944).

5. Our treatment of the historical development of servitudes owes a substantial debt to Uriel Reichman, Servitudes in Residential Private Government Systems 92-187 (unpublished J.S.D. thesis, University of Chicago 1975).

6. Charles J. Gale & Thomas D. Whatley, Law of Easements (1st ed. London 1839). The latest edition is Gale on Easements (Spencer G. Maurice 15th ed. 1986).

7. *Incorporeal hereditaments* is a euphonious collective name for certain intangible rights that, as the term "hereditament" indicates, descended as real property to the primogenitary heir. Although the idea of an incorporeal hereditament originally grew out of feudal ways of thinking (see A.W.B. Simpson, A History of the Land Law 106-107, 121-122 (2d ed. 1986)), the classification proved useful in sorting out those types of medieval rights that ought to descend to the eldest son and those that ought to be treated as personal property and divided among all the children. Incorporeal hereditaments (inherited by the eldest son) included, along with easements and profits, such rights as advowsons (right to appoint the parson of a church), corodies (right to board and lodging, usually in a religious house, assigned to an impoverished relative), peerages, and franchises (rights granted by the crown to hold a fair or market, or to take the chattels of a condemned felon, or to hang convicted thieves). Offices — constable, keeper of a park, falconer, master of the hounds, and such — were also inheritable as incorporeal hereditaments.

There is a modern point to this ancient learning. Some property is inappropriate for common ownership. Single ownership of the right by the eldest son was more efficient (particularly in hanging thieves) than group ownership by all the children. It made sense

rights of way, recognized easements included the right to place clothes on lines over neighboring land, the right to nail fruit trees on a neighbor's wall, and the rights to water cattle at a pond and take water for domestic purposes. Observe that each of these easements, granted by a servient owner, gave a neighbor the right to enter or perform an act on the servient land. They are known as affirmative easements, and in the last 150 years they have grown enormously in both the types and extent of use made by the dominant owner over the servient land.

The early law also recognized a few types of negative easements — easements forbidding one landowner from doing something on his land that might harm a neighbor. But the courts were chary of creating new negative easements, for reasons we will discuss later, at pages 851-854, and strictly fenced them in.

2. Creation of Easements

An *easement,* being an interest in land, is within the Statute of Frauds (so too for *profits*). Creation of an easement generally requires a written instrument signed by the party to be bound thereby. However, in addition to the usual exceptions of fraud, part performance, and estoppel, an easement may, under certain circumstances, be created by implication or by prescription.

Willard v. First Church of Christ, Scientist
Supreme Court of California, 1972
7 Cal. 3d 473, 102 Cal. Rptr. 739, 498 P.2d 987

PETERS, J. In this case we are called upon to decide whether a grantor may, in deeding real property to one person, effectively reserve an interest in the property to another. We hold that in this case such a reservation vests the interest in the third party.

Plaintiffs Donald E. and Jennie C. Willard filed an action to quiet title to a lot in Pacifica against the First Church of Christ, Scientist (the church). After a trial, judgment was entered quieting the Willards' title. The church has appealed.

Genevieve McGuigan owned two abutting lots in Pacifica known as lots 19 and 20. There was a building on lot 19, and lot 20 was vacant. McGuigan was a member of the church, which was located across the street from her lots, and she permitted it to use lot 20 for parking during

to give the easements and profits appurtenant to land to the eldest son, who inherited the land. (Compare the law of heirlooms, which gave heirlooms to the heir; see footnote 20 on page 400.) Why might profits in gross have been assigned to the eldest son and not to all the children? See pages 843-850.

services. She sold lot 19 to one Petersen, who used the building as an office. He wanted to resell the lot, so he listed it with Willard, who is a realtor. Willard expressed an interest in purchasing both lots 19 and 20, and he and Petersen signed a deposit receipt for the sale of the two lots. Soon thereafter they entered into an escrow, into which Petersen delivered a deed for both lots in fee simple.

At the time he agreed to sell lot 20 to Willard, Petersen did not own it, so he approached McGuigan with an offer to purchase it. She was willing to sell the lot provided the church could continue to use it for parking. She therefore referred the matter to the church's attorney, who drew up a provision for the deed that stated the conveyance was "subject to an easement for automobile parking during church hours for the benefit of the church on the property at the southwest corner of the intersection of Hilton Way and Francisco Boulevard . . . such easement to run with the land only so long as the property for whose benefit the easement is given is used for church purposes." Once this clause was inserted in the deed, McGuigan sold the property to Petersen, and he recorded the deed.

Willard paid the agreed purchase price into the escrow and received Petersen's deed 10 days later. He then recorded this deed, which did not mention an easement for parking by the church. While Petersen did mention to Willard that the church would want to use lot 20 for parking, it does not appear that he told him of the easement clause contained in the deed he received from McGuigan.

Willard became aware of the easement clause several months after purchasing the property. He then commenced this action to quiet title against the church. At the trial, which was without a jury, McGuigan testified that she had bought lot 20 to provide parking for the church, and would not have sold it unless she was assured the church could thereafter continue to use it for parking. The court found that McGuigan and Petersen intended to convey an easement to the church, but that the clause they employed was ineffective for that purpose because it was invalidated by the common law rule that one cannot "reserve" an interest in property to a stranger to the title.

The rule derives from the common law notions of reservations from a grant and was based on feudal considerations. A reservation allows a grantor's whole interest in the property to pass to the grantee, but revests a newly created interest in the grantor.[8] (4 Tiffany, The Law of Real Property (3d ed. 1939) §972.) While a reservation could theoretically vest an interest in a third party, the early common law courts vig-

---

8. The effect of a reservation should be distinguished from an exception, which prevents some part of the grantor's interest from passing to the grantee. The exception cannot vest an interest in the third party, and the excepted interest remains in the grantor. (6 Powell, The Law of Real Property (Rohan ed. 1971) §892.) [This citation to Powell is unhelpful. The useful reference is to 3 Powell ¶407. — Eds.]

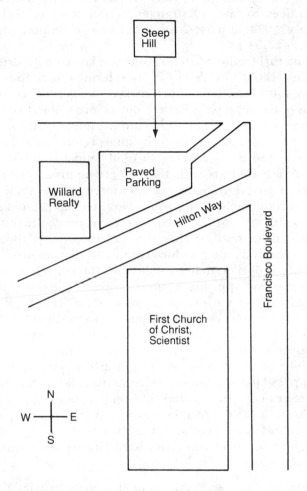

Figure 9-1

orously rejected this possibility, apparently because they mistrusted and wished to limit conveyance by deed as a substitute for livery by seisin. (See Harris, Reservations in Favor of Strangers to the Title (1953) 6 Okla. L. Rev. 127, 132-133.) Insofar as this mistrust was the foundation of the rule, it is clearly an inapposite feudal shackle today. Consequently, several commentators have attacked the rule as groundless and have called for its abolition. (See, e.g., Harris, supra, 6 Okla. L. Rev. at p.154; Meyers & Williams, Oil and Gas Conveyancing; Grants and Reservations by Owners of Fractional Mineral Interests (1957) 43 Va. L. Rev. 639, 650-651; Comment, Real Property: Easements: Creation by Reservation or Exception (1948) 36 Cal. L. Rev. 470, 476; Annot., Reservation or exception in deed in favor of stranger, 88 A.L.R.2d 1199, 1202; cf. 4 Tiffany, supra, §974, at p.54; 2 American Law of Property (Casner ed. 1952) §8.29, at p.254.)

California early adhered to this common law rule. (Eldridge v. See Yup Company (1860) 17 Cal. 44.) In considering our continued adherence to it, we must realize that our courts no longer feel constricted by feudal forms of conveyancing. Rather, our primary objective in construing a conveyance is to try to give effect to the intent of the grantor. . . . In general, therefore, grants are to be interpreted in the same way as other contracts and not according to rigid feudal standards. . . . The common law rule conflicts with the modern approach to construing deeds because it can frustrate the grantor's intent. Moreover, it produces an inequitable result because the original grantee has presumably paid a reduced price for title to the encumbered property. In this case, for example, McGuigan testified that she had discounted the price she charged Petersen by about one-third because of the easement. . . .

In view of the obvious defects of the rule, this court has found methods to avoid it where applying it would frustrate the clear intention of the grantor. In Butler v. Gosling (1900) 130 Cal. 422 [62 P. 596], the court prevented the reserved title to a portion of the property from vesting in the grantee by treating the reservation as an exception to the grant. In Boyer v. Murphy (1927) 202 Cal. 23 [259 P. 38], the court, noting that its primary objective was to give effect to the grantor's intention (id., at pp.28-29), held that the rule was inapplicable where the third party was the grantor's spouse. (See Fleming v. State Bar (1952) 38 Cal. 2d 341, 345, fn. 2 [239 P.2d 866].) Similarily, the . . . courts of other states[9] have found ways of circumventing the rule.

The highest courts of two states have already eliminated the rule

---

9. (See generally Harris, Reservations in Favor of Strangers to the Title, supra, 6 Okla. L. Rev. 127, 139-150.) Some courts, like the court in Butler v. Gosling, supra, mitigate the harshness of the rule by treating the reservation as an exception that retained the interest in the grantor. (See Lemon v. Lemon (1918) 273 Mo. 484, 201 S.W. 103.) While this approach did prevent the reserved interest from passing to the grantee, it did not achieve the grantor's intention of vesting that interest in the third party. Other courts gave effect to the grantor's intention by estopping those who claimed under a chain of title including the deed containing the reservation from challenging it on the basis of the common law rule. (See Beinlein v. Johns (1898) 102 Ky. 570, 19 Ky. L.R. 1969, 44 S.W. 128; Hodge v. Boothby (1861) 48 Me. 68; Dalton v. Eller (1926) 153 Tenn. 418, 284 S.W. 68.) This approach has the effect of emasculating the common law rule without expressly abandoning it. One court found that a reservation created a trust in favor of the stranger (Burns v. Bastien (1935) 174 Okla. 40, 50 P.2d 377), but this approach seems unduly elaborate to achieve the grantor's intent. Finally, several courts, like the court in *Boyer,* supra, will disregard the rule entirely when the stranger is the grantor's spouse. (See Saunders v. Saunders (1940) 373 Ill. 302, 26 N.E.2d 126, 129 A.L.R. 306; Du Bois v. Judy (1920) 291 Ill. 340, 126 N.E. 104; Derham v. Hovey (1917) 195 Mich. 243, 161 N.W. 883, 21 A.L.R. 999; Glasgow v. Glasgow (1952) 221 S.C. 322, 70 S.E.2d 432.) Thus, as in California, the rule has been riddled with exceptions in other states.

altogether, rather than repealing it piecemeal by evasion. In Townsend v. Cable (Ky. 1964) 378 S.W.2d 806, the Court of Appeals of Kentucky abandoned the rule. It said: "We have no hesitancy in abandoning this archaic and technical rule. It is entirely inconsistent with the basic principle followed in the construction of deeds, which is to determine the intention of grantor as gathered from the four corners of the instrument." (Id., at p.808.) (See also Blair v. City of Pikeville (Ky. 1964) 384 S.W.2d 65, 66; Combs v. Hounshell (Ky. 1961) 347 S.W.2d 550, 554.) Relying on *Townsend*, the Supreme Court of Oregon, in Garza v. Grayson (1970) 255 Ore. 413 [467 P.2d 960], rejected the rule because it was "derived from a narrow and highly technical interpretation of the meaning of the terms 'reservation' and 'exception' when employed in a deed" (id., at p.961), and did not sufficiently justify frustrating the grantor's intention. Since the rule may frustrate the grantor's intention in some cases even though it is riddled with exceptions, we follow the lead of Kentucky and Oregon and abandon it entirely.

Willard contends that the old rule should nevertheless be applied in this case to invalidate the church's easement because grantees and title insurers have relied upon it. He has not, however, presented any evidence to support this contention, and it is clear that the facts of this case do not demonstrate reliance on the old rule. There is no evidence that a policy of title insurance was issued, and therefore no showing of reliance by a title insurance company. Willard himself could not have relied upon the common law rule to assure him of an absolute fee because he did not even read the deed containing the reservation. This is not a case of an ancient deed where the reservation has not been asserted for many years. The church used lot 20 for parking throughout the period when Willard was purchasing the property and after he acquired title to it, and he may not claim that he was prejudiced by lack of use for an extended period of time.

The determination whether the old common law rule should be applied to grants made prior to our decision involves a balancing of equitable and policy considerations. We must balance the injustice which would result from refusing to give effect to the grantor's intent against the injustice, if any, which might result by failing to give effect to reliance on the old rule and the policy against disturbing settled titles. The record before us does not disclose any reliance upon the old common law rule, and there is no problem of an ancient title. Although in other cases the balancing of the competing interests may warrant application of the common law rule to presently existing deeds, in the instant case the balance falls in favor of the grantor's intent, and the old common law rule may not be applied to defeat her intent.

Willard also contends that the church has received no interest in this case because the clause stated only that the grant was "subject to" the church's easement, and not that the easement was either excepted or reserved. In construing this provision, however, we must look to the clause as a whole which states that the easement "is given." Even if we assume that there is some ambiguity or conflict in the clause, the trial court found on substantial evidence that the parties to the deed intended to convey the easement to the church. (Coast Bank v. Minderhout, 61 Cal. 2d 311, 315 [38 Cal. Rptr. 505, 392 P.2d 265]; see Estate of Russell, 69 Cal. 2d 200, 206-214 [70 Cal. Rptr. 561, 444 P.2d 353].)

The judgment is reversed.

NOTES AND QUESTIONS

1. The *Willard* case is noted in 61 Cal. L. Rev. 548 (1973); 24 Hastings L.J. 469 (1973); and 13 Santa Clara Law. 344 (1972). For a recent New York case reaffirming the common law rule that a grantor cannot reserve an easement in favor of a third party, see Estate of Thomson v. Wade, 69 N.Y.2d 570, 509 N.E.2d 309, 516 N.Y.S.2d 614 (1987).

Restatement (Third) of Property, Servitudes, §2.6, Reporter's Note (T.D. No. 1, 1989), provides that an easement can be created in favor of a third party, but contrary authority in a number of states is cited. The Restatement (Third) is a project by the American Law Institute to restate the law of servitudes in a unified system and discard limitations unsuited to contemporary land utilization. Professor Susan French is the reporter. See Susan F. French, Design Proposal for the New Restatement of the Law of Property — Servitudes, 21 U.C. Davis L. Rev. 1213 (1988); Susan F. French, Servitudes Reform and the New Restatement of Property: Creation Doctrines and Structural Simplification, 73 Cornell L. Rev. 928 (1988).

2. How would you draft documents so as to carry out Genevieve McGuigan's intent and not violate the common law rule that an easement cannot be reserved in favor of a third party? If the church had lost, would the church's attorney who drew up the deed be liable for malpractice?

3. *Reservations and exceptions.* The court holds that an easement can be reserved in favor of a third party but states in footnote 8 that an easement cannot be excepted in favor of a third party. What is the difference between an exception and a reservation? How did the court determine that Genevieve McGuigan had reserved rather than excepted an easement? (The deed said "subject to an easement.")

A *reservation* is a provision in a deed creating some *new* servitude which did not exist before as an independent interest. For example, *O* conveys Blackacre to *A* reserving a 20-foot wide easement of way along the south boundary of Blackacre. The easement did not exist as an independent interest prior to the conveyance by *O*. An *exception* is a provision in a deed that excludes from the grant some *pre-existing* servitude on the land. For example, after the above conveyance, *A* conveys Black-acre to *B*, except for the easement previously reserved by *O*. An exception may also exclude from the grant some part of the land to which the grantor retains the fee simple (for example, the back 20 acres).

When the grantor attempted to reserve an easement at early common law, there were difficulties. A new right, such as some feudal obligation or the payment of rent, could be reserved if it was to issue out of the land granted, but the English courts held that an easement could not be reserved because it did not issue out of the land granted. English courts ultimately found a way around this obstacle by inventing the *regrant theory*. They held that an easement "reserved" by the grantor was not a reservation at all (which would be void), but a *regrant* of an easement by the grantee to the grantor. Thus a deed from "*O* to *A* and her heirs, reserving an easement in *O*," was treated as if it were two deeds. The deed grants *A* a fee simple; then *A* is treated as granting an easement back to *O*.

The regrant theory may have been a brilliant way around the crabbed interpretation of what could be reserved in a grant, but it brought a new difficulty of its own. Because a reserved easement theoretically involved a regrant by the grantee, the Statute of Frauds required the deed to be signed by the grantee as well as by the grantor. In this country, where deeds are usually signed only by the grantor, this could have caused trouble. But American courts deftly held that the grantee had, by accepting the deed, made it her own and adopted the seal and signature of the grantor! Thus was a legal fiction invented to overcome a faulty premise.

Occasionally a grantor "excepts" an easement in himself when technically he should use the term "reserves." The court will usually give the retained easement effect as a reservation. "The terms *reservation* and *exception* are often used as synonymous, and the intention of the parties, not the language used, is the dominating factor." Nelson v. Bacon, 113 Vt. 161, 169, 32 A.2d 140, 145 (1943).

Now that you understand the difference between a reservation and an exception, does the court's statement in footnote 8 that an exception cannot vest an interest in a third party make sense? If *O* can grant Blackacre (consisting of 50 acres) to *A*, except for 10 acres, which *O* conveys to *B*, and except for a life estate in the remaining 40 acres, which *O* conveys to *C*, why cannot *O* except an easement in favor of *D*? Why can possesssory interests be excepted in favor of a third party but not non-possessory interests?

4. Is the church's easement in the *Willard* case *appurtenant* or *in gross*? An *easement appurtenant* benefits the owner of the easement in the use of land belonging to the owner. There is a dominant tenement as well as a servient tenement, and an easement appurtenant attaches to the dominant tenement and (usually, unless it is "personal") goes with it

to successive owners. If an easement is appurtenant to a dominant tenement, it cannot be detached without the consent of both dominant and servient owners. An *easement in gross* does not benefit the owner of the easement in the use of land belonging to the owner, but benefits the owner without regard to ownership of land. If it is unclear which type of easement is intended by the parties, the law construes in favor of an easement appurtenant. For example, in a case where the sellers reserved an easement "for the watering of livestock owned by the sellers," the court held the easement was appurtenant to the neighboring tract the sellers owned. Nelson v. Johnson, 106 Idaho 385, 679 P.2d 662 (1984). Easements in gross raise special problems which are treated subsequently in this chapter at pages 843-850.

Here's another way of phrasing the question above: If the Christian Science Church sold the church on Hilton Way and Francisco Boulevard to a Methodist Church, and erected a new church a block away to the west on Hilton Way, would the easement belong to the Methodist Church or to the Christian Science Church, or would the easement be extinguished?

An easement can have a duration comparable to any of the possessory estates. An easement can be in fee simple (perpetual duration), or for life, or for a term of years. How would you describe the duration of the easement in *Willard*?

5. *Retroactive overruling.* When a court decides to abandon a common law property rule, as in *Willard,* should it make the new rule retroactive? If the new rule is retroactive, should the court make an exception for persons who relied upon the old rule? If the new rule is not retroactive, should it nonetheless apply to the parties in the case? In Estate of Propst, 50 Cal. 3d 448, 788 P.2d 628, 268 Cal. Rptr. 114 (1990), the court, assuming there had been little reliance on the old rule at issue, overruled the old rule retroactively, excepting persons who showed reliance on it (as in *Willard*). Justice Mosk dissented: "How many persons may be affected by the new rule this court pronounces today is wholly speculative. The only way they can be protected without protracted litigation, after relying on what the judiciary has been declaring for the better part of this century, is to make our current view of the law applicable to this case and thereafter prospective." 50 Cal. 3d at 466-467, 788 P.2d at 639, 268 Cal. Rptr. at 125. See also Tucker v. Badoin, 376 Mass. 907, 918-919, 384 N.E.2d 1195, 1201-1202 (1978) (Kaplan, J., concurring).

In this chapter, you will doubtless find some rules that ought to be discarded. As you appraise them, think about whether they should be eliminated retroactively. For a thoughtful analysis of retroactive overruling, see Roger J. Traynor, Quo Vadis, Prospective Overruling: A Question of Judicial Responsibility, 28 Hastings L.J. 533 (1977).

6. The Comprehensive Environmental Response, Compensation,

and Liability Act (CERCLA), 42 U.S.C. §§9601-9675 (Supp. 1992), imposes strict liability on "owners" of land on which hazardous waste is found (see page 614). Inasmuch as some easement owners, such as utilities and railroads, exercise control over the land to almost the same degree as does the fee simple owner, should these easement owners face CERCLA liability unless they fall within the scope of the innocent owner defense? See Note, Easement Holder Liability Under CERCLA: The Right Way to Deal with Rights of Way, 89 Mich. L. Rev. 1233 (1991), arguing that they should. (If easement owners exercise sufficient control over the property, they usually have the same tort liabilities as owners of a fee simple.)

Suppose that hazardous waste is found under the parking lot in the *Willard* case. Should the church, as well as Willard, be responsible for the clean-up costs?

NOTE: EASEMENT OR FEE SIMPLE?

An easement gives the dominant owner the right to *use* the servient land. A fee simple owner is entitled to *possession* of the land. Sometimes it is difficult to distinguish between use and possession, as when a pipeline company lays pipes through the soil or a railroad company lays tracks.

A surprising amount of litigation involves the question whether a deed, usually of a strip of land, conveys an easement or a fee simple. For example, suppose a grantor conveys to a railroad a strip of land 50 feet wide, from one border of the grantor's tract to the opposite border, on which the railroad lays tracks. When the railroad abandons the railroad tracks some years later, the railroad continues to own the strip if a fee simple was granted, but if an easement was granted, it disappears, relieving the servient tenement of the easement. Although there is sometimes said to be a presumption that a conveyance to a railroad conveys an easement, cases of this sort tend to be decided on the particular facts, including a careful reading of the deed. If the strip is referred to as a "right-of-way" in the granting clause, the court usually finds an easement is granted. But if "right-of-way" is used in another part of the deed (say, in a covenant by the railroad to construct an underpass under the "right-of-way"), the court often finds a fee simple was granted. See Greaves v. McGee, 492 So. 2d 307 (Ala. 1986) (easement); Urbaitis v. Commonwealth Edison, 143 Ill. 2d 458, 575 N.E.2d 548 (1991) (fee simple); Restatement (Third) of Property, Servitudes, §2.2, Comment g (T.D. No. 1, 1989) (discussing relevant factors in construction of deeds). Litigation can be avoided by expressly stating that the grant is of an *easement* or a *fee simple*. A grant of a narrow strip of land "to A and her heirs," rather than "to A in fee simple," will not necessarily avoid litigation, as the words "and her heirs" may be taken as merely fixing, as unlimited in time, the duration of the easement. So too a grant "to *B* Corporation, its successors and assigns."

Judge Posner, comparing the costs that may arise upon termination of the use, favors adherence to the common law presumption of an easement.

> Transaction costs are minimized by undivided ownership of a parcel of land, and undivided ownership is, in turn, facilitated by the automatic reuniting of divided land once the reason for the division has ceased. If the railroad is the owner of a multitude of skinny strips of land now usable only by the owner of the surrounding or adjacent land, then before that land can be put to its best use there must be expensive and time-consuming negotiation — that or the gradual extinction of the railroad's interest through the operation of the doctrine of adverse possession. It is cleaner to wipe out the railroad's interest upon its abandonment of railroad service. [Richard A. Posner, Economic Analysis of Law 76 (4th ed. 1992).]

NOTE: LICENSES

An easement must be distinguished from a license. A *license* is permission given by the occupant of land allowing the licensee to do some act that otherwise would be a trespass. Licenses are very common: The plumber fixing a drain, the guest coming to dinner, the purchaser of a theater ticket all have licenses. This privilege to use the land resembles an easement, but a license is revocable whereas an easement is not. Because a license can be revoked by the licensor at any time, there is some question whether a license is properly called an interest in land. Restatement of Property §512 (1944) states that a license is an interest in land but goes on to say, in Comment e, that a license is not always treated as an interest in land. For example, a license may be created orally and in that respect is not treated as an interest in land subject to the Statute of Frauds.

There are two distinct exceptions to the rule that a license is revocable. First, a license coupled with an interest cannot be revoked. A license coupled with an interest is one that is incidental to ownership of a chattel on the licensor's land. For example, *O* grants to *A* the right to take timber from Blackacre, owned by *O. A* has an interest (a *profit à prendre*) and an irrevocable license to enter the land and take the timber. The irrevocability of a license coupled with an interest bears some resemblance to the doctrine of easements by necessity. (See pages 820-822.) The second exception is a license that becomes irrevocable under the rules of estoppel. A license that cannot be revoked is something very akin to an easement.

Holbrook v. Taylor

Supreme Court of Kentucky, 1976
532 S.W.2d 763

STERNBERG, J. This is an action to establish a right to the use of a roadway, which is 10 to 12 feet wide and about 250 feet long, over the unenclosed, hilly woodlands of another. The claimed right to the use of the roadway is twofold: by prescription and by estoppel. Both issues are heatedly contested. The evidence is in conflict as to the nature and type of use that had been made of the roadway. The lower court determined that a right to the use of the roadway by prescription had not been established, but that it had been established by estoppel. The landowners, feeling themselves aggrieved, appeal. We will consider the two issues separately.

In Grinestaff v. Grinestaff, Ky., 318 S.W.2d 881 (1958), we said that an easement may be created by express written grant, by implication, by prescription, or by estoppel. It has long been the law of this commonwealth that

> (an) easement, such as a right of way, is created when the owner of a tenement to which the right is claimed to be appurtenant, or those under whom he claims title, have openly, peaceably, continuously, and under a claim of right adverse to the owner of the soil, and with his knowledge and acquiescence, used a way over the lands of another for as much as 15 years.

Flener v. Lawrence, 187 Ky. 384, 220 S.W. 1041 (1920); Rominger v. City Realty Company, Ky., 324 S.W.2d 806 (1959).

In 1942 appellants purchased the subject property. In 1944 they gave permission for a haul road to be cut for the purpose of moving coal from a newly opened mine. The roadway was so used until 1949, when the mine closed. During that time the appellants were paid a royalty for the use of the road. In 1957 appellants built a tenant house on their property and the roadway was used by them and their tenant. The tenant house burned in 1961 and was not replaced. In 1964 the appellees bought their three-acre building site, which adjoins appellants, and the following year built their residence thereon. At all times prior to 1965, the use of the haul road was by permission of appellants. There is no evidence of any probative value which would indicate that the use of the haul road during that period of time was either adverse, continuous, or uninterrupted. The trial court was fully justified, therefore, in finding that the right to the use of this easement was not established by prescription.

As to the issue of estoppel, we have long recognized that a right to the use of a roadway over the lands of another may be established by estoppel. In Lashley Telephone Co. v. Durbin, 190 Ky. 792, 228 S.W. 423 (1921), we said:

> Though many courts hold that a licensee is conclusively presumed as a matter of law to know that a license is revocable at the pleasure of the licensor, and if he expend money in connection with his entry upon the land of the latter, he does so at his peril . . . , yet it is the established rule in this state that where a license is not a bare, naked right of entry, but includes the right to erect structures and acquire an interest in the land in the nature of an easement by the construction of improvements thereon, the licensor may not revoke the license and restore his premises to their former condition after the licensee has exercised the privilege given by the license and erected the improvements at considerable expense. . . .

In Gibbs v. Anderson, 288 Ky. 488, 156 S.W.2d 876 (1941), Gibbs claimed the right, by estoppel, to the use of a roadway over the lands of Anderson. The lower court denied the claim. We reversed. Anderson's immediate predecessor in title admitted that he had discussed the passway with Gibbs before it was constructed and had agreed that it might be built through his land. He stood by and saw Gibbs expend considerable money in this construction. We applied the rule announced in Lashley Telephone Co. v. Durbin, supra, and reversed with directions that a judgment be entered granting Gibbs the right to the use of the passway.

In McCoy v. Hoffman, Ky., 295 S.W.2d 560 (1956), the facts are that Hoffman had acquired the verbal consent of the landowner to build a passway over the lands of the owner to the state highway. Subsequently, the owner of the servient estate sold the property to McCoy, who at the time of the purchase was fully aware of the existence of the roadway and the use to which it was being put. McCoy challenged Hoffman's right to use the road. The lower court found that a right had been gained by prescription. In this court's consideration of the case, we affirmed, not on the theory of prescriptive right but on the basis that the owner of the servient estate was estopped. After announcing the rule for establishing a right by prescription, we went on to say:

> . . . On the other hand, the right of revocation of the license is subject to the qualification that where the licensee has exercised the privilege given him and erected improvements or made substantial expenditures on the faith or strength of the license, it becomes irrevocable and continues for so long a time as the nature of the license calls for. In effect, under this condition the license becomes in reality a grant through estoppel. . . .

In Akers v. Moore, Ky., 309 S.W.2d 758 (1958), this court again considered the right to the use of a passway by estoppel. Akers and others had used the Moore branch as a public way of ingress and egress from their property. They sued Moore and others who owned property along the branch seeking to have the court recognize their right to the use of the roadway and to order the removal of obstructions which had been placed in the roadway. The trial court found that Akers and others had acquired a prescriptive right to the use of the portion of the road lying on the left side of the creek bed, but had not acquired the right to the use of so much of the road as lay on the right side of the creek bed. Consequently, an appeal and a cross-appeal were filed. Considering the right to use of the strip of land between the right side of the creek bed and the highway, this court found that the evidence portrayed it very rough and apparently never improved, that it ran alongside the house in which one of the protestors lived, and that by acquiescence or by express consent of at least one of the protestors the right side of the roadway was opened up so as to change the roadway from its close proximity to the Moore residence. The relocated portion of the highway had only been used as a passway for about six years before the suit was filed. The trial court found that this section of the road had not been established as a public way by estoppel. We reversed. In doing so, we stated:

> We consider the fact that the appellees, Artie Moore, et al., had stood by and acquiesced in (if in fact they had not affirmatively consented to) the change being made and permitted the appellants to spend money in fixing it up to make it passable and use it for six years without objecting. Of course, the element of time was not sufficient for the acquisition of the right of way by adverse possession. But the law recognizes that one may acquire a license to use a passway or roadway where, with the knowledge of the licensor, he has in the exercise of the privilege spent money in improving the way or for other purposes connected with its use on the faith or strength of the license. Under such conditions the license becomes irrevocable and continues for so long a time as its nature calls for. This, in effect, becomes a grant through estoppel. Gibbs v. Anderson, 288 Ky. 488, 156 S.W.2d 876; McCoy v. Hoffman, Ky., 295 S.W.2d 560. It would be unconscionable to permit the owners of this strip of land of trivial value to revoke the license by obstructing and preventing its use.

In the present case the roadway had been used since 1944 by permission of the owners of the servient estate. The evidence is conflicting as to whether the use of the road subsequent to 1965 was by permission or by claim of right. Appellees contend that it had been used by them and others without the permission of appellants; on the other hand, it is contended by appellants that the use of the roadway at all times was by their permission. The evidence discloses that during the period of preparation for the construction of appellees' home and during the time the house was being built, appellees were permitted to use the roadway as ingress and egress for workmen, for hauling machinery and material to the building site, for construction of the dwelling, and for making improvements generally to the premises. Further, the evidence reflects that after construction of the residence, which cost $25,000, was completed, appellees continued to regularly use the roadway as they had been doing. Appellant J.S. Holbrook testified that in order for appellees to get up to their house he gave them permission to use and repair the roadway. They widened it, put in a culvert and graveled part of it with "red dog," also known as cinders, at a cost of approximately $100. There is no other location over which a roadway could reasonably be built to provide an outlet for appellees.

No dispute had arisen between the parties at any time over the use of the roadway until the fall of 1970. Appellant J. S. Holbrook contends that he wanted to secure a writing from the appellees in order to relieve him from any responsibility for any damage that might happen to anyone on the subject road. On the other hand, Mrs. Holbrook testified that the writing was desired to avoid any claim which may be made by appellees of a right to the use of the roadway. Appellees testified that the writing was an effort to force them to purchase a small strip of land over which the roadway traversed, for the sum of $500. The dispute was not resolved and appellants erected a steel cable across the roadway to prevent its use and also constructed "no-trespassing" signs. Shortly thereafter, the suit was filed to require the removal of the obstruction and to declare the right of appellees to the use of the roadway without interference.

The use of the roadway by appellees to get to their home from the public highway, the use of the roadway to take in heavy equipment and material and supplies for construction of the residence, the general improvement of the premises, the maintenance of the roadway, and the construction by appellees of a $25,000 residence, all with the actual consent of appellants or at least with their tacit approval, clearly demonstrates the rule laid down in Lashley Telephone Co. v. Durbin, supra, that the license to use the subject roadway may not be revoked.

The evidence justifies the finding of the lower court that the right to the use of the roadway had been established by estoppel.

The judgment is affirmed.

Shepard v. Purvine, 196 Or. 348, 369, 248 P.2d 352, 361-362 (1952). "These people were close friends and neighbors, and they were not dealing at arm's length. One's word was considered as good as his bond. Under the circumstances, for plaintiffs to have insisted upon a deed would have been embarrassing; in effect it would have been expressing a doubt as to their friend's integrity. We do not believe the evidence warrants a conclusion that plaintiffs were negligent in not insisting upon a formal transfer of the rights accorded. An oral license promptly acted upon in the manner plaintiffs acted is just as valid, binding, and irrevocable as a deeded right of way."

Henry v. Dalton, 98 R.I. 150, 156-158, 151 A.2d 362, 366 (1959).
"We are of the opinion that in reason and justice the better rule is expressed in the case of Crosdale v. Lanigan, 129 N.Y. 604, 29 N.E. 824.
There the plaintiff was required to remove a wall built on the property
of the defendant pursuant to a license. The court stated the rule at page
610 of 129 N.Y., at page 825 of 29 N.E. as follows: '. . . a parol license to
do an act on the land of the licensor, while it justifies anything done by
the licensee before revocation, is, nevertheless, revocable at the option
of the licensor, and this, although the intention was to confer a continuing right and money had been expended by the licensee upon the faith
of the license. This is plainly the rule of the statute. It is also, we believe,
the rule required by public policy. It prevents the burdening of lands
with restrictions founded upon oral agreements, easily misunderstood.
It gives security and certainty to titles, which are most important to be
preserved against defects and qualifications not founded upon solemn
instruments. The jurisdiction of courts to enforce oral contracts for the
sale of land, is clearly defined and well understood, and is indisputable;
but to change what commenced in a license into an irrevocable right, on
the ground of equitable estoppel, is another and quite different matter.
It is far better, we think, that the law requiring interests in land to be
evidenced by deed, should be observed, than to leave it to the chancellor
to construe an executed license as a grant, depending upon what, in his
view, may be equity in the special case. . . .'

"Counsel for the complainants urge that the statute of frauds was
conceived and is designed to protect against fraud and should not be
used to assist in the perpetration of fraud. We are in accord with this
contention, but are not convinced that in the circumstances of the instant
case the respondent's revocation of the complainants' license is fraudulent within any acceptable definition of that term. The right which complainants seek to establish in the land of the respondent is essentially an
easement and should be the subject of a grant, expressed in the solem-
nity of a written instrument. It is no hardship for one in the position of
these complainants either to secure an easement in perpetuity in the
manner provided by the statute, or, such being refused, to weigh
the advantages inuring to them as against the uncertainty implicit in the
making of expenditures on the basis of a revocable license."

NOTES AND QUESTIONS

1. Restatement (Third) of Property, Servitudes, §2.10 (T.D. No. 1,
1989), provides that a servitude may be created by estoppel. Comment e
says, "Normally the change in position that triggers application of the
rule stated in this subsection is an investment in improvements either to
the servient estate or to other land of the investor."

2. Suppose that Taylor's house burns down. Can Taylor build a new house using the right of way across Holbrook's land? Restatement of Property §519(4) (1944) says the licensee may continue the use "to the extent necessary to realize upon his expenditures." Comment g explains that the license is irrevocable "to the extent necessary to prevent the licensee from being unfairly deprived of the fruits of expenditures made by him."

3. Where the facts justify an application of estoppel, should the court give the servient landowner damages rather than denying all relief? Remember that the court has the choice of giving the servient owner an injunction, damages, or nothing. If it is considered unfair for the landowner to revoke permission to cross, is it fair for the appellees to gain the benefit without paying anything for it? Would an award of damages be an efficient solution? See Stewart E. Sterk, Neighbors in American Land Law, 87 Colum. L. Rev. 55, 77-78 (1987).

Van Sandt v. Royster

Supreme Court of Kansas, 1938
148 Kan. 495, 83 P.2d 698

ALLEN, J. The action was brought to enjoin defendants from using and maintaining an underground lateral sewer drain through and across plaintiff's land. The case was tried by the court, judgment was rendered in favor of defendants, and plaintiff appeals.

In the city of Chanute, Highland avenue, running north and south, intersects Tenth street running east and west. In the early part of 1904 Laura A.J. Bailey was the owner of a plot of ground lying east of Highland avenue and south of Tenth street. Running east from Highland avenue and facing north on Tenth street the lots are numbered respectively, 19, 20, and 4. In 1904 the residence of Mrs. Bailey was on lot 4 on the east part of her land.

In the latter part of 1903 or the early part of 1904, the city of Chanute constructed a public sewer in Highland avenue, west of lot 19. About the same time a private lateral drain was constructed from the Bailey residence on lot 4 running in a westerly direction through and across lots 20 and 19 to the public sewer.

On January 15, 1904, Laura A.J. Bailey conveyed lot 19 to John J. Jones, by general warranty deed with the usual covenants against encumbrances, and containing no exceptions or reservations. Jones erected a dwelling on the north part of the lot. In 1920 Jones conveyed the north 156 feet of lot 19 to Carl D. Reynolds; in 1924 Reynolds conveyed to the plaintiff, who has owned and occupied the premises since that time.

In 1904 Laura A.J. Bailey conveyed lot 20 to one Murphy, who built

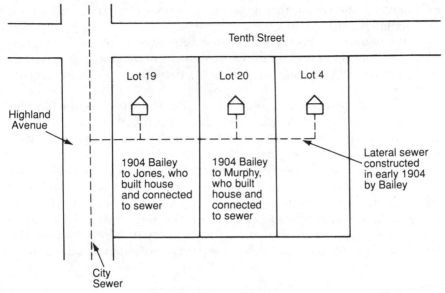

Tenth Street

Lot 19   Lot 20   Lot 4

Highland
Avenue

1904 Bailey   1904 Bailey   Lateral sewer
to Jones, who   to Murphy,   constructed
built house   who built   in early 1904
and connected   house and   by Bailey
to sewer   connected
                  to sewer

City
Sewer

Figure 9-2

a house thereon, and by mesne conveyances the title passed to the defendant, Louise H. Royster. The deed to Murphy was a general warranty deed without exceptions or reservations. The defendant Gray has succeeded to the title to lot 4 upon which the old Bailey home stood at the time Laura A.J. Bailey sold lots 19 and 20.

In March, 1936, plaintiff discovered his basement flooded with sewage and filth to a depth of six or eight inches, and upon investigation he found for the first time that there existed on and across his property a sewer drain extending in an easterly direction across the property of Royster to the property of Gray. The refusal of defendants to cease draining and discharging their sewage across plaintiff's land resulted in this lawsuit. . . .

The drain pipe in the lateral sewer was several feet under the surface of the ground. There was nothing visible on the ground in the rear of the houses to indicate the existence of the drain or the connection of the drain with the houses.

As a conclusion of law the court found that "an appurtenant easement existed in the said lateral sewer as to all three of the properties involved in the controversy here." Plaintiff's prayer for relief was denied and it was decreed that plaintiff be restrained from interfering in any way with the lateral drain or sewer.

Plaintiff contends that the evidence fails to show that an easement was ever created in his land, and, assuming there was an easement created as alleged, that he took the premises free from the burden of the easement for the reason that he was a bona fide purchaser, without notice, actual or constructive.

Defendants contend: (1) That an easement was created by implied reservation on the severance of the servient from the dominant estate of the deed from Mrs. Bailey to Jones; (2) there is a valid easement by prescription.

In finding No. 11, the court found that the lateral sewer "was an appurtenance to the properties belonging to plaintiff and Louise Royster, and the same is necessary to the reasonable use and enjoyment of the said properties of the parties."

As an easement is an interest which a person has in land in the possession of another, it necessarily follows that an owner cannot have an easement in his own land. (Johnston v. City of Kingman, 141 Kan. 131, 39 P.2d 924; Ferguson v. Ferguson, 106 Kan. 823, 189 Pac. 925.)

However, an owner may make use of one part of his land for the benefit of another part, and this is very frequently spoken of as a quasi easement.

> When one thus utilizes part of his land for the benefit of another part, it is frequently said that a quasi easement exists, the part of the land which is benefited being referred to as the "quasi dominant tenement" and the part which is utilized for the benefit of the other part being referred to as the "quasi servient tenement." The so-called quasi easement is evidently not a legal relation in any sense, but the expression is a convenient one to describe the particular mode in which the owner utilizes one part of the land for the benefit of the other. . . .
>
> If the owner of land, one part of which is subject to a quasi easement in favor of another part, conveys the quasi dominant tenement, an easement corresponding to such quasi easement is ordinarily regarded as thereby vested in the grantee of the land, provided, it is said, the quasi easement is of an apparent continuous and necessary character. [2 Tiffany on Real Property, 2d ed., 1272, 1273.]

Following the famous case of Pyer v. Carter, 1 Hurl & N. 916, some of the English cases and many early American cases held that upon the transfer of the quasi-servient tenement there was an implied reservation of an easement in favor of the conveyor. Under the doctrine of Pyer v. Carter, no distinction was made between an implied reservation and an implied grant.

The case, however, was overthrown in England by Suffield v. Brown, 4 De G.J. & S. 185, and Wheeldon v. Burrows, L.R. 12 Ch. D. 31. In the former case the court said:

> It seems to me more reasonable and just to hold that if the grantor intends to reserve any right over the property granted, it is his duty to reserve it expressly in the grant, rather than to limit and cut down the operation of a plain

grant (which is not pretended to be otherwise than in conformity with the contract between the parties), by the fiction of an implied reservation. If this plain rule be adhered to, men will know what they have to trust, and will place confidence in the language of their contracts and assurances. . . . But I cannot agree that the grantor can derogate from his own absolute grant so as to claim rights over the thing granted, even if they were at the time of the grant continuous and apparent easements enjoyed by an adjoining tenement which remains the property of him the grantor. [Pp.190, 194.]

Many American courts of high standing assert that the rule regarding implied grants and implied reservations is reciprocal and that the rule applies with equal force and in like circumstances to both grants and reservations. (Washburn on Easements, 4th ed. 75; Miller v. Skaggs, 79 W. Va. 645, 91 S.E. 536, Ann. Cas. 1918 D. 929.)

On the other hand, perhaps a majority of the cases hold that in order to establish an easement by implied reservation in favor of the grantor the easement must be one of strict necessity, even when there was an existing drain or sewer at the time of the severance.

Thus in Howley v. Chaffee et al., 88 Vt. 468, 474, 93 Atl. 120, L.R.A. 1915 D. 1010, the court said:

With the character and extent of implied grants, we now have nothing to do. We are here only concerned with determining the circumstances which will give rise to an implied reservation. On this precise question the authorities are in conflict. Courts of high standing assert that the rule regarding implied grants and implied reservations of "visible servitudes" is reciprocal, and that it applies with equal force and in like circumstances to both grants and reservations. But upon a careful consideration of the whole subject, studied in the light of the many cases in which it is discussed, we are convinced that there is a clear distinction between implied grants and implied reservations, and that this distinction is well founded in principle and well supported by authority. It is apparent that no question of public policy is here involved, as we have seen is the case where a way of necessity is involved. To say that a grantor reserves to himself something out of the property granted, wholly by implication, not only offends the rule that one shall not derogate from his own grant, but conflicts with the grantor's language in the conveyance, which, by the rule, is to be taken against him, and is wholly inconsistent with the theory on which our registry laws are based. If such an illogical result is to follow an absolute grant, it must be by virtue of some legal rule of compelling force. The correct rule is, we think, that where, as here, one grants a parcel of land by metes and bounds, by a deed containing full covenants of warranty and without any express reservation, there can be no reservation by implication, unless the easement claimed is one of strict necessity, within the meaning of that term as explained in Dee v. King, 73 Vt. 375.

See, also, Brown v. Fuller, 165 Mich. 162, 130 N.W. 621, 33 L.R.A., n.s., 459, Ann. Cas. 1912 C 853. The cases are collected in 58 A.L.R. 837.

We are inclined to the view that the circumstance that the claimant of the easement is the grantor instead of the grantee, is but one of many factors to be considered in determining whether an easement will arise by implication. An easement created by implication arises as an inference of the intentions of the parties to a conveyance of land. The inference is drawn from the circumstances under which the conveyance was made rather than from the language of the conveyance. The easement may arise in favor of the conveyor or the conveyee. In the Restatement of Property, Tentative Draft No. 8, section 28, the factors determining the implication of an easement are stated:

> Sec. 28. Factors Determining Implication of Easements or Profits. In determining whether the circumstances under which a conveyance of land is made imply an easement or a profit, the following factors are important: (a) whether the claimant is the conveyor or the conveyee, (b) the terms of the conveyance, (c) the consideration given for it, (d) whether the claim is made against a simultaneous conveyee, (e) the extent of necessity of the easement or the profit to the claimant, (f) whether reciprocal benefits result to the conveyor and the conveyee, (g) the manner in which the land was used prior to its conveyance, and (h) the extent to which the manner of prior use was or might have been known to the parties.

Comment j, under the same section, reads:

> The extent to which the manner of prior use was or might have been known to the parties. The effect of the prior use as a circumstance in implying, upon a severance of possession by conveyance, an easement or a profit results from an inference as to the intention of the parties. To draw such an inference, the prior use must have been known to the parties at the time of the conveyance, or, at least, have been within the possibility of their knowledge at the time. Each party to a conveyance is bound not merely to what he intended, but also to what he might reasonably have foreseen the other party to the conveyance expected. Parties to a conveyance may, therefore, be assumed to intend the continuance of uses known to them which are in a considerable degree necessary to the continued usefulness of the land. Also they will be assumed to know and to contemplate the continuance of reasonably necessary uses which have so altered the premises as to make them apparent upon reasonably prudent investigation. The degree of necessity required to imply an easement in favor of the conveyor is greater than that required in the case of the conveyee (see comment b). Yet, even in the case of the conveyor, the implication from necessity will be aided by a previous use made apparent by the physical adaptation of the premises to it.

Illustrations:

9. A is the owner of two adjacent tracts of land, Blackacre and Whiteacre. Blackacre has on it a dwelling house. Whiteacre is unimproved. Drainage

from the house to a public sewer is across Whiteacre. This fact is unknown to *A,* who purchased the two tracts with the house already built. By reasonable effort, *A* might discover the manner of drainage and the location of the drain. *A* sells Blackacre to *B,* who has been informed as to the manner of drainage and the location of the drain and assumes that *A* is aware of it. There is created by implication an easement of drainage in favor of *B* across Whiteacre.

10. Same facts as in illustration 9, except that both *A* and *B* are unaware of the manner of drainage and the location of the drain. However, each had reasonable opportunity to learn of such facts. A holding that there is created by implication an easement of drainage in favor of *B* across Whiteacre is proper.

At the time John J. Jones purchased lot 19 he was aware of the lateral sewer, and knew that it was installed for the benefit of the lots owned by Mrs. Bailey, the common owner. The easement was necessary to the comfortable enjoyment of the grantor's property. If land may be used without an easement, but cannot be used without disproportionate effort and expense, an easement may still be implied in favor of either the grantor or grantee on the basis of necessity alone. This is the situation as found by the trial court.

Neither can it be claimed that plaintiff purchased without notice. At the time plaintiff purchased the property he and his wife made a careful and thorough inspection of the property. They knew the house was equipped with modern plumbing and that the plumbing had to drain into a sewer. Under the facts as found by the court, we think the purchaser was charged with notice of the lateral sewer. It was an apparent easement as that term is used in the books. (Wiesel v. Smira, 49 R.I. 246, 142 Atl. 148, 58 A.L.R. 818; 19 C.J. 868.)

The author of the annotation on Easements by Implication in 58 A.L.R. 832, states the rule as follows:

> While there is some conflict of authority as to whether existing drains, pipes, and sewers may be properly characterized as apparent, within the rule as to apparent or visible easements, the majority of the cases which have considered the question have taken the view that appearance and visibility are not synonymous, and that the fact that the pipe, sewer, or drain may be hidden underground does not negative its character as an apparent condition; at least, where the appliances connected with and leading to it are obvious.

As we are clear that an easement by implication was created under the facts as found by the trial court, it is unnecessary to discuss the question of prescription.

The judgment is affirmed.

NOTES AND QUESTIONS: IMPLIED EASEMENTS

1. Easements are implied in two basic situations. In the first situation the easement is implied on the basis of an apparent and continuous (or permanent) use of a portion of the tract existing when the tract is divided. The existing use is often described as a "quasi-easement." The easement is implied to protect the probable expectations of the grantor and grantee that the existing use will continue after the transfer. An *easement implied from a prior existing use* was involved in Van Sandt v. Royster.

In the second situation the easement is implied when the court finds the claimed easement is necessary to the enjoyment of the claimant's land and that the necessity arose when the claimed dominant parcel was severed from the claimed servient parcel. This kind of implied easement is known as an *easement by necessity* and is involved in the next case, Othen v. Rosier.

Necessity is an important circumstance in implying an easement on the basis of an existing use, because it probably affects the intention of the parties as to whether the existing use is to continue. Because necessity is a factor in implying an easement from a prior existing use, the distinction between that kind of implied easement and an implied easement by necessity has sometimes been overlooked. Failure to keep the two bases for implication separate can lead to a confusion of tongues. See Restatement (Third) of Property, Servitudes, §2.12, Comment e and Reporter's Note (T.D. No. 1, 1989) (discussing reasonable necessity requirement for easements implied from prior use); id. §2.15, Comment d and Reporter's Note (discussing easements by necessity). The Restatement (Third) notes that a number of jurisdictions, including New York, follow the old rule that strict necessity is required for implied easements in favor of the grantor.

If a court implies an easement on the basis of an existing use, and the easement is hidden (such as a pipeline), should the easement be valid against a subsequent purchaser of the servient land who has no notice of the easement? See Joel Eichengrun, The Problem of Hidden Easements and the Subsequent Purchaser Without Notice, 40 Okla. L. Rev. 3 (1987).

2. *Servitudes implied from a map.* See 3 Richard R. Powell, The Law of Real Property ¶409 (rev. ed. 1992):

> Where a conveyance of land describes the parcel as bounded by a street designated in the conveyance, or refers to a map on which spaces for streets, parks, or other common uses are shown, but the conveyance says nothing about the creation of an easement or a dedication to a public use, the conveyee of the land acquires an easement with respect to the street or the areas shown on the map.

Accord, Restatement (Third) of Property, Servitudes, supra, §2.13. Easements are not implied when the map is equivocal, but the use of broken lines to define a street or the notation "proposed road" will not prevent the implication of an easement from the plan if other circumstances indicate that an easement is intended.

3. If the dominant tenement and the servient tenement come into the same ownership, the easement is extinguished altogether. It will not be revived by a severance of the united title into the former dominant and servient tenements. (When the united title is subsequently redivided, a new easement by implication can arise if the circumstances at that time indicate a new easement was intended.)

Look back at Willard v. First Church of Christ, Scientist, page 791. Suppose that after the case the church buys lot 20 from Willard. Thereafter, the church sells lot 20 to A by a deed that does not mention an easement for parking. Does the church have an implied easement for parking in lot 20? Would it matter if the city zoning ordinance requires a certain number of off-street parking spaces for churches and other traffic generators and the sale of lot 20 without an easement for parking puts the church in violation of the zoning ordinance? See 3 Powell, supra, ¶411.

Othen v. Rosier

Supreme Court of Texas, 1950
148 Tex. 485, 226 S.W.2d 622

BREWSTER, J., delivered the opinion of the Court.

Petitioner, Albert Othen, brought this suit to enforce a roadway easement on lands of respondents, Estella Rosier et al., claiming the easement both of necessity and by prescription.

The land of both parties is a part of the Tone Survey of 2493 acres, all of which was formerly owned by one Hill. [The Rosiers own tracts of 100 acres and 16.31 acres, over which Othen claims an easement. Along the west side of the Rosiers' 100 acres runs Belt Line Road, a public highway running north and south. Othen owns tracts of 60 acres and 53 acres, lying to the east of, and contiguous to, the Rosiers' land (see Figure 9-3).

The chronological order of the conveyances of these tracts is as follows. First, Hill conveyed the 100-acre tract on August 26, 1896; by mesne conveyances this tract came into the hands of the Rosiers in 1924. Second, Hill conveyed the 60-acre tract in 1897, and by mesne conveyances Othen acquired it in 1904. These two conveyances left Hill owning the 53-acre tract and the 16.31-acre tract (and possibly other land). On the same day, January 26, 1899, Hill conveyed the 53-acre tract and the

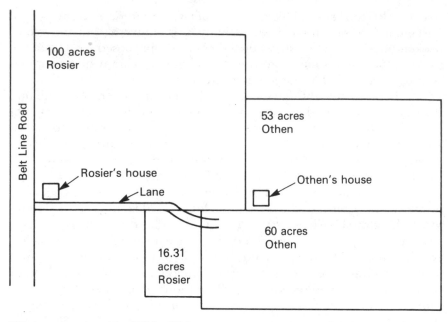

100 acres Rosier

Belt Line Road

53 acres
Othen

Rosier's house

Lane

Othen's house

16.31
acres
Rosier

60 acres
Othen

100 acres conveyed by Hill in 1896.
 60 acres conveyed by Hill in 1897.
 53 acres and 16.31 acres conveyed by Hill in 1899.

Figure 9-3

16.31-acre tract to separate purchasers, who conveyed the 53 acres to Othen in 1913 and the 16.31 acres to the Rosiers in 1924.]

    ... The Tone Survey touches three roads: the Belt Line Road, which runs along its west side; the Duncanville Road, which borders it on the south; and the Fish Creek Road, which is its north boundary. But Othen's 113 acres is not contiguous to any of them; so he must cross somebody else's land to get out to a highway. That he had accomplished before the happening which precipitated this litigation by going through a gate in the west line of his 60 acres and in the east line of Rosiers' 16.31 acres, a short but unproved distance south of the south line of Rosiers' 100 acres; thence west-northwesterly across the 16.31 acres into a fenced lane which runs along the south side of Rosiers' 100 acres; thence through this lane to a gate, which opens into the Belt Line Road. Near this gate and in the southwest corner of the 100 acres was the Rosiers' dwelling house, orchard, stock lots and barns. The Rosiers travel and use the lane above described for such purposes as go with the operation of a farm, as well as for their stock to travel to and from the 16.31 acres, which they use as a pasture and from which they get fire wood. On the

814

16.31 acres is a tenant house, which has been occupied some of the 18 or 20 years previous to the trial by tenants of the Rosiers; and they have made the same use of the lane as Othen has made. The south fence of this lane was built about 1895. Its north fence and the outside gate were constructed about 1906. Before Othen bought his 60 acres in 1904 he had lived on it for two years as a tenant and had moved away for about a year; and he has continuously used the disputed roadway to get to and from the highway from and to his home.

It seems undisputed that the Rosiers made whatever repairs were necessary to keep the land usable. And, so far as the record shows, nobody else recognized any obligation or claimed any right so to keep it. The surface waters flowing into the lane had cut out a large ditch which threatened to encroach across the roadway and render it impassable unless a bridge should be built across it, and these waters threatened erosion damage to Rosiers' cultivated land. To remedy that situation the Rosiers caused a levee 300 feet long to be constructed as close as possible to the south fence of the lane, with something like half of it in the lane and the other half curving southeasterly into the 16.31 acres. This levee impounded the waters draining southward off Rosiers' 100 acres and made the lane so muddy that for weeks at a time it was impassable except by horseback, thereby, Othen alleged, depriving him of ingress and egress to and from his farm. So he filed this suit praying a temporary writ of injunction enjoining the Rosiers from further maintaining this levee and a "mandatory writ of injunction commanding and enjoining and restraining the said defendant from further interfering with" his "use of such easement and roadway" and for damages.

The trial court found that Othen had an easement of necessity and adjudged it to him "upon, over and across" land of the Rosiers beginning at the northeast corner of the 16.31 acres and extending westward "along the said 16.31 acre tract and having a width of approximately 40 feet" to a point in its north boundary immediately east of the northwest corner of the 16.31 acres, thence across that boundary line and westward along the south boundary line of Rosiers' 100 acres to its southwest corner and into the Belt Line Road. The judgment further ordered the Rosiers "to take such action as is necessary to put said easement and roadway, so described, in as usable a condition as same was prior to the erection of said levee."

The Court of Civil Appeals first affirmed the judgment in so far as it decreed Othen a roadway easement of necessity but reversed the injunction phase of it because that order is too vague and uncertain to be enforceable. However, on rehearing the majority concluded that Othen has no easement either of necessity or by prescription and rendered judgment for the Rosiers, Chief Justice Bond dissenting. 221 S.W.2d 594. That conclusion is attacked here in two points of error.

In support of his claim to an easement of necessity, Othen quotes from 15 Tex. Jur., Sec. 16. p.785, as follows:

> Furthermore, the grantor impliedly reserves for himself a right of way where he sells land surrounded by other land of which he is owner, and to which he can have access or egress only through the granted premises, and the servient estate is charged with the burden in the hands of any vendee holding under the conveyance.[10]

That statement is in line with the recent holding by this court in Bains v. Parker, 143 Texas 57, 182 S.W.2d 397: "Where a vendor retains a tract of land which is surrounded partly by the tract conveyed and partly by the lands of a stranger, there is an implied reservation of a right of way by necessity over the land conveyed where grantor has no other way out." In 28 C.J.S., Easements, Secs. 34 and 35, pp.694 et seq., it is made clear that before an easement can be held to be created by implied reservation it must be shown: (1) that there was a unity of ownership of the alleged dominant and servient estates; (2) that the roadway is a necessity, not a mere convenience; and (3) *that the necessity existed at the time of severance of the two estates.* And see 17 Am. Jur., Easements, Secs. 43 and 49, pp.953 and 963.

Under the foregoing authorities, Othen's claim to an implied reservation of an easement in a roadway means that when Hill, the original owner, sold the 116.31 acres to the Rosiers it was then necessary, not merely convenient, for him to travel over it from the 113 acres now owned by Othen in order to get to and from the Belt Line Road. In determining that question we shall ignore the Duncanville Road to the South, which was established in 1910, as well as the Fish Creek Road to the north, although the record is silent as to when the latter came into existence.

As already stated, the entire Tone Survey of 2493 acres was owned by one Hill, in whom was unity of ownership of the lands now owned by the parties to this suit. On August 26, 1896, he sold the 100 acres in question to Rosiers' predecessors in title, retaining the south 60 acres now owned by Othen, which he conveyed on February 20, 1897. In the deed of date August 26, 1896, did he impliedly reserve the roadway easement from the 60 acres, which he retained over and across the 16.31 acres which he did not convey until January 26, 1899, thence on and along the south side of the 100 acres to the Belt Line Road? Obviously, no such easement arose as to the 16.31 acres over which the trial court decreed Othen a roadway, because Hill did not part with his title to it

---

10. Blackstone put it this way: "[I]f a man grants me a piece of ground in the middle of his field, he at the same time tacitly and impliedly gives me a way to come to it; and I may cross his land for that purpose without trespass." 2 William Blackstone, Commentaries *37 — EDS.

until two years and five months after he sold the 100 acres and about
two years after he sold the 60 acres which Othen now owns; one cannot
be said to have an easement in lands, the fee simple title to which is in
himself. Alley v. Carleton, 29 Texas 74, 94 Am. Dec. 260. Under the
record before us we cannot hold that petitioner has shown any implied
easement as to the 100 acres by reason of the deed of August 26, 1896,
because the record nowhere shows that the roadway along the south line
of the 100 acres was a necessity on the date of that deed, rather than a
mere convenience. The burden to prove that was on Othen. Bains v.
Parker, supra. There was testimony that it was the only outlet to a public
road since about 1900 and for the "last 40 years"; *but there was none as to
the situation on August 26, 1896.* One Posey did testify that the owner of
the "Othen land" (necessarily the 60 acres) in 1897 "came out up across
the south side of the place to the road there," but he did not testify that
it was then the only roadway out. On that proposition his testimony was:
"Q. Now, then, *is* there any other outlet from Mr. Othen's place to a
highway, outside of the road — to a public road? A. Well, I don't know
of any." (Italics ours.) The record does not show just how much of the
Tone Survey Hill owned when he conveyed the 100 acres on August 26,
1896, but it does appear from a stipulation of the parties that he owned
as much as 1350 acres of it until January 26, 1899; and Othen's 53 acres
and Rosiers' 16.31 acres were a part of that tract. So, for all the record
shows, Hill may easily have been able to cross the 53 acres and around
north of the 100 acres on to the Belt Line Road, or he may as easily have
been able to go from the 16.31 acres southwesterly to that road across
land which he still owned. Certainly Othen should have excluded any
such possibility by proof if he would raise an implied reservation in derogation of the warranties in Hill's deed of date August 26, 1896. Rights
claimed in derogation of the warranties are implied with great caution,
hence they should be made clearly to appear. Sellers v. Texas Cent. Ry.
Co., 81 Texas 458, 17 S.W. 32, 13 L.R.A. 657; Scarborough v. Anderson
Bros. Const. Co. (Civ. App.), 90 S.W.2d 305 (er. dism.).

What we have said determines Othen's claim to a way of necessity;
such an easement necessarily can arise only from an implied grant or
implied reservation. 17 Am. Jur., p. 959, Sec. 48. This results from [the]
rule that the mere fact that the claimant's land is completely surrounded
by the land of another does not, of itself, give the former a way of necessity over the land of the latter, where there is no privity of ownership.
Neblett v. R. S. Sterling Inv. Co. (Civ. App.), 233 S.W. 604 (er. ref.);
Parker v. Bains (Civ. App.), 194 S.W.2d 569 (er. ref., N.R.E.); Brundrett
v. Tarpley (Civ. App.), 50 S.W.2d 401; Texas & N.O.R.R. Co. v. Millard
(Civ. App.), 181 S.W.2d 842.

It is dependent upon an implied grant or reservation, and cannot exist unless
it is affirmatively shown that there was formerly unity of ownership of the

alleged dominant and servient estates, for no one can have a way of necessity over the land of a stranger. Necessity alone, without reference to any relations between the respective owners of the land, is not sufficient to create such a right. [Ward v. Bledsoe (Civ. App.), 105 S.W.2d 1116.]

Petitioner's other point complains of the holding of the Court of Civil Appeals that, as a matter of law, he has no easement by prescription.

An important essential in the acquisition of a prescriptive right is an adverse use of the easement.

Generally, the hostile and adverse character of the user necessary to establish an easement by prescription is the same as that which is necessary to establish title by adverse possession. If the enjoyment is consistent with the right of the owner of the tenement, it confers no right in opposition to such ownership.

17 Am. Jur., Easements, Sec. 63, p.974, citing cases from 22 jurisdictions, among which are Weber v. Chaney (Civ. App.), 5 S.W.2d 213 (er. ref.), and Callan v. Walters (Civ. App.), 190 S.W. 829. Therefore, the same authority declares in Sec. 67, at page 978,

The rule is well settled that use by express or implied permission or license, no matter how long continued, cannot ripen into an easement by prescription, since user as of right, as distinguished from permissive user, is lacking,

citing, among other cases, Klein v. Gehrung, 25 Texas Supp. 232, 78 Am. Dec. 565.

In Klein v. Gehrung, it is said: "The foundation of prescriptive title is the presumed grant of the party whose rights are adversely affected; but where it appears that the enjoyment has existed by the consent or license of such party, no presumption of grant can be made."

In Weber et ux. v. Chaney, supra, the Webers sued to require Chaney to reopen a road through his farm to public use. Before Chaney closed it such of the public as had occasion to do so used the road as if it had been an established highway. Chaney, his family, tenants and employees likewise used it. Although Chaney never made any objection to the public using the road, he at all times maintained three closed gates across it and the public usually closed them after passing through. It was held that this use by the public was a permissive use which, in the absence of any adverse claim of right against Chaney, could never ripen into a prescriptive right against him so as to constitute the road a public highway.

Callan v. Walters, supra, holds that where both the owner and the claimant were using a common stairway, each to get into his own building, the claimant's use was not adverse because not exclusive. "The use of a way over the land of another when the owner is also using the same is not such adverse possession as will serve as notice of a claim of right, for the reason that the same is not inconsistent with a license from the owner."

In Sassman v. Collins, 53 Texas Civ. App. 71, 115 S.W. 337 (er. ref.), Collins sued to enforce a roadway across Sassman's land, alleging that he had an easement therein both of necessity and by prescription. Collins and others did use the roadway to get to a public road but Sassman and his predecessors in title likewise used it for the same purpose. The court held that under those circumstances the use of the roadway by the claimant and others is presumed to be with the consent of the owner and not adverse.

In Tolbert et al. v. McClellan (Civ. App.), 241 S.W. 206, it was sought to enforce the public right to a road across McClellan's land by prescription based on 30 years' use. It was shown that the road was entered through gaps in the fence around McClellan's farm; and that during the greater part but not all of the 30 years these gaps were closed by gates provided by McClellan. It was held that the use made of the road by the public was only permissive and did not exclude any individual right of McClellan inconsistent therewith. . . .

There is a criticism of the foregoing authorities in Foster et al. v. Patton (Civ. App.), 104 S.W.2d 944 (er. dism.), wherein it is said that a use by the owner should not be regarded as of itself sufficient to show that a corresponding user by the claimant is merely permissive. However, as the opinion itself frankly recognizes, the holding is dictum, so we must give effect to the authorities above discussed.

It is undisputed that the road along the Rosiers' 100 acres has been fenced on both sides since about 1906; that the gate opening from the lane into the Belt Line Road was erected at the same time and has been kept closed by the Rosiers and Othen as well as by all parties using the lane as an outlet to the road; that the Rosiers and their tenants have used the lane for general farm purposes as well as to haul wood from the 16.31 acres and to permit their livestock to get to and from the pasture. Under those facts, we conclude that Othen's use of the roadway was merely permissive, hence constituted only a license, which could not and did not ripen into a prescriptive right.

But Othen insists that he had prescriptive title of 10 years to the easement before the lane was fenced and the gate opening into the Belt Line Road was erected in 1906, because "at least since 1895 and probably since 1893 said roadway has been established and claimed by petitioner and others." Othen testified that about 1900 he moved onto the 113 acres in question as a tenant and lived there two years, moved away for about 11 months, then "bought it and moved back." It is obvious that he did not use the roadway in any way for any period of 10 years prior to 1906. The testimony as to its use by Othen's predecessors is, in our opinion, too vague and uncertain to amount to any evidence of prescriptive right to the roadway decreed by the trial court. For example, when Othen was asked to "tell the court what the condition of that passageway was there," he answered: "Well, in that day and time it was just prairie and there were some hog wallows which would hold water. You would just pick your place round about; if there was a hog wallow, go around it and come on in. But that was the general direction through there." Another witness, asked whether in 1901 there was a road "by the side of the present Rosier property," replied: "It was on the present Rosier property, and at that time went up through the edge of the field." When asked by Othen's counsel, "Do you know anything about where this road used to run?", Mrs. Rosier said: "Well, it didn't run up exactly next to the Belt Line like it is running now." It cannot be said that this showed only a slight divergence in the directions taken by the roadway before 1904, therefore Othen did not discharge his burden of showing that his predecessors' adverse possession was in the same place and within the definite lines claimed by him and fixed by the trial court. . . .

Moreover, since Hill did not part with his title to Othen's alleged dominant estate until 1897 (as to the 60 acres) and until 1899 (as to the 53 acres) and did not part with his title to 16.31 acres of the Rosiers' alleged servient estate until 1899, Othen could not under any circumstances have perfected prescriptive title to a roadway easement on the 16.31 acres prior to 1906.

> Since a person cannot claim adversely to himself, the courts uniformly maintain that the prescriptive period does not begin to run while the dominant and servient tracts are under the same ownership. [17 Am. Jur., Easements, Sec. 69, p.980.]

It follows that the judgment of the Court of Civil Appeals is affirmed.

NOTES, QUESTIONS, AND PROBLEMS: EASEMENTS BY NECESSITY

1. Is an easement by necessity implied because of public policy or because it effectuates the intent of the parties? In the early English cases, it was said that one who grants a thing must be understood to have granted that without which the granted thing cannot exist. By the seventeenth century, an easement by necessity came to be supported by a public policy that no land be made inaccessible. In the nineteenth century, when courts sought to ground rights in the contract between the parties, the easement by necessity was said to carry out the presumed intent of the parties. In most cases, it does not matter which justification

is given, but if the parties expressly provide that no way of necessity exists, the court must decide whether such a provision is valid. See Sayre v. Dickerson, 278 Ala. 477, 179 So. 2d 57 (1965) (holding express agreement landlocking land enforceable where the land is accessible by water).

There is some conflict in the cases over the degree of necessity required for an easement by necessity. Most courts, like the court in Othen v. Rosier, require strict necessity, but some have granted an easement by necessity where access to the land exists but it is claimed to be inadequate, difficult, or costly. In a few jurisdictions a surface way of necessity will not be implied if the tract has access by navigable water.

On easements by necessity, see 3 Richard R. Powell, The Law of Real Property ¶410 (rev. ed. 1992); Stewart E. Sterk, Neighbors in American Land Law, 87 Colum. L. Rev. 55 (1987) (attempting to ground easements by necessity, implication, and estoppel in a social obligation of neighbors to cooperate).

2. *A* owns five adjoining tracts of forest land, numbered 1 through 5. All five lots had previously been owned by *O* as a single tract; *A* purchased each lot from *O* in a separate transaction, lot 1 first, lot 2 second, lot 3 third, lot 4 fourth, and finally lot 5. Lots 1 and 2 are bounded by a public road on the north. Lots 3 and 4 are bounded by a public road on the south. Lot 5 has no access to a public road except through one of the other four lots, thus:

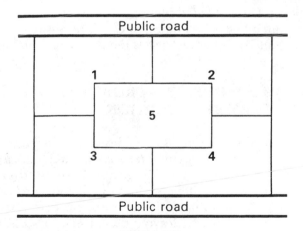

Figure 9-4

A dies intestate. Her five children, *B, C, D, E,* and *F,* are her heirs. In the decree of distribution settling *A*'s estate, the court assigns lot 1 to *B,* lot 2 to *C,* lot 3 to *D,* lot 4 to *E,* and lot 5 to *F.* Nothing is said in the decree about lot 5 having an easement of way. Sometime later *F* sues the owners of lots 1 through 4, claiming an easement by necessity. What result? See 2 American Law of Property §8.91 (1952). Cf. Horner v. Heersche, 202 Kan. 250, 447 P.2d 811 (1968); McQuinn v. Tantalo, 41 A.D.2d 575, 339 N.Y.S.2d 541 (1973).

3. An easement by necessity endures only so long as it is necessary. If the dominant owner secures another way out from the landlocked parcel, the easement by necessity ceases. Thus if *A*, owner of a landlocked parcel with an easement by necessity over *B*'s land, acquires an easement over *C*'s land enabling *A* to reach a public road, the easement by necessity disappears.

In Van Sandt v. Royster, page 806, suppose that the city constructs a public sewer in Tenth Street, and that the owner of lot 4 can connect with it. Does the owner of lot 4 lose the implied sewer easement over lots 19 and 20?

4. In some states, mainly in the West, statutes give an owner of landlocked land the right to condemn an easement across neighboring land upon showing the requisite necessity. The condemnation is a judicial proceeding, and the landowner must pay damages to the owner of the land where the easement is sought. Under these statutes, it does not matter how the landlocking occurred; prior common ownership of the dominant and servient estates is not required.

Why should the servient owner of a common law easement by necessity receive no compensation whereas the servient owner of a privately condemned easement by necessity receives compensation from the benefitted owner?

In Leo Sheep Co. v. United States, 440 U.S. 668 (1979), the court held that the United States had no easement by necessity to reach landlocked government lands because it has the power of eminent domain.

NOTES, QUESTIONS, AND PROBLEMS: EASEMENTS BY PRESCRIPTION

1. As mentioned in Chapter 2 (see footnote 11 on page 127), easements may be acquired by prescription, which in many ways is similar to adverse possession but in some ways distinctly different. Adverse possession involves a statute of limitations running on the right to bring an action to recover *possession* of land; the statute operates to extinguish the remedy of the previous owner, leaving the adverse possessor in indefeasible possession. The result is that the adverse possessor has a new title based on his possession. A statute of limitations upon the recovery of possession does not cover actions concerning easements, which involve *use* and not possession of land. Yet the reasons underlying the protection of long-continued adverse possession apply also to long-continued use. Inasmuch as legislatures enacted no legislation to protect ancient easements, courts developed the doctrine of prescription. Pre-

scription rests upon the idea, taken from Roman law, that rights can be acquired simply by the passage of time.

The earliest type of prescriptive easement was the easement based upon a use from time immemorial. In 1275, to settle old claims to earlier possession, Parliament enacted a statute prohibiting challenges to rights of possession enjoyed since the accession to the throne of Richard I (the Lionheart) in 1189. This legislation applied only to writs of right to recover seisin, but the courts thereafter by analogy held that any continuous use in the nature of an easement or profit from 1189 was unchallengeable. The year 1189 was fixed as the time beyond which legal memory could not go, and the claimant of an easement by prescription would allege use since "the memory of man runneth not to the contrary." As the year 1189 receded into history, it became more and more difficult to prove that the claimant and his predecessors had enjoyed the use since 1189. In time, "as parliament failed to intervene to amend the law, the judges set their ingenuity to work, by fictions and presumptions, to atone for the supineness of the legislature, and to amend, so far as in them lay, the law."[11] They first set down the rule that if a use had existed so long as any living person could remember, it was presumed to have existed from the year 1189. Later, by analogy to a statute of limitations enacted in 1623 providing a 20-year limitation on suits in ejectment, the judges held that, if a use had continued for 20 years, it presumptively had existed since 1189. However, these presumptions did not provide an effective system of prescription because they were only presumptions and could be overcome by evidence showing that some time since 1189 (perhaps 25 years before the lawsuit) the use could not or did not exist. And so, "endowed with a great power of imagination for the purpose of supporting ancient uses,"[12] the judges invented the *fiction of the lost grant*. If a use was shown to have existed for 20 years, it was presumed that a grant of an easement had been made and that the grant had been lost. The presumption of grant could not be rebutted by evidence that no grant had in fact been made. Thus was the 20 years' adverse use clothed with a rightful beginning and the necessity of proof of use from 1189 obviated.

In this country it would have been impossible to require a continuous use since 1189, and American courts rejected the theory that prescriptive easements rest upon use from time immemorial. They developed the law of prescription, applying by analogy the statutes of limitation relating to the recovery of possession. Courts set the same period for prescriptive easements as the statutes fixed for recovery of possession, and generally required the same manner of use as is required for adverse possession: open and notorious, continuous, adverse, and

11. Bryant v. Foot, (1867) L.R. 2 Q.B. 161, 181.
12. Neaverson v. Peterborough R.D.C., [1902] 1 Ch. 557, 573.

under claim of right. The fiction of the lost grant — an ingenious invention to overcome the onerous burden of proving use from time immemorial, never required in the United States — should not have crossed the Atlantic. Once prescriptive easements were put on the same basis as adverse possession (the running of the statute of limitations upon a cause of action), the lost grant theory should have been seen as irrelevant.[13] But, in slavish adherence to the verbal formulation of eighteenth-century English law, and unmindful of its historical justification, some American courts adopted the fiction of the lost grant, although the majority rejected it.

The lost grant theory draws a confusing distinction between acquiescence and permission. Under lost grant theory, the owner of land is presumed to consent or acquiesce in the use; after all, the owner (or his predecessor) is thought to have granted the easement. On the other hand, if the use is made with the permission of the owner, the use is not adverse. To secure a prescriptive easement under lost grant theory, the claimant must show that the use was not permissive and also that the owner acquiesced (did not object). Language that the owner must acquiesce in the easement sometimes appears, like a pentimento, in opinions in jurisdictions that have erased the lost grant theory.

Consider the fiction of the lost grant in relation to the following problem: To reach her land more easily, in 1975 A makes a road across O's land. In 1984 O writes A a letter saying: "You are hereby notified that the portion of my land which you made into a road is my private property. No person has the right to cross this land, and you are liable to me in damages. I hereby forbid you to pass over any portion of my land, especially that portion which you unlawfully made into a road." A ignores O's letter and continues to use the road for the prescriptive period of 20 years. In 1995 does A have a prescriptive easement? See Dartnell v. Bidwell, 115 Me. 227, 98 A. 743 (1916) (holding that a letter interrupts prescription because it rebuts any claim of acquiescence or grant). Would a letter to a possessor stop adverse possession from running?

In a jurisdiction not following the fiction of the lost grant, to prevent a prescriptive easement from being acquired, the owner must effectively interrupt or stop the adverse use. Suppose, under the preceding facts, that in 1984 O had erected a fence across the road, and that A tore down

13. To illustrate, a prescriptive easement for parking vehicles obtained against a tenant is not valid against the landlord because actions in ejectment and trespass (the usual methods of preventing a prescriptive easement) are available only to the owner of a possessory interest (the tenant). Dieterich Intl. v. J.S.&J. Servs., 3 Cal. App. 4th 1601, 5 Cal. Rptr. 2d 388 (1992). (Compare adverse possession, Problem 3, page 150.) Under a lost grant theory, the landlord would be barred simply by the passage of time if the landlord were capable of making a grant. See Jerome J. Curtis, Jr., Reviving the Lost Grant, 23 Real Prop., Prob. & Tr. J. 535 (1988).

the fence and continued to use the road. Does *A* acquire a prescriptive easement in 1995? See Lofland v. Truitt, 260 A.2d 909 (Del. Ch. 1969); Caswell v. Bisnett, 50 A.D. 672, 375 N.Y.S.2d 218 (1975), appeal denied, 38 N.Y.2d 709, 346 N.E.2d 558, 382 N.Y.S.2d 1028 (1976).

2. Where *A* acquires a prescriptive easement over *O*'s land, should *A* have to pay *O* damages? This question arose in Warsaw v. Chicago Metallic Ceilings, Inc., 35 Cal. 3d 564, 676 P.2d 584, 199 Cal. Rptr. 773 (1984). Although six of the seven judges agreed that any change in the no-compensation rule must come from the legislature, the judges divided on the soundness of the no-compensation rule. Four members of the court thought the rule sound because (1) prescription protected a long use or possession against largely unmeritorious claims of an "alleged owner," (2) the rule reduced litigation, and (3) land use historically has been favored over disuse. Three members of the court thought that allowing persons to acquire prescriptive rights without compensation had no justification. See Thomas W. Merrill, Property Rules, Liability Rules, and Adverse Possession, 79 Nw. U. L. Rev. 1122 (1984-1985); Comment, Compensation for the Involuntary Transfer of Property Between Private Parties: Application of a Liability Rule to the Law of Adverse Possession, 79 Nw. U. L. Rev. 759 (1984), both discussed in footnote 19 on page 140.

Compare the law of nuisance, for example, Note 3 on pages 974-975, and the law of mistaken improver, pages 150-151, both of which give a court power to grant damages or an injunction. See John W. Weaver, Easements are Nuisances, 25 Real Prop., Prob. & Tr. J. 103 (1990) (arguing for the application to easements of the rules developed in nuisance law for determining when an injunction or damages should be granted).

3. In Othen v. Rosier the court presumed that the use of the road by Othen was permissive rather than adverse because it was not exclusive. Why should this be presumed? In order to gain title by adverse possession, a person must show exclusive possession for the required period. There is good reason for this requirement when one is claiming exclusive ownership of the land ousting the legal owner. But why should it apply so as to bar a claim to a nonexclusive prescriptive easement to be used by the servient owner as well? The majority of courts requires exclusive use for prescription, but defines it differently from the adverse possession requirement. "Exclusivity does not require a showing that only the claimant made use of the way, but that the claimant's right to use the land does not depend upon a like right in others." Page v. Bloom, 223 Ill. App. 3d 18, 20, 584 N.E.2d 813, 815 (1991). See Note, Exclusiveness in the Law of Prescription, 8 Cardozo L. Rev. 611 (1987).

Consider also the case of a common driveway lying one-half on *A*'s land and one-half on *B*'s. If, after the prescriptive period has passed, *A* erects a fence in the middle of the driveway, *B* probably can get it removed. Even though the common driveway began as a permissive and not wrongful use, most courts hold that *B*'s use of a common driveway was presumptively adverse to *A* and *A*'s use presumptively adverse to *B*. Does the common driveway case differ so significantly from the use by Othen of Rosier's road that a different presumption should apply? See Causey v. Lanigan, 208 Va. 587, 159 S.E.2d 655 (1968).

4. Adjacent to Conrad Hilton's home is a golf club. Every day several golf balls are driven onto Hilton's property, and the players come onto his property to retrieve them. If this continues, will the golf club acquire a prescriptive easement over Hilton's property? See MacDonald Properties, Inc. v. Bel-Air Country Club, 72 Cal. App. 3d 693, 140 Cal. Rptr. 367 (1977). If so, what should Hilton do to prevent a prescriptive easement from arising?

5. *Public prescriptive easements.* In most states a public prescriptive easement can be obtained by long continuous use by the public under a claim of right. The landowner must be put on notice, by the kind and extent of use, that an adverse right is being claimed by the general public, not by individuals.[14] Where a public road is being claimed, the same requirements generally apply as are applied to a private prescriptive easement.

Some courts use the theory of implied dedication, rather than prescription, for public easements. This theory owes something to the lost grant fiction, for it seeks a substitute for a grant in an implied dedication. It may be used where the landowner evidences an intent to dedicate and the state accepts by maintaining the land used by the public. Or implied dedication theory may be used as a substitute for prescription.

In states bordering the sea, the availability of coastal beaches for public use is a matter of considerable importance. The state holds, in public trust, the beach from the water to the mean high-tide line (the foreshore). The dry sand portion of the beach between the mean high-tide line and the vegetation line is subject to private ownership.[15] Public access requires both a way of access from inland to the coast and a lateral easement up and down the beach. The prescriptive easement doctrine has not been notably successful in providing public access, largely be-

14. In Rockefeller Center, in New York City, a private street called Rockefeller Plaza is situated between the RCA Building and the sunken skating rink. In order to preserve Rockefeller Center's right of ownership of the street, each year the street is closed to all traffic, even pedestrian, for one day — a Sunday in July is usually chosen as interfering least with tenants and visitors. It is believed by lawyers for Rockefeller Center that this formality is necessary to prevent the public from acquiring a permanent right of way in the street.

15. In Maine and Massachusetts, private ownership extends to the mean low tide, subject to the public right to fish, fowl, and navigate on the foreshore. See Bell v. Town of Wells, 557 A.2d 168 (Me. 1989) (holding that a public easement in the foreshore does not include sunbathing or general recreation, and that a statute defining public rights in intertidal lands to include recreational purposes is an unconstitutional taking of property); Symposium, Public Access and the New England Shoreline, 42 Me. L. Rev. 1 (1990).

cause most courts presume that public use of beaches is with the permission of the owner, and the burden of proving adverse use cannot be met. See City of Daytona Beach v. Tona-Rama, Inc., 294 So. 2d 73 (Fla. 1974). In a few states, suits for prescriptive easements for beach access have been successful. See Gion v. City of Santa Cruz, 2 Cal. 3d 29, 465 P.2d 50, 84 Cal. Rptr. 162 (1970) (using implied dedication theory, and holding there was no presumption either of permissive or adverse use);[16] Concerned Citizens of Brunswick County Taxpayers Assn. v. Holden Beach Enterprises, 329 N.C. 37, 404 S.E.2d 677 (1991) (holding pathway to beach could shift over prescriptive period so long as there was substantial identity of use; barricades placed by owner did not destroy the public's continuity of use because they were ineffective in stopping the public), noted in 70 N.C. L. Rev. 1289 (1992).

Because beach access is usually presumed to be with the permission of the owner and because each individual beach access must be litigated separately under the prescriptive easement doctrine, courts in some jurisdictions have turned to other doctrines with greater potential for opening the beaches. In Florida, Oregon, and Texas, courts have roused, from a sleep of some centuries, the medieval doctrine of customary rights — uses that existed for so long that "the memory of man runneth not to the contrary" — and have held that long usage of beaches by the public is protected as a customary right. City of Daytona Beach v. Tona-Rama, Inc., supra; State ex rel. Thornton v. Hay, 254 Or. 584, 462 P.2d 671 (1969); Matcha v. Mattox, 711 S.W.2d 95 (Tex. Civ. App. 1986).

Another method of recognizing a public interest in beaches is the public trust doctrine, discussed in the following case. See generally Gilbert L. Finnell, Jr., Public Access to Coastal Public Property: Judicial Theories and the Takings Issue, 67 N.C. L. Rev. 627 (1989).

Matthews v. Bay Head Improvement Association
Supreme Court of New Jersey, 1984
95 N.J. 306, 47 A.2d 355

SCHREIBER, J. The public trust doctrine acknowledges that the ownership, dominion and sovereignty over land flowed by tidal waters, which

---

16. The California legislature, believing this decision would cause landowners to erect fences excluding the public, repudiated it. Cal. Civ. Code §1009 (West 1982), enacted in 1971, abolishes implied dedication of land more than 1000 yards from the ocean, and provides that a landowner may prevent implied dedication either by posting annually a sign ("Right to pass by permission of owner, revocable at any time") or recording a similar notice in the public records. The landowner's act granting permission defeats any claim of public adverse use.

extend to the mean high water mark, is vested in the State in trust for the people. The public's right to use the tidal lands and water encompasses navigation, fishing and recreational uses, including bathing, swimming and other shore activities. Borough of Neptune City v. Borough of Avon-by-the-Sea, 61 N.J. 296, 309, 294 A.2d 47 (1972). In *Avon* we held that the public trust applied to the municipally-owned dry sand beach immediately landward of the high water mark. The major issue in this case is whether, ancillary to the public's right to enjoy the tidal lands, the public has a right to gain access through and to use the dry sand area not owned by a municipality but by a quasi-public body.

The Borough of Point Pleasant instituted this suit against the Borough of Bay Head and the Bay Head Improvement Association (Association), generally asserting that the defendants prevented Point Pleasant inhabitants from gaining access to the Atlantic Ocean and the beachfront in Bay Head. The proceeding was dismissed as to the Borough of Bay Head because it did not own or control the beach. Subsequently, . . . Stanley Van Ness, as Public Advocate, joined as plaintiff-intervenor. When the Borough of Point Pleasant ceased pursuing the litigation, the Public Advocate became the primary moving party. The Public Advocate asserted that the defendants had denied the general public its right of access during the summer bathing season to public trust lands along the beaches in Bay Head and its right to use private property fronting on the ocean incidental to the public's right under the public trust doctrine. The complaint was amended on several occasions, eliminating the Borough of Point Pleasant as plaintiff and adding more than 100 individuals, who were owners or had interests in properties located on the oceanfront in Bay Head, as defendants. . . .

Facts

The Borough of Bay Head (Bay Head) borders the Atlantic Ocean. Adjacent to it on the north is the Borough of Point Pleasant Beach, on the south the Borough of Mantoloking, and on the west Barnegat Bay. Bay Head consists of a fairly narrow strip of land, 6,667 feet long (about 1¼ miles). A beach runs along its entire length adjacent to the Atlantic Ocean. There are 76 separate parcels of land that border the beach. All except six are owned by private individuals. Title to those six is vested in the Association.

The Association was founded in 1910 and incorporated as a non-profit corporation in 1932. . . . Its constitution delineates the Association's object to promote the best interests of the Borough and "in so doing to own property, operate bathing beaches, hire life guards, beach cleaners and policemen. . . ."

Nine streets in the Borough, which are perpendicular to the beach, end at the dry sand. The Association owns the land commencing at the end of seven of these streets for the width of each street and extending through the upper dry sand to the mean high water line, the beginning of the wet sand area or foreshore. In addition, the Association owns the fee in six shore front properties, three of which are contiguous and have a frontage aggregating 310 feet. Many owners of beachfront property executed and delivered to the Association leases of the upper dry sand area. These leases are revocable by either party to the lease on thirty days' notice. Some owners have not executed such leases and have not permitted the Association to use their beaches. . . .

The Association controls and supervises its beach property between the third week in June and Labor Day. It engages about 40 employees, who serve as lifeguards, beach police and beach cleaners. . . . Beach police are stationed at the entrances to the beaches where the public streets lead into the beach to ensure that only Association members or their guests enter. Some beach police patrol the beaches to enforce its membership rules.

Membership is generally limited to residents of Bay Head. Class A members are property owners. Class B are non-owners. . . . Upon application residents are routinely accepted. . . .

Except for fishermen, who are permitted to walk through the upper dry sand area to the foreshore, only the membership may use the beach between 10:00 A.M. and 5:30 P.M. during the summer season. The public is permitted to use the Association's beach from 5:30 P.M. to 10:00 A.M. during the summer and, with no hourly restrictions, between Labor Day and mid-June.

No attempt has ever been made to stop anyone from occupying the terrain east of the high water mark. During certain parts of the day, when the tide is low, the foreshore could consist of about 50 feet of sand not being flowed by the water. The public could gain access to the foreshore by coming from the Borough of Point Pleasant Beach on the north or from the Borough of Mantoloking on the south.

The Public Trust

In Borough of Neptune City v. Borough of Avon-by-the-Sea, 61 N.J. 296, 303, 294 A.2d 47 (1972), Justice Hall alluded to the ancient principle "that land covered by tidal waters belonged to the sovereign, but for the common use of all the people." The genesis of this principle is found in Roman jurisprudence, which held that "[b]y the law of nature" "the air, running water, the sea, and consequently the shores of the sea" were "common to mankind." Justinian, Institutes 2.1.1 (T. Sandars trans. 1st Am. ed. 1876). No one was forbidden access to the sea, and everyone could use the seashore "to dry his nets there, and haul them from the sea. . . ." Id., 2.1.5. The seashore was not private property, but "subject to the same law as the sea itself, and the sand or ground beneath it." Id.

This underlying concept was applied in New Jersey in Arnold v. Mundy, 6 N.J.L. 1 (Sup. Ct. 1821).

The defendant in *Arnold* tested the plaintiff's claim of an exclusive right to harvest oysters by taking some oysters that the plaintiff had planted in beds in the Raritan River adjacent to his farm in Perth Amboy. The oyster beds extended about 150 feet below the ordinary low water mark. The tide ebbed and flowed over it. The defendant's motion for a nonsuit was granted. The Supreme Court denied the plaintiff's subsequent motion to set aside the nonsuit.

Chief Justice Kirkpatrick, in an extensive opinion, . . . concluded that all navigable rivers in which the tide ebbs and flows and the coasts of the sea, including the water and land under the water, are "common to all the citizens, and that each [citizen] has a right to use them according to his necessities, subject only to the laws which regulate that use. . . ." Id. at 93. Regulation included erecting docks, harbors and wharves, and improving fishery and oyster beds. This common property . . . [belonged] to the Crown of England, and upon the Revolution these royal rights became vested in the people of New Jersey. Later, in Illinois Central R.R. v. Illinois, 146 U.S. 387, 453, 13 S. Ct. 110, 118, 36 L. Ed. 1018, 1043 (1892), the Supreme Court, in referring to the common property, stated that "[t]he State can no more abdicate its trust over the property in which the whole people are interested . . . than it can abdicate its police powers. . . ." [17]

In *Avon,* Justice Hall reaffirmed the public's right to use the waterfront as announced in Arnold v. Mundy. He observed that the public has a right to use the land below the mean average high water mark where the tide ebbs and flows. These uses have historically included navigation and fishing. In *Avon* the public's rights were extended "to recreational uses, including bathing, swimming and other shore activities." 61 N.J. at 309, 294 A.2d 47. Compare Blundell v. Catterall, 5 B. & Ald. 268, 106 Eng. Rep. 1190 (K.B. 1821) (holding no right to swim in common property) with Martin v. Waddell's Lessee, 41 U.S. (16 Pet.) 367, 10 L. Ed. 997 (1842) (indicating right to bathe in navigable waters). The Florida Supreme Court has held:

> The constant enjoyment of this privilege [bathing in salt waters] of thus using the ocean and its fore-shore for ages without dispute should prove sufficient to establish it as an American common law right, similar to that of fishing in the sea, even if this right had not come down to us as a part of the English

17. In Illinois Central Railroad Co. v. Illinois, the Illinois legislature in 1886 granted to the railroad in fee simple submerged lands comprising virtually the entire Chicago waterfront. Four years later, regretting the grant, the legislature revoked it. The Supreme Court upheld the revocation, explaining that the legislature did not have the power to convey the entire city waterfront free of trust, thus barring all future legislatures from protecting the public interest. — EDs.

common law, which it undoubtedly has. [White v. Hughes, 139 Fla. 54, 59, 190 So. 446, 449 (1939).] . . .

Extension of the public trust doctrine to include bathing, swimming and other shore activities is consonant with and furthers the general welfare. The public's right to enjoy these privileges must be respected.

In order to exercise these rights guaranteed by the public trust doctrine, the public must have access to municipally-owned dry sand areas as well as the foreshore. The extension of the public trust doctrine to include municipally-owned dry sand areas was necessitated by our conclusion that enjoyment of rights in the foreshore is inseparable from use of dry sand beaches. See Lusardi v. Curtis Point Property Owners Ass'n, 86 N.J. 217, 228, 430 A.2d 881 (1981). In *Avon* . . . the Court depended on the public trust doctrine, impliedly holding that full enjoyment of the foreshore necessitated some use of the upper sand, so that the latter came under the umbrella of the public trust.

In Van Ness v. Borough of Deal, 78 N.J. 174, 393 A.2d 571 (1978), we stated that the public's right to use municipally-owned beaches was not dependent upon the municipality's dedication of its beaches to use by the general public. The Borough of Deal had dedicated a portion of such beach for use by its residents only. We found such limited dedication "immaterial" given the public trust doctrine's requirement that the public be afforded the right to enjoy all dry sand beaches owned by a municipality. 78 N.J. at 179-80, 393 A.2d 571.

Public Rights in Privately-Owned Dry Sand Beaches

In *Avon* and *Deal* our finding of public rights in dry sand areas was specifically and appropriately limited to those beaches owned by a municipality. We now address the extent of the public's interest in privately-owned dry sand beaches. This interest may take one of two forms. First, the public may have a right to cross privately owned dry sand beaches in order to gain access to the foreshore. Second, this interest may be of the sort enjoyed by the public in municipal beaches under *Avon* and *Deal*, namely, the right to sunbathe and generally enjoy recreational activities. . . .

Exercise of the public's right to swim and bathe below the mean high water mark may depend upon a right to pass across the upland beach. Without some means of access the public right to use the foreshore would be meaningless. To say that the public trust doctrine entitles the public to swim in the ocean and to use the foreshore in connection therewith without assuring the public of a feasible access route would seriously impinge on, if not effectively eliminate, the rights of the public trust doctrine. This does not mean the public has an unrestricted right to cross at will over any and all property bordering on the common property. The public interest is satisfied so long as there is reasonable access to the sea.

Judge Best, in his dissent in Blundell v. Catterall, 5 B. & Ald. 268, 275, 106 Eng. Rep. 1190, 1193 (K.B. 1821), stated that passage to the seashore was essential to the exercise of that right. He believed that bathing in the tidal waters was an essential right similar to that of navigation and served the general welfare by promoting health and the ability to swim. 5 B. & Ald. at 278-79, 106 Eng. Rep. at 1194 (Best, J., dissenting). . . . Judge Best would have held on principles of public policy "that the interruption of free access to the sea is a public nuisance. . . . The principle of exclusive appropriation must not be carried beyond things capable of improvement by the industry of man. If it be extended so far as to touch the right of walking over these barren sands, it will take from the people what is essential to their welfare, whilst it will give to individuals only the hateful privilege of vexing their neighbours." Id. at 287, 106 Eng. Rep. at 1197. . . .

The bather's right in the upland sands is not limited to passage. Reasonable enjoyment of the foreshore and the sea cannot be realized unless some enjoyment of the dry sand area is also allowed.[18] The complete pleasure of swimming must be accompanied by intermittent periods of rest and relaxation beyond the water's edge. See State ex rel. Thornton v. Hay, 254 Or. 584, 599-602, 462 P.2d 671, 678-79 (1969) (Denecke, J., concurring). The unavailability of the physical situs for such rest and relaxation would seriously curtail and in many situations eliminate the right to the recreational use of the ocean. This was a principal reason why in Avon and Deal we held that municipally-owned dry sand beaches "must be open to all on equal terms. . . ." Avon, 61 N.J. at 308, 294 A.2d 47. We see no reason why rights under the public trust doctrine to use of the upland dry sand area should be limited to municipally-owned property. It is true that the private owner's interest in the upland dry sand area is not identical to that of a municipality. Nonetheless, where use of dry sand is essential or reasonably necessary for enjoyment of the ocean, the doctrine warrants the public's use of the upland dry sand area subject to an accommodation of the interests of the owner.

We perceive no need to attempt to apply notions of prescription, City of Daytona Beach v. Tona-Rama, Inc., 294 So. 2d 73 (Fla. 1974), dedication, Gion v. City of Santa Cruz, 2 Cal. 3d 29, 465 P.2d 50, 84 Cal. Rptr. 162 (1970), or custom, State ex rel. Thornton v. Hay, 254 Or. 584, 462 P.2d 671 (1969), as an alternative to application of the public trust doctrine. Archaic judicial responses are not an answer to a modern social problem. Rather, we perceive the public trust doctrine not to be "fixed

---

18. Some historical support for this proposition may be found in an analogous situation where fishermen, in exercising the right of public fishery in tidal waters, were permitted to draw nets on the beach above the ordinary high water mark in the act of fishing. S. Moore & H. Moore, The History and Law of Fisheries 96 (1903).

or static," but one to "be molded and extended to meet changing conditions and needs of the public it was created to benefit." *Avon,* 61 N.J. at 309, 294 A.2d 47.

Precisely what privately-owned upland sand area will be available and required to satisfy the public's rights under the public trust doctrine will depend on the circumstances. Location of the dry sand area in relation to the foreshore, extent and availability of publicly-owned upland sand area, nature and extent of the public demand, and usage of the upland sand land by the owner are all factors to be weighed and considered in fixing the contours of the usage of the upper sand.

Today, recognizing the increasing demand for our State's beaches and the dynamic nature of the public trust doctrine, we find that the public must be given both access to and use of privately-owned dry sand areas as reasonably necessary. While the public's rights in private beaches are not co-extensive with the rights enjoyed in municipal beaches, private landowners may not in all instances prevent the public from exercising its rights under the public trust doctrine. The public must be afforded reasonable access to the foreshore as well as a suitable area for recreation on the dry sand.

The Beaches of Bay Head

The Bay Head Improvement Association, which services the needs of all residents of the Borough for swimming and bathing in the public trust property, owns the streetwide strip of dry sand area at the foot of seven public streets that extends to the mean high water line. It also owns the fee in six other upland sand properties connected or adjacent to the tracts it owns at the end of two streets. In addition, it holds leases to approximately 42 tracts of upland sand area. The question that we must address is whether the dry sand area that the Association owns or leases should be open to the public to satisfy the public's rights under the public trust doctrine. Our analysis turns upon whether the Association may restrict its membership to Bay Head residents and thereby preclude public use of the dry sand area. . . .

The Association's activities paralleled those of a municipality in its operation of the beachfront. . . . When viewed in its totality — its purposes, relationship with the municipality, communal characteristic, activities, and virtual monopoly over the Bay Head beachfront — the quasi-public nature of the Association is apparent. The Association makes available to the Bay Head public access to the common tidal property for swimming and bathing and to the upland dry sand area for use incidental thereto, preserving the residents' interests in a fashion similar to *Avon.* . . .

Accordingly, membership in the Association must be open to the public at large. In this manner the public will be assured access to the common beach property during the hours of 10:00 A.M. to 5:30 P.M. between mid-June and September, where they may exercise their right to swim and bathe and to use the Association's dry sand area incidental to those activities. . . .

The Public Advocate has urged that all the privately-owned beachfront property likewise must be opened to the public. Nothing has been developed on this record to justify that conclusion. We have decided that the Association's membership and thereby its beach must be open to the public. That area might reasonably satisfy the public need at this time. We are aware that the Association possessed, as of the initiation of this litigation, about 42 upland sand lots under leases revocable on 30 days' notice. If any of these leases have been or are to be terminated, or if the Association were to sell all or part of its property, it may necessitate further adjudication of the public's claims in favor of the public trust on part or all of these or other privately-owned upland dry sand lands depending upon the circumstances.

. . . It is not necessary for us to determine under what circumstances and to what extent there will be a need to use the dry sand of private owners who either now or in the future may have no leases with the Association. Resolution of the competing interests, private ownership and the public trust, may in some cases be simple, but in many it may be most complex. In any event, resolution would depend upon the specific facts in controversy. . . .

We realize that considerable uncertainty will continue to surround the question of the public's right to cross private land and to use a portion of the dry sand as discussed above. Where the parties are unable to agree as to the application of the principles enunciated herein, the claim of the private owner shall be honored until the contrary is established.

. . . Judgment is entered for the plaintiff against the Association. Judgment of dismissal against the individual property owners is affirmed without prejudice. No costs.

NOTES

1. Matthews v. Bay Head Improvement Assn. is noted in 10 Colum. J. Envtl. L. 35 (1985); 15 Rutgers L.J. 813 (1984); and 15 Seton Hall L. Rev. 344 (1985).

2. The public trust doctrine extends to all land covered by the ebb and flow of the tide and, in addition, all inland lakes and rivers that are navigable. Phillips Petroleum Co. v. Mississippi, 484 U.S. 469 (1988). As trustee, the state has the duty to act in the best interests of the public. The public trust in such lands and waters can be extinguished only by a conveyance that benefits the public. If the conveyance does not benefit the public (as perhaps later declared by a court), the state may revoke

the grant. National Audubon Soc. v. Superior Court, 33 Cal. 3d 419, 658 P.2d 709, 189 Cal. Rptr. 346 (1983).

After public trust lands have been conveyed and filled in, the land may remain subject to the public trust. For example, in the nineteenth century a substantial amount of Boston harbor was filled in (including the Back Bay and two-thirds of the land area in the present city of Boston). In the 1970s, the owner of a parcel of land at the end of a solid-fill wharf sought to register a fee simple title. When the Commonwealth of Massachusetts challenged the title registration, the court held that the tidelands could not be permanently conveyed to private interests, but were burdened by an implied condition subsequent that the property be used for the public purpose for which it was originally granted. Boston Waterfront Dev. Corp. v. Commonwealth, 378 Mass. 629, 393 N.E.2d 356 (1979). See William L. Lahey, Lauren S. Zurier & Kenneth W. Salinger, Expanding Public Access by Codifying the Public Trust Doctrine: The Massachusetts Experience, 42 Me. L. Rev. 65 (1990).

For discussion of how the public trust doctrine is applied in the various states, see David D. Slade, Putting the Public Trust Doctrine to Work (1990). See also Joseph L. Sax, Liberating the Public Trust Doctrine from Its Historical Shackles, 14 U.C. Davis L. Rev. 185 (1980); Joseph L. Sax, The Public Trust Doctrine in Natural Resource Law: Effective Judicial Intervention, 68 Mich. L. Rev. 471 (1970); Symposium on the Public Trust and the Waters of the American West, 19 Envtl. L. 425 (1989).

3.   Scope of Easements

Brown v. Voss

Supreme Court of Washington, 1986
105 Wash. 2d 366, 715 P.2d 514

BRACHTENBACH, J. The question posed is to what extent, if any, the holder of a private road easement can traverse the servient estate to reach not only the original dominant estate, but a subsequently acquired parcel when those two combined parcels are used in such a way that there is no increase in the burden on the servient estate. The trial court denied the injunction sought by the owners of the servient estate. The Court of Appeals reversed. Brown v. Voss, 38 Wash. App. 777, 689 P.2d 1111 (1984). We reverse the Court of Appeals and reinstate the judgment of the trial court.

A portion of an exhibit [Figure 9-5] depicts the involved parcels.

In 1952 the predecessors in title of parcel A granted to the predecessor owners of parcel B a private road easement across parcel A for "ingress to and egress from" parcel B. Defendants acquired parcel A in

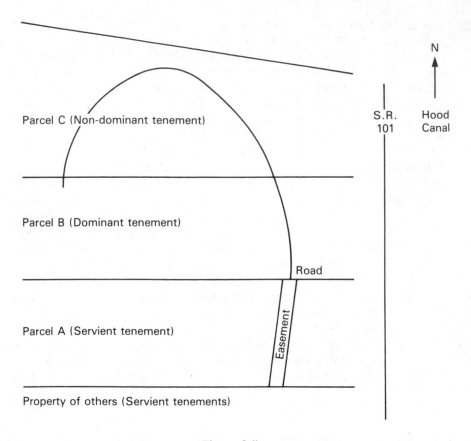

Figure 9-5

1973. Plaintiffs bought parcel B on April 1, 1977 and parcel C on July 31, 1977, but from two different owners. Apparently the previous owners of parcel C were not parties to the easement grant.

When plaintiffs acquired parcel B a single family dwelling was situated thereon. They intended to remove that residence and replace it with a single family dwelling which would straddle the boundary line common to parcels B and C.

Plaintiffs began clearing both parcels B and C and moving fill materials in November 1977. Defendants first sought to bar plaintiffs' use of the easement in April 1979 by which time plaintiffs had spent more than $11,000 in developing their property for building.

Defendants placed logs, a concrete sump and a chain link fence within the easement. Plaintiffs sued for removal of the obstructions, an injunction against defendants' interference with their use of the easement and damages. Defendants counterclaimed for damages and an injunction against plaintiffs using the easement other than for parcel B.

The trial court awarded each party $1 in damages. The award against the plaintiffs was for a slight inadvertent trespass outside the easement.

The trial court made the following findings of fact:

VI

The plaintiffs have made no unreasonable use of the easement in the development of their property. There have been no complaints of unreasonable use of the roadway to the south of the properties of the parties by other neighbors who grant[ed] easements to the parties to this action to cross their properties to gain access to the property of the plaintiffs. Other than the trespass there is no evidence of any damage to the defendants as a result of the use of the easement by the plaintiffs. There has been no increase in volume of travel on the easement to reach a single family dwelling whether built on tract B or on tracts B and C. There is no evidence of any increase in the burden on the subservient estate from the use of the easement by the plaintiffs for access to parcel C.

VIII

If an injunction were granted to bar plaintiffs' access to tract C across the easement to a single family residence, Parcel C would become landlocked; plaintiffs would not be able to make use of their property; they would not be able to build their single family residence in a manner to properly enjoy the view of the Hood Canal and the surrounding area as originally anticipated at the time of their purchase and even if the single family residence were constructed on parcel B, if the injunction were granted, plaintiffs would not be able to use the balance of their property in parcel C as a yard or for any other use of their property in conjunction with their home. Conversely, there is and will be no appreciable hardship or damage to the defendants if the injunction is denied.

IX

If an injunction were to be granted to bar the plaintiffs' access to tract C, the framing and enforcing of such an order would be impractical. Any violation of the order would result in the parties back in court at great cost but with little or no damages being involved.

X

Plaintiffs have acted reasonably in the development of their property. Their trespass over a "little" corner of the defendants' property was inadvertent, and de minimis. The fact that the defendants' counter claim seeking an injunction to bar plaintiffs' access to parcel C was filed as leverage against the original plaintiffs' claim for an interruption of their easement rights, may be considered in determining whether equitable relief by way of an injunction should be granted.

Relying upon these findings of fact, the court denied defendants' request for an injunction and granted the plaintiffs the right to use the easement for access to parcels B & C "as long as plaintiffs' properties (B and C) are developed and used solely for the purpose of a single family residence." Clerk's Papers, at 10.

The Court of Appeals reversed, holding [that an injunction must issue]. . . .

The easement in this case was created by express grant. Accordingly, the extent of the right acquired is to be determined from the terms of the grant properly construed to give effect to the intention of the parties. See Zobrist v. Culp, 95 Wash. 2d 556, 561, 627 P.2d 1308 (1981); Seattle v. Nazarenus, 60 Wash. 2d 657, 665, 374 P.2d 1014 (1962). By the express terms of the 1952 grant, the predecessor owners of parcel B acquired a private road easement across parcel A and the right to use the easement for ingress to and egress from parcel B. Both plaintiffs and defendants agree that the 1952 grant created an easement appurtenant to parcel B as the dominant estate. Thus, plaintiffs, as owners of the dominant estate, acquired rights in the use of the easement for ingress to and egress from parcel B.

However, plaintiffs have no such easement rights in connection with their ownership of parcel C, which was not a part of the original dominant estate under the terms of the 1952 grant. As a general rule, an easement appurtenant to one parcel of land may not be extended by the owner of the dominant estate to other parcels owned by him, whether adjoining or distinct tracts, to which the easement is not appurtenant. E.g., Heritage Standard Bank & Trust Co. v. Trustees of Schs., 84 Ill. App. 3d 653, 40 Ill. Dec. 104, 405 N.E.2d 1196 (1980); Kanefsky v. Dratch Constr. Co., 376 Pa. 188, 101 A.2d 923 (1954); S.S. Kresge Co. of Mich. v. Winkleman Realty Co., 260 Wis. 372, 50 N.W.2d 920 (1952); 28 C.J.S. Easements §92, at 772-73 (1941).

Plaintiffs, nonetheless, contend that extension of the use of the easement for the benefit of nondominant property does not constitute a misuse of the easement, where as here, there is no evidence of an increase in the burden on the servient estate. We do not agree. If an easement is appurtenant to a particular parcel of land, any extension thereof to other parcels is a misuse of the easement. Wetmore v. Ladies of Loretto, Wheaton, 73 Ill. App. 2d 454, 220 N.E.2d 491 (1966). See also, e.g., Robertson v. Robertson, 214 Va. 76, 197 S.E.2d 183 (1973); Penn Bowling Rec. Ctr., Inc. v. Hot Shoppes, Inc., 179 F.2d 64 (D.C. Cir. 1949). As noted by one court in a factually similar case, "[I]n this context this classic rule of property law is directed to the rights of the respective parties rather than the actual burden on the servitude." National Lead Co. v. Kanawha Block Co., 228 F. Supp. 357, 364 (S.D. W. Va. 1968), aff'd, 409 F.2d 1309 (4th Cir. 1969). Under the express language of the 1952 grant, plaintiffs only have rights in the use of the easement for the benefit of parcel B. Although, as plaintiffs contend, their planned use of the easement to gain access to a single family residence located partially on parcel B and partially on parcel C is perhaps no more than technical misuse of the easement, we conclude that it is misuse nonetheless.

However, it does not follow from this conclusion alone that defendants are entitled to injunctive relief. Since the awards of $1 in damages were not appealed, only the denial of an injunction to defendants is in issue. Some fundamental principles applicable to a request for an injunction must be considered. (1) The proceeding is equitable and addressed to the sound discretion of the trial court. (2) The trial court is vested with a broad discretionary power to shape and fashion injunctive relief to fit the *particular facts, circumstances, and equities of the case before it.* Appellate courts give great weight to the trial court's exercise of that discretion. (3) One of the essential criteria for injunctive relief is actual and substantial injury sustained by the person seeking the injunction.

The trial court found as facts, upon substantial evidence, that plaintiffs have acted reasonably in the development of their property, that there is and was no damage to the defendants from plaintiffs' use of the easement, that there was no increase in the volume of travel on the easement, that there was no increase in the burden on the servient estate, that defendants sat by for more than a year while plaintiffs expended more than $11,000 on their project, and that defendants' counterclaim was an effort to gain "leverage" against plaintiffs' claim. In addition, the court found from the evidence that plaintiffs would suffer considerable hardship if the injunction were granted whereas no appreciable hardship or damages would flow to defendants from its denial. Finally, the court limited plaintiffs' use of the combined parcels solely to the same purpose for which the original parcel was used — i.e., for a single family residence.

Neither this court nor the Court of Appeals may substitute its effort to make findings of fact for those supported findings of the trial court. . . . Therefore, the only valid issue is whether, under these established facts, as a matter of law, the trial court abused its discretion in denying defendants' request for injunctive relief. Based upon the equities of the case, as found by the trial court, we are persuaded that the trial court acted within its discretion. The Court of Appeals is reversed and the trial court is affirmed.

DORE, J. (dissenting). The majority correctly finds that an extension of this easement to nondominant property is a misuse of the easement. The majority, nonetheless, holds that the owners of the servient estate are not entitled to injunctive relief. I dissent.

The comments and illustrations found in the Restatement of Property §478 (1944) address the precise issue before this court. Comment *e* provides in pertinent part that "if one who has an easement of way over

Whiteacre appurtenant to Blackacre uses the way with the purpose of going to Greenacre, the use is improper even though he eventually goes to Blackacre rather than to Greenacre." Illustration 6 provides:

> 6. By prescription, *A* has acquired, as the owner and possessor of Blackacre, an easement of way over an alley leading from Blackacre to the street. He buys Whiteacre, an adjacent lot, to which the way is not appurtenant, and builds a public garage one-fourth of which is located on Blackacre and three-fourths of which is located on Whiteacre. *A* wishes to use the alley as a means of ingress and egress to and from the garage. He has no privilege to use the alley to go to that part of the garage which is built on Whiteacre, and he may not use the alley until that part of the garage built on Blackacre is so separated from the part built on Whiteacre that uses for the benefit of Blackacre are distinguishable from those which benefit Whiteacre.

The majority grants the privilege to extend the agreement to nondominant property on the basis that the trial court found no appreciable hardship or damage to the servient owners. However, as conceded by the majority, any extension of the use of an easement to benefit a nondominant estate constitutes a misuse of the easement. Misuse of an easement is a trespass. Raven Red Ash Coal Co. v. Ball, 184 Va. 534, 39 S.E.2d 231 (1946); Selvia v. Reitmeyer, 156 Ind. App. 203, 295 N.E.2d 869 (1973). The Browns' use of the easement to benefit parcel C, especially if they build their home as planned, would involve a continuing trespass for which damages would be difficult to measure. Injunctive relief is the appropriate remedy under these circumstances. *Selvia,* at 212, 295 N.E.2d 869; Gregory v. Sanders, 635 P.2d 795, 801 (Wyo. 1981). In Penn Bowling Rec. Ctr., Inc. v. Hot Shoppes, Inc., 179 F.2d 64, 66 (D.C. Cir. 1949) the court states:

> It is contended by appellant that since the area of the dominant and nondominant land served by the easement is less than the original area of the dominant tenement, the use made by appellant of the right of way to serve the building located on the lesser area is not materially increased or excessive. It is true that where the nature and extent of the use of an easement is, by its terms, unrestricted, the use of the dominant tenement may be increased or enlarged. . . . But the owner of the dominant tenement may not subject the servient tenement to use or servitude in connection with other premises to which the easement is not appurtenant. See Williams v. James, Eng. Law. Rep. (1867), 2 C.P. 577. And when an easement is being used in such a manner, an injunction will be issued to prevent such use. Cleve et al. v. Nairin, 204 Ky. 342, 264 S.W. 741 [(1924)]; Diocese of Trenton v. Toman et al., 74 N.J. Eq. 702, 70 A. 606 [(1908)]; Shock v. Holt Lumber Co. et al., 107 W. Va. 259, 148 S.E. 73 [(1929)]. Appellant, therefore, may not use the easement to serve both the dominant and nondominant property, even though the area thereof is less than the original area of the dominant tenement.

See also Kanefsky, v. Dratch Constr. Co., 376 Pa. 188, 101 A.2d 923 (1954). Thus, the fact that an extension of the easement to nondominant property would not increase the burden on the servient estate does not warrant a denial of injunctive relief.

The Browns are responsible for the hardship of creating a land-locked parcel. They knew or should have known from the public records that the easement was not appurtenant to parcel C. See Seattle v. Naza-renus, 60 Wash. 2d 657, 670, 374 P.2d 1014 (1962). In encroachment cases this factor is significant. As stated by the court in Bach v. Sarich, 74 Wash. 2d 575, 582, 445 P.2d 648 (1968): "The benefit of the doctrine of balancing the equities, or relative hardship, is reserved for the inno-cent defendant who proceeds without knowledge or warning that his structure encroaches upon another's property or property rights."

In addition, an injunction would not interfere with the Browns' right to use the easement as expressly granted, i.e., for access to parcel B. An injunction would merely require the Browns to acquire access to parcel C if they want to build a home that straddles parcels B and C. One possibility would be to condemn a private way of necessity over their existing easement in an action under RCW 8.24.010. See Brown v. McAnally, 97 Wash. 2d 360, 644 P.2d 1153 (1982).

I would affirm the Court of Appeals decision as a correct applica-tion of the law of easements. If the Browns desire access to their land-locked parcel they have the benefit of the statutory procedure for condemnation of a private way of necessity.

NOTES, QUESTIONS, AND PROBLEM

1. Brown v. Voss is noted in 62 Wash. L. Rev. 295 (1987). See also Robert Kratovil, Easement Law and Service of Nondominant Tene-ments: Time for a Change, 24 Santa Clara L. Rev. 649 (1984).

2. In Penn Bowling Recreation Center, Inc. v. Hot Shoppes, Inc., 179 F.2d 64 (D.C. Cir. 1949), Penn Bowling had an easement of way for ingress and egress to its property across land owned by Hot Shoppes. Penn Bowling bought an adjacent lot and erected a building on both the dominant and adjacent property housing a bowling alley and luncheon-ette. The luncheonette was on the nondominant property. The right of way was used as a backdoor entrance to the building, and for bringing supplies to the luncheonette and removing garbage. The court enjoined the use of the easement for the luncheonette, and held that any use by the dominant tenement could be prohibited until the building was so altered that the easement could not be used by the nondominant part. Accord, DND Neffson Co. v. Galleria Partners, 155 Ariz. 148, 745 P.2d 206 (Ariz. App. 1987).

When an easement is wrongfully extended to a nondominant tract, which is the best remedy — an injunction, as in *Penn Bowling,* or damages, as in Brown v. Voss? For matters bearing on the answer, see footnote 17 on page 137 and the discussion in Note 3 on pages 974-975.

3. Suppose that the owner of the dominant tenement wants to subdivide her land into 100 subdivision tracts. Will each tract have the right to use the easement over the servient tenement? Restatement of Property §484 (1944) says the answer depends in part upon whether subdivision is a "normal development of the use of the dominant tenement," which the parties are assumed to anticipate. Other factors include the foreseeability and amount of the increased burden on the servient estate. See Hill v. Allan, 259 Cal. App. 2d 470, 66 Cal. Rptr. 676 (1968) (permitting access for 24 additional homes on 120-acre tract); Cox v. Glenbrook Co., 78 Nev. 254, 371 P.2d 647, 10 A.L.R.3d 947 (1962) (refusing to declare in advance the point where the additional homes would become unreasonable).

4. A private easement of way does not usually permit the easement owner to install on the easement aboveground or underground utilities, such as electrical lines and sewer pipes. Most courts hold such uses are not reasonably foreseeable by the parties. Kuras v. Kope, 205 Conn. 332, 533 A.2d 1202, 79 A.L.R.4th 585 (1987); Ward v. McGlory, 358 Mass. 322, 265 N.E.2d 78 (1970).

Compare Witteman v. Jack Barry Cable TV, 183 Cal. App. 3d 1101, 228 Cal. Rptr. 584 (1986), holding that where a landowner had granted a utility easement to a telephone company "for the transmission of electrical energy and for telephone lines," the telephone company could license a cable television company to string cable television lines on the telephone poles. The court stressed that the scope of the easement "encompasses normal technological evolution" in transmitting telephonic communication.

5. *O* grants *A* an easement of way over Blackacre to reach adjacent land owned by *A*. The easement location is fixed by mutual agreement. Subsequently *O* proposes to change the location of the easement, at *O*'s expense, in order to facilitate development of *O*'s land. *A* objects. What result?

The general rule is that the location of an easement, once fixed by the parties, cannot be changed by the servient owner without permission of the dominant owner. Does this make sense? Why should not the servient owner be permitted to relocate an easement if it can be done without substantially lessening the utility of the servitude or increasing the burdens on the dominant owner? Should rights of dominant and servient owners be construed so as to maximize the utility of the servitude and minimize interference with use of the servient estate?

6. A prescriptive easement is not as broad in scope as an easement created by grant, by implication, or by necessity. Although the uses of a prescriptive easement are not confined exactly to the actual uses made

during the prescriptive period, the uses made of a prescriptive easement must be consistent with the general kind of use by which the easement was created and be a foreseeable evolution of the old use. For example, a prescriptive easement acquired by pedestrian traffic or by herding livestock with men and horses across land has been held not usable by motor vehicles. "Anyone who does not think there is a significant difference between horses and motorcycles may wish to ponder why it is that carriages in Central Park are pulled by horses, not Hondas." Connolly v. McDermott, 162 Cal. App. 3d 973, 978, 208 Cal. Rptr. 796, 799 (1984). See also 3 Richard R. Powell, The Law of Real Property ¶416 (rev. ed. 1992); Annot., 79 A.L.R.4th 604 (1990).

Miller v. Lutheran Conference & Camp Association

Supreme Court of Pennsylvania, 1938
331 Pa. 241, 200 A. 646, 130 A.L.R. 1245

STERN, J. This litigation is concerned with interesting and somewhat novel legal questions regarding rights of boating, bathing and fishing in an artificial lake.

Frank C. Miller, his brother Rufus W. Miller, and others, who owned lands on Tunkhannock Creek in Tobyhanna Township, Monroe County, organized a corporation known as the Pocono Spring Water Ice Company, to which, in September, 1895, they made a lease for a term of ninety-nine years of so much of their lands as would be covered by the backing up of the water as a result of the construction of a 14-foot dam which they proposed to erect across the creek. The company was to have "the exclusive use of the water and its privileges." It was chartered for the purpose of "erecting a dam . . . , for pleasure, boating, skating, fishing and the cutting, storing and selling of ice." The dam was built, forming "Lake Naomi," somewhat more than a mile long and about one-third of a mile wide.

By deed dated March 20, 1899, the Pocono Spring Water Ice Company granted to "Frank C. Miller, his heirs and assigns forever, the exclusive right to fish and boat in all the waters of the said corporation at Naomi Pines, Pa." On February 17, 1900, Frank C. Miller (his wife Katherine D. Miller not joining) granted to Rufus W. Miller, his heirs and assigns forever, "all the one-fourth interest in and to the fishing, boating, and bathing rights and privileges at, in, upon and about Lake Naomi . . . ; which said rights and privileges were granted and conveyed to me by the Pocono Spring Water Ice Company by their indenture of the 20th day of March, A.D. 1899." On the same day, Frank C. Miller and Rufus W. Miller executed an agreement of business partnership, the purpose of which was the erection and operation of boat and bath houses on

Lake Naomi, 1918

Naomi Lake and the purchase and maintenance of boats for use on the lake, the houses and boats to be rented for hire and the net proceeds to be divided between the parties in proportion to their respective interests in the bathing, boating and fishing privileges, namely, three-fourths to Frank C. Miller and one-fourth to Rufus W. Miller, the capital to be contributed and the losses to be borne in the same proportion. In pursuance of this agreement the brothers erected and maintained boats and bath houses at different points on the lake, purchased and rented out boats, and conducted the business generally, from the spring of 1900 until the death of Rufus W. Miller on October 11, 1925, exercising their control and use of the privileges in an exclusive, uninterrupted and open manner and without challenge on the part of anyone.[19]

Discord began with the death of Rufus W. Miller, which terminated the partnership. Thereafter Frank C. Miller, and the executors and

19. In the early 1900s Rufus Miller, a prominent Philadelphia minister in the Reformed Church, established Pocono Pines Assembly on the shore of Lake Naomi (named for Ruth's mother-in-law in the Bible). The Assembly was a religious camp providing vacations each summer for members of the Reformed Church and other like-minded Protestants in eastern Pennsylvania. The Assembly vacationers used the lake for many years with the permission of the Miller brothers. After Rufus died in 1925, the Assembly, in financial distress, sold its lakefront property to the Lutheran Conference and Camp Association, which renamed the property Lutherland and planned to bring to the lake each summer between 1300 and 2000 Lutherans from New York, New Jersey, and Pennsylvania. Frank and Katherine objected to the use of the lake by the Lutherans. The sale had been arranged by Rufus's children to carry on his religious work, and the lawsuit resulted in an irreparable split in the Miller families. See Emma Miller Waygood, Changing Times in the Poconos (1972). — EDS.

heirs of Rufus W. Miller, went their respective ways, each granting licenses without reference to the other. Under date of July 13, 1929, the executors of the Rufus W. Miller estate granted a license for the year 1929 to defendant, Lutheran Conference and Camp Association, which was the owner of a tract of ground abutting on the lake for a distance of about 100 feet, purporting to grant to defendant, its members, guests and campers, permission to boat, bathe and fish in the lake, a certain percentage of the receipts therefrom to be paid to the estate. Thereupon Frank C. Miller and his wife Katherine D. Miller, filed the present bill in equity, complaining that defendant was placing diving floats on the lake and "encouraging and instigating visitors and boarders" to bathe in the lake, and was threatening to hire out boats and canoes and in general to license its guests and others to boat, bathe and fish in the lake. The bill prayed for an injunction to prevent defendant from trespassing on the lands covered by the waters of the lake, from erecting or maintaining any structures or other encroachments thereon, and from granting any bathing licenses. The court issued the injunction.

It is the contention of plaintiffs that, while the privileges of boating and fishing were granted in the deed from the Pocono Spring Water Ice Company to Frank C. Miller, no *bathing* rights were conveyed by that instrument. In 1903 all the property of the company was sold by the sheriff under a writ of fi. fa. on a mortgage bond which the company had executed in 1898. As a result of that sale the Pocono Spring Water Ice Company was entirely extinguished, and the title to its rights and property came into the ownership of the Pocono Pines Ice Company, a corporation chartered for "the supply of ice to the public." In 1928 the title to the property of the Pocono Pines Ice Company became vested in Katherine D. Miller. Plaintiffs therefore maintain that the bathing rights, never having passed to Frank C. Miller, descended in ownership from the Pocono Spring Water Ice Company through the Pocono Pines Ice Company to plaintiff Katherine D. Miller, and that Frank C. Miller could not, and did not, give Rufus W. Miller any title to them. They further contend that even if such bathing rights ever did vest in Frank C. Miller, all of the boating, bathing and fishing privileges were easements in gross which were inalienable and indivisible, and when Frank C. Miller undertook to convey a one-fourth interest in them to Rufus W. Miller he not only failed to transfer a legal title to the rights but, in attempting to do so, extinguished the rights altogether as against Katherine D. Miller, who was the successor in title of the Pocono Spring Water Ice Company. It is defendant's contention, on the other hand, that the deed of 1899 from the Pocono Spring Water Ice Company to Frank C. Miller should be construed as transferring the bathing as well as the boating and fishing privileges, but that if Frank C. Miller did not obtain them by grant he and Rufus W. Miller acquired them by prescription, and that all of these rights were alienable and divisible. . . .

Coming to the merits of the controversy, it is initially to be observed that no boating, bathing or fishing rights can be, or are, claimed by defendant as a riparian owner. Ordinarily, title to land bordering on a navigable stream extends to low water mark subject to the rights of the public to navigation and fishery between high and low water, and in the case of land abutting on creeks and non-navigable rivers to the middle of the stream, but in the case of a non-navigable lake or pond where the land under the water is owned by others, no riparian rights attach to the property bordering on the water, and an attempt to exercise any such rights by invading the water is as much a trespass as if an unauthorized entry were made upon the dry land of another: Baylor v. Decker, 133 Pa. 168; Smoulter v. Boyd, 209 Pa. 146, 152; Gibbs v. Sweet, 20 Pa. Superior Ct. 275, 283; Fuller v. Cole, 33 Pa. Superior Ct. 563; Cryer v. Sawkill Pines Camp, Inc., 88 Pa. Superior Ct. 71.

It is impossible to construe the deed of 1899 from the Pocono Spring Water Ice Company to Frank C. Miller as conveying to the latter any privileges of bathing. It is clear and unambiguous. It gives to Frank C. Miller the exclusive right to *fish and boat. Expressio unius est exclusio alterius.* No *bathing* rights are mentioned. This omission may have been the result of oversight or it may have been deliberate, but in either event the legal consequence is the same. It is to be noted that the mortgagee to whom the company mortgaged all its property in 1898 executed in 1902 a release of the fishing and boating rights to the company and to Frank C. Miller, thus validating the latter's title to these rights under the company's deed of 1899, but in this release also the bathing rights are omitted.

But, while Frank C. Miller acquired by grant merely boating and fishing privileges, the facts are amply sufficient to establish title to the bathing rights by prescription. True, these rights, not having been granted in connection with, or to be attached to, the ownership of any land, were not easements appurtenant but in gross. There is, however, no inexorable principle of law which forbids an adverse enjoyment of an easement in gross from ripening into a title thereto by prescription. In Tinicum Fishing Co. v. Carter, 61 Pa. 21, it was questioned whether a fishing right could be created by prescription, although there is an intimation (p. 40) that some easements in gross might so arise if there be evidence sufficient to establish them. Certainly the casual use of a lake during a few months each year for boating and fishing could not develop into a title to such privileges by prescription. But here the exercise of the bathing right was not carried on sporadically by Frank C. Miller and his assignee Rufus W. Miller for their personal enjoyment but systematically for commercial purposes in the pursuit of which they conducted an extensive and profitable business enterprise. The circumstances thus presented must be viewed from a realistic standpoint. Naomi Lake is situated in the Pocono Mountains district, has become a summer resort for campers and boarders, and, except for the ice it furnishes, its bathing and boating facilities are the factors which give it its prime importance and value. They were exploited from the time the lake was created, and are recited as among the purposes for which the Pocono Spring Water Ice Company was chartered. From the early part of 1900 down to at least the filing of the present bill in 1929, Frank C. Miller and Rufus W. Miller openly carried on their business of constructing and operating bath houses and licensing individuals and camp associations to use the lake for bathing. This was known to the stockholders of the Pocono Spring Water Ice Company and necessarily also to Katherine D. Miller, the wife of Frank C. Miller; no objection of any kind was made, and Frank C. Miller and Rufus W. Miller were encouraged to expend large sums of money in pursuance of the right of which they considered and asserted themselves to be the owners. Under such circumstances it would be highly unjust to hold that a title by prescription to the bathing rights did not vest in Frank C. Miller and Rufus W. Miller which is just as valid, as far as Katherine D. Miller is concerned, as that to the boating and fishing rights which Frank C. Miller obtained by express grant.

We are thus brought to a consideration of the next question, which is whether the boating, bathing and fishing privileges were assignable by Frank C. Miller to Rufus W. Miller. What is the nature of such rights? In England it has been said that easements in gross do not exist at all, although rights of that kind have been there recognized. In this country such privileges have sometimes been spoken of as licenses, or as contractual in their nature, rather than as easements in gross. These are differences of terminology rather than of substance. We may assume, therefore, that these privileges are easements in gross, and we see no reason to consider them otherwise. It has uniformly been held that a profit in gross — for example, a right of mining or fishing — may be made assignable: Funk v. Haldeman, 53 Pa. 229; Tinicum Fishing Co. v. Carter, 61 Pa. 21, 39; see cases cited 19 C.J. 870, note 25. In regard to easements in gross generally, there has been much controversy in the courts and by textbook writers and law students as to whether they have the attribute of assignability. There are dicta in Pennsylvania that they are non-assignable: Tinicum Fishing Co. v. Carter, supra, 38, 39; Lindenmuth v. Safe Harbor Water Power Corporation, 309 Pa. 58, 63, 64; Commonwealth v. Zimmerman, 56 Pa. Superior Ct. 311, 315, 316. But there is forcible expression and even definite authority to the contrary: Tide Water Pipe Co. v. Bell, 280 Pa. 104, 112, 113; Dalton Street Railway Co. v. Scranton, 326 Pa. 6, 12. Learned articles upon the subject are to be found in 32 Yale Law Journal 813; 38 Yale Law Journal 139; 22 Michigan Law Review 521; 40 Dickinson Law Review 46. There does not seem to be any reason why the law should prohibit the assignment of an easement in gross if the parties to its creation evidence their intention to make it assignable. Here, as in Tide Water Pipe Company v. Bell, supra, the rights of fishing and boating were conveyed to the grantee — in this case Frank C. Miller — "his heirs and assigns," thus showing that the grantor, the Pocono Spring Water Ice Company, intended to attach the attribute of assignability to the privileges granted. Moreover, as a practical matter, there is an obvious difference in this respect between easements for personal enjoyment and those designed for commercial exploitation; while there may be little justification for permitting assignments in the former case, there is every reason for upholding them in the latter.

The question of assignability of the easements in gross in the present case is not as important as that of their divisibility. It is argued by plaintiffs that even if held to be assignable such easements are not divisible, because this might involve an excessive user or "surcharge of the easement" subjecting the servient tenement to a greater burden than originally contemplated. The law does not take that extreme position. It does require, however, that, if there be a division, the easements must be used or exercised as an entirety. This rule had its earliest expression in Mountjoy's Case, which is reported in Co. Litt. 164b, 165a. It was there said, in regard to the grant of a right to dig for ore, that the grantee, Lord Mountjoy, "must assign his whole interest to one, two, or more; but then, if there be two or more, they could make no division of it, but work together with one stock." In Caldwell v. Fulton, 31 Pa. 475, 477, 478, and in Funk v. Haldeman, 53 Pa. 229, that case was followed, and it was held that the right of a grantee to mine coal or to prospect for oil might be assigned, but if to more than one they must hold, enjoy and convey the right as an entirety, and not divide it in severalty. There are cases in other jurisdictions which also approve the doctrine of Mountjoy's Case, and hold that a mining right in gross is essentially integral and not susceptible of apportionment; an assignment of it is valid, but it cannot be aliened in such a way that it may be utilized by grantor and grantee, or by several grantees, separately; there must be a joint user, nor can one of the tenants alone convey a share in the common right: Grubb v. Baird, Federal Case No. 5849 (Circuit Court, Eastern District of Pennsylvania); Harlow v. Lake Superior Iron Co., 36 Mich. 105, 121; Stanton v. T.L. Herbert & Sons, 141 Tenn. 440, 211 S.W. 353.

These authorities furnish an illuminating guide to the solution of the problem of divisibility of profits or easements in gross. They indicate that much depends upon the nature of the right and the terms of its creation, that "surcharge of the easement" is prevented if assignees exercise the right as "one stock," and that a proper method of enjoyment of the easement by two or more owners of it may usually be worked out in any given instance without insuperable difficulty.

In the present case it seems reasonably clear that in the conveyance of February 17, 1900, it was not the intention of Frank C. Miller to grant, and of Rufus W. Miller to receive, a separate right to subdivide and sublicense the boating, fishing and bathing privileges on and in Lake Naomi, but only that they should together use such rights for commercial purposes, Rufus W. Miller to be entitled to one-fourth and Frank C. Miller to three-fourths of the proceeds resulting from their combined exploitation of the privileges. They were to hold the rights, in the quaint phraseology of Mountjoy's Case, as "one stock." Nor do the technical rules that would be applicable to a tenancy in common of a corporeal hereditament apply to the control of these easements in gross. Defendant contends that, as a tenant in common of the privileges, Rufus W. Miller individually was entitled to their use, benefit and possession and to exercise rights of ownership in regard thereto, including the right to license third persons to use them, subject only to the limitation that he must not thereby interfere with the similar rights of his co-tenant. But the very nature of these easements prevents their being so exercised, inasmuch as it is necessary, because of the legal limitations upon their divisibility, that they should be utilized in common, and not by two owners severally, and, as stated, this was evidently the intention of the brothers.

Summarizing our conclusions, we are of opinion (1) that Frank C. Miller acquired title to the boating and fishing privileges by grant and he and Rufus W. Miller to the bathing rights by prescription; (2) that he made a valid assignment of a one-fourth interest in them to Rufus W. Miller; but (3) that they cannot be commercially used and licenses thereunder granted without the common consent and joinder of the present owners, who with regard to them must act as "one stock." It follows that the executors of the estate of Rufus W. Miller did not have the right, in and by themselves, to grant a license to defendant.

The decree is affirmed; costs to be paid by defendant.

NOTES AND QUESTIONS

1. In England, an easement in gross is not recognized. There must be a dominant tenement. Profits, on the other hand, can exist in gross. See Michael F. Sturley, Easements in Gross, 96 L.Q. Rev. 557 (1980). In England, Frank and Rufus's executor would have a license to boat and fish. The license would be irrevocable if given as part of a contract for consideration or if estoppel applied. Under such circumstances, the license would be very like an easement, though not called such. See Robert Megarry & H.W.R. Wade, The Law of Real Property 798-808, 834-835 (5th ed. 1984).

2. Where an easement is appurtenant, the burden on the servient tenement is limited by the needs of the dominant tenement. An easement in gross has no such limitation; therefore, American courts have

attempted to prevent the burden on the servient tenement from increasing beyond what was intended by the original parties.

Some early cases held that an easement in gross was not transferable. Such a rule proved inconvenient when railroad or utility companies, holding easements in gross, attempted to transfer them. So the law changed. Restatement of Property §489 (1944) says that an easement in gross can be assigned if of a commercial character (used primarily for economic benefit rather than personal satisfaction). More recent cases permit any easement in gross to be assignable if the parties so intended. About the only easements in gross that are not assignable under modern cases are recreational easements (easements for hunting, fishing, boating, and camping). Restricting their assignability appears to rest on the courts' fear of burdening the servient land beyond the original contemplation of the parties. See Note, The Easement in Gross Revisited: Transferability and Divisibility Since 1945, 39 Vand. L. Rev. 109 (1986).

3. In *Miller* the court declined to regulate the amount of use by declaring the easement nonassignable. Instead it applied the "one stock" rule of the law of profits. This means Frank and Rufus's executor must use the lake as one person; either one can veto the other's use. Is it sound to apply this rule to easements?

Since Frank and Rufus's executor are tenants in common in the easement, why not give Frank the same rights as Mrs. Swartzbaugh had when her husband leased the land over her objections? See page 363.

The rights of riparian owners to take water out of a stream are, in most states, governed by a reasonable use principle ("fair participation"). See pages 40-41. Why not apply the reasonable use principle to solve problems involving common ownership of profits or easements? See Richard A. Epstein, Why Restrain Alienation?, 85 Colum. L. Rev. 970, 978-984 (1985).

4. Termination of Easements

An easement is extinguished when title to the dominant estate and title to the servient estate are held by the same person (see Note 3, page 813). A corollary of this principle is that an easement is terminated if it is released to the owner of the servient estate. An easement may also be extinguished by the servient owner's use of his land in a manner that wrongfully and physically prevents the easement from being used for the period of the statute of limitations. See Spiegel v. Ferraro, 73 N.Y.2d 622, 541 N.E.2d 15, 543 N.Y.S.2d 15 (1989).

In addition, an easement can be abandoned by an *act* of the dominant owner indicating an intention never to make use of the easement again. Mere nonuse for an extended period does not constitute an abandonment, however. See Lague, Inc. v. Royea, 152 Vt. 499, 568 A.2d 357

(1989). A look at the cases shows that courts rarely find on equivocal evidence an intention to abandon an easement. See 3 Richard R. Powell, The Law of Real Property ¶423 (rev. ed. 1992).

Abandoned railroad easements. The National Trails System Act, 16 U.S.C. §§1241-1251 (1988), authorizes the Interstate Commerce Commission to preserve for possible future railroad use rights-of-way not currently in railroad service by allowing interim use of the land as recreational trails. Congress believed abandonment would defeat the rails-to-trails system, and so it provided, in §1247(d) of the act, that interim trail use "shall not be treated, for any purposes of any law or rule of law, as an abandonment of the use of such rights-of-way for railroad purposes." The act was upheld by a unanimous Supreme Court in Preseault v. Interstate Commerce Commission, 494 U.S. 1 (1990). The Court held that the statute was not an unconstitutional taking of the reverter rights of the servient owners because compensation was available in the U.S. Claims Court under the Tucker Act. See Note 5 on page 1241.

5. Negative Easements

A negative easement is the right of the dominant owner to stop the servient owner from doing something on the servient land. Prior to Queen Victoria's reign, English courts had recognized four types of negative easements: the right to stop your neighbor from (1) blocking your windows, (2) interfering with air flowing to your land in a defined channel, (3) removing the support of your building (usually by excavating or removing a supporting wall), and (4) interfering with the flow of water in an artificial stream.[20] If the judges had let the list of negative easements expand naturally with the changes taking place in urban development, the excessive complexity characterizing the law of servitudes may never have developed. But the expansion of the English law of easements was curbed in the first half of the nineteenth century.

Judges, for several reasons, were not disposed to permit the creation of new types of easements, negative easements in particular. First, England was without an effective system of public records of land titles until 1925, and the purchaser of land was bound by its servitudes regardless of notice, actual or constructive. The purchaser could protect himself by viewing the land, but negative easements were not so easy to discover as affirmative easements, such as an easement of way. To ex-

---

20. All landowners have the duty, imposed by law, of supporting adjoining *land* (see pages 962-963) and of not interfering unreasonably with the flow of water in adjacent *natural* streams (see pages 40-41). Landowners can bargain among themselves for additional rights and duties respecting support of buildings and not interfering with artificial streams. These bargains, creating recognized negative easements, are enforceable against successor owners.

pand the list of negative easements would increase the risk to the purchaser that the land was subject to undiscoverable rights. Thus, to keep land titles unencumbered, judges did not favor negative easements.

Second, the traditional negative easements could arise by prescription in England; for example, a person whose windows had not been blocked by a neighbor for 20 years received a prescriptive easement for light over the neighbor's land.[21] If new types of negative easements could arise by prescription, the servient owner's rights to change the land use would be unduly restricted. A neighbor, sensing some harm from a change on the neighboring land, might claim, "You cannot do act X on your land because it has never been done before. I have a prescriptive right to prevent it." Judicial recognition of such claims would hopelessly cloud the conditions under which development could take place.

The final objection to negative easements was conceptual. From the time of the Year Books (see footnote 13 on page 33), English judges had a hard time deciding whether negative obligations should be analyzed as easements or as covenants. An easement could be created only by grant.[22] From this it was deduced that a right in land could not be an easement unless it could be pictured as an intelligible object of a grant. English judges found it difficult to picture, in their minds, a negative right being granted from A to B. Judges could imagine an affirmative easement (for example, a right of way) being granted from A to B, because B was given the right to do an affirmative act on A's land. On the other hand, a negative easement resembled an obligation of A. If A purported to grant to B the right not to have a piggery on A's land, B's rights depended on the behavior of A. A negative right thus seemed more naturally to be acquired by a covenant, that is, by a promise by A that A would not establish a piggery on A's land.

For these reasons the English law courts in the nineteenth century called a halt to the creation of negative easements other than the four traditional kinds. They refused to recognize any new negative servitudes as easements.

Two of the conditions that influenced, and perhaps justified, the English law of servitudes did not exist in the United States in the nine-

---

21. This doctrine, known as the doctrine of ancient lights, has never been accepted in the United States. American courts have held that negative easements cannot be acquired by prescription. Analogizing to statutes of limitations, which set time periods on causes of action, the courts have reasoned that prescription does not apply unless the servient owner has a cause of action against the user. Since a landowner has no cause of action against a neighbor for erecting a building with windows overlooking his land, the neighbor can acquire no prescriptive right to unobstructed light and air. Hence the doctrine of ancient lights has been rejected in this country.

22. A grant — a sealed writing at early law — was used to convey nonpossessory interests, whereas a feoffment with livery of seisin was used to convey freehold possessory estates. See pages 626-627, 797.

teenth century, when the English law crossed the Atlantic. In all American states a recording system existed to protect subsequent purchasers against unrecorded claims; during the post-Civil War industrialization period, reliance on record searches became universally common in this country. An effective recording system is of the greatest importance because it provides information about existing servitudes at small cost and protects against hidden claims — which English judges rightly feared. Subsequent purchasers were further protected in this country by rejection of the English idea that negative easements could be created by prescription. American courts held that prescription does not apply until the rights of the "servient owner" are interfered with and a cause of action against the "dominant owner" arises.

The third objection to negative easements — that they cannot be conceptualized as the subject of a grant — could also have been overcome. This is merely a peculiar and entirely unnecessary way of looking at the matter. Any negative restriction can be cast in terms of either a promise or a grant. "A promises B that A will not put a piggery on A's land," or "A grants to B the right not to have a piggery on A's land." B has a right; A has a duty not to establish a pig farm. Whether rights are created in the form of a grant or in the form of a promise, the resulting legal relationship (right in B, duty in A) is the important thing. Unless there is some overriding policy reason, a right created by promise should be treated the same way as a right created by grant.

American courts thus might have rejected the artificial English barriers to the creation of servitudes. They might have fashioned a law that enforced all servitudes of whatever type against subsequent purchasers with notice, in more or less the same manner as they enforce other interests in land against subsequent purchasers with notice. In short, they might have relied upon the market system to ensure that the bargains creating these servitudes were advantageous to affected parties and hence economically efficient. And courts might have relied on the recording system to protect subsequent purchasers and to find parties from whom releases could be obtained, thus clearing servitudes from the land. And courts might have concentrated their talents on removing obsolete servitudes when the market did not function to remove them. But alas, they did not.

In the main, American courts accepted the English restrictions on creating new types of easements. Nonetheless, although the list of four negative easements is seemingly closed in England, it is not necessarily closed in the United States. Now and then a new type of negative easement is recognized. In Petersen v. Friedman, 162 Cal. App. 2d 245, 328 P.2d 264 (1958), the court enforced an express easement of unobstructed view of the San Francisco bay over a neighbor's house, compelling the neighbor to remove obstructing television aerials. In England, the right to an unspoiled view cannot exist as an easement. Gale on Easements 27 (Spencer G. Maurice 15th ed. 1986). A solar easement, preventing a person from blocking a neighbor's solar collector, has also been recognized in this country. See also Manitowoc Remanufacturing, Inc. v. Vocque, 307 Ark. 271, 819 S.W.2d 275 (1991) (implying, when a tract was divided, a negative easement that the owner of the part of the tract on which a dike was erected would not remove the dike, which protected the dominant part of the land from flooding).

The most noteworthy new negative easement is the conservation easement, developed in the last 40 years to preserve scenic and historic areas and open space. An owner of land can give a public body or a private charitable organization a conservation easement, preventing the servient owner from building on the land except as specified in the grant. The value of the conservation easement (which is usually the development value of the land) is deductible as a charitable gift on the federal income tax return. Because of doubts about the validity and transferability of negative easements in gross at common law, statutes have been enacted in almost all states authorizing conservation easements. Conservation easements are perpetual in duration, are transferable, and can be in gross. See 3 Richard R. Powell, The Law of Real Property ¶414[5] (rev. ed. 1992); Andrew Dana & Michael Ramsey, Conservation Easements and the Common Law, 8 Stan. Envtl. L.J. 2 (1989); Comment, Conservation Easements: Michigan's Land Preservation Tool of the 1990s, 68 U. Det. L. Rev. 193 (1991). See also Uniform Conservation Easement Act (1981).

Although the English law courts closed the books on negative easements 150 years ago, chancery soon thereafter began to enforce negative covenants between the parties as equitable servitudes (see page 861). Equitable servitudes became the equivalent of negative easements, but subject to a different set of rules developed in chancery. The American courts followed suit. Today there is little pressure on the courts to expand the traditional list of negative easements because negative restrictions on land can be, and usually are, treated as equitable servitudes. American courts frequently refer to equitable servitudes as negative easements, acknowledging both the similarity of these interests and equity's circumvention of the law.

B. Covenants Running with the Land

1. Historical Background

a. Covenants Enforceable at Law: Real Covenants

Thwarted by the law courts' refusal to recognize new types of negative easements, landowners turned — in the early nineteenth century — to the law of contracts. They sought judicial recognition of a contract right respecting land use enforceable not only against the promisor landowner, but against his successors in title as well.

Why were landowners so interested in imposing restrictions on the use of land? Suppose that O owns a large tract of land on which he wants to put several different uses — a factory, a residence, and a market. If O wishes to maximize the value of all parts of his tract, he will locate these uses so as to minimize the harms they might impose on each other, taking into consideration the interrelationships among the various activities. Because a factory produces smoke and a grocery produces traffic, O may place them at some distance from each other and from the residence; he may even provide a green belt of trees to serve as a buffer zone.

Similarly, bargains between neighboring property owners can operate to allocate resources efficiently by arranging land uses so as to minimize conflicts. For example, if A (owner of a residence on Whiteacre) and B (owner of a vacant lot, Blackacre) agree that a factory should not be built on Blackacre, presumably the agreement between A and B maximizes their well-being (and society's too, if there are no third-party effects that A and B have neglected to take into account). If A pays B $1,000 for B's promise, the gain to A from not having a factory for a neighbor is likely to be greater than $1,000, and the loss to B of the opportunity of putting a factory on his land is likely to be less than $1,000; otherwise, we can presume that A and B would not have reached their bargain. Both A and B, then, are better off. So too if A, rather than giving B $1,000, agrees instead by a reciprocal promise not to use Whiteacre for a factory. Here the value of both Whiteacre and Blackacre for residential use is presumably greater than the value of the opportunities for industrial use that have been forgone.

Thus bargains among neighbors of the sort just discussed can serve to minimize the harmful impacts ("external costs") that arise from conflicting resource uses. Such bargains, though, are less likely to be struck if only the original promisor is bound and only the original promisee benefitted. The promisee wants assurances that he and his successors in interest will be protected against the original promisor and his successors in interest. What is needed, then, is some sort of *property right* that is enforceable by and against subsequent purchasers of Whiteacre and Blackacre. A mere contract right — the right of the original promisee to sue the original promisor alone — will seldom be sufficient to enable the market to allocate conflicting land uses efficiently. Do you see why? The answer relates to the discussion of transaction costs at pages 51-52. See also James E. Krier, Book Review, 122 U. Pa. L. Rev. 1664, 1678-1680 (1974).

In the early nineteenth century, contract rights and duties were not generally assignable. Promises were not enforceable against a person who was not a party to the contract. The law had, however, developed one exception to the rule of nonassignability. *Where there is privity of estate,* the judges held, the contract is enforceable against assignees. It had long been established that privity of estate existed between a landlord and a tenant and that covenants in leases would run with the land. But it was unclear, at the beginning of the nineteenth century, whether privity of estate might exist in other circumstances.

The requirement of privity of estate for the burden of a covenant to run developed from Spencer's Case, 5 Co. 16a, 77 Eng. Rep. 72 (1583). In this famous case Spencer and his wife conveyed a house and lot to *A* for a term of 21 years, and *A* covenanted on behalf of himself, his executors, administrators, and assigns to build a brick wall on the lot conveyed. *A* assigned his term to *B*. *B* refused to build the brick wall, and Spencer and his wife sued *B* on the covenant. Although there is some doubt from the report as to who won, the case is famous because the judges laid down three propositions about the running of the burden of covenants. First, a covenant relating to something not in esse (e.g., to build a wall) will not bind assignees of the covenantor unless the covenantor expressly agrees not only for himself but also "for his assigns," so as to show an intent to bind successors. A covenant relating to something in esse will bind the assigns, without expressly mentioning them, if there is other evidence suggesting such an intent.[23] Second, for the burden of the covenant to run it must "touch and concern" the land (more about this later). Third, the judges laid down the requirement that there must be privity of estate for a covenant to run. What the judges had in mind by privity of estate was unclear and has been debated ever since. Did it refer to a landlord-tenant (tenurial) relationship? Or to mutual interests in the land conveyed? Or to a successive relationship between a grantor and a grantee? On the facts of Spencer's Case, privity

23. The requirement that the document specify expressly that the assigns of the covenantor are bound if the promise relates to something not in esse has been abolished in almost all states for covenants running with a fee simple. The covenanting parties must show only an intention to bind assigns. However, Note, Covenants Running with the Land: Viable Doctrine or Common-Law Relic?, 7 Hofstra L. Rev. 139, 156 n.105 (1978), finds that assigns must be expressly bound in Georgia, Texas, California, Montana, North Dakota, and South Dakota. The last four states have statutes enacting the first proposition in Spencer's Case.

of estate could have meant any one of those three relationships, since all were present.

Landowners in England attempted to persuade the law courts to read Spencer's Case to permit covenants between neighboring owners to run to successors, but these attempts ultimately failed. The courts concluded that privity of estate, required for the burden of a covenant to run at law to successors, was satisfied only by a landlord-tenant relationship. Keppell v. Bailey, 39 Eng. Rep. 1042 (Ch. 1834). To this day, the burden of a covenant between landowners will not run at law in England.

Unlike the English courts, American courts did not define privity of estate to mean only a landlord-tenant relationship. They permitted, under varying circumstances, covenants to run in favor of and against successor owners. They developed the American *real covenant,* a promise respecting the use of land that runs with the land *at law.* The cases on real covenants are in some disarray and are often obscure and disputed, but you will be able to understand the issues and the confusion if you pay close attention to the following analytic model.

Suppose that *B,* owner of Blackacre, has promised *A,* owner of Whiteacre, that Blackacre shall not be used for industrial purposes. *B* sells Blackacre to *C,* and *A* sells Whiteacre to *D. C* constructs a factory on Blackacre. *D* sues *C* for damages. Will the covenant run to *C* and *D*? Let us begin with a diagram:

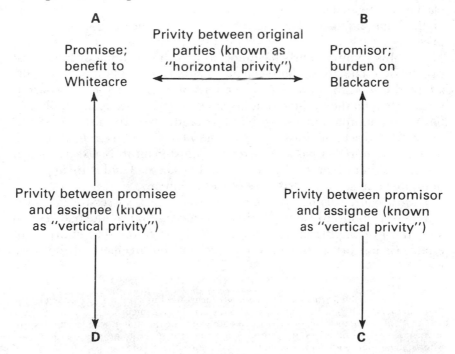

Figure 9-6

If *A*, before any assignment, sues *B*, *A* is suing on the contract. There is privity of contract between *A* and *B*, and the law of contracts governs. No question arises whether a covenant runs. The question whether a covenant runs arises only when a person who is not a party to the covenant is suing or being sued.

Note that there are two ends of the covenant, the benefit end originally held by *A* and the burden end originally held by *B*.[24] If *A* conveys Whiteacre to *D*, and *B* still owns Blackacre and constructs the factory, and *D* sues *B*, *D* must allege that the *benefit* runs to *D*. The burden remains with *B*, the original promisor. If *B* conveys Blackacre to *C*, who constructs the factory, and *A*, still owning Whiteacre, sues *C*, *A* must allege that the *burden* runs to *C*. If, as in the diagram above, both Whiteacre and Blackacre are conveyed to *D* and *C* respectively, and *D* sues *C*, *D* must allege that *both the burden and the benefit run*. It is important to keep in mind whether the running of the benefit or the running of the burden is involved in the case because the test for running of the burden is traditionally more onerous than the test for running of the benefit.

Note that in the above diagram we have two types of privity of estate that we shall discuss: (1) *horizontal privity,* meaning privity of estate between the original covenanting parties; and (2) *vertical privity,* meaning privity of estate between one of the covenanting parties and a successor in interest. These are called horizontal and vertical privity because, probably, countless law professors have put the above diagram on the blackboard to analyze the issues; as a result the terms have become part of the legal language. First, let us explore the meaning of horizontal privity.

In this country courts have not limited the meaning of horizontal privity of estate to landlord-tenant relationships. They have usually adopted one of the other interpretations of Spencer's Case. Massachusetts early took the position that horizontal privity means that both parties have a mutual interest in the same land, apart from the covenant. Morse v. Aldrich, 56 Mass. (19 Pick.) 449 (1837). Thus, referring back to our diagram, if *A* has an easement appurtenant in Blackacre, and *B* promises *A* not to construct a factory on Blackacre, *A* and *B* are in privity of estate because of the existence of the easement.

Most courts define horizontal privity to be a successive (grantor-grantee) relationship.[25] Thus, if in our diagram *B*'s promise had been in a deed conveying Blackacre from *A* to *B*, *A* and *B* would be in privity of estate. Giving privity this meaning prevents enforcement of the cove-

---

24. The benefited parcel is, in analogous terms used in speaking of easements, the dominant tenement. The burdened parcel is the servient tenement.

25. This is the meaning of privity of estate when the question is whether a successor adverse possessor can tack on the period of a prior adverse possessor (see page 149), and when the question is whether covenants for title run with the land (see page 647).

nant against successors only when the covenant was not created in conjunction with the transfer of some other interest in land.

The Restatement of Property, synthesizing these two positions, declared that there must be either a mutual *or* successive relationship between the promisor and promisee for the *burden* of a covenant to run at law. Restatement of Property §534 (1944). The Restatement went on to say, in accordance with most authority, that horizontal privity is not required for the *benefit* to run. Id. §548. The policy of the Restatement was to put various obstacles in the way of the burden running at law, but to permit the benefit to run freely. (Does that attitude make sense?)

The Restatement's requirement of horizontal privity of estate was sharply denounced by Judge Charles Clark, the foremost authority on running covenants at the time. See Charles E. Clark, Real Covenants and Other Interests Which "Run with Land" 137-143, 206-262 (2d ed. 1947). Judge Clark maintained that horizontal privity was not required at all and should not be, because such a requirement could be easily evaded by using a straw. In his view only vertical privity was (or should be) required for a covenant to run at law. Vertical privity means succession by the plaintiff or defendant to the estate of one of the parties to the covenant. Recent analyses conclude that the privity requirement persists in many states, but it is often unclear what type of privity is required; sometimes decisions within one jurisdiction appear to be inconsistent. See 5 Richard R. Powell, The Law of Real Property ¶673[2] [c] (rev. ed. 1992) (documenting the confusion in many states); Ralph A. Newman & Frank R. Losey, Covenants Running with the Land, and Equitable Servitudes; Two Concepts, or One?, 21 Hastings L.J. 1319 (1970); Note, supra footnote 23, at 170. The Restatement (Third) of Property, Servitudes, §2.4 (T.D. No. 1, 1989), takes the position that horizontal privity of estate is not required for a covenant to run.

A real covenant can be a negative promise (a promise not to do an act) or an affirmative promise (a promise to do an act). A real covenant subjects the promisor (or successor) to personal liability for damages, with a damage award collectible out of all the promisor's (or successor's) assets.

PROBLEMS AND NOTES

1. *A* and *B*, neighboring landowners, decide that they will mutually restrict their lots to single-family residential use. They sign an agreement wherein each promises on behalf of herself, and her heirs and assigns, that her lot will be used for single-family residential purposes only. This agreement is recorded in the county courthouse under the name of each signer. *B* sells her lot to *C*. *C* builds an apartment house on his lot. *A* sues *C* for damages. What result? Suppose that *A* rather

than *C* had built the apartment house. Is *C* entitled to damages against *A*? See William B. Stoebuck, Running Covenants: An Analytical Primer, 52 Wash. L. Rev. 861, 877-881 (1977).

Suppose that, in order to preserve *A*'s view over *B*'s lot, *A* and *B* agree that no building taller than 20 feet will be erected on *B*'s lot. This agreement is recorded. Thereafter *B* sells her lot to *C*, who erects a 30-foot building. *A* argues that the agreement creates a negative easement. What result in a suit by *A* against *C* for damages?

2. *Vertical privity.* The authorities appear to agree that vertical privity of estate is required for a covenant to run at law. What does vertical privity mean? It is best understood by referring to Professor Powell's vivid metaphor. A real covenant, Powell says, is like "a bird riding on a wagon." 5 Richard R. Powell, The Law of Real Property ¶670[2] (rev. ed. 1992). The wagon is the estate, and wherever the estate goes the covenant goes with it. A real covenant thus does not run with the land, as the common expression has it; *it runs with an estate in land.*

For the burden to run, Restatement of Property §535 (1944) says the successor must have an *estate of the same duration* as the promisor had.[26] If the promisor had a fee simple, the successor must have a fee simple. This meaning of privity of estate is consistent with landlord-tenant law, where a covenant made by a tenant will run only to an assignee of the tenant's whole estate, who is then said to be in privity of estate with the landlord (see pages 475-477).

Now consider the following problems:

O, owner of a two-acre tract, conveys one acre of the tract to *A*. The deed, which is duly recorded, contains covenants by *A*, and her heirs and assigns, that the one-acre tract will be used for residential purposes only and that *A*, and her heirs and assigns, will keep the trees on *A*'s lot trimmed so that they do not shade the solar collector on *O*'s house.

(a) *B*, an adverse possessor, ousts *A* and remains in adverse possession for the period of the statute of limitations. *B* then opens a restaurant on the premises and lets the trees grow to shade *O*'s solar collector. *O* sues *B* for damages. What result? See Lawrence Berger, A Policy Analysis of Promises Respecting the Use of Land, 55 Minn. L. Rev. 167, 190-193 (1970).

(b) *A* leases her tract to *C* for two years. *C* opens a nursery school and refuses to cut the trees on *O*'s demand. *O* sues *C* for damages. What result? Should the landlord, *A*, or the tenant, *C*, be liable in damages? See Berger, supra, at 203-207; Susan F. French, Toward a Modern Law of Servitudes: Reweaving the Ancient Strands, 55 S. Cal. L. Rev. 1261, 1273-1275, 1294-1300 (1982).

Suppose that neither the events in (a) nor in (b), above, happen, but that *A*, the promisor, subsequently conveys her entire estate to *D*. Unless

---

26. Restatement §547 (1944) says that the *benefit* runs to a successor of *any interest* in the land, and not only to a successor of the whole estate.

A's continuing liability on the covenant is clearly bargained for, *A* no longer remains liable on the covenant even though there is privity of contract between *O* and *A*. Unlike the case in landlord-tenant law, where the covenantor would remain liable to the landlord after an assignment of the leasehold, the liability on a covenant attached to a fee simple ceases when the fee simple is transferred. The covenantor, *A*, has lost all control of the land when she assigns her entire interest, and it would be unfair to penalize *A* for the conduct of some future owner. Therefore, after assignment of the original covenantor's entire estate, it is usually held that liability on the covenant for damages rests only on those in privity of estate. See 2 American Law of Property §9.18 (1952); Curtis J. Berger, Some Reflections on a Unified Law of Servitudes, 55 S. Cal. L. Rev. 1323, 1335-1337 (1982).

b. Covenants Enforceable in Equity: Equitable Servitudes

Although in England the law courts, bound by the learning of the past, failed to respond positively to market demands for servitudes enforceable against successor owners, the chancellor, by design or by result, came to the aid of the market in the famous case of Tulk v. Moxhay.

Tulk v. Moxhay
Court of Chancery, England, 1848
2 Phillips 774, 41 Eng. Rep. 1143

In the year 1808 the Plaintiff, being then the owner in fee of the vacant piece of ground in Leicester Square, as well as of several of the houses forming the Square, sold the piece of ground by the description of "Leicester Square garden or pleasure ground, with the equestrian statue then standing in the centre thereof, and the iron railing and stone work round the same," to one Elms in fee: and the deed of conveyance contained a covenant by Elms, for himself, his heirs, and assigns, with the Plaintiff, his heirs, executors, and administrators,

> that Elms, his heirs, and assigns should, and would from time to time, and at all times thereafter at his and their own costs and charges, keep and maintain the said piece of ground and square garden, and the iron railing round the same in its then form, and in sufficient and proper repair as a square garden and pleasure ground, in an open state, uncovered with any buildings, in neat and ornamental order; and that it should be lawful for the inhabitants of Leicester Square, tenants of the Plaintiff, on payment of a reasonable rent for the same, to have keys at their own expense and the privilege of admission therewith at any time or times into the said square garden and pleasure ground.

The piece of land so conveyed passed by divers mesne conveyances into the hands of the Defendant, whose purchase deed contained no similar covenant with his vendor: but he admitted that he had purchased with notice of the covenant in the deed of 1808.

The Defendant having manifested an intention to alter the character of the square garden, and asserted a right, if he thought fit, to build upon it, the Plaintiff, who still remained owner of several houses in the square, filed this bill for an injunction; and an injunction was granted by the Master of the Rolls to restrain the Defendant from converting or using the piece of ground and square garden, and the iron railing round the same, to or for any other purpose than as a . . . square garden and pleasure ground in an open state, and uncovered with buildings. . . .

THE LORD CHANCELLOR [Cottenham]. . . . That this Court has jurisdiction to enforce a contract between the owner of land and his neighbour purchasing a part of it, that the latter shall either use or abstain from using the land purchased in a particular way, is what I never knew disputed. Here there is no question about the contract: the owner of certain houses in the square sells the land adjoining, with a covenant from the purchaser not to use it for any other purpose than as a square garden. And it is now contended, not that the vendee could violate the contract, but that he might sell the piece of land, and that the purchaser from him may violate it without this Court having any power to interfere. If that were so, it would be impossible for an owner of land to sell part of it without incurring the risk of rendering what he retains worthless. It is said that, the covenant being one which does not run with the land, this court cannot enforce it; but the question is, not whether the covenant runs with the land, but whether a party shall be permitted to use the land in a manner inconsistent with the contract entered into by his vendor, and with notice of which he purchased. Of course, the price would be affected by the covenant, and nothing could be more inequitable than the original purchaser should be able to sell the property the next day for a greater price, in consideration of the assignee being allowed to escape from the liability which he had himself undertaken.

That the question does not depend upon whether the covenant runs with the land is evident from this, that if there was a mere agreement and no covenant, this Court would enforce it against a party purchasing with notice of it; for if an equity is attached to the property by the owner, no one purchasing with notice of that equity can stand in a different situation from the party from whom he purchased. . . .

I think the cases cited before the Vice-Chancellor and this decision of the Master of the Rolls perfectly right, and, therefore, that this motion must be refused, with costs.

Leicester Square, 1852

It is said that "an injunction is for sale," meaning the person who holds it may sell it to the enjoined party if the price is right. And this is what happened after the decision in Tulk v. Moxhay.

At the time of Tulk v. Moxhay, Leicester Square was changing from a residential to a commercial area, and the central garden had become an unkempt receptacle for rubbish. In 1851 James Wyld, a geographer, purchased the garden from Moxhay's widow. With the consent of the Tulk family, who received an option to purchase an undivided half of the garden at the end of 10 years, Wyld erected in the garden a building to house a 60-foot high plaster scale model of the earth. This building, called "Wyld's Monster Globe" in the etching above, dwarfed the surrounding houses. After 10 years this was pulled down, and John A. Tulk, grandson of the plaintiff in Tulk v. Moxhay, exercised the option to purchase. John A. Tulk hoped to convert the garden to building land, as Moxhay had tried to do formerly. After much public outcry, the garden was acquired by the government for a public park in 1874. Leicester Square today is the center of London's cinema district. For more on the history of Leicester Square, see 1 Zechariah Chafee & Sidney P. Simpson, Cases on Equity 704 (1934).

NOTES, QUESTIONS, AND PROBLEM

1. Examine each of the covenants made by Elms. How would you classify the rights and duties intended by the deed of conveyance? Is the covenant sued on really an easement of view in promissory form?

The chancellor reasoned that it would be inequitable for Elms, who bought the land at a price reflecting the burdens, to be able to charge his purchaser the price of unburdened land. He therefore enforced the negative covenant. Does this reasoning suggest that the other covenants should also be enforceable against the defendant? Although in a few cases after Tulk v. Moxhay the court suggested it was prepared to enforce affirmative covenants, in 1881 it was settled in England that only negative covenants are enforceable as equitable servitudes. Haywood v. Brunswick Permanent Benefit Bldg. Soc., (1881) 8 Q.B.D. 403. An equitable servitude was viewed as an interest in property analogous to a negative easement. In the United States, as we shall see, affirmative obligations have been enforced as equitable servitudes.

2. An equitable servitude is a covenant respecting the use of land enforceable against successor landowners in equity regardless of its enforceability at law. Equity requires that the parties intend the promise to run, that a subsequent purchaser have actual or constructive notice of the covenant,[27] and that the covenant touch and concern the land (of which more later). Horizontal privity of estate — the largest obstacle to running covenants at law — is of no importance in equity. Nor is vertical privity required for the *burden* to run. All subsequent possessors are bound by the servitude, just as they are bound by an easement. However, for a person other than the original covenantee to enforce the *benefit*, in some jurisdictions the beneficiary must show that he acquired title to his land from the covenantee, either before or after the covenant was made. In this sense, vertical privity may be required for enforcement of the benefit in equity. See pages 877-879 and the discussion in Neponsit Property Owners' Assn., Inc. v. Emigrant Indus. Sav. Bank at pages 885-886.

3. *The property theory of equitable servitudes.* Although an equitable servitude started out as a promise enforced in equity, in the course of time it turned into an interest in land. Unlike a real covenant, which attaches to an estate in land, an equitable servitude " 'sinks its tentacles into the soil,' burdening the land itself and not the estate." 5 Richard R. Powell, The Law of Real Property ¶670[2] (rev. ed. 1992). In this respect it is like an easement.

---

27. Covenants run in equity against successors who have given no consideration (donees, heirs, will beneficiaries), even though they have no notice. See William B. Stoebuck, Running Covenants: An Analytical Primer, 52 Wash. L. Rev. 861, 901 (1977).

There was, in earlier years, considerable debate over whether equitable restrictions on land are enforced as contracts, creating only contract rights, or whether they create servitudes burdening land and are property rights. All recent writers and almost all modern cases support the property theory, which has been helped along by courts calling an equitable servitude a negative easement. See id. The property theory facilitates the holding that, after the original promisor has conveyed the burdened land, the promisor cannot be sued on the covenant. (Compare the similar rule with respect to real covenants discussed at pages 860-861.) Concomitantly, the original promisor may not enforce restrictions after he has conveyed the benefited land.[28] See Annot., 51 A.L.R.3d 556 (1991). The property theory also supports the holding that, if the government condemns the burdened land, the government must pay the benefited owner damages for loss of the servitude. Southern California Edison Co. v. Bourgerie, 9 Cal. 3d 169, 507 P.2d 964, 107 Cal. Rptr. 76 (1973); Mercantile-Safe Deposit & Trust Co. v. Baltimore, 308 Md. 627, 521 A.2d 734 (1987). Nonetheless, even though an equitable servitude is a property interest, it arises out of a contract and many contract doctrines are applicable to it.

Consider the contract theory and the property theory in this context. It is said that a promise requires consideration for enforcement, but that an owner of land may give another an interest in the land. No consideration is required for a gift.

Suppose that O, owner of Blackacre, delivers a signed instrument to A, owner of adjacent Whiteacre, reading: "I, O, hereby promise A, her heirs and assigns, on behalf of myself, my heirs and assigns, that no billboard will be erected on Blackacre." No consideration is given by A. Subsequently O conveys Blackacre to B, and B, with knowledge of the instrument, begins to erect a billboard on Blackacre. Is A entitled to enjoin B?

4. The traditional difference between real covenants and equitable servitudes relates to the remedy sought. The remedy for breach of a real covenant is damages in a suit at law. The remedy for breach of an equitable servitude is an injunction or enforcement of a lien in a suit in equity.

Refer back to Problems 1 and 2 at pages 859-861. If injunctive relief had been sought there, what result?

Does the plaintiff in land-use cases usually want an injunction or damages? Is continued observance of the covenant more valuable than monetary compensation?

If, in the United States, a court acting in equity were to grant dam-

---

28. But compare B.C.E. Dev., Inc. v. Smith, 215 Cal. App. 3d 1142, 264 Cal. Rptr. 55 (1989), permitting a developer to enforce architectural restrictions after sale of all lots, where expressly given that right.

ages for breach of a covenant in any case where an injunction could have been awarded, even though damages would not be allowed at law, the real covenant would disappear.

> The modern union of law and equity, as well as the judicial confusion over which covenants should run at law and which should run in equity, have caused courts, in general, to grant the relief they feel is appropriate without regard to the real or equitable nature of the covenant. In most cases, the appropriate relief has been an injunction against future breaches and, if necessary, damages for past breaches. [5 Powell, supra, ¶676.]
> Actions at law for damages based on theories of real covenants have almost been replaced in the courts by suits in equity. In large part this is because modern covenants most frequently regulate residential subdivisions, which are best preserved by injunctive relief, and these covenants usually meet the requirements for running with the land in equity. [Id., ¶670[2].]

For a comprehensive treatment of the history of real covenants and equitable servitudes, with suggestions for their unification, see Uriel Reichman, Toward a Unified Concept of Servitudes, 55 S. Cal. L. Rev. 1179 (1982). For a thorough examination of running covenants in North Carolina, see Thomas E. Roberts, Private Land Use Controls: Enforcement Problems with Real Covenants and Equitable Servitudes in North Carolina, 22 Wake Forest L. Rev. 749 (1987).

2.   Creation of Covenants

A real covenant must be created by a written instrument signed by the covenantor. It is an interest in land within the meaning of the Statute of Frauds. If the deed creating a real covenant is signed by the grantor only, and it contains a promise by the grantee, the promise is enforceable against the grantee. The grantee is bound by the act of accepting such a deed. See Restatement (Third) of Property, Servitudes, §2.7 (T.D. No. 1, 1989). A real covenant cannot arise by estoppel, implication, or prescription, as can an easement.

Similarly, an equitable servitude is an interest in land. But unlike a real covenant, it may be implied in equity under certain limited circumstances. An equitable servitude, which arises out of a promise, cannot be obtained by prescription.

Sanborn v. McLean
Supreme Court of Michigan, 1925
233 Mich. 227, 206 N.W. 496, 60 A.L.R. 1212

Wiest, J. Defendant Christina McLean owns the west 35 feet of lot 86 of Green Lawn subdivision, at the northeast corner of Collingwood av-

Corner House
Lot 86 of Green Lawn Subdivision
Collingwood Avenue at Second Boulevard
Detroit 1987

enue and Second boulevard, in the city of Detroit, upon which there is a dwelling house, occupied by herself and her husband, defendant John A. McLean. The house fronts Collingwood avenue. At the rear of the lot is an alley. Mrs. McLean derived title from her husband and, in the course of the opinion, we will speak of both as defendants. Mr. and Mrs. McLean started to erect a gasoline filling station at the rear end of their lot, and they and their contractor, William S. Weir, were enjoined by decree from doing so and bring the issues before us by appeal. Mr. Weir will not be further mentioned in the opinion.

Collingwood avenue is a high-grade residence street between Woodward avenue and Hamilton boulevard, with single, double, and apartment houses, and plaintiffs who are owners of land adjoining, and in the vicinity of defendants' land, and who trace title, as do defendants, to the proprietors of the subdivision, claim that the proposed gasoline station will be a nuisance per se, is in violation of the general plan fixed for use of all lots on the street for residence purposes only, as evidenced by restrictions upon 53 of the 91 lots fronting on Collingwood avenue, and that defendants' lot is subject to a reciprocal negative easement barring a use so detrimental to the enjoyment and value of its neighbors. Defendants insist that no restrictions appear in their chain of title and

they purchased without notice of any reciprocal negative easement, and
deny that a gasoline station is a nuisance per se. We find no occasion to
pass upon the question of nuisance, as the case can be decided under
the rule of reciprocal negative easement.

This subdivision was planned strictly for residence purposes, except
lots fronting Woodward avenue and Hamilton boulevard. The 91 lots
on Collingwood avenue were platted in 1891, designed for and each one
sold solely for residence purposes, and residences have been erected
upon all of the lots. Is defendants' lot subject to a reciprocal negative
easement? If the owner of two or more lots, so situated as to bear
the relation, sells one with restrictions of benefit to the land retained, the
servitude becomes mutual, and, during the period of restraint, the
owner of the lot or lots retained can do nothing forbidden to the owner
of the lot sold. For want of a better descriptive term this is styled a reciprocal negative easement. It runs with the land sold by virtue of express
fastening and abides with the land retained until loosened by expiration
of its period of service or by events working its destruction. It is not
personal to owners but operative upon use of the land by any owner
having actual or constructive notice thereof. It is an easement passing its
benefits and carrying its obligations to all purchasers of land subject to
its affirmative or negative mandates. It originates for mutual benefit and
exists with vigor sufficient to work its ends. It must start with a common
owner. Reciprocal negative easements are never retroactive; the very nature of their origin forbids. They arise, if at all, out of a benefit accorded
land retained, by restrictions upon neighboring land sold by a common
owner. Such a scheme of restrictions must start with a common owner;
it cannot arise and fasten upon one lot by reason of other lot owners
conforming to a general plan. If a reciprocal negative easement attached
to defendants' lot it was fastened thereto while in the hands of the common owner of it and neighboring lots by way of sale of other lots with
restrictions beneficial at that time to it. This leads to inquiry as to what
lots, if any, were sold with restrictions by the common owner before the
sale of defendants' lot. While the proofs cover another avenue we need
consider sales only on Collingwood.

December 28, 1892, Robert J. and Joseph R. McLaughlin, who were
then evidently owners of the lots on Collingwood avenue, deeded lots 37
to 41 and 58 to 62, inclusive, with the following restrictions:

> No residence shall be erected upon said premises, which shall cost less
> than $2,500 and nothing but residences shall be erected upon said premises.
> Said residences shall front on Helene (now Collingwood) avenue and be
> placed no nearer than 20 feet from the front street line.

July 24, 1893, the McLaughlins conveyed lots 17 to 21 and 78 to 82,
both inclusive, and lot 98 with the same restrictions. Such restrictions

were imposed for the benefit of the lands held by the grantors to carry out the scheme of a residential district, and a restrictive negative easement attached to the lots retained, and title to lot 86 was then in the McLaughlins. Defendants' title, through mesne conveyances, runs back to a deed by the McLaughlins dated September 7, 1893, without restrictions mentioned therein. Subsequent deeds to other lots were executed by the McLaughlins, some with restrictions and some without. Previous to September 7, 1893, a reciprocal negative easement had attached to lot 86 by acts of the owners, as before mentioned, and such easement is still attached and may now be enforced by plaintiffs, provided defendants, at the time of their purchase, had knowledge, actual or constructive, thereof. The plaintiffs run back with their title, as do defendants, to a common owner. This common owner, as before stated, by restrictions upon lots sold, had burdened all the lots retained with reciprocal restrictions. Defendants' lot and plaintiff Sanborn's lot, next thereto, were held by such common owner, burdened with a reciprocal negative easement and, when later sold to separate parties, remained burdened therewith and right to demand observance thereof passed to each purchaser with notice of the easement. The restrictions were upon defendants' lot while it was in the hands of the common owners, and abstract of title to defendants' lot showed the common owners and the record showed deeds of lots in the plat restricted to perfect and carry out the general plan and resulting in a reciprocal negative easement upon defendants' lot and all lots within its scope, and defendants and their predecessors in title were bound by constructive notice under our recording acts. The original plan was repeatedly declared in subsequent sales of lots by restrictions in the deeds, and while some lots sold were not so restricted the purchasers thereof, in every instance, observed the general plan and purpose of the restrictions in building residences. For upward of 30 years the united efforts of all persons interested have carried out the common purpose of making and keeping all the lots strictly for residences, and defendants are the first to depart therefrom.

When Mr. McLean purchased on contract in 1910 or 1911, there was a partly built dwelling on lot 86, which he completed and now occupies. He had an abstract of title which he examined and claims he was told by the grantor that the lot was unrestricted. Considering the character of use made of all the lots open to a view of Mr. McLean when he purchased, we think he was put thereby to inquiry, beyond asking his grantor whether there were restrictions. He had an abstract showing the subdivision and that lot 86 had 97 companions; he could not avoid noticing the strictly uniform residence character given the lots by the expensive dwellings thereon, and the least inquiry would have quickly developed the fact that lot 86 was subjected to a reciprocal negative easement, and he could finish his house and, like the others, enjoy the benefits of the easement. We do not say Mr. McLean should have asked his neighbors about restrictions, but we do say that with the notice he had from a view of the premises on the street, clearly indicating the residences were built and the lots occupied in strict accordance with a general plan, he was put to inquiry, and had he inquired he would have found of record the reason for such general conformation, and the benefits thereof serving the owners of lot 86 and the obligations running with such service and available to adjacent lot owners to prevent a departure from the general plan by an owner of lot 86.

While no case appears to be on all fours with the one at bar the principles we have stated, and the conclusions announced, are supported by Allen v. City of Detroit, 167 Mich. 464 (36 L.R.A. [N.S.] 890); McQuade v. Wilcox, 215 Mich. 302 (16 A.L.R. 997); French v. White Star Refining Co., 229 Mich. 474; Silberman v. Uhrlaub, 116 N.Y. App. Div. 869 (102 N.Y. Supp. 299); Boyden v. Roberts, 131 Wis. 659 (111 N.W. 701); Howland v. Andrus, 80 N.J. Eq. 276 (83 Atl. 982).

We notice the decree in the circuit directed that the work done on the building be torn down. If the portion of the building constructed can be utilized for any purpose within the restrictions it need not be destroyed.

With this modification the decree in the circuit is affirmed, with costs to plaintiffs.

NOTES AND QUESTIONS

1. In McQuade v. Wilcox, 215 Mich. 302, 183 N.W. 771 (1921), Mary Wilcox, the owner of a large tract of land, divided it into lots for residential subdivision. By each deed, save the deed to lot 2, Wilcox restricted the lot sold to a single-family residential dwelling, and by the same instrument restricted her remaining lots to the same use. After she had sold almost all the other lots in the subdivision, and after expensive residences had been built on them, Wilcox sold lot 2, a 4-acre lot on which was her home, to a purchaser who wanted to convert it into a restaurant. Wilcox's deed conveying lot 2 contained no restrictions, and the purchaser had no actual notice of the restrictions on lot 2 appearing in the earlier deeds to the other lots. The court held, as did Guillette v. Daly Dry Wall, Inc., page 725, that the recording of the deeds to the other lots, which contained a restriction on lot 2, gave constructive notice to the purchaser of lot 2 that lot 2 was restricted.

If prior deeds by the McLaughlins to other lots in Green Lawn subdivision gave constructive notice of their contents to the purchaser of lot 86, why did the court talk of "inquiry notice" in Sanborn v. McLean? Would the defendants McLean have found any restriction on lot 86 had they searched the title to other lots in Green Lawn subdivision?

2. On what constitutes a scheme or plan, from which restrictions

will be implied in equity, see 5 Richard R. Powell, The Law of Real Property ¶672 (rev. ed. 1992); Restatement (Third) of Property, Servitudes, §2.14 (T.D. No. 1, 1989).

3. A majority of courts imply negative restrictions from a common scheme, as was done in Sanborn v. McLean. But a few jurisdictions take the Statute of Frauds more seriously. They hold that an equitable servitude will not be implied from the existence of restrictions on other lots in a subdivision, from an oral promise of the developer to restrict the remaining lots, or from a general scheme of restrictions not included, by recitation or incorporation, in the deed to the lot alleged to be burdened with the servitude. Riley v. Bear Creek Planning Comm., 17 Cal. 3d 500, 551 P.2d 1213, 131 Cal. Rptr. 381 (1976) (objecting to implied covenants, which are not in recorded deeds, because of "the vagaries of proof by extrinsic evidence of actual notice on the part of" subsequent grantees); Werner v. Graham, 181 Cal. 174, 183 P. 945 (1919); Sprague v. Kimball, 213 Mass. 380, 100 N.E. 622 (1913).

4. Suppose that, in the conveyance of a lot or in a recorded declaration of restrictions, the developer retains a right to modify the restrictions imposed upon subsequently sold lots. Does this provision negate the existence of a scheme? See Nelle v. Loch Haven Homeowners' Assn., Inc., 413 So. 2d 28 (Fla. 1982); Restatement (Third) of Property, Servitudes, supra, §2.14, Comment h.

After the developer sells all the lots and has no economic interest to protect, the right to modify the restrictions ceases. See Armstrong v. Roberts, 254 Ga. 15, 325 S.E.2d 769 (1985).

Snow v. Van Dam
Supreme Judicial Court of Massachusetts, 1935
291 Mass. 477, 197 N.E. 224

Bill in equity, filed in the Supreme Court on June 13, 1933.

By order of Walsh, J., there were entered an interlocutory decree confirming a master's report, and a final decree "permanently" enjoining the defendants "from erecting, using or maintaining any building" "for other than dwelling house purposes" on the land of the defendant Van Dam. The defendants appealed from the final decree. . . .

LUMMUS, J. This suit, although brought in Middlesex County, relates to land on the seashore at Brier Neck in Gloucester in Essex County, title to which, after the decision in Luce v. Parsons, 192 Mass. 8, was registered on September 5, 1906, in the name of one Luce, from whom title soon passed to one Shackelford. The tract so registered was bounded northerly by a line through a pond not far northerly from a county road called Thatcher Road, which ran through the tract from west to east; easterly by land of other owners; southerly by the Atlantic

Ocean, where there was a fine bathing beach; and westerly by Witham Road. The entrance to the tract was at the north-westerly corner, where is situated the lot now owned by the defendant Van Dam, which is the larger part of a triangular piece of land lying north of Thatcher Road and enclosed by Thatcher Road, Witham Road and another road.

The northerly part of the tract, including the lot of the defendant Van Dam, is low and marshy. When the tract was registered in 1906, this northerly part was deemed unsuitable for building and worthless, and consequently was not divided into lots on the earlier plans. Thatcher Road is a public way on which electric cars used to run. There is no summer residence on the north side of that way, and only one bounding on that way on the south side.

From Thatcher Road, going south, there is a fairly sharp ascent to the top of a low hill, from which there is a gentle slope southward to the beach. This hill and slope were in 1906, and still are, well adapted to summer residences. In 1907 the whole tract, except the part north of Thatcher road, was divided into building lots. By later plans some of the lots were further subdivided and the boundaries of others were changed. In all, about a hundred building lots were laid out. Each of the plaintiffs owns one of these building lots, either on the hill or on the southerly slope, on which he has built a summer residence.

Between July 8, 1907, and January 23, 1923, almost all the lots into which the part of the tract south of Thatcher Road was divided, including the lots of most of the plaintiffs, were sold at various times by the general owner of the tract to various persons. With negligible exceptions, the deeds contained uniform restrictions, of which the material one is that "only one dwelling house shall be erected or maintained thereon at any given time which building shall cost not less than $2500 and no outbuilding containing a privy shall be erected or maintained on said parcel without the consent in writing of the grantor or their [sic] heirs." The entire unsold remainder of the land south of Thatcher Road was conveyed, on June 15, 1923, by Shackelford, the general owner of the unsold parts of the tract, to J. Richard Clark, subject to similar restrictions.

The low and marshy land north of Thatcher Road was first divided, on a revised plan of 1919, into three parcels, called C, D and E. The revised plan covered the whole Brier Neck tract. On January 23, 1923, about five months before the deed to J. Richard Clark, already mentioned, said Shackelford conveyed said lots C, D and E to one Robert C. Clark, subject to the following restrictions:

> Only one dwelling house may be maintained on each of said parcels of land at any given time, which dwelling shall cost not less than Twenty-five Hundred Dollars ($2500) unless plans and specifications for a dwelling house of less cost shall be approved in writing by the grantor of said parcels of land,

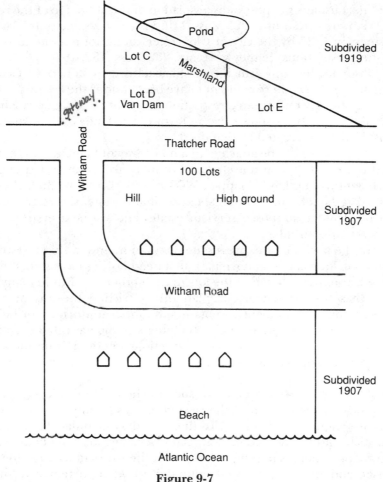

Figure 9-7

and no outbuilding containing a privy shall be maintained on either of said parcels of land without the consent in writing of the grantor. . . .

Lot D is the lot of which the larger part is now owned by the defendant Van Dam, having been conveyed to him by Robert C. Clark on February 18, 1933, subject to the restrictions contained in the deed to him "in so far as the same may be now in force and applicable." This phrase did not purport to create any new restriction, and could have no such effect. Sargent v. Leonardi, 223 Mass. 556, 558, 559. The defendants have erected on lot D a large building to be used for the sale of ice cream and dairy products and the conducting of the business of a common victualler. The plaintiffs bring this suit for an injunction, claiming a violation of the restrictions. We think that the erection of a building to be

873

used for business purposes was a violation of the language of the restriction. Powers v. Radding, 225 Mass. 110, 114. The zoning of the land for business in 1927 by the city of Gloucester could not operate to remove existing restrictions. Jenney v. Hynes, 282 Mass. 182, 194.

Prior to the conveyance from Shackelford to Robert C. Clark on January 23, 1923, there could not have been, under the law of this Commonwealth, any enforceable restriction upon lot D. Sprague v. Kimball, 213 Mass. 380. If any now exists in favor of the lands of the plaintiffs, it must have been created by that deed.

A restriction, to be attached to land by way of benefit, must not only tend to benefit that land itself . . . , but must also be intended to be appurtenant to that land. Clapp v. Wilder, 176 Mass. 332, 339. If not intended to benefit an ascertainable dominant estate, the restriction will not burden the supposed servient estate, but will be a mere personal contract on both sides. . . .

In the absence of express statement, an intention that a restriction upon one lot shall be appurtenant to a neighboring lot is sometimes inferred from the relation of the lots to each other. . . . But in many cases there has been a scheme or plan for restricting the lots in a tract undergoing development to obtain substantial uniformity in building and use. The existence of such a building scheme has often been relied on to show an intention that the restrictions imposed upon the several lots shall be appurtenant to every other lot in the tract included in the scheme. . . .

In some cases the absence of such a scheme has made it impossible to show that the burden of the restriction was intended to be appurtenant to neighboring land. . . . In the present case, unless the lots of the plaintiffs and the defendant Van Dam were included in one scheme of restrictions, there is nothing to show that the restrictions upon the lot of the defendant Van Dam were intended to be appurtenant to the lots of the plaintiffs.

What is meant by a "scheme" of this sort? In England, where the idea has been most fully developed, it is established that the area covered by the scheme and the restrictions imposed within that area must be apparent to the several purchasers when the sales begin. The purchasers must know the extent of their reciprocal rights and obligations, or, in other words, the "local law" imposed by the vendor upon a definite tract. Reid v. Bickerstaff, [1909] 2 Ch. 305. Kelly v. Barrett, [1924] 2 Ch. 379, 399, et seq. Where such a scheme exists, it appears to be the law of England and some American jurisdictions that a grantee subject to restrictions acquires by implication an enforceable right to have the remaining land of the vendor, within the limits of the scheme, bound by similar restrictions. . . . Sanborn v. McLean, 233 Mich. 227. . . . But it was settled in this Commonwealth by Sprague v. Kimball, 213 Mass. 380, that the statute of frauds prevents the enforcement against the vendor, or any purchaser from him of a lot not expressly restricted, of any implied or oral agreement that the vendor's remaining land shall be bound by restrictions similar to those imposed upon lots conveyed. Only where . . . the vendor binds his remaining land by writing, can reciprocity of restriction between the vendor and the vendee be enforced.

law (in writing)

Nevertheless, the existence of a "scheme" continues to be important in Massachusetts for the purpose of determining the land to which the restrictions are appurtenant. Sometimes the scheme has been established by preliminary statements of intention to restrict the tract, particularly in documents of a public nature . . . or in a recorded plan. Sprague v. Kimball, 213 Mass. 380, 383. Oliver v. Kalick, 223 Mass. 252. More often it is shown by the substantial uniformity of the restrictions upon the lots included in the tract. Nottingham Patent Brick & Tile Co. v. Butler, 15 Q.B.D. 261, 269, affirmed, 16 Q.B.D. 778. In some jurisdictions the logic of the English rule, that the extent and character of the scheme must be apparent when the sale of the lots begins, has led to rulings that the restrictions imposed in later deeds are not evidence of the existence or nature of the scheme. Werner v. Graham, 181 Cal. 174, 183-186. Sailer v. Podolski, 12 Buch. 459, 464. See also Nashua Hospital Association v. Gage, 85 N.H. 335, 340, 341. In the present case there is no evidence of a scheme except a list of conveyances of different lots *here* from 1907 to 1923 with substantially uniform restrictions. Although the point has not been discussed by this court, the original papers show, more clearly than the reports, that subsequent deeds were relied on to show a scheme existing at the time of the earlier conveyances to the parties or their predecessors in title, in Hills v. Metzenroth, 173 Mass. 423, Bacon v. Sandberg, 179 Mass. 396, Stewart v. Finkelstone, 206 Mass. 28, and Storey v. Brush, 256 Mass. 101. See also Hazen v. Mathews, 184 Mass. 388, 393. Apparently in Massachusetts a "scheme" has legal effect if definitely settled by the common vendor when the sale of lots begins, even though at that time evidence of such settlement is lacking and a series of subsequent conveyances is needed to supply it. In Bacon v. Sandberg, 179 Mass. 396, 398, it was said, "the criterion in this class of cases is the intent of the grantor in imposing the restrictions."

Neither the restricting of every lot within the area covered, nor absolute identity of restrictions upon different lots, is essential to the existence of a scheme. . . . But extensive omissions or variations tend to show that no scheme exists, and that the restrictions are only personal contracts. . . .

The existence of a "scheme" is important in the law of restrictions for another purpose, namely, to enable the restrictions to be made appurtenant to a lot within the scheme which has been earlier conveyed by the common vendor. In the present case the lots of some of the plaintiffs were sold before, and the lots of others after, the conveyance from Shackelford to Robert C. Clark on January 23, 1923, which first imposed a restriction upon the lot now owned by the defendant Van Dam. The plaintiffs whose lots were sold before January 23, 1923, cannot claim succession to any rights of Shackelford or of land then retained by him. In general, an equitable easement or restriction cannot be created in favor of land owned by a stranger. Hazen v. Mathews, 184 Mass. 388. Compare Vogeler v. Alwyn Improvement Corp. 247 N.Y. 131; Lister v. Vogel, 110 N.J. Eq. 35. Nevertheless an earlier purchaser in a land development has long been allowed to enforce against a later purchaser the restrictions imposed upon the latter by the deed to him in pursuance of a scheme of restrictions. . . . Earlier as well as later purchasers of lots within the area covered by the scheme acquire such an interest in the restrictions that the common vendor cannot release them. Hopkins v. Smith, 162 Mass. 444. Ivarson v. Mulvey, 179 Mass. 141. Goulding v. Phinney, 234 Mass. 411, 413.

The rationale of the rule allowing an earlier purchaser to enforce restrictions in a deed to a later one pursuant to a building scheme, is not easy to find. De Gray v. Monmouth Beach Club House Co., 5 Dick. (N.J.) 329, 335-341. The simple explanation that the deed to the earlier purchaser, subject to restrictions, implied an enforceable agreement on the part of the vendor to restrict in like manner all the remaining land included in the scheme (Dean Stone, now Mr. Justice Stone, in 19 Colum. L. Rev. 177, 187), cannot be accepted in Massachusetts without conflict with Sprague v. Kimball, 213 Mass. 380. In Bristol v. Woodward, 251 N.Y. 275, 288, Cardozo, C.J., said,

> If we regard the restriction from the point of view of contract, there is trouble in understanding how the purchaser of lot A can gain a right to enforce the restriction against the later purchaser of lot B without an extraordinary extension of Lawrence v. Fox (20 N.Y. 268). . . . Perhaps it is enough to say that the extension of the doctrine, even if illogical, has been made too often and too consistently to permit withdrawal or retreat.

It follows from what has been said, that if there was a scheme of restrictions, existing when the sale of lots began in 1907, which scheme included the lands of the plaintiffs and of the defendant Van Dam, and if the restrictions imposed upon the land of the defendant Van Dam in 1923 were imposed in pursuance of that scheme, then all the plaintiffs are entitled to relief, unless some special defence is shown. The burden is upon the plaintiffs to show the existence of such a scheme. Lowell Institution for Savings v. Lowell, 153 Mass. 530, 533. American Unitarian Association v. Minot, 185 Mass. 589, 595. In our opinion they have done so. Unquestionably there was a scheme which included all the land south of Thatcher Road. The real question is, whether in its origin it included the land north of that road, where is situated the lot of the defendant Van Dam. That lot lies at the gateway of the whole development. One must pass it to visit any part of Brier Neck. The use made of that lot tends strongly to fix the character of the entire tract. It is true, that the land north of Thatcher Road was not divided into lots until 1919, but it was shown on all the plans from the beginning. The failure to divide it sooner was apparently due to a belief that it could not be sold, not to an intent to reserve it for other than residential purposes. We think that the scheme from the beginning contemplated that no part of the Brier Neck tract should be used for commercial purposes. When the lot of the defendant Van Dam was restricted in 1923, the restriction was in pursuance of the original scheme and gave rights to earlier as well as to later purchasers. . . .

held scheme enforced

Ordered accordingly.

NOTES, QUESTIONS, AND PROBLEM

1. There are two current theories by which a prior purchaser in a subdivision can enforce an agreement subsequently made by his grantor and a subsequent purchaser, with an intention to benefit the land previously sold. The first is the theory adopted in Sanborn v. McLean, page 866. It goes as follows: At the time the prior purchaser acquires his land, he receives an implied reciprocal servitude in the common grantor's remaining land. When the common grantor later sells a tract from his remaining land, the prior purchaser is enforcing this servitude against the subsequent purchaser with notice. This theory could not be used by the Massachusetts court in Snow v. Van Dam because Massachusetts does not imply negative reciprocal servitudes. Nor can it be used where the developer does not have a scheme of reciprocal restrictions.

theory 1

The second theory is that equity is enforcing a contract for the benefit of third-party beneficiaries. In Snow v. Van Dam, for instance, Shackelford conveyed lots C, D, and E to Robert C. Clark, subject to express restrictions imposed in the conveyance from Shackelford to Clark. It could be said that these express restrictions were for the benefit of the neighbors on the south side of Thatcher Road and that equity was merely permitting them to enforce the restrictions as third-party beneficiaries. The Massachusetts court could not openly accept that theory in 1935, however, because it did not then generally permit third-party beneficiaries to recover on contracts.[29]

theory 2

The idea that third parties should be able to sue on contracts made for their benefit took more than a century to develop fully; the conceptual obstacle was lack of privity of contract. Under mid-nineteenth cen-

29. Massachusetts did not formally allow recovery by third-party beneficiaries of all types until 1982. Finally, in that year, Rae v. Air-Speed, Inc., 386 Mass. 187, 435 N.E.2d 628 (1982), adopted the rule of the Restatement (Second) of Contracts §302 (1981).

tury law, if *A* made a promise to *B* for the benefit of *C*, only *B* and not *C* could enforce the contract. In Lawrence v. Fox, 20 N.Y. 268 (1859), the New York court decided that *C* could sue if *C* was a creditor of *B*, thus permitting creditor third-party beneficiaries to recover. Subsequently contract law has moved in this century to extend Lawrence v. Fox to all types of third-party beneficiaries. Restatement (Second) of Contracts, supra footnote 29, §302, permits any intended beneficiary to enforce a contract. Restatement of Property §541 (1944) adopted a third-party beneficiary doctrine to allow enforcement by any intended beneficiary of a covenant respecting the use of land. Under that doctrine, in Snow v. Van Dam, the owners on the south side of Thatcher Road could enforce the covenants in the Shackelford-to-Clark deed as third-party beneficiaries. Similarly, under Restatement (Third) of Property, Servitudes, §2.6 (T.D. No. 1, 1989), any intended beneficiary can enforce a servitude.

Although modern third-party beneficiary theory makes a good deal of sense, some American jurisdictions hem it in, when it comes to enforcing promises respecting land use, with a requirement that the third-party beneficiary be in privity of estate with the original promisee. It is a "commonly accepted principle," says 2 American Law of Property §9.30 at 425 (1952), "that the enforcement of an equitable servitude is limited to those landowners who can trace title to the promisee either prior to or subsequent to the date of the agreement." This limitation does not cause any difficulty when subdivision restrictions are sued on by neighbors in the subdivision, because they received their titles from the developer or other original promisees, but it does prevent enforcement by someone to whom the original promisee has never conveyed land. See Brown v. Heirs of Fuller, 347 A.2d 127 (Me. 1975).

Now that contract law has thrown off limitations on enforcement of contracts by third-party beneficiaries, is there any reason a third-party beneficiary of a promissory servitude should be able to enforce the promise only if the intended beneficiary is in privity of estate with the promisee? Observe that privity of estate in this context means that the beneficiary can trace title to the promisee, not that the beneficiary succeeded to land already benefited by a covenant. It thus differs slightly from the usual meaning of vertical privity, discussed earlier at pages 860, 864.

2. To test your understanding of the discussion above, take the following problem. Hardcastle Barnes owns a lot immediately to the south of Walter Zamiarski's lot. Barnes and Zamiarski are friendly neighbors. When Barnes sells his lot to Stanley Lewek he places a restriction in the deed for the benefit of Zamiarski's lot. The restriction provides: "Said parties of the second part [grantees] further covenant and agree that neither they nor their assigns shall or will erect or permit on any portion of said premises any building whatsoever within 10 feet of the northerly line of said premises." The restricted lot subsequently comes into the

hands of Thaddeus Kozial who wants to build within 10 feet of the northerly line. Zamiarski seeks an injunction. What result? In Zamiarski v. Kozial, 18 A.D.2d 297, 239 N.Y.S.2d 221 (1963), the court, holding that third-party beneficiary theory is not limited by any concept of privity of estate, granted Zamiarski an injunction. A more recent New York Court of Appeals case, however, without mentioning *Zamiarski*, states that vertical privity of estate with the covenantee is necessary for enforcement of the benefit. Malley v. Hanna, 65 N.Y.2d 289, 480 N.E.2d 1068, 491 N.Y.S.2d 286 (1985).

3. Recall the common law rule that an easement may not be created in favor of a third party. Willard v. First Church of Christ Scientist, page 791. Why do courts permit equitable servitudes to be created for the benefit of third parties but not easements?

Neponsit Property Owners' Association, Inc. v. Emigrant Industrial Savings Bank

Court of Appeals of New York, 1938
278 N.Y. 248, 15 N.E.2d 793

LEHMAN, J. The plaintiff, as assignee of Neponsit Realty Company, has brought this action to foreclose a lien upon land which the defendant owns. The lien, it is alleged, arises from a covenant, condition or charge contained in a deed of conveyance of the land from Neponsit Realty Company to a predecessor in title of the defendant. The defendant purchased the land at a judicial sale. The referee's deed to the defendant and every deed in the defendant's chain of title since the conveyance of the land by Neponsit Realty Company purports to convey the property subject to the covenant, condition or charge contained in the original deed. . . .

It appears that in January, 1911, Neponsit Realty Company, as owner of a tract of land in Queens county, caused to be filed in the office of the clerk of the county a map of the land. The tract was developed for a strictly residential community, and Neponsit Realty Company conveyed lots in the tract to purchasers, describing such lots by reference to the filed map and to roads and streets shown thereon. In 1917, Neponsit Realty Company conveyed the land now owned by the defendant to Robert Oldner Deyer and his wife by deed which contained the covenant upon which the plaintiff's cause of action is based.

That covenant provides:

And the party of the second part for the party of the second part and the heirs, successors and assigns of the party of the second part further covenants that the property conveyed by this deed shall be subject to an annual charge in such an amount as will be fixed by the party of the first part, its successors and assigns, not, however exceeding in any year the sum of four ($4.00) Dol

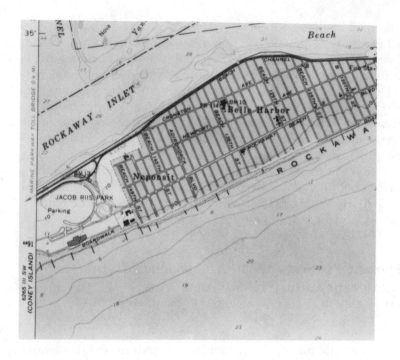

lars per lot 20 × 100 feet. The assigns of the party of the first part may include a Property Owners' Association which may hereafter be organized for the purposes referred to in this paragraph, and in case such association is organized the sums in this paragraph provided for shall be payable to such association. The party of the second part for the party of the second part and the heirs, successors and assigns of the party of the second part covenants that they will pay this charge to the party of the first part, its successors and assigns on the first day of May in each and every year, and further covenants that said charge shall on said date in each year become a lien on the land and shall continue to be such lien until fully paid. Such charge shall be payable to the party of the first part or its successors or assigns, and shall be devoted to the maintenance of the roads, paths, parks, beach, sewers and such other public purposes as shall from time to time be determined by the party of the first part, its successors or assigns. And the party of the second part by the acceptance of this deed hereby expressly vests in the party of the first part, its successors and assigns, the right and power to bring all actions against the owner of the premises hereby conveyed or any part thereof for the collection of such charge and to enforce the aforesaid lien therefor.

These covenants shall run with the land and shall be construed as real covenants running with the land until January 31st, 1940, when they shall cease and determine.

Every subsequent deed of conveyance of the property in the defendant's chain of title, including the deed from the referee to the defendant, contained, as we have said, a provision that they were made subject to covenants and restrictions of former deeds of record.

There can be no doubt that the Neponsit Realty Company intended that the covenant should run with the land and should be enforceable by a property owners association against every owner of property in the residential tract which the realty company was then developing. The language of the covenant admits of no other construction. Regardless of the intention of the parties, a covenant will run with the land and will be enforceable against a subsequent purchaser of the land at the suit of one who claims the benefit of the covenant, only if the covenant complies with certain legal requirements. These requirements rest upon ancient rules and precedents. The age-old essentials of a real covenant, aside from the form of the covenant, may be summarily formulated as follows: (1) it must appear that grantor and grantee intended that the covenant should run with the land; (2) it must appear that the covenant is one "touching" or "concerning" the land with which it runs; (3) it must appear that there is "privity of estate" between the promisee or party claiming the benefit of the covenant and the right to enforce it, and the promisor or party who rests under the burden of the covenant. (Clark on Covenants and Interests Running with Land, p.74.) Although the deeds of Neponsit Realty Company conveying lots in the tract it developed "contained a provision to the effect that the covenants ran with the land, such provision in the absence of the other legal requirements is insufficient to accomplish such a purpose." (Morgan Lake Co. v. N.Y., N.H. & H.R.R. Co., 262 N.Y. 234, 238.) In his opinion in that case, Judge Crane posed but found it unnecessary to decide many of the questions which the court must consider in this case.

The covenant in this case is intended to create a charge or obligation to pay a fixed sum of money to be "devoted to the maintenance of the roads, paths, parks, beach, sewers and such other public purposes as shall from time to time be determined by the party of the first part [the grantor], its successors or assigns." It is an affirmative covenant to pay money for use in connection with, but not upon, the land which it is said is subject to the burden of the covenant. Does such a covenant "touch" or "concern" the land? These terms are not part of a statutory definition, a limitation placed by the State upon the power of the courts to enforce covenants *intended* to run with the land by the parties who entered into the covenants. Rather they are words used by courts in England in old cases to describe a limitation which the courts themselves created or to formulate a test which the courts have devised and which the courts voluntarily apply. (Cf. Spencer's Case, Coke, vol. 3, part 5, p.16; Mayor of Congleton v. Pattison, 10 East, 316.) In truth the test so formulated is too vague to be of much assistance and judges and academic scholars alike have struggled, not with entire success, to formulate a test at once more satisfactory and more accurate. "It has been found impossible to state any absolute tests to determine what covenants touch and concern land and what do not. The question is one for the court to determine in the exercise of its best judgment upon the facts of each case." (Clark, op. cit. p.76.)

Even though that be true, a determination by a court in one case upon particular facts will often serve to point the way to correct decision in other cases upon analogous facts. Such guideposts may not be disregarded. It has been often said that a covenant to pay a sum of money is a personal affirmative covenant which usually does not concern or touch the land. Such statements are based upon English decisions which hold in effect that only covenants, which compel the covenanter to submit to some *restriction on the use* of his property, touch or concern the land, and that the burden of a covenant which requires the covenanter to do an affirmative act, even on his own land, for the benefit of the owner of a "dominant" estate, does not run with his land. (Miller v. Clary, 210 N.Y. 127.) In that case the court pointed out that in many jurisdictions of this country the narrow English rule has been criticized and a more liberal and flexible rule has been substituted. In this State the courts have not gone so far. We have not abandoned the historic distinction drawn by the English courts. So this court has recently said:

> Subject to a few exceptions not important at this time, there is now in this State a settled rule of law that a covenant to do an affirmative act, as distinguished from a covenant merely negative in effect, does not run with the land so as to charge the burden of performance on a subsequent grantee [citing cases]. This is so though the burden of such a covenant is laid upon the very parcel which is the subject-matter of conveyance. [Guaranty Trust Co. v. N.Y. & Queens County Ry. Co., 253 N.Y. 190, 204, opinion by Cardozo, Ch. J.]

Both in that case and in the case of Miller v. Clary (supra) the court pointed out that there were some exceptions or limitations in the application of the general rule. Some promises to pay money have been enforced, as covenants running with the land, against subsequent holders of the land who took with notice of the covenant. (Cf. Greenfarb v. R.S.K. Realty Corp., 256 N.Y. 130; Morgan Lake Co. v. N.Y., N.H. & H.R.R. Co., supra.) It may be difficult to classify these exceptions or to formulate a test of whether a particular covenant to pay money or to perform some other act falls within the general rule that ordinarily an affirmative covenant is a personal and not a real covenant, or falls outside the limitations placed upon the general rule. At least it must "touch" or "concern" the land in a substantial degree, and though it may be inexpedient and perhaps impossible to formulate a rigid test or definition which will be entirely satisfactory or which can be applied mechanically in all cases, we should at least be able to state the problem and find a reasonable method of approach to it. It has been suggested that a covenant which runs with the land must affect the legal relations — the advantages and the burdens — of the parties to the covenant, as owners of particular parcels of land and not merely as members of the community in general, such as taxpayers or owners of other land. (Clark, op. cit. p.76. Cf. Professor Bigelow's article on The Contents of Covenants in Leases, 12 Mich. L. Rev. 639; 30 Law Quarterly Review 319.) That method of approach has the merit of realism. The test is based on the effect of the covenant rather than on technical distinctions. Does the covenant impose, on the one hand, a burden upon an interest in land, which on the other hand increases the value of a different interest in the same or related land?[30]

Even though we accept that approach and test, it still remains true that whether a particular covenant is sufficiently connected with the use of land to run with the land, must be in many cases a question of degree. A promise to pay for something to be done in connection with the promisor's land does not differ essentially from a promise by the promisor to do the thing himself, and both promises constitute, in a substantial sense, a restriction upon the owner's right to use the land, and a burden upon the legal interest of the owner. On the other hand, a covenant to perform or pay for the performance of an affirmative act disconnected with the use of the land cannot ordinarily touch or concern the land in any substantial degree. Thus, unless we exalt technical form over substance, the distinction between covenants which run with land and covenants which are personal, must depend upon the effect of the covenant on the legal rights which otherwise would flow from ownership of land and which are connected with the land. The problem then is: Does the covenant in purpose and effect *substantially* alter these rights?

Looking at the problem presented in this case . . . and stressing the intent and substantial effect of the covenant rather than its form, it seems clear that the covenant may properly be said to touch and concern the land of the defendant and its burden should run with the land. True, it calls for payment of a sum of money to be expended for "public purposes" upon land other than the land conveyed by Neponsit Realty Company to [defendant's] predecessor in title. By that conveyance the grantee, however, obtained not only title to particular lots, but an easement or right of common enjoyment with other property owners in roads, beaches, public parks or spaces and improvements in the same

---

30. A fuller statement of Professor Bigelow's test for touch and concern, alluded to by the court, runs as follows: "[I]f the covenantor's legal interest in land is rendered less valuable by the covenant's performance, then the burden of the covenant satisfies the requirement that the covenant touch and concern land. If, on the other hand, the covenantee's legal interest in land is rendered more valuable by the covenant's performance, then the benefit of the covenant satisfies the requirement that the covenant touch and concern land." 5 Richard R. Powell, The Law of Real Property ¶673[2][a] (rev. ed. 1992). This test may have the virtue of realism, as Judge Lehman suggests, but does it escape the vice of circularity? — Eds.

Houses in Neponsit, 1980

tract. For full enjoyment in common by the defendant and other property owners of these easements or rights, the roads and public places
must be maintained. In order that the burden of maintaining public
improvements should rest upon the land benefited by the improvements, the grantor exacted from the grantee of the land with its appurtenant easement or right of enjoyment a covenant that the burden of
paying the cost should be inseparably attached to the land which enjoys
the benefit. It is plain that any distinction or definition which would exclude such a covenant from the classification of covenants which "touch"
or "concern" the land would be based on form and not on substance.

Another difficulty remains. Though between the grantor and the
grantee there was privity of estate, the covenant provides that its benefit
shall run to the assigns of the grantor who "may include a Property
Owners' Association which may hereafter be organized for the purposes
referred to in this paragraph." The plaintiff has been organized to receive the sums payable by the property owners and to expend them for
the benefit of such owners. Various definitions have been formulated of
"privity of estate" in connection with covenants that run with the land,
but none of such definitions seems to cover the relationship between the
plaintiff and the defendant in this case. The plaintiff has not succeeded
to the ownership of any property of the grantor. It does not appear that
it ever had title to the streets or public places upon which charges which
are payable to it must be expended. It does not appear that it owns any
other property in the residential tract to which any easement or right of
enjoyment in such property is appurtenant. It is created solely to act as
the assignee of the benefit of the covenant, and it has no interest of its
own in the enforcement of the covenant.

The arguments that under such circumstances the plaintiff has no
right of action to enforce a covenant running with the land are all based
upon a distinction between the corporate property owners association
and the property owners for whose benefit the association has been
formed. If that distinction may be ignored, then the basis of the arguments is destroyed. How far privity of estate in technical form is necessary to enforce in equity a restrictive covenant upon the use of land,
presents an interesting question. Enforcement of such covenants rests
upon equitable principles (Tulk v. Moxhay, 2 Phillips, 774; Trustees of
Columbia College v. Lynch, 70 N.Y. 440; Korn v. Campbell, 192 N.Y.
490), and at times, at least, the violation "of the restrictive covenant may
be restrained at the suit of one who owns property, or for whose benefit
the restriction was established, irrespective of whether there were privity
either of estate or of contract between the parties, or whether an action
at law were maintainable." (Cheseboro v. Moers, 233 N.Y. 75, 80.) The
covenant in this case does not fall exactly within any classification of "restrictive" covenants, which have been enforced in this State (Cf. Korn v.
Campbell, 192 N.Y. 490), and no right to enforce even a restrictive cov-

enant has been sustained in this State where the plaintiff did not own property which would benefit by such enforcement so that some of the elements of an equitable servitude are present. In some jurisdictions it has been held that no action may be maintained without such elements. (But cf. Van Sant v. Rose, 260 Ill. 401.) We do not attempt to decide now how far the rule of Trustees of Columbia College v. Lynch (supra) will be carried, or to formulate a definite rule as to when, or even whether, covenants in a deed will be enforced, upon equitable principles, against subsequent purchasers with notice, at the suit of a party without privity of contract or estate. (Cf. Equitable Rights and Liabilities of Strangers to a Contract, by Harlan F. Stone, 18 Columbia Law Review, 291.) There is no need to resort to such a rule if the courts may look behind the corporate form of the plaintiff.

The corporate plaintiff has been formed as a convenient instrument by which the property owners may advance their common interests. We do not ignore the corporate form when we recognize that the Neponsit Property Owners' Association, Inc., is acting as the agent or representative of the Neponsit property owners. As we have said in another case: when Neponsit Property Owners' Association, Inc., "was formed, the property owners were expected to, and have looked to that organization as the medium through which enjoyment of their common right might be preserved equally for all." (Matter of City of New York [Public Beach], 269 N.Y. 64, 75.) Under the conditions thus presented we said: "it may be difficult, or even impossible, to classify into recognized categories the nature of the interest of the membership corporation and its members in the land. The corporate entity cannot be disregarded, nor can the separate interests of the members of the corporation" (p.73). Only blind adherence to an ancient formula devised to meet entirely different conditions could constrain the court to hold that a corporation formed as a medium for the enjoyment of common rights of property owners owns no property which would benefit by enforcement of common rights and has no cause of action in equity to enforce the covenant upon which such common rights depend. Every reason which in other circumstances may justify the ancient formula may be urged in support of the conclusion that the formula should not be applied in this case. In substance if not in form the covenant is a restrictive covenant which touches and concerns the defendant's land, and in substance, if not in form, there is privity of estate between the plaintiff and the defendant. . . .

The order [denying a motion by defendant for judgment on the pleadings] should be affirmed.

NOTES AND QUESTIONS

1. In *Neponsit* the plaintiff brought an action to foreclose a lien. The lien was imposed by Neponsit Realty Company to secure the promise to pay money. In mortgage law, a mortgage lien is enforceable against the property even though a subsequent purchaser does not assume the debt and has no personal liability. The court in *Neponsit* appeared to assume that, contrary to general lien theory, a lien to secure a covenant to pay money to maintain common facilities cannot be enforced unless the successor owner is liable on the covenant. See Allison Dunham, Promises Respecting the Use of Land, 8 J.L. & Econ. 133, 147-148 (1965). Is this consistent with the release of the original covenantor from liability when the covenantor transfers his entire interest in the land (see pages 860-861, 865)?

2. Covenants restricting the use of land have almost always been held to touch and concern land. These negative covenants directly affect the uses to which the land can be put and substantially affect its value.

On the other hand, courts have been wary of enforcing affirmative covenants against successors. Three reasons inform this caution. First, courts are reluctant to issue orders to perform a series of acts requiring continuing judicial supervision. Second, enforcing an affirmative covenant, which requires the covenantor to maintain property or pay money, may impose a large personal liability on a successor. (Compare the hedging of real covenants, which impose personal liability, by the courts and the first Restatement of Property (pages 858-860).) Enforcement of a negative covenant restricting use of land limits the successor's loss to the investment in the land itself. Third, an affirmative obligation, unlimited in time, resembles a feudal service or perpetual rent.[31]

Oceanside Community Assn. v. Oceanside Land Co., 147 Cal. App. 3d 166, 195 Cal. Rptr. 14 (1983), is illustrative. This case involved Oceana, a residential development of 932 residences on individual lots with a central club house, swimming pool, recreation areas, and landscaped areas. The Oceanside Community Association (homeowners association) maintained these common areas, which it had leased from the developer, out of assessments against homeowner members. In addition, there was an adjacent golf course, which the developer built and maintained. The developer covenanted with the homeowners that the land would be maintained as a golf course for 99 years, that homeowners were entitled to play at 75 percent of the rate charged the public, and

---

31. In the settlement of this country, perpetual rents (often called quit rents, because they were in lieu of feudal obligations) were sometimes reserved by the crown or the proprietaries of the original colonies. After the Revolution, legislation was enacted to transfer these quit rents to the states and make them redeemable. But some perpetual ground rents survived in New York, Pennsylvania, and Maryland. It took an uprising of the farmers against descendants of the Dutch patroons to eliminate these feudal rents in New York in the nineteenth century. See 2 American Law of Property §9.41 (1952); William R. Vance, The Quest for Tenure in the United States, 33 Yale L.J. 248 (1923).

that these covenants ran with the land. The developer used the golf course as an inducement to purchasers.

Subsequently the developer sold the golf course to the Smiths. They operated the golf course for a few years and then sold it to Phil Plies. Plies refused to maintain the golf course and barricaded its entrance. After Plies ran into financial difficulty, the golf course was sold to Pine Tree Motel, Inc. The homeowners association sued Pine Tree Motel asking for an injunction requiring it to maintain the golf course. The court denied the injunction, because (1) it thought holding Pine Tree personally liable for the substantial cost of renovation would be inequitable when the damage occurred before it acquired the property, and (2) restoring a golf course was complicated and court supervision of such a process would be difficult. Nonetheless, the court concluded that the 932 Oceana residences were losing $10 a month in benefits and imposed an equitable lien against the land in the amount of $9,320 (932 residences multiplied by $10) each month the land was not being renovated or maintained as a golf course. The Oceana homeowners were granted the right to foreclose the lien whenever the conditions were not met. By this remedy, the court limited Pine Tree's loss to its investment in the golf course and avoided a personal judgment collectible out of all the defendant's assets.

3. Sometimes it is hard to tell whether the obligation is affirmative or negative. In Ezer v. Fuchsloch, 99 Cal. App. 3d 849, 160 Cal. Rptr. 486, 13. A.L.R.4th 1333 (1979), the subdivider recorded a declaration of restrictions that provided that "no tree, shrub, or other landscaping be planted that may at present or in the future obstruct the view [of the ocean] from any lot." Is this a negative covenant that changes into an affirmative covenant as the trees grow? On complaint of an uphill neighbor, the court ordered the defendants, who had bought into the subdivision, to cut down to the level of the roof of their house all trees and shrubs and thereafter to keep their trees and shrubs cut so that they did not grow above the rooftop. The court rejected an argument that the trees had an independent right to exist paramount to the rights of the covenanting parties and their successors.

4. In Streams Sports Club, Ltd. v. Richmond, 99 Ill. 2d 182, 457 N.E.2d 1226 (1983), the condominium agreement included a covenant to pay annual dues of $216 to a profitmaking sports club owned by the developer, located adjacent to the condominium. The obligation to pay dues was secured by a lien on the condominium unit. The condominium declaration stated that the covenant ran with the land. The developer subsequently sold the sports club to Streams Sports Club. Sometime later Donna Richmond bought a condominium unit from one of the original purchasers. Richmond was not sportsminded and did not want to belong to the sports club. The court held that the covenant touched and concerned the land because the owners have the right to enjoy the club

facilities.[32] Accord, Homsey v. University Gardens Racquet Club, 730 S.E.2d 763 (Tex. Civ. App. 1987).

Compare Chesapeake Ranch Club, Inc. v. C.R.C. United Members, Inc., 60 Md. App. 609, 483 A.2d 1334 (1984), holding that the burden of a covenant to pay membership dues for the use of social and recreational facilities did not run with the land. The court reasoned that the covenants did not necessarily increase the value of the individual lots because some buyers would not want to use the facilities. Accord, Ebbe v. Senior Estates Golf & Country Club, 61 Or. App. 398, 657 P.2d 696 (1983) (covenant to pay $1,000 initiation fee to golf club did not touch and concern land).

Eagle Enterprises, Inc. v. Gross
Court of Appeals of New York, 1976
39 N.Y.2d 505, 349 N.E.2d 816, 384 N.Y.S.2d 717

GABRIELLI, J. In 1951, Orchard Hill Realties, Inc., a subdivider and developer, conveyed certain property in the subdivision of Orchard Hill in Orange County to William and Pauline Baum. The deed to the Baums contained the following provision:

> The party of the first part shall supply to the party of the second part, seasonably, from May 1st to October 1st, of each year, water for domestic use only, from the well located on other property of the party of the first part, and the party of the second part agrees to take said water and to pay the party of the first part, a fee of Thirty-five ($35.00) dollars per year, for said water so supplied.

In addition, the deed also contained the following:

> It is expressly provided that the covenants herein contained shall run with the land . . . and shall bind and shall enure to the benefit of the heirs, distributees, successors, legal representatives and assigns of the respective parties hereto.

Appellant is the successor in interest of Orchard Hill Realties, Inc., and respondent, after a series of intervening conveyances, is the successor in interest of the Baums. . . .

32. After this case the owners of another condominium — built by the same developer and subject to a similar covenant — amended the condominium agreement, by unanimous vote, to eliminate the covenant, relieving the owners of liability for annual dues to Streams Club, Ltd. The court held the condominium owners could thus defeat the club's claim, on the ground that the covenant was in the condominium declaration of ownership, which could be amended by three-fourths of the owners. Streams Club, Ltd. v. Thompson, 180 Ill. App. 3d 830, 536 N.E.2d 459 (1989).

According to the stipulated facts, respondent has refused to accept and pay for water offered by appellant since he has constructed his own well to service what is now a year-round dwelling. Appellant, therefore, instituted this action to collect the fee specified in the covenant . . . for the supply of water which, appellant contends, respondent is bound to accept. The action was styled as one "for goods sold and delivered" even though respondent did not utilize any of appellant's water. Two of the lower courts found that the covenant "ran" with the land and, hence, was binding upon respondent as successor to the Baums, but the Appellate Division reversed and held that the covenant could not be enforced against respondent. We must now decide whether the promise of the original grantees to accept and make payment for a seasonal water supply from the well of their grantor is enforceable against subsequent grantees and may be said to "run with the land." We agree with the determination of the Appellate Division and affirm its order.

Regardless of the express recital in a deed that a covenant will run with the land, a promise to do an affirmative act contained in a deed is generally not binding upon subsequent grantees of the promisor unless certain well-defined and long established legal requisites are satisfied (Nicholson v. 300 Broadway Realty Corp., 7 NY2d 240, 244; Neponsit Prop. Owners' Assn. v. Emigrant Ind. Sav. Bank, 278 NY 248, 254-255). . . . In the landmark *Neponsit* case (supra), we adopted and clarified the following test, originating in the early English decisions, for the enforceability of affirmative covenants (cf. Spencer's Case, 77 Eng. Rep. 72 [1583]), and reaffirmed the requirements that in order for a covenant to run with the land, it must be shown that:

(1) The original grantee and grantor must have intended that the covenant run with the land.

(2) There must exist "privity of estate" between the party claiming the benefit of the covenant and the right to enforce it and the party upon whom the burden of the covenant is to be imposed.

(3) The covenant must be deemed to "touch and concern" the land with which it runs.

(See, also, Nicholson v. 300 Broadway Realty Corp., supra; Restatement Property, §§531, 534, 537, 538; 13 NY Jur, Covenants and Restrictions, §8, p248.)

Even though the parties to the original deed expressly state in the instrument that the covenant will run with the land, such a recital is insufficient to render the covenant enforceable against subsequent grantees if the other requirements for the running of an affirmative covenant are not met. . . . Thus, although the intention of the original parties here is clear and privity of estate exists, the covenant must still satisfy the requirement that it "touch and concern" the land.

It is this third prong of the tripartite rule which presents the obstacle to appellant's position and which was the focus of our decisions in *Neponsit* and Nicholson v. 300 Broadway Realty Corp. (7 NY2d 240, 244, supra). . . .

The covenants in issue in *Neponsit* required the owners of property in a development to pay an annual charge for the maintenance of roads, paths, parks, beaches, sewers and other public improvements. The court concluded that the covenant substantially affected the promisor's legal interest in his property since the latter received an easement in common and a right of enjoyment in the public improvements for which contribution was received by all the landowners in the subdivision (supra, pp259-260).

A close examination of the covenant in the case before us leads to the conclusion that it does not substantially affect the ownership interest of landowners in the Orchard Hill subdivision. The covenant provides for the supplying of water for only six months of the year; no claim has been advanced by appellant that the lands in the subdivision would be waterless without the water it supplies. Indeed, the facts here point to the converse conclusion since respondent has obtained his own source of water. The record, based on and consisting of an agreed stipulation of facts, does not demonstrate that other property owners in the subdivision would be deprived of water from appellant or that the price of water would become prohibitive for other property owners if respondent terminated appellant's service. Thus, the agreement for the seasonal supply of water does not seem to us to relate in any significant degree to the ownership rights of respondent and the other property owners in the subdivision of Orchard Hill. The landowners in *Neponsit* received an easement in common to utilize public areas in the subdivision; this interest was in the nature of a property right attached to their respective properties. The obligation to receive water from appellant resembles a personal, contractual promise to purchase water rather than a significant interest attaching to respondent's property. It should be emphasized that the question whether a covenant is so closely related to the use of the land that it should be deemed to "run" with the land is one of degree, dependent on the particular circumstances of a case. . . .

There is an additional reason why we are reluctant to enforce this covenant for the seasonal supply of water. The affirmative covenant is disfavored in the law because of the fear that this type of obligation imposes an "undue restriction on alienation or an onerous burden in perpetuity" (Nicholson v. 300 Broadway Realty Corp., 7 NY2d 240, 246, supra). In *Nicholson*, the covenant to supply heat was not interdicted by this concern because it was conditioned upon the continued existence of the buildings on both the promisor's and the promisee's properties. Similarly, in *Neponsit,* the original 1917 deed containing the covenant to pay an annual charge for the maintenance of public areas expressly provided for its own lapse in 1940. Here, no outside limitation has been placed on the obligation to purchase water from appellant. Thus, the covenant falls prey to the criticism that it creates a burden in perpetuity, and purports to bind all future owners, regardless of the use to which the land is put. Such a result militates strongly against its enforcement. On this ground also, we are of the opinion that the covenant should not be enforced as an exception to the general rule prohibiting the "running" of affirmative covenants.

Accordingly, the order of the Appellate Division should be affirmed, with costs.

QUESTION AND NOTES

1. Reverse the parties in *Eagle Enterprises*. If Eagle Enterprises had refused to supply Gross with water at $35 a year, would the covenant touch and concern and be enforceable?

2. The touch and concern requirement has been criticized for being vague and unpredictable, for interfering with freedom of contract, and for being economically inefficient. See Richard A. Epstein, Notice and Freedom of Contract in the Law of Servitudes, 55 S. Cal. L. Rev. 1353, 1360-1364 (1982) ("denies the original parties their contractual freedom by subordinating their desires to the interests of future third parties"; produces high transaction costs when the servitude is created, because of unpredictability; and gives incentives to seek more objectionable devices, such as an option to repurchase, a defeasible fee, or a long-term lease). But the requirement also has its defenders. See Gregory S. Alexander, Freedom, Coercion, and the Law of Servitudes, 73 Cornell L. Rev. 883, 890-898 (1988) (favors retaining the touch and concern requirement "to protect subsequent purchasers who have behaved foolishly and to prevent promisors and other successors from behaving opportunistically"); Uriel Reichman, Judicial Supervision of Servitudes, 7 J. Legal Stud. 139, 150-161 (1978) (arguing that the touch and concern requirement helps ward off economic inefficiencies and protects individual freedom from modern variations of feudal servitudes); Jeffrey E. Stake, Toward an Economic Understanding of Touch and Concern, 1988 Duke L.J. 925, 971-974 (arguing that the test permits courts to identify economic inefficiencies and that its obscurity is a virtue in this regard); Stewart E. Sterk, Freedom from Freedom of Contract: The Enduring Value of Servitude Restrictions, 70 Iowa L. Rev. 615, 661 (1985) (advocating retention of the touch and concern test as a "check against externalities, inadequate foresight, and intergenerational imposition").

See also Davidson Bros. v. Katz, 121 N.J. 196, 579 A.2d 288 (1990), which discards the touch and concern doctrine as a substantive limit on running covenants and holds that a covenant not to compete runs to successors, discussed in Paula A. Franzese, "Out of Touch": The Diminished Viability of the Touch and Concern Requirement in the Law of Servitudes, 21 Seton Hall L. Rev. 235 (1991).

Restatement (Third) of Property, Servitudes, §3.2 (T.D. No. 2, 1991) "supersedes" the touch and concern requirement with more specific tests, as indicated below.

Restatement (Third) of Property, Servitudes, §§3.2-3.7
(T.D. No. 2, 1991)

§3.2 Touch and Concern Doctrine Superseded

Neither the burden nor the benefit of a covenant is required to touch or concern land in order for the covenant to be valid as a servitude. Whether a servitude is valid is to be determined under the general rule stated in §3.1 and the particular rules stated in §§3.4 through 3.10.

Comment:

a. Effect of supersedure. Under traditional servitudes law, the question whether a valid covenant running with the land had been created was posed as a question whether the burden or benefit touched or concerned the land. The primary effect of the rule stated in this section is to reformulate the inquiry so that the appropriate question is whether the servitude arrangement violates public policy. Servitudes that formerly were held invalid for failure to touch or concern land remain invalid under the rules stated in this Chapter if they impose unreasonable restraints on alienation, undue restraints on trade, or if they are unconscionable or lack a rational justification.

b. Historical note and rationale. Throughout the nineteenth and early twentieth centuries, the touch and concern doctrine played an important role in servitudes law by providing courts with a flexible, discretionary power to disallow and terminate servitudes. The doctrine was particularly useful in that era because it permitted courts to invalidate servitudes they found unwise or pernicious without articulating the policy reasons for their decisions, and it permitted them to terminate obsolete and unwise servitudes without explicitly developing termination doctrines, or acknowledging what they were doing. The vagueness of the doctrine's content afforded a wide range of judicial discretion in policing servitudes. . . .

As the need for the touch and concern doctrine has decreased, criticism of the doctrine has increased. Its vagueness, its obscurity, its intent-defeating character, and its growing redundancy have become increasingly apparent. Although courts still use the rhetoric of touch and concern, they increasingly determine the validity of servitudes on the basis of the rules stated in this Chapter. They look to the legitimacy and importance of the purposes to be served by the servitude in the particular context, the fairness of the arrangement, its impact on alienability and marketability of the property, its impact on competition, and the degree to which it interferes with rights to personal autonomy and freedom from discrimination. In modern law there is no need to use the obsolete and confusing rhetoric of touch and concern to determine whether the parties were successful in creating an interest that runs with the land. . . .

d. *Modern uses of touch and concern doctrine.* Today, most of the cases in which failure to touch or concern the land is invoked as the primary basis for refusing to enforce a servitude involve monetary obligations and tying arrangements. Although there are good reasons why some of these servitudes should not be enforced, they do not apply to all monetary obligations and tying arrangements. The touch and concern doctrine does not provide the means to discriminate between those which should and should not be enforced, which leads to apparently incomprehensible distinctions in cases and to invalidation of some legitimate servitudes. Monetary obligations and tying arrangements that should not be enforced are captured by the rules stated in §3.5 on indirect restraints on alienation lacking rational justification, §3.6 on unreasonable restraints of trade, and §3.7 on unconscionable servitude arrangements.

§3.3 Rule Against Perpetuities Inapplicable

The rule against perpetuities does not apply to servitudes or powers to create servitudes.

§3.4 Direct Restraints on Alienation

A servitude that imposes a direct restraint on alienation of the burdened estate is invalid if the restraint is unreasonable. Reasonableness is determined by weighing the utility of the restraint against the injurious consequences of enforcing the restraint.

Comment:

a. *Historical note.* . . .

b. *Scope.* . . .

c. *Determining reasonableness.* Determining reasonableness of a restraint on alienation requires balancing the utility of the purpose served by the restraint against the harm that is likely to flow from its enforcement. Restraints on alienation of land are used to accomplish a wide variety of purposes of differing utility. They are used to retain land in families and to preserve affordable housing. They are used to control entry into cooperative, condominium, and subsidized housing developments that require particular financial qualifications. They are also used to control entry into communities, like retirement communities, developed for specialized purposes. Entry controls may be used for legitimate purposes or for the purpose of effecting illegal discrimination. Restraints on alienation are used to further the conservation, preservation, and charitable purposes to which land is devoted. They are also imposed to facilitate land development and create investment opportunities.

The harmful effects that may flow from restraints on alienation include impediments to the operation of a free market in land, limiting the prospects for improvement, development, and redevelopment of land, and limiting the mobility of landowners and would-be purchasers. Other harmful consequences include the demoralization costs associated with subordinating the desires of current landowners to the desires of past owners, and frustrating the expectations that normally flow from land ownership. Harmful consequences also may flow from enforcement of restraints on alienation that place one person in a position to take unfair advantage of another's need or desire to transfer property. . . .

§3.5 Indirect Restraints on Alienation

A servitude is not invalid because it indirectly restrains alienation by limiting the use that can be made of property, by reducing the amount realizable by the owner on sale or other transfer of the property, or by otherwise reducing the value of the property, unless there is no rational justification for the servitude.

§3.6 Unreasonable Restraints on Trade or Competition

A servitude that imposes an unreasonable restraint on trade or competition is invalid.

Comment:

a. Historical note and rationale. Land use restrictions designed to protect a business against competition met with a hostile reaction in the Massachusetts court in the late nineteenth century. Justice Holmes initiated a line of decisions holding that the burden of covenants not to compete would not run with the land because the benefit did not touch or concern the land of the covenantee. . . .

Massachusetts has since overruled its old cases, and the predominant rule in the United States today is that stated in this section. The validity of covenants against competition is to be determined by the common law of unreasonable restraints on trade and competition and under statutory antitrust and competition laws. Legislation governing restraints of trade is beyond the scope of this Restatement.

   b. Unreasonable restraints on trade and competition. The common law of unreasonable restraints on competition looks to the purpose, the geographic extent, and the duration of the restraint to determine whether it is reasonable. Covenants against competition that are tied to ownership of a particular parcel of land are seldom unreasonable because the impact is limited to one piece of land. The owner is free to engage in the activity elsewhere. However, if the restricted land is extensive, or it is the only land available in a community for a particular use, the restriction is unreasonable if it will tend toward a monopoly or substantially restrict competition in the relevant market.

§3.7 Unconscionability

A servitude is invalid if it is unconscionable.

   The Washington Post, July 2, 1992, Home Section, at 14, carried a story on Sherwood Forest subdivision near Annapolis, where all houses must be painted green. In addition, cats are not permitted; dogs are permitted but *not* in the summer (they must be put in kennels). How would these restrictions fare under the Restatement (Third) of Property? Would the restrictions in the following story be allowed?

Wilderness Subdivision OK's Nudity, Bans Mowers
L.A. Times, June 28, 1992, at A23

SADIEVILLE, KY. (AP) — Residents of a new environmentally conscious subdivision near Lexington are permitted to go fishing naked, but they'd better not mow their lawns.

   Those are among the rules owners must agree to in writing to buy one of the $25,000 to $35,000 lots in the woods northwest of Lexington. Another rule requires household cats to wear bells so wildlife know they're coming.

   "My lawyer told me, 'It's the only document I've ever seen that makes it legal to go around naked as long as your cat wears a bell,' " said developer Deborah Reed, a writer, dancer and part-time farmer who bought the land in 1987.

The rules, called restrictive covenants, tell residents what they may and may not do while living in the 40-acre Wood Sorrel development.

"Coming from a farming background, I got to have a great deal of respect for nature's balancing act," Reed said. "That's really what this is all about."

Two homes are completed. Three of the seven plots have been sold.

Reed, who lives at the development, said she walks among jumpy squirrels instead of dodging speeding motorists and hears songbirds instead of traffic.

Deer, raccoons and orioles dart across the only road, a dirt path called Gold Tooth Woman Lane, and take cover among oak and hickory trees.

Restrictions are placed on pesticide use and on hunting, as well as on embarrassing or annoying behavior.

Planting grass or mowing native ground cover are banned.

Nudity is allowed, including while fishing at the development's stocked lake.

"I am looking for people who want a greater interaction with their environment and who are willing to make fewer demands and place less stress on the environment," Reed said.

Caullett v. Stanley Stilwell & Sons, Inc.

Superior Court of New Jersey, Appellate Division, 1961
67 N.J. Super. 111, 170 A.2d 52

FREUND, J. This is an action in the nature of a bill to quiet title to a parcel of land in the Township of Holmdel. Defendant appeals from the entry of summary judgment in favor of plaintiffs.

Defendant, a developer, by warranty deed conveyed the subject property, consisting of a lot approximately one acre in size, to the plaintiffs for a consideration of $4,000. The deed was delivered on January 13, 1959. Following the collapse of negotiations directed towards agreement on the construction by defendant of a dwelling on the transferred premises, the present suit was instituted.

The focal point of the action is a recital in the deed, inserted under the heading of "covenants, agreements and restrictions," to the effect that: "(i) The grantors reserve the right to build or construct the original dwelling or building on said premises." The item is one of those designated in the instrument as "covenants running with the land . . . [which] shall bind the purchasers, their heirs, executors, administrators and assigns."

In support of their motion for summary judgment, plaintiffs set forth that no contract exists or ever did exist between the parties for the construction of a dwelling or building on the premises. The principal officer of the defendant corporation, in a countering affidavit, stated that one of the foremost considerations in fixing the price of the lot, and one of the primary conditions of the sale as it was effected, was the understanding that when the purchasers declared themselves ready and able to build, defendant would act as general contractor.

The trial judge held that the provision in question was unenforceable and should properly be stricken from the deed. He granted plaintiffs the relief demanded in their complaint, namely, an adjudication that: (1) defendant has no claim, right or interest in and to the lands by virtue of the clause in question; (2) defendant has no interest, right or cause of action against plaintiffs by virtue of the covenant; and (3) the clause in question is stricken from the deed and declared null, void and of no further force and effect.

The central issue argued on the appeal is whether the recital constitutes an enforceable covenant restricting the use of plaintiffs' land. Defendant urges that it comprises an ordinary property restriction, entered into for the benefit of the grantor and his retained lands. Plaintiffs maintain that the clause is too vague to be capable of enforcement and that, in any event, it amounts to no more than a personal covenant which in no way affects or burdens the realty and has no place in an instrument establishing and delimiting the title to same.

While restrictive covenants are to be construed realistically in the light of the circumstances under which they were created, . . . counter considerations, favoring the free transferability of land, have produced the rule that incursions on the use of property will not be enforced unless their meaning is clear and free from doubt. . . . Thus, if the covenants or restrictions are vague or ambiguous, they should not be construed to impair the alienability of the subject property.

Approached from a direction compatible with the constructional principles set forth above, it is clear that the deed item in question is incapable of enforcement and is therefore not restrictive of plaintiffs' title. The clause is descriptive of neither the type of structure to be built, the cost thereof, or the duration of the grantees' obligation. While it might conceivably have been intended to grant to defendant a right of first refusal on construction bids on the property, this is by no means its palpable design. What, for example, would be its effect were plaintiffs to erect a structure by their own hands? . . .

Moreover, assuming arguendo that the clause is sufficiently definite to give defendant a primary option to build whenever plaintiffs should decide to construct a dwelling or building on the premises, it still cannot operate either as a covenant running with the land at law, or as an equitable servitude enforceable against the original grantee and all successors, having notice, to his interest.

In the first place, it is clear to us that the item in question does not satisfy the primary requirement of covenants directly restrictive of title

to land — that they "touch and concern" the subject property. To constitute a real rather than a personal covenant, the promise must exercise
direct influence on the occupation, use or enjoyment of the premises. It
must be a promise "respecting the use of the land," that is, "a use of
identified land which is not merely casual and which is not merely an
incident in the performance of the promise." 5 Restatement, Property,
Scope Note to Part III, pp.3147-48 (1944).

Thus, to qualify as a covenant properly affecting the subject property, the deed provision must define in some measurable and reasonably
permanent fashion the proscriptions of and limitations upon the uses to
which the premises may be put. Typical provisions, some of them included in the deed of the parties herein, limit the property to residential
purposes, provide minimum setback and acreage requirements, proscribe certain architectural forms, and limit the number or set the minimum cost of future dwellings to be constructed on the land.

The provision here in issue is not of the variety described above. It
pertains to the use of plaintiffs' land only in the very incidental fashion
that refusal to allow defendant to build the original structure would
seemingly preclude plaintiffs from constructing at all. This is at best a
personal arrangement between the two parties, designed to insure defendant a profit on the erection of a dwelling in return, allegedly, for a
comparatively low sales price on the land. While there is nothing in our
law precluding such an arrangement, as a contract *inter partes,* this form
of contract, contemplating a single personal service upon the property,
does not affect the title. And the stipulation between the parties in their
instrument to the effect that this was a covenant running with the land
cannot override the inherently personal nature of their arrangement
under established legal principles.

We note, in addition, that even if the deed clause were to be construed as directly restricting plaintiffs' use of their land, i.e., prohibiting
erection of a structure until such time as the owner shall permit such
construction to be performed by the grantor, the clause would nonetheless comprise neither a legal restriction nor an equitable servitude upon
the estate. This is so because whatever the effect of the burden of the
covenant, its benefit is clearly personal to the grantor, securing to him a
mere commercial advantage in the operation of his business and not
enhancing or otherwise affecting the use or value of any retained lands.

Generally prerequisite to a conclusion that a covenant runs with the
land at law is a finding that both burdened and benefited properties exist
and were intended to be so affected by the contracting parties. Where,
however, the *benefit* attaches to the property of one of the parties, the
fact that the *burden* is in gross, i.e., personal, does not preclude the covenant from running with the land conveyed. National Union Bank at
Dover v. Segur, 38 N.J.L. 173 (Sup. Ct. 1877). There is no public policy
opposed to the running of a benefit, since a continuing benefit is pre-

sumed to help rather than hinder the alienability of the property to which it is attached. 5 Powell, Real Property, §675, p.173; 5 Restatement, Property, supra, §543, comment (c), pp.3255-56. When, however, as here, the *burden* is placed upon the land, and the *benefit* is personal to one of the parties and does not extend to his or other lands, the burden is generally held not to run with the land at law. The policy is strong against hindering the alienability of one property where no corresponding enhancement accrues to surrounding lands. See 5 Restatement, Property, supra, §537, pp.3218-24; 2 American Law of Property, §9.13, pp.373-76 (1952).

Nor can the covenant be enforced as an equitable servitude where the benefit is in gross and neither affects retained land of the grantor nor is part of a neighborhood scheme of similar restrictions. Purporting to follow the case of Tulk v. Moxhay, 2 Phil. 774, 41 Eng. Rep. 1143 (Ch. 1848), our courts have consistently enforced the covenantal rights of an owner of benefited property against a successor, with notice, to the burdened land, even though the covenant did not run with the land at law. . . . However, the right to urge enforcement of a servitude against the burdened land "depends primarily on the covenant's having been made for the benefit" of other land, either retained by the grantor or part of a perceptible neighborhood scheme. . . . Where the benefit is purely personal to the grantor, and has not been directed towards the improvement of neighboring properties, it cannot pass as an incident to any of his retained land and therefore is not considered to burden the conveyed premises but only, at best, to obligate the grantee personally. See 2 Tiffany, Real Property, §399, pp.1441-42 (1920).

The latter doctrine has recently come under considerable criticism, see 2 American Law of Property, supra, §9.32, pp.428-30, and has even been rejected in some jurisdictions, thus permitting attachment of an equitable servitude even though the benefit is in gross. See, e.g., Pratte v. Balatsos, 99 N.H. 430, 113 A.2d 492 (Sup. Ct. 1955). But the law in this jurisdiction, as last authoritatively declared, is that "from the very nature of the equitable restriction arising from a restrictive covenant," the "existence of the dominant estate is . . . essential to the validity of the servitude granted. . . ." Welitoff v. Kohl, 105 N.J. Eq. 181, 189, 147 A. 390, 393, 66 A.L.R. 1317 (E.&A. 1929).

We therefore conclude that the clause in question, even were we to assume both its clarity and its direct operation upon the use of plaintiffs' land, cannot comprise an impairment of plaintiffs' title, because of the indisputably personal nature of the benefit conferred thereby. An intention to dispense broader land use benefits, in the form of a neighborhood scheme, cannot here be found, as in effect conceded by defendant and as expressly stipulated in the parties' deed. . . .

The judgment of the trial court is affirmed.

NOTES AND QUESTIONS

1. Because the English courts viewed an equitable servitude as an "equitable interest analogous to a negative easement," they held that the burden of a restrictive covenant will not run in equity if the benefit is in gross. London County Council v. Allen, [1914] 3 K.B. 642. In that country, as noted on page 849, a dominant tenement is required for an easement. Hence by analogy to easements a dominant tenement is required for an equitable servitude.[33]

If the reason for the rule in England is by analogy to the law of easements, such a reason could not support the rule in this country. In the United States an easement in gross can be created, and the burden will run with the servient land. Example: O, owner of Blackacre, grants a billboard company an easement to erect advertising signs on Blackacre. The easement, benefiting the billboard company in its business and not as an owner of land, is in gross. O transfers Blackacre to A. If A has notice of the easement, A is bound.

Nonetheless, even though an analogy to easement law does not support the rule that the burden of a covenant will not run when the benefit is in gross, there may be a policy objection to the burden running when the covenant does not benefit other land. Are the information and transaction costs of transferring the benefit to the servient owner, thus removing the burden, greater when the benefit is in gross than when it is appurtenant?

2. Restatement (Third) of Property, Servitudes, §2.6, Comment d (T.D. No. 1, 1989), provides that benefits in gross are freely permitted and the burden will run when the benefit is in gross. The Reporter's Note cites case authority for the enforcement of covenants in gross by homeowners associations, by business corporations desirous of restricting competition or assuring markets, by government bodies, and by charitable associations holding conservation or historic preservation servitudes.

3. Conservation servitudes cast in covenant form run into the rule that if the benefit is in gross, as is usual with such servitudes, the burden will not run. This problem has largely been obviated by statutes author-

---

33. The rule that a dominant tenement is required for an easement in England is tempered by a generous definition of a dominant tenement. "A dominant tenement may be wholly incorporeal, or partly corporeal and partly incorporeal, as where it consists of the whole undertaking of a waterworks company and thus comprises both physical land and rights over the land of others, such as the right to lay pipes." Robert Megarry & H.W.R. Wade, The Law of Real Property 835 (5th ed. 1984). Similarly, a dominant tenement has been broadly defined for the running of an equitable servitude. A covenant by the owner of a public house to buy ale, wine, and liquor only from a particular brewery, which is for the benefit of the brewing business, has been held to run with the burdened land, the public house. John Bros. Abergarw Brewery Co. v. Holmes, [1900] 1 Ch. 188.

izing conservation servitudes in gross, discussed at page 854. See Gerald Korngold, Privately Held Conservation Servitudes: A Policy Analysis in the Context of In Gross Real Covenants and Easements, 63 Tex. L. Rev. 433 (1984).

For a discussion of the New York conservation easements statute (N.Y. Envtl. Conserv. Law §49-0301 (McKinney 1992)), which exempts conservation easements (in the form of easement or covenant) from a wide variety of common law doctrines that have traditionally defeated servitude enforcement (including privity, touch and concern, no easement in third parties, no negative easements, no affirmative covenants, no covenants in gross), see Dorothy Glancy, Preserving Rockefeller Center, 24 Urb. Law. 423, 448-450 (1992). Professor Glancy also examines the complex agreements between the city and the owners of the Center providing for continuing landmark maintenance of Rockefeller Center. Id. at 451-466.

4. You are counsel for a city. A developer has asked for a variance from the zoning ordinance in an apartment district. The city is willing to grant the variance if the developer will give the city a covenant running with the land limiting the use of five apartments to families of low income. Advise the city as to what rules in this chapter might impede the enforcement by the city of low-income housing covenants.

Mass. Ann. Laws ch. 184, §§31, 32 (Supp. 1992) provide that no covenant limiting the use of land to low- or moderate-income housing, or restricting its sale price to ensure its future affordability by low- or moderate-income purchasers, held by a governmental body or charitable corporation or trust with the purpose of creating affordable housing, "shall be unenforceable on account of lack of privity of estate or contract or lack of benefit to particular land or on account of the benefit being assignable or being assigned to any other government body or to any charitable corporation or trust with like purposes." The act provides that an owner, after moving in, may procure the release of the covenant by purchasing the restriction at fair market value; the purchase money is returned to the original program to fund more low-income housing.

In Bennett v. Commissioner of Food & Agriculture, 411 Mass. 1, 576 N.E.2d 1365 (1991), the court enforced the running of the burden of a conservation easement in gross where the beneficiary was a public body. The court gave notice that it might discard other restrictive rules relating to servitudes:

> What we decide here does not, of course, endorse the enforcement of all easements in gross. It does, however, prompt us to observe that certain common law rules concerning the creation, validity, and enforcement of servitudes may no longer be sound and that we are willing to reconsider them in appropriate cases. Any change affecting substantive rights would presumably be made applicable prospectively, that is, to instruments executed after the

date of this opinion . . . or any prior date on which fair warning was given so that no one could reasonably have relied on prior law. [411 Mass. at 7 n.4, 576 N.E.2d at 1368 n.4.]

NOTE: DEFEASIBLE FEES AS LAND-USE CONTROL DEVICES

Defeasible fees (determinable fee, fee simple subject to condition subsequent, and fee simple subject to executory limitation, see pages 236-238, 280) may be employed to control land use. A defeasible fee differs from a servitude in that the remedy for its breach is forfeiture, whereas the remedy for breach of a servitude is damages, injunction, or enforcement of a lien.

Defeasible fees were popular land-use control devices in the late nineteenth and early twentieth centuries before the modern development of equitable servitudes. But they are infrequently used today to control land use except in gifts for charitable purposes. A purchaser of land will likely object to a condition with a forfeiture remedy, both because it makes the purchaser's capital investment risky and because it may make the land unmortgageable and therefore unimprovable.

A defeasible fee can be used to create a right of enforcement in a third party or in a person who owns no land. In view of this, does it make sense to deny enforcement of a covenant by a third-party beneficiary (see pages 877-878) or by a person owning no land?

See Gerald Korngold, For Unifying Servitudes and Defeasible Fees: Property Law's Functional Equivalents, 66 Tex. L. Rev. 533 (1988), arguing that defeasible fees should be integrated with servitudes in a rational system and damages or injunction (rather than forfeiture) given for breach of condition except in unusual cases.

3. Scope of Covenants

Shelley v. Kraemer
Supreme Court of the United States, 1948
334 U.S. 1

MR. CHIEF JUSTICE VINSON delivered the opinion of the Court.

These cases present for our consideration questions relating to the validity of court enforcement of private agreements, generally described as restrictive covenants, which have as their purpose the exclusion of persons of designated race or color from the ownership or occupancy of real property. Basic constitutional issues of obvious importance have been raised.

The first of these cases comes to this Court on certiorari to the Supreme Court of Missouri. On February 16, 1911, thirty out of a total of thirty-nine owners of property fronting both sides of Labadie Avenue between Taylor Avenue and Cora Avenue in the city of St. Louis, signed an agreement, which was subsequently recorded, providing in part:

> . . . the said property is hereby restricted to the use and occupancy for the term of Fifty (50) years from this date, so that it shall be a condition all the time and whether recited and referred to as [sic] not in subsequent convey- ances and shall attach to the land as a condition precedent to the sale of the same, that hereafter no part of said property or any portion thereof shall be, for said term of Fifty-years, occupied by any person not of the Caucasian race, it being intended hereby to restrict the use of said property for said period of time against the occupancy as owners or tenants of any portion of said prop- erty for resident or other purpose by people of the Negro or Mongolian Race.

The entire district described in the agreement included fifty-seven parcels of land. The thirty owners who signed the agreement held title to forty-seven parcels, including the particular parcel involved in this case. . . .

On August 11, 1945, pursuant to a contract of sale, petitioners Shel- ley, who are Negroes, for valuable consideration received from one Fitz- gerald a warranty deed to the parcel in question. The trial court found that petitioners had no actual knowledge of the restrictive agreement at the time of the purchase.

On October 9, 1945, respondents, as owners of other property sub- ject to the terms of the restrictive covenant, brought suit in the Circuit Court of the city of St. Louis praying that petitioners Shelley be re- strained from taking possession of the property and that judgment be entered divesting title out of petitioners Shelley and revesting title in the immediate grantor or in such other person as the court should di- rect. . . .

The Supreme Court of Missouri . . . directed the trial court to grant the relief for which respondents had prayed. That court held the agree- ment effective and concluded that enforcement of its provisions violated no rights guaranteed to petitioners by the Federal Constitution. At the time the court rendered its decision, petitioners were occupying the property in question.

The second of the cases under consideration comes to this Court from the Supreme Court of Michigan. The circumstances presented do not differ materially from the Missouri case. In June, 1934, one Fergu- son and his wife, who then owned the property located in the city of Detroit which is involved in this case, executed a contract providing in part:

> This property shall not be used or occupied by any person or persons except those of the Caucasian race.

It is further agreed that this restriction shall not be effective unless at least eighty percent of the property fronting on both sides of the street in the block where our land is located is subjected to this or a similar restriction.

The agreement provided that the restrictions were to remain in effect until January 1, 1960. The contract was subsequently recorded; and similar agreements were executed with respect to eighty percent of the lots in the block in which the property in question is situated.

By deed dated November 30, 1944, petitioners, who were found by the trial court to be Negroes, acquired title to the property and thereupon entered into its occupancy. On January 30, 1945, respondents, as owners of property subject to the terms of the restrictive agreement, brought suit against petitioners in the Circuit Court of Wayne County. After a hearing, the court entered a decree directing petitioners to move from the property within ninety days. Petitioners were further enjoined and restrained from using or occupying the premises in the future. On appeal, the Supreme Court of Michigan affirmed, deciding adversely to petitioners' contentions that they had been denied rights protected by the Fourteenth Amendment.

Petitioners have placed primary reliance on their contentions, first raised in the state courts, that judicial enforcement of the restrictive agreements in these cases has violated rights guaranteed to petitioners by the Fourteenth Amendment of the Federal Constitution and Acts of Congress passed pursuant to that Amendment.[34] Specifically, petitioners urge that they have been denied the equal protection of the laws, deprived of property without due process of law, and have been denied privileges and immunities of citizens of the United States. We pass to a consideration of those issues.

I

Whether the equal protection clause of the Fourteenth Amendment inhibits judicial enforcement by state courts of restrictive covenants based on race or color is a question which this Court has not heretofore been called upon to consider. . . .

It cannot be doubted that among the civil rights intended to be protected from discriminatory state action by the Fourteenth Amendment are the rights to acquire, enjoy, own and dispose of property. Equality in the enjoyment of property rights was regarded by the framers of that

---

34. The first section of the Fourteenth Amendment provides: "All persons born or naturalized in the United States, and subject to the jurisdiction thereof, are citizens of the United States and of the State wherein they reside. No State shall make or enforce any law which shall abridge the privileges or immunities of citizens of the United States; nor shall any State deprive any person of life, liberty, or property, without due process of law; nor deny to any person within its jurisdiction the equal protection of the laws."

Amendment as an essential pre-condition to the realization of other basic civil rights and liberties which the Amendment was intended to guarantee. Thus, §1978 of the Revised Statutes, derived from §1 of the Civil Rights Act of 1866 which was enacted by Congress while the Fourteenth Amendment was also under consideration, provides:

> All citizens of the United States shall have the same right, in every State and Territory, as is enjoyed by white citizens thereof to inherit, purchase, lease, sell, hold, and convey real and personal property.

This Court has given specific recognition to the same principle. Buchanan v. Warley, 245 U.S. 60 (1917).

It is likewise clear that restrictions on the right of occupancy of the sort sought to be created by the private agreements in these cases could not be squared with the requirements of the Fourteenth Amendment if imposed by state statute or local ordinance. We do not understand respondents to urge the contrary. In the case of Buchanan v. Warley, supra, a unanimous Court declared unconstitutional the provisions of a city ordinance which denied to colored persons the right to occupy houses in blocks in which the greater number of houses were occupied by white persons, and imposed similar restrictions on white persons with respect to blocks in which the greater number of houses were occupied by colored persons. . . .

But the present cases, unlike . . . [Buchanan v. Warley], do not involve action by state legislatures or city councils. Here the particular patterns of discrimination and the areas in which the restrictions are to operate, are determined, in the first instance, by the terms of agreements among private individuals. Participation of the State consists in the enforcement of the restrictions so defined. The crucial issue with which we are here confronted is whether this distinction removes these cases from the operation of the prohibitory provisions of the Fourteenth Amendment.

Since the decision of this Court in the Civil Rights Cases, 109 U.S. 3 (1883), the principle has become firmly embedded in our constitutional law that the action inhibited by the first section of the Fourteenth Amendment is only such action as may fairly be said to be that of the States. That Amendment erects no shield against merely private conduct, however discriminatory or wrongful.

We conclude, therefore, that the restrictive agreements standing alone cannot be regarded as violative of any rights guaranteed to petitioners by the Fourteenth Amendment. So long as the purposes of those agreements are effectuated by voluntary adherence to their terms, it would appear clear that there has been no action by the State and the provisions of the Amendment have not been violated.

But here there was more. These are cases in which the purposes of the agreements were secured only by judicial enforcement by state courts of the restrictive terms of the agreements. . . .

II

That the action of state courts and judicial officers in their official capacities is to be regarded as action of the State within the meaning of the Fourteenth Amendment, is a proposition which has long been established by decisions of this Court. . . .

The short of the matter is that from the time of the adoption of the Fourteenth Amendment until the present, it has been the consistent ruling of this Court that the action of the States to which the Amendment has reference includes action of state courts and state judicial officials. . . .

III

Against this background of judicial construction, extending over a period of some three-quarters of a century, we are called upon to consider whether enforcement by state courts of the restrictive agreements in these cases may be deemed to be the acts of those States; and, if so, whether that action has denied these petitioners the equal protection of the laws which the Amendment was intended to insure.

We have no doubt that there has been state action in these cases in the full and complete sense of the phrase. The undisputed facts disclose that petitioners were willing purchasers of properties upon which they desired to establish homes. The owners of the properties were willing sellers; and contracts of sale were accordingly consummated. It is clear that but for the active intervention of the state courts, supported by the full panoply of state power, petitioners would have been free to occupy the properties in question without restraint.

. . . The judicial action in each case bears the clear and unmistakable imprimatur of the State. We have noted that previous decisions of this Court have established the proposition that judicial action is not immunized from the operation of the Fourteenth Amendment simply because it is taken pursuant to the state's common-law policy. Nor is the Amendment ineffective simply because the particular pattern of discrimination, which the State has enforced, was defined initially by the terms of a private agreement. State action, as that phrase is understood for the purposes of the Fourteenth Amendment, refers to exertions of state power in all forms. And when the effect of that action is to deny rights subject to the protection of the Fourteenth Amendment, it is the obligation of this Court to enforce the constitutional commands.

We hold that in granting judicial enforcement of the restrictive agreements in these cases, the States have denied petitioners the equal protection of the laws and that, therefore, the action of the state courts cannot stand. We have noted that freedom from discrimination by the States in the enjoyment of property rights was among the basic objectives sought to be effectuated by the framers of the Fourteenth Amendment. That such discrimination has occurred in these cases is clear. Because of the race or color of these petitioners they have been denied rights of ownership or occupancy enjoyed as a matter of course by other citizens of different race or color.

. . . Upon full consideration, we have concluded that in these cases the States have acted to deny petitioners the equal protection of the laws guaranteed by the Fourteenth Amendment. . . .

For the reasons stated, the judgment of the Supreme Court of Missouri and the judgment of the Supreme Court of Michigan must be reversed.

Reversed.

NOTES, PROBLEMS, AND QUESTIONS

1. In Barrows v. Jackson, 346 U.S. 249 (1953), the Supreme Court held that a court cannot give money damages against a seller who breaches a covenant not to convey to a nonwhite. Such action is state action. Is there unconstitutional state action if a court gives effect to discriminatory provisions cast in terms of a defeasible estate rather than a covenant? Suppose, for example, that a will devises property to a trust company, with instructions to pay the income from the property to County School Foundation "so long as County School admits only members of the White Race, and if County School should admit any person not a member of the White Race, all the income shall be paid to the Methodist Home." Some years later, after County School had admitted black students, the trustee seeks a declaratory judgment as to who is entitled to the income. What result? Does it matter whether the language in the will is regarded as a determinable estate or an estate subject to condition subsequent? See pages 236-237 and Hermitage Methodist Home of Virginia v. Dominion Trust Co., 239 Va. 46, 387 S.E.2d 740, cert. denied, 111 S. Ct. 277 (1990). See also Evans v. Abney, 396 U.S. 435 (1970).

2. A covenant with a racially discriminatory effect may violate the federal Fair Housing Act, enacted as Title VIII of the Civil Rights Act of 1968, 42 U.S.C.A. §§3601-3631 (Supp. 1992). This act makes it unlawful to refuse to sell or rent or otherwise make unavailable a dwelling to any person because of race, color, religion, sex, national origin, familial status, or handicap. See pages 441-444.

A deed containing a restrictive covenant against a particular race or religion or ethnic group violates §3604(c) of the Fair Housing Act, which prohibits the printing or publishing of any statement indicating a racial, religious, or ethnic preference with respect to the buyer of a dwelling. In Mayers v. Ridley, 465 F.2d 630 (D.C. Cir. 1972), the court permanently enjoined the District of Columbia recorder of deeds from recording deeds containing racial covenants.

In 1986, in the Senate confirmation hearings on the nomination of Justice William Rehnquist (appointed an associate justice in 1971) to the office of Chief Justice, it was revealed that Justice Rehnquist and his wife had bought a Vermont summer house in 1974. The deed from the seller to the Rehnquists contained a covenant barring sale to "any member of the Hebrew race," copied from the 1961 deed of the original real estate developer. Justice Rehnquist called the restriction "very offensive," said he undoubtedly read the letter from his lawyer noting the restrictive covenant on the property but had no recollection of it, and pointed out that such a covenant had been unenforceable since Shelley v. Kraemer. Senate Comm. on the Judiciary, S. Exec. Rep. No. 18, 99th Cong., 2d Sess. 30-31, 64, 88-90, 107 (1986). Rehnquist told the Senate committee that he had ordered his lawyer to remove the offending language from the deed. If you were Rehnquist's lawyer, how would you remove the covenant from the deed? Should the records be purged of old discriminatory covenants?

Rehnquist Alters Restrictive Deed
N.Y. Times, Nov. 16, 1986, §1, pt. 2, at 50

Chief Justice William H. Rehnquist and his wife, Natalie, have removed a clause in the deed to their summer house in Greensboro, Vt., barring its lease or sale to "any member of the Hebrew race," the Greensboro town clerk's office said Thursday.

The clause in the original deed came to light in a background check of Mr. Rehnquist conducted after President Reagan nominated him to be Chief Justice. Under court decisions at the Federal and state levels, the clause has been unenforceable for years.

The restrictive covenant was removed through a transaction in which the Rehnquists sold the house to their lawyer, David L. Willis of St. Johnsbury, Vt., for $1, and repurchased it from him for $1, said Dougal Stuart, one of Greensboro's three selectmen.

Mr. Stuart said simply removing the phrase from older records would not have been possible. "If it's in the book, it's in the book," he said.

The covenant might have been removed by negotiation with the principal parties, he added, but that was impossible now "because the people who put it in originally are dead."

The transaction took place Sept. 1, he said. Chief Justice Rehnquist was sworn in Sept. 26.

The restriction in the Rehnquists' 1974 deed to the house in Greensboro was copied from a 1961 deed to the property. The deed recorded in September does not mention "the Hebrew race," according to Mr. Stuart, but it lists the1961 deed and notes, "reference may be had to the above-mentioned deed and its record and to all prior deeds and their records for a more complete and particular description of the lands and premises hereby conveyed."

3. The most common running covenant in the United States restricts the use of land to "a single-family dwelling." What constitutes single-family use has sometimes been litigated when nontraditional families try to move into a house in a single-family neighborhood. A few courts have held that a single-family dwelling covenant requires only that the house be architecturally designed to look like a dwelling for one family, and does not require that the occupants be related by blood or marriage. Other courts have held that the covenant requires only that a group of persons live as a single housekeeping unit, or that the external effects (e.g., noise and parking) do not exceed traditional one-family use. Some courts define family as persons related by blood or marriage. The results may be affected by the particular wording of the covenant. For example, a covenant "for residential use" only (rather than "a single-family dwelling") might permit use by a nontraditional family. See Gerald Korngold, Single Family Use Covenants: For Achieving a Balance Between Traditional Family Life and Individual Autonomy, 22 U.C. Davis L. Rev. 951 (1989).

Much of the litigation in recent years has involved group homes for mentally retarded persons or the disabled, with decisions divided on whether such use violated the covenants. Some states have enacted statutes denying enforcement of covenants barring group homes for the disabled. Retroactive application to existing covenants of such a statute was held unconstitutional, as an impairment of contract in violation of the contracts clause of the state constitution, in Clem v. Christole, Inc., 582 N.E.2d 780 (Ind. 1991), but upheld against such an argument in Crane Neck Assn., Inc. v. New York City/Long Island County Servs. Group, 61 N.Y.2d 154, 460 N.E.2d 1336, 472 N.Y.S.2d 901, 41 A.L.R.4th 1204 (1984).

The 1988 amendments to the federal Fair Housing Act are likely to open more single-family areas to group homes. Among other things, the amendments make it unlawful to discriminate because of a handicap. See 42 U.S.C. §3604(f), on page 443, and footnote 18 on page 446. The House committee report on the amendments states

This provision is intended to prohibit special restrictive covenants or other terms or conditions, or denials of service because of an individual's handicap and which have the effect of excluding, for example, congregate living arrangements for persons with handicaps.

. . . The Act is intended to prohibit the application of special requirements through land-use regulations, restrictive covenants, and conditional or special use permits that have the effect of limiting the ability of such individuals to live in the residence of their choice in the community. [H.R. Rep. No.

100-711, 100th Cong., 2d Sess. 23 (1988), reprinted in 1988 U.S. Code Cong. & Adm. News 2184-2185.]

See Rhodes v. Palmetto Pathway Homes, Inc., 303 S.C. 308, 400 S.E.2d 484 (1991), holding that the 1988 amendments to the Fair Housing Act preclude the enforcement of a single-family covenant against a group home for retarded persons. For the effect of the 1988 amendments on zoning ordinance prohibitions of group homes, see pages 1091-1105.

4. Greenwood Subdivision has the following covenant, imposed in 1953 by the original developer:

> The premises shall be used for a single-family residential dwelling only. No business of any kind shall be conducted on the premises. The premises shall not be used as a place for care or treatment of the sick or the mentally or physically disabled.

Suppose that AIDS Services Foundation, a charitable organization providing shelter and services to persons with AIDS, finds a house in Greenwood Subdivision suitable for use as a group home for eight persons with AIDS. AIDS Services Foundation consults you respecting whether it can use the house to care for persons with AIDS if it buys it. What is your advice? See Baxter v. City of Belleville, 720 F. Supp. 720 (S.D. Ill. 1989).

Could AIDS Services Foundation use the house for a hospice for persons dying of AIDS? Could the house be used as a nursing home?

5. Dogwood Hills, a large subdivision, has a restrictive covenant on all lots prohibiting the use of land for anything but single-family residences. A religious congregation buys a lot in Dogwood Hills and proposes to erect a house of worship. The neighbors sue for an injunction. Does an injunction constitute state action in violation of the freedom of religion clause of the First Amendment? Can the neighbors ban a church by private covenant under circumstances where a city could not exclude churches from residential areas? See Note, Restrictive Covenants and Religious Uses: The Constitutional Interplay, 29 Syracuse L. Rev. 993 (1978).

4. Termination of Covenants

Western Land Co. v. Truskolaski
Supreme Court of Nevada, 1972
88 Nev. 200, 495 P.2d 624

BATJER, J. The respondents, homeowners in the Southland Heights subdivision in southwest Reno, Nevada, brought an action in the district court to enjoin the appellant from constructing a shopping center on a 3.5-acre parcel of land located within the subdivision at the northeast corner of Plumas and West Plum Lane. In 1941 the appellant subdivided this 40-acre development, and at that time it subjected the lots to certain restrictive covenants which specifically restricted the entire 40 acres of the subdivision single-family dwellings and further prohibited any stores, butcher shops, grocery or mercantile business of any kind. . The district court held these restrictive covenants to be enforceable, and enjoined the appellant from constructing a supermarket or using the 3.5 acres in any manner other than that permitted by the covenants. The appellant contends that the district court erred in enforcing these covenants because the subdivision had so radically changed in recent years as to nullify their purpose. We agree with the holding of the district court that the restrictive covenants remain of substantial value to the homeowners in the subdivision, and that the changes that have occurred since 1941 are not so great as to make it inequitable or oppressive to restrict the property to single-family residential use.

In 1941 the Southland Heights subdivision was outside of the Reno city limits. The property surrounding the subdivision was primarily used for residential and agricultural purposes, with very little commercial development of any type in the immediate area. At that time Plumb Lane extended only as far east as Arlington Avenue.

By the time the respondents sought equitable relief in an effort to enforce the restrictive covenants, the area had markedly changed. In 1941 the city of Reno had a population of slightly more than 20,000; that figure had jumped to approximately 95,100 by 1969. One of the significant changes, as the appellant aptly illustrates, is the increase in traffic in the surrounding area. Plumb Lane had been extended to Virginia Street, and in 1961 the city of Reno condemned 1.04 acres of land on the edge of the subdivision to allow for the widening of Plumb Lane into a four-lane arterial boulevard. A city planner, testifying for the appellant, stated that Plumb Lane was designed to be and now is the major east-west artery through the southern portion of the city. A person who owns property across Plumas from the subdivision testified that the corner of Plumb Lane and Plumas is "terribly noisy from 5:00 P.M. until midnight." One of the findings of the trial court was that traffic on Plumb Lane had greatly increased in recent years.

Another significant change that had occurred since 1941 was the increase in commercial development in the vicinity of the subdivision. On the east side of Lakeside Drive, across from the subdivision property, is a restaurant and the Lakeside Plaza Shopping Center. A supermarket, hardware store, drug store, flower shop, beauty shop and a dress shop are located in this shopping center. Still further east of the subdivision, on Virginia Street, is the Continental Lodge, and across Virginia Street is the Park Lane Shopping Center.

Even though traffic has increased and commercial development has occurred in the vicinity of the subdivision, the owners of land within Southland Heights testified to the desirability of the subdivision for res-

idential purposes. The traffic density within the subdivision is low, resulting in a safe environment for the children who live and play in the
area. Homes in Southland Heights are well cared for and attractively
landscaped.

The trial court found that substantial changes in traffic patterns and
commercial activity had occurred since 1941 in the vicinity of the subdivision. Although it was shown that commercial activity outside of the
subdivision had increased considerably since 1941, the appellant failed
to show that the area in question is now unsuitable for residential purposes.

Even though nearby avenues may become heavily traveled thoroughfares, restrictive covenants are still enforceable if the single-family
residential character of the neighborhood has not been adversely affected, and the purpose of the restrictions has not been thwarted. Burden v. Lobdell, 93 Ill. App. 2d 476, 235 N.E.2d 660 (1968); Gonzales v.
Gackle Drilling Company, 67 N.M. 130, 353 P.2d 353 (1960); Continental Oil Co. v. Fennemore, 38 Ariz. 277, 299 P. 132 (1931). Although
commercialization has increased in the vicinity of the subdivision, such
activity has not rendered the restrictive covenants unenforceable because they are still of real and substantial value to those homeowners
living within the subdivision. West Alameda Heights H. Assn. v. Board
of Co. Comrs., 169 Colo. 491, 458 P.2d 253 (1969); Burden v. Lobdell,
supra; Hogue v. Dreeszen, 161 Neb. 268, 73 N.W.2d 159 (1955).

The appellant asks this court to reverse the judgment of the district
court and declare as a matter of law that the objects and purposes for
which the restrictive covenants were originally imposed have been
thwarted, and that it is now inequitable to enforce such restrictions
against the entity that originally created them. This we will not do. The
record will not permit us to find as a matter of law that there has been
such a change in the subdivision or for that matter in the area to relieve
the appellant's property of the burden placed upon it by the covenants.
There is sufficient evidence to sustain the findings of the trial court that
the objects and purposes of the restrictions have not been thwarted, and
that they remain of substantial value to the homeowners in the subdivision.

The case of Hirsch v. Hancock, 173 Cal. App. 2d 745, 343 P.2d 959
(1959) as well as the other authorities relied upon by the appellant [Key
v. McCabe, 54 Cal. 2d 736, 356 P.2d 169, 8 Cal. Rptr. 425 (1960); Strong
v. Hancock, 201 Cal. 530, 258 P. 60 (1927); Downs v. Kroeger, 200 Cal.
743, 254 P. 1101 (1927)], are inapposite for in those cases the trial court
found many changes within as well as outside the subdivision and concluded from the evidence that the properties were entirely unsuitable
and undesirable for residential use and that they had no suitable economic use except for business or commercial purposes, and the appellate courts in reviewing those cases held that the evidence supported the
findings and sustained the judgments of the trial courts.

On the other hand, in the case of West Alameda Heights H. Assn. v. Board of Co. Comrs., supra, upon facts similar to those found in this case, the trial court decided that the changed conditions in the neighborhood were such as to render the restrictive covenants void and unenforceable. The appellate court reversed and held that the trial court misconceived and misapplied the rule as to change of conditions and said, 169 Colo. at 498, 458 P.2d at 256: "As long as the original purpose of the covenants can still be accomplished and substantial benefit will inure to the restricted area by their enforcement, the covenants stand even though the subject property has a greater value if used for other purposes."

There is substantial evidence in the record to support the trial court's findings of fact and conclusions of law that the covenants were of real and substantial value to the residents of the subdivision. Where the evidence is conflicting and the credibility of the witnesses is in issue, the judgment will not be disturbed on appeal if the evidence is substantially in support of the judgment of the lower court. Here the appellant has not carried its burden of showing that the subdivision is not now suitable for residential purposes because of changed conditions.

In another attempt to show that the restrictive covenants have outlived their usefulness, the appellant points to actions of the Reno city council. On August 1, 1968, the council adopted a Resolution of Intent to reclassify this 3.5-acre parcel from R-1 [residential] to C-1(b) [commercial]. The council never did change the zoning, but the appellant contends that since the council did indicate its willingness to rezone, it was of the opinion that the property was more suitable for commercial than residential use. This argument of the appellant is not persuasive. A zoning ordinance cannot override privately-placed restrictions, and a trial court cannot be compelled to invalidate restrictive covenants merely because of a zoning change. Rice v. Heggy, 158 Cal. App. 2d 89, 322 P.2d 53 (1958).

Another of the appellant's arguments regarding changed conditions involves the value of the property for residential as compared to commercial purposes. A professional planning consultant, testifying for the appellant, stated that the land in question is no longer suitable for use as a single-family residential area. From this testimony the appellant concludes that the highest and best use for the land is non-residential. Even if this property is more valuable for commercial than residential purposes, this fact does not entitle the appellant to be relieved of the restrictions it created, since substantial benefit inures to the restricted area by their enforcement. West Alameda Heights H. Assn. v. Board of Co. Comrs., supra; Cawthon v. Anderson, 211 Ga. 77, 84 S.E.2d 66 (1954).

In addition to the alleged changed circumstances, the appellant contends that the restrictive covenants are no longer enforceable because they have been abandoned or waived due to violations by homeowners

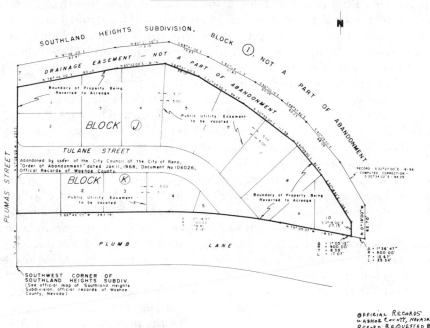

MAP OF REVERSION TO ACREAGE
OF A PORTION OF SOUTHLAND HEIGHTS
SUBDIVISION, RENO, NEVADA

SCALE: 1"= 50' ········ MARCH, 1968

On May 16, 1968, Western Land Company filed with the county recorder this map abandoning the Southland Heights subdivision map as applied to the acreage litigated in Western Land Co. v. Truskolaski. Earlier that spring the city council of Reno had approved the abandonment and reversion of Tulane Street and also had approved the abandonment of the subdivision map applied to this acreage. The utility companies also had consented to the abandonment of the public utility easements. This abandonment procedure was undertaken pursuant to Nev. Stat. §278.490 (1991), which permits the abandonment of a subdivision map by the owner of the subdivided land. After the decision in Western Land Co. v. Truskolaski, what is the status of this acreage? Does the original subdivision map apply? Can it be re-subdivided in a different manner for residential use?

915

in the area. Paragraph 3 of the restrictive agreement provides that no residential structure shall be placed on a lot comprising less than 6,000 square feet. Both lot 24 and lot 25 of block E contain less than 6,000 square feet and each has a house located on it. This could hardly be deemed a violation of the restrictions imposed by the appellant inasmuch as it was the appellant that subdivided the land and caused these lots to be smaller than 6,000 feet. Paragraph 7 of the agreement provides that a committee shall approve any structure which is moved onto the subdivision, or if there is no committee, that the structure shall conform to and be in harmony with existing structures. The appellant did show that two houses were moved on to lots within the subdivision, but the appellant failed to show whether a committee existed and if so approved or disapproved, or whether the houses failed to conform or were out of harmony with the existing structures. Finally, in an effort to prove abandonment and waiver, the appellant showed that one house within the subdivision was used as a painting contractor's office for several years in the late 1940's, and that more recently the same house had been used as a nursery for a baby sitting business. However, the same witnesses testified that at the time of the hearing this house was being used as a single-family residence.

Even if the alleged occurrences and irregularities could be construed to be violations of the restrictive covenants they were too distant and sporadic to constitute general consent by the property owners in the subdivision and they were not sufficient to constitute an abandonment or waiver. In order for community violations to constitute an abandonment, they must be so general as to frustrate the original purpose of the agreement. Thodos v. Shirk, 248 Iowa 172, 79 N.W.2d 733 (1956).

Affirmed.

NOTES AND QUESTION

1. For an argument that courts should honor freedom of contract and specifically enforce covenants in spite of a change of conditions (leaving it to the parties to bargain), see Richard A. Epstein, Notice and Freedom of Contract in the Law of Servitudes, 55 S. Cal. L. Rev. 1353, 1364-1368 (1982). Professor Epstein subsequently modified his view to take account of the holdout, which he believes is best dealt with by a provision in the covenants that they may be released by a majority of beneficiaries. Richard A. Epstein, Covenants and Constitutions, 73 Cornell L. Rev. 906, 920-926 (1988). For replies, see Stewart E. Sterk, Foresight and Servitudes, 73 Cornell L. Rev. 956 (1988); Stewart E. Sterk, Freedom from Freedom of Contract: The Enduring Value of Servitude Restrictions, 70 Iowa L. Rev. 615, 652-654 (1985).

2. The change of conditions doctrine is accepted by Restatement of Property §564 (1944). Comment d states that denial of an injunction

because of a change in conditions does not extinguish the obligation and does not foreclose an award of damages for breach of covenant. The possibility of a damage award as an alternative to specific performance has rarely been mentioned in cases denying an injunction, perhaps because the plaintiff could not prove damages. The damages remedy for breach of a restrictive covenant has the backing of some commentators when multiple parties have the benefit of a covenant, making voluntary release impracticable. See Curtis J. Berger, Some Reflections on a Unified Law of Servitudes, 55 S. Cal. L. Rev. 1323, 1330-1332 (1982); Glen O. Robinson, Explaining Contingent Rights: The Puzzle of "Obsolete" Covenants, 91 Colum. L. Rev. 546, 548-560, 570-576 (1991) (a revealing search into theoretical justifications for the change of conditions doctrine); Carol M. Rose, Servitudes, Security, and Assent: Some Comments on Professors French and Reichman, 55 S. Cal. L. Rev. 1403, 1411-1415 (1982); Note, Termination of Servitudes: Expanding the Remedies for "Changed Conditions," 31 UCLA L. Rev. 226 (1983).

3. Massachusetts has moved to make damages rather than an injunction the only remedy in some cases. Mass. Ann. Laws ch. 184, §30 (1987) (enacted 1961) provides that no restriction shall be enforced or declared to be enforceable unless it is determined that the restriction is, at the time of the proceeding, of actual and substantial benefit to a person claiming rights of enforcement. Further, even if a restriction is found to be of such benefit, it shall not be enforced except by award of money damages if any of several enumerated conditions are found to exist. Those conditions are as follows:

(1) changes in the character of the properties affected or their neighborhood, in available construction materials or techniques, in access, services or facilities, in applicable public controls of land use or construction, or in any other conditions or circumstances, which reduce materially the need for the restriction or the likelihood of the restriction accomplishing its original purposes or render it obsolete or inequitable to enforce except by award of money damages, or (2) conduct of persons from time to time entitled to enforce the restriction has rendered it inequitable to enforce except by award of money damages, or (3) in case of a common scheme the land of the person claiming rights of enforcement is for any reason no longer subject to the restriction or the parcel against which rights of enforcement are claimed is not in a group of parcels still subject to the restriction and appropriate for accomplishment of its purpose, or (4) continuation of the restriction on the parcel against which enforcement is claimed or on parcels remaining in a common scheme with it or subject to like restrictions would impede reasonable use of land for purposes for which it is most suitable, and would tend to impair the growth of the neighborhood or municipality in a manner inconsistent with the public interest or to contribute to deterioration of properties or to result in decadent or substandard areas or blighted open areas, or (5) enforcement, except by award of money damages, is for any other reason inequitable or not in the public interest.

In Blakeley v. Gorin, 365 Mass. 590, 313 N.E.2d 903 (1974), the court held the statute constitutional. The court reasoned that the statute did not take property (the benefit of a restrictive covenant) but merely altered the remedies by which such restrictions may be enforced in certain circumstances. The court emphasized

> that the rights of the [covenant beneficiaries] . . . are to be recognized in full and fair money damages; that the rights they assert relate, not directly to ownership or use of their own land, but to the control of land use in the surrounding community; that . . . a sophisticated system of statutes and ordinances has arisen for the regulation of land use in the community; and that it is not in the public interest to enforce the restrictions. [365 Mass. at 600-601, 313 N.E.2d at 910.]

But compare Pulos v. James, 261 Ind. 279, 302 N.E.2d 768 (1973), holding unconstitutional as a taking of property a statute authorizing the planning commission to vacate any outmoded plat, including any recorded covenant or restriction applying to the platted acreage.

4. In Western Land Co. v. Truskolaski, the court says (at page 914), "A zoning ordinance cannot override privately-placed restrictions, and a trial court cannot be compelled to invalidate restrictive covenants merely because of a zoning change." Most zoning ordinances are organized on the principle of preventing the "heavyweight" from harming the "lightweight." Apartments are excluded from single-family areas (but not vice versa); commercial uses are excluded from residential areas (but not vice versa). Therefore, rezoning of a parcel with a single-family covenant to commercial use does not bring the covenant into conflict with the zoning. Under the zoning ordinance single-family use is permitted; under the covenant single-family use is required. Enforcement of the covenant does not violate the zoning ordinance.

Suppose that the zoning ordinance permits only commercial uses in a commercial district and is in direct conflict with the private covenant. Which should prevail? The cases are few. See Note, Legal and Policy Conflicts Between Deed Covenants and Subsequently Enacted Zoning Ordinances, 24 Vand. L. Rev. 1031 (1971). Restatement of Property §568 (1944) takes the position that the zoning ordinance supersedes the covenant when they are in direct conflict. See 5 Richard R. Powell, The Law of Real Property ¶679[4] (rev. ed. 1992).

Rick v. West

New York Supreme Court, Westchester County, 1962
34 Misc. 2d 1002, 228 N.Y.S.2d 195

[Chester Rick owned 62 acres of vacant land, which he subdivided in 1946. A declaration of covenants, restricting the land to single-family dwellings, was filed in the courthouse. In 1956 Rick sold to Catherine West a half-acre lot, upon which she built a house. In 1957 the land was zoned for residential use. Subsequently Rick contracted for the sale of 45 acres to an industrialist, the sale being conditioned upon rezoning of the tract to industrial use. The town board rezoned the 45 acres, but West would not release the covenant in her favor and the sale fell through. In 1959, unable to sell more than a few lots, Rick conveyed the remaining acreage to the plaintiffs. In 1961 the plaintiffs contracted to sell 15 acres from the tract to Peekskill Hospital, but again West refused to consent to release of the covenant. The plaintiffs sued, claiming the covenant was no longer enforceable because of a change of conditions. The court held for the defendant, stating that there was no evidence of any substantial change in the general neighborhood and no change at all within the plaintiffs' tract.]

Hoyt, J. The parcel in question would doubtless by its topography and proximity to fast-growing suburban areas make a desirable location for the hospital. The hospital authorities would like to acquire it, and the plaintiffs would like to sell it, and it may be asked why should defendant owning a most respectable, but modest, home be permitted to prevent the sale, or in any event why should the covenants be not determined nonenforcable and the defendant relegated to pecuniary damages.

Plaintiffs' predecessor owned the tract free and clear of all restrictions. He could do with the parcel as he saw best. He elected to promote a residential development and in the furtherance of his plan, and as an inducement to purchasers he imposed the residential restrictions. The defendant relied upon them and has a right to continue to rely thereon. It is not a question of balancing equities or equating the advantages of a hospital on this site with the effect it would have on defendant's property. Nor does the fact that defendant is the only one of the few purchasers from plaintiffs' predecessor in title who has refused to release the covenants make defendant's insistence upon the enforcement of the covenants no less deserving of the court's protection and safeguarding of her rights.

The opinion of Judge Cardozo in Evangelical Lutheran Church of the Ascension, of Snyder, N.Y. v. Sahlem (254 N.Y. 161, 166, 168) is quoted at length since the questions therein presented are so similar to those in the case at bar.

> By the settled doctrine of equity, restrictive covenants in respect of land will be enforced by preventive remedies while the violation is still in prospect, unless the attitude of the complaining owner in standing on his covenant is unconscionable or oppressive. Relief is not withheld because the money damage is unsubstantial or even none at all. . . .
>
> Here, in the case at hand, no process of balancing the equities can make

the plaintiff's the greater when compared with the defendant's, or even place the two in equipoise. The defendant, the owner, has done nothing but insist upon adherence to a covenant which is now as valid and binding as at the hour of its making. His neighbors are willing to modify the restriction and forego a portion of their rights. He refuses to go with them. Rightly or wrongly he believes that the comfort of his dwelling will be imperilled by the change, and so he chooses to abide by the covenant as framed. The choice is for him only. Neither at law nor in equity is it written that a license has been granted to religious corporations, by reason of the high purpose of their being, to set covenants at naught. Indeed, if in such matters there can be degrees of obligation, one would suppose that a more sensitive adherence to the demands of plighted faith might be expected of them than would be looked for of the world at large. Other owners may consent. One owner, the defendant, satisfied with the existing state of things, refuses to disturb it. He will be protected in his refusal by all the power of the law.

For the reasons stated in the above-quoted portion of Judge Cardozo's opinion, and since section 346 of the Real Property Law provides no basis for awarding pecuniary damages when the restriction is not outmoded and when it affords real benefit to the person seeking its enforcement, no consideration can or should be given to any award of pecuniary damages to the defendant in lieu of the enforcement of the restrictions. . . .

NOTES AND QUESTIONS

1. For fascinating stories of holdouts in New York City, see Andrew Alpern & Seymour Durst, Holdouts! (1984). The book discusses numerous instances where skyscrapers were built over and around business establishments — especially bars — owned by stubborn proprietors. Examples: Hurley's at 49th Street and Sixth Avenue, which stood up to the Rockefellers, and P.J. Clarke's midtown on Third Avenue. Also compare London, which has many interesting variations in cityscape resulting from holdouts, with Paris, where holdouts were not permitted against the grand redevelopment plans of Baron Haussmann.

If Mass. Ann. Laws ch. 184, §30, set forth on page 917, had been applicable to Chester Rick's subdivision, would Catherine West be entitled to damages only? As a matter of fairness and efficiency, *should* she have been entitled to damages only? (We asked the same sort of question after Brown v. Voss, see Note 2 on pages 841-842, and the same considerations apply.) More generally, given damages as a possible remedy, what need is there for the doctrine of change of conditions? Why not allow parties to breach restrictive covenants whenever they wish, but hold them liable for any resulting diminution in the value of other lots

"Talk about argument, cajolery, threats!"

in the restricted tract? See Richard A. Posner, Economic Analysis of Law 67-68 (4th ed. 1992).

A related point: Can you imagine situations where restrictive covenants should *not* be enforced unless the parties who seek enforcement pay compensation to the parties who maintain that changed conditions have rendered the restrictions unenforceable? Is such a remedy of "reverse damages" even conceivable? (It is. See the discussion in Note 3 on page 985.)

2. Some states have statutes requiring re-recordation of covenants after a period of time. Thirty years is the usual period selected. If not re-recorded, they cannot be enforced after the period has passed. See, e.g., Mass. Ann. Laws ch. 184, §27 (1987).

Subdivision covenants commonly provide that after a relatively long initial period (say 25 or 30 years), the covenants may be altered by a majority or greater vote. Uniform Planned Community Act §2-118 (1980) permits termination of servitudes in a planned development at any time with the assent of 80 percent of the unit owners in a homeowners association.

3. An easement can be terminated by an act of abandonment with the intention of giving up the easement (see pages 850-851). Comparable doctrines terminating covenants include abandonment, acquiescence in breaches, waiver, and estoppel. In applying these doctrines, but not the change in conditions doctrine, courts sometimes weigh the relative hardship to the parties. See 5 Richard R. Powell, The Law of Real Property ¶679 (rev. ed. 1992).

5.   Enforcement by Homeowners Associations

In the last 30 years, homeowners associations have grown greatly in number and spread to all corners of the United States. A large number of persons have moved into new housing developments in the suburbs with homeowners associations enforcing covenants on use. An even larger number have moved into condominiums with similar homeowners associations regulating the affirmative obligations of and negative restrictions on the unit owners. Professor French reports that in 1988, "thirty million people, or more than twelve percent of the population, lived in common interest communities. Of those communities, fifty-four percent were condominiums, five percent cooperatives, and the remaining forty-one percent were subdivisions or planned unit developments." See Susan F. French, The Constitution of a Private Residential Government Should Include a Bill of Rights, 27 Wake Forest L. Rev. 345, 347-348 (1992). The result has been a tremendous increase in litigation over promissory servitudes.

Condominiums. The condominium form of shared ownership, known for centuries in Europe, was virtually unheard of in the United

States until the 1960s, when it rather suddenly became very popular. Scholars have attributed this to various causes: the rising cost of single-family homes; the availability of shared amenities (swimming pools, tennis courts, clubhouses, playgrounds) at lower cost; the tax subsidy to owner-occupied housing (deductibility of mortgage interest and real property taxes and failure to include the imputed rental value of owner-occupied housing in taxable personal income); the increasing liquidity among apartment dwellers permitting a greater proportion to invest in equity ownership (as seen among two-earner childless couples and the elderly); the belief that real estate is an inflation-proof investment; the availability of FHA mortgage insurance on condominiums, eliminating risk to lenders; the fear of rent control by investors in housing. See Henry B. Hansmann, Condominium and Cooperative Housing: Transactional Efficiency, Tax Subsidies, and Tenure Choice, 20 J. Legal Stud. 25 (1991).

The basic idea of a condominium is simple. Each unit (or interior space) in a condominium is owned separately *in fee simple* by an individual owner.[35] The exterior walls, the land beneath, the hallways, and other common areas are owned by the unit owners as *tenants in common*. Because each unit is owned separately, each owner obtains mortgage financing by a separate mortgage on his individual unit. Real estate taxes are assessed or allocated to each unit separately. The failure of one unit owner to pay mortgage interest or taxes does not jeopardize the other unit owners.

The condominium form of ownership can be adapted to residential or commercial use, and can apply to units in highrise buildings or to lateral developments such as townhouses and detached dwellings. The declaration of condominium, filed before the first sale is made, will provide for an association of unit owners to make and enforce rules, to manage the common areas, and to set maintenance charges levied against unit owners. Each purchaser, by accepting a deed, becomes an association member and must abide by its bylaws. All 50 states have some form of condominium statute governing this type of shared ownership.

Each condominium unit owner is liable for a monthly charge to maintain common facilities and insure against casualty and liability. The condominium documents fix the fraction of each unit owner's pro rata burden of common expenses. This fraction also may govern the unit owner's voice in management and may be used by the tax assessor in apportioning the project's total value among the separate units. The association may also have the right to make improvements and assess the unit owners their fractional share. Enforcement of condominium obligations may be covered by the state condominium statute. If not, en-

---

35. In rare cases, as in Laguna Royale Owners Association v. Darger, which follows, the project may be based on a long-term lease, and the unit owners may own a leasehold rather than a fee.

forcement raises all the legal problems associated with enforcement of covenants, previously discussed in this chapter.

The condominium statute or documents should state what procedures are to be followed if the condominium building is destroyed. A common solution is for the unit owner to receive an undivided fractional interest in the property upon the building's destruction. See generally Robert G. Natelson, Law of Property Owners Associations (1989); Patrick J. Rohan & Melvin A. Reskin, Condominium Law and Practice (1988). See also Uniform Condominium Act (1977, amended 1980); Uniform Common Interest Ownership Act (1982).

Laguna Royale Owners Association v. Darger
Court of Appeal of California, Fourth District, 1981
119 Cal. App. 3d 670, 174 Cal. Rptr. 136

KAUFMAN, J. Defendants Stanford P. Darger and Darlene B. Darger (the Dargers) were the owners of a leasehold condominium in Laguna Royale, a 78-unit community apartment complex on the ocean front in South Laguna Beach. The Dargers purported to assign three one-quarter undivided interests in the property to three other couples: Wendell P. Paxton and Daila D. Paxton, Keith I. Gustaveson and Elsie Gustaveson, and Keith C. Brown and Geneva B. Brown (collectively the other defendants) without the approval of Laguna Royale Owners Association (Association). Association instituted this action to obtain a declaration that the assignments from the Dargers to defendants were invalid because they were made in violation of a provision of the instrument by which the Dargers acquired the property, prohibiting assignment or transfer of interests in the property without the consent and approval of Association's predecessor in interest. Following trial to the court judgment was rendered in favor of Association invalidating the assignments from the Dargers to the other defendants. Defendants appeal.

Facts

The Laguna Royale development is built on land leased by the developer from the landowner in a 99-year ground lease executed in 1961. As the units were completed, the developer sold each one by executing a Subassignment and Occupancy Agreement with the purchaser. This document conveyed an undivided $\frac{1}{78}$ interest in the leasehold estate for a term of 99 years, a right to exclusive use of a designated unit and one or more garage spaces and a right to joint use of common areas and facilities; it also contained certain restrictions. The restriction pertinent to this action is paragraph 7, which provides in relevant part: "7. Subassignee [the purchaser] shall not assign or otherwise transfer this agreement, . . . nor shall subassignee sublet . . . without the consent of and approval of Lessee. . . ."

Upon the sale of all units and completion of the project, the developer entered into an "Assignment Agreement" with the Association, transferring and assigning to the Association all the developer's rights, powers and duties under the Subassignment and Occupancy Agreements, including inter alia the "right to approve or disapprove assignments or transfers of interests in Laguna Royale pursuant to Paragraph 7 of the Subassignment and Occupancy Agreements."

In 1965, Ramona G. Sutton acquired unit 41, consisting of some 3,000 square feet, by a Subassignment and Occupancy Agreement with the developer. In 1973 the Dargers purchased unit 41 from the executrix of Mrs. Sutton's estate. As owner of a unit in the project, the Dargers automatically became members of the Association and were bound by the Association's bylaws.

The Dargers reside in Salt Lake City, Utah, where Mr. Darger became a vice president of a large banking chain not long after the Dargers acquired their unit at Laguna Royale. The responsibilities of Mr Darger's new position made it difficult for them to get away, and they attempted unsuccessfully to lease their unit through real estate agents in Laguna Beach. On October 30, 1973, Mr. Darger wrote to Mr. Yount, then chairman of the board of governors of the Association, in which he stated in part:

> It has been suggested that we might sell shares in our apartment to two or three other couples here. These associates would be aware of the restrictions regarding children under 16 living there, as well as the restrictions regarding pets, and would submit themselves to the regular investigation of the Board given prospective purchasers and lessees. I would expect that the apartment will remain vacant most of the time, as now, and not more than one of the families will occupy the apartment at one time. . . .

[After several letters between the Dargers and the Association, the Association in 1976 refused consent to transfer of the Dargers' unit in undivided shares to four couples.]

By a letter from its attorney to the Dargers dated March 16, 1976, Association advised the Dargers that it would not consent to the requested transfer. It was denied that written and verbal approvals had been given the Dargers in the past, and it was stated in relevant part:

> The reason the Association will not consent to your requested transfer is that the Board feels it is obligated to protect and preserve the private single family residential character of Laguna Royale, together with the use and quiet enjoyment of all apartment owners of their respective apartments and the common facilities, taking into consideration the close community living circumstances of Laguna Royale.
>
> The Board feels strongly about its power of consent to assignments and

other transfers of leasehold interests and considers the protection and preservation of that power to be critical in maintaining the character of Laguna
Royale for the benefit of all owners as a whole. A four family ownership of a
single apartment, with the guests of each owner potentially involved, would
compound the use of the apartment and common facilities well beyond the
normal and usual private single family residential character to the detriment
of other owners and would frustrate effective controls over general security,
guest occupants and rule compliance, as has been the case in the past.

Provision 7 of the Subassignment and Occupancy Agreement, under
which all apartment leasehold interests are held, requires the unqualified
consent to any transfer. . . .

After consultation with legal counsel the Dargers proceeded nevertheless, and on June 11 they executed instruments purporting to assign
undivided one-fourth interests in the property to themselves and the
other three couples. The instruments were recorded on June 30, and on
July 3, 1976, the Dargers informed Association by letter of the transfers
enclosing on Association's forms a separate "Request for Approval Of
Sale Or Lease" and financial statement prepared and executed by each
of the other couples. . . .

After unsuccessfully demanding that the other defendants retrans-
fer their purported interests to the Dargers, the Association filed this
action.

At trial the testimony confirmed that no more than one family of
defendants used the property at a time and, although the matter was not
examined in detail, answers to questions by one or more defendants indicated that 13-week periods had been agreed upon for exclusive use by
each of the four families. It was also indicated that for substantial periods during the year, no use at all was being made of the unit. The
evidence also showed that a number of Laguna Royale units were owned
by several unrelated persons, but that in each case the owners used the
unit "as family."

No formal findings were made. However, in its notice of intended
decision the court stated in relevant part:

> The Court . . . finds that the plaintiff association acted reasonably in refusing
> to grant consent to the proposed transfer by Darger to the other defendants.
> Plaintiff is entitled to a declaration that the assignments by Darger to the
> other defendants are invalid. Plaintiff is awarded attorney fees in the amount
> of $2500.

Judgment was entered accordingly.

Contentions, Issues and Discussion

Defendants contend paragraph 7 of the Subassignment and Occupancy
Agreement prohibiting assignments or transfers without the consent of

Laguna Royale Condominium, 1992

Association is invalid because it is in violation of their constitutional rights to associate with persons of their choosing (U.S. Const., 1st amend.; Cal. Const., art I, §1), [and] because it constitutes an unlawful restraint on alienation (Civ. Code, §711). . . . Failing those, defendants contend finally that if by its finding that Association acted reasonably in refusing to approve the transfers, the court meant to indicate that Association had the duty to act reasonably in withholding consent and did so, that determination is not supported by substantial evidence and is contrary to law.

Association contends that the prohibition against transfer or assignment without its consent is not invalid on any of the bases urged by defendants. It argues primarily that its right to withhold approval or consent is absolute, that in exercising its power it is not required to adhere to a standard of reasonableness but may withhold approval or consent for any reason or for no reason at all. Secondarily, it argues that the evidence supports the finding it acted reasonably in disapproving the transfers to the other defendants.

We reject Association's contention that its right to give or withhold approval or consent is absolute. We likewise reject defendants' contention that the claimed right to approve or disapprove transfers is an invalid restraint on alienation because it is repugnant to the conveyance of a fee. We hold that in exercising its power to approve or disapprove transfers or assignments Association must act reasonably, exercising its power in a fair and nondiscriminatory manner and withholding approval only for a reason or reasons rationally related to the protection, preservation and proper operation of the property and the purposes of Association as set forth in its governing instruments. We hold that the restriction on transfer contained in paragraph 7 of the Subassignment and Occupancy Agreement (hereafter simply paragraph 7), thus limited, does not violate defendants' constitutional rights of association and is not invalid as an unreasonable restraint on alienation. However, we conclude that in view of the present provisions of Association's bylaws, its refusal to consent to the transfers to defendants was unreasonable as a matter of law. Accordingly, we reverse the judgment with directions to enter judgment for defendants. . . .

As indicated, the initial positions of the parties are at opposite extremes. Association contends that the Subassignment and Occupancy Agreement constitutes a sublease and that under the law applicable to leasehold interests, when a lease contains a provision permitting subletting only upon consent of the lessor, the lessor is under no obligation to give consent and, in fact, may withhold consent arbitrarily. . . . Defendants on the other hand contend that the Subassignment and Occupancy Agreement conveys, in essence, a fee, and that under California law when a fee simple interest is granted, any restriction on the subsequent conveyance of the grantee's interest contained in the original grant is repugnant to the interest conveyed and is therefore void. . . .

We reject the extreme contentions of both parties; the rules of law they propose, borrowed from the law of landlord and tenant developed during the feudal period in English history (see Green v. Superior Court (1974) 10 Cal. 3d 616, 622, 111 Cal. Rptr. 704, 517 P.2d 1168), are entirely inappropriate tools for use in affecting an accommodation of the competing interests involved in the use and transfer of a condominium. Even assuming the continued vitality of the rule that a lessor may arbitrarily withhold consent to a sublease (but see Note, Effect of Leasehold Provision Requiring the Lessor's Consent to Assignment (1970) 21 Hast. L.J. 516), there is little or no similarity in the relationship between a condominium owner and his fellow owners and that between lessor and lessee or sublessor and sublessee. Even when the right to the underlying land is no more than an undivided interest in a ground lease or sublease, ownership of a condominium constitutes a statutorily recognized estate in real property (see Civ. Code, §783), and in our society the right freely to use and dispose of one's property is a valued and protected right. (U.S. Const., amends. 5 and 14; Cal. Const., art. I, §7, subd. (a); see 5 Witkin, Summary of Cal. Law (8th ed. 1974) Constitutional Law, §273, p.3563.) Ownership and use of condominiums is an increasingly significant form of "home ownership" which has evolved in recent years to meet the desire of our people to own their own dwelling place, in the face of heavy concentrations of population in urban areas, the limited availability of housing, and, thus, the impossibly inflated cost of individual homes in such areas.

On the other hand condominium living involves a certain closeness to and with one's neighbors, and, as stated in Hidden Harbour Estates, Inc. v. Norman (Fla. App. 1975) 309 So. 2d 180, 181-182:

> [I]nherent in the condominium concept is the principle that to promote the health, happiness, and peace of mind of the majority of the unit owners since they are living in such close proximity and using facilities in common, each unit owner must give up a certain degree of freedom of choice which he might otherwise enjoy in separate, privately owned property.

(See also White Egret Condominium v. Franklin (Fla. 1979) 379 So. 2d 346, 350; Seagate Condominium Association, Inc. v. Duffy (Fla. App. 1976) 330 So. 2d 484, 486.) Thus, it is essential to successful condominium living and the maintenance of the value of these increasingly significant property interests that the owners as a group have the authority to regulate reasonably the use and alienation of the condominiums. . . .

Nor does the right of Association reasonably to approve or disapprove the assignment or transfer of the Dargers' ownership interest violate defendants' constitutional right to associate freely with persons of their choosing. Preliminarily, there is considerable doubt of whether the actions of Association constitute state action so as to bring into play the constitutional guarantees. (Cf. Moose Lodge No. 107 v. Irvis (1972) 407

U.S. 163, 173, 92 S. Ct. 1965, 1971, 32 L. Ed. 2d 627, 637; Newby v. Alto Riviera Apartments (1976) 60 Cal. App. 3d 288, 293-295, 131 Cal. Rptr. 547; see generally 5 Witkin, Summary of Cal. Law (8th ed. 1974) Constitutional Law, §338, pp. 3631-3632.) In any event, however, the constitutionally guaranteed freedom of association, like most other constitutionally protected rights, is not absolute but is subject to reasonable restriction in the interests of the general welfare. (Village of Belle Terre v. Boraas (1974) 416 U.S. 1, 9, 94 S. Ct. 1536, 1541, 39 L. Ed. 2d 797 804; White Egret Condominium v. Franklin, supra, 379 So. 2d. at pp.349-351.) Moreover, it may be persuasively argued that if any constitutional right is at issue it is the due process right of an owner of property to use and dispose of it as he chooses. . . . And, of course, property rights are subject to reasonable regulation to promote the general welfare. . . . Finally, any determination of the validity or invalidity of Association's right to approve or disapprove assignments or transfers of the Dargers' interest will of necessity impinge upon someone's constitutional freedom of association. A determination that the power granted the Association is invalid would adversely affect the constitutional right of association of the remaining owners at least as much as a contrary determination would affect the same right of the Dargers. (Cf. Presbytery of Riverside v. Community Church of Palm Springs (1979) 89 Cal. App. 3d 910, 925, 152 Cal. Rptr. 854.)

Having concluded that a reasonable restriction on the right of alienation of a condominium is lawful, we must now determine whether Association's refusal to approve the transfer of the Dargers' interest to the other defendants was reasonable in the circumstances of the case at bench. The criteria for testing the reasonableness of an exercise of such a power by a owner's association are (1) whether the reason for withholding approval is rationally related to the protection, preservation or proper operation of the property and the purposes of the Association as set forth in its governing instruments and (2) whether the power was exercised in a fair and nondiscriminatory manner. . . .

To determine whether or not Association's disapproval of the transfers to the other defendants was reasonable it is necessary to isolate the reason or reasons approval was withheld. Aside from the assertion that it had the power to withhold approval arbitrarily, essentially three reasons were given by the Association for its refusal to approve the transfers: (1) the multiple ownership of undivided interests; (2) the use the defendants proposed to make of the unit would violate a bylaw restricting use of all apartments to "single family residential use"; and (3) the use proposed would be inconsistent with "the private single family residential character of Laguna Royale, together with the use and quiet enjoyment of all apartment owners of their respective apartments and the common facilities, taking into consideration the close community living circumstances of Laguna Royale." As to (3) Association asserted:

> A four family ownership of a single apartment, with the guests of each owner potentially involved, would compound the use of the apartment and common facilities well beyond the normal and usual private single family residential character to the detriment of other owners and would frustrate effective controls over general security, guest occupants and rule compliance. . . .

We examine each of these reasons in light of the indicia of reasonableness referred to above.

Insofar as approval was withheld based on multiple ownership alone, Association's action was clearly unreasonable. In the first place, multiple ownership has no necessary connection to intensive use. Twenty, yea a hundred, persons could own undivided interests in a condominium for investment purposes and lease the condominium on a long-term basis to a single occupant whose use of the premises would probably be less intense in every respect than that considered "normal and usual." Secondly, the Association bylaws specifically contemplate multiple ownership; in Section 7 of Article III, dealing with voting at meetings, it is stated:

> Where there is more than one record owner of a unit, any or all of the record owners may attend [the meeting] but only one vote will be permitted for said unit. In the event of disagreement among the record owners of a unit, the vote for that unit shall be cast by a majority of the record owners.

Finally the evidence is uncontroverted that a number of units are owned by several unrelated persons. Although those owners at the time of trial used their units "as a family," there is nothing in the governing instruments as they presently exist that would prevent them from changing the character of their use.

We turn to the assertion that the use of the premises proposed by defendants would be in violation of section 1 of article VIII of the bylaws which provides: "All apartment unit uses are restricted and limited to single family residential use and shall not be used or occupied for any other purpose." . . . Actually, there is no evidence that defendants proposed to use the property other than for single family residential purposes. It is uncontroverted that they planned to and did use the property one family at a time for residential purposes. Thus, the proposed use was not in violation of the restriction to single family residential use. (White Egret Condominium v. Franklin, supra, 379 So. 2d at p.352.)

The reasonableness of Association's disapproval of the transfers from the Dargers to the other defendants must stand or fall in the final analysis on the third reason offered by the Association for its action: the prospect that defendants' proposed use of the apartment and common facilities would be so greatly in excess of that considered "usual and normal" as to be inconsistent with the quiet enjoyment of the premises by the other occupants and the maintenance of security.

There can be no doubt that the reason given is rationally related to the proper operation of the property and the purposes of the Association as set forth in its governing instruments. The bylaws provide that . . . the Board is empowered to "prescribe reasonable regulations pertaining to . . . [r]egulating the purchase and/or lease of an apartment to a buyer or sublessee who has no children under 16 years of age that will occupy the apartment temporarily or full time as a resident." This power is said by the bylaws to be given the Board in recognition of "the prime importance of both security and quiet enjoyment of the Apartments owned by each member, and of the common recreation areas. . . ."

The difficulty with upholding the Association's disapproval of the transfers by the Dargers to the other defendants is twofold. First, no evidence was introduced to establish that the intensity or nature of the use proposed by defendants would in fact be inconsistent with the peaceful enjoyment of the premises by the other occupants or impair security. We may take judicial notice as a matter of common knowledge that the use of a single apartment by four families for 13 weeks each during the year would create some problems not presented by the use of a single, permanent resident family. The moving in and out would, of course, be more frequent, and it might be that some temporary residents would not be as considerate of their fellow occupants as more permanent residents. However, we are not prepared to take judicial notice that the consecutive use of unit 41 by these four families, one at a time, would be so intense or disruptive as to interfere substantially with the peaceful enjoyment of the premises by the other occupants or the maintenance of building security.

Secondly, and most persuasive, a provision of the bylaws, subdivision (A) of section 1 of article VIII, provides:

> Residential use and purpose, as used herein and as referred to in the lease, subassignment and occupancy agreement pertaining to and affecting each apartment unit in LAGUNA ROYALE shall be and is hereby deemed to exclude and prohibit the rental of any apartment unit for a period of time of less than ninety (90) days, as it is deemed and agreed that rentals of apartment units for less than ninety (90) day periods of time are contrary to the close community apartment character of LAGUNA ROYALE; interfere with and complicate the orderly administration and process of the security system and program and maintenance program of LAGUNA ROYALE, and interfere with the orderly management and administration of the common areas and facilities of LAGUNA ROYALE. Accordingly, no owner shall rent an apartment unit for a period of time of less than ninety (90) days.

The point is self-evident: under the present bylaws the Dargers could effect the same *use* of the property as is proposed by defendants by simply leasing to each couple for a period of 90 days each year.

Under these circumstances we are constrained to hold that Board's refusal to approve the transfers to the other defendants on the basis of the prospect of intensified use was unreasonable as a matter of law. . . .

Disposition

The judgment is reversed with directions to the trial court to enter judgment for the defendants.

GARDNER, P.J., dissenting. I dissent.

Stripped to its essentials, this is a case in which the other owners of a condominium are attempting to stop the owner of one unit from embarking on a time sharing enterprise. The majority properly conclude that the owners as a group have the authority to regulate reasonably the use and alienation of the units. The majority then conclude that the Board's refusal to approve this transfer was unreasonable as a matter of law. To the contrary, I would find it to be entirely reasonable and would affirm the judgment of the trial court.

The use of a unit on a time sharing basis is inconsistent with the quiet enjoyment of the premises by the other occupants. Time sharing is a remarkable gimmick. P.T. Barnum would have loved it. It ordinarily brings enormous profits to the seller and in this case would bring chaos to the other residents. Here we have only four occupants but if this transfer is permitted there is nothing to stop a more greedy occupant of a unit from conveying to 52 or 365 other occupants.

If as an occupant of a condominium I must anticipate that my neighbors are going to change with clocklike regularity I might just as well move into a hotel — and get room service.

NOTES AND QUESTIONS

1. Many condominium and cooperative agreements attempt to control entry by giving the homeowners association (or any member of the association) a preemptive right to buy any unit that is put up for sale. For example, if a member wishes to sell his unit and finds a purchaser, the association (or one of its members) is given a stated period of time in which it can match the price offered and buy the unit for itself. In a few early cases, before condominiums became so popular, it was found that preemptive options in condominiums were subject to the Rule against Perpetuities (see page 312). But all recent cases and other authorities hold that preemptive options in condominium agreements are not subject to the Rule against Perpetuities but are instead subject to the rule prohibiting unreasonable restraints upon alienation. Restatement (Third) of Property, Servitudes, §3.3, Reporter's Note (T.D. No. 2,

1991) (citing cases). Uniform Statutory Rule Against Perpetuities §4(1) (1986) exempts all commercial transactions from the Rule.

A preemptive option in a condominium agreement or homeowners association has generally been held reasonable if the preemption is limited in time and gives the association the right either to match a bona fide offer or to purchase at the market price. See Restatement (Third) of Property, supra, §3.4, Reporter's Note. Restatement (Second) of Property, Donative Transfers, §4.4 (1983), approves. Cases have upheld preemptions limited in time from 1 month to 12 months.

Should the Laguna Royale Owners Association have retained a preemptive option to purchase the Dargers' apartment if the purchasers proposed by the Dargers were not satisfactory?

2. *New York's cooperative apartments.* New York City is probably the only housing market in the country with a substantial number of cooperative apartments. In a housing cooperative, the title to the land and building is held by a corporation; the residents own all the shares of stock in the corporation and control it through an elected board of directors. Each resident also has a long-term renewable lease of an apartment unit. Hence, residents are both owners of the cooperative corporation (by virtue of share ownership) and tenants of the corporation.

The cooperative property is usually subject to one blanket mortgage securing the money lender for the money borrowed to buy the land and erect the building. If one cooperator fails to pay his share of the mortgage interest or taxes, the other cooperators must make it up or the entire property may be foreclosed upon. Thus, in a cooperative more than a condominium, the investment of one person depends upon the financial stability of others.

As a result, members of a cooperative have a strong incentive to screen applicants to insure that they can carry their share of the collective mortgage. Financial screening also provides an opportunity for social screening. New York courts have held that cooperative boards can deny entry to anyone for any reason and without giving any reason, provided the board does not violate federal and state civil rights laws. Weisner v. 791 Park Ave. Corp., 6 N.Y.2d 426, 160 N.E.2d 720, 190 N.Y.S.2d 70 (1959). Because cooperatives give the ability to screen prospective members, and because of long experience with the cooperative form of housing, cooperatives continue to flourish in New York City despite the growth of condominiums in all the rest of the country. (In a condominium in New York, the boards typically can prevent entry only by exercising a preemptive option; they rarely screen applicants by social criteria.)

Tenants in upper east side cooperatives in Manhattan place a premium on having neighbors of high status or well-seasoned money in conservative surroundings. As a result of their screening procedures, numerous prominent persons have been excluded from cooperative apartments. The actor Peter Lawford and his wife, Patricia, a sister of President Kennedy, were refused permission to buy a 16-room cooperative "because of his occupation, acting, and her affiliations with the Democratic party. . . . The city's Commission on Human Rights was asked to intervene, but declined. It noted that there was nothing in the law to prevent a person's being denied living quarters because he is an actor or a Democrat." N.Y. Times, Apr. 7, 1964, §1, at 41. Other notables rejected by cooperatives include Barbra Streisand, Gloria Vanderbilt, ex-President Richard Nixon, and Prince Saud al-Faisal of Saudi Arabia. See N.Y. Times, Nov. 2, 1986, §8, at 1.

3. *Time-share estates.* New forms of property interests may be created by time-sharing. Usually these agreements relate to the sharing by several persons of a resort condominium unit for separate periods of the year. The right to occupy a unit for a time period may be coupled with an estate or interest in the condominium (for example, the occupants own the unit as tenants in common with designated rights of occupancy), or the right to occupy may be merely a license given by the developer for a period of years.

Time-share estates are governed by rules laid down in statutes providing for such estates in a manner similar to the governance of condominium shares. See Model Real Estate Time-Share Act (1980, amended 1982); Note, Timesharing and Realty Interests Under the Martin Act: Consumer or Investor Protection?, 17 Fordham Urb. L.J. 505 (1989).

4. What standards of review should a court use in passing on the validity of an association regulation? Courts have generally applied a standard of reasonableness. See Johnson v. Hobson, 505 A.2d 1313 (D.C. App. 1986); Note, Judicial Review of Condominium Rulemaking, 94 Harv. L. Rev. 647, 658-667 (1981). This is a more demanding standard than is applied to legislation and city ordinances, which — under the due process and equal protection clauses of the Fourteenth Amendment — are required only to be rationally related to a legitimate state interest. Why is a homeowners association held to a higher standard than is a city? What standard was applied in Laguna Royale Owners Association v. Darger, page 924?

The reasonableness standard has been opposed by a number of commentators in recent years. They see homeowners associations essentially as consensual regimes, which people may enter or leave as they choose, and in which they voluntarily participate. In this view, courts should rarely intrude into the internal regulations of these private associations. See Robert C. Ellickson, Cities and Homeowners Associations, 130 U. Pa. L. Rev. 1519 (1982); Gerald E. Frug, Cities and Homeowners Associations: A Reply, 130 U. Pa. L. Rev. 1589 (1982) (replying to Ellickson); Robert C. Ellickson, A Reply to Michelman and Frug, 130 U. Pa. L. Rev. 1602 (1982); Richard A. Epstein, Covenants and Constitutions,

73 Cornell L. Rev. 906 (1988); Uriel Reichman, Residential Private Governments: An Introductory Survey, 43 U. Chi. L. Rev. 253 (1976); Uriel Reichman, Judicial Review of Servitudes, 7 J. Legal Stud. 139 (1978). See also Note, The Rule of Law in Residential Associations, 99 Harv. L. Rev. 472 (1985).

Other commentators believe that homeowners regimes are not entirely voluntary. For lack of a satisfactory array of options, they argue, home buyers are coerced into accepting obligations they do not want to get the property they do want. Once inside the enclave, members are coerced by the power of the association to make rules. These scholars fear the exclusiveness, regimentation, and loss of personal autonomy that may result from giving the associations a strong form of group autonomy. They would require homeowners associations to justify their regulations by a standard of reasonableness similar to substantive due process. See Gregory S. Alexander, Dilemmas of Group Autonomy: Residential Associations and Community, 75 Cornell L. Rev. 1 (1989) (arguing that communitarian theory justifies judicial review for substantive reasonableness); Gregory S. Alexander, Freedom, Coercion and the Law of Servitudes, 73 Cornell L. Rev. 883 (1988); Glen O. Robinson, Explaining Contingent Rights: The Puzzle of "Obsolete" Covenants, 91 Colum. L. Rev. 546, 577-579 (1991) (replying to Alexander).

For a summary and further debate, see Gerald Korngold, Resolving the Flaws of Residential Servitudes and Owners Associations: For Reformation Not Termination, 1990 Wis. L. Rev. 513; James L. Winokur, The Mixed Blessings of Promissory Servitudes: Toward Optimizing Economic Utility, Individual Liberty, and Personal Identity, 1989 Wis. L. Rev. 1; James L. Winokur, Reforming Servitude Regimes: Toward Associational Federalism and Community, 1990 Wis. L. Rev. 537.

See also Todd Brower, Communities Within the Community: Consent, Constitutionalism, and Other Failures of Legal Theory in Residential Associations, 7 J. Land Use & Envtl. L. 203 (1992); Robert G. Natelson, Consent, Coercion and "Reasonableness" in Private Law: The Special Case of the Property Owners Association, 51 Ohio St. L.J. 41 (1990); Note, Community Association Use Restrictions: Applying the Business Judgment Doctrine, 64 Chi.-Kent L. Rev. 653 (1988).

Nahrstedt v. Lakeside Village Condominium Association, Inc.

Court of Appeal of California, Second District, 1992
11 Cal. Rptr. 2d 299, hearing granted by the
California Supreme Court, Nov. 19, 1992

CROSKEY, J. This action concerns (1) a plaintiff who wishes to continue living with her three pet cats in the condominium she owns, (2) a provision in the recorded covenants, conditions and restrictions ("CC & Rs") governing that condominium, which prohibits owners of the units in her condominium project from keeping most types of pets, and (3) the authority of the Board of Directors of her homeowners association to levy monetary fines on homeowners who violate that pet restriction. Plaintiff has filed this action to obtain, among other things, a declaration that she (1) is entitled to keep her pets in her condominium, notwithstanding the CC & Rs and (2) has no legal obligation to pay the fines which have been assessed against her for her refusal to move her cats out of her condominium. This case comes to us on an appeal from a judgment of dismissal which was entered after the trial court sustained, without leave to amend, demurrers to all five causes of action in plaintiff's original complaint. . . .

We conclude that plaintiff has stated at least three causes of action and should have been given leave to amend her complaint in order to state additional causes of action if she can. Therefore, the judgment of dismissal will be reversed and the cause remanded for further proceedings.

Procedural and Factual Background

1. The Parties

Plaintiff resides in the Lakeside Village Condominiums in Culver City. She filed her complaint on February 20, 1990 and names as defendants the Lakeside Village Condominium Association ("Condominium Association"), the Homeowners Association, and certain persons alleged in the complaint to be employees, agents, officers and directors of the Homeowners Association and the Condominium Association.

2. The Complaint

We describe here, in turn, the essential allegations of each of the . . . causes of action in the complaint. . . .

a. Plaintiff's first cause of action is for invasion of privacy. In it she alleges that Article VII, section 11 of the CC & Rs for the condominium project provides in part:

No animals (which shall mean dogs and cats), livestock, reptiles or poultry shall be kept in any unit except that usual and ordinary domestic fish and birds (and [sic] inside bird cages) may be kept as household pets within any unit; provided (a) they are not kept, bred or raised for commercial purposes or in unreasonable numbers; and (b) prior written approval of the Board [of Directors of the Condominium Association] is first obtained. As used herein, "unreasonable numbers" shall be determined by the Board, but in no event shall such term be construed so as to permit the maintenance by any owner

**Lakeside Village Condominiums
Culver City**

of more than two (2) pets per unit. The Association shall have the right to prohibit maintenance of any pet which constitutes, in the opinion of the Board, a nuisance to any other owner.

Plaintiff alleges that her three cats at all times remain inside her unit and are noiseless and not a nuisance; that beginning in July 1988 defendants peered into and entered her condominium without a compelling reason to do so and in violation of the California Constitution's provision for privacy, found in Article 1, section 1 thereof; that defendants have harassed plaintiff by assessing penalties against her in increasingly large amounts, (beginning with $25/month and increasing in steps to $500/ month), to penalize her for keeping her pet cats; and that the assessments are in violation of the CC & Rs and in violation of her right to privacy.

b. Plaintiff's second cause of action is for declaratory relief. She alleges that the "cat provision" in the CC & Rs is overly broad and, as applied to her, violates her constitutional right to privacy; that the requisite state action is present because of the small claims court actions brought against her for the fines levied on her; that the cat provision is "unreasonable" under Civil Code section 1354;[36] that the defendants

36. At the time this action was filed, Civil Code section 1354 stated: "The covenants and restrictions in the declaration [of CC & Rs] shall be enforceable equitable servitudes, unless unreasonable, and shall inure to the benefit of and bind all owners of separate interests in the project. Unless the declaration states otherwise, these servitudes may be enforced by any owner of a separate interest or by the association, or by both." An amendment to section 1354, effective July 1, 1991, provides that "In any action to enforce the

believe the cat provision is constitutional and enforceable; and that an actual controversy exists between herself and defendants regarding said provision.

    c. Plaintiff's third and fourth causes of action are for intentional and negligent infliction of emotional distress, respectively. In the former, she alleges that defendants have assessed fines against her as a penalty for keeping her cats; that the cats are not a nuisance, are clean, are kept inside her unit and have not been the object of complaints by any of her close neighbors; that defendants' acts in assessing her fines which are unauthorized, have been designed to inflict emotional distress upon her and have done so; that as a result, plaintiff has had to seek medical attention; that the fines have been designed to force her to sell her condominium at an unreasonable price or remove her cats from her home; and that defendants' acts are intentional and malicious.

    d. In the cause of action for negligent infliction of emotional distress, plaintiff alleges that defendants knew or should have known that she is excitable emotionally, that she is susceptible to being easily upset, and that she is susceptible of obsessing about defendants' unfair and unprovoked actions. Plaintiff further alleges that she is entitled to live in her home undisturbed and unharassed; that defendants' acts were negligent; that as a proximate result of said negligence, she suffered "profound shock to her nervous system, resulting in physical injuries, for which she has sought the help of physicians [and] psychologists"; and that she has incurred expenses associated therewith.

    e. Plaintiff's fifth cause of action is labeled one "to invalidate penal assessments levied in excess of authority and for damages." In this cause of action, plaintiff alleges that although the CC & Rs do provide for certain charges and assessments (i.e., regular monthly assessments, special assessments for capital improvements, and emergency assessments), no other assessments are provided for in the CC & Rs. . . .

3.   The Cause of Action for Declaratory Relief

a. Introduction
    . . . In Wilshire Condominium Assn., Inc. v. Kohlbrand (Fla. Ct. of Appeal 1979) 368 So. 2d 629, the court examined a condominium regulation which permitted purchasers of condominium units to keep the dogs that they owned when they moved into the unit but forbade them from replacing such pets when the pets died or otherwise left the unit. The court adopted a "reasonableness" test in examining the challenged

---

declaration, the prevailing party shall be awarded reasonable attorney's fees and costs." Section 1354 is found in title 6 of part 4 of division 2 of the Civil Code. Title 6 is entitled "Common Interest Developments." A common interest development is any of the following: community apartment project, condominium project, planned development and stock cooperative. (Civ. Code §1351.)

restriction. The court found that the restriction was "reasonably consistent with principles that promote the health, happiness and peace of mind of unit owners living in close proximity." The court did not explain why the replacement dogs would impinge on the health, happiness and peace of mind of unit owners but the dogs originally owned by buyers would not.

In Dulaney Towers Maintenance v. O'Brey (Md. Ct. of Special Appeals 1980) 418 A.2d 1233, the court considered a restriction that permitted unit owners to keep one dog or one cat. The defendants kept two dogs in their unit and were sued. The court found the restriction reasonable. It noted that courts have often upheld restrictions regulating dogs and stated that communal living requires giving fair consideration to the rights and privileges of all occupants of the condominium project so as to provide a harmonious atmosphere.

Neither Wilshire Condominium nor Dulaney Towers is helpful to the resolution of the case before us because (1) neither case addressed the reasonableness of a blanket restriction against keeping any cats in a condominium unit, (2) neither addressed a statutory limitation on condominium restrictions similar to the one in Civil Code section 1354, and (3) neither examined the particular facts of the case before it to see if the challenged restrictions were reasonable as applied to those facts. This latter characteristic runs contrary to the approach taken by our California courts in examining challenged provisions in condominium and "planned community" CC & Rs to see if they are enforceable under Civil Code section 1354. For example, in Bernardo Villas Management Corp. v. Black (1987) 190 Cal. App. 3d 153, 235 Cal. Rptr. 509, and Portola Hills Community Assn. v. James (1992) 4 Cal. App. 4th 289, 5 Cal. Rptr. 2d 580, the courts found that the CC & R restrictions sought to be enforced by homeowner management groups were unreasonable when they were applied to the circumstances of the homeowners who were challenging them.

In Bernardo Villas, the provisions being challenged precluded residents from parking trucks in the project except on a temporary basis for the purpose of loading or unloading the trucks. The provisions also restricted the project's carports to passenger automobiles and non-powered vehicles, such as bicycles. The defendants in the case parked their new pickup truck, which they used solely for their personal transportation, in their carport space. The management of the project sued to enjoin them from doing so and to recover $2,060 in fines it had imposed on the defendants for violating the truck restriction.

In its opinion, the court applied Civil Code section 1354. It stated:

> the trial court properly found the restriction unreasonable as applied to clean noncommercial pickup trucks. The court correctly concluded the parking of such vehicles in condominium carports was not aesthetically unpleasant to

reasonable persons and did not interfere with other owners' use and enjoyment of their property. [Bernardo Villas Management Corp. v. Black, supra, 190 Cal. App. 3d at pp.154-155, 235 Cal. Rptr. 509.]

Also instructive is Portola Hills Community Assn. v. James, supra, 4 Cal. App. 4th 289, 5 Cal. Rptr. 2d 580. There, the challenged CC & R provision was a total ban on satellite dishes in the "planned community" of Portola Hills. The plaintiff was the body having the right to enforce the CC & Rs. The defendant installed a satellite dish in his back yard. The trial court found from the evidence that the dish was installed in such a manner that it was not visible to other residents of the community or to the public and therefore the defendant did not have to remove the dish. On review, the Portola Hills court agreed with the trial court's conclusion. Its opinion begins: "Is a private restriction prohibiting a homeowner from installing a satellite dish in his yard unreasonable? In this case it is." (Id. at p.291, 5 Cal. Rptr. 2d 580.) Thereafter in its opinion, the court stated: "With [the finding of nonvisibility] established, the question becomes whether the ban against a satellite dish that cannot be seen promotes any legitimate goal of the association. It clearly does not. Accordingly, the restriction is unreasonable as a matter of law." (Id. at p.293, 5 Cal. Rptr. 2d 580.)

b. The Standard to be Applied by the Trial Court

The question of whether the pet restriction at issue in the case before us is an enforceable equitable servitude under Civil Code section 1354 is a mixed issue of law and fact which can only be resolved in the context of the particular circumstances of this case. (Portola Hills Community Assn. v. James, supra, 4 Cal. App. 4th at p.293, 5 Cal. Rptr. 2d 580; Bernardo Villas Management Corp. v. Black, supra, 190 Cal. App. 3d at p.154, 235 Cal. Rptr. 509.) In *Portola Hills* and *Bernardo Villas*, the courts did not address the question of law (i.e., the reasonableness of the restrictions being challenged), until the question of fact (the circumstances of the particular homeowners who were challenging the restrictions) was determined.

So also here, the enforceability of the pet restriction will be decided in the trial court after the taking of evidence as to the relevant circumstances of this case. Restrictions in CC & Rs regarding the ownership and possession of pets are reasonable and therefore are enforceable under Civil Code section 1354 when they prohibit conduct which, while otherwise lawful, in fact interferes with, or has a reasonable likelihood of interfering with, the rights of other condominium owners to the peaceful and quiet enjoyment of their property.

Defendants argue that the blanket pet restriction they seek to enforce against plaintiff is reasonable and enforceable because it avoids a situation where they must always take a "wait and see" position on pets and then litigate over pets that are causing problems in the condominium project. We reject this contention. First, it runs contrary to the philosophy of *Portola Hills* and *Bernardo Villas*, which is to judge situations on their own specific facts. Plaintiff's condominium home is her castle and her enjoyment of it should be by the least restrictive means possible, conducive with a harmonious communal living arrangement. Second, if carried to its logical conclusion, defendants' argument could be used to support all-inclusive bans on such diverse things as stereo equipment, social gatherings and visitors between the ages of two and eighteen. We cannot envision the courts finding that blanket restrictions against such things are reasonable; yet it is certainly conceivable that allowing Fluffin, Muffin and Ruffin[37] to live inside plaintiff's condominium will pose less of a threat to the peace and quiet of the parties' communal living arrangement than would stereo equipment, parties or young visitors. . . .

4.   The Cause of Action for Invasion of Privacy

Although some of the allegations in plaintiff's cause of action for invasion of privacy are more properly placed in her cause of action for declaratory relief and others are more properly included in a cause of action for trespass, the cause of action for invasion of privacy does indeed survive a general demurrer because it does state a cause of action. . . .

Plaintiff should have been given an opportunity to revise the invasion of privacy cause of action by limiting it to the allegations regarding defendants' peering into and entering her home. She should also have been given the opportunity to advance these allegations as a basis for a cause of action for trespass. . . .

5.   The Cause of Action for Intentional Infliction of Emotional Distress

To state a cause of action for intentional infliction of emotional distress, the plaintiff must allege conduct by the defendants that is "extreme and outrageous" and that is performed "with the intention of causing, or reckless disregard of the probability of causing, emotional distress." (Cervantez v. J.C. Penney Co. (1979) 24 Cal. 3d 579, 593, 156 Cal. Rptr. 198, 595 P.2d 975.) "Conduct to be outrageous must be so extreme as to exceed all bounds of that usually tolerated in a civilized community. [Citations.]" (Ibid.)

---

37. The Los Angeles Times, in a story entitled Cat Fight, Dec. 24, 1992, at J1, reported that the actual names of the cats are Boo-Boo, Dockers, and Tulip. The Times reported that Ms. Nahrstedt had spent $25,000 in legal fees. "I will not get rid of these cats," she said. "They're my babies. I chose to have cats instead of babies. . . . If they were attacking your children, you'd go out and hire an attorney and do the same thing." — EDS.

In the instant case, the conduct alleged by plaintiff which she claims constitutes an intentional infliction of emotional distress is defendants' assessment of fines against her so as "to force plaintiff to sell her unit at unreasonable prices or alternatively to force plaintiff to remove her cats . . . from the premises," cats which she describes as clean, living inside her condominium only and not constituting a nuisance. We have no trouble concluding, as a matter of law, that this conduct is not so extreme and outrageous as to permit recovery in a cause of action for intentional infliction of emotional distress. (Fuentes v. Perez (1977) 66 Cal. App. 3d 163, 172, 136 Cal. Rptr. 275.) . . .

6. The Cause of Action for Negligent Infliction of Emotional Distress

Unlike a cause of action for intentional infliction of emotional distress, a cause of action for the negligent infliction of emotional distress is not an independent tort but rather is the tort of negligence, involving the usual issues of duty of care, breach of duty, causation and damages. (6 Witkin, Summary of Cal. Law (9th ed. 1988) Torts, §838, p.195.) The totality of plaintiff's complaint shows that her cause of action for negligent infliction of emotional distress is based on defendants' entering plaintiff's home without her permission and on their imposing fines on her and threatening to impose a lien on her home.

Defendants contend they have a duty to enforce the restrictions in the CC & Rs and therefore this cause of action cannot be maintained. But the gist of a cause of action for negligence is that the defendant owes the plaintiff a duty to act carefully when he or she undertakes to act. As persons connected with the enforcement of the CC & Rs, defendants have a duty to plaintiff to enforce the CC & Rs in an appropriate manner. Plaintiff alleges that entering her home, levying fines on her and threatening to impose a lien on her home are inappropriate.

Under Molien v. Kaiser Foundation Hospitals (1980) 27 Cal. 3d 916, 167 Cal. Rptr. 831, 616 P.2d 813, plaintiff is the direct victim of defendants' allegedly negligent enforcement of the CC & Rs. It was reasonably foreseeable that said negligent enforcement of the pet restriction would cause her emotional distress. Plaintiff has stated a cause of action for negligent infliction of emotional distress.

7. The Cause of Action for Invalidation of the Fines . . .

[The court held that the Homeowners Association had authority under the condominium CC & Rs to levy fines only with respect to use of the common areas of the condominium project. It had no authority to levy fines to regulate conduct within the owners' units.]

Disposition

The judgment of dismissal is reversed and, as to Homeowners Association, a writ of mandate shall issue directing the trial court to vacate its order sustaining demurrers without leave to amend and to enter a new and different order. The cause is remanded to the trial court for further proceedings consistent with the views expressed herein. Costs on appeal to plaintiff.

HINZ, J., dissenting.
I respectfully dissent.
. . . The courts should leave the enforcement of covenants and restrictions to the homeowners associations unless there are constitutional principles at stake, enforcement is arbitrary, or the association fails to follow its own procedures. Thus it is appropriate for the courts to have the power to rule on these matters at the demurrer stage.

Among many other tasks, a homeowners association must enforce CC & Rs. Such an association owes a fiduciary duty to members, who can sue the association if it fails to perform its enforcement obligations. (Cohen v. Kite Hill Community Assn. (1983) 142 Cal. App. 3d 642, 651, 191 Cal. Rptr. 209.) As Duffey v. Superior Court (1992) 3 Cal. App. 4th 425, 434, 4 Cal. Rptr. 2d 334 stated, even limited or "small" litigation undertaken pursuant to that enforcement duty can be expensive. The money to pay for such litigation comes from mandatory fees paid by each and every property owner. Not only from the standpoint of an already overburdened court system, but from the standpoint of property owners who rely on the enforcement of CC & Rs when they contracted to buy and as they continue to own and live in their property, it is vital to resolve any litigation stemming from such enforcement as early as possible.[38]

To find otherwise would only encourage prolonged litigation, which would burden both the courts and all parties untenably. (Compare, in a different context involving a member's dispute with a voluntary association, the rule in Berke v. TRI Realtors (1989) 208 Cal. App. 3d 463, 467, 257 Cal. Rptr. 738 regarding the balancing test that arises if an organization's challenged action contravenes its by-laws: whether judicial relief is available depends on the interest in protecting the aggrieved party's rights balanced against the infringement on the organization's autonomy and the burdens on the courts that will result from judicial attempts to settle internal disputes.). . .

Legal rules borrowed from real property principles developed dur-

---

38. The majority's new rule will place a tremendous burden on both the condominium owners and the courts by requiring a trial in virtually every lawsuit over the validity of such restrictions. All the pet owner must do to force a trial under the majority rule is allege the pets are noiseless and are not a nuisance. Suppose a third of the condominium owners want to keep three cats or a dozen cats or the same number of dogs or other pets. Is the result the same? Would each of these instances be another jury trial?

ing feudal times may prove inappropriate tools as this court, in the late 20th century, tries to accommodate competing interests involved in the use of a condominium. (Laguna Royale Owners Assn. v. Darger (1981) 119 Cal. App. 3d 670, 681, 174 Cal. Rptr. 136.) What is true of the law is even more true of metaphor. An Englishman's home may be a castle. Increasingly, however, a Californian's home is a condominium, and I must question the majority opinion's attempt to recast the respondent's incidents of ownership by calling a condominium a "castle." I have never seen a condominium that even remotely resembled a castle. As a frequently quoted portion of the *Laguna Royale Owners Assn.* opinion reasons, condominium living involves increased density, shared and intensified use of common areas and facilities, and a heightened proximity to neighbors. Therefore it necessarily involves the principle that to promote the health, happiness, and peace of mind of the majority of the unit owners, individual unit owners must relinquish a degree of freedom of choice that they might otherwise enjoy in separate, privately owned property. . . .

It does not help the decision of this case for the majority opinion to create fanciful names, not alleged in the complaint, for the owner's three cats. Cat occupancy can create offensive and unpleasant odor, additional sewage, trash, and litter and resulting problems relating to its disposal, the potential for diseases, allergies, and pests that affect neighbors, caterwauling and other noise, and can attract other cats from outside the condominium during mating season. Other difficulties could doubtless lengthen this catalogue of cat problems. It is nonetheless sufficient to make a restriction against cat occupancy "reasonable."

. . . The other condominium residents at Lakeside Village apparently desired pet-free living. Plaintiff consented to that restriction. I see no reason why this reasonable restriction should not be enforced, and would affirm the sustaining of the demurrer.

NOTES

1. If Natore Nahrstedt recovers damages, what is the liability of the property owners association, association officials, and unit owners for paying the damages? What is the personal liability of the board members and officers who authorized the actions against Ms. Nahrstedt?

The result [of the recent cases on association officials' duties] has been a body of law looking superficially like that applied to officials of business corporations. Thus, the judges have imposed upon POA officials a duty of *good faith* and duties of *obedience,* such as the obligation to follow the by laws and other rules of the association. . . . The courts have required the exercise of *reasonable care* in the conduct of association business, by, for example, insisting that the board of directors exercise appropriate supervision over the affairs of the association. . . . Finally, the courts have imposed certain *fiduciary obligations* upon association officials, including limitations on self-dealing, and other obstacles to loyalty. [Robert G. Natelson, Law of Property Owners Associations §10.1 (1989).]

2. A review of cases involving homeowners associations in recent years reveals that the amount of litigation involving condominium homeowners associations is several times greater than the litigation involving associations of owners of detached single-family dwellings. Most of the cases involve suits against the builder for faulty construction,[39] tort suits by a unit owner against the association (burglary, criminal attack, biting by a neighbor's dog),[40] or suits by the association against a member for objectionable activity (unauthorized building extensions, awnings, roof materials, fences, landscaping, satellite dishes, blocking views, tinkering with a car in the driveway, parking on the street instead of in a closed garage).

Here is a sampling of recent cases.

O'Buck v. Cottonwood Village Condominium Association, 750 P.2d 813 (Alaska 1988). The condominium association, responding to a serious problem of roof leakage, removed all television antennas from the roof, repaired the roof for $155,000, prohibited reinstallation of antennas, and made cable television available to the units at $10 per month per set. The O'Bucks, who had four television sets, frequently tuned to different programs, objected primarily because they did not want to pay the cable television monthly charges. The Supreme Court of Alaska held the association rule was reasonable.

"In evaluating the reasonableness of a condominium association rule, it is necessary to balance the importance of the rule's objective against the importance of the interest infringed upon. In a case where a rule seriously curtails an important civil liberty — such as, for example, freedom of expression — we will look with suspicion on the rule and require a compelling justification. The antenna ban in the instant case curtails no significant interests. The only loss suffered is that the O'Bucks and the other owners must now pay a small monthly fee to receive television, and even this cost is offset to a degree by the savings from the lack of need to install and maintain an antenna."

The court also rejected the O'Bucks' claim of an easement that entitled them to install a television antenna on the roof, even though Alaska statutes gave each apartment owner an easement over common areas and the condominium declaration designated the roof as a com-

---

39. See Natelson, supra, §§9.0-9.15.
40. See Eric T. Freyfogle, A Comprehensive Theory of Condominium Tort Liability, 39 U. Fla. L. Rev. 877 (1987); Katherine Rosenberry & Clifford J. Treese, Purchasing Insurance for the Common Interest Community, 27 Wake Forest L. Rev. 397 (1992).

mon area. The court affirmed the lower court's award of $8,000 to the association, to cover 80 percent of the association's legal fees in fighting the O'Bucks.

Trustees of the Prince Condominium Trust v. Prosser, 412 Mass. 723, 592 N.E.2d 1301 (1992). The homeowners association sued to enforce a lien for monthly charges against a unit owner who refused to pay until his claim for loss of an assigned parking space was offset. The court held for the plaintiff and refused to permit the offset. "A system that would tolerate a unit owner's refusal to pay an assessment because the unit owner asserts a grievance, even a seemingly meritorious one, would threaten the financial integrity of the entire condominium operation. For the same reason that taxpayers may not lawfully decline to pay lawfully assessed taxes because of some grievance or claim against the taxing governmental unit, a condominium unit owner may not decline to pay lawful assessments."

Accord, Abbey Park Homeowners v. Bowen, 508 So. 2d 554 (Fla. App. 1987) (association's failure to maintain common areas not a defense in suit to enforce monthly assessment).

Duffey v. Superior Court, 3 Cal. App. 4th 425, 4 Cal. Rptr. 2d 334 (1992). The Duffeys and the Mehrenses, two neighbors of the Bertrams, complained to the homeowners association when the Bertrams proposed to erect a patio cover blocking their ocean views. The association sued for a declaratory judgment, asking the court to determine whether the covenants prohibited the Bertrams' patio cover, joining the Bertrams and the neighbors as parties. The neighbors moved to be dismissed from the case. The court granted their motion.

"Homeowner associations have the responsibility of enforcing a development's declaration of restrictions (Cohen v. Kite Hill Community Assn., 142 Cal. App. 3d 642, 191 Cal. Rptr. 209 (1983) [association could be held liable for failing to enforce architectural standards in CC & Rs]; see also Sproul & Rosenberry, Advising Cal. Condominium and Homeowners Associations (Cont. Ed. Bar 1991), §1.2, p.5). This duty exists independently of what any given group of owners, such as the complaining neighbors in this case, might think or assert. The Duffeys' and the Mehrenses' written objection to the Bertrams' proposed construction is thus quite irrelevant to the question of what the association must do about that construction. If the Bertrams' construction is, indeed, contrary to the CC & Rs, the association would still have the responsibility of trying to prevent it even if the Duffeys and the Mehrenses *favored* it. . . .

"Homeowner associations play an increasingly important role in the daily lives of Californians. It is common knowledge that much of the new housing developed in recent years — including single-family detached dwellings — is subject to CC & Rs enforceable by such associations. Some large homeowner associations have budgets which put them on a par with small cities and towns. In many areas of our state homeowner associations have practically become a 'quasibranch' of municipal government. (Cf. Sproul and Rosenberg, §6.5, p.252 [noting both associations and local governments can 'be responsible for providing services such as road maintenance, street lighting, parks, recreation, and utilities']; see also Cohen v. Kite Hill Community Assn., supra, 142 Cal. App. 3d 642, 652, 191 Cal. Rptr. 209 ['approval of a fence not in conformity with the Declaration is analogous to the administrative award of a zoning variance'].)

"Given this role, it would be incongruous indeed if the expression of opinion to a homeowner association by one neighbor about another neighbor's proposed construction were cause to name the objecting neighbor in a lawsuit. Merely standing up at a homeowners' or board of directors' meeting to argue that one's neighbors' plan to paint their garage door dayglo orange with magenta polka dots is prohibited by the CC & Rs should not land one in a lawsuit. Even a 'small' lawsuit for declaratory relief can be expensive.

"The tactic employed by this homeowner association of naming objecting neighbors in a declaratory relief lawsuit only sows the seeds of destruction of its own declarations. If every neighbor who demands enforcement of the CC & Rs winds up in court, no one will demand enforcement, and landscape and construction standards will effectively cease to exist. It is difficult to imagine a denser pall cast over association governance than the prospect of being named in a lawsuit for simply insisting the association do its job."

David Willman, Woman Faces Fine for Kissing Her Date

L.A. Times, June 16, 1991, at A3

A 51-year-old woman who said she only kissed her date good night outside her condominium has been threatened by her homeowners' association with a fine if she does "bad things" again.

At first, Helen (Kim) Garrett said, she thought the warning letter in her mailbox was a prank. Now, she says, she is angry enough to consider selling or suing.

The "courtesy notice" she received from the owners' association was brief and to the point:

"DESCRIPTION OF VIOLATION: RESIDENT SEEN PARKING IN CIRCULAR DRIVEWAY KISSING AND DOING BAD THINGS FOR OVER 1 HOUR." The association, it warned, would "demand a fine" if it happened again.

But Garrett says she only kissed a man good night in his car.

Garrett, a grandmother and financial consultant, says she grew up near Memphis in what she describes as a "strict Baptist" home. She has lived in her condo for two years and has made California her home for a decade. She considers herself "an educated woman of high moral values."

Representatives of the Town Square association and the owner, Vanco Properties in Long Beach, did not return calls.

Garrett said that on the evening of May 22, she and a friend pulled into the public driveway of her complex and came to an idling stop. She said she leaned to her left, kissed him, opened the door of his vehicle and walked to an indoor elevator. Her friend drove away. It all took no more than a minute.

Still, Garrett says she considers it no laughing matter that the letter was posted publicly at the complex. She says that when she called Vanco Properties she was "given the option" of attending what she understood to be an arbitration to try to get the warning overturned.

"I could go in and let a bunch of people decide whether I can kiss someone good night," Garrett said. "It's ridiculous."

"I feel controlled, I feel watched," she said. "If they can judge my morals, which are not wrong, they can just keep passing rules. It will be like Russia."

10

"Judicial Zoning": Nuisances Private and Public

The law of nuisance has been characterized as a process of "judicial zoning." See J.H. Beuscher & Jerry W. Morrison, Judicial Zoning Through Recent Nuisance Cases, 1955 Wis. L. Rev. 440. The description is inspired by the observation that courts, working within the hospitable boundaries of nuisance law, operate as central administrators of land-use practices; proceeding in an ad hoc (but not unprincipled) way, judges try to resolve land-use conflicts in a manner that accommodates the divergent needs and wants of a given community. Utility, fairness, expectations, and incentives are considered and shaped in an effort to promote constructive patterns of land use for the area in question. Judges strive, in short, to allocate resources justly and efficiently in the absence of private arrangements like servitudes or public controls like zoning, and sometimes despite their presence. So runs the argument behind the characterization. As you read the cases that follow, consider how well they fit the judicial zoning generalization. Consider also the institutional strengths and weaknesses of courts as land-use administrators.

A. An Introduction to the Substantive Law

Morgan v. High Penn Oil Co.
Supreme Court of North Carolina, 1953
238 N.C. 185, 77 S.E.2d 682

Civil action to recover temporary damages for a private nuisance, and to abate such nuisance by injunction.

The salient facts appear in the numbered paragraphs which immediately follow. . . .

2. The land of the plaintiffs is a composite tract, which they acquired by two separate purchases antedating 3 August, 1945. It contains a dwelling-house, a restaurant, and accommodations for thirty-two habitable trailers. The dwelling-house existed at the time of the purchases of the plaintiffs, and has been occupied by them as

their home since 3 August, 1945. The plaintiffs constructed the restaurant and the trailer accommodations immediately after they established their residence on the premises, and have been renting these improvements since their completion to third persons. They have been supplementing their income from these sources by taking lodgers in their dwelling. . . .

5. The High Penn Oil Company operated [an] oil refinery at virtually all times between 10 October, 1950, and the date of the rendition of the judgement in this action. . . .

9. The oil refinery is approximately 1,000 feet from the dwelling of the plaintiffs.

10. These structures are situated within a radius of one mile of the oil refinery: a church; at least twenty-nine private dwellings; four tourist and trailer camps; a grocery store; two restaurants; a nursery appropriated to the propagation of young trees, shrubs, and plants; three motor vehicle service stations; two motor vehicle repair shops; a railroad track; the terminus of a gasoline pipe line; numerous large storage tanks capable of storing sixty million gallons of gasoline; and the headquarters of at least four motor truck companies engaged in the transportation of petroleum products and other property for hire. Railway tank cars and motor tank trucks are filled with gasoline at the storage tanks for conveyance to various places at virtually all hours of the day and night. . . .

16. The evidence of the plaintiffs tended to show that for some hours on two or three different days during each week of its operation by the High Penn Oil Company, the oil refinery emitted nauseating gases and odors in great quantities; that the nauseating gases and odors invaded the nine acres owned by the plaintiffs and the other lands located within "a mile and three-quarters or two miles" of the oil refinery in such amounts and in such densities as to render persons of ordinary sensitiveness uncomfortable and sick; that the operation of the oil refinery thus substantially impaired the use and enjoyment of the nine acres by the plaintiffs and their renters; and that the defendants failed to put an end to the atmospheric pollution arising out of the operation of the oil refinery after notice and demand from the plaintiffs to abate it. The evidence of the plaintiffs tended to show, moreover, that the oil refinery was the only agency discharging gases or odors in annoying quantities into the air in the Friendship section. . . .

18. [The jury found the refinery to be a nuisance and set damages at $2,500. The trial judge entered a judgment to that effect and further enjoined the defendant from continuing the nuisance. The defendant appealed.]

ERVIN, J.[1] . . . The High Penn Oil Company contends that the evi-

___

1. "Ervin, J." refers to Sam J. Ervin, Jr. In 1954, a year after the decision in the *Morgan* case, Sam Ervin was elected to the U.S. Senate; 20 years after that he presided over the Senate Select Committee on Presidential Campaign Activities. "[T]o millions of Americans he was the hero of the unfolding drama of the Watergate affair that led, even-

dence is not sufficient to establish either an actionable or an abatable private nuisance. This contention rests on a twofold argument somewhat alternative in character. The High Penn Oil Company asserts primarily that private nuisances are classified as nuisances *per se* or at law, and nuisance *per accidens* or in fact; that when one carries on an oil refinery upon premises in his rightful occupation, he conducts a lawful enterprise, and for that reason does not maintain a nuisance *per se* or at law; that in such case the oil refinery can constitute a nuisance *per accidens* or in fact to the owner of neighboring land if, and only if, it is constructed or operated in a negligent manner; that there was no testimony at the trial tending to show that the oil refinery was constructed or operated in a negligent manner; and that consequently the evidence does not suffice to establish the existence of either an actionable or an abatable private nuisance. The High Penn Oil Company insists secondarily that the plaintiffs in a civil action can recover only on the case presented by their complaint; that the complaint in the instant action states a cause of action based solely on negligence; that there was no testimony at the trial indicating that the oil refinery was constructed or operated in a negligent manner; and that consequently the evidence is not sufficient to warrant the relief sought and obtained by the plaintiffs, even though it may be ample to establish a nuisance.

The case on appeal discloses some substantial reasons for contesting the soundness of the thesis of the High Penn Oil Company that there was no testimony at the trial tending to show that the oil refinery was constructed or operated in a negligent manner. Even expert witnesses for the defendants testified in substance on cross-examination that the oil refinery would not emit gases or odors in annoying quantities if it were "operated properly." We would be compelled, however, to reject the argument of the High Penn Oil Company on the present aspect of the appeal even if we should accept at face value its thesis that there was no testimony at the trial tending to show that the oil refinery was constructed or operated in a negligent manner.

The High Penn Oil Company asserts with complete correctness that private nuisances may be classified as nuisances *per se* or at law, and nuisances *per accidens* or in fact. A nuisance *per se* or at law is an act, occupation, or structure which is a nuisance at all times and under any circumstances, regardless of location or surroundings. . . . Nuisances *per accidens* or in fact are those which become nuisances by reason of their location, or by reason of the manner in which they are constructed, maintained, or operated. . . . The High Penn Oil Company also asserts with complete correctness that an oil refinery is a lawful enterprise and for that reason cannot be a nuisance *per se* or at law. . . . The High Penn

---

tually, to the resignation of President Nixon in 1974." N.Y. Times, Apr. 24, 1985, at B12 (obituary).

Oil Company falls into error, however, when it takes the position that an oil refinery cannot become a nuisance *per accidens* or in fact unless it is constructed or operated in a negligent manner.

Negligence and nuisance are distinct fields of tort liability. . . . While the same act or omission may constitute negligence and also give rise to a private nuisance *per accidens* or in fact, and thus the two torts may coexist and be practically inseparable, a private nuisance *per accidens* or in fact may be created or maintained without negligence. . . . Most private nuisances *per accidens* or in fact are intentionally created or maintained, and are redressed by the courts without allegation or proof of negligence. . . .

The law of private nuisance rests on the concept embodied in the ancient legal maxim *Sic utere tuo ut alienum non laedas,* meaning, in essence, that every person should so use his own property as not to injure that of another. . . . As a consequence, a private nuisance exists in a legal sense when one makes an improper use of his own property and in that way injures the land or some incorporeal right of one's neighbor. . . .

Much confusion exists in respect to the legal basis of liability in the law of private nuisance because of the deplorable tendency of the courts to call everything a nuisance, and let it go at that. . . . The confusion on this score vanishes in large part, however, when proper heed is paid to the sound propositions that private nuisance is a field of tort liability rather than a single type of tortious conduct; that the feature which gives unity to this field of tort liability is the interest invaded, namely, the interest in the use and enjoyment of land; that any substantial nontrespassory invasion of another's interest in the private use and enjoyment of land by any type of liability forming conduct is a private nuisance; that the invasion which subjects a person to liability for private nuisance may be either intentional or unintentional; that a person is subject to liability for an intentional invasion when his conduct is unreasonable under the circumstances of the particular case; and that a person is subject to liability for an unintentional invasion when his conduct is negligent, reckless or ultrahazardous. See Scope and Introduction Note to Chapter 40, American Law Institute's Restatement of the Law of Torts. . . .

An invasion of another's interest in the use and enjoyment of land is intentional in the law of private nuisance when the person whose conduct is in question as a basis for liability acts for the purpose of causing it, or knows that it is resulting from his conduct, or knows that it is substantially certain to result from his conduct. Restatement of the Law of Torts, section 825. . . . A person who intentionally creates or maintains a private nuisance is liable for the resulting injury to others regardless of the degree of care or skill exercised by him to avoid such injury. . . . One of America's greatest jurists, the late Benjamin N. Cardozo, made this illuminating observation on this aspect of the law:

Nuisance as a concept of the law has more meanings than one. The primary meaning does not involve the element of negligence as one of its essential factors. One acts sometimes at one's peril. In such circumstances, the duty to desist is absolute whenever conduct, if persisted in, brings damage to another. Illustrations are abundant. One who emits noxious fumes or gases day by day in the running of his factory may be liable to his neighbor though he has taken all available precautions. He is not to do such things at all, whether he is negligent or careful. [McFarlane v. City of Niagara Falls, 247 N.Y. 340, 160 N.E. 391.]

When the evidence is interpreted in the light most favorable to the plaintiffs, it suffices to support a finding that in operating the oil refinery the High Penn Oil Company intentionally and unreasonably caused noxious gases and odors to escape onto the nine acres of the plaintiffs to such a degree as to impair in a substantial manner the plaintiffs' use and enjoyment of their land. This being so, the evidence is ample to establish the existence of an actionable private nuisance, entitling the plaintiffs to recover temporary damages from the High Penn Oil Company. . . .

When the evidence is taken in the light most favorable to the plaintiffs, it also suffices to warrant the additional inferences that the High Penn Oil Company intends to operate the oil refinery in the future in the same manner as in the past; that if it is permitted to carry this intent into effect, the High Penn Oil Company will hereafter cast noxious gases and odors onto the nine acres of the plaintiffs with such recurring frequency and in such annoying density as to inflict irreparable injury upon the plaintiffs in the use and enjoyment of their home and their other adjacent properties; and that the issuance of an appropriate injunction is necessary to protect the plaintiffs against the threatened irreparable injury. This being true, the evidence is ample to establish the existence of an abatable private nuisance, entitling the plaintiffs to such mandatory or prohibitory injunctive relief as may be required to prevent the High Penn Oil Company from continuing the nuisance. . . .

The contention of the High Penn Oil Company that the complaint states a cause of action based solely on negligence is untenable. To be sure, the plaintiffs assert that the defendants were "negligent and careless" in specified particulars in constructing and operating the oil refinery. When the complaint is construed as a whole, however, it alleges facts which show a private nuisance resulting from an intentional and unreasonable invasion of the plaintiffs' interest in the use and enjoyment of their land. . . .

For the reasons given, the evidence is sufficient to withstand the motion of the High Penn Oil Company for a compulsory nonsuit. . . .

NOTES AND QUESTIONS

1. *Private and public nuisance.* A private nuisance arises from unreasonable interference with the use and enjoyment of land. A public nuisance is different — an act that interferes with general community interests or the comfort of the public at large. Air pollution, loud noises, houses of prostitution, public gaming, harboring vicious animals, and storing dangerous explosives could all be public nuisances (they could also be private nuisances if they interfered with the use and enjoyment of land). At English common law, public nuisances were crimes subject to prosecution. Common law crimes no longer exist in the United States, but English history introduced a peculiarity into public nuisance law that persists today. We take it up later.

2. *The language of nuisance.* Nuisance law has been littered with Latin phrases, which thankfully are dying away. Their main purpose was probably to lend an air of rigor and precision to a seeming morass of cases.

> There is perhaps no more impenetrable jungle in the entire law than that which surrounds the word "nuisance." It has meant all things to all people and has been applied indiscriminately to everything from an alarming advertisement to a cockroach baked in a pie. There is general agreement that it is incapable of any exact or comprehensive definition. Few terms have afforded so excellent an illustration of the familiar tendency of the courts to seize upon a catchword as a substitute for any analysis of a problem; the defendant's interference with the plaintiff's interests is characterized as a "nuisance," and there is nothing more to be said. [William L. Prosser & W. Page Keeton, The Law of Torts 616-617 (5th ed. 1984).]

The opinion in the *Morgan* case shares this lament but manages nevertheless to substitute many catchwords for a little analysis. Notice, for example, the reference to nuisances *per se* and *per accidens*. If nuisance *per se* (or absolute nuisance) means anything, it means liability no matter how reasonable the defendant's conduct. That generalization, though, is not very useful. Abnormal and unduly hazardous activities (such as storage of explosives) have been held nuisances *per se*, as have activities (like a rendering plant in the middle of a town) unsuited to their surroundings — and in both these general instances questions of reasonableness are obviously involved. Activities designated nuisances by statute are also often called nuisances *per se*, and in these instances the phrase is more concrete: The legislative designation might be regarded as conclusive, foreclosing any consideration of reasonableness. Perhaps it is this restricted meaning that the opinion in *Morgan* contemplated in implying that nuisances *per se* are unlawful enterprises. Such instances aside, the phrase *nuisance per se* seems to be conclusory, empty of analytic content. This hardly means the phrase is insignificant. A conclusion (for whatever reason) that an activity is an absolute nuisance will usually result in liability no matter how careful the defendant has been, so long as the activity in question has interfered with the use and enjoyment of the plaintiff's land.

The opinion in *Morgan* makes reference to another phrase of nuisance law — *Sic utere tuo ut alienum non laedes.* Can one take seriously the court's suggestion that the concept "embodied" in this language supports the entire law of private nuisance? Could the language possibly help the court in determining the rights of plaintiff and defendant? Black's Law Dictionary, after translating the *sic utere* apothegm, quotes some comments that have been made about it: "Mere verbiage"; "No help to decision"; "Utterly useless as a legal maxim"; "It is a mere begging of the question; it assumes the very point in controversy." Black's Law Dictionary (rev. ed. 1968).[2] See also 2 John Austin's Jurisprudence 795, 829 (Robert Campbell 3d ed. 1869) ("A party may damage the property of another where the law permits; and he may not where the law prohibits; so that the maxim can never be applied till the law is ascertained; and, when it is, the maxim is superfluous.").

Suppose *A* and *B*, neighbors, are engaged in conflicting land uses, such that *A*'s use interferes with *B*'s use. If a court, for reasons suggested by the *sic utere* maxim, enjoins *A* at *B*'s behest, does not *B*'s use now interfere with *A*'s? Given this sort of interaction, what principle(s) of resolution might be chosen? Compare Ronald Coase, The Problem of Social Cost, 3 J.L. & Econ. 1 (1960), with Richard A. Epstein, Nuisance Law: Corrective Justice and Its Utilitarian Constraints, 8 J. Legal Stud. 49 (1979). See also page 53.

3. *Some history.* Commentators attribute much of the vagueness and confusion of nuisance law to its origins. What we today call the law of private nuisance developed in England as a means of redress for activities conducted solely on the defendant's land that nevertheless interfered with the use and enjoyment of plaintiff's land. (Thus a famous early nuisance suit — William Aldred's Case, 9 Co. Rep. 57b, 77 Eng. Rep. 816 (K.B. 1611) — grew out of Aldred's claim that the hogsty of his neighbor, one Benton, caused "unhealthy odors . . . such that Aldred . . . could not come and go without being subjected to continuous annoyance. . . ." Judgment for plaintiff.) At about the same time, however, the law of public nuisance was also developing in England, and, as mentioned above, it included all sorts of annoyances to the community at large. Often these had no relation whatsoever to interferences with land use; still they were called nuisances, and it was easy enough for less than careful judges to begin labeling any unpleasant thing a nuisance even

---

2. Unhappily, subsequent editions of Black's omit the quotations, no doubt to make room for all the new words that have entered the legal lexicon.

though it was neither an offense against the public nor an interference with use and enjoyment of land. Hence the confusion. That a public nuisance can also be a private nuisance only makes matters worse. Still, properly speaking, a private nuisance is an unreasonable interference with use and enjoyment of land, and a public nuisance an invasion of public rights. See Prosser & Keeton, supra, at 616-619.

The history of nuisance law — its social as opposed to doctrinal history — sheds still some other light on our concerns in this chapter. In its formative years — medieval times in England — nuisance law operated to protect the economic status quo: Activities on one's property were permitted only to the extent that they did not impair a neighbor's use and enjoyment, and impairment was measured in the terms of a rural, conservative society. The notion of reciprocal, conflicting interests in the use of resources, so common to us today, was foreign to the early English mind. Nuisance, reflecting this, worked as a check on economic expansion, especially so in that liability was strict: The gravity of the harm to the plaintiff was an issue, but not the reasonableness of the defendant's conduct. *Sic utere tuo* . . . was taken in its most literal sense.

It is probably the case that England and the law of nuisance alike could survive in such a rigid regimen because pressures for economic (especially industrial) growth were small relative to the amount of space available. Even in these early times, nuisance had a zoning function; acting under it, judges ordered offensive trades to the outskirts of towns and cities where they would cause less harm. But the Industrial Revolution changed the balance of pressure and space. It became impossible to accommodate economic growth simply by sending industries elsewhere; it also became important — this was the changing social impulse — to accommodate, indeed to encourage, industrialization. The law of nuisance helped this happen, among other ways, by developing a standard of reasonableness that considered not only the injury to the plaintiff but the social utility of the defendant's activity as well. By mid-nineteenth century, English courts were reflecting this new approach. One could still see their work as judicial zoning, but zoning that took account of new circumstances. People in industrial locales could not assert extreme rights without regard to the nature of the area and the needs of business. What was a nuisance in one place might not be in another.

This, at least, is one view. For interesting and somewhat varying accounts of the social history of nuisance law in England, see Joel F. Brenner, Nuisance Law and the Industrial Revolution, 3 J. Legal Stud. 403 (1974); John P. McLaren, Nuisance Law and the Industrial Revolution — Some Lessons from Social History, 3 Oxford J. Legal Stud. 155 (1983). An essay that explores similar themes in the American setting, and from the standpoint of ideology and intellectual history, is Robert G. Bone, Normative Theory and Legal Doctrine in American Nuisance Law: 1850 to 1920, 59 S. Cal. L. Rev. 1101 (1986).

4. *Unreasonableness.* As the foregoing discussion suggests, issues of "unreasonableness" have come to play an important role in the law of nuisance. Precisely what that role amounts to, however, is obscure. The opinion in *Morgan* states the textbook rules: An interference with use and enjoyment of land, in order to give rise to liability, must be substantial; it must also be *either* intentional and unreasonable, *or* the unintentional result of negligent, reckless, or abnormally dangerous activity. See Restatement (Second) of Torts §§821F, 822 (1979).

Regarding the question of unreasonableness, the case of unintentional nuisance seems clear enough. Liability here is based on traditional tort categories — negligence, recklessness, abnormally dangerous activities — all of which "embody in some degree the concept of unreasonableness." Id. §821B, Comment e, at 90. The intentional nuisance is another matter, and an important one given that most modern-day nuisances are intentional in the sense that the *Morgan* case and the Restatement use that term. Thus situations giving rise to allegations of nuisance today typically involve interference with use and enjoyment of land — from air and water pollution, noise, odors, vibrations, flooding, excessive light (or inadequate light) — that continues over time and is known by the defendant to result from its activities. Despite the presence of intent in these instances, nuisance liability arises only if the resulting interference is substantial and unreasonable.

What does *unreasonable* mean in this context of an intentional tort? On one view, the term has a function here that is quite different from the role it plays in the law of negligence. Rather than inviting a comparison of whether the social beliefs of the defendant's conduct outweigh its expected costs, the relevant inquiry is said to concern the *level* of interference that results from the conduct — particularly, whether the interference crosses some threshold that marks the point of liability. For example, in Jost v. Dairyland Power Coop., 45 Wis. 2d 164, 172 N.W.2d 647 (1969), the court upheld the exclusion of evidence offered by the defendant to show that the utility of its operations outweighed the gravity of the harm caused to the plaintiffs. Of the defendant's operation, a power plant, the court said, "Whether its economic or social importance dwarfed the claim of a small farmer is of no consequence in this lawsuit." 45 Wis. 2d at 176, 172 N.W.2d at 653.

The view of the *Jost* case is not uniformly followed, a fact revealed by the Restatement's position that, to determine unreasonableness in a case of intentional nuisance, the court is to consider whether "the gravity of the harm outweighs the utility of the actor's conduct. . . ." Restatement (Second) of Torts, supra, §826(1). See also id. §827 (factors relevant to gravity of the harm are the extent and character of the harm, the social value of the plaintiff's use, its suitability to the locality in question, and the burden on the plaintiff of avoiding the harm); §828 (factors relevant to utility of the actor's conduct are its social value, its suitability to the locality in question, and the impracticality of the defendant preventing the harm). Do not these considerations suggest essentially a negligence calculus? The Restatement seems to think so. See id. §822, Comment k, at 114-115.

Which view of unreasonableness did the court in *Morgan* adopt?

5. *More on unreasonableness: trespass compared.* Typically, an intentional tort results in liability without regard to the amount of harm or the reasonableness of the activity causing it. Trespass, involving a *physical invasion* of land, is a case in point. While liability for unintentional trespass is virtually identical to that for unintentional nuisance,[3] the two torts differ markedly if the element of intent is present. In such an instance, trespass is treated like the other intentional torts; nuisance, on the other hand, is usually subjected to inquiries about reasonableness and amount of harm. Thus, unless the plaintiff can show a physical invasion by a tangible thing (that is, a trespass), the defendant can escape liability for intentional conduct on grounds of reasonableness or amount of harm that would be irrelevant if there has been a physical invasion by a tangible thing. This seems anomalous. Is there any sense to a system of rules that treats the intentional release of contaminated water onto neighboring land one way (trespass) and the intentional release of polluting gases another way (nuisance)? Some torts scholars have thought not, and at their urging the Restatement added a provision that an intentional invasion is "unreasonable" for purposes of nuisance law if, (1) as before, the gravity of the harm caused outweighs the utility of the actor's conduct; *or* if, (2) alternatively, "the harm caused by the conduct is serious and the financial burden of compensating for this and similar harm to others would not make the continuation of the conduct not feasible." Restatement (Second) of Torts, supra, §826(b). See also id. §829A ("an intentional invasion of another's interest in the use and enjoyment of land is unreasonable if the harm resulting from the invasion is severe and greater than the other should be required to bear without compensation"). Is alternative (2) a restatement of the threshold-level

---

3. See Restatement (Second) of Torts §165 (1965):

> One who recklessly or negligently, or as a result of an abnormally dangerous activity, enters land in the possession of another or causes a thing or third person so to enter is subject to liability to the possessor if, but only if, his presence or the presence of the thing or the third person upon the land causes harm to the land, to the possessor, or to a thing or a third person in whose security the possessor has a legally protected interest.

See also Restatement (Second) of Torts, supra, §821D, Comment e, at 102 (commenting on the similarity of the two torts). Since a physical invasion — e.g., by polluted water — can also interfere with use and enjoyment of land and thus be a nuisance, the choice of theory with regard to unintentional conduct is usually a matter of indifference, statutes of limitations and variations in the interest protected aside. See W. Page Keeton, Trespass, Nuisance, and Strict Liability, 59 Colum. L. Rev. 457, 465, 474 (1959).

test of liability? Do the remedies available to a plaintiff differ under the two alternatives? See Jeff L. Lewin, Compensated Injunctions and the Evolution of Nuisance Law, 71 Iowa L. Rev. 775, 779-785 (1986).

Why should an activity that causes serious harm be excused from liability under alternative (2) if the obligation to pay would make continuation of the activity "not feasible"? Why should it be excused under alternative (1) simply because the utility of the conduct in question outweighs the harm it causes?

Section 826(b) of the Restatement moves intentional nuisance in the doctrinal direction of intentional trespass, though still there are differences. (Do you see them?) At times one finds a court taking the opposite approach, treating an intentional trespass like an intentional nuisance. A case in point is Martin v. Reynolds Metals Co., 221 Or. 86, 342 P.2d 790 (1959), cert. denied, 362 U.S. 918 (1960). The plaintiffs in *Martin* were cattle ranchers who alleged that their herds were poisoned by fumes from the defendant's aluminum plant. The trial court found the defendant liable on a *trespass* theory; on appeal the defendant argued that trespass was inappropriate because there had been no physical invasion of the plaintiffs' land. The court rejected the argument, choosing "in this atomic age" to define a trespass "as any intrusion which invades the possessor's protected interest in exclusive possession, whether that intrusion is by visible or invisible pieces of matter or by energy which can be measured only by the mathematical language of the physicist." 221 Or. at 93-94, 342 P.2d at 793-794. But then, having found an intentional trespass, the court went on to apply a balancing test of reasonableness in order to determine liability. Trespass and nuisance were harmonized, but by subjecting both to the utilitarian calculus of intentional nuisance. Compare Wilson v. Interlake Steel Co., 32 Cal. 3d 229, 649 P.2d 922, 185 Cal. Rptr. 280 (1982), holding that excessive noise alone will not support a trespass action absent some kind of physical invasion or physical damage to property. Intangible intrusions, the court said, must be approached on a nuisance theory. See generally Annot., 2 A.L.R.4th 1054 (1980).

As anomalous as it may at first seem, might the trespass-nuisance dichotomy in fact be sensible — at least as to the typical trespass (where A enters B's land) and the typical nuisance (where pollution, say, from A's operations interferes with neighbors B, C, D, . . . N)? Is there a way to generalize the difference between the typical fact settings of the two torts, so as to arrive at better doctrine? See Thomas W. Merrill, Trespass, Nuisance, and the Costs of Determining Property Rights, 14 J. Legal Stud. 13 (1985).

The questions just raised are closely related to issues concerning appropriate remedies in nuisance cases, a matter considered in the next section of this chapter.

PROBLEMS

In which of the following situations would defendant be liable?

1. Defendant operates a halfway house for parolees and prisoners; the purpose of the operation is to ease the painful and difficult transition from incarceration to freedom. Defendant tries, although not always with success, to exclude from residency people with records of sex and drug offenses. Plaintiffs establish that since the halfway house began operations, property values in the area have declined and neighbors have suffered fear and apprehension. See Arkansas Release Guidance Found. v. Needler, 252 Ark. 194, 477 S.W.2d 821 (1972); Nicholson v. Connecticut Halfway House, 153 Conn. 507, 218 A.2d 383 (1966); Annot., 21 A.L.R.3d 1058 (1968).

2. Defendant operates an amusement park located near plaintiff's drive-in theater. Nighttime operations of the park, bright lights in particular, interfere with use of the drive-in. See Amphitheaters, Inc. v. Portland Meadows, 184 Or. 336, 198 P.2d 847 (1948).

3. Defendant, the next-door neighbor of plaintiff, builds a high fence on his property that obstructs plaintiff's view and reduces the light and air her home receives. Defendant's motive in building and maintaining the fence is pure spite. See Hornsby v. Smith, 191 Ga. 491, 13 S.E.2d 20 (1941); Annot., 133 A.L.R. 691 (1941). Suppose plaintiff's objection to the fence is simply that it is ugly. See Haehlen v. Wilson, 11 Cal. App. 2d 437, 54 P.2d 62 (1936). Suppose the problem is that the fence cuts off the sunlight from plaintiff's solar collector. See Sher v. Leiderman, 181 Cal. App. 3d 867, 226 Cal. Rptr. 698 (1986); Prah v. Maretti, 108 Wis. 2d 223, 321 N.W.2d 182 (1982); Judith Alden, Declaring Solar Access Interference a Private Nuisance, 10 Temp. Envtl. L. & Tech. J. 93 (1991).

4. Defendant keeps wrecked automobiles, scrap metal, and rubbish on his property, much to the dismay of his neighbors. See Allison v. Smith, 695 P.2d 791 (Colo. Ct. App. 1984); Ness v. Albert, 665 S.W.2d 1 (Mo. Ct. App. 1983); George P. Smith II & Griffin W. Fernandez, The Price of Beauty: An Economic Approach to Aesthetic Nuisance, 15 Harv. Envtl. L. Rev. 53 (1991).

NOTE: LATERAL AND SUBJACENT SUPPORT

From the perspective of property, the law of private nuisance is regarded as defining one of a number of so-called rights incident to land ownership; other rights commonly placed in the category are freedom from trespass, water rights, and the right to support. See, e.g., 6A American Law of Property (1954 & Supp. 1977). Trespass was touched upon above (see Note 5, page 960), and we introduced the law of water rights in Chapter 1, Note 2, page 40. The subject here is support, lateral and subjacent. Our brief summary is drawn from 5 Richard R. Powell, The Law of Real Property ch. 63 (rev. ed. 1992).

Lateral support refers to that provided one piece of land by the parcels of land surrounding it; subjacent support refers to support from underneath as opposed to the sides. The common law right of lateral support imposes a duty on neighboring land to provide the support that the subject parcel would need and receive under *natural* conditions; ordinarily, then, there is no right to support of *structures* on the land. A cause of action for interference with the right to lateral support does not arise until subsidence actually occurs or is threatened, and then it runs against the excavator (who may, of course, be a predecessor of the present possessor). Liability is absolute; negligence need not be shown. If, however, the supported land had been built upon in such a way that subsidence would not have occurred but for the improvements, there is no liability without negligence, at least so long as the excavator gives notice of his plans. Generally speaking, there is also no liability, absent negligence, if subsidence of improved or unimproved land is shown to have been caused by withdrawal of fluids (e.g., groundwater) or their release as a result of excavation. And see footnote 21 on page 40.

The right of lateral support can be waived; it can also be expressly expanded, as by grant of a right to additional support. Moreover, a number of jurisdictions have statutes that enlarge or otherwise modify the common law right, in recognition of its unsuitability to modern, dense, high-rise building practices.

Issues of subjacent support arise when one person owns surface rights and another person owns some kind of subsurface rights, such as a mineral interest. The situation is analogous to that of lateral support, and the law pretty much tracks that outlined above.

Could problems of lateral and subjacent support be handled satisfactorily simply through application of nuisance law? Are there any fundamental differences in the bodies of doctrine? Cf. Richard A. Epstein, Nuisance Law: Corrective Justice and Its Utilitarian Constraints, 8 J. Legal Stud. 49, 94-96 (1979).

B. Remedies (and More on the Substantive Law)

Estancias Dallas Corp. v. Schultz
Court of Civil Appeals of Texas, 1973
500 S.W.2d 217

STEPHENSON, J. This is an appeal from an order of the trial court granting a permanent injunction. Trial was by jury and judgment was rendered upon the jury verdict. The parties will be referred to here as they were in the trial court.

Plaintiffs, Thad Schultz and wife, brought this suit asking that defendant, Estancias Dallas Corporation, be permanently enjoined from operating the air conditioning equipment and tower on the property next to plaintiffs' residence. The jury found: that the noise emitted solely from defendant's air conditioning equipment constitutes a nuisance; that the nuisance began May 1, 1969; that it is permanent; that the nuisance has been continuous since it began; that Mrs. Schultz has been damaged $9000 and Thad Schultz $1000, considering material personal discomfort, inconvenience, annoyance and impairment of health as the elements of damages. The jury failed to find that the nuisance proximately caused material personal discomfort, inconvenience, annoyance, and impairment of health to either plaintiff. The jury also failed to find that there was any unreasonable delay by plaintiffs in calling the nuisance to the attention of the defendant.

Defendant's first two points of error, briefed together, are that the trial court erred in granting the injunction because plaintiffs failed to secure a jury finding that the nuisance in question was a proximate cause of their alleged discomfort and because the trial court failed to balance the equities in its favor.

We proceed to consider first the matter as to balancing the equities. Even though this matter has arisen many times, we have found little in-depth writing on the subject. The case cited most frequently in this state is Storey v. Central Hide & Rendering Co., 148 Tex. 509, 226 S.W.2d 615 (1950). The rule of law was clearly established in this case that even though a jury finds facts constituting a nuisance, it was held that there should be a balancing of equities in order to determine if an injunction should be granted. The Supreme Court then stated certain guidelines for the trial courts to follow in making such determinations by quoting as follows from 31 Tex. Jur. §35 Nuisances:

> According to the doctrine of "comparative injury" or "balancing of equities" the court will consider the injury which may result to the defendant and the public by granting the injunction as well as the injury to be sustained by the complainant if the writ be denied. If the court finds that the injury to the

complainant is slight in comparison to the injury caused the defendant and the public by enjoining the nuisance, relief will ordinarily be refused. It has been pointed out that the cases in which a nuisance is permitted to exist under this doctrine are based on the stern rule of necessity rather than on the right of the author of the nuisance to work a hurt, or injury to his neighbor. The necessity of others may compel the injured party to seek relief by way of an action at law for damages rather than by a suit in equity to abate the nuisance.

"Some one must suffer these inconveniences rather than that the public interest should suffer. . . . These conflicting interests call for a solution of the question by the application of the broad principles of right and justice, leaving the individual to his remedy by compensation and maintaining the public interests intact; this works hardships on the individual, but they are incident to civilization with its physical developments, demanding more and more the means of rapid transportation of persons and property."

On the other hand, an injunction may issue where the injury to the opposing party and the public is slight or disproportionate to the injury suffered by the complainant. [226 S.W.2d at 618-619.] . . .

There is no specific mention in the judgment that the trial court balanced the equities. However, that question was raised by the pleadings, evidence was heard, and there is an implied finding that the trial court balanced the equities in favor of plaintiffs by entering the judgment granting the injunction. We do not find that the trial court abused its discretion in balancing the equities in favor of plaintiffs.

It is significant that the Supreme Court of Texas in the *Storey* case, supra, placed great emphasis upon public interest. Also, in all of the other cases cited above, the appellate courts in their opinions refer to the benefit to the public generally in permitting a nuisance to continue through the balancing of equities. We find little or no testimony in the record before us reflecting benefit to the public generally. There is no evidence that there is a shortage of apartments in the City of Houston and that the public would suffer by having no place to live.

Our record shows that this apartment complex was completed about March or April of 1969 with about 155 rentable apartments in eight buildings. The air conditioning unit complained of here served the entire complex. This unit is located at the back side of defendant's property, about five and one-half feet from plaintiffs' property line, about fifty-five feet from plaintiffs' back door, and about seventy feet from plaintiffs' bedroom. According to much of the testimony, the unit sounds like a jet airplane or helicopter. The plaintiffs testified: That this was a quiet neighborhood before these apartments were constructed. That they can no longer do any entertaining in their backyard because of the noise. That they cannot carry on a normal conversation in their home with all their doors and windows closed. That the noise interferes with their sleep at night. Several of the neighbors gave similar testimony.

Plaintiffs testified that the value of their land before was $25,000 and $10,000 after the noise began. One of the neighbors, a real estate broker, placed the value at $25,000 before and $12,500 after. A witness who qualified an an expert metallurgical consultant testified as to the results of tests made at various points as to the sound factors in decibels before and after defendant made changes in an effort to reduce the noise.

A witness testified: That he was the original owner of the apartments. That it cost about $80,000 to construct this air conditioning system and that separate units for the eight buildings would have cost $40,000 more. That it would now cost $150,000 to $200,000 to change to that system. That these apartments could not be rented without air conditioning.

Applying the rules of law set forth above in the quotation from the *Storey* case, supra (226 S.W.2d at 619), the nuisance in this case will not be permitted to exist " 'based on the stern rule of necessity rather than on the right of the author of the nuisance to work a hurt, or injury to his neighbor.' " There is not evidence before us to indicate the " 'necessity of others . . . compel[s] the injured party to seek relief by way of an action at law for damages rather than by a suit in equity to abate the nuisance.' " Furthermore, although plaintiffs had a count in their pleading seeking damages, in response to a motion made by defendant, the court forced plaintiffs to elect at the close of their evidence. Thus, defendant's own trial tactics prevented the development of a full record upon which we could predicate the doctrine of balancing the equities.

Plaintiffs were not required to recover damages for a temporary nuisance, that is, for the time when the nuisance began until the date of the trial, in order to secure a permanent injunction. They were entitled to such injunction based upon the affirmative answers given by the jury as set out above. The failure on the part of the jury to give an affirmative answer to the proximate cause issues related to the damage issues or to a temporary nuisance and did not alter the situation. . . .

Affirmed.

NOTES AND QUESTIONS

1. Allegations of nuisance based on air-conditioning noise are not uncommon, judging by the collection of cases in Annot., 79 A.L.R.3d 320 (1977). As Havelock Ellis put it, "what we call 'Progress' is the exchange of one Nuisance for another Nuisance." Havelock Ellis, Impressions and Comments 5 (1914).

2. Why was a nuisance found in the *Estancias* case? The plaintiffs had suffered past damages — up to the date of trial — of $10,000

($9,000 damage to Mrs. Schultz, $1,000 to Thad Schultz). As to future damages, if the air-conditioning noise were allowed to continue presumably these were reflected ("capitalized") in the $12,500 to $15,000 reduction in property value suggested by the evidence. The defendant had tried, unsuccessfully, to abate the air-conditioning noise. If a quiet system (separate air-conditioning units for each apartment) had been installed at the time the defendant's apartment building was originally constructed, it would have cost an additional $40,000; to change to such a system later would cost at least $150,000. The apartments could not be rented without air conditioning.

Do these numbers show that the utility of the defendant's conduct outweighed the gravity of the harm to the plaintiffs? Or might it be that the apartment building simply should not have been built in this neighborhood? Suppose the area were zoned for apartments. Should that matter? See Note, Zoning Ordinances and Common-Law Nuisance, 16 Syracuse L. Rev. 860 (1965).

3. Do you find credible the high costs of noise abatement suggested by the defendant's evidence in the *Estancias* case? In any event, why not simply limit the plaintiffs' remedy, and the defendant's liability, to damages? Presumably the defendant would then, as to the future, abate the noise if that were cheaper than paying damages or pay damages and continue with the present system if that proved the less costly alternative. The conflict between plaintiffs and defendant would be resolved at least cost, and the plaintiffs — at worst — would be compensated for any hardship caused by the noise. The result, in short, would be efficient (meaning the cost of conflict would be minimized) and fair (meaning the injury would be redressed). Do you agree? But would the plaintiffs then be relegated to a series of lawsuits for damages? See Comment, Equity and the Eco-System: Can Injunctions Clear the Air?, 68 Mich. L. Rev. 1254, 1280 (1970).

4. Given the facts in *Estancias,* might not the injunction affirmed by the court be equally (if not more) effective than damages in accomplishing the ends of fairness and efficiency just discussed? The argument would run as follows: The granting of an injunction to the Schultzes need not represent the final resolution of the conflict between them and the defendant; the parties can bargain over whether the injunction will be enforced. Put another way, "injunctions are for sale by the plaintiff; the plaintiff expects to demand enforcement of the injunction only if the defendant refuses to pay a good round price for the plaintiff's consent to its dissolution." W. Page Keeton & Clarence Morris, Notes on "Balancing the Equities," 18 Tex. L. Rev. 412, 416 (1940). See also Note, Injunction Negotiations: An Economic, Moral, and Legal Analysis, 27 Stan. L. Rev. 1563 (1975) ("the enjoined party may, and often will, attempt to buy off the injunction").

Assume for now that we could count on such post-injunction bargaining by the parties in the *Estancias* case.[4] On that assumption, what, if any, are the advantages of injunctive relief as opposed to an award of damages?

5. Note the discussion in *Estancias* of the doctrine of "balancing the equities." The doctrine, sometimes called comparative hardship or equitable hardship, has an apparent efficiency objective — to avoid the greater harm (or social cost). Why is that objective not served by the nuisance calculus itself, which compares the utility of the conduct to the gravity of the harm it causes? There is some claim that the doctrine is also used to avoid the extortion problem. See, e.g., Note, Injunction Negotiations, supra, at 1577-1580. Why was the doctrine not applied in *Estancias*? Should it have been?

"Balancing the equities" figures prominently in the *Boomer* case, considered after the following problem.

PROBLEM

A lives next door to a parcel of land that has just been purchased by *B Co.* as the site for a waste dump for toxic chemicals. *A* brings suit to enjoin *B* from going forth with its plans on the ground that the dump is a prospective nuisance. Hornbook law has it that a defendant may be restrained from entering into an activity where it is highly probable that it will lead to harmful results — a nuisance — but not where the harmful results "are merely uncertain or contingent." Suppose that in the case in question the harmful results are uncertain, but that if they do occur they will be devastatingly severe. Should injunctive relief be granted? On what reasoning? See Village of Wilsonville v. SCA Servs., Inc., 86 Ill. 2d 1, 426 N.E.2d 824 (1981) (majority and concurring opinions).

---

4. In fact, no bargaining occurred. Inquiring of counsel, we learned that there was at first some thought that the defendant would simply try to buy the plaintiffs' property (apparently the cheapest alternative, judging from the evidence) — but this didn't happen. Instead, the offensive air-conditioning equipment was moved from the back of the defendant's building to the front. The plaintiffs would probably have resisted negotiations in any event. They had turned down a pre-trial settlement offer of $12,500, and their lawyer thought it unlikely that they would have sold their property after judgment, because they were an elderly couple who had lived in the neighborhood for many years.

On the general question of bargaining in situations like *Estancias,* recall the discussion in footnote 17 on page 137. We shall return to the matter shortly. See Note 3 on page 974.

Boomer v. Atlantic Cement Co.
Court of Appeals of New York, 1970
26 N.Y.2d 219, 257 N.E.2d 870, 309 N.Y.S.2d 312

BERGAN, J. Defendant operates a large cement plant near Albany. These are actions for injunction and damages by neighboring land owners alleging injury to property from dirt, smoke, and vibration emanating from the plant. A nuisance has been found after trial, temporary damages have been allowed; but an injunction has been denied.

The public concern with air pollution arising from many sources in industry and in transportation is currently accorded ever wider recognition accompanied by a growing sense of responsibility in State and Federal Governments to control it. Cement plants are obvious sources of air pollution in the neighborhoods where they operate.

But there is now before the court private litigation in which individual property owners have sought specific relief from a single plant operation. The threshold question raised by the division of view on this appeal is whether the court should resolve the litigation between the parties now before it as equitably as seems possible; or whether, seeking promotion of the general pubic welfare, it should channel private litigation into broad public objectives.

A court performs its essential function when it decides the rights of parties before it. Its decision of private controversies may sometimes greatly affect public issues. Large questions of law are often resolved by the manner in which private litigation is decided. But this is normally an incident to the court's main function to settle controversy. It is a rare exercise of judicial power to use a decision in private litigation as a purposeful mechanism to achieve direct public objectives greatly beyond the rights and interests before the court.

Effective control of air pollution is a problem presently far from solution even with the full public and financial powers of government. In large measure adequate technical procedures are yet to be developed and some that appear possible may be economically impracticable.

It seems apparent that the amelioration of air pollution will depend on technical research in great depth; on a carefully balanced consideration of the economic impact of close regulation; and of the actual effect on public health. It is likely to require massive public expenditure and to demand more than any local community can accomplish and to depend on regional and interstate controls.

A court should not try to do this on its own as a by-product of private litigation and it seems manifest that the judicial establishment is neither equipped in the limited nature of any judgment it can pronounce nor prepared to lay down and implement an effective policy for the elimination of air pollution. This is an area beyond the circumference of one private lawsuit. It is a direct responsibility for government and should not thus be undertaken as an incident to solving a dispute between property owners and a single cement plant — one of many — in the Hudson River valley.

The cement making operations of defendant have been found by the court at Special Term to have damaged the nearby properties of plaintiffs in these two actions. That court, as it has been noted, accordingly found defendant maintained a nuisance and this has been affirmed at the Appellate Division. The total damage to plaintiffs' properties is, however, relatively small in comparison with the value of defendant's operation and with the consequences of the injunction which plaintiffs seek.

The ground for the denial of injunction, notwithstanding the finding both that there is a nuisance and that plaintiffs have been damaged substantially, is the large disparity in economic consequences of the nuisance and of the injunction. This theory cannot, however, be sustained without overruling a doctrine which has been consistently reaffirmed in several leading cases in this court and which has never been disavowed here, namely that where a nuisance has been found and where there has been any substantial damage shown by the party complaining an injunction will be granted.

The rule in New York has been that such a nuisance will be enjoined although marked disparity be shown in economic consequence between the effect of the injunction and the effect of the nuisance.

The problem of disparity in economic consequence was sharply in focus in Whalen v. Union Bag & Paper Co., 208 N.Y. 1, 101 N.E. 805. A pulp mill entailing an investment of more than a million dollars polluted a stream in which plaintiff, who owned a farm, was "a lower riparian owner." The economic loss to plaintiff from this pollution was small. This court, reversing the Appellate Division, reinstated the injunction granted by the Special Term against the argument of the mill owner that in view of "the slight advantage to plaintiff and the great loss that will be inflicted on defendant" an injunction should not be granted (p.2, 101 N.E. p.805). "Such a balancing of injuries cannot be justified by the circumstances of this case," Judge Werner noted (p.4, 101 N.E. p.805). He continued: "Although the damage to the plaintiff may be slight as compared with the defendant's expense of abating the condition, that is not a good reason for refusing an injuncton" (p.5, 101 N.E. p.806).

Thus the unconditional injunction granted at Special Term was reinstated. The rule laid down in that case, then, is that whenever the damage resulting from a nuisance is found not "unsubstantial," viz., $100 a year, injunction would follow. This states a rule that had been followed in this court with marked consistency. . . .

Although the court at Special Term and the Appellate Division held that injunction should be denied, it was found that plaintiffs had been damaged in various specific amounts up to the time of the trial and damages to the respective plaintiffs were awarded for those amounts. The effect of this was, injunction having been denied, plaintiffs could maintain successive actions at law for damages thereafter as further damage was incurred.

The court at Special Term also found the amount of permanent damage attributable to each plaintiff, for the guidance of the parties in the event both sides stipulated to the payment and acceptance of such permanent damage as a settlement of all the controversies among the parties. The total of permanent damages to all plaintiffs thus found was $185,000. The basis of adjustment has not resulted in any stipulation by the parties.

This result at Special Term and at the Appellate Division is a departure from a rule that has become settled; but to follow the rule literally in these cases would be to close down the plant at once. This court is fully agreed to avoid that immediately drastic remedy; the difference in view is how best to avoid it.[5]

One alternative is to grant the injunction but postpone its effect to a specified future date to give opportunity for technical advances to permit defendant to eliminate the nuisance; another is to grant the injunction conditioned on the payment of permanent damages to plaintiffs which would compensate them for the total economic loss to their property present and future caused by defendant's operations. For reasons which will be developed the court chooses the latter alternative.

If the injunction were to be granted unless within a short period — e.g., 18 months — the nuisance be abated by improved methods, there would be no assurance that any significant technical improvement would occur.

The parties could settle this private litigation at any time if defendant paid enough money and the imminent threat of closing the plant would build up the pressure on defendant. If there were no improved techniques found, there would inevitably be applications to the court at Special Term for extensions of time to perform on showing of good faith efforts to find such techniques.

Moreover, techniques to eliminate dust and other annoying by-products of cement making are unlikely to be developed by any research the defendant can undertake within any short period, but will depend on the total resources of the cement industry nationwide and throughout the world. The problem is universal wherever cement is made.

For obvious reasons the rate of the research is beyond control of defendant. If at the end of 18 months the whole industry has not found

---

5. Respondent's investment in the plant is in excess of $45,000,000. There are over 300 people employed there.

a technical solution a court would be hard put to close down this one cement plant if due regard be given to equitable principles.

On the other hand, to grant the injunction unless defendant pays plaintiffs such permanent damages as may be fixed by the court seems to do justice between the contending parties. All of the attributions of economic loss to the properties on which plaintiffs' complaints are based will have been redressed.

The nuisance complained of by these plaintiffs may have other public or private consequences, but these particular parties are the only ones who have sought remedies and the judgment proposed will fully redress them. The limitation of relief granted is a limitation only within the four corners of these actions and does not foreclose public heath or other public agencies from seeking proper relief in a proper court.

It seems reasonable to think that the risk of being required to pay permanent damages to injured property owners by cement plant owners would itself be a reasonable effective spur to research for improved techniques to minimize nuisance.

The power of the court to condition on equitable grounds the continuance of an injunction on the payment of permanent damages seems undoubted. . . .

The damage base here suggested is consistent with the general rule in those nuisance cases where damages are allowed. "Where a nuisance is of such a permanent and unabatable character that a single recovery can be had, including the whole damage past and future resulting therefrom, there can be but one recovery" (66 C.J.S. Nuisances §140, p.947). It has been said that permanent damages are allowed where the loss recoverable would obviously be small as compared with the cost of removal of the nuisance (Kentucky-Ohio Gas Co. v. Bowling, 264 Ky. 470 477, 95 S.W.2d 1). . . .

Thus it seems fair to both sides to grant permanent damages to plaintiffs which will terminate this private litigation. The theory of damage is the "servitude on land" of plaintiffs imposed by defendant's nuisance. (See United States v. Causby, 328 U.S. 256, 261, 262, 267, 66 S. Ct. 1062, 90 L. Ed. 1206, where the term "servitude" addressed to the land was used by Justice Douglas relating to the effect of airplane noise on property near an airport.)

The judgment, by allowance of permanent damages imposing a servitude on land, which is the basis of the actions, would preclude future recovery by plaintiffs or their grantees.

This should be placed beyond debate by a provision of the judgment that the payment by defendant and the acceptance by plaintiffs of permanent damages found by the court shall be in compensation for a servitude on the land. . . .

The orders should be reversed, without costs, and the cases remitted to Supreme Court, Albany County to grant an injunction which shall be vacated upon payment by defendant of such amounts of permanent damage to the respective plaintiffs as shall for this purpose be determined by the court.

JASEN, J. (dissenting). I agree with the majority that a reversal is required here, but I do not subscribe to the newly enunciated doctrine of assessment of permanent damages, in lieu of an injunction, where substantial property rights have been impaired by the creation of a nuisance. . . .

I see grave dangers in overruling our long-established rule of granting an injunction where a nuisance results in substantial continuing damage. In permitting the injunction to become inoperative upon the payment of permanent damages, the majority is, in effect, licensing a continuing wrong. It is the same as saying to the cement company, you may continue to do harm to your neighbors so long as you pay a fee for it. Furthermore, once such permanent damages are assessed and paid, the incentive to alleviate the wrong would be eliminated, thereby continuing air pollution of an area without abatement. . . .

NOTES AND QUESTIONS

1. For illuminating discussion of the background and aftermath of *Boomer,* see Symposium on Nuisance Law: Twenty Years after *Boomer v. Atlantic Cement Co.,* 54 Alb. L. Rev. 169-399 (1990); Daniel A. Farber, Reassessing *Boomer:* Justice, Efficiency, and Nuisance Law, in Property Law and Legal Education 7 (Peter Hay & Michael H. Hoeflich eds. 1988). Farber notes two points in particular: First, the consequences of the nuisance in *Boomer* were much more serious than the opinion of the N.Y. Court of Appeals suggests. The cement company had a quarry a half mile from its plant, and blasting operations at the quarry frightened neighborhood children, cracked the walls, ceilings, and exteriors of homes in the vicinity, and filled the air with fine dust that covered everything. Second, on remand the trial court awarded damages in amounts that came to considerably more than the $185,000 mentioned in the Court of Appeals opinion:

> The trial judge agreed with the plaintiffs that damages would not be limited to the decrease in fair market value. On the other hand, he also rejected the plaintiffs' theory that damages should be awarded under a "contract price theory," that is, for the amount Atlantic would have had to pay to persuade the plaintiffs themselves to agree to lift a permanent injunction. . . . By the time of the judge's decision, all but one of the cases had settled. In the remaining case, the judge found the decline in market value to be $140,000, and awarded $175,000 in damages.

. . . We know from [subsequent proceedings] that Atlantic's total liability, including the settlements, ultimately came to $710,000, some four times the amount mentioned in the Court of Appeals decision denying permanent injunctive relief. [Id. at 11-12.]

2. *The liability issue.* But why was a nuisance even found in *Boomer*? In a subsequent case, Copart Indus., Inc. v. Consolidated Edison Co., 41 N.Y.2d 564, 362 N.E.2d 968, 394 N.Y.S.2d 169 (1977), the N.Y. Court of Appeals confronted a set of facts essentially identical to those in *Boomer,* yet found no nuisance. The court in *Copart* claimed to follow the Restatement. It considered the liability category of abnormally dangerous conditions to be inapplicable and concluded that neither intent nor negligence had been established. *Boomer* was distinguished on the ground that it involved an intentional and unreasonable invasion.

Do you agree with that characterization of the *Boomer* case? Notice the statement in *Boomer* that the trial court based liability simply on the fact that the plaintiffs' property had been damaged. See also the opinion below, 55 Misc. 2d 1023, 287 N.Y.S.2d 112 (Sup. Ct. 1967). Given that, which of the theories of nuisance liability discussed earlier (see pages 959-961) might *Boomer* reflect? For a suggested answer, and a criticism of *Copart,* see Comment, Internalizing Externalities: Nuisance Law and Economic Efficiency, 53 N.Y.U. L. Rev. 219 (1978).

Assume that in *Boomer* the costs of pollution abatement would exceed the benefits. Is this a reason to find no liability on the part of the defendant? On the assumption stated, are there reasons (apart from fairness) for holding the defendant liable? See Guido Calabresi & Jon T. Hirschoff, Toward a Test for Strict Liability in Torts, 81 Yale L.J. 1055 (1972).

3. *The remedy issue: injunctions.* Is it not an accurate characterization of *Boomer* to say that the court, in essence, denied injunctive relief, and that it did so by "balancing the equities"? What do you think of the method of striking the balance? Consider the following from Mahoney v. Walter, 205 S.E.2d 692, 698 (W. Va. 1974):

One of the chief problems with this doctrine [of balancing the equities] is that it compares the general loss to the public, such as loss of jobs, while it only considers specific loss to the private land owner, i.e., the specific money damage to his property, notwithstanding he may be damaged in many general ways which cannot be translated into specific damages.

See also Comment, Equity and the Eco-System: Can Injunctions Clear the Air?, 68 Mich. L. Rev. 1254, 1284 n.158 (1970):

Most cases in which injunctions are sought involve injury to only one or a few persons, but in the air pollution context many are being injured. If the plaintiff were to bring a class action, the weighing of the benefit which would result from granting the injunction would include all the members of the class. Class actions are sometimes difficult to bring, however, and it therefore seems appropriate as a general rule that if a judge can recognize harm to third persons from granting an injunction, he should be able to consider harm to third persons from not granting the injunction.

Is balancing the equities a sensible (or necessary) way to reach a decision about granting or denying injunctive relief; should one look instead at factors other than those suggested by the balancing doctrine (which are what)?

In the discussion after the *Estancias* case we considered in a preliminary way the issue of damages versus injunctive relief (see Note 4 on pages 967-968). But *Estancias* was a case involving just a few parties, whereas in *Boomer* there was a sizable number of plaintiffs, and perhaps a larger number of plaintiffs in the wings. Is this a difference that matters? See the Note on "Externalities" in Chapter 1 (page 49) and consider some findings reported in a series of articles by Hoffman and Spitzer. The first article concluded, on the basis of a set of experiments, that in two-party situations like *Estancias* the parties will likely bargain to efficient outcomes, whereas in many-party situations like *Boomer* post-litigation bargaining difficulties could well arise. Surprisingly, however, the subsequent studies, based on further experiments, suggested that even in situations involving up to forty parties post-litigation bargaining can be expected to lead to efficient solutions with no problems of free-riding or holding out whatsoever![6]

Can you, then, fashion a functional notion of just when a court should grant, and when deny, injunctive relief? How does it differ from the doctrinal approach of balancing the equities? See Richard A. Posner, Economic Analysis of Law 70-71 (4th ed. 1992).

Understand that the question of injunctive relief is not all black and white — a court's injunction need not ban an activity altogether. Indeed, it is quite common for courts to fashion specific orders to fit particular cases. Thus a defendant might be required to install a certain kind of noise abatement technology or reduce air pollution emissions to a stated level and so forth. On this point, and for a collection of cases on the contemporary standing of the doctrine of balancing the equities, see Annot., 40 A.L.R.3d 601 (1971).

4. *The remedy issue: permanent damages.* Notice the nature of the relief

_____

6. See Elizabeth Hoffman & Matthew L. Spitzer, The Coase Theorem: Some Experimental Tests, 25 J.L. & Econ. 73 (1982); Elizabeth Hoffman & Matthew L. Spitzer, Experimental Law and Economics: An Introduction, 85 Colum. L. Rev. 991 (1985); Elizabeth Hoffman & Matthew L. Spitzer, Experimental Tests of the Coase Theorem with Large Bargaining Groups, 15 J. Legal Stud. 149 (1986). For comments on the limitations of experimental studies such as these, see Mark Kelman, Comment on Hoffman and Spitzer's *Experimental Law and Economics,* 85 Colum. L. Rev. 1037 (1985); Stewart E. Sterk, Neighbors in American Land Law, 87 Colum. L. Rev. 55, 72-74 (1987).

awarded in *Boomer*. Does the fact that a court can award permanent damages dispel the concern, mentioned in the discussion after *Estancias*, that denial of injunctive relief relegates plaintiffs to a series of lawsuits? Do permanent damages have any other advantages? Any disadvantages? On the last question, consider the reasons why the damages might fail to give the aggrieved parties "full" compensation. See Farber, supra, at 14-19. Consider also the observation of the dissenting judge in *Boomer,* who argued that an award of permanent damages destroys any incentive on the part of the defendant to abate its pollution in the future — presumably even if new, cost-effective technology is developed. Is there any solution to this problem, other than periodic or temporary damages (which, of course, will give rise to a multiplicity of actions)? Do periodic damages generate incentive problems of their own? See Posner, supra, at 65; William F. Baxter & Lillian R. Altree, Legal Aspects of Airport Noise, 15 J.L. & Econ. 1 (1972).

Spur Industries, Inc. v. Del E. Webb Development Co.

Supreme Court of Arizona, 1972
108 Ariz. 178, 494 P.2d 700

CAMERON, J. From a judgment permanently enjoining the defendant, Spur Industries, Inc., from operating a cattle feedlot near the plaintiff Del E. Webb Development Company's Sun City, Spur appeals. Webb cross-appeals. Although numerous issues are raised, we feel that it is necessary to answer only two questions. They are:

1. Where the operation of a business, such as a cattle feedlot is lawful in the first instance, but becomes a nuisance by reason of a nearby residential area, may the feedlot operation be enjoined in an action brought by the developer of the residential area?

2. Assuming that the nuisance may be enjoined, may the developer of a completely new town or urban area in a previously agricultural area be required to indemnify the operator of the feedlot who must move or cease operation because of the presence of the residential area created by the developer?

The facts necessary for a determination of this matter on appeal are as follows. The area in question is located in Maricopa County, Arizona, some 14 or 15 miles west of the urban area of Phoenix, on the Phoenix-Wickenburg Highway, also known as Grand Avenue. About two miles south of Grand Avenue is Olive Avenue which runs east and west. 111th Avenue runs north and south as does the Agua Fria River immediately to the west. See Exhibits A and B.

Farming started in this area about 1911. In 1929, with the completion of the Carl Pleasant Dam, gravity flow water became available to the

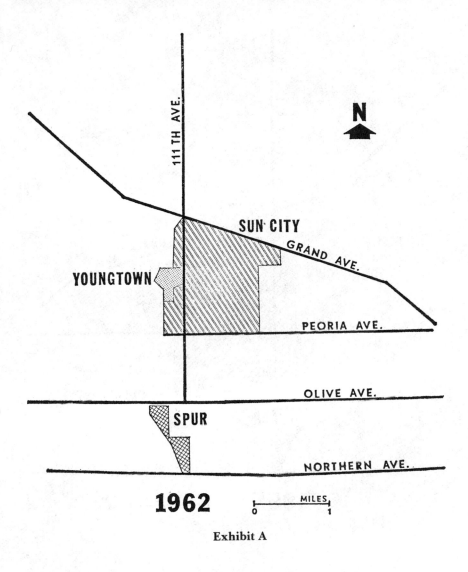

Exhibit A

property located to the west of the Agua Fria River, though land to the east remained dependent upon well water for irrigation. By 1950, the only urban areas in the vicinity were the agriculturally related communities of Peoria, El Mirage, and Surprise located along Grand Avenue. Along 111th Avenue, approximately one mile south of Grand Avenue and 1½ miles north of Olive Avenue, the community of Youngtown was commenced in 1954. Youngtown is a retirement community appealing primarily to senior citizens.

In 1956, Spur's predecessors in interest, H. Marion Welborn and the Northside Hay Mill and Trading Company, developed feedlots

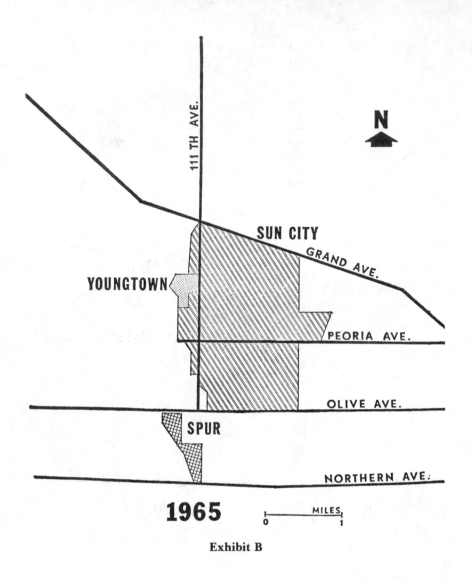

1965

MILES
0 ——————— 1

Exhibit B

about ½ mile south of Olive Avenue, in an area between the confluence of the usually dry Agua Fria and New Rivers. The area is well suited for cattle feeding and in 1959, there were 25 cattle feeding pens or dairy operations within a 7 mile radius of the location developed by Spur's predecessors. In April and May of 1959, the Northside Hay Mill was feeding between 6,000 and 7,000 head of cattle and Welborn approximately 1,500 head on a combined area of 35 acres.

In May of 1959, Del Webb began to plan the development of an urban area to be known as Sun City. For this purpose, the Marinette and the Santa Fe Ranches, some 20,000 acres of farmland, were purchased for $15,000,000 or $750.00 per acre. This price was considerably less than the price of land located near the urban area of Phoenix, and along with the success of Youngtown was a factor influencing the decision to purchase the property in question.

By September 1959, Del Webb had started construction of a golf course south of Grand Avenue and Spur's predecessors had started to level ground for more feedlot area. In 1960, Spur purchased the property in question and began a rebuilding and expansion program extending both to the north and south of the original facilities. By 1962, Spur's expansion program was completed and had expanded from approximately 35 acres to 114 acres.

Accompanied by an extensive advertising campaign, homes were first offered by Del Webb in January 1960 and the first unit to be completed was south of Grand Avenue and approximately 2½ miles north of Spur. By 2 May 1960, there were 450 to 500 houses completed or under construction. At this time, Del Webb did not consider odors from the Spur feed pens a problem and Del Webb continued to develop in a southerly direction, until sales resistance became so great that the parcels were difficult if not impossible to sell. . . .

By December 1967, Del Webb's property had extended south to Olive Avenue and Spur was within 500 feet of Olive Avenue to the north. . . . Del Webb filed its original complaint alleging that in excess of 1,300 lots in the southwest portion were unfit for development for sale as residential lots because of the operation of the Spur feedlot.

Del Webb's suit complained that the Spur feeding operation was a public nuisance because of the flies and the odor which were drifting or being blown by the prevailing south to north wind over the southern portion of Sun City. At the time of the suit, Spur was feeding between 20,000 and 30,000 head of cattle, and the facts amply support the finding of the trial court that the feed pens had become a nuisance to the people who resided in the southern part of Del Webb's development. The testimony indicated that cattle in a commercial feedlot will produce 35 to 40 pounds of wet manure per day, per head, or over a million pounds of wet manure per day for 30,000 head of cattle, and that despite the admittedly good feedlot management and good housekeeping practices by Spur, the resulting odor and flies produced an annoying if not unhealthy situation as far as the senior citizens of southern Sun City were concerned. There is no doubt that some of the citizens of Sun City were unable to enjoy the outdoor living which Del Webb had advertised and that Del Webb was faced with sales resistance from prospective purchasers as well as strong and persistent complaints from the people who had purchased homes in that area. . . .

It is noted, however, that neither the citizens of Sun City nor Youngtown are represented in this lawsuit and the suit is solely between Del E. Webb Development Company and Spur Industries, Inc.

May Spur Be Enjoined?

The difference between a private nuisance and a public nuisance is generally one of degree. A private nuisance is one affecting a single individual or a definite small number of persons in the enjoyment of private rights not common to the public, while a public nuisance is one affecting the rights enjoyed by citizens as a part of the public. To constitute a public nuisance, the nuisance must affect a considerable number of people or an entire community or neighborhood. . . .

Where the injury is slight, the remedy for minor inconveniences lies in an action for damages rather than in one for an injunction. . . . Moreover, some courts have held, in the "balancing of conveniences" cases, that damages may be the sole remedy. See Boomer v. Atlantic Cement Co., 26 N.Y.2d 219, 309 N.Y.S.2d 312, 257 N.E.2d 870, 40 A.L.R.3d 590 (1970), and annotation comments, 40 A.L.R.3d 601.

Thus, it would appear from the admittedly incomplete record as developed in the trial court, that, at most, residents of Youngtown would be entitled to damages rather than injunctive relief.

We have no difficulty, however, in agreeing with the conclusion of the trial court that Spur's operation was an enjoinable public nuisance as far as the people in the southern portion of Del Webb's Sun City were concerned.

§36-601, subsec. A reads as follows:

> §36-601. Public nuisances dangerous to public health
> A. The following conditions are specifically declared public nuisances dangerous to the public health:
>   1. Any condition or place in populous areas which constitutes a breeding place for flies, rodents, mosquitoes and other insects which are capable of carrying and transmitting disease-causing organisms to any person or persons.

By this statute, before an otherwise lawful (and necessary) business may be declared a public nuisance, there must be a "populous" area in which people are injured:

> . . . [I]t hardly admits a doubt that, in determining the question as to whether a lawful occupation is so conducted as to constitute a nuisance as a matter of fact, the locality and surroundings are of the first importance. (Citations omitted.) A business which is not per se a public nuisance may become such by being carried on at a place where the health, comfort, or inconvenience of a populous neighborhood is affected. . . . What might amount to a serious nuisance in one locality by reason of the density of the population, or character of the neighborhood affected, may in another place and under different surroundings be deemed proper and unobjectionable. . . . [MacDonald v. Perry, 32 Ariz. 39, 49-50, 255 P. 494, 497 (1927).]

It is clear that as to the citizens of Sun City, the operation of Spur's feedlot was both a public and a private nuisance. They could have successfully maintained an action to abate the nuisance. Del Webb, having shown a special injury in the loss of sales, had standing to bring suit to enjoin the nuisance. . . . The judgment of the trial court permanently enjoining the operation of the feedlot is affirmed.

Must Del Webb Indemnify Spur?

A suit to enjoin a nuisance sounds in equity and the courts have long recognized a special responsibility to the public when acting as a court of equity. . . .

In addition to protecting the public interest, however, courts of equity are concerned with protecting the operator of a lawful, albeit noxious, business from the result of a knowing and willful encroachment by others near his business.

In the so-called coming to the nuisance cases, the courts have held that the residential landowner may not have relief if he knowingly came into a neighborhood reserved for industrial or agricultural endeavors and has been damaged thereby. . . .

Were Webb the only party injured, we would feel justified in holding that the doctrine of "coming to the nuisance" would have been a bar to the relief asked by Webb, and, on the other hand, had Spur located the feedlot near the outskirts of a city and had the city grown toward the feedlot, Spur would have to suffer the cost of abating the nuisance as to those people locating within the growth pattern of the expanding city: "The case affords, perhaps, an example where a business established at a place remote from population is gradually surrounded and becomes part of a populous center, so that a business which formerly was not an interference with the rights of others has become so by the encroachment of the population. . . ." City of Ft. Smith v. Western Hide & Fur Co., 153 Ark. 99, 103, 239 S.W. 724, 726 (1922).

We agree, however, with the Massachusetts court that: "The law of nuisance affords no rigid rule to be applied in all instances. It is elastic. It undertakes to require only that which is fair and reasonable under all the circumstances. In a commonwealth like this, which depends for its material prosperity so largely on the continued growth and enlargement of manufacturing of diverse varieties, 'extreme rights' cannot be enforced. . . ." Stevens v. Rockport Granite Co., 216 Mass. 486, 488, 104 N.E. 371, 373 (1914).

There was no indication in the instant case at the time Spur and its predecessors located in western Maricopa County that a new city would spring up, full-blown, alongside the feeding operation and that the developer of that city would ask the court to order Spur to move because of the new city. Spur is required to move not because of any wrongdoing

on the part of Spur, but because of a proper and legitimate regard of
the courts for the rights and interests of the public.

Del Webb, on the other hand, is entitled to the relief prayed for (a
permanent injunction), not because Webb is blameless, but because of
the damage to the people who have been encouraged to purchase homes
in Sun City. It does not equitably or legally follow, however, that Webb,
being entitled to the injunction, is then free of any liability to Spur if
Webb has in fact been the cause of the damage Spur has sustained. It
does not seem harsh to require a developer, who has taken advantage of
the lesser land values in a rural area as well as the availability of large
tracts of land on which to build and develop a new town or city in the
area, to indemnify those who are forced to leave as a result.

Having brought people to the nuisance to the foreseeable detriment
of Spur, Webb must indemnify Spur for a reasonable amount of the cost
of moving or shutting down. It should be noted that this relief to Spur
is limited to a case wherein a developer has, with foreseeability, brought
into a previously agricultural or industrial area the population which
makes necessary the granting of an injunction against a lawful business
and for which the business has no adequate relief.

It is therefore the decision of this court that the matter be remanded
to the trial court for a hearing upon the damages sustained by the defendant Spur as a reasonable and direct result of the granting of the permanent injunction. Since the result of the appeal may appear novel and
both sides have obtained a measure of relief, it is ordered that each side
will bear its own costs.

Affirmed in part, reversed in part, and remanded for further proceedings consistent with this opinion.

NOTES AND QUESTIONS

1. *More on public nuisance.* We introduced the subject of public nuisance in Note 1, page 956. A public nuisance, according to the Restatement, "is an unreasonable interference with a right common to the
general public." Circumstances said to bear on the issue of unreasonableness are: whether the conduct in question significantly interferes
with public health, safety, peace, comfort, or convenience; whether the
conduct is proscribed by statute or ordinance (as in *Spur*); whether the
conduct is of a continuing nature or has produced a permanent or long-
lasting effect. See Restatement (Second) of Torts §821B (1979). Essentially, though, the underlying bases of liability for public nuisance are
the same as those for private nuisance — there must be substantial harm
caused by intentional and unreasonable conduct or by conduct that is
negligent, reckless, or abnormally dangerous. And, as with private nuisance, unreasonableness turns heavily on considerations of gravity and

utility. Thus, as one early public nuisance case is said to have put it, *"Le utility del chose excusera le noisomeness del stink."* Quoted in id. §826, Comment a, at 120.

Note, then, that the difference between public and private nuisance lies in the interests protected: public nuisance protects public rights; private nuisance protects rights in the use and enjoyment of land. In *Spur* the court states (at page 981) that as to the citizens of Sun City the defendant's feedlot was both a public and a private nuisance. This reflects the reasoning of most courts; they take the position that interference with the use and enjoyment of land such as occurred in *Spur* is a private nuisance no matter how many landowners are involved. The interference can also be a public nuisance if it interferes with a general public right, again as in *Spur*.

The distinction between private and public nuisance can be important in several respects. First, since a private nuisance arises from interference with the use and enjoyment of land, *only* owners of interests in land can bring suit. Second, since a public nuisance arises from interference with public rights, any member of the affected public can sue, but usually *only* if the person bringing suit can show "special injury" (or "special damage," or "particular damage") — injury or damage of a kind different from that suffered by other members of the public.

The special injury requirement is a remnant of English history. The original remedies for public nuisances were criminal prosecutions or abatement actions initiated by public officials. No private cause of action was recognized until 1536 and then only if the plaintiff suffered harm over and above that caused to other members of the community. The justifications for the rule are said to be that it is needed to protect the defendant from a multiplicity of actions (could this concern not be handled through class actions or by limiting the plaintiff's remedy to abatement?) and that redress of wrongs to the general public should be left to public officials. Moreover, some commentators make the dubious assertion "that any harm or interference shared by the public at large will normally be, if not entirely theoretical or potential, at least minor, petty and trivial so far as the individual is concerned." Id. §821C, Comment a, at 95.

The restriction on standing to sue imposed by the special injury rule has often been criticized, especially by environmentalists, and, perhaps in response, the law has been liberalized by statute, judicial decision, and the Restatement. See, e.g., id. §821C (suits for damages may be brought only by persons suffering special injury; abatement actions may be brought by those same persons, by public officials, *and* by any person who "has standing to sue as a representative of the general public, as a citizen in a citizen's action or as a member of a class in a class action"). The Restatement's objective is to leave courts free to proceed with recent developments expanding citizen access to courts. Motivating concerns are probably that special injury can be difficult to prove (especially if harm is only threatened and has not yet occurred) and that public prosecution can be inhibited by political pressure, inertia, and lack of resources. For a good overview, see John E. Bryson & Angus Macbeth, Public Nuisance, the Restatement (Second) of Torts, and Environmental Law, 2 Ecology L.Q. 241 (1972).

2. *"Coming to the nuisance."* Note the discussion in *Spur* of the "coming to the nuisance" defense. See page 981. Though there are cases to the contrary, the prevailing view is that moving into the vicinity of a nuisance does not completely bar a suit for damages or injunctive relief, but it is a "relevant factor" (much like the factors, suggested earlier in this chapter, that an area is zoned for the activity in question or has come to be commonly used for such an activity). See Restatement (Second) of Torts, supra, §840D. What role does this "relevant factor" play? Does it matter whether the plaintiff knew of the nuisance prior to moving into the area? Whether the defendant could foresee future settlement in the vicinity? Whether the plaintiff bought property before the nuisance came into being, but developed it after? What the plaintiff paid for the property? Is "coming to the nuisance" concerned with fairness or with efficiency?

The answer to the last question is that both concerns have played a role in doctrinal development. As to the first series of questions, all the factors mentioned — perhaps others as well — have a bearing. Working out the role of "coming to the nuisance" in particular cases, then, can be a complicated business from both fairness and efficiency points of view. See, e.g., Robert C. Ellickson, Alternatives to Zoning: Covenants, Nuisance Rules, and Fines as Land Use Controls, 40 U. Chi. L. Rev. 681, 758-761 (1973); Edward H. Rabin, Nuisance Law: Rethinking Fundamental Assumptions, 63 Va. L. Rev. 1299, 1321-1329 (1977).

Recall the principle of first in time that figured so prominently in Chapter 1. Is "coming to the nuisance" yet another application? See Lawrence Berger, An Analysis of the Doctrine that "First in Time is First in Right," 64 Neb. L. Rev. 349, 378-381 (1985); Donald Wittman, First Come, First Served: An Economic Analysis of "Coming to the Nuisance," 9 J. Legal Stud. 557 (1980).

Did the court in *Spur* end up taking "coming to the nuisance" into account, or not? In any event, is the resolution in *Spur* preferable to a judgment that denies all relief by virtue of the plaintiff's moving into the area or to one that grants it notwithstanding that fact? Compare Pendoley v. Ferreira, 345 Mass. 309, 187 N.E.2d 142 (1963) (piggery; injunction granted but time provided for defendant to make new arrangements).[7]

_____

7. An alternative solution to cases like *Spur* is suggested by "right to farm" statutes designed to protect established agricultural uses from encroachment by urban develop-

3. *Four rules.* A conventional view of long standing held that nuisance claims could be resolved in one of three ways: abate the activity in question by granting the plaintiff injunctive relief (the *Morgan* and *Estancias* cases, pages 951 and 964); let the activity continue if the defendant pays damages (the *Boomer* case, page 969); let the activity continue by denying all relief (the converse of the first alternative). *Spur* adds a new possibility, a fourth rule of decision that is the converse of the second alternative: abate the activity if the plaintiff pays damages.[8]

This "rule four" has an interesting intellectual history: An Arizona court and two Ivy League scholars came up with it at more or less the same time, but through very different approaches. The court in *Spur*, it appears, developed the rule out of the logic of necessity. None of the three traditional approaches yielded a result the court regarded as appropriate. Hence rule four. In the same year, Calabresi and Melamed, working at Harvard, developed the rule as the logical product of a modeling exercise. They reasoned that an entitlement exists (for example, an entitlement to use the air resource) that can be located in either the plaintiff or the defendant (the receptor or the polluter) and that can be protected by an injunction or so-called property rule that permits violation of the entitlement only if one gets the permission of its owner, or — alternatively — by damages, a so-called liability rule that permits violation of the entitlement if one pays a judicially determined sum to its owner. Given that the entitlement can be in either of two parties and that it can be protected by either of two means, there must be four possible outcomes or rules of decision rather than the three traditionally relied on by the courts. Hence rule four again. See Guido Calabresi & A. Douglas Melamed, Property Rules, Liability Rules, and Inalienability: One View of the Cathedral, 85 Harv. L. Rev. 1089 (1972).[9]

---

ment. A typical statute provides that no nuisance action may be brought against an "agricultural operation" if the operation has been lawfully ongoing for a year or more prior to the action and if the conditions complained of in the action have existed substantially unchanged since the date the agricultural operation began. John E. Cribbet, Concepts in Transition: The Search for a New Definition of Property, 1986 U. Ill. L. Rev. 1, 19-20, reports that some 35 states have enacted such legislation since 1979.

8. The approach taken in *Spur* could work by degrees. The courts could adopt a doctrine of "comparative nuisance," akin to the contributory or comparative negligence doctrine of standard tort law, and apportion costs between the parties according to degrees of comparative responsibility. Under such an approach, a court might provide injunctive relief but also require a plaintiff whose share of responsibility for the nuisance was (say) 20 percent to pay 20 percent of the defendant's compliance costs. If the suit were for damages, the defendant's liability would be reduced in the same manner. See Jeff L. Lewin, *Boomer* and the American Law of Nuisance: Past, Present, and Future, 54 Alb. L. Rev. 189, 276-291 (1990); Jeff L. Lewin, Comparative Nuisance, 50 U. Pitt. L. Rev. 1009 (1989).

9. A central topic in Calabresi & Melamed is the law of nuisance — and *Spur*, of course, is itself a nuisance case — but the conceptions developed in the article can illuminate any number of legal topics. We first mentioned them, for example, in the context of adverse possession (see footnote 19 on pages 140-141), and they were brought into play

Calabresi and Melamed claim that with the full complement of four rules one can go a long way toward achieving both efficiency and fairness in any given nuisance dispute (subject, of course, to the inherent limitations of judicial intervention). Their case turns in substantial part on matters we raised in discussing the *Estancias* and *Boomer* cases, having to do with the various advantages and disadvantages of damages and injunctive relief. Given that discussion, can you work out guidelines indicating when a judge should be inclined to employ each of the four rules? For commentary and elaboration, see Calabresi & Melamed, supra; A. Mitchell Polinsky, Resolving Nuisance Disputes: The Simple Economics of Injunctive and Damage Remedies, 32 Stan. L. Rev. 1075 (1980).

Did the court in *Spur* give Del Webb a *choice* either to pay damages to the defendant or to tolerate the presence of its feedlot? Compare the opinion in the *Boomer* case at pages 972-973. Could the parties, after the decision, agree that Spur need not abate? If so, would Del Webb, in conducting negotiations, take into account the situation of the real parties in interest?[10]

On the merits and demerits of the novel approach taken by the court in *Spur*, see Jeff L. Lewin, Compensated Injunctions and the Evolution of Nuisance Law, 71 Iowa L. Rev. 775 (1986); R.E. Hawkins, "In and Of Itself": Some Thoughts on the Assignment of Property Rights in Nuisance Cases, 36 U. Toronto Fac. L. Rev. 209 (1978).

NOTE: NUISANCE LAW AND ENVIRONMENTAL CONTROLS

As much of the material in this chapter suggests, nuisance law has an obvious bearing on environmental problems — pollution, for example, interferes with use and enjoyment of land as well as with public rights and thus seems a natural target for control as a nuisance. And so

---

again when we considered the problem of changed conditions in the law of servitudes (see Note 1 on page 921).

10. In fact, the case was settled in another fashion, as the editors learned by inquiring of counsel. Spur moved its feedlot away and Del Webb paid an undisclosed amount to compensate for the costs of relocation, loss of profits, and related expenses. The property where the feedlot had been located was pretty much idle as of mid-1980; a small part of it was being used for farming.

Pending at the time of the *Spur* litigation reported in the principal case was a suit by residents of Sun City seeking damages from Spur for maintaining a nuisance. After the main decision in *Spur*, the feedlot company cross-complained against Del Webb, seeking indemnification for any damages for which Spur might be held liable in the residents' suit. The trial court granted a motion by Del Webb to dismiss the cross-complaint, but the Arizona Supreme Court reversed, holding that Spur might indeed be entitled to recover. See Spur Feeding Co. v. Superior Court, 109 Ariz. 105, 505 P.2d 1377 (1973). The residents' lawsuit was subsequently settled for an undisclosed amount.

it has been. *Aldred's Case,* see page 957, is an early (seventeenth century) example, commonly regarded as the first instance of air pollution litigation; *Boomer* and *Spur* are contemporary cases in point; other instances have figured in this chapter as well.

That the law of nuisance has a place in environmental control seems clear, but there are a number of reasons to conclude that its contributions must be limited ones. Nuisance litigation is an expensive, cumbersome, and somewhat fortuitous means for resolving modern environmental problems, typified as they are by continuing and multiple causes, widespread effects and multiple victims, and scientifically complex issues as to cause, effect, and remedy. Potential plaintiffs, each usually bearing only a small part of the social costs of a large problem, have weak incentives to bring expensive lawsuits that promise limited rewards and difficult problems of proof; judges are poorly equipped to deal in a competent fashion with issues that demand considerable scientific expertise and are probably even less able to devise and oversee an ongoing program of technological controls; arguably, judges also lack the (political) competence to make the large-scale value judgments implicit in far-reaching environmental controls — judgments better left to more politically accountable government branches.

The shortcomings of nuisance litigation as a means of environmental control could, perhaps, be overcome to some degree through such techniques as class actions, provision of attorneys' fees to plaintiffs bringing suit "in the public interest," special environmental courts, and so on. The general conclusion, though, is that nuisance litigation is ill-suited to other than small-scale, incidental, localized, scientifically uncomplicated pollution problems. Indeed, judges themselves at times reveal a marked reluctance to use nuisance suits as the means for an ambitious program of environmental control — see once again the opinion in *Boomer.*

An alternative to judicial resolution of pollution problems is legislative and administrative intervention — the mainstay of environmental control efforts for many years. Air and water pollution were the subjects of royal proclamations in fourteenth-century England and of some parliamentary action not long thereafter; primitive legislative programs to control these same problems existed in the United States at least by the 1800s. By and large, American efforts began at the local level and were followed by state legislation as the dimensions of pollution problems, and knowledge about them, expanded. While there were some early federal pollution control programs, they were generally modest, intended in most instances merely to provide support for state activities. The federal presence was not really felt at all until about 1950; especially since 1970, however, the national government has occupied a dominant position. Today there are federal programs on virtually every aspect of environmental problems (air and water pollution, noise, pesticides, solid waste, and toxic pollutants are examples). State and local programs still operate, but largely within a framework of requirements set at the national level.

To date, virtually all legislative-administrative efforts to control environmental problems — at any level of government — have taken the form of *regulation*. A regulatory program (sometimes called in the trade a program of command and control) typically proceeds by prohibiting certain activities, requiring installation of prescribed technologies, and setting standards limiting emissions from pollution sources. Once established, the measures are backed up by civil and criminal sanctions.

Regulation, then, proceeds by telling pollution sources how much, and sometimes how, to control. *Incentive systems* stand in sharp contrast. Rather than command, they induce. The classic example is the emission or effluent fee — a charge on each unit of air or water pollution, set so as to yield an appropriate level of control in the aggregate (the higher the charge, the less pollution). A variant — marketable or transferable rights — sets a fixed number of pollution rights, distributes them by one means or another, and then permits trading in the rights thereafter (the fewer the rights, the less pollution).

As should be clear, incentive systems are much more decentralized than regulation; pollution sources are left largely to do as they wish, provided that they pay the price of the fee or that they hold the required rights. The advocates of incentive systems have maintained for years that a primary advantage of the decentralized approach is its promise of achieving desired levels of pollution control at lower cost than under regulation. The argument is straightforward: Sources with low control costs will control to greater degrees than sources facing higher costs, with the result that the total outlay for a given level of quality will be minimized. (Can you see why?) Advocates also argue that incentive systems encourage more technological innovation than does regulation. But proponents of regulation have arguments of their own. The regulatory approach, for example, is said to be more direct, more certain, and easier to monitor. It avoids the problem of "commodifying" environmental quality (recall the discussion of commodification in connection with the sale of body parts; see page 91). And it is the more acceptable alternative politically.

And so it has been, until very recently. While regulation remains the dominant approach to environmental problems in the United States (and elsewhere), incentive systems — marketable rights in particular — have made substantial inroads that may prove to be of enormous significance. The most notable instance is found in the acid rain provisions of the 1990 amendments to the federal Clean Air Act, which set up a system of pollution allowances that can be banked and traded by sources of sulfur dioxide (primarily power plants). See 42 U.S.C. §§7651-7651*o* (Supp. II 1990). For a quick picture of the program, see Roger W. Findley & Daniel A. Farber, Environmental Law in a Nutshell 163-166 (3d ed. 1992), observing that "[s]ulfur dioxide allowances became truly marketable when the Chicago Board of Trade voted to create a private market for them. Implementation of the program is now well underway. The success or failure of the program in controlling acid rain may determine the future of the concept of marketable permits."

No one maintains that command-and-control regulation should be abandoned as a means of environmental policy, though there are those who come close to taking that position. See, e.g., Terry L. Anderson & Donald R. Leal, Free Market Environmentalism (1991). The point, rather, is that regulation should not be regarded as the exclusive means. And this is an observation that pertains to more than pollution problems. Recall, for instance, the discussion of transferable fishing rights discussed in Chapter 1, at page 55.

11

Legislative Zoning: Processes, Practices, and Problems

A. *Introduction*

1. Historical Background

Prior to the 1900s, land use was controlled primarily — if not quite exclusively — through the bodies of doctrine on servitudes and nuisance considered in Chapters 9 and 10. These still play very important roles today, of course, but they have been diminished at least in relative terms by the growth of zoning. "The restrictive covenant and common-law nuisance doctrine were together not strong enough to hold the forces of change at bay in big cities. The 20th century tried zoning." Lawrence M. Friedman, A History of American Law 678 (2d ed. 1985).

To say that zoning is a twentieth-century development is not to say that there had been no earlier legislative controls on land use. What came before, however, was piecemeal and limited — local regulations aimed at a narrow range of particular urban problems of the times, like the location and operation of stables, slaughterhouses, and pool halls. See John Delafons, Land Use Control in the United States 20 (2d ed. 1969). These were little more than legislative applications of the nuisance law typically administered by courts; indeed, justification for the early ordinances was often articulated in precisely such terms — they were mere nuisance controls. Later, the nuisance rationale would be raised in partial support of comprehensive zoning efforts.

The word *comprehensive* is a hallmark; it suggests the systematic approach that distinguishes zoning from the piecemeal regulations of the nineteenth century. Initial steps in the zoning direction were modest. Early in the 1900s a few large cities established building height restrictions that applied in specified districts; their purpose was to enhance public health and safety. Between 1909 and 1915, however, Los Angeles in particular went much further, enacting a series of ordinances that divided the entire city into zones and specified the sorts of industrial activities permitted in each. See National Commission on Urban Problems, Building the American City 200 (1969). Despite this precedent, New York City is generally credited with the first comprehensive zoning program. Its ordinance of 1916 classified uses and assigned them to zones; in addition, restrictions on structural height and bulk were established.

The background of the New York ordinance is an interesting one, treated at length in Stanislaw J. Makielski, The Politics of Zoning (1966), and Seymour I. Toll, Zoned American (1969). By the time of World War I, New York City had experienced a period of rapid and haphazard growth. Skyscrapers as high as 55 stories sprouted like so many mushrooms in Manhattan, to the great annoyance of residents whose properties were being cut off from light and air. Garment manufacturers were moving their lofts into the vicinity of fashionable Fifth Avenue stores, and at lunch time the immigrant workers from these sweatshops would mingle with the wealthy patrons of local merchants. This was thought to be bad for business. Important interests, then, had a stake in controlling the course of development. Reformers — perhaps disinterested but zealous nevertheless — also saw the need for change. The mayor set up a Committee on City Planning which in turn appointed several advisory commissions. In 1916 one of these reported:

> New York City has certainly reached a point beyond which continued unplanned growth cannot take place without inviting social and economic disaster. It is too big a city, the social and economic interests involved are too great to permit the continuance of the laissez faire methods of earlier days. There is too much at stake to permit a habit of thought as to private property rights to stand in the way of a plan that is essential to the health, order and welfare of the entire city and to the conservation of property values. [Quoted in Delafons, supra, at 21.]

The New York zoning ordinance followed a few months later.

Zoning spread rapidly in the years after 1916 — especially so after the appearance of a Standard State Zoning Enabling Act issued in 1922 by an Advisory Committee on Zoning that had been appointed by Secretary of Commerce Herbert Hoover. With the growth of zoning came constitutional attacks — assertions that the new controls effected takings of property without compensation or worked deprivations of property without due process of law. By the mid-1920s, however, state courts were generally sympathetic to height and area restrictions, because of the close relation of these controls to accepted police power goals like fire prevention; the U.S. Supreme Court had also approved height restrictions. On the question of use restrictions, however, the state courts were sharply divided, and there was little guidance from the Supreme Court. While it had upheld use controls in the past, the cases were narrow precedent because they involved no more than local regulation of traditional nuisances such as stables and places of prostitution. Broad comprehensive zoning remained to be tested in the nation's highest court.

The ordinance of a tiny suburb of Cleveland, Ohio, gave the Court an opportunity to pronounce judgment on the new social engineering. In 1924, a federal district court had found the ordinance unconstitutional:

> The plain truth is that the true object of the ordinance in question is to place all the property in an undeveloped area of 16 square miles in a straitjacket. The purpose to be accomplished is really to regulate the mode of living of persons who may hereafter inhabit it. In the last analysis, the result to be accomplished is to classify the population and segregate them according to their income or situation in life. The true reason why some persons live in a mansion and others in a shack, why some live in a single-family dwelling and others in a double-family dwelling, why some live in a two-family dwelling and others in an apartment, or why some live in a well-kept apartment and others in a tenement, is primarily economic. It is a matter of income and wealth, plus the labor and difficulty of procuring adequate domestic service. Aside from contributing to these results and furthering such class tendencies, the ordinance has also an esthetic purpose; that is to say, to make this village develop into a city along lines now conceived by the village council to be attractive and beautiful. . . . Whether these purposes and objects would justify the taking of plaintiff's property as and for a public use need not be considered. It is sufficient to say that, in our opinion, and as applied to plaintiff's property, it may not be done without compensation under the guise of exercising the police power. [Ambler Realty Co. v. Village of Euclid, 297 F. 307, 316 (N.D. Ohio 1924).]

The judge knew his decision was an important one. "This case," he said, "is obviously destined to go higher." 297 F. at 308.

Village of Euclid v. Ambler Realty Co.
Supreme Court of the United States, 1926
272 U.S. 365

MR. JUSTICE SUTHERLAND delivered the opinion of the Court.

The Village of Euclid is an Ohio municipal corporation. It adjoins and practically is a suburb of the City of Cleveland. Its estimated population is between 5,000 and 10,000, and its area from twelve to fourteen square miles, the greater part of which is farm lands or unimproved acreage. It lies, roughly, in the form of a parallelogram measuring approximately three and one-half miles each way. East and west it is traversed by three principal highways: Euclid Avenue, through the southerly border, St. Clair Avenue, through the central portion, and Lake Shore Boulevard, through the northerly border in close proximity to the shore of Lake Erie. The Nickel Plate railroad lies from 1,500 to 1,800 feet north of Euclid Avenue, and the Lake Shore railroad 1,600 feet farther to the north. The three highways and the two railroads are substantially parallel.

Appellee is the owner of a tract of land containing 68 acres, situated in the westerly end of the village, abutting on Euclid Avenue to the south and the Nickel Plate railroad to the north. Adjoining this tract, both on the east and on the west, there have been laid out restricted residential plats upon which residences have been erected.

On November 13, 1922, an ordinance was adopted by the Village Council, establishing a comprehensive zoning plan for regulating and restricting the location of trades, industries, apartment houses, two-family houses, etc., the lot area to be built upon, the size and height of buildings, etc.

The entire area of the village is divided by the ordinance into six classes of use districts, denominated U-1 to U-6, inclusive; three classes of height districts, denominated H-1 to H-3, inclusive; and four classes of area districts, denominated A-1 to A-4, inclusive. The use districts are classified in respect of the buildings which may be erected within their respective limits, as follows: U-1 is restricted to single family dwellings, public parks, water towers and reservoirs, suburban and interurban electric railway passenger stations and rights of way, and farming, noncommercial greenhouse nurseries and truck gardening; U-2 is extended to include two-family dwellings; U-3 is further extended to include apartment houses, hotels, churches, schools, public libraries, museums, private clubs, community center buildings, hospitals, sanitariums, public playgrounds and recreation buildings, and a city hall and courthouse; U-4 is further extended to include banks, offices, studios, telephone exchanges, fire and police stations, restaurants, theatres and moving picture shows, retail stores and shops, sales offices, sample rooms, wholesale stores for hardware, drugs and groceries, stations for gasoline and oil (not exceeding 1,000 gallons storage) and for ice delivery, skating rinks and dance halls, electric substations, job and newspaper printing, public garages for motor vehicles, stables and wagon sheds (not exceeding five horses, wagons or motor trucks) and distributing stations for central store and commercial enterprises; U-5 is further extended to include billboards and advertising signs (if permitted), warehouses, ice and ice cream manufacturing and cold storage plants, bottling works, milk bottling and central distribution stations, laundries, carpet cleaning, dry cleaning and dyeing establishments, blacksmith, horseshoeing, wagon and motor vehicle repair shops, freight stations, street car barns, stables and wagon sheds (for more than five horses, wagons or motor trucks), and wholesale produce markets and salesrooms; U-6 is further extended to include plants for sewage disposal and for producing gas, garbage and refuse incineration, scrap iron, junk, scrap paper and rag storage, aviation fields, cemeteries, penal and correctional institutions, insane and feeble minded institutions, storage of oil and gasoline (not to exceed 25,000 gallons), and manufacturing and industrial operations of any kind other than, and any public utility not included in, a class U-1, U-2, U-3, U-4 or U-5 use. There is a seventh class of uses which is prohibited altogether.

Class U-1 is the only district in which buildings are restricted to those enumerated. In the other classes the uses are cumulative; that is to say, uses in class U-2 include those enumerated in the preceding class, U-1; class U-3 includes uses enumerated in the preceding classes, U-2 and U-1; and so on. In addition to the enumerated uses, the ordinance provides for accessory uses, that is, for uses customarily incident to the principal use, such as private garages. Many regulations are provided in respect of such accessory uses.

The height districts are classified as follows: In class H-1, buildings are limited to a height of two and one-half stories or thirty-five feet; in class H-2, to four stories or fifty feet; in class H-3, to eighty feet. To all of these, certain exceptions are made, as in the case of church spires, water tanks, etc.

The classification of area districts is: In A-1 districts, dwellings or apartment houses to accommodate more than one family must have at least 5,000 square feet for interior lots and at least 4,000 square feet for corner lots; in A-2 districts, the area must be at least 2,500 square feet for interior lots, and 2,000 square feet for corner lots; in A-3 districts, the limits are 1,250 and 1,000 square feet, respectively; in A-4 districts, the limits are 900 and 700 square feet, respectively. The ordinance contains, in great variety and detail, provisions in respect of width of lots, front, side and rear yards, and other matters, including restrictions and regulations as to the use of bill boards, sign boards and advertising signs. . . .

Appellee's tract of land comes under U-2, U-3, and U-6. The first strip of 620 feet immediately north of Euclid Avenue falls in class U-2, the next 130 feet to the north, in U-3, and the remainder in U-6. The uses of the first 620 feet, therefore, do not include apartment houses, hotels, churches, schools, or other public and semi-public buildings, or other uses enumerated in respect to U-3 to U-6, inclusive. The uses of the next 130 feet include all of these, but exclude industries, theatres, banks, shops, and the various other uses set forth in respect of U-4 to U-6, inclusive.

Annexed to the ordinance, and made a part of it, is a zone map, showing the location and limits of the various use, height and area districts, from which it appears that the three classes overlap one another; that is to say, for example, both U-5 and U-6 use districts are in A-4 area

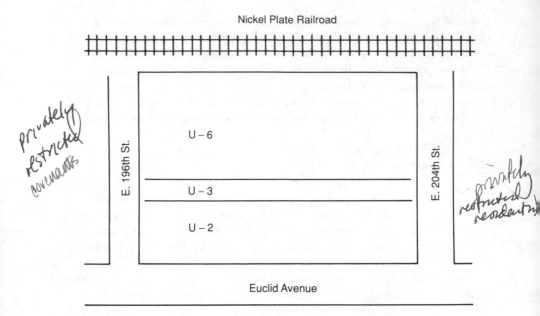

Nickel Plate Railroad

U – 6

E. 196th St.

E. 204th St.

U – 3

U – 2

Euclid Avenue

Ambler Realty Property   U-1
Figure 11-1

districts, but the former is in H-2 and the latter in H-3 height districts. . . .

The lands lying between the two railroads for the entire length of the village area and extending some distance on either side to the north and south, having an average width of about 1,600 feet, are left open, with slight exceptions, for industrial and all other uses. This includes the larger part of appellee's tract. . . .

The enforcement of the ordinance is entrusted to the inspector of buildings, under rules and regulations of the board of zoning appeals. Meetings of the board are public, and minutes of its proceedings are kept. It is authorized to adopt rules and regulations to carry into effect provisions of the ordinance. Decisions of the inspector of buildings may be appealed to the board by any person claiming to be adversely affected by any such decision. The board is given power in specific cases of practical difficulty or unnecessary hardship to interpret the ordinance in harmony with its general purpose and intent, so that the public health, safety and general welfare may be secure and substantial justice done. Penalties are prescribed for violations, and it is provided that the various provisions are to be regarded as independent and the holding of any provision to be unconstitutional, void or ineffective shall not affect any of the others.

The ordinance is assailed on the grounds that it is in derogation of

996

§1 of the Fourteenth Amendment to the Federal Constitution in that it deprives appellee of liberty and property without due process of law and denies it the equal protection of the law, and that it offends against certain provisions of the Constitution of the State of Ohio. The prayer of the bill is for an injunction restraining the enforcement of the ordinance and all attempts to impose or maintain as to appellee's property any of the restrictions, limitations or conditions. The court below held the ordinance to be unconstitutional and void, and enjoined its enforcement. 297 Fed. 307.

Before proceeding to a consideration of the case, it is necessary to determine the scope of the inquiry. The bill alleges that the tract of land in question is vacant and has been held for years for the purpose of selling and developing it for industrial uses, for which it is especially adapted, being immediately in the path of progressive industrial development; that for such uses it has a market value of about $10,000 per acre, but if the use be limited to residential purpose the market value is not in excess of $2,500 per acre; that the first 200 feet of the parcel back from Euclid Avenue, if unrestricted in respect of use, has a value of $150 per front foot, but if limited to residential uses, and ordinary mercantile business be excluded therefrom, its value is not in excess of $50 per front foot.

It is specifically averred that the ordinance attempts to restrict and control the lawful uses of appellee's land so as to confiscate and destroy a great part of its value; that it is being enforced in accordance with its terms; that prospective buyers of land for industrial, commercial and residential uses in the metropolitan district of Cleveland are deterred from buying any part of this land because of the existence of the ordinance and the necessity thereby entailed of conducting burdensome and expensive litigation in order to vindicate the right to use the land for lawful and legitimate purposes; that the ordinance constitutes a cloud upon the land, reduces and destroys its value, and has the effect of diverting the normal industrial, commercial and residential development thereof to other and less favorable locations.

The record goes no farther than to show, as the lower court found, that the normal, and reasonably to be expected, use and development of that part of appellee's land adjoining Euclid Avenue is for general trade and commercial purposes, particularly retail stores and like establishments, and that the normal, and reasonably to be expected, use and development of the residue of the land is for industrial and trade purposes. Whatever injury is inflicted by the mere existence and threatened enforcement of the ordinance is due to restrictions in respect of these and similar uses; to which perhaps should be added — if not included in the foregoing — restrictions in respect of apartment houses. Specifically, there is nothing in the record to suggest that any damage results from the presence in the ordinance of those restrictions relating to churches, schools, libraries and other public and semipublic buildings. It is neither alleged nor proved that there is, or may be, a demand for any part of appellee's land for any of the last named uses; and we cannot assume the existence of facts which would justify an injunction upon this record in respect of this class of restrictions. For present purposes the provisions of the ordinance in respect of these uses may, therefore, be put aside as unnecessary to be considered. It is also unnecessary to consider the effect of the restrictions in respect of U-1 districts, since none of appellee's land falls within that class.

We proceed, then, to a consideration of those provisions of the ordinance to which the case as it is made relates, first disposing of a preliminary matter.

A motion was made in the court below to dismiss the bill on the ground that, because complainant [appellee] had made no effort to obtain a building permit or apply to the zoning board of appeals for relief as it might have done under the terms of the ordinance, the suit was premature. The motion was properly overruled. The effect of the allegations of the bill is that the ordinance of its own force operates greatly to reduce the value of appellee's lands and destroy their marketability for industrial, commercial and residential uses; and the attack is directed, not against any specific provision or provisions, but against the ordinance as an entirety. Assuming the premises, the existence and maintenance of the ordinance, in effect, constitutes a present invasion of appellee's property rights and a threat to continue it. Under these circumstances, the equitable jurisdiction is clear. . . .

It is not necessary to set forth the provisions of the Ohio Constitution which are thought to be infringed. The question is the same under both Constitutions, namely, as stated by appellee: Is the ordinance invalid in that it violates the constitutional protection "to the right of property in the appellee by attempted regulations under the guise of the police power, which are unreasonable and confiscatory"?

Building zone laws are of modern origin. They began in this country about twenty-five years ago. Until recent years, urban life was comparatively simple; but with the great increase and concentration of population, problems have developed, and constantly are developing, which require, and will continue to require, additional restrictions in respect of the use and occupation of private lands in urban communities. Regulations, the wisdom, necessity and validity of which, as applied to existing conditions, are so apparent that they are now uniformly sustained, a century ago, or even half a century ago, probably would have been rejected as arbitrary and oppressive. Such regulations are sustained, under the complex conditions of our day, for reasons analogous to those which justify traffic regulations, which, before the advent of automobiles and rapid transit street railways, would have been condemned as fatally arbitrary and unreasonable. And in this there is no inconsistency, for while the meaning of constitutional guaranties never varies, the scope of their application must expand or contract to meet the new and different conditions which are constantly coming within the field of their operation. In a changing world, it is impossible that it should be otherwise. But although a degree of elasticity is thus imparted, not to the *meaning,* but to the *application* of constitutional principles, statutes and ordinances, which, after giving due weight to the new conditions, are found clearly not to conform to the Constitution, of course, must fall.

The ordinance now under review, and all similar laws and regulations, must find their justification in some aspect of the police power, asserted for the public welfare. The line which in this field separates the legitimate from the illegitimate assumption of power is not capable of precise delimitation. It varies with circumstances and conditions. A regulatory zoning ordinance, which would be clearly valid as applied to the great cities, might be clearly invalid as applied to rural communities. In solving doubts, the maxim *sic utere tuo ut alienum non laedas,* which lies at the foundation of so much of the common law of nuisances, ordinarily will furnish a fairly helpful clew. And the law of nuisances, likewise, may be consulted, not for the purpose of controlling, but for the helpful aid of its analogies in the process of ascertaining the scope of, the power. Thus the question whether the power exists to forbid the erection of a building of a particular kind or for a particular use, like the question whether a particular thing is a nuisance, is to be determined, not by an abstract consideration of the building or of the thing considered apart, but by considering it in connection with the circumstances and the locality. . . . A nuisance may be merely a right thing in the wrong place — like a pig in the parlor instead of the barnyard. If the validity of the legislative classification for zoning purposes be fairly debatable, the legislative judgment must be allowed to control. . . .

There is no serious difference of opinion in respect of the validity of laws and regulations fixing the height of buildings within reasonable limits, the character of materials and methods of construction, and the adjoining area which must be left open, in order to minimize the danger of fire or collapse, the evils of over-crowding, and the like, and excluding from residential sections offensive trades, industries and structures likely to create nuisances. . . .

Here, however, the exclusion is in general terms of all industrial establishments, and it may thereby happen that not only offensive or dangerous industries will be excluded, but those which are neither offensive nor dangerous will share the same fate. But this is no more than happens in respect of many practice-forbidding laws which this Court has upheld although drawn in general terms so as to include individual cases that may turn out to be innocuous in themselves. . . . The inclusion of a reasonable margin to insure effective enforcement, will not put upon a law, otherwise valid, the stamp of invalidity. Such laws may also find their justification in the fact that, in some fields, the bad fades into the good by such insensible degrees that the two are not capable of being readily distinguished and separated in terms of legislation. In the light of these considerations, we are not prepared to say that the end in view was not sufficient to justify the general rule of the ordinance, although some industries of an innocent character might fall within the proscribed class. It can not be said that the ordinance in this respect "passes the bounds of reason and assumes the character of a merely arbitrary fiat." Purity Extract Co. v. Lynch, 226 U.S. 192, 204. Moreover, the restrictive provisions of the ordinance in this particular may be sustained upon the principles applicable to the broader exclusion from residential districts of all business and trade structures, presently to be discussed.

It is said that the Village of Euclid is a mere suburb of the City of Cleveland; that the industrial development of that city has now reached and in some degree extended into the village and, in the obvious course of things, will soon absorb the entire area for industrial enterprises; that the effect of the ordinance is to divert this natural development elsewhere with the consequent loss of increased values to the owners of the lands within the village borders. But the village, though physically a suburb of Cleveland, is politically a separate municipality, with powers of its own and authority to govern itself as it sees fit within the limits of the organic law of its creation and the State and Federal Constitutions. Its governing authorities, presumably representing a majority of its inhabitants and voicing their will, have determined, not that industrial development shall cease at its boundaries, but that the course of such development shall proceed within definitely fixed lines. If it be a proper exercise of the police power to relegate industrial establishments to localities separated from residential sections, it is not easy to find a sufficient reason for denying the power because the effect of its exercise is to divert an industrial flow from the course which it would follow, to the injury of the residential public if left alone, to another course where such injury will be obviated. It is not meant by this, however, to exclude the possibility of cases where the general public interest would so far outweigh the interest of the municipality that the municipality would not be allowed to stand in the way.

We find no difficulty in sustaining restrictions of the kind thus far reviewed. The serious question in the case arises over the provisions of the ordinance excluding from residential districts, apartment houses, business houses, retail stores and shops, and other like establishments. This question involves the validity of what is really the crux of the more recent zoning legislation, namely, the creation and maintenance of residential districts, from which business and trade of every sort, including hotels and apartment houses, are excluded. Upon that question this Court has not thus far spoken. The decisions of the state courts are numerous and conflicting; but those which broadly sustain the power greatly outnumber those which deny altogether or narrowly limit it; and it is very apparent that there is a constantly increasing tendency in the direction of the broader view. . . .

The matter of zoning has received much attention at the hands of commissions and experts, and the results of their investigations have been set forth in comprehensive reports. These reports, which bear every evidence of painstaking consideration, concur in the view that the segregation of residential, business, and industrial buildings will make it easier to provide fire apparatus suitable for the character and intensity of the development in each section; that it will increase the safety and security of home life; greatly tend to prevent street accidents, especially to children, by reducing the traffic and resulting confusion in residential sections; decrease noise and other conditions which produce or intensify nervous disorders; preserve a more favorable environment in which to rear children, etc. With particular reference to apartment houses, it is pointed out that the development of detached house sections is greatly retarded by the coming of apartment houses, which has sometimes resulted in destroying the entire section for private house purposes; that in such sections very often the apartment house is a mere parasite, constructed in order to take advantage of the open spaces and attractive surroundings created by the residential character of the district. Moreover, the coming of one apartment house is followed by others, interfering by their height and bulk with the free circulation of air and monopolizing the rays of the sun which otherwise would fall upon the smaller homes, and bringing, as their necessary accompaniments, the disturbing noises incident to increased traffic and business, and the occupation, by means of moving and parked automobiles, of larger portions of the streets, thus detracting from their safety and depriving children of the privilege of quiet and open spaces for play, enjoyed by those in more favored localities, — until, finally, the residential character of the neighborhood and its desirability as a place of detached residences are utterly destroyed. Under these circumstances, apartment houses, which in a different environment would be not only entirely unobjectionable but highly desirable, come very near to being nuisances.

If these reasons, thus summarized, do not demonstrate the wisdom or sound policy in all respects of those restrictions which we have indicated as pertinent to the inquiry, at least, the reasons are sufficiently cogent to preclude us from saying, as it must be said before the ordinance can be declared unconstitutional, that such provisions are clearly arbitrary and unreasonable, having no substantial relation to the public health, safety, morals, or general welfare. . . .

It is true that when, if ever, the provisions set forth in the ordinance in tedious and minute detail, come to be concretely applied to particular premises, including those of the appellee, or to particular conditions, or to be considered in connection with specific complaints, some of them, or even many of them, may be found to be clearly arbitrary and unreasonable. But where the equitable remedy of injunction is sought, as it is here, not upon the ground of a present infringement or denial of a specific right, or of a particular injury in process of actual execution, but upon the broad ground that the mere existence and threatened enforcement of the ordinance, by materially and adversely affecting values and curtailing the opportunities of the market, constitute a present and irreparable injury, the court will not scrutinize its provisions, sentence by sentence, to ascertain by a process of piecemeal dissection whether there may be, here and there, provisions of a minor character, or relating to matters of administration, or not shown to contribute to the injury complained of, which, if attacked separately, might not withstand the test of constitutionality. In respect of such provisions, of which specific complaint is not made, it cannot be said that the land owner has suffered or is threatened with an injury which entitles him to challenge their constitutionality. . . .

The relief sought here is . . . an injunction against the enforcement of any of the restrictions, limitations or conditions of the ordinance. And the gravamen of the complaint is that a portion of the land of the appellee cannot be sold for certain enumerated uses because of the general and broad restraints of the ordinance. What would be the effect of a restraint imposed by one or more of the innumerable provisions of the ordinance, considered apart, upon the value or marketability of the lands is neither disclosed by the bill nor by the evidence, and we are afforded no basis, apart from mere speculation, upon which to rest a conclusion that it or they would have any appreciable effect upon those matters. Under these circumstances, therefore, it is enough for us to determine, as we do, that the ordinance in its general scope and dominant features, so far as its provisions are here involved, is a valid exercise of authority, leaving other provisions to be dealt with as cases arise directly involving them.

And this is in accordance with the traditional policy of this Court. In the realm of constitutional law, especially, this Court has perceived the embarrassment which is likely to result from an attempt to formulate rules or decide questions beyond the necessities of the immediate issue. It has preferred to follow the method of a gradual approach to the general by a systematically guarded application and extension of constitutional principles to particular cases as they arise, rather than by out of hand attempts to establish general rules to which future cases must be fitted. This process applies with peculiar force to the solution of questions arising under the due process clause of the Constitution as applied to the exercise of the flexible powers of police, with which we are here concerned.

Decree reversed.

Mr. Justice Van Devanter, Mr. Justice McReynolds and Mr. Justice Butler, dissent.

NOTES AND QUESTIONS

1. As mentioned earlier, the New York City ordinance of 1916 and the Standard Act of 1922 triggered a rapid increase in zoning. By 1925, for example, 368 municipalities had zoning ordinances. The decision in *Euclid* appears to have had an even greater impact: by 1930 over 1,000 cities had zoning, and by 1967 the number was over 9,000. "Today, zoning is virtually universal in the metropolitan areas of the United States, where more than 97 percent of cities having a population over 5,000 employ it. Of cities with over 250,000 population only Houston, Texas, has not enacted a zoning ordinance." Robert C. Ellickson, Alternatives to Zoning: Covenants, Nuisance Rules, and Fines as Land Use Controls, 40 U. Chi. L. Rev. 681, 692 (1973). Whether the growth of zoning is a good thing is an open question. As we shall see later, there are those who believe that we should move back toward the old controls that Houston is starting only now to abandon — primarily covenants and nuisance law.

2. "Historically, the village of Euclid was founded by some land surveyors who liked the location they had surveyed and named the town after their favorite mathematician. Today, 'cooky cutter' zoning that divides the municipality into rigid zones with rectangular lots in each zone, as was done in the village of Euclid, is derisively referred to as 'Euclidean zoning.' " Robert Kratovil, Zoning: A New Look, 11 Creighton L. Rev. 433, 434 n.6 (1977).

Euclidean zoning is typically "cumulative," which is to say that use districts are graded such that "higher" uses are permitted in areas zoned for "lower" uses, but not vice versa; thus one can put a house in an industrial zone, but not a factory in a residential zone. Single-family dwellings are usually classified as the highest use, and zones for such dwellings are often exclusive. Some cities have other exclusive or noncumulative zones (for example, *only* heavy industry may be permitted in certain areas) or partially noncumulative ones (heavy and light industry and some commercial offices may be permitted in certain areas, while all other, "higher," uses are excluded). The modern trend is away from cumulative zoning, the idea being that an apartment in a factory zone is as unhealthy as a factory in an apartment zone. See generally 2 Robert M. Anderson, American Law of Zoning §9.14 (3d ed. 1986).

3. Justice Sutherland, the author of the majority opinion in the *Euclid* case, was a famous judicial conservative; he wrote the opinion of the Court in Adkins v. Children's Hospital, 261 U.S. 525 (1923), invalidating a minimum wage law for women. "A mass of reports, opinions of special

observers and students of the subject, and the like" had been submitted in *Adkins*. Sutherland said he found these "interesting but only mildly persuasive." 261 U.S. at 560. According to Alfred McCormack, A Law Clerk's Recollections, 46 Colum. L. Rev. 710, 712 (1946), Sutherland was writing a majority opinion in *Euclid* that would hold the zoning ordinance unconstitutional; conversations with dissenters on the Court "shook his convictions and led him to request a reargument, after which he changed his mind and the ordinance was upheld."

4. The Ambler Realty Company property involved in the *Euclid* case was eventually zoned for industrial use. General Motors built a factory on the land. Charles M. Haar & Michael A. Wolf, Land-Use Planning 190 (4th ed. 1989).

5. Look at the last few sentences of the opinion by the lower court in *Euclid*, mentioning the "taking" of property for a "public use" upon payment of "compensation." The judge had in mind the Fifth Amendment to the U.S. Constitution, which provides in part that private property shall not "be taken for public use, without just compensation." How could one say that Ambler Realty's property had been "taken" by Euclid's zoning ordinance? Was it because the property's value was so severely impacted? Given the reduction in value, why did the Supreme Court not find a "taking"? We explore these matters in the next chapter. Suffice it to say for now that zoning ordinances are routinely upheld in the face of takings allegations, especially if they are controlling nuisance-like conditions or so long as they leave the property owner with some reasonable use.

6. Notice that the appellee in *Euclid* had not challenged any specific provisions of the ordinance in question but rather attacked the zoning law in its entirety. The Supreme Court in turn held zoning *in general* to be constitutional but added that concrete applications of specific provisions could prove to be arbitrary and unreasonable; such problems would be dealt with as they arose. Two years later the Court decided Nectow v. City of Cambridge, 277 U.S. 183 (1928). The zoning ordinance at issue there put a 100-foot strip of the plaintiff's land into a residential district, the balance of the land being unrestricted. A master appointed by the trial court found that as a result of the zoning no practical use could be made of the strip, and also found that placing the strip in a residential district did not promote health, safety, or welfare. On this record, the Court found the zoning as applied to the plaintiff's land to be unconstitutional.

When zoning is declared unconstitutional as applied to a specific lot, what uses are then permitted on the lot? Is the lot unrestricted, does the city have a reasonable time to rezone it, or should the court decree provide what uses are permitted? See Union Oil Co. of California v. City of Worthington, 62 Ohio St. 2d 263, 405 N.E.2d 277 (1980); AMG Assocs. v. Township of Springfield, 65 N.J. 101, 319 A.2d 705 (1974).

After *Nectow*, the Supreme Court went out of the zoning business for nearly half a century, leaving the policing of zoning laws to state and lower federal courts; in recent years, however, the Court has become active in the area once again. We shall have occasion to consider some of its opinions in the balance of this chapter.

2. Some Zoning Fundamentals

The text that follows provides a brief introduction to the structure of authority that underlies the zoning process.

a. Enabling Legislation

Zoning is an exercise of the police power — essentially, the power of government to protect health, safety, welfare, and morals. Generally speaking, the police power is held to reside in the state, but in the case of zoning the virtually universal practice is a delegation of authority from the state legislature to municipalities or other political subdivisions. In some states such a delegation might be unnecessary, on the ground that cities have home-rule powers under state statutory or constitutional law. The point is not particularly important for our purposes, though, inasmuch as all states have adopted enabling acts that delegate zoning authority to local governments. "A general State enabling act is always advisable, and while the power to zone may, in some States, be derived from . . . home rule, still it is seldom that the home-rule powers will cover all the necessary provisions for successful zoning."

The quoted language is from an explanatory note to the Standard State Zoning Enabling Act mentioned earlier.[1] The Standard Act was adopted at one time or another in all 50 states and is still in effect (with modifications) in many of them. A few states — most notably California, New Jersey, and Pennsylvania — have in recent years enacted tailor-made statutes that depart significantly from the Standard Act; even these, however, reflect its continuing influence.

> It is . . . remarkable that this law, drafted to deal with the world of the 1920s, has not only survived so long, but has served to authorize so many of the new control devices which have become popular in recent years. . . . The reason is simple — the Standard Act dealt with many of the basics of the situation. [1 Norman Williams, Jr. & John M. Taylor, American Planning Law §18.01 at 462 (rev. ed. 1988).]

1. Standard State Zoning Enabling Act, explanatory note 1, reprinted in American Law Institute, A Model Land Development Code 210 (Tent. Draft No. 1, 1968). See page 992.

The central sections of the Standard Act provide as follows:

Section 1. Grant of Power — Empowers municipalities to "regulate and restrict the height, number of stories, and size of buildings and other structures, the percentage of lot that may be occupied, the size of yards, courts, and other open spaces, the density of population, and the location and use of buildings, structures, and land for trade, industry, residence, or other purposes."

Section 2. Districts — Permits division of municipalities into districts (zones) of appropriate number, shape, and area, and provides that regulations may vary from district to district.

Section 3. Purposes in View — Requires that regulations be "made in accordance with a comprehensive plan and designed to lessen congestion in the streets; to secure safety from fire, panic, and other dangers; to promote health and the general welfare; to provide adequate light and air; to prevent the overcrowding of land; to avoid undue concentration of population; to facilitate the adequate provision of transportation, water, sewerage, schools, parks, and other public requirements. Such regulations shall be made with reasonable consideration, among other things, to the character of the district and its peculiar suitability for particular uses, and with a view to conserving the value of buildings and encouraging the most appropriate use of land throughout [the] municipality."

Section 4. Method of Procedure — Requires the enactment of procedures by which to establish, enforce, and change regulations.

Section 5. Changes — Permits modification and repeal of regulations.

Section 6. Zoning Commission — Requires appointment of a zoning commission to recommend district boundaries and regulations.

Section 7. Board of Adjustment — Authorizes appointment of a board of adjustment to hear appeals and make special exceptions to regulations "in appropriate cases and subject to appropriate conditions and safeguards . . . ," and also to permit "such variance from the terms of the ordinance as will not be contrary to the public interest, where, owing to special conditions, a literal enforcement of the provisions of the ordinance will result in unnecessary hardship, and so that the spirit of the ordinance shall be observed and substantial justice done."

Section 8. Enforcement and Remedies — Declares that violations of regulations shall be misdemeanors punishable by fine or imprisonment; civil penalties are also authorized.

Section 9. Conflict with Other Laws — Provides that in instances of conflict between zoning regulations and other laws controlling land use, the more stringent shall apply.

Bear in mind that, notwithstanding "so standardized a statutory framework, the actual systems of law vary so sharply as between the different states" as to suggest "that the wording in the enabling act is far

from being the most important element in the system of legal controls."
1 Williams & Taylor, supra, at 462.

b. The Comprehensive Plan

Notice the provision in Section 3 of the Standard Act stating that
zoning regulations shall be "in accordance with a comprehensive plan."
A comprehensive plan is a statement of the local government's objectives
and standards for development. Usually made up of maps, charts, and
descriptive text, it shows — at least in a general way — the boundaries
of height, area, bulk, and use zones, and the locations of streets, bridges,
parks, public buildings, and the like. The plan is based on surveys and
studies of the city's present situation and future needs, the idea being to
anticipate change and promote harmonious development. To require
some sort of master plan and regulations "in accordance" with it, as enabling legislation typically does, reflects the view that zoning itself is but
a means of giving effect to a larger planning enterprise that has led to
formulation of the comprehensive plan.[2]

By and large, this view of the planning process has not been taken
too seriously by the courts. Some have held that absent a specific statutory requirement (and the language of Section 3 of the Standard Zoning
Act is hardly that), the plan need not be written down in a document
separate from the zoning ordinance itself; some have considered that
the purposes recited in the zoning ordinance's preamble are themselves
evidence of a plan to which the ordinance conforms; some have found
the scheme of regulations in the zoning ordinance to amount to a plan
which the regulation implements. "The zoning ordinance itself may be-
speak the scheme; there need be no extrinsic guide." Ward v. Montgomery Township, 28 N.J. 529, 536, 147 A.2d 248, 252 (1959). If zoning
regulations are subsequently amended, they are often considered as
working an implicit and automatic change in the plan on which they are
based! Mott's Realty Corp. v. Town Plan & Zoning Commn., 152 Conn.
535, 209 A.2d 179 (1965). Even when a formal, written plan exists, it is
hardly clear that zoning regulations inconsistent with it are invalid.
"What is mandated," one court has said, "is that there be comprehen-
siveness of planning, rather than special interest, irrational ad hocery.
The obligation is support of comprehensive planning, not slavish servi-

---

2. Most states have separate enabling legislation for planning and for zoning. A Stan-
dard City Planning Enabling Act, drafted in 1928 as part of the effort by the United States
Department of Commerce leading to the Standard State Zoning Enabling Act, has pro-
vided the model for planning legislation. The Act is reprinted in American Law Institute,
A Model Land Development Code, supra footnote 1, at 222. See Charles M. Haar, "In
Accordance with a Comprehensive Plan," 68 Harv. L. Rev. 1154, 1155 (1955).

tude to any particular comprehensive plan. Indeed sound planning inherently calls for recognition of the dynamics of change." Town of Bedford v. Village of Mt. Kisco, 33 N.Y.2d 178, 188, 306 N.E.2d 155, 159, 351 N.Y.S.2d 129, 136 (1973). The emphasis, in short, has been on whether the zoning ordinance is a comprehensive plan, not whether it is "in accordance" with such a plan. Little more has been required than that zoning be reasonable and impartial. See Haar, supra footnote 2; 1 Robert M. Anderson, American Law of Zoning §5.04 (3d ed. 1986).

The role to be played by the comprehensive plan has long been a subject of debate. The plan, of course, should never be the final, conclusive word; it "may be just as arbitrary and irresponsible as the municipal zoning ordinance if that plan reflects no more than the municipality's arbitrary desires." Richard F. Babcock, The Zoning Game 123 (1966). Independent constraints, then, must be applied to exercises of the zoning power. This is not to say, though, that zoning should go forth without the considered foresight that a well-conceived planning process can provide. Planning is claimed to be especially important today, in light of increasing urbanization and growing public concern with environmental quality. See Daniel R. Mandelker, The Role of the Local Comprehensive Plan in Land Use Regulation, 74 Mich. L. Rev. 899 (1976). A few courts, perhaps agreeing with this view, have given the comprehensive plan a significant role in the zoning process, but decisions holding to the old line — the plan is of minor importance — continue to appear.[3]

Beginning about 20 years ago, some states adopted so-called consistency statutes that change the familiar "in accordance" language of Section 3 of the Standard Act and require instead that local zoning ordinances be consistent with, or implement, an adopted comprehensive plan. The effect of these statutes is still somewhat uncertain. Consistency doctrine at its strongest makes planning mandatory, specifies with some precision the nature of the required plan, and subjects virtually all zoning decisions to the plan's dictates. The plan might be enforceable through citizen suits, and remedies for inconsistency might include injunctions against development. But not all states that have adopted the doctrine carry it to its extremes as to each or any of these elements; moreover, much can turn on the degree of judicial scrutiny applied in reviewing zoning actions alleged to be inconsistent with the comprehensive plan. The more the judiciary defers, the less the impact of consistency requirements.[4] See generally Joseph F. DiMento, The Consistency

3. Compare Baker v. City of Milwaukie, 271 Or. 500, 533 P.2d 772 (1975) (holding that a city can be compelled to conform its zoning ordinance to the plan and to suspend the issuance of building permits in violation of the plan), with West Hill Citizens for Controlled Dev. Density v. King County Council, 29 Wash. App. 168, 627 P.2d 1002 (1981) (explicitly rejecting *City of Milwaukie* and holding that the comprehensive plan is merely a "blueprint"; strict adherence is not required and ordinances in conflict with the plan are not necessarily void).

4. Questions regarding judicial review of zoning decisions will be considered at var-

Doctrine in Its Adolescence: More Questions About the Role of Comprehensive Plans, 5 Zoning & Plan. L. Rep. 49 (1982).

The debate over comprehensive planning that began long ago now centers on the wisdom of consistency doctrine. Skeptics regard planning as a troubled science at best and worry that consistency requirements will only aggravate its shortcomings. See A. Dan Tarlock, Consistency with Adopted Land Use Plans as a Standard of Judicial Review: The Case Against, 9 Urb. L. Ann. 69 (1975). Enthusiasts, of course, believe that good planning is important — and possible — and that carefully implemented consistency requirements can have a positive impact on the land-use decision process. See Joseph F. DiMento, Improving Development Control Through Planning: The Consistency Doctrine, 5 Colum. J. Envtl. L. 1 (1978), and, generally, Joseph F. DiMento, The Consistency Doctrine and the Limits of Planning (1980). Ironically, some planners have become increasingly despairing of their ability to formulate adequate comprehensive plans in the face of rapid change and are searching for more flexible techniques.

c. Zoning Ordinances and Subdivision Controls

We need not say too much about zoning ordinances; the *Euclid* case and the materials above give a pretty good picture. The ordinance is simply a set of regulations enacted by the local legislative body and enforced by local officials. Zoning ordinances typically specify the uses to which designated areas may be put, the types and sizes of structures that may be built within those areas, and the placement of the structures (setbacks, sidelots, and so forth). Minimum lot size and floor space requirements are commonly specified for residential dwellings; controls on advertising often appear with regard to commercial zones. Special districts, with their own peculiar structural restrictions, are often established for airports, floodplains, and areas of historical importance.

Zoning regulations are enforced in large part through review by local officials of plans for proposed developments; permits for new construction or remodeling are granted only if proposals conform to the applicable zoning restrictions. The denial of a building permit or certificate of occupancy is the chief means of enforcing zoning regulations. Many ordinances provide criminal penalties for proceeding without appropriate approvals, but orders of compliance are the more commonly used enforcement tool. It is not unusual for private citizens to complain to local officials that the zoning laws are not being enforced; if the complaints go unheeded, property owners injured by nonenforcement may

---

ious points throughout this chapter. See generally Daniel R. Mandelker & A. Dan Tarlock, Shifting the Presumption of Constitutionality in Land-Use Law, 24 Urb. Law. 1 (1992).

usually sue for an injunction or for mandamus against the passive officials. Most cities have some sort of administrative body — a board of adjustment or of zoning appeals — to review the decisions of local officials and to grant exceptions of one sort or another (considered later) in special cases. Generally speaking, however, the board is not empowered to amend the zoning ordinance. Actions of the board and of the local legislative body are subject to judicial review.

Related to zoning ordinances is another means used to implement planning — subdivision controls. Subdivision ordinances set out standards and procedures to govern the breaking up of tracts of land into lots (for sale before or after development). The purpose of subdivision regulation is to ensure that appropriate attention is paid to such factors as light and air, transportation flows, recreational needs, and water and sanitary facilities. Suppose a developer's subdivision proposal complies with all the specific requirements set out in the subdivision ordinance, but the local regulatory authority identifies other problems with the proposal. May the authority withhold approval? As a general matter, the answer is no. See, e.g., Richardson v. City of Little Rock Planning Commn., 295 Ark. 189, 747 S.W.2d 116 (1988) (approval could not be denied on any grounds other than the minimum standards of the subdivision ordinance); Reed v. Planning & Zoning Commn. of Chester, 208 Conn. 431, 544 A.2d 1213 (1988) (approval could not be denied on ground of inadequate road access when road access was not a requirement specified in regulations). For criticism of such cases, see Laurie Reynolds, Local Subdivision Regulation: Formulaic Constraints in an Age of Discretion, 24 Ga. L. Rev. 525 (1990), arguing that some discretion in the application of subdivision ordinances is necessary given the complexities of urbanization. (As we shall see, the question of discretion arises repeatedly in the zoning context. Discretion provides flexibility but invites abuse by those in authority. Fixed standards help avoid abuse but may prove unduly rigid in the face of changing circumstances.)

An important objective of subdivision regulation is to see to it that necessary public services and public improvements will be provided before a proposal is approved. Thus a typical subdivision ordinance may authorize the local authority to require that the developer not only design the subdivision in accordance with specified standards but also provide (or make in-lieu payments to provide) streets, sidewalks, lighting, gutters, sewers, recreation areas, schools, and other public facilities — on-site and off-site. Most recently, some localities have started charging so-called impact fees calculated as a function of the type, scale, and location of a development, and intended to mitigate the burdens it will place on the larger community.

The justification offered for "exactions," a generic label for all of the foregoing conditions and requirements, is this: Since homeowners could be subjected to special assessments by the city in order to provide the facilities in question, an equivalent is to put the burden on developers, who will in turn pass the costs on to buyers. But is the matter as simple as that? See Robert C. Ellickson & A. Dan Tarlock, Land-Use Controls 735-737, 754-756 (1981), discussing uncertainties in the passing on of costs, and also considering questions of equity as between the residents of established neighborhoods in the area, on the one hand, and the residents of new developments on the other.

Exactions have proved to be controversial. Some of them have been challenged as illegal taxes and others as unconstitutional takings of property. In reviewing exactions, most courts have in the past applied one or another variant of the same test, essentially asking whether there is a "rational nexus" (a reasonable relationship) between the particular requirement and the needs created by the new subdivision. The standing of this test is now in question, thanks to the Supreme Court's decision in Nollan v. California Coastal Commn., 483 U.S. 825, which we take up in Chapter 12. (See pages 1217-1224.) Judicial decisions have been mixed in any event, primarily because some courts approach exactions with more liberality than others. See generally Richard R. Roddewig, Recent Developments in Land Use, Planning and Zoning Law, 22 Urb. Law. 719, 779-794 (1990); Stewart E. Sterk, *Nollan*, Henry George, and Exactions, 88 Colum. L. Rev. 1731 (1988) (discussing concerns with exactions).

B. The Nonconforming Use

PA Northwestern Distributors, Inc. v. Zoning Hearing Board

Supreme Court of Pennsylvania, 1991
526 Pa. 186, 584 A.2d 1372

LARSEN, J. This appeal presents an issue of first impression to this Court, i.e., whether a zoning ordinance which requires the amortization and discontinuance of a lawful preexisting nonconforming use is confiscatory and violative of the constitution as a taking of property without just compensation.

On May 4, 1985, after obtaining the necessary permits and certificates to conduct its business on leased premises, appellant, PA Northwestern Distributors, Inc., opened an adult book store in Moon Township, Pennsylvania. Four days later, the Moon Township Board of Supervisors published a public notice of its intention to amend the Moon Township Zoning Ordinance to regulate "adult commercial enterprises." On May 23, 1985, following a public hearing on the matter, the

Moon Township Board of Supervisors adopted Ordinance No. 243, effective on May 28, 1985, which ordinance imposes extensive restrictions on the location and operation of "adult commercial enterprises." Section 805 of the ordinance provides as follows:

Amortization. Any commercial enterprise which would constitute a pre-existing use and which would be in conflict with the requirements set forth in this amendment to the Moon Township Zoning Ordinance has 90 days from the date that the ordinance becomes effective to come into compliance with this ordinance. This 90-day grace period is designed to be a period of amortization for those pre-existing businesses which cannot meet the standards set forth in this amendment to the Moon Township Zoning Ordinance.

Appellant's adult book store, by definition, is an adult commercial enterprise under the ordinance, and it does not and cannot meet the place restrictions set forth in the ordinance in that it is not located within an area designated for adult commercial enterprises.[5] The Zoning Officer of Moon Township notified appellant that it was out of compliance with the ordinance. Appellant filed an appeal to the Zoning Hearing Board of the Township of Moon, appellee herein. The appeal was limited to challenging the validity of the amortization provision set forth in the ordinance.

Following a hearing, the Zoning Hearing Board upheld the validity of the amortization provision as applied, and appellant filed an appeal to the Court of Common Pleas of Allegheny County. No further evidence was taken, and appellant's appeal was dismissed. On appeal, Commonwealth Court affirmed, 124 Pa. Cmwlth. 228, 555 A.2d 1368, basing its decision on Sullivan v. Zoning Board of Adjustment, 83 Pa. Commw. 228, 478 A.2d 912 (1984). We granted appellant's petition for allowance of appeal, and we now reverse. . . .

In the case of *Sullivan,* supra, the Commonwealth Court determined that provisions for the amortization of nonconforming uses are constitutional exercises of the police power so long as they are reasonable. It was the opinion of the Commonwealth Court in that case, that the "distinction between an ordinance restricting future uses and one requiring the termination of present uses within a reasonable period of time is merely one of degree. . . ." 83 Pa. Commw. at 244, 478 A.2d at 920. To determine whether the amortization provisions are reasonable, the Commonwealth Court stated:

5. Section 803 of the ordinance requires that no adult commercial enterprise can operate within 500 feet of a pre-existing school, hospital, nursing home, group care facility, park, church, establishment selling alcoholic beverages, or another adult commercial enterprise. Section 804 requires that no adult commercial enterprise can operate within 1,000 feet of an area zoned residential. Appellant's adult book store is located closer to a school, a church and a residential district than permitted under these place restrictions.

Each case in this class must be determined on its own facts; and the answer to the question of whether the provision is reasonable must be decided by observing its impact upon the property under consideration. The true issue is that of whether, considering the nature of the present use, the length of the period for amortization, the present characteristics of and the foreseeable future prospects for development of the vicinage and other relevant facts and circumstances, the beneficial effects upon the community that would result from the discontinuance of the use can be seen to more than offset the losses to the affected landowner. [83 Pa. Commw. at 247, 478 A.2d at 920.]

Following this standard, the Zoning Hearing Board herein heard evidence regarding the impact upon the property in question with respect to the nature of the present use, the period for amortization, the characteristics of the vicinage, etc., and determined that the amortization provision was reasonable as applied. In this regard the Zoning Hearing Board stated that the "real and substantial benefits to the Township of elimination of the nonconforming use from this location . . . more than offset the losses to the affected landowner." Opinion of the Board at 13 (May 20, 1987).

If the Commonwealth Court opinion in *Sullivan*, supra, had been a correct statement of the law in this Commonwealth, we would be constrained to find that appellee herein had not committed an error of law or an abuse of discretion. For the following reasons, however, we find that *Sullivan* is not a correct statement of the law regarding amortization provisions in this Commonwealth.

In this Commonwealth, all property is held in subordination to the right of its reasonable regulation by the government, which regulation is clearly necessary to preserve the health, safety, morals, or general welfare of the people. Anstine v. Zoning Board of Adjustment, 411 Pa. 33, 190 A.2d 712 (1963). Moreover, "a presumption of validity attaches to a zoning ordinance which imposes the burden to prove its invalidity upon the one who challenges it." National Land and Investment Co. v. Easttown Township Board of Adjustment, 419 Pa. 504, 522, 215 A.2d 597, 607 (1965). This Court has noted, however, that the presumption of a zoning ordinance's validity must be tempered by the Court's appreciation of the fact that zoning involves governmental restrictions upon a property owner's *constitutionally guaranteed* right to use his or her property, unfettered by governmental restrictions, except where the use violates any law, the use creates a nuisance, or the owner violates any covenant, restriction or easement.[6]

---

6. At the hearing before the Zoning Hearing Board herein, no evidence was presented to show that appellant's adult book store had violated any law, created a nuisance in the community, or violated any covenant, restriction or easement. In fact, evidence presented at the hearing tended to show that appellant was operating its adult book store well within the parameters of the law in that prosecutions against appellant's employees for violations of the obscenity law, 18 Pa. C.S.A. §5903, had resulted in acquittals. Hearing Transcript at 45-46 (Nov. 13, 1986).

Many other jurisdictions have upheld the validity of amortization provisions in zoning ordinances, finding that it is appropriate to balance the property interests of the individual with the health, safety, morals or general welfare of the community at large, and that, where reasonable, amortization provisions succeed in effectuating orderly land use planning and development in a way that the natural attrition of nonconforming uses cannot. See cases collected at Annotation, Validity of Provisions for Amortization of Nonconforming Uses, 22 A.L.R. 3d (1968 & Supp. 1990). See also Katarincic, Elimination of Non-Conforming Uses, Buildings, and Structures by Amortization — Concept Versus Law, 2 Duq. L. Rev. 1 (1963).

Although this Court has never before considered the validity of an amortization provision in a zoning ordinance, it has long been the law of this Commonwealth that municipalities lack the power to compel a change in the nature of an existing lawful use of property. . . . In addition, municipalities may not prevent the owner of nonconforming property from making those necessary additions to an existing structure as are needed to provide for its natural expansion, so long as such additions would not be detrimental to the public welfare, safety, and health.

A lawful nonconforming use establishes in the property owner a vested property right which cannot be abrogated or destroyed, unless it is a nuisance, it is abandoned, or it is extinguished by eminent domain. See Gross v. Zoning Board of Adjustment, 424 Pa. 603, 227 A.2d 824 (1967). This determination is compelled by our constitution which recognizes the "inherent and indefeasible" right of our citizens to possess and protect property, Pa. Const. art. I, §1, and requires that just compensation be paid for the taking of private property, Pa. Const. art. I, §10. As we emphasized in Andress v. Zoning Board of Adjustment, 410 Pa. 77, 82-84, 188 A.2d 709, 711-12 (1963):

> The natural or zealous desire of many zoning boards to protect, improve and develop their community, to plan a city or a township or a community that is both practical and beautiful, and to conserve the property values as well as the "tone" of that community is commendable. But they must remember that property owners have certain rights which are ordained, protected and preserved in our Constitution and which neither zeal nor worthwhile objectives can impinge upon or abolish. . . .

Although at times it may be difficult to discern whether zoning legislation is merely regulating as opposed to "taking," this Court has stated that "[a] 'taking' is not limited to an actual physical possession or seizure of the property; if the *effect* of the zoning law or regulation is to deprive a property owner of the lawful use of his property it amounts to a 'taking,' for which he must be justly compensated." Cleaver v. Board of Adjustment, 414 Pa. 367, 372, 200 A.2d 408, 412 (1964) (emphasis in original).

The effect of the amortization provision herein is to deprive appellant of the lawful use of its property in that the ordinance forces appellant to cease using its property as an adult book store within 90 days. Appellee argues that appellant is free to relocate to one of the few sites in the Township of Moon that complies with the place restrictions of the ordinance, or to change its use to sell some other commodity, in an attempt to convince this Court that the ordinance has not effectuated a "taking" of appellant's property without just compensation. The Pennsylvania Constitution, Pa. Const. art I, §1, however, protects the right of a property owner to use his or her property in any lawful way that he or she so chooses. If government desires to interfere with the owner's use, where the use is lawful and is not a nuisance nor is it abandoned, it must compensate the owner for the resulting loss. A gradual phasing out of nonconforming uses which occurs when an ordinance only restricts future uses differs in significant measure from an amortization provision which restricts future uses *and* extinguishes a lawful nonconforming use on a timetable which is not of the property owner's choosing.

The language of the Missouri Supreme Court in Hoffman v. Kinealy, 389 S.W.2d 745, 753 (Mo. 1965), is apropos to the issue of this case:

> [I]t would be a strange and novel doctrine indeed which would approve a municipality taking private property for public use without compensation if the property was not too valuable and the taking was not too soon, and prompts us to repeat the caveat of Mr. Justice Holmes in Pennsylvania Coal Co. v. Mahon, 260 U.S. 393, 416, 43 S. Ct. 158, 160, 67 L. Ed. 322, 326, 28 A.L.R. 1321, that "[we] are in danger of forgetting that a strong public desire to improve the public condition is not enough to warrant achieving the desire by a shorter cut than the constitutional way of paying for the change." . . .

Thus, we hold that the amortization and discontinuance of a lawful pre-existing nonconforming use is per se confiscatory and violative of the Pennsylvania Constitution, Pa. Const. art. I, §1. There are important policy considerations which support this determination. If municipalities were free to amortize nonconforming uses out of existence, future economic development could be seriously compromised. As one commentator has noted:

> The law of zoning should be designed to protect the reasonable expectations of persons who plan to enter business or make improvements on property. The possibility that the municipality could by zoning force removal of installations or cessation of business might serve to deter such investors. [Note, Nonconforming Uses: A Rationale and an Approach, 102 U. Pa. L. Rev. 91, 103 (1953).]

This commentator also notes that forced destruction will often result in economic waste. Id. at 104.

It is clear that if we were to permit the amortization of nonconforming uses in this Commonwealth, *any* use could be amortized out of existence without just compensation. Although such a zoning option seems reasonable when the use involves some activity that may be distasteful to some members of the public, *no* use would be exempt from the reach of amortization, and *any* property owner could lose the use of his or her property without compensation. Even a homeowner could find one day that his or her "castle" had become a nonconforming use and would be required to vacate the premises within some arbitrary period of time, *without just compensation*. Such a result is repugnant to a basic protection accorded in this Commonwealth to vested property interests.

Accordingly, we find that the amortization provision, Section 805, of Ordinance No. 243 of the Township of Moon is unconstitutional on its face, and we reverse the order of the Commonwealth Court, which affirmed the order of the Court of Common Pleas of Allegheny County dismissing appellant's appeal from the decision of the Zoning Hearing Board of the Township of Moon.

NIX, C.J., concurring. While I agree with the result reached by the majority, that Section 805 of Ordinance No. 243 is invalid in this case, I must disagree with the finding that any provision for the amortization of nonconforming uses would be per se confiscatory and unconstitutional. I would uphold the Commonwealth Court's decision relying on Sullivan v. Zoning Board of Adjustment, 83 Pa. Commw. 228, 478 A.2d 912 (1984), and hold that a reasonable amortization provision is valid if it reflects the consideration of certain factors. The instant provision, however, falls short of the reasonableness requirements and therefore must be struck down.

The weight of authority supports the conclusion that a reasonable amortization provision would not be unconstitutional. See generally 22 A.L.R.3d 1134 (1968). It has been stated that a blanket rule against amortization provisions should be rejected because such a rule has a debilitating effect on effective zoning, unnecessarily restricts a state's police power, and prevents the operation of a reasonable and flexible method of eliminating nonconforming uses in the public interest. Lachapelle v. Goffstown, 107 N.H. 485, 225 A.2d 624 (1967). The New Hampshire court found acceptable amortization provisions which were reasonable as to time and directed toward some reasonable aspect of land use regulation under properly delegated police power. Id. Other cases have considered several factors in determining the reasonableness of these provisions. Those factors weigh any circumstance bearing upon a balancing of public gain against private loss, including the length of the amortization period in relation to the nature of the nonconforming use, Gurnee v. Miller, 69 Ill. App. 2d 248, 215 N.E.2d 829 (1966); Eutaw Enterprises, Inc. v. Baltimore, 241 Md. 686, 217 A.2d 348 (1966); length of time in relation to the investment, id.; and the degree of offensiveness of the nonconforming use in view of the character of the surrounding neighborhood. See City of Los Angeles v. Gage, 127 Cal. App. 2d 442, 274 P.2d 34, 43-44 (1954); Grant v. Baltimore, 212 Md. 301, 129 A.2d 363 (1957); Lachapelle v. Goffstown, supra. . . .

I believe that a per se prohibition against amortization provisions is too restrictive. A community should have a right to change its character without being locked into pre-existing definitions of what is offensive. As this Court has also noted, "nonconforming uses, inconsistent with a basic purpose of zoning, represent conditions which should be reduced to conformity as speedily as is compatible with the law and the Constitution." Hanna v. Board of Adjustment of Borough of Forest Hills, 408 Pa. 306, 312-13, 183 A.2d 539, 543 (1962). I believe that amortization provisions are an effective method of reconciling interests of the community with those of property owners. Where the provisions are reasonable in consideration of the elements herein discussed, they provide adequate notice to the property owner so that no deprivation of property or use thereof is suffered, yet they simultaneously afford a township the opportunity to alter the character of its neighborhoods when the alteration takes the form of a reasonable land use regulation.

In this case, however, the amortization provision is not a reasonable one because it fails to provide adequate time for elimination of the nonconforming use. The period allowed for the dissolution of appellant's business is ninety days. Certainly ninety days is an insufficient period of time to allow a merchant to close a business. Any contractual obligations appellant has incurred in anticipation of operating the business probably cannot be terminated within such a short period of time without severe hardship on appellant's part. Three months also would not permit appellant to obtain an alternative means of income. Moreover, forcing appellant to liquidate his enterprise within ninety days could prevent him from obtaining a reasonable return on his investment. I therefore agree that the instant provision is confiscatory.[7]

PROBLEMS, NOTES, AND QUESTIONS

1. Should nonconforming uses be protected? Consider this problem. *A* and *B* each have $50,000 to invest. *A* purchases a vacant lot for $50,000. Ten years later the city passes a zoning ordinance zoning *A*'s land for single-family dwellings. The value of *A*'s land is reduced to $12,500 by this action. In Village of Euclid v. Ambler Realty Co., page

---

7. Zoning measures designed to control the location of adult bookstores and the like can give rise to First Amendment concerns. We address these later. See pages 1078-1079. — EDS.

993, the Supreme Court approved a zoning ordinance that allegedly reduced the value of vacant land by three-fourths. Hence *A* has no constitutional complaint.

B purchases a vacant lot next to *A*'s lot for $10,000 and builds and equips a store on the premises for $40,000, for a total investment of $50,000. The store earns *B* a 10-percent net profit each year after paying all business expenses including *B*'s salary. After 10 years the city passes a zoning ordinance zoning *B*'s land for single-family dwellings. The value of *B*'s land, like *A*'s land, is reduced by three-fourths. If this ordinance requires *B* to discontinue his nonconforming use immediately, the courts almost surely would declare it unconstitutional as a taking of *B*'s property. Why should this be so? Is *B* harmed more than *A*? If the ordinance were retroactive, would you prefer to be in *A*'s shoes or *B*'s?

2. The right to maintain a nonconforming use "runs with the land"; hence it survives a change of ownership. If a nonconforming use is abandoned, however, it may be terminated, as it may be if brought to an end by an act of God. Changes and enlargements in use can also result in termination.[8] And wisely or not, ordinances sometimes limit the right to repair nonconforming structures in order to promote their withering away.

Suppose that in 1989 *X* purchases a gasoline and service station from *Y*; *Y*'s use of the property for those purposes predated a 1986 zoning ordinance limiting the area to exclusive residential use. After purchase, *X* remodels the station and leases it to a machine shop operator; the service facilities are used by *X* to fuel and service trucks that *X* uses in a delivery business. In 1992 *X* terminates the lease to the machine shop and leases the property to *Z* for use as a gasoline and service station. Are *X* and *Z* entitled to a permit for the gasoline and service station operations? Would it matter that *X* had leased the property to the machine shop because, at that time, no other suitable tenants could be found? See Miorelli v. Zoning Hearing Bd. of Hazleton, 30 Pa. Commw. 330, 373 A.2d 1158 (1977).

Suppose that *X* purchases agricultural land in 1990 and uses it for a scrap and salvage yard. In 1992 a zoning ordinance is enacted to restrict the land to residential use. Shortly thereafter *X* seeks a permit to install a machine that crushes and bales large amounts of scrap metal; the machine would increase the scale and speed of *X*'s operation and make it possible to process new kinds of scrap. Is *X* entitled to the permit? Would it matter that *X* wishes to install the new machine because demand is outstripping the capabilities of his present facilities? See Township of

8. What if the proposed change in use would be to a less offensive nonconforming use — say from a foundry to an automobile repair shop? Must it be permitted? See Adolphson v. Zoning Bd. of Appeals of Fairfield, 205 Conn. 703, 535 A.2d 799 (1988) (yes).

Kelly v. Zoning Hearing Bd. of Kelly Township, 36 Pa. Commw. 509, 388 A.2d 347 (1978).

3. Would a longer period have mattered in the *PA Northwestern* case? Should it have? The court in the *Sullivan* case (quoted on page 1012) reasoned that "the distinction between an ordinance restricting future uses and one requiring the termination of present uses within a reasonable period of time is merely one of degree." Isn't that correct? If it is, doesn't it follow that amortization should be accepted in principle, the only issue being whether the ordinance allows the use in question a sufficient period of time to phase out of existence? After all, a sufficient period of time can reduce the degree of difference to, essentially, zero.

Courts approving the amortization technique claim to require a reasonable period for the particular nonconforming use in question. In practice, however, there appears to be considerable deference to rough-and-ready lines. For any given use, one can find cases upholding, and other cases invalidating, periods ranging from 1 to 30 or more years. See, e.g., 1 Robert M. Anderson, American Law of Zoning §6.74 (3d ed. 1986). This kind of (apparent) sloppiness threatens to make amortization especially vulnerable to challenge. See Craig A. Peterson & Claire McCarthy, Amortization of Legal Land Use Nonconformities as Regulatory Takings: An Uncertain Future, 35 Wash. U. J. Urb. & Contemp. L. 37 (1989); Osborne M. Reynolds, Jr., The Reasonableness of Amortization Periods for Nonconforming Uses — Balancing the Private Interest and the Public Welfare, 34 Wash. U. J. Urb. & Contemp. L. 99 (1988).

Factors usually listed as relevant to an assessment of the reasonableness of a particular amortization period are the nature of the use in question, the amount invested in it, the number of improvements, the public detriment caused by the use, the character of the surrounding neighborhood, and the amount of time needed to "amortize" the investment. Would you add to the list? May an amortization period be based on the depreciation regulations of the Internal Revenue Service, and a nonconforming use forced out when it is fully amortized for tax purposes? See National Advertising Co. v. County of Monterey, 1 Cal. 3d 875, 464 P.2d 33, 83 Cal. Rptr. 577, cert. denied, 398 U.S. 946 (1970) (yes). Must the amortization period permit the owner of improvements sufficient time to depreciate his property entirely? See Art Neon Co. v. City and County of Denver, 488 F.2d 118 (10th Cir. 1973), cert. denied, 417 U.S. 932 (1974) (use may be terminated prior to full depreciation); Modjeska Sign Studios, Inc. v. Berle, 43 N.Y.2d 468, 373 N.E.2d 255 (1977) (same).

4. *Vested rights.* Related to the law of nonconforming uses is the more general doctrine of vested rights. In the case of nonconforming uses, a pre-existing operation is protected; plans to engage in some particular use are insufficient. In the case of vested rights doctrine, a pro-

posed use might be protected if sufficient commitments have been made — plans drawn, permits obtained, the site prepared, construction begun — in reliance on existing zoning requirements that are subsequently changed in a way that invalidates the proposed use. Vested rights doctrine varies in practice from jurisdiction to jurisdiction (some of which have statutes or ordinances on the question), but the critical variables include how far the developer has gone in obtaining governmental approvals, how much money has been sunk in good faith, and on what the money has been spent.[9] See generally 1 Anderson, supra, §§6.20-6.34.

Another theory, estoppel, is sometimes mentioned in cases where developers rely reasonably and to their detriment on the issuance of a permit and proceed to make substantial expenditures. Whether estoppel differs in any significant way from vested rights doctrine is a matter of conjecture. See, e.g., Richard B. Cunningham & David H. Kremer, Vested Rights, Estoppel, and the Land Development Process, 29 Hastings L.J. 623 (1978); Donald G. Hagman, Estoppel and Vesting in the Age of Multi-Land Use Permits, 11 Sw. U. L. Rev. 545 (1979).

Consider a problem that can arise under either theory — vested rights or estoppel. Suppose a local official erroneously issues a building permit, such that, say, the proposed construction would violate setback requirements. Construction proceeds considerably before the error is discovered. Must the developer demolish and start again to comply with the applicable requirements, or, rather, must neighbors live with a misplaced building? The cases go both ways, but neither way seems very satisfactory. An alternative approach would allow local authorities to enforce the regulations but require compensation to the developer to cover any loses sustained in good faith. See the discussion in Robert C. Ellickson & A. Dan Tarlock, Land-Use Controls 210-212 (1981). Something like this was considered in Allen v. City & County of Honolulu, 58 Haw. 432, 571 P.2d 328 (1977), but rejected on the ground that it would inhibit cities from exercising discretion. The approach was approved in J&B Dev. Co. v. King County, 100 Wash. 2d 299, 669 P.2d 468 (1983), but that case was recently overruled in Taylor v. Stevens County, 111 Wash. 2d 159, 759 P.2d 447 (1988), the court concluding that the compensation requirement exposed local authorities to virtually unlimited liability.

---

9. Some jurisdictions require expenditures on actual construction before rights vest, and even then — as mentioned in the text — the expenditures must be in good faith. For example, in Parkview Assocs. v. City of New York, 71 N.Y.2d 274, 519 N.E.2d 1372 (1988), the court held that the city could enforce zoning limitations even though the developer had carried out substantial construction in reliance on an erroneously issued building permit. Why? Because reasonable diligence would have revealed the zoning limitations to anyone proceeding in good faith.

C. Achieving Flexibility in Zoning

By binding limited classes of uses into tightly drawn districts, Euclidean zoning can work inequitable hardships and promote inefficient patterns of land use; it can also inhibit socially and aesthetically desirable diversity. See Jane Jacobs, The Death and Life of Great American Cities 152-177, 222-269 passim (1961). On a variety of grounds, then, there must be means for providing flexibility in zoning. The approach to nonconforming uses, considered in the last section, could be regarded as one way of doing so; this section surveys a number of others. They range from modest techniques by which to modify traditional zoning regulations, to distinctly non-Euclidean approaches to public control of land use. As you study the materials that follow, note the differing requirements of each of the flexibility devices and the differing methods (and decisionmakers) by which the devices are administered. Keep especially in mind that the power to regulate "flexibly" can be the power to favor, or disfavor, for illegitimate reasons. How might abuses of power best be controlled?

1. Variances and Special Exceptions

Recall that Section 7 of the Standard State Zoning Enabling Act authorizes appointment of a board of adjustment that may, "in appropriate cases and subject to appropriate conditions and safeguards, make special exceptions to the terms of the ordinance in harmony with its general purpose and intent . . . ," and may authorize "in specific cases such variance from the terms of the ordinance as will not be contrary to the public interest, where, owing to special conditions, a literal enforcement of the provisions of the ordinance will result in unnecessary hardship, and so that the spirit of the ordinance shall be observed and substantial justice done." This section thus authorizes two rather different means of promoting flexibility: the special exception (or special-use permit or conditional-use permit) and the variance.

Commons v. Westwood Zoning Board of Adjustment
Supreme Court of New Jersey, 1980
81 N.J. 597, 410 A.2d 1138

SCHREIBER, J. We are again called upon to examine the proceedings before and findings of a board of adjustment which denied a zoning variance for construction of a single-family residence on an undersized lot. See N.J.S.A. 40:55-39(c). Plaintiffs, Gordon L. Commons, Helen T. Commons and Leo Weingarten, filed a complaint to review the denial of the variance by the Borough of Westwood Zoning Board of Adjustment. The Superior Court, Law Division, and the Appellate Division affirmed the board's action. We granted plaintiffs' petition for certification. 79 N.J. 482, 401 A.2d 237 (1979).

The facts developed at the hearings before the Board of Adjustment were substantially undisputed. The property in question is a vacant lot, designated as Lot 20 in Block 208 on the tax map of the Borough of Westwood. Located in an established residential area consisting of one and two-family dwellings, this lot is the only undeveloped property in the neighborhood. Plaintiffs Gordon and Helen Commons are the present owners. They and their predecessors in title have owned this plot since 1927. Plaintiff Weingarten, a builder, contracted to purchase the property on the condition that he could construct a one-family residence on the lot.

A variance from the borough's zoning ordinance was necessary for two reasons. The land was located in a District B residential zone requiring a minimum frontage of 75 feet and a minimum area of 7500 square feet. The lot, however, has a frontage on Brickell Avenue of only 30 feet and a total area of 5190 square feet.

When adopted in 1933, the borough's zoning ordinance contained no minimum frontage or area provisions. However, a 1947 amendment required that one-family houses be located on lots with a frontage of at least 75 feet and an area of no less than 7500 square feet. At the time the amendment was adopted there were approximately 32 homes in the immediate area. Only seven satisfied the minimum frontage requirement. The nonconforming lots had frontages varying from 40 to 74 feet. This situation has remained virtually unchanged, only two homes having been constructed thereafter, one in 1948 with a frontage of 70 feet and one in 1970 with a frontage of 113 feet.

Weingarten proposed to construct a single-family, one and one-half story "raised ranch" with four bedrooms, a living room, dining room, kitchen, two baths and a one-car garage. Weingarten had no architectural design of the proposed house, but submitted a plan for a larger home which he claimed could be scaled down. The proposed home would have an approximate width of 19 feet, 18 inches and a depth of 48 feet. It would be centered on the 30-foot lot so as to provide five-foot side yards, the minimum required by the zoning ordinance. The proposed setback would also conform with the zoning plan. Weingarten further explained that the proposed residence would be roughly 18 feet from the house belonging to Robert Dineen located on adjacent land to the north, and 48 feet from the two-family residence owned by David

Butler on the property to the south. The Dineen property has a 50-foot frontage, and the Butler frontage measures 74.5 feet.

The proposed home would be offered for sale for about $55,000. That price compared favorably with the market values of other near-by homes which a local realtor, Thomas Reno, estimated at between $45,000 and $60,000. Reno testified that the proposed home would not impair the borough's zoning plan because the house would be new, its value would compare favorably with other homes, its setback from the street would be at least as great as others, and the distances between the adjoining houses on each side would be substantial.

In 1974, plaintiff Gordon Commons had offered to sell the lot to Dineen for $7,500. Negotiations terminated, however, after Dineen countered with a $1,600 proposal, the assessed value of the property. When Weingarten contracted to purchase the land, he sought, albeit unsuccessfully, to purchase from Butler a 10-foot strip, adjacent to the south side of the lot.

Many neighbors opposed the application for a variance. Butler testified that a house on a 30-foot lot would be aesthetically displeasing, would differ in appearance by having a garage in front rather than alongside the dwelling, and would impair property values in the neighborhood. Another property owner, whose home was across the street, expressed her concern about privacy, reasoning that the occupants of a four-bedroom residence on a small lot would cause a spillover effect in terms of noise and trespassing.

The board of adjustment denied the variance, finding "that the applicant failed to demonstrate any evidence to establish hardship" and "that the granting of the variance would substantially impair the intent and purpose of the Zone Plan and Zoning Ordinance of the Borough of Westwood." The trial court, after reviewing the testimony, affirmed because it felt that to permit the variance "would be detrimental to the entire area wherein the property in question is situated." The Appellate Division, holding that the board of adjustment had not acted arbitrarily, affirmed in a brief per curiam opinion.

The variance application was filed and heard when N.J.S.A. 40:55-39(c) was effective. That statute has been replaced with N.J.S.A. 40:55D-70(c) of the Municipal Land Use Law, N.J.S.A. 40:55D-1 et seq. Since these provisions are substantially the same and we are remanding this matter to the board of adjustment, we shall consider the issues in the light of the current statute.

I

N.J.S.A. 40:55D-70(c) provides that a board of adjustment shall have power to grant a variance where by reason of the narrowness of the land or other extraordinary and exceptional situation of the property, the strict application of a zoning ordinance would result in exceptional and undue hardship upon the developer of the property.[10] In addition, the statute's negative criteria must be satisfied, that is that the variance can be granted "without substantial detriment to the public good and will not substantially impair the intent and purpose of the zone plan and zoning ordinance." As in Chirichello v. Monmouth Beach Zoning Bd. of Adjustment, 78 N.J. 544, 397 A.2d 646 (1978), where the proposed residence conformed to the use requirement of the zoning ordinance but had insufficient frontage and area, we are called upon to consider and analyze the "undue hardship" concept and the negative criteria.

"Undue hardship" involves the underlying notion that no effective use can be made of the property in the event the variance is denied. Use of the property may of course be subject to reasonable restraint. As Justice Pashman observed in Taxpayers Association of Weymouth Tp., Inc. v. Weymouth Tp., 80 N.J. 6, 20, 364 A.2d 1016, 1023 (1976), cert. den. 430 U.S. 977, 97 S. Ct. 1672, 52 L. Ed. 2d 373 (1977), "[z]oning is inherently an exercise of the State's police power" and the property owner's use of the land is subject to regulation "which will promote the public health, safety, morals and general welfare. . . ." N.J.S.A. 40:55D-2(a). Put another way an "owner is not entitled to have his property zoned for its most profitable use." Bow & Arrow Manor v. West Orange, 63 N.J. 335, 350, 307 A.2d 563, 571 (1973). See Shell Oil Co. v. Shrewsbury Zoning Bd. of Adjustment, 64 N.J. 334, 316 A.2d 5 (1974). However, when the regulation renders the property unusable for any purpose, the analysis calls for further inquiries which may lead to a conclusion that the property owner would suffer an undue hardship.

It is appropriate to consider first the origin of the existing situation. If the property owner or his predecessors in title created the nonconforming condition, then the hardship may be deemed to be self-imposed. To measure this type of impact it is necessary to know when the zoning ordinance limitations were adopted and the status of the property with respect to those limitations at that time. Thus, if the lot had contained a 75-foot frontage and despite the existence of that requirement, the owner sold a 40-foot strip of the land, he or his successors in title would have little cause to complain. Likewise no undue hardship is

10. The statute refers to situations in which a denial would "result in peculiar and exceptional practical difficulties to, or exceptional and undue hardship upon the developer of such property." N.J.S.A. 40:55D:70(c). In Chirichello v. Monmouth Beach Zoning Bd. of Adjustment, 78 N.J. 544, 552, 397 A.2d 646, 650 (1978), we referred to the language as indicating "two different standards, difficulties or hardship," and noted that "the two in large measure are overlapping and complementary. Clearly, peculiar and exceptional practical difficulties may well bear upon the exceptional and undue hardship visited upon the owner of the property."

suffered by an owner of a lot with a 35-foot frontage who acquired an adjoining 40-foot strip so that the lot complied with the ordinance and then sold a part of the land. These examples serve to illustrate the nature of a self-inflicted hardship which would not satisfy the statutory criteria.

Related to a determination of undue hardship are the efforts which the property owner has made to bring the property into compliance with the ordinance's specifications. Attempts to acquire additional land would be significant if it is feasible to purchase property from the adjoining property owners. Endeavors to sell the property to the adjoining landowners, the negotiations between and among the parties, and the reasonableness of the prices demanded and offered are also relevant considerations. See Gougeon v. Stone Harbor Bd. of Adjustment, 52 N.J. 212, 224, 245 A.2d 7 (1968), where it was held that if an owner of land refused to sell at a "fair and reasonable" price he would not be considered to be suffering an "undue hardship." If on the other hand the owner is willing to sell at a "fair and reasonable" price and the adjoining property owners refuse to make a reasonable offer, the "undue hardship" would exist.

When an undue hardship is found to exist, the board of adjustment must be satisfied that the negative criteria are satisfied before granting a variance. Thus the grant of the variance must not substantially impinge upon the public good and the intent and purpose of the zone plan and ordinance. As we observed in *Chirichello*, "the variance may be granted only if the spirit of the ordinance and the general welfare are observed." 78 N.J. at 552, 397 A.2d at 650. In this respect attention must be directed to the manner in and extent to which the variance will impact upon the character of the area. We have frequently observed that the applicant carries the burden of establishing the negative criteria by a fair preponderance of the evidence, but that "[t]he less of an impact, the more likely the restriction is not that vital to valid public interests." Chirichello v. Monmouth Zoning Bd. of Adjustment, 78 N.J. at 561, 397 A.2d at 654. See Fobe Associates v. Demarest, 74 N.J. 519, 547, 379 A.2d 31 (1977).

There lurks in the background of cases of this type the possibility that denial of a variance will zone the property into inutility so that "an exercise of eminent domain [will be] . . . called for and compensation must be paid." Harrington Glen, Inc. v. Leonia Bd. of Adjustment, 52 N.J. 22, 33, 243 A.2d 233, 239 (1968). When that occurs all the taxpayers in the municipality share the economic burden of achieving the intent and purpose of the zoning scheme. Compared to this result is the denial of a variance conditioned upon the sale of the property at a fair market value to the adjoining property owners. They will perhaps receive the more direct benefit of the land remaining undeveloped and it may therefore be fairer for them to bear the cost. In this respect we made the following pertinent comments in *Chirichello*:

> It would certainly be consonant with the interest of all parties to deny a variance conditioned on the purchase of the land by adjoining property owners at a fair price. The immediate benefit to the adjoining property owners of maintenance of the zoning scheme and aesthetic enjoyment of surrounding vacant land adjacent to their homes is self-evident. The owner of the odd lot would suffer no monetary damage having received the fair value of the land. Of course, if the owner refused to sell, then he would have no cause for complaint. Or if the adjoining owners would not agree to purchase, then perhaps the variance should be granted, less weight being given to their position particularly when the land in question will have been rendered useless. In either event the use of a conditional variance, the condition bearing an overall reasonable relationship to the purposes of the zoning ordinance, may lead to a satisfactory solution. See Harrington Glen, Inc. v. Leonia Bd. of Adj., supra; Houdaille Const. Materials, Inc. v. Tewksbury Tp. Bd. of Adj., 92 N.J. Super. 293, 223 A.2d 210 (App. Div. 1966); Cohen v. Fair Lawn, 85 N.J. Super. 234, 237-238, 204 A.2d 375 (App. Div. 1964).
>
> Hearings before the board of adjustment serve as the focal point for resolution of conflicting interests between public restraints on the use of private property and the owner's right to utilize his land as he wishes. A third interest which frequently makes its appearance is represented by other property owners in the immediate vicinity whose major objective is the more limited self-interest of taking whatever position they believe will enhance the value of their property or coincide with their personal preferences. The board of adjustment must settle these disputes by engaging in a "discretionary weighing," a function inherent in the variance process. [78 N.J. at 555-556, 397 A.2d at 651-52.]

We have referred to the fair market value and the fair and reasonable price of the property with respect to considerations of offers to purchase and sell the property as well as the possibility of conditioning the variance. We believe that the preferred method to determine value is on the assumption that a variance had been granted so that a home could be constructed on the lot. See Gougeon v. Stone Harbor Bd. of Adjustment, 52 N.J. at 224, 245 A.2d 7, and Chirichello v. Monmouth Beach Zoning Bd. of Adjustment, 78 N.J. at 562, 397 A.2d 646 (Pashman, J., concurring). It is possible that other methods of valuation may be feasible. However, the parties have not briefed or argued the issue and accordingly we do not foreclose such possibilities.

II

Here, the board of adjustment concluded that "the applicant failed to demonstrate *any* evidence to establish hardship on the part of the applicant." (Emphasis supplied.) The record does not support that conclusion. Until the 1947 amendment to the zoning ordinance the plaintiffs or their predecessors in title could have constructed a one-family house on the lot. Ownership commenced in 1927 when the Borough of Westwood had no zoning ordinance. Furthermore, an attempt, albeit unsuccessful, had been made to acquire an additional ten-foot strip from Mr. Butler, owner of the property bordering to the south. A 40-foot frontage would have at least brought the property into conformity with one home in the neighborhood and within close proximity of the size of the lots of two other houses. In addition there had been discussions concerning the possible sale of the property to a neighbor, there being a substantial divergence in the offering and asking prices. Lastly, one could reasonably conclude that, if a variance were not granted, the land would be zoned into inutility. In view of all the above, it cannot be said that there was *not any* evidence to establish hardship.

Passing to the negative criteria, the board of adjustment made only the conclusive statement that the variance would substantially impair the intent and purpose of the zone plan and ordinance. The manner in which the variance would cause that effect is not explained. The board found that the lot was the only 30-foot parcel in the block, that the applicant builder had never constructed a house on a 30-foot lot, and that the proposed house would be 19 feet in width. How these facts relate to the zone plan is not made clear. The proposed use, side yards and setback meet the requirements of the ordinance. The proposed sales price of the home would be within the range of the value of the houses in the neighborhood. The total acreage of the land, exceeding 5,000 square feet, is comparable to 17 other properties in the neighborhood.

Perhaps the proposed house would be smaller in size than others. But in and of itself that would not justify a denial of a variance. Size of the house does not violate any of the traditional zoning purposes of light, air and open space which are reflected in the ordinance. We have recognized that minimum lot size "may be closely related to the goals of public health and safety" but that minimum floor area requirements "are not per se related to public health, safety or morals." Home Builders League of South Jersey, Inc. v. Berlin Tp., 81 N.J. 127, 139, 142, 405 A.2d 381, 388, 389 (1979).

It is possible that the board of adjustment was concerned with the appearance of the house and its relationship to the neighborhood from an aesthetic and economic viewpoint. These are proper zoning purposes, for the appearance of a house may be related to the character of the district. N.J.S.A. 40:55D-62(a). In *Home Builders League of South Jersey, Inc.*, 81 N.J. at 145, 405 A.2d 381, we recognized that conserving the value of the surrounding properties and aesthetic considerations are appropriate desiderata of zoning. Thus, if the size and layout of the proposed house would have adversely affected the character of the neighborhood, both with respect to a "desirable visual environment," N.J.S.A. 40:55D-2(i), and the value of the neighborhood properties, a board may justly conclude that a variance should not be granted.

The board's resolution does not address these problems. They are brought into sharp focus when an articulation of findings and reasoning must be made. We have frequently advised boards of adjustment to make findings predicated upon factual support in the record and directed to the issues involved. We refer again to Justice Francis's statements in *Harrington Glen, Inc.,* 52 N.J. at 28, 243 A.2d at 236:

> Denial of a variance on a summary finding couched in the conclusionary language of the statute is not adequate. There must be a statement of the specific findings of fact on which the Board reached the conclusion that the statutory criteria for a variance were not satisfied. Unless such findings are recited, a reviewing court cannot determine fairly whether the Board acted properly and within the limits of its authority in refusing a variance.

In this connection boards should be mindful that they may receive assistance from other municipal employees. The board would not have been amiss here in calling the municipal building inspector to testify to construction requirements. The board or its counsel may also have addressed inquiries with respect to the size and appearance of the other homes, and the aesthetic and economic impact upon those homeowners. We do not mean to imply that the burden of proof is not upon the applicant. It is, but in performing its function as a governmental body, the board may take some action which may be of assistance to it. The difficulty in this case also rests with the applicants. They did not submit a plan of the proposed house, demonstrate compliance with the municipality's building code, and adequately describe the appearance and type of structure. It is essential in a case of this type that the proponent submit a detailed plan of the proposed house. Under all these circumstances we believe fairness calls for a remand to the board of adjustment so that the record may be supplemented, the matter reconsidered, and adequate findings made.

Reversed and remanded to the Borough of Westwood Zoning Board of Adjustment.

NOTES AND QUESTIONS

1. Should the detriment-to-public-welfare element of variance requirements be balanced against hardship to the property owner, or should the mere existence of any detriment to the neighborhood foreclose issuance of a variance? Which approach would best provide equitable relief for the owner? Which would best promote efficient land use? Is it relevant that an approach not based on balancing would probably be the easiest to administer?

2. Suppose that an owner wishes to enclose his front porch with glass to prevent drafts and reduce heating costs and respiratory infec-

tions of his children. Because the enclosure will extend the front of his house 4 feet beyond the required 25-foot setback, the enclosure requires a variance. Should a variance be granted on the ground of practical difficulties or unnecessary hardship? See Fuhst v. Foley, 45 N.Y.2d 441, 382 N.E.2d 756 (1978). Suppose that the owner wants to add a porch onto the back of his house for use by an invalid child. The home itself already violates side-yard requirements, and the porch would simply extend the line of the existing violation. High shrubbery protects the privacy of neighboring lots, and there is no evidence that the porch will affect their value. Adding the porch elsewhere is not feasible. Should a variance be granted on grounds of practical difficulty or unnecessary hardship? See Aronson v. Board of Appeals of Stoneham, 349 Mass. 593, 211 N.E.2d 228 (1965) (no; existing violations cannot be made a basis for further violations, and "hardship" does not include personal infirmity). Cf. Crossley v. Town of Pelham, 133 N.H. 215, 578 A.2d 319 (1990) (opinion by Souter, J., now on the U.S. Supreme Court, holding irrelevant hardships that are a product of personal circumstances).

3. Note the discussion in *Commons* of the concept of self-imposed hardship. See pages 1024-1025. Suppose that undeveloped property is purchased by someone who knows or should know that the land cannot be developed in accordance with zoning restrictions unless a variance is subsequently granted. Does purchase with knowledge of a hardship preclude issuance of a variance? See Conley v. Town of Brookhaven Zoning Bd. of Appeals, 40 N.Y.2d 309, 353 N.E.2d 594 (1976); H.A. Steen Indus. v. Zoning Hearing Bd. of Bensalem Township, 48 Pa. Commw. 469, 410 A.2d 386 (1980); Swift v. Zoning Hearing Bd. of East Hempfield, 33 Pa. Commw. 442, 382 A.2d 150 (1978). See generally 3 Robert M. Anderson, American Law of Zoning §§20.44, 20.45 (3d ed. 1986).

4. The *Commons* case involved a so-called area variance, having to do with setback requirements and the like, as opposed to a use variance relaxing restrictions on permissible uses in a particular area (e.g., allowing a commercial use in a residential zone). The burden of proof is said to be greater for a use variance than for an area variance. Can you see why? See Silverstone v. District of Columbia Bd. of Zoning Adjustment, 372 A.2d 1286 (D.C. App. 1977); Board of Adjustment of New Castle County v. Kwik-Check Realty, Inc., 389 A.2d 1289 (Del. 1978).

May zoning authorities decide in a particular case to relax the burden on someone seeking a use variance, and then grant the requested relief? In Village Board v. Jarrold, 53 N.Y.2d 254, 423 N.E.2d 385, 440 N.Y.S.2d 908 (1981), the zoning board granted a variance to conduct commercial activity on land zoned for residential uses after hearing testimony from several witnesses — including an architect and a real estate broker — that residential construction on the lot in question would entail special costs and make a house on the land unsalable at a reasonable price. No figures were provided regarding construction costs or market value. The court reversed the board's decision, holding that a use variance may be granted only upon a demonstration, by dollars and cents proof, that permissible uses would not provide a reasonable return on the value of the property in question. Zoners have discretion, the court said, but a minimum showing is necessary. Concrete figures are needed not only to overturn denial of a variance on appeal, but also to support the grant of one. Otherwise judicial review would be meaningless, zoning authority could be corrupted, and piecemeal exemptions could change the character of the zoned neighborhood.

In one respect at least, the decision in *Jarrold* is typical and that in *Commons* uncommon: According to conventional wisdom, issuance of variances is reversed far more often than denial. This is not to say that variance administration is policed as closely as it should be. "The criteria for obtaining a variance are rigorous. If the courts really superintended their issuance, more than ninety percent of the variances granted would probably be found invalid. . . . Illegal issuance is a widespread phenomenon nationwide." Donald G. Hagman & Julian C. Juergensmeyer, Urban Planning and Land Development Control Law 173 (2d ed. 1986). See also Jesse Dukeminier & Clyde L. Stapleton, The Zoning Board of Adjustment: A Case Study in Misrule, 50 Ky. L.J. 273 (1962); Ronald M. Shapiro, The Zoning Variance Power — Constructive in Theory, Destructive in Practice, 29 Md. L. Rev. 3 (1969).

Cope v. Inhabitants of the Town of Brunswick

Supreme Court of Maine, 1983
464 A.2d 223

WATHEN, J. The plaintiffs, Mitchell and David Cope, appeal from a decision of the Superior Court (Cumberland County) which affirmed a decision of the Brunswick Zoning Board of Appeals (the Board) denying plaintiffs a zoning exception to construct eight multi-unit apartment buildings within the Town of Brunswick. On appeal, the plaintiffs assert inter alia that the Brunswick zoning ordinance is facially unconstitutional. Specifically, they argue that the ordinance improperly delegates to the Board the authority to permit the use of land for the construction of an apartment building. We conclude that the ordinance is in part unconstitutional and therefore sustain the appeal.

On March 16, 1982, plaintiffs filed an application with the Brunswick Codes Enforcement Officer requesting that the Board grant them an exception under the Brunswick zoning ordinance permitting them to construct eight six-unit apartment buildings on a twenty-one acre parcel of land located near Jordan Avenue in the Town of Brunswick. The land, an undeveloped and wooded lot, is classified under the Brunswick ordinance for "suburban A residential" use. Under section 402 of the ordinance, multi-unit apartment buildings are permitted in suburban A residential zones, "only as an exception granted by the Board of Appeals."[11]

Section 1107 of the ordinance prescribes the criteria that an applicant must fulfill to qualify for an exception.

> *Section 1107 Exceptions.* The Board of Appeals may grant an exception to the Ordinance and allow the uses in the zones designated as "XA" in Sec. 402. An appellant who seeks a use by exception shall submit to the Board diagrams or photographs, which become part of the record, illustrating the proof required by this section. He must prove the following:
>
> (1) *Certain Requirements Met.* That the use requested meets the requirements of this Ordinance set forth in Chapters 5-8.
>
> (2) *Use Not Adverse.* That the use requested will not adversely affect the health, safety, or general welfare of the public.
>
> (3) *Purpose Upheld.* That the use requested will not tend to defeat the purpose of this Ordinance as set forth in Section 101 or of the Comprehensive Plan for the development of the Town of Brunswick.
>
> (4) *Value Maintained.* That the use requested will not tend to devaluate or alter the essential characteristics of the surrounding property.

Following a public hearing held on March 30 and April 10, 1982, the Board found that plaintiffs' project was in compliance with the ordinance in all respects, with the exception of subsections (2) and (4) of section 1107. The Board found that the proposed use would pose problems that would endanger the safety of the public and that the project would "drastically change the basic characteristics of the existing neighborhood from one of a small quiet not very heavily travelled area to one more dense and heavily travelled."

The board denied plaintiffs' application for an exception and plaintiffs appealed to Superior Court pursuant to Rule 80B of the Maine Rules of Civil Procedure. On appeal, the Superior Court upheld the constitutionality of the Brunswick ordinance and affirmed the Board's denial of plaintiffs' application for a use exception.

The issue before us arises from the fact that local zoning boards, like municipalities, have no inherent authority to regulate the use of private property. Instead, the power of a town, and therefore that of the local zoning board of appeals, is conferred upon the town by the State. Sec 30 M.R.S.A. §2411 (1978 and Supp. 1982-1983) (granting municipality authority to establish board of appeals); 30 M.R.S.A. §4962 (1978 and Supp. 1982-1983) (governing zoning ordinances). This power may not be delegated from the legislature to the municipality or from the

---

11. The ordinance permits apartment buildings only as an exception and then only in areas zoned for urban residential, suburban residential, downtown commercial, and highway commercial.

municipality to a local administrative body without a sufficiently detailed statement of policy to:

> furnish a guide which will enable those to whom the law is to be applied to reasonably determine their rights thereunder, and so that the determination of those rights will not be left to the purely arbitrary discretion of the administrator. [Stucki v. Plavin, 291 A.2d 508, 510 (Me. 1972).]

The present case calls into question the constitutionality of two of the standards contained in section 1107 of the ordinance. Under the ordinance, the Board is directed to base its decision upon a determination of whether the proposed use would "adversely affect the health, safety or general welfare of the public," and whether the use would "alter the essential characteristics of the surrounding property." Upon the authority of prior decisions of this Court, we hold that the ordinance improperly delegates legislative authority to the Board and is therefore void.

In Waterville Hotel Corp. v. Board of Zoning Appeals, 241 A.2d 50 (Me. 1968), this Court struck down a provision of a zoning ordinance which vested absolute power in the Board of Zoning Appeals to approve or disapprove "all major changes of uses of land, buildings or structures. . . ." The land owner in that case sought to construct a service station in a "Commercial C" zone. Although the landowner satisfied all of the specific requirements of the zoning ordinance, the Board of Appeals denied him a building permit on the ground that the proposed use would be inimical of public safety. Id. at 51. In striking down that portion of the ordinance making all major changes in the uses of land "subject to the approval of the Board of Zoning Appeals," we stated:

> The legislative body may specify conditions under which certain uses may exist and may delegate to the Board discretion in determining whether or not the conditions have been met. The legislative body cannot, however, delegate to the Board a discretion which is not limited by legislative standards. It cannot give the Board discretionary authority to approve or disapprove applications for permits as the Board thinks best serves the public interest without establishing standards to limit and guide the Board. [Id. at 52.]

Although a provision in the Waterville ordinance required the Board to exercise its power "in harmony with the comprehensive plan for municipal development and the purpose and intent of this ordinance, in accordance with the public interest and in support and furtherance of the health, safety and general welfare of the residents of the municipality," this Court held that such general language did not provide sufficient guidance to meet constitutional requirements. Id. at 53.

In Stucki v. Plavin, 291 A.2d 508 (Me. 1972), we held to be facially unconstitutional an ordinance which provided that the less restrictive regulations would apply to a lot split by two zones "provided, however, that such extension of use into the more restricted portion *shall meet the approval* of the Board of Zoning Appeals." Id. at 509 (emphasis added).

Similarly, we held a provision of a town zoning ordinance unconstitutional in Town of Windham v. LaPointe, 308 A.2d 286 (Me. 1973), which vested unguided authority in the selectmen and planning board to approve or disapprove of the location of proposed trailer parks. In striking down that ordinance, the Court noted:

> Such broad delegation of power breeds selectivity in the enforcement of the law. When no standards are provided to guide the discretion of the enforcement authority, the fact that the law might be applied in a discriminatory manner settles its constitutionality. [Id. at 293.]

Defendants seek to avoid the implications of the foregoing decisions by relying upon the later decision of Barnard v. Zoning Board of Appeals of the Town of Yarmouth, 313 A.2d 741 (Me. 1974). The ordinance at issue in that case provided that the Board of Appeals had authority to grant variances, "where necessary to avoid undue hardship, provided there is no substantial departure from the intent of the ordinances." Although acknowledging that the standard was broadly stated, we concluded that it was nonetheless sufficient to guide the Board in granting or denying *variances.* Id. at 748.

Contrary to defendants' assertion, *Barnard* does not represent a departure from our earlier decisions. The standard provided by the ordinance in *Barnard* was sufficient because it related to the granting of a variance and described only the negative findings which were required to be made before the prohibited use could be allowed by variance. In determining absence of a "substantial departure from the intent of the ordinances," it would be the other provisions of the ordinance which would provide substantive guidance for the decision. Moreover, *Barnard* does not have application in judging the sufficiency of standards to permit use by exception as opposed to use by variance. A use by exception, such as the apartment complex proposed in this case, differs substantially from a use by variance:

> A special exception use differs from a variance in that a variance is authority extended to a landowner to use his property in a manner prohibited by the ordinance (absent such variance) while a special exception allows him to put his property to a use which the ordinance expressly permits. [*Stucki*, 291 A.2d at 511.]

An exception is a conditional use under a zoning ordinance and results from a legislative determination that such use will not ordinarily be detrimental or injurious to the neighborhood within the zone. *Community School, Inc. v. Zoning Board of Appeals of the Town of Camden*, 369 A.2d 1146, 1149 (Me. 1977). Whether the use will generally comply with the health, safety and welfare of the public and the essential character of the area is a legislative question. The delegation is improper if the Board is permitted to decide that same legislative question anew, without specific guidelines which permit the Board to determine what unique or distinctive characteristics of a particular apartment building will render it detrimental or injurious to the neighborhood. . . .

We therefore conclude that the relevant portions of subsections (2) and (4) of section 1107 of the Brunswick zoning ordinance upon which the Board relied in denying the permit to plaintiffs are facially unconstitutional. Those standards refer only to the same general considerations which the legislative body was required to address and resolve in enacting the ordinance. As we have previously stated: "[t]here should be no discretion in the Board of Appeals as to whether or not to grant the permit if the conditions stated in the ordinance exist. That determination should be made by the legislators." *Stucki*, 291 A.2d at 511. To permit the broad legislative judgment to be delegated to the Board "would be equivalent to conferring upon the board of appeals the power to rescind the ordinance with respect to such uses." Phillips Petroleum Company [v. Zoning Board of Appeals of the City of Bangor, 260 A.2d 434, 435 (Me. 1970)].

Stated simply, by enacting the ordinance, the voters of Brunswick determined that an apartment building was generally suitable for location in a suburban residential zone. The ordinance did not provide the Board with any basis for determining that a particular location was unsuitable because of the existence of certain characteristics which rendered the general legislative determination inapplicable. Since the Board found that plaintiffs were in compliance with all requirements of the ordinance except for those which we now find to be invalid, a permit for the exception should issue.

The entry is: Judgment reversed.

Remanded to the Superior Court for an appropriate order sustaining the appeal and directing issuance of the permit.

NOTES AND QUESTIONS

1. See Daniel R. Mandelker, Delegation of Power and Function in Zoning Administration, 1963 Wash. U. L.Q. 60, 62-63 (emphasis added):

Confusion about the role of exceptions and variances is endemic to zoning, reflecting the confusion over underlying purposes, and shows little sign of being resolved. The variance is an *administratively-authorized* departure from the terms of the zoning ordinance, granted in cases of unique and individual hardship, in which a strict application of the terms of the ordinance would be unconstitutional. The grant of the variance is meant to avoid an unfavorable holding on constitutionality.

By way of contrast, an exception is a use *permitted by the ordinance* in a district in which it is not necessarily incompatible, but where it might cause harm if not watched. Exceptions are authorized under conditions which will insure their compatibility with surrounding uses. Typically, a use which is the subject of a special exception demands a large amount of land, may be public or semipublic in character and might often be noxious or offensive. Not all of these characteristics will apply to every excepted use, however. Hospitals in residential districts are one example, because of the extensive area they occupy, and because of potential traffic and other problems which may affect a residential neighborhood. A filling station in a light commercial district is another example because of its potentially noxious effects.

2. The theory of special exceptions (also called conditional uses) is clear enough; practice under the theory varies. One approach, illustrated by the *Cope* case, reflects an effort by zoners to use special exceptions as an essentially discretionary device: Listed uses will be granted an exception only if very general criteria — no adverse effects on health, welfare, and safety, for example — are found to be met. The approach gives zoners considerable leverage over applicants and also, obviously, invites abuse. Hence the reaction of the court in *Cope*, shared by a number of jurisdictions. See, e.g., Town of Westford v. Kilburn, 131 Vt. 120, 300 A.2d 523 (1973) (general welfare test for granting exceptions held to be too vague to serve as a guide). But some states do tolerate the sorts of standards at issue in *Cope*. See, e.g., Coronet Homes, Inc. v. McKenzie, 84 Nev. 250, 439 P.2d 219 (1968).

An alternative approach to special exceptions reduces discretion by listing detailed criteria regarding such things as design, location, hours of operation, standards of performance, and the like in the ordinance; if the proposed use meets the criteria, an exception must be granted. See, e.g., Value Oil Co. v. Town of Irvington, 152 N.J. Super, 354, 377 A.2d 1225 (1977) (holding that additional general criterion of public welfare is defined by the specific factors, so that when the latter are met the former is as well). A variant of this approach permits denial of an exception even when the specific criteria are met, but puts on the zoning authorities the burden of demonstrating why the use will have an adverse affect on welfare. See, e.g., Appeal of Fleming, 44 Pa. Commw. 641, 405 A.2d 1309 (1979). Since the detailed-criteria approach to special exceptions helps control abuse, why not use it as the chief means of providing more flexibility in Euclidean zoning, and extend it even to cases typically handled through variances?

3. Some jurisdictions have attempted to rely on special exceptions

as *the* approach to zoning. For example, in Rockhill v. Chesterfield Township, 23 N.J. 117, 128 A.2d 473 (1957), an entire town was zoned for agriculture and residences, but special uses were authorized if broad standards — such as "beneficial to the general development" of the community — were satisfied. The court invalidated the approach, calling it the antithesis of zoning, hardly adequate to control local discretion. See, to the same effect, People v. Perez, 214 Cal. App. 2d 881, 29 Cal. Rptr. 781 (1963).

2.   Zoning Amendments and the Spot Zoning Problem

Fasano v. Board of County Commissioners of Washington County
Supreme Court of Oregon, 1973
264 Or. 574, 507 P.2d 23

HOWELL, J. The plaintiffs, homeowners in Washington county, unsuccessfully opposed a zone change before the Board of County Commissioners of Washington County. Plaintiffs applied for and received a writ of review of the action of the commissioners allowing the change. The trial court found in favor of plaintiffs, disallowed the zone change, and reversed the commissioners' order. The Court of Appeals affirmed, 489 P.2d 693 (1971), and this court granted review.

The defendants are the Board of County Commissioners and A.G.S. Development Company. A.G.S., the owner of 32 acres which had been zoned R-7 (Single Family Residential), applied for a zone change to P-R (Planned Residential), which allows for the construction of a mobile home park. The change failed to receive a majority vote of the Planning Commission. The Board of County Commissioners approved the change and found, among other matters, that the change allows for "increased densities and different types of housing to meet the needs of urbanization over that allowed by the existing zoning."

The trial court, relying on its interpretation of Roseta v. County of Washington, 254 Or. 161, 458 P.2d 405, 40 A.L.R.3d 364 (1969), reversed the order of the commissioners because the commissioners had not shown any change in the character of the neighborhood which would justify the rezoning. The Court of Appeals affirmed for the same reason, but added the additional ground that the defendants failed to show that the change was consistent with the comprehensive plan for Washington county.

According to the briefs, the comprehensive plan of development for Washington county was adopted in 1959 and included classifications in the county for residential, neighborhood commercial, retail commercial, general commercial, industrial park and light industry, general and heavy industry, and agricultural areas.

The land in question, which was designated "residential" by the comprehensive plan, was zoned R-7, Single Family Residential.

Subsequent to the time the comprehensive plan was adopted, Washington county established a Planned Residential (P-R) zoning classification in 1963. The P-R classification was adopted by ordinance and provided that a planned residential unit development could be established and should include open space for utilities, access, and recreation; should not be less than 10 acres in size; and should be located in or adjacent to a residential zone. The P-R zone adopted by the 1963 ordinance is of the type known as a "floating zone," so-called because the ordinance creates a zone classification authorized for future use but not placed on the zoning map until its use at a particular location is approved by the governing body. The R-7 classification for the 32 acres continued until April 1970 when the classification was changed to P-R to permit the defendant A.G.S. to construct the mobile home park on the 32 acres involved.

The defendants argue that (1) the action of the county commissioners approving the change is presumptively valid, requiring plaintiffs to show that the commissioners acted arbitrarily in approving the zone change; (2) it was not necessary to show a change of conditions in the area before a zone change could be accomplished; and (3) the change from R-7 to P-R was in accordance with the Washington county comprehensive plan.

We granted review in this case to consider the questions — by what standards does a county commission exercise its authority in zoning matters; who has the burden of meeting those standards when a request for change of zone is made; and what is the scope of court review of such actions?

Any meaningful decision as to the proper scope of judicial review of a zoning decision must start with a characterization of the nature of that decision. The majority of jurisdictions state that a zoning ordinance is a legislative act and is thereby entitled to presumptive validity. This court made such a characterization of zoning decisions in Smith v. County of Washington, 241 Or. 380, 406 P.2d 545 (1965). . . .

At this juncture we feel we would be ignoring reality to rigidly view all zoning decisions by local governing bodies as legislative acts to be accorded a full presumption of validity and shielded from less than constitutional scrutiny by the theory of separation of powers. Local and small decision groups are simply not the equivalent in all respects of state and national legislatures. There is a growing judicial recognition of this fact of life: "It is not part of the legislative function to grant permits, make special exceptions, or decide particular cases. Such activities are not legislative but administrative, quasi-judicial, or judicial in character.

To place them in the hands of legislative bodies, whose acts as such are not judicially reviewable, is to open the door completely to arbitrary government." Ward v. Village of Skokie, 26 Ill. 2d 415, 186 N.E.2d 529, 533 (1962) (Klingbiel, J., specially concurring).

The Supreme Court of Washington, in reviewing a rezoning decision, recently stated: ". . . in its role as a hearing and fact-finding tribunal, the planning commission's function more nearly than not partakes of the nature of an administrative, quasi-judicial proceeding. . . ." Chrobuck v. Snohomish County, 78 Wash. 2d 884, 480 P.2d 489, 495-496 (1971).

Ordinances laying down general policies without regard to a specific piece of property are usually an exercise of legislative authority, are subject to limited review, and may only be attacked upon constitutional grounds for an arbitrary abuse of authority. On the other hand, a determination whether the permissible use of a specific piece of property should be changed is usually an exercise of judicial authority and its propriety is subject to an altogether different test. An illustration of an exercise of legislative authority is the passage of the ordinance by the Washington County Commission in 1963 which provided for the formation of a planned residential classification to be located in or adjacent to any residential zone. An exercise of judicial authority is the county commissioners' determination in this particular matter to change the classification of A.G.S. Development Company's specific piece of property. The distinction is stated, as follows, in Comment, Zoning Amendments — The Product of Judicial or Quasi-Judicial Action, 33 Ohio St. L.J. 130 (1972):

> . . . Basically, this test involves the determination of whether action produces a general rule or policy which is applicable to an open class of individuals, interests, or situations, or whether it entails the application of a general rule or policy to specific individuals, interests, or situations. If the former determination is satisfied, there is legislative action; if the latter determination is satisfied, the action is judicial. [33 Ohio St. L.J. at 137.]

We reject the proposition that judicial review of the county commissioners' determination to change the zoning of the particular property in question is limited to a determination whether the change was arbitrary and capricious.

In order to establish a standard of review, it is necessary to delineate certain basic principles relating to land use regulation.

The basic instrument for county or municipal land use planning is the "comprehensive plan." Haar, In Accordance with a Comprehensive Plan, 68 Harv. L. Rev. 1154 (1955); 1 Yokley, Zoning Law and Practice, §3-2 (1965); 1 Rathkopf, The Law of Zoning and Planning, §9-1 (3d ed. 1969). The plan has been described as a general plan to control and direct the use and development of property in a municipality. Nowicki v. Planning and Zoning Board, 148 Conn. 492, 172 A.2d 386, 389 (1961).

In Oregon the county planning commission is required by ORS 215.050 to adopt a comprehensive plan for the use of some or all of the land in the county. Under ORS 215.110(1), after the comprehensive plan has been adopted, the planning commission recommends to the governing body of the county the ordinances necessary to "carry out" the comprehensive plan. The purpose of the zoning ordinances, both under our statute and the general law of land use regulation, is to "carry out" or implement the comprehensive plan. 1 Anderson, American Law of Zoning, §1.12 (1968). Although we are aware of the analytical distinction between zoning and planning, it is clear that under our statutes the plan adopted by the planning commission and the zoning ordinances enacted by the county governing body are closely related; both are intended to be parts of a single integrated procedure for land use control. The plan embodies policy determinations and guiding principles; the zoning ordinances provide the detailed means of giving effect to those principles. . . .

We believe that the state legislature has conditioned the county's power to zone upon the prerequisite that the zoning attempt to further the general welfare of the community. . . . In other words, except as noted later in this opinion, it must be proved that the change is in conformance with the comprehensive plan.

In proving that the change is in conformance with the comprehensive plan in this case, the proof, at a minimum, should show (1) there is a public need for a change of the kind in question, and (2) that need will be best served by changing the classification of the particular piece of property in question as compared with other available property.

In the instant case the trial court and the Court of Appeals interpreted prior decisions of this court as requiring the county commissions to show a change of conditions within the immediate neighborhood in which the change was sought since the enactment of the comprehensive plan, or a mistake in the comprehensive plan as a condition precedent to the zone change.

In Smith v. Washington County, supra, the land in question was designated residential under the comprehensive plan, and the county commissioners enacted an amendatory ordinance changing the classification to manufacturing. The court held that the change constituted spot zoning and was invalid. We stated: ". . . Once a [zoning scheme] is adopted, changes in it should be made only when such changes are consistent with the over-all objectives of the plan *and in keeping with changes in the character of the area or neighborhood to be covered thereby.* . . ." (Emphasis added.) 241 Or. at 384, 406 P.2d at 547.

In Roseta v. Washington County, supra, the land in question was classified as residential under the comprehensive plan and had been originally zoned as R-10, Single Family Residential. The county commissioners granted a zone change to A-1, Duplex Residential. We held that the commissioners had not sustained the burden of proving that the change was consistent with the comprehensive plan and reversed the order allowing the zone change. In regard to defendants' argument that the change was consistent with the comprehensive plan because the plan designated the area as "residential" and the term included both single family dwellings and duplex residences, we stated: ". . . However, the ordinance established a distinction between the two types of use by classifying one area as R-10 and another area as A-1. It must be assumed that the Board had some purpose in making a distinction between these two classifications. It was for defendant to prove that this distinction was not valid or that the change in the character of the use of the . . . parcel was not inconsistent with the comprehensive plan." 254 Or. at 169, 458 P.2d 405, at 409. . . .

However, *Roseta* should not be interpreted as establishing a rule that a physical change of circumstances within the rezoned neighborhood is the only justification for rezoning. The county governing body is directed by ORS 215.055 to consider a number of other factors when enacting zoning ordinances,[12] and the list there does not purport to be exclusive. The important issues, as *Roseta* recognized, are compliance with the statutory directive and consideration of the proposed change in light of the comprehensive plan.

Because of the action of the commission in this instance is an exercise of judicial authority, the burden of proof should be placed, as is usual in judicial proceedings, upon the one seeking change. The more drastic the change, the greater will be the burden of showing that it is in conformance with the comprehensive plan as implemented by the ordinance, that there is a public need for the kind of change in question, and that the need is best met by the proposal under consideration. As the degree of change increases, the burden of showing that the potential impact upon the area in question was carefully considered and weighed will also increase. If other areas have previously been designated for the particular type of development, it must be shown why it is necessary to introduce it into an area not previously contemplated and why the property owners there should bear the burden of the departure.

---

12. At the time of the *Fasano* case, ORS 215.055 provided as "Standards for plan": "(1) The plan and all legislation and regulations authorized by ORS 215.010 to 215.233 shall be designed to promote the public health, safety and general welfare and shall be based on the following considerations, among others: The various characteristics of the various areas in the county, the suitability of the areas for particular land uses and improvements, the land uses and improvements in the areas, trends in land improvement, density of development, property values, the needs of economic enterprises in the future development of the areas, needed access to particular sites in the areas, natural resources of the county and prospective needs for development thereof, and the public need for healthful, safe, aesthetic surroundings and conditions." — Eds.

Although we have said in *Roseta* that zoning changes may be justified without a showing of a mistake in the original plan or ordinance, or of changes in the physical characteristics of an affected area, any of these factors that are present in a particular case would, of course, be relevant. Their importance would depend upon the nature of the precise change under consideration.

By treating the exercise of authority by the commission in this case as the exercise of judicial rather than of legislative authority and thus enlarging the scope of review on appeal, and by placing the burden of the above level of proof upon the one seeking change, we may lay the court open to criticism by legal scholars who think it desirable that planning authorities be vested with the ability to adjust more freely to changed conditions. However, having weighed the dangers of making desirable change more difficult against the dangers of the almost irresistible pressures that can be asserted by private economic interests on local government, we believe that the latter dangers are more to be feared.

What we have said above is necessarily general, as the approach we adopt contains no absolute standards or mechanical tests. We believe, however, that it is adequate to provide meaningful guidance for local governments making zoning decisions and for trial courts called upon to review them. With future cases in mind, it is appropriate to add some brief remarks on questions of procedure. Parties at the hearing before the county governing body are entitled to an opportunity to be heard, to an opportunity to present and rebut evidence, to a tribunal which is impartial in the matter — i.e., having had no pre-hearing or ex parte contacts concerning the question at issue — and to a record made and adequate findings executed. Comment, Zoning Amendments — The Product of Judicial or Quasi-Judicial Action, 33 Ohio St. L.J. 130-143 (1972).

When we apply the standards we have adopted to the present case, we find that the burden was not sustained before the commission. The record now before us is insufficient to ascertain whether there was a justifiable basis for the decision. The only evidence in the record, that of the staff report of the Washington County Planning Department, is too conclusory and superficial to support the zoning change. It merely states:

> The staff finds that the requested use does conform to the residential designation of the Plan of Development. It further finds that the proposed use reflects the urbanization of the County and the necessity to provide increased densities and different types of housing to meet the needs of urbanization over that allowed by the existing zoning. . . .

Such generalizations and conclusions, without any statement of the facts on which they are based, are insufficient to justify a change of use. Moreover, no portions of the comprehensive plan of Washington County are before us, and we feel it would be improper for us to take judicial notice of the plan without at least some reference to its specifics by counsel.

As there has not been an adequate showing that the change was in accord with the plan, or that the factors listed in ORS 215.055 were given proper consideration, the judgment is affirmed.

Arnel Development Co. v. City of Costa Mesa
Supreme Court of California, 1980
28 Cal. 3d 511, 620 P.2d 565, 169 Cal. Rptr. 904

TOBRINER, J. Plaintiff Arnel proposed to construct a 50-acre development consisting of 127 single-family residences and 539 apartment units. Objecting to this proposal, a neighborhood association circulated an initiative rezoning the Arnel property and two adjoining properties (68 acres in all) to single-family residential use. When the voters approved the initiative, Arnel instituted the instant action. The superior court upheld the initiative: the Court of Appeal reversed. We transferred the cause here on our own motion to examine further the holding of the Court of Appeal that the rezoning of specific, relatively small parcels of privately owned property is essentially adjudicatory in nature, and thus cannot be enacted by initiative.

As we shall explain, California precedent has settled the principle that zoning ordinances, whatever the size of parcel affected, are legislative acts. We find no warrant for departing from that principle. A decision that some zoning ordinances, depending on the size and number of parcels affected and perhaps on other factors, are adjudicative acts would unsettle well established rules which govern the enactment of land use restrictions, creating confusion which would require years of litigation to resolve. Since such a decision is unnecessary to protect either the rights of the landowners or the public interest in orderly community planning and development, we adhere to established precedent and conclude, accordingly, that the ordinance rezoning plaintiffs' property was a legislative act. . . .

Numerous California cases have settled that the enactment of a measure which zones or rezones property is a legislative act. California courts have so held in cases permitting zoning by initiative, in cases upholding zoning referendums, and in cases involving other issues which distinguish between adjudicative and legislative acts. . . .

The cases draw no distinctions based on the size of the area or the number of owners. Some of the cases involved measures which rezoned a substantial part of the city, some rezoned areas roughly comparable to the 68 acres at issue here, many involved parcels much smaller than 68 acres. . . . Thus whatever the legal controversy and whatever the size or ownership of the land involved, every California decision on point has held that the enactment or amendment of a zoning ordinance is a legislative act. . . .

Plaintiffs suggest that the foregoing principle — that rezoning is a legislative act — operates in the present case to deny them due process of law under the United States and California Constitutions. Both federal and state precedent refute this contention.

In Eastlake v. Forest City Enterprises, Inc. (1976) 426 U.S. 668, 96 S. Ct. 2358, 49 L. Ed. 2d 132, the United States Supreme Court rejected contentions identical to those urged by plaintiffs. There the City Council of Eastlake rezoned eight acres to permit construction of multifamily housing. The proposed zoning change, however, did not receive the approval of 55 percent of the voters as required by the Eastlake City Charter. Rejecting the Ohio Supreme Court's conclusion that the referendum requirement was an unconstitutional delegation of legislative power, the United States Supreme Court held the use of a referendum to bar a zoning change did not violate the due process clause of the Fourteenth Amendment.

A number of passages in the majority opinion of Chief Justice Burger bear closely on the present case. First, that opinion notes that the Ohio Supreme Court held that the rezoning of a single eight-acre parcel is a legislative act. The United States Supreme Court accepted that classification. . . . Nowhere does the opinion suggest that the Ohio courts erred in treating the rezoning of a single lot as legislative, or even that the classification raised a significant constitutional question.

Second, the Ohio court had expressed the fear that voters would not be able to apply land use standards fairly and consistently. The United States Supreme Court replied: "there is no more advance assurance that a legislative body will act by conscientiously applying consistent standards than there is with respect to voters. . . . The critical constitutional inquiry, rather, is whether the zoning restriction produces arbitrary or capricious results." (P.676, fn. 10, 96 S. Ct. p.2363, fn. 10.)

Finally, the dissenting opinion of Justice Stevens in *Eastlake* presented the argument that due process required a hearing for the rezoning of small parcels of property, and that the charter referendum requirement thus denied due process. The majority rejected that argument in a footnote. The court stated that:

> The fears expressed in dissent rest on the proposition that the procedure at issue here is "fundamentally unfair" to landowners; this fails to take into account the mechanisms for relief potentially available to property owners whose desired land use changes are rejected by the voters. First, if hardship is occasioned by zoning restrictions, *administrative* relief is potentially available. Indeed, the very purpose of "variances" allowed by zoning officials is to avoid "practical difficulties and unnecessary hardship." 8E McQuillan, Municipal Corporations §25.159, p.511 (3d ed. 1965). As we noted . . . remedies

remain available under the Ohio Supreme Court's holding and provide a
means to challenge unreasonable or arbitrary action. Euclid v. Ambler Realty
Co., 272 U.S. 365 [47 S. Ct. 114, 71 L. Ed. 303] (1926). [(P.679, fn. 13, 96 S.
Ct. p.2365, fn. 13.)]

Both of the propositions stated in the Supreme Court's footnote
apply to the present case. Plaintiffs here retain the right to seek administrative relief from the zoning imposed by the initiative. They also retain the right to seek judicial invalidation of zoning which is arbitrary
and unreasonable, which bears no reasonable relationship to the regional welfare, or which deprives them of substantially all use of their
land. . . . We conclude in accord with the *Eastlake* decision, that classification of the rezoning ordinance as a legislative act, thus permitting its
enactment by initiative, does not violate the federal Constitution.

When we turn from the federal Constitution to the California Constitution, the force of precedent is even clearer. The California decisions
cited previously in this opinion hold that amendment of a zoning ordinance is a legislative act and consequently that zoning by initiative does
not violate due process.

We can appreciate the view that in a case in which, unlike the present case, proposed legislation affects only a few persons, the legislative
body should grant those persons a hearing if practicable. To elevate this
precatory suggestion to a constitutional command, however, would radically constrain the power of legislative bodies. The rationale of our decision could not be confined to zoning cases. . . . Thus whenever a
legislative body enacted legislation which affected relatively few persons,
that legislation would be invalid unless the persons affected received notice and hearing before the enacting body. We find no warrant for such
a radical curtailment of the authority traditionally enjoyed by legislatures.

We conclude that no constitutional requirement compels us to depart from the California doctrine that rezoning is a legislative act. We
recognize, however, that the courts of some other states, basing their
decisions on nonconstitutional grounds, have held that in some instances
a zoning ordinance is an adjudicative decision.[13] The Court of Appeal,
as we noted earlier, adopted that view, holding specifically that the rezoning of relatively small parcels of land is adjudicative in character. We

13. See West v. City of Portage (Mich. 1974) 221 N.W.2d 303; Fasano v. Board of
County Commissioners of Washington County (Or. 1973) 507 P.2d 23; Leonard v. City of
Bothell (Wash. 1976) 557 P.2d 1306. Similar views are advocated in Glenn, State Law
Limitations on the Use of Initiatives and Referenda in Connection with Zoning Amend-
ments (1978) 51 So. Cal. L. Rev. 265; Hile, Zoning by Initiative in California: A Critical
Analysis (1979) 12 Loyola L.A.L. Rev. 903; Kahn, In Accordance with a Constitutional
Plan: Procedural Due Process and Zoning Decisions (1979) 6 Hastings Const. L.Q. 1011.

therefore explain our reasons for rejecting that view and adhering to the settled California position.

From the doctrine that zoning ordinances are legislative, but variances and similar administrative decisions are adjudicative,[14] derive a number of rules which facilitate the making of land use decisions and simplify litigation challenging those decisions. Among those rules are: (1) Zoning ordinances, but not administrative decisions, can be enacted by initiative. (2) Zoning ordinances, but not administrative decisions, are subject to referendum. (3) A zoning ordinance is reviewable by ordinary mandamus, an administrative decision by administrative mandamus. (4) A zoning ordinance, unlike an administrative decision, does not require explicit findings. (5) A zoning ordinance is valid if it is reasonably related to the public welfare; administrative decisions must implement established standards and rest upon findings supported by substantial evidence. Under the views advanced by plaintiffs, however, the application of these rules is uncertain until a reviewing court finds whether the decision is legislative or an adjudicative act. Plaintiffs propose, however, no test to distinguish legislative and adjudicative actions with reasonable certainty. . . .

Plaintiffs alternatively urge that the present initiative is adjudicatory because it assertedly affects only three landowners. But this is a very myopic view of the matter; the proposed construction of housing for thousands of people affects the prospective tenants, the housing market, the residents living nearby, and the future character of the community. The number of landowners whose property is actually rezoned is as unsuitable a test as the size of the property rezoned. Yet without some test which distinguishes legislative from adjudicative acts with clarity and reasonable certainty, municipal governments and voters will lack adequate guidance in enacting and evaluating land-use decisions.

In summary, past California land-use cases have established generic classifications, viewing zoning ordinances as legislative and other decisions, such as variances and subdivision map approvals, as adjudicative. This method of classifying land-use decisions enjoys the obvious advantage of economy; the municipality, the proponents of a proposed measure, and the opponents of the measure can readily determine if notice, hearings, and findings are required, what form of judicial review is appropriate, and whether the measure can be enacted by initiative or overturned by referendum.

To depart from past precedent and embark upon a case by case determination, on the other hand, would incur substantial administrative cost. Such a rule would expose the municipality to the uncertainty

---

14. A holding that rezoning of relatively small parcels is an adjudicative act would necessarily imply that decisions presently considered adjudicative, such as the grant of a use permit or the approval of a subdivision map, would henceforth be classifed as legislative acts if they affected a relatively large parcel of property.

of whether a proposed measure would be held to be legislative or adjudicative: it would entail cost to the litigants, and it would burden the courts with the resolution of these issues.

Plaintiffs argue, however, that the administrative cost which would be entailed by departure from precedent in this case is justified to protect the rights of landowners. We believe, however, that those rights are adequately protected under existing law. . . .

Although from the landowner's view a "hearing" before the electorate may be less satisfactory than a hearing before a planning commission or city council, as a practical matter the initiative is unlikely to be employed in matters which could fairly be characterized as adjudicative in character. An initiative petition requires valid signatures of 10 percent of the registered voters. (Elec. Code, §4011.) Having accomplished that feat, the proponents must then be prepared to wage an expensive campaign to persuade the majority of the voters to support the measure. In consequence of these requirements, the initiative can be and is employed to support or oppose major projects which affect hundreds or thousands of persons and often present questions of policy concerning the quality of life and the future development of the city; it is not likely to be employed in matters which affect only an individual landowner and raise no policy issues.

Neither do we believe departure from settled precedent is necessary to protect the public interest in rational and orderly land-use planning. Zoning changes must conform to the city's general plan (see Gov. Code, §65860), which must in turn conform to requirements established by state statute. . . . The spectre of a few voters imposing their selfish interests upon an objecting city and region has no basis in reality.

In conclusion, the current California rule that rezoning is a legislative act is well settled by precedent and comports with both federal and state constitutional requirements. The cost of departing from settled precedent in this setting is apparent; the benefits questionable and perhaps nonexistent. We therefore adhere to the rule that a zoning ordinance is a legislative act and, as such, may be enacted by initiative. . . .

[The dissenting opinion of Richardson, J., joined by Clark, J., is omitted.]

NOTES AND QUESTIONS

1. We consider floating zones and planned residential (or unit) developments, both mentioned in the *Fasano* case, beginning at page 1056.

2. *Spot zoning.* See Donald G. Hagman & Julian C. Juergensmeyer, Urban Planning and Land Development Control Law 136-137 (2d ed. 1986):

To the popular mind, spot zoning means the improper permission to use an "island" of land for a more intensive use than permitted on adjacent properties. The popular definition needs several qualifications. Some courts use the term spot zoning to describe a certain set of facts so that the term is neutral with respect to validity or invalidity. Other courts use the term spot zoning to describe a set of facts where the zoning as applied is invalid. . . .

Spot zoning is invalid where some or all of the following factors are present:

1. a small parcel of land is singled out for special and privileged treatment;
2. the singling out is not in the public interest but only for the benefit of the landowner;
3. the action is not in accord with a comprehensive plan.

The list is not meant to suggest that the three tests are mutually exclusive. If spot zoning is invalid, usually all three elements are present, or said another way, the three statements may be merely nuances of one another.

Spot zoning usually arises from legislative zoning amendments, although administrative variances and special exceptions are sometimes invalidated by reference to the same concept. See 1 Robert M. Anderson, American Law of Zoning §5.12, 3 id. §20.04 (3d ed. 1986). And although spot zoning usually involves preferential treatment, the phrase may be used in connection with restrictions that single out particular parcels to the *detriment* of their owners — a kind of "reverse" spot zoning. More commonly, though, instances of especially detrimental treatment are simply overturned as "arbitrary and capricious."

The underlying concern in spot zoning cases is that special favors have been granted in response to bribes or more subtle influences, such as political pressure. Neither, of course, is unheard of. For example, the L.A. Times, Aug. 20, 1980, §1, at 3, reported that a Los Angeles city councilman voted four times in one month to change the zoning on various parcels owned by his chief deputy in order to permit more extensive development. Another article in the L.A. Times, Dec. 6, 1978, §1, at 1, reported that "Los Angeles City Councilman Arthur K. Snyder sought $500 campaign contributions from persons who had zoning matters before the Planning Committee, which he chairs." One of the zoning lobbyists, known as expediters, who received an invitation to the councilman's dinner said: "It's a good business relationship to see the people you are dealing with at City Hall. It's easier if you know them on a first-name basis." See also Jerry Carroll, San Jose Councilman Indicted for Bribery, S.F. Chronicle, Nov. 11, 1979, at 1, describing payments of $30,000 made by a developer to members of the San Jose City Council in an effort to secure a zoning amendment. " 'I thought that's just the way business is done in San Jose,' " the developer said.

See also Clan Crawford, Jr., Strategy and Tactics in Municipal Zoning ch. 11 (1969), discussing "Persuasive Techniques Before the City Council."

3. *Legislative or quasi-judicial?* The traditional reasonableness standard for judicial review of legislative regulation of economic activities — including zoning regulations — is extraordinarily permissive, amounting to virtual deference on the part of the courts. Hence the zoning amendment process may be particularly vulnerable to such abuses as spot zoning if courts regard rezoning as "legislative." No doubt this concern underlies the rule, common but not universal, that zoning amendments must be justified by showing a mistake in the original ordinance or a change in conditions subsequent to its enactment. See 1 Anderson, supra, §5.11.

Fasano illustrates a different approach to the problem, rejecting the requirements (though not the relevance) of mistake or change and substituting more intensive judicial review when zoning amendments are of an essentially "adjudicative" nature. Is that a good idea? In thinking about the matter, consider the opinion in *Arnel* and note also such issues as the following: Exactly what standards should be applied if intensive judicial review is to be the norm? Is judicial scrutiny the best way to control abuse, or does the amendment process itself provide a better means? Does the *Fasano* approach accommodate the need for flexibility, and for expertise, in zoning administration? Does the judiciary have the necessary capabilities? According to Robert C. Ellickson & A. Dan Tarlock, Land-Use Controls 41-42 (Supp. 1984):

> Recent academic writings have been highly critical of the *Fasano* approach. Professor Jan Krasnowiecki, in Abolish Zoning, 31 Syracuse L. Rev. 719 (1980), has concluded that the advance planning and zoning of developing communities is impossible. He proposes that local governments have the authority to make case-by-case decisions on proposed projects, with "a statutory presumption that any housing project must be approved unless the approving agency gives persuasive reasons why it should not." A state statute would list the only harmful spillovers with which an agency could be concerned. Krasnowiecki thinks the *Fasano* court was right to regard zoning amendments as being quasi-judicial in character. Yet he concludes that it then erred when it embraced "the old concept of the comprehensive plan, thus transforming what should have been the beginning of a flexible zoning system into one of the most powerful antigrowth weapons ever devised in zoning history." Id. at 748-749.
>
> Professor Carol Rose, in Planning and Dealing: Piecemeal Land Controls as a Problem of Local Legitimacy, 71 Cal. L. Rev. 839 (1983), describes the *Fasano* approach as "plan jurisprudence." Rose asserts that modern planning theory and actual local planning practice both deny that the comprehensive plan can play the role that *Fasano* asks it to play. . . . Rose suggests that the legitimacy of a local land-use decision be judged not according to its consistency with a comprehensive plan, but rather according to whether the local

agency mediated and accommodated conflicting local interests. Thus, while most commentators have deplored the "lawless" state of variance administration, Rose applauds the tendency of members of variance boards to mediate informally the disputes that come before them.

Professor Rose addresses the *Fasano* issue again in a subsequent article. See Carol M. Rose, New Models for Local Land Use Decisions, 79 Nw. U. L. Rev. 1155, 1157-1164 (1984-1985). She agrees that it is problematic to view small-scale land-use decisions as legislative products likely to enjoy the protections of the political process. But viewing the decisions as adjudicative is also troublesome. There are the familiar problems of standards and the need for flexibility, and also a number of procedural difficulties. Local governmental authorities are always involved in the zoning process at some point, and they do — and should — make contact with their constituents in the community. They also take positions on land-use issues when they campaign. But can they then, by prevailing standards of appropriate *judicial* conduct, subsequently make legitimate adjudicative decisions (and if they can't, who can)? And what about the nitty-gritty? If there are hearings, must witnesses be sworn? Subject to cross-examination? On these latter points, the courts of at least one state, Kentucky, have answered in the negative. See id. at 1164 n.47.

The Oregon Supreme Court subsequently retreated from the position it had adopted in *Fasano*. See Neuberger v. City of Portland, 288 Or. 155, 603 P.2d 771 (1979), characterized as "overruling" *Fasano*, "at least in part," because of "extensive legislative and administrative activity in the land use area since *Fasano* was decided — seeming to imply that the time has come for Oregon courts to defer more to other branches of government in the area of land use law." Norvell v. Portland Metro. Area Local Govt. Boundary Commn., 43 Or. App. 849, 852, 604 P.2d 896, 899 (1979).

4. *Rezoning by referendum, initiative, and other popular measures.* In the case of a referendum, the local governing body approves an ordinance and then refers it to the electorate for a final decision. An initiative goes right from a qualifying petition, initiatied by citizens, to the ballot. *Arnel* involved a rezoning initiative, and gave rise to the legislative-adjudicative issue because referendums and initiatives are reserved for legislative functions. If small-scale rezoning is essentially adjudicative — the central questions in *Fasano* and *Arnel* alike — then neither method of popular lawmaking can be used. The court in *Arnel* relied on City of Eastlake v. Forest City Enterprises, Inc., 426 U.S. 668 (1976). The issue in *Eastlake* was whether a city charter provision requiring popular ratification of zoning changes was an unconstitutional delegation of legislative power to the populace, and the Supreme Court held it was not. The legislative power cannot be delegated by the legislature to a regulatory body; it

may, however, be reserved by the people — because it derives from them. If the ordinance that results from the process is standardless, arbitrary, and unreasonable, then it can be attacked on those grounds in state courts, as a violation of the due process principles established in the *Euclid* case (page 993).

Notwithstanding *Eastlake,* the states themselves differ on the availability of initiatives and referendums for small-scale rezonings. At least one state, in a novel approach to the dilemma, has held that such rezoning is legislative for purposes of the popular measures, but quasi-judicial when the issue is the applicable standard of judicial review. See Margolis v. District Court, 638 P.2d 297 (Colo. 1981). For a brief overview of recent decisions, see Edward H. Ziegler, Jr., Limitations on Use of Initiative and Referendum Measures in Controlling Land Use Disputes, 13 Zoning & Plan. L. Rep. 17 (1990).

What is the concern with small-scale rezoning by popular procedures? Ronald H. Rosenberg, Referendum Zoning: Legal Doctrine and Practice, 53 U. Cin. L. Rev. 381 (1984), reports on a study of one Ohio county. Typically, Rosenberg found, the issues at stake were poorly presented to the public, giving at best only a superficial understanding. Voter turnout was generally very low, and the procedures used meant that in some instances a small handful of neighbors had effective veto power. Hence small-scale rezonings can be "conspicuously undemocratic," and large rezonings are too complex to be decided on a yes-or-no basis. Moroever, in both cases the popular procedures tend to discourage full and open discussion in a public forum — such as before the legislative body — and to devalue expert input. See id. at 431-433. For similar sentiments, see David L. Callies, Nancy C. Neuffer & Carlito P. Caliboso, Ballot Box Zoning: Initiative, Referendum and the Law, 39 Wash. U. J. Urb. & Contemp. L. 53 (1991).

The Supreme Court's decision in *Eastlake* distinguished the situation where the power of popular approval is given to a narrow segment of the community, such as those living near the precise area to be zoned or rezoned. Measures like these have been invalidated, but neighborhood consent requirements persist and are sometimes upheld. See Robert C. Ellickson & A. Dan Tarlock, Land-Use Controls 300-304 (1981).

3.   Contract and Conditional Rezoning

Collard v. Incorporated Village of Flower Hill
Court of Appeals of New York, 1981
52 N.Y.2d 594, 421 N.E.2d 818, 439 N.Y.S.2d 326

JONES, J. . . . [In 1976 a landowner applied for a rezoning that would permit the land to be used for business. The application was granted subject to a number of conditions expressed in a declaration of covenants entered into and recorded by the landowner. One of the conditions provided that no structures then on the land were to be altered without consent of the local legislative body. The appellants later purchased the land in question.]

Appellants, after acquiring title, made application in late 1978 to the village board for approval to enlarge and extend the existing structure on the premises. Without any reason being given that application was denied. Appellants then commenced this action to have the board's determination declared arbitrary, capricious, unreasonable, and unconstitutional and sought by way of ultimate relief an order directing the board to issue the necessary building permits.

Asserting that the board's denial of the application was beyond review as to reasonableness, respondent moved to dismiss the complaint for failure to state a cause of action. Special Term denied the motion. . . . The Appellate Division, 75 A.D.2d 631, 427 N.Y.S.2d 301, reversed and dismissed the complaint. . . . We now affirm.

At the outset this case involves the question of the permissibility of municipal rezoning conditioned on the execution of a private declaration of covenants restricting the use to which the parcel sought to be rezoned may be put. Prior to our decision in Church v. Town of Islip, 8 N.Y.2d 254, 203 N.Y.S.2d 866, 168 N.E.2d 680, in which we upheld rezoning of property subject to reasonable conditions, conditional rezoning had been almost uniformly condemned by courts of all jurisdictions — a position to which a majority of States appear to continue to adhere. Since *Church*, however, the practice of conditional zoning has become increasingly widespread in this State, as well as having gained popularity in other jurisdictions (see, e.g., Scrutton v. County of Sacramento, 275 Cal. App. 2d 412, 79 Cal. Rptr. 872; Goffinet v. County of Christian, 30 Ill. App. 3d 1089, 333 N.E.2d 731; City of Greenbelt v. Bresler, 248 Md. 210, 236 A.2d 1; Sylvania Elec. Prods. v. City of Newton, 344 Mass. 428, 183 N.E.2d 118; Gladwyne Colony v. Lower Merion Twp., 409 Pa. 441, 187 A.2d 549).

Because much criticism has been mounted against the practice, both by commentators and the courts of some of our sister States,[15] further exposition is in order.

15. See, e.g., Babcock, The Zoning Game, chs. 1, 3; Bassett, Zoning, ch. 9; Crolly, The Rezoning of Properties Conditioned on Agreements with Property Owners — Zoning by Contract, N.Y.L.J., March 9, 1961, p.4, col. 1; Scott, Toward a Strategy for Utilization of Contract and Conditional Zoning, 51 J. Urban L. 94; Trager, Contract Zoning, 23 Md. L. Rev. 121; Note, Three Aspects of Zoning: Unincorporated Areas — Exclusionary Zoning — Conditional Zoning, 6 Real Prop., Prob. & Tr. J. 178 (1971); Comment, The Use and Abuse of Contract Zoning, 12 U.C.L.A. L. Rev. 897. For judicial criticism, see, e.g., Allred v. City of Raleigh, 277 N.C. 530, 178 S.E.2d 432; Baylis v. City of Baltimore, 219 Md. 164, 148 A.2d 429; City of Farmers Branch v. Hawnco, Inc., 435 S.W.2d 288 [Tex. Civ. App.]; Ford Leasing Dev. Co. v Board of County Comrs., 186 Colo. 418, 528 P.2d

Probably the principal objection to conditional rezoning is that it constitutes illegal spot zoning, thus violating the legislative mandate requiring that there be a comprehensive plan for, and that all conditions be uniform within, a given zoning district. When courts have considered the issue . . . , the assumptions have been made that conditional zoning benefits particular landowners rather than the community as a whole and that it undermines the foundation upon which comprehensive zoning depends by destroying uniformity within use districts. Such unexamined assumptions are questionable. First, it is a downward change to a less restrictive zoning classification that benefits the property rezoned and not the opposite imposition of greater restrictions on land use. Indeed, imposing limiting conditions, while benefiting surrounding properties, normally adversely affects the premises on which the conditions are imposed. Second, zoning is not invalid per se merely because only a single parcel is involved or benefited; the real test for spot zoning is whether the change is other than part of a well-considered and comprehensive plan calculated to serve the general welfare of the community. Such a determination, in turn, depends on the reasonableness of the rezoning in relation to neighboring uses — an inquiry required regardless of whether the change in a zone is conditional in form. Third, if it is initially proper to change a zoning classification without the imposition of restrictive conditions notwithstanding that such change may depart from uniformity, then no reason exists why accomplishing that change subject to condition should automatically be classified as impermissible spot zoning.

Both conditional and unconditional rezoning involve essentially the same legislative act — an amendment of the zoning ordinance. The standards for judging the validity of conditional rezoning are no different from the standards used to judge whether unconditional rezoning is illegal. If modification to a less restrictive zoning classification is warranted, then a fortiori conditions imposed by a local legislature to minimize conflicts among districts should not in and of themselves violate any prohibition against spot zoning.

Another fault commonly voiced in disapproval of conditional zoning is that it constitutes an illegal bargaining away of a local government's police power. . . . Because no municipal government has the power to make contracts that control or limit it in the exercise of its legislative powers and duties, restrictive agreements made by a municipality in conjunction with a rezoning are sometimes said to violate public policy. While permitting citizens to be governed by the best bargain they can strike with a local legislature would not be consonant with notions of

---

237; Hartnett v. Austin, 93 So. 2d 86 [Fla.]; Haymon v. City of Chattanooga, 513 S.W.2d 185 [Tenn. App.]; Houston Petroleum Co. v. Automotive Prods. Credit Assn., 9 N.J. 122, 87 A.2d 319; Sandenburgh v. Michigamme Oil Co., 249 Mich. 372, 228 N.W. 707; Ziemer v. County of Peoria, 33 Ill. App. 3d 612, 338 N.E.2d 145.

good government, absent proof of a contract purporting to bind the local legislature in advance to exercise its zoning authority in a bargained-for manner, a rule which would have the effect of forbidding a municipality from trying to protect landowners in the vicinity of a zoning change by imposing protective conditions based on the assertion that that body is bargaining away its discretion, would not be in the best interests of the public. The imposition of conditions on property sought to be rezoned may not be classified as a prospective commitment on the part of the municipality to zone as requested if the conditions are met; nor would the municipality necessarily be precluded on this account from later reversing or altering its decision.

Yet another criticism leveled at conditional zoning is that the State enabling legislation does not confer on local authorities authorization to enact conditional zoning amendments. On this view any such ordinance would be ultra vires. While it is accurate to say there exists no explicit authorization that a legislative body may attach conditions to zoning amendments (see, e.g., Village Law, §7-700 et seq.), neither is there any language which expressly forbids a local legislature to do so. Statutory silence is not necessarily a denial of the authority to engage in such a practice. Where in the face of nonaddress in the enabling legislation there exists independent justification for the practice as an appropriate exercise of municipal power, that power will be implied. Conditional rezoning is a means of achieving some degree of flexibility in land-use control by minimizing the potentially deleterious effect of a zoning change on neighboring properties; reasonably conceived conditions harmonize the landowner's need for rezoning with the public interest and certainly fall within the spirit of the enabling legislation.

One final concern of those reluctant to uphold the practice is that resort to conditional rezoning carries with it no inherent restrictions apart from the restrictive agreement itself. This fear, however, is justifiable only if conditional rezoning is considered a contractual relationship between municipality and private party, outside the scope of the zoning power — a view to which we do not subscribe. When conditions are incorporated in an amending ordinance, the result is as much a "zoning regulation" as an ordinance, adopted without conditions. Just as the scope of all zoning regulation is limited by the police power, and thus local legislative bodies must act reasonably and in the best interests of public safety, welfare and convenience . . . , the scope of permissible conditions must of necessity be similarly limited. If, upon proper proof, the conditions imposed are found unreasonable, the rezoning amendment as well as the required conditions would have to be nullified, with the affected property reverting to the preamendment zoning classification.

Against this backdrop we proceed to consideration of the contentions advanced by appellants in the appeal now before us. It is first useful to delineate arguments which they do not advance. Thus, they do not challenge the conditional zoning change made in 1976 at the behest of their predecessors in title; no contention is made that the village board was not authorized to adopt the resolution of October 4, 1976, conditioned as it was on the execution and recording of the declaration of covenants, or that the provisions of that declaration were in 1976 arbitrary, capricious, unreasonable or unconstitutional. The reason may be what is apparent, namely, that any successful challenge to the adoption of the 1976 resolution would cause appellants' premises to revert to their pre-1976 zoning classification — a consequence clearly unwanted by them.

The focus of appellants' assault is the provision of the declaration of covenants that no structure may be extended or enlarged "without the prior consent of the Board of Trustees of the Village." Appellants would have us import the added substantive prescription — "which consent may not be unreasonably withheld." Their argument proceeds along two paths; first, that as a matter of construction the added prescription should be read into the provision; second, that because of limitations associated with the exercise of municipal zoning power the village board would have been required to include such a prescription.

Appellants' construction argument must fail. The terminology employed in the declaration is explicit. The concept that appellants would invoke is not obscure and language to give it effect was readily available had it been the intention of the parties to include this added stipulation. Appellants point to no canon of construction in the law of real property or of contracts which would call for judicial insertion of the missing clause. Where language has been chosen containing no inherent ambiguity or uncertainty, courts are properly hesitant, under the guise of judicial construction, to imply additional requirements to relieve a party from asserted disadvantages flowing from the terms actually used.

The second path either leads nowhere or else goes too far. If it is appellants' assertion that the village board was legally required to insist on inclusion of the desired prescription, there is no authority in the court to reform the zoning enactment of 1976 retroactively to impose the omitted clause. Whether the village board at that time would have enacted a different resolution in the form now desired by appellants is open only to speculation; the certainty is that they did not then take such legislative action. On the other hand, acceptance of appellants' proposition would produce as the other possible consequence the conclusion that the 1976 enactment was illegal, throwing appellants unhappily back to the pre-1976 zoning of their premises, a destination which they assuredly wish to sidestep. . . .

For the reasons stated the Board of Trustees of the Incorporated Village of Flower Hill may not now be compelled to issue its consent to the proposed enlargement and extension of the existing structure on the premises or in the alternative give an acceptable reason for failing to do so. Accordingly, the order of the Appellate Division should be affirmed, with costs.

NOTES AND QUESTIONS

1. There is disagreement about the difference (if any) between contract and conditional rezoning, and about the validity of each technique. If there is a real line between the two, it seems to be this: Under conditional rezoning, the property owner agrees to certain conditions as a prerequisite to the zoning change, but the local government makes no commitments; with contract rezoning, the property owner and the government enter into a reciprocal agreement, the owner covenanting to restrict the use of the property in exchange for the government's promise to rezone. Contract rezoning was once regarded as illegal per se, so advocates of the technique came up with the label "conditional" rezoning to help avoid invalidity. Conditional rezoning can be as binding in practice, and perhaps legally as well, as the contract rezoning still formally rejected by some courts. In practice, zoners might find it politically embarrassing not to rezone once a landowner has complied with the required conditions. Beyond this, compliance might give rise to vested rights. See Note 4 on page 1019.

The modern trend, with a few exceptions, is to approve of conditional rezoning in general, although particular applications might be invalidated. For an overview, see 1 Patrick J. Rohan, Zoning and Land Use Controls §5.01 (1992). See also Judith Wegner, Moving Toward the Bargaining Table: Contract Zoning, Development Agreements, and the Theoretical Foundations of Government Land Use Deals, 65 N.C. L. Rev. 957 (1987).

2. Where conditional (or contract) rezoning is considered per se invalid, zoners have to resort to other familiar devices — such as special exceptions — to accomplish the ends in mind. The problem is that the alternative devices might not fit the problem as well, or might take more time and trouble to execute. As *Collard* suggests, one concern with contract and conditional rezoning is piecemeal deterioration in the comprehensive plan; another is fear of abuse and favoritism. Are the alternatives to contract and conditional rezoning — special exceptions again, for example — less vulnerable to these concerns? Does *Collard* dismiss the concerns too quickly in the case of conditional rezoning?

3. Was the benefit of the covenant in *Collard* appurtenant to land, or was it in gross? If the benefit was in gross, would the burden run to Collard? See Note 1 on page 901.

4. Suppose a landowner wishes to use his lot in a residential zone for a corner grocery. The neighbors do not object to the grocery, but say they will fight any other kind of business at the site. How should the

landowner go about securing permission from the local government to use his lot as a grocery, but only as a grocery? In Dexter v. Town Bd. of Town of Gates, 36 N.Y.2d 102, 324 N.E.2d 870, 365 N.Y.S.2d 506 (1975), the town board rezoned the petitioner's lot from residential to commercial, with the condition that the lot could be used only for a market by Wegman Enterprises (the petitioner). The court held that the condition was improper in that it was personal to the petitioner, did not relate to the use of the property, and was prima facie evidence of spot zoning.

5. Under conditional and contract rezoning, developers are sometimes permitted to disregard regulatory limitations in exchange for one or another kind of "exaction." See pages 1010-1011 and 1 Rohan, supra, §5.04[5]. This approach, called "incentive zoning," is discussed in Jerold S. Kayden, Zoning for Dollars: New Rules for an Old Game? Comments on the *Municipal Art Society* and *Nollan* Cases, 39 Wash. U. J. Urb. & Contemp. L. 3 (1991).

4.   Floating Zones, Cluster Zones, and Planned Unit Developments (PUDs)

Cheney v. Village 2 at New Hope, Inc.
Supreme Court of Pennsylvania, 1968
429 Pa. 626, 241 A.2d 81

ROBERTS, J. Under traditional concepts of zoning the task of determining the type, density and placement of buildings which should exist within any given zoning district devolves upon the local legislative body. In order that this body might have to speak only infrequently on the issue of municipal planning and zoning, the local legislature usually enacts detailed requirements for the type, size and location of buildings within each given zoning district, and leaves the ministerial task of enforcing these regulations to an appointed zoning administrator, with another administrative body, the zoning board of adjustment, passing on individual deviations from the strict district requirements, deviations known commonly as variances and special exceptions. At the same time, the overall rules governing the dimensions, placement, etc. of primarily public additions to ground, e.g., streets, sewers, playgrounds, are formulated by the local legislature through the passage of subdivision regulations. These regulations are enforced and applied to individual lots by an administrative body usually known as the planning commission.

This general approach to zoning fares reasonably well so long as development takes place on a lot-by-lot basis, and so long as no one cares that the overall appearance of the municipality resembles the design achieved by using a cookie cutter on a sheet of dough. However, with the increasing popularity of large scale residential developments, particularly in suburban areas, it has become apparent to many local municipalities that land can be more efficiently used, and developments more aesthetically pleasing, if zoning regulations focus on density requirements rather than on specific rules for each individual lot. Under density zoning, the legislature determines what percentage of a particular district must be devoted to open space, for example, and what percentage used for dwelling units. The task of filling in the particular district with real houses and real open spaces then falls upon the planning commission usually working in conjunction with an individual large scale developer. See Chrinko v. South Brunswick Twp., Planning Bd., 77 N.J. Super. 594, 187 A.2d 221 (1963). The ultimate goal of this so-called density or cluster concept of zoning is achieved when an entire self-contained little community is permitted to be built within a zoning district, with the rules of density controlling not only the relation of private dwellings to open space, but also the relation of homes to commercial establishments such as theaters, hotels, restaurants, and quasi-commercial uses such as schools and churches. The present controversy before this Court involves a frontal attack upon one of these zoning districts, known in the trade as a Planned Unit Development (hereinafter PUD).

Spurred by the desire of appellant developer to construct a Planned Unit Development in the Borough of New Hope, in December of 1964 Borough Council began considering the passage of a new zoning ordinance to establish a PUD district in New Hope. After extensive consultation with appellant, council referred the matter to the New Hope Planning Commission for further study. This body, approximately six months after the project idea was first proposed, formally recommended to council that a PUD district be created. Council consulted with members of the Bucks County Planning Commission on the text of the proposed ordinance, held public hearings, and finally on June 14, 1965 enacted ordinance 160 which created the PUD district, and ordinance 161 which amended the Borough zoning map, rezoning a large tract of land known as the Rauch farm from low density residential to PUD. Pursuant to the procedural requirements of ordinance 160, appellant presented plans for a Planned Unit Development on the Rauch tract to the Borough Planning Commission. These plans were approved on November 8, 1965, and accordingly four days later two building permits, known as zoning permits 68 and 69, were issued to appellant. . . .

Subsequently, permit number 75 was issued. Appellees, all neighboring property owners opposing the issuance of these permits, appealed to the zoning board of adjustment. The board, after taking extensive testimony, upheld ordinances 160 and 161 and accordingly affirmed the issuance of the permits. Appellees then appealed to the Bucks County Court of Common Pleas. That tribunal took no additional testimony, but reversed the board, holding the ordinances invalid for failure to conform to a comprehensive plan and for vesting too much discretion in the New Hope Planning Commission. This Court granted certiorari. . . .

[W]e hold that no error of law or abuse of discretion was committed by the New Hope Board of Adjustment, and that therefore the Court of Common Pleas of Bucks County must be reversed.

I

Approximately one year before the PUD seed was planted in New Hope, Borough Council had approved the New Hope Comprehensive Plan. This detailed land use projection clearly envisioned the Rauch tract as containing only single family dwellings of low density. The court below therefore concluded that the enactment of ordinance 160, and more specifically the placing of a PUD district on the Rauch tract by ordinance 161 was not "in accordance with a comprehensive plan," as required by the Act of February 1, 1966, P.L. (1965) — §3203, 53 P.S. §48203. See also Eves v. Zoning Bd. of Adjustment, 401 Pa. 211, 164 A.2d 7 (1960).

The fallacy in the court's reasoning lies in its mistaken belief that a comprehensive plan, once established, is forever binding on the municipality and can never be amended. Cases subsequent to Eves have made it clear, however, that these plans may be changed by the passage of new zoning ordinances, provided the local legislature passes the new ordinance with some demonstration of sensitivity to the community as a whole, and the impact that the new ordinance will have on this community. . . .

Given this rule of law allowing post-plan zoning changes, and the presumption in favor of an ordinance's validity . . . , we are not in a position, having reviewed the record in the present case, to say that the zoning board committed an abuse of discretion or an error of law when it concluded that ordinances 160 and 161 were properly passed. Presented as it was with evidence that the PUD district had been under consideration by council for over six months and had been specifically recommended by the borough planning commission, a body specially equipped to view proposed ordinances as they relate to the rest of the community, we hold that the board, within its sound discretion, could have concluded that council passed the ordinances with the proper overall considerations in mind. The PUD district established by ordinance 160 is not the type of use which by its very nature could have no place in the middle of a predominantly residential borough. It is not a steel mill, a fat rendering plant, or a desiccated egg factory. It is, in fact, nothing more than a miniature residential community.

Closely tied to the comprehensive plan issue is the argument raised by appellees that ordinances 160 and 161 constitute spot zoning outlawed by Eves, supra. Given the fact situation in Eves, however, as well as the post-*Eves* cases, we do not believe that there is any spot zoning here. In *Eves,* the municipality created a limited industrial district, F-1, which, by explicit legislative pronouncement, was not to be applied to any particular tract until the individual land owner requested that his own tract be so re-zoned. The obvious evil in this procedure did *not* lie in the fact that a limited industrial district might be placed in an area previously zoned, for example, residential. The evil was the *pre-ordained* uncertainty as to where the F-1 district would crop up. The ordinance all but invited spot zoning where the legislature could respond to private entreaties from land owners and re-zone tracts F-1 without regard to the surrounding community. In *Eves,* it was almost impossible for the F-1 districts to conform to a comprehensive plan since tracts would be re-zoned on a strictly ad hoc basis.

Quite to the contrary, no such "floating zone" exists in the present case. On the very day that the PUD district was created by ordinance 160, it was brought to earth by ordinance 161; and, as discussed supra, this *was* done "in accordance with a comprehensive plan." . . .

II

The court below next concluded that even if the two ordinances were properly *passed,* they must fall as vesting authority in the planning commission greater than that permitted under Pennsylvania's zoning enabling legislation. More specifically, it is now contended by appellees that complete project approval by the planning commission under ordinance 160 requires that commission to encroach upon legislative territory whenever it decides where, within a particular PUD district, specific types of building should be placed.

In order to appreciate fully the arguments of counsel on both sides it is necessary to explain in some detail exactly what is permitted within a PUD district, and who decides whether a particular land owner has complied with these requirements. Admittedly the range of permissible uses within the PUD district is greater than that normally found in a traditional zoning district. Within a New Hope PUD district there may be: single family attached or detached dwellings; apartments; accessory private garages; public or private parks and recreation areas including golf courses, swimming pools, ski slopes, etc. (so long as these facilities do not produce noise, glare, odor, air pollution, etc., detrimental to existing or prospective adjacent structures); a municipal building; a school; churches; art galleries; professional offices; certain types of signs; a theatre (but not a drive-in); motels and hotels; and a restaurant. The ordinance then sets certain overall density requirements. The PUD district may have a maximum of 80% of the land devoted to residential uses, a maximum of 20% for the permitted commercial uses and enclosed recreational facilities, and must have a minimum of 20% for open spaces.

The residential density shall not exceed 10 units per acre, nor shall any such unit contain more than two bedrooms. All structures within the district must not exceed maximum height standards set out in the ordinance. Finally, although there are not traditional "set back" and "side yard" requirements, ordinance 160 does require that there be 24 feet between structures, and that no townhouse structure contain more than 12 dwelling units.

The procedure to be followed by the aspiring developer reduces itself to presenting a detailed plan for his planned unit development to the planning commission, obtaining that body's approval and then securing building permits. Of course, the planning commission may not approve any development that fails to meet the requirements set forth in the ordinance as outlined above.

We begin with the observation that there is nothing in the borough zoning enabling act which would prohibit council from creating a zoning district with this many permissible uses. The applicable section of the borough code is the Act of February 1, 1966, P.L. (1965) — §3201, 53 P.S. §48201. Under this section, council is given the power to regulate and restrict practically all aspects of buildings themselves, open spaces, population density, location of structures, etc., the only limitation on this power being that it be exercised so as to promote the "health, safety, morals or the general welfare" of the borough. Under the same act, section 1601, 53 P.S. §46601, empowers council to adopt ordinances to govern the use of public areas, such as streets, parks, etc., again with the only limitation being that such ordinances create "conditions favorable to the health, safety, morals and general welfare of the citizens." Thus, if council reasonably believed that a given district could contain *all* types of structures, without *any* density requirements whatsoever, so long as this did not adversely affect health, safety and morals, such a district could be created. In fact, it is common knowledge that in many industrial and commercial districts just such a wide range of uses is permitted. Given such broad power to zone, we cannot say that New Hope Borough Council abrogated its legislative function by creating a PUD district permitting the mixture of uses outlined supra, especially given the density requirements.

We must next examine the statutory power of the borough planning commission to determine whether such an administrative body may regulate the internal development of a PUD district. The Act of February 1, 1966, P.L. (1965) — §1155, 53 P.S. §46155, requires that all plans for land "laid out in building lots" be approved by the planning commission before they may be recorded. Thus, the traditional job of the commission has been to examine tract plans to determine whether they conform to the applicable borough ordinances. The ordinances most frequently interpreted and applied to the planning commission are those dealing with streets, sewers, water and gas mains, etc., i.e., the so-called public improvements. However, the statute contains no language which would prohibit the planning commission from approving plans with reference to ordinances dealing with permissible building uses as well. The primary reason that planning commissions have not traditionally interpreted this type of ordinance is that such regulations do not usually come into play until the landowner wishes to begin the actual construction of a particular building. By this time, the relevant subdivision plan has already been approved by the commission; thus the task of examining the plans for a particular structure to see whether it conforms to the regulations for the zoning district in which it will be erected devolves upon the local building inspector who issues the building permit.

However, in the case of PUD the entire development (including specific structures) is mapped out and submitted to the administrative agency at once. Accordingly, the requirements set forth in a PUD ordinance must relate not only to those areas traditionally administered by the planning commission, but also to areas traditionally administered by the building inspector. Therefore, quite logically, the job of approving a particular PUD should rest with a single municipal body. The question then is simply which one: Borough Council (a legislative body), the Planning Commission (an administrative body), or the Zoning Board of Adjustment (an administrative body)?

There is no doubt that it would be statutorily permissible for council itself to pass a PUD ordinance and simultaneous zoning map amendment so specific that no details would be left for any administrator. The ordinance could specify where each building should be placed, how large it should be, where the open spaces are located, etc. But what would be the practical effect of such an ordinance? One of the most attractive features of Planned Unit Development is its flexibility; the chance for the builder and the municipality to sit down together and tailor a development to meet the specific needs of the community and the requirements of the land on which it is to be built. But all this would be lost if the Legislature let the planning cement set before any developer could happen upon the scene to scratch his own initials in that cement. Professor Krasnowiecki has accurately summed up the effect on planned unit development of such legislative planning. The picture, to be sure, is not a happy one:

> The traditional refuge of the courts, the requirement that all the standards be set forth in advance of application for development, does not offer a practical solution to the problem. The complexity of pre-established regulations that would automatically dispose of any proposal for planned unit development, when different housing types and perhaps accessory commercial areas are envisaged, would be quite considerable. Indeed as soon as various housing types are permitted, the regulations that would govern their design and distribution on every possible kind of site, their relationship to each other and their relationship to surrounding properties must be complex

unless the developer's choice in terms of site, site plan, and design and distribution of housing is reduced close to zero. It is not likely ... that local authorities would want to adopt such a set of regulations. [Krasnowiecki, Planned Unit Development: A Challenge to Established Theory and Practice of Land Use Control, 114 U. Pa. L. Rev. 47, 71 (1965).]

Left with Professor Krasnowiecki's "Hobson's choice" of no developer leeway at all, or a staggering set of legislative regulations sufficient to cover every idea the developer might have, it is not likely that Planned Unit Development could thrive, or even maintain life, if the local legislature assumed totally the role of planner.

The remaining two municipal bodies which could oversee the shaping of specific Planned Unit Developments are both administrative agencies, the Zoning Board of Adjustment and the Planning Commission. As this Court views both reality and zoning enabling act, the Zoning Board of Adjustment is not the proper body. . . . Zoning boards are accustomed to focusing on one lot at a time. They traditionally examine hardship cases and unique uses proposed by landowners. As Professor Krasnowiecki has noted: "To suggest that the board is intended, or competent, to handle large scale planning and design decisions is, I think, far fetched." Technical Bulletin 52, Urban Land Institute, p.38 (1965). We agree.

Thus, the borough planning commission remains the only other body both qualified and statutorily permitted to approve PUD. Of course, we realize that a planning commission is not authorized to engage in actual re-zoning of land. But merely because the commission here has the power to approve more than one type of building for a particular lot within the PUD district does not mean that the commission is usurping the zoning function. Indeed, it is acting in strict *accordance* with the applicable zoning ordinance, for that ordinance, No. 160, *permits* more than one type of building for a particular lot. To be sure, if the commission approved a plan for a PUD district where 30% of the land were being used commercially, *then* we would have an example of illegal re-zoning by an administrator. But no one argues in the present case that appellant's plan does not conform to the requirements of ordinance 160.

Nor is this Court sympathetic to appellees' argument that ordinance 160 permits the planning commission to grant variances and special exceptions. We fail to see how a development such as appellant's that meets every single requirement of the applicable zoning ordinance can be said to be the product of a variance or a special exception. The very essence of variances and special exceptions lies in their *departure* from ordinance requirements, not in their compliance with them. We therefore conclude that the New Hope Planning Commission has the power to approve development plans submitted to it under ordinance 160. . . .

NOTES AND QUESTIONS

1. *Floating zones.* The floating zone represents a relatively new method — postdating the standard techniques of variances, special exceptions, and rezoning — by which to deal with the rigidities of typical Euclidean zoning. The floating zone achieves flexibility by, in essence, defining a zone but reserving the decision about its location for the future. Two steps are usually involved: First, the city creates (but does not locate) a use district by an ordinance that specifies standards and criteria to govern the uses permitted in the zone. Second, and later in time, the zone is attached to a particular area through a zoning amendment, ordinarily at the request of a property owner or developer.

Floating zones have been challenged on a number of grounds, most of them predictable and some of them suggested in the *Cheney* case: failure to comply with a comprehensive plan; spot zoning; lack of authorization by enabling legislation; unlawful delegation of legislative authority. Judicial results are mixed, though it should be noted that invalidation on some of the foregoing grounds is not a general condemnation of floating zones, but only of particular applications.

The *Eves* case discussed at some length in *Cheney* struck down a floating zone on broad grounds, finding it to represent "the antithesis of zoning." In the view of the *Eves* court, zoning contemplates division of a community into districts, in accordance with a comprehensive plan. Because the floating zone in question would be precisely located only at the request of particular landowners on a case-by-case basis, it was clear to the court that at the time of enactment of the floating zone ordinance there was in fact no orderly plan of development in mind. The court's reasoning was formalistic, but its concerns were real ones: political influence could be exercised too easily in the location of the floating zone; piecemeal placements of floating zones could encourage spot zoning; notice of the nature of a neighborhood would not be provided to people when they purchased property.[16]

While the *Cheney* case claims only to distinguish *Eves*, perhaps it should be read to have rejected it. The court's discussion of comprehensive planning suggests this, as does its reliance on the fact that the new zone was enacted, and its location settled, on the same day. Why should that matter? In both *Cheney* and *Eves*, after all, the desires of particular

---

16. Contrast the leading decision upholding floating zones, Rodgers v. Village of Tarrytown, 302 N.Y. 115, 96 N.E.2d 731 (1951). The floating zone approved there was regarded as being in accordance with a comprehensive plan because it was established and located with careful attention to the nature of the area and to reasonably foreseeable community needs. Spot zoning was not involved, the court held, because the floating zone was located pursuant to a comprehensive plan and not simply for the benefit of individual landowners.

landowners played an instrumental part, and this was the core concern in *Eves*. The timing in *Cheney* seems irrelevant.

Is the floating zone technique any more (or less) subject to abuse than the more standard approaches of variances, special exceptions, and rezoning? Does it provide more flexibility? How does the technique differ from these other devices? See 2 Patrick J. Rohan, Zoning and Land Use Controls §§13.01-13.03 (1992).

2. *Cluster zones and PUDs.* Cluster zoning is a flexibility device whereby a developer is permitted to construct dwellings in a pattern not in literal compliance with the area restrictions of a zoning ordinance. Residences in a cluster zone are typically relieved from observing the usual frontage or setback regulations and side- or rear-yard requirements. Overall population density is generally no greater in a cluster zone than in other residential areas, however, because open spaces are preserved as an element of the cluster. A central idea of the concept is to provide some of the amenities of a rural environment in an otherwise urban setting.

PUDs are similar to cluster zones. While the terms are often used interchangeably, planned unit developments generally contemplate, as in *Cheney*, a mix of residential, commercial, and sometimes even industrial uses. Cluster zones, then, involve area variations; PUDs involve area and use variations.

Both cluster zones and PUDs can be accomplished in a number of ways: through special exceptions issued by a board of adjustment; through subdivision controls administered by a planning board; through floating zones created, ultimately, by the local legislative body. (Which technique was under review in *Cheney*?) The floating zone is the most common approach, and cluster zones and PUDs have been challenged with all the arguments leveled at floating zones. Generally speaking, though, the courts have been tolerant, so long as adequate standards are specified in the ordinance in question. For a good brief overview, see 2 Robert M. Anderson, American Law of Zoning §§11.01-11.06, 11.12-11.24 (3d ed. 1986).

D. Expanding the Aims (and Exercising the Muscle) of Zoning

> The best laid schemes o' mice an' men
>   Gang aft a-gley,
> An' lea'e us nought but grief an' pain
>   For promised joy! —
>
>   *Robert Burns,*
>   To a Mouse (1785)

Recall the early objectives of zoning, at least as stated by the Supreme Court in Euclid v. Ambler, the first case in this chapter. The central idea seemed to be little more than the control of nuisances, though in a comprehensive fashion. Thus the height, spacing, and location of buildings were controlled, justifiably, as means to provide light and air, to help avoid and control the dangers of fire, to prevent overcrowding, and to exclude offensive industries from areas where people lived. Ends and means alike appeared to be innocuous and relatively unintrusive.

But the picture painted by the Court in *Euclid* was somewhat misleading. Recall, for example, that the Euclid ordinance excluded apartment buildings from areas zoned for single-family dwellings, a result the trial court characterized as economic segregation but that the Supreme Court managed to justify in the same terms as it did the more benign aspects of Euclidean zoning. The facts and holding in the case, then, could be read as a generous endorsement of social engineering in the name of public health, safety, and welfare.

It is beside the point whether zoning authorities actually read the case this way; the point is that they came to act as though they did. Over the years after *Euclid* the aims of zoning gradually expanded, no doubt for a host of reasons — population growth, increased pressures on the public fisc, the rise of activist government generally, the appearance of counter-culture groups, an expanding environmental consciousness, a changing moral climate, and so on. Zoning authorities began taking initiatives that the Court in *Euclid* would never have imagined (and others that the Court could have foreseen but chose to ignore).

There are any number of ways to organize a study of the new initiatives and judicial reaction to them. We shall concentrate on the rise of aesthetics as a factor in zoning, on efforts to control household composition, and on efforts to control the nature and size of local populations. All of the developments in question can be seen as yet more measures to correct for market failure of one sort or another. But the market failure argument has a flip-side: The government can fail as well. In particular, it can abuse the power that zoning provides. So, what is the reach of "public health, safety, and welfare," and how are the courts to judge the ambitions of modern-day zoners?

1.   Aesthetic Regulation

State ex rel. Stoyanoff v. Berkeley
Supreme Court of Missouri, 1970
458 S.W.2d 305

PRITCHARD, Commissioner. Upon summary judgment the trial court issued a peremptory writ of mandamus to compel appellant to issue a residential building permit to respondents. The trial court's judgment is that the below-mentioned ordinances are violative of Section 10, Article I of the Constitution of Missouri, 1945, V.A.M.S., in that restrictions placed by the ordinances on the use of property deprive the owners of their property without due process of law. Relators' petition pleads that they applied to appellant Building Commissioner for a building permit to allow them to construct a single family residence in the City of Ladue, and that plans and specifications were submitted for the proposed residence, which was unusual in design, "but complied with all existing building and zoning regulations and ordinances of the City of Ladue, Missouri."

It is further pleaded that relators were refused a building permit for the construction of their proposed residence upon the ground that the permit was not approved by the Architectural Board of the City of Ladue. Ordinance 131, as amended by Ordinance 281 of that city, purports to set up an Architectural Board to approve plans and specifications for buildings and structures erected within the city and in a preamble to

> conform to certain minimum architectural standards of appearance and conformity with surrounding structures, and that unsightly, grotesque and unsuitable structures, detrimental to the stability of value and the welfare of surrounding property, structures and residents, and to the general welfare and happiness of the community, be avoided, and that appropriate standards of beauty and conformity be fostered and encouraged.

It is asserted in the petition that the ordinances are invalid, illegal and void, "are unconstitutional in that they are vague and provide no standard nor uniform rule by which to guide the architectural board," that the city acted in excess of statutory powers (§89.020, RS Mo 1959, V.A.M.S.) in enacting the ordinances, which "attempt to allow respondent to impose aesthetic standards for buildings in the City of Ladue, and are in excess of the powers granted the City of Ladue by said statute."

Relators filed a motion for summary judgment and affidavits were filed in opposition thereto. Richard D. Shelton, Mayor of the City of Ladue, deposed that the facts in appellant's answer were true and correct, as here pertinent: that the City of Ladue constitutes one of the finer suburban residential areas of Metropolitan St. Louis, the homes therein are considerably more expensive than in cities of comparable size, being homes on lots from three fourths of an acre to three or more acres each; that a zoning ordinance was enacted by the city regulating the height, number of stories, size of buildings, percentage of lot occupancy, yard sizes, and the location and use of buildings and land for trade, industry, residence and other purposes; that the zoning regulations were made in accordance with a comprehensive plan "designed to promote the health and general welfare of the residents of the City of Ladue," which in furtherance of said objectives duly enacted said Ordinances numbered 131 and 281. Appellant also asserted in his answer that these ordinances were a reasonable exercise of the city's governmental, legislative and police powers, as determined by its legislative body, and as stated in the above-quoted preamble to the ordinances. It is then pleaded that relators' description of their proposed residence as " 'unusual in design' is the understatement of the year. It is in fact a monstrosity of grotesque design, which would seriously impair the value of property in the neighborhood."

The affidavit of Harold C. Simon, a developer of residential subdivisions in St. Louis County, is that he is familiar with relators' lot upon which they seek to build a house, and with the surrounding houses in the neighborhood; that the houses therein existent are virtually all two-story houses of conventional architectural design, such as Colonial, French Provincial or English; and that the house which relators propose to construct is of ultramodern design which would clash with and not be in conformity with any other house in the entire neighborhood. It is Mr. Simon's opinion that the design and appearance of relators' proposed residence would have a substantial adverse effect upon the market values of other residential property in the neighborhood, such average market value ranging from $60,000 to $85,000 each.

As a part of the affidavit of Russell H. Riley, consultant for the city planning and engineering firm of Harland Bartholomew & Associates, photographic exhibits of homes surrounding relators' lot were attached. . . . [The surrounding houses consisted of a conventional frame residence, several of a Colonial style, and one of a Tudor style.] In substance Mr. Riley went on to say that the City of Ladue is one of the finer residential suburbs in the St. Louis area. . . . The homes are considerably more expensive than average homes found in a city of comparable size. The ordinance which has been adopted by the City of Ladue is typical of those which have been adopted by a number of suburban cities in St. Louis County and in similar cities throughout the United States, the need therefor being based upon the protection of existing property values by preventing the construction of houses that are in complete conflict with the general type of houses in a given area. The intrusion into this neighborhood of relators' unusual, grotesque and nonconforming structure would have a substantial adverse effect on market values of other homes in the immediate area. According to Mr. Riley the standards of Ordinance 131, as amended by Ordinance 281, are usually and customarily applied in city planning work and are:

(1) whether the proposed house meets the customary architectural requirements in appearance and design for a house of the particular type which is proposed (whether it be Colonial, Tudor English, French Provincial, or Mod-

ern), (2) whether the proposed house is in general conformity with the style and design of surrounding structures, and (3) whether the proposed house lends itself to the proper architectural development of the City; and that in applying said standards the Architectural Board and its Chairman are to determine whether the proposed house will have an adverse effect on the stability of values in the surrounding area.

Photographic exhibits of relators' proposed residence were also attached to Mr. Riley's affidavit. They show the residence to be of a pyramid shape, with a flat top, and with triangular shaped windows or doors at one or more corners . . . .

[R]elators' position is that "the creation by the City of Ladue of an architectural board for the purpose of promoting and maintaining 'general conformity with the style and design of surrounding structures' is totally unauthorized by our Enabling Statute." (§§89.020, 89.040, RS Mo 1959, V.A.M.S.) It is further contended by relators that Ordinances 131 and 281 are invalid and unconstitutional as being an unreasonable and arbitrary exercise of the police power (as based entirely on aesthetic values); and that the same are invalid as an unlawful delegation of legislative powers (to the Architectural Board).

Section 89.020 provides . . . [for regulation of lot size; height, size, spacing, and use of buildings; and population density — all for the purpose of promoting health, safety, and welfare.] Section 89.040 provides . . . [that regulations be made in accordance with a comprehensive plan and designed "to promote health *and the general welfare. . . . Such regulations shall be made with reasonable consideration, among other things, to the character of the district and its peculiar suitability for particular uses, and with a view to conserving the values of buildings and encouraging the most appropriate use of land throughout such municipality.*" (Italics added by the court.)]

Relators say that "Neither Sections 89.020 or 89.040 nor any other provision of Chapter 89 mentions or gives a city the authority to regulate architectural design and appearance. There exists no provision providing for an architectural board and no entity even remotely resembling such a board is mentioned under the enabling legislation." Relators conclude that the City of Ladue lacked any power to adopt Ordinance 131 as amended by Ordinance 281 "and its intrusion into this area is wholly unwarranted and without sanction in the law." As to this aspect of the appeal relators rely upon the 1961 decision of State ex rel. Magidson v. Henze, Mo. App., 342 S.W.2d 261. That case had the identical question presented. An Architectural Control Commission was set up by an ordinance of the City of University City. In its report to the Building Commissioner, the Architectural Control Commission disapproved the Magidson application for permits to build four houses. It was commented that the proposed houses did not provide for the minimum number of square feet, and "In considering the existing character of this

A 1992 rendering by architect Shinji Isozaki, showing what the Stoyanoff house might have looked like

neighborhood, the Commission is of the opinion that houses of the character proposed in these plans are not in harmony with and will not contribute to nor protect the general welfare of this neighborhood" (loc. cit. 264). The court held that §89.020, RS Mo 1949, V.A.M.S., does not grant to the city the right to impose upon the landowner aesthetic standards for the buildings he chooses to erect.

As is clear from the affidavits and attached exhibits, the City of Ladue is an area composed principally of residences of the general types of Colonial, French Provincial and English Tudor. The city has a comprehensive plan of zoning to maintain the general character of buildings therein. The *Magidson* case, supra, did not consider the effect of §89.040, supra, and the italicized portion relating to the character of the district, its suitability for particular uses, and the conservation of the values of buildings therein. These considerations, sanctioned by statute, are directly related to the general welfare of the community. . . . In Marrs v. City of Oxford (D.C.D. Kan.) 24 F.2d 541, 548, it was said, "The stabilizing of property values, and giving some assurance to the public that, if property is purchased in a residential district, its value as such will be preserved, is probably the most cogent reason back of zoning ordinances." The preamble to Ordinance 131, quoted above in part, demonstrates that its purpose is to conform to the dictates of §89.040, with reference to preserving values of property by zoning procedure and restrictions on the use of property. This is an illustration of what was referred to in Deimeke v. State Highway Commission, Mo., 444 S.W.2d 480, 484, as a growing number of cases recognizing a change in the scope of the term "general welfare." In the *Deimeke* case on the same page it is said, "Property use which offends sensibilities and debases property values affects not only the adjoining property owners in that vicinity but the general public as well because when such property values are destroyed or seriously impaired, the tax base of the community is affected and the public suffers economically as a result."

Relators say further that Ordinances 131 and 281 are invalid and unconstitutional as being an unreasonable and arbitrary exercise of the police power. It is argued that a mere reading of these ordinances shows that they are based entirely on aesthetic factors in that the stated purpose of the Architectural Board is to maintain "conformity with surrounding structures" and to assure that structures "conform to certain minimum architectural standards of appearance." The argument ignores the further provisos in the ordinance: ". . . and that unsightly, grotesque and unsuitable structures, *detrimental to the stability of value and the welfare of surrounding property, structures, and residents,* and *to the general welfare and happiness of the community,* be avoided, and that appropriate standards of beauty and conformity be fostered and encouraged." (Italics added.) Relators' proposed residence does not descend to the " 'patently offensive character of vehicle graveyards in close proximity to such highways' " referred to in the *Deimeke* case, supra (444 S.W.2d 484). Nevertheless, the aesthetic factor to be taken into account by the Architectural Board is not to be considered alone. Along with that inherent factor is the effect that the proposed residence would have upon the property values in the area. In this time of burgeoning urban areas, congested with people and structures, it is certainly in keeping with the ultimate ideal of general welfare that the Architectural Board, in its function, preserve and protect existing areas in which structures of a general conformity of architecture have been erected. The area under consideration is clearly, from the record, a fashionable one. In State ex rel. Civello v. City of New Orleans, 154 La. 271, 97 So. 440, 444, the court said, "If by the term 'aesthetic considerations' is meant a regard merely for outward appearances, for good taste in the matter of the beauty of the neighborhood itself, we do not observe any substantial reason for saying that such a consideration is not a matter of general welfare. The beauty of a fashionable residence neighborhood in a city is for the comfort and happiness of the residents, and it sustains in a general way the value of property in the neighborhood." . . .

The denial by appellant of a building permit for relators' highly modernistic residence in this area where traditional Colonial, French Provincial and English Tudor styles of architecture are erected does not appear to be arbitrary and unreasonable when the basic purpose to be served is that of the general welfare of persons in the entire community.

In addition to the above-stated purpose in the preamble to Ordinance 131, it establishes an Architectural Board of three members, all of whom must be architects. Meetings of the Board are to be open to the public, and every application for a building permit, except those not affecting the outward appearance of a building, shall be submitted to the Board along with plans, elevations, detail drawings and specifications, before being approved by the Building Commissioner. The Chairman of the Board shall examine the application to determine if it conforms to proper architectural standards in appearance and design and will be in general conformity with the style and design of surrounding structures and conducive to the proper architectural development of the city. If he so finds, he approves and returns the application to the Building Commissioner. If he does not find conformity, or has doubt, a full meeting of the Board is called, with notice of the time and place thereof given to the applicant. The Board shall disapprove the application if it determines the proposed structure will constitute an unsightly, grotesque or unsuitable structure in appearance, detrimental to the welfare of surrounding property or residents. If it cannot make that decision, the application shall be returned to the Building Commissioner either with or without suggestions or recommendations, and if that is done without disapproval, the Building Commissioner may issue the permit. If the Board's disapproval is given and the applicant refuses to comply with recommendations, the Building Commissioner shall refuse the permit. Thereafter provisions are made for an appeal to the Council of the city for review of the decision of the Architectural Board. Ordinance 281 amends Ordinance 131 only with respect to the application initially being submitted to and considered by all members of the Architectural Board.

Relators claim that the above provisions of the ordinance amount to an unconstitutional delegation of power by the city to the Architectural Board. It is argued that the Board cannot be given the power to determine what is unsightly and grotesque and that the standards, "whether the proposed structure will conform to proper architectural standards in appearance and design, and will be in general conformity with the style and design of surrounding structures and conducive to the proper architectural development of the City . . ." and "the Board shall disapprove the application if it determines that the proposed structure will constitute an unsightly, grotesque or unsuitable structure in appearance, detrimental to the welfare of surrounding property or residents . . . ," are inadequate. . . . Ordinances 131 and 281 are sufficient in their general standards calling for a factual determination of the suitability of any proposed structure with reference to the character of the surrounding neighborhood and to the determination of any adverse effect on the general welfare and preservation of property values of the community. Like holdings were made involving Architectural Board ordinances in State ex rel. Saveland Park Holding Corp. v. Wieland, 269 Wis. 262, 69 N.W.2d 217, and Reid v. Architectural Board of Review of the City of Cleveland Heights, 119 Ohio App. 67, 192 N.E.2d 74.

The judgment is reversed.

NOTES AND QUESTIONS: AESTHETIC ZONING; ZONING AND THE FIRST AMENDMENT

1. *Aesthetic zoning in general.*[17] Notice that the court in *Stoyanoff* did not rest its decision on the legitimacy of aesthetics as a zoning objective, relying instead largely on protection of property values. (To the same effect are the *Saveland Park* and *Reid* cases cited above by the court. *Reid* in particular is remarkably similar to *Stoyanoff*.) The approach is typical and owes to a long line of early cases holding that aesthetic ends alone could not support zoning measures. Some courts would admit them as a "secondary purpose," but most, if they wished to sustain the ordinance in question, pursued the property value rationale.

What appears to be an aesthetically aimed regulation is often upheld because it "protects property values," and therefore need not depend for its validity on its curbing a "merely aesthetic" nuisance. It should be clearly understood that this is escapist reasoning that evades the real issues.

The effect on market value, after all, is derivative or symptomatic — not primary or of the essence. If the activities curbed by the regulation would otherwise make the surrounding property less valuable, it must be because those activities would radiate some kind of undesirable impact.

If that impact is received and felt through visual sensibility, then the "economic" interest in question simply masks what has been referred to above as an "aesthetic" interest. In other words, without the aesthetic nuisance, there would be no market devaluation.

The decline in market value, therefore, ought to be regarded as a kind of socially computerized, objective evidence that the regulated activity is by a social consensus deemed intrinsically ugly, negatively suggestive, or destructive of prior existing beauty. [Frank Michelman, Toward a Practical Standard for Aesthetic Regulation, Prac. Law., Vol. 15, No. 2, Feb. 1969, at 36, 37.]

17. There is an extensive bibliography on the matters discussed here. Readings of interest, beyond those cited in the discussion in the text, include John J. Costonis, Law and Aesthetics: A Critique and a Reformulation of the Dilemmas, 80 Mich. L. Rev. 355 (1982); James P. Karp, The Evolving Meaning of Aesthetics in Land-Use Regulation, 15 Colum. J. Envtl. L. 307 (1990); James C. Smith, Law, Beauty, and Human Stability: A Rose Is a Rose Is a Rose, 78 Cal. L. Rev. 787 (1990) (reviewing John J. Costonis, Icons and Aliens: Law, Aesthetics, and Environmental Change (1989)); Note, Beyond the Eye of the Beholder: Aesthetics and Objectivity, 71 Mich. L. Rev. 1438 (1973).

Courts today are more inclined to accept the legitimacy of zoning based exclusively on aesthetic considerations. A survey in 1980 found a "new majority" of 16 jurisdictions adhering to that view, with another 16 states accepting zoning based "partially" on aesthetics, 9 rejecting the aesthetic rationale, and 10 with no decisions on the question. Samuel Bufford, Beyond the Eye of the Beholder: A New Majority of Jurisdictions Authorize Aesthetic Regulation, 48 UMKC L. Rev. 127, 127 (1980). A subsequent judicial survey counted (the court including itself) 18 states accepting aesthetic regulation, 17 waffling on the issue, 7 opposed, and 9 yet to take any position at all. See State v. Jones, 305 N.C. 520, 290 S.E.2d 675 (1982). But the topic remains a tender one. The court in State v. Jones, for example, insisted that the legitimacy of aesthetics depended on "the facts and circumstances of each case." And the court's decision was regarded as very noteworthy — judging at least by the amount of law review commentary devoted to it. See, e.g., 18 Wake Forest L. Rev. 1167 (1982); 61 N.C. L. Rev. 942 (1983); 14 N.C. Cent. L. Rev. 239 (1983). See also Village of Hudson v. Albrecht, Inc., 9 Ohio St. 3d 69, 458 N.E.2d 852 (1984), acknowledging the "legitimate governmental interest in maintaining the aesthetics of a community" but working to find that the ordinance in question was based on other considerations as well.[18]

Even those who have advocated dealing openly with aesthetic purposes in zoning — rather than relying on property values or some other manufactured grounds — have noted "the sound judicial skepticism" underlying the view that rejects aesthetics as an exclusive consideration. See Jesse Dukeminier, Zoning for Aesthetic Objectives: A Reappraisal, 20 Law & Contemp. Probs. 218 (1955). See also Stephen F. Williams, Subjectivity, Expression, and Privacy: Problems of Aesthetic Regulation, 62 Minn. L. Rev. 1, 58 (1977) ("merit in the intuitive judicial anxiety about purely aesthetic purposes"). What are the concerns?

One problem is *vagueness.* Aesthetic standards are commonly expressed in amorphous terms that can easily lead to arbitrary treatment. Is *Stoyanoff* a case in point? Can abuse be controlled — was it in *Stoyanoff*? — by the common device of an architectural review board (usually but not always made up entirely of architects) charged to make aesthetic

18. Aesthetic considerations are an important factor in historic zoning and historic preservation legislation, and in these contexts the courts have felt less inhibition in admitting the legitimacy of aesthetic objectives. See generally Carol M. Rose, Preservation and Community: New Directions in the Law of Historic Preservation, 33 Stan. L. Rev. 473 (1981); Note, The Legal History of Zoning for Aesthetic Purposes, 8 Ind. L. Rev. 1028, 1038-1041 (1975); Symposium, Perspectives on Historic Preservation, 8 Conn. L. Rev. 199-248 (1976). But see United Artists Theater Circuit, Inc. v. Philadelphia Historical Commn., 528 Pa. 12, 595 A.2d 6 (1991), invalidating as an unconstitutional taking the historical designation of United Artists' Boyd Theater building in Philadelphia. The court held that, under Pennsylvania law, neither aesthetic reasons nor the conservation of property values qualify as justifications for use of the police power. Compare Penn Central Transp. Co. v. City of New York, at page 1203.

judgments in a professional and disinterested manner?[19] Consider in this respect the views of the architects whose criticism of modern architecture brought on the postmodernist architectural movement. See Robert Venturi, Denise Scott Brown & Steven Izenour, Learning from Las Vegas 189 (1972):

> The courts have ruled that beauty is an urban amenity to be sought through the police powers, review boards, and other regulatory measures; but they have omitted to set the standards by which beauty may be defined or the processes through which it may be equitably judged to be present. Local authorities have reacted by appointing "experts" (usually local architects) who use their own discretion in assigning beauty or lack of it to the works of others. The limits set on capriciousness, authoritarianism, or venality in such a system are those internal to the individual review board members. This is rule by man rather than rule by law.
>
> In proceedings based solely on taste, the supplicant architect is left perplexed, and often thousands of dollars are lost as he makes frustrating attempts, scheming rather than designing, to anticipate or to follow the dicta of "experts" whose tastes and philosophies differ from his own or are so capricious as to be incomprehensible to him.
>
> Aesthetically too, the aim is not achieved. Any artist could have told the lawmakers that you cannot legislate beauty and that attempts to do so by the use of experts will result not only in gross injustice but in an ugly deadness in the environment.
>
> Beauty escapes in the pursuit of safety, which promotes a simplistic sameness over a varied vitality. It withers under the edicts of today's aging architectural revolutionaries who man the review boards and who have achieved aesthetic certainty.

Philadelphia architects Robert Venturi and his wife, Denise Scott Brown, are contemporary architecture's most influential thinkers and among its most adventurous designers. In his book, Complexity and Contradiction in Architecture (1966), Venturi, tired of the spare aesthetics of glass boxes, parodied the famous dictum of Mies van der Rohe, "less is more," with his own mot, "less is a bore." The postmodern architectural movement was thus born. In 1991 Venturi received the Pritzker Prize, architecture's equivalent of the Nobel. See Diana Ketcham, Robert Venturi & Denise Scott Brown: More *Is* More, Art News, Apr. 1992, at 90.

Venturi and Scott Brown have been tireless critics of design review boards. In a conference in Austin, Texas in 1984, Scott Brown fired another shot:

19. In 1937, 30 cities had design review requirements in their zoning ordinances; by 1969, 550 cities had them. See James L. Bross, Taking Design Review Beyond the Beauty Part: Aesthetics in Perspective, 9 Envtl. L. 211, 212 n.6 (1979). According to one survey, architects constitute 97 percent of the membership on 221 design review boards. American Institute of Architects, Design Review Boards: A Handbook for Communities 9 (1974).

Design review, from our personal experiences as people at the cutting edge of art — it kills us. I believe that Frank Lloyd Wright would not have had a single building built, nor Le Corbusier, if there had been design review and fine arts boards in cities where they would have had to present their work.

Where there are design review boards, what is accepted is the going and the slightly old-fashioned and the mediocre. Where you have design review, you have the avoidance of risk. You will get nothing bad, but you will get little that's new. [The Land, The City, and the Human Spirit 128 (Larry P. Fuller ed. 1985).]

In the 1980s San Francisco — the most narcissistic of American cities — became unhappy with what it called the "Manhattanization" of its skyline (forgetting, for the moment, that Chicago, not New York, invented the skyscraper). In 1985 San Francisco adopted an ordinance requiring design approval of every high-rise building by a design review board of outside experts. In the first year the board rejected all designs by San Francisco architects. Developers then sought out national firms, the most noted of which won approval. Still, according to one report, everyone — supporters and opponents alike — remained dissatisfied. "[T]he new buildings are unusually tame, even dull, in the opinion of architecture critics." Pushed by the developers to design for board approval, the architects took little architectural risk. N.Y. Times, Dec. 5, 1987, §1, at 8.

2. *First Amendment concerns.* A simple way to remedy the problem of vagueness in aesthetic zoning ordinances is to specify precisely what structures must look like. An ordinance, for example, could spell everything out: white stucco walls, red tile roofs, Spanish balconies, and so on. Or a variety of carefully specified styles could be permitted. An obvious difficulty is that either approach would undercut the legitimate motivations behind design review by mandating, in essence, not good original architecture but typical tract communities. A related difficulty is that design specification tends to interfere with *expression and related First Amendment values.*

Whether architectural expression is protected by the First Amendment seems to be an open question, but it is a common view that design regulation, because it implicates expressive values, should at least be subject to close scrutiny. See Samuel C. Poole III & Ilene Katz Kobert, Architectural Appearance Review Regulations and the First Amendment: The Constitutionally Infirm "Excessive Difference" Test, 12 Zoning & Plan. L. Rep. 89 (1989); Note, Aesthetic Regulation and the First Amendment, 3 Va. J. Natl. Resources L. 237 (1984); Note, Architectural Expression: Police Power and the First Amendment, 16 Urb. L. Ann. 273 (1979).

3. The argument for close scrutiny does not apply, of course, to all aesthetic regulation. A requirement that junkyards be screened from

public view for aesthetic reasons hardly impinges on freedom of expression, whereas controls like those in *Stoyanoff* quite clearly do to some degree.[20] By the same token, controls motivated by other than aesthetic concerns *can* impact on First Amendment values. Consider some instances:

Signs and billboards. In Metromedia, Inc. v. City of San Diego, 453 U.S. 490 (1981), the Court confronted an ordinance — motivated by aesthetic *and* safety concerns — that (1) allowed on-site signs advertising goods or services available on the premises on which the sign was located, (2) banned off-site signs advertising goods or services available elsewhere, and (3) banned noncommercial signs everywhere in the locality (subject to certain exceptions). The case resulted in five separate opinions and no majority; the plurality opinion held the ordinance unconstitutional because, given the on-site advertising exemption, the ordinance favored commercial over noncommercial speech, and because, given the exceptions for certain noncommercial signs, it favored some noncommercial messages over others. See Note, Making Sense of Billboard Law: Justifying Prohibitions and Exemptions, 88 Mich. L. Rev. 2482 (1990).

For a time before *Metromedia,* commercial billboard regulations generally withstood First Amendment challenges simply because the U.S. Supreme Court refused to extend constitutional protection to commercial speech, a situation that changed in the mid-1970s. See Comment, *Metromedia, Inc. v. City of San Diego*: Municipal Billboard Regulation and the First Amendment, 23 Urb. L. Ann. 361, 369-375 (1982). Billboard and sign controls are permissible after *Metromedia,* but there is much uncertainty regarding the range of alternative measures open to zoners. On one view, the only clear holding in the case is that off-site commercial billboards may be totally banned. See Theodore Y. Blumoff, After *Metromedia*: Sign Controls and the First Amendment, 28 St. Louis U. L.J. 171, 199 (1984). But see Rzadkowolski v. Village of Lake Orion, 845 F.2d 653 (6th Cir. 1988) (upholding an ordinance that allowed only on-site signs with messages, commercial or noncommercial, related to activities conducted on the premises); Bell v. Township of Stafford, 110 N.J. 384, 541 A.2d 692 (1988) (invalidating an ordinance prohibiting billboards, signboards, and off-site advertising signs).

Members of City Council of Los Angeles v. Taxpayers for Vincent, 466 U.S. 789 (1984), was the Court's first post-*Metromedia* sign control case. The ordinance in question, which prohibited the posting of signs on public property, was upheld against the challenge of a group cam-

20. Some architectural design controls use so-called anti-difference regulations to promote homogeneity, while others use anti-similarity regulations to avoid it. See Note, You Can't Build That Here: The Constitutionality of Aesthetic Zoning and Architectural Review, 58 Fordham L. Rev. 1013, 1019 (1990). Is one of these more troublesome than the other from a free-expression point of view? See Poole & Kobert, supra, at 93-95.

What is a "sign"?

A question for semiotics mavens: Does the illustration above depict a "sign"? To what does an ordinance regulating "signs" apply? To a giant model of an iguana perched on the roof of a bar in Manhattan? To a sculpture, 30 feet high, made of brushed aluminum cylinders? To colossal toothbrushes and teeth placed outside a dentist's office? See Russ VerSteeg, Iguanas, Toads and Toothbrushes: Land-Use Regulation of Art as Signage, 25 Ga. L. Rev. 437 (1991) (citing and discussing cases in point).

———————

paigning for a political candidate. The Court held that the ordinance was content-neutral and furthered a legitimate governmental objective — aesthetic interests — unrelated to suppression of free expression, and in a manner no more restrictive than necessary. The majority rejected the claim that posting political signs on public property is a uniquely important mode of communication, notwithstanding the historic concern for inexpensive forms of expression on topics important to a large segment of the public. In the view of Professor Weinstein, the case shows that a majority "of the Court will clearly defer to a legislative enactment that incidentally restricts freedom of expression in pursuit of aesthetic objectives, as long as the municipality does not appear to be judging speech on the basis of its content or restricting a form of expression for which there are no adequate alternatives." Alan Weinstein, Billboards, Aesthetics, and the First Amendment: Municipal Sign Regulation After *Metromedia*, Land Use L. & Zoning Dig., Aug. 1984, at 4, 7.

Suppose an ordinance permits on-site commercial signs but prohibits the posting of prices on such signs. Constitutional? See H&H Operations v. City of Peachtree, 248 Ga. 500, 283 S.E.2d 867 (1981), cert. denied, 456 U.S. 961 (1982) (no). Suppose an ordinance prohibits the posting of "For Sale" or "Sold" signs in an effort to stem white flight from integrated neighborhoods. Constitutional? See Linmark Assocs. v. Township of Willingboro, 431 U.S. 85 (1977) (no); City of Chicago v. Gordon, 146 Ill. App. 3d 898, 497 N.E.2d 442 (1986) (ban on outdoor advertising in residential districts held unconstitutional as applied to "For Sale" signs, citing *Linmark* and *Metromedia*). Suppose an ordinance permits, in residential neighborhoods, only name plates, "For Sale" and "For Rent" signs, identification signs for churches, schools, and public buildings, and signs identifying home professional offices. Constitutional as applied to political signs? See Farrell v. Township of Teaneck, 126 N.J. Super. 460, 315 A.2d 424 (1974) (no). Suppose a sign ordinance prohibits all signs but permits applications for "variations" from the prohibition. A resident wishes to place in her front yard a sign declaring "Say No to War in the Persian Gulf, Call Congress Now." She applies for a variation, which is denied. Constitutional? See Gilleo v. City of Ladue, 774 F. Supp. 1559 (E.D. Mo. 1991) (no). Suppose a District of Columbia ordinance prohibits displaying within 500 feet of a foreign embassy any sign that "tends to bring the foreign government into 'public odium' or 'public disrepute.'" Constitutional? See Boos v. Barry, 485 U.S. 312 (1988) (no).

Adult entertainment. Government controls based on the *content* of communication are said to be subject to closer judicial scrutiny than controls that simply regulate the time, place, and manner of communication without regard to content. Yet several Supreme Court decisions regarding zoning controls on adult entertainment call the assertion into question. In recent years the Court has approved two distinct approaches to control — in each instance against strong dissents that the zoning measures were obviously not content-neutral because they imposed selective limitations on movie theater location based exclusively on the content of the films shown. Young v. American Mini Theatres, Inc., 427 U.S. 50 (1976), upheld a Detroit ordinance that *dispersed* adult theaters by requiring that they not locate within 500 feet of a residential area nor within 1,000 feet of any two other regulated uses (adult bookstores, cabarets, and so forth). City of Renton v. Playtime Theatres, Inc., 475 U.S. 41 (1986), upheld the ordinance of a Seattle suburb that effectively *concentrated* adult theaters in about 5 percent of the city's total land area. The Court explained in *Renton* that both measures *seemed* to be content based, but in fact were time, place, and manner restrictions aimed not at content but at the secondary effects of adult theaters on the quality of urban life — a substantial interest. The Court found that neither ordinance unreasonably limited alternative avenues of communication. It contrasted Schad v. Mount Ephraim, 452 U.S. 61 (1981), invalidating an ordinance that banned live entertainment (including nude dancers) throughout the Borough of Mount Ephraim. The borough had failed to justify the "substantial restriction" there.[21] The Renton and Detroit ordinances survived because they were "narrowly tailored" to affect only entertainment demonstrated to have the unwanted secondary effects.

Subsequent to the *Mini Theatres* case, many municipalities enacted pornography zoning laws modeled on the Detroit dispersion technique. See Fredric A. Strom, Zoning Control of Sex Business (1977); Norman Marcus, Zoning Obscenity: Or, The Moral Politics of Porn, 27 Buffalo L. Rev. 1 (1978). *Renton* now endorses the opposite approach as well. See generally Comment, Zoning Adult Entertainment: A Reassessment of *Renton*, 79 Cal. L. Rev. 119 (1991); Note, Zoning and the First Amendment Rights of Adult Entertainment, 22 Val. U. L. Rev. 695 (1988).

Religious establishments. Suppose that a zoning ordinance excludes churches from residential areas. Is the ordinance unconstitutional as a significant burden on the free exercise of religion? Is it subject, at least, to close judicial scrutiny to discern whether a compelling governmental interest justifies the exclusion? See Laurie Reynolds, Zoning the Church:

---

21. Compare Barnes v. Glen Theatre, 111 S. Ct. 2456 (1991), upholding an Indiana public indecency law proscribing public nudity across the board and thus requiring female dancers who would otherwise be nude to wear pasties and a G-string. "It is without cavil that the public indecency statute is 'narrowly tailored'; Indiana's requirement that the dancers wear at least pasties and a G-string is modest, and the bare minimum necessary to achieve the state's purpose." 111 S. Ct. at 2463.

The Court of Appeals had held the Indiana statute unconstitutional, relying in part on *Schad*. See Miller v. Civil City of South Bend, 904 F.2d 1081 (7th Cir. 1990). For students interested in the general subject — public censorship of erotica — Judge Posner's concurring opinion in *Miller* is must reading. See 904 F.2d at 1089-1104. See also Comment, Nude Dancing and the First Amendment, 59 U. Cin. L. Rev. 1275 (1991).

The Police Power Versus the First Amendment, 64 B.U. L. Rev. 767 (1985). Or suppose a historic preservation ordinance limits the freedom of a religious group to alter its place of worship. Constitutional? See Richard F. Babcock & David A. Theriaque, Landmarks Preservation Ordinances: Are the Religion Clauses Violated by Their Application to Religious Properties?, 7 J. Land Use & Envtl. L. 165 (1992).

2.　Controls on Household Composition

Village of Belle Terre v. Boraas
Supreme Court of the United States, 1974
416 U.S. 1

MR. JUSTICE DOUGLAS delivered the opinion of the Court.

Belle Terre is a village on Long Island's north shore of about 220 homes inhabited by 700 people. Its total land area is less than one square mile. It has restricted land use to one-family dwellings excluding lodging houses, boarding houses, fraternity houses, or multiple-dwelling houses. The word "family" as used in the ordinance means,

> [o]ne or more persons related by blood, adoption, or marriage, living and cooking together as a single housekeeping unit, exclusive of household servants. A number of persons but not exceeding two (2) living and cooking together as a single housekeeping unit though not related by blood, adoption, or marriage shall be deemed to constitute a family.

Appellees the Dickmans are owners of a house in the village and leased it in December 1971 for a term of 18 months to Michael Truman. Later Bruce Boraas became a colessee. Then Anne Parish moved into the house along with three others. These six are students at nearby State University at Stony Brook and none is related to the other by blood, adoption, or marriage. When the village served the Dickmans with an "Order to Remedy Violations" of the ordinance, the owners plus three tenants thereupon brought this action under 42 U.S.C. §1983 for an injunction and a judgment declaring the ordinance unconstitutional. The District Court held the ordinance constitutional, 367 F. Supp. 136, and the Court of Appeals reversed, one judge dissenting, 476 F.2d 806. The case is here by appeal, 28 U.S.C. §1254(2); and we noted probable jurisdiction, 414 U.S. 907.

This case brings to this Court a different phase of local zoning regulations from those we have previously reviewed. Euclid v. Ambler Realty Co., 272 U.S. 365, involved a zoning ordinance classifying land use in a given area into six categories. . . .

The main thrust of the case in the mind of the Court was in the exclusion of industries and apartments, and as respects that it commented on the desire to keep residential areas free of "disturbing noises"; "increased traffic"; the hazard of "moving and parked automobiles"; the "depriving children of the privilege of quiet and open spaces for play, enjoyed by those in more favored localities." Id., at 394. The ordinance was sanctioned because the validity of the legislative classification was "fairly debatable" and therefore could not be said to be wholly arbitrary. Id., at 388.

Our decision in Berman v. Parker, 348 U.S. 26, sustained a land-use project in the District of Columbia against a landowner's claim that the taking violated the Due Process Clause and the Just Compensation Clause of the Fifth Amendment. The essence of the argument against the law was, while taking property for ridding an area of slums was permissible, taking it "merely to develop a better balanced, more attractive community" was not, id., at 31. We refused to limit the concept of public welfare that may be enhanced by zoning regulations. We said:

> Miserable and disreputable housing conditions may do more than spread disease and crime and immorality. They may also suffocate the spirit by reducing the people who live there to the status of cattle. They may indeed make living an almost insufferable burden. They may also be an ugly sore, a blight on the community which robs it of charm, which makes it a place from which men turn. The misery of housing may despoil a community as an open sewer may ruin a river.
>
> We do not sit to determine whether a particular housing project is or is not desirable. The concept of the public welfare is broad and inclusive. . . . The values it represents are spiritual as well as physical, aesthetic as well as monetary. It is within the power of the legislature to determine that the community should be beautiful as well as healthy, spacious as well as clean, well-balanced as well as carefully patrolled. [Id., at 32-33.]

If the ordinance segregated one area only for one race, it would immediately be suspect under the reasoning of Buchanan v. Warley, 245 U.S. 60, where the Court invalidated a city ordinance barring a black from acquiring real property in a white residential area by reason of an 1866 Act of Congress, 14 Stat. 27, now 42 U.S.C. §1982, and an 1870 Act, §17, 16 Stat. 144, now 42 U.S.C. §1981, both enforcing the Fourteenth Amendment. 245 U.S., at 78-82. See Jones v. Mayer Co., 392 U.S. 409.

In Seattle Trust Co. v. Roberge, 278 U.S. 116, Seattle had a zoning ordinance that permitted a " 'philanthropic home for children or for old people' " in a particular district " 'when the written consent shall have been obtained of the owners of two-thirds of the property within four hundred (400) feet of the proposed building.' " Id., at 118. The Court held that provision of the ordinance unconstitutional, saying that the existing owners could "withhold consent for selfish reasons or arbitrarily and may subject the trustee [owner] to their will or caprice." Id., at 122. Unlike the billboard cases (e.g., Cusack Co. v. City of Chicago, 242 U.S. 526), the Court concluded that the Seattle ordinance was invalid since the proposed home for the aged poor was not shown by its maintenance and construction "to work any injury, inconvenience or annoyance to the community, the district or any person." 278 U.S., at 122.

The present ordinance is challenged on several grounds: that it interferes with a person's right to travel; that it interferes with the right to migrate to and settle within a State; that it bars people who are uncongenial to the present residents; that it expresses the social preferences of the residents for groups that will be congenial to them; that social homogeneity is not a legitimate interest of government; that the restriction of those whom the neighbors do not like trenches on the newcomers' rights of privacy; that it is of no rightful concern to villagers whether the residents are married or unmarried; that the ordinance is antithetical to the Nation's experience, ideology, and self-perception as an open, egalitarian, and integrated society.

We find none of these reasons in the record before us. It is not aimed at transients. Cf. Shapiro v. Thompson, 394 U.S. 618. It involves no procedural disparity inflicted on some but not on others such as was presented by Griffin v. Illinois, 351 U.S. 12. It involves no "fundamental" right guaranteed by the Constitution, such as voting, Harper v. Virginia Board, 383 U.S. 663; the right of association, NAACP v. Alabama, 357 U.S. 449; the right of access to the courts, NAACP v. Button, 371 U.S. 415; or any rights of privacy, cf. Griswold v. Connecticut, 381 U.S. 479; Eisenstadt v. Baird, 405 U.S. 438, 453-454. We deal with economic and social legislation where legislatures have historically drawn lines which we respect against the charge of violation of the Equal Protection Clause if the law be " 'reasonable, not arbitrary' " (quoting Royster Guano Co. v. Virginia, 253 U.S. 412, 415) and bears "a rational relationship to a [permissible] state objective." Reed v. Reed, 404 U.S. 71, 76.

It is said, however, that if two unmarried people can constitute a "family," there is no reason why three or four may not. But every line drawn by a legislature leaves some out that might well have been included. That exercise of discretion, however, is a legislative, not a judicial, function.

It is said that the Belle Terre ordinance reeks with an animosity to unmarried couples who live together. There is no evidence to support it; and the provision of the ordinance bringing within the definition of a "family" two unmarried people belies the charge.

The ordinance places no ban on other forms of association, for a "family" may, so far as the ordinance is concerned, entertain whomever it likes.

The regimes of boarding houses, fraternity houses, and the like present urban problems. More people occupy a given space; more cars rather continuously pass by; more cars are parked; noise travels with crowds.

A quiet place where yards are wide, people few, and motor vehicles restricted are legitimate guidelines in a land-use project addressed to family needs. This goal is a permissible one within Berman v. Parker, supra. The police power is not confined to elimination of filth, stench, and unhealthy places. It is ample to lay out zones where family values, youth values, and the blessings of quiet seclusion and clean air make the area a sanctuary for people. . . .

MR. JUSTICE MARSHALL, dissenting. This case draws into question the constitutionality of a zoning ordinance of the incorporated village of Belle Terre, New York, which prohibits groups of more than two unrelated persons, as distinguished from groups consisting of any number of persons related by blood, adoption, or marriage, from occupying a residence within the confines of the township. Lessor-appellees, the two owners of a Belle Terre residence, and three unrelated student tenants challenged the ordinance on the ground that it establishes a classification between households of related and unrelated individuals, which deprives them of equal protection of the laws. In my view, the disputed classification burdens the students' fundamental rights of association and privacy guaranteed by the First and Fourteenth Amendments. Because the application of strict equal protection scrutiny is therefore required, I am at odds with my Brethren's conclusion that the ordinance may be sustained on a showing that it bears a rational relationship to the accomplishment of legitimate governmental objectives.

I am in full agreement with the majority that zoning is a complex and important function of the State. It may indeed be the most essential function performed by local government, for it is one of the primary means by which we protect that sometimes difficult to define concept of quality of life. I therefore continue to adhere to the principle of Euclid v. Ambler Realty Co., 272 U.S. 365 (1926), that deference should be given to governmental judgments concerning proper land-use allocation. That deference is a principle which has served this Court well and which is necessary for the continued development of effective zoning and land-use control mechanisms. Had the owners alone brought this suit alleging that the restrictive ordinance deprived them of their property or was an irrational legislative classification, I would agree that the ordinance would have to be sustained. Our role is not and should not be to sit as a zoning board of appeals.

I would also agree with the majority that local zoning authorities may properly act in furtherance of the objectives asserted to be served by the ordinance at issue here: restricting uncontrolled growth, solving traffic problems, keeping rental costs at a reasonable level, and making the community attractive to families. The police power which provides the justification for zoning is not narrowly confined. See Berman v. Parker, 348 U.S. 26 (1954). And, it is appropriate that we afford zoning authorities considerable latitude in choosing the means by which to implement such purposes. But deference does not mean abdication. This Court has an obligation to ensure that zoning ordinances, even when adopted in furtherance of such legitimate aims, do not infringe upon fundamental constitutional rights.

When separate but equal was still accepted constitutional dogma, this Court struck down a racially restrictive zoning ordinance. Buchanan v. Warley, 245 U.S. 60 (1917). I am sure the Court would not be hesitant to invalidate that ordinance today. The lower federal courts have considered procedural aspects of zoning, and acted to insure that land-use controls are not used as means of confining minorities and the poor to the ghettos of our central cities. These are limited but necessary intrusions on the discretion of zoning authorities. By the same token, I think it clear that the First Amendment provides some limitation on zoning laws. It is inconceivable to me that we would allow the exercise of the zoning power to burden First Amendment freedoms, as by ordinances that restrict occupancy to individuals adhering to particular religious, political, or scientific beliefs. Zoning officials properly concern themselves with the uses of land — with, for example, the number and kind of dwellings to be constructed in a certain neighborhood or the number of persons who can reside in those dwellings. But zoning authorities cannot validly consider who those persons are, what they believe, or how they choose to live, whether they are Negro or white, Catholic or Jew, Republican or Democrat, married or unmarried.

My disagreement with the Court today is based upon my view that the ordinance in this case unnecessarily burdens appellees' First Amendment freedom of association and their constitutionally guaranteed right to privacy. Our decisions establish that the First and Fourteenth Amendments protect the freedom to choose one's associates. NAACP v. Button, 371 U.S. 415, 430 (1963). Constitutional protection is extended, not only to modes of association that are political in the usual sense, but also to those that pertain to the social and economic benefit of the members. Id., at 430-431; Brotherhood of Railroad Trainmen v. Virginia Bar, 377 U.S. 1 (1964). See United Transportation Union v. State Bar of Michigan, 401 U.S. 576 (1971); Mine Workers v. Illinois State Bar Assn., 389 U.S. 217 (1967). The selection of one's living companions involves similar choices as to the emotional, social, or economic benefits to be derived from alternative living arrangements.

The freedom of association is often inextricably entwined with the constitutionally guaranteed right of privacy. The right to "establish a home" is an essential part of the liberty guaranteed by the Fourteenth Amendment. Meyer v. Nebraska, 262 U.S. 390, 399 (1923); Griswold v. Connecticut, 381 U.S. 479, 495 (1965) (Goldberg, J., concurring). And the Constitution secures to an individual a freedom "to satisfy his intellectual and emotional needs in the privacy of his own home." Stanley v. Georgia, 394 U.S. 557, 565 (1969); see Paris Adult Theatre I v. Slaton, 413 U.S. 49, 66-67 (1973). Constitutionally protected privacy is, in Mr. Justice Brandeis' words, "as against the Government, the right to be let alone . . . the right most valued by civilized man." Olmstead v. United States, 277 U.S. 438, 478 (1928) (dissenting opinion). The choice of household companions — of whether a person's "intellectual and emotional needs" are best met by living with family, friends, professional associates, or others — involves deeply personal considerations as to the kind and quality of intimate relationships within the home. That decision surely falls within the ambit of the right to privacy protected by the Constitution. See Roe v. Wade, 410 U.S. 113, 153 (1973); Eisenstadt v. Baird, 405 U.S. 438, 453 (1972); Stanley v. Georgia, supra, at 564-565; Griswold v. Connecticut, supra, at 483, 486; Olmstead v. United States, supra, at 478 (Brandeis, J., dissenting); Moreno v. Department of Agriculture, 345 F. Supp. 310, 315 (DC 1972), aff'd, 413 U.S. 528 (1973).

The instant ordinance discriminates on the basis of just such a personal lifestyle choice as to household companions. It permits any number of persons related by blood or marriage, be it two or twenty, to live in a single household, but it limits to two the number of unrelated persons bound by profession, love, friendship, religious or political affiliation, or mere economics who can occupy a single home. Belle Terre imposes upon those who deviate from the community norm in their choice of living companions significantly greater restrictions than are applied to residential groups who are related by blood or marriage, and compose the established order within the community. The village has, in effect, acted to fence out those individuals whose choice of lifestyle differs from that of its current residents.

This is not a case where the Court is being asked to nullify a township's sincere efforts to maintain its residential character by preventing the operation of rooming houses, fraternity houses, or other commercial or high-density residential uses. Unquestionably, a town is free to restrict such uses. Moreover, as a general proposition, I see no constitutional infirmity in a town's limiting the density of use in residential areas by zoning regulations which do not discriminate on the basis of constitutionally suspect criteria. This ordinance, however, limits the density of occupancy of only those homes occupied by unrelated persons. It thus reaches beyond control of the use of land or the density of population, and undertakes to regulate the way people choose to associate with each other within the privacy of their own homes.

It is no answer to say, as does the majority, that associational interests are not infringed because Belle Terre residents may entertain whomever they choose. Only last Term Mr. Justice Douglas indicated in concurrence that he saw the right of association protected by the First

Amendment as involving far more than the right to entertain visitors. He found that right infringed by a restriction on food stamp assistance, penalizing households of "unrelated persons." As Mr. Justice Douglas there said, freedom of association encompasses the "right to invite the stranger into one's home" not only for "entertainment" but to join the household as well. Department of Agriculture v. Moreno, 413 U.S. 528, 538-545 (1973) (concurring opinion). I am still persuaded that the choice of those who will form one's household implicates constitutionally protected rights.

Because I believe that this zoning ordinance creates a classification which impinges upon fundamental personal rights, it can withstand constitutional scrutiny only upon a clear showing that the burden imposed is necessary to protect a compelling and substantial governmental interest, Shapiro v. Thompson, 394 U.S. 618, 634 (1969). And, once it be determined that a burden has been placed upon a constitutional right, the onus of demonstrating that no less intrusive means will adequately protect the compelling state interest and that the challenged statute is sufficiently narrowly drawn, is upon the party seeking to justify the burden. See Memorial Hospital v. Maricopa County, 415 U.S. 250 (1974); Speiser v. Randall, 357 U.S. 513, 525-526 (1958).

A variety of justifications have been proffered in support of the village's ordinance. It is claimed that the ordinance controls population density, prevents noise, traffic and parking problems, and preserves the rent structure of the community and its attractiveness to families. As I noted earlier, these are all legitimate and substantial interests of government. But I think it clear that the means chosen to accomplish these purposes are both overinclusive and underinclusive, and that the asserted goals could be as effectively achieved by means of an ordinance that did not discriminate on the basis of constitutionally protected choices of lifestyle. The ordinance imposes no restriction whatsoever on the number of persons who may live in a house, as long as they are related by marital or sanguinary bonds — presumably no matter how distant their relationship. Nor does the ordinance restrict the number of income earners who may contribute to rent in such a household, or the number of automobiles that may be maintained by its occupants. In that sense the ordinance is underinclusive. On the other hand, the statute restricts the number of unrelated persons who may live in a home to no more than two. It would therefore prevent three unrelated people from occupying a dwelling even if among them they had but one income and no vehicles. While an extended family of a dozen or more might live in a small bungalow, three elderly and retired persons could not occupy the large manor house next door. Thus the statute is also grossly overinclusive to accomplish its intended purposes.

There are some 220 residences in Belle Terre occupied by about 700 persons. The density is therefore just above three per household.

The village is justifiably concerned with density of population and the related problems of noise, traffic, and the like. It could deal with those problems by limiting each household to a specified number of adults, two or three perhaps, without limitation on the number of dependent children.[22] The burden of such an ordinance would fall equally upon all segments of the community. It would surely be better tailored to the goals asserted by the village than the ordinance before us today, for it would more realistically restrict population density and growth and their attendant environmental costs. Various other statutory mechanisms also suggest themselves as solutions to Belle Terre's problems — rent control, limits on the number of vehicles per household, and so forth, but, of course, such schemes are matters of legislative judgment and not for this Court. Appellants also refer to the necessity of maintaining the family character of the village. There is not a shred of evidence in the record indicating that if Belle Terre permitted a limited number of unrelated persons to live together, the residential, familial character of the community would be fundamentally affected.

By limiting unrelated households to two persons while placing no limitation on households of related individuals, the village has embarked upon its commendable course in a constitutionally faulty vessel. Cf. Marshall v. United States, 414 U.S. 417, 430 (1974) (dissenting opinion). I would find the challenged ordinance unconstitutional. But I would not ask the village to abandon its goal of providing quiet streets, little traffic, and a pleasant and reasonably priced environment in which families might raise their children. Rather, I would commend the village to continue to pursue those purposes but by means of more carefully drawn and even-handed legislation.

I respectfully dissent.

NOTES AND QUESTION

1. In Moore v. City of East Cleveland, 431 U.S. 494 (1977), the Supreme Court limited the holding in *Belle Terre*. *Moore* invalidated a single-family zoning ordinance which defined "family" to include no more than one set of grandchildren. Mrs. Moore was convicted of violating the ordinance and sentenced to jail because she had living with her a son and two grandsons who were not brothers. The plurality opinion distinguished *Belle Terre* on the ground that Belle Terre's ordinance applied only to unrelated individuals:

22. By providing an exception for dependent children, the village would avoid any doubts that might otherwise be posed by the constitutional protection afforded the choice of whether to bear a child. See Molino v. Mayor & Council of Glassboro, 116 N.J. Super. 195, 281 A.2d 401 (1971); cf. Cleveland Board of Education v. LaFleur, 414 U.S. 632 (1974).

But one overriding factor sets this case apart from *Belle Terre*. The ordinance there affected only *unrelated* individuals. It expressly allowed all who were related by "blood, adoption, or marriage" to live together, and in sustaining the ordinance we were careful to note that it promoted "family needs" and "family values." . . .

East Cleveland, in contrast, has chosen to regulate the occupancy of its housing by slicing deeply into the family itself. This is no mere incidental result of the ordinance. On its face it selects certain categories of relatives who may live together and declares that others may not. In particular, it makes a crime of a grandmother's choice to live with her grandson in circumstances like those presented here.

When a city undertakes such intrusive regulation of the family, neither *Belle Terre* nor *Euclid* governs; the usual judicial deference to the legislature is inappropriate. "This Court has long recognized that freedom of personal choice in matters of marriage and family life is one of the liberties protected by the Due Process Clause of the Fourteenth Amendment." . . . Of course, the family is not beyond regulation. . . . But when the government intrudes on choices concerning family living arrangements, this Court must examine carefully the importance of the governmental interests advanced and the extent to which they are served by the challenged regulation. . . .

When thus examined, this ordinance cannot survive. The city seeks to justify it as a means of preventing overcrowding, minimizing traffic and parking congestion, and avoiding an undue financial burden on East Cleveland's school system. Although these are legitimate goals, the ordinance before us serves them marginally, at best. For example, the ordinance permits any family consisting only of husband, wife, and unmarried children to live together, even if the family contains a half dozen licensed drivers, each with his or her own car. At the same time it forbids an adult brother and sister to share a household, even if both faithfully use public transportation. The ordinance would permit a grandmother to live with a single dependent son and children, even if his school-age children number a dozen, yet it forces Mrs. Moore to find another dwelling for her grandson John, simply because of the presence of his uncle and cousin in the same household. We need not labor the point. [The ordinance] has but a tenuous relation to alleviation of the conditions mentioned by the city. . . .

Substantive due process has at times been a treacherous field for this Court. There *are* risks when the judicial branch gives enhanced protection to certain substantive liberties without the guidance of the more specific provisions of the Bill of Rights. As the history of the *Lochner* era demonstrates, there is reason for concern lest the only limits to such judicial intervention become the predilections of those who happen at the time to be Members of this Court. That history counsels caution and restraint. But it does not counsel abandonment, nor does it require what the city urges here: cutting off any protection of family rights at the first convenient, if arbitrary boundary — the boundary of the nuclear family.

Appropriate limits on substantive due process come not from drawing arbitrary lines but rather from careful "respect for the teachings of history [and] solid recognition of the basic values that underlie our society." . . . Our decisions establish that the Constitution protects the sanctity of the family precisely because the institution of the family is deeply rooted in this Nation's history and tradition. It is through the family that we inculcate and pass down many of our most cherished values, moral and cultural.

Ours is by no means a tradition limited to respect for the bonds uniting the members of the nuclear family. The tradition of uncles, aunts, cousins, and especially grandparents sharing a household along with parents and children has roots equally venerable and equally deserving of constitutional recognition. Over the years millions of our citizens have grown up in just such an environment, and most, surely, have profited from it. Even if conditions of modern society have brought about a decline in extended family households, they have not erased the accumulated wisdom of civilization, gained over the centuries and honored throughout our history, that supports a larger conception of the family. Out of choice, necessity, or a sense of family responsibility, it has been common for close relatives to draw together and participate in the duties and the satisfactions of a common home. [431 U.S. at 498-505. Chief Justice Burger and Justices Stewart, White, and Rehnquist dissented.]

2. On issues of household composition, some state courts have taken a less deferential position than that of the Supreme Court in *Belle Terre;* they have found one basis or another — including the state's own constitution — to narrow the territory left open by the Court. A prominent example is McMinn v. Town of Oyster Bay, 66 N.Y.2d 544, 488 N.E.2d 1240, 498 N.Y.S.2d 128 (1985). The ordinance in *McMinn* restricted single-family housing to any number of people related by blood, marriage, or adoption, or to two people not so related but both over the age of 62. The court invalidated the ordinance because it infringed on the due process protections of the New York constitution. The objectives of the ordinance — to preserve the character of single-family neighborhoods, control density, reduce traffic and noise — were acceptable, but the means were not. Occupancy restrictions based on biological or legal relationships, the court said, had no reasonable tie to the city's objectives. The ordinance was overinclusive (prohibiting occupancy by a young unmarried couple) and underinclusive (permitting a dozen distantly related people to live together). The court was mindful of *Belle Terre* and *Moore,* but said neither case set out the definition of "family" minimally necessary under the federal Constitution. In any event, the definition in the ordinance was incompatible with the state constitution and earlier state cases prohibiting definitions of "family" that excluded households that were families in all but the biological sense. See also Baer v. Town of Brookhaven, 73 N.Y.2d 942, 537 N.E.2d 619, 540 N.Y.S.2d 234 (1989) (involving an ordinance that defined "family" as one or more persons related by blood, adoption, or marriage, or a group of no more than four unrelated persons living and cooking together as a single

housekeeping unit; the court brushed *Belle Terre* aside, cited *McMinn,* and held that the ordinance violated the state constitution).

Cases to similar effect are City of Santa Barbara v. Adamson, 27 Cal. 3d 123, 610 P.2d 436, 164 Cal. Rptr. 539 (1980) (ordinance allowing no more than five unrelated persons to live together was an invasion of privacy unjustified by any compelling governmental interest; less restrictive alternatives were available; *Moore* was read by the court as undermining *Belle Terre,* and California's right of privacy is broader than the federal right in any event); Charter Township of Delta v. Dinolfo, 419 Mich. 253, 351 N.W.2d 831 (1984) (the ordinance was underinclusive and overinclusive; less restrictive alternatives were available; *Belle Terre* was not accepted as a guide to the state constitution).

Compare City of Ladue v. Horn, 720 S.W.2d 745 (Mo. App. 1986), upholding an ordinance — as applied to an unmarried couple living together with three children from earlier marriages — that defined "family" as two or more persons related by blood, marriage, or adoption. The court relied on *Belle Terre* and deferred to the legislative definition set forth in the ordinance. The ordinance was rationally related to public health, safety, and welfare, needed to pass only that "relaxed test" of judicial review, and was thus constitutional notwithstanding the availability of less restrictive alternatives. The state constitution and earlier state cases endorsed "traditional notions of family. . . . There is no doubt that there is a governmental interest in marriage and in preserving the integrity of the biological or legal family. There is no concomitant governmental interest in keeping together a group of unrelated persons, no matter how closely they simulate a family." 720 S.W.2d at 751-752.

Ladue probably represents the majority view. A few states following the more activist minority position sketched above have proceeded on other than constitutional grounds. For example, in Borough of Glassboro v. Vallorosi, 117 N.J. 421, 568 A.2d 888 (1990), the Supreme Court of New Jersey held that a group of ten unrelated college students living together were a "family" within the definition of a local ordinance that limited houses and duplexes in residential zones to "one or more persons occupying a dwelling unit as a single non-profit housekeeping unit, who are living together as a stable and permanent living unit, being a traditional family unit or the functional equivalency [sic] thereof." (The stated purpose of the ordinance was to confine college students to dormitories and to districts zoned for apartments, in order to preserve "family living style" and neighborhood character.)

The court noted that its earlier decisions had declined to follow *Belle Terre;* restrictions based upon legal or biological relationships were not to be tolerated. On the other hand, localities were allowed to restrict uses in certain residential zones to single housekeeping units, as the Glassboro ordinance did.

But the standard for determining whether a use qualifies as a single house-keeping unit must be functional, and hence capable of being met by either related or unrelated persons.

. . . The uncontradicted testimony [here] reflects a plan by ten sophomore college students to live together for three years under conditions that correspond substantially to the ordinance's requirement of a "stable and permanent living unit." . . . The students ate together, shared household chores, and paid expenses from a common fund. [117 N.J. at 431-432, 568 A.2d at 894 (1990).]

A related approach is to view certain restrictive definitions of family as unauthorized by state enabling legislation. See, e.g., City of Des Plaines v. Trottner, 34 Ill. 2d 432, 216 N.E.2d 116 (1966). Subsequent to the decision in *Trottner,* the Illinois legislature authorized a restrictive definition of "family." One commentator speculates that the possibility of such legislative overrides "may explain why the courts of other states have taken a constitutional approach in invalidating 'family' definitions." See Comment on *McMinn,* Land Use L. & Zoning Dig., Jan. 1985, at 17, 18. The Comment goes on to say that the constitutional approach "is regrettable because communities have heavily relied on the authority to define a 'family' to control density. In adopting 'family' definitions, communities are typically pursuing the public purposes of maintaining neighborhood character, preventing overcrowding, and decreasing traffic congestion." Id.

Do you think that's what communities are up to?[23]

Elliott v. City of Athens

United States Court of Appeals, Eleventh Circuit, 1992
960 F.2d 975

ANDERSON, J. This case presents a challenge to a local zoning ordinance of the City of Athens, Georgia, pursuant to the 1988 amendments to the Fair Housing Act, 42 U.S.C.A. §3601, et seq. (hereinafter referred to as the "FHA" or the "Act"). Appellants seek to establish a group home for recovering alcoholics in an area of Athens zoned for single-family occupancy. The district court held that there was no violation of the FHA, and appellants appealed.

I. Facts

Appellants, John D. Elliott and C. Leonard Davis, are owners of a single lot located at 490-490½ Ruth Street in Athens, Georgia, which contains

---

23. On the meaning of "family," recall the discussion of tenant succession rights under rent control regulations (Note 2 on page 554) and the matter of restrictive covenants limiting neighborhoods to "single-family dwellings" (Note 3 on page 909).

two detached houses. Appellants sought to sell the property to The Potter's House, a division of the Atlanta Mission, for use as an alcohol and drug rehabilitation center. The sale was contingent on obtaining approval for the proper zoning to accommodate The Potter's House.

The City of Athens, Georgia, is divided into various zoning districts with local ordinances defining the permitted uses for each zone. Within the city limits, there are three types of single-family residential districts (RS-10, RS-15, and RS-20), two types of multi-family residential districts (RM-1 and RM-2), and several types of general residential, commercial, industrial, and governmental districts.

The property at issue is located in an area zoned RS-10 for single-family use pursuant to the local ordinance.[24] Under the ordinance, a family is defined as:

> One (1) or more persons occupying a single dwelling unit, provided that unless all members are related by blood, marriage or adoption, no such family shall contain over four (4) persons. Domestic servants employed on the premises may be housed on the premises without being counted as a separate family or families. In addition, a related family may have up to two (2) unrelated individuals living with them. The term "family" does not include any organization or institutional group.

Athens, Ga., Code §9-1-4 (1987). Thus, under the ordinance an unlimited number of related persons may reside together, while a maximum of four unrelated individuals may occupy a single residence. Although the zoning ordinance permits only one single-family structure per lot, a grandfather clause allows the two structures on the Ruth Street property to remain as they were built prior to the adoption of the ordinance. As a result, two "families" or a maximum of eight unrelated persons are permitted to reside on the property.

The City of Athens adopted its definition of "family," which restricts the number of unrelated persons who may live together, in order to regulate the large student population from the University of Georgia campus located in Athens and to protect the single-family character of the neighborhoods surrounding the university. The City was attempting

---

24. The following are permitted uses in an RS-10 zone: "(1) Single-family; (2) Parks and recreational areas publicly owned and operated; (3) Horticulture activities and the raising of farm animals, including horses, for noncommercial purposes; (4) Governmental buildings — federal, state and local; (5) Subdivision recreational areas owned, operated, and maintained by homeowners' associations exclusively for the use of residents and their guests; (6) Family day care homes; (7) Accessory uses as defined by section 9-1-4 and in accordance with section 9-1-14, except limited to one hundred (100) feet of setback if located in the front yard." [Athens, Ga., Code §9-1-143 (1987) (RS-10 Single-Family Residential District (10,000 square feet)).]

to prevent the adverse effects that can occur when an area increases its population density because of a large demand for rental apartments for students. The City was concerned particularly with overcrowding, traffic, noise, and the excess demand on city services such as transportation and water.

In this case, the proposed purchaser of the Ruth Street property, The Potter's House, operates an alcohol and drug rehabilitation center for men at its farm facility in Jefferson, Georgia. The male residents of The Potter's House are employed in one of the four stores operated by The Potter's House or in some part of the farm operation. Reverend Jack Lindsay, director of The Potter's House, sought to purchase the Ruth Street property for use as a group-residence home, or "half-way" house, for men who had finished the program at the farm facility but were not yet ready to live on their own. The Athens residence home would thus serve as a second stage in the rehabilitation process, providing structure and support to those program participants who had completed the first part of the program.

The Potter's House planned to accommodate twelve male program participants[25] and at least one staff member at the Ruth Street property. Thus, the planned occupancy was in excess of the eight permitted residents under the ordinance. The program participants would be employed outside the property and would be subject to program rules prohibiting the use of alcohol and overnight female visitation. These participants would pay $75.00 per week in exchange for their food, clothing, shelter, and supervision.

In order to carry out their project, appellants approached the City of Athens planning department to have the property rezoned to multi-family designation which would permit the proposed use for the half-way house. The planning department advised appellants that the proposed use of the Ruth Street property would be considered, under a "similar use" provision, as a boarding house.[26] Members of the planning department then studied the impact the proposed zoning change would have on the neighborhood and the demand for municipal services. While the planning department determined that the proposed group

---

25. The parties stipulated at trial that the persons who would reside at the Ruth Street property are handicapped within the meaning of 42 U.S.C. §3602(h) and are not a threat to the community under 42 U.S.C. §3604(f)(9). [The relevant language of 42 U.S.C. §§3602(h) & 3604(f)(9) appears in footnote 18 on page 446. — Eds.]

26. The definition of boarding house is: "A dwelling in which meals and lodging or just lodging are [is] furnished for compensation to more than four (4) but not more than twenty (20) persons. Provisions for meals may be made, provided cooking is done in a central kitchen and not in individual rooms or suites. For purposes of zoning, a boarding or rooming house shall be a multiple dwelling." [Athens, Ga., Code §9-1-4 (1987).]

home would not burden the provision of municipal services such as transportation, water, and sewage, the department nonetheless recommended denial of the proposed change, stating as its reasons that the rezoning would set a negative precedent for the neighborhood and would constitute spot zoning.

Thereafter, the appellants requested that the City either issue an interpretation of the current ordinance which would permit the intended use under the current definition of "family" or amend the ordinance so that it would conform to the provisions of the FHA amendments.

After the City failed to issue the requested interpretation of the current ordinance or to amend the ordinance, the appellants instituted suit in the district court on November 6, 1989. Appellants sought declaratory and injunctive relief on the grounds that the City's actions violated the Fair Housing Act and their rights of substantive due process and equal protection.[27] More particularly, appellants alleged that handicapped persons were denied the opportunity to reside within single-family residential neighborhoods in the City of Athens, Georgia, and that the City refused to make reasonable accommodations in its rules, policies, practices, or services, when such accommodations may be necessary to afford handicapped persons equal opportunity to use and enjoy a dwelling. See 42 U.S.C. §3604(f).

After a bench trial, the court entered judgment against the appellants. The court held that the City of Athens had set reasonable restrictions on the maximum number of unrelated persons who may occupy a single dwelling unit and, therefore, is exempt from the instant FHA claim under 42 U.S.C.A. §3607(b)(1). In addition, the court held that appellants had not established a prima facie case of discriminatory effect. The district court did not address the "reasonable accommodations" issue. On appeal, appellants challenge the district court's conclusions regarding their FHA claims. Because we conclude that the Athens ordinance falls within the exemption contained in §3607(b)(1), we need not address the issues of discriminatory effect and "reasonable accommodations."

II. Discussion

A. Overview of Fair Housing Act and Exemptions

The Fair Housing Act, 42 U.S.C. §§3601 et seq., enacted as Title VIII of the Civil Rights Act of 1968, was designed to prohibit discrimination on the basis of race, color, religion, or national origin in the sale, rental, and financing of housing and to assure fair housing practices. In

---

27. Appellants do not pursue their constitutional claims on appeal.

1974, sex was added as a protected class but otherwise the statute remained basically unchanged until 1988. See 42 U.S.C. §3604(a). In 1988, Congress amended the Fair Housing Act to extend its protection to handicapped persons. Fair Housing Amendments Act of 1988, P.L. No. 100-430, 102 Stat. 1619 (1988) ("FHAA"). Congress recognized that discrimination against the handicapped is "most often the product, not of invidious animus, but rather of thoughtlessness and indifference — of benign neglect." Alexander v. Choate, 469 U.S. 287, 105 S. Ct. 712, 717, 83 L. Ed. 2d 661 (1985). The House Report states:

> The Fair Housing Amendments Act, like Section 504 of the Rehabilitation Act of 1973, as amended, is a clear pronouncement of a national commitment to end the unnecessary exclusion of persons with handicaps from the American mainstream. It repudiates the use of stereotypes and ignorance, and mandates that persons with handicaps be considered as individuals. Generalized perceptions about disabilities and unfounded speculations about threats to safety are specifically rejected as grounds to justify exclusion. [H.R. Rep. No. 711, 100th Cong., 2d Sess. 18, reprinted in 1988 U.S.C.C.A.N. 2173, 2179 (hereinafter "House Report").]

In general, the Fair Housing Act makes it unlawful

> (1) To discriminate in the sale or rental, or to otherwise make unavailable or deny, a dwelling to any buyer or renter because of a handicap. . . .
> (2) To discriminate against any person in the terms, conditions, or privileges of sale or rental of a dwelling, or in the provision of services or facilities in connection with such dwelling, because of a handicap. . . . [42 U.S.C. §§3604(f)(1) and (2).]

The FHA, however, contains a number of exemptions, which, if applicable, remove the alleged violation from the coverage of the Act. See 42 U.S.C. §3604 ("except as exempted by section[ ] . . . 3607 of this title, it shall be unlawful . . . ."). In this case, appellees claim that the exemption relating to maximum occupancy limitations is applicable. This exemption provides: "Nothing in this subchapter limits the applicability of any reasonable local, state, or federal restrictions regarding the maximum number of occupants permitted to occupy a dwelling." 42 U.S.C. §3607(b)(1).

While we conclude that the exemption applies in this case,[28] we note

_____

28. Because we conclude that the city's action in this case falls within the maximum occupancy limitation exemption, we need not decide the precise contours of the proof which a plaintiff must adduce in order to establish a violation under the Act. See Metropolitan Housing Development Corp. v. Village of Arlington Heights, 558 F.2d 1283 (7th Cir. 1977) (racial discrimination), cert. denied, 434 U.S. 1025, 98 S. Ct. 752, 54 L. Ed. 2d 772 (1978); United States v. City of Black Jack, Missouri, 508 F.2d 1179 (8th Cir. 1974) (racial discrimination), cert. denied, 422 U.S. 1042, 95 S. Ct. 2656, 45 L. Ed. 2d 694 (1975); Familystyle of St. Paul v. City of St. Paul, Minn., 728 F. Supp. 1396 (D. Minn. 1990) (discrimination against the handicapped), aff'd, 923 F.2d 91 (8th Cir. 1991); Association of

that any exemptions contained in the Act are to be construed narrowly. See United States v. Columbus Country Club, 915 F.2d 877, 883 (3d Cir. 1990), cert. denied, 111 S. Ct. 2797, 115 L. Ed. 2d 971 (1991); United States v. Hughes Memorial Home, 396 F. Supp. 544, 550 (W.D. Va. 1975) ("In view of the Supreme Court's holding that the Fair Housing Act must be accorded a generous construction, the general principle requiring the strict reading of exemptions from the Act applies here with even greater force.") (citation omitted). In fact, none of the few courts that have considered the exemptions have found them applicable. See, e.g., United States v. Columbus Country Club, supra (religious organization exemption and private club exemption); United States v. Hughes Memorial Home, 396 F. Supp. 544 (W.D. Vir. 1975) (religious organization exemption); Park Place Home Brokers v. P-K Mobile Home Park, 773 F. Supp. 46 (N.D. Ohio 1991) (housing for older persons exemption); Lanier v. Fairfield Communities, Inc., 776 F. Supp. 1533 (M.D. Fla. 1990) (housing for older persons). Acknowledging the narrowness of the exemption, we turn to §3607.

B.   Maximum Occupancy Limitation Exemption

In this appeal, appellants present only two arguments to support their position that the exemption is inapplicable: first, appellants argue that the ordinance is not a maximum occupancy limitation because it does not apply to all occupants, but only to those occupants who are unrelated; and second, appellants argue that the exemption does not apply because the ordinance is unreasonable.

1. The Athens Ordinance Is a Maximum Occupancy Limitation

Appellants argue that the district court erred in holding that the ordinance falls within the exemption contained in 42 U.S.C. §3607 (b)(1). Appellants argue that the ordinance at issue cannot be characterized as a maximum occupancy limitation within the meaning of §3607. Appellants urge that §3607(b)(1) pertains only to restrictions setting a "maximum number of occupants" and that the ordinance in this case does not set an absolute maximum because there is no limit placed on the number of family members who may reside together; here the limitation is only on unrelated persons. Appellants suggest that the only

Relatives and Friends of AIDS Patients (A.F.A.P.S.) v. Regulations & Permits Admin. (A.R.P.E.), 740 F. Supp. 95 (D. Puerto Rico 1990) (same); Baxter v. City of Belleville, Ill., 720 F. Supp. 720 (S.D. Ill. 1989); see also Alexander v. Choate, 469 U.S. 287, 105 S. Ct. 712, 83 L. Ed. 2d 661 (1985) (addressing an alleged violation of §504 of the Rehabilitation Act of 1973).

maximum occupancy limitation that Congress contemplated was a limitation on the number of persons per square foot of dwelling space. Such a limitation would apply to all persons living together, whether related or not. In support of their argument, appellants cite the following passage of the House Report, stating that the maximum occupancy limitation exemption is:

> not intended to limit the applicability of any reasonable local, State, or Federal restrictions on the maximum number of occupants permitted to occupy a dwelling unit. A number of jurisdictions limit the number of occupants per unit based on a minimum number of square feet in the unit or the sleeping areas of the unit. Reasonable limitations by governments would be allowed to continue, as long as they were *applied to all occupants,* and *did not operate to discriminate on the basis of race, color, religion, sex, national origin, handicap or familial status.* [House Report at 31; 1988 U.S.C.C.A.N. at 2192 (1988) (emphasis added).]

In addressing appellants' argument that the ordinance restricts only unrelated occupants, cases that examine discrimination, under a constitutional analysis rather than under the FHA, are helpful. In Moore v. City of East Cleveland, Ohio, 431 U.S. 494, 97 S. Ct. 1932, 52 L. Ed. 2d 531 (1977), the Supreme Court held that an ordinance that limited occupancy to members of a single family, but that defined family so narrowly that a grandmother was not permitted to live with her grandson, violated the Due Process Clause of the Fourteenth Amendment. In reaching its decision, the Court emphasized its reasons for protecting family living situations:

> Our decisions establish that the Constitution protects the sanctity of the family precisely because the institution of the family is deeply rooted in this Nation's history and tradition. It is through the family that we inculcate and pass down many of our most cherished values, moral and cultural. [97 S. Ct. at 1938 (footnotes omitted).]

Moore distinguished Village of Belle Terre v. Boraas, 416 U.S. 1, 94 S. Ct. 1536, 39 L. Ed. 2d 797 (1974), because the zoning ordinance there affected only *unrelated* individuals, and did not limit the number of family members permitted to live together. In *Belle Terre,* the Supreme Court rejected a constitutional challenge to a zoning ordinance which limited single family dwellings to a maximum of two unrelated persons or to any number of persons related by blood, adoption or marriage. Six students at a nearby college sought to live in a house together and were denied permission. The Supreme Court held that the zoning ordinance was rationally related to legitimate interests relating to density, traffic, and quiet, open spaces for families.

Reading *Belle Terre* and *Moore* together, it is apparent that Supreme

Court precedent sanctions zoning limitations based upon the number of unrelated persons living together as a means of furthering the state's legitimate interest in controlling density, notwithstanding the absence of a similar limitation on related persons. In light of this legal reality, and in light of the prevalence of zoning regulations which limit unrelated persons without a simultaneous limitation upon related persons, see *Moore*, 431 U.S. at 513-21, 97 S. Ct. at 1942-47 (Stevens, J., concurring),[29] we decline to accept appellants' construction of congressional intent. We do not believe that Congress intended that the maximum occupancy limitation exemption would apply *only* to a limitation on the maximum number of persons per square foot of dwelling space. A careful reading of the legislative history demonstrates that Congress was merely giving examples of the type of restrictions on occupancy that would be reasonable. See House Report at 31; 1988 U.S.C.C.A.N. at 2192 ("*A number of jurisdictions* limit the number of occupants per unit based on a minimum number of square feet in the unit or the sleeping areas of the unit.") (emphasis added). The list of reasonable restrictions listed in the House Report is not meant to be exhaustive.

In the instant case, the City of Athens was attempting to prevent overcrowding in the area surrounding the university without restricting family members unnecessarily. At trial, the City presented evidence that limiting unrelated individuals was the most workable solution in order to maintain the residential character of the neighborhood. The City felt that a restriction based on square footage, applicable to both related and unrelated persons, would not be feasible because too low a number would cause a family to move if a child were born while too high a number would defeat the ability of the City to protect single-family neighborhoods.

Our reasoning finds support in Doe v. City of Butler, Pa., 892 F.2d 315, 321 (3d Cir. 1989). There, the Third Circuit concluded that a zoning regulation was rationally related to legitimate state interests in controlling density, notwithstanding the fact that the regulation limited to six the number of unrelated persons who could occupy a single dwelling unit while imposing no limitation upon the number of related persons. The court rejected the argument that the zoning restriction was not related to density control because there were no limits placed on the occupancy of related persons. Applying reasoning similar to our own, the Third Circuit stated: "If the absence of an occupancy limitation on the members of a family who can live together is boot-strapped into the argument that therefore there can be no occupancy limitation for unrelated persons living together, there could never be such an occupancy

29. The record establishes that the zoning limitation in this case is commonplace. A majority of counties and municipalities limit the number of unrelated persons who may reside in a dwelling.

limitation and *Belle Terre* would be meaningless." 892 F.2d at 321. In other words, *Moore* and *Belle Terre,* read together, indicate that a feasible method of controlling density is to place occupancy limitations on unrelated persons but not on related persons.

Having concluded that the Athens zoning restriction is a maximum occupancy limitation, we turn to appellant's argument that the Athens ordinance is unreasonable.

2. Reasonableness of the Athens Ordinance

The §3607(b)(1) exemption applies only to *reasonable* restrictions regarding the maximum number of occupants permitted to occupy a dwelling. Appellants argue that the Athens, Georgia, ordinance is unreasonable because it has a disparate impact on handicapped individuals. In determining the reasonableness of the ordinance, this court must strike a balance between a municipality's interest in maintaining the residential character of a particular area and the interests of the handicapped in remaining free from a zoning restriction having some disparate impact.[30] Courts have long recognized that local governments have broad power in zoning. See Village of Euclid v. Ambler Realty Co., 272 U.S. 365, 395, 47 S. Ct. 114, 121, 71 L. Ed. 303 (1926) ("[B]efore [a zoning] ordinance can be declared unconstitutional, [it must be shown to be] clearly arbitrary and unreasonable, having no substantial relation to the public health, safety, morals, or general welfare.").

We turn then to the evidence of discrimination adduced by appellants at trial. The only evidence of disparate impact[31] upon handicapped

---

30. In Alexander v. Choate, 469 U.S. 287, 105 S. Ct. 712, 83 L. Ed. 2d 661 (1985), the Supreme Court recognized the need to balance the interests of the handicapped against those of the recipients of federal funds in the context of §504 of the Rehabilitation Act of 1973, 87 Stat. 394, as amended, 29 U.S.C. §794:

> [Southeastern Community College v. Davis, 442 U.S. 397, 99 S. Ct. 2361, 60 L. Ed. 2d 980 (1979)] . . . struck a balance between the statutory rights of the handicapped to be integrated into society and the legitimate interests of federal grantees in preserving the integrity of their programs: while a grantee need not be required to make "fundamental" or "substantial" modifications to accommodate the handicapped, it may be required to make "reasonable" ones. [*Alexander,* 469 U.S. at 300, 105 S. Ct. at 720.]

While we are construing the FHA and not the Rehabilitation Act of 1973, the above cases are still useful to our analysis. Because the legislative history likens the purposes of the FHA amendments to that of the Rehabilitation Act of 1973, see House Report at 18, we look to cases interpreting the Rehabilitation Act in order to construe the FHA. Nonetheless, we note that "too facile an assimilation of [§504] law into [the Fair Housing Act] must be resisted." Alexander v. Choate, 105 S. Ct. at 716 n.7 (assimilation of Title VI into §504).

31. The district court concluded that the City did not intend to discriminate against handicapped persons, and appellants do not challenge this conclusion on appeal. Appellants assert only that the City's application of the zoning ordinance has a disparate impact on handicapped persons.

persons adduced by appellants was the fact that appellants' proposed use for handicapped persons was rejected and the testimony of Reverend Lindsay that a group home for recovering alcoholics in Athens, Georgia, could not be economically feasible with fewer than 12 residents. There was no attempt to establish that the ordinance had a harsher effect on handicapped persons wanting to live in group homes than on college students or other non-handicapped persons desiring to live in group homes. While we assume *arguendo* that the ordinance had some disparate impact upon handicapped persons, we conclude that the evidence of disparate impact upon handicapped persons is extremely weak.

Weighed against the foregoing rather slim evidence of disparate impact upon handicapped persons are the City's very substantial interests in controlling density, traffic, and noise in its single family residential districts, and in preserving the residential character of such districts. The City's purpose in adopting the zoning restriction at issue was to control the large University of Georgia student population. The City adopted its definition of "family" in the ordinance in order to protect the character of single-family neighborhoods and regulate the negative effects emanating from the student population such as overcrowding, traffic, and noise.

At trial, the City presented the testimony of Mr. Leon Eplan, a land use planner and currently the Commissioner of Planning and Development for the City of Atlanta, Georgia. Eplan testified about the effects that a large student population can have on the surrounding residential neighborhood absent measures aimed at restricting occupancy. Eplan cited the Home Park area surrounding Georgia Tech University in Atlanta, Georgia, as an example of an area that has gone from being primarily residential to an area that has increased in density, is primarily rental property, and is no longer suitable for single-family dwellings because of the increased noise and traffic. As the student population grew, the residents found it profitable to rent to students. At the time that this demand for off-campus housing grew, there was no city ordinance in place that would limit the density in the area. Thus, the neighborhood has changed its character dramatically over the years.

As noted above, and as the district court found, see District Court Opinion at 7, the most practical means of accomplishing the City's legitimate interests was a limitation on the number of unrelated persons permitted to occupy a single dwelling. The Athens restriction has the following primary effects in the affected single family residential districts: (1) to control the number of college students who may rent a single dwelling; (2) to exclude boarding houses; and (3) to exclude fraternity and sorority houses. All are clearly legitimate and serve important interests of the City. In addition, of course, the restriction had the incidental effect of excluding group homes such as the one proposed by appellants, at least those which cannot be economically operated with the permitted number of residents.

In considering whether the City's legitimate interests outweigh the disparate impact upon handicapped persons, it is also relevant that there are other areas in the City that would be available for group homes. The City presented evidence at trial that such a group home would be permitted to operate in the following zones: R.M. 1 and R.M. 2 (both multi-family residential zones); O.I. (office institutional); O.I.B. (office institutional and limited commercial); L.B. (local business); G.B. (general business); C.B.D. (central business district); and H.B. (highway business). R2-168-174. Thus, it appears that group homes of the kind appellants propose would be permitted in other residential areas of the city, as well as non-residential areas.

The Athens ordinance on its face does not draw a line between handicapped individuals and non-handicapped individuals. Rather, the legislative line was drawn between related and unrelated individuals, a distinction which Supreme Court precedent clearly permits. See *Moore* and *Belle Terre,* supra. While a local government cannot exclude handicapped individuals on the premise that "they can go elsewhere,"[32] the Fair Housing Act amendments do not require a local government to permit handicapped individuals to live wherever they desire. The Act provides only that handicapped individuals be given meaningful access to housing in a nondiscriminatory fashion. While it may be true that handicapped individuals have a greater need to reside in group settings, the City of Athens has other zones that permit such access for handicapped and other individuals.

We conclude that the zoning restriction as applied in this case is reasonable, and thus the exemption is applicable. Appellants have adduced only weak evidence of disparate impact upon handicapped persons. On the other hand, the City has adduced evidence of strong and legitimate interests in controlling density, traffic, and noise in its single-family residential districts, and in preserving the residential character thereof. The City not only demonstrated that its restriction upon the number of unrelated persons who may occupy a dwelling is the only practical method of serving its legitimate interests but also adduced evidence that comparable restrictions are commonplace in the zoning regulations of counties and municipalities. The exemption contained in §3607(b)(1) relating to maximum occupancy limitations is an attempt on the part of Congress to advance the interests of the handicapped without

32. See Michael P. Seng, Discrimination against Families with Children and Handicapped Persons under the 1988 Amendments to the Fair Housing Act, 22 J. Marshall L. Rev. 541, 560 (1989).

interfering seriously with reasonable local zoning. In this case, the City has preserved meaningful access for group homes for handicapped persons in its residential areas. We conclude that the zoning restriction, as applied under the circumstances of this case, is reasonable, and thus that the §3607(b)(1) exemption is applicable.

Finally, appellants argue that the fact that the ordinance has some disparate impact upon handicapped persons means, *ipso facto,* that the ordinance is unreasonable. Our research has uncovered no support in the case law for that proposition. To the contrary, the relevant case law suggests otherwise. . . .

For the foregoing reasons, the Athens, Georgia, zoning ordinance was reasonable as applied in this case. We conclude that §3607(b)(1) exempts the City's action from the coverage of the Act.[33] Accordingly, the judgment of the district court is Affirmed.

[The dissenting opinion of Kravitch, J., is omitted.]

NOTES: GROUP HOMES

1. "Group homes" is a generic term for any number of small, decentralized treatment facilities housing foster children, the mentally ill, the developmentally disabled, juvenile offenders, ex-drug addicts, alcoholics, and so on. Such people were once congregated in large public institutions, but group homes have become very common in recent

---

33. . . . In City of Cleburne v. Cleburne Living Center, 473 U.S. 432, 105 S. Ct. 3249, 87 L. Ed. 2d 313 (1985), the Supreme Court held that a city's refusal to grant a special use permit to allow construction of a group home for the mentally retarded violated the equal protection clause of the fourteenth amendment. In *Cleburne,* the city required special use permits for the operation of group homes for the handicapped but did not require permits for other uses such as hospitals and nursing homes in the same area. The city attempted to justify its requirement on the grounds that it was concerned with the negative attitude of property owners, that students from a school across the street from the proposed site might harass the residents, and that the location was on "a five hundred year flood plain." In addition, the city did put forth some concerns about population density, but failed "to explain why apartment houses, fraternity and sorority houses, hospitals and the like, may freely locate in the area without a permit." 105 S. Ct. at 3260. The Court rejected the City's arguments and concluded that the reasons given for the special use permits were not rationally related to a legitimate government purpose. 105 S. Ct. at 3258.

The present case can be distinguished from *Cleburne* in two respects. First, this case does not involve the requirement of a special use permit for the operation of The Potter's House. Group homes for the handicapped are not singled out and treated differently than any other dwelling that would house a large number of unrelated persons. See also Doe v. City of Butler, Pa., 892 F.2d 315 (3d Cir. 1989) (distinguishing *Cleburne* on same ground). Second, while in *Cleburne,* there were other group dwellings in the same area, there is no evidence in the present case that the City of Athens has recently permitted other groups to locate in a single-family zone. Therefore, the City's concerns relating to density are more credible as the ordinance has been applied across the board to uphold the residential character of the Ruth Street neighborhood. Thus, the City of Athens ordinance does not appear to rest on an irrational fear of the handicapped such that the FHA is violated. . . .

years because they are less expensive than centralized facilities and are thought to provide more humane and effective treatment.

Neighbors, of course, dislike group homes — the NIMBY (Not In My Back Yard) phenomenon.[34] A circular mailed out by a Michigan group listed some of the reasons neighbors give for not wanting a group home on their street. The reasons were portrayed like this:

> Our road is too wide / Our road is too narrow
> It's too dangerous in the country / It's too dangerous in the city
> The residents might hurt my kids / My kids might hurt the residents
> Our street ends in a cul-de-sac / Our street is a thru street

Other sorts of reasons were: we don't have sidewalks; there's water (someone else said quicksand) nearby; we let our dogs run free; the retarded stay up and scream all night; dust in our neighborhood would be a health hazard to the residents of the home.

2. Conditional or special use permits (see pages 1030-1036) are a common means by which communities try to control the location of group homes. A number of state court decisions have found that denial of a permit to a group home could not be upheld in light of other uses that were allowed or because prejudice motivated the decision. See Martin Jaffe, Group Homes and Family Values, Land Use L. & Zoning Dig., Mar. 1982, at 4, 7-8. The Fair Housing Act can also provide grounds to attack special exception requirements. See, e.g., Stewart B. McKinney Found. v. Town Plan & Zoning Commn., 790 F. Supp. 1197 (D. Conn. 1992) (special exception for use of two-family residence as home for HIV-infected persons); Baxter v. City of Belleville, 720 F. Supp. 720 (S.D. Ill. 1989) (similar).

Another common technique, illustrated by the *Elliott* case, aims to exclude group homes from areas zoned for single-family residences on the ground that the occupants exceed the number of unrelated persons allowed to live together as a family unit. Recall the discussion in Note 2

---

34. See Peter W. Salsich, Jr., Group Homes, Shelters and Congregate Housing: Deinstitutionalization Policies and the NIMBY Syndrome, 21 Real Prop., Prob. & Tr. J. 413 (1986).

NIMBY is only one — but probably the best known — of the LULU acronyms (a LULU is a Locally Undesirable Land Use). Others include:

NOPE (Nowhere On Planet Earth)
NIABY (Not In Anyone's Back Yard)
NIMTOO (Not In My Term Of Office)
NIRPBY (Never In Rich People's Back Yards)
LASBY (Look At Several Back Yards)
GUMBY (Gotta Use Many Back Yards)
YIMBY (Yes In Many Back Yards)

See Herbert Inhaber, Of NIMBYs, LULUs, and NIMTOOs, The Public Interest, Spring 1992, at 52, 64 (adding DAD: Decide, Announce, and Defend); Denis Binder, Cutting the Nimbian Knot: A Primer, 40 DePaul L. Rev. 1009 (1991).

on page 1089. A number of state court cases have reasoned that group homes house the functional equivalent of families and thus may not be excluded, but there are also decisions to the contrary. See Salsich, supra footnote 34, at 419-424; Annot., 32 A.L.R.4th 1018, 1022-1026 (1984 & Supp. 1992). Again, the Fair Housing Act can have a bearing. See, e.g., Oxford House-Evergreen v. City of Plainfield, 769 F. Supp. 1329 (D.N.J. 1991) (residence for nine recovering alcoholics; zoning ordinance limited number of occupants to six).[35]

3. Many states — on the order of half of them — deal with group homes through legislation, which typically preempts local zoning controls over group homes of specified types. State statutes vary in approach: They might prohibit discrimination against the developmentally disabled and certain other groups, or establish policies in favor of group homes, or define group homes as "residential uses" or their occupants as a "family" for purposes of local zoning ordinances, or specify that group homes are a permissible use in all zones. The statutes might restrict the number of occupants permitted in a group home and might require dispersal of the homes throughout neighborhoods in order to avoid group home ghettos. Much of the state legislation is modeled on a statute drafted by the American Bar Association's Commission on the Mentally Disabled. See Robert J. Hopperton, A State Legislative Strategy for Ending Exclusionary Zoning of Community Homes, 19 Urb. L. Ann. 47 (1980) (an appendix to the article sets out the ABA's model statute).

4. All zoning is exclusionary, by definition: Its central purpose is to minimize or eliminate unwanted effects — externalities — in a given district, whether the effects be caused by typical nuisances (*Euclid*'s pig in a parlor), by apartments or commercial uses in a high-class single-family residential zone, or by group homes. Commonly, however, zoning measures like these aim not to ban uses (nuisances aside), but rather to relegate them to what the zoners regard as their proper place in the community. Contrast another kind of exclusionary zoning, the kind to which that phrase particularly refers today: measures whose purpose or effect is essentially to close an entire community to unwanted groups — typically people of low income who might put a heavy burden on the public fisc yet at the same time contribute little to it, resulting in increased property taxes and reduced land values throughout the community. The attitude here is, "Let them go elsewhere, to some other city." A related zoning technique, growth controls, aims to limit access to everyone, rich and poor alike, again probably as a means to enhance

35. The Fair Housing Act can also preclude enforcement of private single-family restrictive covenants against group homes. See the discussion in Note 3 on pages 909-910. All in all, the act has figured in a great deal of recent litigation. A LEXIS search conducted in late 1992 disclosed about two dozen federal district court cases, in addition to those cited above and in footnote 28 on page 1095.

(certain) property values. The next section considers these two kinds of measures.

3. Exclusionary Zoning and Growth Controls

Southern Burlington County NAACP
v. Township of Mount Laurel

Supreme Court of New Jersey, 1975
67 N.J. 151, 336 A.2d 713, appeal dismissed and cert. denied,
423 U.S. 808 (1975)

HALL, J. This case attacks the system of land use regulation by defendant Township of Mount Laurel on the ground that low and moderate income families are thereby unlawfully excluded from the municipality. . . .

The implications of the issue presented are indeed broad and far-reaching, extending much beyond these particular plaintiffs and the boundaries of this particular municipality. . . .

Plaintiffs represent the minority group poor (black and Hispanic)[36] seeking such quarters. But they are not the only category of persons barred from so many municipalities by reason of restrictive land use regulations. We have reference to young and elderly couples, single persons and large, growing families not in the poverty class, but who still cannot afford the only kinds of housing realistically permitted in most places — relatively high-priced, single-family detached dwellings on sizeable lots and, in some municipalities, expensive apartments. We will, therefore, consider the case from the wider viewpoint that the effect of Mount Laurel's land use regulation has been to prevent various categories of persons from living in the township because of the limited extent of their income and resources. In this connection, we accept the presentation of the municipality's counsel at oral argument that the regulatory scheme was not adopted with any desire or intent to exclude prospective residents on the obviously illegal bases of race, origin or believed social incompatibility. . . .

36. Plaintiffs fall into four categories: (1) present residents of the township residing in dilapidated or substandard housing; (2) former residents who were forced to move elsewhere because of the absence of suitable housing; (3) nonresidents living in central city substandard housing in the region who desire to secure decent housing and accompanying advantages within their means elsewhere; (4) three organizations representing the housing and other interests of racial minorities. The township originally challenged plaintiffs' standing to bring this action. The trial court properly held (119 N.J. Super. at 166, 290 A.2d 465) that the resident plaintiffs had adequate standing to ground the entire action and found it unnecessary to pass on that of the other plaintiffs. The issue has not been raised on appeal. . . .

I

The Facts

Mount Laurel is a flat, sprawling township, 22 square miles, or about 14,000 acres, in area, on the west central edge of Burlington County. . . .

In 1950, the township had a population of 2817, only about 600 more people than it had in 1940. It was then, as it had been for decades, primarily a rural agricultural area with no sizeable settlements or commercial or industrial enterprises. The populace generally lived in individual houses scattered along country roads. There were several pockets of poverty, with deteriorating or dilapidated housing (apparently 300 or so units of which remain today in equally poor condition). After 1950, as in so many other municipalities similarly situated, residential development and some commerce and industry began to come in. By 1960 the population had almost doubled to 5249 and by 1970 had more than doubled again to 11,221. These new residents were, of course, "outsiders" from the nearby central cities and older suburbs or from more distant places drawn here by reason of employment in the region. The township is now definitely a part of the outer ring of the South Jersey metropolitan area, which area we define as those portions of Camden, Burlington and Gloucester Counties within a semicircle having a radius of 20 miles or so from the heart of Camden city. And 65% of the township is still vacant land or in agricultural use.

The growth of the township has been spurred by the construction or improvement of main highways through or near it. . . . This highway network gives the township a most strategic location from the standpoint of transport of goods and people by truck and private car. There is no other means of transportation.

The location and nature of development have been, as usual, controlled by the local zoning enactments. The general ordinance presently in force, which was declared invalid by the trial court, was adopted in 1964. We understand that earlier enactments provided, however, basically the same scheme but were less restrictive as to residential development. The growth pattern dictated by the ordinance is typical.

Under the present ordinance, 29.2% of all the land in the township, or 4,121 acres, is zoned for industry. This amounts to 2,800 more acres than were so zoned by the 1954 ordinance. . . .

Only industry meeting specified performance standards is permitted. The effect is to limit the use substantially to light manufacturing, research, distribution of goods, offices and the like. Some nonindustrial uses, such as agriculture, farm dwellings, motels, a harness racetrack, and certain retail sales and service establishments, are permitted in this zone. At the time of trial no more than 100 acres . . . were actually occupied by industrial uses. They had been constructed in recent years, mostly in several industrial parks, and involved tax ratables of about 16 million dollars. The rest of the land so zoned has remained undeveloped. If it were fully utilized, the testimony was that about 43,500 industrial jobs would be created, but it appeared clear that, as happens in the case of so many municipalities, much more land has been so zoned than the reasonable potential for industrial movement or expansion warrants. At the same time, however, the land cannot be used for residential development under the general ordinance.

The amount of land zoned for retail business use under the general ordinance is relatively small — 169 acres, or 1.2% of the total. . . .

While the greater part of the land so zoned appears to be in use, there is no major shopping center or concentrated retail commercial area — "downtown" — in the township.

The balance of the land area, almost 10,000 acres, has been developed until recently in the conventional form of major subdivisions. The general ordinance provides for four residential zones, designated R-1, R-1D, R-2 and R-3. All permit only single-family, detached dwellings, one house per lot — the usual form of grid development. Attached townhouses, apartments (except on farms for agricultural workers) and mobile homes are not allowed anywhere in the township under the general ordinance. This dwelling development, resulting in the previously mentioned quadrupling of the population, has been largely confined to the R-1 and R-2 districts in two sections — the northeasterly and southwesterly corners adjacent to the turnpike and other major highways. The result has been quite intensive development of these sections, but at a low density. The dwellings are substantial; the average value in 1971 was $32,500 and is undoubtedly much higher today.

The general ordinance requirements, while not as restrictive as those in many similar municipalities, nonetheless realistically allow only homes within the financial reach of persons of at least middle income. The R-1 zone requires a minimum lot area of 9,375 square feet, a minimum lot width of 75 feet at the building line, and a minimum dwelling floor area of 1,100 square feet if a one-story building and 1,300 square feet if one and one-half stories or higher. Originally this zone comprised about 2,500 acres. Most of the subdivisions have been constructed within it so that only a few hundred acres remain (the testimony was at variance as to the exact amount). The R-2 zone, comprising a single district of 141 acres in the northeasterly corner, has been completely developed. While it only required a minimum floor area of 900 square feet for a one-story dwelling, the minimum lot size was 11,000 square feet; otherwise the requisites were the same as in the R-1 zone.

The general ordinance places the remainder of the township, outside of the industrial and commercial zones and the R-1D district (to be mentioned shortly), in the R-3 zone. This zone comprises over 7,000 acres — slightly more than half of the total municipal area — practically all of which is located in the central part of the township extending southeasterly to the apex of the triangle. The testimony was that about 4,600 acres of it then remained available for housing development. Ordinance requirements are substantially higher, however, in that the minimum lot size is increased to about one-half acre (20,000 square feet). (We understand that sewer and water utilities have not generally been installed, but, of course, they can be.) Lot width at the building line must be 100 feet. Minimum dwelling floor area is as in the R-1 zone. Presently this section is primarily in agricultural use; it contains as well most of the municipality's substandard housing.

The R-1D district was created by ordinance amendment in 1968. The area is composed of a piece of what was formerly R-3 land in the western part of that zone. The district is a so-called "cluster" zone. See generally 2 Williams, American Planning Law: Land Use and the Police Power, §§47.01-47.05 (1974). . . . Here [the] concept is implemented by reduction of the minimum lot area from 20,000 square feet required in the R-3 zone to 10,000 square feet (12,000 square feet for corner lots) but with the proviso that one-family houses — the single permitted dwelling use — "shall not be erected in excess of an allowable development density of 2.25 dwelling units per gross acre." The minimum lot width at the building line must be 80 feet and the minimum dwelling floor area is the same as in the R-3 zone. The amendment further provides that the developer must set aside and dedicate to the municipality a minimum of 15% and a maximum of 25% of the total acreage for such public uses as may be required by the Planning Board, including "but not limited to school sites, parks, playgrounds, recreation areas, public buildings, public utilities." Some dwelling development has taken place in this district, the exact extent of which is not disclosed by the record. It is apparent that the dwellings are comparable in character and value to those in the other residential zones. The testimony was that 486 acres remained available in the district.

A variation from conventional development has recently occurred in some parts of Mount Laurel, as in a number of other similar municipalities, by use of the land use regulation device known as "planned unit development" (PUD). This scheme differs from the traditional in that the type, density and placement of land uses and buildings, instead of being detailed and confined to specified districts by local legislation in advance, is determined by contract, or "deal," as to each development between the developer and the municipal administrative authority, under broad guidelines laid down by state enabling legislation and an implementing local ordinance. The stress is on regulation of density and permitted mixture of uses within the same area, including various kinds of living accommodations with or without commercial and industrial enterprises. The idea may be basically thought of as the creation of "new towns" in virgin territory, full-blown or in miniature, although most frequently the concept has been limited in practice, as in Mount Laurel, to residential developments of various sizes having some variety of housing and perhaps some retail establishments to serve the inhabitants.

New Jersey passed such enabling legislation in 1967, which closely follows a model act found in 114 U. Pa. L. Rev. 140 (1965), and Mount Laurel adopted the implementing enactment as a supplement to its general zoning ordinance in December of that year. While the ordinance was repealed early in 1971, the township governing body in the interim had approved four PUD projects, which were specifically saved from extinction by the repealer.[37]

These projects, three in the southwesterly sector and one in the northeasterly sector, are very substantial and involve at least 10,000 sale and rental housing units of various types to be erected over a period of years. Their bounds were created by agreement rather than legislative specification on the zoning map, invading industrial, R-1, R-1D, R-3 and even flood plain zones. If completed as planned, they will in themselves ultimately quadruple the 1970 township population, but still leave a good part of the township undeveloped. (The record does not indicate how far development in each of the projects has progressed.) While multi-family housing in the form of rental garden, medium rise and high rise apartments and attached townhouses is for the first time provided for, as well as single-family detached dwellings for sale, it is not designed to accommodate and is beyond the financial reach of low and moderate income families, especially those with young children. The aim is quite the contrary; as with the single-family homes in the older conventional subdivisions, only persons of medium and upper income are sought as residents.

A few details will furnish sufficient documentation. Each of the resolutions of tentative approval of the projects contains a similar fact finding to the effect that the development will attract a highly educated and trained population base to support the nearby industrial parks in the township as well as the business and commercial facilities. The approvals also sharply limit the number of apartments having more than one bedroom. Further, they require that the developer must provide in its leases that no school-age children shall be permitted to occupy any one-bedroom apartment and that no more than two such children shall re-

---

37. . . . This court has never passed upon the PUD enabling legislation, any local implementing ordinance or any municipal approval of a PUD project. The basic legal questions . . . , which include among others the matter of what requirements a municipal authority may, in effect, impose upon a developer as a condition of approval, are serious and not all easy of solution. We refer to the Mount Laurel PUD projects as part of the picture of land use regulation in the township and its effect. It may be noted that, at a hearing on the PUD ordinance, the then township attorney stated that ". . . providing for apartments in a PUD ordinance in effect would seem to overcome any court objection that the Township was not properly zoning in denying apartments." [On cluster zoning and PUDs, see pages 1056-1064. — Eds.]

side in any two-bedroom unit. The developer is also required, prior to the issuance of the first building permit, to record a covenant, running with all land on which multi-family housing is to be constructed, providing that in the event more than .3 school children per multi-family unit shall attend the township school system in any one year, the developer will pay the cost of tuition and other school expenses of all such excess numbers of children. In addition, low density, required amenities, such as central air conditioning, and specified developer contributions help to push rents and sales prices to high levels. These contributions include fire apparatus, ambulances, fire houses, and very large sums of money for educational facilities, a cultural center and the township library.[38]

Still another restrictive land use regulation was adopted by the township through a supplement to the general zoning ordinance enacted in September 1972 creating a new zone, R-4, Planned Adult Retirement Community (PARC). The supplementary enactment designated a sizeable area as the zone — perhaps 200 acres — carved out of the R-1D and R-3 districts in the southwesterly sector. The enactment recited a critical shortage of adequate housing in the township suitable "for the needs and desires of senior citizens and certain other adults over the age of 52." The permission was essentially for single ownership development of the zone for multi-family housing (townhouses and apartments), thereafter to be either rented or sold as cooperatives or condominiums. The extensive development requirements detailed in the ordinance make it apparent that the scheme was not designed for, and would be beyond the means of, low and moderate income retirees. The highly restricted nature of the zone is found in the requirement that all permanent residents must be at least 52 years of age (except a spouse, immediate family member other than a child, live-in domestic, companion or nurse). Children are limited to a maximum of one, over age 18, residing with a parent and there may be no more than three permanent residents in any one dwelling unit.[39]

All this affirmative action for the benefit of certain segments of the population is in sharp contrast to the lack of action, and indeed hostility, with respect to affording any opportunity for decent housing for the township's own poor living in substandard accommodations, found largely in the section known as Springville (R-3 zone). The 1969 Master Plan Report recognized it and recommended positive action. The continuous official reaction has been rather a negative policy of waiting for dilapidated premises to be vacated and then forbidding further occupancy. An earlier non-governmental effort to improve conditions had

38. The current township attorney, at oral argument, conceded, without specification, that many of these various conditions which had been required of developers were illegal.

39. This court has not yet passed on the validity of any land use regulation which restricts residence on the basis of occupant age.

been effectively thwarted. In 1968 a private non-profit association sought to build subsidized, multi-family housing in the Springville section with funds to be granted by a higher level governmental agency. Advance municipal approval of the project was required. The Township Committee responded with a purportedly approving resolution, which found a need for "moderate" income housing in the area, but went on to specify that such housing must be constructed subject to all zoning, planning, building and other applicable ordinances and codes. This meant single-family detached dwellings on 20,000 square foot lots. (Fear was also expressed that such housing would attract low income families from outside the township.) Needless to say, such requirements killed realistic housing for this group of low and moderate income families.

The record thoroughly substantiates the findings of the trial court that over the years Mount Laurel "has acted affirmatively to control development and to attract a selective type of growth" and that "through its zoning ordinances has exhibited economic discrimination in that the poor have been deprived of adequate housing and the opportunity to secure the construction of subsidized housing, and has used federal, state, county and local finances and resources solely for the betterment of middle and upper-income persons."

There cannot be the slightest doubt that the reason for this course of conduct has been to keep down local taxes on *property* (Mount Laurel is not a high tax municipality) and that the policy was carried out without regard for non-fiscal considerations with respect to *people*, either within or without its boundaries. This conclusion is demonstrated not only by what was done and what happened, as we have related, but also by innumerable direct statements of municipal officials at public meetings over the years which are found in the exhibits. . . .

This policy of land use regulation for a fiscal end derives from New Jersey's tax structure, which has imposed on local real estate most of the cost of municipal and county government and of the primary and secondary education of the municipality's children. The latter expense is much the largest, so, basically, the fewer the school children, the lower the tax rate. Sizeable industrial and commercial ratables are eagerly sought and homes and the lots on which they are situate are required to be large enough, through minimum lot sizes and minimum floor areas, to have substantial value in order to produce greater tax revenues to meet school costs. Large families who cannot afford to buy large houses and must live in cheaper rental accommodations are definitely not wanted, so we find drastic bedroom restrictions for, or complete prohibition of, multi-family or other feasible housing for those of lesser income.

This pattern of land use regulation has been adopted for the same purpose in developing municipality after developing municipality. Almost every one acts solely in its own selfish and parochial interest and in effect builds a wall around itself to keep out those people or entities not adding favorably to the tax base, despite the location of the municipality or the demand for varied kinds of housing. There has been no effective intermunicipal or area planning or land use regulation. All of this is amply demonstrated by the evidence in this case as to Camden, Burlington and Gloucester counties. . . .

One incongruous result is the picture of developing municipalities rendering it impossible for lower paid employees of industries they have eagerly sought and welcomed with open arms (and, in Mount Laurel's case, even some of its own lower paid municipal employees) to live in the community where they work.

The other end of the spectrum should also be mentioned because it shows the source of some of the demand for cheaper housing than the developing municipalities have permitted. Core cities were originally the location of most commerce and industry. Many of those facilities furnished employment for the unskilled and semi-skilled. These employees lived relatively near their work, so sections of cities always have housed the majority of people of low and moderate income, generally in old and deteriorating housing. Despite the municipally confined tax structure, commercial and industrial ratables generally used to supply enough revenue to provide and maintain municipal services equal or superior to those furnished in most suburban and rural areas.

The situation has become exactly the opposite since the end of World War II. Much industry and retail business, and even the professions, have left the cities. Camden is a typical example. The testimonial and documentary evidence in this case as to what has happened to that city is depressing indeed. For various reasons, it lost thousands of jobs between 1950 and 1970, including more than half of its manufacturing jobs (a reduction from 43,267 to 20,671, while all jobs in the entire area labor market increased from 94,507 to 197,037). A large segment of retail business faded away with the erection of large suburban shopping centers. The economically better situated city residents helped fill up the miles of sprawling new housing developments, not fully served by public transit. In a society which came to depend more and more on expensive individual motor vehicle transportation for all purposes, low income employees very frequently could not afford to reach outlying places of suitable employment and they certainly could not afford the permissible housing near such locations. These people have great difficulty in obtaining work and have been forced to remain in housing which is overcrowded, and has become more and more substandard and less and less tax productive. There has been a consequent critical erosion of the city tax base and inability to provide the amount and quality of those governmental services — education, health, police, fire, housing and the like — so necessary to the very existence of safe and decent city life. This category of city dwellers desperately needs much better housing and living conditions than is available to them now, both in a rehabilitated city and in outlying municipalities. They make up, along with the other classes of persons earlier mentioned who also cannot afford the only generally permitted housing in the developing municipalities, the acknowledged great demand for low and moderate income housing.

II

The Legal Issue

The legal question before us, as earlier indicated, is whether a developing municipality like Mount Laurel may validly, by a system of land use regulation, make it physically and economically impossible to provide low and moderate income housing in the municipality for the various categories of persons who need and want it and thereby, as Mount Laurel has, exclude such people from living within its confines because of the limited extent of their income and resources. Necessarily implicated are the broader questions of the right of such municipalities to limit the kinds of available housing and of any obligation to make possible a variety and choice of types of living accommodations.

We conclude that every such municipality must, by its land use regulations, presumptively make realistically possible an appropriate variety and choice of housing. More specifically, presumptively it cannot foreclose the opportunity of the classes of people mentioned for low and moderate income housing and in its regulations must affirmatively afford that opportunity, at least to the extent of the municipality's fair share of the present and prospective regional need therefor. These obligations must be met unless the particular municipality can sustain the heavy burden of demonstrating peculiar circumstances which dictate that it should not be required so to do.[40]

We reach this conclusion under state law and so do not find it necessary to consider federal constitutional grounds urged by plaintiffs. We begin with some fundamental principles as applied to the scene before us.

Land use regulation is encompassed within the state's police power. . . .

It is elementary theory that all police power enactments, no matter at what level of government, must conform to the basic state constitutional requirements of substantive due process and equal protection of the laws. . . .

It is required that, affirmatively, a zoning regulation, like any police power enactment, must promote public health, safety, morals or the

---

40. While, as the trial court found, Mount Laurel's actions were deliberate, we are of the view that the identical conclusion follows even when municipal conduct is not shown to be intentional, but the effect is substantially the same as if it were.

general welfare. (The last term seems broad enough to encompass the others.) Conversely, a zoning enactment which is contrary to the general welfare is invalid. . . .

Indeed these considerations are specifically set forth in the zoning enabling act as among the various purposes of zoning for which regulations must be designed. N.J.S.A. 40:55-32. Their inclusion therein really adds little; the same requirement would exist even if they were omitted. If a zoning regulation violates the enabling act in this respect, it is also theoretically invalid under the state constitution. We say "theoretically" because, as a matter of policy, we do not treat the validity of most land use ordinance provisions as involving matters of constitutional dimension; that classification is confined to major questions of fundamental import. . . .

We consider the basic importance of housing and local regulations restricting its availability to substantial segments of the population to fall within the latter category.

The demarcation between the valid and the invalid in the field of land use regulation is difficult to determine, not always clear and subject to change. This was recognized almost fifty years ago in the basic case of Village of Euclid v. Ambler Realty Co., 272 U.S. 365, 47 S. Ct. 114, 71 L. Ed. 303 (1926). . . .

This court has also said as much and has plainly warned, even in cases decided some years ago sanctioning a broad measure of restrictive municipal decisions, of the inevitability of change in judicial approach and view as mandated by change in the world around us. . . .

The warning implicates the matter of *whose* general welfare must be served or not violated in the field of land use regulation. Frequently the decisions in this state . . . have spoken only in terms of the interest of the enacting municipality, so that it has been thought, at least in some quarters, that such was the only welfare requiring consideration. It is, of course, true that many cases have dealt only with regulations having little, if any, outside impact where the local decision is ordinarily entitled to prevail. However, it is fundamental and not to be forgotten that the zoning power is a police power of the state and the local authority is acting only as a delegate of that power and is restricted in the same manner as is the state. So, when regulation does have a substantial external impact, the welfare of the state's citizens beyond the borders of the particular municipality cannot be disregarded and must be recognized and served. . . .

This brings us to the relation of housing to the concept of general welfare just discussed and the result in terms of land use regulation which that relationship mandates. There cannot be the slightest doubt that shelter, along with food, are the most basic human needs. . . .

It is plain beyond dispute that proper provision for adequate housing of all categories of people is certainly an absolute essential in promotion of the general welfare required in all local land use regulation. Further the universal and constant need for such housing is so important and of such broad public interest that the general welfare which developing municipalities like Mount Laurel must consider extends beyond their boundaries and cannot be parochially confined to the claimed good of the particular municipality. It has to follow that, broadly speaking, the presumptive obligation arises for each such municipality affirmatively to plan and provide, by its land use regulations, the reasonable opportunity for an appropriate variety and choice of housing, including, of course, low and moderate cost housing, to meet the needs, desires and resources of all categories of people who may desire to live within its boundaries. Negatively, it may not adopt regulations or policies which thwart or preclude that opportunity.

It is also entirely clear, as we pointed out earlier, that most developing municipalities, including Mount Laurel, have not met their affirmative or negative obligations, primarily for local fiscal reasons. . . .

In sum, we are satisfied beyond any doubt that, by reason of the basic importance of appropriate housing and the long-standing pressing need for it, especially in the low and moderate cost category, and of the exclusionary zoning practices of so many municipalities, conditions have changed, and . . . judicial attitudes must be altered . . . to require, as we have just said, a broader view of the general welfare and the presumptive obligation on the part of developing municipalities at least to afford the opportunity by land use regulations for appropriate housing for all.

We have spoken of this obligation of such municipalities as "presumptive." The term has two aspects, procedural and substantive. Procedurally, we think the basic importance of appropriate housing for all dictates that, when it is shown that a developing municipality in its land use regulations has not made realistically possible a variety and choice of housing, including adequate provision to afford the opportunity for low and moderate income housing or has expressly prescribed requirements or restrictions which preclude or substantially hinder it, a facial showing of violation of substantive due process or equal protection under the state constitution has been made out and the burden, and it is a heavy one, shifts to the municipality to establish a valid basis for its action or non-action. . . .

The substantive aspect of "presumptive" relates to the specifics, on the one hand, of what municipal land use regulation provisions, or the absence thereof, will evidence invalidity and shift the burden of proof and, on the other hand, of what bases and considerations will carry the municipality's burden and sustain what it has done or failed to do. Both kinds of specifics may well vary between municipalities according to peculiar circumstances.

We turn to application of these principles in appraisal of Mount Laurel's zoning ordinance, useful as well, we think, as guidelines for future application in other municipalities.

The township's general zoning ordinance (including the cluster zone provision) permits, as we have said, only one type of housing — single-family detached dwellings. This means that all other types — multi-family including garden apartments and other kinds housing more than one family, town (row) houses, mobile home parks — are prohibited.[41] Concededly, low and moderate income housing has been intentionally excluded. While a large percentage of the population living outside of cities prefers a one-family house on its own sizeable lot, a substantial proportion do not for various reasons. Moreover, single-family dwellings are the most expensive type of quarters and a great number of families cannot afford them. Certainly they are not pecuniarily feasible for low and moderate income families, most young people and many elderly and retired persons, except for some of moderate income by the use of low cost construction on small lots.

As previously indicated, Mount Laurel has allowed some multi-family housing by agreement in planned unit developments, but only for the relatively affluent and of no benefit to low and moderate income families. And even here, the contractual agreements between municipality and developer sharply limit the number of apartments having more than one bedroom.[42] While the township's PUD ordinance has been repealed, we mention the subject of bedroom restriction because, assuming the overall validity of the PUD technique . . . , the measure could be reenacted and the subject is of importance generally. The design of such limitations is obviously to restrict the number of families in the municipality having school age children and thereby keep down local education costs. Such restrictions are so clearly contrary to the general welfare as not to require further discussion. Cf. Molino v. Mayor and Council of Borough of Glassboro, 116 N.J. Super. 195, 281 A.2d 401 (Law Div. 1971).

Mount Laurel's zoning ordinance is also so restrictive in its minimum lot area, lot frontage and building size requirements, earlier detailed, as to preclude single-family housing for even moderate income

41. Zoning ordinance restriction of housing to single-family dwellings is very common in New Jersey. Excluding six large, clearly rural townships, the percentage of remaining land zoned for multi-family use is only just over 1% of the net residential land supply in 16 of New Jersey's 21 counties. . . . Pennsylvania has held it unconstitutional for a developing municipality to fail to provide for apartments anywhere within it. Appeal of Girsh, 437 Pa. 237, 263 A.2d 395 (1970).

42. Apartment bedroom restrictions are also common in municipalities of the state which do allow multi-family housing. About 60% of the area zoned to permit multi-family dwellings is restricted to efficiency or one-bedroom apartments; another 20% permits two-bedroom units and only the remaining 20% allows units of three bedrooms or larger. . . .

families. Required lot area of at least 9,375 square feet in one remaining regular residential zone and 20,000 square feet (almost half an acre) in the other, with required frontage of 75 and 100 feet, respectively, cannot be called small lots and amounts to low density zoning, very definitely increasing the cost of purchasing and improving land and so affecting the cost of housing.[43] As to building size, the township's general requirements of a minimum dwelling floor area of 1,100 square feet for all one-story houses and 1,300 square feet for all of one and one-half stories or higher is without regard to required minimum lot size or frontage or the number of occupants. . . . Again it is evident these requirements increase the size and so the cost of housing. The conclusion is irresistible that Mount Laurel permits only such middle and upper income housing as it believes will have sufficient taxable value to come close to paying its own governmental way.

Akin to large lot, single-family zoning restricting the population is the zoning of very large amounts of land for industrial and related uses. Mount Laurel has set aside almost 30% of its area, over 4,100 acres, for that purpose; the only residential use allowed is for farm dwellings. In almost a decade only about 100 acres have been developed industrially. Despite the township's strategic location for motor transportation purposes, as intimated earlier, it seems plain that the likelihood of anywhere near the whole of the zoned area being used for the intended purpose in the foreseeable future is remote indeed and that an unreasonable amount of land has thereby been removed from possible residential development, again seemingly for local fiscal reasons.

Without further elaboration at this point, our opinion is that Mount Laurel's zoning ordinance is presumptively contrary to the general welfare and outside the intended scope of the zoning power in the particulars mentioned. A facial showing of invalidity is thus established, shifting to the municipality the burden of establishing valid superseding reasons for its action and non-action. We now examine the reasons it advances.

The township's principal reason in support of its zoning plan and ordinance housing provisions, advanced especially strongly at oral argument, is the fiscal one previously adverted to, i.e., that by reason of New Jersey's tax structure which substantially finances municipal governmental and educational costs from taxes on local real property, every municipality may, by the exercise of the zoning power, allow only such uses and to such extent as will be beneficial to the local tax rate. In other words, the position is that any municipality may zone extensively to seek and encourage the "good" tax ratables of industry and commerce and limit the permissible types of housing to those having the fewest school children or to those providing sufficient value to attain or approach paying their own way taxwise.

43. These restrictions are typical throughout the state. . . .

We have previously held that a developing municipality may properly zone for and seek industrial ratables to create a better economic
balance for the community vis-à-vis educational and governmental costs
engendered by residential development, provided that such was ". . .
done reasonably as part of and in furtherance of a legitimate comprehensive plan for the zoning of the entire municipality." Gruber v. Mayor
and Township Committee of Raritan Township, 39 N.J. 1, 9-11, 186
A.2d 489, 493 (1962). We adhere to that view today. But we were not
there concerned with, and did not pass upon, the validity of municipal
exclusion by zoning of types of housing and kinds of people for the same
local financial end. We have no hesitancy in now saying, and do so emphatically, that, considering the basic importance of the opportunity for
appropriate housing for all classes of our citizenry, no municipality may
exclude or limit categories of housing for that reason or purpose. While
we fully recognize the increasingly heavy burden of local taxes for municipal governmental and school costs on homeowners, relief from the
consequences of this tax system will have to be furnished by other
branches of government. It cannot legitimately be accomplished by restricting types of housing through the zoning process in developing municipalities.

The propriety of zoning ordinance limitations on housing for ecological or environmental reasons seems also to be suggested by Mount
Laurel in support of the one-half acre minimum lot size in that very
considerable portion of the township still available for residential development. It is said that the area is without sewer or water utilities and that
the soil is such that this plot size is required for safe individual lot sewage
disposal and water supply. The short answer is that, this being flat land
and readily amenable to such utility installations, the township could require them as improvements by developers or install them under the
special assessment or other appropriate statutory procedure. The
present environmental situation of the area is, therefore, no sufficient
excuse in itself for limiting housing therein to single-family dwellings on
large lots. Cf. National Land and Investment Co. v. Kohn, 419 Pa. 504,
215 A.2d 597 (1965). This is not to say that land use regulations should
not take due account of ecological or environmental factors or problems.
Quite the contrary. Their importance, at last being recognized, should
always be considered. Generally only a relatively small portion of a developing municipality will be involved, for, to have a valid effect, the
danger and impact must be substantial and very real (the construction
of every building or the improvement of every plot has some environmental impact) — not simply a makeweight to support exclusionary
housing measures or preclude growth — and the regulation adopted
must be only that reasonably necessary for public protection of a vital
interest. Otherwise difficult additional problems relating to a "taking"
of a property owner's land may arise.

By way of summary, what we have said comes down to this. As a developing municipality, Mount Laurel must, by its land use regulations, make realistically possible the opportunity for an appropriate variety and choice of housing for all categories of people who may desire to live there, of course including those of low and moderate income. It must permit multi-family housing, without bedroom or similar restrictions, as well as small dwellings on very small lots, low cost housing of other types and, in general, high density zoning, without artificial and unjustifiable minimum requirements as to lot size, building size and the like, to meet the full panoply of these needs. Certainly when a municipality zones for industry and commerce for local tax benefit purposes, it without question must zone to permit adequate housing within the means of the employees involved in such uses. (If planned unit developments are authorized, one would assume that each must include a reasonable amount of low and moderate income housing in its residential "mix," unless opportunity for such housing has already been realistically provided for elsewhere in the municipality.) The amount of land removed from residential use by allocation to industrial and commercial purposes must be reasonably related to the present and future potential for such purposes. In other words, such municipalities must zone primarily for the living welfare of people and not for the benefit of the local tax rate.

We have earlier stated that a developing municipality's obligation to afford the opportunity for decent and adequate low and moderate income housing extends at least to ". . . the municipality's fair share of the present and prospective regional need therefore." Some comment on that conclusion is in order at this point. Frequently it might be sounder to have more of such housing, like some specialized land uses, in one municipality in a region than in another, because of greater availability of suitable land, location of employment, accessibility of public transportation or some other significant reason. But, under present New Jersey legislation, zoning must be on an individual municipal basis, rather than regionally. So long as that situation persists under the present tax structure, or in the absence of some kind of binding agreement among all the municipalities of a region, we feel that every municipality therein must bear its fair share of the regional burden. (In this respect our holding is broader than that of the trial court, which was limited to Mount Laurel-related low and moderate income housing needs.)

The composition of the applicable "region" will necessarily vary from situation to situation and probably no hard and fast rule will serve to furnish the answer in every case. Confinement to or within a certain county appears not to be realistic, but restriction within the boundaries of the state seems practical and advisable. (This is not to say that a developing municipality can ignore a demand for housing within its boundaries on the part of people who commute to work in another state.) Here we have already defined the region at present as "those portions of Camden, Burlington and Gloucester Counties within a semicircle having a radius of 20 miles or so from the heart of Camden City." The concept of "fair share" is coming into more general use and, through the expertise of the municipal planning adviser, the county planning boards and the state planning agency, a reasonable figure for Mount Laurel can be determined, which can then be translated to the allocation of sufficient land therefor on the zoning map. . . .

There is no reason why developing municipalities like Mount Laurel, required by this opinion to afford the opportunity for all types of housing to meet the needs of various categories of people, may not become and remain attractive, viable communities providing good living and adequate services for all their residents in the kind of atmosphere which a democracy and free institutions demand. They can have industrial sections, commercial sections and sections for every kind of housing from low cost and multi-family to lots of more than an acre with very expensive homes. Proper planning and governmental cooperation can prevent over-intensive and too sudden development, insure against future suburban sprawl and slums and assure the preservation of open space and local beauty. We do not intend that developing municipalities shall be overwhelmed by voracious land speculators and developers if they use the powers which they have intelligently and in the broad public interest. Under our holdings today, they can be better communities for all than they previously have been.

III

The Remedy

[T]he trial court invalidated the zoning ordinance in toto and ordered the township to make certain studies and investigations and to present to the court a plan of affirmative public action designed "to enable and encourage the satisfaction of the indicated needs" for township related low and moderate income housing. Jurisdiction was retained for judicial consideration and approval of such a plan and for the entry of a final order requiring its implementation.

We are of the view that the trial court's judgment should be modified in certain respects. We see no reason why the entire zoning ordinance should be nullified. Therefore we declare it to be invalid only to the extent and in the particulars set forth in this opinion. The township is granted 90 days from the date hereof, or such additional time as the trial court may find it reasonable and necessary to allow, to adopt amendments to correct the deficiencies herein specified. It is the local function and responsibility, in the first instance at least, rather than the court's, to decide on the details of the same within the guidelines we have laid down. If plaintiffs desire to attack such amendments, they may do so by supplemental complaint filed in this cause within 30 days of the final adoption of the amendments.

We are not at all sure what the trial judge had in mind as ultimate action with reference to the approval of a plan for affirmative public action concerning the satisfaction of indicated housing needs and the entry of a final order requiring implementation thereof. Courts do not build housing nor do municipalities. That function is performed by private builders, various kinds of associations, or, for public housing, by special agencies created for that purpose at various levels of government. The municipal function is initially to provide the opportunity through appropriate land use regulations and we have spelled out what Mount Laurel must do in that regard. It is not appropriate at this time, particularly in view of the advanced view of zoning law as applied to housing laid down by this opinion, to deal with the matter of the further extent of judicial power in the field or to exercise any such power. . . . The municipality should first have full opportunity to itself act without judicial supervision. We trust it will do so in the spirit we have suggested, both by appropriate zoning ordinance amendments and whatever additional action encouraging the fulfillment of its fair share of the regional need for low and moderate income housing may be indicated as necessary and advisable. (We have in mind that there is at least a moral obligation in a municipality to establish a local housing agency pursuant to state law to provide housing for its resident poor now living in dilapidated, unhealthy quarters.) The portion of the trial court's judgment ordering the preparation and submission of the aforesaid study, report and plan to it for further action is therefore vacated as at least premature. Should Mount Laurel not perform as we expect, further judicial action may be sought by supplemental pleading in this cause.

The judgment of the Law Division is modified as set forth herein.

NOTES AND QUESTIONS

1. *The general picture.* Exclusionary zoning is not a thing just of the 1970s and '80s. For the last 40 years at least, suburban communities have resorted to various measures in an effort to restrict or bar particular uses — such as apartments, small houses on small lots, mobile homes — and to limit or foreclose entry by particular people, especially the poor and racial minorities. (More recently, some communities, to control growth generally, have tried to exclude everybody. See the Note on Growth Controls on page 1130.)

Growth controls aside for now, simple prejudice has much to do with exclusionary efforts, but — as the court in *Mount Laurel* indicates — fiscal concerns are also a powerful motivation. Ideally, *all* communities want low property taxes. Citizens obviously would rather spend their money in other ways, and they like the fact that low property taxes buoy up property values. Public officials want contented citizens who will keep them in office.

The straightforward way to achieve relatively low taxes is to have a handsome tax base (valuable property, especially nonresidential property), well-to-do residents, and low demand for such public services as water and sewer, schools, police and fire departments, public assistance programs, and so on. Translated into policy, this means measures to ensure a community of substantial and desirable industrial uses and expensive homes located in a low-density manner (say on large lots). With such a policy in place, residents will necessarily tend to have high incomes and, as a result, will probably be white; the typical family will have few children. Most of the workers in the local industries will be unable to live in the community or in other suburbs nearby (the other suburbs will be using exclusionary measures to pursue their own fiscal aims). They will reside in the central city.

2. *Exclusionary zoning before* Mount Laurel. Putting aside blatant efforts to exclude racial minorities and the poor,[44] and focusing on residential uses, there are essentially three techniques a community might use to exclude people whose characteristics (low income, high service demand) would interfere with the ideal fiscal picture: controls on minimum housing cost, minimum housing size, and minimum lot size. (Related techniques include prohibitions on mobile homes and on multifamily housing.)

The few early efforts to set *minimum housing-cost* requirements were invalidated by the courts. See, e.g., County Commrs. of Anne Arundel County v. Ward, 186 Md. 330, 46 A.2d 684 (1946); Appeal from Ordinance, Borough of Speers, 28 Wash. Co. 221 (Pa. Quar. Sess. 1948). *Minimum floor-area* requirements, often set without regard to the number of residents in a dwelling (and therefore lacking any apparent health and safety rationale), met with a more mixed judicial reaction, and the cases sustaining such measures tend to be dated. See generally Annot., 87 A.L.R.4th 294 (1991 & Supp. 1992).

Minimum lot-size requirements have fared the best of the three techniques. See, e.g., County Commrs. of Queen Anne's County v. Miles, 246 Md. 355, 228 A.2d 450 (1967) (upholding five-acre minimum, but where the municipality had provided for smaller lot sizes in other areas; low density was held to advance municipal concerns with sanitation,

---

44. As the *Elliott* case on page 1091 should suggest, racially discriminatory exclusionary zoning practices violate the federal Fair Housing Act. See Town of Huntington v. Huntington Branch, NAACP, 488 U.S. 15 (1988) (per curiam), aff'g 844 F.2d 926 (2d Cir. 1988). The ordinance at issue in *Huntington* prohibited apartments everywhere but in the town's urban renewal area, located in the central city and occupied mostly by minority residents. The town had denied a developer's request that the ordinance be amended to allow construction of subsidized multifamily housing in a white neighborhood. On the Fair Housing Act generally, see pages 441-461.

traffic problems, and protection of historic areas); Steel Hill Dev., Inc. v. Town of Sanbornton, 469 F.2d 956 (1st Cir. 1972) (upholding three- and six-acre minimums in rural resort area); Nopro Co. v. Town of Cherry Hills Village, 180 Colo. 217, 504 P.2d 344 (1972) (upholding two-and-a-half acre requirement for lots in village center). But in National Land & Inv. Co. v. Kohn, 419 Pa. 504, 215 A.2d 597 (1965), the court threw out a four-acre minimum in the face of arguments that it was designed to deal with sewage treatment and traffic problems, and to preserve the area's character. The real purpose, the court said, was to avoid economic burdens on the city. See also Appeal of Kit-Mar Builders, Inc., 439 Pa. 466, 268 A.2d 765 (1970) (two- and three-acre minimums; same holding). See generally Note, Judicial Acquiescence in Large Lot Zoning: Is It Time to Rethink the Trend?, 16 Colum. J. Envtl. L. 183 (1991) (majority upholds minimum lot-size regulations); Annots., 1 A.L.R.5th 622, 2 A.L.R.5th 553 (1992).

3. *The* Mount Laurel *case.* Notice that *Mount Laurel* is based on state, not federal, constitutional law. See Richard F. Babcock & Charles L. Siemon, The Zoning Game Revisited 210 (1985):

> [Justice] Hall was especially shrewd in his treatment of the constitutional issues. The plaintiffs had challenged the regulations under both the federal and New Jersey constitutions. He expressly based his opinion on the New Jersey Constitution, knowing that the U.S. Supreme Court could not then take the case for review; a state Supreme Court is the final arbiter of that state's constitution.

Justice Hall was aware that several decisions of the U.S. Supreme Court made federal constitutional law an uneasy basis for exclusionary zoning claims.[45]

Would you consider that the courts are capable of managing the concept of a "fair share of regional needs" developed in *Mount Laurel*? Some observers have thought not. See, e.g., Jerome G. Rose, Is the Decision Based on Wishful Thinking?, in After *Mount Laurel:* The New Suburban Zoning 183, 188 (Jerome G. Rose & Robert E. Rothman eds. 1977):

> The implementation of this decision requires studies and reports based upon interpretations of such indeterminate and ambiguous concepts as "fair

---

45. For example, the Supreme Court held in Lindsey v. Normet, 405 U.S. 56 (1972), that housing is not a fundamental right, and in San Antonio Indep. School Dist. v. Rodriguez, 411 U.S. 1 (1973), that wealth is not necessarily a suspect classification for purposes of the Equal Protection Clause of the U.S. Constitution.

On state courts turning to state constitutions to reach beyond Supreme Court interpretations of the federal Constitution, recall the discussion in Note 2 on page 1089. See also W. John Moore, In Whose Court, 23 Natl. J. 2396 (1991) ("state courts have sometimes simply ignored Supreme Court rulings, relying on the language of their states' constitutions to carve out exceptions to high court dogma").

share," "region," "future housing need," and "presumptively realistic efforts
to make possible an appropriate variety and choice of housing." Each concept
must be quantified, for each municipality, in terms of numbers of housing
units. This computation will be based upon underlying premises and theories
of extrapolation about which competent and honest professional planners
may differ. These differences in professional judgment can cause a wide disparity in the proposed number of housing units necessary to meet the requirements of the decision. It will be possible for a municipality to argue that
with a minimum contribution of new housing, its zoning ordinance has met
the prescribed standard of validity. A developer restricted by the ordinance
will disagree, and the statistical issues will be joined and argued in the courts.
The process of litigation has rarely been an inducement to housing construction.

See also Note, The Inadequacy of Judicial Remedies in Cases of Exclusionary Zoning, 74 Mich. L. Rev. 760 (1976); Note, Zoning for the Regional Welfare, 89 Yale L.J. 748 (1980). For a picture of some of the
complications entailed in fair-share housing allocation, see David Listo-
kin, Fair Share Housing Allocation (1976).

The line of thinking reflected above continues by asserting that state
or regional legislative and administrative bodies are best equipped to
deal with the problem of housing allocation. The argument to the contrary is two-fold. First, "rather than being a hopelessly vague and imprecise concept, the fair share principle can be consistently and equitably
applied and can therefore guide judicial supervision of local zoning
plans as well as provide a workable standard for local planning officials
who wish to comply voluntarily with their regional mandate." Developments in the Law — Zoning, 91 Harv. L. Rev. 1427, 1640-1641 (1978);
see also id. at 1644-1652; Conrad Bagne, The Parochial Attitudes of
Metropolitan Governments: An Argument for a Regional Approach to
Urban Planning and Development, 22 St. Louis U. L.J. 271 (1978). Second, whether or not state and regional bodies are best equipped to handle problems of exclusionary zoning, the fact is they have not been
responsive. See, e.g., Harold A. McDougall, The Judicial Struggle
Against Exclusionary Zoning: The New Jersey Paradigm, 14 Harv. C.R.-
C.L. L. Rev. 625, 651-653 (1979).

4. *After* Mount Laurel. It appears that the idea behind *Mount Laurel*
was essentially one of deregulation: Remove obstacles that local governments had put in the way of less costly housing and let the market respond. Newly constructed housing, even of modest residences, might be
beyond the reach of low-income people, but the increased supply would
let used housing trickle down to them at affordable prices.

Things did not work out quite that way. The New Jersey Supreme
Court itself seemed to draw away from the bold activist ambitions of
Mount Laurel. See Oakwood at Madison, Inc. v. Township of Madison,
72 N.J. 481, 371 A.2d 1192 (1977) (refusing to require judicial fair-share

quotas for low-cost housing, apparently regarding allocation of fair shares as a complex task better handled by legislative and administrative bodies). And communities engaged in a close reading of the *Mount Laurel* opinion. They saw, for example, that it applied only to "developing" communities. (Justice Hall later said "he had to make this exception to secure, for his unanimous judgment, two justices who were worried about small towns that were not in the path of the outward population explosion from the central cities." Babcock & Siemon, supra, at 210. A number of communities claimed that they were not "developing," and in some cases they won lawsuits on this ground. See, e.g., Pascack Assn., Ltd. v. Township of Washington, 74 N.J. 470, 379 A.2d 6 (1977). Other communities, noting Justice Hall's sympathy for environmental protection, pleaded that their local ecology was too sensitive to fall fully under *Mount Laurel*'s dictates. Still others fudged, changing their ordinances in such a way as to create the appearance, but not the reality, of compliance. The lower courts in New Jersey reviewed many of these cosmetic exercises with a deferential eye.

A host of questions developed in the wake of *Mount Laurel*: Was it even economically feasible to provide low-income housing opportunities outside urban areas? Was the developing-communities exception a mistake? Did an exclusionary motive have to be proved, or was an exclusionary effect sufficient? How far should the fair-share concept reach? What remedies should be available? And so on.

Meanwhile, the Township of Mount Laurel itself was shirking the obligations put on it by the court. Its new ordinance was upheld by the court below, see 161 N.J. Super. 317, 391 A.2d 935 (1978), but discarded as a complete failure in Southern Burlington County NAACP v. Township of Mount Laurel, 92 N.J. 158, 456 A.2d 390 (1983) — popularly known as *Mount Laurel II*.

Mount Laurel II (whose 120 pages in the Atlantic Reporter make the length of the opinion in the first case look like child's play) consolidated six cases and gave the court a chance to address at least some of the issues mentioned above. The court had learned, it said, that without a strong judicial hand there would not be more housing but only paper, process, and litigation. It also learned, or so it seems, that its original idea of deregulation and an unconstrained market was wrong; rather the need was for measures that *required* the production of low- and moderate-income housing. The court held, among other rulings, as follows:

Essentially, *every* municipality — not just developing ones — must provide a realistic opportunity for decent housing for its poor, except where (as in many urban areas) the poor represent a disproportionately large percentage of the population as compared to the rest of the region. Good faith attempts on the part of municipalities would be insufficient; each community must provide its fair share, expressed in terms of number of units needed immediately and in the future. It would not be enough for municipalities to remove barriers to low-cost construction; they were to undertake affirmative measures and to assist developers in obtaining state and federal aid. Affirmative measures might include inclusionary zoning devices — such as altering density limits in exchange for a developer's commitment to construct certain amounts of low- and moderate-income housing. (See Note 7 below.) Zones for mobile homes were to be created if necessary to meet the fair-share obligation. All future *Mount Laurel* litigation would be assigned to a group of three judges, a measure intended in part to ease the difficulties of calculating fair shares. Finally, the opinion confirmed a "builder's remedy" under which the trial court could allow a developer to go forth with a low-income project even though the municipality had not granted a permit.

On *Mount Laurel II,* see, e.g., Jerome G. Rose, The *Mount Laurel II* Decision: Is It Based on Wishful Thinking?, 12 Real Est. L.J. 115 (1983); Babcock & Siemon, supra, at 211-233; Symposium, 15 Rutgers L.J. 513 (1984); Symposium, 14 Seton Hall L. Rev. 829 (1984).

The end of the story? Hardly. Several years after *Mount Laurel II,* the New Jersey legislature enacted its own response to the ongoing problem of exclusionary zoning (the court had invited legislative action in its opinion). See the Fair Housing Act of 1985, N.J. Stat. Ann. §§52-27D-301 to 52-27D-329 (1986 & Supp. 1992), held constitutional in Hills Dev. Co. v. Bernards Township, 103 N.J. 1, 510 A.2d 621 (1986) (*Mount Laurel III,* of course). The legislation limits the availability of the builder's remedy discussed above; pending cases can under certain conditions be transferred to a Council on Affordable Housing created by the act and charged with the task of identifying and enforcing *Mount Laurel II* obligations.

A particularly interesting feature of the Fair Housing Act provides for regional contribution agreements whereby suburbs may, with Council approval, compensate cities for agreeing to absorb up to half of the suburbs' fair-share obligation. The legislation itself states that the purpose of this transfer option is to make use of the existing housing stock; suburban contributions will make it possible to rehabilitate substandard housing — presumably in the central cities. For commentary, see Harold A. McDougall, From Litigation to Legislation in Exclusionary Zoning Law, 22 Harv. C.R.-C.L. L. Rev. 623, 635-642 (1987).[46]

---

46. New Jersey is not the only state to enact exclusionary zoning legislation, nor was it the first. Massachusetts made the initial move with its Low and Moderate Income Housing Act of 1969. See Note, Anti-Snob Zoning in Massachusetts: Assessing One Attempt at Opening the Suburbs to Affordable Housing, 78 Va. L. Rev. 535 (1992). The Massachusetts law allows sponsors of low- or moderate-income housing projects to appeal local denials of development permission to a state committee, which can overturn local decisions found to be unreasonable in light of local and regional needs. George Judson, Housing Law Challenges Power of Zoning Boards, N.Y. Times, Nov. 5, 1991, at B5, reports that

Items from the news. An article by Robert Hanley, Housing the Poor in Suburbia: A Vision Lags in Jersey, N.Y. Times, June 1, 1987, at B1, reported that the Fair Housing Act was gutting *Mount Laurel,* whose aspirations had "gone largely unfulfilled." The suburbs were simply ignoring the state's Council on Affordable Housing; bills that would undercut its work were being proposed by suburban legislators. The builder's remedy was essentially dead. And the transfer option, according to critics, "turns the [*Mount Laurel*] doctrine upside down." The idea of *Mount Laurel* was to keep the poor from being locked into urban slums. The Fair Housing Act alters the effort to one aimed at reviving inner cities.

Two and a half years later, Hanley reported: "After 18 years of litigation and two landmark court rulings, New Jersey's *Mount Laurel* open-housing doctrine is embroiled in lawsuits again. . . ." All of the litigation involved the transfer option. Robert Hanley, Open Housing Is Mired in Lawsuits Again, N.Y. Times, Jan. 2, 1990, at B1. About a year later, an article in the Philadelphia Inquirer noted that the stated purpose of New Jersey's law "was to provide actual houses for real families — not to merely put meaningless numbers on a piece of paper." The article continued:

> In truth, though, 15 years after New Jersey's Supreme Court ordered local municipalities to provide for more affordable housing, meaningless numbers are all that most of the state's 567 towns have produced.
>
> Nearly a decade ago, experts projected that the court's ruling designed to give all residents a fair chance for a home in the suburbs would require the construction of 254,000 affordable homes statewide by now.
>
> The state has fallen 246,000 homes short of that goal. . . .
>
> To date, records show, many communities have in fact devoted less energy to constructing homes for low- and moderate-income families than to looking for creative ways to get around the ruling. For example:
>
> — Edison Township in Middlesex County claimed that 430 beds for Medicaid and Medicare patients were actually affordable homes. The state's Council on Affordable Housing (COAH) rejected the proposal. . . .
> — Princeton Township in Mercer County claimed 42 new apartments for graduate students at Princeton University as homes. The COAH rejected the proposal. . . .
> — Franklin Township in Somerset County claimed 71 apartments in an existing public housing project as new units. The town argued that because the federal government had repaired them, they should be counted as new houses. The state agreed.

[Alan Sipress, Despite Ruling, Affordable Homes Still Scarce in N.J., Phila. Inq., Nov. 25, 1990, at 1-A.]

Connecticut, New Hampshire, and Rhode Island have recently adopted zoning appeal laws similar in some respects to the Massachusetts legislation.

For more thoroughgoing accounts of progress since *Mount Laurel,* see, e.g., Martha Lamar, Alan Mallach & John M. Payne, *Mount Laurel at Work: Affordable Housing in New Jersey, 1983-1988,* 41 Rutgers L. Rev. 1197 (1989) (basically upbeat assessment); John M. Payne, Title VIII and *Mount Laurel:* Is Affordable Housing Fair Housing?, 6 Yale L. & Poly. Rev. 361 (1988) (prospects promising in long run); Colloquium, *Mount Laurel* and the Fair Housing Act: Success or Failure?, 19 Fordham Urb. L.J. 59-86 (1991) (mixed reviews).

5. *Other states.* Exclusionary zoning can be practiced anywhere, and not all state courts respond in the activist fashion of the New Jersey Supreme Court in *Mount Laurel.* Some, quite to the contrary, continue to honor the convention that zoning ordinances (exclusionary ordinances included) are presumed to be constitutional. The rational basis test of judicial review is applied and many measures survive. Others adopt a middle ground, say by maintaining the presumption of validity but judging the rationality of the measure in question with reference to regional as opposed to purely local interests. Still others are true to the spirit, but not necessarily the letter, of *Mount Laurel.*

As an instance of the latter, consider Britton v. Town of Chester, 134 N.H. 434, 595 A.2d 492 (1991). In *Britton,* the plaintiffs consisted of (1) a group of low- and moderate-income people who had been unsuccessful in finding decent affordable housing in the town, and (2) a builder who had been unsuccessful in getting permission from the local zoning authorities to develop an affordable housing complex on 23 acres of land he owned in the town. At the time the lawsuit was filed, the local zoning regulations permitted single-family residences on two-acre lots, duplexes on three-acre lots, and excluded multifamily housing from all five zoning districts in the town. The last provision was changed in 1986 to permit multifamily housing, but only if the housing were part of a planned residential development (PRD) that included single-family residences and duplexes as well.

The Supreme Court of New Hampshire accepted a master's finding that, despite the 1986 amendment, the zoning requirements placed unreasonable barriers in the way of affordable housing. In reality, for example, only a little less than 2 percent of the land in the town had been made available for PRDs. Beyond this, the new ordinance gave zoning authorities a "blank check," letting them impose expensive approval requirements without reference to any objective standards. "The master found such subjective review for developing multi-family housing to be a substantial disincentive to the creation of such units, because it would escalate the economic risks of developing affordable housing to the point where these projects would not be realistically feasible." 134 N.H. at 439, 595 A.2d at 495. The court held that the ordinance was unlawful as applied, and provided a builder's remedy:

We have previously addressed the issue of whether municipalities are required to consider regional needs when enacting zoning ordinances which control growth. In Beck v. Town of Raymond, 118 N.H. 793, 394 A.2d 847 (1978), we held that "[growth] controls must not be imposed simply to exclude outsiders, . . . especially outsiders of any disadvantaged social or economic group" [citing *Mount Laurel*]. We reasoned that "each municipality [should] bear its fair share of the burden of increased growth." . . . Today, we pursue the logical extension of the reasoning in *Beck* and apply its rationale and high purpose to zoning regulations which wrongfully exclude persons of low- or moderate-income from the zoning municipality. . . .

Although we determine that the "builder's remedy" is appropriate in this case, we do not adopt the *Mount Laurel* analysis for determining whether such a remedy will be granted. Instead, we [follow the rule of a number of states — Illinois, Michigan, Ohio, Pennsylvania, and Virginia — that] eliminates the calculation of arbitrary mathematical quotas which *Mount Laurel* requires. . . . Once an existing zoning ordinance is found invalid in whole or in part, whether on constitutional grounds or, as here, on grounds of statutory construction and application, the court may provide relief in the form of a declaration that the plaintiff builder's proposed use is reasonable, and the municipality may not interfere with it. . . . The plaintiff must bear the burden of proving reasonable use by a preponderance of the evidence. . . .

The zoning ordinance evolved as an innovative means to counter the problems of uncontrolled growth. It was never conceived to be a device to facilitate the use of governmental power to prevent access to a municipality by "outsiders of any disadvantaged social or economic group." . . . The town of Chester has adopted a zoning ordinance which is blatantly exclusionary. This court will not condone the town's conduct. [134 N.H. at 440-445, 595 A.2d at 495-498.][47]

6. *Exclusionary zoning and the Tiebout Hypothesis.* Are restrictions on exclusionary zoning definitely a good thing? Consider the following from Robert C. Ellickson & A. Dan Tarlock, Land-Use Controls 812 (1981):

A number of urban economists have suggested that specialization among suburbs is efficiency-enhancing. The seminal article is by Professor Charles Tiebout, A Pure Theory of Local Expenditures, 64 J. Pol. Econ. 416 (1956). The Tiebout Hypothesis (developed with the aid of several simplifying assumptions) is that consumers benefit from being able to "vote with their feet" among municipalities offering varying packages of public goods and taxation policies. For example, families most concerned with schooling would settle in jurisdictions with excellent schools; elderly individuals worried about public safety would pick locations with excellent police services; and so on. Under

47. See also Brian W. Blaesser et al., Advocating Affordable Housing in New Hampshire: The *Amicus Curiae* Brief of the American Planning Association in *Wayne Britton v. Town of Chester*, in Symposium on Growth Management and Exclusionary Zoning, 40 Wash. U. J. Urb. & Contemp. L. at 3 (1991).

Tiebout's assumptions, the specialization of municipalities and the competition among them would enhance the efficiency of metropolitan organization because people would tend to get the public goods they most preferred.

The Tiebout Hypothesis may be contrasted with what might be called a "Waring Blender model," which would call for all land uses and all types of households to be represented in each neighborhood in proportion to their representation in the entire metropolitan area. . . . Note that the Waring Blender model produces great diversity *within* neighborhoods, but no diversity *between* neighborhoods, and thus may limit the variety of residential choices available to households.

An efficient Tiebout outcome requires that everybody living in a locality pay the same amount of taxes (called head taxes) for public goods provided by the local government. (Can you see why?) Local governments in the United States do not rely much on head taxes, but zoning regulations, by effectively setting minimum values on property in the area, can help ensure that residents pay taxes in proportion to the services or public goods they receive. For this reason, exclusionary zoning practices can have efficiency-enhancing properties. Unfortunately, however, they can also have very undesirable effects. First, they distribute wealth away from people with low incomes. Second, they generate spillovers (negative externalities) between communities, and these can result in *in*efficiencies that more than outweigh the efficiency gains of specialization. Such as what? For discussion and a review of the literature, see Michael H. Schill, Deconcentrating the Inner City Poor, 67 Chi.-Kent L. Rev. 795, 811-821 (1991); Michael H. Schill, The Federal Role in Reducing Regulatory Barriers to Affordable Housing in the Suburbs, 7 J.L. & Poly. 703, 716-722 (1992) (also discussing the case for increased *federal* oversight of suburban exclusionary practices).

7. *Inclusionary zoning.* Inclusionary zoning consists of any number of devices designed to require or encourage developers to supply low- and moderate-income housing. Examples: (1) A requirement — conditioning a building permit on the builder's agreement to provide a certain number of units for lease at below-market rents. (As an extreme example, recall the *Seawall* case discussed on pages 558-559.) The courts have divided on the legality of such measures. (2) An incentive — lifting density limits in exchange for the builder's agreement to build more low-income units. Can you see how inclusionary zoning might backfire, becoming exclusionary in effect? See Robert C. Ellickson, The Irony of "Inclusionary" Zoning, 54 S. Cal. L. Rev. 1167 (1981).

NOTE: GROWTH CONTROLS

Growth controls aim — nominally anyway — to keep out everybody; the idea is to stop or slow development. For example, a munici-

Drawing by H. Martin; © 1970
The New Yorker Magazine, Inc.

pality might put a moratorium on building permits, or time their issuance, or establish a quota.

Associated Home Builders v. City of Livermore, 18 Cal. 3d 582, 557 P.2d 473, 135 Cal. Rptr. 41 (1976), involved the first technique. The court there upheld a plan that stopped all development until school, sewage, and water supply problems were solved. But moratoriums have become somewhat more vulnerable as a consequence of several U.S. Supreme Court cases decided in 1987 (and considered in the next chapter). For discussion, see Richard J. Roddewig, Recent Developments in Land Use, Planning and Zoning Law, 22 Urb. Law. 719, 768-779 (1990).

In Golden v. Planning Bd. of Ramapo, 30 N.Y.2d 359, 285 N.E.2d 291, 334 N.Y.S.2d 138, appeal dismissed, 409 U.S. 1003 (1972), the town of Ramapo used timing controls that required developers to accumulate points before a project could go forth. Points were awarded based on the availability of sewage systems, schools, roads, parks, fire departments, and so on. An eager developer could earn points faster by providing some of these. The court approved the scheme, regarding it not as exclusionary but as a means to phase development and provide a balanced community and efficient land use. For a discussion of the significance of the case and a review of statewide (as opposed to local) growth controls used in various jurisdictions, see Note, *Golden v. Planning Bd. of*

Ramapo Revisited: Old Lessons for New Problems, 12 Pace L. Rev. 107 (1992).

Finally, the use of quotas is illustrated by Construction Indus. Assn. v. City of Petaluma, 522 F.2d 897 (9th Cir. 1975), cert. denied, 424 U.S. 934 (1976). The city first established a moratorium in order to give planners a chance to study problems brought on by a booming population, then set up a system that allowed only a certain number of units to be constructed each year. The court, aware that the plan had exclusionary effects, upheld it nevertheless as rationally related to the social and environmental welfare of the community.

According to one recent study, growth controls have proliferated over the last decade. In California alone, more than 200 growth control ordinances have appeared on city ballots since 1981; 70 percent of those proposed in the last several years have been approved. When they are challenged, "success is rare." See Note, That Old Due Process Magic: Growth Control and the Federal Constitution, 88 Mich. L. Rev. 1245, 1247 (1990).

Should the courts be so deferential, simply because growth controls do not on their face exclude low-income people? What impact do they have on the surrounding region?[48] On the poor? (Most studies find, unsurprisingly, that growth controls increase housing prices.)

How are growth controls likely to affect the value of *un*developed land? Does this tell you anything about the politics of growth-control measures? See Robert C. Ellickson, Suburban Growth Controls: An Economic and Legal Analysis, 86 Yale L.J. 385 (1977). On growth controls generally, see the articles collected in Growth Management and the Environment in the 1990s, 24 Loy. L.A. L. Rev. 905-1245 (1991).

E.   Is Zoning Necessary?

William Fischel, in his study The Economics of Zoning Laws (1985), devotes a chapter midway through to the question whether zoning matters. He anticipates that his readers, having worked through 230 pages of the book, will say it "had darn well *better*. . . ." (Id. at 231.) Your sentiments are no doubt the same.

Relax. Zoning will undoubtedly remain a standard part of the American land-use picture into the foreseeable future. Whether it need

---

48. See Julia Hayward Biggs, No Drip, No Flush, No Growth: How Cities Can Control Growth Beyond Their Boundaries by Refusing to Extend Utility Services, 22 Urb. Law. 285 (1990); Susan M. Wachter & Man Cho, Interjurisdictional Price Effects of Land Use Controls, in Symposium on Growth Management and Exclusionary Zoning, 40 Wash. U. J. Urb. & Contemp. L. 49 (1991).

(or should) remain, however, raises a nice set of questions: What are the costs and benefits of zoning? What are the alternatives? Can standard practices and alternative approaches be melded into some improved approach to land-use problems? Do we have any theory to draw upon? Any evidence? This brief section addresses some of these questions, though hardly in exhaustive fashion (for those who wish to pursue the topic, there is a bibliographic note at the end; it isn't exhaustive either).

To get the inquiry going, recall the conventional justification for zoning. The following is from Daniel R. Mandelker, The Zoning Dilemma 23-24 (1971):

> [T]he exercise of the zoning function is predicated on a "gap hypothesis." While the zoning ordinance contains the legislative allocation of land uses on a community scale, the implementation of the development pattern contemplated by the ordinance is left to private initiative. In other words, there is a gap between the adoption of the zoning framework and its execution in the market place. Implementation of the ordinance depends on an appropriate private market response, both at the right place and at the right time.
>
> But why, if we rely on the private market to implement the zoning ordinance, do we need the zoning ordinance in the first place? Cannot the market be trusted to make land use allocations which are appropriate for the community? In the absence of a zoning ordinance, the community land development pattern would be a summation of a series of development decisions made individually by private entrepreneurs, acting to maximize their own opportunity gains and to minimize their own opportunity costs. Why not assume that the sum of these individual development decisions represents a collective public interest which we can legally sanction? The answer lies in whether we perceive the land market as making perfect or imperfect allocations through the pricing system. We might achieve a helpful perspective on this problem by noting, as we have stated, that each entrepreneur in that market need consider only his own opportunity costs and gains. He is not compelled by the private market to consider the externalities which his own development decision may visit on others. . . . A zoning ordinance based on the separation of land use incompatibilities must therefore intervene to prevent the visitation of externalities which the private market cannot prevent. By making district allocations predicated on land use separation, zoning ordinances correct for the externalities which the private market need not consider.

1. Criticisms of Zoning: A Summary

As imperfect as the land market might be, we should not overlook that zoning is not so perfect either. As you have seen throughout this chapter (and as Professor Mandelker, a noted scholar in the fields of land use and zoning, well knows), zoning is fraught with problems and abuses of its own. One question, then, is whether zoning is more or less imperfect, from relevant perspectives, than its alternatives. Another question is what those alternatives are. The market, after all, is not the only other choice. Between its marked decentralization and the highly centralized approach of zoning rest other methods, studied earlier, like nuisance law and covenants.

Let us consider here an aspect of the first question by drawing together what are said to be the central vices of zoning. Our source is a leading work on the subject of this Note, Robert C. Ellickson, Alternatives to Zoning: Covenants, Nuisance Rules, and Fines as Land Use Controls, 40 U. Chi. L. Rev. 681 (1973). Evaluating zoning from the viewpoints of efficiency and equity, Ellickson reaches some rather discouraging conclusions. While zoning does reduce social costs by segregating incompatible uses, it often goes too far. For example, small, single-family neighborhoods are protected by prohibiting apartments in the area. This often means that apartment dwellers must live at a distance from their work, "impos[ing] substantially higher commuting costs on a large segment of the population, and aggravat[ing] their city's traffic, noise, and pollution problems." Id. at 695. As other examples of measures that result in more costs than they abate, Ellickson cites minimum lot-size and maximum building-size (bulk) controls. The first encourage sprawl, the second ugly and inefficient buildings.

The costs of shortcomings like the foregoing are aggravated, Ellickson argues, by the high administrative costs of zoning — the direct public expense of running the system, the indirect private expense borne by citizens who must learn what the regulations require, apply for permits, seek exceptions and amendments. And for all of its net costs, Ellickson finds zoning to be inequitable. It works unfair redistributions of wealth, promotes economic and racial segregation, and invites and responds to special influence.

> The problems just illustrated have not won zoning many friends other than the 9,000 governments that employ it. Most critics of zoning focus their attack on specific flaws. Jane Jacobs attacked zoning's lack of flexibility while ignoring, for example, the compensation problem. Civil rights groups are disturbed by the exclusionary use of zoning, but rarely condemn the resulting efficiency losses. Without an overall framework for evaluating land use control systems, critics may propose reforms that sensibly ameliorate their particular concerns, but exacerbate other problems. For example, a suggestion to upgrade the staff and procedures of the land planning structure is sound only if the benefit from these changes will exceed the required increase in administrative costs. Similarly, more frequent compensation for losses inflicted by zoning decisions will solve equity problems and tend to make planners more concerned about efficiency, but again at the expense of increased administrative costs. Shifting land use planning power to state or regional units would reduce the present evils of parochialism and balkanization, but

larger units are less responsive and less locally knowledgeable than smaller ones and may draft crude ordinances. A tiered system, with the state handling statewide issues and localities handling local issues, is possible, but increased costs of defining and policing jurisdictional limits would result. Whether any of these narrow reforms is sound depends ultimately on the relative size of the efficiency gains and losses and the effect of the reform on the fairness of the system.

Most of the zoning reforms that have been proposed do not address the three fundamental weaknesses of the institution: (1) exclusive reliance on mandatory public standards, (2) concentration on prospective development with little attention to existing land use problems, and (3) sharp and frequent variability of regulations among zones. [Id. at 705-706.]

2. Is Zoning Necessary — In Principle?

Ellickson concludes that zoning is "out of control and must be severely curtailed, if not entirely replaced." Id. at 781. Land use should be regulated instead by a system that would rely heavily on less centralized means, primarily convenants and nuisance law. With some revamping of present doctrine, plus a few additions to it, such a system could, Ellickson believes, be put into operation. His proposal is rich in detail and deserves more attention than space allows here, but we can sketch the high points.

Consensual arrangements such as convenants can be relied upon to some degree as fruitful mechanisms for land-use control, especially in relatively undeveloped areas and in situations where there are no third-party effects likely to be ignored by covenantors. Where these conditions do not prevail, more coercive devices are necessary. Here Ellickson would rely chiefly on nuisance law, reformulated in such a way as to promote fairness and efficiency. (See Chapter 10.) Private nuisance law would be suitable for "localized spillovers" — those concerning no more than a few dozen parties. In the case of "pervasive nuisances" — those causing widespread injury that is usually insubstantial as to any one victim — a more centralized system of fines would apply. The fines would be assessed by local public authorities — "nuisance boards" — and would complement the more typical nuisance remedies available to people suffering substantial harm from pervasive nuisances. (The boards would have primary jurisdiction over nuisance cases and power to award injunctions and damages.) Fines could prove unsuitable for some pervasive nuisances; for example, there may be no objective way to arrive at an appropriate schedule of fines by which to regulate subdivision design or aesthetic blight. In such instances Ellickson would provide, but only reluctantly, for mandatory enforcement of minimum standards. Of all of present-day zoning, only that remnant would remain.

3.   Is Zoning Necessary — In Practice?

If Ellickson's proposal strikes you as unrealistic, consider that an even more decentralized, laissez-faire system operated in Houston for some years and was widely (but not universally) regarded as a success. See Bernard H. Siegan, Non-Zoning in Houston, 13 J.L. & Econ. 71 (1970). The city had typical subdivision controls and building codes, but not a zoning ordinance. It also had a city planning department that functioned much like such departments in other large cities, making studies and recommendations for the location of streets, parks, public buildings, utilities, and so forth. There were some zoning-like public restrictions in Houston, but they were modest. There were no specific constraints on the uses that could be made of property, but the subdivision regulations, applicable to some but not all development, provided for minimum lot widths, minimum lot areas, and setback lines.

Nuisance law figures prominently in Ellickson's proposal, discussed above; by way of contrast, restrictive covenants were the linchpin of Houston's system. Typically the covenants were privately drafted, but under a special state statute the city had the power to enforce the covenants "to about the same extent as if it were the owner of property benefited by them." Siegan, supra, at 77. There is evidence that this enforcement power was not essential; the covenants would probably be observed or privately enforced in any event.

The following discussion suggests some of Siegan's central observations and conclusions regarding Houston (id. at 91, 128-129, 141-144):

> How does Houston compare in appearance with zoned cities? Has the absence of zoning created ugliness and visual disorder and disarray? Although some have attempted to answer these questions,[49] it would seem impossible to evaluate the aesthetics and physical composition of over 450 square miles of real estate and compare such a determination with a similar area elsewhere. There certainly are a great many areas of single-family occupancy that look identical to the "idyllic" areas of the zoned cities. There are also mixtures of uses available for those wishing to demonstrate the ill effects of non-zoning. Frequently, however, the same mixtures exist in cities that are zoned.[50] . . .

49. Irvin Stander, Land Use Controls in Houston, Texas, The Legal Intelligencer, Sept. 14, 1967, finds the city unattractive; M.W. Lee, Zoning: Myth or Magic, The Real Estate Appraiser, at 2 (Apr. 1964) finds the city attractive.

50. An illustration of this can be seen in a photograph published in House and Home Magazine, May 1967, at 10, showing a gas station next to an apartment building. The legend below the photo seems to attribute such a mixture of uses to "no zoning." The same sight would hardly attract much attention in many zoned cities, since it is not uncommon for apartments to be permitted next to commercial uses for a variety of "sound" planning reasons. For example, under the Chicago zoning ordinance, gas stations and apartments are both permitted in six of its eleven business and commercial zones. Similar provisions

In many respects it is apparent that Houston, a non-zoned city, does not differ from what it would be if it were zoned. However, there are at least three characteristics of the non-zoned city that distinguish it from the zoned city, and they are as follows:

1. The relative absence of restrictions on apartment development has allowed the market to satisfy the demand for apartments to a much greater degree than could occur under zoning controls. Rents are probably less as a consequence for most tenants. Among the beneficiaries are those tenants of lesser income levels who have been able to afford new apartments but probably would have been unable to do so if Houston had been zoned.

2. More areas adjoining major thoroughfares (that is, arterial and collector streets) are being used, or will be used, for all varieties of commercial and multiple-family purposes than would be the case under zoning.

3. There are probably more non-home uses in "interior" single-family areas than would be present if these areas had been zoned for single-family.

Some or all of the foregoing may have occurred at the expense of some single-family values. In general, however, the value of most homes is no more affected than they would be under the "protection" of zoning. The greater likelihood is that on the whole property values have been augmented. . . .

These in brief are the conclusions drawn from this examination of Houston's system of non-zoning, with appropriate comparisons with, and conclusions about zoning:

1. Economic forces tend to make for a separation of uses even without zoning. Business uses will tend to locate in certain areas, residential in others, and industrial in still others. Apartments, however, may be built in almost any area except within an industrial one. There is also a tendency for further separation within a category; light industrial uses do not want to adjoin heavy industrial uses, and vice versa. Different kinds of business uses require different locations. Expensive homes will separate from less expensive ones, town-houses, duplexes, etc. It is difficult to assess the effectiveness of zoning in furthering this process. It is highly successful in this respect in the "bedroom" suburbs, but much less so in the larger cities.

2. When these economic forces do not guarantee that there will be a separation, and separation is vital to maximize profits (or promote one's tastes and desires), property owners will enter into agreements to provide such protection. The restrictive covenants covering home and industrial subdivisions are the most prominent example of this. Adjoining property owners (such as those on a strip location) can also make agreements not to sell for a use that will be injurious to one or both.

3. Because many of the early restrictive covenants in Houston were (a) limited in duration, or (b) legally insufficient, or (c) not enforced by owners, zoning would have kept more areas as strictly single-family. The covenants created subsequent to 1950 were more durable and as a practical matter will remain in force for long periods. They may be as effective as zoning in maintaining single-family homogeneity.

_____

can be found in the zoning ordinances of Dallas and Los Angeles, and probably most large cities.

4. When covenants expire, land and properties will be used as economic pressures dictate. Most business uses will not locate on interior streets because they require favorable traffic conditions available only on major thoroughfares. Within recent years, the most important factor influencing diversity in non-restricted interior areas is the strong demand for multiple-family accommodations. But this demand does not extend to all sections of the city. Accordingly, some areas fronting on interior streets will remain relatively free of diverse uses after their covenants expire.

5. A non-zoned city is a cosmopolitan collection of property uses. The standard is supply and demand, and if there is economic justification for the use, it is likely to be forthcoming. Zoning restricts the supply of some uses, and thereby prevents some demands from being satisfied. It may likewise impede innovation. However, in general, zoning in the major cities, which contain diverse life styles, has responded and accommodated to most consumer demands. This has not occurred usually in the more homogeneous suburbs.

6. Zoning is a legislative function. As such, political, economic and social pressures of many, or even a relatively few, often influence or control zoning decisions. These pressures may even be more important than the provisions of the zoning ordinance. Such forces play no part in a non-zoned city.

7. The most measurable influence of zoning is its effect on multiple family dwellings. If Houston had adopted zoning in 1962, this would probably have resulted in higher rents and a lesser number and variety of apartments and, in consequence, some tenants would have been priced out of the new apartment market. Most adversely affected would be tenants of average incomes.

8. The experience of the FHA suggests that the appreciation over the years in values of new and existing single-family homes has not differed in Houston from those of zoned cities.

9. The role of planning under zoning is a curious one. The original zoning ordinance will largely freeze the existing pattern of land use. All subsequent decisions on the ordinance will be made through the legislative process, which would seem inherently more responsive to political and economic opinion and pressures than the recommendations of the planners. As one result, changes in zoning in the major cities seem to follow a more chaotic than orderly pattern.

10. In Houston, the level of control over land use and development has not increased appreciably over the years. The most significant policy adopted in recent years has been the city's enforcement since 1965 of the restrictive covenants in residential subdivisions. By contrast, zoning has tended to give the municipality greater and more minute control. One reason is that the failure of existing controls has usually led to more severe controls, not lesser ones.

Much criticism has been levelled at zoning within recent years. It might almost seem from reading the commentaries, that no matter how bad the Houston system, it could hardly be worse than what is described as having occurred under zoning. Yet it is clear that the critics are not moved to study the Houston system. Instead, they advocate additional government controls over the use and development of property. The dogma persists that if zoning does not work, it is desirable to try more of it. Given the history of zoning, the new efforts will lead in their turn to even more controls.

The experience of Houston should not be ignored by those seeking to solve problems stemming from property use and developments by the use of zoning techniques. Instead of newer and stronger controls, the reverse approach may be in order. About 40 years have elapsed since the Commerce Department persuaded state legislatures to enact legislation authorizing zoning ordinances. The changes that have occurred since then have often not been for the better; the opposite is nearer the truth. Government has acquired more powers when less was warranted. Zoning in this respect has not differed from the usual pattern of government regulation. The example of Houston is sufficiently clear, however, to warrant at least an exception to the rule in the area of zoning.

NOTES: MORE ON HOUSTON, AND A BRIEF BIBLIOGRAPHY

1. *On Houston.* An expanded version of Siegan's study is Land Use Without Zoning (1972). William A. Fischel, The Economics of Zoning Laws 233 (1985), says Siegan's work

is most useful as an antidote to assertions about the absolute necessity of zoning in our complex, interdependent, urban society. Houston functions well enough to attract plenty of immigrants. Other cities of comparable size seem to have at least as many urban problems.

Yet the real question is not whether Houston works but whether it works as well as it would under zoning. I admit that the question is a very difficult one, but the evidence that Siegan presents is not entirely convincing. Housing prices may indeed be lower in Houston. Maybe that's because of nuisances that zoning would have prevented. We so often concentrate on zoning as excessively raising the price of housing that we forget that housing might be priced too low if it is devalued by the threat of uncompensated nuisances.

The other problem with the study is that Houston is a large central city. . . . [C]entral cities generally are less restrictive than suburbs. The more important question about zoning is its effect on the suburbs. Since Houston's municipal boundaries encompass both the downtown and, to an extent unusual among large metropolitan areas, most of its suburbs, it is hard to say what the effect of nonzoning would be in independent suburban districts.

For better or worse, Houston is now headed in the direction of conventional zoning. In 1991 the city established a planning and zoning commission responsible for creating a new master plan for the city and a zoning code to implement the plan. "The creation of the code will eliminate Houston's controversial distinction as the only major city in the

United States without zoning." Houston Establishes Planning and Zoning Commission, 14 Zoning & Plan. L. Rep. 119 (1991). See also Lisa Belkin, Houston Journal: Now That City's Grown, They Plan, N.Y. Times, Feb. 10, 1991, at A14, reporting that "[e]ven the strongest supporters of zoning say it will be years before dramatic changes will be seen in most neighborhoods."

Professor John Mixon of the University of Houston Law Center was actively involved in the Houston developments. See his Neighborhood Zoning for Houston, 31 S. Tex. L. Rev. 1 (1990).

2. *A brief bibliography.* See, in addition to the works cited throughout this section (most of which themselves contain useful bibliographies) the following: Orlando E. Delogu, Local Land Use Controls: An Idea Whose Time Has Passed, 36 Me. L. Rev. 261 (1984); Douglas W. Kmiec, Deregulating Land Use: An Alternative Free Enterprise Development System, 130 U. Pa. L. Rev. 28 (1981); Jan. Z. Krasnowiecki, Abolish Zoning, 31 Syracuse L. Rev. 719 (1980); Zoning and the American Dream: Promises Still to Keep (Charles M. Haar & Jerold S. Kayden eds. 1989); Note, A Walk Along Willow: Patterns of Land Use Coordination in Pre-Zoning New Haven (1870-1926), 101 Yale L.J. 617 (1991).

12
Eminent Domain and the Problem of Regulatory Takings

Unsatisfied with private arrangements (servitudes) and nuisance law as means of land-use control, the government might and often does embark on more activist courses — leaving property in the hands of its owners but regulating its use, or taking property from its owners and reallocating it to governmentally preferred uses.[1] The first approach, *regulating,* is illustrated by the method of zoning, studied in the last chapter. The second approach, *taking,* is the method of eminent domain, to be considered here.

That the government has the power of eminent domain is, as we shall see, a point long beyond dispute. There are constraints, however. The Fifth Amendment enjoins, "nor shall private property be taken for public use, without just compensation."[2] As it happens, this language limits not only the government's right literally to take property through the power of eminent domain, but its freedom to regulate property as well. In regulating through zoning or other means, the government might at times be said to have expropriated what it claimed only to control; so too in carrying out the myriad other activities that attend the modern state.[3] Some of the most intractable issues in the jurisprudence of property concern the matter of just when — under what circumstances — such governmental activities should be regarded as takings.

---

1. Reallocation might be part of a grand scheme (for example, an urban renewal program intended to upgrade a slum area) or might instead involve a narrow, self-serving transfer (say the government wants a piece of land for a post office).

2. Virtually all state constitutions have similar language; in any event, the Fifth Amendment applies to the states through the due process clause of the Fourteenth Amendment.

3. Thus we saw takings issues arise, for example, in connection with zoning (recall the discussion of nonconforming uses beginning on page 1011), in connection with the right to exclude (see footnote 48 on page 100), and in connection with rent controls (see pages 556-559). Some of these matters will be revisited in this chapter.

A.   The Power of Eminent Domain: Sources and Rationales

Eminent domain is the power of government to force transfers of property from owners to itself.[4] Notice that the Fifth Amendment does not grant the taking power, but only confirms it — "a tacit recognition of a pre-existing power. . . ." United States v. Carmack, 329 U.S. 230, 241-242 (1946). The origins of eminent domain,[5] it appears, can be traced back to ancient Rome, where property could be taken for public projects (the evidence suggests that owners received compensation). English sovereigns enjoyed similar powers; indeed, they had no obligation to pay compensation (save in limited instances regarding seizure of provisions for the use of the royal household — a prerogative later abolished). By the time of the American Revolution, the power of the British government to take private property for public uses was well established, notwithstanding Sir William Blackstone's overstatement that "So great . . . is the regard of the law for private property, that it will not authorize the least violation of it; no, not even for the general good of the whole community." 1 William Blackstone, Commentaries*139. While never required to do so, the British Parliament has commonly paid compensation in the course of appropriating land for public purposes.

Early American practice regarding eminent domain was heavily influenced by the precedent of English experience. The power of government to take private property was recognized, though compensation was hardly universal in colonial times (a perhaps insignificant matter, given abundant land and very meager public development). Gradually, however, statutes came to provide for compensation, and some judges required it even in the absence of legislation. Constitutional provisions began to appear in the late 1700s, and by the end of the first half of the nineteenth century a trend in this direction had developed. Such provisions eventually became the norm; by the time the United States Constitution was held to require compensation by the states, it appears they were already providing it on their own — through constitutional or judge-made law.

Various rationales for the taking power have been offered over the

4. Or to other entities commonly invested with the power of eminent domain, such as public utilities and public schools, or, at times, to other private parties. See, e.g., the *Midkiff* case on page 1146.

5. For extended discussion, see 1 Phillip Nichols, The Law of Eminent Domain §§1.1-1.3 (rev. 3d ed. 1992). See also Fred P. Bosselman, David L. Callies & John Banta, The Taking Issue ch. 6 (1973); Morton J. Horwitz, The Transformation of American Law 63-66 (1977); James W. Ely, Jr., "That due satisfaction may be made:" the Fifth Amendment and the Origins of the Compensation Principle, 36 Am. J. Legal Hist. 1 (1992); Note, The Origins and Original Significance of the Just Compensation Clause of the Fifth Amendment, 94 Yale L.J. 694 (1985).

years. Early civil law scholars like Grotius and Pufendorf (to whom you were introduced in Chapter 1 — see page 24) argued essentially that sovereign states had original and absolute ownership of property, prior to possession by citizens; individual possession derived from grants from the state and was held subject to an implied reservation that the state might resume its ownership. Another rationale is that eminent domain is the natural consequence of royal prerogatives that inhered in the concept of feudalism; on this view, the taking power is a remnant of feudal tenures. Finally, it has been argued, especially by natural law theorists, that eminent domain is an inherent attribute of sovereignty, necessary to the very existence of government.

Each of these notions has been reflected to some degree in American law, the last being the most common rationale today. Notice that none of the rationales really explains the obligation to compensate, as opposed to the power to take. In fact, there is very little historical evidence on the motivations behind the requirement of just compensation. Various accounts attribute it to a moral imperative of the natural law view of eminent domain; to English practice; to the views of Blackstone, at one time as influential in America as in England, in favor of "full indemnification"; and to a shift from traditional republican ideology to a liberalism that carried with it distrust of legislatures and a concern for individual rights. Related to the last point is speculation that James Madison, in drafting the Fifth Amendment, inserted the compensation requirement to guard the propertied classes from egalitarian redistributions of wealth.

NOTES AND QUESTIONS

1. *The power to take.* Richard Posner sketches a functional justification for the taking power, a justification that stresses efficiency. See Richard A. Posner, Economic Analysis of Law 56-57 (4th ed. 1992):

> A good economic argument for eminent domain, although one with greater application to railroads and other right-of-way companies than to the government, is that it is necessary to prevent monopoly. Once the railroad or pipeline has begun to build its line, the cost of abandoning it for an alternative route becomes very high. Knowing this, people owning land in the path of the advancing line will be tempted to hold out for a very high price — a price in excess of the opportunity cost of the land. (This is a problem of bilateral monopoly. . . .) Transaction costs will be high, land-acquisition costs high, and for both reasons the right-of-way company will have to raise the price of its services. The higher price will induce some consumers to shift to substitute services. Right-of-way companies will therefore have a smaller output; as a result they will need, and buy, less land than they would have bought at prices equal to the opportunity costs of the land. Higher land prices will also give

the companies an incentive to substitute other inputs for some of the land they would have bought. As a result of all this, land that would have been more valuable to a right-of-way company than to its present owners will remain in its existing, less valuable uses, and this is inefficient. . . .

This analysis shows that the distinction between conflicting claims to a resource and conflicting or incompatible uses of resources is not fundamental. What is fundamental is the distinction between settings of low transaction costs and of high transaction costs. In the former, the law should require the parties to transact in the market; it can do this by making the present owner's property right absolute (or nearly so), so that anyone who thinks the property is worth more has to negotiate with the owner. But in settings of high transaction costs people must be allowed to use the courts to shift resources to a more valuable use, because the market is by definition unable to perform this function in those settings. This distinction is only imperfectly reflected in the law. While some government takings of land do occur in high-transaction-cost settings — taking land for a highway, or for an airport or military base that requires the assembly of a large number of contiguous parcels (does this mean that private developers should be given eminent domain powers to assemble land for shopping centers and resort communities?) — many others do not (public schools, post offices, government office buildings).

Look at Posner's parenthetical question — should private developers facing land assembly problems be given the power of eminent domain? — from the other side: Should the government be denied the power, leaving it to cope with assembly problems just as private developers must? (Private developers use buying agents, option agreements, and straw transactions in their efforts — apparently often successful — to deal with the problem of holdouts.) See Patricia Munch, An Economic Analysis of Eminent Domain, 84 J. Pol. Econ. 473 (1976) (suggesting that the government could cope effectively and that eminent domain has not been proven to be the most efficient means for handling assembly problems); Thomas W. Merrill, The Economics of Public Use, 72 Cornell L. Rev. 61, 81-82 (1986) (assembly through voluntary transactions is usually an unattractive alternative for the government because it often seeks to acquire larger, more site-dependent parcels than do private developers, and because it would have greater difficulty maintaining the secrecy necessary for effective use of assembly techniques and controlling the opportunities for corruption that would arise).

2. *The duty to compensate.* Posner also suggests an economic rationale for the compensation obligation: "[I]t prevents the government from overusing the taking power. If there were no such requirement, the government would have an incentive to substitute land for other inputs that were socially cheaper but more costly to the government." Posner, supra, at 58. But there might be more to it than that. See William A. Fischel & Perry Shapiro, Takings, Insurance, and Michelman: Comments on Economic Interpretations of "Just Compensation" Law, 17 J. Legal Stud. 269 (1988):

In a world lacking any compensation requirement, the obvious fear is that private investors will be inhibited by the thought that government will snatch away or unthinkingly destroy the fruits of their venture. The fears of what will happen at the end of the process work themselves into the calculation of property owners at the beginning of that process, so that too little capital will be invested in productive enterprises. The compensation requirement thus serves the dual purpose of offering a substantial measure of protection to private entitlements, while disciplining the power of the state, which would otherwise overexpand unless made to pay for the resources that it consumes. [Id. at 269-270.]

Professors Fischel and Shapiro go on to discuss (which is not to say endorse) challenges to this "conventional economic wisdom," in particular the argument that compensation for takings can be *in*efficient in that it encourages landowners to overinvest in capital on their land without regard to its value for efficient government projects (an analogy would be unconditional payments for losses from hurricane damage; owners of shoreland would build on their property without thinking about predictable weather losses). The problem, it has been suggested, might best be handled by a private insurance market. The premium paid by insured property owners would force them to consider costs presently ignored. Id. at 270-271. For an overview of the debate — which, so far as we know, remains unresolved — see Michael H. Schill, Intergovernmental Takings and Just Compensation: A Question of Federalism, 137 U. Pa. L. Rev. 829, 851-856 (1989).

An alternative view of the duty to compensate is framed in terms of fairness. The question to be answered is this: "[I]s it fair to effectuate this social measure without granting this claim to compensation for private loss thereby inflicted?" Frank Michelman, Property, Utility, and Fairness: Comments on the Ethical Foundations of "Just Compensation" Law, 80 Harv. L. Rev. 1165, 1172 (1967). Michelman's is a classic but difficult treatment, built on careful attention to principles of efficiency and fairness and on their interplay. We can leave the article for now, returning to it when, in the final section of this chapter, we address the rules of decision used by the courts to identify regulatory takings — the central inquiry in Michelman's discussion.

Can you think of other grounds for requiring compensation? What about the argument that it protects against exploitation of relatively powerless groups and individuals? For discussion, see Daniel A. Farber, Economic Analysis and Just Compensation, 12 Intl. Rev. L. & Econ. 125 (1992); Daniel A. Farber, Public Choice and Just Compensation, 9 Const. Commentary 279 (1992); William A. Fischel & Perry Shapiro, A Constitutional Choice Model of Compensation for Takings, 9 Intl. Rev. L. & Econ. 115 (1989); Saul Levmore, Just Compensation and Just Politics, 22 Conn. L. Rev. 285 (1990); Saul Levmore, Takings, Torts, and Special Interests, 77 Va. L. Rev. 1333 (1991).

Bear all of the foregoing in mind as you consider the materials in the balance of this chapter.

B.   The Public-Use Puzzle (and a Note on Just Compensation)

The Fifth Amendment's mention of "public use" is read to mean that property may be taken *only* for such uses; the government may not condemn for "private" purposes, however willing it might be to pay compensation for the forced transfer. Quite obviously, then, the reach of the eminent domain power hinges directly on the breadth or narrowness of meaning attached to "public use."

Hawaii Housing Authority v. Midkiff
Supreme Court of the United States, 1984
467 U.S. 229

JUSTICE O'CONNOR delivered the opinion of the Court.
      The Fifth Amendment of the United States Constitution provides, in pertinent part, that "private property [shall not] be taken for public use, without just compensation." These cases present the question whether the Public Use Clause of that Amendment, made applicable to the States through the Fourteenth Amendment, prohibits the State of Hawaii from taking, with just compensation, title in real property from lessors and transferring it to lessees in order to reduce the concentration of ownership of fees simple in the State. We conclude that it does not.
      The Hawaiian Islands were originally settled by Polynesian immigrants from the eastern Pacific. These settlers developed an economy around a feudal land tenure system in which one island high chief, the ali'i nui, controlled the land and assigned it for development to certain subchiefs. The subchiefs would then reassign the land to other lower ranking chiefs, who would administer the land and govern the farmers and other tenants working it. All land was held at the will of the ali'i nui and eventually had to be returned to his trust. There was no private ownership of land. . . .
      Beginning in the early 1800's, Hawaiian leaders and American settlers repeatedly attempted to divide the lands of the kingdom among the crown, the chiefs, and the common people. These efforts proved largely unsuccessful, however, and the land remained in the hands of a few. In the mid-1960's, after extensive hearings, the Hawaii Legislature discovered that, while the State and Federal Governments owned almost 49%

of the State's land, another 47% was in the hands of only 72 private landowners. . . . The legislature further found that 18 landholders, with tracts of 21,000 acres or more, owned more than 40% of this land and that, on Oahu, the most urbanized of the islands, 22 landowners owned 72.5% of the fee simple titles. . . . The legislature concluded that concentrated land ownership was responsible for skewing the State's residential fee simple market, inflating land prices, and injuring the public tranquility and welfare.

To redress these problems, the legislature decided to compel the large landowners to break up their estates. The legislature considered requiring large landowners to sell lands which they were leasing to homeowners. However, the landowners strongly resisted this scheme, pointing out the significant federal tax liabilities they would incur. Indeed, the landowners claimed that the federal tax laws were the primary reason they previously had chosen to lease, and not sell, their lands. Therefore, to accommodate the needs of both lessors and lessees, the Hawaii Legislature enacted the Land Reform Act of 1967 (Act), Haw. Rev. Stat., ch. 516, which created a mechanism for condemning residential tracts and for transferring ownership of the condemned fees simple to existing lessees. By condemning the land in question, the Hawaii Legislature intended to make the land sales involuntary, thereby making the federal tax consequences less severe while still facilitating the redistribution of fees simple. . . .

Under the Act's condemnation scheme, tenants living on single-family residential lots within developmental tracts at least five acres in size are entitled to ask the Hawaii Housing Authority (HHA) to condemn the property on which they live. When 25 eligible tenants,[6] or tenants on half the lots in the tract, whichever is less, file appropriate applications, the Act authorizes HHA to hold a public hearing to determine whether acquisition by the State of all or part of the tract will "effectuate the public purposes" of the Act. If HHA finds that these public purposes will be served, it is authorized to designate some or all of the lots in the tract for acquisition. It then acquires, at prices set either by condemnation trial or by negotiation between lessors and lessees,[7] the former fee owners' full "right, title, and interest" in the land.

After compensation has been set, HHA may sell the land titles to tenants who have applied for fee simple ownership. HHA is authorized to lend these tenants up to 90% of the purchase price, and it may condition final transfer on a right of first refusal for the first 10 years following sale. If HHA does not sell the lot to the tenant residing there, it may

6. An eligible tenant is one who, among other things, owns a house on the lot, has a bona fide intent to live on the lot or be a resident of the State, shows proof of ability to pay for a fee interest in it, and does not own residential land elsewhere nearby.

7. In either case, compensation must equal the fair market value of the owner's leased fee interest. The adequacy of compensation is not before us.

lease the lot or sell it to someone else, provided that public notice has been given. However, HHA may not sell to any one purchaser, or lease to any one tenant, more than one lot, and it may not operate for profit. In practice, funds to satisfy the condemnation awards have been supplied entirely by lessees. While the Act authorized HHA to issue bonds and appropriate funds for acquisition, no bonds have issued and HHA has not supplied any funds for condemned lots. . . .

In April 1977, HHA held a public hearing concerning the proposed acquisition of some of appellees' lands. HHA made the statutorily required finding that acquisition of appellees' lands would effectuate the public purposes of the Act. Then, in October 1978, it directed appellees to negotiate with certain lessees concerning the sale of the designated properties. Those negotiations failed, and HHA subsequently ordered appellees to submit to compulsory arbitration.

Rather than comply with the compulsory arbitration order, appellees filed suit, in February 1979, in United States District Court, asking that the Act be declared unconstitutional and that its enforcement be enjoined. The District Court temporarily restrained the State from proceeding against appellees' estates. Three months later, while declaring the compulsory arbitration and compensation formulae provisions of the Act unconstitutional,[8] the District Court refused preliminarily to enjoin appellants from conducting the statutory designation and condemnation proceedings. Finally, in December 1979, it granted partial summary judgment to appellants, holding the remaining portion of the Act constitutional under the Public Use Clause. See 483 F. Supp. 62 (Haw. 1979). The District Court found that the Act's goals were within the bounds of the State's police powers and that the means the legislature had chosen to serve those goals were not arbitrary, capricious, or selected in bad faith.

The Court of Appeals for the Ninth Circuit reversed. 702 F.2d 788 (CA9 1983). . . . [It] determined that the Hawaii Land Reform Act could not pass the requisite judicial scrutiny of the Public Use Clause. It found that the transfers contemplated by the Act were unlike those of takings previously held to constitute "public uses" by this Court. The court further determined that the public purposes offered by the Hawaii Legislature were not deserving of judicial deference. The court concluded that the Act was simply "a naked attempt on the part of the state of

8. As originally enacted, lessor and lessee had to commence compulsory arbitration if they could not agree on a price for the fee simple title. Statutory formulae were provided for the determination of compensation. The District Court declared both the compulsory arbitration provision and the compensation formulae unconstitutional. No appeal was taken from these rulings, and the Hawaii legislature subsequently amended the statute to provide only for mandatory negotiation and for advisory compensation formulae. These issues are not before us.

Hawaii to take the private property of *A* and transfer it to *B* solely for *B*'s private use and benefit." Id., at 798. One judge dissented.

On applications of HHA and certain private appellants who had intervened below, this Court noted probable jurisdiction. . . . We now reverse. . . .

The starting point for our analysis of the Act's constitutionality is the Court's decision in Berman v. Parker, 348 U.S. 26, 75 S. Ct. 98, 99 L. Ed. 27 (1954). In *Berman,* the Court held constitutional the District of Columbia Redevelopment Act of 1945. That Act provided both for the comprehensive use of the eminent domain power to redevelop slum areas and for the possible sale or lease of the condemned lands to private interests. In discussing whether the takings authorized by that Act were for a "public use," id., at 31, 75 S. Ct., at 101, the Court stated

> We deal, in other words, with what traditionally has been known as the police power. An attempt to define its reach or trace its outer limits is fruitless, for each case must turn on its own facts. The definition is essentially the product of legislative determinations addressed to the purposes of government, purposes neither abstractly nor historically capable of complete definition. Subject to specific constitutional limitations, when the legislature has spoken, the public interest has been declared in terms well-nigh conclusive. In such cases the legislature, not the judiciary, is the main guardian of the public needs to be served by social legislation, whether it be Congress legislating concerning the District of Columbia . . . or the States legislating concerning local affairs. . . . This principle admits of no exception merely because the power of eminent domain is involved. . . . [Id., at 32, 75 S. Ct., at 102 (citations omitted).]

The Court explicitly recognized the breadth of the principle it was announcing, noting:

> Once the object is within the authority of Congress, the right to realize it through the exercise of eminent domain is clear. For the power of eminent domain is merely the means to the end. . . . Once the object is within the authority of Congress, the means by which it will be attained is also for Congress to determine. Here one of the means chosen is the use of private enterprise for redevelopment of the area. Appellants argue that this makes the project a taking from one businessman for the benefit of another businessman. But the means of executing the project are for Congress and Congress alone to determine, once the public purpose has been established. [Id., at 33, 75 S. Ct., at 102.]

The "public use" requirement is thus coterminous with the scope of a sovereign's police powers.

There is, of course, a role for courts to play in reviewing a legislature's judgment of what constitutes a public use, even when the eminent domain power is equated with the police power. But the court in *Berman* made clear that it is "an extremely narrow" one. Id., at 32, 75 S. Ct., at 102. The court in *Berman* cited with approval the Court's decision in Old Dominion Co. v. United States, 269 U.S. 55, 66, 46 S. Ct. 39, 40, 70 L. Ed. 162 (1925), which held that deference to the legislature's "public use" determination is required "until it is shown to involve an impossibility." The *Berman* Court also cited to United States ex rel. TVA v. Welch, 327 U.S. 546, 552, 66 S. Ct. 715, 718, 90 L. Ed. 843 (1946), which emphasized that "[a]ny departure from this judicial restraint would result in courts deciding on what is and is not a governmental function and in their invalidating legislation on the basis of their view on that question at the moment of decision, a practice which has proved impracticable in other fields." In short, the Court has made clear that it will not substitute its judgment for a legislature's judgment as to what constitutes a public use "unless the use be palpably without reasonable foundation." United States v. Gettysburg Electric R. Co., 160 U.S. 668, 680, 16 S. Ct. 427, 429, 40 L. Ed. 576 (1896).

   To be sure, the Court's cases have repeatedly stated that "one person's property may not be taken for the benefit of another private person without a justifying public purpose, even though compensation be paid." Thompson v. Consolidated Gas Corp., 300 U.S. 55, 80, 57 S. Ct. 364, 376, 81 L. Ed. 510 (1937). . . . Thus, in Missouri Pacific R. Co. v. Nebraska, where the "order in question was not, *and was not claimed to be,* . . . a taking of private property for a public use under the right of eminent domain," the Court invalidated a compensated taking of property for lack of a justifying public purpose. 164 U.S. 403, 416, 17 S. Ct. 130, 135, 41 L. Ed. 2d 489 (1896) (emphasis added). But where the exercise of the eminent domain power is rationally related to a conceivable public purpose, the Court has never held a compensated taking to be proscribed by the Public Use Clause. See Berman v. Parker, supra; Rindge v. Los Angeles, 262 U.S. 700, 43 S. Ct. 689, 67 L. Ed. 1186 (1923); Block v. Hirsh, 256 U.S. 135, 41 S. Ct. 458, 65 L. Ed. 865 (1921); cf. Thompson v. Consolidated Gas Corp., supra (invalidating an *uncompensated* taking).

   On this basis, we have no trouble concluding that the Hawaii Act is constitutional. The people of Hawaii have attempted, much as the settlers of the original 13 Colonies did,[9] to reduce the perceived social and economic evils of a land oligopoly traceable to their monarchs. The land

---

   9. After the American Revolution, the colonists in several states took steps to eradicate the feudal incidents with which large proprietors had encumbered land in the colonies. See, e.g., Act of May 1779, 10 Henning's Statutes At Large 64, ch. 13, §6 (1822) (Virginia statute); Divesting Act of 1779, 1775-1781, Pa. Acts 258, ch. 139 (1782) (Pennsylvania statute). Courts have never doubted that such statutes served a public purpose. See, e.g., Wilson v. Iseminger, 185 U.S. 55, 60-61, 22 S. Ct. 573, 574-575, 46 L. Ed. 804 (1902); Stewart v. Gorter, 70 Md. 242, 243, 16 A. 644, 645 (Md. 1889).

oligopoly has, according to the Hawaii Legislature, created artificial deterrents to the normal functioning of the State's residential land market and forced thousands of individual homeowners to lease, rather than buy, the land underneath their homes. Regulating oligopoly and the evils associated with it is a classic exercise of a State's police powers. . . . We cannot disapprove of Hawaii's exercise of this power.

Nor can we condemn as irrational the Act's approach to correcting the land oligopoly problem. The Act presumes that when a sufficiently large number of persons declare that they are willing but unable to buy lots at fair prices the land market is malfunctioning. When such a malfunction is signalled, the Act authorizes HHA to condemn lots in the relevant tract. The Act limits the number of lots any one tenant can purchase and authorizes HHA to use public funds to ensure that the market dilution goals will be achieved. This is a comprehensive and rational approach to identifying and correcting market failure.

Of course, this Act, like any other, may not be successful in achieving its intended goals. But "whether *in fact* the provision will accomplish its objectives is not the question: the [constitutional requirement] is satisfied if . . . the . . . [state] Legislature *rationally could have believed* that the [Act] would promote its objective." Western & Southern Life Ins. Co. v. State Bd. of Equalization, 451 U.S. 648, 671-672, 101 S. Ct. 2070, 2084-2085, 68 L. Ed. 2d 514 (1981). . . . When the legislature's purpose is legitimate and its means are not irrational, our cases make clear that empirical debates over the wisdom of takings — no less than debates over the wisdom of other kinds of socioeconomic legislation — are not to be carried out in the federal courts. Redistribution of fees simple to correct deficiencies in the market determined by the state legislature to be attributable to land oligopoly is a rational exercise of the eminent domain power. Therefore, the Hawaii statute must pass the scrutiny of the Public Use Clause.

The Court of Appeals read our cases to stand for a much narrower proposition. First, it read our "public use" cases, especially *Berman,* as requiring that government possess and use property at some point during a taking. Since Hawaiian lessees retain possession of the property for private use throughout the condemnation process, the court found that the Act exacted takings for private use. 702 F.2d, at 796-797. Second, it determined that these cases involved only "the review of . . . *congressional* determination[s] that there was a public use, *not* the review of . . . state legislative determination[s]." Id., at 798 (emphasis in original). Because state legislative determinations are involved in the instant cases, the Court of Appeals decided that more rigorous judicial scrutiny of the public use determinations was appropriate. The court concluded that the Hawaii Legislature's professed purposes were mere "statutory rationalizations." Ibid. We disagree with the Court of Appeals' analysis.

The mere fact that property taken outright by eminent domain is transferred in the first instance to private beneficiaries does not condemn that taking as having only a private purpose. The Court long ago rejected any literal requirement that condemned property be put into use for the general public. "It is not essential that the entire community, nor even any considerable portion, . . . directly enjoy or participate in any improvement in order [for it] to constitute a public use." Rindge Co. v. Los Angeles, 262 U.S., at 707, 43 S. Ct., at 692. "[W]hat in its immediate aspect [is] only a private transaction may . . . be raised by its class or character to a public affair." Block v. Hirsh, 256 U.S., at 155, 41 S. Ct., at 459. As the unique way titles were held in Hawaii skewed the land market, exercise of the power of eminent domain was justified. The Act advances its purposes without the State taking actual possession of the land. In such cases, government does not itself have to use property to legitimate the taking; it is only the taking's purpose, and not its mechanics, that must pass scrutiny under the Public Use Clause.

Similarly, the fact that a state legislature, and not the Congress, made the public use determination does not mean that judicial deference is less appropriate. Judicial deference is required because, in our system of government, legislatures are better able to assess what public purposes should be advanced by an exercise of the taking power. State legislatures are as capable as Congress of making such determinations within their respective spheres of authority. See Berman v. Parker, 348 U.S., at 32, 75 S. Ct., at 102. Thus, if a legislature, state or federal, determines there are substantial reasons for an exercise of the taking power, courts must defer to its determination that the taking will serve a public use.

The State of Hawaii has never denied that the Constitution forbids even a compensated taking of property when executed for no reason other than to confer a private benefit on a particular private party. A purely private taking could not withstand the scrutiny of the public use requirement; it would serve no legitimate purpose of government and would thus be void. But no purely private taking is involved in this case. The Hawaii Legislature enacted its Land Reform Act not to benefit a particular class of identifiable individuals but to attack certain perceived evils of concentrated property ownership in Hawaii — a legitimate public purpose. Use of the condemnation power to achieve this purpose is not irrational. Since we assume for purposes of this appeal that the weighty demand of just compensation has been met, the requirements of the Fifth and Fourteenth Amendments have been satisfied. Accordingly, we reverse the judgment of the Court of Appeals, and remand these cases for further proceedings in conformity with this opinion.

NOTES AND QUESTIONS

1. *Public use in general.* See Lawrence Berger, The Public Use Requirement in Eminent Domain, 57 Or. L. Rev. 203, 205, 209 (1978):

> The precise meaning of the "public use" requirement has varied over time and according to the type of taking involved. The conventional statement of the historical case development holds that there are two basic opposing views of the meaning of "public use": (1) that the term means advantage or benefit to the public (the so-called broad view); and (2) that it means actual use or right to use of the condemned property by the public (the so-called narrow view). The conventional wisdom goes on to say that right after the Revolution the broad view dominated the courts; that later the narrow view came into fashion; and that later still and to date, the broad — and according to many — the enlightened view has returned to favor. Actually, the history is somewhat more complicated. . . .
>
> While the narrow view of public use held considerable sway, especially in the latter half of the nineteenth century, it never completely took over the field. The two doctrines competed, leaving the commentators in hopeless confusion as to what the "true rule" (for in those days they believed in such things) was. And no wonder the difficulty, for each view as applied to particular cases obviously led to at least what were then regarded as unacceptable results. Thus the narrow use by the public rule would have allowed condemnation for the purpose of erecting a privately owned theater or hotel, something which no one then (or perhaps even now) would seriously advocate. And the broad public advantage test would have allowed a toy manufacturer who provided substantial employment in the vicinity to condemn land for the construction of a plant, likewise then unthinkable.
>
> Thus by the beginning of the twentieth century, doctrine was in a shambles and predictability of result at a minimum. . . .

Even today the limits of the public-use test are hardly clear. Jurisdictions differ, for example, on the question whether a city may condemn land for an industrial park, or to provide a right of way for the owners of landlocked property.

2. *Public use — ends or means?* What *should* the public-use test be? The question can be approached in two ways. One way, suggested in the excerpt from Berger set out above, focuses on the contemplated *ends* of an act of condemnation. If the ends are sufficiently "public" in one sense or another, the test is passed. Notice that if the relevant sense of "public" is the broad test of "public benefit" to which Professor Berger refers, then really there is no test at all. Essentially, the public-benefit test permits an act of condemnation so long as the objective it serves is in the public interest, as an exercise of the police power must be. Yet this suggests that what the government is doing by way of eminent domain it could just as well do by way of the police power; recall the statement in

Midkiff that the public-use requirement of the Taking Clause is "co-terminous with the scope of a sovereign's police powers." Page 1149.

> This pronouncement has dismayed commentators because the outer limit of the police power has traditionally marked the line between *noncompensable* regulation and compensable takings of property. . . . Legitimately exercised, the police power requires no compensation. Thus, if public use is truly co-terminous with the police power, a state could freely choose between compensation and noncompensation any time its actions served a "public use." [Thomas W. Merrill, The Economics of Public Use, 72 Cornell L. Rev. 61, 70 (1986).]

See also Richard A. Epstein, Takings: Private Property and the Power of Eminent Domain 170 (1985) (a public-benefit test makes the public-use requirement wholly empty).

In an effort to avoid the sweeping breadth of either of the two traditional tests of public use, Professor Epstein has argued that public use must involve provision of "public goods" in the technical economic conception — a limited category[10] — or at least provision of goods, like highways and parks, open to the public at large without discrimination. See id. at 166-169. Ironically, even this view could end up being extraordinarily encompassing rather than tightly restrictive. Can you see how?

Another restrictive view was expressed long ago by Justice Woodbury, who thought that the end in question, however public by any test of use or benefit, should represent a pressing need rather than a mere convenience. See West River Bridge Co. v. Dix, 47 U.S. (6 How.) 507, 539, 545-546 (1848) (concurring opinion). But Justice Woodbury also expressed the idea that public uses should be ones "difficult to be provided for without this power of eminent domain," 47 U.S. at 546, suggesting attention to *means*.

The case for a public-use test focused on governmental means is developed by Professor Merrill in his article on The Economics of Public Use, supra. A test oriented toward ends, Professor Merrill argues, requires a conception of the functions of government — an exercise in high political theory that courts, probably rightly, wish not to pursue. In consequence, the courts defer to legislative judgments, emptying the public-use test in the process. A test that looks at means, on the other hand, puts the judiciary in a familiar role: Courts, as we shall see in the next section of this chapter, commonly must decide whether the govern-

---

10. Pure public goods have two characteristics: Once the good is provided, it is impossible to prevent anyone from consuming it; and consumption by one person does not diminish or otherwise affect the ability of others to consume as well. Can you think of examples of pure public goods? Do you see why markets have difficulty supplying them? The latter question was addressed indirectly in connection with the reading from Demsetz on page 42 and the Note on "Externalities" that follows it.

ment may properly proceed by regulating under the police power, or whether instead the government must use the taking power and bear the burden of compensation. What the courts decide in such cases is a question of legitimate means. Merrill believes that if the courts can deal with that question of means, then they can deal with another: whether the government may condemn or must instead resort to voluntary transactions in the market. The public-use test, Merrill argues, should be formulated to answer the question. His view, simply stated, is that "public use" could be applied in such a way as to endorse condemnation through the power of eminent domain only when transaction costs are sufficiently high — picture the assembly problem referred to on pages 1143-1144 — to frustrate voluntary transactions in the market because sellers have the power to hold out for prices they would not be able to obtain under competitive conditions.

This is Merrill's basic model, similar to Justice Woodbury's notion that eminent domain should be used only when purchase through the market is unduly burdensome.[11] One of its most interesting features is a self-regulating quality. Because eminent domain entails costs that market exchange does not — legislative authorization, judicial proceedings, professional appraisals (see page 1165) — the government will have a healthy incentive to *avoid* eminent domain whenever possible (whenever, then, transaction costs are relatively low). Accordingly, the pattern of judicial deference that has developed under the traditional ends-oriented tests of public use is in Merrill's view entirely appropriate in many instances. He develops a refined model, however, to take exceptions into account. For example, we shall see (in the Note on "Just Compensation," page 1162) that the compensation awarded in eminent domain proceedings is the objective or fair market value of the condemned property. Suppose, however, that the property's owner places on it a large subjective premium, say out of sentimental value. Here the self-regulating nature of the basic model would break down because the government will have an incentive to buy the property on the cheap through eminent domain. The problem could be dealt with in various ways, one of which is close judicial scrutiny under the guise of public use whenever there is a suspicion of large losses to be borne by the condemnee.

Merrill develops several other exceptions in his refined model — the most important one involving instances where circumstances suggest that a few individuals have captured the legislative process and induced condemnation to facilitate private gains (see the *Poletown* case set out

11. Merrill's model exploits the distinction between "property rules" and "liability rules" to which you were introduced in footnote 19 on page 140. Can you see that when the power of eminent domain is exercised, an owner's interest is protected only by a liability rule, and that Merrill suggests a public-use test that would at times protect that interest with a property rule instead?

below). Here again, close judicial scrutiny under the guise of public use might well be appropriate.

3. Midkiff *in particular.* In *Midkiff,* did the court approach the issue of public use as a question of ends, or means? Does it matter? See Merrill, supra, at 113-114. Epstein, supra, at 161, says that Berman v. Parker, cited in *Midkiff,* gave the public-use limitation a mortal blow, and that *Midkiff* has now driven the point home. The case, he says, is straightforward and quite incorrect in its holding. "The statute allows tenants as a class to take the reversion from the landlord. These takings do not become something else simply because a large number of tenants is involved." Id. at 181. Most of the considerable commentary generated by *Midkiff* agrees that "under the Court's analysis, it will be the truly rare taking that will not be for a public use." David R. Burch, Linda J. Bozung, Anita P. Miller & G. Richard Hill, Land Use Controls: Public Use and Private Beneficiaries, 16 Urb. Law. 713, 714 (1984).[12]

But what's new? A student writing in 1949 observed "that so far as the federal courts are concerned neither state legislators nor Congress need be concerned about the public use test in any of its ramifications." Note, The Public Use Limitation on Eminent Domain: An Advance Requiem, 58 Yale L.J. 599, 613-614 (1949).

4. *Another view.* Merrill, supra, at 95-109, sets out the results of a survey of all state and federal public-use cases decided since Berman v. Parker in 1954. In over 15 percent of these, the courts found no public use — a high percentage given the conventional wisdom about almost complete judicial deference. *All* the federal cases, however, found a public use; the federal courts were markedly deferential. One in six of the state decisions, on the other hand, found no public use. Moreover, the pattern in state cases is in the direction of decreasing deference; the percentage of decisions finding no public use has grown regularly, from 11.8 percent in 1954-1960 to almost twice that in 1981-1985.[13]

But consider the following:

Poletown Neighborhood Council v. City of Detroit, 410 Mich. 616, 304 N.W.2d 455 (1981). Detroit planned to condemn a residential

12. For a sampling of commentary on *Midkiff,* see 71 Cornell L. Rev. 428 (1986), 1985 Ariz. St. L.J. 237, 15 Envtl. L. 565 (1985), 25 Natural Resources J. 773 (1985), and 60 Notre Dame Law. 388 (1985).

Related to the issue of public use is the propriety of a delegation of eminent domain power from the government to private corporations and individuals engaged in "public services" (e.g., common carriers, public utilities). That such delegation is generally permitted is "well settled." 1A Philip Nichols, The Law of Eminent domain §3.21[2] (rev. 3d ed. 1992).

13. Merrill speculates that the pattern of deference by *federal* courts may be appropriate, at least where the courts are reviewing takings by the federal government, because the federal government is probably less subject to capture by small factions than are state governments. Hence close public-use reviews may be unnecessary. Merrill, supra, at 115.

neighborhood (not a slum or blighted area), clear the land, and convey it to General Motors as a site for construction of an assembly plant. Residents of the neighborhood sued to enjoin the project on the ground that it would take property for a private not a public use.

"What plaintiffs-appellants . . . challenge is the constitutionality of using the power of eminent domain to condemn one person's property to convey it to another private person in order to bolster the economy. They argue that whatever incidental benefit may accrue to the public, assembling land to General Motors' specifications for conveyance to General Motors for its uncontrolled use in profit making is really a taking for private use and not a public use because General Motors is the primary beneficiary of the condemnation.

"The defendants-appellees contend, on the other hand, that the controlling public purpose in taking this land is to create an industrial site which will be used to alleviate and prevent conditions of unemployment and fiscal distress. The fact that it will be conveyed to and ultimately used by a private manufacturer does not defeat this predominant public purpose.

"There is no dispute about the law. All agree that condemnation for a public use or purpose is permitted. All agree that condemnation for a private use or purpose is forbidden. Similarly, condemnation for a private use cannot be authorized whatever its incidental public benefit and condemnation for a public purpose cannot be forbidden whatever the incidental private gain. The heart of this dispute is whether the proposed condemnation is for the primary benefit of the public or the private user.

"The Legislature has determined that governmental action of the type contemplated here meets a public need and serves an essential public purpose. The Court's role after such a determination is made is limited. . . .

"In the court below, the plaintiffs-appellants challenged the necessity for the taking of the land for the proposed project. In this regard the city presented substantial evidence of the severe economic conditions facing the residents of the city and state, the need for new industrial development to revitalize local industries, the economic boost the proposed project would provide, and the lack of other adequate available sites to implement the project. . . .

"In the instant case the benefit to be received by the municipality invoking the power of eminent domain is a clear and significant one and is sufficient to satisfy this Court that such a project was an intended and a legitimate object of the Legislature when it allowed municipalities to exercise condemnation powers even though a private party will also, ultimately, receive a benefit as an incident thereto.

"The power of eminent domain is to be used in this instance primarily to accomplish the essential public purpose of alleviating unemployment and revitalizing the economic base of the community. The benefit to a private interest is merely incidental.

"Our determination that this project falls within the public purpose, as stated by the Legislature, does not mean that every condemnation proposed by an economic development corporation will meet with similar acceptance simply because it may provide some jobs or add to the industrial or commercial base. If the public benefit was not so clear and significant, we would hesitate to sanction approval of such a project. The power of eminent domain is restricted to furthering public uses and purposes and is not to be exercised without substantial proof that the public is primarily to be benefited. Where, as here, the condemnation power is exercised in a way that benefits specific and identifiable private interests, a court inspects with heightened scrutiny the claim that the public interest is the predominant interest being advanced. Such public benefit cannot be speculative or marginal but must be clear and significant if it is to be within the legitimate purpose as stated by the Legislature. We hold this project is warranted on the basis that its significance for the people of Detroit and the state has been demonstrated. . . ."

There were two dissenting opinions in *Poletown*. One distinguished the slum clearance cases relied on by the city, which upheld condemnation for renewal purposes despite the fact that the property taken was eventually transferred to private parties. "The public purpose that has been found to support the slum clearance cases is the benefit to the public health and welfare that arises from the elimination of existing blight. . . ." In such cases, resale to a private party was not a primary purpose but was, rather, " 'incidental and ancillary to the primary and real purpose of clearance.' . . . However, in the present case the transfer of the property to General Motors cannot be considered incidental to the taking. It is only through the acquisition and use of the property by General Motors that the 'public purpose' of promoting employment can be achieved. Thus, it is the economic benefits of the project that are incidental to the private use of the property."

The second dissenting opinion called the case "extraordinary."

"The reverberating clang of its economic, sociological, political, and jurisprudential impact is likely to be heard and felt for generations. By its decision, the Court has altered the law of eminent domain in this state in a most significant way and, in my view, seriously jeopardized the security of all private property ownership. . . .

"The real controversy which underlies this litigation concerns the propriety of condemning private property for conveyance to another private party because the use of it by the new owner promises greater public 'benefit' than the old use. The controversy arises in the context of economic crisis. While unemployment is high throughout the nation, it is of calamitous proportions throughout the state of Michigan, and particularly in the City of Detroit, whose economic lifeblood is the now foundering automobile industry. It is difficult to overstate the magnitude of the crisis. Unemployment in the state of Michigan is at 14.2%. In the City of Detroit it is at 18%, and among black citizens it is almost 30%. The high cost of doing business in Michigan generally has driven many manufacturers out of this state to the so-called sunbelt states on a continuing basis during the past several years. Nowhere is the exodus more steady or more damaging than from the Metropolitan Detroit area. . . .

"A new national administration and a reconstituted Congress are struggling to find acceptable means to assist the American automotive industry to compete with the overseas automobile manufacturing competition which is largely accountable for domestic automobile industry losses. To meet that competition, domestic manufacturers are finding it necessary to construct new manufacturing facilities in order to build redesigned, lighter and more economical cars. That means new factories and new factory locations. . . .

"It was in this economic context, fueled with talk of removal of its long-established Cadillac and Fisher Body manufacturing operations from the Detroit area and the construction of a new 3-million-square-foot plant in a sunbelt state, that in 1980 General Motors made its first overture to the City of Detroit about finding a suitable plant site in the city. . . .

"It was, of course, evident to all interested observers that the removal by General Motors of its Cadillac manufacturing operations to a more favorable economic climate would mean the loss to Detroit of at least 6,000 jobs as well as the concomitant loss of literally thousands of allied and supporting automotive design, manufacture and sales functions. There would necessarily follow, as a result, the loss of millions of dollars in real estate and income tax revenues. The darkening picture was made even bleaker by the operation of other forces best explained by the social sciences, including the city's continuing loss of its industrial base and the decline of its population.

"Thus it was to a city with its economic back to the wall that General Motors presented its highly detailed 'proposal' for construction of a new plant in a 'green field' location in the city of Detroit. In addition to the fact that Detroit had virtually no 'green fields,' the requirements of the 'proposal' were such that it was clear that no existing location would be suitable unless the city acquired the requisite land one way or another and did so within the General Motors declared time schedule. . . .

"In a most impressive demonstration of governmental efficiency, the City of Detroit set about its task of meeting General Motors' specifications. . . .

"Behind the frenzy of official activity was the unmistakable guiding and sustaining, indeed controlling, hand of the General Motors Corporation. The city administration and General Motors worked in close contact during the summer and autumn of 1980 negotiating the specifics for the new plant site. . . .

"The evidence is that what General Motors wanted, General Motors got. The corporation conceived the project, determined the cost, allocated the financial burdens, selected the site, established the mode of financing, imposed specific deadlines for clearance of the property and taking title, and even demanded 12 years of tax concessions. . . .

"Stripped of the justifying adornments which have universally attended public description of this controversy, the central jurisprudential issue is the right of government to expropriate property from those who do not wish to sell for the use and benefit of a strictly private corporation."

The *Poletown* case is discussed in Peter E. Millspaugh, Eminent Domain: Is It Getting Out of Hand?, 11 Real Est. L.J. 99 (1982); Thomas Ross, Transferring Land to Private Entities by the Power of Eminent Domain, 51 Geo. Wash. L. Rev. 355 (1983); Note, Public Use, Private Use, and Judicial Review in Eminent Domain, 58 N.Y.U. L. Rev. 409 (1983). Popular accounts include Jeanie Wylie, Poletown: Community Betrayed (1989); and a film, Poletown Lives! (16 mm. and video cassette, 52 mins., available from Information Factory, 3512 Courville Street, Detroit, Michigan 48224).

In contrast to *Poletown*, see In re City of Seattle, 96 Wash. 2d 616, 638 P.2d 549 (1981), involving the city's efforts to condemn land for its Westlake Project, designed to forestall central city decay by developing a retail shopping center, public square, park, museum, and off-street parking. Held: The public-use requirement was not satisfied, because the project was for both public *and* private purposes. But Seattle subsequently managed anyway. It had already acquired some of the land it needed (apparently through voluntary transactions or by condemnation without objection), and it sold this to a developer (who already owned some other land necessary to the project) on condition that the developer follow the project's plan. Then the city sought to condemn adjacent property to be used for the public park it had originally contemplated. The owner of the property objected that its land was to be used for the identical project invalidated by In re City of Seattle. Held: The city could go forward, because the condemned land would be used only for a public park. "It does not follow . . . that the park is not a public use simply because it will be compatible with and incidentally benefit the Westlake Project retail development. Public parks will almost always benefit private properties that are adjacent to them." In re City of Seattle, 104 Wash. 2d 621, 625, 707 P.2d 1348, 1350 (1985).

City of Oakland v. Oakland Raiders, 32 Cal. 3d 60, 646 P.2d 835, 183 Cal. Rptr, 673 (1982). In 1980 the owners of the Oakland Raiders professional football team decided to move the franchise to Los Angeles. Oakland thereafter sought to keep the team by acquiring it through eminent domain. On the issue of public use, the court said:

"Is it possible for City to prove that its attempt to take and operate the Raiders' football franchise is for a valid public use? . . .

"No case anywhere of which we are aware has held that a municipality can acquire and operate a professional football team, although we are informed that the City of Visalia owns and operates a professional Class A baseball franchise in the California League; apparently, its right to do so never has been challenged in court. In our view, several decisions concerning recreation appear germane. In City of Los Angeles v. Superior Court (1959) 51 Cal. 2d 423, 434, 333 P.2d 745, we noted that a city's acquisition of a baseball field, with recreational facilities to be constructed thereon to be used by the city, was 'obviously for proper public purposes.' Similarly, in County of Alameda v. Meadowlark Dairy Corp. (1964) 227 Cal. App. 2d 80, 84, 38 Cal. Rptr. 474, the court upheld a county's acquisition by eminent domain of lands to be used for a county fair, reasoning that 'Activities which promote recreation of the public constitute a public purpose.' (Id., at p.85, 38 Cal. Rptr. 474.) Considerably earlier, in Egan v. San Francisco (1913) 165 Cal. 576, 582, 133 P. 294, in sustaining a city's power to build an opera house, we declared: 'Generally speaking, anything calculated to promote the education, the recreation or the pleasure of the public is to be included within the legitimate domain of public purposes.'

"The examples of Candlestick Park in San Francisco and Anaheim Stadium in Anaheim, both owned and operated by municipalities, further suggest the acceptance of the general principle that providing access to recreation to its residents in the form of spectator sports is an appropriate function of city government. In connection with the latter stadium, the appellate court upheld the power of the City of Anaheim to condemn land for parking facilities at the stadium on the ground that 'the acquisition, construction, and operation of a stadium by a county or city represents a legitimate public purpose.' (City of Anaheim v. Michel [1968] 259 Cal. App. 2d 835, 839, 66 Cal. Rptr. 543.) . . .

"Is the obvious difference between managing and owning the facility in which the game is played, and managing and owning the team which plays in the facility, legally substantial? To date, respondents have not presented a valid legal basis for concluding that it is, but we do not foreclose the trial court's reaching a different conclusion on a fuller record. . . ."

The court remanded for a hearing on the public-use question and the trial court thereafter dismissed the action on other grounds without reaching the issue. The dismissal was reversed by the court of appeal and the case once again remanded for a hearing. Subsequently, the court of appeal ruled that the taking would violate the commerce clause.

See City of Oakland v. Oakland Raiders, 174 Cal. App. 3d 414, 220 Cal. Rptr. 153 (1985), cert. denied, 478 U.S. 1007 (1986). So the Raiders stayed in Los Angeles, but the California Supreme Court's decision caused Jim Murray, the well-known sports columnist, to wonder whether Brooklyn could reclaim the Dodgers. L.A. Times, June 24, 1982, §3, at 1.

Question: Recall the discussion in Note 2 on page 1153. What would Professor Merrill say of the *Poletown* and *Raiders* cases? See Thomas W. Merrill, The Economics of Public Use, 72 Cornell L. Rev. 61, 109-113 (1986) (correct results under the basic model but probably not under the refined model).

NOTE: "JUST COMPENSATION"

Why is "public use" a matter of concern to property owners, given that they are entitled to "just compensation" if their property is taken? The answer lies in part in the measure of what they receive. See, e.g., Coniston Corp. v. Village of Hoffman Estates, 844 F.2d 461, 464 (7th Cir. 1988) (Posner, J.):

> "[J]ust compensation" has been held to be satisfied by payment of market value. . . . Compensation in the constitutional sense is therefore not full compensation, for market value is not the value that every owner of property attaches to his property but merely the value that the marginal owner attaches to *his* property. Many owners are "intramarginal" meaning that because of relocation costs, sentimental attachments, or the special suitability of the property for their particular (perhaps idiosyncratic) needs, they value their property at more than its market value (i.e., it is not "for sale"). Such owners are hurt when the government takes their property and gives them just its market value in return. The taking in effect confiscates the additional (call it "personal") value that they obtain from the property, but this limited confiscation is permitted provided the taking is for a public use.

Earlier we briefly considered the reasons for the just-compensation requirement (see Note 2 on pages 1144-1145). One reason, as the word *just* suggests, must surely be justice or fairness. "The constitutional requirement of just compensation derives as much content from the basic equitable principles of fairness . . . as it does from technical concepts of property law." United States v. Fuller, 409 U.S. 488, 490 (1973).[14] Given Judge Posner's remarks in the *Hoffman Estates* case, is fair market value fair? (Fair to whom? In United States v. Commodities Trading Corp.,

---

14. The compensation practices of a number of countries are considered in a recent two-volume work, Compensation for Expropriation: A Comparative Study (Gavin M. Erasmus ed. 1990).

339 U.S. 121, 123 (1950), the Court said the question is this: "What compensation is 'just' both to an owner whose property is taken and to the public that must pay the bill?")

What about efficiency? Does not the market-value measure of just compensation promote or at least tolerate transfers of property from higher- to lower-valued uses?[15]

Concerns from the standpoint of fairness and efficiency alike could be remedied, at least in part, by including in just compensation the "personal value" mentioned by Judge Posner, but the Supreme Court has rejected the idea:

> Because of serious practical difficulties in assessing the worth an individual places on particular property at a given time, we have recognized the need for a relatively objective working rule. . . . The Court therefore has employed the concept of fair market value to determine the condemnee's loss. Under this standard, the owner is entitled to receive "what a willing buyer would pay in cash to a willing seller" at the time of the taking. [United States v. 564.54 Acres of Land, 441 U.S. 506, 511 (1979), quoting United States v. Miller, 317 U.S. 369, 374 (1943).]

What are these "practical difficulties," and how might the legal system deal with them? See Richard A. Posner, Economic Analysis of Law 522 (4th ed. 1992); Thomas W. Merrill, The Economics of Public Use, 72 Cornell L. Rev. 61, 82-85, 90-92 (1986). Professor Ellickson has suggested a system of bonuses to compensate for losses of personal value. To limit the administrative costs of such a system, the bonuses could be defined in legislative schedules.[16]

Matters of detail. The law of just compensation is busy and complex. Consider just a few nice issues:

Suppose that the government condemns part of a tract of land and that the government's use of that land will reduce (increase) the value of the rest of the tract remaining in the condemnee's hands. How is just

---

15. An empirical study of eminent domain suggests that high-value parcels condemned under eminent domain systematically receive more than fair market value, while low-value parcels systematically receive less. Can you imagine why? See Patricia Munch, An Economic Analysis of Eminent Domain, 84 J. Pol. Econ. 473 (1976).

16. See Robert C. Ellickson, Alternatives to Zoning: Covenants, Nuisance Rules, and Fines as Land Use Controls, 40 U. Chi. L. Rev. 681, 736-737 (1973). Compare the approach taken in Canada, where allowances over and above market value have been made to compensate for the compulsory nature of the taking; moreover, if a condemnee can prove that her use of a tract of land generates "special advantages" not captured in fair market value, she is entitled to compensation for these (sentimental value is not compensable). See generally Eric C. Todd, The Law of Expropriation and Compensation in Canada (1976). Also compare England, where condemnees used to be awarded fair market value plus 10 percent to soften the blow of compulsory taking. The approach has been abandoned, but people displaced from dwellings are entitled to home loss payments ascertained by an arbitrary formula. See Keith Davies, Law of Compulsory Purchase and Compensation 136, 219 (4th ed. 1984).

compensation computed? See 3 Philip Nichols, The Law of Eminent Domain §8A.03 (rev. 3d ed. 1992).[17] Is compensation due if the government's use does not reduce the value of the condemnee's remaining land, but does reduce the rate at which it appreciates? See State v. Doyle, 735 P.2d 733 (Alaska 1987).

May a city downzone property, restricting its permissible uses, so as to be liable in a subsequent condemnation action only for fair market value in light of the restrictive zoning? See Riggs v. Township of Long Beach, 109 N.J. 601, 538 A.2d 808 (1988). Suppose that there has been no downzoning, but that future zoning changes, reasonably likely to occur, will increase the value of condemned property. How might this bear on the measure of just compensation? See Developments in the Law — Zoning, 91 Harv. L. Rev. 1427, 1498-1499 (1978).

Sometimes the federal government condemns property owned by a state or city. Until 1984, the courts in such cases usually measured compensation in terms of "substitute facilities" doctrine: The state or city was entitled not merely to market value but to the cost of obtaining or constructing the equivalent of what had been taken. In United States v. 50 Acres of Land, 469 U.S. 24 (1984), the Court held that the substitute-facilities measure is not required when the market value of the condemned property is ascertainable, even if the condemnee has a duty to replace the condemned facility and the cost of the substitute will exceed compensation measured in market-value terms. The idea was to treat public condemnees like private ones. Is that a *good* idea? See Michael H. Schill, Intergovernmental Takings and Just Compensation: A Question of Federalism, 137 U. Pa. L. Rev. 829 (1989).

C. Physical Occupations and Regulatory Takings

At the outset of this chapter we alluded to governmental actions that, though not intended to take property, might nonetheless be held by the

---

17. Compensation practice can give rise to public-use issues. For example, a Florida statute provides that if less than all of a parcel of land is taken by eminent domain, and the partial taking results in damages to a business owned by the condemnee and operated on the remaining land, then the government must pay not only for the land taken but also for any consequential business damages. (The rule applies *only* to partial takings.) Suppose that the government needs only part of a parcel for a project, but proposes to condemn *all* of the parcel because the fair market value of the whole is less than the sum of the fair market value of the part needed plus the business damages that would be caused by a partial taking. Is the public-use requirement violated? See Department of Transp. v. Fortune Fed. Sav. & Loan, 532 So. 2d 1267 (Fla. 1988) (no), discussed in Note, Eminent Domain Revisited: Business Owners Beware!, 18 Stetson L. Rev. 707 (1989).

courts to have done so; these cases, we said, present some of the most difficult issues in the law of property. The materials that follow should justify the assertion. Before getting to them, however, it is useful to have in mind a far simpler matter — the general method of straightforward condemnation under the power of eminent domain.

If the government wishes to condemn private property for public use, it must comply with procedures designed to assure owners due process of law. The first step is usually the filing of a petition in court (some jurisdictions require the government to attempt a negotiated purchase before initiating a condemnation action), followed by notice to all persons with an interest in the property in question. Thereafter, a trial is held, at which the government must establish its authority to condemn (which means, in some jurisdictions, that the government must show that a taking is "necessary"). The court can give the government permission to enter and inspect the subject property; it may require the government to make a deposit as security for the eventual condemnation, in an amount based on the compensation estimated to be awarded at the end of the proceedings. Jurisdictions differ on the availability of a jury trial in condemnation actions (none is required under the United States Constitution). If there is a jury trial, it is typically the jury that determines just compensation; issues of public use and necessity are decided by the court. At the conclusion of a successful condemnation action (or within a prescribed time thereafter), the government must pay the compensation awarded plus interest, if any, accrued from the time of the taking. Generally, condemnees may not recover attorneys' fees or other litigation expenses. Dissatisfied condemnees may, of course, appeal.

In a straightforward condemnation action, then, there is no question that the government is taking property (though there might well be questions about whether the taking is for a public use and about the measure of compensation). The cases that follow are different: The central question in each is *whether* a taking has occurred. Consider some of the tests courts have constructed to resolve the issue.

1. Rules of Decision

Loretto v. Teleprompter Manhattan CATV Corp.
Supreme Court of the United States, 1982
458 U.S. 419

JUSTICE MARSHALL delivered the opinion of the Court.

This case presents the question whether a minor but permanent physical occupation of an owner's property authorized by government constitutes a "taking" of property for which just compensation is due under the Fifth and Fourteenth Amendments of the Constitution. New

York law provides that a landlord must permit a cable television company to install its cable facilities upon his property. N.Y. Exec. Law §828(1) (McKinney Supp. 1981-1982). In this case, the cable installation occupied portions of appellant's roof and the side of her building. The New York Court of Appeals ruled that this appropriation does not amount to a taking. 53 N.Y.2d 124, 423 N.E.2d 320 (1981). Because we conclude that such a physical occupation of property is a taking, we reverse.

Appellant Jean Loretto purchased a five-story apartment building located at 303 West 105th Street, New York City, in 1971. The previous owner had granted appellees Teleprompter Corporation and Teleprompter Manhattan CATV (collectively Teleprompter) permission to install a cable on the building and the exclusive privilege of furnishing cable television (CATV) services to the tenants. The New York Court of Appeals described the installation as follows:

> On June 1, 1970 TelePrompter installed a cable slightly less than one-half inch in diameter and of approximately 30 feet in length along the length of the building about 18 inches above the roof top, and directional taps, approximately 4 inches by 4 inches by 4 inches, on the front and rear of the roof. By June 8, 1970 the cable had been extended another 4 to 6 feet and cable had been run from the directional taps to the adjoining building at 305 West 105th Street. [Id., at 135, 423 N.E.2d, at 324.]

Teleprompter also installed two large silver boxes along the roof cables. The cables are attached by screws or nails penetrating the masonry at approximately two-foot intervals, and other equipment is installed by bolts.

Initially, Teleprompter's roof cables did not service appellant's building. They were part of what could be described as a cable "highway" circumnavigating the city block, with service cables periodically dropped over the front or back of a building in which a tenant desired service. Crucial to such a network is the use of so-called "crossovers" — cable lines extending from one building to another in order to reach a new group of tenants. Two years after appellant purchased the building, Teleprompter connected a "noncrossover" line — i.e., one that provided CATV service to appellant's own tenants — by dropping a line to the first floor down the front of appellant's building.

Prior to 1973, Teleprompter routinely obtained authorization for its installations from property owners along the cable's route, compensating the owners at the standard rate of 5% of the gross revenues that Teleprompter realized from the particular property. To facilitate tenant access to CATV, the State of New York enacted §828 of the Executive Law, effective January 1, 1973. Section 828 provides that a landlord may not "interfere with the installation of cable television facilities upon his

Loretto's Apartment House
303 West 105th Street, New York City
Note the cable television line, a little left of center, dropping down the front of
the building to the first floor.

property or premises," and may not demand payment from any tenant for permitting CATV, or demand payment from any CATV company "in excess of any amount which the [State Commission on Cable Television] shall, by regulation, determine to be reasonable." The landlord may, however, require the CATV company or the tenant to bear the cost of installation and to indemnify for any damage caused by the installation. Pursuant to §828(1)(b), the State Commission has ruled that a onetime $1 payment is the normal fee to which a landlord is entitled. . . . The Commission ruled that this nominal fee, which the Commission concluded was equivalent to what the landlord would receive if the property were condemned pursuant to New York's Transportation Corporations Law, satisfied constitutional requirements "in the absence of a special showing of greater damages attributable to the taking."

Appellant did not discover the existence of the cable until after she had purchased the building. She brought a class action against Teleprompter in 1976 on behalf of all owners of real property in the State on which Teleprompter has placed CATV components, alleging that Teleprompter's installation was a trespass and, insofar as it relied on §828, a taking without just compensation. She requested damages and injunctive relief. Appellee the City of New York, which has granted Teleprompter an exclusive franchise to provide CATV within certain areas of Manhattan, intervened. The Supreme Court, Special Term, granted summary judgment to Teleprompter and the city, upholding the constitutionality of §828 in both crossover and noncrossover situations. 98 Misc. 2d 944, 415 N.Y.S.2d 180 (1979). The Appellate Division affirmed without opinion. 73 App. Div. 2d 849, 422 N.Y.S.2d 550 (1979).

On appeal, the Court of Appeals, over dissent, upheld the statute. 53 N.Y.2d 124, 423 N.E.2d 320 (1981). The court concluded that the law requires the landlord to allow both crossover and noncrossover installations but permits him to request payment from the CATV company under §828(1)(b), at a level determined by the State Cable Commission, only for noncrossovers. The court then ruled that the law serves a legitimate police power purpose — eliminating landlord fees and conditions that inhibit the development of CATV, which has important educational and community benefits. Rejecting the argument that a physical occupation authorized by government is necessarily a taking, the court stated that the regulation does not have an excessive economic impact upon appellant when measured against her aggregate property rights, and that it does not interfere with any reasonable investment-backed expectations. Accordingly, the court held that §828 does not work a taking of appellant's property. Chief Judge Cooke dissented, reasoning that the physical appropriation of a portion of appellant's property is a taking without regard to the balancing analysis courts ordinarily employ in evaluating whether a regulation is a taking.

In light of its holding, the Court of Appeals had no occasion to determine whether the $1 fee ordinarily awarded for a noncrossover installation was adequate compensation for the taking. Judge Gabrielli, concurring, agreed with the dissent that the law works a taking but concluded that the $1 presumptive award, together with the procedures permitting a landlord to demonstrate a greater entitlement, affords just compensation. . . .

The Court of Appeals determined that §828 serves the legitimate public purpose of "rapid development of and maximum penetration by a means of communication which has important educational and community aspects," 53 N.Y.2d, at 143-144, 423 N.E.2d, at 329, and thus is within the State's police power. We have no reason to question that determination. It is a separate question, however, whether an otherwise valid regulation so frustrates property rights that compensation must be paid. We conclude that a permanent physical occupation authorized by government is a taking without regard to the public interests that it may serve. Our constitutional history confirms the rule, recent cases do not question it, and the purposes of the Takings Clause compel its retention.

In Penn Central Transportation Co. v. New York City, [438 U.S. 104 (1978) (considered at page 1203)], the Court surveyed some of the general principles governing the Takings Clause. The Court noted that no "set formula" existed to determine, in all cases, whether compensation is constitutionally due for a government restriction of property. Ordinarily, the Court must engage in "essentially ad hoc, factual inquiries." Id., at 124. But the inquiry is not standardless. The economic impact of the regulation, especially the degree of interference with investment-backed expectations, is of particular significance.

> So, too, is the character of the government action. A "taking" may more readily be found when the interference with property can be characterized as a physical invasion by government, than when interference arises from some public program adjusting the benefits and burdens of economic life to promote the common good. [Id.]

As *Penn Central* affirms, the Court has often upheld substantial regulation of an owner's use of his own property where deemed necessary to promote the public interest. At the same time, we have long considered a physical intrusion by government to be a property restriction of an unusually serious character for purposes of the Takings Clause. Our cases further establish that when the physical intrusion reaches the extreme form of a permanent physical occupation, a taking has occurred. In such a case, "the character of the government action" not only is an important factor in resolving whether the action works a taking but also is determinative.

When faced with a constitutional challenge to a permanent physical occupation of real property, this Court has invariably found a taking. As early as 1872, in Pumpelly v. Green Bay Co., 13 Wall. 166, this Court held that the defendant's construction, pursuant to state authority, of a dam which permanently flooded plaintiff's property constituted a taking. A unanimous Court stated, without qualification, that "where real estate is actually invaded by superinduced additions of water, earth, sand, or other material, or by having any artificial structure placed on it, so as to effectually destroy or impair its usefulness, it is a taking, within the meaning of the Constitution." Id., at 181. Seven years later, the Court reemphasized the importance of a physical occupation by distinguishing a regulation that merely restricted the use of private property. In Northern Transportation Co. v. Chicago, 99 U.S. 635 (1879), the Court held that the city's construction of a temporary dam in a river to permit construction of a tunnel was not a taking, even though the plaintiffs were thereby denied access to their premises, because the obstruction only impaired the use of plaintiffs' property. The Court distinguished earlier cases in which permanent flooding of private property was regarded as a taking, e.g., *Pumpelly*, supra, as involving "a physical invasion of the real estate of the private owner, and a practical ouster of his possession." In this case, by contrast, "[n]o entry was made upon the plaintiffs' lot." 99 U.S., at 642.

Since these early cases, this Court has consistently distinguished between flooding cases involving a permanent physical occupation, on the one hand, and cases involving a more temporary invasion, or government action outside the owner's property that causes consequential damages within, on the other. A taking has always been found only in the former situation. . . .

More recent cases confirm the distinction between a permanent physical occupation, a physical invasion short of an occupation, and a regulation that merely restricts the use of property. In United States v. Causby, 328 U.S. 256 (1946), the Court ruled that frequent flights immediately above a land-owner's property constituted a taking, comparing such overflights to the quintessential form of a taking:

> If, by reason of the frequency and altitude of the flights, respondents could not use this land for any purpose, their loss would be complete. It would be as complete as if the United States had entered upon the surface of the land and taken exclusive possession of it. [Id., at 261.] . . .

Although this Court's most recent cases have not addressed the precise issue before us, they have emphasized that physical *invasion* cases are special and have not repudiated the rule that any permanent physical *occupation* is a taking. The cases state or imply that a physical invasion is subject to a balancing process, but they do not suggest that a permanent physical occupation would ever be exempt from the Takings Clause. . . .

In Kaiser Aetna v. United States, 444 U.S. 164 (1979), the Court held that the Government's imposition of a navigational servitude requiring public access to a pond was a taking where the landowner had reasonably relied on Government consent in connecting the pond to navigable water. The Court emphasized that the servitude took the landowner's right to exclude, "one of the most essential sticks in the bundle of rights that are commonly characterized as property." Id., at 176. The Court explained:

> This is not a case in which the Government is exercising its regulatory power in a manner that will cause an insubstantial devaluation of petitioner's private property; rather, the imposition of the navigational servitude in this context will result in an *actual physical invasion* of the privately owned marina. . . . And even if the Government physically invades only an easement in property, it must nonetheless pay compensation. See United States v. Causby, 328 U.S. 256, 265 (1946); Portsmouth Co. v. United States, 260 U.S. 327 (1922). [Id., at 180 (emphasis added).]

Although the easement of passage, not being a permanent occupation of land, was not considered a taking per se, *Kaiser Aetna* reemphasizes that a physical invasion is a government intrusion of an unusually serious character.[18]

Another recent case underscores the constitutional distinction between a permanent occupation and a temporary physical invasion. In PruneYard Shopping Center v. Robins, 447 U.S. 74 (1980), the Court upheld a state constitutional requirement that shopping center owners permit individuals to exercise free speech and petition rights on their property, to which they had already invited the general public. The Court emphasized that the State Constitution does not prevent the owner from restricting expressive activities by imposing reasonable time, place, and manner restrictions to minimize interference with the owner's commercial functions. Since the invasion was temporary and limited in nature, and since the owner had not exhibited an interest in excluding all persons from his property, "the fact that [the solicitors] may have 'physically invaded' [the owners'] property cannot be viewed as determinative." Id., at 84.

18. See also Andrus v. Allard, 444 U.S. 51 (1979). That case held that the prohibition of the sale of eagle feathers was not a taking as applied to traders of bird artifacts. "The regulations challenged here do not compel the surrender of the artifacts, and there is no physical invasion or restraint upon them. . . . In this case, it is crucial that appellees retain the rights to possess and transport their property, and to donate or devise the protected birds. . . . [L]oss of future profits — unaccompanied by any physical property restriction — provides a slender reed upon which to rest a takings claim." Id., at 65-66.

In short, when the "character of the governmental action," *Penn Central*, 438 U.S., at 124, is a permanent physical occupation of property, our cases uniformly have found a taking to the extent of the occupation, without regard to whether the action achieves an important public benefit or has only minimal economic impact on the owner.

The historical rule that a permanent physical occupation of another's property is a taking has more than tradition to commend it. Such an appropriation is perhaps the most serious form of invasion of an owner's property interests. . . .

Property rights in a physical thing have been described as the rights "to possess, use and dispose of it." United States v. General Motors Corp., 323 U.S. 373, 378 (1945). To the extent that the government permanently occupies physical property, it effectively destroys *each* of these rights. First, the owner has no right to possess the occupied space himself, and also has no power to exclude the occupier from possession and use of the space. The power to exclude has traditionally been considered one of the most treasured strands in an owner's bundle of property rights.[19] See *Kaiser Aetna*, 444 U.S., at 179-180; see also Restatement of Property §7 (1936). Second, the permanent physical occupation of property forever denies the owner any power to control the use of the property; he not only cannot exclude others, but can make no nonpossessory use of the property. Although deprivation of the right to use and obtain a profit from property is not, in every case, independently sufficient to establish a taking, see Andrus v. Allard, supra, at 66, it is clearly relevant. Finally, even though the owner may retain the bare legal right to dispose of the occupied space by transfer or sale, the permanent occupation of that space by a stranger will ordinarily empty the right of any value, since the purchaser will also be unable to make any use of the property.

Moreover, an owner suffers a special kind of injury when a *stranger* directly invades and occupies the owner's property. . . . [P]roperty law has long protected an owner's expectation that he will be relatively undisturbed at least in the possession of his property. To require, as well, that the owner permit another to exercise complete dominion literally adds insult to injury. See Michelman, Property, Utility, and Fairness: Comments on the Ethical Foundations of "Just Compensation" Law, 80

---

19. The permanence and absolute exclusivity of a physical occupation distinguish it from temporary limitations on the right to exclude. Not every physical *invasion* is a taking. As PruneYard Shopping Center v. Robins, 447 U.S. 74 (1980), Kaiser Aetna v. United States, 444 U.S. 164 (1979), and the intermittent flooding cases reveal, such temporary limitations are subject to a more complex balancing process to determine whether they are a taking. The rationale is evident: they do not absolutely dispossess the owner of his rights to use, and exclude others from, his property.

The dissent objects that the distinction between a permanent physical occupation and a temporary invasion will not always be clear. This objection is overstated, and in any event is irrelevant to the critical point that a permanent physical occupation *is* unquestionably a taking. . . .

Harv. L. Rev. 1165, 1228, and n.110 (1967). Furthermore, such an occupation is qualitatively more severe than a regulation of the *use* of property, even a regulation that imposes affirmative duties on the owner, since the owner may have no control over the timing, extent, or nature of the invasion. See n.22, infra.

The traditional rule also avoids otherwise difficult line-drawing problems. Few would disagree that if the State required landlords to permit third parties to install swimming pools on the landlords' rooftops for the convenience of the tenants, the requirement would be a taking. If the cable installation here occupied as much space, again, few would disagree that the occupation would be a taking. But constitutional protection for the rights of private property cannot be made to depend on the size of the area permanently occupied. Indeed, it is possible that in the future, additional cable installations that more significantly restrict a landlord's use of the roof of his building will be made. Section 828 requires a landlord to permit such multiple installations.

Finally, whether a permanent physical occupation has occurred presents relatively few problems of proof. The placement of a fixed structure on land or real property is an obvious fact that will rarely be subject to dispute. Once the fact of occupation is shown, of course, a court should consider the *extent* of the occupation as one relevant factor in determining the compensation due. For that reason, moreover, there is less need to consider the extent of the occupation in determining whether there is a taking in the first instance.

Teleprompter's cable installation on appellant's building constitutes a taking under the traditional test. The installation involved a direct physical attachment of plates, boxes, wires, bolts, and screws to the building, completely occupying space immediately above and upon the roof and along the building's exterior wall.[20]

In light of our analysis we find no constitutional difference between a crossover and a noncrossover installation. The portions of the installation necessary for both crossovers and noncrossovers permanently appropriate appellant's property. Accordingly, each type of installation is a taking.

Appellees raise a series of objections to application of the traditional

---

20. It is constitutionally irrelevant whether appellant (or her predecessor in title) had previously occupied this space, since a "landowner owns at least as much of the space above the ground as he can occupy or use in connection with the land." United States v. Causby, supra, at 264.

The dissent asserts that a taking of about one-eighth of a cubic foot of space is not of constitutional significance. The assertion appears to be factually incorrect, since it ignores the two large silver boxes that appellant identified as part of the installation. Although the record does not reveal their size, appellant states that they are approximately $18'' \times 12'' \times 6''$, and appellees do not dispute this statement. The displaced volume, then, is in excess of 1½ cubic feet. In any event, these facts are not critical; whether the installation is a taking does not depend on whether the volume of space it occupies is bigger than a breadbox.

rule here. Teleprompter notes that the law applies only to buildings used as rental property, and draws the conclusion that the law is simply a permissible regulation of the use of real property. We fail to see, however, why a physical occupation of one type of property but not another type is any less a physical occupation. Insofar as Teleprompter means to suggest that this is not a permanent physical invasion, we must differ. So long as the property remains residential and a CATV company wishes to retain the installation, the landlord must permit it.[21]

Teleprompter also asserts the related argument that the State has effectively granted a tenant the property right to have a CATV installation placed on the roof of his building, as an appurtenance to the tenant's leasehold. The short answer is that §828(1)(a) does not purport to give the *tenant* any enforceable property rights with respect to CATV installation, and the lower courts did not rest their decisions on this ground. Of course, Teleprompter, not appellant's tenants, actually owns the installation. Moreover, the government does not have unlimited power to redefine property rights. See Webb's Fabulous Pharmacies, Inc. v. Beckwith, 449 U.S. 155, 164 (1980) ("a State, by ipse dixit, may not transform private property into public property without compensation").

Finally, we do not agree with appellees that application of the physical occupation rule will have dire consequences for the government's power to adjust landlord-tenant relationships. This Court has consistently affirmed that States have broad power to regulate housing conditions in general and the landlord-tenant relationship in particular without paying compensation for all economic injuries that such regulation entails. See, e.g., Heart of Atlanta Motel, Inc. v. United States, 379 U.S. 241 (1964) (discrimination in places of public accommodation); Queenside Hills Realty Co. v. Saxl, 328 U.S. 80 (1946) (fire regulation); Bowles v. Willingham, 321 U.S. 503 (1944) (rent control); Home Building & Loan Assn. v. Blaisdell, 290 U.S. 398 (1934) (mortgage moratorium); Edgar A. Levy Leasing Co. v. Siegel, 258 U.S. 242 (1922) (emergency housing law); Block v. Hirsh, 256 U.S. 135 (1921) (rent control). In none of these cases, however, did the government authorize the permanent occupation of the landlord's property by a third party. Consequently, our holding today in no way alters the analysis governing the State's power to require landlords to comply with building codes and provide utility connections, mailboxes, smoke detectors, fire extinguishers, and the like in the common area of a building. So long as these regulations do not require the landlord to suffer the physical occupation of a portion of his building by a third party, they will be analyzed under the multifactor inquiry generally applicable to nonpossessory govern-

---

21. It is true that the landlord could avoid the requirements of §828 by ceasing to rent the building to tenants. But a landlord's ability to rent his property may not be conditioned on his forfeiting the right to compensation for a physical occupation. . . .

mental activity. See Penn Central Transportation Co. v. New York City, 438 U.S. 104 (1978).[22]

Our holding today is very narrow. We affirm the traditional rule that a permanent physical occupation of property is a taking. In such a case, the property owner entertains a historically rooted expectation of compensation, and the character of the invasion is qualitatively more intrusive than perhaps any other category of property regulation. We do not, however, question the equally substantial authority upholding a State's broad power to impose appropriate restrictions upon an owner's *use* of his property.

Furthermore, our conclusion that §828 works a taking of a portion of appellant's property does not presuppose that the fee which many landlords had obtained by Teleprompter prior to the law's enactment is a proper measure of the value of the property taken. The issue of the amount of compensation that is due, on which we express no opinion, is a matter for the state courts to consider on remand. . . .

JUSTICE BLACKMUN, with whom JUSTICE BRENNAN and JUSTICE WHITE join, dissenting. . . .

In a curiously anachronistic decision, the Court today acknowledges its historical disavowel of set formulae in almost the same breath as it constructs a rigid per se takings rule: "a permanent physical occupation authorized by government is a taking without regard to the public interests that it may serve." To sustain its rule against our recent precedents, the Court erects a strained and untenable distinction between "temporary physical invasions," whose constitutionality concededly "is subject to a balancing process," and "permanent physical occupations," which are "taking[s] without regard to other factors that a court might ordinarily examine."

In my view, the Court's approach "reduces the constitutional issue

---

22. If §828 required landlords to provide cable installation if a tenant so desires, the statute might present a different question from the question before us, since the landlord would own the installation. Ownership would give the landlord rights to the placement, manner, use, and possibly the disposition of the installation. The fact of ownership is, contrary to the dissent, not simply "incidental"; it would give a landlord (rather than a CATV company) full authority over the installation except only as government specifically limited that authority. The *landlord* would decide how to comply with applicable government regulations concerning CATV and therefore could minimize the physical, esthetic, and other effects of the installation. Moreover, if the landlord wished to repair, demolish, or construct in the area of the building where the installation is located, he need not incur the burden of obtaining the CATV company's cooperation in moving the cable.

In this case, by contrast, appellant suffered injury that might have been obviated if she had owned the cable and could exercise control over its installation. The drilling and stapling that accompanied installation apparently caused physical damage to appellant's building. Appellant, who resides in the building, further testified that the cable installation is "ugly." Although §828 provides that a landlord may require "reasonable" conditions that are "necessary" to protect the appearance of the premises and may seek indemnity for damage, these provisions are somewhat limited. Even if the provisions are effective, the inconvenience to the landlord of initiating the repairs remains a cognizable burden.

to a formalistic quibble" over whether property has been "permanently occupied" or "temporarily invaded." Sax, Takings and the Police Power, 74 Yale L.J. 36, 37 (1964). The Court's application of its formula to the facts of this case vividly illustrates that its approach is potentially dangerous as well as misguided. Despite its concession that "States have broad power to regulate . . . the landlord-tenant relationship . . . without paying compensation for all economic injuries that such regulation entails," the Court uses its rule to undercut a carefully considered legislative judgment concerning landlord-tenant relationships. I therefore respectfully dissent. . . .

The Court's recent Takings Clause decisions teach that *nonphysical* government intrusions on private property, such as zoning ordinances and other land-use restrictions, have become the rule rather than the exception. Modern government regulation exudes intangible "externalities" that may diminish the value of private property far more than minor physical touchings. . . .

Precisely because the extent to which the government may injure private interests now depends so little on whether or not it has authorized a "physical contact," the Court has avoided per se takings rules resting on outmoded distinctions between physical and nonphysical intrusions. As one commentator has observed, a takings rule based on such a distinction is inherently suspect because "its capacity to distinguish, even crudely, between significant and insignificant losses is too puny to be taken seriously." Michelman, Property, Utility, and Fairness: Comments on the Ethical Foundations of "Just Compensation" Law, 80 Harv. L. Rev. 1165, 1227 (1967).

Surprisingly, the Court draws an even finer distinction today — between "temporary physical invasions" and "permanent physical occupations." When the government authorizes the latter type of intrusion, the Court would find "a taking without regard to the public interests" the regulation may serve. Yet an examination of each of the three words in the Court's "permanent physical occupation" formula illustrates that the newly created distinction is even less substantial than the distinction between physical and nonphysical intrusions that the Court already has rejected.

First, what does the Court mean by "permanent"? Since all "temporary limitations on the right to exclude" remain "subject to a more complex balancing process to determine whether they are a taking," the Court presumably describes a government intrusion that lasts forever. But as the Court itself concedes, §828 does not require appellant to permit the cable installation forever, but only "[s]o long as the property remains residential and a CATV company wishes to retain the installation." This is far from "permanent."

. . . If §828 authorizes a "permanent" occupation, and thus works a taking "without regard to the public interests that it may serve," then all other New York statutes that require a landlord to make physical attachments to his rental property also must constitute takings, even if they serve indisputably valid public interests in tenant protection and safety.[23]

The Court denies that its theory invalidates these statutes, because they "do not require the landlord to suffer the physical occupation of a portion of his building by a third party." But surely this factor cannot be determinative, since the Court simultaneously recognizes that temporary invasions by third parties are not subject to a per se rule. Nor can the qualitative difference arise from the incidental fact that, under §828, Teleprompter, rather than appellant or her tenants, owns the cable installation. If anything, §828 leaves appellant better off than do other housing statutes, since it ensures that her property will not be damaged esthetically or physically, without burdening her with the cost of buying or maintaining the cable.

In any event, under the Court's test, the "third party" problem would remain even if appellant herself owned the cable. So long as Teleprompter continuously passed its electronic signal through the cable, a litigant could argue that the second element of the Court's formula — a "physical touching" by a stranger — was satisfied and that §828 therefore worked a taking. Literally read, the Court's test opens the door to endless metaphysical struggles over whether or not an individual's property has been "physically" touched. . . .

Third, the Court's talismanic distinction between a continuous "occupation" and a transient "invasion" finds no basis in either economic logic or Takings Clause precedent. In the landlord-tenant context, the Court has upheld against takings challenges rent control statutes permitting "temporary" physical invasions of considerable economic magnitude. . . .

In sum, history teaches that takings claims are properly evaluated under a multifactor balancing test. By directing that all "permanent physical occupations" automatically are compensable, "without regard to whether the action achieves an important public benefit or has only minimal economic impact on the owner," the Court does not further equity so much as it encourages litigants to manipulate their factual allegations to gain the benefit of its per se rule. I do not relish the prospect of distinguishing the inevitable flow of certiorari petitions attempting to shoehorn insubstantial takings claims into today's "set formula." . . .

For constitutional purposes, the relevant question cannot be solely

23. See, e.g., N.Y. Mult. Dwell. Law §35 (McKinney 1974) (requiring entrance doors and lights); §36 (windows and skylights for public halls and stairs); §50-a (Supp. 1982) (locks and intercommunication systems); §50-c (lobby attendants); §51-a (peepholes); §51-b (elevator mirrors); §53 (fire escapes); §57 (bells and mail receptacles); §67(3) (fire sprinklers). See also Queenside Hills Realty Co. v. Saxl, 328 U.S. 80 (1946) (upholding constitutionality of New York fire sprinkler provision). . . .

whether the State has interfered in some minimal way with an owner's use of space on her building. Any intelligible takings inquiry must also ask whether the *extent* of the State's interference is so severe as to constitute a compensable taking in light of the owner's alternative uses for the property. Appellant freely admitted that she would have had no other use for the cable-occupied space, were Teleprompter's equipment not on her building.

The Court's third and final argument is that §828 has deprived appellant of her "power to exclude the occupier from possession and use of the space" occupied by the cable. This argument has two flaws. First, it unjustifiably assumes that appellant's tenants have no countervailing property interest in permitting Teleprompter to use that space.[24] Second, it suggests that the New York legislature may not exercise its police power to affect appellant's common-law right to exclude Teleprompter even from one-eighth cubic foot of roof space. . . .

This Court now reaches back in time for a per se rule that disrupts that legislative determination.[25] . . . I would affirm the judgment and uphold the reasoning of the New York Court of Appeals.

NOTES AND QUESTIONS

1. On remand in *Loretto*, the New York Court of Appeals sustained the validity of the statutory provisions empowering the Commission on Cable Television to set compensation for the takings in question at $1. Loretto v. Teleprompter Manhattan CATV Corp., 58 N.Y.2d 143, 446 N.E.2d 428, 459 N.Y.S.2d 743 (1983). The Commission concluded that $1 was sufficient compensation because the presence of cable TV usually increases a building's value.

2. *"Per se" (or "categorical") rules.* As Justice Blackmun observes in his dissenting opinion (at page 1175), the majority in *Loretto* decided the case in terms of a per se or categorical rule: A permanent physical occupation authorized by the government is a taking, period. As we shall see — and as Justice Marshall suggests at page 1169, where he notes that there is no "set formula" and mentions "ad hoc, factual inquiries" — not

___

24. It is far from clear that, under New York law, appellant's tenants would lack all property interests in the few square inches on the exterior of the building to which Teleprompter's cable and hardware attach. Under modern landlord-tenant law, a residential tenancy is not merely a possessory interest in specified space, but also a contract for the provision of a package of services and facilities necessary and appurtenant to that space. . . .

25. Happily, the Court leaves open the question whether §828 provides landlords like appellant sufficient compensation for their actual losses. . . . If, after the remand following today's decision, this minor physical invasion is declared to be a taking deserving little or no compensation, the net result will have been a large expenditure of judicial resources on a constitutional claim of little moment.

all takings cases are decided in terms of such categorical rules, but some are, and cases involving physical occupation are not the only instance. More on this as we go along, but do start thinking about the virtues and vices of categorical takings rules as compared to an ad hoc approach. See generally Frank Michelman, Takings, 1987, 88 Colum. L. Rev. 1600 (1988); Susan Rose-Ackerman, Against Ad Hocery: A Comment on Michelman, 88 Colum. L. Rev. 1697 (1988); Frank Michelman, A Reply to Susan Rose-Ackerman, 88 Colum. L. Rev. 1712 (1988). These three essays are part of a larger collection appearing in a symposium on The Jurisprudence of Takings. An overview of the collection is provided by William A. Fischel, Introduction: Utilitarian Balancing and Formalism in Takings, 88 Colum. L. Rev. 1581 (1988).

   3. *Permanent physical occupation.* The particular categorical rule of *Loretto* is described as "anachronistic" and "aberrational" in John J. Costonis, Presumptive and Per Se Takings: A Decisional Model for the Taking Issue, 58 N.Y.U. L. Rev. 465, 529 (1985). Notwithstanding, the fact remains that *Loretto* represents little more than the U.S. Supreme Court's endorsement of a rule of long standing. If government action is pictured as having worked a permanent physical occupation, it appears that there is always a taking, no matter how inconsequential or trivial the invasion. See, e.g., Frank Michelman, Property, Utility, and Fairness: Comments on the Ethical Foundations of "Just Compensation" Law, 80 Harv. L. Rev. 1165, 1184-1185 (1967):

> At one time it was commonly held that, in the absence of explicit expropriation, a compensable "taking" could occur *only* through physical encroachment and occupation. The modern significance of physical occupation is that courts, while they sometimes do hold nontrespassory injuries compensable, *never* deny compensation for a physical takeover. The one incontestable case for compensation (short of formal expropriation) seems to occur when the government deliberately brings it about that its agents, or the public at large, "regularly" use, or "permanently" occupy, space or a thing which theretofore was understood to be under private ownership. This may be true although the invasion is practically trifling from the owner's point of view: a marginally encroaching sidewalk, for example, or the installation of utility lines underneath a road where the public already owns an easement of way across the surface. Moreover, compensation may be due although the actual harm to the complainant is indistinguishable from noncompensable harm to him which results from activity on the part of the government identical in every respect save that it apparently does not invade "his" sector of space.[26]

   In the last sentence just quoted, Michelman is referring to the flight nuisance cases — the *Causby* case discussed in *Loretto* at page 1170 is an

---

26. Compare the analogous situation of a physical invasion — an encroachment — by one *private* party upon another. Where the damage caused by such an encroachment is so minor as to be trivial, many courts simply deny all relief. See the discussion at pages 150-151. Why should the result be different when the government is the encroaching party?

example — holding that noise and vibration damages caused by direct overflights, but *only* direct overflights, are compensable as takings by physical invasion. This distinction between overflights and other flights has been rejected in some jurisdictions. See, e.g., Martin v. Port of Seattle, 64 Wash. 2d 309, 391 P.2d 540 (1964), cert. denied, 379 U.S. 989 (1965). A possible (but improbable) reason for the result in *Martin* is the Washington Constitution's requirement of compensation for "damaging" as well as for "taking" property. The constitutions of several dozen states have similar provisions, but the conventional wisdom is that the language has little if any significance. In some states the courts have rejected the overflight prerequisite notwithstanding the absence of a "damaging" clause. See, e.g., Thornburg v. Port of Portland, 233 Or. 178, 376 P.2d 100 (1962).

Is there any reason why damages from aircraft overflights should be compensable but exactly equivalent damages from other flights not compensable? See the discussion in Richard A. Posner, Economic Analysis of Law 60 (4th ed. 1992).

4. If *Loretto* added anything new, it is the distinction between permanent occupations, as to which the finding of a taking necessarily follows, and the temporary invasions that the Court says call for a balancing process. The distinction had been hinted at, but left uncrystallized, in the *Kaiser Aetna* and *PruneYard* cases discussed by the Court in its opinion. (See page 1171.) Why should permanent occupations be treated one way and temporary invasions another way, especially where, as in *Loretto,* the permanent occupation may have, at most, trivial effects on any interest of the property owner? The majority in *Loretto* claims that its per se rule for permanent occupations avoids "difficult line-drawing problems." Do you agree? See the dissenting opinion of Justice Blackmun.

5. *The right to exclude again.* We introduced the right to exclude in Chapter 1, at pages 92-102. *Loretto,* taking its lead from *Kaiser Aetna* and other cases, describes the power to exclude as "one of the most treasured strands in an owner's bundle of property rights." (See page 1172; see also page 1171, quoting *Kaiser Aetna*.) If the right to exclude is entitled to such solicitude, why isn't something like rent control a taking by physical occupation? See the Court's discussion on page 1174. Recall that the constitutionality of a rent control ordinance was recently considered by the Court in Yee v. City of Escondido, 112 S. Ct. 1522 (1992), discussed in Chapter 6 at pages 557-558. Here is a passage of interest from *Yee*:

> Petitioners' final line of argument rests on a footnote in *Loretto,* in which we rejected the contention that "the landlord could avoid the requirements of [the statute forcing her to permit cable to be permanently placed on her property] by ceasing to rent the building to tenants." We found this possibility insufficient to defeat a physical taking claim, because "a landlord's ability to rent his property may not be conditioned on his forfeiting the right to com-

pensation for a physical occupation." *Loretto* [footnote 21 on page 1174]. Petitioners argue that if they have to leave the mobile home park business in order to avoid the strictures of the Escondido ordinance, their ability to rent their property has in fact been conditioned on such a forfeiture. This argument fails at its base, however, because there has simply been no compelled physical occupation giving rise to a right to compensation that petitioners could have forfeited. Had the city required such an occupation, of course, petitioners would have a right to compensation, and the city might then lack the power to condition petitioners' ability to run mobile home parks on their waiver of this right. . . . But because the ordinance does not effect a physical taking in the first place, this footnote in *Loretto* does not help petitioners.

With respect to physical takings, then, this case is not far removed from FCC v. Florida Power Corp., 480 U.S. 245 (1987), in which . . . [w]e rejected the respondent's claim that "it is a taking under *Loretto* for a tenant invited to lease at a rent of $7.15 to remain at the regulated rent of $1.79." . . . We explained that "it is the invitation, not the rent, that makes the difference. The line which separates [this case] from *Loretto* is the unambiguous distinction between a . . . lessee and an interloper with a government license." [112 S. Ct. at 1530-1531.][27]

Hadacheck v. Sebastian

Supreme Court of the United States, 1915
239 U.S. 394

MR. JUSTICE MCKENNA delivered the opinion of the Court.

Habeas corpus prosecuted in the Supreme Court of the State of California for the discharge of plaintiff in error from the custody of defendant in error, Chief of Police of the City of Los Angeles.

Plaintiff in error, to whom we shall refer as petitioner, was convicted of a misdemeanor for the violation of an ordinance of the City of Los Angeles which makes it unlawful for any person to establish or operate a brick yard or brick kiln, or any establishment, factory or place for the manufacture or burning of brick within described limits in the city. . . .

The petition sets forth . . . that petitioner is the owner of a tract of land within the limits described in the ordinance upon which tract of land there is a very valuable bed of clay, of great value for the manufacture of brick of a fine quality, worth to him not less than $100,000 per acre or about $800,000 for the entire tract for brick-making purposes,

---

27. Elsewhere in *Yee* the Court quotes *Florida Power* for the proposition that the "element of required acquiescence is at the heart of the concept of occupation." 112 S. Ct. at 1528. Compare the *Seawall* case, discussed in Chapter 6 at pages 558-559.

Suppose a rent control ordinance does not require property owners to be landlords and lease at controlled rents, but does foreclose them, once they enter the system, from getting out of it (say by demolishing the rented premises). Does denial of a right of exit work a taking by physical occupation? See Fresh Pond Shopping Center, Inc. v. Callahan, 464 U.S. 875 (1983) (Rehnquist, J., dissenting from dismissal of appeal). — EDS.

and not exceeding $60,000 for residential purposes or for any purpose other than the manufacture of brick. That he has made excavations of considerable depth and covering a very large area of the property and that on account thereof the land cannot be utilized for residential purposes or any purpose other than that for which it is now used. That he purchased the land because of such bed of clay and for the purpose of manufacturing brick; that it was at the time of purchase outside of the limits of the city and distant from dwellings and other habitations and that he did not expect or believe, nor did other owners of the property in the vicinity expect or believe, that the territory would be annexed to the city. That he has erected expensive machinery for the manufacture of bricks of fine quality which have been and are being used for building purposes in and about the city.

That if the ordinance be declared valid he will be compelled to entirely abandon his business and will be deprived of the use of his property.

That the manufacture of brick must necessarily be carried on where suitable clay is found and the clay cannot be transported to some other location, and, besides, the clay upon his property is particularly fine and clay of as good quality cannot be found in any other place within the city where the same can be utilized for the manufacture of brick. That within the prohibited district there is one other brick yard besides that of plaintiff in error.

That there is no reason for the prohibition of the business; that its maintenance cannot be and is not in the nature of a nuisance . . . , and cannot be dangerous or detrimental to health or the morals or safety or peace or welfare or convenience of the people of the district or city.

That . . . no noises arise therefrom, and no noxious odors, and that by the use of certain means (which are described) provided and the situation of the brick yard an extremely small amount of smoke is emitted from any kiln and what is emitted is so dissipated that it is not a nuisance nor in any manner detrimental to health or comfort. That during the seven years which the brick yard has been conducted no complaint has been made of it, and no attempt has ever been made to regulate it.

That the city embraces 107.62 square miles in area and 75% of it is devoted to residential purposes; that the district described in the ordinance includes only about three square miles, is sparsely settled and contains large tracts of unsubdivided and unoccupied land; and that the boundaries of the district were determined for the sole and specific purpose of prohibiting and suppressing the business of petitioner and that of the other brick yard.

That there are and were at the time of the adoption of the ordinance in other districts of the city thickly built up with residences brick yards maintained more detrimental to the inhabitants of the city. That a petition was filed, signed by several hundred persons, representing such brick yards to be a nuisance and no ordinance or regulation was passed in regard to such petition and the brick yards are operated without hindrance or molestation. That other brick yards are permitted to be maintained without prohibition or regulation.

That no ordinance or regulation of any kind has been passed at any time regulating or attempting to regulate brick yards or inquiry made whether they could be maintained without being a nuisance or detrimental to health.

That the ordinance does not state a public offense and is in violation of the constitution of the State and the Fourteenth Amendment to the Constitution of the United States.

That the business of petitioner is a lawful one, none of the materials used in it are combustible, the machinery is of the most approved pattern and its conduct will not create a nuisance.

There is an allegation that the ordinance if enforced fosters and will foster a monopoly and protects and will protect other persons engaged in the manufacture of brick in the city, and discriminates and will discriminate against petitioner in favor of such other persons who are his competitors, and will prevent him from entering into competition with them.

The petition, after almost every paragraph, charges a deprivation of property, the taking of property without compensation, and that the ordinance is in consequence invalid.

We have given this outline of the petition as it presents petitioner's contentions, with the circumstances (which we deem most material) that give color and emphasis to them.

But there are substantial traverses made by the return to the writ, among others, a denial of the charge that the ordinance was arbitrarily directed against the business of petitioner, and it is alleged that there is another district in which brick yards are prohibited.

There was a denial of the allegations that the brick yard was conducted or could be conducted sanitarily or was not offensive to health. And there were affidavits supporting the denials. In these it was alleged that the fumes, gases, smoke, soot, steam and dust arising from petitioner's brick-making plant have from time to time caused sickness and serious discomfort to those living in the vicinity.

There was no specific denial of the value of the property or that it contained deposits of clay or that the latter could not be removed and manufactured into brick elsewhere. There was, however, a general denial that the enforcement of the ordinance would "entirely deprive petitioner of his property and the use thereof."

How the Supreme Court dealt with the allegations, denials and affidavits we can gather from its opinion. The court said, through Mr. Justice Sloss, 165 California, p.416:

The district to which the prohibition was applied contains about three square miles. The petitioner is the owner of a tract of land, containing eight acres, more or less, within the district described in the ordinance. He acquired his land in 1902, before the territory to which the ordinance was directed had been annexed to the city of Los Angeles. His land contains valuable deposits of clay suitable for the manufacture of brick, and he has, during the entire period of his ownership, used the land for brickmaking, and has erected thereon kilns, machinery and buildings necessary for such manufacture. The land, as he alleges, is far more valuable for brickmaking than for any other purpose.

The court considered the business one which could be regulated and that regulation was not precluded by the fact "that the value of investments made in the business prior to any legislative action will be greatly diminished," and that no complaint could be based upon the fact that petitioner had been carrying on the trade in that locality for a long period.

And, considering the allegations of the petition, the denials of the return and the evidence of the affidavits, the court said that the latter tended to show that the district created had become primarily a residential section and that the occupants of the neighboring dwellings are seriously incommoded by the operations of petitioner; and that such evidence, "when taken in connection with the presumptions in favor of the propriety of the legislative determination, overcame the contention that the prohibition of the ordinance was a mere arbitrary invasion of private right, not supported by any tenable belief that the continuance of the business was so detrimental to the interests of others as to require suppression."

The court, on the evidence, rejected the contention that the ordinance was not in good faith enacted as a police measure and that it was intended to discriminate against petitioner or that it was actuated by any motive of injuring him as an individual.

The charge of discrimination between localities was not sustained. ... "The facts before us," the court finally said, "would certainly not justify the conclusion that the ordinance here in question was designed, in either its adoption or its enforcement, to be anything but what it purported to be, viz., a legitimate regulation, operating alike upon all who came within its terms."

We think the conclusion of the court is justified by the evidence and makes it unnecessary to review the many cases cited by petitioner in which it is decided that the police power of a state cannot be arbitrarily exercised. The principle is familiar, but in any given case it must plainly appear to apply. It is to be remembered that we are dealing with one of the most essential powers of government, one that is the least limitable. It may, indeed, seem harsh in its exercise, usually is on some individual, but the imperative necessity for its existence precludes any limitation upon it when not exerted arbitrarily. A vested interest cannot be asserted against it because of conditions once obtaining. Chicago & Alton R.R. v. Tranbarger, 238 U.S. 67, 78. To so hold would preclude development and fix a city forever in its primitive conditions. There must be progress, and if in its march private interests are in the way they must yield to the good of the community. The logical result of petitioner's contention would seem to be that a city could not be formed or enlarged against the resistance of an occupant of the ground and that if it grows at all it can only grow as the environment of the occupations that are usually banished to the purlieus.

The police power and to what extent it may be exerted we have recently illustrated in Reinman v. Little Rock, 237 U.S. 171. The circumstances of the case were very much like those of the case at bar and give reply to the contentions of petitioner, especially that which asserts that a necessary and lawful occupation that is not a nuisance *per se* cannot be made so by legislative declaration. There was a like investment in property, encouraged by the then conditions; a like reduction of value and deprivation of property was asserted against the validity of the ordinance there considered; a like assertion of an arbitrary exercise of the power of prohibition. Against all of these contentions, and causing the rejection of them all, was adduced the police power. There was a prohibition of a business, lawful in itself, there as here. It was a livery stable there; a brick yard here. They differ in particulars, but they are alike in that which cause and justify prohibition in defined localities — that is, the effect upon the health and comfort of the community.

The ordinance passed upon prohibited the conduct of the business within a certain defined area in Little Rock, Arkansas. This Court said of it: granting that the business was not a nuisance *per se,* it was clearly within the police power of the State to regulate it, "and to that end to declare that in particular circumstances and in particular localities a livery stable shall be deemed a nuisance in fact and in law." And the only limitation upon the power was stated to be that the power could not be exerted arbitrarily or with unjust discrimination. There was a citation of cases. We think the present case is within the ruling thus declared.

There is a distinction between Reinman v. Little Rock and the case at bar. There a particular business was prohibited which was not affixed to or dependent upon its locality; it could be conducted elsewhere. Here, it is contended, the latter condition does not exist, and it is alleged that the manufacture of brick must necessarily be carried on where suitable clay is found and that the clay on petitioner's property cannot be transported to some other locality. This is not urged as a physical impossibility but only, counsel say, that such transportation and the transportation of the bricks to places where they could be used in construction work would be prohibitive "from a financial standpoint." But upon the evidence the Supreme Court considered the case, as we understand its opinion, from the standpoint of the offensive effects of the operation of a brick yard

and not from the deprivation of the deposits of clay, and distinguished
Ex parte Kelso, 147 California 609, wherein the court declared invalid
an ordinance absolutely prohibiting the maintenance or operation of a
rock or stone quarry within a certain portion of the city and county of
San Francisco. The court there said that the effect of the ordinance was
"to absolutely deprive the owners of real property within such limits of
a valuable right incident to their ownership, — viz., the right to extract
therefrom such rock and stone as they might find it to their advantage
to dispose of." The court expressed the view that the removal could be
regulated but that "an absolute prohibition of such removal under the
circumstances," could not be upheld.

In the present case there is no prohibition of the removal of the
brick clay; only a prohibition within the designated locality of its manufacture into bricks. And to this feature of the ordinance our opinion is
addressed. Whether other questions would arise if the ordinance were
broader, and opinion on such questions, we reserve. . . .

In his petition and argument something is made of the ordinance
as fostering a monopoly and suppressing his competition with other
brickmakers. The charge and argument are too illusive. It is part of the
charge that the ordinance was directed against him. The charge, we have
seen, was rejected by the Supreme Court, and we find nothing to justify
it. . . .

Judgment affirmed.

NOTES AND QUESTIONS

1. Consolidated Rock Prods. Co. v. City of Los Angeles, 57 Cal. 2d
515, 370 P.2d 342, 20 Cal. Rptr. 638, appeal dismissed, 371 U.S. 36
(1962), involved a zoning ordinance that prohibited rock and gravel operations on the plaintiff's property. The trial court had found that the
property in question was of great value if used as a gravel pit but virtually valueless in any other use; that a residential community with a
"national reputation as a haven for sufferers from respiratory ailments"
had grown up around the gravel pit; and that dust and noise pollution
from the gravel operations could be satisfactorily controlled. Held: The
ordinance was not a taking but a valid exercise of the police power to
control activities injurious to the public. See, to the same effect, Goldblatt v. Town of Hempstead, 369 U.S. 590 (1962).

2. *Another categorical rule?* Recall the categorical rule of *Loretto* and
like cases: If government action is seen to work a permanent physical
occupation, then a taking *always* follows. See Note 3 on page 1179. In
contrast, if the government action in question is depicted as a nuisance-
control measure, then it has long been thought that a taking *never* follows. The underlying notion is that the government is curbing a public

bad rather than expropriating a public good. See Ernst Freund, The Police Power §511 (1904):

> If we differentiate eminent domain and police power as distinct powers of government, the difference lies neither in the form nor in the purpose of taking, but in the relation which the property affected bears to the danger or evil which is to be provided against.
>
> Under the police power, rights of property are impaired not because they become useful or necessary to the public, or because some public advantage can be gained by disregarding them, but because their free exercise is believed to be detrimental to public interests; it may be said that the state takes property by eminent domain because it is useful to the public, and under the police power because it is harmful, or as Justice Bradley put it, because "the property itself is the cause of the public detriment."
>
> From this results the difference between the power of eminent domain and the police power, that the former recognizes a right to compensation, while the latter on principle does not.

Though not completely without defenders, the nuisance or public-bad test has been rather roundly criticized as a basis for deciding when a regulation amounts to a taking. See in particular Frank Michelman, Property, Utility, and Fairness: Comments on the Ethical Foundations of "Just Compensation" Law, 80 Harv. L. Rev. 1165, 1196-1197 (1967):

> The idea is that compensation is required when the public helps itself to good at private expense, but not when the public simply requires one of its members to stop making a nuisance of himself.
>
> For illustration of this approach, let us compare a regulation forbidding continued operation of a brick works which has been annoying residential neighbors with one forbidding an owner of rare meadowland to develop it so as to deprive the public of the benefits of drainage and wildlife conservation. According to the theories we are now to consider, a person affected by the second regulation would have the stronger claim to compensation. But even as to him, the matter is not free of ambiguity. To see this clearly, we can take as a third example a regulation forbidding the erection of billboards along the highway. Shall we construe this regulation as one which prevents the "harms" of roadside blight and distraction, or as one securing the "benefits" of safety and amenity? Shall we say that it prevents the highway abutter from inflicting injury on passing motorists, or that it enhances the value of the public's highway facility? This third example serves to expose one basic difficulty with the method of classifying regulations as compensable or not according to whether they prevent harms or extract benefits. Such a method will not work unless we can establish a benchmark of "neutral" conduct which enables us to say where refusal to confer benefits (not reversible without compensation) slips over into readiness to inflict harms (reversible without compensation).

A wonderful example of the "basic difficulty" identified by Michelman is Just v. Marinette County, 56 Wis. 2d 7, 201 N.W.2d 761 (1972), finding that an ordinance regulating wetlands development did not work a taking. As the court saw the case, the issue was whether the ordinance was designed to control a public harm or create a public benefit. Held: The purpose and effect were to control a public harm, not to extract a benefit. The ordinance simply limited land uses that were not "natural and indigenous" (the neutral benchmark). The court contrasted cases finding a taking where an ordinance prohibited bathing, swimming, and boating (is boating a "natural use"?), and where an ordinance limited building height (are high buildings a "natural use"?). See, to the same effect as *Just*, Graham v. Estuary Properties, Inc., 39 So. 2d 1374 (Fla. 1981); Sibson v. State, 115 N.H. 124, 336 A.2d 239 (1972), overruled in part by Burrows v. Keene, 121 N.H. 590, 432 A.2d 15 (1981). Contra, State v. Johnson, 265 A.2d 711 (Me. 1970). State courts have divided on the question whether wetlands regulation works a taking. See generally Annot., 19 A.L.R.4th 756 (1983).

A caveat: Having said all of this, we must now add a warning of sorts. The categorical rule that nuisance controls are never takings has been qualified (though not abolished) by the Supreme Court's decision in Lucas v. South Carolina Coastal Council, 112 S. Ct. 2886 (1992). Indeed, *Lucas* announces yet another categorical rule, but one that brings into play background material that has yet to be considered. Hence we save the case for later. See page 1241.

3. *Hadacheck* is very similar on its facts to the *Spur* case, page 976. In *Spur* the feedlot in question was held to be a nuisance, but the court concluded that, as a matter of fairness, the costs of moving or shutting down the feedlot operation should be borne by others. Why did considerations of fairness not compel the same result in *Hadacheck*? Is it not one thing to say that the government can control nuisances and quite another to say that compensation is never required in the course of doing so? See Lawrence Berger, A Policy Analysis of the Taking Problem, 49 N.Y.U. L. Rev. 165, 175 (1974):

> This [nuisance] approach assumes that if the harm [from the nuisance] is great enough, no compensation should be necessary. But why should that be? A result of no compensation will seem fair only when the regulated owner could reasonably have foreseen at the time he purchased or improved the property that the regulation would be imposed; in that event, the price he paid would reflect that expectation. He would have such expectation when, for example, there is a continuing and long standing consensus about the moral obloquy of the activity such as to warn the prospective actor that what he is about to do is against the law. On the other hand, he would be much less likely to foresee future regulation of a brickyard originally constructed in an undeveloped area.

PROBLEM

Miller owns a large number of ornamental red cedar trees infected with red cedar rust, a fungus which has no effect on cedars but can infect and kill apple trees. Pursuant to a Cedar Rust Act, the state orders Miller to cut down his trees in order to protect nearby apple orchards (apple growing is a principal agricultural industry in the state). The state is willing to pay Miller for the minor expense of cutting down the trees but not for the value of the standing trees nor for the decrease in market value resulting to Miller's property if the trees are removed. Miller claims a taking. What result? See Miller v. Schoene, 276 U.S. 272 (1928). See also Empire Kosher Poultry, Inc. v. Hallowell, 816 F.2d 907 (3d Cir. 1987); Department of Agric. & Consumer Servs. v. Mid-Florida Growers, Inc., 521 So. 2d 101 (Fla.), cert. denied, 488 U.S. 870 (1988).

Pennsylvania Coal Co. v. Mahon
Supreme Court of the United States, 1922
260 U.S. 393

MR. JUSTICE HOLMES delivered the opinion of the Court.

This is a bill in equity brought by the defendants in error to prevent the Pennsylvania Coal Company from mining under their property in such way as to remove the supports and cause a subsidence of the surface and of their house. The bill sets out a deed executed by the Coal Company in 1878, under which the plaintiffs claim. The deed conveys the surface, but in express terms reserves the right to remove all the coal under the same, and the grantee takes the premises with the risk, and waives all claim for damages that may arise from mining out the coal. But the plaintiffs say that whatever may have been the Coal Company's rights, they were taken away by an Act of Pennsylvania, approved May 27, 1921, P.L. 1198, commonly known there as the Kohler Act. The Court of Common Pleas found that if not restrained the defendant would cause the damage to prevent which the bill was brought, but denied an injunction, holding that the statute if applied to this case would be unconstitutional. On appeal the Supreme Court of the State agreed that the defendant had contract and property rights protected by the Constitution of the United States, but held that the statute was a legitimate exercise of the police power and directed a decree for the plaintiffs. A writ of error was granted bringing the case to this Court.

The statute forbids the mining of anthracite coal in such way as to cause the subsidence of, among other things, any structure used as a human habitation, with certain exceptions, including among them land where the surface is owned by the owner of the underlying coal and is distant more than one hundred and fifty feet from any improved prop-

Justice Oliver Wendell Holmes

erty belonging to any other person. As applied to this case the statute is admitted to destroy previously existing rights of property and contract. The question is whether the police power can be stretched so far.

Government hardly could go on if to some extent values incident to property could not be diminished without paying for every such change in the general law. As long recognized, some values are enjoyed under an implied limitation and must yield to the police power. But obviously the implied limitation must have its limits, or the contract and due process clauses are gone. One fact for consideration in determining such limits is the extent of the diminution. When it reaches a certain magnitude, in most if not in all cases there must be an exercise of eminent domain and compensation to sustain the act. So the question depends upon the particular facts. The greatest weight is given to the judgment of the legislature, but it always is open to interested parties to contend that the legislature has gone beyond its constitutional power.

This is the case of a single private house. No doubt there is a public interest even in this, as there is in every purchase and sale and in all that happens within the commonwealth. Some existing rights may be modified even in such a case. Rideout v. Knox, 148 Mass. 368. But usually in ordinary private affairs the public interest does not warrant much of this kind of interference. A source of damage to such a house is not a public nuisance even if similar damage is inflicted on others in different places. The damage is not common or public. Wesson v. Washburn Iron Co., 13 Allen 95, 103. The extent of the public interest is shown by the statute to be limited, since the statute ordinarily does not apply to land when the surface is owned by the owner of the coal. Furthermore, it is not justified as a protection of personal safety. That could be provided for by notice. Indeed the very foundation of this bill is that the defendant gave timely notice of its intent to mine under the house. On the other hand the extent of the taking is great. It purports to abolish what is recognized in Pennsylvania as an estate in land — a very valuable estate — and what is declared by the court below to be a contract hitherto binding the plaintiffs. If we were called upon to deal with the plaintiffs' position alone, we should think it clear that the statute does not disclose a public interest sufficient to warrant so extensive a destruction of the defendant's constitutionally protected rights.

But the case has been treated as one in which the general validity of the act should be discussed. The Attorney General of the State, the City of Scranton, and the representatives of other extensive interests were allowed to take part in the argument below and have submitted their contentions here. It seems, therefore, to be our duty to go farther in the statement of our opinion, in order that it may be known at once, and that further suits should not be brought in vain.

It is our opinion that the act cannot be sustained as an exercise of the police power, so far as it affects the mining of coal under streets or cities in places where the right to mine such coal has been reserved. As said in a Pennsylvania case, "For practical purposes, the right to coal consists in the right to mine it." Commonwealth v. Clearview Coal Co., 256 Pa. St. 328, 331. What makes the right to mine coal valuable is that it can be exercised with profit. To make it commercially impracticable to mine certain coal has very nearly the same effect for constitutional purposes as appropriating or destroying it. This we think that we are warranted in assuming that the statute does.

It is true that in Plymouth Coal Co. v. Pennsylvania, 232 U.S. 531, it was held competent for the legislature to require a pillar of coal to be left along the line of adjoining property, that, with the pillar on the other side of the line, would be a barrier sufficient for the safety of the employees of either mine in case the other should be abandoned and allowed to fill with water. But that was a requirement for the safety of employees invited into the mine, and secured an average reciprocity of advantage that has been recognized as a justification of various laws.

The rights of the public in a street purchased or laid out by eminent domain are those that it has paid for. If in any case its representatives have been so short sighted as to acquire only surface rights without the right of support, we see no more authority for supplying the latter without compensation than there was for taking the right of way in the first place and refusing to pay for it because the public wanted it very much. The protection of private property in the Fifth Amendment presupposes that it is wanted for public use, but provides that it shall not be taken for such use without compensation. A similar assumption is made in the decisions upon the Fourteenth Amendment. Hairston v. Danville & Western Ry. Co., 208 U.S. 598, 605. When the seemingly absolute protection is found to be qualified by the police power, the natural tendency of human nature is to extend the qualification more and more until at last private property disappears. But that cannot be accomplished in this way under the Constitution of the United States.

The general rule at least is, that while property may be regulated to a certain extent, if regulation goes too far it will be recognized as a taking. It may be doubted how far exceptional cases, like the blowing up of a house to stop a conflagration, go — and if they go beyond the general rule, whether they do not stand as much upon tradition as upon principle. Bowditch v. Boston, 101 U.S. 16. In general it is not plain that a man's misfortunes or necessities will justify his shifting the damages to his neighbor's shoulders. Space v. Lynn & Boston R.R. Co., 172 Mass. 488, 489. We are in danger of forgetting that a strong public desire to improve the public condition is not enough to warrant achieving the desire by a shorter cut than the constitutional way of paying for the change. As we already have said, this is a question of degree — and therefore cannot be disposed of by general propositions. But we regard this as going beyond any of the cases decided by this Court. The late decisions upon laws dealing with the congestion of Washington and New York, caused by the war, dealt with laws intended to meet a temporary emergency and providing for compensation determined to be reasonable by an impartial board. They went to the verge of the law but fell far short of the present act. Block v. Hirsh, 256 U.S. 135. Marcus Brown Holding Co. v. Feldman, 256 U.S. 170. Levy Leasing Co. v. Siegel, 258 U.S. 242.

We assume, of course, that the statute was passed upon the conviction that an exigency existed that would warrant it, and we assume that an exigency exists that would warrant the exercise of eminent domain. But the question at bottom is upon whom the loss of the changes desired should fall. So far as private persons or communities have seen fit to take the risk of acquiring only surface rights, we cannot see that the fact that their risk has become a danger warrants the giving to them greater rights than they bought.

Decree reversed.

MR. JUSTICE BRANDEIS, dissenting.

The Kohler Act prohibits, under certain conditions, the mining of anthracite coal within the limits of a city in such a manner or to such an extent "as to cause the . . . subsidence of any dwelling or other structure used as a human habitation, or any factory, store, or other industrial or mercantile establishment in which human labor is employed." Coal in place is land; and the right of the owner to use his land is not absolute. He may not so use it as to create a public nuisance; and uses, once harmless, may, owing to changed conditions, seriously threaten the public welfare. Whenever they do, the legislature has power to prohibit such uses without paying compensation; and the power to prohibit extends alike to the manner, the character and the purpose of the use. Are we justified in declaring that the Legislature of Pennsylvania has, in restricting the right to mine anthracite, exercised this power so arbitrarily as to violate the Fourteenth Amendment?

Every restriction upon the use of property imposed in the exercise of the police power deprives the owner of some right theretofore enjoyed, and is, in that sense, an abridgement by the State of rights in property without making compensation. But restriction imposed to protect the public health, safety or morals from dangers threatened is not a taking. The restriction here in question is merely the prohibition of a noxious use. The property so restricted remains in the possession of its owner. The State does not appropriate it or make any use of it. The State merely prevents the owner from making a use which interferes with paramount rights of the public. Whenever the use prohibited ceases to be noxious, — as it may because of further change in local or social conditions, — the restriction will have to be removed and the owner will again be free to enjoy his property as heretofore.

Justice Louis Dembitz Brandeis

The restriction upon the use of this property can not, of course, be lawfully imposed, unless its purpose is to protect the public. But the purpose of a restriction does not cease to be public, because incidentally some private persons may thereby receive gratuitously valuable special benefits. Thus, owners of low buildings may obtain, through statutory restrictions upon the height of neighboring structures, benefits equivalent to an easement of light and air. Furthermore, a restriction, though imposed for a public purpose, will not be lawful, unless the restriction is an appropriate means to the public end. But to keep coal in place is surely an appropriate means of preventing subsidence of the surface; and ordinarily it is the only available means. Restriction upon use does not become inappropriate as a means, merely because it deprives the owner of the only use to which the property can then be profitably put. The liquor and the oleomargarine cases settled that. Mugler v. Kansas, 123 U.S. 623; Powell v. Pennsylvania, 127 U.S. 678. Nor is a restriction imposed through exercise of the police power inappropriate as a means, merely because the same end might be effected through exercise of the power of eminent domain, or otherwise at public expense. Every restriction upon the height of buildings might be secured through acquiring by eminent domain the right of each owner to build above the limiting height; but it is settled that the State need not resort to that power. If by mining anthracite coal the owner would necessarily unloose poisonous gasses, I suppose no one would doubt the power of the State to prevent the mining, without buying his coal fields. And why may not the State, likewise, without paying compensation, prohibit one from digging so deep or excavating so near the surface, as to expose the community to like dangers? In the latter case, as in the former, carrying on the business would be a public nuisance.

It is said that one fact for consideration in determining whether the limits of the police power have been exceeded is the extent of the resulting diminution in value; and that here the restriction destroys existing rights of property and contract. But values are relative. If we are to consider the value of the coal kept in place by the restriction, we should compare it with the value of all other parts of the land. That is, with the value not of the coal alone, but with the value of the whole property. The rights of an owner as against the public are not increased by dividing the interests in his property into surface and subsoil. The sum of the rights in the parts can not be greater than the rights in the whole. The estate of an owner in land is grandiloquently described as extending *ab orco usque ad coelum*. But I suppose no one would contend that by selling his interest above one hundred feet from the surface he could prevent the State from limiting, by the police power, the height of structures in a city. And why should a sale of underground rights bar the State's power? For aught that appears the value of the coal kept in place by the restriction may be negligible as compared with the value of the whole property, or even as compared with that part of it which is represented by the coal remaining in place and which may be extracted despite the statute. Ordinarily a police regulation, general in operation, will not be held void as to a particular property, although proof is offered that owing to conditions peculiar to it the restriction could not reasonably be applied. But even if the particular facts are to govern, the statute should, in my opinion, be upheld in this case. For the defendant has failed to adduce any evidence from which it appears that to restrict its mining operations was an unreasonable exercise of the police power. Where the surface and the coal belong to the same person, self-interest would ordinarily prevent mining to such an extent as to cause a subsidence. It was, doubtless, for this reason that the legislature, estimating the degrees of danger, deemed statutory restriction unnecessary for the public safety under such conditions.

It is said that this is a case of a single dwelling house; that the restriction upon mining abolishes a valuable estate hitherto secured by a contract with the plaintiffs; and that the restriction upon mining cannot be justified as a protection of personal safety, since that could be provided for by notice. The propriety of deferring a good deal to tribunals on the spot has been repeatedly recognized. . . . May we say that notice would afford adequate protection of the public safety where the legislature and the highest court of the State, with greater knowledge of local conditions, have declared, in effect, that it would not? If public safety is imperiled, surely neither grant, nor contract, can prevail against the exercise of the police power. . . .

This case involves only mining which causes subsidence of a dwelling house. But the Kohler Act contains provisions in addition to that quoted above; and as to these, also, an opinion is expressed. These provisions deal with mining under cities to such an extent as to cause subsidence of —

(a) Any public building or any structure customarily used by the public as a place of resort, assemblage, or amusement, including, but not being limited to, churches, schools, hospitals, theatres, hotels, and railroad stations.

(b) Any street, road, bridge or other public passageway, dedicated to public use or habitually used by the public.

(c) Any track, roadbed, right of way, pipe, conduit, wire, or other facility, used in the service of the public by any municipal corporation or public service company as defined by the Public Service Company Law.

A prohibition of mining which causes subsidence of such structures and facilities is obviously enacted for a public purpose and it seems, likewise, clear that mere notice of intention to mine would not in this connection secure the public safety. Yet it is said that these provisions of the act cannot be sustained as an exercise of the police power where the right to mine such coal has been reserved. The conclusion seems to rest upon the assumption that in order to justify such exercise of the police power there must be "an average reciprocity of advantage" as between the owner of the property restricted and the rest of the community; and that here such reciprocity is absent. Reciprocity of advantage is an important consideration, and may even be an essential, where the State's power is exercised for the purpose of conferring benefits upon the property of a neighborhood, as in drainage projects, Wurts v. Hoagland, 114 U.S. 606; Fallbrook Irrigation District v. Bradley, 164 U.S. 112; or upon adjoining owners, as by party wall provisions, Jackman v. Rosenbaum Co., [260 U.S.] 22. But where the police power is exercised, not to confer benefits upon property owners, but to protect the public from detriment and danger, there is, in my opinion, no room for considering reciprocity of advantage. There was no reciprocal advantage to the owner prohibited from using his oil tanks in 248 U.S. 498; his brickyard, in 239 U.S. 394; his livery stable, in 237 U.S. 171; his billiard hall, in 225 U.S. 623; his oleomargarine factory, in 127 U.S. 678; his brewery, in 123 U.S. 623; unless it be the advantage of living and doing business in a civilized community. That reciprocal advantage is given by the act to the coal operators.

NOTES AND QUESTIONS

1. *Takings tests.* We have thus far seen two categorical tests or rules of decision for takings cases: Permanent physical occupations are always takings; nuisance-control measures are never takings (but remember the caveat on page 1188). *Pennsylvania Coal* is the classic statement of a different sort of test, softer around its edges, concerned with differences of degree rather than differences in kind, inquiring whether — on balance — matters have gone "too far." The test says, in essence, that when governmental regulation of a use that is not a nuisance works too great a burden on property owners, it cannot go forth without compensation. Notice, though, that the regulation itself might provide implicit compensation by way of what Justice Holmes called, on page 1192, "an average reciprocity of advantage." The idea, of course, is that the apparent losers under a government program might not be losers at all (or not, at least, big losers) because they are simultaneously benefitted by the very action that burdens them. Watch for this idea as it plays into later cases. See generally Richard A. Epstein, Takings: Private Property and the Power of Eminent Domain 195-197 (1985).

2. *Diminution in value.* The rule of decision in *Pennsylvania Coal* is usually referred to as the diminution-in-value test. What is its point? Is it concerned with efficiency, with justice, or with both?[28]

28. Some observers see a *balancing* test in *Pennsylvania Coal.* The idea here is that one should compare the public benefits of governmental activity against the private harms it

Notice Justice Brandeis's response to the majority opinion of Justice Holmes. His first argument is straightforward. The Kohler Act was merely controlling a nuisance, hence no compensation was required. His second argument attacks the diminution-in-value test head-on: diminution relative to what?

The question is an important one. Contemporary takings cases most commonly arise from governmental regulatory activities that involve neither permanent physical occupations nor any pretense of nuisance controls, so the diminution-in-value test has a dominant role to play.[29] The problem is the extraordinary ambiguity of the test. See, e.g., Rose, supra footnote 28, at 566-569. How much of a loss of value is too much? Is loss to be measured in absolute terms, or rather in relative ones? If the latter, relative to what?

Consider how Holmes and Brandeis differed in their approach to the last question in particular. Pennsylvania law recognizes three separate estates in mining property: in the surface, in the minerals, and in support of the surface. See id. at 563-564, 565-567; E.F. Roberts, Mining with Mr. Justice Holmes, 39 Vand. L. Rev. 287 (1986). Holmes saw the Kohler Act as purporting to "abolish" the third estate entirely. See page 1191. Brandeis, on the other hand, reasoned that the "rights of an owner as against the public are not increased by dividing the interests in his property"; the Kohler Act did not take all of a smaller thing (the third estate) but only a part "of the whole property." See pages 1195-1196.

Which view is correct? The question — referred to in the literature as the issue of *conceptual severance* — is seemingly crucial but also, thus far, seemingly unresolved. Simply note it for now; it plays into later cases.

Conceptual severance aside, there are other puzzles about the diminution-in-value test. For example, Bruce A. Ackerman, Private Property and the Constitution 142 (1977), observes that when courts apply the test they actually frame the inquiry not in terms of absolute or relative value lost but rather in terms of absolute value left. Is that sensible?

---

works on claimants. If claimants would lose a lot more than the public would gain, a taking should be found, otherwise not. The test fares pretty well in efficiency terms, but begs the question of fairness. As to each point, do you see why? In any event, were there in Holmes's view any *public* benefits in the Kohler Act? That question is addressed in the *Keystone* case, to which we shall turn momentarily. See also Carol M. Rose, *Mahon* Reconstructed: Why the Takings Issue Is Still a Muddle, 57 S. Cal. L. Rev. 561, 571-581 (1984).

29. Which is not to say that it has been much of a constraint on regulatory activity. For example, so far as we know the Supreme Court never once in the years 1922-1991 found a taking in *Pennsylvania Coal*'s diminution-in-value terms. Moreover, it retreated from the case in 1987, as you are about to see.

For interesting background on *Pennsylvania Coal*, see Joseph F. DiMento, Mining the Archives of *Pennsylvania Coal*: Heaps of Constitutional Mischief, 11 J. Legal Hist. 396 (1990); Lawrence M. Friedman, A Search for Seizure: *Pennsylvania Coal Co. v. Mahon* in Context, 4 Law & Hist. Rev. 1 (1986).

Another example: Should diminution in value figure in cases involving permanent physical occupations? Finally, should it figure in cases involving nuisance controls? Here we have to repeat our caveat about the *Lucas* case, which suggests, as you shall see, that diminution in value *is* of some relevance in nuisance-control cases. Consider also the following:

Keystone Bituminous Coal Association v. DeBenedictis, 480 U.S. 470 (1987). *Keystone* is *Pennsylvania Coal* redux. In 1966 Pennsylvania enacted legislation designed, as was the Kohler Act, to control subsidence from coal mining. The legislation, here called the Subsidence Act, requires mine operators to keep up to 50 percent of their coal in place, and to repair surface damage caused by subsidence even if surface owners have waived their rights (as they are permitted to do under Pennsylvania law if the state's Department of Environmental Resources (DER) consents). Petitioners, an association of coal mine operators and four mining corporations, challenged the constitutionality of the legislation, claiming, among other things, that it worked a taking of their property. The Court, in an opinion by Justice Stevens, disagreed.

"Petitioners assert that disposition of their takings claim calls for no more than a straightforward application of the Court's decision in Pennsylvania Coal Co. v. Mahon. Although there are some obvious similarities between the cases, we agree with the Court of Appeals and the District Court that the similarities are far less significant than the differences, and that *Pennsylvania Coal* does not control this case.

". . . First, unlike the Kohler Act, the character of the governmental action involved here leans heavily against finding a taking; the Commonwealth of Pennsylvania has acted to arrest what it perceives to be a significant threat to the common welfare. Second, there is no record in this case to support a finding, similar to the one the Court made in *Pennsylvania Coal*, that the Subsidence Act makes it impossible for petitioners to profitably engage in their business, or that there has been undue interference with their investment-backed expectations.

"Unlike the Kohler Act, which was passed upon in *Pennsylvania Coal*, the Subsidence Act does not merely involve a balancing of the private economic interests of coal companies against the private interests of the surface owners. The Pennsylvania legislature specifically found that important public interests are served by enforcing a policy that is designed to minimize subsidence in certain areas. . . .

"None of the indicia of a statute enacted solely for the benefit of private parties identified in Justice Holmes' opinion are present here. First, Justice Holmes explained that the Kohler Act was a 'private benefit' statute since it 'ordinarily does not apply to land when the surface is owned by the owner of the coal.' [See page 1191.] The Subsidence Act, by contrast, has no such exception. The current surface owner may only waive the protection of the Act if the DER consents. Moreover, the

Court was forced to reject the Commonwealth's safety justification for the Kohler Act because it found that the Commonwealth's interest in safety could as easily have been accomplished through a notice requirement to landowners. The Subsidence Act, by contrast, is designed to accomplish a number of widely varying interests, with reference to which petitioners have not suggested alternative methods through which the Commonwealth could proceed. . . .

"Thus, the Subsidence Act differs from the Kohler Act in critical and dispositive respects. With regard to the Kohler Act, the Court believed that the Commonwealth had acted only to ensure against damage to some private landowners' homes. Justice Holmes stated that if the private individuals needed support for their structures, they should not have 'take[n] the risk of acquiring only surface rights.' [See page 1193.] Here, by contrast, the Commonwealth is acting to protect the public interest in health, the environment, and the fiscal integrity of the area. That private individuals erred in taking a risk cannot estop the Commonwealth from exercising its police power to abate activity akin to a public nuisance. . . .

"The Court's hesitance to find a taking when the State merely restrains uses of property that are tantamount to public nuisances is consistent with the notion of 'reciprocity of advantage' that Justice Holmes referred to in *Pennsylvania Coal*. [See page 1192.] Under our system of government, one of the State's primary ways of preserving the public weal is restricting the uses individuals can make of their property. While each of us is burdened somewhat by such restrictions, we, in turn, benefit greatly from the restrictions that are placed on others.

". . . [T]he public interest in preventing activities similar to public nuisances is a substantial one, which in many instances has not required compensation. The Subsidence Act, unlike the Kohler Act, plainly seeks to further such an interest. Nonetheless, we need not rest our decision on this factor alone, because petitioners have also failed to make a showing of diminution of value sufficient to satisfy the test set forth in *Pennsylvania Coal* and our other regulatory takings cases. . . .

"The posture of the case [— the claim that the mere enactment of the Subsidence Act, without regard to its particular applications, constitutes a facially unconstitutional taking —] is critical because we have recognized an important distinction between a claim that the mere enactment of a statute constitutes a taking and a claim that the particular impact of government action on a specific piece of property requires the payment of just compensation. . . . Petitioners thus face an uphill battle in making a facial attack on the Act as a taking.

"The hill is made especially steep because petitioners have not claimed, at this stage, that the Act makes it commercially impracticable for them to continue mining their bituminous coal interests in western Pennsylvania. [They] have not even pointed to a single mine that can no longer be mined for profit. . . .

"Instead, petitioners have sought to narrowly define certain segments of their property and assert that, when so defined, the Subsidence Act denies them economically viable use. They advance two alternative ways of carving their property in order to reach this conclusion. First, they focus on the specific tons of coal that they must leave in the ground under the Subsidence Act, and argue that the Commonwealth has effectively appropriated this coal since it has no other useful purpose if not mined. Second, they contend that the Commonwealth has taken their separate legal interest in property — the 'support estate.'

"Because our test for regulatory taking requires us to compare the value that has been taken from the property with the value that remains in the property, one of the critical questions is determining how to define the unit of property 'whose value is to furnish the denominator of the fraction.' Michelman, Property, Utility, and Fairness: Comments on the Ethical Foundations of 'Just Compensation' Law, 80 Harv. L. Rev. 1165, 1192 (1967). [The Court then cited Penn Central Transportation Co. v. New York City, considered at page 1203 in this book, for the proposition that takings jurisprudence 'does not divide a single parcel into discrete segments and attempt to determine whether rights in a particular segment have been entirely abrogated.' Instead, the Court considers rights in the parcel as a whole.]

". . . The 27 million tons of coal [that must be left in place under the Subsidence Act] do not constitute a separate segment of property for takings law purposes. Many zoning ordinances place limits on the property owner's right to make profitable use of some segments of his property. A requirement that a building occupy no more than a specified percentage of the lot on which it is located could be characterized as a taking of the vacant area as readily as the requirement that coal pillars be left in place. . . . There is no basis for treating the less than 2% of petitioners' coal as a separate parcel of property.

"We do not consider Justice Holmes' statement that the Kohler Act made mining of 'certain coal' commercially impracticable as requiring us to focus on the individual pillars of coal that must be left in place. That statement is best understood as referring to the Pennsylvania Coal Company's assertion that it could not undertake profitable anthracite coal mining in light of the Kohler Act. There were strong assertions in the record to support that conclusion. . . .

"When the coal that must remain beneath the ground is viewed in the context of any reasonable unit of petitioners' coal mining operations and financial-backed expectations, it is plain that petitioners have not come close to satisfying their burden of proving that they have been denied the economically viable use of that property. . . .

"Pennsylvania property law is apparently unique in regarding the support estate as a separate interest in land that can be conveyed apart from either the mineral estate or the surface estate. Petitioners therefore argue that even if comparable legislation in another State would not constitute a taking, the Subsidence Act has that consequence because it entirely destroys the value of their unique support estate. It is clear, however, that our takings jurisprudence forecloses reliance on such legalistic distinctions within a bundle of property rights. . . .

"The Court of Appeals, which is more familiar with Pennsylvania law than we are, concluded that as a practical matter the support estate is always owned by either the owner of the surface or the owner of the minerals. . . .

"Thus, in practical terms, the support estate has value only insofar as it protects or enhances the value of the estate with which it is associated. Its value is merely a part of the entire bundle of rights possessed by the owner of either the coal or the surface. Because petitioners retain the right to mine virtually all of the coal in their mineral estates, the burden the Act places on the support estate does not constitute a taking. Petitioners may continue to mine coal profitably even if they may not destroy or damage surface structures at will in the process.

"But even if we were to accept petitioners' invitation to view the support estate as a distinct segment of property for 'takings' purposes, they have not satisfied their heavy burden of sustaining a facial challenge to the Act. Petitioners have acquired or retained the support estate for a great deal of land, only part of which is protected under the Subsidence Act. . . . The record is devoid of any evidence on what percentage of the purchased support estates, either in the aggregate or with respect to any individual estate, has been affected by the Act. Under these circumstances, petitioners' facial attack under the Takings Clause must surely fail."

Chief Justice Rehnquist, joined by Justices Powell, O'Connor, and Scalia, dissented in the *Keystone* case, finding it "strikingly similar" to *Pennsylvania Coal*; "the holding in *Pennsylvania Coal* today discounted by the Court has for 65 years been the foundation of our 'regulatory takings' jurisprudence."

The Kohler Act, in the view of the Chief Justice, clearly had been intended to serve public interests, yet it was invalidated. Beyond this, the Chief Justice saw the Subsidence Act as more than a nuisance-control measure. In any event, the majority defined the nuisance exception too broadly: "our cases have never applied the nuisance exception to allow complete extinction of the value of a parcel of property." Finally, as to the coal that had to be left in place, there was in the Chief Justice's judgment "no question that this coal is an identifiable and separable property interest. Unlike many property interests, the 'bundle' of rights in this coal is sparse. . . . From the relevant perspective — that of the property owners — this interest has been destroyed every bit as much as if the government had proceeded to mine the coal for its own use." And there was the matter of the support estate. "I see no reason for refusing to evaluate the impact of the Subsidence Act on the support estate alone,

for Pennsylvania has clearly defined it as a separate estate in property.
. . . In these circumstances, where the estate defined by state law is both
severable and of value in its own right, it is appropriate to consider the
effect of regulation on that particular property interest."

"In sum," the Chief Justice said, "I would hold that Pennsylvania's
Bituminous Mine Subsidence and Land Conservation Act effects a taking of petitioners' property without providing just compensation. Specifically, the Act works to extinguish petitioners' interest in at least 27
million tons of coal by requiring that coal to be left in the ground, and
destroys their purchased support estates by returning to them financial
liability for subsidence."

NOTES AND QUESTIONS

1. *Keystone* clearly rejects conceptual severance (page 1198), does it
not? See Frank Michelman, Takings, 1987, 88 Colum. L. Rev. 1600,
1615-1616 (1988).[30] What about the categorical rule regarding nuisance
controls discussed in Note 2 on page 1186? Is it confirmed or undermined by the decision in *Keystone*? See Yancey v. United States, 915 F.2d
1534, 1540 (Fed. Cir. 1990); Michelman, supra, at 1603 n.19.

2. Notice the reference in *Keystone* to a new term of art: "investment-backed expectations." See page 1199. The phrase owes, in a sense,
to the case that follows (which talks about reciprocity of advantage and
conceptual severance as well).

Penn Central Transportation Co.
v. City of New York
Supreme Court of the United States, 1978
438 U.S. 104

[In 1967, New York City's Landmarks Preservation Commission (the
Commission), acting under the authority of the city's Landmarks Preservation Law, designated Grand Central Terminal a landmark. The
Terminal, owned by the Penn Central Transportation Co. and its affiliates, is one of New York City's most famous buildings, "a magnificent

---

30. In Allingham v. City of Seattle, 109 Wash. 2d 947, 749 P.2d 160 (1988), the court
considered a Greenbelt Ordinance requiring that up to 70 percent of the area of certain
privately owned lots be retained in or restored to a natural state. The city argued that the
ordinance was not a taking because the balance of each lot could be put to profitable use.
In the city's view, it was free to regulate away *all* rights of ownership to a *part* of the
property, so long as the rest remained usable. The court disagreed and invalidated the
ordinance. Suppose the ordinance touched only 50 percent of the land, or only 10 percent,
or only 5 percent. Would it work a taking? On this question the decision is opaque. On
what does the answer turn?

example of the French beaux arts style." Designation as a landmark re-sulted in restrictions upon the use of the Terminal. In particular, any changes in its exterior architectural features had to be approved in ad-vance by the Commission. But designation also had an advantage. Un-der the landmarks law, owners who have not developed their property to the full extent permitted by zoning regulations are allowed to transfer development rights to contiguous parcels on the same city block and, in some cases, to other parcels, provided all lots are in the same ownership. At the time of the case, Penn Central owned a number of properties in midtown Manhattan.

In 1968 Penn Central, in order to increase its income, entered into a renewable long-term lease with UGP, a British corporation; under the terms of the lease, UGP was to construct a multistory office building above Grand Central Terminal. UGP would pay an annual rent of $1 million during construction and at least $3 million a year thereafter.

Penn Central and UGP applied to the Commission for permission to build atop the Terminal. Two separate plans by architect Marcel Breuer were submitted; both of them — called Breuer I and Breuer II revised — were turned down by the Commission. Of Breuer I the Com-mission said, "to balance a 55-story office tower above a flamboyant Beaux-Arts facade seems nothing more than an aesthetic joke." Breuer II provoked an even sterner reaction: "To protect a Landmark, one does not tear it down. To perpetuate its architectural features, one does not strip them off." Penn Central and UGP then brought suit in state court, claiming that the application of the landmarks law had taken their prop-erty. The trial court granted injunctive and declaratory relief, but its judgment was reversed by the intermediate appellate court. The New York Court of Appeals affirmed, finding no taking because the law had not transferred control but only restricted it. The case then went to the U.S. Supreme Court, which affirmed in an opinion by Justice Brennan, portions of which follow.]

[T]his Court, quite simply, has been unable to develop any "set formula" for determining when "justice and fairness" require that economic injuries caused by public action be compensated by the gov-ernment, rather than remain disproportionately concentrated on a few persons. . . . Indeed, we have frequently observed that whether a partic-ular restriction will be rendered invalid by the government's failure to pay for any losses proximately caused by it depends largely "upon the particular circumstances [in that] case." United States v. Central Eureka Mining Co., 357 U.S. 155, 168 (1958).

In engaging in these essentially ad hoc, factual inquiries, the Court's decisions have identified several factors that have particular significance. The economic impact of the regulation on the claimant and, particu-larly, the extent to which the regulation has interfered with distinct investment-backed expectations are, of course, relevant considerations.

Breuer I

Breuer II

So, too, is the character of the governmental action. A "taking" may more readily be found when the interference with property can be characterized as a physical invasion by government . . . than when interference arises from some public program adjusting the benefits and burdens of economic life to promote the common good. . . .

In contending that the New York City law has "taken" their property in violation of the Fifth and Fourteenth Amendments, appellants make a series of arguments. . . .

They first observe that the airspace above the Terminal is a valuable property interest. . . . They urge that the Landmarks Law has deprived them of any gainful use of their "air rights" above the Terminal and that, irrespective of the value of the remainder of their parcel, the city has "taken" their right to this superjacent airspace, thus entitling them to "just compensation" measured by the fair market value of these air rights.

Apart from our own disagreement with the appellants' characterization of the effect of the New York City law, the submission that appellants may establish a "taking" simply by showing that they have been denied the ability to exploit a property interest that they heretofore had believed was available for development is quite simply untenable. . . . "Taking" jurisprudence does not divide a single parcel into discrete segments and attempt to determine whether rights in a particular segment have been entirely abrogated. In deciding whether a particular governmental action has effected a taking, this Court focuses rather both on the character of the action and on the nature and extent of the interference with rights in the parcel as a whole. . . .[31]

Secondly, appellants, focusing on the character and impact of the New York City law, argue that it effects a "taking" because its operation has significantly diminished the value of the Terminal site. Appellants concede that the decisions sustaining other land-use regulations, which, like the New York City law, are reasonably related to the promotion of the general welfare, uniformly reject the proposition that diminution in property value, standing alone, can establish as "taking," see Euclid v. Ambler Realty Co., 272 U.S. 365 (1926) (75% diminution in value caused by zoning law); Hadacheck v. Sebastian, 239 U.S. 394 (1915) (87½% diminution in value), and that the "taking" issue in these contexts is resolved by focusing on the uses the regulations permit. Appellants, moreover, also do not dispute that a showing of diminution in property value would not establish a "taking" if the restriction had been imposed as a result of historic-district legislation, see generally Maher v.

31. [This observation disposes] of any contention that might be based on Pennsylvania Coal Co. v. Mahon, 260 U.S. 393 (1922), that full use of air rights is so bound up with the investment-backed expectations of appellants that governmental deprivation of these rights invariably — i.e., irrespective of the impact of the restriction on the value of the parcel as a whole — constitutes a "taking." . . .

New Orleans, 516 F.2d 1051 (CA5 1975), but appellants argue that New York City's regulation of individual landmarks is fundamentally different from zoning or from historic-district legislation because the controls imposed by New York City's law apply only to individuals who own selected properties.

Stated baldly, appellants' position appears to be that the only means of ensuring that selected owners are not singled out to endure financial hardship for no reason is to hold that any restriction imposed on individual landmarks pursuant to the New York City scheme is a "taking" requiring the payment of "just compensation." Agreement with this argument would, of course, invalidate not just New York City's law, but all comparable landmark legislation in the Nation. We find no merit in it.

It is true, as appellants emphasize, that both historic-district legislation and zoning laws regulate all properties within given physical communities whereas landmark laws apply only to selected parcels. But, contrary to appellants' suggestions, landmark laws are not like discriminatory, or "reverse spot," zoning: that is, a land-use decision which arbitrarily singles out a particular parcel for different, less favorable treatment than the neighboring ones. See 2 A. Rathkopf, The Law of Zoning and Planning 26-4 and 26-4–26-5, n.6 (4th ed. 1978). In contrast to discriminatory zoning, which is the antithesis of land-use control as part of some comprehensive plan, the New York City law embodies a comprehensive plan to preserve structures of historic or aesthetic interest wherever they might be found in the city, and as noted, over 400 landmarks and 31 historic districts have been designated pursuant to this plan.

Equally without merit is the related argument that the decision to designate a structure as a landmark "is inevitably arbitrary or at least subjective, because it is basically a matter of taste," thus unavoidably singling out individual landowners for disparate and unfair treatment. The argument has a particularly hollow ring in this case. For appellants not only did not seek judicial review of either the designation or of the denials of the certificates of appropriateness and of no exterior effect, but do not even now suggest that the Commission's decisions concerning the Terminal were in any sense arbitrary or unprincipled. But, in any event, a landmark owner has a right to judicial review of any Commission decision, and, quite simply, there is no basis whatsoever for a conclusion that courts will have any greater difficulty identifying arbitrary or discriminatory action in the context of landmark regulation than in the context of classic zoning or indeed in any other context.

Next, appellants observe that New York City's law differs from zoning laws and historic-district ordinances in that the Landmarks Law does not impose identical or similar restrictions on all structures located in particular physical communities. It follows, they argue, that New York City's law is inherently incapable of producing the fair and equitable distribution of benefits and burdens of governmental action which is characteristic of zoning laws and historic-district legislation and which they maintain is a constitutional requirement if "just compensation" is not to be afforded. It is, of course, true that the Landmarks Law has a more severe impact on some landowners than on others, but that in itself does not mean that the law effects a "taking." Legislation designed to promote the general welfare commonly burdens some more than others. The owners of the brickyard in *Hadacheck*, of the cedar trees in Miller v. Schoene, and of the gravel and sand mined in Goldblatt v. Hempstead, were uniquely burdened by the legislation sustained in those cases.[32] Similarly, zoning laws often affect some property owners more severely than others but have not been held to be invalid on that account. For example, the property owner in *Euclid* who wished to use its property for industrial purposes was affected far more severely by the ordinance than its neighbors who wished to use their land for residences.

In any event, appellants' repeated suggestions that they are solely burdened and unbenefited is factually inaccurate. This contention overlooks the fact that the New York City law applies to vast numbers of structures in the city in addition to the Terminal — all the structures contained in the 31 historic districts and over 400 individual landmarks, many of which are close to the Terminal. Unless we are to reject the judgment of the New York City Council that the preservation of landmarks benefits all New York citizens and all structures, both economically and by improving the quality of life in the city as a whole — which we are unwilling to do — we cannot conclude that the owners of the Terminal have in no sense been benefited by the Landmarks Law. . . .

Appellants' final broad-based attack would have us treat the law as an instance, like that in United States v. Causby [see pages 1179-1180] in which government, acting in an enterprise capacity, has appropriated part of their property for some strictly governmental purpose. Apart from the fact that *Causby* was a case of invasion of airspace that destroyed

---

32. Appellants attempt to distinguish these cases [discussed in this book at pages 1181, 1186, and 1189 respectively] on the ground that, in each, government was prohibiting a "noxious" use of land and that in the present case, in contrast, appellants' proposed construction above the Terminal would be beneficial. We observe that the uses in issue . . . were perfectly lawful in themselves. They involved no "blameworthiness, . . . moral wrongdoing or conscious act of dangerous risk-taking which induce[d society] to shift the cost to a pa[rt]icular individual." Sax, Takings and the Police Power, 74 Yale L.J. 36, 50 (1964). These cases are better understood as resting not on any supposed "noxious" quality of the prohibited uses but rather on the ground that the restrictions were reasonably related to the implementation of a policy — not unlike historic preservation — expected to produce a widespread public benefit and applicable to all similarly situated property.

Nor, correlatively, can it be asserted that the destruction or fundamental alteration of a historic landmark is not harmful. The suggestion that the beneficial quality of appellants' proposed construction is established by the fact that the construction would have been consistent with applicable zoning laws ignores the development in sensibilities and ideals reflected in landmark legislation like New York City's. . . .

the use of the farm beneath and this New York City law has in nowise impaired the present use of the Terminal, the Landmarks Law neither exploits appellants' parcel for city purposes nor facilitates nor arises from any entrepreneurial operations of the city. The situation is not remotely like that in *Causby* where the airspace above the property was in the flight pattern for military aircraft. The Landmarks Law's effect is simply to prohibit appellants or anyone else from occupying portions of the airspace above the Terminal, while permitting appellants to use the remainder of the parcel in a gainful fashion. . . .

Rejection of appellants' broad arguments is not, however, the end of our inquiry, for all we thus far have established is that the New York City law is not rendered invalid by its failure to provide "just compensation" whenever a landmark owner is restricted in the exploitation of property interests, such as air rights, to a greater extent than provided for under applicable zoning laws. We now must consider whether the interference with appellants' property is of such a magnitude that "there must be an exercise of eminent domain and compensation to sustain [it]." Pennsylvania Coal Co. v. Mahon, 260 U.S., at 413. That inquiry may be narrowed to the question of the severity of the impact of the law on appellants' parcel, and its resolution in turn requires a careful assessment of the impact of the regulation on the Terminal site.

. . . [T]he New York City law does not interfere in any way with the present uses of the Terminal. Its designation as a landmark not only permits but contemplates that appellants may continue to use the property precisely as it has been used for the past 65 years: as a railroad terminal containing office space and concessions. So the law does not interfere with what must be regarded as Penn Central's primary expectation concerning the use of the parcel. More importantly, on this record, we must regard the New York City law as permitting Penn Central not only to profit from the Terminal but also to obtain a "reasonable return" on its investment.

Appellants, moreover, exaggerate the effect of the law on their ability to make use of the air rights above the Terminal in two respects. First, it simply cannot be maintained, on this record, that appellants have been prohibited from occupying *any* portion of the airspace above the Terminal. While the Commission's actions in denying applications to construct an office building in excess of 50 stories above the Terminal may indicate that it will refuse to issue a certificate of appropriateness for any comparably sized structure, nothing the Commission has said or done suggests an intention to prohibit *any* construction above the Terminal. The Commission's report emphasized that whether any construction would be allowed depended upon whether the proposed addition "would harmonize in scale, materials, and character with [the Terminal]." Since appellants have not sought approval for the construction of

a smaller structure, we do not know that appellants will be denied any
use of any portion of the airspace above the Terminal.

Second, to the extent appellants have been denied the right to build
above the Terminal, it is not literally accurate to say that they have been
denied *all* use of even those pre-existing air rights. Their ability to use
these rights has not been abrogated; they are made transferable to at
least eight parcels in the vicinity of the Terminal, one or two of which
have been found suitable for the construction of new office buildings.
Although appellants and others have argued that New York City's transferable development-rights program is far from ideal, the New York
courts have supportably found that, at least in the case of the Terminal,
the rights afforded are valuable. While these rights may well not have
constituted "just compensation" if a "taking" had occurred, the rights
nevertheless undoubtedly mitigate whatever financial burdens the law
has imposed on appellants and, for that reason, are to be taken into
account in considering the impact of regulation.

[Justice Rehnquist, joined by Chief Justice Burger and Justice Stevens, dissented in the *Penn Central* case. The New York City law, the
dissenting opinion argued, was unlike typical zoning restrictions, which
usually benefit as well as burden restricted lots, creating the "average
reciprocity of advantage" mentioned by Justice Holmes in *Pennsylvania
Coal* (see page 1192). Instead, under the city's law just a few buildings
were singled out and subjected to large burdens with no comparable
reciprocal benefits. Penn Central's valuable air rights had been destroyed, and without any nuisance-control justification. Hence there was
a taking. The transferable development rights made available to Penn
Central under the New York City law could perhaps be of sufficient
value to constitute just compensation, but the record on appeal was too
slim to tell. So the dissenting justices would "remand to the Court of
Appeals for a determination of whether TDR's constitute 'a full and perfect equivalent for the property taken.' "]

NOTES AND QUESTIONS

1. *The* Penn Central *case.* The decision in *Penn Central* stimulated a
good deal of commentary, much of it very enthusiastic — e.g., Norman
Marcus, The Grand Slam Grand Central Terminal Decision: A *Euclid*
for Landmarks, Favorable Notice for TDR and a Resolution of the Reg-
ulatory/Taking Impasse, 7 Ecology L.Q. 730 (1978) — and some of it
far less so. Among the latter see The Supreme Court, 1977 Term, 92
Harv. L. Rev. 57, 228-232 (1978), noting that the majority in *Penn Central* rejected a number of traditional taking tests, particularly the nuisance-control and reciprocity tests:

Until *Penn Central,* courts have required compensation more readily when, as in this case, the regulation is aimed at providing amenities such as historic preservation rather than protecting the public health or safety; when the prohibited use bears no resemblance whatever to common law nuisance; and when the law benefits a much larger group than it burdens. These factors are inextricably bound up in the goals of "fairness and justice" which have shaped, and indeed must shape, takings law.

Regarding the nuisance-control test, what do you make of the Court's footnote 32 on page 1209? See James E. Krier, The Regulation Machine, 1 Sup. Ct. Econ. Rev. 1, 7 (1982):

[T]he Court noted that to promote the public health, safety, welfare, and morals, laws prohibiting certain land uses have been upheld, even though they "destroyed . . . recognized real property interests." In this connection, the Court cited and discussed a number of cases conventionally gathered together in the nuisance-control pigeonhole. But these cases, according to the Court, did not rest "on any supposed 'noxious' quality of the prohibited uses but rather on the ground that the restrictions were reasonably related to the implementation of a policy" expected to promote the public good. Then comes the alternative pleading: it could not, in any event, "be asserted that the destruction or fundamental alteration of a historic landmark is not harmful," that is, nuisance-like.

This last remark saves the Court from an embarrassing problem, but it also brings into play the nuisance test, which the Court claimed to abjure. *Any* exercise of the police power, to be valid, must bear some rational relationship to health, safety, and so on. It hardly follows that by passing the easy rational-basis test a measure then becomes immune from a taking challenge as well. If this were so, then the diminution-in-value test would be virtually meaningless. Yet, by the Court's own analysis, that test seems to label some otherwise valid laws as "takings," because they leave too little value, while others are regarded as "not takings," even though they leave no value at all. Only by resort to some such concept as nuisance or noxiousness can we tell losses of value that count from losses of value that do not.

2. *"Reasonable return," "reasonable expectations," and "distinct investment-backed expectations."* The majority opinion in *Penn Central* adds something new to the conventional collection of takings tests, but just what is less than clear. The "distinct investment-backed expectations" formulation is obviously drawn from Professor Michelman's influential essay on takings, particularly the portion dealing with diminution in value. See Frank Michelman, Property, Utility, and Fairness: Comments on the Ethical Foundations of "Just Compensation" Law, 80 Harv. L. Rev. 1165, 1229-1234 (1967). Is the test in *Penn Central* different from the diminution-in-value test? Michelman saw the latter as calling for compensation when a claimant is deprived of "distinctly perceived, sharply crystallized, investment-backed expectations." Id. at 1223. His

discussion suggests that *Pennsylvania Coal* (see page 1189) is a case in point, for in *Pennsylvania Coal* the claimant had a distinct interest — the support estate — that was wiped out by the Kohler Act. But what then of the distinct interest of Penn Central in the air rights above Grand Central Terminal? See Note, Vertical and Horizontal Aspects of Takings Jurisprudence: Is Airspace Property?, 7 Cardozo L. Rev. 489, 510-516 (1986).

Do people who inherit property, or receive it as a gift, have *investment-backed* expectations?

On the test in *Penn Central* generally, see Daniel R. Mandelker, Investment-Backed Expectations: Is There a Taking?, 31 Wash. U. J. Urb. & Contemp. L. 3 (1987).

The concept of "reasonable return on investment" gives rise to familiar problems (see the discussion of rent controls at pages 555-556). The New York Court of Appeals, in its opinion leading up to the Supreme Court's decision in *Penn Central*, also relied on reasonable return, though it regarded it as "an elusive concept, incapable of easy definition. For the reasonableness of the return must be based on the value of the property, and the value of the property necessarily depends on the return permitted or available. The inevitable circularity of reasoning is obvious." Penn Central Transp. Co. v. City of New York, 42 N.Y.2d 324, 331, 366 N.E.2d 1271, 1275, 397 N.Y.S.2d 914, 918 (1977), citing Curtis J. Berger, The Accommodation Power in Land Use Controversies: A Reply to Professor Costonis, 76 Colum. L. Rev. 799, 818-819 (1976). See also The Supreme Court, 1977 Term, supra, at 231.

3. *TDRs.* Transferable development rights (TDRs) like those involved in Penn Central represent a relatively new, very important, and very controversial approach to land-use planning. The concept, still evolving, has many variants and has spawned an enormous literature.[33] Here we can do little more than introduce the subject and suggest a few issues.

Essentially, the TDR approach severs development rights from other rights in land and treats them as a separate item. The right to develop is restricted at particular sites or in so-called conservation areas, but owners of the restricted land are given TDRs that can be used for development, beyond that which would otherwise be permitted, on receiving lots or in so-called transfer areas. Depending on the method used, recipients of TDRs may sell their rights or use them on land they own (in a transfer area, for example). The idea, of course, is to ease the burdens of land-use restrictions by providing some form of compensation.

TDRs have already been put to a variety of uses: to preserve historic

---

33. "It appears that more has been published about TDR than all other land use techniques combined." Marcus, supra, at 748 n.94.

sites, as in *Penn Central;* to preserve farmland and open space; to create incentives for low-income housing; to regulate land use generally. Whatever its purpose, the approach gives rise to a number of issues. Where should development be restricted, and where permitted? How many rights should there be, and how should they be allocated? How is their marketability to be assured? The central question for our purposes concerns the bearing of TDRs on the takings issue.

Notice that the Court in *Penn Central* left unresolved the question whether TDRs can provide the "just compensation" required if a taking has occurred. See page 1211. It appears to be the Court's view, however, that TDRs can ease the burden of a regulation such that it will not amount to a taking. Can you make sense of that line of thinking? If a given regulation without TDRs would be a taking but the same regulation with TDRs would not be a taking, isn't that just a roundabout way of saying that the TDRs do in fact amount to "just compensation," even though the value of the TDRs may fall short of the fair market value ordinarily required in cases of condemnation? If so, the takings issue and the just-compensation requirement can be made, more or less, to disappear. See Developments in the Law — Zoning, 91 Harv. L. Rev. 1427, 1497-1501 (1978), arguing as follows: In the event of a taking, fair market value must be paid, based on the highest and best use of the property in question. But the standard of highest and best use is a rule of convenience, not a constitutional necessity. Moreover, it is inconsistent with the standard tests in takings law. If a regulation goes too far in diminishing value, "it is hard to see why compensation need be greater than the amount necessary to leave the property holder above the 'too far' point." If a regulation works a disproportionate burden (under some form of balancing or reciprocity test, for example), then compensation need only be in the amount necessary to bring matters into proportion. And compensation need not be in cash. It can take other forms — such as TDRs. See also John J. Costonis, "Fair" Compensation and the Accommodation Power: Antidotes for the Taking Impasse in Land Use Controversies, 75 Colum. L. Rev. 1021 (1975).

Do TDRs let government purchase property on the cheap with "funny money" it mints by unduly restricting development in transfer areas so as to make the TDRs (which would permit more intense development) valuable in those areas? Doesn't this just move the takings issue around, rather than make it go away? See Richard A. Epstein, Takings: Private Property and the Power of Eminent Domain 188-190 (1985); Note, The Unconstitutionality of Transferable Development Rights, 84 Yale L.J. 1101 (1975).

Understand that TDRs are but one means of mitigating the burdens of regulation. A number of other approaches exist, many of them attempting to soften regulatory burdens ("wipeouts") by providing compensation funded through assessments on gains ("windfalls") occasioned

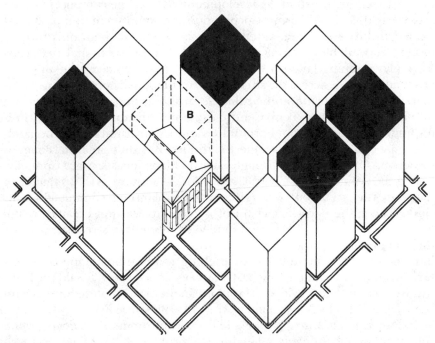

Figure 12-1
Development Rights Transfer

The landmark building (A) utilizes only a fraction of the development rights of
the site, the remainder of which (B) are transferred to various other sites within
a transfer district and appear as additional bulk on top of neighboring
buildings (dark areas).

Source: John Costonis, Space Adrift, 1974, © 1974 (University of Illinois)

by other governmental actions. See Donald G. Hagman & Dean Misczynski, Windfalls for Wipeouts: Land Value Capture and Compensation (1978); David E. Ervin & James B. Fitch, Evaluating Alternative Compensation and Recapture Techniques for Expanded Public Control of Land Use, 19 Natural Resources J. 21 (1979).

Penn Central's TDRs — items from the news. Subsequent to the decision in the *Penn Central* case, the Penn Central Corporation began extensive efforts to sell its transferable development rights. The complication that arose was this: First Boston Corporation, an investment company that wished to buy the TDRs, intended to use some of them on property located several blocks away from Grand Central Terminal, but New York City's zoning laws provide that TDRs may be used only on properties adjacent to, across the street from, or diagonally opposite the landmark site. First Boston argued that its proposal presented no problem in this respect because Penn Central still holds subsurface rights, including railroad tracks, to land around Grand Central, such that the landmark site could be seen as connected to First Boston's site by a "chain of ownership." See Carlyle C. Douglas, Laura Mansnerus & Mary Connelly, Filling the Air at Grand Central, N.Y. Times, Sept. 21, 1986, §4, at 6. In the end, the argument was rejected. The planning commission concluded "that the necessary chain of ownership was not created by the lots that make up Grand Central's rail yard, under the street surface." If the commission had approved the underground approach, "it would have had — quite literally — far-reaching implications. 'One could establish a link or a chain going past Yonkers, conceivably,' " said the commission's chair. See David W. Dunlap, Panel Rejects Plan to Shift Grand Central's Air Rights, N.Y. Times, Aug. 24, 1989, at B3.

4. *A new standard of review?* The majority opinion in *Penn Central* refers to laws "reasonably related to the promotion of the general welfare" (see page 1207). The language suggests the "rational basis" test ordinarily applied by courts as they review government programs regulating economic activity: If the legislature could rationally have decided that its approach to the matter might achieve legitimate state objectives, then the measure will withstand constitutional challenges framed in terms of equal protection or substantive due process. In other words, when reasonable minds could differ about the appropriate means to a given appropriate end, the courts are to defer to the legislative judgment.

Does this lax standard apply to judicial review of measures alleged to be takings? The general view has long been that it does, but now the matter is less than clear. Consider:

Nollan v. California Coastal Commission
Supreme Court of the United States, 1987
483 U.S. 825

Justice Scalia delivered the opinion of the Court. . . .

The Nollans own a beachfront lot in Ventura County, California. A quarter-mile north of their property is Faria County Park, an oceanside public park with a public beach and recreation area. Another public beach area, known locally as "the Cove," lies 1,800 feet south of their lot. A concrete seawall approximately eight feet high separates the beach portion of the Nollans' property from the rest of the lot. The historic mean high tide line determines the lot's oceanside boundary.

The Nollans originally leased their property with an option to buy. The building on the lot was a small bungalow, totaling 504 square feet, which for a time they rented to summer vacationers. After years of rental use, however, the building had fallen into disrepair, and could no longer be rented out.

The Nollans' option to purchase was conditioned on their promise to demolish the bungalow and replace it. In order to do so, under Cal. Pub. Res. Code Ann. §§30106, 30212, and 30600 (West 1986), they were required to obtain a coastal development permit from the California Coastal Commission. On February 25, 1982, they submitted a permit application to the Commission in which they proposed to demolish the existing structure and replace it with a three-bedroom house in keeping with the rest of the neighborhood.

The Nollans were informed that their application had been placed on the administrative calendar, and that the Commission staff had recommended that the permit be granted subject to the condition that they allow the public an easement to pass across a portion of their property bounded by the mean high tide line on one side, and their seawall on the other side. This would make it easier for the public to get to Faria County Park and the Cove. The Nollans protested imposition of the condition, but the Commission overruled their objections and granted the permit subject to their recordation of a deed restriction granting the easement. . . .

[In June 1982 the Nollans filed a petition asking the Ventura County Superior Court to invalidate the access condition, arguing that it could not be imposed absent evidence that their proposed development would have an impact on public access to the beach. The court agreed and remanded to the Commission for a hearing on that issue. The Commission subsequently held a hearing and reaffirmed the condition. The Nollans again petitioned the superior court, arguing that imposition of the condition was a taking. When the court ruled in their favor on other grounds, the Commission took the case to the court of appeal, which reversed, holding among other things that imposition of the access condition was not a taking. The Nollans then appealed to the Supreme Court, raising only the takings question.]

Had California simply required the Nollans to make an easement across their beachfront available to the public on a permanent basis in order to increase public access to the beach, rather than conditioning their permit to rebuild their house on their agreeing to do so, we have no doubt there would have been a taking. To say that the appropriation of a public easement across a landowner's premises does not constitute the taking of a property interest but rather (as Justice Brennan contends) "a mere restriction on its use," is to use words in a manner that deprives them of all their ordinary meaning. Indeed, one of the principal uses of the eminent domain power is to assure that the government be able to require conveyance of just such interests, so long as it pays for them. . . . Perhaps because the point is so obvious, we have never been confronted with a controversy that required us to rule upon it, but our cases' analysis of the effect of other governmental action leads to the same conclusion. We have repeatedly held that, as to property reserved by its owner for private use, "the right to exclude [others is] 'one of the most essential sticks in the bundle of rights that are commonly characterized as property.'" Loretto v. Teleprompter Manhattan CATV Corp., 458 U.S. 419, 433 (1982), quoting Kaiser Aetna v. United States, 444 U.S. 164, 176 (1979). In *Loretto* we observed that where governmental action results in "[a] permanent physical occupation" of the property, by the government itself or by others, see 458 U.S., at 432-433, n.9, "our cases uniformly have found a taking to the extent of the occupation, without regard to whether the action achieves an important public benefit or has only minimal economic impact on the owner," id., at 434-435. We think a "permanent physical occupation" has occurred, for purposes of that rule, where individuals are given a permanent and continuous right to pass to and fro, so that the real property may continuously be traversed, even though no particular individual is permitted to station himself permanently upon the premises.[34] . . .

Given, then, that requiring uncompensated conveyance of the easement outright would violate the Fourteenth Amendment, the question becomes whether requiring it to be conveyed as a condition for issuing a land-use permit alters the outcome. We have long recognized that land-use regulation does not effect a taking if it "substantially advance[s] legitimate state interests" and does not "den[y] an owner economically

34. The holding of PruneYard Shopping Center v. Robins, 447 U.S. 74 (1980), is not inconsistent with this analysis, since there the owner had already opened his property to the general public, and in addition permanent access was not required. The analysis of Kaiser Aetna v. United States, 444 U.S. 164 (1979), is not inconsistent because it was affected by traditional doctrines regarding navigational servitudes. Of course neither of those cases involved, as this one does, a classic right-of-way easement.

viable use of his land," Agins v. Tiburon, 447 U.S. 255, 260 (1980). See also Penn Central Transportation Co. v. New York City, 438 U.S. 104, 127 (1978) ("[A] use restriction may constitute a 'taking' if not reasonably necessary to the effectuation of a substantial government purpose"). Our cases have not elaborated on the standards for determining what constitutes a "legitimate state interest" or what type of connection between the regulation and the state interest satisfies the requirement that the former "substantially advance" the latter.[35] They have made clear, however, that a broad range of governmental purposes and regulations satisfies these requirements. See Agins v. Tiburon, supra, at 260-262 (scenic zoning); Penn Central Transportation Co. v. New York City, supra (landmark preservation); Euclid v. Ambler Realty Co., 272 U.S. 365 (1926) (residential zoning); Laitos & Westfall, Government Interference with Private Interests in Public Resources, 11 Harv. Envtl. L. Rev. 1, 66 (1987). The Commission argues that among these permissible purposes are protecting the public's ability to see the beach, assisting the public in overcoming the "psychological barrier" to using the beach created by a developed shorefront, and preventing congestion on the public beaches. We assume, without deciding, that this is so - - in which case the Commission unquestionably would be able to deny the Nollans their permit outright if their new house (alone, or by reason of the cumulative impact produced in conjunction with other construction) would substantially impede these purposes, unless the denial would interfere so drastically with the Nollans' use of their property as to constitute a taking. See Penn Central Transportation v. New York City, supra.

The Commission argues that a permit condition that serves the same legitimate police-power purpose as a refusal to issue the permit should not be found to be a taking if the refusal to issue the permit would not constitute a taking. We agree. Thus, if the Commission attached to the permit some condition that would have protected the public's ability to see the beach notwithstanding construction of the new house — for example, a height limitation, a width restriction, or a ban on fences — so long as the Commission could have exercised its police power (as we have assumed it could) to forbid construction of the house altogether, imposition of the condition would also be constitutional. Moreover (and here we come closer to the facts of the present case), the condition would be constitutional even if it consisted of the requirement that the Nollans provide a viewing spot on their property for passersby

35. Contrary to Justice Brennan's claim, our opinions do not establish that these standards are the same as those applied to due process or equal protection claims. To the contrary, our verbal formulations in the takings field have generally been quite different. We have required that the regulation "substantially advance" the "legitimate state interest" sought to be achieved, Agins v. Tiburon, 447 U.S. 255, 260 (1980), not that "the State 'could rationally have decided' that the measure adopted might achieve the State's objective.". . .

with whose sighting of the ocean their new house would interfere. Although such a requirement, constituting a permanent grant of continuous access to the property, would have to be considered a taking if it were not attached to a development permit, the Commission's assumed power to forbid construction of the house in order to protect the public's view of the beach must surely include the power to condition construction upon some concession by the owner, even a concession of property rights, that serves the same end. If a prohibition designed to accomplish that purpose would be a legitimate exercise of the police power rather than a taking, it would be strange to conclude that providing the owner an alternative to that prohibition which accomplishes the same purpose is not.

The evident constitutional propriety disappears, however, if the condition substituted for the prohibition utterly fails to further the end advanced as the justification for the prohibition. When that essential nexus is eliminated, the situation becomes the same as if California law forbade shouting fire in a crowded theater, but granted dispensations to those willing to contribute $100 to the state treasury. While a ban on shouting fire can be a core exercise of the State's police power to protect the public safety, and can thus meet even our stringent standards for regulation of speech, adding the unrelated condition alters the purpose to one which, while it may be legitimate, is inadequate to sustain the ban. Therefore, even though, in a sense, requiring a $100 tax contribution in order to shout fire is a lesser restriction on speech than an outright ban, it would not pass constitutional muster. Similarly here, the lack of nexus between the condition and the original purpose of the building restriction converts that purpose to something other than what it was. The purpose then becomes, quite simply, the obtaining of an easement to serve some valid governmental purpose, but without payment of compensation. Whatever may be the outer limits of "legitimate state interests" in the takings and land-use context, this is not one of them. In short, unless the permit condition serves the same governmental purpose as the development ban, the building restriction is not a valid regulation of land use but "an out-and-out plan of extortion." J.E.D. Associates, Inc. v. Atkinson, 121 N.H. 581, 584, 432 A.2d 12, 14-15 (1981). . . .[36]

The Commission claims that it concedes as much, and that we may sustain the condition at issue here by finding that it is reasonably related

---

36. One would expect that a regime in which this kind of leveraging of the police power is allowed would produce stringent land-use regulation which the State then waives to accomplish other purposes, leading to lesser realization of the land-use goals purportedly sought to be served than would result from more lenient (but nontradeable) development restrictions. Thus, the importance of the purpose underlying the prohibition not only does not *justify* the imposition of unrelated conditions for eliminating the prohibition, but positively militates against the practice.

to the public need or burden that the Nollans' new house creates or to which it contributes. We can accept, for purposes of discussion, the Commission's proposed test as to how close a "fit" between the condition and the burden is required, because we find that this case does not meet even the most untailored standards. The Commission's principal contention to the contrary essentially turns on a play on the word "access." The Nollans' new house, the Commission found, will interfere with "visual access" to the beach. That in turn (along with other shorefront development) will interfere with the desire of people who drive past the Nollans' house to use the beach, thus creating a "psychological barrier" to "access." The Nollans' new house will also, by a process not altogether clear from the Commission's opinion but presumably potent enough to more than offset the effects of the psychological barrier, increase the use of the public beaches, thus creating the need for more "access." These burdens on "access" would be alleviated by a requirement that the Nollans provide "lateral access" to the beach.

Rewriting the argument to eliminate the play on words makes clear that there is nothing to it. It is quite impossible to understand how a requirement that people already on the public beaches be able to walk across the Nollans' property reduces any obstacles to viewing the beach created by the new house. It is also impossible to understand how it lowers any "psychological barrier" to using the public beaches, or how it helps to remedy any additional congestion on them caused by construction of the Nollans' new house. We therefore find that the Commission's imposition of the permit condition cannot be treated as an exercise of its land-use power for any of these purposes.[37] Our conclusion on this point is consistent with the approach taken by every other court that has considered the question, with the exception of the California state courts. . . .

Justice Brennan argues that imposition of the access requirement is not irrational. In his version of the Commission's argument, the reason for the requirement is that in its absence, a person looking toward the

---

37. As Justice Brennan notes, the Commission also argued that the construction of the new house would " 'increase private use immediately adjacent to public tidelands,' " which in turn might result in more disputes between the Nollans and the public as to the location of the boundary. That risk of boundary disputes, however, is inherent in the right to exclude others from one's property, and the construction here can no more justify mandatory dedication of a sort of "buffer zone" in order to avoid boundary disputes than can the construction of an addition to a single-family house near a public street. Moreover, a buffer zone has a boundary as well, and unless that zone is a "no-man's land" that is off limits for both neighbors (which is of course not the case here) its creation achieves nothing except to shift the location of the boundary dispute further on to the private owner's land. It is true that in the distinctive situation of the Nollans' property the seawall could be established as a clear demarcation of the public easement. But since not all of the lands to which this land-use condition applies have such a convenient reference point, the avoidance of boundary disputes is, even more obviously than the others, a made-up purpose of the regulation.

beach from the road will see a street of residential structures including the Nollans' new home and conclude that there is no public beach nearby. If, however, that person sees people passing and repassing along the dry sand behind the Nollans' home, he will realize that there is a public beach somewhere in the vicinity. The Commission's action, however, was based on the opposite factual finding that the wall of houses completely blocked the view of the beach and that a person looking from the road would not be able to see it at all.

Even if the Commission had made the finding that Justice Brennan proposes, however, it is not certain that it would suffice. We do not share Justice Brennan's confidence that the Commission "should have little difficulty in the future in utilizing its expertise to demonstrate a specific connection between provisions for access and burdens on access" that will avoid the effect of today's decision. We view the Fifth Amendment's Property Clause to be more than a pleading requirement, and compliance with it to be more than an exercise in cleverness and imagination. As indicated earlier, our cases describe the condition for abridgment of property rights through the police power as a "*substantial* advanc[ing]" of a legitimate state interest. We are inclined to be particularly careful about the adjective where the actual conveyance of property is made a condition to the lifting of a land-use restriction, since in that context there is heightened risk that the purpose is avoidance of the compensation requirement, rather than the stated police-power objective.

We are left, then, with the Commission's justification for the access requirement unrelated to land-use regulation:

> Finally, the Commission notes that there are several existing provisions of pass and repass lateral access benefits already given by past Faria Beach Tract applicants as a result of prior coastal permit decisions. The access required as a condition of this permit is part of a comprehensive program to provide continuous public access along Faria Beach as the lots undergo development or redevelopment.

That is simply an expression of the Commission's belief that the public interest will be served by a continuous strip of publicly accessible beach along the coast. The Commission may well be right that it is a good idea, but that does not establish that the Nollans (and other coastal residents) alone can be compelled to contribute to its realization. Rather, California is free to advance its "comprehensive program," if it wishes, by using its power of eminent domain for this "public purpose," see U.S. Const., Amdt. 5; but if it wants an easement across the Nollans' property, it must pay for it.

Reversed.

[There were three dissenting opinions in the *Nollan* case — written by Justice Brennan (joined by Justice Marshall), by Justice Blackmun, and by Justice Stevens (joined by Justice Blackmun) — expressing, among other points, the view that the majority had imposed an unwarranted and discredited standard of precision for a state's exercise of the police power. But even under the majority's tight standard the permit condition in question directly responded to the burden on access that would be created by the Nollans' development, and implicated none of the concerns underlying takings doctrine.]

NOTES AND QUESTIONS

1. An op-ed piece written shortly after *Nollan* says the case indicates the Supreme Court's intention to apply more intensive judicial scrutiny to land-use regulations than it has in the past. "Where such regulations were previously thought to be clothed with a presumption of validity, invulnerable to constitutional attack unless there was no conceivable underlying justification, the Court will now require a substantial justification." Charles M. Haar & Jerold S. Kayden, Private Property vs. Public Use, N.Y. Times, July 29, 1987, §1, at 23.

Is that so clear? See Frank Michelman, Takings, 1987, 88 Colum. L. Rev. 1600, 1605-1614 (1988); Comment, The First Applications of the *Nollan* Nexus Test: Observations and Comments, 13 Harv. Envtl. L. Rev. 585 (1989) (discussing the wide variety of readings given to *Nollan* by scholars and judges alike).

What sort of scrutiny *should* courts give to state and local land-use decisions?

2. *Nollan* is obviously bad news for local and state governments.[38]

---

38. Consider, for example, its impact on the exactions discussed in Chapter 11 at pages 1010-1011. See, e.g., Stewart E. Sterk, *Nollan*, Henry George, and Exactions, 88 Colum. L. Rev. 1731 (1988). Or its impact on the TDRs discussed in Note 3 on page 1213. See, e.g., John A. Humbach, Law and a New Land Ethic, 74 Minn. L. Rev. 339, 352 n.39 (1989). Or its impact on rent controls. In Chapter 6, and then again in this chapter, we talked about constitutional attacks on rent controls, focusing in particular on claims of taking by physical occupation and the Supreme Court's discussion of such claims in Yee v. City of Escondido, 112 S. Ct. 1522 (1992). (See pages 557-558, 1180-1181.) But rent controls can work *regulatory* takings as well, and *Yee* suggests that as to challenges framed in those terms the Court will give careful scrutiny to the question "whether there is a sufficient nexus between the effect of the ordinance and the objectives it is supposed to advance." 112 S. Ct. at 1530 (citing *Nollan*).

Nollan also brings into play (though not explicitly) a matter we do not pursue here — the doctrine of unconstitutional conditions. The doctrine holds that the government may not offer a privilege conditioned on the recipient's surrender of a constitutional right, even where the government has no obligation to offer the privilege in the first place. For discussion particularly connected to *Nollan*, see, e.g., Vicki Been, "Exit" as a Constraint on Land Use Exactions: Rethinking the Unconstitutional Conditions Doctrine, 91 Colum. L. Rev. 473 (1991); Stewart E. Sterk, Competition Among Municipalities as a Constraint on Land Use Exactions, 45 Vand. L. Rev. 831 (1992) (responding to Professor Been's article); Richard A. Epstein, The Supreme Court, 1987 Term — Foreword: Unconstitutional Conditions, State Power, and the Limits of Consent, 102 Harv. L. Rev. 4, 60-64 (1988).

Is it good news for property owners? See The Supreme Court, 1986 Term — Leading Cases, 101 Harv. L. Rev. 119, 249 (1987).

NOTES: ACADEMIC PERSPECTIVES ON TAKINGS

Legal scholars have struggled for decades to make sense of takings jurisprudence. Here we can sketch the ideas of only a few of them, drawn as contrasting samples from a large (and growing) literature. Because our discussion is necessarily brief, you might wish to pursue in the original works any line of analysis that strikes you as particularly provocative. In the originals, by the way, you will find citations and commentary that provide a good annotated bibliography on the subject.[39]

1. Let us start with one of the earlier of contemporary essays on the problem, Joseph L. Sax, Takings and the Police Power, 74 Yale L.J. 36 (1964). Sax distinguished between government-as-enterpriser and government-as-arbiter. In the first capacity government builds roads and bridges, operates schools and airports, and so forth; in the second capacity government resolves disputes among owners that arise when their uses of property conflict. According to Sax's argument, the government should be obligated to compensate when it acquires (directly or indirectly) private property in order to carry out entrepreneurial functions — for example, when it physically takes land for an airport, or when it runs an airport the noise from which reduces neighboring property values. But when the government merely resolves disputes among competing private parties, no compensation is due — no matter how severe a loss might result to one party or the other as a result of the government's decision (embodied, say, in a land-use regulation). This approach, Sax thought, would satisfactorily guard against arbitrary or unfair government action, a central purpose he attributes to just compensation requirements.

Sax formulated his views in a second article, Takings, Private Property and Public Rights, 81 Yale L.J. 149 (1971). Drawing on the concept of externalities, he concluded that when government acts to control spillover effects, it should not be required to compensate. Thus, the government could, without paying compensation, prohibit mining to protect

---

39. So too for any number of significant articles postdating the work discussed in the text. See, for example, and in addition to the literature cited elsewhere in this chapter, Stephen R. Munzer, A Theory of Property 419-469 (1990); Gregory S. Alexander, Takings and the Post-Modern Dialectic of Property, 9 Const. Commentary 259 (1992); Glynn S. Lunney, Jr., A Critical Reexamination of the Takings Jurisprudence, 90 Mich. L. Rev. 1892 (1992); Gary Minda, The Dilemmas of Property and Sovereignty in the Postmodern Era: The Regulatory Takings Problem, 62 U. Colo. L. Rev. 599 (1991); Jeremy Paul, The Hidden Structure of Takings Law, 64 S. Cal. L. Rev. 1393 (1991); Andrea L. Peterson, The Takings Clause: In Search of Underlying Principles (pts. 1 & 2), 77 Cal. L. Rev. 1299 (1989), 78 Cal. L. Rev. 53 (1990).

neighboring residential areas suffering drainage from the mine; conversely, it could prohibit (again without compensation) residential uses that required freedom from drainage. Each of these uses, after all, imposes spillovers. If, on the other hand, the government controls property uses that do not produce external costs, there should be compensation measured by the value of the highest and best use that could be made of the property without producing spillovers.

2. An essay that has proved remarkably influential is Frank Michelman, Property, Utility, and Fairness: Comments on the Ethical Foundations of "Just Compensation" Law, 80 Harv. L. Rev. 1165 (1967). Michelman's analysis, built in part on philosophical theories of property,[40] begins by developing a utilitarian compensation principle:

> A strictly utilitarian argument leading to the specific identification of "compensable" occasions would have a quasi-mathematical structure. Let us define three quantities to be known as "efficiency gains," "demoralization costs," and "settlement costs." "Efficiency gains" we define as the excess of benefits produced by a measure over losses inflicted by it, where benefits are measured by the total number of dollars which prospective gainers would be willing to pay to secure adoption, and losses are measured by the total number of dollars which prospective losers would insist on as the price of agreeing to adoption. "Demoralization costs" are defined as the total of (1) the dollar value necessary to offset disutilities which accrue to losers and their sympathizers specifically from the realization that no compensation is offered, and (2) the present capitalized dollar value of lost future production (reflecting either impaired incentives or social unrest) caused by demoralization of uncompensated losers, their sympathizers, and other observers disturbed by the thought that they themselves may be subjected to similar treatment on some other occasion. "Settlement costs" are measured by the dollar value of the time, effort, and resources which would be required in order to reach compensation settlements adequate to avoid demoralization costs. Included are the costs of settling not only the particular compensation claims presented, but also those of all persons so affected by the measure in question or similar measures as to have claims not obviously distinguishable by the available settlement apparatus.
>
> A measure attended by positive efficiency gains is, under utilitarian ethics, prima facie desirable. But felicific calculation under the definition given for efficiency gains is imperfect because it takes no account of demoralization costs caused by a capricious redistribution, or alternatively, of the settlement costs necessary to avoid such demoralization costs. When pursuit of efficiency gains entails capricious redistribution, either demoralization costs or settlement costs must be incurred. It follows that if, for any measure, both demoralization costs and settlement costs (whichever were chosen) would exceed efficiency gains, the measure is to be rejected; but that otherwise, since either demoralization costs or settlement costs must be paid, it is the lower of these

40. Including the theories of Locke, Hume, and Bentham, briefly introduced in Chapter 1. See pages 15-18, 56-57.

two costs which should be paid. The compensation rule which then clearly emerges is that compensation is to be paid whenever settlement costs are lower than both demoralization costs and efficiency gains. But if settlement costs, while lower than demoralization costs, exceed efficiency gains, then the measure is improper regardless of whether compensation is paid. The correct utilitarian statement, then, insofar as *the issue of compensability* is concerned, is that compensation is due whenever demoralization costs exceed settlement costs, and not otherwise. [Id. at 1214-1215.]

Michelman goes on to subject the utilitarian compensation principle to a principle of fairness. Drawing on early work by the philosopher John Rawls, later elaborated in A Theory of Justice (1971), Michelman argues that a decision not to compensate on utilitarian grounds "is not unfair so long as the disappointed claimant ought to be able to appreciate how such decisions might fit into a consistent practice which holds forth a lesser long term risk to people like him than would any consistent practice which is naturally suggested by the opposite decision." Michelman, supra, at 1223. Often the utilitarian approach and the fairness approach lead to common results; at times, though, they have divergent implications. See id. at 1223-1224.

One of the many interesting features of Michelman's analysis is that it tends to make sense of the rules of decision considered earlier in this chapter — the judicial tests concerned with physical occupation, diminution in value, and so forth. In the case of a physical occupation, for example, settlement costs are likely to be low, and demoralization costs (absent compensation) to be high; moreover, it would be difficult to explain the justice of a decision not to compensate.

3. In the view of Bruce A. Ackerman, Private Property and the Constitution (1977), all of the work discussed above represents what he calls "Scientific Policymaking" — the use of technical concepts to assess legal rules in terms of abstract general principles. Most of the work, moreover, reflects Scientific Policymaking of a Utilitarian sort (the capitalization is Ackerman's), and one of Ackerman's contributions is the development of a contrasting, Kantian perspective. That much of his discussion we leave entirely to you (see in particular his Chapter 4). What we can do here is suggest how Ackerman, by constructing an Ordinary Observer's conception of property, is able to find some coherence in present takings law.

The Ordinary Observer is someone who thinks about law the way ordinary (lay) people do. Because, unlike Scientific Policymakers, ordinary people do not use technical concepts to assess legal rules in terms of general principles, neither will the Ordinary Observer. Rather, he or she looks at how people in our culture are socialized regarding property. Layman, as Ackerman calls the typical citizen, is taught at an early age to distinguish between things that are his and things that are not. If something belongs to him, others are generally under an obligation to ask his permission to use it, unless they have some very compelling reason. Layman, in contrast, may use his things in any number of ways without anybody's permission, though he is to refrain from uses unduly harmful to others. So an Ordinary Observer, rather than entertaining complicated notions about "bundles of rights," says that something is Layman's property when "(a) Layman may, without negative social sanction, use the thing in lots more ways than others can; and (b) others need a specially compelling reason if they hope to escape the negative social sanctions that are normally visited upon those who use another's things without receiving his permission." Id. at 99-100.

Given this conception of property, Ackerman can argue that takings law makes some sense after all. Suppose, for example, that a person has some "thing" that all regard as his in the Ordinary sense — it is "property" that he "owns." Then the government enacts a regulation that destroys or reduces the value of the property, or actually transfers the property to itself or someone else. In the latter case, the transfer, a taking results for the Ordinary Observer (and according to conventional law): The person no longer has his thing at all. In the case of a regulation that merely reduces value, however, the person still has the property, and thus no taking has occurred — unless, perhaps, the property's value has been so utterly destroyed that it would be a "bad joke" to say that he still has a thing that has in fact been rendered virtually useless. (By this reasoning Ackerman can explain cases that deny compensation where the value of property is reduced from $100 million to $20 million, yet grant it where the reduction is from $100 to $20, even though the first loss is magnitudes larger and the percentage diminution in the two cases the same.) Even where value is utterly destroyed, however, there is no taking for the Ordinary Observer, nor under conventional law, if the property owner has been using his thing in ways that well-socialized people should recognize as unduly harmful — for example, to create a nuisance.

To say that Ackerman is able, through the eyes of an Ordinary Observer, to give a convincing account of takings law is not to say that he endorses the approach. For critical commentary on Ackerman's book see Richard A. Epstein, The Next Generation of Legal Scholarship? (Book Review), 30 Stan. L. Rev. 635 (1978); James E. Krier & Gary T. Schwartz, Talking About Taking (Book Review), 87 Yale L.J. 1295 (1978); Philip Soper, On the Relevance of Philosophy to Law: Reflections on Ackerman's Private Property and the Constitution, 79 Colum. L. Rev. 44 (1979).

4. Richard A. Epstein, Takings: Private Property and the Power of Eminent Domain (1985), pursues an essentially libertarian line of think-

ing. The basic argument is that any governmental modifications of rights of possession, use, and disposition of property are takings, with the exception of nuisance controls. The position is not quite so rigid as it seems, however; there is room for the police power. Some of the takings that result under the analysis can be approved without *explicit* compensation because they carry *implicit* compensation with them. The government's action, though it burdens claimants, might provide offsetting compensation by restricting the rights of other people to the advantage of the claimants. (The idea is akin to the notion of a "reciprocity of advantage" discussed earlier, see page 1197.) Still, Epstein ends up with a body of law very different from what exists today. "Under Epstein's reading of the takings clause, progressive income taxation, welfare, and the National Labor Relations Act are all unconstitutional. . . . For most reviewers, these conclusions are so antithetical to conventional wisdom that they discredit the entire book." Thomas W. Merrill, Rent Seeking and the Compensation Principle (Book Review), 80 Nw. U. L. Rev. 1561, 1562 (1986) (citing many other reviews).

2.   Matters of Remedy

What should be the remedy for physical occupations and regulatory takings? Logic would suggest a straightforward answer: The remedy should be compensation. After all, if the government takes property — condemns it — under the power of eminent domain, the obligation to pay just compensation follows. Should it not follow as well where the government takes property by other means? The suit for compensation would usually proceed by way of a so-called inverse condemnation action. As its name suggests, inverse condemnation is simply the opposite of a government eminent domain proceeding: The claimant rather than the government institutes the suit, alleging that a taking has occurred and seeking recompense for it. A forced purchase, rather than a forced sale, is the claimant's objective.

Though one would logically expect compensation through inverse condemnation to be commonplace, for many years it was not. To be sure, the remedy was routinely granted as to takings by physical occupation (including in that category loss of access, destruction of property, or an actual transfer of title, possession, or control to the government), but it was typically denied as to regulatory takings. Instead, the courts awarded declaratory or injunctive relief invalidating the regulation or its application. If the government wished to proceed thereafter, it either had to bring an eminent domain proceeding or amend the regulation to avoid the taking problem. If the government chose the latter alternative, losses sustained by the claimant during the period the regulation was in effect went uncompensated.

This, at least, is the conventional wisdom. It is disputed by some observers,[41] but that no longer matters.

First English Evangelical Lutheran Church of Glendale v. County of Los Angeles
Supreme Court of the United States, 1987
482 U.S. 304

CHIEF JUSTICE REHNQUIST delivered the opinion of the Court.

In this case the California Court of Appeal held that a landowner who claims that his property has been "taken" by a land-use regulation may not recover damages for the time before it is finally determined that the regulation constitutes a "taking" of his property. We disagree, and conclude that in these circumstances the Fifth and Fourteenth Amendments to the United States Constitution would require compensation for that period.

In 1957, appellant First English Evangelical Lutheran Church purchased a 21-acre parcel of land in a canyon along the banks of the Middle Fork of Mill Creek in the Angeles National Forest. The Middle Fork is the natural drainage channel for a watershed area owned by the National Forest Service. Twelve of the acres owned by the church are flat land, and contained a dining hall, two bunkhouses, a caretaker's lodge, an outdoor chapel, and a footbridge across the creek. The church operated on the site a campground, known as "Lutherglen," as a retreat center and a recreational area for handicapped children.

In July 1977, a forest fire denuded the hills upstream from Lutherglen, destroying approximately 3,860 acres of the watershed area and creating a serious flood hazard. Such flooding occurred on February 9 and 10, 1978, when a storm dropped 11 inches of rain in the watershed. The runoff from the storm overflowed the banks of the Mill Creek, flooding Lutherglen and destroying its buildings.

In response to the flooding of the canyon, appellee County of Los Angeles adopted Interim Ordinance No. 11,855 in January 1979. The ordinance provided that "[a] person shall not construct, reconstruct, place or enlarge any building or structure, any portion of which is, or will be, located within the outer boundary lines of the interim flood protection area located in Mill Creek Canyon. . . ." The ordinance was ef-

---

41. See in particular Michael M. Berger & Gideon Kanner, Thoughts on *The White River Junction Manifesto*: A Reply to the "Gang of Five's" Views on Just Compensation for Regulatory Taking of Property, 19 Loy. L.A. L. Rev. 685 (1986), urging the view that in "a consistent line of United States Supreme Court decisions during the last half-century . . . the Court concluded that the primary remedy in 'taking cases' (both physical and regulatory) is just compensation." Id. at 703. See also Note 2 on page 1238, discussing state supreme court cases to the same effect.

fective immediately because the county determined that it was "required for the immediate preservation of the public health and safety. . . ." The interim flood protection area described by the ordinance included the flat areas on either side of Mill Creek on which Lutherglen had stood.

The church filed a complaint in the Superior Court of California a little more than a month after the ordinance was adopted. As subsequently amended, the complaint alleged two claims against the county and the Los Angeles County Flood Control District. The first alleged that the defendants were liable . . . for dangerous conditions on their upstream properties that contributed to the flooding of Lutherglen. As a part of this claim, appellant also alleged that "Ordinance No. 11,855 denies [appellant] all use of Lutherglen." The second claim sought to recover from the Flood District in inverse condemnation and in tort for engaging in cloud seeding during the storm that flooded Lutherglen. Appellant sought damages under each count for loss of use of Lutherglen. The defendants moved to strike the portions of the complaint alleging that the county's ordinance denied all use of Lutherglen, on the view that the California Supreme Court's decision in Agins v. Tiburon, 24 Cal. 3d 266, 598 P.2d 25 (1979), aff'd on other grounds, 447 U.S. 255 (1980), rendered the allegation "entirely immaterial and irrelevant [, with] no bearing upon any conceivable cause of action herein." . . .

In Agins v. Tiburon, supra, the Supreme Court of California decided that a landowner may not maintain an inverse condemnation suit in the courts of that State based upon a "regulatory" taking. In the court's view, maintenance of such a suit would allow a landowner to force the legislature to exercise its power of eminent domain. Under this decision, then, compensation is not required until the challenged regulation or ordinance has been held excessive in an action for declaratory relief or a writ of mandamus and the government has nevertheless decided to continue the regulation in effect. Based on this decision, the trial court in the present case granted the motion to strike the allegation that the church had been denied all use of Lutherglen. It explained that "a careful rereading of the Agins case persuades the Court that when an ordinance, even a non-zoning ordinance, deprives a person of the total use of his lands, his challenge to the ordinance is by way of declaratory relief or possibly mandamus." Because the appellant alleged a regulatory taking and sought only damages, the allegation that the ordinance denied all use of Lutherglen was deemed irrelevant. [The trial court granted defendants' motion for judgment on the pleadings on the second cause of action and ultimately dismissed the entire complaint.]

On appeal, the California Court of Appeal . . . [also] relied on . . . Agins in rejecting the cause of action, declining appellant's invitation to reevaluate Agins in light of this Court's opinions in San Diego Gas & Electric Co. v. San Diego, 450 U.S. 621 (1981). The court found itself obligated to follow Agins "because the United States Supreme Court has not yet ruled on the question of whether a state may constitutionally limit the remedy for a taking to nonmonetary relief. . . ." . . . The Supreme Court of California denied review.

. . . Appellant asks us to hold that the Supreme Court of California erred in Agins v. Tiburon in determining that the Fifth Amendment, as made applicable to the States through the Fourteenth Amendment, does not require compensation as a remedy for "temporary" regulatory takings — those regulatory takings which are ultimately invalidated by the courts. Four times this decade, we have considered similar claims and have found ourselves for one reason or another unable to consider the merits of the Agins rule. See MacDonald, Sommer & Frates v. Yolo County, 106 S. Ct. 2561 (1986); Williamson County Regional Planning Commn. v. Hamilton Bank, 473 U.S. 172 (1985); San Diego Gas & Electric Co., supra; Agins v. Tiburon, supra. . . . [W]e find the constitutional claim properly presented in this case, and hold that on these facts the California courts have decided the compensation question inconsistently with the requirements of the Fifth Amendment. . . .[42]

We reject appellee's suggestion that, regardless of the state court's treatment of the question, we must independently evaluate the adequacy of the complaint and resolve the takings claim on the merits before we can reach the remedial question. However "cryptic" — to use appellee's description — the allegations with respect to the taking were, the California courts deemed them sufficient to present the issue. We accordingly have no occasion to decide whether the ordinance at issue actually denied appellant all use of its property or whether the county might avoid the conclusion that a compensable taking had occurred by establishing that the denial of all use was insulated as a part of the State's authority to enact safety regulations. See, e.g., Goldblatt v. Hempstead, 369 U.S. 590 (1962); Hadacheck v. Sebastian, 239 U.S. 394 (1915); Mugler v. Kansas, 123 U.S. 623 (1887). These questions, of course, remain open for decision on the remand we direct today. We now turn to the question of whether the Just Compensation Clause requires the government to pay for "temporary" regulatory takings.

Consideration of the compensation question must begin with direct reference to the language of the Fifth Amendment, which provides in relevant part that "private property [shall not] be taken for public use, without just compensation." As its language indicates, and as the Court has frequently noted, this provision does not prohibit the taking of pri-

---

42. Our cases have . . . required that one seeking compensation must "seek compensation through the procedures the State has provided for doing so" before the claim is ripe for review. Williamson County Regional Planning Commn. v. Hamilton Bank, 473 U.S. 172, 194 (1985). It is clear that appellant met this requirement. Having assumed that a taking occurred, the California court's dismissal of the action establishes that "the inverse condemnation procedure is unavailable. . . ." Id., at 197. The compensation claim is accordingly ripe for our consideration.

vate property, but instead places a condition on the exercise of that power. See . . . Hurley v. Kincaid, 285 U.S. 95, 104 (1932). . . . This basic understanding of the Amendment makes clear that it is designed not to limit the governmental interference with property rights per se, but rather to secure *compensation* in the event of otherwise proper interference amounting to a taking. Thus, government action that works a taking of property rights necessarily implicates the "constitutional obligation to pay just compensation." Armstrong v. United States, 364 U.S. 40, 49 (1960).

   We have recognized that a landowner is entitled to bring an action in inverse condemnation as a result of " 'the self-executing character of the constitutional provision with respect to compensation. . . .' " United States v. Clarke, 445 U.S. 253, 257 (1980), quoting 6 P. Nichols, Eminent Domain §25.41 (3d rev. ed. 1972). As noted in Justice Brennan's dissent in *San Diego Gas & Electric Co.*, 450 U.S., at 654-655, it has been established at least since Jacobs v. United States, 290 U.S. 13 (1933), that claims for just compensation are grounded in the Constitution itself:

> The suits were based on the right to recover just compensation for property taken by the United States for public use in the exercise of its power of eminent domain. *That right was guaranteed by the Constitution.* The fact that condemnation proceedings were not instituted and that the right was asserted in suits by the owners did not change the essential nature of the claim. The form of the remedy did not qualify the right. It rested upon the Fifth Amendment. Statutory recognition was not necessary. A promise to pay was not necessary. Such a promise was implied because of the duty imposed by the Amendment. *The suits were thus founded upon the Constitution of the United States.* [Id., at 16. (Emphasis added.)]

Jacobs, moreover, does not stand alone, for the Court has frequently repeated the view that, in the event of a taking, the compensation remedy is required by the Constitution.

   It has also been established doctrine at least since Justice Holmes' opinion for the Court in Pennsylvania Coal Co. v. Mahon, 260 U.S. 393 (1922), that "[t]he general rule at least is, that while property may be regulated to a certain extent, if regulation goes too far it will be recognized as a taking." Id., at 415. While the typical taking occurs when the government acts to condemn property in the exercise of its power of eminent domain, the entire doctrine of inverse condemnation is predicated on the proposition that a taking may occur without such formal proceedings. In Pumpelly v. Green Bay Co., 13 Wall. 166, 177-178 (1872), construing a provision in the Wisconsin Constitution identical to the Just Compensation Clause, this Court said:

> It would be a very curious and unsatisfactory result if . . . it shall be held that if the government refrains from the absolute conversion of real property to

the uses of the public it can destroy its value entirely, can inflict irreparable and permanent injury to any extent, can, in effect, subject it to total destruction without making any compensation, because, in the narrowest sense of that word, it is not *taken* for the public use.

Later cases have unhesitatingly applied this principle. See, e.g., Kaiser Aetna v. United States, 444 U.S. 164 (1979); United States v. Dickinson, 331 U.S. 745, 750 (1947); United States v. Causby, 328 U.S. 256 (1946).

While the Supreme Court of California may not have actually disavowed this general rule in *Agins,* we believe that it has truncated the rule by disallowing damages that occurred prior to the ultimate invalidation of the challenged regulation. The Supreme Court of California justified its conclusion at length in the *Agins* opinion, concluding that:

> In combination, the need for preserving a degree of freedom in the land-use planning function, and the inhibiting financial force which inheres in the inverse condemnation remedy, persuade us that on balance mandamus or declaratory relief rather than inverse condemnation is the appropriate relief under the circumstances. [Agins v. Tiburon, 24 Cal. 3d, at 276-277, 598 P.2d, at 31.]

We, of course, are not unmindful of these considerations, but they must be evaluated in the light of the command of the Just Compensation Clause of the Fifth Amendment. The Court has recognized in more than one case that the government may elect to abandon its intrusion or discontinue regulations. See e.g., Kirby Forest Industries, Inc. v. United States, 467 U.S. 1 (1984); United States v. Dow, 357 U.S. 17, 26 (1958). Similarly, a governmental body may acquiesce in a judicial declaration that one of its ordinances has effected an unconstitutional taking of property; the landowner has no right under the Just Compensation Clause to insist that a "temporary" taking be deemed a permanent taking. But we have not resolved whether abandonment by the government requires payment of compensation for the period of time during which regulations deny a landowner all use of his land.

In considering this question, we find substantial guidance in cases where the government has only temporarily exercised its right to use private property. In United States v. Dow, supra, at 26, though rejecting a claim that the Government may not abandon condemnation proceedings, the Court observed that abandonment "results in an alteration in the property interest taken — from [one of] full ownership to one of temporary use and occupation. . . . In such cases compensation would be measured by the principles normally governing the taking of a right to use property temporarily." Each of the cases cited by the *Dow* Court involved appropriation of private property by the United States for use during World War II. Though the takings were in fact "temporary," there was no question that compensation would be required for the Government's interference with the use of the property; the Court was concerned in each case with determining the proper measure of the monetary relief to which the property holders were entitled.

These cases reflect the fact that "temporary" takings which, as here, deny a landowner all use of his property, are not different in kind from permanent takings, for which the Constitution clearly requires compensation. Cf. *San Diego Gas & Electric Co.*, 450 U.S., at 657 (Brennan, J., dissenting) ("Nothing in the Just Compensation Clause suggests that 'takings' must be permanent and irrevocable"). It is axiomatic that the Fifth Amendment's just compensation provision is "designed to bar Government from forcing some people alone to bear public burdens which, in all fairness and justice, should be borne by the public as a whole." Armstrong v. United States, 364 U.S., at 49. In the present case the interim ordinance was adopted by the county of Los Angeles in January 1979, and became effective immediately. Appellant filed suit within a month after the effective date of the ordinance and yet when the Supreme Court of California denied a hearing in the case on October 17, 1985, the merits of appellant's claim had yet to be determined. The United States has been required to pay compensation for leasehold interests of shorter duration than this. The value of a leasehold interest in property for a period of years may be substantial, and the burden on the property owner in extinguishing such an interest for a period of years may be great indeed. Where this burden results from governmental action that amounted to a taking, the Just Compensation Clause of the Fifth Amendment requires that the government pay the landowner for the value of the use of the land during this period. Cf. United States v. Causby, 328 U.S., at 261 ("It is the owner's loss, not the taker's gain, which is the measure of the value of the property taken"). Invalidation of the ordinance or its successor ordinance after this period of time, though converting the taking into a "temporary" one, is not a sufficient remedy to meet the demands of the Just Compensation Clause.

Appellee argues that requiring compensation for denial of all use of land prior to invalidation is inconsistent with this Court's decisions in Danforth v. United States, 308 U.S. 271 (1939), and Agins v. Tiburon, 447 U.S. 255 (1980). In *Danforth*, the landowner contended that the "taking" of his property had occurred prior to the institution of condemnation proceedings, by reason of the enactment of the Flood Control Act itself. He claimed that the passage of that Act had diminished the value of his property because the plan embodied in the Act required condemnation of a flowage easement across his property. The Court held that in the context of condemnation proceedings a taking does not occur until compensation is determined and paid, and went on to say that "[a] reduction or increase in the value of property may occur by reason of legislation for or the beginning or completion of a project," but "[s]uch changes in value are incidents of ownership. They cannot be considered as a 'taking' in the constitutional sense." *Danforth,* supra, at 285. *Agins* likewise rejected a claim that the city's preliminary activities constituted a taking, saying that "[m]ere fluctuations in value during the process of governmental decisionmaking, absent extraordinary delay, are 'incidents of ownership.' " See 447 U.S., at 263, n.9.

But these cases merely stand for the unexceptional proposition that the valuation of property which has been taken must be calculated as of the time of the taking, and that depreciation in value of the property by reason of preliminary activity is not chargeable to the government. Thus, in *Agins,* we concluded that the preliminary activity did not work a taking. It would require a considerable extension of these decisions to say that no compensable regulatory taking may occur until a challenged ordinance has ultimately been held invalid.[43]

Nothing we say today is intended to abrogate the principle that the decision to exercise the power of eminent domain is a legislative function, " 'for Congress and Congress alone to determine.' " Hawaii Housing Authority v. Midkiff, 467 U.S. 229, 240 (1984), quoting Berman v. Parker, 348 U.S. 26, 33 (1954). Once a court determines that a taking has occurred, the government retains the whole range of options already available — amendment of the regulation, withdrawal of the invalidated regulation, or exercise of eminent domain. Thus we do not, as the Solicitor General suggests, "permit a court, at the behest of a private person, to require the . . . Government to exercise the power of eminent domain. . . ." We merely hold that where the government's activities have already worked a taking of all use of property, no subsequent action by the government can relieve it of the duty to provide compensation for the period during which the taking was effective.

We also point out that the allegation of the complaint which we treat as true for purposes of our decision was that the ordinance in question denied appellant all use of its property. We limit our holding to the facts presented, and of course do not deal with the quite different questions that would arise in the case of normal delays in obtaining building permits, changes in zoning ordinances, variances, and the like which are not before us. We realize that even our present holding will undoubtedly

---

43. *Williamson County Regional Planning Commn.* is not to the contrary. There, we noted that "no constitutional violation occurs until just compensation has been denied." 473 U.S., at 194, n.13. This statement, however, was addressed to the issue of whether the constitutional claim was ripe for review and did not establish that compensation is unavailable for government activity occurring before compensation is actually denied. Though, as a matter of law, an illegitimate taking might not occur until the government refuses to pay, the interference that effects a taking might begin much earlier, and compensation is measured from that time. See Kirby Forest Industries, Inc. v. United States, 467 U.S. 1, 5 (1984) (where Government physically occupies land without condemnation proceedings, "the owner has a right to bring an 'inverse condemnation' suit to recover the value of the land *on the date of the intrusion by the Government*").

lessen to some extent the freedom and flexibility of land-use planners and governing bodies of municipal corporations when enacting land-use regulations. But such consequences necessarily flow from any decision upholding a claim of constitutional right; many of the provisions of the Constitution are designed to limit the flexibility and freedom of governmental authorities and the Just Compensation Clause of the Fifth Amendment is one of them. As Justice Holmes aptly noted more than 50 years ago, "a strong public desire to improve the public condition is not enough to warrant achieving the desire by a shorter cut than the constitutional way of paying for the change." Pennsylvania Coal Co. v. Mahon, 260 U.S., at 416.

Here we must assume that the Los Angeles County ordinances have denied appellant all use of its property for a considerable period of years, and we hold that invalidation of the ordinance without payment of fair value for the use of the property during this period of time would be a constitutionally insufficient remedy. The judgment of the California Court of Appeal is therefore reversed, and the case is remanded for further proceedings not inconsistent with this opinion.

[Justice Stevens dissented on four grounds, as to the first and third of which Justices Blackmun and O'Connor joined. First, Justice Stevens expressed the view that the Court's decision would generate a great deal of unproductive litigation, with a significant impact on land-use regulation. He stressed the fact that the Court had *not* held that the flood protection regulation worked a taking, and stated the view that under the Court's precedents, such as *Keystone* (see page 1199), no such holding would be forthcoming; the regulation was a valid health and safety measure.

Second, Justice Stevens argued that the duration of a restriction should be relevant to the question whether it works a regulatory taking. "Why," he asked, "should there be a constitutional distinction between a permanent restriction that only reduces the economic value of the property by a fraction — perhaps one-third — and a restriction that merely postpones the development of a property for a fraction of its useful life — presumably far less than a third? In the former instance, no taking has occurred; in the latter case, the Court now proclaims that compensation for a taking must be provided." Similarly, the Justice wondered why "normal delays" are not compensable under the majority's view, whereas compensation must be provided for "delays involved in obtaining a court declaration that the regulation constitutes a taking," even though the second period may be no longer than the first.

Third, litigants should not be allowed to challenge a regulation as a temporary taking without explaining why a state court declaration invalidating the offending regulation would not provide an adequate remedy. Even if state courts adhere to a rule of never granting monetary relief for temporary regulatory takings, property owners should be required to exhaust their state remedies before raising the question whether the net result of the state proceedings amounted to a temporary taking without just compensation.

Fourth, Justice Stevens expressed the concern that the Court's decision would inhibit orderly, fully informed planning on the part of government agencies. "The policy implications of today's decision are obvious and, I fear, far reaching. Cautious local officials and land-use planners may avoid taking any action that might later be challenged and thus give rise to a damage action. Much important regulation will never be enacted,[44] even perhaps in the health and safety area."]

NOTES AND QUESTIONS

1. *After* First English. The Supreme Court's decision in *First English* was limited to the question of remedy *if* a regulatory taking occurs. The Court did not hold that the Los Angeles County ordinance actually *was* a taking; that issue was remanded to the court of appeal. See page 1231. The subsequent proceedings are reported in First English Evangelical Lutheran Church v. County of Los Angeles, 210 Cal. App. 3d 1353, 258 Cal. Rptr. 893 (1989), cert. denied, 493 U.S. 1056 (1990). The court found that the ordinance did not work a taking. "It did not deny First English 'all use' of the property and the uses it did deny could be constitutionally prohibited under the County's power to protect public safety." 210 Cal. App. 3d at 1367, 258 Cal. Rptr. at 902. The court of appeal's decision was "[e]specially heartening to municipal attorneys. . . . It has done a great deal to eliminate misconceptions about the implications of the Supreme Court's decision." Richard J. Roddewig, Recent Developments in Land Use, Planning and Zoning Law, 22 Urb. Law. 719, 769 (1990).

Misconceptions like what? Does *First English* make vulnerable the development moratoria and other growth controls discussed in Chapter 11 at pages 1130-1132? See Roddewig, supra, at 769-779; Thomas E. Roberts & Thomas C. Shearer, Report of the Subcommittee on Land-Use Litigation and Damages: Regulation, Property Rights, and Remedies, 23 Urb. Law. 785, 788-794 (1991). Does the case revitalize "conceptual severance," a notion the Court's earlier decisions in *Penn Central* and

---

44. It is no answer to say that "[a]fter all, if a policeman must know the Constitution, then why not a planner?" San Diego Gas & Electric Co. v. San Diego, 450 U.S. 621, 661, n.26 (1981) (Brennan, J., dissenting). To begin with, the Court has repeatedly recognized that it itself cannot establish any objective rules to assess when a regulation becomes a taking. . . . How then can it demand that land planners do any better? . . . As one commentator concluded: "The chaotic state of taking law makes it especially likely that availability of the damages remedy will induce land-use planning officials to stay well back of the invisible line that they dare not cross." Johnson, Compensation for Invalid Land-Use Regulations, 15 Ga. L. Rev. 559, 594 (1981).

Keystone had seemingly put to rest? Recall the discussion at pages 1203 and 1212-1213, and see Frank Michelman, Takings, 1987, 88 Colum. L. Rev. 1600, 1614-1621 (1988) (discussing, among other things, the strategic significance of conceptual severance, which is what?); Margaret J. Radin, The Liberal Conception of Property: Cross Currents in the Jurisprudence of Takings, 88 Colum. L. Rev. 1667, 1674-1678 (1988).

2. *Before* First English. See Gene R. Rankin, The First Bite at the Apple: State Supreme Court Takings Jurisprudence Antedating *First English*, 22 Urb. Law. 417 (1990):

> When the U.S. Supreme Court, in First English Evangelical Lutheran Church v. County of Los Angeles, decided that regulation of land could constitute a taking, and that such a taking (even if temporary) should be compensated, at least eight states[45] responded with, "So, what else is new?" These eight states had decided, as long as two decades ago, that their state constitutions required that damages be paid where a regulation goes too far, and seven required compensation for temporary takings.
>
> These eight states are rather far-flung, and range from the intensely urbanized to the predominantly rural. In at least four instances, they border states which took a position directly opposite. In at least two instances, they are states which historically have taken the side of the community against the developer.
>
> The point they bring home is that the cutting edge of land-use decisions is found in the state supreme court where, for a number of reasons, issues of local government, of land and of its regulation seem to be better understood than they are in Washington, D.C. . . .
>
> My suspicion is that all of our institutions are beginning to come to grips with the notion that our resources are not unlimited. Just as there is not enough land for all to use as freely as they might (hence more complex regulations), there is also not enough land for us to go off somewhere else when a community overreaches itself and takes by regulating. The lesson is, I think, a healthy one. It is by no means resolved, even though the U.S. Supreme Court finally figured it out in *First English*. [Id. at 417, 429.]

3. *The pros and cons of the compensation remedy.* As indicated on page 1233, the California Supreme Court had concluded in Agins v. City of Tiburon that to charge the government with the duty to compensate for regulatory takings would inhibit community planning and chill exercises of the police power. Regulators would become not simply cautious, but too cautious. Judicial imposition of a compensation requirement, moreover, would usurp the legislature's power to make decisions about public expenditures. Scholarly commentary adds to the list of concerns, the following being the chief points: If compensation is required, there arises the problem of determining just what interest the government has

---

45. Arizona, New Hampshire, New Jersey, North Dakota, Oregon, Rhode Island, Texas, and Wisconsin. — EDS.

"purchased"; where the overly harsh regulation is later repealed, the claimant in the inverse condemnation suit will have received an undeserved windfall (an observation that obviously assumes compensation awards are based on permanent losses); cases involving physical invasion or property destruction are off the point because they, unlike regulatory takings, are more likely to involve irreparable losses.

Justice Brennan, dissenting in *San Diego Gas & Elec. Co.*, responded to these and other concerns, and the majority opinion in *First English* echoes some of his points. Regulatory action can destroy use and enjoyment of property just as effectively as physical occupation or destruction, Brennan argued, and in the latter cases compensation has always been required. Logic, then, requires that overzealous regulation also be compensable, especially because invalidation of itself fails to compensate for losses that were wrongfully imposed. The government should have the duty to pay compensation for losses accruing from the time a regulation effected a taking until the time the regulation is rescinded or amended. (Alternatively, the government could condemn the property or, presumably, leave the regulation in place and be liable for an award based on the permanent, not temporary, loss of value.) Policy considerations of the sort expressed in *Agins,* Brennan said, could not work to limit the express guarantees of the Fifth Amendment. In any event, the concerns were unpersuasive. The threat of governmental financial liability for unconstitutional exercises of the police power would help produce more rational land-use controls, ones that more carefully weighed costs against benefits. It would also encourage state and local officials to err on the constitutional side of police power regulation.

Do other arguments, pro or con, occur to you? Where do you come out in the debate?[46]

4. *Procedural matters.* Consider a few statements from *First English*, and some problems to which they give rise:

(a) "[T]he Just Compensation Clause of the Fifth Amendment requires that the government pay the landowner for the value of the use of the land during this period" of a regulatory taking. (Page 1234.) But what precisely is the measure of damages?

There are various possibilities, such as fair rental value, option price, interest on lost profits, before-and-after valuation, and benefit to

---

46. The arguments sketched in the text have been stated and restated in the literature over a period beginning well before the decision in *First English* and continuing up to the present. For a recent summary, see Theodore M. Cooperstein, Sensing Leave for One's Takings: Interim Damages and Land Use Regulation, 7 Stan. Envtl. L.J. 49, 52-60 (1987-1988). Cooperstein, who surveyed local land-use planners as part of his study, concludes that denial of a compensation remedy in the past did not provide planners with as much freedom as one might suppose (because there was still landowner resistance), and that availability of the remedy after *First English* will have no chilling effect. "Without any noticeable harm to land use planning and local government processes," he says, "the pragmatic concerns of those who oppose interim damages evaporate." Id. at 70.

the government. In *Wheeler v. City of Pleasant Grove*, 896 F.2d 1347 (11th Cir. 1990), the court calculated damages based on "the market rate [of] return computed over the period of the temporary taking on the difference between the property's fair market value without the regulatory restriction and its fair market value with the restriction." 896 F.2d at 1350. Accord, *Front Royal & Warren County Indus. Park Corp. v. Town of Front Royal*, 749 F. Supp. 1439 (W.D. Va. 1990).

(b) "Though, as a matter of law, an illegitimate taking might not occur until the government refuses to pay, the interference that effects a taking might begin much earlier, and compensation is measured from that time." (Footnote 43 on page 1235.) Does the cause of action for a regulatory taking accrue on the date the offending regulation is enacted, or when the government refuses to pay, or on some other date? In any event, may a suit for compensation be barred by a statute of limitations running from that date? See *Scott v. City of Sioux City*, 432 N.W.2d 144 (Iowa 1988); *Millison v. Wilzack*, 77 Md. App. 676, 551 A.2d 899 (1989).

(c) "[In] *Williamson County Regional Planning Commn.* . . . we noted that 'no constitutional violation occurs until just compensation has been denied.' " (Again, footnote 43 on page 1235.) What this means, among other things, is that inverse condemnation suits seeking compensation for regulatory takings are generally to be pursued in the first instance in state courts. Constitutional challenges in the federal courts are usually not ripe until a state denies compensation, because states are free to take property for legitimate governmental purposes, provided only that they pay.[47]

Here is a related matter: Suppose a *federal* regulation, otherwise legitimate, so burdens some claimant as to work a taking. Is the regulation to be invalidated as unconstitutional? The answer is no, if compensation

---

47. For a discussion of complications, see Thomas E. Roberts, Fifth Amendment Taking Claims in Federal Court: The State Compensation Requirement and Principles of Res Judicata, 24 Urb. Law. 479 (1992).

Notice our statement in the text: "states are free to take property *for legitimate governmental purposes*, provided only that they pay." Suppose the governmental purpose is illegitimate — the alleged taking would not be for a public use, say, or the legislative objective is unconstitutional. Invalidation of the measure in question can follow as a matter of course, but is relief in damages available? See *Wheeler v. City of Pleasant Grove*, 833 F.2d 267, 270 n.3 (11th Cir. 1987), discussing 42 U.S.C. §1983 (1988), which provides for civil rights suits seeking damages for deprivation of constitutional rights under color of state law:

Technically, the fifth amendment's just compensation clause is not applicable where there has been no "public use." Such may be the case where . . . the land use regulation that effected the taking was not enacted in furtherance of the public health, safety, morals, or general welfare. The affected landowner may nevertheless have a damage cause of action under section 1983 since the taking may violate his fourteenth amendment rights to due process.

See also *Coniston Corp. v. Village of Hoffman Estates*, 844 F.2d 461, 464 (7th Cir. 1988), and, generally, Michael M. Berger, The Civil Rights Act: An Alternative Remedy for Property Owners Which Avoids Some of the Procedural Traps and Pitfalls in Traditional "Takings" Litigation, 12 Zoning & Plan. L. Rep. 121 (1989).

is available under the Tucker Act, 28 U.S.C. §1491 (1988). See, e.g., Preseault v. ICC, 494 U.S. 1 (1990).

5. *The Tucker Act and the Court of Federal Claims.* The Tucker Act provides jurisdiction in the U.S. Court of Federal Claims for damage claims against the federal government founded on the Constitution, a regulation, or an express or implied contract. If a regulation works a taking, then the claim for compensation is founded on the Constitution and within the court's jurisdiction (unless Congress has provided otherwise).

The Court of Federal Claims came about as part of a reorganization and renaming of the former Court of Claims, established in 1855 to provide a forum for monetary claims against the federal government. Appeals from the court's decisions go to the Federal Circuit, also established as part of the reorganization. Cases like *Preseault,* supra, effectively move a large number of takings cases against the federal government into the Court of Federal Claims — a point that would perhaps be unremarkable were it not for the fact that the court is thought by some observers to have "tilted ideologically to the right." W. John Moore, Just Compensation, Natl. J., June 13, 1992, at 1404, 1405. " 'The opinions there smack of a certain philosophy, which is a minimalist government approach' to problems," according to one environmental lawyer worried about the court's impact on environmental regulation. Id. Most if not all of the judges on the court were appointed by Presidents Reagan and Bush. Id. at 1406.

For a favorable review of recent decisions by the Court of Federal Claims and the Federal Circuit, see Roger J. Marzulla & Nanci G. Marzulla, Regulatory Takings in the United States Claims Court: Adjusting the Burdens That in Fairness and Equity Ought to Be Borne by Society as a Whole, 40 Cath. U. L. Rev. 549 (1991). From the article one can gather two particularly interesting tendencies in the decisions: (1) conceptual severance is taken seriously; (2) the nuisance exception is not.[48]

Prescient? Consider the following and judge for yourself.

3. Reprise

Lucas v. South Carolina Coastal Council
Supreme Court of the United States, 1992
112 S. Ct. 2886

JUSTICE SCALIA delivered the opinion of the Court.

In 1986, petitioner David H. Lucas paid $975,000 for two residen-

---

48. Recall our discussion of these matters earlier in this chapter. See, e.g., Note 2 on pages 1186-1188, Note 2 on pages 1197-1198, Note 1 on page 1203, and Note 1 on pages 1211-1212.

tial lots on the Isle of Palms in Charleston County, South Carolina, on which he intended to build single-family homes. In 1988, however, the South Carolina Legislature enacted the Beachfront Management Act, S.C. Code §48-39-250 et seq. (Supp. 1990) (Act), which had the direct effect of barring petitioner from erecting any permanent habitable structures on his two parcels. A state trial court found that this prohibition rendered Lucas's parcels "valueless." This case requires us to decide whether the Act's dramatic effect on the economic value of Lucas's lots accomplished a taking of private property under the Fifth and Fourteenth Amendments requiring the payment of "just compensation."

I

A

South Carolina's expressed interest in intensively managing development activities in the so-called "coastal zone" dates from 1977 when, in the aftermath of Congress's passage of the federal Coastal Zone Management Act of 1972, 86 Stat. 1280, as amended, 16 U.S.C. §1451 et seq., the legislature enacted a Coastal Zone Management Act of its own. In its original form, the South Carolina Act required owners of coastal zone land that qualified as a "critical area" (defined in the legislation to include beaches and immediately adjacent sand dunes) to obtain a permit from the newly created South Carolina Coastal Council (respondent here) prior to committing the land to a "use other than the use the critical area was devoted to on [September 28, 1977]."

In the late 1970's, Lucas and others began extensive residential development of the Isle of Palms, a barrier island situated eastward of the City of Charleston. Toward the close of the development cycle for one residential subdivision known as "Beachwood East," Lucas in 1986 purchased the two lots at issue in this litigation for his own account. No portion of the lots, which were located approximately 300 feet from the beach, qualified as a "critical area" under the 1977 Act; accordingly, at the time Lucas acquired these parcels, he was not legally obliged to obtain a permit from the Council in advance of any development activity. His intention with respect to the lots was to do what the owners of the immediately adjacent parcels had already done: erect single-family residences. He commissioned architectural drawings for this purpose.

The Beachfront Management Act brought Lucas's plans to an abrupt end. Under that 1988 legislation, the Council was directed to establish a "baseline" connecting the landward-most "point[s] of erosion . . . during the past forty years" in the region of the Isle of Palms that includes Lucas's lots. In action not challenged here, the Council fixed this baseline landward of Lucas's parcels. That was significant, for under the Act construction of occupiable improvements[49] was flatly prohibited seaward of a line drawn 20 feet landward of, and parallel to, the baseline. The Act provided no exceptions.

B

Lucas promptly filed suit in the South Carolina Court of Common Pleas, contending that the Beachfront Management Act's construction bar effected a taking of his property without just compensation. Lucas did not take issue with the validity of the Act as a lawful exercise of South Carolina's police power, but contended that the Act's complete extinguishment of his property's value entitled him to compensation regardless of whether the legislature had acted in furtherance of legitimate police power objectives. Following a bench trial, the court agreed. Among its factual determinations was the finding that "at the time Lucas purchased the two lots, both were zoned for single-family residential construction and . . . there were no restrictions imposed upon such use of the property by either the State of South Carolina, the County of Charleston, or the Town of the Isle of Palms." The trial court further found that the Beachfront Management Act decreed a permanent ban on construction insofar as Lucas's lots were concerned, and that this prohibition "deprive[d] Lucas of any reasonable economic use of the lots, . . . eliminated the unrestricted right of use, and render[ed] them valueless." The court thus concluded that Lucas's properties had been "taken" by operation of the Act, and it ordered respondent to pay "just compensation" in the amount of $1,232,387.50.

The Supreme Court of South Carolina reversed. It found dispositive what it described as Lucas's concession "that the Beachfront Management Act [was] properly and validly designed to preserve . . . South Carolina's beaches." 304 S.C. 376, 379, 404 S.E.2d 895, 896 (1991). Failing an attack on the validity of the statute as such, the court believed itself bound to accept the "uncontested . . . findings" of the South Carolina legislature that new construction in the coastal zone — such as petitioner intended — threatened this public resource. Id., at 383, 404 S.E.2d, at 898. The Court ruled that when a regulation respecting the use of property is designed "to prevent serious public harm," id., at 383, 404 S.E.2d, at 899 (citing, inter alia, Mugler v. Kansas, 123 U.S. 623, 8 S. Ct. 273, 31 L. Ed. 205 (1887)), no compensation is owing under the Takings Clause regardless of the regulation's effect on the property's value.

---

49. The Act did allow the construction of certain nonhabitable improvements, e.g., "wooden walkways no larger in width than six feet," and "small wooden decks no larger than one hundred forty-four square feet."

Two justices dissented. They acknowledged that our *Mugler* line of cases recognizes governmental power to prohibit "noxious" uses of property — i.e., uses of property akin to "public nuisances" — without having to pay compensation. But they would not have characterized the Beachfront Management Act's "*primary* purpose [as] the prevention of a nuisance." 304 S.C., at 395, 404 S.E.2d, at 906 (Harwell, J., dissenting). To the dissenters, the chief purposes of the legislation, among them the promotion of tourism and the creation of a "habitat for indigenous flora and fauna," could not fairly be compared to nuisance abatement. Id., at 396, 404 S.E.2d, at 906. As a consequence, they would have affirmed the trial court's conclusion that the Act's obliteration of the value of petitioner's lots accomplished a taking.

We granted certiorari.

II

As a threshold matter, we must briefly address the Council's suggestion that this case is inappropriate for plenary review. . . .

[The Court rejected the argument that the case was not ripe for review. The South Carolina Supreme Court had decided Lucas's takings claim on the merits. While it was true that Lucas might be able to obtain a permit for *future* construction, the judgment below had disposed of his takings claim with respect to *past* deprivations, and hence review was appropriate. (Here the Court cited the *First English* case; see page 1229 of this book.) Questions left unaddressed by the South Carolina Supreme Court as a consequence of its categorical disposition could be considered on remand.]

III

A

Prior to Justice Holmes' exposition in Pennsylvania Coal Co. v. Mahon, 260 U.S. 393, 43 S. Ct. 158, 67 L. Ed. 322 (1922), it was generally thought that the Takings Clause reached only a "direct appropriation" of property, Legal Tender Cases, 12 Wall. 457, 551, 20 L. Ed. 287 (1871), or the functional equivalent of a "practical ouster of [the owner's] possession." Transportation Co. v. Chicago, 99 U.S. 635, 642, 25 L. Ed. 336 (1879). . . . Justice Holmes recognized in *Mahon,* however, that if the protection against physical appropriations of private property was to be meaningfully enforced, the government's power to redefine the range of interests included in the ownership of property was necessarily constrained by constitutional limits. . . . These considerations gave birth in that case to the oft-cited maxim that, "while property may be regulated

to a certain extent, if regulation goes too ...
taking."

Nevertheless, our decision in *Mahon* offerea ...cognized as a
and under what circumstances, a given regulatio... into when,
going "too far" for purposes of the Fifth Amendmen... seen as
of succeeding "regulatory takings" jurisprudence, we ha... years
chewed any " 'set formula' " for determining how far is too... ... es-
ring to "engag[e] in . . . essentially ad hoc, factual inquir... ...fer-
Central Transportation Co. v. New York City, 438 U.S. 104, 12... ...n
Ct. 2646, 2659, 57 L. Ed. 2d 631 (1978) (quoting Goldblatt v. He...
stead, 369 U.S. 590, 594, 82 S. Ct. 987, 990, 8 L. Ed. 2d 130 (1962)). Se...
Epstein, Takings: Descent and Resurrection, 1987 Sup. Ct. Rev. 1, 4. We
have, however, described at least two discrete categories of regulatory
action as compensable without case-specific inquiry into the public interest advanced in support of the restraint. The first encompasses regulations that compel the property owner to suffer a physical "invasion" of
his property. In general (at least with regard to permanent invasions),
no matter how minute the intrusion, and no matter how weighty the
public purpose behind it, we have required compensation [citing *Loretto*,
reproduced at page 1165].

The second situation in which we have found categorical treatment
appropriate is where regulation denies all economically beneficial or
productive use of land. . . .[50] As we have said on numerous occasions,
the Fifth Amendment is violated when land-use regulation "does not
substantially advance legitimate state interests *or denies an owner economically viable use of his land.*" [Agins v. City of Tiburon, 447 U.S. 255, 260
(1980).][51]

---

50. We will not attempt to respond to all of Justice Blackmun's mistaken citation of
case precedent. . . . The cases say, repeatedly and unmistakably, that " '[t]he test to be
applied in considering [a] facial [takings] challenge is fairly straightforward. A statute regulating the uses that can be made of property *effects a taking if it "denies an owner economically
viable use of his land."* ' " . . .
    Justice Blackmun describes that rule (which we do not invent but merely apply today)
as "alter[ing] the long-settled rules of review" by foisting on the State "the burden of showing [its] regulation is not a taking." This is of course wrong. Lucas had to do more than
simply file a lawsuit to establish his constitutional entitlement; he had to show that the
Beachfront Management Act denied him economically beneficial use of his land. Our
analysis presumes the unconstitutionality of state land-use regulation only in the sense that
any rule-with-exceptions presumes the invalidity of a rule that violates it. . . .
    51. Regrettably, the rhetorical force of our "deprivation of all economically feasible
use" rule is greater than its precision, since the rule does not make clear the "property
interest" against which the loss of value is to be measured. When, for example, a regulation
requires a developer to leave 90% of a rural tract in its natural state, it is unclear whether
we would analyze the situation as one in which the owner has been deprived of all economically beneficial use of the burdened portion of the tract, or as one in which the owner has
suffered a mere diminution in value of the tract as a whole. (For an extreme — and, we
think, unsupportable — view of the relevant calculus, see Penn Central Transportation
Co. v. New York City, 42 N.Y.2d 324, 333-334, 397 N.Y.S.2d 914, 920, 366 N.E.2d 1271,
1276-1277 (1977), aff'd, 438 U.S. 104, 98 S. Ct. 2646, 57 L. Ed. 2d 631 (1978), where the

...et forth the justification for this rule. Perhaps it is simply, ...rennan suggested, that total deprivation of beneficial use is, ...We landowner's point of view, the equivalent of a physical appr... See San Diego Gas & Electric Co. v. San Diego, 450 U.S., at ... . Ct., at 1304 (Brennan, J., dissenting). "[F]or what is the la ...he profits thereof[?]" 1 E. Coke, Institutes ch. 1, §1 (1st Am. 2). Surely, at least, in the extraordinary circumstance when *no* ...ctive or economically beneficial use of land is permitted, it is less ...istic to indulge our usual assumption that the legislature is simply adjusting the benefits and burdens of economic life," *Penn Central Transportation Co.*, 438 U.S., at 124, 98 S. Ct., at 2659, in a manner that secures an "average reciprocity of advantage" to everyone concerned. Pennsylvania Coal Co. v. Mahon, 260 U.S., at 415, 43 S. Ct., at 160. And the *functional* basis for permitting the government, by regulation, to affect property values without compensation — that "Government hardly could go on if to some extent values incident to property could not be diminished without paying for every such change in the general law," id., at 413, 43 S. Ct., at 159 — does not apply to the relatively rare situations where the government has deprived a landowner of all economically beneficial uses.

On the other side of the balance, affirmatively supporting a compensation requirement, is the fact that regulations that leave the owner of land without economically beneficial or productive options for its use — typically, as here, by requiring land to be left substantially in its natural state — carry with them a heightened risk that private property is being pressed into some form of public service under the guise of mitigating serious public harm.... As Justice Brennan explained: "From the government's point of view, the benefits flowing to the public from preservation of open space through regulation may be equally great as from creating a wildlife refuge through formal condemnation

---

state court examined the diminution in a particular parcel's value produced by a municipal ordinance in light of total value of the taking claimant's other holdings in the vicinity.) Unsurprisingly, this uncertainty regarding the composition of the denominator in our "deprivation" fraction has produced inconsistent pronouncements by the Court. Compare Pennsylvania Coal Co. v. Mahon, 260 U.S. 393, 414, 43 S. Ct. 158, 160, 67 L. Ed. 322 (1922) (law restricting subsurface extraction of coal held to effect a taking), with Keystone Bituminous Coal Assn. v. DeBenedictis, 480 U.S. 470, 497-502, 107 S. Ct. 1232, 1248-1251, 94 L. Ed. 2d 472 (1987) (nearly identical law held not to effect a taking); see also id., at 515-520, 107 S. Ct., at 1257-1260 (Rehnquist, C.J., dissenting); Rose, *Mahon* Reconstructed: Why the Takings Issue is Still a Muddle, 57 S. Cal. L. Rev. 561, 566-569 (1984). The answer to this difficult question may lie in how the owner's reasonable expectations have been shaped by the State's law of property — i.e., whether and to what degree the State's law has accorded legal recognition and protection to the particular interest in land with respect to which the takings claimant alleges a diminution in (or elimination of) value. In any event, we avoid this difficulty in the present case, since the "interest in land" that Lucas has pleaded (a fee simple interest) is an estate with a rich tradition of protection at common law, and since the South Carolina Court of Common Pleas found that the Beachfront Management Act left each of Lucas's beachfront lots without economic value.

or increasing electricity production ...
private property." *San Diego Gas & Elec...*
S. Ct., at 1304 (Brennan, J., dissenting). Th... project that floods
both state and federal, that provide for the ... U.S., at 652, 101
impose servitudes on private scenic lands pre... s on the books,
uses, or to acquire such lands altogether, suggest t...t domain to
lence in this setting of negative regulation and appropr...lopmental

We think, in short, that there are good reasons for d... equiva-
expressed belief that when the owner of real property has b...
upon to sacrifice *all* economically beneficial uses in the name of t...ed
mon good, that is, to leave his property economically idle, he has ...
fered a taking.[52]

B

The trial court found Lucas's two beachfront lots to have been rendered valueless by respondent's enforcement of the coastal-zone construction ban. Under Lucas's theory of the case, which rested upon our "no economically viable use" statements, that finding entitled him to compensation. Lucas believed it unnecessary to take issue with either the purposes behind the Beachfront Management Act, or the means chosen by the South Carolina Legislature to effectuate those purposes. The South Carolina Supreme Court, however, thought otherwise. In its view, the Beachfront Management Act was no ordinary enactment, but involved an exercise of South Carolina's "police powers" to mitigate the

---

52. Justice Stevens criticizes the "deprivation of all economically beneficial use" rule as "wholly arbitrary," in that "[the] landowner whose property is diminished in value 95% recovers nothing," while the landowner who suffers a complete elimination of value "recovers the land's full value." This analysis errs in its assumption that the landowner whose deprivation is one step short of complete is not entitled to compensation. Such an owner might not be able to claim the benefit of our categorical formulation, but, as we have acknowledged time and again, "[t]he economic impact of the regulation on the claimant and . . . the extent to which the regulation has interfered with distinct investment-backed expectations" are keenly relevant to takings analysis generally. Penn Central Transportation Co. v. New York City, 438 U.S. 104, 124, 98 S. Ct. 2646, 2659, 57 L. Ed. 2d 631 (1978). It is true that in at least *some* cases the landowner with 95% loss will get nothing, while the landowner with total loss will recover in full. But that occasional result is no more strange than the gross disparity between the landowner whose premises are taken for a highway (who recovers in full) and the landowner whose property is reduced to 5% of its former value by the highway (who recovers nothing). Takings law is full of these "all-or-nothing" situations.

Justice Stevens similarly misinterprets our focus on "developmental" uses of property (the uses proscribed by the Beachfront Management Act) as betraying an "assumption that the only uses of property cognizable under the Constitution are *developmental* uses." We make no such assumption. Though our prior takings cases evince an abiding concern for the productive use of, and economic investment in, land, there are plainly a number of noneconomic interests in land whose impairment will invite exceedingly close scrutiny under the Takings Clause. See, e.g., Loretto v. Teleprompter Manhattan CATV Corp., 458 U.S. 419, 436, 102 S. Ct. 3164, 3176, 73 L. Ed. 2d 868 (1982) (interest in excluding strangers from one's land).

st that petitioner's use of his land might occa-
404 S.E.2d, at 899. By neglecting to dispute the
harm to the in the Act[53] or otherwise to challenge the legisla-
sion. 304 petitioner "concede[d] that the beach/dune area of
findings s shores is an extremely valuable public resource; that
ture's new construction, *inter alia*, contributes to the erosion and
South of this public resource; and that discouraging new construc-
the ose proximity to the beach/dune area is necessary to prevent a
de public harm." Id., at 382-383, 404 S.E.2d, at 898. In the court's
w, these concessions brought petitioner's challenge within a long line
of this Court's cases sustaining against Due Process and Takings Clause
challenges the State's use of its "police powers" to enjoin a property
owner from activities akin to public nuisances. See Mugler v. Kansas, 123
U.S. 623, 8 S. Ct. 273, 31 L. Ed. 205 (1887) (law prohibiting manufacture
of alcoholic beverages); Hadacheck v. Sebastian, 239 U.S. 394, 36 S. Ct.
143, 60 L. Ed. 348 (1915) (law barring operation of brick mill in residential area); Miller v. Schoene, 276 U.S. 272, 48 S. Ct. 246, 72 L. Ed. 568
(1928) (order to destroy diseased cedar trees to prevent infection of
nearby orchards); Goldblatt v. Hempstead, 369 U.S. 590, 82 S. Ct. 987,
8 L. Ed. 2d 130 (1962) (law effectively preventing continued operation
of quarry in residential area).

It is correct that many of our prior opinions have suggested that
"harmful or noxious uses" of property may be proscribed by government regulation without the requirement of compensation. For a number of reasons, however, we think the South Carolina Supreme Court
was too quick to conclude that that principle decides the present case.
The "harmful or noxious uses" principle was the Court's early attempt
to describe in theoretical terms why government may, consistent with
the Takings Clause, affect property values by regulation without incurring an obligation to compensate — a reality we nowadays acknowledge
explicitly with respect to the full scope of the State's police power. . . .
We made this very point in *Penn Central Transportation Co.*, where, in the
course of sustaining New York City's landmarks preservation program
against a takings challenge, we rejected the petitioner's suggestion that
Mugler and the cases following it were premised on, and thus limited by,
some objective conception of "noxiousness":

> [T]he uses in issue in *Hadacheck, Miller,* and *Goldblatt* were perfectly lawful in
> themselves. They involved no "blame-worthiness, . . . moral wrongdoing or

---

53. The legislature's express findings include [mention of the importance of the
beach/dune system as a storm barrier, a basis for tourism, a habitat for plants and animals,
and a recreational resource. The legislature further found that beach/dune vegetation is
unique and important to the preservation of the system; that the beaches are eroding; that
development has been sited too close to the system; and that seawalls and other means to
control erosion have been ineffective. Erosion is a natural process that becomes a problem
only when development occurs in close proximity to the beach/dune system.]

conscious act of dangerous risk-taking which induce[d society] to shift the cost to a pa[rt]icular individual." Sax, Takings and the Police Power, 74 Yale L.J. 36, 50 (1964). These cases are better understood as resting not on any supposed "noxious" quality of the prohibited uses but rather on the ground that the restrictions were reasonably related to the implementation of a policy — not unlike historic preservation — expected to produce a widespread public benefit and applicable to all similarly situated property. [438 U.S., at 133-134, n.30, 98 S. Ct., at 2664, n.30.]

"Harmful or noxious use" analysis was, in other words, simply the progenitor of our more contemporary statements that "land-use regulation does not effect a taking if it 'substantially advance[s] legitimate state interests.' . . ." Nollan [v. California Coastal Commn., 483 U.S. 825, 834, 107 S. Ct. 3141, 3147 (1987)] (quoting Agins v. Tiburon, 447 U.S., at 260, 100 S. Ct., at 2141). . . .

The transition from our early focus on control of "noxious" uses to our contemporary understanding of the broad realm within which government may regulate without compensation was an easy one, since the distinction between "harm-preventing" and "benefit-conferring" regulation is often in the eye of the beholder. It is quite possible, for example, to describe in *either* fashion the ecological, economic, and aesthetic concerns that inspired the South Carolina legislature in the present case. One could say that imposing a servitude on Lucas's land is necessary in order to prevent his use of it from "harming" South Carolina's ecological resources; or, instead, in order to achieve the "benefits" of an ecological preserve.[54] . . . Whether one or the other of the competing characterizations will come to one's lips in a particular case depends primarily upon one's evaluation of the worth of competing uses of real estate. . . . A given restraint will be seen as mitigating "harm" to the adjacent parcels or securing a "benefit" for them, depending upon the observer's evaluation of the relative importance of the use that the restraint favors. See Sax, Takings and the Police Power, 74 Yale L.J. 36, 49 (1964)

54. In the present case, in fact, some of the "[South Carolina] legislature's 'findings'" to which the South Carolina Supreme Court purported to defer in characterizing the purpose of the Act as "harm-preventing," 304 S.C. 376, 385, 404 S.E.2d 895, 900 (1991), seem to us phrased in "benefit-conferring" language instead. . . . It would be pointless to make the outcome of this case hang upon this terminology, since the same interests could readily be described in "harm-preventing" fashion.

Justice Blackmun, however, apparently insists that we *must* make the outcome hinge (exclusively) upon the South Carolina Legislature's other, "harm-preventing" characterizations, focusing on the declaration that "prohibitions on building in front of the setback line are necessary to protect people and property from storms, high tides, and beach erosion." He says "[n]othing in the record undermines [this] assessment," apparently seeing no significance in the fact that the statute permits owners of *existing* structures to remain (and even to rebuild if their structures are not "destroyed beyond repair," S.C. Code Ann. §48-39-290(B)), and in the fact that the 1990 amendment authorizes the Council to issue permits for new construction in violation of the uniform prohibition, see S.C. Code §48-39-290(D)(1) (Supp. 1991).

("[T]he problem [in this area] is not one of noxiousness or harm-creating activity at all; rather it is a problem of inconsistency between perfectly innocent and independently desirable uses"). Whether Lucas's construction of single-family residences on his parcels should be described as bringing "harm" to South Carolina's adjacent ecological resources thus depends principally upon whether the describer believes that the State's use interest in nurturing those resources is so important that *any* competing adjacent use must yield.[55]

When it is understood that "prevention of harmful use" was merely our early formulation of the police power justification necessary to sustain (without compensation) *any* regulatory diminution in value; and that the distinction between regulation that "prevents harmful use" and that which "confers benefits" is difficult, if not impossible, to discern on an objective, value-free basis; it becomes self-evident that noxious-use logic cannot serve as a touchstone to distinguish regulatory "takings" — which require compensation — from regulatory deprivations that do not require compensation. A *fortiori* the legislature's recitation of a noxious-use justification cannot be the basis for departing from our categorical rule that total regulatory takings must be compensated. If it were, departure would virtually always be allowed. The South Carolina Supreme Court's approach would essentially nullify *Mahon's* affirmation of limits to the noncompensable exercise of the police power. Our cases provide no support for this: None of them that employed the logic of "harmful use" prevention to sustain a regulation involved an allegation that the regulation wholly eliminated the value of the claimant's land. See *Keystone Bituminous Coal Assn.*, 480 U.S., at 513-514, 107 S. Ct., at 1257 (Rehnquist, C.J., dissenting).[56]

Where the State seeks to sustain regulation that deprives land of all economically beneficial use, we think it may resist compensation only if the logically antecedent inquiry into the nature of the owner's estate shows that the proscribed use interests were not part of his title to begin

---

55. In Justice Blackmun's view, even with respect to regulations that deprive an owner of all developmental or economically beneficial land uses, the test for required compensation is whether the legislature has recited a harm-preventing justification for its action. Since such a justification can be formulated in practically every case, this amounts to a test of whether the legislature has a stupid staff. We think the Takings Clause requires courts to do more than insist upon artful harm-preventing characterizations.

56. E.g., Mugler v. Kansas, 123 U.S. 623, 8 S. Ct. 273, 31 L. Ed. 205 (1887) (prohibition upon use of a building as a brewery; other uses permitted); Plymouth Coal Co. v. Pennsylvania, 232 U.S. 531, 34 S. Ct. 359, 58 L. Ed. 713 (1914) (requirement that "pillar" of coal be left in ground to safeguard mine workers; mineral rights could otherwise be exploited); Reinman v. Little Rock, 237 U.S. 171, 35 S. Ct. 511, 59 L. Ed. 900 (1915) (declaration that livery stable constituted a public nuisance; other uses of the property permitted); Hadacheck v. Sebastian, 239 U.S. 394, 36 S. Ct. 143, 60 L. Ed. 348 (1915) (prohibition of brick manufacturing in residential area; other uses permitted); Goldblatt v. Hempstead, 369 U.S. 590, 82 S. Ct. 987, 8 L. Ed. 2d 130 (1962) (prohibition on excavation; other uses permitted).

with.[57] This accords, we think, with our "takings" jurisprudence, which has traditionally been guided by the understandings of our citizens regarding the content of, and the State's power over, the "bundle of rights" that they acquire when they obtain title to property. It seems to us that the property owner necessarily expects the uses of his property to be restricted, from time to time, by various measures newly enacted by the State in legitimate exercise of its police powers. . . . And in the case of personal property, by reason of the State's traditionally high degree of control over commercial dealings, he ought to be aware of the possibility that new regulation might even render his property economically worthless (at least if the property's only economically productive use is sale or manufacture for sale), see Andrus v. Allard, 444 U.S. 51, 66-67, 100 S. Ct. 318, 327, 62 L. Ed. 2d 210 (1979) (prohibition on sale of eagle feathers). In the case of land, however, we think the notion pressed by the Council that title is somehow held subject to the "implied limitation" that the State may subsequently eliminate all economically valuable use is inconsistent with the historical compact recorded in the Takings Clause that has become part of our constitutional culture.[58]

Where "permanent physical occupation" of land is concerned, we have refused to allow the government to decree it anew (without compensation), no matter how weighty the asserted "public interests" involved, Loretto v. Teleprompter Manhattan CATV Corp., 458 U.S., at 426, 102 S. Ct., at 3171 — though we assuredly *would* permit the govern-

57. Drawing on our First Amendment jurisprudence, see, e.g., Employment Division, Department of Human Resources of Oregon v. Smith, 494 U.S. 872, 878-879, 110 S. Ct. 1595, 1600, 108 L. Ed. 2d 876 (1990), Justice Stevens would "loo[k] to the *generality* of a regulation of property" to determine whether compensation is owing. The Beachfront Management Act is general, in his view, because it "regulates the use of the coastline of the entire state." There may be some validity to the principle Justice Stevens proposes, but it does not properly apply to the present case. The equivalent of a law of general application that inhibits the practice of religion without being aimed at religion, see Oregon v. Smith, supra, is a law that destroys the value of land without being aimed at land. Perhaps such a law — the generally applicable criminal prohibition on the manufacturing of alcoholic beverages challenged in *Mugler* comes to mind — cannot constitute a compensable taking. See 123 U.S., at 655-656, 8 S. Ct., at 293-294. But a regulation *specifically directed to land use* no more acquires immunity by plundering landowners generally than does a law specifically directed at religious practice acquire immunity by prohibiting all religions. Justice Stevens' approach renders the Takings Clause little more than a particularized restatement of the Equal Protection Clause.

58. After accusing us of "launch[ing] a missile to kill a mouse," Justice Blackmun expends a good deal of throw-weight of his own upon a noncombatant, arguing that our description of the "understanding" of land ownership that informs the Takings Clause is not supported by early American experience. That is largely true, but entirely irrelevant. The practices of the States *prior* to incorporation of the Takings and Just Compensation Clauses, see Chicago, B.&Q. R. Co. v. Chicago, 166 U.S. 226, 17 S. Ct. 581, 41 L. Ed. 979 (1897) — which, as Justice Blackmun acknowledges, occasionally included *outright physical appropriation* of land without compensation — were out of accord with *any* plausible interpretation of those provisions. Justice Blackmun is correct that early constitutional theorists did not believe the Takings Clause embraced regulations of property at all, but even he does not suggest (explicitly, at least) that we renounce the Court's contrary conclusion in *Mahon*. . . .

ment to assert a permanent easement that was a pre-existing limitation upon the landowner's title. . . . We believe similar treatment must be accorded confiscatory regulations, i.e., regulations that prohibit all economically beneficial use of land: Any limitation so severe cannot be newly legislated or decreed (without compensation), but must inhere in the title itself, in the restrictions that background principles of the State's law of property and nuisance already place upon land ownership. A law or decree with such an effect must, in other words, do no more than duplicate the result that could have been achieved in the courts — by adjacent landowners (or other uniquely affected persons) under the State's law of private nuisance, or by the State under its complementary power to abate nuisances that affect the public generally, or otherwise.[59]

On this analysis, the owner of a lake bed, for example, would not be entitled to compensation when he is denied the requisite permit to engage in a landfilling operation that would have the effect of flooding others' land. Nor the corporate owner of a nuclear generating plant, when it is directed to remove all improvements from its land upon discovery that the plant sits astride an earthquake fault. Such regulatory action may well have the effect of eliminating the land's only economically productive use, but it does not proscribe a productive use that was previously permissible under relevant property and nuisance principles. The use of these properties for what are now expressly prohibited purposes was *always* unlawful, and (subject to other constitutional limitations) it was open to the State at any point to make the implication of those background principles of nuisance and property law explicit. . . . In light of our traditional resort to "existing rules or understandings that stem from an independent source such as state law" to define the range of interests that qualify for protection as "property" under the Fifth (and Fourteenth) amendments, . . . this recognition that the Takings Clause does not require compensation when an owner is barred from putting land to a use that is proscribed by those "existing rules or understandings" is surely unexceptional. When, however, a regulation that declares "off-limits" all economically productive or beneficial uses of land goes beyond what the relevant background principles would dictate, compensation must be paid to sustain it.[60]

59. The principal "otherwise" that we have in mind is litigation absolving the State (or private parties) of liability for the destruction of "real and personal property, in cases of actual necessity, to prevent the spreading of a fire" or to forestall other grave threats to the lives and property of others. Bowditch v. Boston, 101 U.S. 16, 18-19, 25 L. Ed. 980 (1880). . . .

60. Of course, the State may elect to rescind its regulation and thereby avoid having to pay compensation for a permanent deprivation. See First English Evangelical Lutheran Church [of Glendale v. County of Los Angeles, 482 U.S. 304, 321, 107 S. Ct. 2378, 2389 (1987)]. But "where the [regulation has] already worked a taking of all use of property, no subsequent action by the government can relieve it of the duty to provide compensation for the period during which the taking was effective." Ibid.

The "total taking" inquiry we require today will ordinarily entail (as the application of state nuisance law ordinarily entails) analysis of, among other things, the degree of harm to public lands and resources, or adjacent private property, posed by the claimant's proposed activities, see, e.g., Restatement (Second) of Torts §§826, 827, the social value of the claimant's activities and their suitability to the locality in question, see, e.g., id., §§828(a) and (b), 831, and the relative ease with which the alleged harm can be avoided through measures taken by the claimant and the government (or adjacent private landowners) alike, see, e.g., id., §§827(e), 828(c), 830. The fact that a particular use has long been engaged in by similarly situated owners ordinarily imports a lack of any common-law prohibition (though changed circumstances or new knowledge may make what was previously permissible no longer so, see Restatement (Second) of Torts, supra, §827, comment g). So also does the fact that other landowners, similarly situated, are permitted to continue the use denied to the claimant.

It seems unlikely that common-law principles would have prevented the erection of any habitable or productive improvements on petitioner's land. . . . The question, however, is one of state law to be dealt with on remand. We emphasize that to win its case South Carolina must do more than proffer the legislature's declaration that the uses Lucas desires are inconsistent with the public interest, or the conclusory assertion that they violate a common-law maxim such as *sic utere tuo ut alienum non laedas*. As we have said, a "State, by *ipse dixit*, may not transform private property into public property without compensation. . . ." Webb's Fabulous Pharmacies, Inc. v. Beckwith, 449 U.S. 155, 164, 101 S. Ct. 446, 452, 66 L. Ed. 2d 358 (1980). Instead, as it would be required to do if it sought to restrain Lucas in a common-law action for public nuisance, South Carolina must identify background principles of nuisance and property law that prohibit the uses he now intends in the circumstances in which the property is presently found. Only on this showing can the State fairly claim that, in proscribing all such beneficial uses, the Beachfront Management Act is taking nothing.[61]

The judgment is reversed and the cause remanded for proceedings not inconsistent with this opinion.

[Justice Kennedy concurred in the judgment, mentioning several points: (1) The majority opinion established a framework for remand but did not decide the ultimate question of whether a temporary taking

---

61. Justice Blackmun decries our reliance on background nuisance principles at least in part because he believes those principles to be as manipulable as we find the "harm prevention"/"benefit conferral" dichotomy. There is no doubt some leeway in a court's interpretation of what existing state law permits — but not remotely as much, we think, as in a legislative crafting of the reasons for its confiscatory regulation. We stress that an affirmative decree eliminating all economically beneficial uses may be defended only if an *objectively reasonable application* of relevant precedents would exclude those beneficial uses in the circumstances in which the land is presently found.

had actually occurred. (2) The finding that Lucas's property had no value was "curious." "I share the reservations of some of my colleagues about a finding that a beach front lot loses all value because of a development restriction." (3) "The finding of no value must be considered under the Takings Clause by reference to the owner's reasonable, investment-backed expectations. . . . There is an inherent tendency towards circularity in this synthesis, of course; for if the owner's reasonable expectations are shaped by what courts allow as a proper exercise of governmental authority, property tends to become what courts say it is. Some circularity must be tolerated in these matters, however, as it is in other spheres. . . . The definition, moreover, is not circular in its entirety. The expectations protected by the Constitution are based on objective rules and customs that can be understood as reasonable by all parties involved." (4) "In my view, reasonable expectations must be understood in light of the whole of our legal tradition. The common law of nuisance is too narrow a confine for the exercise of regulatory power in a complex and interdependent society."

Justice Souter filed a separate statement saying he would dismiss the writ of certiorari as having been improvidently granted. "The petition for review was granted on the assumption that the state by regulation had deprived the owner of his entire economic interest in the subject-property. Such was the state trial court's conclusion, which the state supreme court did not review. It is apparent now that in light of our prior cases . . . the trial court's conclusion is highly questionable. . . . [T]he Court is certainly right to refuse to take up the issue, which is not fairly included within the question presented. . . . This alone is enough to show that there is little utility in attempting to deal with this case on the merits."

In addition to the foregoing, there were two dissenting opinions, which follow.]

JUSTICE BLACKMUN, dissenting.

Today the Court launches a missile to kill a mouse.

. . . Relying on an unreviewed (and implausible) state trial court finding that this restriction left Lucas' property valueless, this Court granted review to determine whether compensation must be paid in cases where the State prohibits all economic use of real estate. According to the Court, such an occasion never has arisen in any of our prior cases, and the Court imagines that it will arise "relatively rarely" or only in "extraordinary circumstances." Almost certainly it did not happen in this case.

Nonetheless, the Court presses on to decide the issue . . . and creates simultaneously a new categorical rule and an exception (neither of which is rooted in our prior case law, common law, or common sense). I protest not only the Court's decision, but each step taken to reach it. More fundamentally, I question the Court's wisdom in issuing sweeping new rules to decide such a narrow case. . . .

My fear is that the Court's new policies will spread beyond the narrow confines of the present case. For that reason, I, like the Court, will give far greater attention to this case than its narrow scope suggests — not because I can intercept the Court's missile, or save the targeted mouse, but because I hope perhaps to limit the collateral damage. . . .

If the state legislature is correct that the prohibition on building in front of the setback line prevents serious harm, then, under this Court's prior cases, the Act is constitutional. . . . The Court consistently has upheld regulations imposed to arrest a significant threat to the common welfare, whatever their economic effect on the owner. . . .

Petitioner never challenged the legislature's findings that a building ban was necessary to protect property and life. Nor did he contend that the threatened harm was not sufficiently serious to make building a house in a particular location a "harmful" use, that the legislature had not made sufficient findings, or that the legislature was motivated by anything other than a desire to minimize damage to coastal areas. . . .

Nothing in the record undermines the General Assembly's assessment that prohibitions on building in front of the setback line are necessary to protect people and property from storms, high tides, and beach erosion. Because that legislative determination cannot be disregarded in the absence of such evidence, . . . and because its determination of harm to life and property from building is sufficient to prohibit that use under this Court's cases, the South Carolina Supreme Court correctly found no taking.

. . . The Court creates its new taking jurisprudence based on the trial court's finding that the property had lost all economic value.[62] This finding is almost certainly erroneous. Petitioner still can enjoy other attributes of ownership, such as the right to exclude others, "one of the most essential sticks in the bundle of rights that are commonly characterized as property." Kaiser Aetna v. United States, 444 U.S. 164, 176, 100 S. Ct. 383, 391, 62 L. Ed. 2d 332 (1979). Petitioner can picnic, swim, camp in a tent, or live on the property in a movable trailer. State courts frequently have recognized that land has economic value where the only residual economic uses are recreation or camping. . . . Petitioner also retains the right to alienate the land, which would have value for neighbors and for those prepared to enjoy proximity to the ocean without a house. . . .

Clearly, the Court was eager to decide this case.

. . . The Court also alters the long-settled rules of review.

---

62. Respondent contested the findings of fact of the trial court in the South Carolina Supreme Court, but that court did not resolve the issue. This Court's decision to assume for its purposes that petitioner had been denied all economic use of his land does not, of course, dispose of the issue on remand.

The South Carolina Supreme Court's decision to defer to legislative judgments in the absence of a challenge from petitioner comports with one of this Court's oldest maxims: "the existence of facts supporting the legislative judgment is to be presumed." United States v. Carolene Products Co., 304 U.S. 144, 152, 58 S. Ct. 778, 783, 82 L. Ed. 1234 (1938). . . .

Accordingly, this Court always has required plaintiffs challenging the constitutionality of an ordinance to provide "some factual foundation of record" that contravenes the legislative findings. O'Gorman & Young [v. Hartford Fire Ins. Co., 282 U.S. 251, 258, 51 S. Ct. 130, 132 (1931)]. In the absence of such proof, "the presumption of constitutionality must prevail." Id., at 257, 51 S. Ct., at 132. We only recently have reaffirmed that claimants have the burden of showing a state law constitutes a taking. See *Keystone Bituminous Coal*, 480 U.S., at 485, 107 S. Ct., at 1242. . . .

Rather than invoking these traditional rules, the Court decides the State has the burden to convince the courts that its legislative judgments are correct. Despite Lucas' complete failure to contest the legislature's findings of serious harm to life and property if a permanent structure is built, the Court decides that the legislative findings are not sufficient to justify the use prohibition. Instead, the Court "emphasize[s]" the State must do more than merely proffer its legislative judgments to avoid invalidating its law. In this case, apparently, the State now has the burden of showing the regulation is not a taking. The Court offers no justification for its sudden hostility toward state legislators, and I doubt that it could.

The Court does not reject the South Carolina Supreme Court's decision simply on the basis of its disbelief and distrust of the legislature's findings. It also takes the opportunity to create a new scheme for regulations that eliminate all economic value. From now on, there is a categorical rule finding these regulations to be a taking unless the use they prohibit is a background common-law nuisance or property principle. . . .

This Court repeatedly has recognized the ability of government, in certain circumstances, to regulate property without compensation no matter how adverse the financial effect on the owner may be. More than a century ago, the Court explicitly upheld the right of States to prohibit uses of property injurious to public health, safety, or welfare without paying compensation: "A prohibition simply upon the use of property for purposes that are declared, by valid legislation, to be injurious to the health, morals, or safety of the community, cannot in any just sense, be deemed a taking or an appropriation of property." Mugler v. Kansas, 123 U.S. 623, 668-669, 8 S. Ct. 273, 301, 32 L. Ed. 205 (1887). On this basis, the Court upheld an ordinance effectively prohibiting operation of a previously lawful brewery, although the "establishments will become of no value as property. . . ."

Mugler was only the beginning in a long line of cases. . . . In Hadacheck v. Sebastian, 239 U.S. 394, 36 S. Ct. 143, 60 L. Ed. 348 (1915), the Court upheld an ordinance prohibiting a brickyard, although the owner had made excavations on the land that prevented it from being utilized for any purpose but a brickyard. In Miller v. Schoene, 276 U.S. 272, 48 S. Ct. 246, 72 L. Ed. 568 (1928), the Court held that the Fifth Amendment did not require Virginia to pay compensation to the owner of cedar trees ordered destroyed to prevent a disease from spreading to nearby apple orchards. . . .

More recently, in *Goldblatt*, the Court upheld a town regulation that barred continued operation of an existing sand and gravel operation in order to protect public safety. 369 U.S., at 596, 82 S. Ct., at 991.[63] . . . In 1978, the Court declared that "in instances in which a state tribunal reasonably concluded that 'the health, safety, morals, or general welfare' would be promoted by prohibiting particular contemplated uses of land, this Court has upheld land-use regulation that destroyed . . . recognized real property interests." *Penn Central Transp. Co.*, 438 U.S., at 125, 98 S. Ct., at 2659. In First Lutheran Church v. Los Angeles County, 482 U.S. 304, 107 S. Ct. 2378, 96 L. Ed. 2d 250 (1987), the owner alleged that a floodplain ordinance had deprived it of "all use" of the property. The Court remanded the case for consideration whether, even if the ordinance denied the owner all use, it could be justified as a safety measure.[64] And in *Keystone Bituminous Coal*, the Court summarized over 100 years of precedent: "the Court has repeatedly upheld regulations that destroy or adversely affect real property interests."[65]

The Court recognizes that "our prior opinions have suggested that 'harmful or noxious uses' of property may be proscribed by government regulation without the requirement of compensation," but seeks to reconcile them with its categorical rule by claiming that the Court never has upheld a regulation when the owner alleged the loss of all economic value. Even if the Court's factual premise were correct, its understanding of the Court's cases is distorted. In none of the cases did the Court

---

63. That same year, an appeal came to the Court asking "[w]hether zoning ordinances which altogether destroy the worth of valuable land by prohibiting the only economic use of which it is capable effect a taking of real property without compensation." The Court dismissed the appeal for lack of a substantial federal question. Consolidated Rock Products Co. v. Los Angeles, 57 Cal. 2d 515, 20 Cal. Rptr. 638, 370 P.2d 342, appeal dism'd, 371 U.S. 36, 83 S. Ct. 145, 9 L. Ed. 2d 112 (1962).

64. On remand, the California court found no taking in part because the zoning regulation "involves this highest of public interests — the prevention of death and injury." First Lutheran Church v. Los Angeles, 210 Cal. App. 3d 1353, 1370, 258 Cal. Rptr. 893, 904 (1989), cert. denied, 493 U.S. 1056, 110 S. Ct. 866, 107 L. Ed. 2d 950 (1990).

65. The Court's suggestion that Agins v. Tiburon, 447 U.S. 255, 100 S. Ct. 2138, 65 L. Ed. 2d 106 (1980), a unanimous opinion, created a new per se rule, only now discovered, is unpersuasive. In *Agins*, the Court stated that "no precise rule determines when property has been taken" but instead that "the question necessarily requires a weighing of public and private interest." Id., at 260-262, 100 S. Ct., at 2141-2142. . . .

suggest that the right of a State to prohibit certain activities without paying compensation turned on the availability of some residual valuable use. Instead, the cases depended on whether the government interest was sufficient to prohibit the activity, given the significant private cost.

These cases rest on the principle that the State has full power to prohibit an owner's use of property if it is harmful to the public. . . . It would make no sense under this theory to suggest that an owner has a constitutionally protected right to harm others, if only he makes the proper showing of economic loss.[66] . . .

Ultimately even the Court cannot embrace the full implications of its per se rule: it eventually agrees that there cannot be a categorical rule for a taking based on economic value that wholly disregards the public need asserted. Instead, the Court decides that it will permit a State to regulate all economic value only if the State prohibits uses that would not be permitted under "background principles of nuisance and property law."[67]

Until today, the Court explicitly had rejected the contention that the government's power to act without paying compensation turns on whether the prohibited activity is a common-law nuisance.[68] The brewery closed in *Mugler* itself was not a common-law nuisance, and the Court specifically stated that it was the role of the legislature to determine what measures would be appropriate for the protection of public health and safety. See 123 U.S., at 661, 8 S. Ct., at 297. In upholding the state action in *Miller*, the Court found it unnecessary to "weigh with nicety the question whether the infected cedars constitute a nuisance according to common law; or whether they may be so declared by statute." 276 U.S., at 280, 48 S. Ct., at 248. Instead the Court has relied in

---

66. "Indeed, it would be extraordinary to construe the Constitution to require a government to compensate private landowners because it denied them 'the right' to use property which cannot be used without risking injury and death." *First Lutheran Church*, 210 Cal. App. 3d, at 1366, 258 Cal. Rptr., at 901-902.

67. Although it refers to state nuisance and property law, the Court apparently does not mean just any state nuisance and property law. Public nuisance was first a common-law creation, see Newark, The Boundaries of Nuisance, 65 L.Q. Rev. 480, 482 (1949) (attributing development of nuisance to 1535), but by the 1800s in both the United States and England, legislatures had the power to define what is a public nuisance, and particular uses often have been selectively targeted. See Prosser, Private Action for Public Nuisance, 52 Va. L. Rev. 997, 999-1000 (1966); J.F. Stephen, A General View of the Criminal Law of England 105-107 (2d ed. 1890). The Court's references to "common-law" background principles, however, indicate that legislative determinations do not constitute "state nuisance and property law" for the Court.

68. Also, until today the fact that the regulation prohibited uses that were lawful at the time the owner purchased did not determine the constitutional question. The brewery, the brickyard, the cedar trees, and the gravel pit were all perfectly legitimate uses prior to the passage of the regulation. . . . This Court explicitly acknowledged in *Hadacheck* that "[a] vested interest cannot be asserted against [the police power] because of conditions once obtaining. To so hold would preclude development and fix a city forever in its primitive conditions." 239 U.S., at 410, 36 S. Ct., at 145 (citation omitted).

the past, as the South Carolina Court has done here, on legislative judgments of what constitutes a harm.[69]

The Court rejects the notion that the State always can prohibit uses it deems a harm to the public without granting compensation because "the distinction between 'harm-preventing' and 'benefit-conferring' regulation is often in the eye of the beholder." Since the characterization will depend "primarily upon one's evaluation of the worth of competing uses of real estate," the Court decides a legislative judgment of this kind no longer can provide the desired "objective, value-free basis" for upholding a regulation. The Court, however, fails to explain how its proposed common law alternative escapes the same trap.

The threshold inquiry for imposition of the Court's new rule, "deprivation of all economically valuable use," itself cannot be determined objectively. As the Court admits, whether the owner has been deprived of all economic value of his property will depend on how "property" is defined. The "composition of the denominator in our 'deprivation' fraction," [see footnote 51 at page 1246] is the dispositive inquiry. Yet there is no "objective" way to define what that denominator should be. "We have long understood that any land-use regulation can be characterized as the 'total' deprivation of an aptly defined entitlement. . . . Alternatively, the same regulation can always be characterized as a mere 'partial' withdrawal from full, unencumbered ownership of the landholding affected by the regulation. . . ." Michelman, Takings, 1987, 88 Colum. L. Rev. 1600, 1614 (1988).

The Court's decision in *Keystone Bituminous Coal* illustrates this principle perfectly. In *Keystone,* the Court determined that the "support estate" was "merely a part of the entire bundle of rights possessed by the owner." 480 U.S., at 501, 107 S. Ct., at 1250. Thus, the Court concluded that the support estate's destruction merely eliminated one segment of the total property. The dissent, however, characterized the support estate as a distinct property interest that was wholly destroyed. Id., at 519, 107 S. Ct., at 1260. The Court could agree on no "value-free basis" to resolve this dispute.

Even more perplexing, however, is the Court's reliance on common-

___

69. The Court argues that finding no taking when the legislature prohibits a harmful use, such as the Court did in *Mugler* and the South Carolina Supreme Court did in the instant case, would nullify *Pennsylvania Coal.* Justice Holmes, the author of *Pennsylvania Coal,* joined Miller v. Schoene, 276 U.S. 272, 48 S. Ct. 246, 72 L. Ed. 568 (1928), six years later. In *Miller,* the Court adopted the exact approach of the South Carolina Court: It found the cedar trees harmful, and their destruction not a taking, whether or not they were a nuisance. Justice Holmes apparently believed that such an approach did not repudiate his earlier opinion. Moreover, this Court already has been over this ground five years ago, and at that point rejected the assertion that *Pennsylvania Coal* was inconsistent with *Mugler, Hadacheck, Miller,* or the others in the string of "noxious use" cases, recognizing instead that the nature of the State's action is critical in takings analysis. *Keystone Bituminous Coal,* 480 U.S., at 490, 107 S. Ct., at 1244.

law principles of nuisance in its quest for a value-free taking jurisprudence. In determining what is a nuisance at common law, state courts make exactly the decision that the Court finds so troubling when made by the South Carolina General Assembly today: they determine whether the use is harmful. Common-law public and private nuisance law is simply a determination whether a particular use causes harm. See Prosser, Private Action for Public Nuisance, 52 Va. L. Rev. 997, 997 (1966) ("*Nuisance* is a French word which means nothing more than harm"). There is nothing magical in the reasoning of judges long dead. They determined a harm in the same way as state judges and legislatures do today. If judges in the 18th and 19th centuries can distinguish a harm from a benefit, why not judges in the 20th century, and if judges can, why not legislators? There simply is no reason to believe that new interpretations of the hoary common law nuisance doctrine will be particularly "objective" or "value-free."[70] Once one abandons the level of generality of *sic utere tuo ut alienum non laedas,* one searches in vain, I think, for anything resembling a principle in the common law of nuisance.

Finally, the Court justifies its new rule that the legislature may not deprive a property owner of the only economically valuable use of his land, even if the legislature finds it to be a harmful use, because such action is not part of the "long recognized" "understandings of our citizens." These "understandings" permit such regulation only if the use is a nuisance under the common law. Any other course is "inconsistent with the historical compact recorded in the Takings Clause." It is not clear from the Court's opinion where our "historical compact" or "citizens' understanding" comes from, but it does not appear to be history.

The principle that the State should compensate individuals for property taken for public use was not widely established in America at the time of the Revolution.

> The colonists . . . inherited . . . a concept of property which permitted extensive regulation of the use of that property for the public benefit — regulation that could even go so far as to deny all productive use of the property to the owner if, as Coke himself stated, the regulation "extends to the public benefit . . . for this is for the public, and every one hath benefit by it." [F. Bosselman, D. Callies & J. Banta, The Taking Issue 80-81 (1973), quoting The Case of the King's Prerogative in Saltpetre, 12 Co. Rep. 12-13 (1606) (hereinafter Bosselman).]

---

70. "There is perhaps no more impenetrable jungle in the entire law than that which surrounds the word 'nuisance.' It has meant all things to all people, and has been applied indiscriminately to everything from an alarming advertisement to a cockroach baked in a pie." W. Keeton, D. Dobbs, R. Keeton, D. Owen, Prosser and Keeton on The Law of Torts 616 (5th ed. 1984) (footnotes omitted). . . .

See also Treanor, The Origins and Original Significance of the Just Compensation Clause of the Fifth Amendment, 94 Yale L.J. 694, 697, n.9 (1985).[71]

Even into the 19th century, state governments often felt free to take property for roads and other public projects without paying compensation to the owners.[72] See M. Horwitz, The Transformation of American Law, 1780-1860, pp.63-64 (1977) (hereinafter Horwitz); Treanor, 94 Yale L.J., at 695. As one court declared in 1802, citizens "were bound to contribute as much of [land], as by the laws of the country, were deemed necessary for the public convenience." M'Clenachan v. Curwin, 3 Yeates 362, 373 (Pa. 1802). There was an obvious movement toward establishing the just compensation principle during the 19th century, but "there continued to be a strong current in American legal thought that regarded compensation simply as a 'bounty given . . . by the State' out of 'kindness' and not out of justice." Horwitz 65 (quoting Commonwealth v. Fisher, 1 Pen. & W. 462, 465 (Pa. 1830)). See also State v. Dawson, 3 Hill 100, 103 (S.C. 1836).[73]

Although, prior to the adoption of the Bill of Rights, America was replete with land use regulations describing which activities were considered noxious and forbidden, see Bender, The Takings Clause: Principles or Politics?, 34 Buffalo L. Rev. 735, 751 (1985); L. Friedman, A History of American Law 66-68 (1973), the Fifth Amendment's Takings Clause originally did not extend to regulations of property, whatever the effect.[74] Most state courts agreed with this narrow interpretation of a taking. "Until the end of the nineteenth century . . . jurists held that the

---

71. See generally Sax, 74 Yale L.J., at 56-59. "The evidence certainly seems to indicate that the mere fact that government activity destroyed existing economic advantages and power did not disturb [the English theorists who formulated the compensation notion] at all. . . ."

72. In 1796, the Attorney General of South Carolina responded to property holders' demand for compensation when the State took their land to build a road by arguing that "there is not one instance on record, and certainly none within the memory of the oldest man now living, of any demand being made for compensation for the soil or freehold of the lands." Lindsay v. Commissioners, 2 S.C.L. 38, 49 (1796).

73. Only the constitutions of Vermont and Massachusetts required that compensation be paid when private property was taken for public use; and although eminent domain was mentioned in the Pennsylvania constitution, its sole requirement was that property not be taken without the consent of the legislature. See Grant, The "Higher Law" Background of the Law of Eminent Domain, in 2 Selected Essays on Constitutional Law 912, 915-916 (1938). By 1868, five of the original States still had no just compensation clauses in their constitutions.

74. James Madison, author of the Takings Clause, apparently intended it to apply only to direct, physical takings of property by the Federal Government. See Treanor, The Origins and Original Significance of the Just Compensation Clause of the Fifth Amendment, 94 Yale L.J., 694, 711 (1985). Professor Sax argues that although "contemporaneous commentary upon the meaning of the compensation clause is in very short supply," 74 Yale L.J., at 58, the "few authorities that are available" indicate that the clause was "designed to prevent arbitrary government action," not to protect economic value. Id., at 58-60.

constitution protected possession only, and not value." Siegel, Understanding the Nineteenth Century Contract Clause: The Role of the Property-Privilege Distinction and "Takings" Clause Jurisprudence, 60 S. Cal. L. Rev. 1, 76 (1986); Bosselman 106. Even indirect and consequential injuries to property resulting from regulations were excluded from the definition of a taking. See Bosselman 106; Callender v. Marsh, 1 Pick. 418, 430 (Mass. 1823).

Even when courts began to consider that regulation in some situations could constitute a taking, they continued to uphold bans on particular uses without paying compensation, notwithstanding the economic impact, under the rationale that no one can obtain a vested right to injure or endanger the public. . . .[75]

In addition, state courts historically have been less likely to find that a government action constitutes a taking when the affected land is undeveloped. According to the South Carolina court, the power of the legislature to take unimproved land without providing compensation was sanctioned by "ancient rights and principles." Lindsay v. Commissioners, 2 S.C.L. 38, 57 (1796). "Except for Massachusetts, no colony appears to have paid compensation when it built a state-owned road across unimproved land. Legislatures provided compensation only for enclosed or improved land." Treanor, 94 Yale L.J., at 695 (footnotes omitted). This rule was followed by some States into the 1800s. See Horwitz 63-65.

With similar result, the common agrarian conception of property limited owners to "natural" uses of their land prior to and during much of the 18th century. See id., at 32. Thus, for example, the owner could build nothing on his land that would alter the natural flow of water. Some more recent state courts still follow this reasoning. See, e.g., Just v. Marinette County, 56 Wis. 2d 7, 201 N.W.2d 761, 768 (1972).

Nor does history indicate any common-law limit on the State's power to regulate harmful uses even to the point of destroying all economic value. Nothing in the discussions in Congress concerning the Takings Clause indicates that the Clause was limited by the common-law nuisance doctrine. Common law courts themselves rejected such an understanding. They regularly recognized that it is "for the legislature to interpose, and by positive enactment to prohibit a use of property which would be injurious to the public." [Commonwealth v. Tewksbury, 11 Metc., 55, 57 (Mass. 1846).] Chief Justice Shaw explained in upholding a regulation prohibiting construction of wharves, the existence of a taking did not depend on "whether a certain erection in tide water is a nuisance at common law or not." [Commonwealth v. Alger, 7 Cush. 53, 104 (Mass. 1851).] . . .

In short, I find no clear and accepted "historical compact" or "understanding of our citizens" justifying the Court's new taking doctrine.

75. For this reason, the retroactive application of the regulation to formerly lawful uses was not a controlling distinction in the past. . . .

Instead, the Court seems to treat history as a grab-bag of principles, to be adopted where they support the Court's theory, and ignored where they do not. If the Court decided that the early common law provides the background principles for interpreting the Taking Clause, then regulation, as opposed to physical confiscation, would not be compensable. If the Court decided that the law of a later period provides the background principles, then regulation might be compensable, but the Court would have to confront the fact that legislatures regularly determined which uses were prohibited, independent of the common law, and independent of whether the uses were lawful when the owner purchased. What makes the Court's analysis unworkable is its attempt to package the law of two incompatible eras and peddle it as historical fact.[76] . . .

I dissent.

JUSTICE STEVENS, dissenting. . . .

In its analysis of the merits, the Court starts from the premise that this Court has adopted a "categorical rule that total regulatory takings must be compensated," and then sets itself to the task of identifying the exceptional cases in which a State may be relieved of this categorical obligation. The test the Court announces is that the regulation must do no more than duplicate the result that could have been achieved under a State's nuisance law. Under this test the categorical rule will apply unless the regulation merely makes explicit what was otherwise an implicit limitation on the owner's property rights.

In my opinion, the Court is doubly in error. The categorical rule the Court establishes is an unsound and unwise addition to the law and the Court's formulation of the exception to that rule is too rigid and too narrow.

The Categorical Rule

. . . Although in dicta we have sometimes recited that a law "effects a taking if [it] . . . denies an owner economically viable use of his land," Agins v. Tiburon, 447 U.S. 255, 260, 100 S. Ct. 2138, 2141, 65 L. Ed. 2d 106 (1980), our *rulings* have rejected such an absolute position. We have frequently — and recently — held that, in some circumstances, a law that renders property valueless may nonetheless not constitute a taking. See, e.g., First English Evangelical Lutheran Church of Glendale v. County of Los Angeles, 482 U.S. 304, 313, 107 S. Ct. 2378, 2385, 96 L.

---

76. The Court asserts that all early American experience, prior to and after passage of the Bill of Rights, and any case law prior to 1897 are "entirely irrelevant" in determining what is "the historical compact recorded in the Takings Clause." Nor apparently are we to find this compact in the early federal taking cases, which clearly permitted prohibition of harmful uses despite the alleged loss of all value, whether or not the prohibition was a common-law nuisance, and whether or not the prohibition occurred subsequent to the purchase. I cannot imagine where the Court finds its "historical compact," if not in history.

Ed. 2d 250 (1987); Goldblatt v. Hempstead, 369 U.S. 590, 596, 82 S. Ct. 987, 991, 8 L. Ed. 2d 130 (1962). . . .

In addition to lacking support in past decisions, the Court's new rule is wholly arbitrary. A landowner whose property is diminished in value 95% recovers nothing, while an owner whose property is diminished 100% recovers the land's full value. . . .

Moreover, because of the elastic nature of property rights, the Court's new rule will also prove unsound in practice. In response to the rule, courts may define "property" broadly and only rarely find regulations to effect total takings. This is the approach the Court itself adopts in its revisionist reading of venerable precedents. We are told that — notwithstanding the Court's findings to the contrary in each case — the brewery in *Mugler,* the brickyard in *Hadacheck,* and the gravel pit in *Goldblatt* all could be put to "other uses" and that, therefore, those cases did not involve total regulatory takings.[77]

On the other hand, developers and investors may market specialized estates to take advantage of the Court's new rule. The smaller the estate, the more likely that a regulatory change will effect a total taking. Thus, an investor may, for example, purchase the right to build a multifamily home on a specific lot, with the result that a zoning regulation that allows only single-family homes would render the investor's property interest "valueless."[78] In short, the categorical rule will likely have one of two effects: Either courts will alter the definition of the "denominator" in the takings "fraction," rendering the Court's categorical rule meaningless, or investors will manipulate the relevant property interests, giving the Court's rule sweeping effect. To my mind, neither of these results is desirable or appropriate, and both are distortions of our takings jurisprudence.

Finally, the Court's justification for its new categorical rule is remarkably thin. The Court mentions in passing three arguments in support of its rule; none is convincing. First, the Court suggests that "total deprivation of feasible use is, from the landowner's point of view, the

---

77. Of course, the same could easily be said in this case: Lucas may put his land to "other uses" — fishing or camping, for example — or may sell his land to his neighbors as a buffer. In either event, his land is far from "valueless."

This highlights a fundamental weakness in the Court's analysis: its failure to explain why only the impairment of "*economically* beneficial or productive use" of property is relevant in takings analysis. I should think that a regulation arbitrarily prohibiting an owner from continuing to use her property for bird-watching or sunbathing might constitute a taking under some circumstances; and, conversely, that such uses are of value to the owner. Yet the Court offers no basis for its assumption that the only uses of property cognizable under the Constitution are *developmental* uses.

78. This unfortunate possibility is created by the Court's subtle revision of the "total regulatory takings" dicta. In past decisions, we have stated that a regulation effects a taking if it "denies an owner economically viable use of his *land,*" Agins v. Tiburon, 447 U.S. 255, 260, 100 S. Ct. 2138, 2141, 65 L. Ed. 2d 106 (1980) (emphasis added), indicating that this "total takings" test did not apply to other estates. Today, however, the Court suggests that a regulation may effect a total taking of *any* real property interest.

equivalent of a physical appropriation." This argument proves too much. From the "landowner's point of view," a regulation that diminishes a lot's value by 50% is as well "the equivalent" of the condemnation of half of the lot. Yet, it is well established that a 50% diminution in value does not by itself constitute a taking. See Euclid v. Ambler Realty Co., 272 U.S. 365, 384, 47 S. Ct. 114, 117, 71 L. Ed. 303 (1926) (75% diminution in value). Thus, the landowner's perception of the regulation cannot justify the Court's new rule.

Second, the Court emphasizes that because total takings are "relatively rare" its new rule will not adversely affect the government's ability to "go on." This argument proves too little. Certainly it is true that defining a small class of regulations that are per se takings will not greatly hinder important governmental functions — but this is true of *any* small class of regulations. The Court's suggestion only begs the question of why regulations of *this* particular class should always be found to effect takings.

Finally, the Court suggests that "regulations that leave the owner . . . without economically beneficial . . . use . . . carry with them a heightened risk that private property is being pressed into some form of public service." As discussed more fully below, I agree that the risks of such singling out are of central concern in takings law. However, such risks do not justify a per se rule for total regulatory takings. There is no necessary correlation between "singling out" and total takings: a regulation may single out a property owner without depriving him of all of his property, see e.g., Nollan v. California Coastal Comm'n, 483 U.S. 825, 837, 107 S. Ct. 3141, 3149, 97 L. Ed. 2d 677 (1987); and it may deprive him of all of his property without singling him out, see e.g., Mugler v. Kansas, 123 U.S. 623, 8 S. Ct. 273, 31 L. Ed. 205 (1887); Hadacheck v. Sebastian, 239 U.S. 394, 36 S. Ct. 143, 60 L. Ed. 348 (1915). What matters in such cases is not the degree of diminution of value, but rather the specificity of the expropriating act. For this reason, the Court's third justification for its new rule also fails.

In short, the Court's new rule is unsupported by prior decisions, arbitrary and unsound in practice, and theoretically unjustified. In my opinion, a categorical rule as important as the one established by the Court today should be supported by more history or more reason than has yet been provided.

The Nuisance Exception

Like many bright-line rules, the categorical rule established in this case is only "categorical" for a page or two in the U.S. Reports. No sooner does the Court state that "total regulatory takings must be compensated," than it quickly establishes an exception to that rule.

The exception provides that a regulation that renders property valueless is not a taking if it prohibits uses of property that were not "pre-

viously permissible under relevant property and nuisance principles."
The Court thus rejects the basic holding in Mugler v. Kansas, 123 U.S.
623, 8 S. Ct. 273, 31 L. Ed. 205 (1887). . . .

Under our reasoning in *Mugler*, a state's decision to prohibit or to
regulate certain uses of property is not a compensable taking just because the particular uses were previously lawful. Under the Court's
opinion today, however, if a state should decide to prohibit the manufacture of asbestos, cigarettes, or concealable firearms, for example, it
must be prepared to pay for the adverse economic consequences of its
decision. . . .

The Court's holding today effectively freezes the State's common
law, denying the legislature much of its traditional power to revise the
law governing the rights and uses of property. . . .

Arresting the development of the common law is not only a departure from our prior decisions; it is also profoundly unwise. The human
condition is one of constant learning and evolution — both moral and
practical. Legislatures implement that new learning; in doing so they
must often revise the definition of property and the rights of property
owners. . . .

Of course, some legislative redefinitions of property will effect a
taking and must be compensated — but it certainly cannot be the case
that every movement away from common law does so. There is no reason, and less sense, in such an absolute rule. We live in a world in which
changes in the economy and the environment occur with increasing frequency and importance. . . . The rule that should govern a decision in a
case of this kind should focus on the future, not the past.[79]

The Court's categorical approach rule will, I fear, greatly hamper
the efforts of local officials and planners who must deal with increasingly
complex problems in land-use and environmental regulation. As this
case — in which the claims of an *individual* property owner exceed $1
million — well demonstrates, these officials face both substantial uncertainty because of the ad hoc nature of takings law and unacceptable penalties if they guess incorrectly about that law.

Viewed more broadly, the Court's new rule and exception conflict
with the very character of our takings jurisprudence. We have frequently and consistently recognized that the definition of a taking cannot be reduced to a "set formula" and that determining whether a
regulation is a taking is "essentially [an] ad hoc, factual inquir[y]." . . .

79. Even measured in terms of efficiency, the Court's rule is unsound. The Court
today effectively establishes a form of insurance against certain changes in land-use regulations. Like other forms of insurance, the Court's rule creates a "moral hazard" and inefficiencies: In the face of uncertainty about changes in the law, developers will overinvest,
safe in the knowledge that if the law changes adversely, they will be entitled to compensation. See generally Farber, Economic Analysis and Just Compensation, 12 Int'l Rev. of Law
& Econ. 125 (1992).

The rigid rules fixed by the Court today clash with this enterprise: "fairness and justice" are often disserved by categorical rules.

It is well established that a takings case "entails inquiry into [several factors:] the character of the governmental action, its economic impact, and its interference with reasonable investment-backed expectations." [PruneYard Shopping Center v. Robins, 447 U.S. 74, 83 (1980).] The Court's analysis today focuses on the last two of these three factors: the categorical rule addresses a regulation's "economic impact," while the nuisance exception recognizes that ownership brings with it only certain "expectations." Neglected by the Court today is the first, and in some ways, the most important factor in takings analysis: the character of the regulatory action. . . .

The presumption that a permanent physical occupation, no matter how slight, effects a taking is wholly consistent with this principle. A physical taking entails a certain amount of "singling out." Consistent with this principle, physical occupations by third parties are more likely to effect takings than other physical occupations. . . .

In analyzing takings claims, courts have long recognized the difference between a regulation that targets one or two parcels of land and a regulation that enforces a state-wide policy. . . .

In considering Lucas' claim, the generality of the Beachfront Management Act is significant. The Act does not target particular landowners, but rather regulates the use of the coastline of the entire State. Indeed, South Carolina's Act is best understood as part of a national effort to protect the coastline, one initiated by the Federal Coastal Zone Management Act of 1972. Pursuant to the Federal Act, every coastal State has implemented coastline regulations.[80] Moreover, the Act did not single out owners of undeveloped land. The Act also prohibited owners of developed land from rebuilding if their structures were destroyed. . . . In short, the South Carolina Act imposed substantial burdens on owners of developed and undeveloped land alike. This generality indicates that the Act is not an effort to expropriate owners of undeveloped land.

Admittedly, the economic impact of this regulation is dramatic and petitioner's investment-backed expectations are substantial. Yet, if anything, the costs to and expectations of the owners of developed land are even greater: I doubt, however, that the cost to owners of developed land of renourishing the beach and allowing their seawalls to deteriorate effects a taking. The costs imposed on the owners of undeveloped land, such as petitioner, differ from these costs only in degree, not in kind.

The impact of the ban on developmental uses must also be viewed

---

80. See Zalkin, Shifting Sands and Shifting Doctrines: The Supreme Court's Changing Takings Doctrine and South Carolina's Coastal Zone Statute, 79 Cal. L. Rev. 205, 216-217, nn.46-47 (1991) (collecting statutes).

in light of the purposes of the Act. . . . This is a traditional and important exercise of the State's police power, as demonstrated by Hurricane
Hugo, which in 1989, caused 29 deaths and more than $6 billion in
property damage in South Carolina alone.

In view of all of these factors, even assuming that petitioner's property was rendered valueless, the risk inherent in investments of the sort
made by petitioner, the generality of the Act, and the compelling purpose motivating the South Carolina Legislature persuade me that the
Act did not effect a taking of petitioner's property.

Accordingly, I respectfully dissent.

NOTES AND QUESTIONS

1. *The* Lucas *case.* The long majority and dissenting opinions in *Lucas* provide you with an opportunity to reflect once again on the many
questions we have asked about the sense of the takings tests examined in
this chapter. Consider also the standing of some of the standard rules of
decision. Suppose, for example, that the legislature, in the name of controlling nuisance-like activities, regulates the use of land in a way that
reduces its value severely, but not entirely. Is the measure categorically
not a taking, or does it remain subject to the test announced by Justice
Holmes in *Pennsylvania Coal*? (See Note 1 on page 1197.) What if the
purposes of the measure are not put in something like nuisance-control
terms?[81]

Such matters aside, does *Lucas* amount to much? Is Justice Blackmun right in saying that the majority "launches a missile to kill a
mouse"? Consider two news accounts reporting on the *Lucas* case. The
headline of one said this: "Supreme Court's Takings Analysis in *Lucas*
Expected to Impose Heavy Burden on Regulators." A subheadline of
the other said that the "ruling allows government to go far in regulating
land use."[82]

---

81. See the pre-*Lucas* comments in Frank Michelman, Takings, 1987, 88 Colum. L.
Rev. 1600, 1622 (1988):

> There are . . . signs in recent developments that the Court is finding its open-
> ended balancing posture hard to maintain and so is moving noticeably towards a
> reformalization of regulatory-takings doctrine. Doctrine appears to be moving in the
> direction of resolution into a series of categorical "either-ors": *either* (a) the regulation
> is categorically a taking of property because (i) it works a permanent physical occupa-
> tion (however practically trivial) of private property by the government, or, perhaps,
> specifically undermines a "distinct investment-backed expectation," or (ii) it totally
> eliminates the property's economic value or "viability" to its nominal owner, *or* (b) the
> regulation is categorically not a taking.

But see id. at 1601-1604 (discussing the nuisance-control exception).

82. See, respectively, Envt. Rep. (BNA) Current Developments, July 3, 1992, at 717;
Linda Greenhouse, Justices Ease Way to Challenge Land-Use Rules That Prevent Development, N.Y. Times, June 30, 1992, at A18. Law review commentary on the Supreme

2. *Courts versus legislatures.* See Timothy D. Searchinger, Private Property Rights and Environmental Harm, EDF Letter (A Report to Members of the Environmental Defense Fund), Oct. 1992, at 4:

> The practical effect of this ruling [in *Lucas*] is to transfer authority from legislatures to courts. Essentially, it implies that legislative judgments of harm are not legitimate, but judge-made judgments are. This transfer is a concern because serious environmental harms, such as the ozone hole or degradation of the Chesapeake Bay, often arise from many small, seemingly safe uses of property that only together cause great harm. Environmental protection began with judge-made law, but shifted to legislative statutes long ago precisely because courts have difficulty recognizing and regulating such diffuse sources of harm.

See also the report of an interview with John A. Humbach, a professor of law at Pace University, in News Notes — High Court Takings Analysis Likely to Burden Regulators, Envt. Rep. (BNA) Decisions No. 22 (July 10, 1992) (unpaginated):

> Humbach said that what troubled him about the ruling was that the Supreme Court reassigned from the legislative branch to the courts final authority for determining what land uses are injurious. This is bad, he said, because the courts are not responsive to a voting constituency and are not so well suited to respond to change. In addition, the courts are institutionally isolated from the "tug and pull of the political process," he said.

The thrust of both sets of remarks, in part, is that legislative bodies can be trusted as much as, if not more than, the courts. The Justices in the majority in *Lucas* seem to disagree. In thinking about your own position on the issue, consider Barton H. Thompson, Jr., Judicial Takings, 76 Va. L. Rev. 1449 (1990). Professor Thompson concludes that, "while the legislative, administrative, and judicial processes are different, they suffer in varying degrees from many of the same political imperfections. As a result, there is no justification for exempting the judiciary from those property protections that are necessary where other branches of the government are concerned." Id. at 1541.

3. Lucas *again: not quite the final word.* In Note 1 on page 1197 we described the diminution-in-value test of *Pennsylvania Coal* as noncategorical. Surely, though, a categorical rule lurks at the test's core: *If* a

---

Court's decision in *Lucas* was just starting to appear as this book went to press. For a sampling of the early returns, see, e.g., Lynda L. Butler, Private Land Use, Changing Public Values, and Notions of Relativity, 1992 B.Y.U. L. Rev. 629; David Coursen, *Lucas v. South Carolina Coastal Council*: Indirection in the Evolution of Takings Law, 22 Envtl. L. Rptr. 10778 (News & Analysis 1992): Dialogues, 23 Envtl. L. Rptr. 10003, 10008 (News & Analysis 1993); Symposium, 45 Stan. L. Rev. No. 5 (May 1993) (forthcoming); Comment, 1992 Wis. L. Rev. 1299.

regulation works a taking when it goes "too far," *then* a total wipeout must always be a taking (nuisance-controls somehow aside). Remember, though, that even this hard core of the soft diminution-in-value test is ambiguous absent some definition of the interest to which it applies. This is the "conceptual severance" or part-of-a-whole, all-of-a-part issue. See Note 2 on pages 1197-1198 and footnote 51 on pages 1245-1246.

A petition for certiorari filed with the Court subsequent to *Lucas* presented this question:

> Whether the Fifth Amendment applicable to the States through the Fourteenth Amendment allows denial of just compensation by including non-regulated upland property in the "relevant calculus," when just compensation would be required if the "parcel as a whole" were limited to the regulated wetlands and permit denial prohibited all economic viable use of the wetland property which must remain forever in its natural state.

Result? Certiorari denied. Tull v. Virginia,113 S. Ct. 191 (1992).

4. *The end of the story (for Mr. Lucas).* On remand from the decision in *Lucas,* the South Carolina Supreme Court concluded that there was no common law basis for holding that Mr. Lucas's intended use of his land was not a part of the bundle of rights inhering in his title. The trial court was thus instructed to make findings of damages — for the period beginning with the enactment of the 1988 Beachfront Management Act and running to the date of the court's order — to compensate Mr. Lucas for a temporary taking. Lucas v. South Carolina Coastal Council, 424 S.E.2d 484 (1992).

Table of Cases

Author Index

Subject Index